ETHICAL CONFLICTS
IN PSYCHOLOGY

ETHICAL CONFLICTS
IN PSYCHOLOGY

FOURTH EDITION

DONALD N. BERSOFF

AMERICAN PSYCHOLOGICAL ASSOCIATION
WASHINGTON, DC

Published by
American Psychological Association
750 First Street, NE
Washington, DC 20002
www.apa.org

To order
APA Order Department
P.O. Box 92984
Washington, DC 20090-2984
Tel: (800) 374-2721; Direct: (202) 336-5510
Fax: (202) 336-5502; TDD/TTY: (202) 336-6123
Online: www.apa.org/books/
E-mail: order@apa.org

In the U.K., Europe, Africa, and the Middle East, copies may be ordered from
American Psychological Association
3 Henrietta Street
Covent Garden, London
WC2E 8LU England

Typeset in Berkeley by Circle Graphics, Columbia, MD

Printer: United Book Press, Inc., Baltimore, MD
Cover Designer: Minker Design, Bethesda, MD
Technical/Production Editor: Kathryn Funk

The opinions and statements published are the responsibility of the authors, and such opinions and statements do not necessarily represent the policies of the American Psychological Association.

Library of Congress Cataloging-in-Publication Data

Ethical conflicts in psychology / Donald N. Bersoff.—4th ed.
    p. cm.
 Includes bibliographical references and index.
 ISBN-13: 978-1-4338-0350-5
 ISBN-13: 978-1-4338-0353-6
 ISBN-10: 1-4338-0350-X
 ISBN-10: 1-4338-0353-4
 1. Psychology—Moral and ethical aspects. 2. Psychologists—Professional ethics. 1. Bersoff, Donald N.

BF76.4.E814 2008
174'.915—dc22

                         2007046426

British Library Cataloguing-in-Publication Data
A CIP record is available from the British Library.

Printed in the United States of America
Fourth Edition

503665

To lead a moral life is noble, to get others to lead
a moral life is nobler—and no trouble.
—Mark Twain

Be not too hasty to trust . . . the teachers of morality. . .
they discourse like angels, but they live like men.
—Samuel Johnson, *Rasselas*

◆　　◆　　◆

To my wife, Deborah Leavy, my children, Benjamin, David, and Judith,
and my granddaughter, Aubrey—may she live in a more ethical
and peaceful world than she was born into.

Contents

Preface to the Fourth Edition xv

Preface to the Third Edition xvii

Preface to the Second Edition xix

Preface to the First Edition xxi

Introduction 3

CHAPTER 1. ETHICS CODES AND HOW THEY ARE ENFORCED

Introduction 7
Donald N. Bersoff

A Short History of the Development of APA's Ethics Codes 10
Donald N. Bersoff

Ethical Principles of Psychologists and Code of Conduct 14
American Psychological Association

Examining the Personal–Professional Distinction:
Ethics Codes and the Difficulty of Drawing a Boundary 31
Randolph B. Pipes, Jaymee E. Holstein, and Maria G. Aguirre

Bylaws of the American Psychological Association 38
American Psychological Association

Rules and Procedures (October 1, 2001) 40
Ethics Committee of the American Psychological Association

CHAPTER 2. HOW ETHICS ARE APPLIED

Introduction 67
Donald N. Bersoff

The Failure of Clinical Psychology Graduate Students to Apply
Understood Ethical Principles 69
J. L. Bernard and Carmen S. Jara

Ethics of Practice: The Beliefs and Behaviors of Psychologists as Therapists 74
Kenneth S. Pope, Barbara G. Tabachnick, and Patricia Keith-Spiegel

Ethical Ambiguities in the Practice of Child Clinical Psychology 91
  Carole I. Mannheim, Michael Sancilio, Susan Phipps-Yonas, Donald Brunnquell,
  Peter Somers, Georganne Farseth, and Fred Ninonuevo

Ethical Decision Making and Psychologists' Attitudes Toward Training in Ethics. . 98
  Alexander J. Tymchuk, Robin Drapkin, Susan Major-Kingsley,
  Andrea B. Ackerman, Elizabeth W. Coffman, and Maureen S. Baum

Ethical Dilemmas in Psychological Practice: Results of a National Survey 101
  Leonard J. Haas, John L. Malouf, and Neal H. Mayerson

When Laws and Ethics Collide: What Should Psychologists Do? 109
  Samuel Knapp, Michael Gottlieb, Jason Berman, and Mitchell M. Handelsman

CHAPTER 3. LEARNING ETHICS

Introduction 117
  Donald N. Bersoff

Problems With Ethics Training by "Osmosis" 120
  Mitchell M. Handelsman

Training Ethical Psychologists: An Acculturation Model. 122
  Mitchell M. Handelsman, Michael C. Gottlieb, and Samuel Knapp

Competency Training in Ethics Education and Practice 128
  Cynthia de las Fuentes, Mary E. Willmuth, and Catherine Yarrow

An Historical Overview of Basic Approaches and Issues in Ethical
and Moral Philosophy and Principles: A Foundation for
Understanding Ethics in Psychology 132
  Joanne E. Callan and Megan E. Callan

A Principle-Based Analysis of the 2002 American Psychological
Association Ethics Code 135
  Samuel Knapp and Leon VandeCreek

Ethics and the Professional Practice of Psychologists:
The Role of Virtues and Principles 139
  Augustus E. Jordan and Naomi M. Meara

The Virtue of Principle Ethics 144
  Donald N. Bersoff

Canadian Code of Ethics for Psychologists 148
  Canadian Psychological Association

Navigating the Nuances: A Matrix of Considerations
for Ethical–Legal Dilemmas. 152
  Nancy Downing Hansen and Susan G. Goldberg

CHAPTER 4. CONFIDENTIALITY, PRIVILEGE, AND PRIVACY

Introduction 159
  Donald N. Bersoff

Privacy, Confidentiality, and Privilege in Psychotherapeutic Relationships 161
  Michele Smith-Bell and William J. Winslade

Privacy and Confidentiality in Psychotherapy 166
  Louis Everstine, Diana Sullivan Everstine, Gary M. Heymann, Reiko Homma
  True, David H. Frey, Harold G. Johnson, and Richard H. Seiden

Therapists as Protectors and Policemen: New Roles as a Result of *Tarasoff?* 169
  Donald N. Bersoff

Tarasoff v. Regents of the University of California (*Tarasoff II*) 171

Some Contrarian Concerns About Law, Psychology, and Public Policy 175
  Donald N. Bersoff

Limiting Therapist Exposure to *Tarasoff* Liability: Guidelines
for Risk Containment 180
  John Monahan

Outpatient Psychotherapy With Dangerous Clients: A Model
for Clinical Decision Making 187
  Derek Truscott, Jim Evans, and Sheila Mansell

Confidentiality With Minor Clients: Issues and Guidelines for Therapists 192
  Kathryn E. Gustafson and J. Regis McNamara

Factors Contributing to Breaking Confidentiality With Adolescent Clients:
A Survey of Pediatric Psychologists 197
  Jeremy R. Sullivan, Eleazar Ramirez, William A. Rae, Nancy Peña Razo,
  and Carrie A. George

HIV, Confidentiality, and Duty to Protect: A Decision-Making Model 203
  Tiffany Chenneville

Divergent Ethical Perspectives on the Duty-to-Warn Principle
With HIV Patients 207
  Steven K. Huprich, Kristi M. Fuller, and Robert B. Schneider

CHAPTER 5. MULTIPLE RELATIONSHIPS

Introduction 215
  Donald N. Bersoff

A Preliminary Look at How Psychologists Identify, Evaluate, and Proceed
When Faced With Possible Multiple Relationship Dilemmas 217
  Douglas H. Lamb, Salvatore J. Catanzaro, and Annorah S. Moorman

The Concept of Boundaries in Clinical Practice: Theoretical
and Risk-Management Dimensions 222
  Thomas G. Gutheil and Glen O. Gabbard

Explicit Ambiguity: The 1992 Ethics Code as an Oxymoron 231
  Donald N. Bersoff

Nonromantic, Nonsexual Posttherapy Relationships Between Psychologists
and Former Clients: An Exploratory Study of Critical Incidents 235
  Sharon K. Anderson and Karen S. Kitchener

How Certain Boundaries and Ethics Diminish Therapeutic Effectiveness 242
  Arnold A. Lazarus

Concrete Boundaries and the Problem of Literal-Mindedness:
A Response to Lazarus 245
   Laura S. Brown

Intimate Relationships Between Teaching Assistants and Students:
Ethical and Practical Considerations 248
   Sarah E. Oberlander and Jeffrey E. Barnett

The Current State of Sexual Ethics Training in Clinical Psychology:
Issues of Quantity, Quality, and Effectiveness 250
   Linda M. Housman and Jayne E. Stake

Managing Risk When Contemplating Multiple Relationships 253
   Jeffrey N. Younggren and Michael C. Gottlieb

Criminalization of Psychotherapist–Patient Sex. 262
   Larry H. Strasburger, Linda Jorgenson, and Rebecca Randles

Remediation for Ethics Violations: Focus on Psychotherapists'
Sexual Contact With Clients. 266
   Melissa J. Layman and J. Regis McNamara

CHAPTER 6. PSYCHOLOGICAL ASSESSMENT

Introduction 271
   Donald N. Bersoff

Test Validity and the Ethics of Assessment 273
   Samuel Messick

The Legal Regulation of School Psychology 276
   Donald N. Bersoff and Paul T. Hofer

APA's Guidelines for Test User Qualifications: An Executive Summary 279
   Samuel M. Turner, Stephen T. DeMers, Heather Roberts Fox,
   and Geoffrey M. Reed

Ethical Issues in Testing and Evaluation for Personnel Decisions 283
   Manuel London and Douglas W. Bray

Detroit Edison Co. v. National Labor Relations Board 287

Statement on the Disclosure of Test Data. 289
   Committee on Psychological Tests and Assessment,
   American Psychological Association

Strategies for Private Practitioners Coping With Subpoenas
or Compelled Testimony for Client Records or Test Data 293
   Committee on Legal Issues, American Psychological Association

The Ethical Practice of School Psychology: A Rebuttal and Suggested Model . . . 299
   Donald N. Bersoff

Legal Issues in Computerized Psychological Testing. 303
   Donald N. Bersoff and Paul J. Hofer

Psychological Testing on the Internet: New Problems, Old Issues. 306
   Jack A. Naglieri, Fritz Drasgow, Mark Schmit, Len Handler,
   Aurelio Prifitera, Amy Margolis, and Roberto Velasquez

Practical and Ethical Issues in Teaching Psychological Testing 313
Patricia A. Rupert, Neal F. Kozlowski, Laura A. Hoffman,
Denise D. Daniels, and Jeanne M. Piette

Report of the Presidential Task Force on Psychological Ethics
and National Security 319
American Psychological Association

Psychiatric Participation in Interrogation of Detainees 325
American Psychiatric Association

CHAPTER 7. THERAPY AND OTHER FORMS OF INTERVENTION

Introduction 329
Donald N. Bersoff

Seeking an Understanding of Informed Consent 331
Jeffrey E. Barnett

Informed Consent: Complexities and Meanings 336
Erica H. Wise

Evolving Standards for Informed Consent: Is It Time
for an Individualized and Flexible Approach? 337
Doug Johnson-Greene

Increasingly Informed Consent: Discussing Distinct Aspects
of Psychotherapy at Different Points in Time. 339
Andrew M. Pomerantz

Risk Management With the Suicidal Patient: Lessons From Case Law 342
Dana Royce Baerger

Ethical and Legal Considerations in Marital and Family Therapy 346
Gayla Margolin

National Survey of Ethical Practices Across Rural and Urban Communities 354
Craig M. Helbok, Robert P. Marinelli, and Richard T. Walls

Guidelines for Therapy With Women 361
Task Force on Sex Bias and Sex Role Stereotyping in Psychotherapeutic Practice

Guidelines for Psychotherapy With Lesbian, Gay, and Bisexual Clients 363
Division 44/Committee on Lesbian, Gay, and Bisexual Concerns Joint Task
Force on Guidelines for Psychotherapy With Lesbian, Gay, and Bisexual Clients

Guidelines for Providers of Psychological Services to Ethnic, Linguistic,
and Culturally Diverse Populations 365
American Psychological Association

Guidelines for Psychological Practice With Older Adults 368
American Psychological Association

A Debate on Prescription Privileges for Psychologists 370
Elaine M. Heiby, Patrick H. DeLeon, and Timothy Anderson

Internet-Mediated Psychological Services and the American Psychological
Association Ethics Code 376
Celia B. Fisher and Adam L. Fried

CHAPTER 8. ACADEMIA: RESEARCH, TEACHING, AND SUPERVISION

Introduction 385
Donald N. Bersoff

Ethical Perspectives in Clinical Research 387
David M. Bersoff and Donald N. Bersoff

Science and Ethics in Conducting, Analyzing, and Reporting
Psychological Research 390
Robert Rosenthal

Policy for Protection of Human Research Subjects 398
U.S. Department of Health and Human Services

Empirical Studies of Ethical Issues in Research: A Research Agenda 406
Barbara Stanley, Joan E. Sieber, and Gary B. Melton

Informed Consent for Psychological Research: Do Subjects Comprehend
Consent Forms and Understand Their Legal Rights? 412
Traci Mann

Deception Methods in Psychology: Have They Changed in 23 Years? 415
Joan E. Sieber, Rebecca Iannuzzo, and Beverly Rodriguez

Deception in Research: Distinctions and Solutions From the Perspective
of Utilitarianism 417
David J. Pittenger

Informed Consent and Deception in Psychotherapy Research:
An Ethical Analysis 423
Richard T. Lindsey

Psychological Research Online: Report of Board of Scientific Affairs' Advisory
Group on the Conduct of Research on the Internet 426
*Robert Kraut, Judith Olson, Mahzarin Banaji, Amy Bruckman,
Jeffrey Cohen, and Mick Couper*

Guidelines for Ethical Conduct in the Care and Use of Animals 434
American Psychological Association

Ethical Issues in the Supervision of Student Research:
A Study of Critical Incidents 439
Rodney K. Goodyear, Clyde A. Crego, and Michael W. Johnston

Black and White and Shades of Gray: A Portrait of the Ethical Professor 446
Mary Birch, Deni Elliott, and Mary A. Trankel

CHAPTER 9. FORENSIC SETTINGS

Introduction 453
Donald N. Bersoff

Use and Then Prove, or Prove and Then Use? Some Thoughts on the Ethics
of Mental Health Professionals' Courtroom Involvement 455
David Faust

Reclaiming the Integrity of Science in Expert Witnessing 456
Bruce D. Sales and Daniel W. Shuman

When is an "Expert" an Expert?............................ 457
  Kirk Heilbrun

Competence and Quality in the Performance of Forensic Psychologists....... 459
  Leonard J. Haas

The Expert Witness, the Adversary System, and the Voice of Reason:
Reconciling Impartiality and Advocacy........................... 465
  Daniel W. Shuman and Stuart A. Greenberg

Psychologists and the Judicial System: Broader Perspectives................ 473
  Donald N. Bersoff

Specialty Guidelines for Forensic Psychologists..................... 476
  Committee on Ethical Guidelines for Forensic Psychologists

Guidelines for Child Custody Evaluations in Divorce Proceedings........... 485
  American Psychological Association

Irreconcilable Conflict Between Therapeutic and Forensic Roles........... 492
  Stuart A. Greenberg and Daniel W. Shuman

Compatibility of Therapeutic and Forensic Roles...................... 499
  Terence Heltzel

When Worlds Collide: Therapeutic and Forensic Roles.................. 505
  Stuart A. Greenberg and Daniel W. Shuman

Role Conflicts in Coercive Assessments: Evaluation
and Recommendations...................................... 507
  Jose M. Arcaya

Role Conflict in Forensic Clinical Psychology: Reply to Arcaya............ 510
  Dewey G. Cornell

Estelle v. Smith... 512

Is It Unethical to Offer Predictions of Future Violence?.................. 515
  Thomas Grisso and Paul S. Appelbaum

Conducting Risk Evaluations for Future Violence:
Ethical Practice Is Possible.................................. 518
  Anton O. Tolman and Andrea L. Rotzien

Some Contrarian Concerns About Law, Psychology,
and Public Policy.. 523
  Donald N. Bersoff

Daubert v. Merrell Dow Pharmaceuticals, Inc....................... 526

On Being Ethical in Legal Places............................... 529
  Patricia Anderten, Valerie Staulcup, and Thomas Grisso

CHAPTER 10. THE BUSINESS OF PSYCHOLOGY

Introduction.. 531
  Donald N. Bersoff

The Commerce of Professional Psychology and the New Ethics Code........ 533
  Gerald P. Koocher

Record Keeping Guidelines 536
    Committee on Professional Practice and Standards, Board of
    Professional Affairs, American Psychological Association

HIPAA: Federal Regulation of Healthcare Records. 543
    Donald N. Bersoff

APA and the FTC: New Adventures in Consumer Protection 546
    Gerald P. Koocher

Practicing Psychology in the Era of Managed Care: Implications
for Practice and Training 552
    Lisa M. Sanchez and Samuel M. Turner

Legal Liability and Managed Care. 559
    Paul S. Appelbaum

Managed Outpatient Mental Health Plans: Clinical, Ethical, and Practical
Guidelines for Participation 563
    Leonard J. Haas and Nicholas A. Cummings

Considerations for Ethical Practice in Managed Care 567
    Catherine Acuff, Bruce E. Bennett, Patricia M. Bricklin, Mathilda B. Canter,
    Samuel J. Knapp, Stanley Moldawsky, and Randy Phelps

Index. 581
About the Author 607

Preface to the Fourth Edition

I was enjoying a relatively restful retirement when the publisher of this text, the American Psychological Association (APA), asked me to prepare a fourth edition. I was not sure at the time that another revision was necessary, particularly because the third edition had been published as recently as 2003, soon after the 2002 APA Ethics Code was adopted. It turns out that APA was correct. This is the most substantial revision of any earlier editions. Only about 40% of the original articles that appeared in the first edition published in 1995 are present in this one. About 50% of the 1995 excerpted articles have been deleted; 50% of the current inclusions are new, most published after 2003. Many more articles and materials were published in the last 5 years than could be accommodated in a student-oriented text, but I have expanded the list of references for those who wish to delve more deeply into certain topics.

It is clear that the literature on legal and ethical issues in the professional journals is burgeoning, and the field is in ferment. New *Record Keeping Guidelines* were adopted in February 2007 by APA (and appear here with some judicious editing). The use of the Internet in assessment, therapy, and research has increased substantially, and an advisory group of the APA's Board of Scientific Affairs has issued an important report concerning online research, also included in this edition. Eloquent contrarians Arnold Lazarus and Ofer Zur continue to argue against strict adherence to standards concerning nonsexual multiple relationships with therapy clients. The implications of the Health Insurance Portability and Accountability Act for protecting patient information as well as the security of tests have become more apparent and get greater coverage than in the third edition. A few new decisions by the courts, once again in California, have expanded liability in cases involving psychotherapy patients who threaten potential victims; I discuss the consequences. Perhaps most controversial is the *Report of the American Psychological Association Presidential Task Force on Psychological Ethics and National Security*. The report permits psychologists working for the military to aid in the interrogation of detainees in such prisons as Guantanamo Bay. I have included major portions of that report and in keeping with the title and theme of this text, the American Psychiatric Association's opposing statement. In all, then, I hope this latest edition provides enough controversy and conflict to stimulate debate and discussion among professional psychologists, researchers, students, and their teachers.

As always, I am indebted to the following members of APA's publishing arm: Gary VandenBos, executive director of the Publication and Communications Program; Julia Frank-McNeil, director of APA Books; Susan Reynolds, senior acquisitions editor, APA Books; Ron Teeter, development editor; Debbie Felder, copyeditor; and Katie Funk, production editor.

I wish to thank two bright and motivated research assistants who helped immeasurably in finding relevant articles and getting permission to excerpt and use them—Amanda Davidio Zelechoski and Christina Riggs Romaine. I want to express my gratitude to Kirk Heilbrun, chair of the Department of Psychology at Drexel University, who graciously provided the funds to support the research assistants. My penultimate thanks go to Robin Lewis, my administrative assistant for almost a decade and one half, who keeps me sane and does marvelous work with computers. And, the proverbial last but certainly not least appreciative nod is to the students who have labored through these materials and continue to improve their quality.

Preface to the Third Edition

This is the second revision of this text since the original was published in 1995. This third edition was necessitated by several events that have occurred since 1999, when the second edition was issued. Most important, in August 2002, the American Psychological Association (APA) Council of Representatives, its policymaking body, adopted a new code of ethical conduct that became effective in June 2003. This new code supplants the one adopted a decade earlier. Whether it will be considered a major improvement over the widely criticized 1992 version or merely a "rearrangement of the deck chairs on the Titanic" remains to be seen. Second, in August of 2001, APA's Ethics Committee proposed and the Board of Directors adopted revisions to the Rules and Procedures for adjudicating complaints of unethical conduct against APA members, producing the Rules published in August 2002. Third, the federal government has made known its concern for the privacy of healthcare records. Under the Health Insurance Portability and Accountability Act (HIPAA), it promulgated new regulatory obligations of confidentiality on the practitioner, enforceable as of April 2003. A summary of these obligations is discussed in chapters 4 and 10. Finally, although prior editions noted the impact of the computer on assessment and therapy, the intensity of the impact has been heightened, not only in these two traditional fields, but in research. I try to give readers a sense of the ethical issues raised by the introduction of the computer in psychology's "holy trinity" (assessment, intervention, research).

Both the new Rules and Procedures and the 2002 Ethics Code are reprinted in chapter 1. Much of the language is the same in both (with some very important exceptions). I have retained several articles discussing the 1992 code in this edition because they are still relevant. Where those articles cite standards from the 1992 code, I have indicated in footnotes what the corollary standards are in the 2002 code.

I am once again indebted to those at APA for their rapid decision to publish this updated and significantly revised third edition. Gary VandenBos, executive director of the APA Publications and Communications Program, Julia Frank-McNeil, director, APA Books, and Susan Reynolds, senior acquisitions editor, APA Books, saw the value in a third edition and encouraged me to pursue the project. Development editor Kristine Enderle collaborated most closely with me during the book's evolution. Copy editor Ed Meidenbauer helped me greatly in improving the text's readability.

I wish to thank Heather Hulse and Marchelle Thompson, advanced students in the Law and Psychology Program cosponsored by Villanova Law School and Drexel University's

Department of Psychology, who served as my research assistants. I want to express my appreciation to Kirk Heilbrun, chair of Drexel's department, and Mark Sargent, dean of Villanova's law school, for their generosity in allowing me to use the resources of their respective domains. Finally, I am again thankful for the students who have used these materials in one form or another over the past 15 years and who have improved their usefulness by their tactful but persuasive criticism.

Preface to the Second Edition

I am gratified by the apparent success of the first edition of this text, published in 1995 by the American Psychological Association (APA). I am hopeful that this revision will be as welcomed as the original. I have kept the same format, presenting judiciously edited articles from a wide variety of sources interspersed with original commentary and citations to other published materials. I have also maintained my original intent—to offer conflicting views about fundamental ethical and moral dilemmas, allowing users of this book to ultimately arrive at their own conclusions about their proper resolutions.

Although the format and intent remain the same, I have incorporated some changes in this edition. Like any anxious author, I read the reviews of the first edition of this text and took them to heart. One important criticism was that the book was too ethnocentric. In response, I have included the Canadian Code of Ethics as well as the Canadian Psychological Association's system for ethical decision making. These additions make the book more useful to colleagues in the North and allow readers to contrast the APA and CPA codes with regard to their readability, helpfulness in guiding ethical behavior, and comparability in regulating professional conduct.

Although I have retained some older articles for historical context, the majority of the materials in this second edition were published within the last decade, and about half were published in the past five years. Much of this newer material represents rapidly changing events in psychology. Thus, readers will find more material on managed care, the merits and demerits of tele- (or cyber-) therapy, and updated information about research ethics, among others.

I am indebted to those at APA for their decision to publish a revised and modernized second edition. Gary VandenBos, executive director of the APA Publications and Communications Program, and Julia Frank-McNeil, director, APA Books, saw the value in a second edition and encouraged me to pursue the project. Development editor Margaret Schlegel collaborated most closely with me during the book's publication. If not for her gentle insistence on keeping the book within a manageable and affordable length and her reading and rereading early drafts, this text would not be as concise and affordable as it is. Production editor Rachael Stryker significantly improved the text's language and readability.

This project could not have been completed but for the granting of my sabbatical leave by the former dean of Villanova Law School, Steven P. Frankino. Also vital was the financial sustenance of a summer research grant provided by the school's present dean, Mark Sargent.

I wish to thank Erik Nabors and Kim Picarello, students in the Law and Psychology Program cosponsored by Villanova Law School and the Medical College of Pennsylvania—Hahnemann University, who served as my research assistants. Finally, I am thankful for the students who have used these materials in one form or another over the past decade and who have improved its usefulness through their cogent suggestions.

If students, psychologists, and other readers have suggestions for material to be included in what I hope will be future editions, I would be pleased if you communicate with me.

Preface to the First Edition

This book represents the final common pathway of over 3 decades of professional work. My experiences as a psychologist working with inpatients and outpatients, collecting data from human subjects in research, or scrutinizing the research proposals of others while serving on institutional review boards; my work as an attorney defending psychologists against claims of malpractice and unethical conduct, or acting as a consultant to state psychology licensing boards seeking to discipline errant professionals; and my service to the American Psychological Association (APA) as its legal counsel for 10 years and, currently, as a member of its Board of Directors—all of this has taught me that there is a need to better inculcate ethical values and virtues in all those who practice, teach, and do research in psychology. In particular, however, it was my role as an academician—directing programs in law and psychology, discussing and debating ethical issues with colleagues and graduate students, and, specifically, teaching ethics to graduate students—that led me to develop this book.

As a teacher, I found that books providing narrative overviews of ethics, although educational, did not always stimulate lively discussion, sometimes failed to adequately represent several sides to the ethical conflicts and dilemmas that contemporary psychologists face, and did not easily facilitate a career-long commitment to treating clients, employees, academic institutions, or research participants with fidelity and integrity. In actuality, students who read published materials, such as journal articles or book chapters, seemed more inspired to invest in particular topics. However, many of these excellent selections often either were burdensomely long or contained information irrelevant to psychology graduate students who were taking their first course in ethics. Moreover, readings alone could not provide the structure, context, and balance that students needed to comprehend the breadth of issues in the field, to understand the conflicts inherent in ethical decision making, and to integrate this material in a meaningful way.

As a result, for a number of years I experimented in the classroom with a hybrid approach—attempting to combine the best of both worlds. First, I gleaned materials from a wide variety of sources, including psychology journals and books, law reviews, legal decisions, statutes, and official policy documents of the APA. When appropriate, I presented only excerpts of the publications to focus attention on their most relevant and salient points, which allowed for comprehensive coverage over the course of a semester of the major ethical conflicts in psychology.

To the articles previously published, I added original explanatory writings before or after some readings as well as provided introductions to each of the topics. In this book, my comments within excerpted articles are called *Editor's Notes*, or *Ed. Notes*, whereas my notes before and after articles are offered as *Commentary*. I added these comments to illuminate the issues raised by readings, to provide thought-provoking questions, and, at times, to direct the reader to other important sources. I found that the topical organization helped to structure learning and the brief introductions to the topics provided readers with an overview and context for both the readings and the notes.

I have used successive editions of these materials since 1990, when I began teaching a course in ethics and professional issues through Hahnemann University's Department of Clinical and Health Psychology. Each year I have revised and improved the materials on the basis of informative and candid critiques by students themselves. Once I felt satisfied that they were indeed inculcating sensitivity and awareness of ethical issues and fostering the kind of ethical decision-making strategies that are respectful of the complexity of such issues, I decided to offer them to a broader audience. This book is the result.

Being fully aware of the professional need for guidance in this area, I also designed this book to be of interest and value to psychologists who have finished their formal training and are engaged in teaching, practice, and research. It is in the conduct of day-to-day professional life in psychology that ethical principles become truly compelling. It is then that perception of and sensitivity to ethical issues become paramount and that ethical decision-making skills are put to the test. Most important, it is in these practical situations that ethical problems fully reveal their ambiguity and in which psychologists may feel at sea. At such times, a book such as this can serve as an anchor—allowing psychologists a brief respite on stormy waters to study the scholarly constellations and landmarks before navigating further on their particular ethical voyage. It is my hope that this book will serve this purpose well.

For psychologists as well as students of psychology, the book is particularly timely, as it reflects the major changes that were made by the APA in 1992 to its Ethics Code, when it was renamed the *Ethical Principles of Psychologists and Code of Conduct*. I take complete responsibility for my interpretation of the past and current Ethics Codes and for the views expressed throughout the book, while applauding the APA for courageously publishing a volume that is at times critical of official APA policy. I do wish to emphasize, however, that my past and current affiliations with the APA do not imply APA endorsement of or agreement with the views expressed herein.

I now offer some words of appreciation for those who helped in the development of this book. First and foremost, I owe the greatest debt of gratitude to my students for their thoughtful and honest critiques of the material over the years. I also wish to acknowledge the support of the APA Publications and Communications Program. Executive director Gary VandenBos encouraged me early on to do this project, despite its unusual format. Julia Frank-McNeil, director of acquisitions and development for APA Books, helped shape the contours of the text during its formative stages and secured helpful, early reviews from colleagues whom I can only thank anonymously. Development editor Margaret Schlegel not only applied just the right amount and mixture of positive reinforcement and necessary prodding but also provided essential suggestions for improving the book's organization and structure. Production editor Molly Flickinger significantly improved its language and readability, with the assistance of Sarah Trembath, production assistant. Both Stan Jones, director of the APA Office of Ethics, and Ken Pope, one of the most prolific and thoughtful ethics scholars in psychology, prepared detailed critiques of the content and structure of drafts. Each of these contributions immeasurably enhanced this text. Of course, I am fully accountable for the flaws that remain.

Back home, Steven P. Frankino, dean of the Villanova Law School, sustained me with research grants for four summers while I wrote, edited, and revised the book. The Medical College of Pennsylvania—Hahnemann University, my other academic setting, provided me with Robin Lewis—one of the most efficient, intelligent, and helpful secretaries that a faculty member could hope for. Finally, I wish to thank Lowell Burket, Adam Rosen, Steve Anderer, Drew Messer, Natacha Blain, and Trudi Kirk, all of whom served as my research assistants during the writing of this text and, as such, did the "scut work"—tracking down the materials, securing readable copies, and obtaining the necessary permissions to reprint—that faculty members assiduously attempt to avoid.

If students, psychologists, or other readers have favorite articles relevant to the issues covered in this text that were not included and serve its goals, I would very much like to hear from them. Please provide me with an appropriate reprint or, at least, a citation to the reference. I will be happy to consider your suggestions for future editions.

ETHICAL CONFLICTS
IN PSYCHOLOGY

Introduction

Ethics is the study of those assumptions held by individuals, institutions, organizations, and professions that they believe will assist them in distinguishing between right and wrong and, ultimately, in making sound moral judgments (Bersoff & Koeppl, 1993; Delgado & McAllen, 1982).[1]

Consider the following situations:

1. A male faculty member is supervising the doctoral research of a female graduate student of a similar age. After several months, the student informs the professor that she would like to develop a social relationship with him and asks if they could discuss the matter over dinner.
2. In perusing an academic journal, a young assistant professor discovers that, in an article just published, an older colleague has used the work of another psychologist without proper attribution.
3. A client in serious need of intensive and long-term treatment informs his therapist that although 80% of the therapist's fees are covered by insurance, he is unable because of severe financial problems, to pay the remaining 20% of the fee and requests that the therapist forgive this copayment for the foreseeable future.
4. An industrial psychologist is told by her employer to use a test of questionable validity to assess applicants for unskilled positions in her factory.
5. A forensic psychologist who has tested a criminal defendant to evaluate whether the defendant may be excused from responsibility for a crime because he meets the test of legal "insanity" is asked by the attorney who has retained the psychologist for a hefty fee to testify that the client is, in fact, insane, although the evidence for that assertion is equivocal.

It is unlikely that all of these hypothetical but realistic situations will arise in the course of any single psychologist's work, but they are assuredly problems that confront the everyday academician and professional psychologist. Each requires the psychologist facing that particular situation to make a sound and reasoned moral judgment. But to do so requires a myriad of skills and attributes.

---

[1]Scholars who study ethics may be divided into two classes. *Descriptive ethicists* are concerned with uncovering and delineating the moral tenets of particular groups. They are like empirical scientists, gathering data about ethical beliefs in an objective and rigorous manner. Once descriptive ethicists have identified and analyzed the basic principles of morality, *normative ethicists* attempt to transform these principles into concrete, behavioral prescriptions designed to guide correct conduct. Thus, normative ethicists are more like philosophers or legislators than scientists. Formal codes of ethics are the expressions of normative ethics.

The psychologist must first be sensitive to and appreciate the fact that the situation does indeed raise an ethical and moral issue. He or she must then know what published sources are available to help resolve the situations in an ethical and moral manner. These sources include, but are not limited to, (a) the American Psychological Association's (APA's, 2002) Ethics Code; (b) other APA documents that guide teaching, practice, and research; (c) federal and state laws and regulations that affect one's work;[2] and (d) institutional or organizational policies of one's work setting.

For several reasons, however, such didactic knowledge is not enough. First, although there may be codes, guidelines, laws, and policies that will be helpful in making and evaluating an ethical decision, they are often fraught with ambiguity or written in generalized language that may not explicitly help to resolve an ethical conflict. Second, it is the rule, rather than the exception, that at any point in time more than one principle can be applied or argument made for and against adopting a particular course of action. Third, at their base level, codes and laws are grounded in such fundamental moral principles and duties as refraining from doing harm, recognizing the right of others to self-determination, or acting justly. Thus, at some point—although armed with knowledge of the rules and appreciative of his or her moral obligations (and recognizing that there may be conflicting points of view)—the psychologist must determine how he or she wants to be viewed. An ethical decision may ultimately depend on one's character and ability to act maturely, wisely, and prudently.

PURPOSE OF THE BOOK

The essential purpose of any book about ethics in psychology is to introduce readers to the formal and enforceable documents that regulate professional, scientific, and academic conduct. That is an inescapable obligation that this book seeks to fulfill. In this regard, the book will be useful to psychology graduate students in their ethics courses. In fact, because its content is relatively comprehensive and reflects the major contemporary ethical conflicts in psychology, the book can be used as a primary text in these classes. In addition, because it covers the major changes made in 2002 in the APA Ethics Code as well as the 2001 revision of the Rules and Procedures by which complaints of ethical violations are adjudicated, it can help those who are already psychologists keep abreast of these changing issues.

The book's primary purpose, however, is to help readers develop sensitivity to the ethical aspects of their work as present or future psychologists. It is intended to actuate readers to a deeper level of thought regarding these aspects and to leave them more considerate, critical, and skeptical about their own behavior and the ethical constraints under which they are asked to treat, teach about, and investigate human and animal behavior.

PLAN OF THE BOOK

To accomplish these ends, I have structured and composed this book in a way that should be useful, yet may be unfamiliar, to those in the social and behavioral sciences. I have sought to combine the benefits of historical, classical, and contemporary readings in psychology, law, and ethics with the benefits of narrative structure, engrossing questions and ethical dilemmas, and suggestions for further reading.

---

[2]These laws would include licensure or certification statutes and administrative regulations existing in the jurisdiction in which the psychologist is practicing. Often, these documents contain ethical codes that may vary from that of the APA.

The articles, chapter excerpts, legal decisions, statutes, policy documents, original chapter introductions, editor's notes, and commentaries are organized in a logical progression to teach, juxtapose points of view, stimulate discussion, and analyze and examine contemporary ethical conflicts and issues in psychology. Because I have found that students enjoy and profit from discussing ethical conflicts derived from factual situations, I have included many articles that contain vignettes presenting such conflicts and have developed some original ones as well. I recommend that teachers who use this book take full advantage of the provocative nature of these vignettes to explore the underlying and sometimes competing ethical and moral values they evoke.

The materials are organized into 10 chapters. The first chapter, "Ethics Codes and How They Are Enforced," provides a bit of history and an introduction to the myriad ethical issues facing contemporary psychologists. As a resource, it also includes an unabridged version of the current APA Ethics Code and the Rules and Procedures by which ethical complaints are adjudicated by the APA Ethics Committee, as well as a description of the sanctions the committee may levy should an ethics violation be found.

The materials in chapter 2, "How Ethics Are Applied," reveal the disparity between the lofty ideals underlying ethical codes and the extent to which those ideals are translated into the real-life behavior of psychologists. This chapter also raises issues concerning the conflict between codes of ethics and other constraints on psychologists' conduct.

Although chapter 3 has an unassuming title, "Learning Ethics," it is actually an essential and central part of the book. In fact, some teachers may want to begin their ethics course with this chapter. It presents and defines the fundamental moral principles that should serve as the foundation for any ethical code and offers several different strategies for attempting to resolve ethical dilemmas and conflicts.

Whereas the first three chapters provide a general framework for studying ethical issues, each of the remaining seven chapters examines a central and contemporary topical conflict in ethics. Chapter 4, "Confidentiality, Privilege, and Privacy," defines these essential terms and then tackles such knotty issues as protecting intimate disclosures by violent clients, by children, or by clients infected with the HIV virus. Chapter 5, "Multiple Relationships," shows how unethical behavior can arise through a variety of interactions between psychologists and clients or research participants, presents opposing views on prohibiting sexual intimacies between clients and clinicians, and offers some strategies for avoiding the almost inevitable problems that dual relationships can create. Chapters 6 and 7—"Psychological Assessment" and "Therapy and Other Forms of Intervention," respectively—cover both traditional issues inherent to these topics and more current ones, such as computerized testing and therapy, treating culturally diverse populations, and the move to gain prescription privileges so that psychologists may administer psychotropic medications.

Chapter 8, "Academia: Research, Teaching, and Supervision," includes material related to research with humans and animals generally but concentrates on the ethical dilemmas presented by deception research with humans. It also raises issues that may confront teachers of psychology, who will find that ethics codes follow them behind the ivy-covered facades of their academic institutions. Chapter 9, "Forensic Settings," may appear to focus on a narrow and specialized topic, but it actually raises issues that will increasingly face professionals and academics in psychology. The text concludes with another subject in chapter 10, "The Business of Psychology," that affects a growing number of psychologists. As the government and the courts more often perceive the provision of mental health services as a matter of commerce and profit making than as a component of a learned profession serving the public interest, there is greater scrutiny and regulation of professional practice.

There is more in this text on psychological practice than on psychologists in science or academia. Psychologists who serve clients in schools, hospitals, clinics, counseling centers, or business organizations appear to have greater opportunities to evoke complaints of ethical misconduct because of the nature of the tasks in which they engage. Nevertheless, the book does pay serious attention to the ethics of those who perform research. I have also included excerpts from those rare articles that discuss the ethics of teaching and of the student–professor relationship.

I believe that this book fulfills its intended goals and hope that readers find it not only timely, educational, and interesting but also challenging and engaging.

References

American Psychological Association. (2002). Ethical principles of psychologists and code of conduct. *American Psychologist, 57,* 1060–1073.

Bersoff, D. N., & Koeppl, P. M. (1993). The relation between ethical codes and moral principles. *Ethics & Behavior, 3,* 345–357.

Delgado, R., & McAllen, P. (1982). The moralist as expert witness. *Boston University Law Review, 62,* 869–926.

CHAPTER 1

ETHICS CODES AND HOW THEY ARE ENFORCED

Each profession shares many, varied attributes. They include selective recruitment, lengthy periods of education and training, the development of a shared language (including technical jargon), and controlled entrance into practice. A common characteristic of professions, and of occupations that would like to be perceived as professions, is the development and dissemination of a code of ethics that both emphasizes devotion to fundamental values, such as service to the public and concern for the welfare of those the profession serves, and informs the public of the positive qualities of those who pledge to adhere to the code.

Learning about ethics and the particular code of conduct promulgated by one's professional organization is, thus, one of the major and essential components of a student's socialization into the profession. Ethics teach "the way a group of associates define their special responsibility to one another and to the rest of the social order in which they work" (Erikson, 1967, p. 367). Alternatively, "Ethics is defined as the rules or standards governing the conduct of members of a profession" (Committee on Professional Practice and Standards, 2003, p. 595). The code of ethics itself, which embodies the formal expression of these responsibilities, should, therefore, instruct those who study it how to relate to their colleagues and how to fulfill their professional roles and responsibilities toward those they serve—clients, patients, employers, research participants, students, institutions, and the public at large.

Ideally, a code of ethics should serve as a guide to resolving moral problems that confront the members of the profession that promulgate it, with its primary emphasis on protecting the public that the profession serves. It should be a grand statement of overarching principles that earn the respect of that public by reflecting the profession's moral integrity. Realistically however, what a code of ethics does is validate the most recent views of a majority of professionals empowered by their colleagues to make decisions about ethical issues. Thus, a code of ethics is, inevitably, anachronistic, conservative, ethnocentric, and the product of political compromise. But recognition of that reality should not inhibit the creation of a document that fully realizes and expresses fundamental moral principles.

This chapter contributes to the socialization of psychologists by introducing readers to the profession's code of ethics—its voice of conscience. I begin by providing a brief history of the development of a code of ethics by the American Psychological Association (APA). Few know that APA established the Committee on Scientific and Professional Ethics 14 years before adopting its first ethics code in 1952. In fact, the development of an APA code was hotly debated in the 1940s and 1950s. One antagonist, eminent psychologist Calvin Hall (1952), argued that an ethics code

> plays into the hands of. . . . ; [t]he crooked operator [who] reads the code to see how much he can get away with, and since any code is bound to be filled with ambiguities and omissions, he can rationalize his unethical conduct by pointing to the code and say[ing], "See, it doesn't tell me I can't do this," or "I can interpret this to mean what I want it to mean." (p. 430)

Modern writers (Schwitzgebel & Schwitzgebel, 1980) have complained that ethics codes are "vaguely formulated and rarely enforced. Therefore they provide almost no specific and tangible guidance to either practitioners or clients" (p. 3). In this chapter, I present in its entirety the current version of the APA ethics document enacted in 2002, enforceable as of June 2003 and titled the "Ethical Principles of Psychologists and Code of Conduct." After studying this most recent version of the Code and the material that follows, the reader may want to ask whether the concerns raised by critics of ethics codes in general pertain to this current revision.

If all the APA Ethics Code did was tweak the conscience and instruct its adherents about "dos" and "don'ts," it would be no more than a book of etiquette—a manual for how scientists, academics, and practitioners should behave. But it is more than that. This Code is enforced by an ethics committee established by the APA, a major purpose of which is to adjudicate complaints of unethical behavior brought by colleagues and members of the public against APA members. In cases where the committee, as a result of its adjudication, finds that a member complained about has committed an ethical violation, it may levy sanctions itself and, in serious cases, may recommend to the APA Board of Directors that the psychologist be expelled. In some very serious cases, such organizationally imposed discipline may lead to complementary sanctions by state licensing boards or institutional employers. How the committee works, on what bases it relies to review complaints, the range of sanctions it may levy and what protections complainants and those psychologists they complain about have are all spelled out in the Rules and Procedures adopted by the ethics committee and the board of directors.

Any set of rules that potentially results in a finding that one has committed an ethical violation, that imposes penalties that consequently may damage one's professional reputation and one's economic security or that may result in the loss of one's license to practice or the right to apply for federal research grants must accord with fundamental principles of fairness, or due process. As readers scrutinize the APA's Rules and Procedures, they might ask whether they afford more due process than is necessary: That is, does the APA provide too much protection for alleged ethics violators, or not enough?

In the remaining nine chapters of this volume, I examine the kinds of ethical dilemmas psychologists commonly face. By way of introduction, I begin this chapter with a brief history of the development of the first code of ethics and the issues of concern to our progenitors almost six decades ago. I then summarize a survey of psychologists conducted more recently that describes their most troubling ethical issues. Two categories pertain to practitioners, one to academicians, and one cuts across both domains. Can you speculate as to what those categories are?

In summary, my purposes in this first chapter are to begin the processes of familiarization and socialization into the ethics of psychology and to introduce the reader to the topics addressed in later chapters of this book.

References

Committee on Professional Practice and Standards. (2003). Legal issues in the professional practice of psychology. *Professional Psychology: Research and Practice, 34,* 595–600.

Erikson, K. T. (1967). A comment on disguised observation in sociology. *Social Problems, 14,* 366–373.

Hall, C. S. (1952). Crooks, codes, and cant. *American Psychologist, 7,* 430–431.

Schwitzgebel, R. L., & Schwitzgebel, R. K. (1980). *Law and psychological practice.* New York: Wiley.

A Short History of the Development of APA's Ethics Codes

Donald N. Bersoff

The American Psychological Association (APA) was founded in 1892, but it took 60 years before it produced its first code of ethics (APA, 1953), and that occurred only after considerable debate (see, e.g., Hall, 1952). Although a Committee on Scientific and Professional Ethics was created as early as 1938, it acted informally and in the absence of any written code. It was not until a decade later that the Committee suggested that a formal code be developed. Finally, on September 4, 1952, the APA's Council of Representatives, its legislative body, adopted what it called the *Ethical Standards of Psychologists* as official policy of the APA. The standards that it promulgated were to be provisional and used for only 3 years until the membership of APA voted, principle by principle, to make them permanent.

The group drafting the first code of ethics was denominated the Committee on Ethical Standards for Psychology. Its chair was Nicholas Hobbs, and its seven other members included such luminaries as Stuart Cook, Helen Sargent, and Donald Super. It went about its task in a unique way. An earlier committee headed by Edward Tolman decided that the preparation of ethical standards should be research based:

> Many psychologists responded favorably to the proposed procedure for developing the code, because it rejected an *a priori* approach in favor of an empirical approach in which ethical principles would be based on the raw data of experience of psychologists in solving their ethical problems. (APA, 1953, p. viii)

Thus, in 1948, the then 7,500 APA members were asked in a letter to describe anonymously a situation they knew from personal experience in which a psychologist made a decision having ethical implica-

tions. The drafting committee received more than 1,000 of these reports. It then placed these ethical problems into six categories: (a) Ethical Standards and Public Responsibility, (b) Ethical Standards in Client Relationships, (c) Ethical Standards in Teaching, (d) Ethical Standards in Research, (e) Ethical Standards in Writing and Publishing, and (f) Ethical Standards in Professional Relationships.

Although the APA was by the 1950s becoming more populated by professional psychologists, it is noteworthy that only one category of the standards (client relationships) pertained to clinicians (compare this to the current Code, reprinted later in this chapter).

Drafting of the standards on the basis of the critical incidents gleaned from the 1,000 responses began shortly after 1948 and went through several revisions and publication, category by category, in the *American Psychologist* as well as after presentations at APA conventions. As noted, the final draft was submitted to the Council of Representatives for passage in September 1952.

Recent commentators have raised concerns that the two most recent versions of the Ethics Code are worded vaguely and ambiguously. The committee drafting the original Code not only had similar concerns but, more broadly, "whether to concern itself only with issues that were clearly a matter of ethics, in the sense of bearing moral implications, or whether to extend its concern to include matters of professional practice and of courtesy" (APA, 1953, p. ix). It decided on the latter course but identified these differing layers by the precision with which the standards were drafted:

> In general, principles involving issues with clear ethical import are worded strongly, in such phrases as, "it is unethical," "the psychologist is obligated," "the psychologist should," "the psychologist must." Principles involving issues of

good practice are worded less strongly, in such phrases as, "it is unprofessional," "the psychologist is expected," "good practice requires," "the psychologist should in general." Principles involving issues of courtesy or of etiquette are worded with modifying phrases which clearly indicate their nature, such as "Professional courtesy suggests," "as a matter of courtesy," etc. (APA, 1953, ix).[1]

It would be worthwhile to peruse the original standards, which are too long to reproduce here. Many of those standards would today be considered illegal (e.g., prohibitions on advertising in newspapers or on radio), and although there are cautionary principles regarding dual relationships, there is no explicit bar against sexual relationships with current or former clients, which did not appear until 1979. But, the most singular aspect of the initial Code was that its drafters eschewed an "armchair approach" (Hobbs, 1948, p. 82) in favor of "an empirically developed code" (p. 83) gleaned from critical incidents reported by members of APA itself. Or, as Golann (1969) commented, "The *Ethical Standards of Psychologists* is unique in the sense that it was based on the day-to-day decisions made by psychologists in the practice of their professions, rather than prescribed by a committee" (p. 454).

Nevertheless, as Pope and Vetter (1992) noted, "APA never again conducted a mail survey of a representative sample of the membership as the basis for revising the general code" (p. 398). The last two versions were developed by an appointed task force, although its drafts were published for comment and recommendations by the APA membership. As the 1992 Code was being drafted, however, Pope and Vetter sought to replicate the critical incident method of constructing the original Code. They sent a survey to 1,319 randomly selected APA members and fellows asking them to anonymously describe a recent ethically troubling incident. They received replies from 679 psychologists (return rate = 51%). Before the reader looks below, can you guess what were the five most troubling categories of troubling incidents?

The five categories of most concern (Pope & Vetter, 1992, p. 399) with their percentages are as follows: (a) confidentiality, 18%; (b) blurred, dual, or conflictual relationships, 17%; (c) payment sources, plans, setting, and methods, 14%; (d) academic settings, teaching dilemmas, training, 8%; and (e) forensic psychology, 5%. Readers may want to study the current Code and consider if these concerns are given proper weight in the enforceable standards.

No other category, including sexual issues, ethics codes, ethnicity, treatment records, or supervision received more than 4% of responses. Interestingly, of the five categories with the highest percent of responses, only three—dual relationships, payment issues, and one form of forensic psychology—led to a significant number of complaints to the APA Ethics Committee (see American Psychological Association, Ethics Committee, 2006). Confidentiality and academic issues, rarely, if ever, result in ethics complaints to APA.

References

American Psychological Association. (1953). *Ethical standards of psychologists*. Washington, DC: Author.

American Psychological Association, Ethics Committee. (2006). Report of the Ethics Committee, 2005. *American Psychologist, 61*, 522–529.

Golann, S. E., (1969). Emerging areas of ethical concern. *American Psychologist, 24*, 454–459.

Hall, C. S. (1952). Crooks, codes, and cants. *American Psychologist, 7*, 430–431.

Hobbs, N. (1948). The development of a code of ethical standards for psychology. *American Psychologist, 3*, 80–84.

Pope, K. S., & Vetter, V. A. (1992). Ethical dilemmas encountered by members of the American Psychological Association: A national survey. *American Psychologist, 47*, 397–411.

◆   ◆   ◆

Commentary: Pope and Vetter (1992) provided an introduction to the wide variety of ethical issues that psychologists face as teachers, scholars, and professionals. All these issues are addressed in subsequent chapters of this book in great detail. For additional discussions of

---

[1]Compare this discussion with the statement concerning the use of modifiers in the Introduction and Applicability section of the current Code, reproduced later in this chapter.

the types of conduct that lead to ethical scrutiny, see, e.g., Ford, G. (2001). Ethical reasoning in the mental health professions. *Boca Raton: CRC Press; Hanson, S. L., Kerkhoff, T. R., & Bush, S. S. (2005). Health care ethics for psychologists. Washington, DC: American Psychological Association; Peterson, C. (1996). Common problem areas and their causes resulting in disciplinary actions. In L. Bass, S. DeMers, J. Ogloff, C. Peterson, J. Pettifor, R. Reaves, et al.* (Eds.), Professional conduct and discipline in psychology (pp. 71–89). Washington, DC: American Psychological Association.

Both the Ford (2001) and Bass et al. (1996) texts provide a more extensive history of the development of codes of ethics. The original APA Code adopted in 1952 has had nine descendants including the current Code. See American Psychological Association (2002). Ethical principles of psychologists and code of conduct. American Psychologist, 57, 1060–1073.

The 1992 revision, the current Code's immediate predecessor, was adopted for at least two reasons. First, the Federal Trade Commission expressed serious concerns about the legality of some of the provisions in the 1981 Code. For a discussion of why the U.S. government was interested in APA's Ethics Code, see chapter 10 ("The Business of Psychology"). Second, many of the provisions in the 1981 Code were considered ambiguous. In fact, application of this Code was challenged by a clinician who was disciplined by his state licensure board. In that 1990 case,[2] the board voted to revoke the psychologist's license to practice for violating the 1981 ethical principles. Such action is not atypical. Many state laws regulating psychologists incorporate the APA Ethics Code. Where this is true, if a licensed psychologist violates APA's ethical principles, then he or she is subject to disciplinary action by the relevant state board. See, e.g., Kirkland, K., Kirkland, K. L., & Reaves, R. P. (2004). On the professional use of disciplinary data. Professional Psychology: Research and Practice, 35, 179–184. The most severe form of discipline is revocation of the license to practice, a sanction with serious economic consequences. See, e.g., Schoenfeld, L., Hatch, J., & Gonzalez, J. (2001). Responses of psychologists to complaints filed against them with a state licensing board. Professional Psychology: Research and Practice, 32, 491–495. *Because of the magnitude of the board's decision, the psychologist challenged the board's actions claiming that the various then-enforceable preambles and principles under which he was charged were unconstitutionally vague and did not provide him with proper notice of potential misconduct. Essentially, he alleged that, under the state and federal constitutions, it was fundamentally unfair for the state to deprive him of his right to practice on the basis of standards that were not comprehensible to the reasonably intelligent psychologist, a violation of due process.*

With regard to the preambles to various principles in the 1981 Code, the court agreed. Their language, the court held, failed to inform licensees of what conduct was forbidden. Although it rejected the psychologist's claim that the specific principles under which he was charged were also unconstitutional, the court stated:

> *Psychologists . . . have a right and fundamental need to be guided by Ethical Codes of Conduct of sufficient clarity and specificity to meet applicable constitutional standards and to adequately apprise practitioners of the boundaries of conduct. Although we have concluded that those principles in question meet such standards, suffice it to say that for the most part, it is by the slimmest of margins. (White v. North Carolina State Board, 1990)*

Such indeterminancy disserved organized psychology and its members. Thus, the 1992 Code was awaited with positive anticipation but, unfortunately, proved to be quite controversial. It was formally reviewed by a number of respected psychologists with experience in ethics in a special section of an APA journal. See Keith-Spiegel, P. (Ed). (1994). The 1992 Ethics Code: Boon or bane? Professional Psychology: Research and Practice, 25, 315–387. Whether from the perspective of science, practice, or public interest, most of the commentators applauded the broadened attention to important issues, but they also found that the new Code lacked clarity, contained qualifying language that

---

[2]White v. North Carolina State Board of Examiners of Practicing Psychologists, 97 N.C. App. 144, 388 S.E. 2d 148 (1990), *review denied*, 326 N.C. 601, 393 S.E. 2d 891 (1990).

would make many provisions unenforceable, and would not completely fulfill its mission of protecting the public. This led to the 5-year-long effort, described in the paragraphs that follow, to create a new and improved Ethics Code.

The APA Ethics Code is considered an expression of APA policy. Barring an emergency, all APA policy is adopted by its legislative body, the Council of Representatives. The Council also promulgates Association Rules (ARs)—regulations for administering the APA's governance structure. AR 20-4.1 states:

> The Ethics Committee shall have the responsibility from time to time of initiating a review of the latest formally adopted version of the ethics code . . . and proposing necessary changes or additions. In carrying out such a review, the Ethics Committee may set up such ad hoc committees as it finds necessary.

An Ethics Code Task Force appointed in 1997 by the Ethics Committee drafted the 2002 Code. After some minor amendments, it was adopted unanimously by the Council at the 2002 APA convention and became enforceable as of June 2003. For brief descriptions of the task force, see APA Ethics Committee. (2002). Report of the Ethics Committee, 2001. American Psychologist, 57, 646–653; APA Ethics Committee. (1998). Report of the Ethics Committee, 1997. American Psychologist, 53, 960–980; APA Ethics Committee. (1996). Report of the Ethics Committee, 1995. American Psychologist, 52, 897–905.

There is some consensus that two major purposes for codes of ethics are "(1) to promote optimal behavior by providing aspirational principles that encourage reflection and decision making within a moral framework, and (2) to regulate professional behavior through monitoring and through disciplinary action against those who violate prescriptive and enforceable standards of conduct" (p. 264). Pettifor, J. L. (2004). Professional ethics across national boundaries. European Psychologist, 9, 264–272. See also Fisher, C. B. (2004). Challenges in constructing a cross-national ethics code for psychologists. European Psychologist, 9, 273–277 (the purposes of an ethics code are to establish a profession, socialize a profession, and gain public trust that a profession is populated by members with high standards).

The 2002 Code reorganizes and rewords many of the provisions of the 1992 Code. See Knapp, S., & Vandecreek, L. (2003). An overview of the major changes in the 2002 APA Ethics Code. Professional Psychology: Research and Practice, 34, 301–308. Where discussions of the 1992 provisions appear in the material excerpted throughout the text (and still quite relevant) I have indicated in footnotes the corollary provisions in the 2002 Code. As readers examine this newest code of conduct and the rules and procedures by which they are enforced, they should come to their own conclusions about whether they are comprehensible, a significant improvement over prior efforts, and most importantly, whether the code is useful in resolving ethical dilemmas and whether both documents fulfill the purposes posited by Pettifor.

Ethical Principles of Psychologists and Code of Conduct

American Psychological Association

INTRODUCTION AND APPLICABILITY

The American Psychological Association's (APA's) Ethical Principles of Psychologists and Code of Conduct (hereinafter referred to as the Ethics Code) consists of an introduction, a Preamble, five General Principles (A–E), and specific Ethical Standards. The Introduction discusses the intent, organization, procedural considerations, and scope of application of the Ethics Code. The Preamble and General Principles are aspirational goals to guide psychologists toward the highest ideals of psychology. Although the Preamble and General Principles are not themselves enforceable rules, they should be considered by psychologists in arriving at an ethical course of action. The Ethical Standards set forth enforceable rules for conduct as psychologists. Most of the Ethical Standards are written broadly, in order to apply to psychologists in varied roles, although the application of an Ethical Standard may vary depending on the context. The Ethical Standards are not exhaustive. The fact that a given conduct is not specifically addressed by an Ethical Standard does not mean that it is necessarily either ethical or unethical.

This Ethics Code applies only to psychologists' activities that are part of their scientific, educational, or professional roles as psychologists. Areas covered include but are not limited to the clinical, counseling, and school practice of psychology; research; teaching; supervision of trainees; public service; policy development; social intervention; development of assessment instruments; conducting assessments; educational counseling; organizational consulting; forensic activities; program design and evaluation; and administration. This Ethics Code applies to these activities across a variety of contexts, such as in person, postal, telephone, Internet, and other electronic transmissions. These activities shall be distinguished from the purely private conduct of psychologists, which is not within the purview of the Ethics Code.

Membership in the APA commits members and student affiliates to comply with the standards of the APA Ethics Code and to the rules and procedures used to enforce them. Lack of awareness or misunderstanding of an Ethical Standard is not itself a defense to a charge of unethical conduct.

From *American Psychologist, 57,* 1060–1073. Copyright 2002 by the American Psychological Association.

This version of the APA Ethics Code was adopted by the American Psychological Association's Council of Representatives during its meeting, August 21, 2002, and is effective beginning June 1, 2003. Inquiries concerning the substance or interpretation of the APA Ethics Code should be addressed to the Director, Office of Ethics, American Psychological Association, 750 First Street, NE, Washington, DC 20002-4242. The Ethics Code and information regarding the Code can be found on the APA Web site, http://www.apa.org/ethics. The standards in this Ethics Code will be used to adjudicate complaints brought concerning alleged conduct occurring on or after the effective date. Complaints regarding conduct occurring prior to the effective date will be adjudicated on the basis of the version of the Ethics Code that was in effect at the time the conduct occurred.

The APA has previously published its Ethics Code as follows:

American Psychological Association. (1953). *Ethical standards of psychologists.* Washington, DC: Author.
American Psychological Association. (1959). Ethical standards of psychologists. *American Psychologist, 14,* 279–282.
American Psychological Association. (1963). Ethical standards of psychologists. *American Psychologist, 18,* 56–60.
American Psychological Association. (1968). Ethical standards of psychologists. *American Psychologist, 23,* 357–361.
American Psychological Association. (1977, March). Ethical standards of psychologists. *APA Monitor,* 22–23.
American Psychological Association. (1979). *Ethical standards of psychologists.* Washington, DC: Author.
American Psychological Association. (1981). Ethical principles of psychologists. *American Psychologist, 36,* 633–638.
American Psychological Association. (1990). Ethical principles of psychologists (Amended June 2, 1989). *American Psychologist, 45,* 390–395.
American Psychological Association. (1992). Ethical principles of psychologists and code of conduct. *American Psychologist, 47,* 1597–1611.

Request copies of the APA's Ethical Principles of Psychologists and Code of Conduct from the APA Order Department, 750 First Street, NE, Washington, DC 20002-4242, or phone (202) 336-5510.

The procedures for filing, investigating, and resolving complaints of unethical conduct are described in the current Rules and Procedures of the APA Ethics Committee. APA may impose sanctions on its members for violations of the standards of the Ethics Code, including termination of APA membership, and may notify other bodies and individuals of its actions. Actions that violate the standards of the Ethics Code may also lead to the imposition of sanctions on psychologists or students whether or not they are APA members by bodies other than APA, including state psychological associations, other professional groups, psychology boards, other state or federal agencies, and payors for health services. In addition, APA may take action against a member after his or her conviction of a felony, expulsion or suspension from an affiliated state psychological association, or suspension or loss of licensure. When the sanction to be imposed by APA is less than expulsion, the 2001 Rules and Procedures do not guarantee an opportunity for an in-person hearing, but generally provide that complaints will be resolved only on the basis of a submitted record.

The Ethics Code is intended to provide guidance for psychologists and standards of professional conduct that can be applied by the APA and by other bodies that choose to adopt them. The Ethics Code is not intended to be a basis of civil liability. Whether a psychologist has violated the Ethics Code standards does not by itself determine whether the psychologist is legally liable in a court action, whether a contract is enforceable, or whether other legal consequences occur.

The modifiers used in some of the standards of this Ethics Code (e.g., *reasonably, appropriate, potentially*) are included in the standards when they would (1) allow professional judgment on the part of psychologists, (2) eliminate injustice or inequality that would occur without the modifier, (3) ensure applicability across the broad range of activities conducted by psychologists, or (4) guard against a set of rigid rules that might be quickly outdated. As used in this Ethics Code, the term *reasonable* means the prevailing professional judgment of psychologists engaged in similar activities in similar circumstances, given the knowledge the psychologist had or should have had at the time.

In the process of making decisions regarding their professional behavior, psychologists must consider this Ethics Code in addition to applicable laws and psychology board regulations. In applying the Ethics Code to their professional work, psychologists may consider other materials and guidelines that have been adopted or endorsed by scientific and professional psychological organizations and the dictates of their own conscience, as well as consult with others within the field. If this Ethics Code establishes a higher standard of conduct than is required by law, psychologists must meet the higher ethical standard. If psychologists' ethical responsibilities conflict with law, regulations, or other governing legal authority, psychologists make known their commitment to this Ethics Code and take steps to resolve the conflict in a responsible manner. If the conflict is unresolvable via such means, psychologists may adhere to the requirements of the law, regulations, or other governing authority in keeping with basic principles of human rights.

PREAMBLE

Psychologists are committed to increasing scientific and professional knowledge of behavior and people's understanding of themselves and others and to the use of such knowledge to improve the condition of individuals, organizations, and society. Psychologists respect and protect civil and human rights and the central importance of freedom of inquiry and expression in research, teaching, and publication. They strive to help the public in developing informed judgments and choices concerning human behavior. In doing so, they perform many roles, such as researcher, educator, diagnostician, therapist, supervisor, consultant, administrator, social interventionist, and expert witness. This Ethics Code provides a common set of principles and standards upon which psychologists build their professional and scientific work.

This Ethics Code is intended to provide specific standards to cover most situations encountered by psychologists. It has as its goals the welfare and protection of the individuals and groups with whom psychologists work and the education of members, students, and the public regarding ethical standards of the discipline.

The development of a dynamic set of ethical standards for psychologists' work-related conduct requires a personal commitment and lifelong effort to act ethically; to encourage ethical behavior by students, supervisees, employees, and colleagues; and to consult with others concerning ethical problems.

GENERAL PRINCIPLES

This section consists of General Principles. General Principles, as opposed to Ethical Standards, are aspirational in nature. Their intent is to guide and inspire psychologists toward the very highest ethical ideals of the profession. General Principles, in contrast to Ethical Standards, do not represent obligations and should not form the basis for imposing sanctions. Relying upon General Principles for either of these reasons distorts both their meaning and purpose.

Principle A: Beneficence and Nonmaleficence

Psychologists strive to benefit those with whom they work and take care to do no harm. In their professional actions, psychologists seek to safeguard the welfare and rights of those with whom they interact professionally and other affected persons, and the welfare of animal subjects of research. When conflicts occur among psychologists' obligations or concerns, they attempt to resolve these conflicts in a responsible fashion that avoids or minimizes harm. Because psychologists' scientific and professional judgments and actions may affect the lives of others, they are alert to and guard against personal, financial, social, organizational, or political factors that might lead to misuse of their influence. Psychologists strive to be aware of the possible effect of their own physical and mental health on their ability to help those with whom they work.

Principle B: Fidelity and Responsibility

Psychologists establish relationships of trust with those with whom they work. They are aware of their professional and scientific responsibilities to society

and to the specific communities in which they work. Psychologists uphold professional standards of conduct, clarify their professional roles and obligations, accept appropriate responsibility for their behavior, and seek to manage conflicts of interest that could lead to exploitation or harm. Psychologists consult with, refer to, or cooperate with other professionals and institutions to the extent needed to serve the best interests of those with whom they work. They are concerned about the ethical compliance of their colleagues' scientific and professional conduct. Psychologists strive to contribute a portion of their professional time for little or no compensation or personal advantage.

Principle C: Integrity

Psychologists seek to promote accuracy, honesty, and truthfulness in the science, teaching, and practice of psychology. In these activities psychologists do not steal, cheat, or engage in fraud, subterfuge, or intentional misrepresentation of fact. Psychologists strive to keep their promises and to avoid unwise or unclear commitments. In situations in which deception may be ethically justifiable to maximize benefits and minimize harm, psychologists have a serious obligation to consider the need for, the possible consequences of, and their responsibility to correct any resulting mistrust or other harmful effects that arise from the use of such techniques.

Principle D: Justice

Psychologists recognize that fairness and justice entitle all persons to access to and benefit from the contributions of psychology and to equal quality in the processes, procedures, and services being conducted by psychologists. Psychologists exercise reasonable judgment and take precautions to ensure that their potential biases, the boundaries of their competence, and the limitations of their expertise do not lead to or condone unjust practices.

Principle E: Respect for People's Rights and Dignity

Psychologists respect the dignity and worth of all people, and the rights of individuals to privacy, confidentiality, and self-determination. Psychologists are aware that special safeguards may be necessary to protect the rights and welfare of persons or communities whose vulnerabilities impair autonomous decision making. Psychologists are aware of and respect cultural, individual, and role differences, including those based on age, gender, gender identity, race, ethnicity, culture, national origin, religion, sexual orientation, disability, language, and socioeconomic status, and consider these factors when working with members of such groups. Psychologists try to eliminate the effect on their work of biases based on those factors, and they do not knowingly participate in or condone activities of others based upon such prejudices.

ETHICAL STANDARDS

1. Resolving Ethical Issues

1.01 Misuse of psychologists' work. If psychologists learn of misuse or misrepresentation of their work, they take reasonable steps to correct or minimize the misuse or misrepresentation.

1.02 Conflicts between ethics and law, regulations, or other governing legal authority. If psychologists' ethical responsibilities conflict with law, regulations, or other governing legal authority, psychologists make known their commitment to the Ethics Code and take steps to resolve the conflict. If the conflict is unresolvable via such means, psychologists may adhere to the requirements of the law, regulations, or other governing legal authority.

1.03 Conflicts between ethics and organizational demands. If the demands of an organization with which psychologists are affiliated or for whom they are working conflict with this Ethics Code, psychologists clarify the nature of the conflict, make known their commitment to the Ethics Code, and to the extent feasible, resolve the conflict in a way that permits adherence to the Ethics Code.

1.04 Informal resolution of ethical violations. When psychologists believe that there may have been an ethical violation by another psychologist, they attempt to resolve the issue by bringing it to the attention of that individual, if an informal reso-

lution appears appropriate and the intervention does not violate any confidentiality rights that may be involved. (See also Standards 1.02, Conflicts Between Ethics and Law, Regulations, or Other Governing Legal Authority, and 1.03, Conflicts Between Ethics and Organizational Demands.)

1.05 Reporting ethical violations. If an apparent ethical violation has substantially harmed or is likely to substantially harm a person or organization and is not appropriate for informal resolution under Standard 1.04, Informal Resolution of Ethical Violations, or is not resolved properly in that fashion, psychologists take further action appropriate to the situation. Such action might include referral to state or national committees on professional ethics, to state licensing boards, or to the appropriate institutional authorities. This standard does not apply when an intervention would violate confidentiality rights or when psychologists have been retained to review the work of another psychologist whose professional conduct is in question. (See also Standard 1.02, Conflicts Between Ethics and Law, Regulations, or Other Governing Legal Authority.)

1.06 Cooperating with ethics committees. Psychologists cooperate in ethics investigations, proceedings, and resulting requirements of the APA or any affiliated state psychological association to which they belong. In doing so, they address any confidentiality issues. Failure to cooperate is itself an ethics violation. However, making a request for deferment of adjudication of an ethics complaint pending the outcome of litigation does not alone constitute noncooperation.

1.07 Improper complaints. Psychologists do not file or encourage the filing of ethics complaints that are made with reckless disregard for or willful ignorance of facts that would disprove the allegation.

1.08 Unfair discrimination against complainants and respondents. Psychologists do not deny persons employment, advancement, admissions to academic or other programs, tenure, or promotion, based solely upon their having made or their being the subject of an ethics complaint. This does not preclude taking action based upon the outcome of such proceedings or considering other appropriate information.

2. Competence

2.01 Boundaries of competence. (a) Psychologists provide services, teach, and conduct research with populations and in areas only within the boundaries of their competence, based on their education, training, supervised experience, consultation, study, or professional experience.

(b) Where scientific or professional knowledge in the discipline of psychology establishes that an understanding of factors associated with age, gender, gender identity, race, ethnicity, culture, national origin, religion, sexual orientation, disability, language, or socioeconomic status is essential for effective implementation of their services or research, psychologists have or obtain the training, experience, consultation, or supervision necessary to ensure the competence of their services, or they make appropriate referrals, except as provided in Standard 2.02, Providing Services in Emergencies.

(c) Psychologists planning to provide services, teach, or conduct research involving populations, areas, techniques, or technologies new to them undertake relevant education, training, supervised experience, consultation, or study.

(d) When psychologists are asked to provide services to individuals for whom appropriate mental health services are not available and for which psychologists have not obtained the competence necessary, psychologists with closely related prior training or experience may provide such services in order to ensure that services are not denied if they make a reasonable effort to obtain the competence required by using relevant research, training, consultation, or study.

(e) In those emerging areas in which generally recognized standards for preparatory training do not yet exist, psychologists nevertheless take reasonable steps to ensure the competence of their work and to protect clients/patients, students, supervisees, research participants, organizational clients, and others from harm.

(f) When assuming forensic roles, psychologists are or become reasonably familiar with the judicial or administrative rules governing their roles.

2.02 Providing services in emergencies. In emergencies, when psychologists provide services to individuals for whom other mental health services are not available and for which psychologists have not obtained the necessary training, psychologists may provide such services in order to ensure that services are not denied. The services are discontinued as soon as the emergency has ended or appropriate services are available.

2.03 Maintaining competence. Psychologists undertake ongoing efforts to develop and maintain their competence.

2.04 Bases for scientific and professional judgments. Psychologists' work is based upon established scientific and professional knowledge of the discipline. (See also Standards 2.01e, Boundaries of Competence, and 10.01b, Informed Consent to Therapy.)

2.05 Delegation of work to others. Psychologists who delegate work to employees, supervisees, or research or teaching assistants or who use the services of others, such as interpreters, take reasonable steps to (1) avoid delegating such work to persons who have a multiple relationship with those being served that would likely lead to exploitation or loss of objectivity; (2) authorize only those responsibilities that such persons can be expected to perform competently on the basis of their education, training, or experience, either independently or with the level of supervision being provided; and (3) see that such persons perform these services competently. (See also Standards 2.02, Providing Services in Emergencies; 3.05, Multiple Relationships; 4.01, Maintaining Confidentiality; 9.01, Bases for Assessments; 9.02, Use of Assessments; 9.03, Informed Consent in Assessments; and 9.07, Assessment by Unqualified Persons.)

2.06 Personal problems and conflicts. (a) Psychologists refrain from initiating an activity when they know or should know that there is a substantial likelihood that their personal problems will prevent them from performing their work-related activities in a competent manner.

(b) When psychologists become aware of personal problems that may interfere with their performing work-related duties adequately, they take appropriate measures, such as obtaining professional consultation or assistance, and determine whether they should limit, suspend, or terminate their work-related duties. (See also Standard 10.10, Terminating Therapy.)

3. Human Relations

3.01 Unfair discrimination. In their work-related activities, psychologists do not engage in unfair discrimination based on age, gender, gender identity, race, ethnicity, culture, national origin, religion, sexual orientation, disability, socioeconomic status, or any basis proscribed by law.

3.02 Sexual harassment. Psychologists do not engage in sexual harassment. Sexual harassment is sexual solicitation, physical advances, or verbal or nonverbal conduct that is sexual in nature, that occurs in connection with the psychologist's activities or roles as a psychologist, and that either (1) is unwelcome, is offensive, or creates a hostile workplace or educational environment, and the psychologist knows or is told this or (2) is sufficiently severe or intense to be abusive to a reasonable person in the context. Sexual harassment can consist of a single intense or severe act or of multiple persistent or pervasive acts. (See also Standard 1.08, Unfair Discrimination Against Complainants and Respondents.)

3.03 Other harassment. Psychologists do not knowingly engage in behavior that is harassing or demeaning to persons with whom they interact in their work based on factors such as those persons' age, gender, gender identity, race, ethnicity, culture, national origin, religion, sexual orientation, disability, language, or socioeconomic status.

3.04 Avoiding harm. Psychologists take reasonable steps to avoid harming their clients/patients, students, supervisees, research participants, organizational clients, and others with whom they work, and to minimize harm where it is foreseeable and unavoidable.

3.05 Multiple relationships. (a) A multiple relationship occurs when a psychologist is in a professional role with a person and (1) at the same time is in another role with the same person, (2) at the same time is in a relationship with a person closely associated with or related to the person with whom the psychologist has the professional relationship, or (3) promises to enter into another relationship in the future with the person or a person closely associated with or related to the person.

A psychologist refrains from entering into a multiple relationship if the multiple relationship could reasonably be expected to impair the psychologist's objectivity, competence, or effectiveness in performing his or her functions as a psychologist, or otherwise risks exploitation or harm to the person with whom the professional relationship exists.

Multiple relationships that would not reasonably be expected to cause impairment or risk exploitation or harm are not unethical.

(b) If a psychologist finds that, due to unforeseen factors, a potentially harmful multiple relationship has arisen, the psychologist takes reasonable steps to resolve it with due regard for the best interests of the affected person and maximal compliance with the Ethics Code.

(c) When psychologists are required by law, institutional policy, or extraordinary circumstances to serve in more than one role in judicial or administrative proceedings, at the outset they clarify role expectations and the extent of confidentiality and thereafter as changes occur. (See also Standards 3.04, Avoiding Harm, and 3.07, Third-Party Requests for Services.)

3.06 Conflict of interest. Psychologists refrain from taking on a professional role when personal, scientific, professional, legal, financial, or other interests or relationships could reasonably be expected to (1) impair their objectivity, competence, or effectiveness in performing their functions as psychologists or (2) expose the person or organization with whom the professional relationship exists to harm or exploitation.

3.07 Third-party requests for services. When psychologists agree to provide services to a person or entity at the request of a third party, psychologists attempt to clarify at the outset of the service the nature of the relationship with all individuals or organizations involved. This clarification includes the role of the psychologist (e.g., therapist, consultant, diagnostician, or expert witness), an identification of who is the client, the probable uses of the services provided or the information obtained, and the fact that there may be limits to confidentiality. (See also Standards 3.05, Multiple Relationships, and 4.02, Discussing the Limits of Confidentiality.)

3.08 Exploitative relationships. Psychologists do not exploit persons over whom they have supervisory, evaluative, or other authority such as clients/patients, students, supervisees, research participants, and employees. (See also Standards 3.05, Multiple Relationships; 6.04, Fees and Financial Arrangements; 6.05, Barter With Clients/Patients; 7.07, Sexual Relationships With Students and Supervisees; 10.05, Sexual Intimacies With Current Therapy Clients/Patients; 10.06, Sexual Intimacies With Relatives or Significant Others of Current Therapy Clients/Patients; 10.07, Therapy With Former Sexual Partners; and 10.08, Sexual Intimacies With Former Therapy Clients/Patients.)

3.09 Cooperation with other professionals. When indicated and professionally appropriate, psychologists cooperate with other professionals in order to serve their clients/patients effectively and appropriately. (See also Standard 4.05, Disclosures.)

3.10 Informed consent. (a) When psychologists conduct research or provide assessment, therapy, counseling, or consulting services in person or via electronic transmission or other forms of communication, they obtain the informed consent of the individual or individuals using language that is reasonably understandable to that person or persons except when conducting such activities without consent is mandated by law or governmental regulation or as otherwise provided in this Ethics Code. (See also Standards 8.02, Informed Consent to Research; 9.03, Informed Consent in Assessments; and 10.01, Informed Consent to Therapy.)

(b) For persons who are legally incapable of giving informed consent, psychologists nevertheless (1) provide an appropriate explanation, (2) seek the individual's assent, (3) consider such persons' preferences and best interests, and (4) obtain appropriate permission from a legally authorized person, if

such substitute consent is permitted or required by law. When consent by a legally authorized person is not permitted or required by law, psychologists take reasonable steps to protect the individual's rights and welfare.

(c) When psychological services are court ordered or otherwise mandated, psychologists inform the individual of the nature of the anticipated services, including whether the services are court ordered or mandated and any limits of confidentiality, before proceeding.

(d) Psychologists appropriately document written or oral consent, permission, and assent. (See also Standards 8.02, Informed Consent to Research; 9.03, Informed Consent in Assessments; and 10.01, Informed Consent to Therapy.)

3.11 Psychological services delivered to or through organizations. (a) Psychologists delivering services to or through organizations provide information beforehand to clients and when appropriate those directly affected by the services about (1) the nature and objectives of the services, (2) the intended recipients, (3) which of the individuals are clients, (4) the relationship the psychologist will have with each person and the organization, (5) the probable uses of services provided and information obtained, (6) who will have access to the information, and (7) limits of confidentiality. As soon as feasible, they provide information about the results and conclusions of such services to appropriate persons.

(b) If psychologists will be precluded by law or by organizational roles from providing such information to particular individuals or groups, they so inform those individuals or groups at the outset of the service.

3.12 Interruption of psychological services. Unless otherwise covered by contract, psychologists make reasonable efforts to plan for facilitating services in the event that psychological services are interrupted by factors such as the psychologist's illness, death, unavailability, relocation, or retirement or by the client's/patient's relocation or financial limitations. (See also Standard 6.02c, Maintenance, Dissemination, and Disposal of Confidential Records of Professional and Scientific Work.)

4. Privacy and Confidentiality

4.01 Maintaining confidentiality. Psychologists have a primary obligation and take reasonable precautions to protect confidential information obtained through or stored in any medium, recognizing that the extent and limits of confidentiality may be regulated by law or established by institutional rules or professional or scientific relationship. (See also Standard 2.05, Delegation of Work to Others.)

4.02 Discussing the limits of confidentiality. (a) Psychologists discuss with persons (including, to the extent feasible, persons who are legally incapable of giving informed consent and their legal representatives) and organizations with whom they establish a scientific or professional relationship (1) the relevant limits of confidentiality and (2) the foreseeable uses of the information generated through their psychological activities. (See also Standard 3.10, Informed Consent.)

(b) Unless it is not feasible or is contraindicated, the discussion of confidentiality occurs at the outset of the relationship and thereafter as new circumstances may warrant.

(c) Psychologists who offer services, products, or information via electronic transmission inform clients/patients of the risks to privacy and limits of confidentiality.

4.03 Recording. Before recording the voices or images of individuals to whom they provide services, psychologists obtain permission from all such persons or their legal representatives. (See also Standards 8.03, Informed Consent for Recording Voices and Images in Research; 8.05, Dispensing With Informed Consent for Research; and 8.07, Deception in Research.)

4.04 Minimizing intrusions on privacy. (a) Psychologists include in written and oral reports and consultations, only information germane to the purpose for which the communication is made.

(b) Psychologists discuss confidential information obtained in their work only for appropriate scientific or professional purposes and only with persons clearly concerned with such matters.

4.05 Disclosures. (a) Psychologists may disclose confidential information with the appropriate consent of the organizational client, the individual client/patient, or another legally authorized person on behalf of the client/patient unless prohibited by law.

(b) Psychologists disclose confidential information without the consent of the individual only as mandated by law, or where permitted by law for a valid purpose such as to (1) provide needed professional services; (2) obtain appropriate professional consultations; (3) protect the client/patient, psychologist, or others from harm; or (4) obtain payment for services from a client/patient, in which instance disclosure is limited to the minimum that is necessary to achieve the purpose. (See also Standard 6.04e, Fees and Financial Arrangements.)

4.06 Consultations. When consulting with colleagues, (1) psychologists do not disclose confidential information that reasonably could lead to the identification of a client/patient, research participant, or other person or organization with whom they have a confidential relationship unless they have obtained the prior consent of the person or organization or the disclosure cannot be avoided, and (2) they disclose information only to the extent necessary to achieve the purposes of the consultation. (See also Standard 4.01, Maintaining Confidentiality.)

4.07 Use of confidential information for didactic or other purposes. Psychologists do not disclose in their writings, lectures, or other public media, confidential, personally identifiable information concerning their clients/patients, students, research participants, organizational clients, or other recipients of their services that they obtained during the course of their work, unless (1) they take reasonable steps to disguise the person or organization, (2) the person or organization has consented in writing, or (3) there is legal authorization for doing so.

5. Advertising and Other Public Statements

5.01 Avoidance of false or deceptive statements. (a) Public statements include but are not limited to paid or unpaid advertising, product endorsements, grant applications, licensing applications, other credentialing applications, brochures, printed matter, directory listings, personal resumes or curricula vitae, or comments for use in media such as print or electronic transmission, statements in legal proceedings, lectures and public oral presentations, and published materials. Psychologists do not knowingly make public statements that are false, deceptive, or fraudulent concerning their research, practice, or other work activities or those of persons or organizations with which they are affiliated.

(b) Psychologists do not make false, deceptive, or fraudulent statements concerning (1) their training, experience, or competence; (2) their academic degrees; (3) their credentials; (4) their institutional or association affiliations; (5) their services; (6) the scientific or clinical basis for, or results or degree of success of, their services; (7) their fees; or (8) their publications or research findings.

(c) Psychologists claim degrees as credentials for their health services only if those degrees (1) were earned from a regionally accredited educational institution or (2) were the basis for psychology licensure by the state in which they practice.

5.02 Statements by others. (a) Psychologists who engage others to create or place public statements that promote their professional practice, products, or activities retain professional responsibility for such statements.

(b) Psychologists do not compensate employees of press, radio, television, or other communication media in return for publicity in a news item. (See also Standard 1.01, Misuse of Psychologists' Work.)

(c) A paid advertisement relating to psychologists' activities must be identified or clearly recognizable as such.

5.03 Descriptions of workshops and non-degree-granting educational programs. To the degree to which they exercise control, psychologists responsible for announcements, catalogs, brochures, or advertisements describing workshops, seminars, or other non-degree-granting educational programs ensure that they accurately describe the audience for which the program is intended, the educational objectives, the presenters, and the fees involved.

5.04 Media presentations. When psychologists provide public advice or comment via print,

Internet, or other electronic transmission, they take precautions to ensure that statements (1) are based on their professional knowledge, training, or experience in accord with appropriate psychological literature and practice; (2) are otherwise consistent with this Ethics Code; and (3) do not indicate that a professional relationship has been established with the recipient. (See also Standard 2.04, Bases for Scientific and Professional Judgments.)

5.05 Testimonials. Psychologists do not solicit testimonials from current therapy clients/patients or other persons who because of their particular circumstances are vulnerable to undue influence.

5.06 In-person solicitation. Psychologists do not engage, directly or through agents, in uninvited in-person solicitation of business from actual or potential therapy clients/patients or other persons who because of their particular circumstances are vulnerable to undue influence. However, this prohibition does not preclude (1) attempting to implement appropriate collateral contacts for the purpose of benefiting an already engaged therapy client/patient or (2) providing disaster or community outreach services.

6. Record Keeping and Fees

6.01 Documentation of professional and scientific work and maintenance of records. Psychologists create, and to the extent the records are under their control, maintain, disseminate, store, retain, and dispose of records and data relating to their professional and scientific work in order to (1) facilitate provision of services later by them or by other professionals, (2) allow for replication of research design and analyses, (3) meet institutional requirements, (4) ensure accuracy of billing and payments, and (5) ensure compliance with law. (See also Standard 4.01, Maintaining Confidentiality.)

6.02 Maintenance, dissemination, and disposal of confidential records of professional and scientific work. (a) Psychologists maintain confidentiality in creating, storing, accessing, transferring, and disposing of records under their control, whether these are written, automated, or in any other medium. (See also Standards 4.01, Maintaining Confidentiality, and 6.01, Documentation of Professional and Scientific Work and Maintenance of Records.)

(b) If confidential information concerning recipients of psychological services is entered into databases or systems of records available to persons whose access has not been consented to by the recipient, psychologists use coding or other techniques to avoid the inclusion of personal identifiers.

(c) Psychologists make plans in advance to facilitate the appropriate transfer and to protect the confidentiality of records and data in the event of psychologists' withdrawal from positions or practice. (See also Standards 3.12, Interruption of Psychological Services, and 10.09, Interruption of Therapy.)

6.03 Withholding records for nonpayment. Psychologists may not withhold records under their control that are requested and needed for a client's/patient's emergency treatment solely because payment has not been received.

6.04 Fees and financial arrangements. (a) As early as is feasible in a professional or scientific relationship, psychologists and recipients of psychological services reach an agreement specifying compensation and billing arrangements.

(b) Psychologists' fee practices are consistent with law.

(c) Psychologists do not misrepresent their fees.

(d) If limitations to services can be anticipated because of limitations in financing, this is discussed with the recipient of services as early as is feasible. (See also Standards 10.09, Interruption of Therapy, and 10.10, Terminating Therapy.)

(e) If the recipient of services does not pay for services as agreed, and if psychologists intend to use collection agencies or legal measures to collect the fees, psychologists first inform the person that such measures will be taken and provide that person an opportunity to make prompt payment. (See also Standards 4.05, Disclosures; 6.03, Withholding Records for Nonpayment; and 10.01, Informed Consent to Therapy.)

6.05 Barter with clients/patients. Barter is the acceptance of goods, services, or other nonmonetary remuneration from clients/patients in return for psychological services. Psychologists may barter only if

(1) it is not clinically contraindicated, and (2) the resulting arrangement is not exploitative. (See also Standards 3.05, Multiple Relationships, and 6.04, Fees and Financial Arrangements.)

6.06 Accuracy in reports to payors and funding sources. In their reports to payors for services or sources of research funding, psychologists take reasonable steps to ensure the accurate reporting of the nature of the service provided or research conducted, the fees, charges, or payments, and where applicable, the identity of the provider, the findings, and the diagnosis. (See also Standards 4.01, Maintaining Confidentiality; 4.04, Minimizing Intrusions on Privacy; and 4.05, Disclosures.)

6.07 Referrals and fees. When psychologists pay, receive payment from, or divide fees with another professional, other than in an employer–employee relationship, the payment to each is based on the services provided (clinical, consultative, administrative, or other) and is not based on the referral itself. (See also Standard 3.09, Cooperation With Other Professionals.)

7. Education and Training

7.01 Design of education and training programs. Psychologists responsible for education and training programs take reasonable steps to ensure that the programs are designed to provide the appropriate knowledge and proper experiences, and to meet the requirements for licensure, certification, or other goals for which claims are made by the program. (See also Standard 5.03, Descriptions of Workshops and Non-Degree-Granting Educational Programs.)

7.02 Descriptions of education and training programs. Psychologists responsible for education and training programs take reasonable steps to ensure that there is a current and accurate description of the program content (including participation in required course- or program-related counseling, psychotherapy, experiential groups, consulting projects, or community service), training goals and objectives, stipends and benefits, and requirements that must be met for satisfactory completion of the program. This information must be made readily available to all interested parties.

7.03 Accuracy in teaching. (a) Psychologists take reasonable steps to ensure that course syllabi are accurate regarding the subject matter to be covered, bases for evaluating progress, and the nature of course experiences. This standard does not preclude an instructor from modifying course content or requirements when the instructor considers it pedagogically necessary or desirable, so long as students are made aware of these modifications in a manner that enables them to fulfill course requirements. (See also Standard 5.01, Avoidance of False or Deceptive Statements.)

(b) When engaged in teaching or training, psychologists present psychological information accurately. (See also Standard 2.03, Maintaining Competence.)

7.04 Student disclosure of personal information. Psychologists do not require students or supervisees to disclose personal information in course- or program-related activities, either orally or in writing, regarding sexual history, history of abuse and neglect, psychological treatment, and relationships with parents, peers, and spouses or significant others except if (1) the program or training facility has clearly identified this requirement in its admissions and program materials or (2) the information is necessary to evaluate or obtain assistance for students whose personal problems could reasonably be judged to be preventing them from performing their training- or professionally related activities in a competent manner or posing a threat to the students or others.

7.05 Mandatory individual or group therapy. (a) When individual or group therapy is a program or course requirement, psychologists responsible for that program allow students in undergraduate and graduate programs the option of selecting such therapy from practitioners unaffiliated with the program. (See also Standard 7.02, Descriptions of Education and Training Programs.)

(b) Faculty who are or are likely to be responsible for evaluating students' academic performance do not themselves provide that therapy. (See also Standard 3.05, Multiple Relationships.)

7.06 Assessing student and supervisee performance. (a) In academic and supervisory relationships, psychologists establish a timely and specific process for providing feedback to students and supervisees. Information regarding the process is provided to the student at the beginning of supervision.

(b) Psychologists evaluate students and supervisees on the basis of their actual performance on relevant and established program requirements.

7.07 Sexual relationships with students and supervisees. Psychologists do not engage in sexual relationships with students or supervisees who are in their department, agency, or training center or over whom psychologists have or are likely to have evaluative authority. (See also Standard 3.05, Multiple Relationships.)

8. Research and Publication

8.01 Institutional approval. When institutional approval is required, psychologists provide accurate information about their research proposals and obtain approval prior to conducting the research. They conduct the research in accordance with the approved research protocol.

8.02 Informed consent to research. (a) When obtaining informed consent as required in Standard 3.10, Informed Consent, psychologists inform participants about (1) the purpose of the research, expected duration, and procedures; (2) their right to decline to participate and to withdraw from the research once participation has begun; (3) the foreseeable consequences of declining or withdrawing; (4) reasonably foreseeable factors that may be expected to influence their willingness to participate such as potential risks, discomfort, or adverse effects; (5) any prospective research benefits; (6) limits of confidentiality; (7) incentives for participation; and (8) whom to contact for questions about the research and research participants' rights. They provide opportunity for the prospective participants to ask questions and receive answers. (See also Standards 8.03, Informed Consent for Recording Voices and Images in Research; 8.05, Dispensing With Informed Consent for Research; and 8.07, Deception in Research.)

(b) Psychologists conducting intervention research involving the use of experimental treatments clarify to participants at the outset of the research (1) the experimental nature of the treatment; (2) the services that will or will not be available to the control group(s) if appropriate; (3) the means by which assignment to treatment and control groups will be made; (4) available treatment alternatives if an individual does not wish to participate in the research or wishes to withdraw once a study has begun; and (5) compensation for or monetary costs of participating including, if appropriate, whether reimbursement from the participant or a third-party payor will be sought. (See also Standard 8.02a, Informed Consent to Research.)

8.03 Informed consent for recording voices and images in research. Psychologists obtain informed consent from research participants prior to recording their voices or images for data collection unless (1) the research consists solely of naturalistic observations in public places, and it is not anticipated that the recording will be used in a manner that could cause personal identification or harm, or (2) the research design includes deception, and consent for the use of the recording is obtained during debriefing. (See also Standard 8.07, Deception in Research.)

8.04 Client/patient, student, and subordinate research participants. (a) When psychologists conduct research with clients/patients, students, or subordinates as participants, psychologists take steps to protect the prospective participants from adverse consequences of declining or withdrawing from participation.

(b) When research participation is a course requirement or an opportunity for extra credit, the prospective participant is given the choice of equitable alternative activities.

8.05 Dispensing with informed consent for research. Psychologists may dispense with informed consent only (1) where research would not reasonably be assumed to create distress or harm and involves (a) the study of normal educational practices, curricula, or classroom management methods conducted in educational settings; (b) only anonymous questionnaires, naturalistic observations, or archival research for which disclosure of responses would not place participants at risk of criminal or civil liability or damage their financial standing, employability, or reputation, and confi-

dentiality is protected; or (c) the study of factors related to job or organization effectiveness conducted in organizational settings for which there is no risk to participants' employability, and confidentiality is protected or (2) where otherwise permitted by law or federal or institutional regulations.

8.06 Offering inducements for research participation. (a) Psychologists make reasonable efforts to avoid offering excessive or inappropriate financial or other inducements for research participation when such inducements are likely to coerce participation.

(b) When offering professional services as an inducement for research participation, psychologists clarify the nature of the services, as well as the risks, obligations, and limitations. (See also Standard 6.05, Barter With Clients/Patients.)

8.07 Deception in research. (a) Psychologists do not conduct a study involving deception unless they have determined that the use of deceptive techniques is justified by the study's significant prospective scientific, educational, or applied value and that effective nondeceptive alternative procedures are not feasible.

(b) Psychologists do not deceive prospective participants about research that is reasonably expected to cause physical pain or severe emotional distress.

(c) Psychologists explain any deception that is an integral feature of the design and conduct of an experiment to participants as early as is feasible, preferably at the conclusion of their participation, but no later than at the conclusion of the data collection, and permit participants to withdraw their data. (See also Standard 8.08, Debriefing.)

8.08 Debriefing. (a) Psychologists provide a prompt opportunity for participants to obtain appropriate information about the nature, results, and conclusions of the research, and they take reasonable steps to correct any misconceptions that participants may have of which the psychologists are aware.

(b) If scientific or humane values justify delaying or withholding this information, psychologists take reasonable measures to reduce the risk of harm.

(c) When psychologists become aware that research procedures have harmed a participant, they take reasonable steps to minimize the harm.

8.09 Humane care and use of animals in research.
(a) Psychologists acquire, care for, use, and dispose of animals in compliance with current federal, state, and local laws and regulations, and with professional standards.

(b) Psychologists trained in research methods and experienced in the care of laboratory animals supervise all procedures involving animals and are responsible for ensuring appropriate consideration of their comfort, health, and humane treatment.

(c) Psychologists ensure that all individuals under their supervision who are using animals have received instruction in research methods and in the care, maintenance, and handling of the species being used, to the extent appropriate to their role. (See also Standard 2.05, Delegation of Work to Others.)

(d) Psychologists make reasonable efforts to minimize the discomfort, infection, illness, and pain of animal subjects.

(e) Psychologists use a procedure subjecting animals to pain, stress, or privation only when an alternative procedure is unavailable and the goal is justified by its prospective scientific, educational, or applied value.

(f) Psychologists perform surgical procedures under appropriate anesthesia and follow techniques to avoid infection and minimize pain during and after surgery.

(g) When it is appropriate that an animal's life be terminated, psychologists proceed rapidly, with an effort to minimize pain and in accordance with accepted procedures.

8.10 Reporting research results. (a) Psychologists do not fabricate data. (See also Standard 5.01a, Avoidance of False or Deceptive Statements.)

(b) If psychologists discover significant errors in their published data, they take reasonable steps to correct such errors in a correction, retraction, erratum, or other appropriate publication means.

8.11 Plagiarism. Psychologists do not present portions of another's work or data as their own, even if the other work or data source is cited occasionally.

8.12 Publication credit. (a) Psychologists take responsibility and credit, including authorship credit, only for work they have actually performed or to which they have substantially contributed. (See also Standard 8.12b, Publication Credit.)

(b) Principal authorship and other publication credits accurately reflect the relative scientific or professional contributions of the individuals involved, regardless of their relative status. Mere possession of an institutional position, such as department chair, does not justify authorship credit. Minor contributions to the research or to the writing for publications are acknowledged appropriately, such as in footnotes or in an introductory statement.

(c) Except under exceptional circumstances, a student is listed as principal author on any multiple-authored article that is substantially based on the student's doctoral dissertation. Faculty advisors discuss publication credit with students as early as feasible and throughout the research and publication process as appropriate. (See also Standard 8.12b, Publication Credit.)

8.13 Duplicate publication of data. Psychologists do not publish, as original data, data that have been previously published. This does not preclude republishing data when they are accompanied by proper acknowledgment.

8.14 Sharing research data for verification.
(a) After research results are published, psychologists do not withhold the data on which their conclusions are based from other competent professionals who seek to verify the substantive claims through reanalysis and who intend to use such data only for that purpose, provided that the confidentiality of the participants can be protected and unless legal rights concerning proprietary data preclude their release. This does not preclude psychologists from requiring that such individuals or groups be responsible for costs associated with the provision of such information.

(b) Psychologists who request data from other psychologists to verify the substantive claims through reanalysis may use shared data only for the declared purpose. Requesting psychologists obtain prior written agreement for all other uses of the data.

8.15 Reviewers. Psychologists who review material submitted for presentation, publication, grant, or research proposal review respect the confidentiality of and the proprietary rights in such information of those who submitted it.

9. Assessment

9.01 Bases for assessments. (a) Psychologists base the opinions contained in their recommendations, reports, and diagnostic or evaluative statements, including forensic testimony, on information and techniques sufficient to substantiate their findings. (See also Standard 2.04, Bases for Scientific and Professional Judgments.)

(b) Except as noted in 9.01c, psychologists provide opinions of the psychological characteristics of individuals only after they have conducted an examination of the individuals adequate to support their statements or conclusions. When, despite reasonable efforts, such an examination is not practical, psychologists document the efforts they made and the result of those efforts, clarify the probable impact of their limited information on the reliability and validity of their opinions, and appropriately limit the nature and extent of their conclusions or recommendations. (See also Standards 2.01, Boundaries of Competence, and 9.06, Interpreting Assessment Results.)

(c) When psychologists conduct a record review or provide consultation or supervision and an individual examination is not warranted or necessary for the opinion, psychologists explain this and the sources of information on which they based their conclusions and recommendations.

9.02 Use of assessments. (a) Psychologists administer, adapt, score, interpret, or use assessment techniques, interviews, tests, or instruments in a manner and for purposes that are appropriate in light of the research on or evidence of the usefulness and proper application of the techniques.

(b) Psychologists use assessment instruments whose validity and reliability have been established for use with members of the population tested. When such validity or reliability has not been established, psychologists describe the strengths and limitations of test results and interpretation.

(c) Psychologists use assessment methods that are appropriate to an individual's language preference and competence, unless the use of an alternative language is relevant to the assessment issues.

9.03 Informed consent in assessments.
(a) Psychologists obtain informed consent for assessments, evaluations, or diagnostic services, as described in Standard 3.10, Informed Consent, except when (1) testing is mandated by law or governmental regulations; (2) informed consent is implied because testing is conducted as a routine educational, institutional, or organizational activity (e.g., when participants voluntarily agree to assessment when applying for a job); or (3) one purpose of the testing is to evaluate decisional capacity. Informed consent includes an explanation of the nature and purpose of the assessment, fees, involvement of third parties, and limits of confidentiality and sufficient opportunity for the client/patient to ask questions and receive answers.

(b) Psychologists inform persons with questionable capacity to consent or for whom testing is mandated by law or governmental regulations about the nature and purpose of the proposed assessment services, using language that is reasonably understandable to the person being assessed.

(c) Psychologists using the services of an interpreter obtain informed consent from the client/patient to use that interpreter, ensure that confidentiality of test results and test security are maintained, and include in their recommendations, reports, and diagnostic or evaluative statements, including forensic testimony, discussion of any limitations on the data obtained. (See also Standards 2.05, Delegation of Work to Others; 4.01, Maintaining Confidentiality; 9.01, Bases for Assessments; 9.06, Interpreting Assessment Results; and 9.07, Assessment by Unqualified Persons.)

9.04 Release of test data. (a) The term *test data* refers to raw and scaled scores, client/patient responses to test questions or stimuli, and psychologists' notes and recordings concerning client/patient statements and behavior during an examination. Those portions of test materials that include client/patient responses are included in the definition of *test data*. Pursuant to a client/patient release, psychologists provide test data to the client/patient or other persons identified in the release. Psychologists may refrain from releasing test data to protect a client/patient or others from substantial harm or misuse or misrepresentation of the data or the test, recognizing that in many instances release of confidential information under these circumstances is regulated by law. (See also Standard 9.11, Maintaining Test Security.)

(b) In the absence of a client/patient release, psychologists provide test data only as required by law or court order.

9.05 Test construction. Psychologists who develop tests and other assessment techniques use appropriate psychometric procedures and current scientific or professional knowledge for test design, standardization, validation, reduction or elimination of bias, and recommendations for use.

9.06 Interpreting assessment results. When interpreting assessment results, including automated interpretations, psychologists take into account the purpose of the assessment as well as the various test factors, test-taking abilities, and other characteristics of the person being assessed, such as situational, personal, linguistic, and cultural differences, that might affect psychologists' judgments or reduce the accuracy of their interpretations. They indicate any significant limitations of their interpretations. (See also Standards 2.01b and c, Boundaries of Competence, and 3.01, Unfair Discrimination.)

9.07 Assessment by unqualified persons. Psychologists do not promote the use of psychological assessment techniques by unqualified persons, except when such use is conducted for training purposes with appropriate supervision. (See also Standard 2.05, Delegation of Work to Others.)

9.08 Obsolete tests and outdated test results. (a) Psychologists do not base their assessment or intervention decisions or recommendations on data or test results that are outdated for the current purpose.

(b) Psychologists do not base such decisions or recommendations on tests and measures that are obsolete and not useful for the current purpose.

9.09 Test scoring and interpretation services. (a) Psychologists who offer assessment or scoring services to other professionals accurately describe the purpose, norms, validity, reliability, and applications of the procedures and any special qualifications applicable to their use.

(b) Psychologists select scoring and interpretation services (including automated services) on the basis of evidence of the validity of the program and procedures as well as on other appropriate considerations. (See also Standard 2.01b and c, Boundaries of Competence.)

(c) Psychologists retain responsibility for the appropriate application, interpretation, and use of assessment instruments, whether they score and interpret such tests themselves or use automated or other services.

9.10 Explaining assessment results. Regardless of whether the scoring and interpretation are done by psychologists, by employees or assistants, or by automated or other outside services, psychologists take reasonable steps to ensure that explanations of results are given to the individual or designated representative unless the nature of the relationship precludes provision of an explanation of results (such as in some organizational consulting, preemployment or security screenings, and forensic evaluations), and this fact has been clearly explained to the person being assessed in advance.

9.11 Maintaining test security. The term *test materials* refers to manuals, instruments, protocols, and test questions or stimuli and does not include *test data* as defined in Standard 9.04, Release of Test Data. Psychologists make reasonable efforts to maintain the integrity and security of test materials and other assessment techniques consistent with law and contractual obligations, and in a manner that permits adherence to this Ethics Code.

10. Therapy

10.01 Informed consent to therapy. (a) When obtaining informed consent to therapy as required in Standard 3.10, Informed Consent, psychologists inform clients/patients as early as is feasible in the therapeutic relationship about the nature and anticipated course of therapy, fees, involvement of third parties, and limits of confidentiality and provide sufficient opportunity for the client/patient to ask questions and receive answers. (See also Standards 4.02, Discussing the Limits of Confidentiality, and 6.04, Fees and Financial Arrangements.)

(b) When obtaining informed consent for treatment for which generally recognized techniques and procedures have not been established, psychologists inform their clients/patients of the developing nature of the treatment, the potential risks involved, alternative treatments that may be available, and the voluntary nature of their participation. (See also Standards 2.01e, Boundaries of Competence, and 3.10, Informed Consent.)

(c) When the therapist is a trainee and the legal responsibility for the treatment provided resides with the supervisor, the client/patient, as part of the informed consent procedure, is informed that the therapist is in training and is being supervised and is given the name of the supervisor.

10.02 Therapy involving couples or families.

(a) When psychologists agree to provide services to several persons who have a relationship (such as spouses, significant others, or parents and children), they take reasonable steps to clarify at the outset (1) which of the individuals are clients/patients and (2) the relationship the psychologist will have with each person. This clarification includes the psychologist's role and the probable uses of the services provided or the information obtained. (See also Standard 4.02, Discussing the Limits of Confidentiality.)

(b) If it becomes apparent that psychologists may be called on to perform potentially conflicting roles (such as family therapist and then witness for one party in divorce proceedings), psychologists take reasonable steps to clarify and modify, or withdraw from, roles appropriately. (See also Standard 3.05c, Multiple Relationships.)

10.03 Group therapy.
When psychologists provide services to several persons in a group setting, they describe at the outset the roles and responsibilities of all parties and the limits of confidentiality.

10.04 Providing therapy to those served by others.
In deciding whether to offer or provide services to those already receiving mental health services elsewhere, psychologists carefully consider the treatment issues and the potential client's/patient's welfare. Psychologists discuss these issues with the client/patient or another legally authorized person on behalf of the client/patient in order to minimize the risk of confusion and conflict, consult with the other service providers when appropriate, and proceed with caution and sensitivity to the therapeutic issues.

10.05 Sexual intimacies with current therapy clients/patients.
Psychologists do not engage in sexual intimacies with current therapy clients/patients.

10.06 Sexual intimacies with relatives or significant others of current therapy clients/patients.
Psychologists do not engage in sexual intimacies with individuals they know to be close relatives, guardians, or significant others of current clients/patients. Psychologists do not terminate therapy to circumvent this standard.

10.07 Therapy with former sexual partners.
Psychologists do not accept as therapy clients/patients persons with whom they have engaged in sexual intimacies.

10.08 Sexual intimacies with former therapy clients/patients.
(a) Psychologists do not engage in sexual intimacies with former clients/patients for at least two years after cessation or termination of therapy.

(b) Psychologists do not engage in sexual intimacies with former clients/patients even after a two-year interval except in the most unusual circumstances. Psychologists who engage in such activity after the two years following cessation or termination of therapy and of having no sexual contact with the former client/patient bear the burden of demonstrating that there has been no exploitation, in light of all relevant factors, including (1) the amount of time that has passed since therapy terminated; (2) the nature, duration, and intensity of the therapy; (3) the circumstances of termination; (4) the client's/patient's personal history; (5) the client's/patient's current mental status; (6) the likelihood of adverse impact on the client/patient; and (7) any statements or actions made by the therapist during the course of therapy suggesting or inviting the possibility of a posttermination sexual or romantic relationship with the client/patient. (See also Standard 3.05, Multiple Relationships.)

10.09 Interruption of therapy. When entering into employment or contractual relationships, psychologists make reasonable efforts to provide for orderly and appropriate resolution of responsibility for client/patient care in the event that the employment or contractual relationship ends, with paramount consideration given to the welfare of the client/patient. (See also Standard 3.12, Interruption of Psychological Services.)

10.10 Terminating therapy. (a) Psychologists terminate therapy when it becomes reasonably clear that the client/patient no longer needs the service, is not likely to benefit, or is being harmed by continued service.

(b) Psychologists may terminate therapy when threatened or otherwise endangered by the client/patient or another person with whom the client/patient has a relationship.

(c) Except where precluded by the actions of clients/patients or third-party payors, prior to termination psychologists provide pretermination counseling and suggest alternative service providers as appropriate.

♦ ♦ ♦

Commentary: Review the Introduction and Applicability section of the code. Assume a developmental psychologist has been arrested for fondling youngsters in the basement of his home. These children have never been participants in the psychologist's research. Would the psychologist be subject to the jurisdiction of the Ethics Committee for violating the code of ethics? The following excerpt discusses the ambiguity of this situation.

Examining the Personal–Professional Distinction: Ethics Codes and the Difficulty of Drawing a Boundary

Randolph B. Pipes, Jaymee E. Holstein, and Maria G. Aguirre

[O]ne of the issues that arises when discussing whether any particular behavior on the part of the psychologist is or is not prohibited by the APA Ethics Code is whether the behavior under consideration does or does not fall within the boundaries of the professional role of the psychologist. The Introduction and Applicability section of the 2002 APA Ethics Code states the following:

> The Ethics Code applies only to psychologists' activities that are part of their scientific, educational, or professional roles as psychologists. . . . These activities shall be distinguished from the purely private conduct of psychologists, which is not within the purview of the Ethics Code. (p. 1061)

Thus, in contrast to the constraints (accepted voluntarily as a result of membership) imposed by the APA Ethics Code on psychologists when they are acting within their role as psychologists, no such constraints are imposed or mandated by the Ethics Code when psychologists function outside their roles as psychologists. Within the constraints of their own moral standards, social custom, the law, and any relevant organizational rules (e.g., those dictated by an employer or other professional association), psychologists may, when their professional role is not operative, engage in exploitative relationships and sexual and multiple relationships of their choosing. They may, with impunity from the Code, demean individuals of a particular gender or a particular religion with whom they interact only on a

personal basis. It appears that in those municipalities that do not make it illegal to do so, a psychologist may own an apartment building and refuse to rent to individuals who are, for example, gay. Outside their roles as psychologists, they may (subject to the constraints just listed) break confidences, be verbally abusive to their romantic partners, lie to their friends, evaluate others unfairly, and generally act like a louse.[3] To summarize, other than the exception footnoted, odious behavior outside the psychologist's professional role is not subject to the current Ethics Code. It is important to note that the APA Ethics Code does little to define personal behavior or to explain the distinction between personal behavior and professional behavior. . . .

WHAT IS PERSONAL?
WHAT IS PROFESSIONAL?

The 1992 APA Ethics Code was apparently the first APA Code to draw a distinction between the personal and the professional behavior of psychologists in terms of the applicability of the Code. The Introduction section of this Code states, "These work-related activities can be distinguished from the purely private conduct of a psychologist, which *ordinarily* [italics added] is not within the purview of the Ethics Code" (APA, 1992, p. 1598).

Fisher and Younggren (1997) noted that the issue of whether particularly egregious behavior outside one's role as a psychologist should fall under the purview of the Code was a subject for discussion in

[3]Members of APA may be expelled from the association after being convicted of a felony, even if the felony is unrelated to their role as a psychologist. That is to say, personal behaviors can fall within reach of the association's discipline, even though they are not directly actionable under the Ethical Standards. Felony convictions allow but do not require the association to discipline members. One reason the APA Ethics Code does not include legal violations as a specific standard is that there has been a consensus that an illegal act such as civil disobedience should not automatically subject the APA member to sanctions (C. Fisher, personal communication, November 5, 2003).

future revisions of the Code (for a discussion of changes reflected in the 2002 APA Code, see Fisher, 2003; Knapp & VandeCreek, 2003a, 2003b). In fact, the limitation of the Code's applicability to professional (as opposed to personal) behavior actually appears to have been strengthened in the new (2002) Ethics Code. As noted above, the 2002 APA Code says, "These activities shall be distinguished from the purely private conduct of psychologists, which *is not* [italics added] within the purview of the Ethics Code" (p. 1061). Despite the clear statement about the purview of the Code, Section 2.06 (Personal Problems and Conflicts) suggests that psychologists' personal behaviors might be at least partially at issue when considering whether the Code has been violated. Standard 3.06 (Conflict of Interest) also brings into focus the potential intermingling of personal activity and professional obligations. The distinction between the personal and the professional is made difficult when the Code both places personal behavior off the table for consideration yet recognizes that personal problems, which may at times be evidenced primarily in nonwork-related activities, are likely correlates of poor performance in the work setting. The distinction between the personal and the professional has been implicitly criticized by Payton (1994), who noted the following:

> The distinction [between personal and professional behavior] provokes rethinking of my role. Until now, I have always considered myself a psychologist regardless of my job title. Social acquaintances view me as such. Are there any psychologists who have not been greeted with a "Oh, you can read my mind," when introduced as a psychologist? The new code [i.e., the 1992 Code] frees me to leave my professional identity at the office at the close of business. (p. 319)

Of particular note in Payton's position is the emphasis on the perception of others. From this standpoint, such perception is an important criterion in determining whether psychologists can in fact, in Payton's words, "leave . . . [their] professional identity at the office at the close of business" (p. 319).

In their book on the 1992 Code, Canter, Bennett, Jones, and Nagy (1994) gave the example (still relevant for the 2002 Code) of the psychologist who sits on a library board and makes statements about the effects of certain kinds of books on children. Is such behavior subject to the Ethics Code? On the one hand, the psychologist may argue that she volunteered to be on the board as a private citizen and that as a member of the board she is entitled to express opinions about children's books. On the other hand, an observer might argue that the individuals who made the board appointment were likely aware that the individual was, in fact, a psychologist. Such an observer might also argue that it is a matter of common sense to link the appointment, the role the psychologist plays as a university professor with, for example, a specialty in child psychology, and the opinions being expressed by the psychologist.

Psychologists who substantially quote psychological literature and freely comment on it in public are arguably engaging in activity that is a part of their "scientific, educational, or professional roles as psychologists," even if they do not specifically identify themselves as psychologists (APA, 2002, p. 1061). It is interesting to note that the Canadian Code of Ethics for Psychologists (Canadian Psychological Association, 2000), the Principles of Medical Ethics with Annotations Especially Applicable to Psychiatry (American Psychiatric Association, 2001), and the ethics code of the American Counseling Association (1995) each contain a section that is quite applicable here. Each of these codes notes that professionals have an affirmative duty to indicate when they are speaking as a matter of personal opinion as opposed to speaking as experts. . . .

Even though the APA Ethics Code does not contain a standard requiring that psychologists clarify statements that might be ambiguous along the dimension of speaking privately versus speaking as a professional, such a standard could indeed help prevent misunderstanding. Obviously, claims by psychologists that they are acting as private citizens, in the face of clear and convincing evidence that they were functioning within a professional role, are fraudulent.

Although the purpose of this article is not to suggest new APA ethical standards, we do believe that in making future revisions of the APA Ethics Code, psychologists should consider slightly altering current standards in the area of public statements, so as to provide additional guidance to psychologists seeking to make clear that they are speaking for themselves in a given arena. In turn, such a standard, when applied to a particular situation, would directly address the question of the distinction between the personal and the professional. Not all difficulties in distinguishing between personal and professional behavior can be solved by a statement; nonetheless, in our view, a standard outlining one's obligation to clarify roles would make a reasonable addition to the Ethics Code. Perhaps it would be helpful to point out here that one of the purposes of the APA Code is to set forth enforceable standards, but another purpose is to educate psychologists. By outlining a standard in the area of public statements, the Code would be alerting psychologists to the importance of being clear about one's role (speaking as a professional vs. speaking personally).

Consider two more examples that draw further attention to the issue of the personal and the professional:

> One night, while drinking with friends at a bar, Dr. Rodriguez, a clinical psychologist, sees two of his long-term clients sitting just a few feet away. Even though he knows his clients are there, he becomes very intoxicated, to the point of slurred speech. Is his behavior subject to the Ethics Code? Would it make any difference if one of his clients had a problem with alcohol abuse or if Dr. Rodriguez ran the local alcohol treatment facility? What if the same incident was repeated a number of times?

> Dr. Green, a psychologist who is a statistician, is a player-manager for a softball team and she has invited her doctoral student, Lois, to play on the team with her. On the ball field, and in front of the other players, Dr. Green repeatedly belittles her student's athletic skills. She also frequently makes substitutions in a way that limits Lois's playing time. In the role of doctoral advisor, Dr. Green is supportive and fair. Is Dr. Green's behavior on the softball field subject to the Code?

Explicit guidance concerning such behavior is not in the Code, although Standard 3.04 (APA, 2002) does admonish psychologists to avoid harming students and others with whom they work. It is unlikely that any ethics code will be able to answer clearly questions about all of the many complicated situations that could conceivably arise in distinguishing between the personal and the professional. . . .

Perhaps as much as any area of psychology, feminist theory and practice (e.g., Worell & Johnson, 1997) raises the question of the personal versus the professional life of the psychologist. One of the mantras of feminist psychology has been the belief that "the personal is political." Indeed, the preamble to the Feminist Therapy Code of Ethics (Feminist Therapy Institute, 2000; . . .) includes this very statement. In turn, political issues (e.g., social justice) are seen as part and parcel of the psychological enterprise. One need only pick up any of several books on feminist ethics (e.g., Brabeck, 2000; Rave & Larsen, 1995) to see that personal values and personal identity are inextricably interwoven with the idea of professional values and ethics.

Another example highlighting the ambiguous relationship between the personal and the professional, especially from a feminist perspective,[4] is that of hate speech. Vasquez and de las Fuentes (2000) have discussed the issue of hate speech and the issues involved in balancing the need for autonomy and feminist ethics. They concluded that faculty and student speech codes were needed (and also discussed a number of relevant court cases). As they pointed out, freedom of speech is by no means absolute. At the same time, however, courts have been rather reluctant to endorse speech codes, often

---

[4]It is inaccurate to speak of a single feminist position on, for example, ethics or hate speech. As Enns (1993) has pointed out, there are several schools of feminist thought, not to mention individual variation among feminists.

finding them too broadly drawn. Although the issue of hate speech on campus is not the same as, for example, hate speech in one's personal life, nonetheless, the issue is raised as to the interaction between one's personal life and one's professional life. If a therapist sees a large caseload of clients who identify their ethnicity as African American, should the profession merely say in essence, "we have nothing to say" if the therapist writes letters to the editor that are racist? Is such (perhaps) personal behavior outside the scope of the APA Ethics Code?

. . .

INTERROGATING THE BOUNDARY

. . .

WHY IS IT IMPORTANT TO THINK ABOUT THIS BOUNDARY?

Perhaps one answer that comes to mind when this question is asked can be found in the APA Ethics Code (and discussed above), namely, that one will not be charged with an Ethics Code violation (or at least will not be found guilty of one) if the behavior in question is deemed personal. So, psychologists have a vested interest in this boundary and obviously so does the APA Ethics Committee. More broadly, and more important, thinking about this boundary challenges psychologists to be reflective about the bridge between the personal and the professional. In this sense, the emphasis is not on "What am I free to do in my personal life that is unregulated by the Code?" but rather "What are those enduring values that cut across my professional life and my personal life?" Let us be clear that we take seriously the right of psychologists to lead personal lives free of oversight from APA. There is something very wrong, however, if psychologists drink to intoxication in front of clients who abuse alcohol and their first thought is "Can I be disciplined under the APA Ethics Code?" Using a less extreme example, we know a psychologist who typically avoids going to a particular coffee shop

because a psychotherapy client frequents the shop and, in the view of the psychologist, there are transference issues that might make such visits problematic. No one doubts that the psychologist has a right to go to the coffee shop. It is scarcely plausible that the Code would constrain behavior in such a circumstance. The psychologist's perspective is that this intersection between the personal ("I would like to visit this coffee shop") and the professional ("My client frequents the shop and my professional judgment leads me to think that my going might interfere with therapy at this juncture") calls for sacrificing personal choice.[6] The personal value of freedom to go to a particular coffee shop is ordered and graded, in part, as an outgrowth of a professional value. We believe that psychologists frequently make such choices. In such circumstances, values as psychologists are fused with more personal values. Such fusion strengthens psychologists' identities, contributes to a feeling of wholeness, and brings satisfaction as they pursue in their after-work lives the same values they uphold during the workday.

. . .

WHAT ARE THE IMPLICATIONS OF A FUZZY BOUNDARY?

We briefly highlight three implications. First, issues of character (see discussion above) must surely count in selecting and training future psychologists. If psychologists cannot always distinguish between the personal and the professional, and assuming that there is a reciprocal relationship between elements of the two domains, then how psychologists select students for graduate school becomes critical. They must select individuals whose character includes qualities such as truthfulness, personal responsibility, and integrity. Such character helps ensure ethical behavior whether one is operating in the personal or in the professional realm or somewhere in between.

Second, training in ethics in graduate school should emphasize not just obeying the standards in

---

[6] We leave aside the questions of whether the psychologist's judgment is correct or not and whether the psychologist is actually avoiding the coffee shop because of countertransference issues or out of self-care.

the Ethics Code but should encourage behavior that is consistent with broader aspirational principles. Furthermore, because the personal and the professional do so often become intertwined, a stance of self-reflection and self-knowledge should be modeled and fostered in graduate programs. Among others, Kant (e.g., see Potter, 2002) emphasized the role of self-deception in moral failures. If self-deception is such a danger, then surely a portion of the antidote is self-reflection and self-knowledge.

Third, lifelong personal development of the psychologist is crucial. Personal problems and conflicts (see APA, 2002, Standard 2.06) are recognized as ongoing threats to effective professionalism. Impairment continues to challenge psychologists both at the practical and at the conceptual level. Personal development of psychologists seems like a reasonable tool in the profession's struggles with impairment.

SUMMARY AND RECOMMENDATIONS

. . .

Finally, we would like to propose an idea that would make no change in the standards to which psychologists are held but that would make clear the investment psychologists have in ethical behavior beyond the borders of their professional lives. We propose that the APA consider amending the Introduction and Applicability portion of the Ethics Code so that the General Principles, which are aspirational (not enforceable), can be explicitly discussed as applying to all areas of a member's life, not just to their professional role behaviors. Our proposal is founded on two fundamental assumptions: (a) It is often difficult to distinguish between what is personal and what is professional. Especially in these gray areas, it would be reassuring to know that at least some portion of the Code addressed the behavior even if that portion were not enforceable. (b) There are some broad aspirational values about which psychologists can attain rough consensus as applying to their personal behavior.

Under APA's current Ethics Code, once a behavior has been defined as personal rather than professional, the entire Ethics Code falls silent. However, APA already has in place a mechanism for potentially disciplining members whose personal behavior leads to a felony conviction. Therefore, the issue is not really whether APA is in the business of making judgments about personal behavior, because under certain circumstances, it certainly does make such judgments. We are deeply sympathetic with the argument, rooted in this country's historical emphasis on the right to be let alone, that professional codes of ethics should not dictate one's personal behavior. At the same time, one of the strengths and attractive features of the APA Code is that it does draw a distinction between what is enforceable and what is aspirational. This does not mean that everyone in APA completely agrees with these aspirational principles; but for the most part, these principles are written in a way that makes them palatable to most psychologists. They are undergirded by values of such obvious appeal (e.g., justice, integrity, respect for people's rights and dignity) that it seems plausible psychologists could achieve a consensus on them as aspirational beyond their professional role. In our view, to say that abiding by these values is something to which psychologists aspire in their personal lives seems reasonable, if not obvious.

References

American Counseling Association. (1995). *Code of ethics.* Alexandria, VA: Author.

American Psychiatric Association. (2001). *The principles of medical ethics with annotations specially applicable to psychiatry.* Arlington, VA: Author.

American Psychological Association. (1992). Ethical principles of psychologists and code of conduct. *American Psychologist, 48,* 1597–1611.

American Psychological Association. (2002). Ethical principles of psychologists and code of conduct. *American Psychologist, 57,* 1060–1073.

Brabeck, M. (Ed.). (2000). *Practicing feminist ethics in psychology.* Washington, DC: American Psychological Association.

Canadian Psychological Association. (2000). *Canadian code of ethics for psychologists* (3rd ed.). Retrieved from http://www.cpa.ca/ethics2000.html

Canter, M. B., Bennett, B. E., Jones, S. E., & Nagy, T. F. (1994). *Ethics for psychologists: A commentary on the APA ethics code.* Washington, DC: American Psychological Association.

Enns, C. Z. (1993). Twenty years of feminist counseling and therapy: From naming biases to implementing multifaceted practice. *The Counseling Psychologist,* 21, 3–87.

Feminist Therapy Institute. (2000). *Feminist therapy code of ethics* (Rev. ed.). Retrieved March 25, 2005, from http://www.feministtherapyinstitute.org/ethics.htm

Fisher, C. B. (2003). *Decoding the ethics code: A practical guide for psychologists.* Thousand Oaks, CA: Sage.

Fisher, C. B., & Younggren, J. N. (1997). The value and utility of the 1992 ethics code. *Professional Psychology: Research and Practice,* 28, 582–592.

Knapp, S., & VandeCreek, L. (2003a). *A guide to the 2002 revision of the American Psychological Association's ethics code.* Sarasota, FL: Professional Resource Press.

Knapp, S., & VandeCreek, L. (2003b). An overview of the major changes in the 2002 APA Ethics Code. *Professional Psychology: Research and Practice,* 34, 301–308.

Payton, C. R. (1994). Implications of the 1992 ethics code for diverse groups. *Professional Psychology: Research and Practice,* 25, 317–320.

Peters, J. W. (2005, February 8). Company's smoking ban means off-hours too. *The New York Times,* C5.

Potter, N. (2002). Duties to oneself, motivational internalism, and self-deception in Kant's ethics. In M. Timmons (Ed.), *Kant's metaphysics of morals: Interpretative essays* (pp. 371–389). Oxford, England: Oxford University Press.

Rave, E. J., & Larsen, C. C. (Eds.). (1995). *Ethical decision making in therapy: Feminist perspectives.* New York: Guilford Press.

Vasquez, M. J. T., & de las Fuentes, C. (2000). Hate speech or freedom of expression? Balancing autonomy and feminist ethics in a pluralistic society. In M. M. Brabeck (Ed.), *Practicing feminist ethics in psychology* (pp. 225–247). Washington, DC: American Psychological Association.

Worell, J., & Johnson, N. G. (Eds.). (1997). *Shaping the future of feminist psychology: Education, research, and practice.* Washington, DC: American Psychological Association.

◆　　◆　　◆

Commentary: One of the major changes in the 2002 code is that the General Principles reflect a different set of fundamental values. The 1992 code began with six general unenforceable principles: competence, integrity, professional and scientific responsibility, respect for people's rights and dignity, concern for others' welfare, and social responsibility. The current code replaces that with beneficence and nonmaleficence, fidelity, integrity, justice, and respect for people's rights and dignity. These are one version of what are called prima facie duties or moral values.

Following the 20th-century English philosopher W. D. Ross (see, Ross, W. D. [1930]. The right and the good. Oxford, England: Clarendon), I have suggested a somewhat different listing of similar values and argued that one function a code of ethics should serve is to translate these moral values into enforceable standards. The duties I would list include nonmaleficence, fidelity, beneficence, justice, and autonomy.

Perhaps the bedrock ethical duty required of psychologists is nonmaleficence captured in the Latin phrase primum non nocere—*above all, do no harm. Fidelity most often refers to the obligations of faithfulness and loyalty inherent in the client–clinician relationship, but it may be extended to mean fidelity toward the scientific roots of one's profession. Beneficence is the most commonsense principle; indeed, the concept of psychology as a "helping profession" is its embodiment. Specifically, it refers to the practitioners' responsibility to benefit those they assess and treat and the obligation of investigators to conduct research with scientific or applied value. Justice refers to psychologists' obligation to treat equitably those who serve and, perhaps, the superordinate responsibility to respect the worth and dignity of each individual. Finally—but by no means least important—is the principle of autonomy, guaranteeing people the freedom to think, choose, and act so long as their actions do not infringe unduly on the rights of others. These principles are explicated more fully in chapter 3. For an analysis of how these prima facie duties have been represented in APA's codes, see Bersoff, D. N., & Koeppl, P. M. (1993). The relation between ethical codes and moral principles. Ethics & Behavior, 3, 345–357; Knapp, S., & Vandecreek, L. (2006). A principle-based analysis of the 2002 American Psychological Association ethics code. Psychotherapy: Theory, Research, Practice, Training, 41, 247–256.*

Although the change in the 2002 code adopting a set of fundamental moral principles is a salutary one, the code may still be criticized for failing to give those referring to it help in working out difficult ethical issues:

> *The code, as it now stands, provides no guidance regarding how one is to resolve conflicts among ethical principles. As a*

result, the APA presumably leaves this matter up to the individual's understanding of and background in ethics, which seems to defeat the fundamental purpose of a code of ethics (i.e., to assist the decision-maker to make well-informed and consistent ethical choices). (pp. 131–132)

See Hadjistavropoulos, T., & Malloy, D. (1999), *Ethical principles of the American Psychological Association: An argument for philosophical and practical ranking.* Ethics & Behavior, 9, 127–140.

Similar to the APA, the Canadian code of ethics delineates four ethical principles undergirding its enforceable standards. They are respect for dignity of persons, responsible caring, integrity in relationships, and responsibility to society. In contrast to the APA code, however, the Canadian Psychological Association has ordered these principles, as listed above, "according to the weight each generally should be given when they conflict." Canadian Code of Ethics for Psychologists *(1991; reprinted in the 2nd edition of this text). Note that respect for persons (autonomy) is given the greatest (though not absolute) weight. For an extensive exposition of the development of the Canadian code and a more detailed discussion of its four undergirding principles see* Pettifor, J. L., Sinclair, C., & Strong, T. (2005). The role of dialogue in defining ethical principles: The Canadian code of ethics for psychologists, *Journal of Constructivist Psychology, 18, 183–197.*

The Association of State and Provincial Psychology Boards, an alliance of agencies responsible for the licensure and certification of psychologists in the United States and Canada, has also promulgated a code of conduct. It is reprinted in L. J. Bass, S. T. DeMars, J. R. P. Ogloff, C. Peterson, J. T. Pettifor, R. P. Reaves, et al. (Eds.). (1996). Professional conduct and discipline in psychology. *Washington, DC: American Psychological Association (Appendix).*

The interpretation and enforcement of the Ethics Code are the responsibility of the APA ethics committee. The structure and work of the committee are governed primarily by the APA bylaws, the Association Rules passed by the Council of Representatives, and the Rules and Procedures developed by the ethics committee itself. The two portions of the bylaws relevant to ethics are Article XI, Section 5, and Article II, Sections 16–18. See Bylaws of the American Psychological Association. (Amended January 2002.) *Washington, DC: American Psychological Association.*

Bylaws of the American Psychological Association

American Psychological Association

. . .

[Article XI, Section 5 provides:]

5. The Ethics Committee shall consist of not fewer than eight persons, at least seven of whom shall be Members of the Association, elected from different geographical areas, for terms of not less than three years. Members of the Ethics Committee shall be selected to represent a range of interests characteristic of psychology. The Ethics Committee shall have the power to receive, initiate, and investigate complaints of unethical conduct of Members (to include fellows), Associate members, and Affiliates; to report on types of cases investigated with specific description of difficult or recalcitrant cases; to dismiss or recommend action on ethical cases investigated; to resolve cases by agreement where appropriate; to formulate rules or principles of ethics for adoption by the Association; to formulate rules and procedures governing the conduct of the ethics or disciplinary process for approval by the Board of Directors acting on behalf of Council; and to interpret, apply, and otherwise administer those rules and procedures.

The work of the Ethics Committee, including information and recommendation on all cases before it, shall be kept confidential, except as provided by the Ethics Committee in rules and procedures approved by the Board of Directors, consistent with the objectives of the committee and the interest of the Association.

. . .

[Article II, Sections 16–18 provide:]

16. A Member (to include Fellows), Associate member, or Affiliate may be dropped from membership or otherwise disciplined for conduct which violates the Ethical Principles of the Association, which tends to injure the Association or to affect adversely its reputation, or which is contrary to or destructive of its objects. Allegations of such conduct shall be submitted to the Ethics Committee.

The Ethics Committee shall formulate rules and procedures governing the conduct of the ethics and disciplinary process. However, such rules and procedures and any changes therein must be approved by the Board of Directors acting on behalf of Council. The Ethics Committee, acting at its own discretion or on direction of the Board of Directors, shall review such rules and procedures periodically and may amend them from time to time, subject to the approval of the Board of Directors, provided, however, that no such amendment shall adversely affect the substantive rights of a Member, Associate member, or Affiliate whose conduct is being investigated or against whom formal charges have been filed at the time of amendment.

17. A person who has been dropped from membership pursuant to the rules and procedures of the Ethics Committee may reapply for membership after five years have elapsed from the date of termination of his/her membership. A person who has been permitted to resign under a stipulated agreement may reapply for membership only after the period of time stipulated in the agreement has elapsed, and all other conditions set forth in such agreement have been discharged. In all cases the Member, Associate member, or Affiliate must show that he/she is ethically as well as technically qualified for membership. Such reapplications shall be considered first by the Ethics Committee, which shall make recommendation to the Membership Committee.

18. Resignations of Members, Associate members or Affiliates may be accepted only by the Board of Directors. In the ordinary course, the Board of Directors will, in its discretion, refuse to accept a resignation tendered by a Member, Associate member, or Affiliate while such Member, Associate mem-

ber, or Affiliate is under the scrutiny of the Ethics Committee. . . .

♦   ♦   ♦

Commentary: In 1996, the Board of Directors adopted a resolution defining the meaning of "under scrutiny":

> *A member will be considered to be under the scrutiny of the Ethics Committee:*
>
> *1. When the member is first brought to the Committee's attention as a result of disciplinary or criminal investigations or actions by other bodies, or*
> *2. For other matters, when a complaint or other investigation is not dismissed after an initial review by the Chair [of the Ethics Committee] and [Staff] Director [of the Committee].*
>
> . . .
>
> *The member is no longer under the scrutiny of the Committee when all matters regarding the member that are under the scrutiny of the Committee are closed. (p. 1314)*

See APA Ethics Committee. (1996). Policy on barring resignations during ethics investigations. American Psychologist, 51, 1341.

The policy was modified a year later. Members who are under scrutiny for one or more pending matters may execute an affidavit that would provide for their resignations upon the completion of the pending matters. Upon the effective date of the affidavit, "APA would not exercise jurisdiction over any newly filed ethics complaints against th[ose] member[s]" (APA Ethics Committee, 1998, p. 972), although APA would retain jurisdiction in cases of noncooperation in connection with pending cases. See APA Ethics Committee. (1998). Report of the Ethics Committee, 1997. American Psychologist, 53, 969–980. Now see the newest revision of the rules governing ethics adjudication, reprinted next.

Rules and Procedures
October 1, 2001

Ethics Committee of the American Psychological Association

OVERVIEW

This brief overview is intended only to help the reader understand the structure of these Rules and Procedures (Rules). The overview is not binding on the Ethics Committee or participants in the ethics process and is not an independent source of authority.

These Rules are divided into five parts, which are further subdivided by sections and subsections. The table of contents lists the major section headings.

Parts I and II: General Provisions

Part I describes the objectives and authority of the Ethics Committee. Part II states the Committee's general operating rules. These address such areas as confidentiality and disclosures of information concerning ethics cases; maintenance and disposition of Ethics Committee records; the Committee's jurisdiction, including the time limits within which ethics complaints must be filed; bars to resignation; requests to reopen a closed case; and descriptions of the various sanctions and directives that may be imposed.

Parts III–V: Processing and Review of Complaints and Other Matters by the Ethics Committee

Membership Matters

The Ethics Committee may review applications or reapplications for membership in APA and may review allegations that membership was obtained based upon false or fraudulent information. These procedures are described in Part III.

Investigations of Unethical Conduct

These Rules describe two types of investigations: show cause proceedings and reviews of alleged unethical conduct. The Committee may choose to deal with a matter according to either procedure and may convert an investigation from one type to another as appropriate. A show cause review is commenced based on an adverse action by another body; a review of alleged unethical conduct is initiated by a complainant or the Committee and charges violation of the Ethics Code.

Show Cause Proceedings

The show cause procedure, addressed in Part IV, can be used when another body—including criminal courts, licensing boards, and state psychological associations—has already taken specified serious adverse action against a member. For example, if a member has been convicted of a felony or equivalent criminal offense; has been expelled or suspended by a state psychological association; or has been decertified, unlicensed, or deregistered or had a certificate, license, or registration revoked or suspended by a state or local board, the Committee may open a show cause case. If the respondent does not respond, he or she will be automatically expelled. The respondent may ask that the pending expulsion be reviewed, in which case the respondent will have 60 days to explain why APA should not expel the respondent from membership on the basis of that prior action. The respondent may show that procedures used were not fair and may argue the merits of the previous action. If the respondent asks for a review, the Committee recommends to the Board of Directors whether the respondent should be expelled or allowed to resign under stipulated conditions, reprimanded or censured, or cleared of the charges.

At the outset of the case, instead of contesting the charges, the respondent may offer a resignation, which is deemed a resignation while under ethics investigation.

Time limits for initiating show cause cases are stated in Part II, Section 5.3.4.

Complaints Alleging Violation of the Ethics Code

Investigations detailed in Part V include those brought by members and nonmembers of the Association and those initiated by the Ethics Committee (*sua sponte* complaints). Complaints must be submitted within specified time periods or allege serious misconduct for which a waiver of the time limit may be granted. (See Part II, Section 5.) Even with a waiver of the time limit, the Committee may not find violations for behavior that occurred 10 years or more before the complaint was filed.

Complaints are evaluated initially by the Ethics Office Director, or Investigators acting as the Director's designees, regarding jurisdictional issues such as whether the subject of the complaint, the respondent, is a member, whether the complaint form is correctly completed, and whether the time limits for filing have been met. Then the Chair of the Ethics Committee and Director of the Ethics Office or their designees determine whether there are grounds for action to be taken by the Committee (defined in Part V, Subsection 5.1). If necessary, the Chair and Director conduct a preliminary investigation (described in Part V, Subsection 5.3) to assist in making these threshold determinations. If the Committee has no jurisdiction or if cause for action does not exist, the complaint is dismissed. If the Committee has jurisdiction and cause for action exists, the Director will open a case, issue a specific charge letter, and conduct an investigation. The respondent is afforded an opportunity to comment on all evidence that will be considered by the Committee and upon which the Committee may rely in its review of the complaint. At the conclusion of the investigation, the case is referred to the Committee for review and resolution.

In resolving a case, the Committee may dismiss it; recommend that it be resolved with a reprimand or censure, with or without supplemental directives; recommend to the Board of Directors that the respondent be expelled from membership; or offer

the member the option of resigning subject to stipulated conditions and subject to approval by the Board of Directors.

If the Committee recommends any action other than dismissal or stipulated resignation, the respondent has a right to an independent case review and evaluation or, in the case of a recommendation of expulsion, a formal hearing or an independent adjudication. In an independent adjudication following a recommendation of censure or reprimand, the respondent provides a rationale for nonacceptance of the Committee's recommendation, and a three-member panel, selected by the respondent from six members of the Board of Directors' Standing Hearing Panel, provides the final adjudication based on the written record. The Director implements the final adjudication, whether based on the panel's decision or the respondent's acceptance of the Committee's recommendation.

A formal hearing is an in-person proceeding before a formal hearing committee, which makes an independent recommendation to the Board of Directors. The respondent may elect to have an independent adjudication instead of a formal hearing. The Board reviews the recommendation of the hearing committee, independent adjudication panel, or, if no hearing was requested, the Ethics Committee, and must adopt that recommendation unless specified defects require the matter to be remanded for further actions.

At the outset of the case, instead of contesting the charges, the respondent may offer a resignation, which is deemed a resignation while under ethics investigation.

ADOPTION AND APPLICATION

The revised Rules and Procedures of the Ethics Committee of the American Psychological Association, which are set forth below, were approved by the APA Board of Directors on December 9, 1995, with an effective date of June 1, 1996. Further revisions that allow respondents to resign while under ethics investigation and that call for the automatic expulsion with a right of review for show cause respondents were approved by the APA Board of Directors on August 25, 2001. The newest revisions will apply to all respondents against whom complaints or notices of show cause predicates were received by the APA Ethics Office on or after October 1, 2001. All other aspects of the Rules will be applied to all complaints and cases pending on the effective date of June 1, 1996, except, as provided in Part II, Subsection 1.2 of the 1992 Rules, "no amendment shall adversely affect the rights of a member of the Association whose conduct is being investigated by the Ethics Committee or against whom the Ethics Committee has filed formal charges" as of the effective date. In the event application of the revised Rules and Procedures would adversely affect such rights, the pertinent provisions of the Rules and Procedures in effect at the time the member came under the scrutiny of the Ethics Committee will be applied. Failure by the Committee or APA to follow these Rules and Procedures shall be cause to set aside action taken under these Rules only in the event such failure has resulted in genuine prejudice to the respondent.

PART I. OBJECTIVES AND AUTHORITY OF THE COMMITTEE

1. Objectives

The fundamental objectives of the Ethics Committee (hereinafter the Committee) shall be to maintain ethical conduct by psychologists at the highest professional level, to educate psychologists concerning ethical standards, to endeavor to protect the public against harmful conduct by psychologists, and to aid the Association in achieving its objectives as reflected in its Bylaws.[1]

2. Authority

The Committee is authorized to

2.1 Formulate rules or principles of ethics for adoption by the Association;

2.2 Investigate allegations of unethical conduct of members (to include fellows) and associates (hereinafter members) and, in certain instances, student affiliates and applicants for membership;

2.3 Resolve allegations of unethical conduct and/or recommend such action as is necessary to achieve the objectives of the Association;

2.4 Report on types of complaints investigated with special description of difficult cases;

2.5 Adopt rules and procedures governing the conduct of all the matters within its jurisdiction;

2.6 Take such other actions as are consistent with the Bylaws of the Association, the Association Rules, the Association's Ethics Code, and these Rules and Procedures, and as are necessary and appropriate to achieving the objectives of the Committee;

2.7 Delegate appropriate tasks to subcommittees, ad hoc committees, and task forces of the Ethics Committee; to Committee Associates; or to employees or agents of the Association, as necessary or appropriate. All of these individuals and groups shall in any such event be fully bound by these Rules and Procedures.

PART II. GENERAL OPERATING RULES

1. General Provisions

1.1 APA documents.[2] The Committee shall base its actions on applicable governmental laws and regulations, the Bylaws of the Association, the Association Rules, the Association's Ethics Code, and these Rules and Procedures.

1.2 Applicable ethics code. Conduct is subject to the Ethics Code in effect at the time the conduct occurred. If a course of conduct continued over a period of time during which more than one Ethics Code was in effect, each Ethics Code will be applicable to conduct that occurred during the time period it was in effect.

1.3 Rules and procedures. The Committee may adopt rules and procedures governing the conduct

---

[1] The Ethics Committee seeks to protect the public by deterring unethical conduct by psychologists, by taking appropriate action when an ethical violation has been proved according to these Rules and Procedures, and by setting standards to aid psychologists in understanding their ethical obligations. Of course, in no circumstances can or does the Committee or the Association guarantee that unethical behavior will not occur or that members of the public will never be harmed by the actions of individual psychologists.

[2] For a copy of the relevant sections of the current Bylaws and Association Rules, contact the APA Ethics Office.

of all matters within its jurisdiction, and may amend such rules from time to time upon a two-thirds vote of the Committee members, provided that no amendment shall adversely affect the rights of a member of the Association whose conduct is being investigated by the Ethics Committee or against whom the Ethics Committee has recommended expulsion, stipulated resignation, voiding membership, censure, or reprimand at the time of amendment. Changes to the Rules and Procedures must be ratified by the Board of Directors acting for the Council of Representatives.

1.4 Compliance with time requirements. The APA and the respondent shall use their best efforts to adhere strictly to the time requirements specified in these Rules and Procedures. Failure to do so will not prohibit final resolution unless such failure was unduly prejudicial. Upon request, the Director may extend time limits stated in these Rules for submitting statements or responses if there is good cause to do so. In all cases in which a time limit for submitting a response is stated in these Rules and Procedures, the period specified is the number of days allowed for receipt of the response by the Ethics Office.

1.5 Computation of time. In computing any period of time stated by these Rules, the day of the act, event, or default from which the designated period of time begins to run shall not be included. The last day of the period shall be included unless it is a Saturday, a Sunday, or a legal holiday, in which event the period runs until the end of the next business day.

2. Meetings and Officers

2.1 Frequency and quorum. The Committee shall meet at reasonable intervals as needed. A quorum at such meetings shall consist of the majority of the elected members of the Committee.

2.2 Selection of officers. The Chair and Vice Chair shall be elected annually at a duly constituted meeting.

2.3 Authority. The Vice Chair shall have the authority to perform all the duties of the Chair when the latter is unavailable or unable to perform them and shall perform such other tasks as are delegated by the Chair or by these Rules.

2.4 Majority rule. Except as otherwise noted in these Rules and Procedures, all decisions shall be by majority vote of those elected members present or, in the case of a vote by mail, a majority of those elected members qualified to vote.

2.5 Designation of responsibilities. The Chief Executive Officer of the Association shall designate a staff member to serve as Director of the Ethics Office. Whenever they appear in these Rules, "Chair," "Vice Chair," "Director," and "President" shall mean these individuals or their designees.

2.6 Attendance. Attendance at the Ethics Committee's deliberation of cases is restricted to elected members of the Committee, Committee Associates, the Director of the Ethics Office, the Ethics Office staff, members of the Board of Directors, Legal Counsel of the Association, and other duly appointed persons authorized by the Committee to assist it in carrying out its functions, except when the Committee, by two-thirds vote, authorizes the presence of other persons.

3. Confidentiality and Notifications

3.1 Requirement of confidentiality. All information concerning complaints against members shall be confidential, except that the Director may disclose such information when compelled by a valid subpoena, in response to a request from a state or local board or similar entity,[3] when otherwise required by law, or as otherwise provided in these Rules and Procedures. Such information may also be released when the Chair and the Director agree that release of that information is necessary to protect the interests of (a) the complainant or respondent; (b) other investigative or adjudicative bodies; (c) the Association; or (d) members of the public, and

[3]For purposes of these Rules and Procedures, a reference to state or local boards or similar entities shall include state, local, or provincial licensing boards (whether located in the United States or Canada); state, local, or provincial boards of examiners or education in those cases where the pertinent licensing or certification is secured from such entities; or, in states or provinces with no licensing authority, nonstatutory boards established for similar purposes (such as registering bodies).

release will not unduly interfere with the Association's interest in respecting the legitimate confidentiality interests of participants in the ethics process and its interest in safeguarding the confidentiality of internal peer review deliberation.

3.2 Access by staff, legal counsel, and other duly appointed persons. Information may be shared with Legal Counsel of the Association, with the Chief Executive Officer of the Association, with staff of the Association's Central Office designated by the Chief Executive Officer to assist the Committee with its work, and with other duly appointed persons authorized by the Committee to assist it in carrying out its functions. Subject to the confidentiality provisions in these Rules, these persons are authorized to use this information for the purposes set out in these Rules regardless of whether the person providing the information has executed a release.

3.3 Notification in connection with investigation or final disposition of investigation. Where these Rules provide for notification of final disposition of a matter, this notification shall include the ethical standard(s)[4] that were judged to have been violated and, if violation is found, the standards not violated, and the sanction (including a statement that directives were given), if any. In show cause proceedings under Part IV, this notification shall describe the type of underlying action (e.g., loss of license) without reference to the underlying behavior. In matters in which membership is voided under Part III, Subsection 3.3, the notification shall indicate that membership was voided because it was obtained on the basis of false or fraudulent information. In any of these matters, the rationale may also be included (a) if the notification is required by these Rules, at the discretion of the Board or Committee, (b) if the notification is not required, at the discretion of the entity or person (i.e., the Board, the Committee, or the Director) authorizing the notification, or (c) as set forth in a stipulation.

3.3.1 Respondent. The Director shall inform the respondent of the final disposition in a matter. This notification shall include the rationale for the Association's actions. As used in these Rules and Procedures, the term respondent includes any member, student affiliate, or membership applicant who is under the scrutiny of the Ethics Committee.

3.3.2 Complainant. The Director shall inform the complainant of the final disposition in a matter and of the respondent's resignation while under ethics investigation. The Director may also at any time, as a matter of discretion, provide such information as is necessary to notify the complainant of the status of a case.

3.3.3 Membership. The Director shall report annually to the membership the names of members who have lost membership due to unethical behavior and the names of members who have resigned their membership while under ethics investigation. For those members who lost their membership, the Director will also report the ethical standard(s) violated or the type of underlying action for a show cause case or that membership was voided because it was obtained on the basis of false or fraudulent information. No report to membership shall be made for other stipulated resignations in which such a report was not stipulated.

3.3.4 Council of representatives. The Director shall report annually and in confidence to the Council the names of members who have been allowed to resign under stipulated conditions and who have resigned while under ethics investigation.

3.3.5 Other entities. When the Board of Directors or the Committee determines that further notification is necessary for the protection of the Association or the public or to maintain the standards of the Association, the Director shall communicate the final disposition to those groups and/or individuals so identified. Such notification may be made to (a) affiliated state and regional associations,[5] (b) the American Board of Professional Psychology, (c) state or local boards or similar entities, (d) the Association of State and Provincial Psychology Boards, (e) the Council for the National Register of

---

[4]In this document "ethical standard(s)" refers to the ethical standard(s) in the Ethical Principles of Psychologists and Code of Conduct, the ethical principle(s) in the Ethical Principles of Psychologists, or the enforceable provisions of any subsequent ethics code.

[5]For purposes of these Rules and Procedures, a state association shall include territorial, local, or county psychological associations and, in cases of Canadian members of the Association, provincial psychological associations.

Health Service Providers in Psychology, and/or (f) other appropriate parties.

3.3.6 Other parties informed of the complaint. The Director may inform such other parties as have been informed of any matter reviewed under these Rules of the final disposition of that matter. Parties with knowledge of a matter may have been informed by the Committee, the Director, the respondent, or the complainant.

3.3.7 Notification in cases that have been converted. In any cases that have been converted under Part II, Subsections 7.3 or 7.4, the complainant and other persons informed of the complaint shall be notified of final disposition, including the fact that there has been a stipulated resignation, as set forth in Part IV, Subsection 12.1 and Part V, Subsection 7.6.5.

3.3.8 Disclosure of fact of investigation. The Director may disclose to any of the entities enumerated in Subsection 3.3.5 (a)–(f) of this part the fact that an individual is under ethical investigation in cases deemed to be serious threats to the public welfare (as determined by a two-thirds vote of the Committee), but only when to do so before final adjudication appears necessary to protect the public.

3.3.9 Notification of additional parties at the request of respondent. The Director may notify such additional parties of the final disposition as are requested by the respondent.

3.3.10 Notification of loss of membership upon written request. The Association shall inform any person who submits a written inquiry concerning a psychologist that a former member has lost membership due to unethical behavior, that a former member has resigned while under ethics investigation, or that an individual's membership was voided because it was obtained on the basis of false or fraudulent information. The notification will not include actions that were already decided or were under the scrutiny of the Committee prior to June 1, 1996, or stipulated resignations unless so stipulated.

3.4 Initiation of legal action constitutes waiver. Initiation of a legal action against the Association or any of its agents, officers, directors, employees, or volunteers concerning any matters considered or actions taken by the Ethics Committee or Director shall constitute a waiver by the person initiating such action of any interest in confidentiality recog-

nized in these Rules or other organic documents of the Association with respect to the subject matter of the legal action.

3.5 Communication for investigation or other functions. Nothing in this section shall prevent the Director from communicating any information (including information from the respondent, complainant, or a witness) to the respondent, complainant, witnesses, or other sources of information to the extent necessary to facilitate the performance of any functions set forth in these Rules and Procedures.

4. Records

4.1 Confidentiality of ethics files. Files of the Committee related to investigation and adjudication of cases shall be confidential, within the limitations of Section 3 of this part, and shall be maintained, consistent with these Rules and Procedures.

4.2 Investigation files. Investigation records containing personally identifiable information shall be maintained for at least five years after a matter is closed.

4.3 Files involving loss of membership. In cases in which members have lost membership, records shall be maintained indefinitely, except as provided in Subsection 4.4 of this part.

4.4 Readmission or death of a member. Records concerning members whom the Association has readmitted to membership or determined to be deceased shall be maintained for at least five years after that determination was made.

4.5 Records for educative purposes. Nothing in these Rules and Procedures shall preclude the Committee from maintaining records in a secure place for archival or record keeping purposes, or from using or publishing information concerning ethics matters for educative purposes without identifying individuals involved.

5. Jurisdiction

5.1 Persons. The Committee has jurisdiction over individual members (to include fellows), associate members, and applicants for membership in the American Psychological Association. The

Committee shall also have jurisdiction over student affiliates, but only to the extent that the conduct at issue is not under the direct supervision of the student's educational program or of a training site that is officially approved by the program as part of the student's supervised training.[6]

5.2 Subject matter. The Committee has jurisdiction to achieve its objectives and perform those functions for which it is authorized in these Rules and Procedures and other organic documents of the Association.

5.3 Time limits for complaints and show cause notices

5.3.1 Complaints by members. Except as provided in Subsections 5.3.5 and 5.3.6 of this part, the Committee may consider complaints brought by members of the Association against other members only if the complaint is received less than three years after the alleged conduct either occurred or was discovered by the complainant.

5.3.2 Complaints by nonmembers and student affiliates. Except as provided in Subsections 5.3.5 and 5.3.6 of this part, the Committee may consider complaints brought by nonmembers and student affiliates only if the complaint is received less than five years after the alleged conduct either occurred or was discovered by the complainant.

5.3.3 Sua sponte *complaints.* Except as provided in Subsection 7.4 of this part, the Committee may initiate a *sua sponte* complaint under Part V of these Rules and Procedures only if it does so, or has provided the notice specified in Subsection 5.6.2 of this part, less than one year after it discovered the alleged unethical conduct and less than 10 years after the alleged conduct occurred, except that whether or not such periods have expired, the Committee may initiate a *sua sponte* complaint less than one year after it discovered that any of the following actions had become final, and less than 10 years after the alleged conduct occurred: (a) a felony conviction, (b) a finding of malpractice by a duly authorized tribunal, (c) expulsion or suspension from a state association for unethical conduct, or (d) revocation, suspension, or surrender of a license or certificate, or deregistration for ethical violations by a state or local board or similar entity, or while ethical proceedings before such board were pending.

5.3.4 Show cause notices. The Committee may issue a show cause notice under Part IV of these Rules and Procedures only if it does so, or has provided the notice specified in Subsection 5.6.2 of this part, less than one year after the date it discovered that the applicable predicate for use of show cause procedures (i.e., an event described in Part IV, Section 1) had become final and less than 10 years after the alleged conduct occurred, except this latter time limit shall be 20 years in any matter involving an offense against a minor.

5.3.5 Exceptions to time limits for complaints by members and nonmembers.

5.3.5.1 Threshold Criteria. Any complaint not received within the time limits set forth in this section shall not be considered unless, with respect to complaints subject to Subsections 5.3.1 and 5.3.2 of this part, the Chair and Director (with the vote of the Vice Chair if agreement is not reached by the Chair and Director) determine that each of the following criteria is met:

5.3.5.1.1 The behavior alleged involved one of the following: sexual misconduct; felony conviction; insurance fraud; plagiarism; noncooperation; blatant, intentional misrepresentation; or other behavior likely to cause substantial harm.

5.3.5.1.2 The complaint was received less than 10 years after the alleged conduct occurred.

5.3.5.2 Determination to Supersede Applicable Time Limit. Where the Chair and Director have determined (with the vote of the Vice Chair if agreement is not reached by the Chair and Director) that the threshold criteria in Subsection 5.3.5.1 are met, the applicable limit shall be superseded.

5.3.6 Conduct outside the time limits. The Committee may consider evidence of conduct outside these time limits in connection with the commencement, investigation, review, or disposition of a matter involving conduct that is within the appli-

---

[6]Whether an individual is a member of the Association is determined according to the Bylaws, Association Rules, and other pertinent organic documents of the Association. Under the current rules, nonpayment of dues results in discontinuation of membership only after two consecutive calendar years during which dues to the Association have remained unpaid. For a copy of the relevant sections of the current Bylaws and Association Rules, contact the APA Ethics Office. For purposes of these Rules and Procedures, high school and foreign affiliates are not members of the Association.

cable time limits. However, the Committee may impose sanctions only for conduct that occurred within the time limits. In order for a sanction to be imposed for conduct occurring outside the time limits, the Chair and Director must decide to supersede the time limits applicable to that conduct as stated in Subsection 5.3.5 of this part.

5.3.7 Reopened investigations. In a matter reopened under Part II, Section 6, the investigation shall be considered within the time limits as long as the complaint in the original matter was received, or the original investigation was initiated, in a timely manner or a decision was made to supersede the time limit under Part II, Subsection 5.3.5. The Committee may not proceed with such an investigation, however, if the new evidence is received more than 10 years after the date the alleged unethical behavior occurred (except that this time limit shall be 20 years in any case that was initiated as or converted to a show cause case and involves an offense against a minor).

5.4 Resignation barred

5.4.1 Resignation barred. Except as provided in Subsection 5.4.2 and 11.4 of this part of these Rules, no one under the scrutiny of the Committee will be allowed to resign from the Association either by letter of resignation, by nonpayment of dues, or otherwise.

5.4.2 Resignation under ethics investigation. A respondent may in the alternative accept the opportunity to resign from membership with the understanding that such resignation will be deemed for all purposes a resignation "under ethics investigation." This opportunity is available only if, within the required number of days (60 days in Part IV automatic expulsion cases; 30 days in Part V matters) after receiving his or her first notification of the ethics matter from the APA Ethics Office, the respondent provides to the APA Ethics Office a signed, notarized affidavit indicating acceptance of the opportunity to resign while under ethics investigation. Failure to return the affidavit within the relevant time period will constitute a waiver of the right to resign while under ethics investigation. Resignation shall be effective upon the Committee's timely receipt of the signed notarized affidavit. The Association may inform a complainant, the membership through the dues notice, and anyone who

requests the information from APA that the respondent has so resigned. (See also Part IV, Section 2 and Part V, Subsections 4.3.2, 5.3, and 6.1 of these Rules and Procedures.)

5.5 Concurrent litigation. Civil or criminal litigation involving members shall not bar action by the Committee; the Committee may proceed or may stay the ethics process during the course of litigation. Delay in conducting the investigation by the Committee during the pendency of civil or criminal proceedings shall not constitute waiver of jurisdiction.

5.6 Other concurrent disciplinary proceedings

5.6.1 Concurrent jurisdiction. Disciplinary proceedings or action by another body or tribunal shall not bar action by the Committee; the Committee may proceed or may stay the ethics process during the course of such proceedings. Delay in conducting the investigation by the Committee during the pendency of such proceedings shall not constitute a waiver of jurisdiction. Where the Committee learns that disciplinary action by another authorized tribunal has been stayed, such stay shall neither require nor preclude action by the Committee. When another body or tribunal has investigated the same allegations and found no merit to the allegations, the Ethics Committee may, in its discretion, decide not to open a matter or, if a matter has already been opened, the Ethics Committee may close the matter.

5.6.2 Nonfinal disciplinary action by another body. The Chair, Vice Chair, and Director may decide not to open a *sua sponte* or show cause case when a state or local board or similar entity has taken disciplinary action against an Association member if the action is either not final or the member has not completed all directives, probation, or other requirements and if the behavior at issue is not likely to result in expulsion from the Association. If this decision is made, the member will be notified that the matter is under the scrutiny of the Committee, that the member will be monitored until completion of actions required by the state or local board or similar entity, that failure to complete the action may result in further action by the Committee, and that completion of such requirements may result in the Committee taking no further action.

5.7 Referral and retention of jurisdiction. The Committee may at any time refer a matter to another recognized tribunal for appropriate action. If a case is referred to another tribunal, the Committee may retain jurisdiction and consider the matter independently under these Rules and Procedures.

6. Reopening a Closed Investigation

If significant new evidence of unethical conduct comes to the attention of the Committee after a matter has been closed, the investigation may be reopened and acted upon under regular procedures. If, in the judgment of the Director, such information is furnished, the new evidence shall be submitted to the Committee, which may reopen the investigation if it agrees that the criteria listed below are satisfied. To be considered under this rule, new evidence must meet each of the following criteria:

6.1 The evidence was brought to the attention of the Committee after the investigation was closed;

6.2 The evidence could not with reasonable diligence have been brought to the attention of the Committee before the investigation was closed;

6.3 The evidence was provided to the Committee in a timely manner following its discovery;

6.4 The evidence would probably produce a different result.

7. Choice and Conversion of Procedures

7.1 Choice of procedures. Where a case might be adjudicated according to the show cause procedures in Part IV of these Rules and Procedures, the Chair and the Director shall determine whether to proceed under Part IV or Part V of these Rules and Procedures.

7.2 Conversion of show cause action to *sua sponte* action. The Chair and the Director may convert a proceeding begun by show cause procedures under Part IV to a *sua sponte* action under Part V. In the event of such conversion, the complaint shall be deemed filed in a timely manner if the show cause proceeding was initiated in a timely fashion.

7.3 Conversion to show cause action. Where the predicates for use of show cause procedures stated in Part IV, Section 1 are present, the Chair and the Director may convert a proceeding begun as a *sua sponte,* member, or nonmember complaint under Part V to a show cause proceeding under Part IV if the predicates are based on some or all of the same underlying conduct as was the basis for the original proceeding. In such event, the show cause proceeding shall be deemed initiated in a timely manner as long as the original proceeding was commenced within the time limits applicable to that proceeding or a decision was made to supersede the time limit under Part II, Subsection 5.3.5.

7.4 Conversion of action initiated by a complainant to a *sua sponte* action. The Chair and the Director may convert a proceeding commenced following a complaint submitted by a member or nonmember (including a proceeding in which the complaint is withdrawn) into a *sua sponte* action under Part V, Subsection 2.2. The action will be deemed filed in a timely manner as long as the member or nonmember complaint was received within the time limits applicable to the initial complaint or a decision was made to supersede the time limit in Part II, Subsection 5.3.5.

8. Correspondence and Documentation

8.1 Use of correspondence. The Committee shall conduct as much of its business as is practical through correspondence, including telecopied information.

8.2 Personal response. Although the respondent has the right to consult with an attorney concerning all phases of the ethics process, the respondent must respond to charges and recommendations of the Ethics Committee personally and not through legal counsel or another third party. If the respondent shows good cause as to why he or she cannot respond personally, the Director may waive this requirement.

8.3 Transcription of audiotapes, videotapes, and similar data compilations. It shall be the responsibility of the individual or entity submitting to the Committee an audiotape, videotape, or similar data compilation to provide an accurate transcription of the information it contains. The Director may reject any audiotape, videotape, or similar data compilation provided unaccompanied by a transcription as required in this subsection unless and until such transcription is provided.

8.4 Service of documents. For purposes of notice, service shall be made by delivery to the respondent or the respondent's attorney or by mail or common carrier to the respondent or the respondent's attorney at the respondent's or attorney's last known address. Delivery within this rule means handing the correspondence to the respondent or the attorney or leaving it at the respondent's office or place of abode or the attorney's office with a receptionist, secretary, clerk, or other person in charge thereof, or, if there is no one in charge, leaving it in a mailbox or a conspicuous place at that address. Service by mail is complete upon mailing. Where, after good faith efforts, the Committee has been unable to locate the respondent, it may give notice by publishing in a newspaper of general circulation in the respondent's last known place of domicile a notice to contact the Ethics Office concerning an important matter.

8.5 Material from the public domain. The Committee may consult authoritative resources from the public domain (e.g., the Directory of the American Psychological Association and the National Register of Health Service Providers in Psychology) without providing this material to the respondent.

9. Failure to Cooperate With Ethics Process

Members are required to cooperate fully and in a timely fashion with the ethics process. Failure to cooperate shall not prevent continuation of any proceedings and itself constitutes a violation of the Ethics Code that may warrant being expelled from the Association.

10. Board of Directors' Standing Hearing Panel

The President of the Association shall appoint members of the Standing Hearing Panel. Standing Hearing Panel members shall serve a three-year renewable term. The Standing Hearing Panel shall consist of at least 30 members at least 5 of whom shall be public members, and the remainder shall be members of the Association in good standing, and shall not include any present members of the Ethics Committee.

11. Available Sanctions

On the basis of circumstances that aggravate or mitigate the culpability of the member, including prior sanctions, directives, or educative letters from the Association or state or local boards or similar entities, a sanction more or less severe, respectively, than would be warranted on the basis of the factors set forth below, may be appropriate.

11.1 Reprimand. Reprimand is the appropriate sanction if there has been an ethics violation but the violation was not of a kind likely to cause harm to another person or to cause substantial harm to the profession and was not otherwise of sufficient gravity as to warrant a more severe sanction.

11.2 Censure. Censure is the appropriate sanction if there has been an ethics violation and the violation was of a kind likely to cause harm to another person, but the violation was not of a kind likely to cause substantial harm to another person or to the profession and was not otherwise of sufficient gravity as to warrant a more severe sanction.

11.3 Expulsion. Expulsion from membership is the appropriate sanction if there has been an ethics violation and the violation was of a kind likely to cause substantial harm to another person or the profession or was otherwise of sufficient gravity as to warrant such action.

11.4 Stipulated resignation. A stipulated resignation may be offered by the Committee following a Committee finding that the respondent has committed a violation of the Ethics Code or failed to show good cause why he or she should not be expelled, contingent on execution of an acceptable affidavit and approval by the Board of Directors, under Part IV, Section 12 or Part V, Subsection 7.6.

12. Available Directives

12.1 Cease and desist order. Such a directive requires the respondent to cease and desist specified unethical behavior(s).

12.2 Other corrective actions. The Committee may require such other corrective actions as may be necessary to remedy a violation, protect the interests of the Association, or protect the public. Such a directive may not include a requirement that the respondent make a monetary payment to the Association or persons injured by the conduct.

12.3 Supervision requirement. Such a directive requires that the respondent engage in supervision.

12.4 Education, training, or tutorial requirement. Such a directive requires that the respondent engage in education, training, or a tutorial.

12.5 Evaluation and/or treatment requirement. Such a directive requires that the respondent be evaluated to determine the possible need for treatment and/or, if dysfunction has been established, obtain treatment appropriate to that dysfunction.

12.6 Probation. Such a directive requires monitoring of the respondent by the Committee to ensure compliance with the Ethics Committee's mandated directives during the period of those directives.

13. Matters Requiring the Concurrence of the Chair of the Committee and Director of the Ethics Office

Whenever matters entrusted by these Rules and Procedures to the Chair and Director require the concurrence of those officers before certain action may be taken, either officer in the event of disagreement may refer the matter to the Vice Chair, who, together with the Chair and Director, shall make a final determination by majority vote.

PART III. MEMBERSHIP

1. Applications

1.1 Specific jurisdiction. The Committee has the authority to investigate the preadmission scientific and professional ethics and conduct of all applicants for membership or student affiliation in the Association and to make recommendations as to whether an individual shall become a member or student affiliate. In addition, the Committee has the authority to consider all applications submitted by individuals who were previously denied admission as a result of unethical behavior and to make recommendations as to whether such an individual shall become a member or student affiliate. The Membership Committee shall transmit all applications on which there is an indication of possible preadmission unethical conduct and all applications from individuals who were previously denied admission as a result of unethical behavior or as a result of a recommendation by the Ethics Committee to the Director of the Ethics Office.

1.2 Procedures for review. The Director shall transmit to the Committee a copy of the application and any other materials pertinent to the case. The Director shall take such steps, including contacting the applicant or other sources of information, as are necessary and appropriate to making a fair determination. Upon review, the Committee may recommend to the Membership Committee that the application be granted or to the Board of Directors that the application be denied. If a recommendation is made to deny the application, the applicant shall be informed of the basis for that recommendation and shall have 30 days to submit a written response for consideration by the Board of Directors.

2. Applications for Readmission

2.1 Specific jurisdiction. The Ethics Committee has the authority to review and make recommendations concerning all applications for readmission by persons who have lost membership as a result of unethical behavior, who have resigned while under ethics investigation, or whose membership was voided because it was obtained on the basis of false or fraudulent information. The Membership Committee shall transmit all such applications for readmission to the Director of the Ethics Office.

2.2 Elapsed time for review. Applications for readmission by members who have lost membership due to unethical behavior (including submission of false or fraudulent information in a membership application) shall be considered by the Committee only after five years have elapsed from the date of that action. Applications for readmission by members who have been permitted to resign shall be considered only after the stipulated period or, where no period has been stipulated, three years have elapsed.

2.3 Procedures for review. The Director shall transmit to the Committee a summary of the application for readmission and the record of the previous case against the former member. In all cases, the ex-member must show that he or she is technically and ethically qualified and has satisfied any conditions upon readmission established by the Board. The Committee shall make one of the following recommendations to the Membership Committee and, as it deems appropriate, shall provide the rationale therefor.

    2.3.1 Readmit. Recommend that the former member be readmitted;

    2.3.2 Deny readmission. Recommend that readmission be denied;

    2.3.3 Defer readmission. Recommend that the application for readmission be deferred until certain conditions have been met;

    2.3.4 Investigate further. Charge the Director to investigate issues specified by the Committee and to place the matter before the Committee at a future date.

3. Allegations That Membership Was Obtained Under False or Fraudulent Pretenses

3.1 Specific jurisdiction. The Committee has the authority to investigate allegations that membership was obtained on the basis of false or fraudulent information and to take appropriate action. The Membership Committee shall transmit all such allegations to the Director of the Ethics Office.

3.2 Procedures for review. The respondent will be given notice of the allegations that membership was obtained on the basis of false or fraudulent information, a copy of any evidence relating to these allegations that is submitted to the Committee, and an opportunity to respond in writing. The Director may take any other steps, such as contacting other sources of information, that are considered necessary and appropriate to making a fair determination in the circumstances of the case. The Director shall transmit to the Committee a copy of the membership application and any other materials pertinent to the case.

3.3 Committee's recommendation. Upon completion of this review, the Committee may recommend to the Board of Directors that it void the election to membership in the Association of any person who obtained membership on the basis of false or fraudulent information.

3.4 Procedures subsequent to committee's recommendation to void membership. If the respondent does not accept the Committee's recommendation, the respondent shall, within 30 days of receipt of the recommendation, either submit a written response to the Board of Directors, request a formal hearing in writing, or request an independent adjudication in writing and provide a written rationale for non-acceptance. The respondent's failure to respond within 30 days after notification shall be deemed acceptance of the Committee's recommendation and a waiver of the right to a formal hearing or an independent adjudication. If a written response is submitted, the Ethics Committee shall have 30 days to reply in a written statement to the Board. If a formal hearing is requested, it shall be conducted according to the procedures explained in Part V, Subsections 10.2 through 10.3.4 of these Rules and Procedures. If an independent adjudication is requested, it shall be conducted according to the procedures explained in Part V, Subsections 9.2.2 through 9.2.7 and Subsections 10.3 through 10.3.4.

3.5 Action by the board of directors. Within 180 days after receiving the record, the Committee's recommendation, any written response and statement described in Subsection 3.4, above, or any recommendation from a Hearing Committee or Independent Adjudication Panel, the Board of Directors shall vote whether to void the respondent's membership or not.

PART IV. SHOW CAUSE PROCEDURES BASED UPON ACTIONS BY OTHER RECOGNIZED TRIBUNALS

1. Predicates for Use of Show Cause Procedures

1.1 Felony or equivalent offense. If a member has been convicted of a felony (including any felony as defined by state/provincial law and any other criminal offense with a possible term of incarceration exceeding one year) and such conviction is not under appeal, the show cause process may be used, if determined by the Chair and the Director to be appropriate.

1.2 Expulsion, suspension, unlicensure, decertification, or other actions. If one of the following actions has been taken and is not under appeal, the show cause process may be used, if determined by the Chair and the Director to be appropriate: (a) a member has been expelled or suspended from an affiliated state or regional psychological association; (b) a member has been denied a license, certificate, or registration, has been unlicensed, decertified, or deregistered, has had a license, certificate, or registration revoked or suspended by a state or local board or similar entity, or has voluntarily surrendered a license or certificate of registration as a result of pending allegations. The show cause procedures may also be used if a state or local board or similar entity has taken any of the actions specified in (a) or (b) above and has then in any way stayed or postponed that action.

2. Notice of Automatic Expulsion and Response by Respondent

2.1 The respondent shall be notified by the Director that he or she has been barred from resigning membership in the Association and will be expelled 60 days after receipt of the notice of expulsion unless the respondent exercises the right to request a review of the pending expulsion by submitting in writing within the 60-day period a request for review and a statement showing good cause why he or she should not be expelled from membership in the Association. If no response is received within the 60 days, the right to a review shall be considered waived and the Director shall inform the Membership Office that the respondent has been expelled, effective immediately.

2.2 The respondent may in the alternative accept the opportunity to resign from membership as provided in Part II, Subsection 5.4.2 ("*Resignation Under Ethics Investigation*").

3. Showing by Respondent That Prior Proceeding Lacked Due Process

In addition to a response to the substance of the charges under Section 2 of this part, the respondent may seek within the 60-day period to show that the other recognized tribunal did not follow fair procedure. If the Committee finds merit to this contention, it may exercise its discretion under Part II, Subsection 7.2 of these Rules and convert the matter to a *sua sponte* action under Part V, or it may dismiss the complaint.

4. Investigation

The Committee may conduct a further investigation, including seeking additional information from the respondent or others or requesting that the respondent appear in person. Any evidence not obtained directly from the respondent and relied upon by the Committee in connection with its review and recommendation shall first have been provided to the respondent, who shall have been afforded not less than 15 days to respond thereto in writing.

5. Failure to Return Affidavit

If the respondent elects to resign while under ethics investigation and fails to return the affidavit, the respondent will be considered to have waived the right to resign while under ethics investigation.

6. Review and Recommendation by the Committee Following a Request for Review

Upon receipt of the respondent's request for review and supporting statement and upon conclusion of any necessary further investigation, the case shall be reviewed by the Ethics Committee. Members of the Ethics Committee and Ethics Committee Associates may be assigned to review and summarize the case. Members and Associates may also be assigned to participate on a panel to review the case and make a preliminary recommendation prior to review by the full Ethics Committee. Ethics Committee Associates may also attend and participate in the full Committee meetings, but shall not vote on the full Committee's disposition of a case. When review of a case has been completed, the Committee shall vote to take one of the following actions:

6.1 Remand

6.2 Dismiss the matter

6.3 Recommend one of the following actions to the board of directors:

6.3.1 Reprimand or censure, with or without directives. The Committee may recommend that the respondent be reprimanded or censured, with or without one or more directives.

6.3.2 Expulsion. The Committee may recommend that the respondent be expelled from the Association; or, the Committee may recommend the sanction of stipulated resignation, under the procedure in Subsection 12.2 of this part.

7. Notification of Respondent

The Director shall notify the respondent of the Committee's recommendation and shall provide the respondent the opportunity to file a written response with the Board of Directors.

8. Respondent's Response to Recommendation

Within 15 days of receipt of notification of the Committee's recommendation, the respondent may file a written response with the Board of Directors. The response should be mailed to the Ethics Office.

9. Committee's Statement

The Ethics Committee shall have 15 days from the time it receives the respondent's written response, or from the time such response was due, to file a written statement, if any. A copy will be provided to the respondent.

10. Respondent's Final Response

Within 15 days of receipt of the Ethics Committee's statement, if any, the respondent may submit to the Director a written response to that statement.

11. Review by the Board of Directors

Within 180 days after receiving the record, the Committee's recommendation, any written response by the respondent, any written statement by the Committee, and any final response from the respondent, the Board of Directors shall vote whether to accept the Committee's recommended sanction, to issue a different sanction, or to dismiss the case. The Board may select a sanction more or less severe than that recommended by the Committee, or it may remand the matter to the Ethics Committee for further consideration.

12. Stipulated Resignation After Review and Recommendation

In lieu of the recommendations set forth in Section 6 of this part, with the agreement of the respondent, the Committee may recommend that the respondent be permitted to resign from the Association under stipulations stated by the Committee, according to the following procedure:

12.1 Offer of stipulated resignation by committee. When the Committee finds that another body has taken one of the actions specified in Part IV, Section 1 against a member, the Committee may offer, contingent upon approval by the Board of Directors, the respondent the opportunity to resign from the Association under mutually agreed upon stipulations. Such stipulations shall include the extent to which the stipulated resignation and its basis shall be disclosed and a minimum period of time, after resignation, during which the resigned member shall be ineligible to reapply for membership. The Committee may, in its discretion, also vote to recommend to the Board and inform the respondent of an alternative sanction chosen from among Subsections 11.1–11.3 of Part II of these Rules in the event the respondent does not accept the offer of stipulated resignation.

12.2 Notification of respondent. In such cases, the respondent shall be notified, in writing, of the Committee's offer of stipulated resignation and that he or she may accept the Committee's offer within 30 days of receipt. The respondent shall also be notified of any alternative recommended sanction.

12.3 Acceptance by respondent. Within 30 days, the respondent may accept the offer of stipulated resignation by signing a notarized affidavit of resignation acceptable to both the respondent and the Committee and forwarding the signed notarized affidavit to the Committee. Such resignation shall become effective only with the approval of the Board, as set forth in this section.

12.4 Transmittal to board of directors. If the respondent accepts the stipulated resignation, the Committee shall submit a copy of the affidavit of resignation, with the record in the matter and the rationale for recommending stipulated resignation on the terms set forth in the affidavit, to the Board of Directors.

12.5 Action by board of directors. Within 180 days, the Board of Directors shall take one of the following actions:

12.5.1 Acceptance of stipulated resignation. The Board of Directors shall accept the respondent's resignation on the terms stated in the affidavit of resignation, unless it is persuaded that to do so would not be in the best interest of the Association and/or of the public. If the resignation is accepted by the Board, the Director shall so notify the respondent.

12.5.2 Reprimand or censure. The Board may reject the stipulated resignation and impose a lesser sanction (reprimand or censure with or without directives). If the Board selects this option, the respondent shall be so notified and shall have 30 days to submit a written request seeking reconsideration of the Board's decision. If no such request is submitted, the Board's decision shall become final. If a request for reconsideration is submitted, the Board shall choose from the options set forth in Subsection 12.5 (including adherence to its prior decision).

12.5.3 Remand to the committee. The Board may choose to reject the affidavit of resignation and remand the matter to the Committee for further consideration. If the Board selects this alternative, the Director shall so notify the respondent and the Committee shall then reconsider the matter.

12.6 Rejection of stipulated resignation by respondent. If the respondent fails within 30 days to accept the recommended resolution, or formally notifies the Committee of rejection of the offer of stipulated resignation within the 30-day period, the offer of stipulated resignation shall be deemed rejected. The Committee shall reconsider the matter or, if an alternative recommended sanction has previously been identified by the Committee, such alternative recommended sanction shall automatically become the recommended sanction. The Director shall notify the respondent of the recommendation and of his or her opportunity to file written responses with the Board of Directors, as stated in Section 8 of this part. Sections 8–11 of this part shall also apply.

PART V. COMPLAINTS ALLEGING VIOLATION OF THE ETHICS CODE

1. Initiation of Actions

Ethics proceedings against a member are initiated by the filing of a complaint or, in the case of a *sua sponte* action, by the issuance of a letter notifying the respondent that a *sua sponte* action has been commenced.

2. Complaints

2.1 Complaints submitted by members or nonmembers. Complaints may be submitted by members or nonmembers of the Association.

2.2 *Sua sponte* action. When a member appears to have violated the Association's Ethics Code, the Committee may proceed on its own initiative. The Committee may, at any time, exercise its discretion to discontinue a *sua sponte* action. If the Committee does so, the respondent shall be so notified.

2.3 *Sua sponte* action based upon a member's filing of a capricious or malicious complaint. To prevent abuse of the ethics process, the Committee is empowered to bring charges itself against a complainant if the initial complaint is judged by two thirds of Committee members voting to be (a) frivolous and (b) intended to harm the respondent rather than to protect the public. The filing of such a complaint constitutes a violation of the Ethics Code.

2.4 Countercomplaints. The Committee will not consider a complaint from a respondent member against a complainant member during the course of its investigation and resolution of the initial complaint. Rather, the Committee shall study all sides of the matter leading to the first complaint and consider countercharges only after the initial complaint is finally resolved. The Committee may waive this procedure by a vote of at least two thirds of the voting Committee members and consider both complaints simultaneously.

2.5 Anonymous complaints. The Committee shall not act upon anonymous complaints. If material in the public domain is provided anonymously, the Committee may choose to consider such material in connection with a *sua sponte* matter or other complaint or may initiate a *sua sponte* action but only if the respondent has been provided with a copy of the material and afforded an opportunity to respond to the material.

2.6 Complaints against nonmembers. If the complaint does not involve an individual within the jurisdiction of the Committee, the Director shall inform the complainant and may suggest that the complainant contact another agency or association that may have jurisdiction.

2.7 Consecutive complaints. When a complaint is lodged against a member with respect to whom a case involving similar alleged behavior was previously closed, materials in the prior case may be considered in connection with the new case and may be considered as evidence as long as the Ethics Committee and/or the Board of Directors is informed of the final disposition of the original case.

2.8 Simultaneous complaints. When more than one complaint is simultaneously pending against the same member, the Committee may choose to combine the cases or to keep them separate. In the event the cases are combined, the Committee shall take reasonable steps to ensure that the legitimate confidentiality interests of any complainant, witness, or respondent are not compromised by combination.

3. Procedures for Filing Complaints

A complaint by a member or nonmember shall be comprised of

3.1 A completed APA Ethics Complaint Form;

3.2 Such releases as are required by the Committee;

3.3 A waiver by the complainant of any right to subpoena from APA or its agents for the purposes of private civil litigation any documents or information concerning the case.[7]

3.4 For purposes of determining time limits, a complaint shall be considered filed with APA as soon as a completed complaint form has been received by the Ethics Office. A deficiency or omission in the preparation of the complaint form may, at the discretion of

the Director, be disregarded for purposes of determining compliance with time limits.

4. Preliminary Evaluation of Complaints by the Director

The Director shall review each complaint to determine if jurisdictional criteria are met and if it can be determined whether cause for action exists.

4.1 Lack of jurisdiction. If jurisdictional criteria are not satisfied, the matter shall be closed and the complainant so notified.

4.2 Information insufficient to determine jurisdiction.

4.2.1 Request for supplementation of complaint. If the information is not sufficient to determine whether jurisdictional criteria are met, the Director shall so inform the complainant, who will be given 30 days from receipt of the request to supplement the complaint.

4.2.2 Consequences of failure to supplement complaint. If no response is received from the complainant within 30 days from receipt of the request, the matter may be closed. If at a later date the complainant shows good cause for delay and demonstrates that jurisdictional criteria can be met, the supplemented complaint shall be considered.

4.3 Process with respect to superseding applicable time limit.

4.3.1 Consideration by chair and director. If a complaint otherwise within the jurisdiction of the Ethics Committee appears to have been filed outside the applicable time limit, the Chair and the Director will determine whether the criteria set forth in Part II, Subsection 5.3.5 appear to be satisfied. If they agree that the criteria do not appear to be satisfied, the matter will be closed, unless there are other allegations that are filed in a timely manner, in which case processing of the timely allegations continues under Section 5, below. If they agree that the criteria appear to be satisfied, the Director will contact the respondent according to the procedure in Subsection 4.3.2, below. If they are not in agreement on whether or not those criteria appear to be satisfied, the Vice Chair shall review the matter and cast the deciding vote.

---

[7]This waiver is required to help assure participants in the APA ethics process, including complainants, that the process will not be inappropriately used to gain an advantage in other litigation.

4.3.2 Response by respondent where criteria appear to be satisfied. If a determination is made according to Subsection 4.3.1 above that the criteria of Part II, Subsection 5.3.5 appear to be satisfied, the Director shall notify the respondent and provide the respondent with a copy of the complaint and any other materials the Director deems appropriate.

4.3.2.1 The respondent shall have 30 days from receipt of these materials to address whether the criteria of Part II, Subsection 5.3.5 are met.

4.3.2.2 The respondent may in the alternative accept the opportunity to resign from membership as provided in Part II, Section 5.4.2 ("*Resignation Under Ethics Investigation*").

4.3.3 Determination by chair and director. If the respondent does not provide a response under Subsection 4.3.2, above, the decision made under Subsection 4.3.1, above, shall become final. In any case in which the respondent provides a response, the Chair and the Director shall consider whether the criteria set forth in Part II, Subsection 5.3.5 are satisfied, based upon any materials provided by the complainant and respondent, and any other information available to the Chair and the Director. If they agree that the criteria are not satisfied, the matter will be closed, unless there are other allegations that are filed in a timely manner, in which case processing of the timely allegations continues under Section 5, below. If they agree that the criteria are satisfied, processing continues under Section 5, below. If they are not in agreement on whether or not those criteria are satisfied, the Vice Chair shall review the matter and cast the deciding vote.

5. Evaluation of Complaints by Chair and Director

All complaints not closed by the Director under Section 4 of this part shall be reviewed by the Chair and the Director to determine whether cause for action by the Ethics Committee exists.

5.1 Cause for action defined. Cause for action shall exist when the respondent's alleged actions and/or omissions, if proved, would in the judgment of the decision maker constitute a breach of ethics. For purposes of determining whether cause for action exists, incredible, speculative, and/or internally inconsistent allegations may be disregarded.

5.2 Information insufficient to determine cause for action.

5.2.1 Request for supplementation of complaint. If the information is not sufficient to determine whether a case should be opened, the Director may so inform the complainant, who will be given 30 days from receipt of the request to supplement the complaint. The Chair and Director may additionally, or in the alternative, commence a preliminary investigation under Subsection 5.3 of this part.

5.2.2 Consequences of failure to supplement complaint. If no response is received from the complainant within 30 days, the matter may be closed. If at a later date the complainant shows good cause for delay and responds to the request for supplementation, the supplemented complaint shall be considered.

5.3 Preliminary investigation due to insufficient information. If the Chair and Director agree that they lack sufficient information to determine whether a case should be opened, either in a case initiated by a complainant or in a *sua sponte* action, a preliminary investigation may be initiated.

5.3.1 Notification to respondent. If a preliminary investigation is opened, the Director shall so inform the respondent in writing. The Director will include a copy of all evidence in the file; a copy of the APA Ethics Code; the Committee's Rules and Procedures; and a statement that information submitted by the respondent shall become a part of the record and can be used if further proceedings ensue.

5.3.2 Time for respondent response. The respondent shall have 30 days after receipt of the notification of a preliminary investigation to file an initial response.

5.3.2.1 The respondent may in the alternative accept the opportunity to resign from membership as provided in Part II, Section 5.4.2 ("*Resignation Under Ethics Investigation*").

5.3.3 Information from other sources. Additional information may be requested from the complainant, respondent, or any other appropriate source. The Committee will not rely upon information submitted by such sources unless it has been shared with the respondent and the respondent has been afforded an opportunity to respond thereto.

5.3.4 Action if there continues to be insufficient information. At the conclusion of the preliminary investigation, if the Director and Chair determine that they still lack evidence sufficient to determine whether cause for action exists, the matter shall be closed.

5.4 Determination of cause for action. If the Chair and Director agree that cause for action exists, they shall consider whether to open a formal case under Subsection 5.5, below. If the Chair and Director agree that cause for action does not exist, the matter shall be closed. If the Chair and Director disagree on whether or not there is cause for action by the Committee, the matter shall be reviewed by the Vice Chair, who will cast the deciding vote.

5.5 Decision to open a case. In any case in which the determination has been made that cause for action exists, the Chair and Director shall consider whether (a) there is a reasonable basis to believe the alleged violation cannot be proved by a preponderance of the evidence and (b) the allegations would constitute only minor or technical violations that would not warrant further action, have already been adequately addressed in another forum, or are likely to be corrected. If they agree that one or more of the conditions are met, the matter shall be closed. Otherwise, the matter shall be opened as a case.

5.6 Educative letter. If a matter is closed under Sections 4 or 5 of this part, the Chair and Director may, if appropriate, send an educative letter to the respondent.

5.7 Reconsideration of decision to open. A matter not opened under either Subsection 5.4 or 5.5, above, may be reconsidered by the Committee only if it does so in accordance with Part II, Section 6.

5.8 Supplementary or alternative action. The Chair and Director may recommend that the complainant refer the complaint to an appropriate state psychological association, state board, regulatory agency, subsidiary body of the Association, or other appropriate entity, or they may make such referral on their own initiative. Such referral does not constitute a waiver of jurisdiction over the complaint provided that the Committee opens a formal case within 24 months from the date of referral.

6. Case Investigation

6.1 Issuance of charge letter and response from respondent

6.1.1 Charge letter. If a case is opened, the Director shall so inform the respondent in a charge letter. The charge letter shall contain a concise description of the alleged behaviors at issue and identify the specific section(s) of the Ethics Code that the respondent is alleged to have violated. The Director shall enclose a copy of any completed Ethics Complaint Form and any materials submitted to date by the complainant or on the complainant's behalf that will be included in the record before the Committee; a copy of the APA Ethics Code and the Committee's Rules and Procedures; and a statement that information submitted by the respondent shall become a part of the record, and can be used if further proceedings ensue.

6.1.2 Significance of charge letter. A charge letter does not constitute or represent a finding that any unethical behavior has taken place, or that any allegations of the complaint are or are not likely to be found to be true.

6.1.3 Issuance of new charge letter to conform to evidence discovered during investigation. At any time prior to final resolution by the Committee, in order to make the charges conform to the evidence developed during the investigation, the Director and Chair may determine that a new charge letter should be issued setting forth ethical standard(s) and/or describing alleged behaviors different from or in addition to those contained in the initial charge letter. In a *sua sponte* case, the date of issuance shall, for purposes of applicable time limits, be deemed to relate back to the date of the initial letter notifying the respondent that a *sua sponte* action has been initiated. The new charge letter shall in all other respects be treated exactly as an initial charge letter issued according to Subsection 6.1.1 of this part.

6.1.4 Time for respondent's response. The respondent shall have 30 days after receipt of the charge letter to file an initial response. Any request to extend the time for responding to the charge letter must be made in writing, within the 30 days, and must show good cause for an extension.

6.1.4.1 The respondent may in the alternative accept the opportunity to resign from membership as provided in Part II, Section 5.4.2 ("*Resignation Under Ethics Investigation*").

6.1.5 Personal appearance. The Chair and Director may request the respondent to appear personally before the Committee. The respondent has no right to such an appearance.

6.2 Information from other sources. Additional information may be requested from the complainant, the respondent, or any other appropriate source.

6.3 Referral to committee. When, in the sole judgment of the Chair and Director, the investigation is complete, the case will be referred to the Committee for review and resolution. The Director shall notify the complainant and respondent that the matter has been referred to the Committee.

6.4 Documentation subsequent to investigation and prior to resolution by the committee. Within 30 days after receipt of notification that the case is being referred to the Ethics Committee for review and resolution, the complainant and respondent may submit any additional information or documentation. Any materials submitted in a timely manner by the complainant or on the complainant's or respondent's behalf will be forwarded to the respondent. Within 15 days from receipt of those materials, the respondent may submit any additional information or documentation. All such materials submitted within these time limitations shall be included in the file to be reviewed by the Ethics Committee. Materials submitted outside of the time limit will not be included in the file materials relative to the ethics case and will not be reviewed by the Ethics Committee.

In the sole discretion of the Director, where good cause for noncompliance with these time limits is shown by the complainant or the respondent, the resolution of the case may be postponed until the next scheduled meeting of the Ethics Committee and the information or documentation provided outside of the time limit may be included in the file materials to be reviewed by the Committee at that later time. In the sole discretion of the Director, in the event the respondent fails to comply with these time limits, the information or documentation provided outside of the time limits may be included in the file materials to be reviewed by the Committee and the matter maintained for resolution by the Committee as originally scheduled.

7. Review and Resolution by the Committee

The Ethics Committee may assign a member of the Committee or an Ethics Committee Associate to serve as a case monitor. The monitor may provide assistance to assure that an adequate record is prepared for Ethics Committee review and in such other respects as necessary to further the objectives of these Rules and Procedures.

Upon conclusion of the investigation, the case shall be reviewed by the Ethics Committee. Members of the Ethics Committee and Ethics Committee Associates may be assigned to review and summarize the case. Members and Associates may also be assigned to participate on a panel to review and make a preliminary recommendation prior to review by the full Ethics Committee. Ethics Committee Associates may also attend and participate in the full Ethics Committee meetings, but shall not vote on the full Committee's disposition of a case. When review of a case has been completed, the Ethics Committee shall vote to take one of the following actions described below: remand, dismiss the charges, recommend reprimand or censure, recommend expulsion, or recommend stipulated resignation. In addition to any of these actions, the Committee may vote to issue an educative letter. The Committee may choose to dismiss some charges but find violation and take disciplinary action on the basis of other charges in the charge letter. The respondent shall then be notified of the Committee's action, the ethical standard(s) involved, if any, the rationale for the Committee's decision, any sanction, and any directives.

7.1 Remand. The Committee may remand the matter to the Director for continued investigation or issuance of a new charge letter according to Subsection 6.1.3 of this part.

7.2 Dismiss the charges

7.2.1 No violation. The Committee may dismiss a charge if it finds the respondent has not violated the ethical standard as charged.

7.2.2 Violation would not warrant further action. The Committee may dismiss the complaint if it concludes that any violation it might find (a) would constitute only a minor or technical violation that would not warrant further action, (b) has already been adequately addressed in another forum, or (c) is likely to be corrected.

7.2.3 Insufficient evidence. The Committee may dismiss a charge if it finds insufficient evidence to support a finding of an ethics violation.

7.3 Educative letter. Where the Committee deems it appropriate, the Committee may issue an educative letter, to be shared only with the respondent, concerning the behaviors charged or other matters. An educative letter may be issued whether the Committee dismisses the charges or recommends finding violations.

7.4 Recommend reprimand or censure. If the Committee finds that the respondent has violated the Ethics Code, but decides that the nature of the respondent's behavior is such that the matter would be most appropriately resolved without recommending loss of membership, the Committee will recommend reprimand or censure of the respondent, with or without one or more available directives. See Part II, Subsections 11.1, 11.2, and Section 12.

7.5 Recommend expulsion. The Committee may recommend expulsion if it concludes that there has been an ethics violation, that it was of a kind likely to cause substantial harm to another person or the profession, or that it was otherwise of such gravity as to warrant this action.

7.6 Recommend stipulated resignation. In lieu of the other resolutions set forth in this section, with the agreement of the respondent, the Committee may recommend to the Board that the respondent be permitted to resign under stipulations set forth by the Committee, according to the following procedure:

7.6.1 Offer of stipulated resignation by the committee. When the Committee finds that the respondent has committed a violation of the Ethics Code, the Committee may offer to enter into an agreement with the respondent, contingent upon approval by the Board of Directors, that the respondent shall resign from the Association under mutually agreed upon stipulations. Such stipulations shall include the extent to which the stipulated resignation and underlying ethics violation shall be disclosed and a minimum period of time after resignation during which the respondent shall be ineligible to reapply for membership. The Committee may also vote to recommend and inform the member of an alternative sanction chosen from among Subsections 11.1–11.3 of Part II of these Rules in the event the member does not accept the offer of stipulated resignation.

7.6.2 Notification of respondent. In such cases, the respondent shall be notified, in writing, of the Committee's recommended sanction of stipulated resignation and that he or she may accept the Committee's recommended sanction within 30 days of receipt. The respondent shall also be notified of any alternative recommended sanction.

7.6.3 Acceptance by respondent. Within 30 days, the respondent may accept the recommended sanction of stipulated resignation by executing a notarized affidavit of resignation acceptable both to the respondent and to the Committee and forwarding the executed notarized affidavit to the Committee. Such resignation shall become effective only with the approval of the Board, as set forth in Subsection 7.6.5 of this part.

7.6.4 Transmittal to board of directors. If the respondent accepts the recommended sanction of stipulated resignation, the Committee shall submit a copy of the affidavit of resignation, with the record in the matter and the rationale for recommending stipulated resignation on the terms stated in the affidavit, to the Board of Directors.

7.6.5 Action by board of directors. Within 180 days, the Board of Directors shall accept the respondent's resignation on the terms stated in the affidavit of resignation, unless it is persuaded that to do so would not be in the best interest of the Association and/or of the public. If the resignation is accepted by the Board, the Director shall notify the complainant and respondent of the final disposition of the case.

7.6.6 Rejection of stipulated resignation by respondent. If the respondent fails to accept the determination within 30 days, or formally notifies the

Committee of rejection of the offer of stipulated resignation within the 30-day period, the offer of stipulated resignation shall be deemed rejected. The Committee shall reconsider the matter or, if an alternative recommended sanction has previously been identified by the Committee, such alternative recommended resolution shall automatically become the recommended sanction according to Subsection 7.4 or 7.5 of this part.

7.6.7 *Rejection of stipulated resignation by board.* If the Board rejects the affidavit of resignation under Subsection 7.6.5 of this part, the Committee shall so notify the respondent and reconsider the matter.

8. Procedures Subsequent to Dismissal by Committee

The Committee may reconsider a case dismissed under Subsection 7.2 of this part only if it does so in accordance with Part II, Section 6.

9. Procedures Subsequent to Committee Recommendation of Reprimand or Censure

If the Committee proceeds under Subsection 7.4 of this part, the following procedures shall govern:

9.1 Acceptance of reprimand or censure. If the respondent accepts the Committee's recommended sanction and directives, if any, the right of independent adjudication shall be waived, any directives will be implemented by the Director, and the case will remain open until the directives are met. The respondent's failure to respond within 30 days of notification shall be deemed acceptance of the Committee's recommended sanction and directives.

9.2 Independent adjudication after recommended sanction of reprimand or censure. The method of adjudication for a recommended sanction of reprimand or censure is an independent adjudication based on the written record by a three-person Independent Adjudication Panel.

9.2.1 *Request for independent adjudication and rationale for nonacceptance.* The respondent may exercise his or her right to independent adjudication by furnishing the Committee, within 30 days after notification of the Committee's recommendation, a written request for independent adjudication and rationale for nonacceptance of the recommendation.

9.2.2 *Statement by committee.* Within 30 days of receipt of the respondent's rationale for nonacceptance, the Committee may prepare a statement and provide a copy to the respondent. No statement by the Committee is required.

9.2.3 *Respondent's final response.* Within 15 days of receipt of the Ethics Committee's statement, if any, the respondent may submit to the Director a written response to that statement.

9.2.4 *Selection of independent adjudication panel.*

9.2.4.1 Provision of Standing Hearing Panel List. Within 60 days of receipt of the request for an independent adjudication, the Director shall provide the respondent with the names and curricula vitae of six members of the Board of Directors' Standing Hearing Panel, of whom at least one shall be a public member. The proposed panel members need not include any member having a particular specialty or representing a particular geographic location. The Director shall make inquiry and ensure that proposed panel members do not have a conflict of interest as defined by applicable law and appear otherwise able to apply fairly the APA Ethics Code based solely on the record in the particular case.

9.2.4.2 Designation of Panel Members. Within 15 days after receipt of the six-member list, the respondent shall select three of the six to constitute the Independent Adjudication Panel. The Panel shall include not fewer than two members of the Association. Whenever feasible, the respondent's selection will be honored. If at any time prior to conclusion of the adjudication, any panelist cannot serve on the Independent Adjudication Panel for any reason, the respondent shall be notified promptly and afforded the opportunity within 10 days of receipt of notification to replace that individual from among a list of not fewer than four members of the Board of Directors' Standing Hearing Panel. In the event the respondent fails to notify the Director of his or her initial or replacement selections in a timely fashion, the right to do so is waived, and the President of the Association shall select the member(s), whose name(s) shall then be made known to the respondent.

9.2.4.3 Designation of Chair of Independent Adjudication Panel. The President shall designate one of the three Panel members to serve as Chair.

The Chair of the Panel shall ensure that the Panel fulfills its obligations according to these Rules and Procedures.

9.2.5 Provision of case file to independent adjudication panel. Within 15 days of selection of the Independent Adjudication Panel; receipt of the Committee's statement according to Subsection 9.2.2 of this part, if any; receipt of the respondent's final response according to Subsection 9.2.3 of this part, if any; or if no statement or response is received, the expiration of the time period for such statement or response, whichever occurs latest, the Director will provide the case file to the members of the Independent Adjudication Panel. The case file shall include the complaint and all correspondence and evidence submitted to the Ethics Committee, the respondent's rationale for nonacceptance of the Committee's recommendation, the Committee's statement, if any, and the respondent's final response, if any.

9.2.6 Consideration and vote by independent adjudication panel. Within 60 days of receipt of the case file, the members of the Panel shall confer with each other and, solely on the basis of the documentation provided and deliberations among themselves, shall vote to take one of the following actions:

9.2.6.1 Adopt the Committee's Recommended Sanction and Directives

9.2.6.2 Adopt a Lesser Sanction and/or Less Burdensome Directives

9.2.6.3 Dismiss the Case

9.2.7 Decision of independent adjudication panel. Decisions of the Independent Adjudication Panel will be made by majority vote, and at least two reviewers must agree to written findings, a sanction, if any, and a directive or directives, if any. The Committee bears the burden to prove the charges by a preponderance of the evidence. The panelists' votes and the majority's written decision must be submitted to the Ethics Office within the 60-day period set forth in Subsection 9.2.6 of this part. If no two panelists can agree as to the appropriate outcome or a written decision, the case will be referred back to the Committee for further action.

9.2.8 Finality of decision by independent adjudication panel. The decision of the Independent Adjudication Panel is unappealable. The decision is binding on the Committee and the respondent except that subsequent to the Panel's decision, the Committee may determine that directives are impractical or unduly burdensome and may choose to reduce or dismiss directives required in the Panel's decision. A decision by the Panel either to impose a sanction and/or directive(s) or to dismiss the case will be implemented by the Director as the final adjudication, unless modified by the Committee.

9.2.9 Notification. The Director shall inform the respondent and complainant, if any, of the final disposition. The respondent shall be provided a copy of the majority's written decision.

10. Procedures Subsequent to Committee Recommendation of Expulsion

If the Committee proceeds under Subsection 7.5 of this part, the following procedures shall govern:

10.1 Acceptance of recommendation of expulsion. If the respondent accepts the Committee's recommendation to the Board of Directors that he or she be expelled from membership, the right to a formal hearing shall be waived, and the Committee shall proceed with its recommendation to the Board of Directors according to Subsection 10.3.5 and other subsections of this part. In such event, the recommendation of the Ethics Committee shall be treated as the equivalent of the recommendation of a Formal Hearing Committee that the respondent be expelled from membership. The respondent's failure to respond within 30 days after notification shall be deemed acceptance of the Committee's recommendation.

10.2 Formal hearing after recommendation of expulsion. The method of adjudication for a recommended sanction of expulsion issued under Subsection 7.5 of this part is a formal hearing before a three-member Hearing Committee. Upon request, the respondent will be provided with a copy of the APA Ethics Office "Guidelines for Formal Hearings." These guidelines are for guidance and information purposes only and are not binding on the APA, the Ethics Committee, or hearing participants. The proceedings are governed solely by the Rules and Procedures of the Ethics Committee and the Ethical Principles of Psychologists and Code of

Conduct. Alternatively, a respondent may request an independent adjudication to be provided according to the procedures described in Subsections 9.2.2 through 9.2.7 of this part of these Rules in place of the Subsections 10.2.2 through 10.2.6. The Independent Adjudication Panel will make a recommendation that will be subject to review by the Board of Directors as described in Subsection 10.3.

10.2.1 Request for formal hearing. The respondent may exercise his or her right to a formal hearing by requesting a hearing in writing within 30 days of notification of the Committee's recommendation. Alternatively, the respondent may request an independent adjudication by furnishing the Committee a written request for independent adjudication and a written rationale for nonacceptance of the Committee's recommendation within 30 days after notification of the Committee's recommendation.

10.2.2 Formal hearing date and hearing committee.

10.2.2.1 Establishment of Hearing Date and Provision of Standing Hearing Panel List. Within 60 days after the receipt of the respondent's request for a formal hearing, the Director shall establish the date of the hearing and provide the respondent with the date and the names and curricula vitae of six members of the Board of Directors' Standing Hearing Panel. The six identified members of the Board of Directors' Standing Hearing Panel shall include at least one public member. The proposed panel members need not include any member having a particular specialty or representing a particular geographic location. The Director shall make inquiry and ensure that proposed panel members do not have a conflict of interest as defined by applicable law and appear otherwise able to apply fairly the Ethics Code based solely on the record in the particular case.

10.2.2.2 Designation of Hearing Committee Members. The Hearing Committee shall consist of three individuals, selected from among the six individuals from the Board of Directors' Standing Hearing Panel identified according to Subsection 10.2.2.1 of this part. The Hearing Committee shall include not fewer than two members of the Association. Within 15 days after the receipt of the names and curricula vitae, the respondent shall notify the Director of his or her selections for the

Hearing Committee. Whenever feasible, the respondent's selections will be honored. In the event an individual selected by the respondent cannot serve on the Hearing Committee for any reason, the respondent shall be notified and afforded the opportunity within 10 days of receipt of notification to replace that individual from among a list of not fewer than four members of the Board of Directors' Standing Hearing Panel. If the respondent fails to notify the Director of his or her initial or replacement selections in a timely fashion, the right to do so is waived and the President shall select the Hearing Committee member(s), whose name(s) shall then be made known to the respondent.

10.2.2.3 Voir Dire of Designated Hearing Committee Members. At the time the respondent selects the three designated Hearing Committee members, the respondent may also submit in writing, to the Director, a request to question designated Hearing Committee members with respect to potential conflict of interest. If the President has chosen the three Hearing Committee members, the respondent shall have 15 days after receipt of their names to submit such a request. Upon receipt of such written request, the Director shall convene by telephone conference call, or otherwise, a formal opportunity for such questioning by the respondent or the respondent's attorney. Legal Counsel for the Association shall preside at such voir dire, shall be the sole judge of the propriety and pertinency of questions posed, and shall be the sole judge with respect to the fitness of designated Hearing Committee members to serve. Failure by the respondent to submit a timely request shall constitute a waiver of the privilege to conduct voir dire.

10.2.2.4 Designation of Chair of Hearing Committee. The President shall designate one of the three Hearing Committee members to serve as Chair. The Chair of the Hearing Committee and Legal Counsel for the Association shall assure proper observance of these Rules and Procedures at the formal hearing.

10.2.3 Documents and witnesses

10.2.3.1 Committee. At least 30 days prior to the scheduled date of the formal hearing, the Ethics Committee shall provide the respondent and the Hearing Committee with copies of all documents and other evidence, and the names of all witnesses that may be offered by the Committee in its case in chief.

10.2.3.2 Respondent. At least 15 days prior to the scheduled date of the formal hearing, the respondent shall provide the Ethics Committee and the Hearing Committee with copies of all documents and other evidence, and the names of all witnesses that may be offered by the respondent.

10.2.3.3 Rebuttal Documents and Witnesses. At least 5 days prior to the scheduled date of the formal hearing, the Committee shall provide the respondent and the Hearing Committee with copies of all documents and other evidence, and the names of all witnesses that may be offered in rebuttal.

10.2.3.4 Audiotapes, Videotapes, and Similar Data Compilations. Audiotapes, videotapes, and similar data compilations are admissible at the formal hearing, provided usable copies of such items, together with a transcription thereof, are provided in a timely fashion according to the provisions of this section.

10.2.3.5 Failure to Provide Documents, Other Evidence, and Names of Witnesses in a Timely Fashion in Advance of the Formal Hearing. Failure to provide copies of a document or other evidence or the name of a witness in a timely fashion and consistent with this section and these Rules and Procedures is grounds for excluding such document, other evidence, or witness from evidence at the formal hearing, unless good cause for the omission and a lack of prejudice to the other side can be shown.

10.2.4 Formal hearing procedures

10.2.4.1 Presiding Officers.

10.2.4.1.1 The Chair of the Hearing Committee shall preside at the hearing. The General Counsel of the Association shall designate Legal Counsel to assist the Hearing Committee.

10.2.4.1.2 Legal Counsel for the Hearing Committee shall be present to advise on matters of procedure and admission of evidence and shall represent neither the Ethics Committee nor the respondent at the formal hearing.

10.2.4.2 Legal Representation of the Respondent and Committee

10.2.4.2.1 Respondent. The respondent may choose, at the respondent's own expense, to be represented by a licensed attorney.

10.2.4.2.2 Committee. The General Counsel of the Association may designate Legal Counsel to advise the Ethics Committee. The Chair of the Ethics Committee, the Chair's designee, or Legal Counsel to the Committee presents the Committee's case.

10.2.4.3 Rules of Evidence. Formal rules of evidence shall not apply. All evidence that is relevant and reliable, as determined for the Hearing Committee by Legal Counsel for the Hearing Committee, shall be admissible.

10.2.4.4 Rights of the Respondent and the Committee. Consistent with these Rules and Procedures, the respondent and the Committee shall have the right to present witnesses, documents, and other evidence, to cross-examine witnesses, and to object to the introduction of evidence.

10.2.4.5 Burden of Proof. The Ethics Committee shall bear the burden to prove the charges by a preponderance of the evidence.

10.2.5 Decision of the hearing committee. The decision shall be by a simple majority vote. Within 30 days of the conclusion of the hearing, the Hearing Committee shall submit in writing to the Board of Directors, through the Director, its decision and the rationale for that decision. The Hearing Committee may decide to:

10.2.5.1 Adopt the Committee's Recommendation to the Board of Directors

10.2.5.2 Recommend to the Board of Directors a Lesser Sanction With or Without Directives

10.2.5.3 Dismiss the Charges

10.2.6 Notice to the respondent and the ethics committee. Within 15 days of receipt of the Hearing Committee's decision, a copy of the decision and the rationale for the decision shall be provided to the respondent and the Ethics Committee. If the Hearing Committee determines that the charges must be dismissed, the Ethics Committee will implement this as the final adjudication.

10.3 Proceedings before the board of directors

10.3.1 Referral to Board of Directors. If the Hearing Committee or Independent Adjudication Panel recommends that the respondent be expelled from membership or otherwise disciplined, the matter will be referred to the Board of Directors. The Director shall provide the materials of record to the

Board, including a copy of the Hearing Committee's or Independent Adjudication Panel's decision; the respondent's timely response, if any, under Subsection 10.3.2 of this part; the Ethics Committee's timely statement, if any, under Subsection 10.3.3 of this part; the respondent's timely final response, if any, under Subsection 10.3.4 of this part; and the record.

10.3.2 Respondent's response. Within 30 days of receipt of the Hearing Committee's or Independent Adjudication Panel's decision, the respondent may file a written response with the Board of Directors, through the Ethics Office. A copy of the respondent's written response shall be retained by the Chair of the Ethics Committee.

10.3.3 Ethics committee's statement. Within 15 days of receipt of the respondent's response or the date such response was due, the Ethics Committee may prepare a written statement and provide a copy to the respondent.

10.3.4 Respondent's final response. Within 15 days of receipt of the Ethics Committee's statement, if any, the respondent may file with the Board of Directors, through the Director, a written response to the Ethics Committee's statement. A copy of this response shall be retained by the Chair of the Ethics Committee.

10.3.5 Action by the board of directors. Within 180 days of receipt of the recommendation of the Hearing Committee or Independent Adjudication Panel (or of the Ethics Committee if no subsequent adjudication was held), together with any timely responses thereto and the record, the Board of Directors will consider these materials and will take action as follows:

10.3.5.1 Adopt. The Board of Directors shall adopt the recommendation, unless by majority vote it finds grounds for nonacceptance, as set forth in Subsection 10.3.5.2.

10.3.5.2 Not Adopt After Determining Grounds for Nonacceptance. Only the following shall constitute grounds for nonacceptance of the recommendation by the Board:

10.3.5.2.1 Incorrect Application of Ethical Standard(s). The Ethics Code of the Association was incorrectly applied.

10.3.5.2.2 Erroneous Findings of Fact. The findings of fact were clearly erroneous.

10.3.5.2.3 Procedural Errors. The procedures used were in serious and substantial violation of the Bylaws of the Association and/or these Rules and Procedures.

10.3.5.2.4 Excessive Sanction or Directives. The disciplinary sanction or directives recommended are grossly excessive in light of all the circumstances.

10.3.5.3 Consequences of Nonacceptance. If the Board of Directors finds grounds for nonacceptance, it shall refer the case back to the Ethics Committee. In its discretion, the Ethics Committee may return the matter for reconsideration before a newly constituted Hearing Committee or Independent Adjudication Panel or may continue investigation and/or readjudicate the matter at the Committee level.

10.4 Notification. If the Board of Directors does not adopt the recommendation, it shall notify the Ethics Committee in writing why the decision was not accepted, citing the applicable ground(s) for nonacceptance under Subsection 10.3.5.2 of this part.

10.5 Reconsideration. If a reconsideration is instituted, the procedures of relevant subsections of this part shall apply. Unless any of the following is offered by the respondent, none shall be part of the record before the second Hearing Committee or Independent Adjudication Panel: the original Hearing Committee's or Independent Adjudication Panel's report; the respondent's written responses or Ethics Committee's written statements made under Subsections 10.3.2, 10.3.3, and 10.3.4 of this part; and the Board of Directors' rationale for nonacceptance of the original Hearing Committee's or Independent Adjudication Panel's recommendation. If the respondent offers any portion of any of the foregoing documents as evidence in the reconsideration, the Committee may introduce any portion of any or all of them.

◆　　◆　　◆

Commentary: The most recent set of procedures replaced an earlier version published in 1996. According to the APA Ethics Committee, the following are the primary changes in the current rules:

> *1. Respondents in all cases will be allowed the right to resign from APA at their first notice of an open case or complaint.*

The resignation will be "under ethics investigation," and APA will advise anyone who inquires that the resignation occurred while the former member was under ethics investigation.

2. *Respondents in show cause matters will be expelled automatically if, within 60 days of receiving notice of the matter, the respondent does not exercise his or her right to resign or to have the matter reviewed . . . The charges apply to complaints and notices of show cause proceedings received by the APA Ethics Office on or after October 2001.*

See APA Ethics Committee. (2002). Report of the Ethics Committee, 2001. American Psychologist, 57, 646–653.

Do you think the rules and procedures are comprehensible to the average APA member? Would you know how to navigate your way through the Ethics Committee if you were the unfortunate recipient of an ethics complaint? It takes over a year to adjudicate a formal complaint. Is the process too lengthy, cumbersome, and expensive, or does it provide the appropriate procedural safeguards for both complainants and respondents?

What do you think are the most frequent kinds of cases that the ethics committee is adjudicating currently, in comparison with cases seen 15 year ago? For answers and other interesting data, see these articles, in chronological order:

Ethics Committee of the American Psychological Association. (1988). Trends in ethics cases, common pitfalls, and published resources. American Psychologist, 43, 564–572.

APA Ethics Committee. (1991). Report of the Ethics Committee, 1989 and 1990. American Psychologist, 46, 750–757.

APA Ethics Committee. (1994). Report of the Ethics Committee, 1993. American Psychologist, 49, 659–666.

APA Ethics Committee. (1998). Report of the Ethics Committee, 1997. American Psychologist, 53, 969–980.

APA Ethics Committee. (2002). Report of the Ethics Committee, 2001. American Psychologist, 57, 646–653.

APA Ethics Committee. (2004). Report of the Ethics Committee, 2003. American Psychologist, 59, 434–441.

APA Ethics Committee. (2005). Report of the Ethics Committee, 2004. American Psychologist, 60, 523–528.

APA Ethics Committee. (2006). Report of the Ethics Committee, 2005. American Psychologist, 61, 522–529.

The 2001 report indicated that from 1985 through 2001, APA terminated the membership of 363 members because of ethical violations—about 21 per year. In 2001, the number was 17, 12 through expulsions and 5 through stipulated resignations. In 2005, no member was expelled through a direct complaint to the ethics committee. Five members were automatically expelled, presumably on the basis of adverse adjudications in other forums; 14 resigned while under investigation; and 1 left through a stipulated investigation. What do these data imply about the vigor with which the Ethics Code has been enforced by APA? Keep in mind that from 1956 to 1980 APA dropped from membership only eight psychologists for ethical violations.

CHAPTER 2

HOW ETHICS ARE APPLIED

Suppose you share offices with a close friend and fellow clinician who, like you, is a member of APA. You discover that this office mate has terminated treatments with a female client after two sessions of behavior therapy and that, soon thereafter, he and she have begun a romantic relationship. What should you do? More, interestingly, what *would* you do? If you are like most colleagues, you would probably be among the nearly one third who would not bring his conduct to the attention of any ethics body.

Assume now that you are a psychotherapist asked to consider whether, in the following situations, the psychologists involved acted ethically:

1. A state requires that an applicant for licensure complete 1,500 hours of postdoctoral experience under supervision before becoming eligible to take the licensure examination. An applicant and a licensed psychologist agree that the psychologist will attest in writing that the applicant has completed the requirement even though the applicant has had only 500 hours of supervised experience.
2. At a social gathering attended by people of many professions, a psychologist is overheard discussing one of her patients by name with two of her friends, a physician and an accountant, neither of whom are involved in the case.
3. A patient who has just begun treatment with you tells you that he terminated his professional relationship with his former therapist because the therapist consistently conducted treatment while under the influence of alcohol.

Is there any question that each of these three incidents describes behavior by psychologists that is clearly unethical? Would it surprise you, then, to discover that APA member psychotherapists do not universally agree that the conduct described in these realistic situations is unethical (Pope, Tabachnik, & Keith-Spiegel, 1987)? What about the finding that over 50% of 60 senior psychologists, all of whom had considerable experience with ethics issues, admitted to intentionally violating a law or a formal ethical principle regulating their professional practice (Pope & Bajt, 1988)?

These vignettes and data (or variants thereof) come from research presented throughout this chapter. They may be properly viewed as examples of deplorable and odious behavior. Then again, one could argue that in some instances, violating an ethical rule or even a state or federal law may evidence the proper exercise of professional discretion.

In any event, it is clear that knowledge of ethical provisions and legal rules does not inevitably lead to perfect conformity with these obligations. Thus, putting aside those few colleagues who meet the definition of sociopathy, what stimulates otherwise moral psychologists to take actions that directly contradict what they know they should do?

In some cases, psychologists may violate ethical principles because those principles are vaguely worded. For example, in some informal research, I asked experienced, licensed clinical psychologists to respond to 75 true–false items concerning ethical behavior. To the items I attached the 1989 APA Ethics Code. The directions indicated that respondents could refer to the code at any time to answer the items. Yet, in no instance did any of the test takers answer more than 60% correctly.

One could hypothesize that these surprising results, although from an admittedly unsystematic study, show that the old APA Ethics Code was simply too ambiguous to guide respondents to the presumptively "correct" answer, and that was my guess. But even if an ethical code were written in perfectly clear language, there are plausible and understandable reasons why, at times, psychologists would deliberately violate ethical rules. One of those may be the psychologist's perception that violating the Code will satisfy even higher moral values. Is it appropriate, however, for psychologists to engage in civil disobedience, following in the revered footsteps of Henry David Thoreau and Martin Luther King? Or are psychologists obligated to abide by their association's code of ethics and to seek to change those provisions they find objectionable through an orderly, though slow-moving, democratic process?

In this chapter, I explore such issues, providing a great many vignettes and dilemmas that should provoke discussion and debate and, thus, move the reader beyond merely learning ethical rules and procedural regulations to thinking about the meaning and value of a code of ethics. It is my guess, as well, that readers will leave this chapter with a sense of creative uncertainty. But they should not despair. Ideas for best dealing with this uncertainty follow in chapter 3.

References

Pope, K. S., & Bajt, T. R. (1988). When laws and values conflict: A dilemma for psychologists. *American Psychologist, 43,* 828–829.

Pope, K. S., Tabachnik, B. E., & Keith-Spiegel, P. (1987). Ethics of practice: The beliefs and behaviors of psychologists as therapists. *American Psychologist, 42,* 993–1006.

The Failure of Clinical Psychology Graduate Students to Apply Understood Ethical Principles

J. L. Bernard and Carmen S. Jara

. . . With any ethical violation there are two distinct elements that must be recognized: (a) the extent to which the ethical principle applicable to the situation in question is understandable, and (b) the degree of willingness to do what one understands should be done. Of these, it seems unlikely that a lack of understanding is ordinarily the basis for a violation. . . . Rather, in dealings with educated, highly intelligent professionals, it seems much more likely that the crux of the issue with ethical violations is an unwillingness to conform to the demands of the Ethical Principles . . .

. . . Ethical Principles 7(g)[1] clearly places the responsibility for confronting recognized violations squarely on the members of the profession. To ignore an ethical violation is, then, a violation in itself. In this article we report data on the willingness (or, more appropriately, the lack thereof) of graduate students to honor Principle 7(g) when faced with a hypothetical ethical violation by a fellow student who is also a friend.

METHOD

Questionnaire

Packets were distributed to a nationwide sample of [250] clinical graduate students at APA-approved programs with a request that they be returned to the experimenter anonymously. Each packet consisted of an explanatory cover letter soliciting anonymous cooperation, two scenarios constructed to depict ethical violations, a demographic information sheet that the student could discard if he or she felt that it might compromise confidentiality (none did), a questionnaire on which the student would react to the scenarios, and a stamped envelope for the student to use in returning the packet.

In the first scenario, a clinical graduate student was depicted as being sexually involved with a client from a psychotherapy practicum. In the scenarios in half of the packets, the student therapist was female, and in the other half, male. In the second scenario (again balanced for sex) a clinical graduate student was characterized as a problem drinker/alcoholic who is manifesting poor judgment and erratic behavior in various clinical practica, but thus far concealing it from the clinical faculty. In each case, the reader was asked to assume that he or she had discovered the problem, and that the alleged violator was not only a fellow graduate student, but also a friend. Also, according to the scenarios, not only had the reader discovered the problem, but it had already led to one confrontation with the alleged violator that had not produced results. Two Ethical Principles involved, 2(f) and 6(a) (American Psychological Association, 1981)[2], were then presented verbatim in order to eliminate recall of the principles as a factor in students' deciding how to answer the questionnaire. . . . At this point, the reader was asked two distinct questions. The first, "According to the Ethical Principles, what *should* you do?", was used to assess the degree of understanding that the described behavior constituted an ethical violation requiring some sort of action, and what that action should be. The second question, "Speaking pragmatically, and recognizing that he [she] is a friend and a fellow graduate student, what do you think you probably *would* do?" was used to assess the reader's willingness to do what he or she had already stated should be done. Each of these

From *Professional Psychology: Research and Practice, 17,* 313–315. Copyright 1986 by the American Psychological Association.

[1]*Ed. Note:* See Standards 1.04 and 1.05 of the current (2002) APA Ethics Code.

[2]*Ed. Note:* See Standards 10.05 and 2.06 of the current (2002) APA Ethics Code.

questions was followed by five possible responses to the situation. To illustrate, those for the problem-drinking/alcoholism scenario in which the student was male were (a) "Nothing"; (b) "Suggest he get help for this problem"; (c) "Keep trying to get him to stop drinking"; (d) "Tell him that if he doesn't get his drinking under control you will have to mention it to the Director of Clinical Training or his clinical supervisor"; and (e) "Tell the Director of Clinical Training or his clinical supervisor." We anticipated that essentially all students would recognize that each scenario depicted a violation that called for a particular course of action. However, we hypothesized that although most students would state a willingness to implement whatever course of action they felt was indicated, a significant number would admit that they would probably do something less than that. Thus the data to be analyzed was the difference between what the reader said should be done and what he or she would actually do if confronted with the situation described in the scenarios. We hypothesized further that to the extent that this was true, some of the demographic items (e.g., whether the student had had coursework in ethics, or the sex of the student who was violating the principles) might enable us to discriminate between these two groups.

As a manipulation check, these scenarios had earlier been presented to the members of a state ethics committee with a request that they respond only to the question of what should be done. With the sexual scenario there was complete agreement that "Tell the Director of Clinical Training or the student's supervisor" was the appropriate response. With the problem-drinking/alcoholism scenario with a male student, 3 of 5 committee members gave this same reply, whereas 2 chose a response one step less severe ("Tell the student that if he doesn't get his drinking under control you will have to tell the Director of Clinical training or his/her supervisor"). . . .

RESULTS

. . . First, we analyzed the data by obtaining percentages of clinical graduate students who stated that they would do the same thing that they had already said they should do, and those who stated that they would do something less than they had already stated they should do. (There were no instances of subjects who said that they would do more than they should.) With the sexual scenario, the split was even: 50% said that they would do what they had already said they should do, and 50% said that they would do less. Applying the binomial expansion to these two groups provides a significant normal approximation to distribution of proportions, $Z(1) = 17.39$, $p < .0001$. With the problem-drinking/alcoholism scenario, 45% of the students said that they would do what they had already stated they should do, and the remaining 55% said that they would do less (again, no one said that they would do more). A comparison of these two groups with the same statistics was also highly significant, $Z(1) = 19.94$, $p < .0001$. . . .

. . . No significant differences were obtained for any demographic or scenario variables.

DISCUSSION

In this study we did not assess whether graduate clinical students would conform to some abstract standard for ethical behavior when confronted with an hypothetical violation. Rather, we first asked the student what should be done, and then whether the student would do that or something else. In this way, each student indicated his or her own understanding of how the Ethical Principle pertinent to each scenario should be applied, and then whether that understanding would result in appropriate behavior. For both scenarios, at least half of the students stated that they would not live up to their own interpretation of what the Ethical Principles required of them as professionals. Most simply put, this amounts to saying, "I know what I should do as an ethical psychologist, but I wouldn't do it."

The fact that no significant differences were obtained between these two groups of students on any of the demographic variables suggests that factors such as how far along the student was in training, whether coursework had been taken in ethics or in substance abuse (most respondents had taken a course on ethics), and so on, had no apparent bearing on willingness to put Ethical Principles into action. This may imply that training in ethics is inadequate, or that a willingness to take action when confronted with an ethical violation that involves a colleague/friend is not something that can be taught. Indeed, one fourth-year student who had had coursework in both ethics and substance abuse stated that for both scenarios he believed that he should "Tell the Director of Clinical Training or the student's supervisor"; yet, to the question "What *would* you do?" he replied "Nothing" both times. It seems that psychologists may be teaching the content of the principles without at the same time adequately communicating the importance of their implementation. . . .

All of this points to a need for a thorough, formal, and systematic approach to training in ethics so that the student will understand what the principles demand of the profession. Yet, our data indicate that although such training is important, the problem is not simply that the Ethical Principles "are vaguely formulated" or "provide almost no guidance." The subjects in this study seemed to understand the ethics of their chosen profession; they simply chose not to apply them in a hypothetical situation involving a peer/friend.

Clearly, there is a problem among those who are training for the profession (and one that may equally well apply to those already practicing). That problem is not how to communicate the ethical principles to students more effectively, but rather how to motivate them to implement principles that they apparently understand quite well. . . .

References

American Psychological Association. (1981). *Ethical standards of psychologists*. Washington, DC: Author.

◆   ◆   ◆

Commentary: Bernard and his colleagues (1987) replicated the preceding study with a sample of members belonging to Division 12 (Clinical) of APA. See Bernard, J. L, Murphy, M., & Little, M. (1987). The failure of clinical psychologists to apply understood ethical principles. Professional Psychology: Research and Practice, 18, 489–491. The scenarios in this study were the same as in Bernard and Jara's (1986) study except that in the first scenario the therapist was a male

doctoral-level clinician, and in the second the therapist was a female doctoral-level clinician. Bernard et al. (1987) reported the following results:

. . . With the sexual scenario, 63% of clinicians responding said that they would do what they felt they should do, and 37% said that they would do less than they felt they should do. Applying the binomial expansion to these data provides a significant normal approximation to distribution of proportions: $Z(1) = 9.08$, $p < .001$. With the problem-drinking/alcoholism scenario, 74% of the clinicians responding said that they would do what they had already said they should do, whereas 26% said that they would do less. A comparison of these two groups with the same statistic was also highly significant: $Z(1) = 9.96$, $p < .001$. . . .

When clinical graduate students were surveyed in this manner (Bernard & Jara, 1986), about the same results were obtained with each scenario. Approximately half of the students said that they would do less than they knew they should do whether the violation involved alcoholism or sex. This was not the case with clinical psychologists. With the problem-drinking/alcoholism scenario, 25% of the clinicians said that they would do less than their understanding of Ethical Principles demanded of them. However, with the sexual scenario, one third of the clinicians would not live up to their understanding of what should be done. This is even more puzzling when one considers that although the problem-drinking/ alcoholism scenario requires that the reader interpret the Ethical Principles as they apply to impaired psychologists, sexual intimacies with patients are flatly described as unethical. . . . [I]t is apparent from this survey that although professionals say that they would behave more responsibly than do graduate students, significant numbers of clinical psychologists simply would not do what they know they should do when confronted with an ethical violation by a colleague. Still, it is perhaps encouraging that the proportion of clinicians who would "do the right thing" is substantially higher than obtained with graduate students. This may reflect an increased awareness among professionals that even though reporting the unethical behavior of a colleague is personally repugnant, it is an ethical obligation and should benefit the profession in the long run.

As with the graduate students (Bernard & Jara, 1986), there were no significant differences, on any demographic variable, between those clinicians who would do what they felt they should do and those who would not. This suggests that the decision to report the unethical behavior of a colleague is a matter of personal values to a large extent. Yet, it seems that if psychology is to prosper, the ethics of the profession must be taken more seriously by the large numbers of clinicians who are not willing to report the unethical behavior of a colleague. The problem is, then, how our profession can motivate more clinicians to implement the Ethical Principles that they understand quite well.

It may be that a different thrust is needed in the teaching of ethics in graduate programs. It is vitally important that students learn that the function of an ethics committee is to help violators change their unethical behavior, using rehabilitative rather than punitive means whenever possible. It is also important that they come to recognize that their own professional self-interest is protected by their willingness to behave ethically and to report those psychologists who do not. It seems probable, in retrospect, that if more of us had been willing to report those instances of unethical conduct of which we were aware, our malpractice premiums might be lower today. . . . (pp. 490–491)

In a more recent study, graduate students were confronted with items that identified ethical improprieties by their peers, such as breaching confidentiality or becoming romantically involved with clients (entering

"dual relationships"). Twenty-five percent of the students indicated that they would do nothing. Only 3% said that they would contact an outside agency. On the other hand, 47% said they would consult other students about the problem, 31% would express concerns directly to the faculty, and 28% would directly confront their unethical colleagues. Interestingly, faculty underestimated the extent to which their students would take any action. Conversely, students viewed faculty as being significantly less active than the faculty viewed themselves in dealing with problem students. Nevertheless, although students deserve more credit than their teachers give them and, in many instances, "indicate that their feelings of ethical obligation . . . outweigh sentiments of loyalty to problematic peers" (Mearns & Allen, 1991, p. 198), a great deal of impaired performance and unethical behavior remains unattended to. See Mearns, J., & Allen, G. J. (1991). *Graduate students' experiences in dealing with impaired peers, compared with faculty predictions: An exploratory study.* Ethics & Behavior, 1, 191–202.

As with the Mearns & Allen study, Oliver et al. (2004), however, found that "[c]onsistent with the published literature, students were more likely to report problems in interpersonal functioning than problems in academic functioning or ethical improprieties." (p. 145). Oliver, M., Bernstein, J., Anderson, K., Blashfield, R., & Roberts, M. (2004). *An exploratory examination of student attitudes toward "impaired" peers in clinical psychology training programs.* Professional Psychology: Research and Practice, 35, 141–147. In a recent survey of graduate students' experiences with problematic peers, the authors found that although students tended to believe that they had greater ability to identify their troubled classmates, they "indicated that faculty members held most of the responsibility for dealing with" them (p. 668). The authors also made some helpful recommendations for improving the training of graduate students, for example, develop clear procedures for students to follow when observing problem behaviors in their peers, enhance screening procedures in the selection of graduate students, provide better education concerning stress and distress for graduate students. Rosenberg, J. I., Getzelman, M. A., Arcinue, F., & Oren, C. Z. (2005). *An exploratory look at students' experiences of problematic peers in academic professional psychology pro-*

grams. Professional Psychology: Research and Practice, 36, 665–673. *In the latest survey, 53% of APA student affiliates "said they would not feel safe to pursue appropriate actions if they have firsthand knowledge of sexual contact" between a student and faculty member (p. 727). Many felt that their ethics training in graduate school was either inadequate or barely adequate in providing a decision making model to handle the issue.* Zakrzewski, R. F. (2007). A national survey of American Psychological Association student affiliates' involvement and ethical training in psychology educator–student sexual relationships. Professional Psychology, 37, 724–730.

In the most recent study using the Bernard and Jara drinking scenario described in the first excerpt in this chapter, 95% of doctoral students in a clinical psychology program (N = 256) *"were aware that they should involve the director of training or supervisor in the case of a colleague's continued drinking problem" (p. 296). As before, one half of the sample would do less than they believed they should. The authors distinguish among "ethical decision-making ability" (i.e., identifying the appropriate intervention), "ethical willingness" (i.e., whether participants would do what they should do), and "ethical resoluteness" (i.e., participants' likelihood to intervene in an ethical manner).* See Betan, E. J., & Stanton, A. L. (1999). Fostering ethical willingness: Integrating emotional and contextual awareness with rational analysis. Professional Psychology: Research and Practice, 30, 295–301.

Stephen Behnke, director of the APA Ethics Office, in one of his monthly columns, addressed the problems of conforming to the requirements of Standards 1.04 (Informal Resolution of Ethical Violations) and 1.05 (Reporting Ethical Violations):

> One complexity in putting these standards into practice is the cultural context: As a society, we don't like snitches. . . . A second complexity is that the nature of our relationships may make pointing out a possible ethical violation complicated and professionally (if not personally) risky. Retaliation is especially a concern when there is an imbalance of power between the two individuals involved. Third, often we have limited information that leaves us uncertain about whether what we know is sufficient to raise the specter of an ethical violation. . . . Fourth, responding to ethically problematic behavior may entail a significant commitment. . . . Fifth, . . . our training tends not to prepare us very well to talk about problematic ethical behavior with our colleagues, and we can feel intimidated in the face of an uncertain and possibly defensive or angry response. (p. 73)

Behnke, S. H. (2006, March). Responding to a colleague's ethical transgressions. Monitor on Psychology, 37, 72–73. *For further speculation on the inconsistency between moral judgment and moral behavior see* Bersoff, D. M. (1999). Explaining unethical behavior among people motivated to act prosocially. Journal of Moral Education, 28, 413–428.

Ethics of Practice: The Beliefs and Behaviors of Psychologists as Therapists

Kenneth S. Pope, Barbara G. Tabachnick, and Patricia Keith-Spiegel

The American Psychological Association (APA) has developed elaborate ethical principles and standards of practice to guide the behavior of its membership (APA, 1973, 1981a, 1981b, 1986, 1987a, 1987b; *Standards*, 1985). However, we still lack comprehensive, systematically gathered data about the degree to which members believe in or comply with these guidelines. Consequently, such data are not available to inform either the clinical decisions of individual practitioners or the attempts of the APA to revise, refine, and extend formal standards of practice.

No implication is intended that norms are the equivalent of ethical standards. In many situations, the formulation and dissemination of formal standards are intended to increase ethical awareness and to improve the behaviors of a professional association. For example, many of the standards set forth in the ancient and still honored Hippocratic Oath were held by a minority of the physicians at the time. But those who are charged with developing, disseminating, and enforcing professional codes can function much more effectively if they are aware of the diverse dilemmas confronting the membership and of the membership's varied personal codes and behaviors.

METHOD

Survey Questionnaire

A survey questionnaire, a cover letter, and a return envelope were sent to 1,000 psychologists (500 men and 500 women) randomly selected from the 4,684 members of Division 29 (Psychotherapy) as listed in the 1985 *Directory of the American Psychological Association* (APA, 1985).

The survey questionnaire was divided into three main parts. The first part consisted of a list of 83 behaviors. Participants were asked to rate each of the 83 behaviors in terms of three categories.[1] First, to what extent had they engaged in the behavior in their practice? Participants either could indicate that the behavior was *not applicable* to their practice or they could rate the behavior's occurrence in their practice as *never, rarely, sometimes, fairly often*, or *very often*. Second, to what extent did they consider the practice ethical? In rating whether each behavior was ethical, participants could use five categories: *unquestionably not, under rare circumstances, don't know/not sure, under many circumstances*, and *unquestionably yes*.

The second part of the questionnaire presented 14 resources for guiding or regulating practice. Participants were asked to rate each resource in terms of "the effectiveness . . . in providing education, direction, sanctions, or support to regulate the practice of psychologists (i.e., to promote effective, appropriate, and ethical practice)." Five options were available for rating each of these resources: *terrible, poor, adequate, good*, and *excellent*.

The third part of the questionnaire asked participants to provide information about their own age, sex, primary work setting, and major theoretical orientation.

From *American Psychologist, 42*, 993–1006. Copyright 1987 by the American Psychological Association.

Ed. Note: Some of the material in this article is irrelevant to the major point, that is, the variability in how psychologists judge certain behavior as ethical. But, the senior author of the article required that no editing take place as a condition for its publication. The most important material is in Table 3 and its related discussion.

[1]The third category in the survey asked participants to rate the extent to which they considered each of the behaviors to constitute "good practice." Due to space limitations, analyses of these data and their relationships to the other ratings have been omitted from this article. However, these analyses are being prepared for separate publication.

TABLE 1			
Demographic Characteristics of Psychologists Providing Usable Data			
Characteristic	**Category**	**N**	**%**
Sex	Male	231	50.7
	Female	225	49.3
Age group	45 and under	230	50.4
	Over 45	226	49.6
Primary work setting	Private office	330	72.4
	Clinic	35	7.7
	Hospital	26	5.7
	University	48	10.5
	Other	14	3.1
	No answer	3	0.7

TABLE 2		
Theoretical Orientation of Psychologists Providing Usable Data		
Orientation	**N**	**%**
Psychodynamic	150	32.9
Eclectic	117	25.7
Cognitive	33	7.2
Gestalt	25	5.5
Humanistic	21	4.6
Existential	18	3.9
Systems	17	3.7
Behavioral	12	2.6
Other	53	11.7
No answer	10	2.2

RESULTS

Demographic Characteristics of the Participants and Ratings of the 83 Behaviors

Questionnaires were returned by 456 respondents (45.6%). Table 1 presents descriptions of the respondents in terms of sex, age, and primary work setting. Table 2 presents the theoretical orientations of the respondents. Table 3 presents the percentage of respondents' ratings for each of the 83 behaviors in terms of occurrence in their own practice and the degree to which they believe the behavior to be ethical.[2]

Resources for Regulating Psychology

Table 4 (p. 79) presents the respondents' ratings of each of the 14 resources for regulating psychology. A mixed between-between-within analysis of variance was performed on ratings of the 14 resources. Between-subjects factors were the two age groups and sex. The within subjects factor was composed of the 14 resources. With a Huyn-Feldt adjustment for heterogeneity of covariance, a highly significant dif-

ference in ratings was found as a function of type of resource, $F(13, 4316) = 55.24$, $p < .001$. Type of resource accounted for 14% of the variance in ratings, using h^2.[3] Scheffé-adjusted pairwise comparisons among the 14 means revealed that 48 of the 91 differences were statistically reliable, $p < .01$. Means for the 14 resources and differences among those means appear in Table 5 (p. 79).

On the average, older clinical psychologists rated the resources higher (mean rating = 3.36) than those who were younger (mean rating = 3.17), $F(1, 32) = 8.88$, $p < .01$, $h^2 = .03$. No statistically significant main effect of sex was found.

The interaction between age group and resource was reliable, $F(13, 4316) = 2.29$, $p < .05$, but of small magnitude, $h^2 < .01$. Applying a Scheffé criterion at $a = .01$, differences between younger and older psychologists were statistically reliable for only three resources: state licensing board (older, $M = 3.25$; younger, $M = 2.86$), state ethics committee (older, $M = 3.36$; younger, $M = 2.97$), and local ethics committee (older, $M = 3.12$; younger, $M = 2.77$). None of the other interactions was statistically significant.

---

[2]Duplication of the item "Being sexually attracted to a client" as both Item 66 and Item 82 provided an informal check on reliability. Correlations between Items 66 and 82 were .84 for responses relevant to "your practice" and .83 for "ethical."

On the assumption that there might be some consistency of responses across certain groups of items, 78 of the 83 behaviors were grouped, on an a priori basis, into 10 potential factors. After the data were collected, separate factor analyses were run on the three types of responses ("your practice," "ethical," and "good or poor practice") by choosing transformations that most effectively normalized variables, including log or square root transforms or dichotomization of variables (Tabachnick & Fidell, 1983). Seven factors, involving 45 of the behaviors, emerged. Due to space limitations, these analyses are not presented here, but a summary is available, upon request, from the authors.

[3]Because of the magnitude of the design, an alternative form of η^2 was used in which the denominator is the sum of the effect being described and its error term.

TABLE 3

Percentage of Psychologists (*N* = 465) in Each Category

| | Rating | | | | | | | | | | |
| Item | Occurrence in your practice? | | | | | | Ethical? | | | | |
	1	2	3	4	5*	NA	1	2	3	4	5*
1. Becoming social friends with a former client	42.1	45.2	9.2	1.8	1.1	0.7	6.4	51.1	13.4	21.9	6.8
2. Charging a client no fee for therapy	33.3	47.4	15.8	1.1	1.8	2.9	4.6	25.2	14.5	24.8	29.6
3. Providing therapy to one of your friends	70.4	25.2	2.2	0.2	0.7	2.2	47.6	40.1	2.9	4.4	3.7
4. Advertising in newspapers or similar media	72.4	13.2	10.1	2.4	0.4	5.5	12.9	14.7	17.8	33.3	20.6
5. Limiting treatment notes to name, date, and fee	48.2	18.4	13.8	6.6	12.1	1.5	18.6	22.4	21.7	20.8	14.7
6. Filing an ethics complaint against a colleague	61.6	25.2	7.5	0.7	1.1	10.7	2.4	11.8	3.1	22.8	57.9
7. Telling a client you are angry at him or her	9.6	45.0	36.8	5.7	2.2	0.7	3.1	26.8	8.3	35.5	25.4
8. Using a computerized test interpretation service	39.0	21.7	20.8	7.9	7.5	13.2	2.0	9.0	12.9	39.3	34.9
9. Hugging a client	13.4	44.5	29.8	7.7	4.2	0.2	4.6	41.2	8.3	35.5	9.2
10. Terminating therapy if client cannot pay	36.2	36.2	20.0	3.7	2.0	5.3	12.1	27.4	15.4	32.7	11.0
11. Accepting services from a client in lieu of fee	66.9	27.0	3.5	0.2	0.4	7.9	22.6	39.3	14.5	16.0	6.4
12. Seeing a minor client without parental consent	65.8	22.4	5.5	0.2	0.7	14.0	23.5	45.6	13.4	11.6	3.7
13. Having clients take tests (e.g., MMPI) at home	43.9	27.0	16.0	4.8	3.5	10.7	20.2	25.9	19.5	22.1	10.1
14. Altering a diagnosis to meet insurance criteria	36.4	26.5	27.0	5.5	2.6	2.9	37.3	28.9	16.0	14.0	2.0
15. Telling client: "I'm sexually attracted to you."	78.5	16.2	3.5	0.2	0.2	4.8	51.5	33.1	5.5	6.8	2.4
16. Refusing to let clients read their chart notes	33.1	21.3	13.6	5.7	14.9	23.2	14.5	28.3	14.9	21.5	16.0
17. Using a collection agency to collect late fees	48.0	21.9	19.7	5.9	1.8	8.6	5.0	15.1	15.6	35.5	27.4
18. Breaking confidentiality if client is homicidal	15.6	9.6	6.6	24.6	17.3	35.7	1.1	5.0	3.5	18.9	69.1
19. Performing forensic work for a contingency fee	67.3	7.0	6.8	0.9	0.7	42.1	35.5	11.0	29.8	7.0	10.3
20. Using self-disclosure as a therapy technique	5.9	22.1	38.6	19.7	12.9	0.7	2.2	17.1	7.9	43.0	29.2
21. Inviting clients to an office open house	76.3	9.6	5.0	0.7	2.0	19.3	28.9	25.7	23.2	12.1	8.3
22. Accepting a client's gift worth at least $50	72.1	19.1	2.4	0.4	0.0	16.7	34.2	36.2	15.8	8.6	3.3
23. Working when too distressed to be effective	38.8	48.5	10.5	0.4	0.2	5.3	46.7	38.4	8.6	4.4	1.3
24. Accepting only male or female clients	83.8	3.7	2.4	0.2	1.1	18.2	11.0	16.2	18.6	16.9	34.6
25. Not allowing client access to testing report	45.0	23.5	13.6	5.9	6.6	14.3	21.7	32.9	14.0	20.6	8.8
26. Raising the fee during the course of therapy	27.6	23.9	29.4	11.8	5.7	3.5	8.3	15.8	13.2	32.5	28.9
27. Breaking confidentiality if client is suicidal	16.2	24.6	25.0	9.6	19.3	11.8	2.0	10.1	5.5	23.5	57.5
28. Not allowing clients access to raw test data	32.2	10.5	9.0	7.9	30.0	1.8	12.1	12.9	11.2	22.8	36.8
29. Allowing a client to run up a large unpaid bill	12.5	44.1	34.4	5.7	1.5	2.9	7.2	35.3	22.8	16.9	16.4
30. Accepting goods (rather than money) as payment	65.1	24.8	6.4	0.2	0.4	12.7	15.8	33.8	21.3	18.2	9.6
31. Using sexual surrogates with clients	81.8	5.7	1.1	0.7	0.2	33.1	36.2	25.7	23.7	8.6	4.6
32. Breaking confidentiality to report child abuse	25.0	16.2	15.1	8.3	22.6	29.4	1.3	4.4	5.3	20.8	64.9

(continued)

	TABLE 3 (*cont.*)

	Rating										
	Occurrence in your practice?						Ethical?				
Item	1	2	3	4	5*	NA	1	2	3	4	5*
33. Inviting clients to a party or social event	82.9	13.2	2.2	0.2	0.4	4.6	50.0	34.0	8.1	6.1	1.5
34. Addressing client by his or her first name	2.0	2.6	9.4	20.8	65.1	0	0.7	0.9	2.6	30.7	65.1
35. Crying in the presence of a client	42.5	41.5	12.5	1.8	0.7	4.6	5.9	32.0	14.5	18.4	27.6
36. Earning a salary which is a % of client's fee	46.3	4.4	10.1	3.5	5.3	41.0	12.1	8.1	34.2	16.0	16.4
37. Asking favors (e.g., a ride home) from clients	60.5	35.7	2.4	0	0.2	5.0	27.0	45.2	12.3	10.1	4.4
38. Making custody evaluation without seeing the child	76.8	7.2	1.3	0.2	0.2	36.0	64.0	22.8	5.3	2.4	0.9
39. Accepting a client's decision to commit suicide	73.9	16.4	3.7	0.4	0	15.4	45.2	36.6	8.8	4.8	2.9
40. Refusing to disclose a diagnosis to a client	49.8	30.9	10.1	4.6	2.4	4.2	21.5	43.2	13.2	13.4	6.8
41. Leading nude group therapy or "growth" groups	88.6	2.2	0.9	0.2	0	24.3	59.6	16.4	14.9	3.9	2.9
42. Telling clients of your disappointment in them	46.9	39.0	11.4	1.1	0.4	2.6	19.7	37.1	18.0	15.4	7.9
43. Discussing clients (without names) with friends	22.8	46.3	22.4	5.7	2.0	0.9	32.9	38.6	13.8	9.4	4.6
44. Providing therapy to your student or supervisee	63.8	22.4	6.8	0.9	0.9	12.3	45.8	33.6	6.1	8.8	4.2
45. Giving gifts to those who refer clients to you	78.5	11.4	7.0	1.5	1.1	4.2	47.8	21.7	15.6	10.3	4.2
46. Using a law suit to collect fees from clients	62.7	21.3	10.3	0.2	0.4	15.4	10.1	28.3	19.3	19.7	21.1
47. Becoming sexually involved with a former client	88.2	10.5	0.4	0	0.2	7.5	50.2	34.4	7.2	3.9	3.3
48. Avoiding certain clients for fear of being sued	48.9	30.3	13.4	1.3	0.9	13.8	7.9	23.0	23.7	23.9	19.7
49. Doing custody evaluation without seeing both parents	63.8	16.9	6.6	0.7	0.2	30.5	47.1	31.6	10.7	3.9	2.6
50. Lending money to a client	73.7	23.9	1.5	0	0	4.4	40.6	38.8	10.7	5.9	3.3
51. Providing therapy to one of your employees	79.6	12.9	2.0	0	0.7	15.6	55.0	31.1	6.8	2.9	2.4
52. Having a client address you by your first name	3.5	10.5	21.9	21.9	41.9	0.4	1.3	3.3	7.9	23.5	63.6
53. Sending holiday greeting cards to your clients	61.4	16.2	12.9	3.1	4.8	5.3	10.5	12.9	26.8	20.4	28.5
54. Kissing a client	70.8	23.5	4.4	0.2	0.4	2.2	48.0	36.6	4.6	7.7	2.2
55. Engaging in erotic activity with a client	97.1	2.4	0.2	0	0	3.9	95.0	3.5	0.4	0.4	0.4
56. Giving a gift worth at least $50 to a client	95.0	3.7	0.4	0	0	4.6	69.7	16.0	8.1	2.9	2.6
57. Accepting a client's invitation to a party	59.6	34.9	4.4	0.2	0.4	2.9	25.7	46.1	10.1	10.7	6.8
58. Engaging in sex with a clinical supervisee	95.0	2.9	0.4	0	0	8.8	85.1	9.0	3.5	1.5	0.2
59. Going to client's special event (e.g., wedding)	23.5	50.7	20.4	3.3	1.5	0.4	5.3	34.0	13.8	28.7	17.5
60. Getting paid to refer clients to someone	98.0	0.4	0.2	0	0	7.2	88.4	7.2	3.3	0	0.2
61. Going into business with a client	95.6	1.5	0.2	0	0.2	9.9	78.5	12.7	5.5	1.1	1.1
62. Engaging in sexual contact with a client	97.8	1.5	0.4	0	0	4.2	96.1	2.6	0.2	0.7	0.2
63. Utilizing involuntarily hospitalization	30.5	42.1	16.7	2.4	1.1	17.1	3.1	28.9	8.8	24.3	31.8
64. Selling goods to clients	90.6	5.9	2.0	0	0.4	7.5	71.1	18.4	4.4	2.9	2.0
65. Giving personal advice on radio, t.v., etc.	66.0	18.6	9.2	1.5	0.2	18.6	18.4	28.3	22.1	23.7	6.4
66. Being sexually attracted to a client	9.2	38.8	43.9	5.5	1.3	1.1	11.2	11.0	19.5	19.1	33.3

(continued)

77

TABLE 3 (*cont.*)

Item	Occurrence in your practice?						Ethical?				
	1	2	3	4	5*	NA	1	2	3	4	5*
67. Unintentionally disclosing confidential data	36.0	58.6	3.3	0	0	2.9	75.2	14.3	4.6	1.8	1.8
68. Allowing a client to disrobe	94.5	2.9	1.5	0	0	5.0	81.4	12.1	3.1	1.5	1.3
69. Borrowing money from a client	97.1	1.8	0	0	0	4.4	86.2	10.7	1.1	0.4	0.9
70. Discussing a client (by name) with friends	91.2	7.5	0.4	0.2	0	3.5	94.5	3.5	0.7	0.4	0.4
71. Providing services outside areas of competence	74.8	22.8	1.8	0	0	2.0	80.7	16.9	0.2	0.9	0.7
72. Signing for hours a supervisee has not earned	89.0	7.2	0.9	0	0	9.9	92.5	5.5	0.4	0.4	0.7
73. Treating homosexuality per se as pathological	75.0	12.7	6.4	2.6	1.8	4.4	55.7	12.9	17.3	6.6	5.3
74. Doing therapy while under influence of alcohol	92.8	5.7	0.2	0	0	3.5	89.5	7.7	1.1	0	0.9
75. Engaging in sexual fantasy about a client	27.0	46.3	22.4	2.4	0.7	3.5	18.9	15.1	26.8	13.2	21.9
76. Accepting a gift worth less than $5 from a client	8.6	31.8	45.0	9.4	3.7	0.7	5.0	20.0	16.2	36.4	20.2
77. Offering or accepting a handshake from a client	1.3	3.3	17.5	28.1	48.2	1.1	0.7	1.1	3.3	21.7	71.9
78. Disrobing in the presence of a client	97.8	0.9	0	0.2	0.2	4.6	94.7	3.3	0	0.2	0.7
79. Charging for missed appointments	11.8	15.4	26.3	22.6	22.6	2.4	1.1	6.8	7.2	38.2	45.8
80. Going into business with a former client	83.1	10.1	2.0	0	0.4	15.6	36.8	28.9	17.5	9.0	5.9
81. Directly soliciting a person to be a client	89.3	8.6	0.9	0	0.2	4.4	67.5	22.6	5.7	1.8	1.5
82. Being sexually attracted to a client	9.2	39.5	41.0	6.1	0.9	1.3	9.2	13.4	21.9	18.0	30.0
83. Helping client file complaint re a colleague	52.9	19.4	9.4	1.1	1.1	20.0	6.4	22.6	14.9	29.2	25.2

Note. Rating codes: Occurrence in your practice? 1 = never, 2 = rarely, 3 = sometimes, 4 = fairly often, 5 very often, NA = not applicable; Ethical? 1 = unquestionably not, 2 = under rare circumstances, 3 = don't know/not sure, 4 = under many circumstances, 5 = unquestionably yes.
*Responses 1 through 5 sum to less than 100% due to missing data.

Behaviors Systematically Related to Sex of Psychologist

In order to assess the degree to which male and female psychologists might be differentially engaging in the 83 behaviors, chi-square analyses were performed on these data. To help eliminate seemingly significant findings actually due to chance—in light of the large number of analyses—a very strict significance level ($p < .001$) was used. Table 6 presents the items significantly related to sex, using this criterion.

DISCUSSION

Validity and Interpretation Issues

Caution is essential in interpreting these data. First, this is an initial study, and it awaits attempts at replication. Second, it is unclear how the behaviors and beliefs of this sample of Division 29 members compare with those of the over 60,000 APA members, of the close to 50,000 individuals (both APA and non-APA members) who are licensed or certified by the states to practice psychology (Dörken, Stapp, & VandenBos, 1986), or of the approximately 63% of licensed, doctoral psychologists who identify clinical psychology as their current major field (Stapp, Tucker, & VandenBos, 1985). Third, the behavior of the majority may not reflect what the majority themselves believe to be ethical. For example, almost two thirds of the participants reported that they have disclosed confidential material unintentionally, yet three fourths identify this behavior as unethical. Fourth, specific ethical standards may

TABLE 4

Percentage of Respondents Rating Effectiveness of Sources of Information About Regulating the Practice of Psychologists

Source	Rating				
	Terrible	Poor	Adequate	Good	Excellent
Your graduate program	5.3	19.1	27.0	29.6	18.2
Your internship	2.0	11.4	25.4	35.7	24.1
Agencies for which you've worked	5.0	16.2	31.4	30.7	12.9
State and federal laws	3.9	32.7	39.0	18.4	1.8
Court decisions (case law)	4.6	30.5	29.6	25.4	4.2
State licensing board	5.9	21.7	35.7	25.9	6.8
APA *Ethical Principles*	1.1	5.9	26.3	45.8	19.1
APA Ethics Committee	2.0	11.4	32.9	36.8	12.9
State ethics committee	3.3	20.8	32.9	28.5	7.0
Local ethics committee	6.4	22.8	29.4	20.8	4.8
Published research	7.2	28.5	30.7	21.3	5.0
Published clinical and theoretical work	4.8	20.0	33.1	29.2	7.2
Continuing education programs	2.4	19.1	29.6	33.6	9.2
Colleagues (informal network)	1.1	6.6	18.9	43.4	28.1

Note. Rows may not sum to 100% due to missing data or rounding.

TABLE 5

Means and Mean Differences for Rated Effectiveness of Sources of Information About the Practice of Psychologists

Source	M	Mean differences												
		1	2	3	4	5	6	7	8	9	10	11	12	13
1. Graduate program	3.36													
2. Internship	3.71	.35*												
3. Agencies	3.30	.06	.40*											
4. State and federal laws	2.84	.52*	.87*	.46*										
5. Court decisions	2.98	.38*	.73*	.32	.14									
6. State licensing boards	3.06	.30	.65*	.25	.22	.07								
7. APA *Ethical Principles*	3.77	.41*	.06	.46*	.93*	.79*	.71							
8. APA Ethics Committee	3.47	.11	.24	.17	.63*	.49*	.42*	.29						
9. State ethics committee	3.17	.19	.54*	.14	.33*	.18	.11	.60*	.31					
10. Local ethics committee	2.95	.41*	.76*	.36*	.11	.04	.11	.82*	.53*	.22				
11. Published research	2.84	.52*	.87*	.46*	.00	.14	.22	.93*	.63*	.33*	.11			
12. Published clinical and theoretical work	3.10	.26	.61*	.21	.26	.11	.04	.67*	.38*	.07	.15	.26		
13. Continuing education programs	3.25	.11	.46*	.06	.41*	.26	.19	.52*	.23	.08	.30	.41	.15	
14. Colleagues	3.93	.57*	.22	.62*	1.09*	.94*	.87*	.16	.45*	.76*	.98*	1.09*	.83*	.68*

*p < .01, Scheffé criterion.

TABLE 6

Items Significantly Related to Sex ($p < .001$)

Item	Direction	x^2	df
9. Hugging a client	Female more likely	18.70	4
15. Telling a client: "I'm sexually attracted to you."	Male more likely	16.29	2
52. Having a client address you by your first name	Female more likely	20.00	4
73. Treating homosexuality per se as pathological	Male more likely	19.26	4
75. Engaging in sexual fantasy about a client	Male more likely	40.39	4
81. Directly soliciting a person to be a client	Male more likely	11.24	1

not be reflected in majority belief. Most psychologists, for example, may be unfamiliar with the procedures, research, or complexities of such special areas as treating minors, performing forensic work, engaging in sex with former clients, or working with suicidal clients. As previously mentioned, the formulation and dissemination of formal ethical standards can represent attempts to improve ethical awareness and behavior. Empirical data about the behavior and beliefs of a general sample should inform—not determine—our ethical deliberations. Finally, most of the questionnaire items involve enormously complex issues. The following discussion is meant only to highlight some of the major themes, patterns, and dilemmas emerging from these initial data.

Relationship Between Behavior and Beliefs

The data suggest that the psychologists' behavior was generally in accordance with their ethical beliefs. This inference is based on the fact that for all but four items, the frequency with which the respondents reported engaging in a behavior was less than the frequency of instances in which the behavior was ethical in their judgment. Of the four exceptions, three involved confidentiality: "discussing a client (by name) with friends," "discussing clients (without names) with friends," and "unintentionally disclosing confidential data." The fourth exception was "providing services outside areas of competence."

Behaviors That Are Almost Universal

For 7 of the 83 items, at least 90% of the respondents indicated that they engaged in the behavior, at least on rare occasions (see Table 3). Two of these almost universal behaviors involved self-disclosure to the clients: "using self-disclosure as a therapy technique" and "telling a client that you are angry at him or her." Thus, it appears that the more extreme versions of the therapist as "blank screen" are exceedingly rare among psychologists. Similarly, the models of the therapist as a distant, almost standoffish authority figure—which, like the "blank screen" approach, are derived from the classical psychoanalytic tradition—are infrequently practiced. Fewer than 10% of the respondents indicated that they never engaged in "having a client address you by your first name" (as Table 6 shows, it is mainly male therapists who insist on being addressed by their last names), "addressing your client by his or her first name," "accepting a gift worth less than $5 from a client," and "offering or accepting a handshake from a client." Finally, only 9.2% of the respondents indicated that they had never been sexually attracted to a client. This finding may be compared to a survey of APA Division 42 (Psychologists in Independent Practice) in which 13% indicated that they had never been sexually attracted to a client (Pope, Keith-Spiegel, & Tabachnick, 1986).

Behaviors That Are Rare

One of the most surprising results was that only 1.9% of the respondents reported engaging in sexual contact with a client and that only 2.6% reported engaging in erotic activity (which may or may not involve actual contact) with a client. Previously, there have been three national surveys of sexual intimacies between psychologists and their patients. Holroyd and Brodsky (1977) reported 7.7% respondents "who answered positively any of the questions regarding erotic-contact behaviors or intercourse during treatment." Pope, Levenson, and Schover (1979) found that 7% of the therapists in their survey reported engaging in sexual contact with their clients. Pope et al. (1986) reported that 6.5% of their respondents acknowledged engaging in sexual intimacies with clients.

It is difficult to explain the discrepancy between the current findings and those of the previous three studies. It may be that respondents are now less willing to admit, even on anonymous survey, to a behavior that is a felony in some states, or it may be that these findings are reflective of random sampling error or bias in return rate rather than of a change in behavior.

However, the current findings may indicate an actual decrease in the percentage of psychologists engaging in sexual intimacies with their patients. The increasing publicity given to the Therapist–Patient Sex Syndrome (Pope, 1985, 1986) and other devastating consequences of therapist–patient sexual intimacy (Bouhoutsos, Holroyd, Lerman, Forer, & Greenberg, 1983; Feldman-Summers & Jones, 1984; Pope & Bouhoutsos, 1986), as well as the vivid first-person accounts of patients who have been sexually involved with their therapists (Freeman & Roy, 1976; Plaisil, 1985; Walker & Young, 1986), may be significantly altering the behavior of psychologists who are tempted in this area. Clinical strategies developed to help therapists at risk to refrain from sexual contact with their patients may also be contributing to this decline (Pope, in press).

Some other items concerning sexual behaviors—such as nudity as part of therapy or using sexual surrogates with clients—also had extremely low rates. Engaging in sex with a clinical supervisee was reported by only 3.4% of the respondents. This figure corresponds closely to the 4.0% in a prior survey of APA Division 29 members who reported engaging in sexual intimacies with their clinical supervisees (Pope et al., 1979).

Dishonesty in helping candidates to become degreed or licensed without the requisite supervised experience is relatively rare; it was reported by 8.1%.

A number of the rare practices concerned financial or business practices, such as borrowing money from a client, selling goods to clients, going into business with a client, or giving a gift worth at least $50 to a client. The most infrequently reported behavior was getting paid to refer clients to someone (0.6%). It is heartening to note that psychologists are not putting their judgment and influence up for sale.

Although over a fourth (26.1%) of the respondents advertise in newspapers and similar media,

only 9.7% report directly soliciting a person to be a client. As Table 6 indicates, men were more likely than women to engage in this practice.

Few psychologists blatantly breach the confidentiality of their clients. However, 8.1% have discussed a client (by name) with friends.

Doing therapy while under the influence of alcohol is also rare (5.9%).

For the most part, psychologists are careful to interview the child when making a custody evaluation, although 8.9% fail to do so.

A gender-based criterion for admission to treatment is rare. Accepting only male or female clients was reported by 7.4%.

Although rare, some of these practices—such as discussing clients by name with friends or doing therapy while under the influence of alcohol—so clearly undermine the rights and welfare of patients that they need to be addressed much more forcefully and effectively by the profession.

Difficult Judgments

We defined a difficult judgment as one in which at least 20% of the respondents indicated "don't know/not sure." There were 12 behaviors that posed difficult judgments in terms of whether they were ethical: "performing forensic work for a contingency fee," "accepting goods (rather than money) as payment," "using sexual surrogates with clients," "earning a salary which is a percentage of client fees," "avoiding certain clients for fear of being sued," "sending holiday greeting cards to your clients," "giving personal advice on radio, t.v., etc.," "engaging in sexual fantasy about a client," "being sexually attracted to a client," "limiting treatment notes to name, date, and fee," "inviting clients to an office open house," and "allowing a client to run up a large unpaid bill." It is interesting that one third of these directly concerned financial issues, and one fourth concerned sexual issues. The profession may need to develop practical guidelines in these areas.

Topic Areas

Redlich and Pope (1980) have suggested seven principles for meaningfully coordinating ethical guidelines with other standards of professional practice in a way that can be most useful to psychologists and psychiatrists attempting to carry out their professional tasks responsibly. These are (1) above all, do no harm; (2) practice only with competence; (3) do not exploit; (4) treat people with respect for their dignity as human beings; (5) protect confidentiality; (6) act, except in the most extreme instances, only after obtaining informed consent; and (7) practice, insofar as possible, within the framework of social equity and justice. The first five are ancient and are mentioned explicitly in the Hippocratic Oath. The sixth and seventh are of recent origin, express patients' rights, and have not yet been universally accepted. This seven-part framework organizes the following discussion of the questionnaire items.

1. Do No Harm

Lending money to a client. It is ironic that lending money to a client—an act that might seem to be generous and helpful—would be viewed as so harmful to the therapeutic enterprise as to be clearly unethical by 40.6% of the respondents and unethical under most circumstances by an additional 38.8%. Nevertheless, about one fourth of the respondents acknowledged that they had lent money to a client (23.9% rarely; 1.5% sometimes).

Signing for unearned hours. A clear majority (92.5%) believe that signing for hours that a supervisee has not earned is unethical. Producing graduates and licensees whose credentials were fraudulently obtained may subject numerous future clients to harm.

Filing ethics complaints. The injunction to do no harm can be construed to include the mandate not to remain passively acquiescent when fellow professionals are violating ethical principles and standards of practice. A surprising finding was that one fourth of the respondents reported that they had, on a rare basis, filed an ethics complaint against a colleague. An additional 9.3% reported that they did so more frequently.

The view that it is unethical always (2.4%) or under most circumstances (11.8%) to file an ethical complaint against a colleague may reflect the difficulties experienced by an association (the APA) charged with the task of promoting the profession when it also attempts to monitor and discipline the behavior of its members. Furthermore, the practical steps for

effective peer monitoring may need to be more widely disseminated (see Keith-Spiegel & Koocher, 1985).

Helping a client file an ethics complaint was a behavior performed by over one third of the respondents on a rare (19.4%) or more frequent (11.6%) basis. Over one fourth believed that this action was unethical (6.4%) or unethical under most circumstances (22.6%). Although Principle 7g of the current *Ethical Principles* (APA, 1981a) speaks to this general issue, the *Principles* may need to address more specifically situations in which the allegations of unethical behavior are brought to the attention of psychologists by their clients.

2. Practice Only With Competence

Providing services outside areas of competence. Both the *Ethical Principles of Psychologists* (APA, 1981a) and the *Specialty Guidelines for the Delivery of Services by Clinical Psychologists* (APA, 1981b) make clear statements that psychologists are to practice only within the limits of demonstrable expertise. Nevertheless, almost one fourth of the respondents indicated that they had practiced outside their area of competence either rarely (22.8%) or sometimes (1.8%).

Impaired performance. Psychology has turned increased attention to the impaired or distressed professional (Kilburg, Nathan, & Thoreson, 1986; Laliotis & Grayson, 1985). The results of this survey suggest that those efforts are needed. Over half (59.6%) of the respondents acknowledged having worked—either rarely or more often—when too distressed to be effective. About 1 out of every 15 or 20 (5.7%) respondents acknowledged, on a rare basis, doing therapy while under the influence of alcohol.

Competence in carrying out assessments. In the area of assessment, what seem like efficient and competent short-cuts or innovative strategies to some may seem questionable to others. Sending tests home with clients is said, by its advocates, to be more convenient and to allow clients to fill out the test in more familiar, less stressful surroundings. Critics of the practice argue that psychologists should monitor the administration of such tests—for example, to prevent clients from relying on the advice of friends and family about how to fill out the test. Furthermore, maintain the critics, should the test results become part of important legal proceedings, the psychologist would be unable to testify that the test responses were those of the client unaided by friends or family. The current study indicates that over half of the respondents send such tests home with clients either on a rare (27.0%) or more frequent (24.3%) basis. This practice is viewed as unethical by 20.2% and unethical in most circumstances by 25.9%.

The use of computerized psychological test interpretations has been harshly criticized (Matarazzo, 1986) but seems to have been accepted by the APA, which has issued guidelines for their use (APA, 1986a). The current findings indicate that a majority of the respondents have used such services either rarely (21.7%) or more often (36.2%). Few believe that they are unethical (2.0%) or unethical under most circumstances (9.0%).

The literature in the field of child-custody conflicts indicates that a competent custody evaluation cannot be conducted without interviewing both parents. Shapiro (1984), for example, wrote that "under no circumstances should a report on child custody be rendered to the court, based on the evaluation of only one party to the conflict" (p. 99). About half of the respondents agree that doing a custody evaluation without seeing both parents is unethical. Only 16.9% reported that they had done this rarely, 7.5% more frequently.

3. Do Not Exploit

Sexual issues and physical contact. As mentioned earlier, the rates of sexual contact and erotic activities with patients are significantly lower than in the three previously reported national studies of psychologists. Over 95% of the respondents believed that both of these behaviors were unethical.

About half of the respondents believed that becoming sexually involved with a *former* client was unethical. (This figure may be compared to the 6.4% who believe that becoming friends with a former client is unethical.) These beliefs seem consistent with the harm associated with these relationships (Pope & Bouhoutsos, 1986), with the awarding of general and punitive damages in malpractice suits in which the sexual intimacies occurred only after termination (e.g., *Whitesell v. Green*, 1973), and with a multiyear study of the adjudications of state licensing boards and state ethics committees (Sell,

Gottlieb, & Schoenfeld, 1986). The study found "that psychologists asserting that a sexual relationship had occurred only after the termination of the therapeutic relationship were more likely to be found in violation than those not making that claim" (p. 504). It is also interesting to note that the $25,000 cap on coverage in regard to sexual intimacies in the APA professional liability policy specifies sex with former as well as current clients.

The focus on erotic contact in therapy has raised questions about the legitimacy and effects of ostensibly nonerotic physical contact (Geller, 1980; Holroyd & Brodsky, 1977, 1980). Holroyd and Brodsky (1980) pointed out that it "is difficult to determine where 'nonerotic hugging, kissing, and affectionate touching' leave off and 'erotic contact' begins" (p. 810). About one fourth of our respondents reported kissing their clients, either rarely (23.5%) or more often (5.0%). About half viewed this practice as unethical. An additional 36.6% believed it to be unethical in most circumstances.

Hugging clients was practiced by 44.5% of the respondents on a rare basis, and by an additional 41.7% more frequently. Few (4.6%) believed the practice to be clearly unethical, but 41.2% believed it to be ethical only under rare circumstances.

The findings in the previous two categories may be compared to the results reported by Holroyd and Brodsky (1977) in which 27% of the therapists reported occasionally engaging in nonerotic hugging, kissing, or affectionate touching with opposite-sex patients, and 7% reported doing so frequently or always.

Almost all respondents offered or accepted a handshake from a client, either rarely (48.9%) or more frequently (48.2%). Very few found the behavior to be ethically questionable.

As mentioned earlier, using sexual surrogates with clients was a difficult ethical judgment for almost one fourth of the respondents. A little over one third believed that the behavior was unethical. An additional one fourth believed it was ethical only under rare circumstances. The use of surrogates has been frequently challenged on ethical bases (Redlich, 1977), but so far no complaint has been filed with the APA Ethics Committee concerning the use of a sexual surrogate.

A large majority (85.1%) believe that sexual intimacies with clinical supervisees are unethical, a finding consistent with published analyses of this practice (Pope & Bouhoutsos, 1986; Pope, Schover, & Levenson, 1980).

Over 1 out of every 10 respondents believed that simply "being sexually attracted to a client" was unethical. Approximately an additional one tenth believed that feeling such attraction was ethical under rare circumstances. These findings seem consistent with the results of a prior survey in which 63% of the respondents reported that experiencing sexual attraction to clients made them feel guilty, anxious, or confused (Pope et al., 1986).

Almost half (46.3%) of the respondents reported engaging in sexual fantasy about a client on a rare basis, an additional one fourth (25.5%) more frequently. These figures may be compared to the 28.7% of psychologists in a previous study who answered affirmatively the question, "While engaging in sexual activity with someone other than a client, have you ever had sexual fantasies about someone who is or was a client?" (Pope et al., 1986). Both the current and previous survey found that male psychologists were significantly more likely to engage in sexual fantasies about clients. This difference is consistent with research regarding sexual fantasizing in general, which shows higher rates for men (Pope, 1982).

Financial issues. The vulnerability, dependency, and sometimes confusion of so many who seek help from psychologists call for a strong ethic against financial exploitation, as well as extensive research to determine which financial arrangements work best for therapist and patient. Yet until the 1970s, the subject was virtually absent from the research literature. Volumes attempting comprehensive collection, review, and evaluation of research in psychotherapy (Bergin & Garfield, 1971; Rubinstein & Parloff, 1959; Shlien, 1968; Strupp & Luborsky, 1962) cited no research on financial arrangements, prompting one contributing author to comment:

> As a footnote, I would like to remark that if a Martian read the volumes reporting the first two psychotherapy conferences and if he read all the papers of this conference it would never occur to him that psychotherapy is something done for money. Either therapists believe that money is not a worthwhile research variable or money is part of the new obscenity in which we talk more freely about sex but never mention money. (Colby, 1968, p. 539)

Mintz (1971) likewise labeled fees a "tabooed subject" and suggested that "a varied set of guidelines" concerning fee payment has "functioned to inhibit therapists from inquiring too closely into the financial side of psychotherapeutic practice and into the actual effects it may have on the therapeutic enterprise" (p. 3).

In the last 15 years such factors as the increase in third-party payments have brought financial issues into the open. As the results of this study reveal, psychologists have developed a consensus of opinion about the acceptability of some—but by no means all—of the financial approaches to their work. Over half of the respondents reported altering an insurance diagnosis to meet insurance criteria, either rarely (26.5%) or more frequently (35.1%). This action—which can be legally construed as insurance fraud—is viewed by slightly more than one third as unethical. An additional one fourth viewed it as ethical under rare circumstances. This widespread practice—in light of its legal implications and the use of dishonesty in the therapeutic endeavor—is in need of open discussion among professionals.

Charging for missed appointments seems an acceptable practice to virtually the entire psychological community. Raising a fee during the course of therapy also seems widely accepted. Principle 6d of the *Ethical Principles* (APA, 1981a) stresses that clients must be aware of such financial aspects of the services in advance and that they thus have a right to informed consent to or informed refusal of the financial arrangements.

About half (49.3%) of the respondents have used a collection agency to collect late fees, at least on a rare basis. Only 5% view this practice as unethical.

About one third (21.3% rarely; 10.9% more often) of the respondents have filed a lawsuit to collect fees. One out of 10 (10.1%) view this as unethical. It may be useful for psychologists to be aware that the current APA professional liability policy specifically excludes "disputes concerning fees charged by any Insured, including but not limited to third party reimbursements sought or received by any Insured" (American Home Assurance Company, undated, p. 3). In addition, psychologists must be aware of the ways in which fee-collection attempts that involve third parties (e.g., collection agencies, the courts) affect both the psychological welfare of the clients as well as such aspects of therapy as privacy and confidentiality.

Accepting a salary that is a percentage of client fees—a practice sometimes known as "kick-backs" or "fee-splitting" (Keith-Spiegel & Koocher, 1985)—was reported by 23.3% of the respondents. It is viewed as unethical by 12.1%. This was the item with the lowest response rate by far, suggesting that many respondents may have been unsure of the meaning of the question.

In another area, forensic psychology, psychologists may be tempted to accept a contingency fee. Standard texts have made clear statements concerning the unacceptability of such arrangements. "The psychologist should never accept a fee contingent upon the outcome of a case" (Blau, 1984, p. 336). "The expert witness should never, under any circumstances, accept a referral on a contingent fee basis" (Shapiro, 1984, p. 95). Only about 15% of the respondents report engaging in this practice either rarely (7.0%) or more often (8.4%).

Bartering of services for therapy has customarily been viewed by the profession as a dual relationship, hence unethical. The APA Ethics Committee took up the question of bartering at its February 18–20, 1982 meeting and formally approved a policy statement that "bartering of personal services is a violation of Principle 6a" (APA, 1982). However, about one fourth of the respondents reported that they had engaged in such bartering, at least on a rare basis. Over half viewed the practice as either unethical or unethical under most circumstances.

Other dual relationships. Both sexual intimacy with clients and bartering for services are dual relationships. However, Principle 6a of the *Ethical Principles* (APA, 1981a) lists other dual relation-

ships that are to be avoided: "Examples of such dual relationships include, but are not limited to, research with and treatment of employees, students, supervisees, close friends, or relatives" (p. 636). The current study inquired into three of these areas: therapy with employees, students/supervisees, and friends. The most frequent dual relationship involved students and supervisees (22.4% rarely; 8.6% more frequently), followed by friends (25.2% rarely; 3.1% more frequently) and employees (12.9% rarely; 2.7% more frequently).

Dual relationships can also be initiated once therapy begins, as happens when a therapist engages in sexual contact with a patient. According to the respondents, initiating business relationships with clients (1.5% rarely; 0.4% more frequently) and former clients (10.1% rarely; 2.4% more frequently) is not a widespread practice.

Advertising for and soliciting clients. Currently, advertising per se is not considered unethical, although direct solicitation of clients can be viewed as potentially exploitive (Keith-Spiegel & Koocher, 1985). About one fourth of the respondents report advertising in newspapers and similar media, either rarely (13.2%) or more frequently (12.9%). Fewer than 10% of the respondents (generally male psychologists) directly solicit clients. At least two thirds view this practice as unethical.

4. Treat People With Respect for Their Dignity as Human Beings

To some extent, the history of psychotherapy has reflected the struggle to arrive at the most effective way in which to express respect. For example, Thompson (1950) discussed the ways in which, because of suspicions about countertransference,

> the feeling grew that even a genuine
> objective feeling of friendliness on his
> part was to be suspected. As a result
> many of Freud's pupils became afraid
> to be simply human and show the ordi-
> nary friendliness and interest a thera-
> pist customarily feels for a patient. In
> many cases, out of a fear of showing
> counter-transference, the attitude
> of the analyst became stilted and
> unnatural. (p. 107)

In this study, we found that many of the walls that prevented therapists from engaging in simple human interactions—for example, therapists revealing their emotions—have come down, although therapists are still in a quandary about some of these issues.

An overwhelming majority of the respondents are on a first-name basis with their clients and do not view this as ethically questionable. Three fourths have attended a client's social event, such as a wedding, although only about one third have accepted an invitation to a party. About one fourth view accepting a party invitation as unethical. About the same percentage have invited clients to an office open house, but slightly more (28.9%) view this as unethical.

A large majority (93.3%) use self-disclosure. More specifically, over half tell clients that they are angry with them (89.7%), cry in the presence of a client (56.5%), and tell clients that they are disappointed in them (51.9%). The most questioned of these was telling clients of disappointment: 56.8% viewed it as unethical or unethical under most circumstances.

5. Protect Confidentiality

Breaking confidentiality to prevent harm. The results of this study suggest that psychologists have accepted the legitimacy of breaking confidentiality in order to prevent danger. Fewer than 10% view this action as unethical in cases involving homicide, suicide, or child abuse.

The data also indicate that such situations are a customary part of general practice for psychologists: 78.5% report having broken confidentiality in regard to suicidal clients, 62.2% in cases of child abuse, and 58.1% when the client was homicidal.

Informally or unintentionally breaking confidentiality. About three fourths discuss clients—without names—with friends. Only 8.1% discuss clients—with names—with friends. Surprisingly, over half (61.9%) have unintentionally disclosed confidential data.

The widespread disclosure of confidential information—whether or not with names—is a practice that needs attention from the profession. Discussion of client information with friends seems to be a clear violation of Principle 5a: "Information obtained in clinical or consulting relationships, or evaluative data concerning children, students, employees, or others, is discussed only for professional purposes and only with persons clearly con-

cerned with the case" (APA, 1981a, p. 636). It also appears to violate the *General Guidelines for Providers of Psychological Services:*

> Psychologists do not release confidential information, except with the written consent of the user involved, or of his or her legal representative, guardian, or other holder of the privilege on behalf of the user, and only after the user has been assisted to understand the implications of the release. (APA, 1987, p. 21)

Public psychology. When psychological services are performed in a public forum, of course, there is no confidentiality. Giving personal advice on radio, TV, and so forth, is a very difficult issue. More than one in five indicated that they did not know or were not sure if it was ethical. The *Ethical Principles* (APA, 1981a, p. 635) appear to indicate that giving such advice is not in itself unethical by stating,

> When personal advice is given by means of public lectures or demonstrations, newspaper or magazine articles, radio or television programs, mail, or similar media, the psychologist utilizes the most current relevant data and exercises the highest level of professional judgment.

Surprisingly, over one fourth of the respondents reported giving such advice in the media either rarely (18.6%) or more frequently (10.9%).

6. Acting Only With Informed Consent

Seeing a minor without parental consent. A major ethical, as well as legal, dilemma is faced by many psychologists when the client is not empowered to give adequate consent to treatment (Koocher, 1976; Melton, 1981; Morrison, Morrison, & Holdridge-Crane, 1979; Plotkin, 1981). Over one fourth of the respondents have elected to see a minor without parental consent either rarely (22.4%) or more frequently (6.4%). Over half of the respondents believe such treatment to be either unethical (23.5%) or unethical under most circumstances (45.6%).

Withholding access to data. Should the clients have full access to assessment and treatment data that concern them? On the one hand, access to data about the client's condition may be important to the client's reaching a truly informed decision about initiating or continuing treatment. For example, if clients are not honestly told the diagnosis, it may be hard for them to know whether they want to be treated without knowing what they are to be treated for. On the other hand, psychologists may feel that certain technical terms or raw data may actually exacerbate the client's condition.

About one in five believe that it is unethical to refuse to disclose the diagnosis (21.5%) or to refuse access to a test report (21.7%). Fewer believe that refusing to allow clients to read their chart notes (14.5%) or that denying clients access to raw test data (12.1%) is unethical. Around half of the respondents have denied their clients access to the diagnosis (48.0%), to the testing report (49.6%), to their chart notes (55.5%), or to raw test data (57.4%).

Access to chart notes may have differential meaning and usefulness depending on how much information is contained in the chart. Over half (50.9%) of the respondents indicated that they had, at least rarely, limited treatment notes to name, date, and fee. The *General Guidelines for Providers of Psychological Services* (APA, 1987) mandate that "accurate, current and pertinent records of essential psychological services are maintained" (p. 19). Lack of adequate documentation of assessment, interventions, and responses to interventions have contributed to successful malpractice actions by establishing lack of care. One court held:

> The hospital record maintained by the State was about as inadequate a record as we have ever examined. We [the court] find that . . . the inadequacies in this record militated against proper and competent psychiatric and ordinary medical care. . . . Therefore, to the extent that a hospital record develops information for subsequent treatment, it contributed to the inadequate treatment this claimant received . . . it was so inadequate that even a layman could determine that fact. (*Whitree v. State*, 1968, p. 487)

Interventions against the client's wishes. Some of the most difficult and painful judgments psychologists must make concern under what, if any, condi-

tions informed consent can be waived. One area of such judgments involves involuntary hospitalization, an area filled with controversy. Over half of the respondents have utilized involuntary hospitalization, either rarely (42.1%) or more often (20.2%). Fewer than 5% view it as unethical.

Whether to accept a client's decision to commit suicide is likewise a difficult and painful dilemma for many psychologists. Some have argued that the informed consent of the patient to accept or to refuse treatment in such cases must be absolute (Szasz, 1986). Only about one in five of the respondents has accepted, either rarely (16.4%) or more frequently (4.1%), a client's decision to kill himself or herself. Almost half (45.2%) believe it to be unethical. An additional 36.6% believe it to be unethical under most circumstances.

7. Promoting Equity and Justice

Homosexuality. The profession's struggle to eliminate the stigma and pathologizing of homosexuality has been long, difficult, and not yet complete (Baer, 1981; Malyon, 1986a, 1986b). Slightly more than one in five of the respondents reported treating homosexuality per se as pathological, either rarely (12.7%) or more often (10.8%). However, over half (55.7%) viewed such a practice as unethical.

Sex of client. Whether to make access to one's practice dependent in any way upon the making of discriminations about a potential client's sex, race, religion, and so forth, is another of the very difficult judgments for many psychologists. On the one hand, discrimination as the term is customarily used is abhorrent. On the other hand, psychologists may wish to specialize, and such specialty areas may be founded in part upon such characteristics as sex, race, or religion. Fewer than 10% engaged in this practice either rarely (3.7%) or more often (3.7%).

Financial barriers. To what extent are people without sufficient funds denied access to needed psychological services? Ever since Freud's (1913/1958) statement that "the absence of the regulating effect offered by the payment of a fee makes itself very painfully felt" (pp. 131–132), there have been strong advocates for the therapeutic necessity of charging fees (e.g., Davids, 1964; Kubie, 1950; Menninger, 1961). Such claims have been made in the absence of empirical support, because systematic studies have found, in general, no therapeutic effect exerted by the fee and no harm to the therapy caused by an absence or lowering of the fee (Balch, Ireland, & Lewis, 1977; Pope, Geller, & Wilkinson, 1975; Turkington, 1984).

Almost half (47.4%) of the respondents report providing free therapy on a rare basis, an additional 18.7% more frequently. Over half of the respondents had terminated therapy due to the client's inability to pay, either rarely (36.2%) or more often (25.7%). The potential legal liability of the therapist's terminating therapy for other than "therapeutic" reasons may expose the psychologist to a malpractice suit for "abandonment."

Fear of being sued. Do certain clients whose condition may make therapists wary of being sued find access to therapy shut off? Avoiding certain clients for fear of being sued was acknowledged by 30.3% on a rare basis and by 15.6% more often. Fewer than 10% viewed this practice as unethical.

Resources for Regulating the Practice of Psychology

It is interesting that informal networks of colleagues are viewed as the most effective source of guidance, but it is heartening that both the *Ethical Principles* and the APA Ethics Committee are highly valued resources. The fact that both state and local ethics committees received significantly lower ratings suggests that state and local associations may need to devote increased time, financial backing, and program planning and evaluation to these efforts if they are to be judged as valuable by psychologists.

In light of psychology's identity as an empirically based discipline (Singer, 1980), the low ratings accorded to published research are troubling. It is possible that research too rarely addresses ethical concerns and standards of practice in a way that is useful for psychologists.

CONCLUSION

The lack of comprehensive normative data about the behaviors of psychologists and their relationship to ethical standards leaves psychologists without adequate guidelines to inform their choices (Rosenbaum, 1982). Ethical issues in general may be relatively neglected in the professional literature. For example,

Baldick (1980) reviewed 250 psychotherapy and counseling texts and found that only 2.8% discussed ethical issues encountered in professional practice.

These data would also be useful to psychology in the formulation of formal standards (APA, 1973, 1981a, 1981b, 1986, 1987a, 1987b; *Standards,* 1985) and in the deliberations of the APA Ethics Committee. In this age of increasing accountability, the formal means by which we psychologists hold ourselves accountable for our behavior is the APA Ethics Committee. Although the Committee participates in a variety of tasks, a major activity is the attempt to resolve complaints against APA members. If the Committee can adjudicate these complaints in a sensitive, fair, and informed manner and can demonstrate a legitimate system of accountability, four consequences are likely to follow.

First, those who file complaints may believe that the perceived wrongs have been corrected or at least seriously addressed. The relationship between the psychologist-complainee and the client or colleague may be reestablished on a more positive, constructive level. At a minimum, those who may have been harmed by the unethical actions of a psychologist may feel that they have been heard and respected. Second, the psychologist-complainee may be at less risk for future unethical behavior and at less risk for harming others. Third, the integrity of the profession is affirmed. Fourth, if the profession can demonstrate a sound process of accountability, that task will not fall by default to external agencies, such as the courts and legislatures, that are ill-equipped for such monitoring.

The integrity of psychology is contingent to a great degree on the extent to which we—both as a discipline or profession and as individuals—can regulate our own behavior. Our ability to engage in effective and ethical regulation, in turn, is contingent on our willingness to study our own behavior and our beliefs about that behavior.

References

American Home Assurance Company undated *Psychologists' professional liability policy* [Insurance policy]. New York: Author.

American Psychological Association. (1985). *Standards for educational and psychological testing.* Washington, DC: Author.

American Psychological Association. (1973). Guidelines for psychologists conducting growth groups. *American Psychologist, 28,* 933.

American Psychological Association. (1981a). *Ethical principles of psychologists* (rev. ed.). Washington, DC: Author.

American Psychological Association. (1981b). *Specialty guidelines for the delivery of services by clinical psychologists.* Washington, DC: Author.

American Psychological Association. (1985). *Directory of the American Psychological Association.* Washington, DC: Author.

American Psychological Association. (1986). *Guidelines for computer-based tests and interpretations.* Washington, DC: Author.

American Psychological Association. (1987a). Guidelines for conditions of employment of psychologists. *American Psychologist, 42,* 712–723.

American Psychological Association. (1987b). General guidelines for providers of psychological services. *American Psychologist, 42,* 724–729.

American Psychological Association, Ethics Committee. (1982, February 18–20), *Policy statement.* Statement presented at the meeting of the Ethics Committee of the American Psychological Association, Washington, DC.

Baer, R. (1981). *Homosexuality and American psychiatry.* New York: Basic Books.

Balch, P., Ireland, J. F., & Lewis, S. B. (1977). Fees and therapy: Relation of source of payment to course of therapy at a community mental health center. *Journal of Consulting and Clinical Psychology, 45,* 504.

Baldick, T. L. (1980). Ethical discrimination ability of intern psychologists: A function of training in ethics. *Professional Psychology, 11,* 276–282.

Bergin, A. E., & Garfield, S. L. (Eds.). (1971). *Handbook of psychotherapy and behavior change: An empirical analysis.* New York: Wiley.

Blau, T. H. (1984). *The psychologist as expert witness.* New York: Wiley Interscience.

Bouhoutsos, J. C., Holroyd, J., Lerman, H., Forer, B. R., & Greenberg, M. (1983). Sexual intimacy between psychotherapists and patients. *Professional Psychology: Research and Practice, 14,* 185–196.

Colby, K. (1968). Commentary: Report to plenary session on psychopharmacology in relation to psychotherapy. In J. M. Shlien (Ed.), *Research in psychotherapy* (Vol. 3, pp. 536–540). Washington, DC: American Psychological Association.

Davids, A. (1964). The relationship of cognitive-dissonance theory to an aspect of psychotherapeutic practice. *American Psychologist, 19,* 329–332.

Dörken, H., Stapp, J., & VandenBos, G. R. (1986). Licensed psychologists: A decade of major growth. In H. Dörken (Ed.), *Professional psychology in transition* (pp. 3–19). San Francisco: Jossey-Bass.

Feldman-Summers, S., & Jones, G. (1984). Psychological impacts of sexual contact between therapists or other health care practitioners and their clients. *Journal of Consulting and Clinical Psychology, 52,* 1054–1061.

Freeman, L., & Roy, J. (1976). *Betrayal.* New York: Stein & Day.

Freud, S. (1958). Further recommendations in the technique of psychoanalysis: On beginning the treatment. In J. Strachey (Ed. & Trans.), *The standard edition of the complete psychological works of Sigmund Freud* (Vol. 12). London: Hogarth Press. (Original work published 1913)

Geller, J. D. (1980). The body, expressive movement, and physical contact in psychotherapy. In J. L. Singer & K. S. Pope (Eds.), *The power of human imagination: New methods in psychotherapy* (pp. 347–378). New York: Plenum.

Holroyd, J. C., & Brodsky, A. M. (1977). Psychologists' attitudes and practices regarding erotic and nonerotic physical contact with patients. *American Psychologist, 32,* 843–849.

Holroyd, J. C., & Brodsky, A. M. (1980). Does touching patients lead to sexual intercourse? *Professional Psychology, 11,* 807–811.

Keith-Spiegel, P. C., & Koocher, G. (1985). *Ethics in psychology: Professional standards and cases.* New York: Random House.

Kilburg, R. R., Nathan, P. E., & Thoreson, R. (1986). *Professionals in distress: Issues, syndromes, and solutions in psychology.* Washington, DC: American Psychological Association.

Koocher, G. P. (Ed.). (1976). *Children's rights and the mental health professions.* New York: Wiley.

Kubie, L. S. (1950). *Practical and theoretical aspects of psychoanalysis.* New York: International Universities Press.

Laliotis, D., & Grayson, J. (1985). Psychologist heal thyself: What is available for the impaired psychologist? *American Psychologist, 40,* 84–96.

Malyon, A. K. (1986a). *Brief follow-up to June 24, 1986 meeting with the American Psychiatric Association work group to revise DSM-III.* Unpublished manuscript.

Malyon, A. K. (1986b). *Presentation to the American Psychiatric Association work group to revise DSM-III.* Unpublished manuscript.

Matarazzo, J. D. (1986). Computerized clinical psychological test interpretations: Unvalidated plus all mean and no sigma. *American Psychologist, 41,* 14–24.

Melton, G. B. (1981). Effects of a state law permitting minors to consent to psychotherapy. *Professional Psychology, 12,* 647–654.

Menninger, K. (1961). *Theory of psychoanalytic technique.* New York: Science Editions.

Mintz, N. L. (1971). Patient fees and psychotherapeutic transactions. *Journal of Consulting and Clinical Psychology, 36,* 1–8.

Morrison, K. L., Morrison, J. K., & Holdridge-Crane, S. (1979). The child's right to give informed consent to psychiatric treatment. *Journal of Clinical Psychology, 8,* 43–47.

Plaisil, E. (1985). *Therapist.* New York: St. Martin's/Marek.

Plotkin, R. (1981). When rights collide: Parents, children, and consent to treatment. *Journal of Pediatric Psychology, 6,* 121–130.

Pope, K. S. (1982). *Implications of fantasy and imagination for mental health: Theory, research, and interventions* (Report commissioned by the National Institute of Mental Health, Order No. 82M024784505D). Bethesda, MD: National Institute of Mental Health.

Pope, K. S. (1985, August). *Diagnosis and treatment of Therapist–Patient Sex Syndrome.* Paper presented at the annual meeting of the American Psychological Association, Los Angeles.

Pope, K. S. (1986, May). *Therapist–Patient Sex Syndrome: Research findings.* Paper presented at the annual meeting of the American Psychiatric Association, Washington, DC.

Pope, K. S. (in press). Preventing therapist–patient sexual intimacy: Therapy for a therapist at risk. *Professional Psychology: Research and Practice.*

Pope, K. S., & Bouhoutsos, J. (1986). *Sexual intimacy between therapists and patients.* New York: Praeger.

Pope, K. S., Geller, J. D., & Wilkinson, L. (1975). Fee assessment and outpatient psychotherapy. *Journal of Consulting and Clinical Psychology, 43,* 835–841.

Pope, K. S., Keith-Spiegel, P. C., & Tabachnick, B. (1986). Sexual attraction to clients: The human therapist and the (sometimes) inhuman training system. *American Psychologist, 41,* 147–158.

Pope, K. S., Levenson, H., & Schover, L. R. (1979). Sexual intimacy in psychology training: Results and implications of a national survey. *American Psychologist, 34,* 682–689.

Pope, K. S., Schover, L. S., & Levenson, H. (1980). Sexual behavior between clinical supervisors and trainees:

Implications for standards of professional practice. *Professional Psychology, 11,* 157–162.

Redlich, F. C. (1977). The ethics of sex therapy. In W. H. Masters, V. E. Johnson, & R. D. Kolodny (Eds.), *Ethical issues in sex therapy and research* (pp. 143–157). Boston: Little, Brown.

Redlich, F. C., & Pope, K. S. (1980). Ethics of mental health training. *Journal of Nervous and Mental Disease, 168,* 709–714.

Rosenbaum, M. (Ed.). (1982). *Ethics and values in psychotherapy.* New York: Free Press.

Rubinstein, E. A., & Parloff, M. B. (Eds.). (1959). *Research in psychotherapy.* Washington, DC: National.

Sell, J. M., Gottlieb, M. C., & Schoenfeld, L. (1986). Ethical considerations of social/romantic relationships with present and former clients. *Professional Psychology: Research and Practice, 17,* 504–508.

Shapiro, D. L. (1984). *Psychological evaluation and expert testimony: A practical guide to forensic work.* New York: Van Nostrand.

Shlien, J. M. (Ed.). (1968). *Research in psychotherapy* (Vol. 3). Washington, DC: American Psychological Association.

Singer, J. L. (1980). The scientific basis of psychotherapeutic practice: A question of values and ethics. *Psychotherapy: Theory, Research and Practice, 17,* 372–383.

Stapp, J., Tucker, A., & VandenBos, G. R. (1985). Census of psychological personnel: 1983. *American Psychologist, 40,* 1317–1351.

Strupp, H. H., & Luborsky, L. (Eds.). (1962). *Research in psychotherapy* (Vol. 2). Baltimore, MD: French-Bray.

Szasz, T. (1986). The case against suicide prevention. *American Psychologist, 41,* 806–812.

Tabachnick, B. G., & Fidell, L. S. (1983). *Using multivariate statistics.* New York: Harper & Row.

Thompson, C. (1950). *Psychoanalysis: Evolution and development.* New York: Hermitage House.

Turkington, C. (1984, April). Austin study questions tenet that free therapy lacks value. *APA Monitor,* p. 6.

Walker, E., & Young, T. D. (1986). *A killing cure.* New York: Henry Holt.

Whitesell v. Green, No. 38745 (Dist. Ct. Hawaii filed November 19, 1973).

Whitree v. State (1968). 290 N.Y.S. 2nd 486.

Ethical Ambiguities in the Practice of Child Clinical Psychology

Carole I. Mannheim, Michael Sancilio, Susan Phipps-Yonas, Donald Brunnquell, Peter Somers, Georganne Farseth, and Fred Ninonuevo

This might have happened to you. In 1991 an article appeared in the *Minneapolis Star Tribune* in which it was noted that a licensed psychologist had been disciplined by the Minnesota Board of Psychology because, among other infractions, she had taken a preschool-age client to the restroom during a therapy session; she had also had dinner in the hospital cafeteria with a young adolescent client (who had missed her bus after a session and had to wait an hour in the early evening for the next one). Many practicing child psychologists reacted with surprise, questioning why such behaviors were deemed problematic, much less unethical. Concerns were raised as to whether the state licensing board was sensitive to the problems that surface regularly for practitioners who work with children and adolescents. Although it may seem obvious on an abstract level that developmental factors affect the types of assessment and interventions that can be applied to a client, it does not follow that professionals who work exclusively with adults readily appreciate the added complexities of working with a younger clientele. . . .

. . .

THE MINNESOTA CHILD PSYCHOLOGISTS' SURVEY

The survey instrument for this study was constructed by the Ethics and Standards of Practice Committee of the Minnesota Child Psychologists. . . .

Certain survey items were drafted in parallel forms in order to permit comparisons of the ethical propriety of a particular practice across developmental levels (i.e., preschool, school age, adolescent, and/or adult). . . . [W]e included in the final version of the survey 33 numbered practice behavior items, 22 of which were presented in parallel forms, resulting in a total of 76 items.

To facilitate presentation of the data, we clustered the 76 survey items into four rationally derived thematic groups. These groups, delineated in the Appendix, include the following:

1. Clinical boundary issues involving practices that are not an intrinsic part of clinical intervention but may coincidentally occur within the context of a clinical intervention.
2. Professional relationship issues involving possible dilemmas with multiclient families and potential dual relationships with current and former clients.
3. Confidentiality issues.
4. Forensic opinions pertaining to custody and other placement issues for a child or an adolescent being seen in individual therapy.

Each of the items required ratings on two 5-point Likert-type scales. The first rating scale, My Practice, measured the prevalence of each practice. Here, respondents were directed to identify the frequency with which they personally engaged in the identified practice (*never, rarely, sometimes, fairly often, very often,* and *not applicable*). A second scale, Ethical Propriety, asked respondents to designate "your judgment about the ethics of such a practice, whether you actually do it or not. For example, you may make it a practice never to shake a client's hand, but you might not judge it unethical for another clinician to do so." The response options for this scale included the following: *unquestionably not ethical, ethical under rare circumstances, ethical under some circumstances, ethical under many circumstances,*

From *Professional Psychology: Research and Practice, 33,* 26–29. Copyright 2002 by the American Psychological Association.

and *unquestionably ethical.* Another response option was *don't know/uncertain.*

Three types of ethical ambiguity, all derived from the respondents' ratings of ethical propriety, were investigated in this study:

1. *Individual uncertainty,* the extent to which individuals are unable to decide about the ethical propriety of a practice, was operationally defined as the percentage of *don't know/uncertain* responses to each item.
2. *Group variability,* reflecting the degree of consensus or controversy among those offering an opinion about the ethical propriety of a practice, was indicated by both the standard deviation of the item's ethical ratings and the shape (kurtosis) of the rating distribution.
3. *Situational variability,* or the degree to which ethical propriety is viewed as dependent on the specific circumstances in which the behavior occurs, was reflected in the effect of contextual variables on the ethical ratings for a given professional activity. . . .

Survey participants came from two sources: (a) the roster of licensed psychologists maintained by the Minnesota State Board of Psychology and (b) the roster of school psychologists maintained by the Special Education Division of the Minnesota Department of Families, Children, and Learning. . . . Of the 1,068 surveys sent out, 354 (33%) were returned. The response rates were equivalent across the pools of licensed and school psychologists.

SURVEY FINDINGS

Notwithstanding the size of this data set and the wide array of possible analytical approaches, this article limits its focus to general trends, developmental comparisons, and ethical ambiguity. . . .

Clinical Boundary Issues

When we compared ethical ratings in this category with the developmental level of the client, evidence emerged for a significant age-related gradient on all of the items, with Items 1 and 2 showing significant differences among all age groups. Whether the practice concerned accepting a hug or attending a client's

major life event, the younger the client was, the more the practice in question received positive ethical ratings and fewer negative ratings.

Individual uncertainty, averaging 6.8% across all items in this cluster, was lower than that in the other item clusters, but not uniformly so: Only 3.5% to 4.4% of respondents were unsure about the propriety of accepting client hugs; the percentage rose to 17.1% in the case of assisting preschoolers with toileting. Ethical uncertainty was unrelated to the developmental status of the client except in the single case of restraining out-of-control clients. Here, McNemar's Test revealed greater uncertainty ($p = .02$) about restraining an adolescent (vs. a school-aged) client from damaging property.

In spite of respondents' relative confidence about the ethical propriety of practices in this category, group consensus, . . . was the most fragile among the four content clusters. The likeliest practices to spark ethical controversy included restraining young clients (Items 2a, 2b, and 3c) and escorting preschoolers to the restroom (Item 8a).

Contextual considerations (as measured by endorsement of the middle response option, *ethical under some circumstances*) figured prominently (as the modal response category) in 46% of all 76 practices enumerated in this survey. In the case of clinical boundary practices, 41% of the rated practices produced this modal endorsement, including accepting hugs from clients (Items 1a, 1b), restraining out-of-control clients (Items 2a–2c), rewarding clients with special food-outings (Item 4a), buying fundraiser items from child clients (Item 6a), and giving gifts to child clients (Item 7a).

Professional Relationship Issues

Evidence for an age-related gradient in ethical ratings reappeared in all of the items contained in this cluster, which focused on multiclient families and other potential client conflicts.

Individual uncertainty averaged 9.5% in this cluster. Respondents displayed the least uncertainty about the propriety of social relationships with former clients or their parents (Items 15a–15c) and accepting child clients who had indirect social connections to the psychologist (Items 14a–14c; *don't know* percentages ranged from 2.4 to 5.3). The greatest uncertainty (15.0%–16.2%) was associated with the practice of accepting as a private client someone with whom professional contact was first made in another setting, adding concurrent family therapy when already providing individual therapy to a member of the family, and adding concurrent individual therapy with a family member already being seen in family therapy. Although uncertainty in this cluster was not generally related to the developmental status of the client, more respondents indicated uncertainty about the propriety of diagnostically assessing the parent of a current child or adolescent client than doing the same assessment with a sibling. . . .

In this cluster, ethical confidence better coincided with consensus. Respondents as a group were in close agreement about the ethical impropriety of engaging in social relationships with former clients or with parents of current child clients. . . .

Contextual considerations were perceived as critical in 74% of the 27 items in this cluster, although they played a notably minimal role when respondents evaluated the propriety of social relationships with a client's parents or with a former client.

Confidentiality

Strong evidence for the operation of an age-related gradient reappeared in items constituting this cluster; rating differences suggest that protecting the privacy of adolescent clients is viewed as more ethically imperative than protecting that of younger clients.

Among the practices in this cluster, uncertainty was lowest (at 3.2%–6.5%) about reporting significant behaviors of a young client over the client's objection. Uncertainty was highest about two record-keeping issues: maintaining individual records for each participating member in family therapy (Item 26; 20.9%) and filing parent test data in a child's clinical record (Item 23; 18.8%). Developmental status had no bearing on ethical uncertainty.

Group consensus and controversy were wide-ranging . . . in this cluster. Five practices from this cluster produced the greatest response variability surveywide, including placement of parental data in the child's clinical record; refusal to share the contents of a therapy session with a parent when doing so is viewed as being in the client's best interests; sharing the contents of a therapy session with a par-

ent after informing the child but not obtaining the child's consent; and exchanging information regarding a client with an agency colleague who is working with another member of the client's family, after obtaining a signed release. Other items with similar content also produced rating distributions with relatively high standard deviations, suggesting similarly high levels of potential controversy. Two practices that produced relatively little rating variation concerned the report of dangerous behaviors to parents (Items 18a and 18b).

Few behaviors in this cluster produced high percentages of respondents who perceived situational factors to have a significant influence on ethical propriety. Only 5 of the 20 practices produced modal responses suggesting situational leeway. These included reporting antisocial behavior to parents, honoring a child's request to refuse parental disclosure, engaging in collegial exchanges about client families, and recording parental data in a child's clinical record (Items 18c, 19b, 20b, 21b, and 22).

Forensic Opinions

Forensic practices elicited the highest levels surveywide of individual uncertainty, averaging 17.6% of the sample across the items in this category.

Forensic practice items also elicited the five highest levels of group concurrence about ethical propriety surveywide. Those items pertained to conducting custody evaluations without attempting to see all the parties (Items 32a, 32b, and 32c) and proffering recommendations about visitation or family reunification without attempting to see all the parties (Items 33a and 33b).

Only two of the seven practices in this cluster produced modal endorsements of situationally qualified ethical ratings (Items 24 and 25). The remaining five practices produced the lowest level of endorsement surveywide of contextual qualifiers, suggesting that most survey respondents perceived the ethical propriety of forensic practices to be relatively unamenable to the influence of case-specific factors.

IMPLICATIONS

Were you aware that the majority of your professional colleagues report that they will commonly overrule a young client's objection about reporting dangerous behaviors or instances of personal victimization to the child's parent but will rarely, if ever, otherwise report a young client's disclosures to a parent without first seeking the child's consent or at least informing the client? Such knowledge about normative standards, as Pope et al. (1987) noted 15 years ago, is essential for psychologists to be able to regulate their own professional behavior. Those researchers decried the relative absence of comprehensive data that could inform decision making, and they called for further work. Although the present survey answered that call, the results suggest that little may have changed since that first groundbreaking survey, insofar as actual practice varies so widely among clinicians. With few exceptions, the majority of the psychologists who responded implemented the practices under consideration in this survey at least on occasion. Nevertheless, certain practices (taking adult clients out for food or rewards; maintaining social relationships with former child clients or their parents) appeared to be relatively rare; others (overriding young clients' objections to parental disclosure, as noted previously) appeared commonplace. Although frequency data can assist practitioners in identifying what constitutes standard practice, such data are less useful in informing practitioners about what they should and should not do.

In terms of ratings of ethical propriety, even here their guidance value is far from clear-cut, particularly in the case of boundary-related and professional relationship practices, where situational considerations seemed to hold sway with the largest group of survey respondents. Indeed, situational considerations predominated respondents' ethical ratings in nearly half of the practices surveyed.

One specific contextual variant—developmental status of the client—emerged as a robust factor in the perceived ethical propriety of given practices. In all three practice categories where this factor was varied, evidence of an age-related gradient uniformly appeared. Generally, the younger the client, the greater the leniency when evaluating the propriety of the specified practice. . . .

In light of these data, rigidly holding child practitioners accountable to the same standards designed with an adult clientele in mind may be undesirable, if not inappropriate, from a developmental perspective. Context was less influential when judging the ethical propriety of practices related to client confidentiality and forensic assessments, perhaps because of the abundance of state and federal statutes, as well as rules, regulations, and agency policies relating to these issues. . . .

Given the contextual and conditional instability of ethical perceptions, there should be little wonder that the average practitioner can easily become confused or lack confidence when ethical choices emerge in day-to-day practice. Interestingly, in this survey, consensus and controversy appeared unrelated to the level of individual ethical uncertainty except in the area of forensic practice. There, however, the relationship that emerged was counterintuitive. Those forensic practices enjoying the highest levels of rating consensus also produced the highest levels of ethical uncertainty among responding practitioners. Perhaps the limits of one's competence become more evident in areas of high-profile practice, where the professional community, under the pressure of external scrutiny, has developed relatively unequivocal standards. A practitioner is then likelier to be aware that a standard exists, even if its specifics have never personally been mastered.

What has been referred to as individual uncertainty in this study (expressed in *don't know/uncertain* responses) has been characterized by other researchers (Pope et al., 1987; Tabachnick et al., 1991) as "difficult judgments." It should be noted, however, that the percentages reported in this study may underestimate the actual level of individual uncertainty, because this number reflects only a subset of those not providing a positive or negative ethical rating. An additional subset of participants (ranging from 4.4% to 13.8% across all survey items, with a mean of 8.3%) failed to endorse any response. It appears likely that many, if not most, of these omissions also reflect uncertainty. The correlation (.61) between the subsets suggests considerable overlap. . . .

Notwithstanding any cautionary limitations on the generalizability of our data, this study constitutes an important step in what should become an ongoing process of elaborating and qualifying professional standards so they can more effectively guide both the psychologist engaged in professional practice, as well as the psychologist who has been entrusted with responsibility for professional oversight. These survey results specifically caution psychologists to be mindful of the various contextual factors that may affect the ethical propriety of a specific practice or relationship. They further suggest that psychologists may need to consider developing different sets of standards to address the situational specifics encountered in different types of practices. The robust age-related gradient evident in this study, for example, strongly argues against the blanket application of standards developed with an adult clientele in mind to clinical practice with children. Psychologists who serve children and adolescents may need to construct an independent set of ethical guidelines that, while adhering to the same general principles of their colleagues, more realistically addresses the many special circumstances and considerations that are unique to their work. Because ethical ambiguities and uncertainty are certain to survive the refinement of more population-specific standards, psychologists will also need to recognize that their empirical data can never fully replace the professional decision-making process. The successful application of our aspirational standards to the day-to-day work of clinical practice will most likely remain a complex and stimulating challenge for coming generations of professional practitioners.

References

Pope, K. S., Tabachnick, B. G., & Keith-Spiegel, P. (1987). Ethics of practice: The beliefs and behaviors of psychologists as therapists. *American Psychologist, 42,* 993–1006.

Tabachnick, B. G., Keith-Spiegel, P., & Pope, K. S. (1991). Ethics of teaching: Beliefs and behaviors of psychologists as educators. *American Psychologist, 46,* 506–515.

APPENDIX: SURVEY ITEMS GROUPED THEMATICALLY

Clinical Boundary Issues

1. I accept hugs from clients if they are:
   a. Preschool age
   b. School age
   c. Adolescent
   d. Adult
2. I restrain tantrumming clients who are damaging property if they are:
   a. Preschool age
   b. School age
   c. Adolescent
3. I restrain tantrumming clients who are in danger of hurting themselves or others if they are:
   a. Preschool age
   b. School age
   c. Adolescent
4. I take clients out for food or other rewards during a therapy hour if they are:
   a. Children/adolescents
   b. Adult
5. I accept invitations to clients' outside events (e.g., school plays, recitals, graduations, weddings) if they are:
   a. Children/adolescents
   b. Adult
6. I buy things from clients (e.g., Girl Scout cookies, raffle tickets) if they are:
   a. Children/adolescents
   b. Adult
7. I give gifts to clients for special events (e.g., termination) if they are:
   a. Children/adolescents
   b. Adult
8. I escort clients to the restroom if they are:
   a. Preschool age
   b. School age
   c. Adolescent
9. I assist preschool-aged, outpatient clients with toiletting.

Professional Relationship Issues

10. I take as a separate client for individual therapy a current child or adolescent client's:
    a. Sibling
    b. Parent
    c. Other relative(s)
    d. Close personal friend
11. I take as a separate client for individual therapy a current adult client's:
    a. Child
    b. Spouse or partner

c. Relative(s)

d. Close personal friend

12. I take as a separate client for diagnostic evaluation a current child or adolescent client's:

a. Sibling

b. Parent(s)

c. Other relative(s)

d. Close personal friend

13. I take as a separate client for diagnostic evaluation a current adult client's:

a. Child

b. Spouse or partner

c. Relative(s)

d. Close personal friend

14. I accept as a client, a child:

a. Of a personal friend

b. Of a professional colleague with whom I have periodic professional contact

c. Who attends my child's school, church, etc.

15. I initiate or maintain social relationships with:

a. A former client

b. A parent of a current child client

c. A parent of a former child client

27. I agree to conduct ongoing family therapy when I already have a current psychotherapy relationship with a child or adolescent member of the family.

28. I agree to conduct ongoing family therapy when I already have a current psychotherapy relationship with an adult member of the family.

29. I agree to conduct individual therapy with a child or adolescent member of a family for whom I currently provide family therapy.

30. I agree to conduct individual therapy with an adult member of a family for whom I currently provide family therapy.

31. I accept as private patients, clients with whom I first had professional contact in another, current job setting (full or part-time consultation, etc.).

Confidentiality Issues

16. I disclose information from a *child* client's individual therapy to a parent or legal guardian who requests it:

a. Without informing the child or seeking the child's consent

b. After informing the child but without asking for the child's consent

c. After informing the child and even if the child objects

17. I disclose information from an adolescent client's individual therapy to a parent or legal guardian who requests it:

a. Without informing the adolescent or seeking the adolescent's consent

b. After informing the adolescent but without asking for his/her consent

c. After informing the adolescent and even if the adolescent objects

18. I would report to the parents or legal guardian, over the objections of my child or adolescent client their report of:

a. Behaviors that are dangerous to themselves

b. Behaviors that are dangerous to others

c. Antisocial behaviors

d. Victimization

19. I refuse to disclose information from a *child* client's individual therapy to a parent or legal guardian who requests it when:

a. I believe it is in the child's best interests

b. The child requests that I do so

20. I refuse to disclose information from an adolescent client's individual therapy to a parent or legal guardian who requests it, when:

a. I believe it is in the adolescent's best interests

b. The adolescent requests that I do so

21. I exchange information about my client with colleagues at my agency who work with a family member of my client:

a. Without informing my client

b. With oral permission from my client but without a signed release

c. With a signed release from my client (or my client's legal guardian)

22. I record details of the parent's personal life, such as mental health history, in the child's clinical record.

23. I file parent test data (e.g., MMPI [Minnesota Multiphasic Personality Inventory]) in the child's clinical record.

26. I maintain individual records for each family member participating in ongoing family therapy.

Forensic Issues

24. I offer expert opinions to the Court about *specific* custody/visitation placements for children and adolescents I see in psychotherapy.

25. I offer opinions about other legally mediated matters about children and adolescents I see in psychotherapy, such as out-of-home placements, juvenile court dispositions, personal injury, etc.

32. I perform a custody evaluation without attempting to see:
    a. The child
    b. Either parent
    c. Both parents

33. I make recommendations regarding visitation and/or reunification between a child in out-of-home placement and his or her parent(s) without attempting to see:
    a. The child
    b. The parent(s)

◆　　◆　　◆

Commentary: In a comparable study with adults, researchers varied the age, sex, and diagnostic severity of a hypothetical client and then asked a randomly selected group of licensed psychologists to respond to an edited version of the Pope, Tabachnick, and Keith-Spiegel (1987) survey:

> [D]ifferent combinations of clients' age and sex elicit different ethicality ratings. . . . [P]sychologists consider their own behavior more ethical when it is directed at a younger male client rather than at an older male client. An opposite (but statistically nonsignificant) trend is evident for female clients, such that psychologists consider their own behavior more ethical when it is directed at an older female client rather than a young female client. (p. 524)

Pomerantz, A. M., & Pettibone, J. C. (2005). The influence of client characteristics on psychologists' ethical beliefs: An empirical investigation. Journal of Clinical Psychology, 61, 517–528. *The authors note that the current APA Code (and its immediate predecessors) fail to take into account that "psychologists' ethical beliefs regarding therapist practices may in fact be situational rather than constant" (p. 525). Should it be situational, or would the already lengthy Code become unwieldy?*

Ethical Decision Making and Psychologists' Attitudes Toward Training in Ethics

Alexander J. Tymchuk, Robin Drapkin, Susan Major-Kingsley, Andrea B. Ackerman, Elizabeth W. Coffman, and Maureen S. Baum

Psychologists often face ethical dilemmas without clear decision-making guidelines provided by the profession or by society. Although the American Psychological Association (APA) has established ethical standards, new and sometimes controversial clinical research technologies as well as increased community concern with the protection of individual rights continually pose new and complex ethical dilemmas.

. . .

. . . When psychologists cannot refer to a specific standard, they must rely more heavily on their own value systems and on their own interpretations of the "spirit'" of the APA standards. Such interpretation may lead to variability in professional decision making. . . .

PURPOSE

The present study had three objectives.[1] The first objective was to determine the extent to which a nationwide sample of clinical psychologists concurred in their responses to a set of hypothetical clinical situations. . . .

METHOD

A two-part questionnaire was developed. . . . The second part consisted of 12 vignettes that described a clinical or research situation in which ethical issues were involved (Table 1). These vignettes were typical of ethical problems faced by psychologists. . . .

The questionnaire was mailed to a random sample of 500 members of the Division of Clinical Psychology listed in the Directory of the APA (1976) [return rate = 23%]. . . . The respondents were asked to agree or disagree with the decision described in each hypothetical situation and to indicate the criteria they considered relevant in determining the appropriateness of the hypothetical decision. These criteria included concerns with (a) the interests of the clients, (b) therapeutic leverage, (c) confidentiality, (d) personal freedom, (e) freedom of expression, (f) individual rights, (g) the interests of the community, (h) public policy, (i) standards of morality, (j) the therapist's judgment, (k) informed consent or agreement, (l) financial issues, and (m) state or federal law. Respondents also were given the opportunity to list additional bases for their decision and to comment on each vignette.

FINDINGS

. . . Table 2 summarizes the percentage of responses to each vignette as well as the criteria used. The vignettes are rank ordered according to degree of consensus (from highest to lowest), with the decision described in each situation. Where there is relatively strong consensus regarding the actions of the hypothetical psychologist, there is also strong agreement regarding the criteria on which the respondents base their judgments. Additionally, relatively weak consensus regarding the hypothetical psychologist's actions corresponds with less agreement about the relevant criteria. . . .

In the vignettes that had relatively strong consensus, the issues were current and timely. These vignettes incorporated confidentiality issues, moral

---

From *Professional Psychology, 13*, 412–421. Copyright 1982 by the American Psychological Association.

[1]*Ed. Note:* Only the first objective is discussed in this excerpt.

TABLE 1

Vignettes of Ethical Issues

Vignette	Decision
1. A psychologist at a cocktail party is having a conversation with a woman whom he has just met. He begins to tell her about a client of his, without mentioning names. He reveals to her a set of situations in which the client has recently found himself involved and which the psychologist finds particularly amusing. The woman appears interested in the psychologist's story, until she has heard enough to cause her to believe he is talking about someone she knows. She says, "Are you talking about . . .?" to which the psychologist replies, "Yes, you know him too?" And they both laugh. The next day she calls her ex-husband and asks him if what she hears about him is true. He files a complaint against the psychologist with the local ethics committee.	The psychologist showed a lack of regard for protecting the identity of his client.
2. A psychologist with considerable skill in behavioral engineering is asked by a state institution for the retarded to plan and assist in executing a behavioral program on its adolescent ward. The purpose of this program will be to increase self-help and ward maintenance skills such as bathing, grooming, dressing, feeding, etc. The program will work only on positive incentives, with special treats such as candy, outings, dances, etc. being provided as rewards for those who improve their skills in these areas. The psychologist meets with each adolescent on the ward to explain the program and finds that about 25% of the youngsters do not understand what he is talking about. Even with a film designed to explain his procedures, the psychologist is unable to get his message across to these youngsters.	These youngsters should not be included in the behavior modification program even though the director of the institution wants all the adolescents on the ward to participate.
3. A male clinical psychologist regularly saw a female patient in his apartment to which he had given her a key. Sometimes the therapeutic sessions lasted past midnight. Eventually the patient and her husband accused the therapist of improper relations. The therapist explained that the highly unusual arrangements for psychotherapy resulted from the fact that he had lost control of the relationship and that his patient dominated it.	It would be ethical for a psychologist to see a client on this basis as long as the client had consented to such sessions and was benefiting from the therapy.
. . .	
5. A researcher in autism provides intensive behavioral treatment for one half of the children under age 3 who come to her treatment/research facility. The other children are placed in a control group. Children in the first group receive up to 2 years intensive behavioral treatment. It is known that beyond the age of 5 or 6, the benefits of the treatment program decrease significantly.	This researcher should be obliged to offer 2 years of intensive treatment to the control group children once they have remained in that group for 2 years.
. . .	
7. Current legal developments suggest that rights to treatment for the involuntarily committed include "nutritionally adequate meals," which suggests that contingent availability of meals as reinforcers is unacceptable even if it is deemed therapeutic. A psychologist complies with this requirement by offering his patients nutritious food by taking all the courses and mixing them together in a blender. This blended together meal is freely available to all patients, but patients desiring separate course servings must pay for them with earned tokens.	There is nothing unethical about what the psychologist has done as long as it can be shown that such a program is therapeutically desirable.
8. The parents of a public school child demand that a psychologist in private practice give them a written report since they paid for psychological testing. The psychologist gives them a copy of his report in which actual test scores are included. The parents take the report to the school psychologist who refers it to the APA.	In giving such a report to the parents, the psychologist is unethical and lacking in good judgment.
. . .	
10. A psychologist advertises by mail a service which offers to introduce marriageable clients to each other on a personality analysis basis, thereby increasing the prospects of a compatible relationship. The psychologist does not influence the clients to make any decision to marry but merely obtains from them by mail, information he deems relevant. The data are sorted by computer and used as a basis for arranging introductions of interested clients.	The psychologist's behavior is ethical.
. . .	
12. A client, at the close of one of his therapy sessions with you, mentions that he has a secret plan to kill his roommate and that he has a gun. You have reason to believe he has the potential for violent behavior (that there may be clear and imminent danger) and you wish to spend more therapy time dealing with this issue. Your client states that he will not return next week. Should you tell anyone his "secret?"	As his psychotherapist, you should inform either the police or his roommate.

TABLE 2

Percentage of Responses to the Vignettes

Degree of Consensus	Vignette		Response		
	Number	Description	Agree	Disagree	No Response
High	1	Failure to protect client identity	98	1	1
	3	Ethical with client consent	2	96	2
	12	Inform police or roommate	84	9	7
Moderate	10	Ethical to advise dating service	22	70	8
	7	Ethical if therapeutically desirable	26	68	6
	2	Exclude patients if fail to understand	33	65	2
	5	Must provide treatment and control group	47	42	10
Low	8	Unethical to provide test scores	47	42	10

Note. Portions of this table, irrelevant here, have been omitted.

issues involving the male therapist–female client relationship, and standards for growth groups.

. . . [T]he vignettes with the weakest consensus (where decisions tended to be approximately equally split between agreement and disagreement) focused on three basic areas that differed from those of the other vignettes: test scrutiny and interpretation, research activities, and remuneration (fees).

These specific findings support the hypothesis that strong consensus in professional decision making may be related to the availability of standards and the nature of the particular situation. When professional or legal standards exist and when the issues are current and related to the therapist–client relationship, the decision-making process appears to be facilitated. Psychologists seem to have more difficulty agreeing either on treatment issues that may be closely intertwined with clinical orientation or on issues that are not in the forefront of the discipline, including those related to "business" or "contract" decisions. . . .

References

Directory of the APA. (1976). Washington, DC: American Psychological Association.

Ethical Dilemmas in Psychological Practice: Results of a National Survey

Leonard J. Haas, John L. Malouf, and Neal H. Mayerson

Recent years have been marked by a rise in professional consciousness about ethical and legal responsibilities and by a concurrent rise in public consciousness about legal rights. The result, in part, is a level of concern (and confusion) about proper professional behavior that is unprecedented in all professions and is particularly evident in psychology (Chalk, Frankel, & Chafer, 1980). . . .

The widespread concern about ethical and legal aspects of practice notwithstanding, relatively little is known about the nature of the actual situations that practitioners find ethically, legally, or professionally problematic. Of the few studies addressed to the issue of ethical concerns, researchers in some (e.g., Baldick, 1980) assess subjects' ability to recognize or identify an ethical dilemma. In other surveys (e.g., Tymchuk et al., 1982) researchers assess the extent of respondents' agreement with a particular choice already made for them. In still other surveys (e.g., Jagim, Wittman, & Noll, 1978), researchers assess a limited sample of psychologists. There has been no study to date in which the nature of respondents' choices from among a range of options has been assessed.

In this study we attempt to investigate some of these unknown areas. Practitioners were presented a set of problems that had at least two potentially workable alternative resolutions, and a set of possible reasons for making those choices. In addition, we attempt to assess the perceived utility of various sources of ethics education. With increasing pressure for standardized ethics education in professional psychology training programs, it is vital to know more about the mechanisms through which ethical practitioners acquire what they consider to be valuable ethics training. Answers to questions such as these may help in training of ethically responsible psychologists.

METHOD

Instrument

The questionnaire developed for this study consisted of five sections. . . . The first section concerned demographic and background factors such as age, number of years in practice, and theoretical orientation. In the second section respondents indicated the sources of their training in ethics, number of hours spent in various categories of ethical training (e.g., coursework, discussions with colleagues), and the value of each of these experiences (see Table 2).

The third section contained 10 vignettes, each describing a dilemma of professional ethics. . . . The vignettes were chosen to represent five general categories that are considered to encompass the broad range of professional dilemmas: confidentiality problems, issues of informed consent, loyalty conflicts, exploitation, and whistle-blowing (Haas, 1982). In addition, we selected vignettes that involved a *dilemma*, rather than simply knowledge of the relevant standards: that is, vignettes represented situations in which more than one alternative could be considered acceptable on the basis of recognized ethical principles.

For each vignette, alternative ways to respond were presented: as much as possible, the number of alternatives was restricted and respondents were urged to choose one of them, rather than to "rearrange" the dilemma (e.g., resolving the dilemma by noting that "I would have gotten informed consent beforehand" or making some other shift in the

TABLE 2

Amount and Perceived Utility of Education in Ethics

Source of Education	Hours		Mean Utility[a]	
	M	*N*	Rating	*N*
Discussions with colleagues	79.1	236	4.4	269
Independent reading	31.3	238	4.0	240
Internship supervision	17.1	231	3.8	124
Graduate coursework	11.5	258	4.4	174
Continuing education courses	2.7	233	3.3	26

[a]Mean ratings on a 5-point scale anchored by 1 (*not at all useful*) and 5 (*extremely useful*).

conditions). In several cases it was possible to reduce the behavioral alternatives to two: act or not act. After the alternatives, eight possible reasons for choosing an alternative were presented: upholding the law, upholding the code of ethics, protecting society's interests, protecting client's rights, upholding personal standards, safeguarding the therapy process, financial considerations, and "other." Analysis of these rationales and the categories of moral reasoning that they reflect are presented elsewhere (Haas, Malouf, & Mayerson, 1985). Respondents were asked to indicate their preferred response to each dilemma and the most important reason for making this choice. The vignettes and alternatives are listed in Table 3.

In the fourth session, respondents were asked to rate the frequency with which they had encountered 17 ethical/legal issues in practice (e.g., concern about colleagues' actions, insurance reporting requirements, sexual misconduct) and their rating of the seriousness of each issue (see Table 4). . . .

Procedure

The sample consisted of 600 randomly selected members of Division 29 (Psychotherapy) of the American Psychological Association (APA) chosen from the APA Directory. . . . 500 individuals received questionnaires and 294 individuals returned them, which was a response rate of 59%.

Characteristics of Respondents

Overall, the sample had substantial experience, worked largely in private practice delivering clinical services, and was largely composed of PhD-level practitioners. The sample obtained here is quite similar to the clinician sample described in the APA's national work force survey (Stapp & Fulcher, 1983).

RESULTS

Education in Ethics

Subjects' reports of their education in professional ethics are summarized in Table 2. As the table shows, discussions with colleagues are the most widely reported category of ethics education. Graduate coursework, perhaps not surprisingly, is the fourth-ranked category. Subjects were also asked to rate how useful the various sources of education had been in their understanding, coping with, or preventing ethical dilemmas. The means of these ratings are also reported in Table 2. As shown, all categories were rated above 3, but graduate coursework and collegial discussions were both rated as the most useful. Modal number of hours in formal ethics education (e.g., graduate coursework and continuing education courses) was zero.

Responses to Vignettes of Ethical Dilemmas

In Table 3 we show the percentage of respondents who chose each alternative for each vignette in the order in which they were presented to respondents. As the table shows, highest degrees of consensus regarding the appropriate choice were obtained (in descending order) on issues involving the following: conflict of interest (Vignette 9), mandatory reporting of threatened violence (Vignette 7), a superior's order to refer a client to someone who is considered incompetent (Vignette 1), and confidentiality (Vignettes 5 and 4). The modal responses indicated that subjects favored acting in the client's interest when one's own interests might be better served by another response, reporting threatened violence to the police or the intended victim(s), or both, and the protection of clients' rights to confidentiality.

Lower degrees of consensus were obtained on dilemmas involving the following (in ascending order

TABLE 3

Vignettes and Choices Presented in Questionnaire, and Percentage of Respondents
Endorsing Each Choice

Vignette	Choice	%
1. You are a therapist in a community mental health center. You are about to move to another state, and must terminate or refer your caseload. Your clinical director tells you to refer a particular individual to a therapist whose ability you do not respect.	Refer the patient.	7
	Refer the patient and indicate your reservations to him.	14
	Refuse to refer the patient to that particular therapist.	79
	Other	1
2. A client of yours tells you that she is still quite upset at her previous therapist for, among other things, making sexual advances toward her. This is the third time you have heard such allegations about this particular therapist.	Discuss the patient's anger but do not discuss the issue of professional standards.	10
	Call the previous therapist and tell him that the behavior you have heard about violates professional ethics.	18
	Tell the patient that she has the right to bring her charge to the ethics committee or the state licensing board.	57
	Call the ethics committee or state licensing board.	14
3. A psychologist whom you have met on occasional meetings but do not know well appears in a TV spot endorsing a local health spa. He says, "As a child psychologist I find relaxation important—I go to the Palm Spa to get my head and body together."	Call the psychologist and indicate that you think the ad violates professional standards.	25
	Call the professional standards committee of your psychological association and report the incident.	42
	Do nothing.	33
	Other	0
4. You have been treating a married couple conjointly for about 6 months. The wife arrives early for the session and tells you that she is thinking of leaving her husband as she has been involved with another man. She also asks you not to tell her husband. You have not previously discussed your policy regarding secrets.	Do not agree to keep the secret.	30
	Agree to keep the secret.	65
	Other	5
5. The mother of a 12-year-old boy comes to pick him up after his initial appointment with you. She asks you if he is taking drugs. He has in fact revealed to you that he has been sniffing glue.	Tell her what you know.	25
	Tell her the information is her son's to reveal or not as he sees fit.	72
	Other	5
6. A man with no previous experience in therapy contacts you and asks for sex therapy. While you understand the general principles of sex therapy, you would not consider it your area of expertise. However, he looks like an interesting prospective client.	Accept him as a client.	5
	Accept him as a client only after discussing your qualifications.	45
	Do not accept him as a client and refer him to another therapist.	49
	Other	1
7. You are treating a Vietnam veteran with a history of impulsive antisocial actions. You and he have established a good therapeutic relationship (his first after 3 previous attempts in therapy). At the end of the session, he disclosed that he is planning to kill his current girlfriend, because she has been dating another man.	Contact his girlfriend and/or the police without informing him.	8
	Plan to discuss this further at the next session.	5
	Inform him that you must warn his girlfriend and/or the police.	87
	Other	1
8. During the course of your treatment of a 45-year-old male who has drinking problems, his wife telephones and tells you that he has been sexually molesting his 7-year-old stepdaughter (her daughter of a previous marriage).	Report the case to the child protection bureau.	25
	Encourage her to report the matter to the child protection bureau.	60
	Reflect her concern but take no further action.	11
	Other	4
9. A client of yours who is a CPA suggests that he prepare your tax return in partial payment for therapy. You have been preparing your own taxes and find it increasingly burdensome.	Accept his offer.	7
	Decline his offer.	93
	Other	0

(continued)

TABLE 3 (*cont.*)

Vignette	Choice	%
10. You work in the emergency room of a community mental health center located within a general hospital. You are about to admit a man best diagnosed as a paranoid schizophrenic; his insurance will cover the cost of hospitalization. This diagnosis may make it difficult for him to obtain other kinds of insurance (e.g., life insurance) later. You suspect that learning of this will make him resist hospitalization since he cannot afford it without insurance.	Inform him of the risks involved.	50
	Do not inform him of the risks; diagnose him as indicated.	30
	Do not inform him of the risks; give him a much "milder" diagnosis.	18
	Other	1

of consensus): others' use of professional credentials in advertising for a local business (Vignette 3), treatment of problems beyond one's established expertise (Vignette 6), and reporting of potentially countertherapeutic diagnoses to insurance companies (Vignette 10). Regarding both alleged client–therapist sexual contact (Vignette 2) and alleged client-instigated sexual abuse (Vignette 8), slightly more than a majority of the respondents apparently would *not* report the allegation themselves, but instead would try to encourage the client or a family member of the client to make the report.

Frequency and Seriousness of Ethical Dilemmas Actually Experienced

The 17 areas of potential ethical difficulty presented to subjects are listed, along with the overall ratings for each area of concern, in Table 4. Subjects were asked to rate the frequency with which the issues had presented problems for them during the past year. They

TABLE 4

Mean Ratings of Frequency With Which Areas of Concern Occur and Their Seriousness

Area of Concern	Frequency[a]	Seriousness[b]
1. Confidentiality or privileged communication	3.09	3.94
2. Providing informed consent to clients	2.54	3.33
3. Rights of minors (e.g., in therapy)	2.43	3.52
4. Conflicting interests (employers vs. clients, clients vs. legal system, etc.)	2.41	3.59
5. Personal use of advertising or other means of generating referrals	1.58	2.46
6. Talk shows, interviews, or other personal media appearances	1.67	2.43
7. Colleagues' sexual conduct	2.08	4.12
8. Appropriateness of other actions of colleagues	2.66	3.69
9. Own sexual impulses or conduct	1.69	3.21
10. Legality of own actions	1.82	3.33
11. Own malpractice liability	1.76	3.37
12. Own competence to deal with particular problem or provide requested service	2.43	3.45
13. Insurance company requests (e.g., for information or diagnoses)	2.77	3.15
14. Civil (involuntary) commitment	1.70	3.54
15. Behavior of employees or supervisees	2.11	3.34
16. Testing (e.g., use of test results, appropriateness of test requested)	2.05	3.17
17. Research (e.g., protection of subjects' privacy, minimizing risk)	1.72	3.17

[a]Scale ranges from 1 (*never a concern*) to 5 (*constantly a concern*).
[b]Scale ranges from 1 (*not at all serious*) to 5 (*extremely serious*).

were also asked to rate the overall severity of those problems, irrespective of how often they had personally encountered them. Interestingly, in terms of mean frequency ratings, none of the issues were reported as more than *occasionally a concern*. In contrast, 11 of the 17 issues were rated as *fairly serious* or *extremely serious* by more than 50% of the respondents. The two issues that overall seemed to be considered most serious involved confidentiality, or privileged communication, and sexual conduct of colleagues. The two issues rated least serious (e.g., rated about 2) were media appearances and advertising to obtain referrals.

DISCUSSION

. . . If one defines high agreement as 75% concordance, then there was a high agreement on what to do in only 3 of the 10 vignettes presented. Psychologists in our sample agreed that it would not be appropriate to refer a client to a therapist whom they did not respect, even when requested to do so by their clinical director. They also agreed that it would not be appropriate to trade therapeutic services for other professional services. Last, psychologists are apparently quite aware of their duties to warn in cases of threatened violence of the sexual abuse of children, and they appear willing to act accordingly, in contrast to the sample surveyed by Jagim et al. (1978). However, in the vignette relating to the sexual abuse of a child, there was a clear difference of opinion as to whether the therapist's most appropriate response should be to report or to suggest that someone else report the allegation. Despite the increasing prevalence of mandatory reporting laws (DeKraii & Sales, 1984), this result shows that uncertainty about this complex ethical/legal issue is still widespread.

Results suggest a number of other areas in which high agreement does not exist, as defined by the 75% agreement criterion. One problematic area is the issue of confidentiality within families or couples. Although a majority of respondents would maintain the confidentiality of a spouse or minor child (as shown in the results for Vignettes 4 and 5), a significant minority (30.5% and 23.6%, respectively) would reveal certain

types of information to a spouse or parent. Despite the existence of legal constraints (DeKraii & Sales, 1984), confidentiality within families is clearly a topic in which much is left to the discretion of the therapist (Margolin, 1982). Clearly, practitioners should be aware of the legal standards and in addition carefully think through the ethical and therapeutic implications of their choices.

Another area of apparent low agreement involves unethical behavior of other professionals. Two vignettes (2 and 3) dealt with this topic, one describing a situation in which a psychologist was alleged to have had sexual relations with clients, the other describing a psychologist who publicly endorsed a health spa. In the first case, approximately 90% felt that some action should be taken, and a significant number felt that the client, rather than the current therapist, should report the previous therapist. In the second case, approximately one third of the respondents felt that they should do nothing about reporting the psychologist who endorsed the health spa, even though such behavior is a clear violation of Principle 4 of the *Ethical Principles* (APA, 1981).[1] One issue that can limit the duty to deal with colleagues' questionable behavior is that of client preferences. It is quite likely that those of our respondents who preferred to let the client report in Vignette 2 held the principle of client control of confidential information to be paramount. This confounding principle was not present in Vignette 3, which suggests that many psychologists find it easier to dismiss as trivial those actions that are not obviously harmful rather than risk being considered vigilantes.

Vignette 6, which concerned a therapist's providing sex therapy despite a lack of specialty training, related to the topic of competence. This vignette highlights another area in which much latitude is given the practitioner by the *Ethical Principles*. Although Principle 23 (APA, 1981)[2] specifies that a therapist be competent to provide the services offered, it is primarily the therapist who determines his or her own competence. In the situation described in the survey, about half of the respondents apparently felt that a knowledge of general principles of sex

[1]*Ed. Note:* See Standards 5.01b and 5.02a of the current (2002) APA Ethics Code.

[2]*Ed. Note:* See Standard 2.01 of the current (2002) APA Ethics Code.

therapy was not adequate to establish competence in that area, whereas about 45% of respondents would discuss their qualifications with the client and, apparently, let the client determine the therapist's competence. Clients' ability to make such a determination can be seriously questioned.

The final vignette raises the complicated and multifaceted issue of diagnosis. Should a client be informed of his or her diagnosis if this information would possibly be harmful? Should the therapist change the diagnosis to something more "acceptable"? Should the therapist be more concerned about the consequences of the diagnosis itself or about the consequences of decreased trust in professional diagnoses? Half of our respondents would inform a paranoid schizophrenic patient about the risks involved in reporting an accurate diagnosis on an insurance form, whereas 30% would not discuss this with the client but would submit an accurate diagnosis, regardless of the consequences. Eighteen percent would not inform the client but would give a milder diagnosis. This variability highlights the ambiguity in this area, in that all response alternatives can be justified by existing ethical guidelines.

In relation to subjects' reports of the sources and value of their ethics education, results seem to confirm the appropriateness of the APA decision to require the development of formal coursework in ethics. Even though the major reported source of learning, in terms of reported hours, is discussions with colleagues and the number of hours spent studying ethics in graduate school is relatively low, this latter endeavor was as highly valued as the former. Independent reading was reported as the other main source of ethical training. It is also interesting to note that internship (in which many assume that young clinicians get their ethics education) was not rated particularly highly as a source of ethics education. In addition, it is interesting that reading and discussing issues with colleagues (both seemingly intrinsically motivated activities) are extensively used as a means of self-education in ethics by this sample. This may be a result of the increasing intensity of concern with ethical and legal issues, or reflect feelings of inadequate preparation in these areas. It is likely that the majority of our respondents completed their graduate training before ethics courses were common in training programs. Given the apparent interest in ethics training and the relatively low ratings given continuing education courses, it seems that further development and improvement of continuing education courses would be appropriate.

Of the 17 areas of potential ethical difficulty that were presented to respondents, only one—confidentiality or privileged communication—received a mean frequency rating of over 3 (*occasionally a concern*). All the other issues received lower ratings. The concerns least frequently encountered involved personal use of advertising and media appearances.

Although the frequency of these 17 topics was not reported to be extremely high, respondents did consider several of them to be serious. The sexual conduct of colleagues was rated as the most serious of the issues, followed by confidentiality or privileged communication, appropriateness of other actions of colleagues, and conflicting interests (e.g., employers vs. clients). Of the 17 issues, all but two received mean ratings of higher than 3 (*somewhat serious*). The questions regarding personal use of advertising and personal media appearances were rated between 2 (*slightly serious*) and 3 (*somewhat serious*).

One interpretation of these findings is that psychologists consider many issues important but do not encounter problems with them very often. In one sense, this can be considered a positive finding insofar as it may mean that psychologists, at least relatively experienced ones, feel comfortable with the ethical decisions that they make.

IMPLICATIONS

Three major implications stand out. First, psychology as a profession has few generally agreed-on choices of action in several important and difficult areas of professional decision making. The fact that our respondents, all of whom were experienced clinicians, concurred that certain areas of professional decision making were areas of serious concern and that at the same time they failed to reach consensus as a group on these areas may be a troublesome state of affairs or not, depending on how one construes the task of professional ethics education in psychology. If this task is construed to involve the training of professionals in specific *behaviors* that are considered ethical, then our results are troubling. The implication of these results for professional ethics education is that such efforts must focus on teaching psychologists more effectively which are the right behaviors to choose in a variety of professional decision-making situations. On the other hand, if the task of professional ethics education is to inculcate ethical reasoning *processes,* then our results may be somewhat more heartening. As researchers in moral development have shown (Blasi, 1980), the same reasoning processes may lead to quite divergent behavioral outcomes. This is likely to be the case if professional moral decision making is involved. Psychologists who use the same ethical reasoning processes may arrive at quite different conclusions about the proper action. . . .

A second implication of this study is that work to further develop graduate course work in ethics (as required for APA accreditation) should be pursued, perhaps with particular attention to real-world ethical problems involving confidentiality, competence, and colleagues' behavior. In addition, our findings suggest that continuing education courses could be quite appropriate even for the experienced clinician.

A third implication is that particular areas of professional decision making deserve added scrutiny, debate, and consideration. They are competence (e.g., What is it? How do we measure it?), confidentiality (What are the implications of preserving it? of failing to uphold it?), diagnoses (For whom are they being done? What about the issue of stigma?), and whistle-blowing (What is the most appropriate means of reporting? To whom should complaints be addressed?). Some of these are empirical issues and should be dealt with as such. Others deserve added scrutiny and debate by the profession at large.

References

American Psychological Association. (1981). *Ethical principles of psychologists.* Washington, DC: Author.

Baldick, T. (1980). Ethical discrimination ability of intern psychologists: A function of training in ethics. *Professional Psychology, 11,* 276–282.

Blasi, A. (1980). Bridging moral cognition and moral action: A critical review of the literature. *Psychological Bulletin, 88,* 1–45.

Chalk, R., Frankel, M., & Chafer, S. (1980). *AAAS Professional Ethics Project: Professional ethics activities in the scientific and engineering societies.* Washington,

DC: American Association for the Advancement of Science.

DeKraii, M. B., & Sales, B. D. (1984). Confidential communications of psychotherapists. *Psychotherapy, 21,* 293–318.

Haas, L. J. (1982). *The teaching of ethics in clinical psychology.* Paper presented at the annual convention of the American Psychological Association, Washington, DC.

Jagim, R. D., Wittman, W., & Noll, J. (1978). Mental health professionals' attitudes toward confidentiality, privilege, and third-party disclosure. *Professional Psychology, 9,* 458–466.

Margolin, G. (1982). Ethical and legal considerations in marital and family therapy. *American Psychologist, 37,* 788–801.

Tymchuk, A., Drapkin, R., Major-Kingsley, S., Ackerman, A., Coffman, E., & Baum, M. (1982). Ethical decision making and psychologists' attitudes toward training in ethics. *Professional Psychology, 13,* 412–421.

◆   ◆   ◆

Commentary: As demonstrated by the two excerpts from Tymchuk et al. (1982) and Haas et al. (1986), and by the debate concerning the conflict between law and ethics, there are a number of reasons for the variability that one finds in the application, interpretation, and enforcement of the APA's Ethical Principles. For example, Kimmel (1991) has noted that a "growing body of research suggests that individuals systematically differ in the ways they formulate ethical appraisals of research," traced in part "to the fact that the ethical principles that guide research in the scientific community typically are broadly stated and are all too often ambiguous" (p. 768). In addition, he found that psychologists asked to review the ethical acceptability of hypothetical examples of behavioral research could be differentiated in their judgments largely on the basis of personal characteristics:

> *. . . Psychologists who tended to be more approving in their ethical evaluations (thereby suggesting a greater emphasis on research benefits) were those who (a) were men, (b) had held their highest degree for a longer period of time, (c) had received the degree in a basic psychology area (such as social, experimental, or developmental psychology), and (d) were employed in research-oriented contexts. Psychologists*

who tended to disapprove or reflect conservatism in their judgments (thereby suggesting a greater emphasis on research costs) were those who (a) were women, (b) had held their highest degree for a shorter period of time, (c) had received the degree in an applied psychology area (such as counseling, school, or community psychology), and (d) were employed in service-oriented contexts. (p. 787)

See Kimmel, A. J. (1991). Predictable biases in the ethical decision making of American psychologists. American Psychologist, 46, 786–788.

There are other, more systemic reasons why codes of ethics do not always engage the respect and authority sought for them. Using the vignettes developed by Haas and his colleagues, Smith, McGuire, Abbott, and Blau (1991) surveyed a sample of 102 eclectically oriented clinicians practicing either in private or in community mental health agencies in an attempt to assess the clinicians' reasoning in resolving professional ethical conflicts. The sample was predominantly White, female, and non-doctoral (70%). Smith et al.'s results supported the research by Bernard and his colleagues, presented earlier in this chapter, indicating a discrepancy between what clinicians recognize they should do and what they actually are willing to do:

These findings suggest that clinicians are most likely to act consistently with how they believe they should act when they believe the ethical violation involves one of the relatively clear rules of existing professional codes. This is particularly true when

such professional rules of conduct are further supported by legal statutes or precedents (e.g., clear danger and duty to protect; prohibition against sexual contact with clients). On the other hand, existing professional codes and standards are more often utilitarian guidelines, not rules of conduct. Utilitarian principles suggest that what is ethically correct depends on an assessment of the effects of one's behavior on oneself and others. Such situations demand increased judgment by the clinician and result in greater inconsistency between perceived *should* versus *would* choices. In such conflict situations, what clinicians indicate that they *would* do is affected not only by professional or legal codes of conduct, but also by personal values and practical considerations of the situation. . . .

See Smith, T. S., McGuire, J. M., Abbott, D. W., & Blau, B. I. (1991). Clinical ethical decision making: An investigation of the rationales used to justify doing less than one believes one should. Professional Psychology: Research and Practice, 22, 235–239.

Even after two subsequent revisions of the Ethics Code since Smith et al. was published, "it [is] clear that . . . [the 2002 Code] neither holds all the answers nor specifically addresses every situation or dilemmas that may confront psychologists in their professional activities" (p. 7) nor does it "provide all needed guidance for psychologists facing ethically challenging situations" (p. 8). Barnett, J. E. (2007). The ethical decision-making process in everyday practice. Professional Psychology: Research and Practice, 38, 7–9.

When Laws and Ethics Collide: What Should Psychologists Do?

Samuel Knapp, Michael Gottlieb, Jason Berman, and Mitchell M. Handelsman

. . .

The consistency between ethical and legal requirements generally allows practitioners to adhere to both without disruption of their daily functioning. Nevertheless, circumstances may arise in which a law (broadly defined to include state and federal laws and regulations, binding case law, administrative rules, or court orders) may require psychologists to do something that could harm patients, limit patient autonomy, and/or otherwise offend the personal and professional ethical values of most psychologists (Knapp & VandeCreek, 2006). When such conflicts arise, psychologists need to engage in an ethical decision-making process to evaluate the alternatives available to them and determine the best possible (or least harmful) course of action.

If a conflict arises between a specific law and an enforceable standard of the Ethics Code, Standard 1.02 provides the following guidance:

> If psychologists' ethical responsibilities conflict with law, regulations, or other governing legal authority, psychologists make known their commitment to the Ethics Code and take steps to resolve the conflict. If the conflict is unresolvable via such means, psychologists may adhere to the requirements of the law, regulations, or other governing legal authority.

Nevertheless, Pope and Bajt (1988) surveyed senior-level psychologists, including those knowledgeable about ethics, and found that 57% of the respondents acknowledged intentionally breaking a law or a formal ethical standard at least once "in light of client welfare or another deeper value" (p. 828). Of the 34 instances reported, 7 involved the refusal to report child abuse, 7 entailed illegally divulging confidential information, 3 involved having sex with a patient, 2 concerned unspecified dual relationships, 2 involved refusing to fulfill a legal mandate to warn about a dangerous patient, and the remainder fell into no clear category. . . . These findings demonstrate that the guidance provided in Standard 1.02 is not sufficient in many cases and that ethical decision making is seldom as simple as we would like it to be.

Furthermore, when some legal requirements arise, the Ethics Code may be silent or ambiguous regarding how psychologists should proceed. In these cases, psychologists turn to a variety of additional resources for assistance in their decision making. One resource that is seldom mentioned is that of one's personal values. . . .

The purpose of this article is to show how psychologists' personal values can be of assistance in addressing some of these vexing situations. In this article, we offer a decision-making process for psychologists facing conflicts between the law and their personal ethical values.

A DECISION-MAKING PROCESS

. . .

The APA Ethics Code states, "If this Ethics Code establishes a higher standard of conduct than is required by law, psychologists must meet the higher ethical standard" (p. 1062). In addition, Standard 1.02 instructs us to "adhere to the requirements of the law, regulations, or other governing legal authority." Thus, psychologists who follow the law will not be subject to disciplinary action by the APA Ethics Committee as long as they have taken steps to resolve the law–ethics conflict responsibly. Although this guidance is somewhat helpful, it does not absolve psychologists of the need to choose whether

From *Professional Psychology: Research and Practice, 38*, 54–59. Copyright 2007 by the American Psychological Association.

to violate their ethical values and follow the law or to violate the law to uphold their values.

Using this example as well as others below, we offer a decision-making process for psychologists who may find themselves in a conflict between the law and their personal system of values. . . . First, psychologists should ensure that they understand what the law requires of them. Sometimes psychologists misunderstand or misconstrue their legal requirements and assume a conflict between the law and ethical values when, in fact, no such conflict exists. Second, psychologists should ascertain if they understand their ethical obligations correctly. Third, if a genuine conflict is found to exist, psychologists can seek creative ways to satisfy both their legal and ethical obligations. Fourth, if the conflict between the law and ethics is real and cannot be avoided, psychologists should either obey the law in a manner that minimizes harm to their ethical values or adhere to their ethical values in a manner that minimizes the violation of the law. In either situation, psychologists should anticipate and be prepared to live with the consequences of their decisions. Finally, psychologists can avoid or mitigate many of these ethical conflicts by anticipating potential conflicts between laws and ethics and taking proactive measures. . . .

. . .

When the Conflict Between Law and Ethics Cannot Be Avoided

As with many situations, the response of the psychologist in Example 4 below cannot be determined by relying only on the Ethics Code, which permits disclosure without patient consent if mandated by state law (Standard 4.05b). The psychologist was forced to consult with other sources of moral and ethical guidance (beyond the Ethics Code) if she wanted to act in an ethically praiseworthy manner toward her client and with future psychotherapy patients in mind.

> *Example 4.* A seriously depressed adolescent patient confided to a psychologist that she thought, but was not certain, that her father had sexually abused her. The psychologist lived in a state that mandated the report of all sexual abuse

by a parent against any child under the age of 18. However, the patient stated that she would kill herself if the psychologist reported this to the local child protective services agency. The psychologist had contact with the agency in the past and lacked confidence in its ability to handle the situation with adequate sensitivity to the emotional needs of the child. The patient had not seen her father for many years, and there was no foreseeable likelihood that she would have any future contact with him.

In Example 4, the child presented information that may, upon further inquiry, cause a reasonable psychologist to suspect abuse. If the psychologist did suspect abuse, according to the laws in many states, she would be required to report it. However, the psychologist believed that reporting the abuse would precipitate the suicide that she was trying to prevent. Although the Ethics Code assures the psychologist that she would not be found in violation of the Ethics Code for following the law, this conscientious psychologist wanted to choose the best way to act, consistent with her overall virtuous aims of helping the client stay alive and live well.

The initial reaction of many psychologists may be to engage in dichotomous thinking and to consider either one option (reporting) or another (not reporting), weigh the benefits and risks of each, and decide which one to follow. Nonetheless, it may be prudent to consider a series of sequential steps before deciding how to respond. The first step is for psychologists to consult with knowledgeable colleagues who can provide them with useful information, encourage them to think through the issues (e.g., including ways the psychologists can advance virtuous aims), and challenge their clinical, legal, and ethical assumptions, if necessary. As noted above, sometimes conflicts are more apparent than real and psychologists may have more flexibility in responding than they originally thought, or they may have misinterpreted the ethical issues or legal requirements involved.

In Example 4, the psychologist needed to assess carefully whether the information she was given was sufficient for a reasonable psychologist to suspect abuse or whether more information was needed. Sometimes in cases of abuse it can be difficult to determine whether the requisite threshold of certainty has been reached. The legal standard for reporting in her state ("reason to suspect") is a vague and poorly defined state of mind that exists somewhere between a passing thought and certainty (Levi & Loeben, 2004). Also, creative clinical solutions can often allow psychologists to meet both their legal and ethical obligations. For example, the psychologist first needed to ensure that the threat was not a manipulation motivated by a secondary gain. Assuming the threat was genuine, the psychologist might bring the mother or another trusted relative into the therapy to obtain more information. Additional clinical information from other sources may clarify the extent of the danger of self-harm, make more clear the likelihood that the abuse occurred, or suggest additional options for dealing constructively with the apparent conflict.

If no viable clinical solution emerges, psychologists must determine how to resolve the conflict between providing optimal care and the duty to report on the basis of their individual value systems. The decision-making process of principle-based ethics provides one way to balance the demands of a particular situation. Beauchamp and Childress (2001) would allow the trumping of one moral value over another after a thorough assessment of the dilemma. But doing so requires that the infringement is the least possible, that it is consistent with achieving the primary goal, and that efforts are made to minimize the negative impact of the infringement. The same process might be used when one is considering disobeying a law. The disobedience should be the least possible, consistent with the primary goal, and done with efforts made to limit the negative effects of the infringement. That is, the disobedience to the law should be restricted only to that portion that violates the ethical standards of the psychologist.

The perspective of virtue ethics provides another way for psychologists to address this conundrum. Psychologists relying on virtue ethics would identify the virtues most relevant to this situation (e.g., kindness, fairness, responsibility, trustworthiness, honesty), deliberate or know what actions would be most likely to reach the desired goal (e.g., help the patient live, heal, and eventually flourish), and respond in a manner that a virtuous or morally outstanding person would, given this situation (e.g., rely on collateral sources of information and consult with ethically outstanding colleagues).

If the Decision Is Made Not to Obey the Law

Civil disobedience has a long history, dating from Sophocles (440 BCE/2006), in whose play, *Antigone*, the heroine (Antigone) defies the orders of the tyrant Creon and openly performs a burial ceremony for her brother, Polyneices, even though it means her death. Proponents of civil disobedience may disagree on particulars, but most would agree with Woolman (1772/1971), Gandhi (Fisher, 1983), King (1958), and others that individuals should obey the laws except only under very limited circumstances to comply with a higher value and be willing to accept whatever punishments may occur.

When psychologists are considering disobeying a law, we recommend that they follow the sequential steps enumerated above: (a) Seek consultation to ensure that the law requires them to do what they believe it requires, (b) make certain that they understand their ethical obligations clearly, (c) consider alternatives that would allow them to follow the law while still upholding their values, and (d) contemplate violating a law only if no viable alternative is available. If a decision is made to disobey the law, the psychologist must ask, "If I disobey the law, how can I limit my disobedience to the minimum necessary to fulfill my higher goal?" Or, "How should I act to support or advance the most relevant virtue?" For example, if clinically and ethically indicated, the psychologist may continue treatment with the possibly abused girl until her mental state improves and then involve her in the decision to make a report. Psychologists should document the reasons why they chose the action they did. If there is a disciplinary hearing, the documentation of the circumstances may lead the disciplinary body to mitigate the punishment.

If the Decision Is Made to Obey the Law

If the decision is made to obey the law, the psychologist needs to ask, "How can I minimize the harm to the offended ethical values?" For example, the psychologist can act to minimize the negative impact of the decision by including the patient in the process as much as possible. The psychologist might inform the patient of the legal obligation and give her the opportunity to have input into the manner in which the disclosure is made. Or the psychologist could ask the child protective services agency to interview the girl in her office with the mother present, if that is what the girl prefers.

References

American Psychological Association. (2002). Ethical principles of psychologists and code of conduct. *American Psychologist, 57,* 1060–1073.

Beauchamp, T., & Childress, J. (2001). *Principles of biomedical ethics* (5th ed.). New York: Oxford University Press.

Fisher, L. (1983). *The life of Mahatma Gandhi.* New York: Harper & Row.

Handelsman, M. M., Knapp, S., & Gottlieb, M. C. (2002). Positive ethics. In C. R. Snyder & S. J. Lopez (Eds.), *Handbook of positive psychology* (pp. 731–744). New York: Oxford University Press.

King, M. L. (1958). *Stride toward freedom.* San Francisco: Harper & Row.

Knapp, S., & VandeCreek, L. (2004). A principle-based analysis of the 2002 American Psychological Association's Ethics Code. *Psychotherapy: Theory/Research/Practice/Training, 41,* 247–254.

Levi, B., & Loeben, G. (2004). Index of suspicion: Feeling not believing. *Theoretical Medicine, 25,* 277–310.

Pope, K., & Bajt, T. R. (1988). When laws and values conflict: A dilemma for psychologists. *American Psychologist, 43,* 828–829.

Sophocles. (2006). *Antigone.* Retrieved January 18, 2006, from http://classics.mit.edu/Sophocles/antigone.html (Original work produced *circa* 440 BCE)

Woolman, J. (1971). *The journal and major essays of John Woolman* (P. Moulton, Ed.). New York: Oxford University Press. (Original work published 1772)

◆   ◆   ◆

Commentary: Commenting on Pope and Bajt (1988), cited in the prior excerpt, Ansell and Ross (1990) argued that because psychologists were not involved in drafting child abuse-reporting statutes, no thought was given to their effect on clinical practice:

The ethicist might have assumed that a psychotherapist who suspected a client of child abuse might consider a range of options before rushing to report. These options lie within the clinical function to make a judgment call. To deny the therapists that judgment is a clear usurpation of professional function. Worse, it compels psychologists to turn away from their professional responsibilities to become agents of the police. . . . (p. 399)

See Ansell and Ross (1990). Reply to Pope and Bajt. American Psychologist, 45, 399. They also called upon ethicists to conduct research on the issue. In a response to Ansell and Ross, Kalichman (1990) affirmed that "as many as 60% of psychologists have elected not to report suspected child abuse" (p. 1273), but countered that "disregarding reporting laws is potentially dangerous for practitioners as well as their clients" (p. 1273). Kalichman concluded that it was "paradoxical that ethical psychologists so frequently choose to break the law" (p. 1273). See Kalichman, S. (1991). Reporting laws, confidentiality, and clinical judgment: Reply to Ansell and Ross. American Psychologist, 45, 1273.

About 30 years ago, I published an article in which a well-trained psychologist faithfully followed the then extant version of the APA Ethics Code, resulting in five law suits against the psychologist and/or her employing institution. I attempted to discern the reasons why ethics codes fail to provide adequate bases for behavior. I hypothesized that they (a) are written from the profession's point of view, not the client public; (b) are written too abstractly, merely providing general guides to behavior; (c) may be used to present a misleading picture to the public of an ethical profession, without its members necessarily subscribing to the profession's ethical values; and (d) may be disregarded by the legal system when a profession's claim to autonomy is in conflict with the rights of individuals or the public at large. See Bersoff, D. N. (1975). Professional ethics and legal responsibilities: On the horns of a dilemma. Journal of School Psychology, 13, 359–376. Based on a reading of the 2002 Ethics Code in chapter 1, are these still valid hypotheses?

The inclusion of those affected by professionals' conduct in the development and application of ethics codes remains an idea whose time has not yet come. Recently, however, Prilleltensky and his colleagues reintroduced the idea in an elegant and organized way. They contrast what they call the current restrictive framework of defining ethics with their concept of a participatory framework. In applying ethics under this alternative, power would be shared equally between professionals and clients, ethics would deal not only with the microcosmic, individualistic relationship between professional and client, but also with ethical issues involving social, cultural, and organizational contexts. For a lengthier discussion of these issues see:

Prilleltensky, I., Rossiter, A., & Walsh-Bowers, R. (1996). Preventing harm and promoting ethical discourse in the helping professions: Conceptual, research, analytical, and action frameworks. Ethics & Behavior, 6, 287–306.

Rossiter, A., Walsh-Bowers, R., & Prilleltensky, I. (1996). Learning from broken rules: Individualism, bureaucracy, and ethics. Ethics & Behavior, 6, 307–320.

Walsh-Bowers, R., Rossiter, A., & Prilleltensky, I. (1996). The personal is the organizational in the ethics of hospital social workers. Ethics & Behavior, 9, 321–335.

In response, Checkland (1996) cautioned that the focus of Prilleltensky et al. may not appropriately "distinguish ethics (as that which is concerned primarily with questions of right and wrong) from politics (where our fundamental concern is to contest and clarify the nature of the collective good and bad)" (p. 343). See Checkland, D. (1996). Individualism, subjectivism, democracy, and "helping" professions. Ethics & Behavior, 6, 337–343. In a similar vein, see also Kendler, H. H. (1993). Psychology and the ethics of social policy. American Psychologist, 48, 1046–1053 (arguing that psychology is limited in its ability to identify and support social policies or guide human behavior through ethical principles).

Other authors also have addressed the value of a code of ethics and criticized the method of its development. Pope and Vetter (1992) complained that the revision process that led to the 1992 Code of Conduct was flawed because that code was not drafted in the same way as the original code, that is, "guided by contemporary empirical data about the incidents faced by the full range of APA's current membership" (p. 409). They argued that unless a critical incident or empirical approach is used,

"the code risks losing relevance and applicability" (p. 409). See Pope, K. S., & Vetter, V. A. (1992). Ethical dilemmas encountered by members of the American Psychological Association: A national survey. American Psychologist, 47, 397–411.

Barlow (1989) has asserted that although "respected, quoted, and esteemed by all," ethics codes "have influence, but little, if any actual authority" (p. 9). He believes that, in addition to often containing contradictory principles, such codes have limited moral authority because they undergo regular revision:

> Sponsoring agencies tend to proceed with regard to special interests and a democratic process of voting to affirm the declarations they compose. By nature the statements can be emended, amended, or revised as the voting body decides. This policy allows for important updating and adjustments called for by technological innovation. But it also allows for amended restatement in response to changes in social policy and moral sentiment.
>
> Moreover, contemporary promulgations are often little more than consensus statements affirming no more than what everyone in the group at that moment agrees upon. The larger, more heterogeneous, is the sponsoring body, the more general, simplified, and minimalist is the position taken. A mark is chiseled into the ethical bench, but its reach is usually only as high as the least common denominator. (p. 13)

See Barlow, J. (1989). The practical limits of codes and declarations. In L. P. Bird & J. Barlow (Eds.), Code of medical ethics, oaths, and prayers: An anthology (pp. 9–14). Richardson, TX: Christian Medical and Dental Society.

Welfel and Lipsitz (1984) were in accord with Barlow's (1989) view:

> In recent years, the profession has shown an increased awareness that even thorough familiarity with the code and powerful sanctions against nonconforming psychologists are insufficient in themselves to guar-

antee ethical practice. For example, a number of authors . . . have pointed out that the ethical codes serve only as general guidelines for practice. They suggest that changes in professional practice happen so quickly that not even regular revision of the standards can address every aspect of current practice. They also contend that many ethically sensitive situations arising in the course of practice are difficult to categorize according to the tenets of the code. In some extreme cases, adherence to one portion of the code even seems to result in violation of another portion. Most importantly, they argue that the purpose of the code was never to provide blueprints that would remove all need for the use of judgment by individual psychologists, but rather, to act as a foundation to assist the psychologist in determining the applicability of the Code to his or her unique and often complex situation. (p. 31)

See Welfel, E. R., & Lipsitz, N. E. (1984). The ethical behavior of professional psychologists: A critical analysis of the research. The Counseling Psychologist, 12(3), 31–41.

As chapter 1 indicates, the first APA Ethics Code was published in 1953 and has been revised or amended nine times since. In light of the comments by Barlow (1989) and Welfel and Lipsitz (1984), does this constant revision so distract from the Code's moral authority that it is disobeyed or, at least, ignored?

The other major criticism of the codes of ethics is that they are often vague and ambiguous. In 1994, the 1992 APA Code was reviewed by several authors in a special section of Professional Psychology: Research and Practice (see Volume 28, pp. 315–387). In my summary of their comments I wrote:

Three overarching and related critical themes emerged from the reviewers' articles: (a) The current code [1992] although broader and more explicit [than the 1981 code] paradoxically, lacks clarity and precision; (b) the code is filled with qualifying language that makes it difficult for those charged with enforcement to find viola-

tions; and (c) it is a document designed more to protect psychologists than to protect the public.

. . .

Perhaps the most pointed criticism of the [1992] code concerns the rampant use of qualifying language throughout. As almost all reviewers pointed out, the code is full of such lawyer-driven "weasel words" as reasonable and feasible. . . . (pp. 383–384)

See Bersoff, D. N. (1994). Explicit ambiguity: The 1992 Ethics Code as oxymoron. Professional Psychology: Research and Practice, 25, 382–387.

By my count, the 1992 Code contained the word "reasonable" 40 times and the word "feasible" 15 times, leading critics to suggest that many of the provisions containing such language were diluted to the point of uselessness, could not serve as a strong moral force, and made enforcement difficult. Although many of the members of the Ethics Committee Task Force that wrote the 2002 Code were aware of these criticisms and some members were individuals who authored critical articles, that Code, again by my count, contains the word "reasonable" 39 times, "feasible" 9 times, and some form of the word "appropriate" 29 times.

The 2002 Code's authors, however, supported the use of these terms. As readers will recall from the Introduction to the Code, they offered the following explanation:

The modifiers used in some of the standards of this Ethics Code (e.g., reasonably, appropriate, potentially) are included in the standards when they would (1) allow professional judgment on the part of psychologists, (2) eliminate injustice or inequality that would occur without the modifier, (3) ensure the applicability across a broad range of activities conducted by psychologists, or (4) guard against a set of rigid rules that might be quickly outdated. As used in this Ethics Code the term "reasonable" means the prevailing professional judgment of psychologists engaged in similar activities or circumstances, given the knowledge that the psychologist had or should have had at the time.

Does this explanation and definition address the concerns of the reviewers of the 1992 Code or whether, if the Code is challenged on the grounds of vagueness and lack of fair notice to psychologists, it would pass constitutional muster any better than did the 1981 Code in White v. North Carolina State Board of Examiners of Professional Psychologists (1990; *see chap. 1, this volume*)?

Finally given that the most frequent ethical complaints against psychologists over the past decade are sexual intimacies with clients, incompetent child custody evaluations, and insurance fraud (see chap. 1, this volume), might it not be more effective to draft a seven-word ethics code that simply reads: Psychologists shall not lie, cheat, or steal?

CHAPTER 3

LEARNING ETHICS

Since the late 1970s, every graduate program training professional psychologists that seeks to be accredited by the APA has been required to offer instruction in ethics and to familiarize students with whatever version of the APA Ethics Code is current at the time. APA does not accredit programs that train graduate students solely for research positions, but a great many such programs offer similar instruction in ethics, at the very least concentrating on the ethics of experimentation and scholarship. Does this training ensure that those who complete these programs act ethically as professionals? As the data and material presented in chapters 1 and 2 illustrate, this is often not the case.

As we have begun to explore, there are a variety of reasons for psychologists to act in ways that violate the code of ethics. A few miscreants deliberately flout their professional and scientific responsibilities for personal gain—monetary, reputational, and sexual, among others. For example, the psychologist who, without consulting his or her client, rushes to the media with the news that he or she is the therapist of a famous personage just charged with a heinous crime is acting in a purely self-serving and inexcusable manner. Other psychologists violate ethical principles because of imprudence, ignorance, or insensitivity about the ethical consequences of their behavior. For instance, consider the psychologist who calls child protection services after she learns that the parents she is counseling are punishing their 10-year-old child with a rattan cane. When the parents file an ethics complaint, the psychologist responds that she thought she was mandated by law to report child abuse but never realized that the APA Ethics Code also required her to inform clients of the limits of confidentiality or that failing to do that would damage the development of the therapeutic relationship.

These are relatively simple cases to adjudicate. But there are at least two other kinds of cases that are more complex. In the first case are psychologists who attempt to comply with the rules but, perceiving that they lack the guidance of clearly written, explicit, and precise ethical provisions, rely on their own interpretation of those rules. To illustrate, under the 2002 Ethics Code, psychologists are supposed to discuss the limits of confidentiality with clients very close to the beginning of a therapeutic relationship, "unless it is not feasible or is contraindicated" (APA, 2002, p. 1066). Suppose now that a patient in the third year of intensive psychoanalysis begins to fall behind in paying for his therapy. For several months the analyst and the patient discuss the patient's failure to pay as part of his resistance to therapy. Finally, however, with the unpaid bills mounting, the analyst and the patient agree to terminate therapy. The analyst then turns over the outstanding account to a collection agency. The client complains that his right to confidentiality was violated when the analyst submitted his name to the collection agency without telling him at any time during treatment that she would do so. In response, the analyst explains that her conduct violated no ethical rule because she believed that any discussion of the limits of confidentiality at the outset of treatment would have interfered with transference issues so crucial to successful psychoanalysis. Thus, in her mind, disclosure was "contraindicated." Lacking specific guidance in this situation by those who drafted the Code, the psychologist made a not implausible interpretation of her own.

The most complex situations are those that present ethically sensitive and knowledgeable psychologists with fundamental and profound ethical dilemmas. Psychologists in these cases understand the rules (or the law) but break them because they consider violation to be in the service of higher moral principles. Consider the following case example. A 10th-grade boy is enrolled in research studying violence in adolescents and how it might be prevented through short-term intervention. During an interview portion of the study, the student reveals to the female investigator that he has had many fantasies about harming his next-door neighbor, a slightly older female teenager who refuses to pay him any attention. On further inquiry, the investigator also learns that the student is contemplating the purchase of a gun. The investigator suggests to the student that it would be a good idea to inform his parents of the situation, even though she is aware that he has no history of violent behavior. The student adamantly refuses to inform his parents or to let the investigator do so, warning that he will drop out of the study and treatment if she does not honor his refusal. Believing that preserving confidentiality would, in the long run, be in the student's best interest by not driving him out of needed treatment and would most closely express the psychologists' moral principle of fidelity, the investigator agrees not to tell his parents.

One week later, the psychologist reads in the newspaper that, with a gun bought the day before, her research subject has shot and wounded his teenage neighbor after she ignored him one evening. The parents of the 10th-grade student file a complaint with APA, stating that the psychologist should have informed them of their son's potentially violent and harmful behavior, regardless of his wishes. The psychologist concedes that the Code permits disclosure without consent to protect third parties from harm, but she argues that supporting the boy's right to privacy and autonomy and the need to establish trust in therapy outweighed any putative entitlement in the code of ethics to inform his parents.

Although the psychologist's decision in this case may have contributed to a negative outcome, the situation did present her with a genuine ethical dilemma. It would have been perfectly ethical for her to disclose the student's confidences and even to refuse to abide by his demand for secrecy. Nevertheless, she decided that this course of action conflicted with more universal moral principles—the promotion of autonomy and the development of faithfulness to her subject's expressed interests—that were an inherent part of her value system as a psychologist.

All psychologists will be faced with such dilemmas sometime in their careers. They may find that, by necessity or design, the APA Ethics Code contains few absolute and explicit prohibitions regarding a particular dilemma. The psychologist who wishes to act ethically in an ethically uncertain world needs to have both a philosophical base from which to make decisions and a method for using that base to build workable options.

In this chapter, I offer some frameworks for recognizing a genuine ethical dilemma, for generating possible solutions to it, and, perhaps for arriving at a reasonable resolution in line with the ethical principles of one's professional association and one's personal value system. However, as the authors of material in this chapter argue, acting ethically is not a compartmentalized function. Instead, ethical behavior results from integrating didactic knowledge, including a thorough familiarity with the APA Ethics Code; an understanding of problem-solving and decision-making approaches; a clear conception of the philosophical principles (each of which may compete with one another) that underlie the formal code of ethics; and a basically sound character that leads one to respond with maturity, judgment, discretion, wisdom, and prudence.

In the remainder of this book I concentrate on seven central topics that inevitably confront and test the psychology practitioner, researcher, and professor with ethical dilemmas surrounding confidentiality, multiple relationships, assessment, therapeutic interventions, teaching and doing research in an academic institution, serving as an expert witness, and dealing with the commercial and business aspects of psychology. Because this chapter provides the foundation for ethical decision making under each of these topics, I consider it absolutely crucial to understanding and integrating the material in the remaining chapters of the book.

References

American Psychological Association. (2002). Ethical principles of psychologists and code of conduct. *American Psychologist, 57,* 1060–1073.

Problems With Ethics Training by "Osmosis"

Mitchell M. Handelsman

Ethical training by osmosis refers to the practice of allowing ethics to be taught in the context of supervision, in which a sensitivity to issues will seep through during discussions of cases. In this article I argue that relying on such informal methods to teach ethics is a dangerous practice. . . .

The first argument against training in the context of practica concerns the nature and extent of supervision. "It is usually assumed that adequate supervision will always be provided in the clinic or hospital, but this is far from universally true" (Arnhoff & Jenkins, 1969, p. 441). Often, needs and time constraints of the agency take precedence over careful exploration of ethical issues. Competence of supervisors in ethics is also an issue. Dalton (1984) noted that "students' learning is limited by the supervisor's awareness of ethical dilemmas and assumptions; issues not recognized by the supervisor are not recognized or mentioned by students" (p. 186). The "extended supervision" argument, then, may be an instance of transferring responsibility. . . .

Even if one knows that supervisors do an adequate job of exploring ethical issues (this remains, of course, an empirical question) when such issues arise in the course of clinical work, this method does not guarantee that a broad range of ethical issues will arise. In their survey, Tymchuk et al. (1982) found that 58% of doctoral-level psychologists felt "that they were not well informed enough about ethical issues in psychology" (p. 419). One may overcome such a gap in knowledge by exposure to such issues in a formal way, rather than leaving it up to chance. . . .

There is no doubt that important learning takes place in relation to meaningful events, and ethical issues encountered during clinical practice will remain salient. However, to rely on such learning to take place seems to be a dangerous practice.

Reconceptualizing ethics and its training is needed in training programs. It is necessary to treat ethical thinking as a skill that must be developed and that is not intimately bound to the process of therapy, testing, and so on. . . .

. . .

. . .

Ethics courses can be made more stimulating and relevant by being taught with a variety of methods that blend theory and application. Learning can include general ethical concepts (Solomon, 1984), ethical thinking processes (Tymchuk, 1981), values clarification (Abeles, 1980), use of comprehensive textbooks . . . and exploration of ethical dilemmas. . . .

References

Abeles, N. (1980). Teaching ethical principles by means of values confrontations. *Psychotherapy: Theory, Research and Practice, 17*, 384–391.

Arnhoff, F. N., & Jenkins, J. W. (1969). Subdoctoral education in psychology: A study of issues and attitudes. *American Psychologist, 24*, 430–443.

Dalton, J. H. (1984). Discussing ethical issues in practicum courses. *Teaching of Psychology, 11*, 186–188.

Solomon, R. C. (1984). *Ethics: A brief introduction.* New York: McGraw-Hill.

Tymchuk, A. J. (1981). Ethical decision-making and psychological treatment. *Journal of Psychiatric Treatment and Evaluation, 3*, 507–513.

◆　◆　◆

Commentary: Compare the argument above by Handelsman (1986) to the following, written by Welfel and Lipsitz 2 years earlier:

> In spite of the dramatic increase in availability of ethics courses in graduate programs there has been little systematic

From *Professional Psychology: Research and Practice, 17*, 371–372. Copyright 1986 by the American Psychological Association.

investigation of the impact of such experiences on students. In fact, there is little information regarding exactly what is being taught in those courses. . . .

[The] literature only very weakly supports the interpretation that ethics courses have a positive impact on students. No study has been reported that examines the influence of such training on actual behavior with clients or assesses whether the effects of ethics courses are temporary or permanent. In addition, there are no data to compare whether ethics is best taught in a separate course or integrated into existing courses in the curriculum. Thus, the push to initiate separate ethics courses in graduate programs is based more on the "good hearted assumption" that such courses will have a positive impact than on any scientific data. Given the cost in faculty time and in tuition for such training, systematic research into such courses seems imperative. (p. 37).

See Welfel, E. R., & Lipsitz, N. E. (1984). *The ethical behavior of professional psychologists: A critical analysis of the research.* Counseling Psychologist, 12(3), 31–41. *Nevertheless, as Welfel (1992) later noted, since 1979 APA has mandated that all programs accredited by APA include ethics training for graduate students. By 1990, 69% of these programs taught ethics in a separate required course, usually in classes lasting 20 to 30 hours. She concluded that graduate faculties now view ethics training as their responsibility, rather than that of clinical supervisors.* See Welfel, E. R. (1992). *Psychologists as ethics educator: Successes, failures, and unanswered questions.* Professional Psychology: Research and Practice, 23, 182–189.

A recent study provides some evidence of the effects of ethics education, at least with regard to graduate students' perception of their ability to handle ethical issues. Doctoral students (N = 223) in school psychology from their first to fifth year of training, one-half of whom had taken an ethics course, were asked how prepared they were to tackle 12 ethical issues. In general, those who had taken a course in ethics felt more prepared than their noncourse counterparts to handle such issues as informed consent to research, confidentiality, requests for access to testing material by nonpsychologists, child abuse, and dual relationships. Both groups had the most trouble with three issues: dealing with possible ethical violations by colleagues (40.8% of the course group and 18.6% of the noncourse group felt prepared here); handling potentially violent clients (30% of the course group and 18.6% of the noncourse group felt prepared here); and child custody cases (only 10% of the course group and 7.1% of the noncourse group felt prepared here). The study did not examine how well these students would actually handle the conflicts they felt prepared for.* See Tryon, G. S. (2001). *School psychology students' beliefs about their preparation and concern with ethical issues.* Ethics & Behavior, 11, 375–394.

Much ethics training in courses has been criticized for concentrating on ethics codes and rules rather than on day-to-day ethical dilemmas in professional practice. See Plante, T. G. (1995). *Training child clinical predoctoral interns and postdoctoral fellows in ethics and professional issues: An experimental model.* Professional Psychology: Research and Practice, 26, 616–619. *Other writers, however, exhort trainers to take a very different approach. For example, Pellegrin and Frueh (1994)*

suggest that PhD candidates should receive training in their degree; that is to say, philosophy. Instead of learning only what ethical principles are, PhD candidates should also be well versed in the philosophical issues and debates that are the foundation for the formation of ethical principles. (p. 970)

See Pellegrin, K. L., & Frueh, B. C. (1994). *Why psychologists don't think like philosophers.* American Psychologist, 49, 970.

The following three contemporary articles describe ethics curricula that go far beyond simple concentration on rules and seek to incorporate the criticisms of Plante and Pellegrin and Frueh.

Training Ethical Psychologists: An Acculturation Model

Mitchell M. Handelsman, Michael C. Gottlieb, and Samuel Knapp

How do students develop a sense of themselves as ethical professionals? How do they develop a "professional ethical identity" as a part of the process of becoming psychologists? We ask these questions to help improve ethical behavior in our students and better prepare them to be more responsive to an increasingly complex and diverse professional world.

Becoming an ethical professional is more complex than simply following a set of rules or doing what one sees one's mentors do, and helping students become ethical psychologists involves more than teaching certain professional rules to morally upright people who will easily understand and implement them. The complexities of ethics training were recognized by the ethics workgroup of the Competencies Conference 2002 (2002; de las Fuentes, Willmuth, & Yarrow, 2003).

There are at least three reasons ethics training is not so simple. First, the rules embedded in ethics codes are sometimes vague and conflicting (Keith-Spiegel, 1994). Second, learning about the ethics of the profession of psychology by watching models is incomplete at best (Branstetter & Handelsman, 2000; Handelsman, 1986). Third, ethics is the study of right and wrong but is often taught as the study of wrong. Many ethics courses are devoted to laws, disciplinary codes, and risk management strategies and do not focus on best practices.

If ethics training is limited primarily to learning rules, then students may not appreciate the extent to which the need for sound ethical thinking will permeate their professional lives. The development of an identity as an ethical psychologist is a far more complex matter that deserves greater attention. To do so requires that ethics training be considered in a new way, as a process of acculturation.

Our assumption is that psychology, as a profession and a scientific discipline, represents a discrete culture with its own traditions, values, and methods of implementing its ethical principles. Students who choose to enter graduate training in psychology have already excelled at academic work and may already have been exposed to some of psychology's academic and professional values. However, their knowledge of the culture of psychology is incomplete at best. We believe that psychologists can continue to improve their ability to acculturate students into the ethical values and standards of the discipline.

The "culture" of psychology is larger than ethics, and an acculturation model could be used more broadly than we attempt here. We focus on ethics because it transcends all aspects of the discipline and because ethics training has been neglected relative to other aspects of professional preparation. In this article we propose that ethics training is an acculturation process, and we present some resulting implications and practical suggestions.

THE CULTURE OF PSYCHOLOGY

Berry and Sam (1997) defined *acculturation* as "a set of internal psychological outcomes including a clear sense of personal and cultural identity, good mental health, and the achievement of personal satisfaction in the new cultural context" (p. 299). We suggest that *ethical acculturation* can be defined by substituting the word *ethical* for the word *cultural* in the above definition. The ethical culture of psychology may differ significantly from the value traditions of students, and the new cultural values may be counterintuitive for some trainees. For example, lending money to friends is often a sign of caring and reciprocation; however, lending money to a psychotherapy client may signify something much different.

The culture of psychology is complex and pluralistic but contains agreed-on values, traditions, and

From *Professional Psychology: Research and Practice, 36,* 59–65. Copyright 2005 by the American Psychological Association.

rituals. Among these values are scientific thinking, appreciating the complexity of behavior, scientifically informed practice, the search for truth, lifelong learning, the sharing of knowledge, improving society, tolerance for diversity, and social justice. Obviously, some of these values exist in many scientific disciplines and professions, but the particular combination of elements and the tradition of helping make psychology a distinct professional culture.

As in any profession, the acculturation of psychology students is a complex and lengthy undertaking. To improve this process, we review the highlights of a model of acculturation that may be helpful.

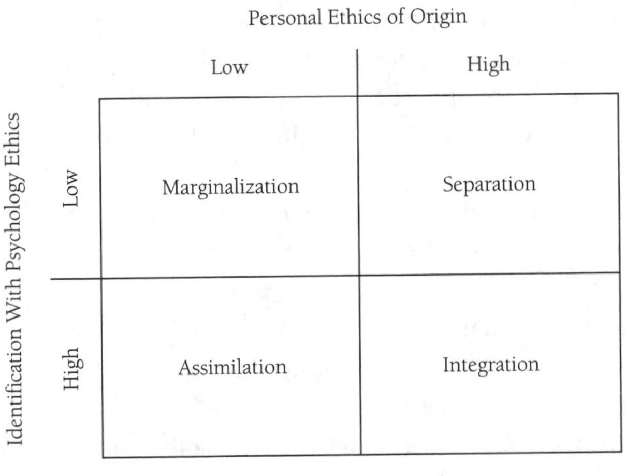

BERRY'S MODEL OF ACCULTURATION

Berry (1980, 2003; Berry & Sam, 1997) conceived of acculturation as a process of adaptation that includes two dimensions that lead to four possible strategies of acculturation or types of adaptation. The first dimension, which Berry and Sam (1997) called *cultural maintenance,* refers to identification with the culture of origin: "Is it considered to be of value to maintain cultural identity and characteristics?" (p. 296). When people enter a new culture (either voluntarily or by force) and need to adapt, they vary in their desire to retain their original cultural values and traditions. At one end of the continuum are those who give up their culture of origin completely. At the other extreme are those who want to fully preserve their heritage.

The second dimension, *contact and participation,* refers to identification with the adopted culture: "Is it considered to be of value to maintain relationships with dominant society?" (Berry & Sam, 1997, p. 296). Individuals high in identification see great value and potential in the traditions of their new culture. Those low in identification refuse to accept a culture of which they are ignorant or in which they place little value.

According to Berry (2003; Berry & Sam, 1997), being relatively high or low in cultural maintenance and in contact and participation leads to four possible strategies of acculturation (see Figure 1). "*Attitudes* towards these four alternatives, and actual *behaviors* exhibiting them, together constitute an individual's acculturation *strategy*" (Berry & Sam, 1997, p. 297). . . .

FIGURE 1. Berry's (1980, 2003; Berry & Sam, 1997) acculturation model applied to ethical identity.

. . . In the next sections we consider each of the four strategies. Although some of the more extreme features of these strategies are presented here, it should be recognized that each strategy comprises a continuum of behaviors.

Integration

People who adopt an *integration* strategy retain important aspects of their heritage but they also adopt what their new culture has to offer. Integration appears to be the most effective acculturation strategy (Berry, 2003; Berry & Sam, 1997). . . . Applied to ethical acculturation, people choosing integration would adopt the ethical values of psychology while understanding and maintaining their own value tradition. . . .

Students and psychologists who often choose among the remaining three strategies may be susceptible to alienation or professional and ethical problems, or both. These strategies may be associated with some implicit misconceptions that we describe. Some, who find themselves with unacceptable value conflicts, may choose to pursue other professions more consistent with their values. Others may continue in the profession but struggle with conflicts that may result in ethical problems.

Assimilation

Berry (2003; Berry & Sam, 1997) called the strategy of relatively high contact and relatively low cultural maintenance *assimilation*. At the extreme of the assimilation strategy, the new culture is adopted totally, and the values and traditions from the culture of origin are discarded. In this mode, students adopt professional standards but do so with little personal sense of a moral base.

Assimilation may be dangerous for students, although it may not be immediately apparent. Trainees may feel so strongly motivated to develop a professional identity that they divorce themselves from the values that had previously guided their personal lives. Perhaps they did not start with a strong personal sense of ethics, or, somewhere in the professional socialization process they may have acquired the belief that their personal values were not relevant to or necessary in their professional lives.

When pursuing an assimilation strategy, external trappings may become more important than substance; this can lead to a false sense of competence. The degree, license, and well-furnished office all signify entry into the profession. Certificates, memberships, and offices in professional associations may be sought because of the purely personal satisfaction they bring rather than the professional accomplishments they are supposed to represent. These outward signs are meaningless and potentially harmful without a firm personal grounding in and an appreciation for the ethics and value traditions of the professional culture.

A misconception implicit in the assimilation strategy might be that "the APA Ethics Code contains all I need to know to practice (teach, do research) ethically." Psychologists may attempt to abide by and apply APA standards or state law without understanding the general principles behind them or without appreciating that the code is not a comprehensive guide for living one's life. This strategy is akin to building a strong structure on a shaky foundation, and it may lead to empty, legalistic, and overly simplistic applications of our ethical principles.

Separation

The *separation* strategy describes relatively high cultural maintenance and relatively low contact and participation. Applied to psychology training, students might have a well-developed ethical sense from their own upbringing, or the values of other professions to which they may have belonged, but

they do not identify as strongly with the values of psychology. . . .

. . .

Problems are easy to foresee for those who actively reject large portions of psychology's professional and ethical culture. Although they may have a very strong personal code of ethics and be very well intentioned, these students may also be unaware of the potential harm that may come from acting on a set of principles or virtues that are inconsistent with the professional context.

Marginalization

Marginalization is the most problematic acculturation strategy, comprising low identification with both cultures. Sometimes this may be a temporary strategy— for example, when people move to a new culture and give up their culture of origin before they attempt to adopt the new culture. However, marginalization may also constitute an enduring state of alienation, or a failure of attempts at other strategies (Berry, 2003). In terms of ethics, psychologists using the marginalization strategy do not have a well-developed personal moral sense; neither have they (yet) internalized a sense of professional ethics. Such persons may be at greatest risk for ethical infractions. The extreme of this dimension is represented by psychopaths, although such persons represent a very small percentage of psychologists. Unfortunately, there seem to be numerous other, less extreme examples.

Unlike psychologists exhibiting integration or assimilation, those exhibiting marginalization will obey ethical standards out of personal convenience rather than a sense of moral commitment. A general misconception implicit in this strategy may be the belief that all ethics codes and standards are equally arbitrary and oppressive. . . .

IMPLICATIONS AND APPLICATIONS OF AN ACCULTURATION MODEL FOR INSTRUCTORS AND SUPERVISORS

. . .

Integration may best occur when instructors and supervisors view ethics not only as a set of prohibitions but also as a way to actualize students' visions of what it means to be a psychologist. Codes of conduct, licensing board rules, and other disciplinary documents are certainly necessary, but they represent only the ethical *floor,* or minimum standards. Teaching these documents by themselves may lead students to separation choices; they may feel that the codes and rules are external to their sense of ethical identity. (After all, applicants do not say they want to become psychologists so they can obey the law.) Taking a positive approach to ethics (Handelsman, Knapp, & Gottlieb, 2002) includes helping students appreciate that ethics is more than the minimum— that ethics means becoming a full member of the culture of psychology.

. . .

Selection of Trainees

First-year graduate students cannot know all that will be expected of them. Students who enter psychology only "because I want to help people" may be especially shocked at the range of values and principles psychologists hold that are irrelevant to, only tangentially related to, or seemingly antithetical to their value of helping. An acculturation framework might help training programs select applicants who are better able to adapt to a new ethical culture. For example, programs could ask applicants to write essays about their preexisting expectations of the ethical culture they are about to enter, their willingness to adopt a new set of values and traditions, or evidence of prior accomplishments that actualize their moral values and indicate their adaptability. These essays or other assessment methods would not be predictors of ethical behavior during one's career; instead, these methods would be more similar to trainability tests (Robertson & Downs, 1979) that may help predict the ability of applicants to learn and adapt to a new ethical culture during graduate training.

First Stages of Ethical Acculturation

New graduate students vary widely in their knowledge and appreciation of psychology ethics. . . . [M]any may not realize that a professional body of ethical standards, literature, and practice exists. These students may experience acculturation stress as they confront the values, traditions, and behaviors of their new culture. . . .

One technique that instructors and supervisors can use with trainees in this early acculturation stage is to ask these questions: "What was the most counterintuitive, shocking, surprising, professional activity that you have learned about so far? What didn't you expect about being, or becoming, a professional psychologist?" When we have asked these questions in ethics courses and workshops, many trainees noted that they were unprepared for how quickly and how much their personal relationships changed. They noted that friends and family treated them as experts even before they had completed a single class. Others said they now felt constrained when they gave advice to friends because that advice could be misconstrued as therapy. Other facets of the profession that are surprising to students are the enormous responsibilities involved in helping people, the varying needs of different populations, and the challenge of reconciling the American Psychological Association's (2002) Ethics Code and the traditions of other cultural groups. Other students were not prepared for the obligation to help clients whom they would not choose to help as friends (e.g., perpetrators and the indigent).

Ethics Courses

Ethics courses present an excellent opportunity for students to explore their acculturation and to begin developing an ethical identity. It may be useful in such courses to have students engage in some reflection about their backgrounds, value traditions, and ethical cultures of origin, before or as they learn the relevant codes and discuss cases. Also, instructors may be more effective when they understand how their instruction fits within the values and skills of their students. One way to accomplish this may be to have trainees write an *ethics autobiography* in which they outline how they came to their present notion of what it means to be an ethical professional. . . .

A variation on the ethics autobiography could be *ethics ethnograms* or *genograms* (de las Fuentes et al., 2003), in which students explore the moral or professional orientation of their family members and other important people in their lives. Having a good sense of where they come from may help students understand and make good use of other class activities, such as studying case vignettes, narrative approaches, first-person accounts of clients, families, and professionals, and exploring the contextual and emotional factors that influence ethical behaviors (Knapp & Sturm, 2002).

Ethics autobiographies or genograms may also make it easier for students to understand that one's ordinary moral sense is not a sufficient basis for ethical behavior in many professional situations (Kitchener, 2000). . . . Understanding one's own implicit moral principles may make it easier to appreciate the philosophical principles behind ethics codes. Having students critique or debate the APA Ethics Code (see, e.g., Keith-Spiegel, 1994) may be an effective way to juxtapose principles from both cultures and thus move students toward integration. . . .

Practicum Supervision

As trainees progress from the classroom to their practicum placements, the acculturation tasks include putting their new ethical identities to the test in real situations. It may be important to prepare students for the types of dissonance that may occur and to encourage openness not only in the classroom but also in their ongoing supervision. Ethics instructors may have a difficult balancing act to perform. On the one hand, it might be useful to try to "immunize" students by warning them that people in complex real life situations do not always live up to their highest professional aspirations. On the other hand, this message may communicate to students that at least some level of ethically questionable activity is tolerated by professionals in positions of authority. Instructors and supervisors may want to reflect on how they first encountered this conflict and how they think about it now.

. . .

Supervisors who take some time to think through ethical problems aloud may help students appreciate how personal and professional principles influence the decision-making process (Knapp & Sturm, 2002). Trainees who practice such integration should become better at making ethical decisions themselves.

Practicum supervisors might want to create an environment in which ethical issues and choices can be discussed openly. Again, it may be useful to approach such discussions as acculturation tasks

rather than indications of ethical weakness or an ineffective ethics course.

. . .

Training Programs

Psychologists can strive to create an ethical culture for colleagues and trainees in academic departments and agencies. The development of an ethical orientation in psychology departments, like the development of a sense of community, is neither random nor accidental (Appleby, 2000). Faculty members who have reflected on their own acculturation appear most likely to be able to create an environment that facilitates an integrated acculturation strategy among their students.

. . .

In addition, departments can foster an ethical environment through rituals (ethics conferences, ethics awards), and the identification of ethical role models (e.g., those who have been especially generous in sharing their skills with less fortunate members of society) and ethical narratives (stories of the virtues that inspired or sustained excellent ethical achievements). Gardner et al. (2001) provided a good model for such an enterprise by looking at the "good work" done in genetics and journalism.

Trainees may experience acculturation stress that is due to a mismatch between the espoused and practiced values in the culture of some training programs. A strong sense of ethical principles and values may be eroded by events in the training program or by the personal behaviors of faculty that do not reflect the highest traditions of the profession. The literature documents unethical conduct in some training programs, ranging from asking teaching assistants to lecture without any preparation to professors and students engaging in sexual relationships with each other (Branstetter & Handelsman, 2000; Glaser & Thorpe, 1986; Hammel, Olkin, & Taube, 1996).

Continuing Acculturation

Development does not and should not end when a degree and a license are earned. As cultures change, the process of shifting values and virtues, and how to implement them, continues throughout one's professional life. . . .

Continuing education efforts can facilitate ongoing ethical acculturation.

CONCLUSION

. . .

The effectiveness of an acculturation model in facilitating ethical behavior is an empirical question. This approach could lead to fewer ethical infractions if the rules and principles are more firmly inculcated and embedded both within students' individual value systems and their professional networks. If so, students may feel less alienated and more likely to act appropriately on their knowledge of ethical principles and rules (cf. Bernard & Jara, 1986). Another prediction stemming from this approach is that students will be able to function better as independent ethical thinkers who are able to handle dilemmas that do not correspond so neatly to adherence to rules.

An acculturation model of ethics training may have more far-reaching results than lowering infractions. First, it could lead to excellent ethical behavior rather than simple rule adherence. Second, it could produce psychologists who are less alienated, better integrated, more professionally active (e.g., in terms of serving on ethics committees), more flexible in their responses to changing societal and professional conditions, and more capable of making greater contributions to society.

References

American Psychological Association. (2002). Ethical principles of psychologists and code of conduct. *American Psychologist, 57*, 1060–1073.

Appleby, D. (2000, November). Academic community building. *APA Monitor, 31*, 38–41.

Bernard, J. L., & Jara, C. S. (1986). The failure of clinical psychology graduate students to apply understood ethical principles. *Professional Psychology: Research and Practice, 17*, 313–315.

Berry, J. W. (1980). Acculturation as varieties of adaptation. In A. M. Padilla (Ed.), *Acculturation: Theory, models, and some new findings* (pp. 9–25). Boulder, CO: Westview Press.

Berry, J. W. (2003). Conceptual approaches to acculturation. In K. M. Chun, P. B. Organista, & G. Marin (Eds.), *Acculturation: Advances in theory, measurement, and applied research* (pp. 17–37). Washington, DC: American Psychological Association.

Berry, J. W., & Sam, D. L. (1997). Acculturation and adaptation. In J. W. Berry, M. H. Segall, & C. Kagitçibasi (Eds.), *Handbook of cross-cultural psychology* (pp. 291–326). Needham Heights, MA: Allyn & Bacon.

Branstetter, S. A., & Handelsman, M. M. (2000). Graduate teaching assistants: Ethical training, beliefs, and practices. *Ethics & Behavior, 10*, 27–50.

Competencies Conference 2002. (2002). *Future directions in education and credentialing in professional psychology*. Retrieved April 20, 2004, from http://www.appic.org/news/3_1_news_Competencies.htm

de las Fuentes, C., Willmuth, M. E., & Yarrow, C. (2003, August). Knowledge is not enough: Training for ethical competence. In N. J. Kaslow (Chair), *2002 Competencies Conference: Update and future directions*. Symposium conducted at the 111th Annual Convention of the American Psychological Association, Toronto, Ontario, Canada.

Gardner, H., Csikszentmihalyi, M., & Damon, W. (2001). *Good work: When excellence and ethics meet*. New York: Basic Books.

Glaser, R. D., & Thorpe, J. S. (1986). Unethical intimacy: A survey of sexual contact and advances between psychology educators and female graduate students. *American Psychologist, 41*, 43–51.

Hammel, G. A., Olkin, R., & Taube, D. O. (1996). Student-educator sex in clinical and counseling psychology doctoral training. *Professional Psychology: Research and Practice, 27*, 93–97.

Handelsman, M. M., Knapp, S., & Gottlieb, M. C. (2002). Positive ethics. In C. R. Snyder & S. J. Lopez (Eds.), *Handbook of positive psychology* (pp. 731–744). New York: Oxford University Press.

Keith-Spiegel, P. (Ed.). (1994). The 1992 Ethics Code: Boon or bane? [Special section]. *Professional Psychology: Research and Practice, 25*(4).

Knapp, S., & Sturm, C. (2002). Ethics education after licensing: Ideas for increasing diversity in content and process. *Ethics and Behavior, 12*, 157–166.

Robertson, I., & Downs, S. (1979). Learning and the prediction of performance: Development of trainability testing in the United Kingdom. *Journal of Applied Psychology, 64*, 42–50.

Competency Training in Ethics Education and Practice

Cynthia de las Fuentes, Mary E. Willmuth, and Catherine Yarrow

The 2002 Competencies Conference was held November 7–9, 2002, in Scottsdale, Arizona. The conference was hosted by the Association of Psychology Postdoctoral and Internship Centers in collaboration with cosponsors from Canada, Mexico, and the United States, including boards, committees, and divisions of the American Psychological Association (APA); education and training groups; credentialing and regulatory bodies; and ethnic minority psychology organizations. . . . The working group in which we participated was charged with addressing the identification, training, and assessment of the development of competence in ethics, legal, public policy, advocacy, and professional issues. Group members spent most of their time discussing training and assessment of competence in ethics. This article presents an overview of the working group's product, enhanced by relevant literature and organized to address (a) the identification of core components of competence in ethics; (b) the critical educational and training experiences needed to develop the knowledge, skills, and attitudes to become a competent ethical psychologist; and (c) the assessment of ethics competency.

IDENTIFICATION OF CORE COMPONENTS OF COMPETENCE IN ETHICS

. . . [T]here was unanimous agreement on the following core components of competence in ethics. Through lively and collegial discussions and debate and the sharing of instructional models and practices, the working group came to a consensus that psychologists and psychologists in training need knowledge and skills for ethical decision making and intervention, including the following abilities:

1. to appraise and adopt or adapt one's own ethical decision-making model and apply it with personal integrity and cultural competence in all aspects of their professional activities;

2. to recognize ethical and legal dilemmas in the course of their professional activities (including the ability to determine whether a dilemma exists through research and consultation);
3. to recognize and reconcile conflicts among relevant codes and laws and to deal with convergence, divergence, and ambiguity; and
4. to raise and resolve ethical and legal issues appropriately.

. . .

The above summarized core components of ethics competency were considered by the working group to be the foundation of ethics education and were discussed as neither sequential in development nor discrete, but as overlapping and essential throughout the professional life of the psychologist.

. . .

GATEKEEPING: PROGRAM RESPONSIBILITIES IN THE SELECTION AND ADJUDICATION OF TRAINEES

Of course, ethics training programs are designed to affect the ethical decision making and behaviors of psychologists and psychologists in training; however, it is naive to assume that training programs can develop a specific moral character in its students, given all of the variables involved in creating moral behavior. Therefore, a comprehensive ethics education program obligates itself to (a) appropriately select candidates whose psychological fitness and moral character are not likely to interfere in their abilities to deliver competent and ethical psychological services and, once students are admitted into a training program, (b) monitor their capacity to process ethical and moral issues and dilemmas cognitively, affectively, and behaviorally. It was the consensus of the working group that training programs and the faculty in them have a responsibility to evaluate

From *Professional Psychology: Research and Practice, 36,* 362–366. Copyright 2005 by the American Psychological Association.

a student's personal and professional competence to practice in the service of protecting the public, the student body, and the profession. Indeed, the APA (2002) code of ethics clearly states that applicants and students may be compelled to disclose elements of their history (those bearing on character and fitness; Johnson & Campbell, 2004)

> if the information is necessary to evaluate or obtain assistance for students whose personal problems could reasonably be judged to be preventing them from performing their training- or professionally related activities in a competent manner or posing a threat to the students or others. (APA, 2002, Section 7.04, pp. 1068–1069)

Additionally, the working group members agreed that programs should develop an ethical training program that includes clear communications about expected conduct, remediation for professionally inappropriate or unethical behavior, termination from the course of study if a remediation plan is not followed or not a viable option (as in the case of impairment or egregious unethical or incompetent behavior), and due process and rights to appeal decisions regarding a change of their status in the training program (see also APA, 2002, Section 7.02: Descriptions of Education and Training Programs). We felt strongly that training programs become emboldened regarding the evaluation and dismissal (if necessary) of students whose conduct, character, or capacity demonstrates an inability to competently and ethically serve the public.

MILIEU AND MODELING

Working group members recalled and discussed many instances from their own training or programs in which ethical standards were required of trainees but not of administrators or educators. Because the most adjudicated offense in psychology is unethical sexual relationships between male therapists and female clients, what attitudes and behaviors are being modeled by psychology faculty who engage in unethical multiple relationships with their students? If people act morally because others have modeled

moral behaviors (Rest, 1983), could not the reverse be true? Can what is taught in the classroom be contradicted by faculty-student relationships outside of the classroom? Are we, as trainers and educators, modeling attitudes and behaviors that imply acceptance of multiple relationships with clients, supervisees, students, research participants, subordinates, and others in positions of lesser power? Kitchener (1992) lamented that "silence best characterizes the discussion of the ethical responsibilities of faculty members toward students in higher education in general and psychology education in particular" (p. 190) and argued that the ethical principles should be the foundation of ethics education in psychology.

. . . The working group members believed that teaching ethical concepts and prohibitions, although essential and generally occurring during most training programs, is not sufficient and does not necessarily translate into ethical behavior. A comprehensive ethics training program includes (a) a living self-reflective application of ethical principles in the training environment demonstrated and modeled for trainees in order for it to become an enduring part of their professional identity and (b) a training that focuses not only on the therapeutic environment but also on the social and cultural contexts within which training occurs (Housman & Stake, 1999).

TRAINING FOR ETHICS COMPETENCE

. . .

The working group discussed our belief that multicultural issues often did not receive the consideration necessary in teaching of ethical behavior and practice. We noted that our ethical codes and ethical practice have evolved in a cultural context and with multicultural influences. We felt that it is essential that all training programs in ethics address the APA's published guidelines on multicultural practice; therapy with gay, lesbian, and bisexual individuals; and therapy with women, in addition to others.

The working group members agreed that training in ethical issues should be infused throughout the training curricula. Although the members agreed that training should be progressive in consideration of trainees' professional development, there was no consensus on a specific sequence for training. The following developmental sequence provides an outline of a set of skills and content areas that programs may consider as they train for ethical competence. The skill sets described below address content and process areas reflecting progressive levels of training.

Beginning students must be able to demonstrate awareness, knowledge, and skills of the following content areas: the development of moral reasoning and moral behavior; values and beliefs as emerging from cultural contexts; ethical codes and practice guidelines; ethical principles, virtues, and orientations; and relevant case law. Beginning students must also be able to demonstrate the following processes skills: the ability to explore one's own moral and ethical values and attitudes, interpersonal skills of flexibility, openness to new ideas and change, nondefensiveness to feedback, and awareness and appreciation of differences in moral and ethical values across cultures.

Teaching Moral Reasoning and Moral Behavior

Ethical behaviors have been seen as arising from several origins, one of which is morals. Although empirical studies have been published that offer a curriculum or model for teaching new professionals how to avoid or address ethically problematic behavior, many authors (e.g., Fly, van Bark, Weinman, Kitchener, & Lang, 1997; Welfel & Kitchener, 1992) have suggested that Rest's (1983, 1986) work provides some guidance. Rest's four stage model of ethical decision making consists of (a) recognition of a moral dilemma and related emotional response, (b) a cognitive understanding of the moral issues involved, (c) a moral course of action that is decided on, and (d) an appropriate ethical behavioral response that is carried out. Fly et al. (1997) suggested that ethics curricula that address all of these stages may be more efficacious in facilitating the ethical development of graduate students as they learn how to avoid ethical transgressions and produce ethical behaviors.

. . .

Ethical Principles and Virtues

An example of principle ethics in psychology was described in Kitchener's (1984) two-level theory of ethical decision making. Kitchener proposed that

Beauchamp and Childress's (1983) five principles (autonomy, nonmalfeasance, beneficence, justice, and fidelity) make up the basis for the critical evaluation of ethical justification in the context of counseling and psychology. Instructors might consider discussing how the above principles have influenced the evolution of APA's (2002) general principles of beneficence and nonmaleficence, fidelity and responsibility, integrity, justice, and respect for people's rights and dignity.

Virtue ethics focus on the character of the individual rather than on the solution to a particular ethical dilemma. According to Meara, Schmidt, and Day (1996), the unique characteristics of virtue ethics is the identification of the motivation, emotion, character, ideals, and moral habits of a person who functions in the traditions and practices of a culture, group, or community. As ethics educators, we should demonstrate to our students that psychologists are informed by both virtues and principles in our professional practice.

. . .

. . . The working group members discussed that psychologists are lifelong learners and as a result they join or form peer networks and consultation-study groups in which they receive and provide consultation and feedback on the competent and ethical delivery of services they provide. To encourage and facilitate this process, those jurisdictions not already doing so should be encouraged to consider providing continuing education credit for participation in peer consultation-study groups. These continuing education practices encourage discussion of the scientific bases of decision making in practice and may make it more likely that a psychologist will access appropriate consultation when confronting an ethical dilemma. In addition, psychologists take advantage of the numerous formal continuing education opportunities available that address the continued development and maintenance of their skills and ethical practice. . . .

ASSESSMENT OF COMPETENCE IN ETHICS

. . .

The working group members thought that multimodal methods of assessment were necessary to ensure that trainees develop ethical practice skills.

Suggestions for modes of assessment included the following methods:

1. Assess for ethical integrity in every course throughout training including monitoring plagiarism, falsification of data, and misrepresentation of one's work or contribution (e.g., in the case of group projects) as these are all reflective of dishonest attitudes and behavior.

2. Assess for ethical competence in clinical training, including violations of confidentiality, sexual and nonsexual boundary violations, compromising the welfare of a client, distortion of information provided to supervisors, and procedural breaches with ethical or legal implications as these transgressions can have harmful effects on clients and reflect a failure to understand or abide by the core ethical values of the profession.

3. Assessments can also be made by the use of a 360°-type of evaluation whereby everyone in the training environment (i.e., peers, support staff, administration, faculty, supervisors, and clients) can evaluate and provide feedback to students and the program regarding students' interpersonal and ethical competence. . . .

4. Assess how trainees respond to actual ethical dilemmas through the use of critical incident methodology. Such a methodology makes note of the processes by which a trainee has (or has not) recognized an ethical or legal dilemma, used (or did not use) consultation and supervision, used appropriate (or inappropriate) cultural and contextual sensitivity, and addressed (or did not address) the matter in an ethical manner. The working group members thought that this approach could be conducted in a transparent, public, and sensitive manner so that all relevant parties can contribute to the discussion and learn from the training moment.

. . .

CONCLUSION

We conclude with a quote from educator and ethicist Melba Vasquez (1992) who wrote "Professionals concerned with the problems of unethical behavior believe that the strongest weapon against professional misconduct may be the education of trainees" (p. 196). The working group underscored this belief and has offered a variety of ways by which ethics education may be improved and the standing of our profession and protection of consumers of psychological services enhanced.

References

American Psychological Association. (2002). Ethical principles of psychologists and code of conduct. *American Psychologist, 57,* 1060–1073.

Beauchamp, T. L., & Childress, J. F. (1983). *Principles of biomedical ethics* (2nd ed.). Oxford, England: Oxford University Press.

Fly, B. J., van Bark, W. P., Weinman, L., Kitchener, K. S., & Lang, P. R. (1997). Ethical transgressions of psychology graduate students: Critical incidents with implications for training. *Professional Psychology: Research and Practice, 28,* 492–495.

Housman, L. M., & Stake, J. E. (1999). The current state of sexual ethics training in clinical psychology: Issues of quantity, quality, and effectiveness. *Professional Psychology: Research and Practice, 30,* 302–311.

Johnson, W. B., & Campbell, C. D. (2004). Character and fitness requirements for professional psychologists: Training directors' perspectives. *Professional Psychology: Research and Practice, 35,* 405–411.

Kitchener, K. S. (1992). Psychologist as teacher and mentor: Affirming ethical values throughout the curriculum. *Professional Psychology: Research and Practice, 23,* 190–195.

Meara, N. M., Schmidt, L. D., & Day, J. D. (1996). Principles and virtues: A foundation for ethical decisions, policies, and character. *The Counseling Psychologist, 24,* 4–77.

Rest, J. R. (1983). Morality. In P. Mussen (Series Ed.) & J. Flavell & E. Markham (Vol. Eds.), *Handbook of child psychology: Vol. 3. Cognitive development* (pp. 556–629). New York: Wiley.

Rest, J. R. (1986). *Moral development: Advances in research and theory.* New York: Praeger.

Vasquez, M. J. T. (1992). Psychologist as clinical supervisor: Promoting ethical practice. *Professional Psychology: Research and Practice, 23,* 196–202.

Welfel, E. R., & Kitchener, K. S. (1992). Introduction to the special section: Ethics education—An agenda for the '90s. *Professional Psychology: Research and Practice, 23,* 179–181.

An Historical Overview of Basic Approaches and Issues in Ethical and Moral Philosophy and Principles: A Foundation for Understanding Ethics in Psychology

Joanne E. Callan and Megan E. Callan

ETHICS THEORIES AND SYSTEMS: PAST AND PRESENT

. . .

Modern and Western Ethical Thought

Modern ethics and moral philosophy, especially in the Western world, have evolved considerably from Greek as well as medieval and Renaissance teachings. In the composite, they are quite diverse and complex. . . .

. . . Among major approaches to ethical inquiry emerging in the 300 to 400 years since the end of the Renaissance in the sixteenth century are those developed or expanded by several well-known theorists, whose works appeared prior to the twentieth century, including Kant, Bentham, and Mills. Following annotations of their contributions to ethics theories are those of more contemporary thinkers.

Immanuel Kant's deontological ethics judge the rightness of an action not only on external factors but on the action itself. In *Groundwork of the Metaphysics of Morals,* Kant (1948) challenged the notion that "action can only be right because it produces good" (Schneewind, 1993, p. 150). He emphasized freedom as essential in any action and individual autonomy as crucial to right actions: "The sole way in which we can be free . . . is if our actions are determined by something within our nature. Before we can know what is good, we must determine what is right" (Schneewind, 1993, p. 151). The central question for Kant is "what ought I to do?" (O'Neill, 1993, p. 175). His writings focus on identifying "the maxims, or fundamental principles of action, that we ought to adopt" (p. 176) and stress the compelling obligations or duty to act in accord with these maxims.

Kant's overarching principle, which he identified as the Categorical Imperative or Universal Law, was that ethics must serve for all (i.e., they must be universal in nature and application). Moreover, the Categorical Imperative prescribes what individuals ought to do without reference to consequence. According to Kant, one should act with regard to only those maxims that would appropriately make universal law. Another Kantian principle emphasized respect for self and others. Arguing against indifference, Kant said: "failure to treat others or oneself as ends is once again seen as a failure of virtue or imperfect obligation" (cited in O'Neill, 1993, p. 179).

Jeremy Bentham (1748–1832), known as the architect of modern Utilitarianism, presented as his major contribution the view that ordinary people can get adequate guidance for action by consciously applying abstract moral principles. His work was complemented by that of John Stuart Mill (1806–1873), and, together, they are viewed as developing the "first detailed and systematic formulation" of Utilitarianism (Arras & Steinbock, 1995, p. 9). Their ethics relied on the principle of utility, or the "greatest happiness" principle, which stated that actions are right in proportion as they tend to promote happiness, and wrong as they tend to produce unhappiness. . . .

Utilitarian as focus on the consequence of actions, choosing between actions on the basis of the outcome that produces the greater happiness; thus, theirs is known as the consequentialist theory or a teleological one (from the Greek *telos* meaning 'end'). . . .

. . .

Although Utilitarian thinking continues to influence ethics and moral philosophy, Arras and

Steinbock (1995) pointed out four objections to it: (1) the value or claim that happiness is the greatest good; (2) the requirement to calculate the probable consequence of every action (since, as these authors point out, such a task is impossible); (3) the responsibility assigned (i.e., that who is responsible is as, or more, important than what the outcome is); and (4) its inadequacy as a theory, given its conflict with some basic moral intuitions or beliefs.

Contemporary Theories

Meta-Ethics. The meta-ethicists, who contributed greatly to the field of ethics from 1930 into the 1970s (Edel, 1987), returned to the study of moral principles. John Rawls, in his influential book *A Theory of Justice* (1971), emphasized principles of right action. Arguing that the right is prior to the good, he assumed a pro-Kantian view against Utilitarianism. Maintaining that a moral person must be guided by a sense of justice, he saw moral feelings as normal and necessary for the development of rules (Wilson, 1993). Although he advocated considering the welfare of the deprived or disadvantaged as well as that of the majority, he wrote that, since the issues are so complex, justice can only be achieved through some kind of contractual agreement on how the basic societal institutions are to be structured. . . .

Ethics of care. More and more, since the 1970s ethics theories and writings have focused on social and political problems rather than on individual autonomy (Battin & Francis, 1988; Edel, 1987; Schneewind, 1993). Several recent developments in ethics thinking reflect this departure from liberal individualism, one of which is the emergence of the *ethics of care.* Indeed, some view today's ethics as being either (a) based theoretically on principles or (b) related to the ethics of care.

Beauchamp and Childress (1994) point to the emphasis in the ethics of care on traits valued in intimate personal relationships, among them sympathy, compassion, fidelity, discernment, and love. They explain that caring refers to "care for, emotional commitment to, and willingness to act on behalf of persons with whom one has a significant relationship" (p. 85), and they noted that "the care ethic provides a needed corrective to two centuries of system-building in ethical theory and to the tendency to

neglect themes such as sympathy, the moral emotions, and women's experiences" (p. 92). These authors also pointed out that, whereas traditional moral theory has focused on matters such as whether to lie or break confidentiality, the ethics of care stresses more "how actions are performed, which motives underlie them, and whether positive relationships are promoted or thwarted" (p. 86) than the actual decision made. Adson (1995) has described operative virtues imperative in ethical behaviors among healing professionals.

Feminist ethics. Congruent with the ethics of care has been the focus of recent moral thinking on concerns for underserved or less protected populations (e.g., minority groups). New approaches for understanding ethics have developed even for majority groups whose needs and issues had not been previously explored; for example, the development of ethics related to women, which received impetus from the feminist movement emerging in the 1960s. Since the sixties, with this impetus from the feminist movement, a number of theorists have contributed to the understanding of ethics regarding women's lives and experiences. Works such as the seminal thinking of Carol Gilligan (1982) raised awareness among ethicists and also among those interested in women's issues and female development about the possible, or actual, differences between how men approach moral issues and how women do. Subsequently, various philosophical approaches to the understanding of ethics as related to women have evolved; based on them, an array of feminist theories have developed. . . .

Applied ethics. Applied ethics has come into its own in the last few decades, with an emphasis on ethics related to professions, business communities, and other systems or venues including public policy. . . .

DEVELOPMENT OF PROFESSIONAL ETHICS

The preceding historical overview notes the common threads as well as differences emerging during this development. It relates the contributions of various earlier systems to current Western ethics and moral thinking as they have developed in the last 300 to 400 years. This brief history underscores the centrality of each civilization's view of humanity and the world with respect to how each has determined moral and ethical thinking (i.e., to how each has viewed right and wrong). Whereas absolutists, for example, view behaviors generally seen as bad or negative (e.g., lying, stealing, and killing) as never justifiable, relativists point to the meaning of a behavior, emphasizing the intention behind it. Generally, as noted above, ethics have been viewed by people as ways of behaving in accord with acceptable standards. As ethics thinking has developed, these ways of behaving and the standards that underlie them have become incorporated as basic principles into ethics theories.

Just as societies have produced their own ethical systems over the years, there has been in this century a developing interest among professions regarding ethics. Increased attention to applied ethics in the last several decades has contributed to the growing emphasis among the various professions in the Western world about ethics, which has led to the development of ethical principles or standards and ethical codes (although it is the case that some professions had begun such work early in the twentieth century). Professional ethics, then, is applied ethics developed to guide ethical behaviors or conduct within professions.

Most professions have now identified ethics principles and guidelines as important. Indeed, a profession's development and also its observance of an ethics code are seen currently as indicators of its having achieved a certain level of maturity. Not only are members of the profession guided by their code, and the next generation of professionals educated and trained by using the code to prepare for future professional activities, ethical codes also serve to inform the public on what they may expect regarding appropriate behavior from professionals. Health care ethics, for example, relies on fundamental principles to guide health care professionals with

regard to what is right and what is wrong. Beauchamp and Childress (1994) have identified four clusters of such basic principles: respect for autonomy, non-maleficence, beneficence, and justice. Edge and Groves (1994) identify seven basic principles of biomedical ethics: autonomy, veracity, beneficence, non-maleficence, confidentiality, justice, and role fidelity.

References

Adson, M. A. (1995). An endangered ethic: The capacity for caring. *Mayo Clinic Proceedings, 70,* 495–500.

Arras, J. D., & Steinbock, B. (1995). *Ethical issues in modern medicine.* Mountain View, CA: Mayfield Publishing.

Battin, M. P., & Francis, L. P. (1988). Foreword. In D. M. Rosenthal & F. Shehad (Eds.), *Applied ethics and ethical theory* (pp. vii–viii). Salt Lake City: University of Utah Press.

Baeuchamp, T., & Childress, J. F. (1994). *The principle of biomedical ethics* (4th ed.). New York: Oxford University Press.

Edel, A. (1987). Ethics applied or conduct enlightened? In J. Howie (Ed.), *Ethical principles and practices* (pp. 24–48). Carbondale: Southern Illinois University Press.

Edge, R. S., & Groves, J. R. (1994). *The ethics of health care: A guide for clinical practice.* Albany, NY: Delmar.

Gilligan, C. (1982). *In a different voice.* Cambridge, MA: Harvard University Press.

Kant, I. (1948). *Groundwork of the metaphysics of morals* (H. J. Paton, Trans.). London: Hutchinson. (Original work published 1785)

O'Neill, O. (1993). Kantian ethics. In P. Singer (Ed.), *A companion to ethics* (pp. 175–185). Cambridge, MA: Basil Blackwell.

Rawls, J. (1971). *A theory of justice.* Cambridge, MA: Harvard University Press.

Schneewind, J. B. (1993). Modern moral philosophy. In P. Singer (Ed.), *A companion to ethics* (pp. 147–157). Cambridge, MA: Basil Blackwell.

Wilson, J. Q. (1993). *The moral sense.* New York: The Free Press.

A Principle-Based Analysis of the 2002 American Psychological Association Ethics Code

Samuel Knapp and Leon VandeCreek

. . .

In this article, we review the enforceable standards of the 2002 APA [American Psychological Association] Ethics Code from the standpoint of principle-based or prima facie ethics. We adopt the position that all the enforceable standards of the Ethics Code should be based upon or linked to some ethical theory, such as principle-based ethics (Ross, 1930/1998).

. . .

Understanding the moral foundations of the Ethics Code is more than an academic exercise; it also has practical implications. Psychologists will be better able to learn the Ethics Code, appreciate its value, and interpret its provisions if they see a connection between the Ethics Code and their intuitive moral sense (Handelsman, Knapp, & Gottlieb, 2002). . . .

[U]nderstanding the moral principles will help professional psychologists to know how to apply the ethical standards in ambiguous situations. Some of the standards of the Ethics Code use the terms "reasonable" or "appropriate" when describing the responsibilities of psychologists. Standards using those or similar qualifiers require psychologists to use their professional judgment and discretion in determining how to fulfill their obligations. Ideally, those decisions will be informed or anchored upon the same moral principles that form the basis of the Ethics Code. Professional psychologists who understand the moral principles behind the Ethics Code will have criteria by which to determine whether their actions are reasonable or appropriate.

. . .

PRINCIPLE-BASED ETHICS

Oxford philosopher Sir William David Ross (1877–1940) developed principle-based or prima facie ethics. Ross (1930/1998) tried to address the shortcomings found in both utilitarian and deontological (Kantian) theories. . . .

. . .

According to Ross (1930/1998), the best ethical theory rests on several, not one, moral principles. Ross referred to these principles as prima facie duties, meaning an obligation that holds unless it is overridden by a superior obligation. Some of these moral duties, according to Ross, are fidelity, gratitude, justice, beneficence, self-improvement, and nonmaleficence. . . .

Ross (1930/1998) allowed that future reflection may result in a different or better list or classification of prima facie duties. Current theorists who apply principle-based ethics to health care do not necessarily agree on the optimal manner to define or categorize these principles. Four moral principles that are especially important in the field of biomedical ethics (respect for patient autonomy, nonmaleficence, beneficence, and justice) have been identified by Beauchamp and Childress (2001). In addition, Kitchener (1984) and Bersoff and Koeppl (1993) have added fidelity as a fifth core moral principle applicable to psychologists. In this article, we identify a sixth moral obligation (generalized beneficence) that corresponds closely to "responsibility to society" found in the ethics code of the Canadian Psychological Association (Canadian Psychological Association, 1991). Furthermore, this sixth moral obligation can be inferred from the General Principles of the APA Ethics Code, which encourage psychologists to be

From *Psychotherapy: Theory, Research, Practice, Training, 41,* 247–254. Copyright 2004 by the Educational Publishing Foundation.

135

"aware of their professional and scientific responsibilities to society," show concern "about the ethical compliance of their colleagues' scientific and professional conduct," and "contribute to a portion of their professional time for little or no compensation or personal advantage" (Principle B).

. . .

Beneficence

According to Ross (1930/1998), beneficence means that "there are other beings in the world whose condition we can make better" (p. 269). Beneficence means promoting the welfare of others. As applied to health care, it means promoting physical or psychological health. "Morality requires not only that we treat people autonomously and refrain from harming them, but also that we contribute to their welfare" (Beauchamp & Childress, 2001, p. 165). Psychologists have a positive obligation to help clients/patients by selecting and conscientiously implementing appropriate services for them. The principle of beneficence can be seen numerous times in the 2002 APA Ethics Code, such as in the standard that requires all psychologists to be competent (Standard 2.01).

Nonmaleficence

"Nonmaleficence asserts an obligation not to inflict harm on others" (Beauchamp & Childress, 2001, p. 113). Psychologists strive toward nonmaleficence when they take care to do no harm. Although this moral principle is often remembered through the phrase *primum non nocere (above all, do no harm)*, nothing in principle-based ethics of Ross's (1930/1998) writing suggests that this moral principle automatically trumps or takes priority over other moral principles. Given the right set of circumstances, another moral principle may trump nonmaleficence.

. . . Nonmaleficence can be found in several standards in the 2002 APA Ethics Code, such as in Standard 3.04, which instructs psychologists to avoid harming those with whom they work.

Justice

The word *justice* can have different meanings for different people. However, we are using the definition of justice as found in the literature on principle-based

ethics. According to Beauchamp and Childress (2001), one meaning of *justice* (i.e., *distributive justice*) "refers to the fair, equitable, and appropriate distribution [of services] determined by norms that structure the terms of social cooperation" (p. 226). The goal of distributive justice is found in the General Principle D of the APA Ethics Code ("Psychologists recognize that fairness and justice entitle all persons to access to and benefit from the contributions of psychology"; APA, 2002). Although it may be laudable for psychologists to work for distributive justice, the failure to do so is not an ethical violation under the APA Ethics Code.

However, justice may also refer to fair or equal treatment or due process when accused of an offense (*procedural justice*). Those aspects of justice also are found in the APA Ethics Code. For example, psychologists have an obligation to treat all individuals fairly, manifested in such obligations as refraining from discrimination against persons because of race, religion, national background, sexual orientation, or other factors listed (Standard 3.01).

Respect for Client/Patient Autonomy

Respect for autonomy means respecting the freedom of others to do as they choose as long as their choices do not restrict or limit the rights of others. "Personal autonomy is, at the minimum, self-rule that is free from both controlling interference by others and from limitations, such as inadequate understanding, that prevent meaningful choice" (Beauchamp & Childress, 2001, p. 58). To the extent possible, psychologists should treat clients/patients as autonomous and independent agents who can participate as full partners in determining treatment goals and methods. Respect for client/patient autonomy can be seen in Standards 3.10 and 10.01, which require psychologists to get the informed consent of their clients/patients.

. . .

Fidelity

The principle of fidelity means that psychologists are faithful to their obligation to serve their clients/patients. They keep promises, tell the truth, and honor their obligations.

The issue of fidelity seems especially critical in psychology because issues like truthfulness and loyalty are basic to trust. While trust is vital to all human relationships, it is particularly vital to client–counselor, researcher–participant, supervisor–supervisee, and consultant–consultee relationships (Kitchener, 1984, p. 51).

Fidelity can also be manifested when psychologists protect client/patient confidentiality (Standard 4.01) and use accurate informed consent procedures (Standard 3.10 and elsewhere).

General Beneficence

Responsibility to the public at large, citizenship, or general beneficence is a sixth moral principle. According to this principle, "psychologists . . . have responsibilities to the societies in which they live and work, such as the neighborhood or city, and to the welfare of all human beings in those societies" (Principle IV: Responsibility to Society; Canadian Psychological Association, 1991). For example, psychologists have a responsibility to act to protect future consumers of psychological services by protecting the integrity of psychological tests (Standards 9.04 and 9.11). In another example, psychologists have a responsibility to act to protect the public when they learn of a psychologist who has committed an ethical violation, subject to certain limitations, such as the need to protect any confidentiality rights involved (Standards 1.04 and 1.05).

. . .

BALANCING MORAL PRINCIPLES

. . . [S]ome of the Standards in the Ethics Code are not based on a single moral principle but are rather derived from balancing two or more moral principles. Consequently, it is necessary to describe how principle-based ethicists (such as Beauchamp and Childress) would balance moral principles. According to principle-based ethics, moral principles are not absolute guides to human behavior and may be superseded by other moral principles in some situations. A prima facie obligation holds unless other obligations override it. According to Ross (1930/1988),

> When I am in a situation . . . in which more than one of these prima facie duties is incumbent on me, what I have

to do is to study the situation as fully as I can until I form the considered opinion (it is never more) that in the circumstances one of them is more incumbent than any other. (p. 268)

Beauchamp and Childress (2001) noted that when a moral principle is overridden, "the infringement selected must be the least possible infringement, commensurate with achieving the primary goal of the action" and "the agent must seek to minimize the negative effects of the infringement" (p. 20).

For example, the informed-consent standards in the APA Ethics Code are based upon the moral obligation to respect client/patient autonomy. Standard 3.10 requires that psychologists receive informed consent from all individuals receiving services. As it applies to psychological assessments, these informed-consent obligations are further amplified in Standard 6.04 (relating to information about fees). However, Standard 9.03a lists several exceptions to the informed-consent requirement for assessments, such as when the purpose of the evaluation is to assess the decisional capacity of the individual being assessed.

The Ethics Code recognizes that respect for client/patient autonomy was not absolute and may sometimes be overridden by beneficence, or the need to act on behalf of the welfare of the client/patient who appears incapable of giving consent. Nonetheless, the Ethics Code suggests that psychologists try to minimize the harm caused by the violation of client/patient autonomy in assessments, and psychologists make some effort to explain the nature of the evaluation in reasonably understandable language (Standard 9.03b).

References

Beauchamp, T., & Childress, J. (2001). *Principles of biomedical ethics* (5th ed.). New York: Oxford University Press.

Bersoff, D., & Koeppl, T. (1993). The relation between ethical codes and moral principles. *Ethics & Behavior, 3*, 345–357.

Canadian Psychological Association. (1991). *Canadian code of ethics for psychologists* (Rev. ed.). Ottawa, Canada: Author.

Handelsman, M., Knapp, S., & Gottlieb, M. (2002). Positive ethics. In C. R. Snyder & S. Lopez (Eds.), *Handbook of positive psychology* (pp. 731–744). New York: Oxford University Press.

Kitchener, K. S. (1984). Intuition, critical evaluation and ethical principles: The foundation of ethical decisions in counseling psychology. *The Counseling Psychologist, 12,* 43–55.

Ross, W. D. (1998). The right and the good. In J. Rachels (Ed.), *Ethical theory* (pp. 265–285). New York: Oxford University Press. (Original work published 1930)

◆　　◆　　◆

Commentary: As did Knapp and VandeCreek with the 2002 Code, after the 1992 Code was published, a coauthor and I attempted to discern to what extent its provisions adopted and implemented the prima facie *duties described in this chapter. See Bersoff, D. N., & Koeppl, P. M. (1993). The relation between ethical codes and moral principles.* Ethics & Behavior, 3, *345–357. We concluded that each of these duties had been translated into some form in the Code. We also concluded, however, that the Code contained very few moral absolutes or deontological provisions. This was especially true with regard to autonomy.*

When it comes to autonomy the [1992] Code . . . is clearly teleological and utilitarian in its approach, consistently balancing autonomy against other interests. This is particularly true when psychologists view autonomy as antagonistic to their perception of their client's best interests; when they believe there are higher values, such as safety of the public that must be satisfied; or when organizational demands conflict with autonomy. (p. 352)

As readers review the 2002 Code, to what extent are the prima facie *values represented, other than in the nonenforceable General Principles? Does our view concerning autonomy still ring true or has it been given greater prominence in the 2002 Code?*

Although most authors stress the importance of employing principle ethics in attempting to resolve ethical conflicts, as the next excerpt indicates, there are competing analyses.

Ethics and the Professional Practice of Psychologists: The Role of Virtues and Principles

Augustus E. Jordan and Naomi M. Meara

Currently, the teaching and practice of ethics in professional psychology tend to focus on the application of ethical principles to situations involving dilemmas. These dilemmas take a variety of forms, but they typically emphasize the competing rights and claims of clients or institutions and the related responsibilities faced by service providers . . . However, philosophical and practical limitations to this approach have been identified. We review some of these limitations and identify an additional approach to ethical analysis called virtue ethics. Our analysis of virtue ethics suggests that this approach offers a supplement to the application of ethical principles in dilemmas. . . .

We believe that the difference between this focus on what we call *principle ethics* (i.e., approaches that emphasize the use of rational, objective, universal, and impartial principles in the ethical analysis of dilemmas) and *virtue ethics* (i.e., characterized by an emphasis on historical virtues) is significant and could have implications for the professional development and practice of psychologists. For example, ethical systems that emphasize universally or prima facie valid principles tend to become salient in the presence of dilemmatic situations and tend to claim objective independence from the people involved. In contrast, virtue ethics focus on the historically formed character of identifiable persons; such character development provides the basis for professional judgment. In addition, principle ethics typically focus on acts and choices. Through the application of what are taken to be objective, rational standards, rules, or codes, they attempt to answer the question "What shall I do?" Virtues, on the other hand, emphasize agents or actors. Through the formation of internal qualities, traits, or mature

habits, virtue ethics attempt to answer the question "Who shall I be?"

. . .

THE LIMITATIONS OF ETHICAL PRINCIPLES AND DILEMMAS

The form of ethics currently reigning as the "paradigmatic center of moral reflection" (Hauerwas, 1981, p. 114) in medical, psychological, and religious contexts is that of principle ethics . . . The prevalent pedagogy of this approach is the evaluation of competing prima facie valid principles in the context of significant quandaries or dilemmas (Beauchamp & Childress, 1983). . . .

All in all, however, the primary content or subject matter of these approaches involves dilemmas cast in the form of brief case histories that typically highlight a significant conflict between the perceived rights, demands, duties, or obligations of several individuals or groups, agencies, or institutions. Such an approach has led some to call this type of ethical discourse *quandary ethics* or *decisionism* (McClendon, 1974; Pincoffs, 1971). The methodology is to sort through the principles involved and then evaluate the actions taken by participants in the case or articulate what actions are appropriate on the basis of relevant but competing principles, or both (Beauchamp & Childress, 1983; Callahan, 1988). . . .

However, others have suggested that principle ethics may be too narrow a characterization of what it means to be engaged in ethical discourse (Dykstra, 1981; Kilpatrick, 1986; Pincoffs, 1971) and thus may be professionally limiting (May, 1984). A narrowing of focus on problem solving in an atmosphere of reasoned deliberation could limit the relevant contextual

From *Professional Psychology: Research and Practice*, 21, 107–114. Copyright 1990 by the American Psychological Association. Table 1 has been omitted.

and methodological resources of the professional psychologist. For instance, Kilpatrick (1986) suggested that "even handed, dispassionate discussion of values . . . may habituate students to the notion that moral questions are merely intellectual problems rather than human problems that naturally call up strong emotion" (p. 189) . . . When this happens, case studies risk becoming primarily abstract thought puzzles to be analyzed according to specified rules. Other critical psychological dimensions, such as human pain, pathos, and historical particularity, tend to be underestimated or forgotten. . . .

. . . By definition, ethical principles seek grounding in a universal context freed from individual bias, and yet the definitive nature of quandaries places principles in direct conflict with each other. . . . To solve this dilemma, appeal must be made to a fundamental moral principle supported by one's moral theory (Steininger et al., 1984). However, different solutions may be achieved, depending on whether one is a utilitarian who emphasizes the public good or a deontologist who advocates a duty to "above all, do no harm" (Jonsen, 1977). Even within a given theoretical orientation, there may exist disagreement regarding the relative weight of competing principles. As Drane (1982) reported, "There is no evident way to determine which principles should take precedence over which others. In such painful dilemmas the psychotherapist simply does the best he (or she) can" (p. 37). The empirical result is that universal principles, as well as their overarching theories, come to be applied idiosyncratically. . . .

. . . As professional psychologists migrate with increasing frequency into large industrial and health maintenance organizations, the likelihood of conflicting principles increases. Professionals, the clients whom they serve, and the service organizations that they create risk becoming hostage to the reasoned, principle based, but potentially controversial choices of these organizations (Eyde & Quaintance, 1988; May, 1984).

VIRTUES AND THE HISTORY OF MORAL DISCOURSE

. . . In contrast to principles, virtues historically have been viewed neither as situation specific nor as uni-versal maxims but rather as character and community specific. Thus they are nurtured habits grown mature in the context of a formative community and a shared set of purpose and assumptions. This process begins in the community of one's childhood and continues throughout life. Professional training and practice introduce new contexts and communities wherein professional virtues can be articulated and nurtured by students and professionals. People socialize one another into a professional culture that they continually construct and shape and from which they seek inspiration and support. As time passes, certain shared assumptions and values are "taken for granted" and form the character of the profession and are part of the individual characters of the professionals. . . .

EMPLOYING VIRTUE ETHICS IN PSYCHOLOGY

. . . Two examples of how specific virtues influence professional practice are offered in this section. The first concerns the use of informed consent in a counseling relationship; the second involves the role of professional virtues in conceptualizing therapeutically relevant constructs such as "genuineness." Although explicitly psychotherapeutic in content, these examples are intended to offer a starting point for more general discussions of potentially relevant virtues for professional psychologists.

Informed Consent
A client's right to informed consent has received increasing attention (Berger, 1982; Burstein, 1987). Respect for the principles of autonomy and beneficence have encouraged therapists to design explicit contracts in response to the rights of clients (Everstine et al., 1980). . . .

There is, however, another layer of ethical concern that is typically overlooked in the midst of such quandaries: Whereas most attention has focused on what information a therapist ought to tell a client, or what information rightly belongs to a client, there is yet a more subtle but equally important ethical issue that concerns *how* the client will be told (May, 1984). As therapists know, how the truth is spoken in therapy is as morally relevant as what truth is spoken.

For example, Everstine et al. (1980) fully illustrated what information ought to be included in an informed consent procedure, but they did not adequately consider the ethical dimension associated with *how* such information is presented. In an effort to address legal and ethical concerns over informed consent, they developed a therapist–client contract that identified clients' legal rights. Issues were explored in depth and clearly delineated. Client autonomy was respected. However, Everstine et al. did not call into question how to present these matters to clients. As they put it, "The form taken by these consent procedures is irrelevant by contrast with the procedure itself. What is important is that specific ground rules be decided upon in advance and endorsed with a signature before the hard work of therapy begins" (p. 832). Such a legalistic procedure, however, may not be in the client's best interests, nor does it adequately reflect the mutual trust and respect or therapist's integrity that are essential for productive therapy. Specifically, at face value, the rights, the contract, and the consent forms provided by Everstine et al. subtly suggest that therapy is first and perhaps foremost a legal transaction of commodities or services. Modern therapy often includes such a transaction, but it is not clear that therapy is best understood, first and foremost, within the limits of such categories. What is more, the forms imply that the client is a passive recipient of these services, for which the client will be billed. Indeed, the client's rights and the therapist's responsibilities are listed in great detail, but little is said of the client's responsibilities, the mutuality of the therapy process, or what "set" such a document provides for the client.

Clearly, Everstine et al. (1980) developed these forms in an environment that presses escalating legal responsibilities on therapists. The prevailing question was, and continues to be, What are therapists legally required to do in order to protect client rights and their own legal culpability? Everstine et al. addressed these issues, and virtue ethics does not deny the importance of the question. But in virtue ethics, such concerns would be seen as an outgrowth of a professional's concern for the integrity of the process and practice of psychotherapy itself and an abiding respect for clients who engage in it. Such concern adds another, equally valid question: Who are thera-

pists required to be in order to competently and credibly inform clients about their rights and responsibilities, as well as concerning the nature and tradition of the practice of psychotherapy? The virtues of prudence and discretion and of fidelity to a particular client with whom the therapist is in a particular relationship are ethically relevant to informed consent. It may be that standardized, legal contracts are necessary and can be presented articulately and sensitively (i.e., professionally) to a depressed client without the need of a lawyer to interpret the contract's legal implications. But this is precisely the point: How professionals present such information is morally relevant without being necessarily rule dependent. The character of the professional is as ethically decisive as the content of the contract.

Genuineness

. . . Rogers (1959; Meador & Rogers, 1984) considered genuineness to be essential to the development of a therapeutic relationship. But apart from a person, how does one define genuineness? For example, to what extent does the therapist reveal personal values, perspectives, and problems to a client or clients (Brammer & Shostrom, 1977)? Such questions have both therapeutic and ethical dimensions that are difficult to differentiate. The therapeutic dimensions usually involve a clinical and empirical evaluation of the effectiveness or curative value of genuineness and related constructs proposed by Rogerians, such as transparency, congruence, realness, and authenticity (Truax & Carkhuff, 1964). Similarly, ethical considerations are typically utilitarian. Genuineness is appropriate insofar as it advances the therapeutic interest of the client and does not violate other relevant ethical principles. The exact parameters and nuances of genuineness that are most effective, however, are difficult to isolate and require continued study.

From the perspective of virtue ethics, genuineness might be approached and defined in a different way. In addition to, and perhaps before, questions concerning the curative value of genuineness in the therapeutic encounter is this question: Is genuineness an essential attribute of being a professional in a therapeutic relationship? Many would argue that genuineness, as articulated by Rogers (1959), is not essential, that it is a technique or approach and not a quality.

Some might further argue that as such it can be therapeutically counterproductive. But beyond such theoretical arguments is a fundamental question: Is there a sense in which one expects professionals *to be*, for example, genuine, trustworthy, or competent in a way that is not completely dependent on therapeutic consequences? These questions place our deliberations regarding effectiveness in a wider context that includes astute considerations of what is meant by *professionalism*.

From this second perspective, the virtue-oriented dimensions of genuineness become salient. Genuineness is a complex concept based on a quality of truthfulness. Genuineness includes both a principle-oriented guide to proper action (e.g., tell the truth) and a virtue-oriented characteristic of professionals (e.g., integrity or trustworthiness). But these two admonitions (i.e., "tell the truth" and "be trustworthy") are not necessarily or logically interdependent. . . . [T]he maintenance of trust sometimes demands of trustworthy therapists a certain measured deliberateness with respect to the truth that they speak. "Measured deliberateness" is not a code for subtle and deceptive manipulations but rather is a reference to three additional virtues: discretion, prudence, and humility. Not speaking or speaking with care and discretion can be just as critical to maintaining integrity and trustworthiness of the therapist as speaking out. . . .

Thus the "genuine" therapist is involved in an intricate interaction that balances honesty and subtle therapeutic manipulation. How the therapist manages this interaction is an ethical, as well as a therapeutic, issue. . . . Rather, ethics from a virtue perspective serves to remind us that professional psychology is a discipline with pervasive moral, as well as scientific, dimensions. These moral dimensions are intimately tied to the character of the professional.

BEYOND PRINCIPLE TO CHARACTER

Last, a focus on virtues, in addition to principles, may offer a tentative response to the problem of individual inconsistencies in the use of ethical principles. Specifically, on what criteria do therapists rely when choosing among rationally justifiable alternatives in a dilemma? . . . .

In such situations, the client and the community rely not simply on a therapist's rational, cognitive processing of universal or prima facie valid principles, nor simply on his or her specific technical skills or legal expertise. Principles, technical skills, and legal knowledge are necessary in evaluating a course of action but are not logically sufficient or necessarily primary. What is demanded of professionals is a dimension of character appropriately understood by way of the virtues. Professionals use words such as *maturity, professional judgment, discretion, wisdom,* or *prudence,* which depend for their exercise not so much on rational, objective principles as on a quality of character identified by the virtues. A serious consideration in psychological training and practice of what constitutes virtuous character will not eliminate professional disagreement about what is proper or ethical, but it could result in the development of professionals who are better prepared to make such judgments. Such professionals might more easily identify their bias, more carefully guard against imposing their values on clients, and be more vigilant in separating personal and cultural preferences from the psychological and therapeutic phenomena. . . .

References

Beauchamp, T. L., & Childress, J. F. (1983). *Principles of biomedical ethics.* New York: Oxford University Press.

Berger, M. (1982). Ethics and the therapeutic relationship: Patient rights and therapist responsibilities. In M. Rosenbaum (Ed.), *Ethics and values in psychotherapy* (pp. 67–95). London: Free Press.

Brammer, L., & Shostrom, E. (1977). *Therapeutic psychology: Fundamentals of counseling and psychotherapy.* Englewood Cliffs, NJ: Prentice-Hall.

Burstein, A. G. (1987). The virtue machine. *American Psychologist, 42,* 199–202.

Callahan, J. C. (1988). *Ethical issues in professional life.* New York: Oxford University Press.

Drane, J. (1982). Ethics and psychotherapy: A philosophical perspective. In M. Rosenbaum (Ed.), *Ethics and values in psychotherapy: A guidebook* (pp. 15–50). New York: Free Press.

Dykstra, C. (1981). *Vision and character: A Christian educator's alternative to Kohlberg.* New York: Paulist Press.

Everstine, L., Everstine, D. S., Heymann, G. M., True, R. M., Johnson, H. G., & Seiden, R. H. (1980). Privacy and confidentiality in psychotherapy. *American Psychologist, 35,* 828–840.

Eyde, L. D., & Quaintance, M. K. (1988). Ethical issues and cases in the practice of personnel psychology. *Professional Psychology: Research and Practice, 19,* 148–154.

Hauerwas, S. (1981). *A community of character.* Notre Dame, IN: University of Notre Dame Press.

Jonsen, A. (1977). Do no harm: Axiom of medical ethics. In S. Spicker & T. Engelhardt, Jr. (Eds.), *Philosophical medical ethics: Its nature and significance* (pp. 27–41). Dordrecht, The Netherlands: Reidel.

Kilpatrick, W. K. (1986). Moral character, story-telling and virtue. In R. Knowles & G. McLean (Eds.), *Psychological foundations of moral education and character development* (pp. 183–199). New York: University Press of America.

May, W. F. (1984). The virtues in a professional setting. *Soundings, 67,* 245–266.

McClendon, J. W. (1974). *Biography as theology: How life stories can remake today's theology.* Nashville, TN: Abingdon.

Meador, B., & Rogers, C. (1984). Person-centered therapy. In R. Corsini (Ed.), *Current psychotherapies* (pp. 142–195). Itasca, IL: Peacock Publishers.

Pincoffs, E. (1971). Quandary ethics. *Mind, 80,* 552–571.

Rogers, C. (1959). Client-centered therapy. In S. Arieti (Ed.), *American handbook of psychiatry* (Vol. 3, pp. 183–200). New York: Basic Books.

Steininger, M., Newell, J., & Garcia, L. (1984). *Ethical issues in psychology.* Homewood, IL: Dorsey.

Traux, C., & Carkhuff, R. (1984). The old and the new: Theory and research in counseling and psychotherapy. *Personnel and Guidance Journal, 42,* 860–866.

◆   ◆   ◆

Commentary: More recently, Meara and her colleagues provided an exegesis on the concept of virtue ethics in a special issue of The Counseling Psychologist *that is well worth studying. They summarized their views, in relevant part:*

> *We have argued that a more complete understanding of professional ethics included, in addition to principle ethics, a cognitive grasp of virtue ethics, and that better ethical practice can be achieved through efforts to develop virtues commensurate with one's professional mission. . . . We have . . . tried to provide a rationale for how integrating principles and virtues can assist professionals in making difficult decisions, setting policies (e.g., revising or interpreting ethics codes), and developing the ethical character of themselves and their professions. We discussed the particular relevance of virtue ethics in enhancing professional competences and sensitivity as well as public trust of professions in a pluralistic, multicultural society. (p. 69)*

Meara, N. M., Schmidt, L. D., & Day, J. D. (1996). Principles and virtues: A foundation for ethical decisions, policies, and character. The Counseling Psychologist, 24, 4–77

The Virtue of Principle Ethics

Donald N. Bersoff

. . .

From empirical and practical perspectives, an argument concerning the relative importance of virtue ethics and principle ethics . . . is inconsequential. The complaints brought before and adjudicated by the American Psychological Association's (APA) Ethics Committee almost exclusively involve behavior that the criminal law would call *malum in se,* that is, conduct that is inherently wrong (Dressler, 1987). Among the primary reasons psychologists are sanctioned by the APA Ethics Committee are because they make false or misleading public statements, engage in sexual intimacies with their clients, or defraud insurance companies (APA Ethics Committee, 1994). In that light, psychology need not go through the endless debate, huge expense, and vast expenditure of time involved in developing, implementing, and enforcing a code of ethics, as it has done every decade in the past half century. It could simply borrow the all-encompassing honor code commandment found at our military academies: Thou shalt not lie, cheat, or steal. Debates about ethics codes or the relative merits of virtue and principle ethics are only relevant at the very outer margins of professional or scholarly conduct.

. . .

Principle ethics encompass five prima facie duties—nonmaleficence, fidelity, beneficence, justice, and autonomy (Beauchamp & Childress, 1994; Bersoff & Koeppl, 1993; Ross, 1930). Like the components of virtue ethics, these prima facie duties provide an array of moral choices and can be applied flexibly in relation to the context of a dilemma. There does not seem to be a great deal of difference between these moral principles and the "four virtues," i.e., prudence, integrity, respectfulness, and benevolence, as Meara et al. define them. Only prudence, which is more categorizable as a means for arriving at an ethi-

cal outcome, is sufficiently different from prima facie duties to merit recognition as a separable concept. Integrity is highly similar to fidelity and justice; benevolence is closely congruent to beneficence; and respectfulness is little different from autonomy.

Although Meara et al. deride the resolution of ethical dilemmas as "abstract thought puzzles," judgment, choice, and the resolution of conflict are some of the inevitable, obligatory, and probably unwelcome tasks confronting human beings (Bersoff & Koeppl, 1993; Hogarth, 1987). The most virtuous, principled, and law-abiding psychologists will be faced with difficult dilemmas throughout their careers for which there are no "cookbooks" prescribing a set of expected behaviors or universally acceptable solutions.

Consider the following facts, for example (adapted from Bersoff, 1995). A tenth grader is enrolled in research studying violence in adolescents and how it might be prevented through short-term intervention. During an interview as part of the study, the student reveals that he has had many fantasies about harming his slightly older female next-door neighbor who refuses to pay him any attention. Upon further inquiry, the psychologist learns that he is contemplating buying a gun but that he has no history of violence. The researcher suggests that she inform his parents of the situation. The young man adamantly refuses to let the researcher do so and warns that he will drop out of the study and treatment if she does not honor his refusal.

On what basis could the psychologist resolve this problem? Recent critics agree that the current APA ethics code (1992) would be an informative but uncertain guide (e.g., Bersoff, 1994; Lakin, 1994; Vasquez, 1994). Under the code, the psychologist has significant discretion to disclose the threat (see the following Principles—5.01, Discussing Limits of Confidentiality; 5.02, Maintaining Confidentiality;

5.05, Disclosures; 6.11, Informed Consent to Research),[1] but the code offers no definitive answers.

Would reliance on virtue ethics be more helpful? We can agree that being motivated to do good, possessing vision and discernment, allowing affect to enter into the process of decision making, understanding oneself, and being connected to the moral sense of the community (the characteristics of virtuous agents) are all laudable characteristics of any psychologist. Further, we would hope that the psychologists will act with prudence, integrity, respectfulness, and benevolence. It is difficult for me, however, to see how these virtues will resolve the dilemma. . . .

For example, under the APA Ethics Code, it would be perfectly ethical for the researcher to disclose the young man's confidences and even to refuse to abide by his demand for secrecy. In fact, it might be prudent (a virtue) for her to do so, particularly because that decision would show respect for predominant community values (a quality of a virtuous agent). Additionally, she could decide that beneficence (a central component of virtue and principle ethics) requires her to protect her research participant from engaging in behavior that will lead him to harming, if not killing, another, and subject him to criminal penalties. Conversely, she could decide to promote the self-determination and sense of accountability of her subject while reinforcing her obligation to remain faithful to his expressed interests without harming innocent victims. . . . Thus she could conclude that disclosure would conflict with what she considers to be the more overriding moral principles of autonomy, fidelity, and nonmaleficence, prima facie obligations that are also an inherent part of her value system. In any event, the psychologist must judge the risks and benefits of her value choices and decide which prima facie duties should take precedence in this case. By adopting some over others and by deciding what she should do, she is also deciding who she should be.

CHARACTER AND COMMUNITY

If virtues "are traits of character," and if "[v]irtue ethics calls upon individuals to aspire toward ideals and develop . . . traits of character that enable them

to achieve these ideals" (Meara et al. 1996), two problems arise. First, I question whether virtue ethics is teachable. Character traits, although potentially malleable, are developed as a result of genetic endowment and life experiences. It is doubtful whether a course in ethics or even 4 years of professional training in which students are sensitized to ethics will produce a virtuous agent able to employ virtuous ideals. Intensive therapy over many years fails to accomplish this goal. Second, if acting ethically depends on character, I wonder if the outcomes will be too individualized and idiosyncratic. An ethical code and ethical conduct, I would assert, relies on consensual decision making about the integrity of the profession, not the singular vagaries of a psychologist's character.

More problematic for me, however, is the heavy reliance on communitarian values. Meara et al. unabashedly assert that "[v]irtue ethics is rooted in community and relies on a community's wisdom and its moral sense." To their credit, they recognize concomitantly that reliance on community can create ethnocentric, even immoral, decisions, but they characterize much of virtue ethics as community based. I see the dangers of a communitarian view as outweighing its benefits. It would be difficult for me to subscribe to a system that led me to act in ways that denied women responsible choices in deciding whether to bear children, that treated those denominated as mentally disabled as incompetent to become involved in decisions regarding their own treatment, that refused to permit the works of Ellison, Salinger, Shakespeare, and Blume in the classrooms of our high schools, that advocated religion in our public institutions, or that perceived single mothers on welfare as the cause of society's violence. These are precisely the views that many communities in the United States hold and act on today.

Meara et al. criticize principles ethics in large part because it holds autonomy and self-determinism in high esteem, because it does not place primacy on religious traditions, and because it depends so highly on rationality. But I value these virtues of principle ethics (Bersoff, 1992) precisely because I want to act with prudence, respect, integrity, and

---

[1]*Ed. Note:* See Standards 4.02, 4.01, 4.05, and 8.02, respectively, of the current (2002) APA Ethics Code.

benevolence. If being virtuous means acting paternalistically, irrationally, and on the basis of faith, I prefer principled iniquity.

References

American Psychological Association Ethics Committee. (1994). Report of the Ethics Committee, 1993. *American Psychologist, 49,* 659–666.

Beauchamp, T. L., & Childress, J. F. (1994). *Principles of biomedical ethics* (3rd ed.). New York: Oxford University Press.

Bersoff, D. N. (1992). Autonomy for vulnerable populations: The Supreme Court's reckless disregard for self-determination and social science. *Villanova Law Review, 37,* 1569–1605.

Bersoff, D. N. (1994). Explicit ambiguity: The 1992 ethics code as an oxymoron. *Professional Psychology: Research and Practice, 25,* 382–387.

Bersoff, D. N. (1995). *Ethical conflicts in psychology.* Washington, DC: American Psychological Association.

Bersoff, D. N., & Koeppl, P. M. (1993). The relation between ethical codes and moral principles. *Ethics & Behavior, 3(3/4),* 345–357.

Dressler, J. (1987). *Understanding criminal law.* New York: Mathew Bender.

Hogarth, R. (1987). *Judgment and choice: The psychology of decision* (2nd ed.). New York: Wiley.

Lakin, M. (1994). Morality in group and family therapies: Multiperson therapies and the 1992 ethics code. *Professional Psychology: Research and Practice, 25,* 344–348.

Meara, N. M., Schmidt, L. D., & Day, J. D. (1996). Principles and virtues: A foundation for ethical decisions, policies, and character. *The Counseling Psychologist, 24,* 4–77.

Ross, W. D. (1930). *The right and the good.* Oxford, England: Clarendon.

Vasquez, M. (1994). Implications of the 1992 ethics code for the practice of individual psychotherapy. *Professional Psychology: Research and Practice, 25,* 321–328.

◆　◆　◆

Commentary: For other contrasting views see these analyses, in order of their appearance:

Miller, D. J. (1991). The necessity of principles in virtue ethics. Professional Psychology: Research and Practice, 22, 107.

Jordan, A. E., & Meara, N. M. (1991). The role of virtues and principles in moral collapse: A response to Miller.

Professional Psychology: Research and Practice, 22, 107–109.

Regardless of the philosophical approach one takes, as the prior excerpts imply, ethics educators are moving away from a "correct answer" approach to resolving ethical dilemmas. It is very difficult to advocate such an approach when there are internal conflicts within ethics codes, between ethics codes of various mental health professions, and between ethics codes and legal requirements. The preferred alternative at the present time is a "problem-solving approach." See, for example, Eberlein, L. (1987). Introducing ethics to beginning psychologists: A problem-solving approach. Professional Psychology: Research and Practice, 18, 353–359.

More specifically, Tymchuk et al. (1982) have argued that

> *the profession . . . needs to attend more closely to decision-making processes and develop decision-making standards that can be applied to situations as they arise. What may be most useful for the professional are broader and more basic decision-making standards rather than specific rules that attempt to define behavior as "right" or "wrong." Models are needed that incorporate a comprehensive range of ethical considerations in order to assist psychologists in the process of making critical decisions. (p. 420)*

See Tymchuk, A. J., Drapkin, R. S., Major-Kingsley, S., Ackerman, A. B., Major, S. M., & Baum, M. S. (1982). Ethical decision making and psychologists' attitudes toward training in ethics. Professional Psychology: Research and Practice, 13, 412–421.

As a general guide to good ethical decision making Rest's (1983) model is useful. See Rest, J. R. (1983). Morality. In J. Flavell & E. Markham (Vol. Eds.) & P. Mussen (General Ed.), Cognitive development: Vol. 4, Manual of child psychology (pp. 520–629). New York: Wiley. He identifies four components of moral behavior. The first requires that one interpret the situation as a moral one, that is, one have moral sensitivity. "For the psychologist, moral sensitivity means the ability to recognize the ethical dimensions of a situation along with its clinical, scholarly, or pragmatic aspects" (p. 179). Welfel, E. R., & Kitchener, K. S. (1992). Introduction to the special section: Ethics education—An agenda for the '90s. Professional Psychology: Research and Practice, 23, *179–181. The second component is moral reasoning, that is, the capacity to differentiate ethical from unethical choices so that the outcome is fair and just. As Welfel & Kitchener acknowledged, "[t]his capacity is informed . . . by one's knowledge of the current code of ethics, the published literature, the philosophical principles underlying the code, and by the individual's level of moral reasoning" (p. 179). The third component involves sorting out competing ethical values and deciding what one intends to do. The final component is the ability and steadfastness to actually implement the moral action one has decided is right. It is this last component that may have been missing in those who failed to take appropriate action in the face of their colleagues' ethical transgressions studied by Bernard & Jara (1986) and Bernard, Murphy, & Little (1987) and referenced in chapter 2.*

A number of more specific decision-making models have been proposed. See, for example, Barnett, J. E., Behnke, S. H., Rosenthal, S. L., & Koocher, G. P. (2007). In case of ethical dilemma, break glass: Commentary on ethical decision making in practice. Professional Psychology: Research and Practice, 38, *7–12; Ford, G. G. (2001). Ethical reasoning in the mental health professions.* Boca Raton, FL: CRC Press *(chap. 6 especially); Kuyken, W. (1999). Power and clinical psychology: A model for resolving power-related ethical dilemmas.* Ethics & Behavior, 9, *21–37; Paul, R., & Elder, L. (2003). Ethical reasoning.* Dillon Beach, CA: Foundation for Critical Thinking; *Treppa, J. A. (1998). A practitioner's guide to ethical decision-making. In R. Anderson, T. Needles, & H. Hall (Eds.),* Avoiding ethical misconduct in psychology specialty areas *(pp. 26–41). Springfield, IL: Charles C Thomas; Koocher, G. P., & Keith-Spiegel, P. K. (1998). Ethics in psychology.* New York: Oxford University Press. *The latter authors suggest the following steps:*

1. *Determine the matter is an ethical one.*
2. *Consult available guidelines that might apply to a specific identification and possible mechanism for resolution.*
3. *Consider, as best as possible, all sources that might influence the kind of decision you will make.*
4. *Consult with a trusted colleague.*
5. *Evaluate the rights, responsibilities, and vulnerability of all affected parties.*
6. *Generate alternative decisions.*
7. *Enumerate the consequences of making each decision.*
8. *Make the decision.*
9. *Implement the decision.*

One of the most respected systems has been developed by the Canadian Psychological Association. It follows next.

Canadian Code of Ethics for Psychologists

Canadian Psychological Association

. . . [P]sychologists will be faced with ethical dilemmas that are difficult to resolve. In these circumstances, psychologists are expected to engage in an ethical decision-making process that is explicit enough to bear public scrutiny. In some cases, resolution might be a matter of personal conscience. However, decisions of personal conscience are also expected to be the result of a decision-making process that is based on a reasonably coherent set of ethical principles and that can bear public scrutiny. If the psychologist can demonstrate that every reasonable effort was made to apply the ethical principles of this *Code* and resolution of the conflict has had to depend on the personal conscience of the psychologist, such a psychologist would be deemed to have followed the *Code*.

THE ETHICAL DECISION-MAKING PROCESS

The ethical decision-making process might occur very rapidly, leading to an easy resolution of an ethical issue. This is particularly true of issues for which clear-cut guidelines or standards exist and for which there is no conflict between principles. On the other hand, some ethical issues (particularly those in which ethical principles conflict) are not easily resolved, might be emotionally distressful, and might require time-consuming deliberation.

The following basic steps typify approaches to ethical decision making:

1. Identification of the individuals and groups potentially affected by the decision.
2. Identification of ethically relevant issues and practices, including the interests, rights, and any relevant characteristics of the individuals and groups involved and of the system or circumstances in which the ethical problem arose.
3. Consideration of how personal biases, stresses, or self-interest might influence the development of or choice between courses of action.
4. Development of alternative courses of action.
5. Analysis of likely short-term, ongoing, and long-term risks and benefits of each course of action on the individual(s)/group(s) involved or likely to be affected (e.g., client, client's family or employees, employee institution, students, research participants, colleagues, the discipline, society, self).
6. Choice of course of action after conscientious application of existing principles, values, and standards.
7. Action, with a commitment to assume responsibility for the consequences of the action.
8. Evaluation of the results of the course of action.
9. Assumption of responsibility for consequences of action, including correction of negative consequences, if any, or re-engaging in the decision-making process if the ethical issue is not resolved.
10. Appropriate action, as warranted and feasible, to prevent future occurrences of the dilemma (e.g., communication and problem solving with colleagues; changes in procedures and practices).

Psychologists engaged in time-consuming deliberation are encouraged and expected to consult with parties affected by the ethical problem, when appropriate, and with colleagues and/or advisory bodies when such persons can add knowledge or objectivity to the decision-making process. Although the decision for action remains with the individual psychologist, the seeking and consideration of such assistance reflects an ethical approach to ethical decision making.

♦   ♦   ♦

Commentary: Gawthrop and Uhlemann (1992) have provided empirical support for the approaches espoused by those urging the use of decision-making systems. They presented a vignette containing an ethical dilemma to undergraduate students who were preparing for careers in mental health professions. The treatment group received a 3-hour workshop on ethical decision making using a problem-solving approach. In comparison with two control groups, the treatment group performed significantly better on a rating scale designed to measure quality of the decision-making process. See Gawthrop, J. C., & Uhlemann, M. R. (1992). Effects of the problem-solving approach in ethics training. Professional Psychology: Research and Practice, 23, 38–42. *The authors offered the following insights on their study and its implications for teaching students about ethics:*

> *The results of this study are consistent with those found in earlier work . . . in that formal exposure to ethics education had a significant positive effect on the dependent variable. In addition, the refinements of the present study made possible several specific conclusions in light of the results.*
>
> *. . . When the brevity of the workshop experience is considered the strength of the observed treatment effect is notable. . . . The results suggest that the problem-solving approach in teaching ethics . . . is effective in fostering quality in ethical decision making and that simply presenting written instructions is not sufficient for eliciting that quality of decision making.*
>
> *It is important to point out that the problem-solving approach . . . was augmented in this study with elements of other ethics teaching models. The workshop goals were to sensitize participants to ethical issues and to maximize the quality of ethical decision making by using reading and discussion of ethical codes and case vignettes, self-generation of ethical dilemmas from experience, and generating and justifying ethical decisions about specific vignettes (Kitchener, 1986). Discussions of ethical dilemmas during the workshops often included an exploration of how values form the basis of codes and decision rationales (Abeles, 1980). The case vignette also served to recognize the contribution made by several teaching models (Eberlein, 1987; Fine & Ulrich, 1988; Kitchener, 1984, 1986; McGovern, 1988) with regard to making participant evaluation and accountability an integral part of ethics education.*
>
> *The present results, in conjunction with findings from earlier studies, permit several suggestions regarding the training of counselors and psychologists in ethical issues. First, it is becoming increasingly clear that the limitations of the informal teaching of ethics need to be accepted (Handelsman, 1986b). The mere provision of ethics information is not sufficient. Rather, the present results support the notion that ethics education be made a formal endeavor in which specific attention is given to the content and process of teaching ethical decision making. Second, the results made it reasonable to suggest that those trainees who do not receive formal exposure to ethics education cannot be assumed to possess the same ethical decision-making skills as trainees who have gone through formal ethics education in which such skills are taught. Third, it seems reasonable to suggest that separate sections of courses or full courses devoted to professional ethics be included in all training programs in the helping professions and that all such courses include the teaching of ethical decision making. Fourth, the results of the present study support the suggestion that educators consider using the problem-solving approach . . . in teaching ethical decision making. . . .*

See Abeles, N. (1980). Teaching ethical principles by means of value confrontations. Psychotherapy: Theory, Research, & Practice, 17, 384–391; Eberlein, L. (1987). Introducing ethics to beginning psychologists: A problem-solving approach. Professional Psychology: Research and Practice, 18, 353–359; Fine, M., & Ulrich, L. (1988). Integrating psychology and philosophy in teaching a graduate course in ethics. Professional Psychology: Research and Practice, 19, 542–546; Handelsman, M. (1986b). Problems with ethics training by "osmosis." Professional Psychology: Research and Practice, 17, 371–372; Kitchener, K. (1984), Intuition, critical evaluation and ethical principles: The foundation of ethical decisions in counseling psychology. Counseling Psychologist, 12(3), 43–55; Kitchener, K. (1986). Teaching applied ethics in counselor education: An integration of psychological processes and philosophical analysis. Journal of Counseling and Development, 64(5), 306–310; McGovern, T. (1988). Teaching the ethical principles of psychology. Teaching of Psychology, 15(1), 22–26.

As a means of consolidating the material studied so far, consider the following cases:

1. Under immense pressure to be a success, a first-year graduate student with considerable academic potential cheats on a final paper in a required course. Such conduct could justify expulsion. What should the professor do?

2. A psychologist tests a 52-year-old resident of an institution for people with mental retardation and finds that the resident's intellectual deficits are not as severe as previously thought. The psychologist recommends that the resident be moved to a group home in the community, not only making the woman more independent but relieving crowded conditions on the ward where she is institutionalized. The shift will save the state about $10,000. When the psychologist reveals the plan to the resident, she becomes depressed and argues that the institution is her home and she does not want to leave it.

3. A psychologist proposes to compare behavioral and pharmacological approaches to the treatment of bulimia. He wants to use a wait-list control group and a placebo group in addition to the two treatment groups.

Identify the ethical dilemmas facing the professor, the clinical psychologist, and the researcher in each of these vignettes adapted from Kitchener's (1984) article: See Kitchener, K. S. (1984). Intuition, critical evaluation and ethical principles: The foundation for ethical decisions in counseling psychologists. Counseling Psychologist, 12(3), 43–55. What provisions in the APA Ethics Code would apply in each vignette? For each situation, specify the relevant philosophical ethical principles from those articulated by Welfel & Kitchener in the previous article and those found in the general principles of the Code. Using any of the decision-making models you have read about in this chapter, what action would you ultimately take in each of these cases? In completing this exercise, consider the following, also from Kitchener (1984):

> The point has been made that neither the identification of ethical principles nor accepting them as prima facie valid relieves the psychologist from the burden of decision making in ethical dilemmas. A dilemma, after all, is a situation in which there are good reasons to take different courses of action. However, we must still ask: Are there better ways to decide what to do when ethical principles conflict? This question is a very complex one and one which is open for debate among twentieth century ethicists (Abelson & Nielsen, 1967). . . .
>
> A second approach is to establish by convention a particular ordering of principles for a set of similar issues. (This ordering may rely on an implicit, but unarticulated theory.) Thus, for example, the APA Ethics Code has established that not doing harm should take precedence over fidelity in regard to the issue of confidentiality, and over beneficence in the area of research. This approach is problematic because preestablished conventions cannot always anticipate issues that arise. In addition, just as with trying to establish a single principle as absolute, establishing a single ordering of principles as absolute may sometimes lead to bad ethical decisions. For

example, if autonomy was always weighed more heavily than beneficence, it would always be unethical to interfere in someone's life against their will. . . .

While the problems of applying ethical principles in decision making need to be acknowledged, this does not keep them from being useful or important. By accepting them as prima facie valid, we imply that their relevance always needs to be considered in ethical situations. Because they are at a more general level than ethical rules, they can be applied across many situations when ethical codes remain silent or conflict. . . .

In addition, they provide a framework and a set of helpful guidelines to use in critical evaluation of our ethical intuitions. What this implies is that our moral insight may be sharpened and our moral intuitions refined and reformulated after careful consideration of our ethical actions in light of ethical principles. Via this kind of feedback process, we may improve as ethical decision makers.

. . . The principles proposed by Beauchamp and Childress . . . have three advantages. First, they offer us a common vocabulary and a set of prima facie valid principles that ought to be relevant whether we are thinking about ethical problems in vocational counseling or behavioral research. Beauchamp and Childress have observed: "Only by examining moral principles and determining how they apply to cases and how they conflict can we bring some order and coherence to the discussion of these problems" (1979, p vii).

Secondly, the principles provide a more general justification for ethical codes and identify areas which ethical codes may need to address. For example, as has been noted, respect for individual autonomy, not harming clients, truthfulness, and justice are minimally addressed by the current APA Code. Furthermore, they may illuminate inconsistencies within the Code itself.

Third, when we moved to the level of ethical principles we move beyond believing that we have fulfilled our ethical responsibility if we have not broken a specific rule in our professional code. If as Drane (1982) and others have argued, the helping professions are involved in ethical issues at their very core, we need to pay attention to more general ethical principles as we evaluate our own ordinary moral judgments as well as those of our colleagues and our profession. (51–53)

The final excerpt consolidates all that has gone before in this chapter.

Navigating the Nuances: A Matrix of Considerations for Ethical–Legal Dilemmas

Nancy Downing Hansen and Susan G. Goldberg

. . .

Contemporary ethical–legal dilemmas are increasingly complex and multifaceted, due, in part, to the often contradictory professional demands resulting from recent changes in health care delivery systems (Appelbaum, 1993; Higuchi, 1994; Newman & Bricklin, 1994) and the more litigious nature of our society (Pope & Vasquez, 1991; Soisson, VandeCreek, & Knapp, 1987). Given the rise in the number of ethics complaints, malpractice claims, and licensing grievances against psychologists (APA, 1994; Stromberg et al., 1988), there are also more risks associated with any given action.

The complexity of contemporary practice necessitates a comprehensive, systematic approach to identifying pertinent legal–ethical variables, issues, and guidelines. Such a systematic approach, or matrix, can then be combined with existing step-by-step decision-making models to improve dilemma resolution. Without a comprehensive organizing schema, professional psychologists cannot be expected to grasp intuitively the distinctions and relationships within the complex web of conflicting demands. . . .

MATRIX OF CONSIDERATIONS

This framework separates the complex web of often interrelated, implicit considerations that confront professional psychologists grappling with ethical–legal quandaries into seven strands: (a) moral principles and personal values; (b) clinical and cultural considerations; (c) ethics codes; (d) agency or employer policies; (e) federal, state, and local statutes; (f) rules and regulations; and (g) case law. Ethics committees, judges, juries, licensing boards, and agencies routinely evaluate actions and omissions by professional psychologists on one or more of these considerations. Sometimes, there are conflicts both within and between dimensions. We believe that in order to master the complexity of contemporary ethical–legal decision making, professional psychologists need to understand and know how to evaluate these different considerations, especially when they are overlapping or conflicting. Without these skills, such dilemmas cannot be resolved in a systematic and prudent manner.

. . .

Consideration I: Moral Principles and Personal Values

The first set of considerations involves the abstract qualities of moral principles and personal values. The moral principles of beneficence, fidelity, autonomy, justice, and nonmalfeasance (Beauchamp & Childress, 1994; Kitchener, 1984; Thompson, 1990) provide a foundational rationale for moral or right choices. On the basis of these moral principles, some authors have promoted *virtue ethics*—character traits and ideals (e.g., prudence, integrity, respectfulness, and benevolence) thought to facilitate the development of ethical psychologists (Jordan & Meara, 1990; Meara, Schmidt, & Day, 1996). In addition to moral principles and virtues, individuals also make decisions based on personal (e.g., religious, political) values.

. . .

Various authors have contended that psychologists rely heavily on personal values in decision making (Abeles, 1980; Eberlein, 1987). Three quarters of a sample of senior psychologists, all of whom were known for their ethics expertise, believed that

From *Professional Psychology: Research and Practice, 30,* 495–503. Copyright 1999 by the American Psychological Association.

formal legal and ethical standards should sometimes be violated on the basis of client welfare or personal values (Pope & Bajt, 1988). Moreover, a majority of these respondents reported having done so.

When psychologists act contrary to moral principles, they often violate ethical standards or legal mandates. When psychologists act contrary to their personal values, they usually do so privately, with the only consequence being heightened anxiety or guilt. . . .

Consideration II: Clinical and Cultural Factors

In the literature, clinical and cultural considerations have often been treated as a part of the general issue of competence (Lakin, 1994), minimized, or ignored entirely (Payton, 1994). Yet, real-world resolution of ethical–legal dilemmas requires careful consideration of both of these interrelated contextual factors.

Clinical perception and judgment (Gambrill, 1990) are central in identifying the salient variables and issues involved in any ethical–legal quandary. Consultation with colleagues is most useful in checking one's clinical judgments, as is knowledge of the relevant literature (e.g., Bongar, 1991). Research suggests this dimension plays an influential role; seasoned professionals frequently disagreed about solutions to ethical vignettes that were closely related to clinical orientation, and, by inference, clinical judgments (Tymchuk et al., 1982).

Cultural considerations are likewise often ignored or minimized when identifying salient variables, issues, and guidelines (Payton, 1994). Even though the *Guidelines for Providers of Psychological Services to Ethnic, Linguistic, and Culturally Diverse Populations* (APA, 1993a) is an aspirational, nonenforceable document, it represents an important step in elucidating relevant cultural considerations. Issues such as the nature of multiple relationships, the use of barter, and the boundaries of confidentiality take on different meaning when viewed from an informed, multicultural perspective (APA, 1993a; Cayleff, 1986). As Pope and Vasquez (1991) stated, "Each therapist must struggle to create an ethical response to an individual client with individual needs within the context of a unique and constantly changing situation" (p. xiii).

Consideration III: Professional Code of Ethics

In this matrix, *ethics* signifies the mandates and limitations on professional conduct that the APA imposes on its members. In this model, ethics is far more limited than Beauchamp and Childress's (1994) broader definition: "various ways of understanding and examining the moral life" (p. 4).

In addition to content-specific, aspirational guidelines (e.g., APA, 1981, 1987, 1993a, and 1993b), the Ethics Code (1992) includes 6 general, aspirational principles and 104 enforceable ethical standards. These documents represent the consensual agreement of organizational representatives on principles and standards of conduct and, as such, are often quite conservative and reactive. In some respects, they do protect professionals who adhere to them. However, they may contain potentially, if not actually, contradictory mandates (Koocher, 1994; Vasquez, 1994), and they often fail to address or anticipate current or emerging issues (Eberlein, 1987, 1988; Lakin, 1994; Pope & Vetter, 1992). Contemporary professional psychology ethics course work and internship training focus primarily on students' understanding and application of the APA code (Plante, 1995; Vanek, 1990).

The Ethics Code applies only to APA members and no one else. If a psychologist violates an ethical standard, the most severe punishment APA can impose is expulsion from its ranks. However, such an expulsion is reported to the psychologist's state licensing board (S. Jones, personal communication, March 11, 1999) and other sanctions may follow. . . .

Consideration IV: Agency or Employer Policies

The fourth set of considerations consists of policies imposed by the psychologist's agency or employer. The literature has recently begun to address the special considerations found in the military (APA, 1994; Johnson, 1995), hospitals (Pope, 1990; Wood, Rogers, McCarthy, & Lewine, 1994), and correctional facilities (Weinberger & Sreenivasan, 1994). In addition, managed care companies increasingly attempt to control practitioners' actions (Appelbaum, 1993; Higuchi, 1994; Koocher, 1994; Newman &

Bricklin, 1994; Vasquez, 1994). Employer policies may address such issues as the sharing of confidential information, record keeping, client access to files, behaviors that must be reported to the employer, and best ways to promote "client" welfare. Often disagreements occur over who is considered the client. Those who propose solutions to these conflicts typically urge more thorough informed consent (APA, 1994). However, when the client (e.g., payor for services) is not the patient, major tensions may arise.

. . .

Consideration V: Federal, State, and Local Statutes

Statutes are general rules created by legislative bodies and consist of federal and state laws, as well as local ordinances. Statutes can both mandate conduct, such as filing a child abuse report, and prohibit behavior, such as having sexual relations with clients. Moreover, they can change from year to year, depending on factors as unpredictable as the political makeup of a legislature.

Although only a few federal statutes regulate professional psychologists, a variety of state statutes affect the practice of psychology (e.g., provisions on confidentiality, privilege, involuntary commitment, age of consent to treatment, access to records, rights of nonclients, duty to protect the client, duty to report certain kinds of abuse . . . and prohibitions on sexual relations with current clients). County, city, and town ordinances may also regulate psychologists. . . .

Statutes usually set forth the penalty for violations, ranging from civil penalties (usually a fine) to criminal penalties (a fine and perhaps incarceration). In addition to such sanctions, psychology boards may revoke a license on conviction of a felony; indeed, this accounts for a significant proportion of state disciplinary actions (Pope & Vasquez, 1991; Stromberg et al., 1988). Likewise, APA bylaws allow for expulsion on the basis of a felony conviction.

. . .

Consideration VI: Rules and Regulations

Any federal, state, or local statute may have implementing rules or regulations that elaborate, explain, and sometimes even modify the law. Most rules and regulations are adopted in accordance with established procedures and carry the force of law. For example, the Department of Health and Human Services Regulations (1997) enumerated the factors involved in implementing the federal law requiring confidentiality in federally funded substance abuse programs (Alcohol and Drug Abuse Amendments of 1983).

One particularly relevant set of rules are those regulations and codes of conduct that implement state licensing laws. Most state boards of psychology have rules regarding how licensees should act, many adapted from the Association of State and Provincial Psychology Boards' (ASPPB) model code of conduct (ASPPB, 1996) or the Ethics Code. In recent years, these rules have become increasingly specific and concrete, sounding more like statutes, featuring "shall" and "shall not" language. . . .

Individuals who violate rules or regulations are subject to several potential sanctions, from fines to criminal penalties. For example, psychologists violating a licensing board's code of conduct may lose their licenses, receive a public or private reprimand, be placed on probation, fined, and/or required to practice under supervision. In addition, just as the disclosure of an Ethics Code violation can trigger a state licensing board investigation, the loss of a psychology license often prompts an APA ethics probe (APA, 1994).

. . .

Consideration VII: Case Law

Case law consists of federal and state court rulings that are found in published reports of decisions. Appellate rulings are more frequently reported than trial decisions, just as federal rulings are more likely to be reported than state decisions. Case law differs from statutes and regulations in that the former is developed on a case-by-case basis, influenced by idiosyncratic circumstances, whereas the latter represent codification of general rules, either by legislatures (statutes) or executive branch officials (regulations). However, case law can interpret and clarify the intent and meaning of statutes, rules, and regulations. Thus, psychologists need to be familiar with statutes, regulations, and any applicable case law interpretations.

Through cases, the law develops by twists and turns and is rarely, if ever, stagnant. Generally, judges rely on precedent, which consists of decisions previously made by the same or a higher court. Courts may also overturn, refine, or explain away an existing ruling, thereby establishing new case law. Because an appellate decision is rendered only after a case has worked its way through lower courts, usually a multiyear process, case law often fails to address the most pressing contemporary dilemmas.

Common law is a particular kind of case law that provides legal rules for situations where there is no relevant legislation. The generally accepted law of contracts, property, and torts (including negligence) is part of the common law, having been developed over several centuries through cases. Although decisions in common law, like other cases, are binding only within a particular court's jurisdiction, most states accept and apply general common law principles, with only minor variations among them.

Torts (i.e., negligent or intentional actions that cause harm) are governed by common law. One kind of tort is malpractice, where a professional negligently treats (or fails to treat) a patient according to accepted standards of care. In a malpractice action, the complaining client will prevail if the jury is persuaded that the clinician had a duty to the client, breached that duty, and his or her actions (or inactions) were the "proximate cause" of harm or injury to the client (Bennett et al., 1990; Stromberg et al., 1988). Clinicians can be sued for malpractice on such grounds as failure to obtain informed consent; improper diagnosis; negligent treatment; failure to prevent harm; sexual relations with a client; and inappropriate referral, supervision, or consultation. Other potential tort areas include suit for breach of privacy, intentional infliction of emotional distress, exercise of undue influence, or defamation.

Clinicians should evaluate the risks of being sued and associated penalties when considering various solutions to an ethical–legal dilemma. For example, the remedy for breaching a contract is an award of damages sufficient to make the plaintiff whole; the remedy for committing a tort may also include a large award of damages for the plaintiff's pain and suffering. Insurance companies often settle cases out of court to save money, even if the insured party (i.e., the psychologist) was not liable. The consequences of being sued, even if the case is settled out of court, may run the gamut from difficulty renewing malpractice insurance to financial ruin. In some jurisdictions . . . , a malpractice settlement or judgment must be reported to the licensing board, which may then initiate its own investigation.

. . .

IMPLICATIONS FOR ETHICS EDUCATORS

Educators who use this model can help ensure that the training in their graduate courses and at their internship sites encompasses all of these considerations, not just the Ethics Code (Plante, 1995; Vanek, 1990). By proactively including the other six considerations—moral principles and personal values; clinical and cultural issues; agency or employer policies; federal, state, and local statutes; associated rules and regulations; and case law—professional psychology graduate students are likely to develop a more coherent, comprehensive, and perhaps even more consistent way of evaluating dilemmas. Graduate educators who use this model would help their students keep pace with the increasing complexity of contemporary clinical practice.

Inclusion of this model in contemporary ethics education may also help to highlight the importance of teaching comprehensive decision-making frameworks (Eberlein, 1987; Fine & Ulrich, 1988; Gawthrop & Uhlemann, 1992; Welfel, 1992), something both graduate students (Tymchuk, 1985) and practitioners (Tymchuk et al., 1982) have historically recommended. . . .

This multidimensional framework needs to be modeled by faculty who appreciate the complexity of the decision-making process and exemplify prudent professional behavior. If this framework is not to become a hollow, abstract conceptualization, it must be coupled with a commitment by faculty and training staff to raise issues when appropriate and to discuss their implications fully.

Finally, ethics educators could test the usefulness of this model through various analogue designs that assess psychologists' judgments when faced with a wide variety of ethical–legal quandaries. A matrix of dilemma content and most salient sets of considerations could be derived, similar to the methods employed by earlier researchers (Haas, Malouf, & Mayerson, 1988; Smith et al., 1991). Psychologists may utilize the seven dimensions of this framework differently, in identifying dilemmas, considering possible solutions, and deciding on a specific action.

References

Abeles N. (1980) Teaching ethical principles by means of value confrontations. *Psychotherapy: Theory, Research and Practice, 17,* 384–391.

Alcohol and Drug Abuse Amendments of 1983, 42 U.S.C. § 290dd-2 (1983).

American Psychological Association. (1981). Specialty guidelines for the delivery of services by clinical psychologists. *American Psychologist, 36,* 640–651.

American Psychological Association. (1987). General guidelines for providers of psychological services. *American Psychologist, 42,* 712–723.

American Psychological Association. (1992). Ethical principles of psychologists and code of conduct. *American Psychologist, 47,* 1597–1611.

American Psychological Association. (1993a). Guidelines for providers of psychological services to ethnic, linguistic, and culturally diverse populations. *American Psychologist, 48,* 45–48.

American Psychological Association. (1993b). Record keeping guidelines. *American Psychologist, 48,* 984–986.

American Psychological Association. (1994). Report of the ethics committee. *American Psychologist, 49,* 659–666.

Appelbaum, P. (1993). Legal liability and managed care. *American Psychologist, 48,* 251–257.

Association of State and Provincial Psychology Boards. (1996). ASPPB code of conduct. In L. J. Bass, S. T. DeMers, J. R. P. Ogloff, C. Peterson, J. L. Pettifor, R. P. Reaves, T. Retfalvi, N. P. Simon, C. Sinclair, & R. M. Tipton (Eds.), *Professional conduct and discipline in psychology* (pp. 165–176). Washington, DC: American Psychological Association.

Beauchamp, T. L., & Childress, J. F. (1994). *Principles of biomedical ethics* (4th ed.). New York: Oxford University Press.

Bennett, B. E., Bryant, B. K., VandenBos, G. R., & Greenwood, A. (1990). *Professional liability and risk management.* Washington, DC: American Psychological Association.

Bongar, B. (1991). *The suicidal patient: Clinical and legal standards of care.* Washington, DC: American Psychological Association.

Cayleff, S. E. (1986). Ethical issues in counseling gender, race, and culturally distinct groups. *Journal of Counseling & Development, 64,* 345–347.

Department of Health and Human Services Regulations, 42 C.F.R. § 2.1, *et seq.* (1997).

Eberlein, L. (1988) The new CPA Code of Ethics for Canadian psychologists: An education and training perspective. *Canadian Psychology, 29,* 206–211.

Fine, M. A., & Ulrich, L. P. (1988). Integrating psychology and philosophy in teaching a graduate course in ethics. *Professional Psychology: Research and Practice, 19,* 542–546.

Gambrill, E. D. (1990). *Critical thinking in clinical practice: Improving the accuracy of judgments and decisions about clients.* San Francisco: Jossey-Bass.

Gawthrop, J. C., & Uhlemann, M. R. (1992). Effects of the problem-solving approach in ethics training. *Professional Psychology: Research and Practice, 23,* 38–42.

Haas, L. J., Malouf, J. L., & Mayerson, N. H. (1988). Personal and professional characteristics as factors in psychologists' ethical decision making. *Professional Psychology: Research and Practice, 19,* 35–42.

Higuchi, S. A. (1994). Recent managed-care legislative and legal issues. In R. L. Lowman & R. J. Resnick (Eds.), *The mental health professional's guide to managed care* (pp. 83–118). Washington, DC: American Psychological Association.

Johnson, W. B. (1995). Perennial ethical quandaries in military psychology: Toward an American Psychological Association–Department of Defense collaboration. *Professional Psychology: Research and Practice, 26,* 281–287.

Jordan, A. E., & Meara, N. M. (1990). Ethics and professional practice of psychologists: The role of virtues and principles. *Professional Psychology: Research and Practice, 21,* 107–114.

Kitchener, K. S. (1984). Intuition, critical evaluation and the ethical principles: The foundation for ethical decisions in counseling psychology. *Counseling Psychologist, 12*(3), 43–55.

Koocher, G. P. (1994). The commerce of professional psychology and the new ethics code. *Professional Psychology: Research and Practice, 25,* 355–361.

Lakin, M. (1994). Morality in group and family therapies: Multiperson therapies and the 1992 ethics code. *Professional Psychology: Research and Practice, 25,* 344–348.

Meara, N. M., Schmidt, L. D., & Day, J. D. (1996). Principles and virtues: A foundation for ethical decisions, policies, and character. *Counseling Psychology, 24,* 4–77.

Newman, R., & Bricklin, P. M. (1994) Parameters of managed mental health care: Legal, ethical, and professional guidelines. In R. L. Lowman & R. G. Resnick (Eds.), *The mental health professional's guide to managed care* (pp. 63–82). Washington, DC: American Psychological Association.

Payton, C. R. (1994). Implications of the 1992 ethics code for diverse groups. *Professional Psychology: Research and Practice, 25,* 317–320.

Plante, T. G. (1995). Training child clinical predoctoral interns and postdoctoral fellows in ethics and professional issues: An experiential model. *Professional Psychology: Research and Practice, 26,* 616–619.

Pope, K. S. (1990). Ethical and malpractice issues in hospital practice. *American Psychologist, 45,* 1066–1070.

Pope, K. S., & Bajt, T. R. (1988). When laws and values conflict: A dilemma for psychologists. *American Psychologist, 43,* 828–829.

Pope, K. S., & Vasquez, M. J. T. (1991). *Ethics in psychotherapy and counseling: A practical guide for psychologists.* San Francisco: Jossey-Bass.

Pope, K. S., & Vetter, V. A. (1992). Ethical dilemmas encountered by members of the American Psychological Association: A national survey. *American Psychologist, 47,* 397–411.

Smith, T. S., McGuire, J. M., Abbott, D. W., & Blau, B. I. (1991). Clinical ethical decision making: An investigation of the rationales used to justify doing less than one believes one should. *Professional Psychology: Research and Practice, 22,* 235–239.

Soisson, E., VandeCreek, L., & Knapp, S. (1987). Thorough record keeping: A good defense in a litigious era. *Professional Psychology: Research and Practice, 18,* 498–502.

Stromberg, C. D., Haggarty, D. J., Leibenluft, R. F., McMillan, M. H., Mishkin, B., Rubin, B. L., & Trilling, H. R. (1988). *The psychologist's legal handbook.* Washington, DC: National Register of Health Service Providers in Psychology.

Thompson, A. (1990). *Guide to ethical practice in psychotherapy.* New York: Wiley.

Tymchuk, A. J. (1985). Ethical decision-making and psychology students' attitudes toward training in ethics. *Professional Practice in Psychology, 6,* 219–232.

Tymchuk, A. J., Drapkin, R. S., Major-Kingsley, S., Ackerman, A. B., Coffman, E. W., & Baum, M. S. (1982). Ethical decision making and psychologists' attitudes toward training in ethics. *Professional Psychology: Research and Practice, 13,* 412–421.

Vanek, C. A. (1990). Survey of ethics education in clinical and counseling psychology. *Dissertation Abstracts International, 52, 5797B* (University Microfilms No. 90–14,449).

Vasquez, M. J. T. (1994). Implications of the 1992 ethics code for the practice of individual psychotherapy. *Professional Psychology: Research and Practice, 25,* 321–328.

Welfel, E. R. (1992). Psychologist as ethics educator: Successes, failures, and unanswered questions. *Professional Psychology: Research and Practice, 23,* 182–189.

Wood, K. A., Rogers, J. H., McCarthy, S. M., & Lewine, R. R. J. (1994). Psychologists in public inpatient settings: Ethical dilemmas. *Professional Psychology: Research and Practice, 25,* 234–240.

♦   ♦   ♦

Commentary: See also, Knapp, S., & VandeCreek, L. (2004). Using case law to teach professional ethics. Teaching of Psychology, 31, 281–284.

CHAPTER 4

CONFIDENTIALITY, PRIVILEGE, AND PRIVACY

Except for the ultimate precept—above all, do no harm—there is probably no ethical value in psychology that is more inculcated than confidentiality. Whether psychologists are engaging in research; assessing children, families, employees, criminal defendants, or others; or providing any of the several forms of psychological intervention—regardless of whether they are employed in private or public settings—they know that they bear responsibility for protecting information disclosed to them in the context of a professional relationship. Yet, there is probably no ethical duty more misunderstood or honored by its breach rather than by its fulfillment.

There is ample evidence that protecting intimate disclosures by patients, clients, and even research subjects is valued in society. Even though the word *privacy* does not appear in the U.S. Constitution, the Supreme Court has recognized it as a fundamental right. In part, the right of privacy means that federal and state governmental agencies are barred from unreasonable gathering, storage, and dissemination of their citizens' private information. Many states have passed even more particularized statutes that regulate the disclosure of psychological information. Some of these laws call for civil or even criminal penalties if psychologists or other professionals breach confidentiality without the informed consent of those they assess, treat, or study. Other states—but not all—have enacted statutes, called privileged communications laws, that permit a client to bar his or her psychologist from testifying about certain matters in legal proceedings. And, of course, medicine and every mental health profession embed in their codes of ethics provisions for protecting confidential communications.

But, to the same degree that this litany of protections evidences the heightened importance of confidentiality and privacy in society, like the ozone layer of the atmosphere, there has been a gradual but constant erosion of these fundamental values, particularly after the destruction of the World Trade Center. As columnist William Safire stated, "after 9/11, the passion went out of advocacy of privacy. The right to be let alone had to be balanced against the right to stay alive" (Safire, 2004, p. A27). As a result, he reported, patients no longer can expect that their medical and mental health histories will remain confidential. But even before 9/11, this was true. For example, when clients seek reimbursement for psychotherapy from their insurers, they are almost compelled to waive their right to bar dissemination to the reimbursing agency of vital and personal information, such as their diagnosis, prognosis, and aspects of their history. Although privileged communications laws sound protective, they most often contain exceptions permitting psychologists to report child abuse, to testify in civil commitment hearings, and to sue for collection of debts. Thus, when read in their entirety, many privilege laws contain more holes than fabric.

To those who view confidentiality as a preeminent value, the most noteworthy and troubling example of its dilution was the decision made by the California Supreme Court in *Tarasoff v. Regents of the University of California* (1976). This was perhaps the most well-known and notorious case in mental health law, and so, in this chapter, I provide extensive material written about the *Tarasoff* case and its ramifications.

Briefly, California's highest court held that psychotherapists have certain obligations to nonpatient third parties whom they may not know and have never seen when their patients disclose believable and serious threats to harm those third parties. In possibly the most quoted line from *Tarasoff*, the court stated: "The protective privilege ends where the public peril begins" (*Tarasoff v. Regents*, 1976, p. 347). Although poetically alliterative, this mandate had stark and even frightening implications. It clearly put mental health professionals on notice that society did not hold confidentiality in as high esteem as do most psychologists. Speaking through its legal system, society told psychologists—including, as you will see, researchers—as well as mental health professionals in general that fidelity to one's client must recede when it is necessary to protect third parties from harm.

There should be many questions rustling around in the reader's mind about the long- and short-term effects of *Tarasoff*. What are the consequences, for example, of establishing a role for psychologists as protectors of private third parties external to therapy? How does this affect the client–clinician relationship? What additional obligations to the client does *Tarasoff* suggest? If clients are told that not everything they say in therapy is confidential, will they be less honest and trusting? What if the client is not threatening to harm another person by force but by infecting a lover with AIDS? If confidentiality is such a core value to the psychological profession and to those it serves, then why does the rest of society seem to hold that value in lesser esteem than psychologists? Is the protection of intimate disclosures to a therapist more important to the therapist than it is to the client? Is, in fact, the profession making too much of confidentiality as an ethical value? And at this point in my litany, the risk-averse reader should be asking how a conscientious therapist (and researcher) can handle the complex treatment, ethical, and legal problems that arise when faced with a dangerous client.

The material in this chapter raises these questions, debates the issues, and, perhaps, even provides some answers. It also has some didactic goals that should not be ignored, such as understanding the distinctions among privacy, privilege, and confidentiality and gaining an appreciation of the confidentiality provisions in the APA Ethics Code. But clearly there are more important lessons to be learned. Perhaps more than any other topic, confidentiality provides a springboard for contemplating the consequences for psychologists torn between their duty and ethical obligations to clients and their responsibilities to the larger society in which they live. A consideration of these dual roles is the overarching purpose of this chapter.

References

Safire, W. (2004, March 10). Privacy in retreat. *The New York Times*, p. A27.

Tarasoff v. Regents of the University of California, 551 P.2d 334 (Cal. 1976).

Privacy, Confidentiality, and Privilege in Psychotherapeutic Relationships

Michele Smith-Bell and William J. Winslade

. . .

PRIVACY

Concept of Privacy

The concept of privacy embraces the idea of limiting the access of others in certain respects (Gavison, 1980), such as limiting the access of others to one's body or mind, including information about the self contained in dreams, fantasies, thoughts, and beliefs. Privacy in the law is sometimes linked to freedom from intrusion by the state or third persons; it also designates a domain of personal associations, abortion, and bodily integrity. Privacy is important because it preserves and protects individuals as they exercise their freedom to develop their personal identity, choose their values, and shape the course of their lives.

Some legal commentators argue for a constitutional right to privacy, seeing personal information as an integral part of an individual's identity and as crucial to most theories of personhood . . .

Constitutional Right to Privacy

The Supreme Court first recognized a constitutional right to privacy in the case of *Griswold* v. *Connecticut* (1965), which struck down a Connecticut statute prohibiting use of contraceptives by married couples. The right to privacy was expanded in the case of *Eisenstadt* v. *Baird* (1972), in which the Supreme Court reversed the defendant's conviction for distributing contraceptives to unmarried persons. In *Roe* v. *Wade* (1973), the Court held that criminal abortion laws, which proscribed abortion except for the purpose of saving the life of the mother, are unconstitutional. However, the *Roe* Court limited the right to privacy by stating that "only personal rights that can be deemed 'fundamental' or 'implicit in the concept of ordered liberty' . . . are included in this guarantee of personal privacy."

The constitutional right to privacy was restricted in the subsequent case of *Whalen v. Roe* (1976), in which the Court ruled that a patient does not have a constitutional right to informational privacy of communications or records generated in the course of medical treatment when the records are adequately protected from unauthorized disclosure. A more recent Supreme Court case further limits the constitutional right to privacy. In *Bowers v. Hardwick* (1985), the Court upheld a Georgia state antisodomy statute, and rejected the assertion that the right to privacy includes the fundamental right of homosexuals to engage in sodomy. Few federal appellate courts or state courts have recognized a constitutional right to privacy for the psychotherapeutic relationship . . .

In California (In re Lifschutz, 1970), a psychotherapist claimed that he had a privacy interest in psychotherapeutic communications with his patients; the court held that only the patient has a constitutionally protected privacy interest in preventing the release of psychotherapeutic communications. In another case (*Caesar v. Mountanos*, 1976), a psychotherapist refused to answer questions about one of his patients even after the patient specifically waived the psychotherapeutic privilege. The court held that the nature of communications between a patient and his therapist brings the relationship within the constitutional right of privacy through the psychotherapist–patient privilege. But on appeal, the court held that the right to privacy may be limited when necessary to advance a compelling

From *American Journal of Orthopsychiatry, 64*, 180–193. Copyright 1994 by the American Orthopsychiatry Association. Adapted with permission of the publisher.

state interest, such as ascertaining truth in court proceedings; moreover, it was held to be the patient's right to waive or assert the privilege.

The case of *Hawaii Psychiatric Society v. Ariyoshi* (1979) supported a constitutional right to privacy. A federal district court enjoined the State of Hawaii from enforcing a statute that permitted the issuance of administrative inspection warrants to review the mental health records of Medicaid patients. The court held that an individual's decision to seek the aid of a psychiatrist, or to communicate certain personal information to that psychiatrist, fell squarely within the constitutional right to privacy. The court balanced the patient's privacy interest against the state's interest in protecting the Medicaid program from fraud; it found that the state failed to show that the issuance of warrants to inspect the confidential medical records of a psychiatrist was necessary to advance a compelling state interest (Smith, 1980). . . .

CONFIDENTIALITY

Distinction From Privacy

Privacy and confidentiality are essential features of the psychotherapeutic relationship, despite the limited recognition of the right to privacy in constitutional law. Both are linked to the general notion of limited access and the exclusion of others; sometimes these concepts are used loosely and interchangeably. For example, privacy and confidentiality both stand as polar opposites to what is public and open to everyone. Nevertheless, it is useful to distinguish these concepts in the context of the psychotherapeutic relationship.

When a person enters into a therapeutic relationship, the client relinquishes his or her personal privacy of thoughts, feelings, beliefs, etc., in exchange for the prospect of therapeutic understanding and assistance. In this respect privacy is an aspect of *individuals*. Once private information has been disclosed to a therapist with an expectation that such information will not ordinarily be disclosed to third parties, it becomes confidential, and one refers to the confidentiality of information in the relationship. Thus, giving a therapist access to private information is necessary by definition for establishing a confidential relationship; and confidentiality is essential. . . .

In some instances, no third parties have access to private information disclosed in confidence to the therapist or even know that the relationship exists at all. Some clients, for example, choose to pay cash for therapy rather than to file an insurance claim (Domb, 1990–1991, citing Sosfin, 1985). Some therapists organize their offices to protect client privacy by the use of separate entrances and exits and of answering machines rather than answering services. The classic image of the exclusive dyadic relationship of the therapist–client, though increasingly rare, is not extinct.

Obstacles to Preservation

Individual and, increasingly, group therapeutic practice often occurs in a larger context of therapist, client, and an array of third parties including family members, employers, insurers, courts, and government agencies. Therapists' general obligation to protect clients' confidential information is overridden by specific obligations to disclose information at the client's request, when the law requires it, or when ethics demands it. For example, a client in a commitment, competency, sanity, or custody proceeding might desire that a therapist testify about disclosures made in therapy. The law might also require disclosures in such contexts even if the client does not consent to them. Legally mandated reporting requirements, such as those concerning child or elder abuse, override confidentiality. Ethics may dictate disclosures in the absence of specific legal authority. Conflicts arise, for example, concerning therapists' obligation to protect third parties threatened by dangerous patients.

The therapeutic consequences of external pressures on the preservation of confidentiality are that therapists may become wary of seeking sensitive information and clients of disclosing it. Even if therapists do not explicitly notify clients of the limits of confidentiality, the style of conducting therapeutic inquiry is influenced by the encroaching shadow of third-party access to information. If therapists inform clients of the limits of confidentiality, clients may then be inhibited in their communication and thereby hamper therapeutic effectiveness. The challenge to policymakers is to balance the need for confidentiality essential to the therapeutic process with the need for access to otherwise confidential information when necessary to protect legitimate public interests.

Patient expectations. Most therapists should be familiar, even if not happy, with the numerous restrictions placed on the right to confidentiality, but studies indicate that patients have greater expectations of privacy and confidentiality (Weiss, 1982). In a 1986 study, a majority of student psychotherapy patients and nonpatients believed that all communications to psychotherapists are confidential; almost all patients wanted to be informed of exceptions to confidentiality; and most reported that they would react negatively to unauthorized breaches of confidentiality that would undermine their right to privacy (VandeCreek, Miars, & Herzog, 1987). . . .

Therapists should, of course, protect confidentiality to the extent permitted by law and required by ethical standards. But in view of clients' sometimes unrealistic expectations about the scope of confidentiality, it is important to clarify its limits at the outset of therapy or at least early on. Therapeutic relationships are often tentative and fragile until a client trusts a therapist. Trust is threatened, if not undermined, if a client feels misled by the therapist, and such a client may withhold information or not cooperate in the therapy in overt or subtle ways—by canceling sessions, coming late, failing to pay, etc. Misunderstandings about confidentiality may even irrevocably rupture a therapeutic relationship. Thus, it is important for therapists to know and disclose what clients can reasonably expect concerning confidentiality. Its precise boundaries may be difficult to mark out in advance, but at least the general issues should be addressed.

When therapists are confronted with a specific conflict between a client's interest in confidentiality and a third party's claim to access, it is almost always appropriate to explore the conflict with the client first. This advances the therapeutic process because it demonstrates respect for both the client and the integrity of the therapeutic relationship. Clients may choose to authorize disclosure even if not legally required to do so. When a client does not want to permit disclosure, therapists have a duty to seek protection of confidentiality to the extent that the law and ethics allow. In specific situations, therapists may find it helpful to consult ethics committees of their professional organizations, ethics consultants or attorneys, or experienced colleagues who are familiar with confidentiality rules and practices. Demands to disclose confidential information are sometimes excessive; it may be possible for the client or the therapist to negotiate a limited disclosure that satisfies both the client and the third party. In other situations a client may have waived or forfeited the right to confidentiality by, for instance, signing a waiver or revealing private information to a third party; the therapist may then have no choice but to disclose otherwise confidential information. The damage to the therapeutic relationship can be minimized, however, if the client has been adequately informed and educated by the therapist early in the relationship.

PRIVILEGE

Concept of Privilege

The concept of privilege should be distinguished from that of confidentiality. Privilege is an exception to the general rule that the public has a right to relevant evidence in a court proceeding; confidentiality refers more broadly to legal rules and ethical standards that protect an individual from the unauthorized disclosure of information. Confidentiality alone is not enough to support a privilege; without a privilege statute or a common-law rule, a therapist may be charged with contempt of court for refusing a court order to testify about a patient's psychotherapeutic communications. Thus, confidentiality is a professional duty to refrain from speaking about certain matters, while privilege is a relief from the duty to speak in a court proceeding about certain matters (Domb, 1990–1991, citing In re Lifschutz, 1970). . . .

Patient Rights

The patient's right to privacy and confidentiality is partially protected by the doctrine of privileged communications. Confidential information that would otherwise be admissible in a judicial proceeding may be withheld if it is classified as a privileged communication. Privilege thus protects patients' privacy and confidentiality and, in doing so, renders them more disposed to seek mental health services. Privilege generally belongs to the patient, who decides whether it will be exercised or waived. Although the holder of the privilege is the patient, in appropriate circumstances the therapist may invoke the privilege on behalf of the patient, unless that privilege has been waived or the communication in question falls within a statutory exception to the privilege (Brakel, Parry, & Weiner, 1985, citing In re Lifschutz, 1970).

To be considered privileged, communications from a patient to a therapist must meet a number of requirements. First, the communications must be to a licensed or certified therapist as described in the state's privilege statute, or to an assistant of the therapist, depending upon state law. Second, a professional relationship must exist between the patient and the therapist. Third, the communications must be related to the provision of professional services. Fourth, the communications must be confidential; they may not be released by the client to a third party (Smith, 1980).

. . .

Criticism of Privilege

. . .

Privilege laws and the general obligation of confidentiality have become increasingly subject to exceptions and limitations, effectively reduced by inconsistent federal and state rules, and threatened by changes in health-care financing. . . . In addition, privilege statutes afford only limited protection to confidentiality because of the narrowness of their application; in the litigation setting, they are often only applicable to psychiatrists and psychologists, thereby decreasing their scope and effectiveness (Brakel, Parry, & Weiner, 1985). The scope of psychotherapeutic privilege is also reduced when it is waived, sometimes unwisely, by patients.

Waiver

Patients waive the privilege for psychotherapeutic communications when they file a tort or Workers' Compensation claim for a psychiatric injury, or when litigants otherwise put their mental states at issue. Unlike exception, in which normally privileged information is not privileged in certain situations prescribed by law (as when a defendant to a criminal charge raises his mental state as a defense), waiver requires action or acquiescence from the patient. . . .

References

Bowers v. Hardwick, 478 U.S. 186. (1985).

Brakel, S. J., Parry, J., & Weiner, B. A. (1985). *The mentally disabled and the law* (3rd ed.). Chicago: American Bar Foundation.

Caesar v. Mountanos, 542 F.2d 1064 (9th Cir. 1976), *cert. denied,* 430 U.S. 954. (1977).

Domb, B. (1990–1991). I shot the sheriff, but only my analyst knows: Shrinking the psychotherapist–patient privilege. *Journal of Law and Health, 5,* 209–236.

Eisenstadt v. Baird, 405 U.S. 438. (1972).

Gavison, R. (1980). Privacy and the limits of the law. *Yale Law Journal, 89,* 421–472.

Griswold v. Connecticut, 381 U.S. 479. (1965).

Hawaii Psychiatric Society v. Ariyoshi, 481 F. Supp. 1028. (D. Hawaii, 1979).

In re Lifschutz, 2 Cal. 3d 415, 467 P.2d 557, 85 Cal. Rptr. 829. (1970).

Roe v. Wade, 410 U.S. 113. (1973).

Smith, S. R. (1980). Constitutional privacy in psychotherapy. *George Washington Law Review, 49,* 1–60.

Sosfin, E. S. (1985). The case for a federal psychotherapist–patient privilege that protects patient identity. *Duke Law Journal,* 1217–1244.

VandeCreek, L., Miars, R. D., & Herzog, C. E. (1987). Client anticipations and preferences for confidentiality of records. *Journal of Counseling Psychology, 34,* 62–67.

Weiss, B. D. (1982). Confidentiality expectations of patients, physicians, and medical students. *Journal of the American Medical Association, 247,* 2695–2697.

Whalen v. Roe, 429 U.S. 589. (1976).

◆　　◆　　◆

Commentary: In discussing the constitutional right to privacy, Smith-Bell and Winslade cite the case of Bowers v. Hardwick, *decided by the U.S. Supreme Court in 1985. As they correctly state, the Court in a 5–4 decision upheld a state statute criminalizing sodomy, rejecting the claim by a homosexual petitioner that such laws violated the right to privacy or liberty under the Due Process Clause. However, in 2003, the Court in Lawrence v. Texas, 539 U.S. 558 (2003), overruled Bowers, and held that statutes that criminalized sodomy between consenting adults of the same sex in the privacy of their home did, indeed, violate the Constitution. As the Court stated, the "right to liberty under the Due Process Clause gives [homosexual persons] the full right to engage in their conduct without the intervention of the government" (p. 578).*

Max Siegel, President of the APA in 1983, subscribed to the "absolute position that psychologists may not break confidentiality of a patient or client under any circumstances" (p. 269). See Siegel, M. (1979). Privacy, ethics, and confidentiality. Professional Psychology, 10, 249–258. The APA has never adopted that view in its ethical codes.

Confidentiality is now covered in seven separate provisions of Section 4 of the 2002 Ethical Principles of Psychologists and Code of Conduct. *This has been pared down from 11 provisions that appeared in the 1992 Code. Provisions concerning maintenance of records and the placing of confidential information in*

databases have been shifted to Section 6 (Record Keeping and Fees; see chapter 10). Standards 4.01 and 4.05 are the major provisions. Standard 4.01 reads in a relevant part, "Psychologists have a primary obligation and take reasonable precautions to protect confidential information . . . recognizing that the extent and limits of confidentiality may be regulated by law, or established by institutional rules or professional or scientific relationships." Compare this with a motion made by a member of the Council of Representatives in debating a very similar provision in the 1992 Code: "Psychologists take the utmost care to respect and protect the confidentiality rights of those with whom they work or consult, and disclose confidential information only when compelled by law." That motion was defeated by a large margin. What version do readers think is preferable?

As you read the material that follows, it may be useful to compare Siegel's view with prevailing sentiments and to ask this: In what ways does the current provision disserve the ethical ideals of self-determination, the independence to decide matters about one's own private interests, and the right to privacy and confidentiality reflected in aspirational Principle E of the 2002 Code?

Privacy and Confidentiality in Psychotherapy

Louis Everstine, Diana Sullivan Everstine, Gary M. Heymann, Reiko Homma True, David H. Frey, Harold G. Johnson, and Richard H. Seiden

. . .

OVERVIEW

. . . [T]he issue is not whether guilt properly falls upon a particular therapist who breaches or declines to breach confidentiality; instead, the issue is one of defining the line between proper and improper conduct. Here in truth is a "doctor's dilemma," created by the tension between two powerful forces that radiate from opposite poles: (a) the client, a private citizen who wishes that the right to privacy be respected and (b) society, which wants to be informed about certain acts or intentions on the part of individual citizens. In choosing a path between these adversaries, a therapist can be excused for seeking the intercession of a guiding star. . . .

DUTY TO WARN

Confusion remains about the case of *Tarasoff v. Board of Regents of the University of California,* confusion that was not dispelled by a final decision handed down by the California Supreme Court in July 1976. Many do not know full details of the events that occurred in 1969 in Berkeley which led to the case being brought. . . .

On August 20, 1969, . . . Prosenjit Poddar, who was a voluntary outpatient at Cowell Memorial Hospital [footnote omitted] on the Berkeley campus informed his therapist, a psychologist, that he was planning to kill a young woman. Poddar did not name the woman, but as established later, the psychologist could easily have inferred who she was [footnote omitted]. The murder was to be carried out when the woman returned to Berkeley from her summer vacation.

Following this session, the psychologist telephoned the campus police to ask them to observe Poddar for possible hospitalization as a person who was "dangerous to himself or others"; he then wrote a letter, containing a formal request for assistance, to the chief of the campus police. The campus officers took Poddar into custody for the purpose of questioning, but later released him when he gave evidence of being "rational." Soon afterward the psychologist's supervisor, Director of the Department of Psychiatry at Cowell Hospital, asked the campus police to return the psychologist's letter, ordered that the letter and therapy notes that had been made in Poddar's case be destroyed, and directed that no further action be taken to hospitalize Poddar. No warning was given either to the intended victim or to her parents. The client, naturally enough, did not resume his therapy.

On October 27, 1969, Prosenjit Poddar killed Tatiana Tarasoff. The victim's parents filed suit against the Board of Regents of the university, several employees of Cowell Hospital, and the chief of the campus police plus four of his officers. A lower court dismissed the suit, the parents appealed, and the California Supreme Court upheld the appeal in 1974 and reaffirmed its decision in 1976. In July 1977, the suit was settled out of court and the Tarasoff family received a substantial award. . . .

A crucial point of the Supreme Court decision was this: It was not the failure of the psychologist or his supervisor to predict violence that made the case a viable one (the psychologist had clearly decided that his client was dangerous), but the failure of the psychologist and his supervisor to provide an adequate warning of violence either to the intended victim or to her parents.

In a brief amicus curiae filed by CSPA [California State Psychological Association] and other professional organizations acting in concert (see Gurevitz, 1977), it was argued that (a) a therapist cannot predict violence with certainty and (b) warning the intended victim would have breached the confidentiality of the therapist–client relationship, thus jeopardizing both the climate of trust that is necessary for therapy to occur and the effectiveness of therapy itself. The Court ignored the first argument because the therapist *had* accurately predicted that a violent act would be committed. The second argument was flatly rejected by the majority[.] . . . And to the contention that the essential nature of psychotherapy is altered by the stated exception to privilege, the Court responded with the view that a therapy relationship, whether effective or not, is of secondary importance to the preservation of life and safety. In its conclusion, the Court affirmed a guiding principle that had weighed heavily in its decision: "The public policy favoring protection of the confidential character of patient–psychotherapist communications must yield to the extent to which disclosure is essential to avert danger to others. The protective privilege ends where the public peril begins" (p. 24) [footnote omitted]. That was the cornerstone of the decision. No psychologist can be immune to the force of this conclusion, and each must ponder its implications.

What is the major impact of *Tarasoff?* In essence, the Court has chosen to make a narrow interpretation of therapist–client privilege, believing that the privilege should be sharply restricted. In deliberating the concept of privilege, the Court took a dim view of the notion that psychotherapy must occur in an atmosphere of secrecy (the canon of sanctum sanctorum). In reaction, Siegel (1976) and others have concluded that by making these value judgments, the Court has struck yet another blow against individual freedom of conscience and has come down hard on the side of conformity. Still others are willing to accept that the "duty to warn" is, at least for the present time and indefinite future, a legal requirement.

Although a therapist, a person is still a citizen, and he or she must protect and contribute to the common good. As a private citizen, the person of good conscience will not hesitate to warn an intended victim. That, as far as can be determined, is the meaning of *Tarasoff.*

EROSION OF THE PROFESSIONAL TRUST RELATIONSHIP

A hallmark of psychotherapy is the establishment of a relationship of trust between client and therapist, and this relationship must be carefully protected through the course of the therapeutic experience. Yet a gradual and continuous weakening has occurred in the confidentiality privilege, one legal mechanism by which this professional trust relationship is implemented in our social system. . . . [I]t is urgent that we make every effort to reestablish and strengthen the sociolegal nature of the trust relationship that is so central to our professional work. . . .

There is a psychotherapist–client privilege. In California law, *psychotherapist* is defined as a clinical psychologist, a school psychologist, a clinical social worker, or a psychiatrist. This privilege is controlled by the client, is not independently held by the psychotherapist, and *must* be breached by the psychotherapist under six legal conditions: (a) when criminal action is involved; (b) when the information is made an issue in a court action; (c) when the information is obtained for the purpose of rendering an expert's report to a lawyer; (d) when the psychotherapist is acting in a court-appointed capacity; (e) when the psychotherapist believes that the client is a danger to himself, herself, or others and feels that it is necessary to prevent an actual threat of danger from being carried out; and when a client is under the age of 16 and the therapist believes that the client has been the victim of a crime (e.g., incest, rape) and judges such disclosure to be in the client's best interest. . . .

CONCLUSIONS AND RECOMMENDATIONS

. . . [W]e have observed a mysterious trend toward legislation that would seriously impair our efforts to strengthen confidentiality. This trend is embodied by the ever more stringent regulations that are being imposed to require the swift and aggressive reporting of an ever widening array of suspected crimes against the person. . . .

. . . We can with confidence put forward the following *prophesies:* (a) More laws will be passed and more court decisions handed down that will mandate respect for privacy and preservation of confidentiality; (b) more laws will be passed and more court decisions handed down which will require that confidentiality be breached and privacy invaded. . . .

References

Gurevitz, H. (1977). *Tarasoff*: Protective privilege versus public peril. *American Journal of Psychiatry, 134,* 289–292.

Siegel, M. (1976, Fall). Confidentiality. *Clinical Psychologist* (Newsletter of Division 12 of the American Psychological Association), pp. 1; 23.

Tarasoff v. Board of Regents of the University of California, Cal. Rptr. 14, No. S.F. 23042 (Cal. Sup. Ct., July 1, 1976) 131.

◆　◆　◆

Commentary: No judicial decision has had more of an impact on professional psychologists (and, in some respects, on researchers as well) than Tarasoff v. Regents of the University of California (1976). *The basic facts of the case are described in the excerpt above by Everstine et al. For additional and interesting facts see Egley, L. C., & Ben-Ari, A. (1994). Making* Tarasoff *practical for various treatment populations.* Journal of Psychiatry and Law, 22, 473–501.

There were actually two decisions rendered by California's Supreme Court: one in 1974 (Tarasoff I) and another in 1976 (Tarasoff II). The defendants, including Dr. Moore (the psychologist who treated Poddar), Dr. Powelson (the psychiatrist who ran the university hospital clinic where Poddar was in outpatient treatment), and the Regents of the University of California (their employer), asserted that Tatiana Tarasoff's parents had no legal claim against them for the death of their daughter because she was not their patient, but a private third party to whom they owed no professional duty. Nevertheless, a majority of the state supreme court held that the parents could sue the defendants for failure to warn Ms. Tarasoff or others of Poddar's threat. The following statement by the court sent psychological shock waves across the psychotherapy landscape—far beyond the borders of California:

> *We shall explain that defendant therapists, merely because Tatiana herself was not their patient, cannot escape liability for failing to exercise due care to warn the endangered Tatiana or those who reasonably could have been expected to notify her of her peril. When a doctor or a psychotherapist, in the exercise of his professional skill and knowledge, determines, or should determine, that a warning is essential to avert danger arising from the medical or psychological condition of his patient, he incurs a legal obligation to give that warning. Primarily, the relationship between defendant therapists and Poddar as their patient imposes the described duty to warn.*

See Tarasoff v. Regents of the University of California, 529 P. 2d 553 (Cal. 1974) (Tarasoff I).

Tarasoff I stimulated a plethora of critical analysis. *See, for example, Slovenko, R. (1975). Psychotherapy and confidentiality.* Cleveland State Law Review, 24, *375–396; Stone, A. (1976). Suing psychotherapists to safeguard society.* Harvard Law Review, 90, 358–378. *The following article addressed the ethical implications of the decision.*

Therapists as Protectors and Policemen: New Roles as a Result of *Tarasoff?*

Donald N. Bersoff

The emphasis on the clinician's duty to disclose threats to potential victims has obscured the concomitant duty of clinicians to disclose to clients the limits of confidentiality. Thus, *Tarasoff* (1974) has relevance in terms of the informed consent doctrine, an emerging rule of law developed in the context of physician–patient malpractice suits. . . . The philosophical underpinning to the informed consent doctrine is that everyone has the right to self-determination and, more specifically, the right to determine what happens to his or her body. As a result, the patient is entitled to all the facts necessary to make an informed, intelligent choice prior to consenting to medical intervention.

Typically, however, the duty to disclose is not absolute. It is tempered by what may be called the materiality rule. Physicians need not disclose risks that are likely to be known to the average patient or are in fact known to the particular patient as a result of past experience. Rather, the extent of disclosure is determined by the materiality of the risk. As defined in a leading case,

> Materiality may be said to be the significance a reasonable person, in what the physician knows or should know is his patient's position, would attach to the disclosed risk or risks in deciding whether to submit or not to submit to surgery or treatment. (*Wilkinson v. Vesey*, 1972, p. 689)

Some of the information falling within the materiality rule and thus necessitating disclosure are inherent and potential hazards of the proposed treatment, alternatives to that treatment, and the results likely if the patient remains untreated.

With this background, the implications of *Tarasoff* with regard to informed consent become self-evident.

The possibility that therapists may be under a duty to make known to both the intended victim and police authorities threats to third persons made by their clients would clearly seem to be a material piece of information requiring disclosure to prospective clients. That such information is material to an individual client is manifest in the consequences of disclosure. Certainly, liberty and privacy interests are at stake (Fleming & Maximov, 1974). Communication of violent threats outside the therapeutic relationship may lead to involuntary incarceration because the standard for emergency commitment in most states is "danger to self or others." Knowledge by the putatively potential victim may lead to abrupt disruption of the relationship between client and third party in instances where such disruption would not, in fact, be warranted. The disclosure clearly violates the confidential association between client and clinician. . . .

It is thus evident that clinicians must now reveal to potential clients the limits of confidentiality. To blithely ensure the secrecy of all communications is to engage in blatant misrepresentation of facts that should now be known to all therapists. To fail to disclose these limits is to hold oneself open to liability under the materiality test. In fact, the failure to disclose the limits of confidentiality in the face of a concomitant duty to disclose threats to third parties may be to entrap the client. Clients, believing that the therapeutic relationship is inviolate, may lay bare heretofore unrevealed secrets, including their most violent urges. Therapists, fearful that their clients' verbal expression of aggression may become manifest in overt behavior, aware of the *Tarasoff* decision, and frightened of the threat to their economic security and professional reputation, may too quickly and frequently inform police officials about the possibility of danger to society. The result will

From *Professional Psychology*, 7, 267–273. Copyright 1976 by the American Psychological Association.

be an increase in involuntary civil commitment of therapy clients who would otherwise have not been incarcerated. . . .

THE DUTY OF DISCLOSURE TO THIRD PERSONS

Tarasoff, important in itself for the implications it has with regard to informed consent, is also important in a larger context. Decisions such as *Tarasoff* make it increasingly clear that therapists not only serve their clients but are also agents of the society in which they work. Psychotherapists have long struggled with the problem of conflicting loyalties to their clients and to society. The traditional cant is that the relationship between client and clinician is an especially private one in which confidentiality is entitled to the utmost respect. The primary allegiance the budding practitioner is told, is to the client. Recently, Bersoff (1978), Halleck (1971), Kittrie (1971), Szasz (1963), and Torrey (1974) have surfaced the many ways in which mental health professionals serve the state and the public, often to the detriment of the individual client. . . .

[W]hile the psychologist in *Tarasoff* was employed by a state agency, the effect of the decision is not limited to those practitioners who work in the government-funded institutions. The therapist in *Tarasoff* was held liable, in part, for breach of a state statute concerning privileged communication that governs the behavior of private, as well as institutional, practitioners. Private therapists who might seek refuge in professional codes of ethics as counterweights in a struggle to protect their clients' confidences will fail to find them safe havens. In fact, the *Tarasoff* court quoted Section 9 of the Principles of Medical Ethics of the American Medical Association to further justify its decision. Section 9 reminds physicians that they may not reveal confidences "unless . . . required to do so by law or unless it becomes necessary in order to protect the welfare of the individual or of the community."[1]

. . . As psychiatrists and psychologists become more identified with the law and its enforcement,

there is the danger of discouraging people from seeking psychotherapy and of trusting those whom society has taught are the most trustworthy of professionals (excluding clergypersons, perhaps). Therapists may find themselves in insolvable conflicts as they attempt to reconcile their own personal morality and training regarding confidentiality, the vague reminders of their professional codes of ethics that warn of the consequences of violating the moral and legal standards of the community, and the developing legal requirements that demand complex decision making and a balancing between client and public interests. In any event, it is evident that there are ever decreasing guarantees to client–clinician privacy and that the therapeutic relationship is not immune from the scrutiny of society. Such limits must clearly be conveyed to the prospective client because failure to do so can result in both loss of liberty and privacy to the client as well as loss to the clinician of reputation and money damages to unwarned victims.

References

Bersoff, D. N. (1978). Coercion and reciprocity in psychotherapy. In C. T. Fischer & S. Brodsky (Eds.), *The Prometheus principle: Informed participation by clients in human services* (pp. 63–90). New Brunswick, NJ: Transaction.

Halleck, S. L. (1971). *The politics of therapy.* New York: Science House.

Kittrie, N. N. (1971). *The right to be different.* Baltimore, MD: Johns Hopkins University Press.

Szasz, T. S. (1963). *Law, liberty, and psychiatry.* New York: Macmillan.

Tarasoff v. Regents of University of California, 13 C.3d 177, 529 P.2d 553, 118 Cal. Rptr. 129 (1974).

Torrey, E. F. (1974). *The death of psychiatry.* Radnor, PA: Chilton.

Wilkinson v. Vesey, 110 R.I. 606, 295 A.2d 676 (1972).

◆　◆　◆

Commentary: In a rare move, the California Supreme Court agreed to hear new arguments and reconsidered its opinion in Tarasoff II.

---

[1]*Ed. Note:* See also Standards 4.02 and 4.05 of the current (2002) APA Ethics Code.

Tarasoff v. Regents of the University of California (*Tarasoff II*)

. . . We shall explain that defendant therapists cannot escape liability merely because Tatiana herself was not their patient. When a therapist determines, or pursuant to the standards of his profession should determine, that his patient presents a serious danger of violence to another, he incurs an obligation to use reasonable care to protect the intended victim against such danger. The discharge of this duty may require the therapist to take one or more of various steps, depending upon the nature of the case. Thus it may call for him to warn the intended victim or others likely to apprise the victim of the danger, to notify the police, or to take whatever other steps are reasonably necessary under the circumstances. . . .

. . .

Although . . . under the common law, as a general rule, one person owed no duty to control the conduct of another . . . nor to warn those endangered by such conduct . . . the courts have carved out an exception to this rule in cases in which the defendant stands in some special relationship to either the person whose conduct needs to be controlled or in a relationship to the foreseeable victim of that conduct. . . . Applying this exception to the present case, we note that a relationship of defendant therapists to either Tatiana or Poddar will suffice to establish a duty of care: as explained in section 315 of the Restatement Second of Torts, a duty of care may arise from either "(a) a special relation . . . between the actor and the third person which imposes a duty upon the actor to control the third person's conduct, or (b) a special relation . . . between the actor and the other which gives to the other a right of protection."

Although plaintiffs' pleadings assert no special relation between Tatiana and defendant therapists, they establish as between Poddar and defendant therapists the special relation that arises between a patient and his doctor or psychotherapist [footnote omitted]. Such a relationship may support affirmative duties for the benefit of third persons. Thus, for example, a hospital must exercise reasonable care to control the behavior of a patient which may endanger other persons [footnote omitted]. A doctor must also warn a patient if the patient's condition or medication renders certain conduct, such as driving a car, dangerous to others [footnote omitted].

Although the California decisions that recognize this duty have involved cases in which the defendant stood in a special relationship *both* to the victim and to the person whose conduct created the danger, we do not think that the duty should logically be constricted to such situations. . . .

. . . "[T]here now seems to be sufficient authority to support the conclusion that by entering into a doctor–patient relationship the therapist becomes sufficiently involved to assume some responsibility for the safety, not only of the patient himself, but also of any third person whom the doctor knows to be threatened by the patient." (Fleming & Maximov, *The Patient or His Victim: The Therapist's Dilemma* (1974) 62 Cal.L.Rev. 1025, 1030.)

Defendants contend, however, that imposition of a duty to exercise reasonable care to protect third persons is unworkable because therapists cannot accurately predict whether or not a patient will resort to violence. In support of this argument amicus representing the American Psychiatric Association and other professional societies cites numerous articles which indicate that therapists, in the present state of the art, are unable reliably to predict violent acts; their forecasts, amicus claims, tend consistently to overpredict violence, and indeed are more often wrong than right. Since predictions of violence are often erroneous, amicus concludes, the courts should not render rulings that

From *Tarasoff v. Regents of the University of California (Tarasoff II)*, 551 P.2d 334 (Cal. 1976).

predicate the liability of therapists upon the validity of such predictions.

The role of the psychiatrist, who is indeed a practitioner of medicine, and that of the psychologist who performs an allied function, are like that of the physician who must conform to the standards of the profession and who must often make diagnoses and predictions based upon such evaluations. Thus the judgment of the therapist in diagnosing emotional disorders and in predicting whether a patient presents a serious danger of violence is comparable to the judgment which doctors and professionals must regularly render under accepted rules of responsibility.

We recognize the difficulty that a therapist encounters in attempting to forecast whether a patient presents a serious danger of violence. Obviously we do not require that the therapist, in making that determination, render a perfect performance: the therapist need only exercise "that reasonable degree of skill, knowledge, and care ordinarily possessed and exercised by members of (that professional specialty) under similar circumstances." . . . Within the broad range of reasonable practice and treatment in which professional opinion and judgment may differ, the therapist is free to exercise his or her own best judgment without liability; proof, aided by hindsight, that he or she judged wrongly is insufficient to establish negligence.

In the instant case, however, the pleadings do not raise any question as to failure of defendant therapists to predict that Poddar presented a serious danger of violence. On the contrary, the present complaints allege that defendant therapists did in fact predict that Poddar would kill, but were negligent in failing to warn.

Amicus contends, however, that even when a therapist does in fact predict that a patient poses a serious danger of violence to others, the therapist should be absolved of any responsibility for failing to act to protect the potential victim. In our view, however, once a therapist does in fact determine, or under applicable professional standards reasonably should have determined, that a patient poses a serious danger of violence to others, he bears a duty to exercise reasonable care to protect the foreseeable victim of that danger. While the discharge of this duty of due care will necessarily vary with the facts

of each case, in each instance the adequacy of the therapist's conduct must be measured against the traditional negligence standard of the rendition of reasonable care under the circumstances. As explained in Fleming and Maximov, *The Patient or His Victim: The Therapist's Dilemma* (1974) 62 Cal.L.Rev. 1025, 1067: " . . . the ultimate question of resolving the tension between the conflicting interests of patient and potential victim is one of social policy, not professional expertise. . . . In sum, the therapist owes a legal duty not only to his patient, but also to his patient's would-be victim and is subject in both respects to scrutiny by judge and jury." . . .

Defendants . . . argue that free and open communication is essential to psychotherapy. . . . The giving of a warning, defendants contend, constitutes a breach of trust which entails the revelation of confidential communications.

We recognize the public interest in supporting effective treatment of mental illness and in protecting the rights of patients to privacy. . . .

We realize that the open and confidential character of psychotherapeutic dialogue encourages patients to express threats of violence, few of which are ever executed. Certainly a therapist should not be encouraged routinely to reveal such threats: such disclosures could seriously disrupt the patient's relationship with his therapist and with the persons threatened. To the contrary, the therapist's obligations to his patient require that he not disclose a confidence unless such disclosure is necessary to avert danger in others, and even then that he do so discreetly, and in a fashion that would preserve the privacy of his patient to the fullest extent compatible with the prevention of the threatened danger. . . .

The revelation of a communication under the above circumstances is not a breach of trust or a violation of professional ethics: as stated in the Principles of Medical Ethics of the American Medical Association (1957), section 9: "A physician may not reveal the confidence entrusted to him in the course of medical attendance . . . *unless he is required to do so by the law or unless it becomes necessary in order to protect the welfare of the individual or of the community.* [Emphasis added.] We conclude that the public policy favoring protection of the confidential character of patient–psychotherapist communications must yield to the extent to which disclosure is essential to avert danger to others. The protective privilege ends where the public peril begins.

Our current crowded and computerized society compels the interdependence of its members. In this risk-infected society we can hardly tolerate the further exposure to danger that would result from a concealed knowledge of the therapist that his patient was lethal. If the exercise of reasonable care to protect the threatened victim requires the therapist to warn the endangered party or those who can reasonably be expected to notify him, we see no sufficient societal interest that would protect and justify concealment. The containment of such risks lies in the public interest. . . .

MOSK, Justice (concurring and dissenting).

I concur in the result in this instance only because the complaints allege that defendant therapists did in fact predict that Poddar would kill and were therefore negligent in failing to warn of that danger. . . .

I cannot concur, however, in the majority's rule that a therapist may be held liable for failing to predict his patient's tendency to violence if other practitioners, pursuant to the "standards of the profession," would have done so. The question is, what standards? . . .

. . . If a psychiatrist does in fact predict violence, then a duty to warn arises. The majority's expansion of that rule will take us from the world of reality into the wonderland of clairvoyance.

CLARK, Justice (dissenting).

Until today's majority opinion, both legal and medical authorities have agreed that confidentiality is essential to effectively treat the mentally ill, and that imposing a duty on doctors to disclose patient threats to potential victims would greatly impair treatment. Further, recognizing that effective treatment and society's safety are necessarily intertwined, the Legislature has already decided effective and confidential treatment is preferred over imposition of a duty to warn.

. . .

Overwhelming policy considerations weigh against imposing a duty on psychotherapists to warn a potential victim against harm. While offering virtually no benefit to society, such a duty will frustrate psychiatric treatment, invade fundamental patient rights and increase violence. . . .

Assurance of confidentiality is important for three reasons. . . .

First, without substantial assurance of confidentiality, those requiring treatment will be deterred from seeking assistance. . . .

Second, the guarantee of confidentiality is essential in eliciting the full disclosure necessary for effective treatment.

Third, even if the patient fully discloses his thoughts, assurance that the confidential relationship will not be breached is necessary to maintain his trust in his psychiatrist—the very means by which treatment is effected. . . .

Given the importance of confidentiality to the practice of psychiatry, it becomes clear the duty to warn imposed by the majority will cripple the use and effectiveness of psychiatry. Many people, potentially violent—yet susceptible to treatment—will be deterred from seeking it; those seeking it will be inhibited from making revelations necessary to effective treatment; and, forcing the psychiatrist to violate the patient's trust will destroy the interpersonal relationship by which treatment is effected. . . .

By imposing a duty to warn, the majority contributes to the danger to society of violence by the mentally ill and greatly increases the risk of civil commitment—the total deprivation of liberty—of those who should not be confined. The impairment of treatment and risk of improper commitment resulting from the new duty to warn will not be limited to a few patients but will extend to a large number of the mentally ill. Although under existing psychiatric procedures only a relatively few receiving treatment will ever present a risk of violence, the number making threats is huge, and it is the latter group—not just the former—whose treatment will be impaired and whose risk of commitment will be increased.

Both the legal and psychiatric communities recognize that the process of determining potential violence in a patient is far from exact, being fraught with complexity and uncertainty. . . .

This predictive uncertainty means that the number of disclosures will necessarily be large. As noted above, psychiatric patients are encouraged to discuss all thoughts of violence, and they often express such thoughts. However, unlike this court, the psychiatrist does not enjoy the benefit of overwhelming hindsight in seeing which few, if any, of his patients will ultimately become violent. Now, confronted by the majority's new duty, the psychiatrist must instantaneously calculate potential violence from each patient on each visit. The difficulties researchers have encountered in accurately predicting violence will be heightened for the practicing psychiatrist dealing for brief periods in his office with heretofore nonviolent patients. And, given the decision not to warn or commit must always be made at the psychiatrist's civil peril, one can expect most doubts will be resolved in favor of the psychiatrist protecting himself.

Neither alternative open to the psychiatrist seeking to protect himself is in the public interest.

◆　　◆　　◆

Commentary: Max Siegel (1979) made the following comments after Tarasoff II *was decided:*

> This was a day in court for the law and not for the mental health professions. If the psychologist had accepted the view of absolute, inviolate confidentiality, he might have been able to keep Poddar in treatment, saved the life of Tatiana Tarasoff, and avoided what was to become the Tarasoff decision. (p. 253)

Siegel, M. (1979). Privacy, ethics, and confidentiality. Professional Psychology, 10, 249–258.

Other commentators have suggested that a good client–clinician relationship is based on trust rather than on confidentiality. Thus, they argue, if trust is maintained, then the therapeutic relationship may endure even after a mandated breach in confidentiality. See Brosig, C. L., & Kalichman, S. C. (1992). Child abuse reporting decisions: Effects of statutory wording of reporting requirements. Professional Psychology: Research and Practice, 23, 486–492; Watson, H., & Levine, M. (1989).

Psychotherapy and mandated reporting of child abuse. American Journal of Orthopsychiatry, 59, 246–256. See also Shuman, D., & Foote, W. (1999). Jaffee v. Redmond's impact: Life after the Supreme Court's recognition of a psychotherapist–patient privilege. Professional Psychology: Research and Practice, 30, 479–487:

> [I]n a series of studies Shuman and Weiner found that, when asked, people expressed concerns with the importance of privilege and confidentiality and clearly preferred them to the alternative, but that in their actions the vast majority sought out therapists when they were in pain and talked to therapists whom they trusted, without regard to the state of the applicable privilege law. (p. 482)

In reviewing cases decided in the decade after Tarasoff II *Mills, Sullivan, and Eth (1987) stated:*

> Two arguments have been proposed to justify the enduring importance of confidentiality. Moral deontologists assert that privacy and absolute control over personal information are among the natural rights of man. They argue that since a breach of confidentiality constitutes an assault on human dignity, it is always wrong. The alternative and more widely held justification for the importance ascribed to confidentiality is based on a utilitarian calculation of effects. . . . This position holds that the consequences of violating confidentiality out-weigh the possible benefits. (p. 69)

Mills, M. J., Sullivan, G., & Eth, S. (1987). Protecting third parties: A decade after Tarasoff. American Journal of Psychiatry, 144, 64–74.

Adopting, for the sake of argument, a utilitarian view, when do readers believe the balance should be tipped in favor of breaching confidentiality? The next excerpt provides one view.

Some Contrarian Concerns About Law, Psychology, and Public Policy

Donald N. Bersoff

It has been my view for over 25 years (Bersoff, 1974), and I agree totally with Chris Slobogin (Reisner, Slobogin, & Rai, 1999) on this, that *Tarasoff* is bad law, bad social science, and bad social policy. It is bad law because there never has been a duty within the Restatement of Torts to protect private third parties from harm unless there are specific conditions and relationships not present in *Tarasoff* (*Tarasoff v. Regents of University of California, 1976*). Remember Poddar was in outpatient therapy not under the control of a hospital and not eligible for involuntary commitment. Second, it is bad social science because the therapist's duty is based on an evaluation of the patient's propensity to act violently. Although more sophisticated research done by the MacArthur Project's Research Network on Mental Health and the Law has improved risk assessment (Monahan et al., 2001), it is still extremely difficult to make accurate assessments in outpatient, nonpsychotic, nonsubstance, abusing populations—the vast majority of patients mental health professionals see. Third, the duty to protect is bad social policy. The crucial fact in this case was not an uttered threat of future violence but that once Poddar knew that his confidences were disclosed by his therapist to the campus police, he never returned for treatment. One wonders if Ms. Tarasoff would be alive today if the psychologist–therapist and his psychiatrist-supervisor were not so quick to call the police but rather worked with their patient for the 2 months between the threat and the killing.

This does not mean that I advocate letting potentially violent patients go unchecked. The truly violent aggressor at some time loses his or her right to absolute protection when he or she threatens to use deadly force. The APA code of ethics (American Psychological Association [APA], 1992), which permits unconsented-to disclosures merely to protect others from harm (left undefined) and not under the more stringent standard required by *Tarasoff* of serious bodily harm, and immunity statutes that protect us from litigation, simply make it too easy to betray our fidelity to our patients and to become society's police force. I think we should be obliged to do all we can to attempt all other viable options before we abrogate the principle of fidelity and unilaterally disclose confidential communications to private third parties.

I would agree in large part with the Supreme Court's view on this issue in *Jaffee v. Redmond* (1996) expressed in a footnote. . . . "[W]e do not doubt that there are situations in which the [psychotherapist–patient] privilege must give way . . . if a serious threat of harm to the patient or others can be averted only by means of a disclosure by the therapist." I find it heartening that Texas in the 1999 case of *Thapar v. Zezulka* rejected the mandatory rule of *Tarasoff* and supported what to me is a more defensible position by recognizing the statutory exception to its privilege statute that allows, but does not require, disclosure and only when the therapist determines that there is a probability of imminent physical injury by the patient to others. This is more in line with the ethical rules binding lawyers. In any event, I would hope that organized mental health would ally themselves with our clients' desire for privacy rather than society's increasingly serious attempts to diminish it. The latest draft of APA's Ethics Code lamely follows the latter trend, I am sad to say.[1]

From *Law and Human Behavior, 26*, 565–574. Copyright 2002 by the American Psychology–Law Society Division 41 of the American Psychological Association.

[1]*Ed* Note: See Standard 4.05 in the current (2002) APA Ethics Code.

References

American Psychological Association. (1992). Ethical principles of psychologists and code of conduct. *American Psychologist, 47*, 1597–1611.

Bersoff, D. N. (1974). Therapists as protectors and policemen: New roles as a result of *Tarasoff. Professional Psychology, 7*, 267–273.

Jaffee v. Redmond, 518 U.S. 1 (1996).

Monahan, J., Steadman, H., Silver, E., Appelbaum, P., Robbins, P. C., Mulvey, E., et al. (2001). *Rethinking risk assessment.* New York: Oxford University Press.

Reisner, R., Slobogin, C., & Rai, A. (1999). *Law and the mental health system* (3rd ed.). St. Paul, MN: West Group.

Tarasoff v. Regents of University of California, 551 P.2d 334 (1976).

Thapar v. Zezulka, 994 S.W.2d 635 (Tex. 1999).

◆　◆　◆

Commentary: In addition to the Mills et al. article, for another useful collection of post-Tarasoff cases, see Fulero, S. M. (1988). Tarasoff: 10 years later. Professional Psychology: Research and Practice, 19, *184–190. For an even more extensive and recent discussion see VandeCreek, L., & Knapp, S. (2001). Tarasoff and beyond (3rd ed.). Sarasota, FL: Professional Resource Press. Among the more noteworthy cases these sources discuss are (a) Bellah v. Greenson, 141 Col. Rptr. 92 (Cal. App. 1977)—in which a California appellate court (but not its Supreme Court) held that the duty to protect does not extend to a patient's suicidal threats; (b) Peck v. Counseling Service of Addison County, 499 A.2d 422 (Vt. 1985)—in which the Vermont Supreme Court extended the duty to a master's-level counselor whose adolescent patient threatened to burn down his father's barn, creating the possibility that the Tarasoff duty may extend to protecting property (or at least damage to property that may also create risk to people); and (c) Hedlund v. Superior Court, 34 Cal.3d 995, 194 Cal. Rptr. 805 (1983)—in which the California Supreme Court held that a foreseeable, innocent bystander who witnesses the violence inflicted by a patient may sue the patient's therapist for negligent infliction of emotional distress in addition to the victim's suit for failure to protect.*

Four more recent cases deserve attention. In Pennsylvania, in what has become a typical scenario, a male patient killed his ex-girlfriend. The state's supreme court followed the rationale of *Tarasoff but with a twist. Recall that in Tarasoff, the California supreme court held that therapists should take whatever reasonable steps were necessary to protect victims, including warning. But in the Pennsylvania case, the court limited therapists' actions solely to warning potential victims. See* Emerich v. Philadelphia Center for Human Development, *720 A.2d 1032 (1998). Bucking the trend factually and legally, however, is* Thapar v. Zezulka, *994 S.W.2d 635 (1999). In that case, a son killed his stepfather. He had communicated the threat to do so to his treating psychiatrist while an inpatient. The psychiatrist never warned any family member. A month after his discharge the son carried out his threat. The Texas supreme court, relying on a state confidentiality statute, held that therapists had the discretion to disclose threats of violence but were not mandated to do so. This holding, incidentally, comports with lawyers' ethical obligations—they may reveal information disclosed by clients to prevent reasonably certain death or substantial bodily harm, but are not required to.*

The most recent important cases are a pair from, once again, California, which like Hedlund, broaden liability. The significant fact in those cases is that the threat did not come from the patient but from the patient's parent. The patient told his father that he was very troubled that his former girlfriend was seeing another man and that he was contemplating causing him harm. Soon after, the father called his son's therapist and informed him of the threat. The therapist recommended admission to a hospital. After 1 day in the hospital he was discharged. On the following day the patient killed the boyfriend and then committed suicide. The patient's parents sued the therapist and the hospital in two separate suits. The therapist asserted that the patient never made a threat that would trigger a required warning or other protective measures. But the California intermediate appellate court held that a "communication from a patient's family member to the patient's therapist, made for the purpose of advancing the patient's therapy, is a 'patient communication' within the meaning [of the relevant California statute— cited and discussed later in this Commentary]" (p. 814). Ewing v. Goldstein, *120 Cal.App.4th 807 (2004). The holding does beg the question of how* broadly "family member" will be defined in later cases or if it might even be extended to include intimate or close friends.

One of the major problems with Tarasoff and similar cases is that the impetus to protect the intended victim is the communication of a serious threat of violence. But the courts have never been clear about what constitutes violence. A threat of murder obviously is, but what about a nonlethal stabbing, a punch in the mouth, a slap on the face, or some other act? Although Ewing enlarges the possibility that confidentiality will be breached, it has one salutary aspect—it does define a serious threat of violence, at least in California. In addition to threatening to take another's life, the court held that the requirement to warn the intended victim and law enforcement authorities would also be triggered by threats of mayhem—depriving potential victims of bodily parts or disabling or disfiguring their facial features—or threats of serious bodily injury—causing loss of consciousness, concussion, bone fracture, or wounds requiring extensive suturing.

In the companion case against the hospital, Ewing v. Northridge Hospital Medical Center, 120 Cal.App.4th 1289 (2004), the court again found the defendants–treaters potentially liable based on the parental communication. But, it made another important holding. The court took issue with that part of the Tarasoff decision that created liability if the therapist should have known that the patient posed a serious threat of violence not only if the therapist actually did know. Interpreting the statute enacted in response to that case, the court held that therapists would be liable only if they failed to warn when patients had, in fact, communicated actual threats of violence against identified victims. Based on that principle, however, the court stated that no expert testimony on that issue was needed:

> [L]iability is not premised on a breach of
> the standard of care. Instead, it rests
> entirely on the fact finder's determination
> that each factual predicate is satisfied: the
> existence of a psychotherapist–patient
> relationship; the psychotherapist's actual
> belief or prediction that the patient poses
> a serious risk of inflicting grave bodily
> injury; a reasonably identifiable victim;
> and the failure to undertake reasonable

efforts to warn the victim and a law enforcement agency. (p. 1302)

For a critical discussion of these cases see Eisner, D. A. (2006). From Tarasoff to Ewing: Expansion of the duty to warn. American Journal of Forensic Psychology, 24, 45–55; Yufik, A. (2005). Revisiting the Tarasoff decision: Risk assessment and liability in clinical and forensic practice. American Journal of Forensic Psychology, 23, 5–21.

Perhaps the dilution of the ethical value of confidentiality exemplified by these cases will ebb as a result of the U.S. Supreme Court's 7–2 decision in Jaffee v. Redmond, 518 U.S. 1 (1996). In holding that the federal rules of evidence require recognition of a psychotherapist–patient privilege in federal cases (all 50 states have some form of this privilege under state law), the Court gave unusually strong support for the principles of fidelity and confidentiality:

> Effective psychotherapy . . . depends
> upon an atmosphere of confidence and
> trust in which the patient is willing to
> make a frank and complete disclosure of
> facts, emotions, memories, and fears. . . .
> [T]he mere possibility of disclosure may
> impede development of the confidential
> relationship necessary for successful
> treatment. . . . (p. 10)

The Court was not prepared to delineate the boundaries of the privilege nor to create exceptions. But in a footnote ending the majority's opinion, it made a statement that could have an impact on the manner in which psychologists and other professionals deal with the duty-to-protect cases: "We do not doubt that there are situations in which the privilege must give way, for example, if a serious threat of harm to the patient or to others can be averted only by means of a disclosure by the therapist" (p. 18). Does this broaden or narrow the duties in Tarasoff-like cases? In answering the question the reader should consider the effect of the word "only" in the footnote.

For some insights on the meaning of Jaffee and its impact on practice see:

DeBell, C., & Jones, R. D. (1997). Privileged communication at last? An overview of Jaffee v. Redmond. Professional Psychology: Research and Practice, 28, 559–566.

Glosoff, H. L., Herlihy, S. B., Herlihy, B., & Spence, E. B. (1997). Privileged communication in the psychologist–clinician relationship. *Professional Psychology: Research and Practice, 28,* 573–581.

Knapp, S., & VandeCreek, L. (1997). Jaffee v. Redmond: *The Supreme Court recognizes a psychotherapist–patient privilege in federal courts.* Professional Psychology: Research and Practice, 28, 567–572.

Shuman, D., & Foote, W. (1999). Jaffee v. Redmond's impact: *Life after the Supreme Court's recognition of a psychotherapist–patient privilege.* Professional Psychology: Research and Practice, 30, 479–487.

In a practical examination of the impact of Jaffee, participants asked to respond to scenarios involving suicidal, gravely disabled, physically abused, and sexually abused patients, and a police officer patient who shot a suspect (the latter being the facts of Jaffee), who were receiving therapy in a privileged communication condition or no privilege condition indicated they were significantly more likely to disclose relevant information when promised confidentiality in the privileged condition.

Marsh, J. E. (2003). Empirical support for the United States Supreme Court's protection of the psychotherapist-patient privilege. *Ethics & Behavior, 13,* 385–400.

Appelbaum and Rosenbaum (1989) raise the intriguing question of whether and under what circumstances researchers may be responsible for preventing violence by a study participant. For example, what if a clinical investigator discovers that a patient-subject harbors homicidal fantasies about an ex spouse? They argue that "[s]ocial and experimental psychologists without clinical training should fall outside the requirements of the duty to protect. . . ." (p. 887). But what, they ask, if a nonclinician researcher heads a project using clinicians as data collectors? What would be the respective obligations of the project director and the data collectors?

Beyond the criterion of the investigator's specialty is the nature of the data collected. Appelbaum and Rosenbaum assert that research projects "using multiple clinical indexes or unstructured interviews . . . would seem susceptible, on the basis of their comparability to the clinical setting, to the imposition of a duty to protect" (p. 888). A third issue may be the nature of the participants. Are there different obligations if the population studied are passive–dependent personalities, child abusers, or violent criminals? There may be some protections with certain populations, as Appelbaum and Rosenbaum describe:

[T]o facilitate research on certain sensitive topics, particularly substance abuse, Congress has permitted the Secretary of Health and Human Services to issue confidentiality certificates. . . . These documents authorize researchers to protect subjects' privacy by withholding "the names or other identifying characteristics" of subjects from "any Federal, State, or local civil, criminal, administrative, legislative, or other proceedings" (42 U.S.C. 242[a]). . . . DHHS has interpreted the statute to mean that researchers holding such certificates are exempt from state and local reporting requirements. . . . The certificates are available to "persons engaged in research on mental health, including research on the use and effect of alcohol and other psychoactive drugs," who make proper application to DHHS. ("Protection of Identity—Research Subjects" [42 C.F.R. Part 2a]. (p. 890))

Appelbaum, P. S., & Rosenbaum, A. (1989). Tarasoff and the researcher: Does the duty to protect apply in the research setting? *American Psychologist, 44,* 885–894.

How helpful is a statute like California's creating immunity from suit under certain conditions:

(a) There shall be no monetary liability on the part of, and no cause of action shall arise against, any person who is a psychotherapist . . . in failing to warn of and protect from a patient's threatened violent behavior or failing to predict and warn of and protect from a patient's violent behavior except where the patient has communicated to the psychotherapist a serious threat of physical violence against a reasonably identifiable victim or victims.

(b) If there is a duty to warn and protect . . . the duty shall be discharged by the psychotherapist making reasonable efforts to communicate the threat to the victim or victims and to a law enforcement agency. [California Civil Code Sec. 43.92.]

Will immunity make it easier for clinicians to breach confidentiality? Do readers agree with Mills et al. (1987: see above) that the law limits the thera-pist's ability to use clinical interventions in working with potentially violent clients? Tarasoff, after all, is a duty-to-protect case, theoretically leaving therapists with more options than merely informing the potential victim or the authorities. One of those options is to civilly commit the client. Although in many cases that may satisfy one's legal obligations under Tarasoff, involuntary hospitalization has its own drawbacks. First, depriving one's clients of liberty over their objec-tions will likely impair the therapeutic relationship. Second, civil commitment necessarily involves breach-ing confidentiality. Third, commitment usually requires not only a finding of potential danger to self and others, but also the presence of serious mental illness. Many outpatient therapy clients may not fit that criterion. Voluntary admission to a hospital, on the other hand, circumvents these pitfalls.

Other options include (a) involving the potential victim in therapy (although that would most likely require the potential victim to be closely related in some way to the client); (b) manipulating the social environment, for example, seeing that the client rids himself or herself of deadly weapons; (c) referring the client for psychotropic medication or for an increased dosage if he or she is already being medicated; and (d) obtaining permission from the client to contact the potential victim, a suggestion that eliminates the invol-untary disclosure of confidential communications. For a review of how courts have interpreted immunity statutes in several states that followed California's lead, see Kachigian, C., & Felthous, A. R. (2004). Court responses to Tarasoff statutes. Journal of the American Academy of Psychiatry & Law, 32, 263–273. The authors conclude "that even in states that have Tarasoff statutes, clinicians must continue to rely on their clinical and ethical judgment, rather than statutory guidance, when considering potential protec-tive disclosures" (p. 263). What follows is a helpful set of recommendations for therapists.

Limiting Therapist Exposure to *Tarasoff* Liability: Guidelines for Risk Containment

John Monahan

. . .

RISK ASSESSMENT

Four tasks form the basis of any professionally adequate risk assessment: The clinician must be educated about what information to gather regarding risk, must gather it, must use this information to estimate risk, and, if the clinician is not the ultimate decision maker, must communicate the information and estimate to those who are responsible for making clinical decisions.

Education

The essence of being a "professional" is having "specialized knowledge" not available to the general public. In this context, specialized knowledge consists of both knowledge of mental disorder in general (e.g., assessment, diagnosis, and treatment) and knowledge of risk assessment in particular. In addition, one should be thoroughly conversant with the laws of the jurisdiction in which one practices regarding the steps to follow when a positive risk assessment is made.

Clinical education. Familiarity with basic concepts in risk assessment (e.g., predictor and criterion variables, true and false positives and negatives, decision rules and base rates) and with key findings of risk assessment research (e.g., past violence as the single best predictor of future violence) is becoming an important aspect of graduate education in psychology, psychiatry, and social work. . . .

It is not enough to learn the basic concepts and classic findings in the field of risk assessment once and consider one's education complete. Research findings evolve and become modified over time, and the conventions of professional practice become more sophisticated. Continuing education in risk assessment through formal programs sponsored by professional or private organizations is one way to keep apprised of developments in the field. Periodically perusing original research journals (e.g., *Law and Human Behavior, Behavioral Sciences and the Law,* the *International Journal of Law and Psychiatry* is another . . .).

Legal education. The standards to which clinicians will be held in making judgments on risk are set largely by state law. In the past, these standards were usually articulated by judges who applied common law tort principles to the context of clinical risk assessment. This is what happened in *Tarasoff* and similar cases in other states. Increasingly, and after intense lobbying by professional mental health organizations, state legislatures are passing statutes to make standards for liability and immunity in this area explicit (Appelbaum, Zonana, Bonnie, & Roth, 1989). These statutes, however, will still require much adjudication to interpret inevitably ambiguous terminology (e.g., what counts as a "serious threat" or a "reasonably identifiable victim" in California's, 1990, statute?). The point here is that there is no national legal standard for what clinicians should do when they assess risk and that it behooves clinicians to know precisely what the legal standards in their own jurisdiction are regarding violence prevention. State mental health professional associations ought to have this information readily available.

Information

Once a clinician knows what information, in general, may be relevant to assessing risk, he or she must take efforts to gather that information in a given case.

From *American Psychologist*, 48, 242–250. Copyright 1993 by the American Psychological Association. Appendix has been omitted.

Most of the *Tarasoff*-like cases on which I have worked have faulted clinicians not for making an inaccurate prediction but for failing to gather information that would have made a reasonable effort at prediction possible. There are generally four sources in which relevant information can be found: in the records of past treatment, in the records of current treatment, from interviewing the patient, and from interviewing significant others. In some criminal contexts (e.g., assessments for suitability for release on parole or from insanity commitment) additional records in the form of police and probation reports, arrest records, and trial transcripts may also be available and should be consulted. But in the civil context, these records are generally not available to clinicians.

Past records. The only cases in which I have been involved that were, in the words of the defense attorneys, "born dead" were those in which the patient had an extensive history of prior violence that was amply documented in reasonably available treatment records, but those records were never requested. In these cases, the clinician has been forced to acknowledge on the witness stand that if he or she had seen the records, preventive action would have been taken.

. . . [A] line has to be drawn as to what constitutes a reasonable effort to obtain records of past treatment. I know of no standard operating procedure on this question. "Records" does not have to mean the entire hospital file; a discharge summary may often suffice. More of a priority might be accorded to requesting the records of patients whose hospitalization was precipitated by a violent incident, or who exhibited violence in the hospital, than to requesting the records of other patients. In the context of long-term hospitalization, of course, there will be more opportunity to obtain records from distant facilities than would be the case for short-term treatment (this opportunity to obtain records is also present for patients with repeated short-term hospitalizations).

Current records. Reading the chart of the current hospitalization when making risk judgments about hospitalized patients is essential. I am continually amazed, however, at how often clinicians peruse the chart as if it were a magazine in a dentist's waiting room. In particular, nursing notes, in which violent acts and threats are often to be found, are frequently glossed over. Yet, I have seen plaintiff's attorneys introduce exhibits consisting of eight-foot-by-four-foot photographic enlargements of pages from nursing notes containing statements such as, "assaulted several other patients without provocation tonight," and "patient threatening to kill spouse as soon as released." These exhibits certainly concentrated the jury's attention.

Inquiries of the patient. Directly asking patients about violent behavior and possible indices of violent behavior (e.g., arrest or hospitalization as "dangerous to others") is surely the easiest and quickest way to obtain this essential information. Open-ended questions such as "What is the most violent thing you have ever done?" or "What is the closest you have ever come to being violent?" may be useful probes, as might "Do you ever worry that you might physically hurt somebody?" The obvious problem, of course, is that patients may lie or distort their history or their current thoughts. This is always a possibility, but often corroborating information will be available from the records (above) or from significant others (below). Quite often, however, patients are remarkably forthcoming about violence. And although there may be reasons to suspect a negative answer in a given case, a positive answer should always be pursued. Unless a question to the patient is ventured, potentially valuable information on risk will not be gained.

Inquiries of significant others. Records are often unavailable, and patients are sometimes not reliable informants. A significant other, usually a family member, is frequently available in the case of inpatient hospitalization, however, either in person (accompanying the patient to treatment or seen later in conjunction with the patient's therapy) or at least by telephone. Asking the significant other about any violent behavior or threats in the event that precipitated hospitalization, or in the past, as well as open-ended questions such as "Are you concerned that X might hurt someone?" with appropriate follow-up questions as to the basis for any expressed concern, may yield useful information.

. . .

Communication

In the individual practice of psychotherapy, the clinician who gathers information on risk is also the clinician who makes decisions based on this information. But in outpatient treatment agencies and in mental hospitals, a division of labor often exists: One person may do the intake, another may be responsible for patient care, a team of several professionals may provide a variety of assessment and treatment modalities, and one person will have formal responsibility for making or approving discharge decisions. Although this division of labor may be an efficient use of resources, it does raise an issue not present in the solo practitioner context: the communication of relevant information from one mental health professional to another. Here, information must be transferred between or among clinicians, and significant information must be made salient to the person responsible for making the ultimate decisions regarding the patient. . . .

Placing all relevant information in the chart, of course, is the primary way of transferring information among treatment professionals. As long as the person ultimately responsible for making the institutionalization or discharge decision reads the entire file, the information is thereby communicated to the person who needs to know it.

In the real world of professional practice, however, information is not always effectively communicated by simply passing on a chart. The ultimate decision maker may be a harried senior staff member whose signature is often a pro forma endorsement of the recommendations of line staff, based only on a brief discharge summary. Or the amount of information in the chart, including information from numerous past hospitalizations, may be literally so voluminous that no final decision maker would be expected to read it verbatim. . . .

It is not sufficient to dump undigested information on the desk of the ultimate decision maker and to claim that he or she assumed the risk of liability by taking possession of the file. Rather, information pertinent to risk should explicitly . . . be brought to the attention of the decision maker. Only by making the information salient can one be assured that the decision maker has had the option to make use of it.

From the decision maker's vantage point, the implications of information overload are equally clear. When the transfer or discharge summary prepared by others makes no explicit positive or negative reference to risk, one should directly ask what information relevant to risk is in the chart and should record the answer.

RISK MANAGEMENT

. . .

Planning

Choice of a plan. For a patient flagged as *high risk*, it is important to explicitly consider preventive action. Such actions usually fall into three categories (see Appelbaum, 1985, p. 426). Following the literature on crime prevention, the first category might be called *incapacitation*, or negating the opportunity for violence in the community by hospitalizing the patient (voluntarily or involuntarily), or if it is hospital violence that is anticipated, negating that opportunity by transferring the patient to a more secure ward until the level of risk is reduced. The second category could be termed *target hardening*, or warning the potential victim when one can be identified, so that the victim can take precautionary measures. The final category might be called *intensified treatment*, in which outpatient status is maintained but sessions are scheduled more frequently, medication is initiated or increased, or joint sessions are held with the patient and others significant to the occurrence of violence, possibly including the potential victim (Wexler, 1981). More creative options may also be possible (Dietz, 1990).

The issue here is not that the clinician must necessarily adopt one of these violence-prevention strategies as part of a risk management plan but that the clinician consciously *consider* such options and make a reasoned and reasonable decision to adopt or not to adopt one of them. If the steps taken to prevent violence are seen as reasonable, the clinician should not be held liable, even if harm occurs.

Second opinions. The problem with choosing a risk management plan, in terms of tort liability, is that because the plan didn't work (or else there would be no law suit), the plaintiff can often retain another mental health professional as an expert witness to say, with the wisdom of hindsight, that any competent clinician would have known that the plan was defective. The more well thought out the preventive measures taken in a case, the more difficulty the plaintiff will have in finding a credible witness who can with integrity make such a claim.

One way for a clinician to immunize himself or herself from this kind of Monday morning quarterbacking is for the clinician to initiate it on Friday afternoon, by consulting with a respected colleague about a difficult case before risk management decisions are made (Rachlin & Schwartz, 1986). Getting a second opinion has two advantages. First, the clinician may learn something. He or she may learn that the consulting colleague does not think that the contemplated actions are reasonable. The clinician may have missed a significant risk or protective risk factor, or may be overreacting to some aspect of the case—we all have blind spots. Or, the planned course of action may be reasonable, but the consultant may have a more creative suggestion.

The second advantage of obtaining a consultation is that it is a concrete way of demonstrating that the clinician took the case seriously and considered a variety of options for violence prevention. If the consultant is an experienced clinician . . . it becomes much more difficult to claim after the fact that "anyone" would have known that the risk management plan was negligent.

There are two clear disadvantages to obtaining consultation, however. The first is that it takes time to familiarize a colleague with a difficult case and to talk through strategy. In many busy practice settings, there is barely enough time to make a reasoned initial decision, much less to review that decision with someone else. The second disadvantage is that in obtaining consultation the clinician may be exposing the chosen consultant to potential liability should the patient commit a violent act (although I emphasize that I know of no cases in which consultants who have not seen the patient have been found to share liability). Perhaps the most equitable ways to obtain consultation are case conferences or grand rounds in which each clinician gets to discuss a difficult case, thereby broadly sharing potential liability with other colleagues, while incurring potential liability from their cases.

Adherence

Without doubt, the single largest category of cases on which I have served as an expert witness have involved patient noncompliance with aftercare recommendations. The typical case is one in which a patient is seriously violent when acutely disordered, is treated in a mental hospital until the disorder is under control, and is discharged with the recommendation to continue treatment as an outpatient. The patient comes to few, if any, appointments and then stops showing up altogether. No one on the hospital staff calls to find out what the problem is or to assess the patient's condition. The patient decompensates over the course of a few weeks or months and, while acutely disordered, kills someone. This situation is even more egregious when the patient is known to have a long history of noncompliance with treatment (typically, with psychotropic medication) and is also known from the record to become disordered when off medication and to become violent when disordered. It does not take the jury long to complete the syllogism and to conclude that the clinician or hospital could and should have avoided the tragedy by pursuing the missed appointments and nonadherence to treatment recommendations.

I know how understaffed many mental health facilities are. It is hard enough to see those people who do show up for aftercare treatment, much less to track down those who do not. Furthermore, unless the former patient satisfies the criteria for civil commitment (or outpatient commitment), there may be little the clinician can legally do to force the patient to comply with treatment recommendations (but see Meichenbaum & Turk, 1987, for an excellent account of *adherence enhancement*). Yet, it is very hard to convince a jury, with the children of the deceased in the front row of the courtroom, that a good faith effort to assure the patient's compliance with treatment was not worth the clinician's time (Klein, 1986).

DOCUMENTATION

It would be an exaggeration to state that in a tort case what is not in the written record does not exist—but not much of an exaggeration. The violent event that gives rise to the suit may occur weeks or months after the patient was last seen. The resolution of the case through settlement or trial will be a minimum of several years from the time of the violent event. Memories fade or become compromised when numerous, or innumerable, other patients are seen in the interval. The record requested by telephone, the questioning of the patient or family member about violence, the hallway conversation with a colleague to communicate information, or the careful consideration of options is unlikely to be retrieved intact from memory; nor would it make much difference if it were. Juries are rightly skeptical of self-interested statements by people who have a lot to lose. "If you did it, why didn't you write it down?" they will reason. "I was busy" is not a credible retort. Unrecorded warnings to a patient's family member that he or she has been threatened with harm are useless when that family member is dead as a result of the threatened violence or is the plaintiff in a suit for damages against the therapist. From the perspective of violence prevention, the suggestions made regarding obtaining and communicating information and developing and monitoring a risk management plan are equally applicable whether or not a record is made. From the perspective of reducing exposure to liability, there is little point in doing any of them unless they are memorialized in ink or on a dated disk (or by a videotaped exit interview; see Poythress, 1990, 1991).

Documenting information received and actions taken, or "building the record," is an essential exposure-limitation technique. When recording information relevant to risk—for example, a statement from a family member that a patient made a violent threat—one should note three things: the *source* of the information (e.g., the name of the family member), the *content* of the information (e.g., the nature and circumstances of the threat), and the *date* on which the information was obtained or communicated. In addition, when noting an action taken in furtherance of a risk reduction plan (e.g., committing or not committing a patient, warning or not warning a potential victim), it is essential to include a statement, however brief, of the *rationale* for the action. A comment in the chart

or discharge summary reading—for example, "Called mother on 6/21. She said that she did not take patient's threats seriously, and that he had always complied with medication in the past"— is worth its weight in gold (perhaps literally) in demonstrating a good faith effort to attend to risk.

POLICY

The time for a clinician to think through difficult issues regarding risk assessment and management is not when a patient makes a threat or misses a follow-up appointment. Rather, general policy choices should be made and reflected upon before the need for them arises in a given case. These policies or guidelines should be committed to writing and should be reviewed by experienced clinicians and lawyers. Staff should be educated in the use of the guidelines, and their compliance should be audited. Finally, forms should be revised to prompt and record the actions contemplated by the policy statement.

Written Guidelines

Memorializing "risk policy" in writing has several virtues (Bennett, Bryant, VandenBos, & Greenwood, 1990). It promotes clarity of thought and thus is conducive to formulating effective procedures, from both the viewpoints of violence prevention and the reduction of exposure to liability. In an organizational context, it allows for consistency of application, so that staff members are not acting at cross purposes ("I thought that it was *your* responsibility to warn the family!"). And it is efficient in the sense that novice clinicians, or clinicians new to the organization, can more quickly be brought up to the level of practitioners experienced in handling potentially violent patients. The guidelines should periodically (e.g., annually) be reviewed, with an eye to revision in light of developments in research, practice, or state law.

The absolutely essential point here is that the guidelines should reflect *the minimal standards necessary for competent professional practice* and not the ideals to which an organization would aspire if it had unlimited resources. . . .

External Review

Experienced clinicians should be the ones to draft risk policy. But the draft should be reviewed by other clinicians from comparable facilities elsewhere (Poythress, 1987). As with securing consultation on difficult cases . . . policy consultation serves two purposes. It allows the drafting clinicians to learn from the experience of others and, thus, to substantively improve the quality of their procedures. If the question of the reasonableness of the policies is later impugned in a tort suit, it is very helpful to announce that they received the blessing of the most relevant slice of the professional community before the events that gave rise to the suit. A leadership role can productively be played by state and local professional organizations in drafting model guidelines in this area. . . . In addition to review by external clinicians, review by house or retained counsel is also essential to make certain that the policies comport with the statutory and case law of the jurisdiction.

Staff Education and Compliance

It is not enough—indeed, it is counterproductive—to draft exemplary guidelines and subject them to clinical and legal review if the guidelines are merely to be filed in some cabinet or entombed in a staff handbook, never to be read. Again, *it is much better to have no policies at all than to have policies that are not followed in actual practice.* . . .

Once the staff have been educated in the use of the guidelines, their compliance should be the subject of periodic "audits." A senior colleague . . . should review files to see whether the guidelines are being followed in practice, whether, for example, records are requested, information is communicated, and all actions are properly documented. Corrective action—including the revision of unworkable policies—should then be taken.

Useful Forms

The creation of user friendly forms for documenting actions called for by policy guidelines can both prompt and memorialize appropriate inquiries and responses. I have seen many a case saved for defendants by clinicians having simply checked off "no" to a list of intake questions, including the items "violent history" and "violent ideation." Expanding that list to incorporate more items contemplated in the risk-policy statement—for example, fill-in-the-blanks for "records requested from_____" "concerns communicated to _____" and "attempted to follow-up by _____ "—would be very useful both in terms of violence prevention and exposure limitations. Forms should facilitate, rather than impede, gathering necessary information, taking appropriate action, and documenting both information and actions. . . .

DAMAGE CONTROL

Risk assessment and risk management involve probabilistic judgments. By definition, these judgments will sometimes be wrong—not wrong in the sense of mistake, but wrong in the sense that low probability events do happen. . . . In the context of being a mental health professional, having a patient kill or severely injure another qualifies as a major life event. I am amazed at how often clinicians panic and take actions that are unwise, unethical, and sometimes illegal. The two most prevalent forms of maladaptive clinician reaction to the stress of patient violence and the fear of liability are tampering with the record and making inculpatory public statements.

Tampering With the Record

In several of the cases on which I have served as an expert witness, a treating clinician has learned of his or her patient's violence from the media and shortly thereafter has gone to the patient's chart and inserted new material tending to support the reasonableness of the decisions that the clinician had made. In each of these cases, to my knowledge, the new material was factually correct. The clinician was not lying about the events that took place, for example, the questioning of family members about the patient's violent history or the attempt to follow up on missed aftercare appointments. But the clinician was lying about the date that these events were recorded: The entries were back-dated to appear as if they had been written before the violent act took place. . . .

If a suit has not been filed, one can argue that the record does not yet constitute evidence and so changing it is not illegal. But once a suit is filed, changing the record can constitute obstruction of justice. If the clinician is asked under oath whether the records—and the dates of entry are part of the records—are accurate and testifies affirmatively and if the late entries come to light, the clinician is guilty of perjury, a criminal offense.

The most likely outcome of tampering with the record . . . is to completely destroy whatever chances one had of winning the case. . . . It is much better to admit that you didn't keep good records and hope that the jury believes you when you tell them what happened than to manufacture good records after the fact at the cost of your own integrity and credibility. . . .

References

Appelbaum, P. (1985). *Tarasoff* and the clinician: Problems in fulfilling the duty to protect. *American Journal of Psychiatry, 142,* 425–429.

Appelbaum, P., Zonana, H., Bonnie, R., & Roth, L. (1989). Statutory approaches to limiting psychiatrist's liability for their patients' violent acts. *American Journal of Psychiatry, 146,* 821–828.

Bennett, B., Bryant, B., VandenBos, G., & Greenwood, A. (1990). *Professional liability and risk management.* Washington, DC: American Psychological Association.

Dietz, P. (1990). Defenses against dangerous people when arrest and commitment fail. In R. Simon (Ed.), *Review of clinical psychiatry and the law* (Vol. 1, pp. 205–219). Washington, DC: American Psychiatric Press.

Klein, J. (1986). The professional liability crisis: An interview with Joel Klein. *Hospital and Community Psychiatry, 37,* 1012–1016.

Meichenbaum, D., & Turk, D. (1987). *Facilitating treatment adherence: A practitioner's guidebook.* New York: Plenum Press.

Poythress, N. (1987). Avoiding negligent release: A risk-management strategy. *Hospital and Community Psychiatry, 38,* 1051–1052.

Poythress, N. (1990). Avoiding negligent release: Contemporary clinical and risk management strategies. *American Journal of Psychiatry, 147,* 994–997.

Poythress, N. (1991). [Letter]. *American Journal of Psychiatry, 148,* 691–692.

Rachlin, S., & Schwartz, H. (1986). Unforeseeable liability for patients' violent acts. *Hospital and Community Psychiatry, 37,* 725–731.

Tarasoff v. Regents of the University of California, 131 Cal. Rptr. 14, 551 P.2d 334 (1976).

◆　◆　◆

Commentary: For the latest research on assessing risk, see Monahan, J., Steadman, H., Silver, E., Appelbaum, P., Robbins, P., Mulvey, E., et al. (2001). Rethinking risk assessment. New York: Oxford University Press.

Outpatient Psychotherapy With Dangerous Clients: A Model for Clinical Decision Making

Derek Truscott, Jim Evans, and Sheila Mansell

. . .

INTERVENTION SELECTION

When a client's potential for violence becomes an issue in outpatient psychotherapy, the therapist rarely has the time to ponder the finer points of ethics, legal duty, diagnosis, and other issues. We propose that the client be thought of as occupying one of four cells in a 2 × 2, Violence Risk X Alliance Strength, table. Interventions are then selected to strengthen the therapeutic alliance and reduce the risk of violence as identified by Botkin and Nietzel (1987) and Monahan (1993), thereby "moving" the client to the lower right cell of low violence risk, strong therapeutic alliance. This formulation is presented in Figure 1.

We assert that attending to the degree of violence risk and the strength of the therapeutic alliance is central both to the effective treatment of these clients and to the protection of their potential victims. The therapeutic alliance should be strengthened as much as possible because it is the foundation on which all treatment interventions are built (Whiston & Sexton, 1993); furthermore, if one acts only to prevent a current violent episode without attending to the therapeutic alliance, it may enrage a client and actually increase the risk of violence while simultaneously deterring the client from seeking further psychotherapeutic services for dealing with any future violent impulses (Weinstock, 1988). If the risk of violence is low, the therapist should attempt to strengthen the alliance and to shift the focus of therapy to deal more specifically with the violent behavior (as one would with any therapeutic issue).

. . .

CASE ILLUSTRATIONS

The following cases illustrate the application of the model to clients at high risk for violent behavior.

. . .

High Risk, Strong Alliance → Low Risk, Strong Alliance

If the risk of violence is high and the therapeutic alliance is strong, therapy should be intensified and the therapeutic alliance should be used to help the client make his or her environment less lethal, thereby assisting the client to control his or her violent behavior (Roth & Meisel, 1977; Wulsin, Bursztajn, & Gutheil, 1983). Sessions can be scheduled more frequently, medication initiated or increased, weapons removed, or joint sessions held

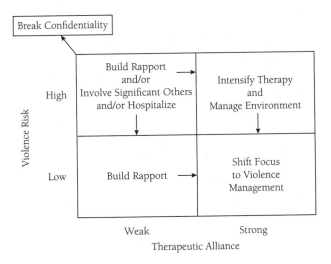

FIGURE 1. Model for decision making with dangerous clients.

From *Professional Psychology: Research and Practice, 26,* 484–490. Copyright 1995 by the American Psychological Association.

with the client and others who are significant to the occurrence of violence (Monahan, 1993).

Case 1. [omitted]

. . .

High Risk, Weak Alliance → Low Risk, Strong Alliance

When a client is at high risk for violence and the therapeutic alliance is weak, the therapist should attempt to strengthen the alliance. If an alliance has not yet been established, the therapist should endeavor to behave in an affiliative, autonomy-granting manner and should refrain from responding in a hostile or controlling manner (Henry & Strupp, 1994). If the therapeutic alliance has already been established and is strained by the current situation, the therapist should openly identify and discuss the client's perception of the alliance, listen nonjudgmentally, identify any misperceptions, and make any necessary adjustments to the therapeutic relationship (Safran, Muran, & Samstag, 1994). The strong reactions that the therapist is likely to feel should be used to help understand the client and to help the client understand the reactions that they arouse in others (Gelso & Carter, 1994). Simultaneously, or in sequence, the therapist should work with the client to alter those aspects of the client's physical and interpersonal environment that are promoting or maintaining violence.

> *Case 2.* . . . After missing numerous sessions, Mr. V. asked for an extra session. . . . One and a half weeks (and four sessions) after asking for an extra session, Mr. V. presented on a Friday afternoon as extremely upset. He was very angry and paced around the office. He reported that his wife had taken all of the belongings from their home, including his clothing and every article of furniture. Mr. V. reported that he had felt suicidal the night before but that he now wanted to kill his wife.

The therapist focused on strengthening the therapeutic alliance by clearing his schedule to spend more than 2 hours with Mr. V. and allowing him

adequate time to emotionally vent in a nonjudgmental atmosphere. The risk of violence was addressed and the relationship was further strengthened by discussing the rationality of his plan, alternate plans, and ways of reducing other stressors. In the interests of strengthening the alliance further still, and to provide an opportunity to reduce any increase in violence risk, the therapist gave Mr. V. his after-hours telephone number and made an appointment for the following Monday.

On Monday, Mr. V. reported feeling settled and had decided to sever all ties with his wife. He attended two more sessions over the next two months and reported that he did not desire any further therapy. A year and a half later, he reported that he was doing well and no harm had come to his (now ex-) wife.

High Risk, Weak Alliance → Low Risk, Weak Alliance

If the alliance cannot be strengthened, the factors promoting violence should be eliminated or significantly reduced so that risk is lessened. This risk reduction will often involve including significant others, such as the client's family members or possibly the police in preventive measures; however, a warning to potential victims should not be issued at this stage. A warning may result in needless emotional distress in the potential victim if the violence is prevented, and this psychic injury could even form the basis for a lawsuit against the therapist (Lewis, 1986). The client should be informed of the limits of confidentiality and the steps that will be taken. Civil commitment proceedings should also be considered—even if there is some doubt as to whether or not the client meets the appropriate criteria—ideally by the client on a voluntary basis. Under this circumstance, the therapist would be responsible for following up to ensure that the client had indeed been committed.

Case 3. [omitted]

. . .

High Risk, Weak Alliance → Break Confidentiality

Only if the therapeutic alliance cannot be strengthened sufficiently enough to implement violence-risk-reducing interventions, or if hospitalization cannot be initiated quickly enough, should potential victims (or their families) and the police be warned, even if there is fear of legal reprisal by the client (Eberlein, 1980). Once confidence is broken, the client's trust in the therapist, and probably in psychotherapy in general, will be lost along with the opportunity for any further therapeutic work. Ideally, permission will be obtained from the client to warn the intended victim(s) or notify the police, thereby circumventing any violation of confidentiality (Fulero, 1988) and loss of trust (Slovenko, 1975). When third parties are involved, only that information necessary to prevent the foreseen violent act should be divulged.

> *Case 4.* Mr. M. telephoned a receptionist and asked to speak with a therapist. After the call was transferred, he proceeded to explain that he had sent his wife and children to a shelter for battered women, that his house had been robbed, and that he was very angry about how he had been treated by the case worker who was handling his Workers' Compensation Board claim. He then issued an ultimatum that he get the money he needed "or else," and he then terminated the telephone call.

Mr. M. telephoned again later that day, and the therapist informed him that he had made enquiries into who would be best able to help him. Mr. M. stated that he would talk to no one else but the therapist and requested a face-to-face meeting. This meeting was arranged and the call was ended. He called again an hour later and asked how things were proceeding. He was much more angry and emotionally upset and spent little time engaged in rational planning. He then issued a veiled threat toward his case worker and hung up. Fifteen minutes later, he called once again and was even more emotional; he stated that he would shoot his case worker and then he hung up.

Mr. M.'s threat was judged to be serious, his history of violence was unknown apart from the implication that he had been violent toward his family, he knew where his intended victim worked, his access to a weapon was unknown, he appeared to be very agitated, he perceived his case worker as the source of his problems, and efforts to dissuade him appeared to be ineffectual in the context of a weak therapeutic alliance.

The therapist informed the police and warned the case worker. Mr. M. was apprehended, and, after two court appearances, he eventually pleaded guilty to criminal charges of uttering a threat to cause death or bodily harm.

References

Botkin, D. J., & Nietzel, M. T. (1987). How therapists manage potentially dangerous clients: Toward a standard of care for psychotherapists. *Professional Psychology: Research and Practice, 18,* 84–85.

Eberlein, L. (1980). Legal duty and confidentiality of psychologists: Tarasoff and Haines. *Canadian Psychology, 21,* 49–58.

Fulero, S. M. (1988). *Tarasoff:* 10 years later. *Professional Psychology, 19,* 184–190.

Gelso, C. J., & Carter, J. A. (1994). Components of the psychotherapy relationship: Their interaction and unfolding during treatment. *Journal of Counseling Psychology, 41,* 296–306.

Henry, W. P., & Strupp, H. H. (1994). The therapeutic alliance as interpersonal process. In A. O. Horvath & L. S. Greenberg (Eds.), *The working alliance: Theory, research, and practice* (pp. 51–84). New York: Wiley.

Lewis, M. B. (1986). Duty to warn versus duty to maintain confidentiality: Conflicting demands on mental health professionals. *Suffolk University Law Review, 20,* 579–615.

Monahan, J. (1993). Limiting therapist exposure to *Tarasoff* liability: Guidelines for risk containment. *American Psychologist, 48,* 242–250.

Roth, L. H., & Meisel, A. (1977). Dangerousness, confidentiality, and the duty to warn. *American Journal of Psychiatry, 134,* 508–511.

Safran, J. D., Muran, J. C., & Samstag, L. W. (1994). Resolving therapeutic alliance ruptures: A task analytic investigation. In A. Horvath & L. S. Greenberg (Eds.), *The working alliance: Theory, research, and practice* (pp. 225–255). New York: Wiley.

Slovenko, R. (1975). Psychotherapy and confidentiality. *Cleveland State Law Review, 24,* 375–391.

Weinstock, R. (1988). Confidentiality and the new duty to protect: The therapist's dilemma. *Hospital and Community Psychiatry, 39,* 607–609.

Whiston, S. C., & Sexton, T. L. (1993). An overview of psychotherapy outcome research: Implications for practice. *Professional Psychology: Research and Practice, 24,* 43–51.

Wulsin, L. R., Bursztajn, H., & Gutheil, T. G. (1983). Unexpected clinical features of the *Tarasoff* decision: The therapeutic alliance and the "duty to warn." *American Journal of Psychiatry, 140,* 601–603.

◆　　◆　　◆

Commentary: According to some research, clinicians treating outpatients were more likely to issue warnings to potential victims than those who worked in institutional settings, who were more likely to choose civil commitment. Institutional clinicians gave warnings only when the violent threat was considered vague or remote. In many cases, when there was a good therapeutic alliance, the threats were dealt with solely within the therapy itself. Compare:

Beck, J. C. (1982). When the patient threatens violence: An empirical study of clinical practice after Tarasoff. American Academy of Psychiatry and Law Bulletin, 10, 189–202 (inpatient);

Wise, T. P. (1978). Where the public peril begins: A survey of psychotherapists to determine the effects of Tarasoff. Stanford Law Review, 31, 165–190 (outpatient).

Using the material concerning the duties generated by Tarasoff and the later cases it spawned, and applying the problem-solving techniques for handling complex ethical dilemmas delineated in chapter 3, how would you handle the following situation?

A woman in her 20s had been involved for almost two years in an abusive relationship. Although the relationship began benignly, once the couple moved in together, over the course of the next year the man inflicted on the woman bruises, a mild concussion, and a broken nose. All injuries were serious enough for the woman to seek treatment in an emergency room. After leaving her husband, the woman now undergoes psychotherapy at a clinic for battered women and presently lives in a safe house connected to the clinic.

Also being seen by the same therapist at the same clinic is another woman who survived an abusive relationship with her husband, albeit only by shooting him during one of his assaults. She was found not guilty of killing and subsequently sought supportive therapy. After several months of treatment she tells her therapist that she has begun a romantic relationship with a wonderful and kind man. This marvelous man, however, is the same one who had abused the therapist's other battering survivor.

This situation is adapted from a 1994 case vignette: Confidentiality and spouse battering. Ethics & Behavior, 4, 161–162. Think through the issues carefully. They are more complex than you may initially think. For three different analyses, from a noted authority on battered spouses, a lawyer, and an ethicist, respectively, see Walker, L. E. A. (1994). The importance of knowing what you know and don't know. Ethics & Behavior, 4, 162–167; Bourne, R. (1994). Rocky Brute: A duty to warn? Ethics & Behavior, 4, 167–170; Ryan, M. A. (1994). Double trouble: "Rocky Brute" and the ethics of confidentiality. Ethics & Behavior, 4, 171–173.

Finally, for an analysis of the therapist's different duties when the client engages in violence impulsively, rather than after disclosure of an articulated plan, see Beck, J. C. (1998). Legal and ethical duties of the clinician treating a patient who is liable to be impulsively violent. Behavioral Sciences and the Law, 16, 375–389.

How does assurance that private information will be protected affect disclosures in therapy? Among pseudopatients (75 undergraduate students), those promised absolute confidentiality were more willing to disclose information than were those in a limited confidentiality group. Although both groups were more willing to disclose information of low severity than high, those in the absolute confidentiality group were significantly more willing to disclose high severity items (like psychotic symptoms). See Nowell, D., & Spruill, J. (1993). If it's not absolutely confidential, will information be disclosed? Professional Psychology: Research and Practice, 24, 367–369. Despite the benefits of absolute assurance that intimate information will be protected, as the authors recognize, it is unethical to promise absolute confidentiality. Standard 4.02 of the APA's 2002 Ethics Code mandates that psychologists discuss confidentiality "at the outset of the relationship" unless "it is not feasible or is contraindicated." Standard 10.01 requires therapists to inform clients of limits to confidentiality "as early as is feasible." Yet, in surveying 204 Midwestern psychologists about what procedures they would follow concerning the mandatory reporting of child abuse, Nicolai and Scott (1994) noted these findings with alarm:

> *Almost 20% of respondents indicated that they sometimes, rarely, or never provide*

this information to clients and that more than 5% misleadingly tell clients that everything disclosed in therapy is confidential. We are disturbed by these and other findings and their implications.

Without explicit presentation of information regarding confidentiality limits, the novice client may well assume that all disclosures, regardless of content, will be kept confidential. Moreover, clinicians who tell clients that everything they say will be held in confidence are clearly putting clients, as well as themselves, at risk. Legal and ethical guidelines for mental health professionals clearly state that clinicians must breach confidentiality when certain information is disclosed by clients in therapy.

(p. 158)

Nicolai, K. M., & Scott, N. A. (1994). Provision of confidentiality information and its relation to child abuse reporting. Professional Psychology: Research and Practice, 25, 154–160.

The following articles address two issues that are perhaps more complex than those difficult issues to which the reader has already been exposed. First, I review the extent to which a minor's confidential communications are protected from disclosure. Second, I present views of potentially conflicting duties and obligations of psychologists who provide services to people infected with HIV or AIDS.

McGuire (1974) asserted that the 1963 APA code of ethics was difficult to understand and apply to the relationship between clinicians and child clients, particularly with regard to confidentiality. Review Standards 3.07, 3.10, and 4.02(a) of the 2002 Ethical Principles and judge whether they offer any greater clarity or guidance to those who work with children than the 1963 Code did. McGuire also conducted a survey of 45 clinicians and found a growing trend among professionals to act as if minors' confidential disclosures could be afforded the same protection as adults'. See McGuire, J. M. (1974). Confidentiality and the child in psychotherapy. Professional Psychology: Research and Practice, 5, 374–379. In light of the following articles, was that trend justified from either a legal or an ethical perspective?

Confidentiality With Minor Clients:
Issues and Guidelines for Therapists

Kathryn E. Gustafson and J. Regis McNamara

. . .

LEGAL CONSIDERATIONS IN CONSENT TO TREATMENT

Increasingly, minors are legally allowed to pursue treatment without parental consent. Most jurisdictions allow minors to consent to treatment without parental knowledge in specific situations in which obtaining parental consent may jeopardize the likelihood that the minor will receive that treatment (Wilson, 1978). These specific situations include counseling or medical care for sexual abuse, substance abuse, pregnancy, sexually transmitted diseases, and contraception.

In addition, the law has recognized four general exceptions to the requirement of parent consent for treatment of minors (Plotkin, 1981). The first, the "mature minor" exception, pertains to minors with sufficient maturity to understand the nature and consequences of treatment. The second, "emancipated minor," refers to minors who are legally entitled to the rights and duties of adulthood for reasons that vary from state to state (e.g., a married minor). "Emergency treatment" is the third circumstance in which parental consent is not necessary. It is assumed that parental consent is implied because of the urgency of the situation. The final exception to obtaining parental consent is when treatment is court ordered.

These exceptions, although originally designed to clarify the rights of minors, have actually confused practitioners because the exceptions are vague, vary from state to state, and are open to a great amount of interpretation. Thus Plotkin (1981) recommended that the age at which individuals may give consent to treatment be lowered according to data in the child development literature.

DEVELOPMENTAL CONSIDERATIONS IN CONSENT TO TREATMENT

There is accumulating evidence that minors of certain ages may have obtained sufficient developmental maturity to make well-informed decisions about psychotherapeutic treatment. Grisso and Vierling (1978) reviewed the cognitive developmental literature and concluded that "there is little evidence that minors of age 15 and above as a group are any less competent to provide consent than are adults" (p. 423). Below age 11, however, minors are not capable of voluntary consent because they do not have the necessary intellectual capabilities, and they have a tendency toward deference to authority. Weithorn (1982) concurred that when children acquire formal operational thinking, between ages 11 and 14, they are able to conceptualize abstract possibilities and hypothetical outcomes of multiple courses of action and therefore are competent to provide consent. . . .

Moreover, by age 15, adolescents are capable of comprehending and exercising their rights. In a therapy analogue, information provided about clients' rights improved 15-year-old, but not 9-year-old, boys' recognition of rights violations and their capacity to protect those rights (Belter & Grisso, 1984). The 15-year-olds in this study performed as well on these variables as did the 21-year-old subjects.

Another important component in informed consent is the ability to identify potential risks and benefits of therapy. Kaser-Boyd, Adelman, and Taylor (1985) found that minors with learning and behavior problems were capable of identifying relevant

From *Professional Psychology: Research and Practice, 18,* 503–508. Copyright 1987 by the American Psychological Association.

therapy risks and benefits. There was a tendency for minors who were older who had had previous therapeutic experience to identify more risks and benefits and to describe these risks and benefits more abstractly. Younger minors and those without previous therapy experience, however, were able to identify risks and benefits that were relevant and practical to their situation.

There is a growing body of evidence that minors can effectively participate in at least some types of treatment decisions. Minors with learning and related behavior problems reported an interest in, and felt competent to participate in, the psychoeducational decisions that affect them, took the steps necessary to get involved, and then felt satisfied with the results of their involvement (Adelman, Lusk, Alvarez, & Acosta, 1985; Taylor, Adelman, & Kaser-Boyd, 1983, 1985). Older students had a greater desire to participate, had a greater tendency to follow through with their plans, and were rated as more effective in doing so by their parents and teachers (Taylor et al., 1985). In addition, adolescents appear to respond more positively to treatment when involved in treatment planning and evaluation (Janzen & Love, 1977) and when they perceive themselves as having a choice about participation (Bastien & Adelman, 1984).

Messenger and McGuire (1981), investigating the child's conception of confidentiality in the therapeutic relationship, also found that older children (ages 12–15) have a significantly better understanding of confidentiality than do younger children (ages 6–8). Thus it appears that children gradually evolve a concept of confidentiality. . . .

DETERMINING THE BEST INTEREST OF THE CHILD

. . . Several authors believe that minors are entitled to the same rights of confidentiality as are adults (Myers, 1982; Patterson, 1971; Wrenn, 1952). As stated by Myers (1982), "the fact of minority in no fashion lessens the importance of the sanctity of confidential communications" (p. 310). Myers maintained that the therapist's duty of confidentiality is not to the parents but to the child because the child is the client. The American Psychiatric Association's Task Force on Confidentiality of Children's and Adolescents' Clinical Records has recommended in their "Model Law of Confidentiality" that the age at which minors may give consent to release confidential information is 12 years or over (American Psychiatric Association, 1979). . . .

Some authors endorse limited confidentiality with minors. Pardue, Whichard, and Johnson (1970) recommended forewarning minors that their parents or guardians might need to become involved, and minors thus informed of this limitation are then free to choose whether to participate in therapy.

Glenn (1980) and Ross (1966) proposed that the determination of whether confidentiality is necessary with minor clients should be decided on an individual, case-by-case basis. Thompson (1983) maintained that "the therapist should decide how the client's guardian is apt to use the disclosed information before deciding whether or not to release it" (p. 99).

There is a paucity of research on what minors perceive as being in their own best interests in regard to confidentiality in the therapeutic relationship. Kobocow et al. (1983) investigated the effects of varying degrees of assurance of confidentiality on self-disclosure in early adolescents. Subjects were reluctant to admit to behaviors that were not socially sanctioned and appeared not to trust the interviewer, even when confidentiality was ensured. Establishing a trusting relationship may be more important than promises of confidentiality when one is dealing with minors (Koocher, 1976, 1983; Ross, 1966). Messenger and McGuire (1981) also suggested that verbal explanations of confidentiality, although necessary, may not be as important as real-life experiences with a therapist who maintains confidentiality. Thus it does appear that confidentiality is important to the older minor.

PROFESSIONAL ATTITUDES AND BEHAVIORS

There is some variability in professionals' consent and confidentiality practices with minor clients. Many therapists apparently provide psychotherapeutic services to minors without parental consent regardless of whether state statutes allow such action (Apsler, cited in Wilson, 1978; Melton, 1981). When providing services to a minor without parental consent, many clinics and practitioners charge either a nominal fee or no fee at all or base the fee on the adolescent's income. Clinics that do not offer such special payment arrangements for minors may discourage minors from seeking treatment because costs would be too exorbitant or because payment by parental insurance would result in parental notification of treatment.

In regard to confidentiality with minor clients, some clinics limit parental access to the minor's treatment records, whereas others allow unlimited parental access to such information (Melton, 1981). McGuire (1974) assessed community mental health professionals' behaviors regarding confidentiality with minors in therapy. He found that the majority of the mental health professionals supported the position that minors should be extended the same rights of confidentiality as adults. Whether this belief was consistent with agency policy or state law was not assessed. . . .

GUIDELINES FOR THERAPISTS

. . .

Whether confidentiality will be ensured may influence the adolescent's decision to enter psychotherapy. An adolescent not guaranteed confidentiality may decide not to enter therapy or may reluctantly participate without disclosing his or her concerns. Thus as with adult clients, ensuring confidentiality serves the interests of society in that it induces individuals in need of treatment to seek that treatment.

Involving adolescents in treatment planning and assuring confidentiality in the relationship may have therapeutic benefits as well. Minors who construe themselves as active participants in a confidential relationship are more likely to be allied with the therapist and hence less likely to resist therapeutic progress.

Moreover, adolescent involvement in treatment decision making, including what information can be revealed to whom, also provides an important social learning experience. It provides them with experience for future decision making and gives them a sense of being active, responsible participants in their own welfare (Weithorn, 1983).

The degree of confidentiality afforded a minor client should be based on consideration of several factors. First, the therapist should consider the age of the client. . . . The therapist should consider the needs and desires of the child, the concerns of the parents, the particular presenting problem, and relevant state statutes in deciding what degree of confidentiality is appropriate with preadolescent children. Second, because age is only a rough indicator of cognitive functioning, the therapist should make an informal assessment of the minor's cognitive capacity, including factors such as intelligence, Piagetian stage, and Kohlbergian reasoning level. . . .

There are a number of strategies that the clinicians can use to optimize the therapeutic experience while simultaneously upholding the rights of both the minor and the parents:

1. Once the therapist has made a decision regarding the degree of confidentiality believed to be necessary and appropriate, the therapist should schedule a pretreatment family meeting with the parents and the adolescent and explain his or her rationale for this decision. The therapist should develop rapport with all family members, and all family members should demonstrate sufficient understanding of the conditions of treatment, including confidentiality. He or she should then prepare a written professional services agreement . . . fully detailing the conditions and the limits of the confidential relationship. All participating parties—parents, the adolescent, and the therapist—should sign the professional services agreement, and it should become part of the minor's permanent file.

   The professional services agreement, as well as open communication and rapport, is likely to discourage parents from demanding information obtained in therapy. In some cases, however, the parents may subsequently demand access to the files. It is unclear whether courts would decide in favor of the parents or uphold the professional service contract. . . .

2. Depending on the nature of the presenting concern and the preferences of the therapist, the parents may be involved in the treatment in different capacities. Indeed, family involvement can be therapeutically beneficial, and it is often the treatment of choice in work with minors. Yet, the

adolescent's communications may still remain confidential. Parents are sometimes involved directly in treatment, such as when an improved parent–adolescent relationship is the ultimate therapeutic goal. Maintaining confidentiality does not necessarily interfere with this goal. In some cases, family relationships have deteriorated to a point to preclude immediate, productive family work. Relationship and communication skills enhancement may first be necessary with the therapist and adolescent before it is extended to the parent and adolescent. At other times, parents may be involved indirectly, such as through monitoring the adolescent's behavior at home for change outside of therapy. In cases in which the adolescent has personal concerns, parent involvement may be even more limited. In those cases, the parents should be cautioned that adolescents often develop a strong trusting relationship with the therapist; the adolescent may reveal more intimate information to the therapist than to the parents. The therapist should explore with the parents whether such a relationship between the therapist and their child is likely to be threatening or to provoke jealousy in the parents. A frank, honest discussion of these feelings can be beneficial. . . .

3. Parents should be encouraged to initiate future family meetings if at any time during treatment they have concerns about the therapeutic process. It should be clear to both the parents and the adolescent (as stated in the professional service agreement) that family sessions will not compromise the confidential relationship between the therapist and the minor. It is important to maintain a relationship with the parents while still maintaining confidentiality of the adolescent's private disclosures. This allows the parents to more adequately assess the competence of the therapist and the effectiveness of therapy.

4. Throughout the duration of treatment, the clinician should make an attempt to provide treatment rationales and explanations that are developmentally appropriate for the adolescent. . . .

5. It is imperative that the clinician be familiar with any relevant statutes in his or her state of residence and adopt policies consistent with these statutes.

Confidentiality with minors is a subject on which the law is unclear (Herr, Arons, & Wallace, 1983). Some states have adopted inconsistent policies in which minors are allowed to consent to treatment and yet parents have access to minors' treatment records or financial responsibility for any fees incurred. Other states' statutes make no mention of the situation in which parents want access but the minor wants confidentiality.

6. If at any time the therapist is confronted with a situation in which he or she is unclear regarding appropriate professional conduct, he or she should first consult a book on ethics . . . as well as a mental health law text. . . . If there is any uncertainty or concern remaining after such a review, appropriate professional and/or legal consultation should be considered. . . .

References

Adelman, H. S., Lusk, R., Alvarez, V., & Acosta, K. (1985). Competence of minors to understand, evaluate, and communicate about their psychoeducational problems. *Professional Psychology: Research and Practice, 16,* 426–434.

American Psychiatric Association. (1979). Task force on confidentiality of children's and adolescents' clinical records. *American Journal of Psychiatry, 136,* 138–144.

Bastien, R. T., & Adelman, H. S. (1984). Noncompulsory versus legally mandated placement, perceived choice, and response to treatment among adolescents. *Journal of Consulting and Clinical Psychology, 52,* 171–179.

Belter, R. W., & Grisso, T. (1984). Children's recognition of rights violations in counseling. *Professional Psychology: Research and Practice, 15,* 899–910.

Glenn, C. M. (1980). Ethical issues in the practice of child psychotherapy. *Professional Psychology, 11,* 613–619.

Grisso, T., & Vierling, L. (1978). Minors consent to treatment: A developmental perspective. *Professional Psychology: Research and Practice, 9,* 412–427.

Herr, S. S., Arons, S., & Wallace, R. E. (1983). *Legal rights and mental health care.* Lexington, MA: Lexington.

Janzen, W. B., & Love, W. (1977). Involving adolescents as active participants in their own treatment plans. *Psychological Reports, 41,* 931–934.

Kaser-Boyd, N., Adelman, H., & Taylor, L. (1985). Minors' ability to identify risks and benefits of therapy. *Professional Psychology: Research and Practice, 16,* 411–417.

Kobocow, B., McGuire, J. M., & Blau, B. (1983). The influence of confidentiality conditions on self-disclosure of early adolescents. *Professional Psychology: Research and Practice, 14,* 435–443.

Koocher, G. P. (1976). A bill of rights for children in psychotherapy. In G. P. Koocher (Ed.), *Children's rights and the mental health professions* (pp. 23–32). New York: Wiley.

Koocher, G. P. (1983). Competence to consent: Psychotherapy. In G. B. Melton, G. P. Koocher, & M. J. Saks (Eds.), *Children's competence to consent* (pp. 111–128). New York: Plenum.

McGuire, J. M. (1974). Confidentiality and the child in psychotherapy. *Professional Psychology, 5,* 374–379.

Melton, G. B. (1981). Effects of a state law permitting minors to consent to psychotherapy. *Professional Psychology, 12,* 647–654.

Messenger, C., & McGuire, J. (1981). The child's conception of confidentiality in the therapeutic relationship. *Psychotherapy: Theory, Research & Practice, 18,* 123–130.

Myers, J. E. B. (1982). Legal issues surrounding psychotherapy with minor clients. *Clinical Social Work Journal, 10,* 303–314.

Pardue, J., Whichard, W., & Johnson, E. (1970). Limited confidential information in counseling. *Personnel and Guidance Journal, 49,* 14–20.

Patterson, C. H. (1971). Are ethics different in different settings? *Personnel and Guidance Journal, 50,* 254–259.

Ross, A. O. (1966). Confidentiality in child therapy: A reevaluation. *Mental Hygiene, 50,* 360–366.

Taylor, L., Adelman, H. S., & Kaser-Boyd, N. (1983). Perspective of children regarding their participation in psychoeducational treatment decision making. *Professional Psychology: Research and Practice, 14,* 882–884.

Taylor, L., Adelman, H. S., & Kaser-Boyd, N. (1985). Minors; attitudes and competence toward participation in psychoeducational decisions. *Professional Psychology: Research and Practice, 16,* 226–235.

Thompson, A. (1983). *Ethical concerns in psychotherapy and their legal ramifications.* New York: University Press of America.

Weithorn, L. A. (1982). Developmental factors and competence to make informed treatment decisions. *Child and Youth Services, 5,* 85–100.

Weithorn, L. A. (1983). Involving children in decisions affecting their own welfare: Guidelines for professionals. In G. B. Melton, G. P. Koocher, & M. J. Saks (Eds.), *Children's competence to consent* (pp. 235–260). New York: Plenum.

Wilson, J. (1978). *The rights of adolescents in the mental health system.* Lexington, MA: Heath.

Wrenn, C. G. (1952). The ethics of counseling. *Educational and Psychological Measurement, 12,* 161–177.

Factors Contributing to Breaking Confidentiality With Adolescent Clients: A Survey of Pediatric Psychologists

Jeremy R. Sullivan, Eleazar Ramirez, William A. Rae, Nancy Peña Razo, and Carrie A. George

How do psychologists decide whether to break confidentiality in order to inform the parents of risk-taking adolescent clients about the potential harm that may result from the adolescent's behavior? In order to encourage open communication and trust during treatment, psychologists often assure adolescent clients that confidentiality will be maintained, although there is no legal basis for doing so (Rae, 2001). Parents have the legal privilege to all information about their adolescent, yet in practice this privilege is usually voluntarily waived in order to facilitate the therapy process. Rather than being based on law, this decision is based on the psychologist's desire to build and maintain an honest therapeutic relationship with the adolescent, in which the client feels safe in revealing sensitive information (Gustafson & McNamara, 1987). However, it is clear that psychologists have an ethical and legal responsibility to break confidentiality when a client's behavior is deemed dangerous enough to constitute potential harm to the client or others (American Psychological Association [APA], 1992).

The decision to break confidentiality appears to be one of the most frequently encountered and serious ethical issues in the practice of professional psychology (Haas, Malouf, & Mayerson, 1986; Jacob-Timm, 1999; Pope & Vetter, 1992), and psychologists seem willing to break confidentiality in order to protect the client or others from harm (Pomerantz, Ross, Gfeller, & Hughes, 1998; Rae & Worchel, 1991). However, very little is known regarding the importance that psychologists place on various factors or considerations when faced with the ethical dilemma of whether to break confidentiality and risk damaging the therapeutic relationship. Clinicians working with adolescents and their families are especially likely to encounter this issue, as adolescent clients are likely to engage in a range of what the psychologist may consider to be potentially dangerous behaviors, thereby making confidentiality a particularly salient issue with this client population (Powell, 1984).

. . .

Pediatric psychologists working with risk-taking adolescents are likely to be faced with the decision to break confidentiality to tell parents about adolescent risk-taking behavior in order to protect the teenager from harm. The pediatric psychologist must assess the potential of danger to the adolescent, but it is often difficult to determine if the adolescent's behavior presents a genuine risk of danger to self or others. It is important to note that although psychologists are both legally and ethically bound to protect their clients from harm, and although both legal and ethical guidelines are critical sources of guidance and accountability for practicing psychologists, laws are prescriptive, whereas ethical principles allow for individual differences in decision making. With that said, the purpose of the present investigation was to identify which considerations most contribute to pediatric psychologists' decisions to break confidentiality and report risk-taking behavior to parents when working with adolescent clients in the context of a therapeutic relationship.

THE SURVEY OF ETHICAL DILEMMAS IN REPORTING ADOLESCENT RISK-TAKING BEHAVIOR

This study is based on a section of the Survey of Ethical Dilemmas in Reporting Adolescent Risk-Taking Behavior, which was designed to assess

From *Professional Psychology: Research and Practice, 33,* 396–401. Copyright 2002 by the American Psychological Association.

psychologists' ethical attitudes and beliefs about the treatment of risk-taking adolescents. In the first part of the survey, participants were asked to read a vignette and then rate the degree to which they believed it was ethical to break confidentiality with an adolescent client engaging in risky and potentially dangerous behaviors (i.e., cigarette smoking, sexual activity, alcohol use, drug use, and suicidal behavior) with varying degrees of frequency, intensity, and duration. The results of the first part of the survey are presented elsewhere (Rae, Sullivan, Razo, George, & Ramirez, 2002) and are briefly summarized later in this article.

In the second part of the survey, on which the present study is based, respondents were asked to indicate the importance of 13 factors when faced with the decision of whether to break confidentiality to report adolescent risk-taking behavior to parents. For this section, participants rated their responses on a 5-point scale, ranging from 1 (*extremely unimportant*) to 5 (*extremely important*). This section was independent of the first section, as the items were not based on the vignette, and participants were not asked to consider any specific risk-taking

behaviors; rather, the items were designed to assess the importance of *general* considerations when deciding whether to break confidentiality. . . . All 13 items are provided in Table 1. . . .

[The survey was mailed to 200 members of Division 54 (Society of Pediatric Psychology) of APA, with a 43% response rate. The authors performed a factor analysis of the responses to the 13 items. They identified two: Factor 1 was named Negative Nature of the Behavior (items 1, 5, 10, 11, 12); Factor 2 was named Maintaining the Therapeutic Process (items 2, 7, 8, 9), with the remaining items having insufficient loadings on any factors.]

. . .

IMPLICATIONS FOR TRAINING AND PRACTICE

Interestingly, the two factors identified in the present study may be seen as competing. That is, there is a tension or push–pull relationship between the factors, such that the Negative Nature of the Behavior factor may push one toward a decision to break confidentiality, whereas the Maintaining the

---

TABLE 1

Item Responses: Percentages and Means

Item	% response					*M*	*SD*
	1	2	3	4	5		
1. Apparent seriousness of the risk-taking behavior	1	4	1	19	74	4.61	0.82
2. The negative effects of reporting on the family	7	24	10	42	18	3.39	1.23
3. Confidence that risky behavior has actually occurred	1	3	4	41	50	4.37	0.81
4. Upholding the law	8	19	10	32	31	3.59	1.32
5. Protecting the adolescent	1	1	5	14	78	4.66	0.76
6. Avoiding legal problems for the adolescent	11	28	16	34	11	3.05	1.23
7. Not disrupting the process of therapy	5	28	10	43	14	3.31	1.18
8. Potential for risk-taking behavior to stop without telling parents	3	8	12	46	28	3.92	1.00
9. Likelihood that family will continue treatment after breaking confidentiality	10	28	18	34	11	3.08	1.20
10. Frequency of risk-taking behavior	3	1	0	43	53	4.42	0.81
11. Intensity of risk-taking behavior	3	1	1	22	73	4.61	0.82
12. Duration of risk-taking behavior	3	3	1	37	57	4.42	0.88
13. Gender of the client	53	23	12	10	3	1.86	1.13

Note. Item response: 1 = *extremely unimportant.* 2 = *somewhat unimportant.* 3 = *not sure.* 4 = *somewhat important.* 5 = *extremely important.* Percentages that do not add up to exactly 100 are the result of missing data and rounding.

Therapeutic Process factor may pull one away from breaking confidentiality. Although there was more consensus among respondents with regard to the importance assigned to the items within the Negative Nature of the Behavior factor, and although this factor accounted for a greater share of the variance among items, we feel that both factors have important and unique clinical and training implications. . . .

Negative Nature of the Behavior

The presence of the Negative Nature of the Behavior factor suggests the importance of comprehensively and systematically assessing the degree of potential risk to adolescent clients (and others) that results from their behaviors. This assessment would take into account psychology's knowledge base regarding the nature and consequences of different risk-taking behaviors given the developmental context of adolescence and would likely facilitate planning for intervention and treatment. A systematic process such as this . . . would include (at the very least) an assessment of the frequency, intensity, and duration of the behavior, as well as a consideration of the potential effect of the behavior on the adolescent and others.

With regard to training, the importance of the Negative Nature of the Behavior factor suggests that psychologists-in-training would benefit from developing an informed knowledge base on normative adolescent risk-taking behavior. This knowledge base would stem from empirical data on normative risk-taking behavior during adolescence (e.g., prevalence rates of different risk-taking behaviors) and would facilitate comparisons between normative behavior and the specific client's behavior in order to determine the extent to which the client's behavior deviates from the norm. . . . The purpose of developing such a knowledge base would be to facilitate empirically based decision making as opposed to relying solely on intuition or "what feels right" when faced with the difficult decision of whether to break confidentiality with a specific adolescent client.

The great importance that respondents assigned to items composing the Negative Nature of the Behavior factor (e.g., frequency, intensity, and duration of the risk-taking behavior) is consistent with

findings from the first part of the survey (Rae et al., 2002), which examined the influences of frequency, intensity, duration, and type of risk-taking behavior on the perceived ethicality of breaking confidentiality with a fictitious adolescent client described in a vignette. The five domains of risk-taking behavior examined in the first part of the survey, and the levels of intensity within each domain, were as follows: smoking (one cigarette, more than a pack of cigarettes), alcohol use (one drink, four or more drinks), drug use (marijuana, amphetamines, inhalants, hallucinogens), sexual behavior (sexual activity with steady partner, sexual activity with multiple partners, sexual activity without protection when HIV-positive), and suicidal behavior (suicidal ideation, suicide gesture, suicide attempt). At each level of intensity within each of the five behavioral domains (with the exception of suicide gesture and suicide attempt), there were four levels of frequency/duration: once several months ago, monthly for several months, weekly for several months, and nearly daily for the last year.

Briefly, results from this previous study indicated that across all five domains of risk-taking behavior, psychologists found it more ethical to break confidentiality as the behaviors increased in intensity and frequency/duration. Thus, respondents were generally unlikely to find it ethical to break confidentiality when the behaviors were of low intensity and low frequency/duration. However, when the adolescent in the vignette was reported to be HIV-positive and admitted to engaging in sexual activity without using protection, and when the adolescent admitted to attempting suicide, respondents were likely to find it ethical to report these behaviors even when they were of relatively low levels of frequency/duration. Conversely, even at high rates of frequency/duration, respondents were unlikely to find it ethical to report the client's smoking more than a pack of cigarettes, using marijuana, and sexual activity with either a steady partner or with multiple partners. Thus, especially intense or severe behaviors appeared to warrant disclosure regardless of frequency and duration, whereas behaviors thought to be common among adolescents were unlikely to lead to disclosure even at high levels of frequency and duration. Finally, respondents were most likely to find it ethical to report suicidal behavior, followed by drug use, sexual behavior, and alcohol use, with cigarette smoking representing the behavior least likely to warrant breaking confidentiality.

. . . Although all of the behaviors included in the survey could be described as risky or dangerous, the extent to which respondents felt that breaking confidentiality was warranted varied as did the intensity and frequency/duration of the behaviors. Although there is no consensus on how to determine whether a certain behavior is potentially dangerous enough to warrant breaking confidentiality, an assessment of the frequency, intensity, and duration of the client's behavior would appear to be a reasonable starting point. The information gained from this assessment can then be used to compare the client's behavior with data regarding typical adolescent behavior in order to reach an informed, empirically based decision.

Maintaining the Therapeutic Process

The emergence of the Maintaining the Therapeutic Process factor suggests the importance of identifying methods with which to maintain the therapeutic relationship even when confidentiality must be broken. Psychologists may fear that once confidentiality has been broken, the adolescent will no longer trust the psychologist and will therefore disclose less information during therapy sessions. Further, psychologists may fear that breaking confidentiality will result in the family's terminating treatment and will cause the family (especially the adolescent) to be less likely to seek help for psychological or behavioral concerns in the future. At the same time, the psychologist may feel pressure from parents to reveal what their adolescent has been up to. These issues point to the importance of a frank and thorough discussion of the limits of confidentiality early in the therapeutic relationship (APA, 1992; Melton, Ehrenreich, & Lyons, 2001). The psychologist should delineate specific behaviors that would warrant breaking confidentiality in order to make the discussion concrete. This process should involve both the adolescent client and the client's parents, and the psychologist should always ensure that everyone comprehends the limits of confidentiality, perhaps by asking follow-up questions to check for

understanding (Ford, Thomsen, & Compton, 2001; Gustafson & McNamara, 1987). Including the limits of confidentiality on the consent form to be signed by the parents and adolescent may also serve to avoid misunderstandings (Rae, 2001). Additionally, confidentiality issues should be revisited periodically or as new issues arise in order to ensure continued understanding by the client.

. . . Two possible alternatives to the psychologist's breaking confidentiality and informing parents privately about their adolescent's behavior include (a) encouraging the client to inform parents himself or herself in the presence of the psychologist and (b) the psychologist's informing the parents in the presence of the client. These options may serve to minimize the adolescent's feelings of resentment toward the psychologist, because in both situations the adolescent is present, and he or she may therefore feel less betrayed or besieged by the psychologist and parents.

Taylor and Adelman (1989) provided useful guidelines for resolving the ethical dilemma of breaking confidentiality with minor clients; these suggestions involve (a) explaining to the client exactly why confidentiality must be broken, (b) discussing some of the possible consequences that may result from breaking confidentiality, and (c) determining how confidentiality may be broken in a way that minimizes negative outcomes for the client. Attending to these guidelines may help clinicians incorporate the act of breaking confidentiality into the therapeutic process. The identification of additional methods with which to maximize adolescents' involvement in breaking confidentiality, and thereby increase the likelihood that the therapeutic relationship will be maintained, is desirable.

Finally, psychologists may benefit from recognizing that the Maintaining the Therapeutic Process factor may tempt them to refrain from breaking confidentiality even in the presence of extremely dangerous behaviors, when breaking confidentiality would appear to be warranted, out of concern that such disclosure will destroy the therapeutic relationship. Under these circumstances, psychologists must realize that although breaking confidentiality may indeed disrupt the process of therapy, the safety of the client (and others) is of primary importance.

Conclusion

In practice, the decision to break confidentiality is multifactored and complex, likely influenced by a combination of the psychologist's own values, the items and factors discussed in the present study, and additional considerations that have yet to be discovered. Given the complexity of this decision (as well as other ethical decisions), ethics training should not attempt to teach students "the answer" to each and every ethical dilemma. To do so would be impossible and would discount the unique complexities involved in individual cases. Rather, ethics training should attempt to teach a process for ethical decision making in which all relevant factors are taken into account within a developmental context. Perhaps the critical rule with regard to ethical decision making and resolving ethical dilemmas is that one should always be able to reasonably defend one's ethical decisions and should be able to show that all relevant factors were considered during the decision-making process. Thus, students should be taught early in their training to document the factors they considered during the ethical decision-making process when faced with ethical dilemmas and to conceptualize how these factors influenced their ultimate decisions. This is especially important when working with risk-taking adolescents, as psychologists may be held liable for not breaking confidentiality and reporting dangerous behavior when this behavior results in harm to the adolescent or others. As noted by Baerger (2001), "mental health professionals will not be held liable for mistakes in judgment, as long as due care was exercised in the decision-making process" (p. 363). In order to benefit from such protection, however, students must be taught to adequately document this decision-making process.

References

American Psychological Association. (1992). Ethical principles of psychologists and code of conduct. *American Psychologist, 47,* 1597–1611.

Baerger, D. R. (2001). Risk management with the suicidal patient: Lessons from case law. *Professional Psychology: Research and Practice, 32,* 359–366.

Ford, C. A., Thomsen, S. L., & Compton, B. (2001). Adolescents' interpretations of conditional confidentiality assurances. *Journal of Adolescent Health, 29,* 156–159.

Gustafson, K. E., & McNamara, J. R. (1987). Confidentiality with minor clients: Issues and guidelines for therapists. *Professional Psychology: Research and Practice, 18,* 503–508.

Haas, L. J., Malouf, J. L., & Mayerson, N. H. (1986). Ethical dilemmas in psychological practice: Results of a national survey. *Professional Psychology: Research and Practice, 17,* 316–321.

Jacob-Timm, S. (1999). Ethically challenging situations encountered by school psychologists. *Psychology in the Schools, 36,* 205–217.

Melton, G. B., Ehrenreich, N. S., & Lyons, P. M. (2001). Ethical and legal issues in mental health services for children. In C. E. Walker & M. C. Roberts (Eds.), *Handbook of clinical child psychology* (3rd ed., pp. 1074–1093). New York: Wiley.

Pomerantz, A., Ross, M. J., Gfeller, J. D., & Hughes, H. (1998). Ethical beliefs of psychotherapists: Scientific findings. *Journal of Contemporary Psychotherapy, 28,* 35–44.

Pope, K. S., & Vetter, V. A. (1992). Ethical dilemmas encountered by members of the American Psychological Association: A national survey. *American Psychologist, 47,* 397–411.

Powell, C. J. (1984). Ethical principles and issues of competence in counseling adolescents. *Counseling Psychologist, 12*(3), 57–68.

Rae, W. A. (2001). Common teen–parent problems. In C. E. Walker & M. C. Roberts (Eds.), *Handbook of clinical child psychology* (3rd ed., pp. 621–637). New York: Wiley.

Rae, W. A., Sullivan, J. R., Razo, N. P., George, C. A., & Ramirez, E. (2002). Adolescent health risk behavior: When do pediatric psychologists break confidentiality? *Journal of Pediatric Psychology, 27,* 541–549.

Rae, W. A., & Worchel, F. F. (1991). Ethical beliefs and behaviors of pediatric psychologists: A survey. *Journal of Pediatric Psychology, 16,* 727–745.

Taylor, L., & Adelman, H. S. (1989). Reframing the confidentiality dilemma to work in children's best interests. *Professional Psychology: Research and Practice, 20,* 79–83.

◆   ◆   ◆

Commentary: See also Sobocinski, M. R. (1990). Ethical principles in the counseling of gay and lesbian adolescents. Issues and autonomy, competence, and confidentiality: Professional Psychology: Research and Practice, 21, 240–247. This important and controversial article presents several vignettes containing ethical dilemmas facing psychologists who work with gay and lesbian youth. Which provisions in the 2002 APA Ethics Code might be helpful in resolving such dilemmas?

Balancing the interests of minors and their parents is a difficult task for practitioners and researchers. Because the law considers children to be generally incompetent in making decisions for themselves, whether they are granted the power to make these decisions is determined by constitutional analyses, case law, and state statutes. For psychologists who work in governmental institutions such as schools or state hospitals or in private institutions such as non-public schools, independent practice, or mental health clinics, it is very risky to serve minors without parental involvement unless there is an explicit statute permit-ting it, for example, 35 Pennsylvania Statute 10101.1, allowing children 14 years of age or older to consent to outpatient and inpatient mental health treatment. In any case, psychologists should clearly delineate expectations among themselves, their minor clients, and the minor's parents. See also Behnke, S. (2005, December). Letter from a reader regarding a minor client and confidentiality. APA Monitor, 36, 78–79. For a more complete discussion of legal issues related to assessment, intervention, and research with minors, see Reschly, D., & Bersoff, D. N. (1999). The legal regulation of school psychology. In C. Reynolds & T. Gutkin (Eds.), Handbook of school psychology (3rd ed., pp. 1077–1112). New York: Wiley.

HIV, Confidentiality, and Duty to Protect: A Decision-Making Model

Tiffany Chenneville

What is your duty as a psychologist when treating a client with HIV? Do *Tarasoff* principles apply? Are ethical guidelines consistent with individual state laws? Questions such as these are all too familiar for mental health professionals who serve clients with HIV. Clinicians may be forced to make difficult decisions about whether to breach confidentiality to protect third parties from HIV exposure. Breaches in confidentiality may result in deterioration of the therapeutic relationship, which may be harmful to the overall well-being of the client. Alternatively, maintaining confidentiality may result in physical, mental, and emotional harm to third parties. This double bind can be extremely burdensome to mental health professionals. Decisions are complicated further by the fact that dichotomous choices rarely exist. In reality, the ultimate question is not whether to breach confidentiality. Rather, it becomes how to protect third parties without destroying the therapeutic alliance between clinician and client. To make responsible decisions, clinicians must carefully examine the various legal and therapeutic factors involved in situations in which clients are at risk for transmitting a potentially lethal virus.

As of December 1999, well over one-half million (733,374) diagnosed AIDS cases had been reported to the Centers for Disease Control and Prevention (CDC; 1999). Not included in this number are the large and growing number of individuals diagnosed with HIV, the virus that causes AIDS. As a result, mental health professionals can expect to encounter clients with HIV. Given the discrimination that individuals with HIV have faced, confidentiality is an extremely important issue. Individuals with HIV may be hesitant to seek needed treatment without the assurance of confidentiality. However, individuals with HIV who engage in unsafe sexual practices or IV drug use may be considered "dangerous" (broadly defined). This reality can become an issue for clinicians who are knowledgeable about their clients' sexual behavior.

ETHICAL ISSUES

A consensus generally exists regarding the importance of confidentiality within therapeutic relationships. Without an assurance of confidentiality, clients may be hesitant to seek treatment because of fear of stigmatization. Furthermore, mental health professionals generally agree that effective treatment may necessitate full disclosure and that confidentiality is important for the maintenance of the therapeutic relationship.

Confidentiality is particularly important in the area of HIV. Individuals at risk for HIV infection may fear discrimination, lifestyle exposure (e.g., sexual orientation, drug use habits or practices), social rejection, or disruption of existing relationships. These fears may discourage individuals from being tested for HIV or from receiving appropriate medical treatment, psychological treatment, or both. Also, given the correlation between HIV exposure risk and domestic abuse (Molina & Basinait-Smith, 1998), it is possible that fear of relationship violence may result in hesitancy to seek treatment if confidentiality is not ensured.

. . .

DECISION-MAKING MODEL

The following decision-making model is based on a review of the literature in this area. It takes into account the major premises outlined in the *Tarasoff* decision while emphasizing professional ethics and

From *Professional Psychology: Research and Practice, 31,* 661–670, Copyright 2000 by the American Psychological Association.

the best interest of the client. In addition, this model takes into account differences in statutory and case law, representing an expansion of models currently available. Indeed, the APA's HIV/AIDS Office for Psychology Education and Ad Hoc Committee on Psychology and AIDS dictate that psychologists "should abide by state laws and regulations" and "should determine what state statutes and case law require, and permit, in the state in which they practice" (APA, 2000). This model also provides specific information on how to proceed in situations in which disclosure is warranted. . . .

Step 1: Determine Whether Disclosure Is Warranted

The first step of the decision-making model involves determining whether disclosure is warranted. As discussed above, making this determination requires an assessment of the foreseeability of harm (i.e., What are the sexual or IV drug use practices of the client?) and the identifiability of the victim (i.e., Are the identities of sexual or needle-sharing partners known?). The following is a list of questions for mental health professionals to consider when determining foreseeability of harm:

> To what extent is the client sexually active or engaged in needle-sharing practices?
>
> How often does the client engage in sexual relations or needle-sharing practices and with whom?
>
> Does the client take precautions against HIV transmission during sexual relations and needle-sharing practices? For example,
>
> Does the client use condoms?
> Does the client clean needles before and after use?
>
> What personality characteristics exist that may increase risk? For example,
>
> Is the client impulsive?
> Is the client aggressive?
> Is the client submissive?
> Is the client shy or timid?

> Has the client been diagnosed with an Axis I or Axis II disorder?
>
> If so, what symptoms are likely to increase risk of danger to others?
>
> Does the client use substances (e.g., alcohol) that decrease inhibitions?
>
> What motivation exists for the client's unwillingness to self-disclose?
>
> Is the client afraid to disclose HIV status because of fear of rejection, discrimination, and so forth?
>
> Is the client intentionally trying to harm others?

If harm is foreseen on the basis of an examination of the aforementioned factors, then it is necessary to determine whether you can identify a third party at risk. The question is whether you, as a clinician, can identify with relative accuracy the identity of one or more potential victims. If you are able to identify a potential victim, then it is necessary to assess the therapeutic alliance. This assessment may be done through a formal or informal examination of the extent to which there is trust, understanding, acceptance, shared goals, perceived effectiveness, and shared values within the therapeutic relationship (see Truscott, Evans, & Mansell, 1995, for specific guidelines on conducting formal and informal assessments of the therapeutic alliance). Keeping in mind the client's best interest, the initial and primary goal of the therapist should be to guide clients to disclose their HIV status to sexual or needle-sharing partners on their own. Not only will this protect the therapeutic relationship but it also may instill in the client a sense of responsibility and personal control. If the client's self-disclosure can be accomplished, there will be no need for a breach in confidentiality. If you are unable to identify a potential victim, it still is advisable that you work with the client to reduce behaviors that increase the risk of transmitting the virus to others.

Step 2: Refer to Professional Ethical Guidelines

The second step of the decision-making model involves an examination of professional ethical guidelines. Mental health professionals who are members of the APA should refer to Ethical Standards 5.02 and 5.05 (APA, 1992)[1]. Depending on the discipline, it may be necessary to consult the ethical guidelines set forth by other professional organizations such as the American Medical Association or the National Association of Social Workers.

Step 3: Refer to State Guidelines

The third step of the decision-making model involves an examination of state guidelines. Statutory laws specify one of the following: permissive disclosure, required disclosure, or mandatory confidentiality. Again, readers are referred to Appendix A for a list of statutes pertaining to confidentiality and exceptions to confidentiality by state and to the following website: www.law.stetson.edu/law.

Permissive disclosure. If state law outlines "permissive disclosure" (i.e., disclosure is allowed but not mandated), mental health professionals need to consider the potential impact of disclosure on the client, the client's amenability to treatment directed at containing the endangering behavior, and the client's willingness to disclose his or her health status to potential victims. The APA (2000), as outlined in a recommendation made by the HIV/AIDS Office for Psychology Education, supports the presumption that "confidentiality on behalf of the client shall be maintained except in extraordinary circumstances wherein individuals are unwilling or incapable of reducing the risk of infection to sexual or needle-sharing partners." In terms of assessing the potential impact of disclosure on the client, mental health professionals need to consider the therapeutic relationship, the emotional well-being of the client, and the potential harm to the client (e.g., in cases in which domestic violence is likely; see Molina & Basinait-Smith, 1998). When assessing a client's amenability to treatment directed at containing endangering behavior, it is important for mental health professionals to consider the client's motivation for engaging in high-risk behaviors. In addition, it is important to consider the attitudes and behavioral characteristics that support at-risk behaviors

and the likelihood that they are amenable to treatment efforts. In terms of assessing a client's willingness to disclose his or her health status to a potential victim, it is important to consider the client's motivation for maintaining confidentiality of health status (e.g., fear of discrimination, loss of relationship). Finally, if it is determined that disclosure is necessary after considering the aforementioned factors, mental health professionals should refer to the steps outlined in the next section of this article.

Required disclosure. If state law requires disclosure, mental health professionals should first encourage the client to disclose his or her HIV status to potential victims. Verification and documentation of self-disclosure are critical at this juncture. If the client refuses to self-disclose, an attempt should be made by the mental health professional to gain the client's consent for disclosure. If the client refuses to consent, the mental health professional must notify the client that information is going to be released. Notification of impending disclosure should be done verbally, preferably in person, and in writing. The basis for the decision (i.e., factors warranting disclosure) and the potential impact on the therapeutic relationship should be discussed with the client. In addition, the client should be given another opportunity to self-disclose. If the client still refuses, thus requiring third-party disclosure, only pertinent information should be provided to potential victims. It is important to remember that the duty outlined in *Tarasoff* is to protect. Protection may or may not include warning. For example, some states consider notification to a local health department to be sufficient protective action. Health officials then become responsible for warning, or otherwise protecting, potential victims in accordance with state regulations. In cases in which protective action requires warning, disclosure should be limited to notifying a potential victim that he or she may have been exposed to HIV without divulging the name of or other personal information about the client. The disclosure process, including notification to the client, should be documented in writing. This documentation is extremely

---

[1]*Ed. Note:* See Standards 4.01 and 4.05 of the current (2002) APA Ethics Code.

important for the protection of the clinician. The date, time, content, and outcome of all conversations pertaining to the topic should be maintained. Also, the reasoning behind the clinician's decision to "protect" should be documented. Finally, an attempt should be made to maintain or repair the therapeutic relationship. If this is not possible, the client should be referred to another mental health professional for continued treatment.

Mandatory confidentiality. If state law requires confidentiality without exceptions, an attempt should be made by the mental health professional to encourage the client to disclose his or her health status to potential victims. If the client refuses to self-disclose, it is important for the mental health professional to address the issues and behaviors that prohibit disclosure. Finally, an attempt should be made to work with the client on changing or altering high-risk behaviors (e.g., encourage the client to use condoms).

References

American Psychological Association. (1992). Ethical principles of psychologists and code of conduct. *American Psychologist, 47*, 1597–1611.

American Psychological Association. (2000). Duty to warn. *HIV/AIDS Office for Psychology Education (HOPE).* Washington, DC: Author. Retrieved January 28, 2000, from the World Wide Web: http://www.apa.org/pi/aids/hope.html

Centers for Disease Control and Prevention. (1999, December). *HIV/AIDS surveillance report* (Vol. 11, No. 2). Atlanta, GA: National Centers for Disease Control and Prevention.

Molina, L. D., & Basinait-Smith, C. (1998). Revisiting the intersection between domestic abuse and HIV risk. *American Journal of Public Health, 88*, 1267–1268.

Truscott, D., Evans, J., & Mansell, S. (1995). Outpatient psychotherapy with dangerous clients: A model for clinical decision making. *Professional Psychology: Research and Practice, 26*, 484–490.

♦ ♦ ♦

Commentary: Apply Chenneville's decision-making model to the following case example, also from her article:

> *You have been seeing Michael Smith in therapy for the past three months. Michael is 33 years old and has been married for 8 years. He has two children, a boy and a girl, ages 3 and 5, respectively. Michael admitted to you in the course of therapy that he had an affair with his neighbor several years ago. His wife never found out about the affair which lasted approximately 6 months. Michael recently discovered that the woman with whom he had an affair died of AIDS. This prompted Michael to have an HIV test, the results of which were positive. Michael told you he has no intention of telling his wife about his test results. (p. 665)*

What factors would you consider in deciding whether to disclose Michael's HIV status to third parties? What additional information might you require to make this decision?

In the following excerpt, the authors present a case study of a 40-year-old gay African American man diagnosed with depression and borderline personality disorder who has been in therapy for 2 years. A former heavy drug user, now drug free for 5 years, he is HIV-positive but with no serious symptoms at present. He reports that he has had sex with gay drug-using partners, some of whom were HIV-positive, but did not reveal his status to any of his partners. Although he never wears a condom during these encounters, most of the time he withdraws prior to ejaculation. What is different about this article is that it presents arguments for both maintaining and breaking confidentiality. As the reader concludes the excerpt, what position seems the most ethical in this case?

Divergent Ethical Perspectives on the Duty-to-Warn Principle With HIV Patients

Steven K. Huprich, Kristi M. Fuller, and Robert B. Schneider

. . .

MAINTAINING CONFIDENTIALITY WHEN A CLIENT IS HIV-POSITIVE AND SEXUALLY ACTIVE

The key question is whether the therapist has a duty to warn an unidentified third party of risk of transmission of HIV where disclosure would violate confidentiality, likely resulting in damage to the therapeutic relationship and possible harm to the client. The best course of action minimizes the harm and maximizes the benefit to all people and relationships involved.

Before facing the dilemma of disclosure, a clinician might explore some alternatives, such as recommending the client inform his friend of his HIV status. The clinician might even offer the client that the at-risk partner be invited in for a session or that the clinician could jointly inform the partner with the client. If the client remained unreceptive to these possibilities, the clinician might suggest the client refrain from engaging in sexual activity with this particular friend. If sexual activity continued to occur, the clinician could advocate the practice of safe sex. . . . Ideally, the client would follow through on these recommendations. But, if he did not, unknown partners should not be informed, nor should steps be taken to identify and inform the third party.

This action is justified under both the utilitarian and deontological frameworks of ethical decision making. Under the perspective of utilitarianism, the ethical decision is that which is in the best interest of the greater number of people and, thus, society. The ethical decision from the deontological point of view is that which is in the greatest interest of the particular person, here the client.

Encouraging the client to inform his friend of his HIV status and, should that fail, to discontinue sexual activity with that friend or practice safer sex would be ethical under both paradigms. This approach would reduce the risk of harm to the unidentified third party and the client, reduce the transmission of HIV, encourage individual responsibility, and maintain both confidentiality and the therapeutic alliance, promoting continued therapy for the client. It is possible that, should the client inform his friend of his HIV status, the friend may react negatively. Such reaction might have adverse consequences for the client. However, steps could be taken to mitigate the potential emotional harm to the client. A session in therapy could be devoted to determining how to tell the friend, anticipating the possible reactions of the friend, and role-playing. The friend's responses and their emotional impact on the client could then be handled in subsequent sessions.

Under the deontological framework, it could be argued that because the client has been diagnosed with borderline personality disorder, revealing his HIV-positive status to the uninfected sexual partner may be extremely traumatic to the client, causing emotional harm and potential for impulsivity, affective disturbance, and possibly suicide. However, it could also be argued that it is in the best interest of the client not to cause harm to another and to expand his sense of individual and moral responsibility. Should his friend become infected with HIV and realize the source of transmission, more severe moral, legal, and emotional consequences might ensue.

Encouraging the client to inform the friend of his HIV-positive status, discontinue sexual relations with the friend, or, at least, practice safe sex with the friend would be congruent with the principles of

Autonomy, Beneficence, Fidelity, Justice, and Nonmaleficence that underlie the APA's [American Psychological Association's] Code of Conduct and Ethical Principles of Psychologists (1992). In doing so, the client would be encouraged to take individual responsibility and have the freedom to choose his response to his friend. Indirectly, the autonomy of the friend would be promoted as well, as the friend would be able to choose whether to continue sexual relations with full knowledge of the client's condition. This course of action would be in the client's best interest insofar as it would encourage personal responsibility and consideration of others while reducing the possibility of harmful consequences that might follow should he transmit HIV to his friend. The friend would benefit from the client either informing him, discontinuing sexual relations with him, or engaging in safe sex, as the risk of transmission of HIV and potential harm to the friend would be reduced. Other people may benefit as well insofar as behaviors reducing the transmission of HIV might follow, limiting others' exposure to HIV. In honoring the capacity of the client to act responsibly, Fidelity is also honored. Fidelity is preserved and modeled in the context of the therapeutic relationship and is encouraged in the client himself.

Furthermore, confidentiality should not be broken through notification of authorities or steps to identify and contact the unidentified third party. If the client were unwilling to either inform his friend of his HIV status or take steps to reduce the risk of transmitting the HIV virus to his friend, the therapist should neither take steps to notify authorities nor take action to try to identify and contact the friend. This position would be ethical from the deontological perspective, where the client would be considered an end in himself. It could be argued that not taking further action to notify the unidentified third party would not fit the utilitarian framework involving the greatest benefit to society insofar as the friend and others might be exposed to the HIV virus. However the therapeutic alliance would most likely be damaged by such actions to warn the third party. Given the client's history and diagnosis, such a rupture to the therapeutic alliance could harm the client, potentially leading to more acting out through unprotected sexual behavior, with the possible effect

of more people exposed to HIV. Furthermore, others may be deterred from utilizing psychological services if they thought confidentiality were in jeopardy.

. . .

It could be argued that this position conflicts with the moral principles of Beneficence, Nonmaleficence, and Paternalism. The therapist might be considered to be passively allowing evil to occur through the actions of the client and undermining benevolence in that good is not being done to the third party and/or society. Further, it could be argued the therapist should take more of a paternalistic role and that it would actually be in the best interest of the client for the therapist to step in and inform the client that confidentiality would need to be broken with the situation reported to the authorities or the unidentified third party.

However, although this course of action may seem sufficient for the short term, it would not provide a long-term solution. The client would most likely lose trust in the therapist, the therapeutic alliance would break down, the client might discontinue therapy, individual functioning likely would not improve, and sexual acting out, including unprotected sex, would possibly increase. Therefore, it would seem preferable to maintain the strength of the therapeutic relationship, continue work on central issues that may be contributing to the client's acting out sexually and prohibiting the client from disclosing his HIV status to his sexual partners, and continue to encourage the client to either disclose his status or reduce the risk of transmission of HIV.

. . .

In a recent case, *Thapar v. Zezulka* (994 S.W.2d 635), decided by the Texas Supreme Court in 1999, the court, in a unanimous decision, held that a mental health professional could not be "liable in negligence for failing to warn the appropriate third parties when a patient makes *specific threats* of harm toward a *readily identifiable* person." Justice Enoch delivered the opinion for the court, stating that "we refrain from imposing on mental-health professionals a duty to warn third parties of a patient's threats." . . .

In *Thapar v. Zezulka* (1999), contrary to the California court *Tarasoff v. Regents of University of California* (1976), the Texas court did not extend a duty to protect third parties. . . .

... [T]he APA has chosen not to impose on mental health professionals a duty to warn. In a 1991 resolution related to HIV/AIDS, "Legal Liability Related to Confidentiality and the Prevention of HIV Transmission," the APA stated that regarding legislation related to confidentiality and the prevention of HIV transmission, "A legal duty to protect third parties from HIV infection should not be imposed." The APA further stated that if such legislation were created, disclosure should be permitted

> only when (a) the provider knows of an *identifiable* third party who the provider has *compelling reason* to believe is at *significant risk* for infection; (b) the provider has a *reasonable belief* that the third party has *no reason* to suspect that he or she is at risk and (c) the client/patient has been urged to inform the third party and has either refused or is considered unreliable in his/her willingness to notify the third party [all italics added]. (APA, 1991)

The APA's position holds confidentiality in the very highest regard, even where risk of harm to a third party is involved. The standards for permitted disclosure to an "identifiable third party" where the mental health professional has "compelling reason" to fear "significant risk" of infection are quite high. Furthermore, the mental health professional must have a "reasonable belief" that the third party has "no reason to suspect" that he or she is at risk. This position seems to shift the burden away from the mental health provider into the hands of the third party. Finally, disclosure is to be the last resort, only after the client has been encouraged to notify the third party.

Applying these standards to the situation at hand, disclosure would not be permitted in the event that the client chose not to inform his friend of his HIV status. In this case, the third party is not identifiable. Also, although the unidentified friend does not know the client is HIV-positive, it is unlikely the third party has "no reason to suspect" he or she is at risk. It is common knowledge that engaging in unsafe sex is a risk factor for contraction of HIV.

In summary, although it would be tragic for the friend to contract the HIV virus, confidentiality should not be broken by attempting to notify either the authorities or the friend. ...

... Although psychologists should be concerned about public health and the transmission of HIV, psychological services play an important role in encouraging individual responsibility and more moral interpersonal functioning and sexual behavior. If the psychologist were to step outside this role of providing a safe place for individual improvement through confidentiality, trust, fidelity, and nondiscrimination, the public would be deterred from the utilization of these services. In the long run, interests of both the client and the public would be undermined should the psychologist's role become one of investigating and policing rather than striving to help the client.

BREAKING CONFIDENTIALITY WHEN A CLIENT IS HIV-POSITIVE AND SEXUALLY ACTIVE

This case presents a fundamental ethical dilemma that should be considered across several related dimensions.

. . .

Ethical Frameworks

... Fine and Ulrich (1988) identified two broad frameworks that inform specific ethical principles. In this moral taxonomy, these two broad frameworks are deontology and utilitarianism. The deontological perspective proceeds from Kant's notion of the categorical imperative, a moral absolute that insists that an individual be treated "as an end and never as a means only" (p. 543). From this perspective, the individual value of all persons is a preeminent concern in ethical decision-making, and "the morality of actions is based on their intrinsic rightness, is independent of the consequences of behaviors, and thus permits no exceptions to the major principles" (p. 543).

In contrast, the more pragmatic utilitarian perspective holds that ethical decision making should be distilled to a cost–benefit analysis that considers the effects of the decision on all concerned parties: "An action is ethically appropriate when it leads to the greatest possible balance of good consequences or to the least possible balance of bad consequences in the world as a whole" (Fine & Ulrich, 1988, p. 543). In reference to *Tarasoff* (1976), Fine and Ulrich (1988) argued that the majority of the justices ruled on utilitarian grounds that in certain circumstances, a clinician's social responsibility supersedes a client's right to confidentiality. They state that a deontological rebuttal to that position "would suggest that one should maintain confidentiality in *all* cases because an individual's right to privacy is a moral absolute and should never be violated" (p. 543).

There seems to be an inherent weakness in the deontological perspective's dilemma-solving ability that proceeds from such idealism. If two moral absolutes are in direct conflict, how does the deontological approach resolve the contradiction? Indeed, the idea of a categorical imperative seems to presuppose that such dilemmas cannot exist, because a moral absolute makes all other consideration moot. Thus, to approach a dilemma from a deontological position seems inherently problematic. At best, one puts oneself in a double bind, pinned between two moral imperatives. In the case at hand, a deontologically inclined clinician would seem to be caught between the rock of the client's absolute right to confidentiality and the hard place of the third party's absolute right to be spared preventable risk of harm.

Approaching this dilemma from a utilitarian perspective, on the other hand, permits the cost–benefit weighing, which becomes necessary when basic principles clash. A utilitarian approach, while it may entail "moral compromise" (Bersoff, 1992), permits a thoroughly analyzed decision. In this case, a utilitarian decision involves weighing two exceedingly important considerations—one specific to the clinical role and the other a more general social responsibility. The first of these, the clinician's duty to maintain confidentiality, is, as Bersoff and Koeppl (1993) recognized, a "bedrock value" in the profession of psychology. Confidentiality is not merely an aspect of the therapeutic relationships; it is foundational to the trust that makes that relationship such a potentially powerful agent of beneficial change. The import of breaking confidentiality cannot, therefore, be easily dismissed. For this reason, the Ethics Code stresses the necessity of making the potential limits of confidentiality as clear as possible to clients at the outset of therapy. Such explicitness can mitigate the destructiveness of a later breach if the clinician deems it necessary.

In deciding whether to breach confidentiality, the clinician must consider not only the decision's intrinsic moral character but also its clinical impact and its effect on the lives of others. Attacking the *Tarasoff* (1976) ruling, former APA president Max Siegel contended that Prosenjit Poddar's psychologist made a profoundly bad decision in breaching confidentiality: "If the psychologist had accepted the view of absolute inviolate confidentiality, he might have been able to keep Poddar in treatment, saved the life of Tatiana Tarasoff, and avoided what was to become the Tarasoff decision" (Siegel, 1979, p. 253). Siegel basically asserted that when the clinician breached confidentiality and destroyed trust he disarmed himself clinically and exacerbated Poddar's "homicidality" by making him less amenable to therapeutic intervention.

In the HIV scenario, the breaching issue is not raised by a threat of deliberate violence but by the threat of harm through irresponsibility; however, the consideration of risk to a third party is essentially the same. In approaching the decision from a utilitarian perspective, one must consider not only the morality of violating trust but also the effects of that violation on the client's behavior. Even if one were clear at the outset of therapy about exceptions to confidentiality, it is possible that a well-intended breach could be destructive not just to the therapeutic relationship. For instance, in this scenario, informing the unsuspecting sex partner about the client's HIV status might well result in the client's stopping his or her therapy, thereby compromising or even negating the therapeutic process. It might also engender a deep distrust of clinicians that could make him unwilling to seek further help from anyone. Furthermore, the client—given his history of impulsivity and affective instability—might angrily react to the breach by becoming even more recklessly promiscuous, thereby imperiling more persons.

. . .

[I]n this case, the issues of immediate risk of harm to the current sexual partner looms. . . . [T]he risk of harm to the current partner seems real and imminent, as the client's characterization of unprotected and anal sex with reliance on withdrawal as being "careful" suggests. From the utilitarian standpoint, this immediacy of risk is a compelling factor.

Given the potential lethality of HIV this danger might well outweigh all other clinical and moral considerations.

Finally, one must judge the trustworthiness of the client's word should he agree to inform the partner himself. His doing so would be the ideal solution, but given his negligence in repeatedly having unprotected sex with an unsuspecting partner, assuming that he would keep his word about disclosure may be naïve. More unsuspecting persons could then be endangered by relying on the client to disclose. If the unknowing partner is not informed and in turn has unsafe sex with others, the danger proceeding from the clinician's not making sure of disclosure is multiplied.

Calculations of all these costs and benefits would no doubt vary among clinicians. In this case, therapists should consider, along with the many issues already discussed, potential countertransference. For example, a client behaving sexually like the one in this case might nonetheless have a record in therapy of keeping commitments and following through with treatment suggestions diligently. If a clinician were still convinced that the client could not be trusted to keep his word to self-disclose, the clinician ought to examine whether some element of homophobia, racism, or perhaps more idiosyncratic countertransferential response might be unduly biasing a decision to breach confidentiality. Conversely, countertransference issues might incline a clinician to ignore or minimize the danger to the third party if acknowledging that danger would threaten a positive image of the client that was excessively important for the clinician to maintain. A truly ethical decision would require such self-scrutiny and contextual analysis. The decision could then proceed to careful consideration of the principles encompassed by the broad ethical frameworks and to the pertinent codes that they generate.

Ethical Principles

. . .

. . . Autonomy, or the human right of self-determination, is central to an informed consent and to all client-centered approaches. However, the principle has a self-limiting aspect: Autonomy is bounded by the point at which it interferes with others' equal rights to self-determination. Clearly, in this case, the client's right to behave sexually as he wishes abuts on his partner's right to know about HIV risk. If the client was not willing or able to identify this boundary himself, the clinician concerned with fully defined autonomy would need to do it for him. Such a decision would exhibit another principle, paternalism, which involves acting on another's behalf when that person is judged incapable of conducting his/her own affairs responsibly. The interrelated principles of nonmaleficence and beneficence—doing no harm and actively seeking to do good, respectively—are clearly basic to the disclosure decision. Again, self-contradiction would be inevitable given that good and harm are inseparable here.

Bersoff and Koeppl (1993) concluded by attacking the "teleological and utilitarian" character of the Ethics Code, implying that the code does not do justice to the grand principles that underlie it. This seems to be a misplaced idealism. The code is intended to apply to the real world, while the principles are explicitly identified as nonenforceable ideals. In actual clinical problems, idealism's purity is constantly stained by complexities and contradictions that make a more pragmatic view not only preferable but necessary. A caveat-ridden code may be more directly helpful precisely because it takes into account more variables—that is, is more utilitarian—than lofty principles.

Ethics Code

Many critics have attacked the ambiguity of the APA Ethics Code. There is no question that the Code is full of qualification and caveats and general wording that leaves much room for interpretation. Certainly, the parts of the code that bear on the ethical dilemma at hand do not point to a clear "correct" answer. Standard 1.14[1] in the General Standards, Avoiding Harm, states that psychologists seek to "minimize harm where it is foreseeable and unavoidable." The guideline refers to the therapeutic relationship, but the wording so strongly suggests a beneficent duty of the clinician toward all people that it is difficult

---

[1]*Ed. Note:* See Standard 3.04 of the current (2002) APA Ethics Code.

to base a nondisclosure decision on this part of the code; indeed, it seems hard not to use it as support for disclosure if weighing of risk to the client and his partner has already inclined one toward a breach.

Standard 5.02, Maintaining Confidentiality, identifies respect for confidentiality as a clinician's "primary obligation." However, Standards 5.03 and 5.05 (Minimizing Intrusions on Privacy Disclosures) balance the scale by permitting the sharing of confidential information "only with persons clearly concerned with such matters" (5.02) and by stating that

> psychologists disclose confidential information without the consent of the individual only as mandated by law, or where permitted by law for a valid purpose, such as . . . (3) to protect the patient or the client or others from harm . . . (5.05)[2]

. . . . The most relevant parts of the APA Ethics Code, despite their attempted comprehensiveness, still do not yield a clear solution to the dilemma.

As a supplement to the Ethics Code for guiding decisions in this kind of scenario, the APA's Public Interest Directorate published its *Resolutions Related to HIV/AIDS* (1998). The Resolutions state the following:

1. A legal duty to protect third parties from HIV infection should not be imposed.
2. If, however, specific legislation is considered, then it should permit disclosure only when (a) the provider knows of an identifiable third party, who the provider has compelling reason to believe is at significant risk for infection; (b) the provider has a reasonable belief that the third party has no reason to suspect that he or she is at risk; and (c) the client/patient has been urged to inform the third party and has either refused or is considered unreliable in his/her willingness to notify the third party.

These Resolutions put the Ethics Code's Standards into specific, relevant form for clinicians faced with an HIV disclosure dilemma, but the basic latitude of choice remains. Again, the stance permits, but does not require, disclosure.

In the end, in the absence of clear, codified directive, utilitarian analysis seems to point toward warning the partner in this case. A clinician guided by the utilitarian framework's logic should certainly inform the client of the decision before contacting the partner. Although the disclosure solution is far from ideal, trusting the client to disclose the information himself would seem unethical, given his pattern of negligence up to this point. Ultimately, after all the invocations of frameworks and principles, consultation of codes and laws, and scrutiny of costs and benefits, an ethical clinician would need to base this extremely difficult decision on relative consideration of human rights. What it comes down to is this: The right of the client's partner to keep his *life* supersedes the right of the client to keep his trust. The latter can be regained (albeit with difficulty); the former cannot.

References

American Psychological Association. (1991). *Legal liability related to confidentiality and the prevention of HIV transmission.* Retrieved from http://www.apa.org/pi/hivres.html

American Psychological Association. (1992). Ethical principles of psychologists and code of conduct. *American Psychologist, 47,* 1597–1611.

American Psychological Association. (1998). *Resolutions related to HIV/AIDS.* Retrieved from http://www.apa.org/pi/hivres.html

Bersoff, D. (1992). Explicit ambiguity: The 1992 ethics code as an oxymoron. *Professional Psychology: Research and Practice, 25,* 382–387.

Bersoff, D., & Koeppl, P. (1993). The relation between ethical codes and moral principles. *Ethics & Behavior, 3,* 345–357.

Fine, M., & Ulrich, L. (1988). Integrating psychology and philosophy in teaching a graduate course in ethics. *Professional Psychology: Research and Practice, 19,* 542–546.

Siegel, M. (1979). Privacy, ethics, and confidentiality. *Professional Psychology: Research and Practice, 10,* 249–258.

Tarasoff v. Regents of University of California, 131 Cal. Rptr. 14, 551 P.2d 334 (1976).

Thapar v. Zezulka, 994 S.W.2d 635 (Tex. 1999).

---

[2]*Ed. Note:* See Standards 4.01, 4.04, and 4.05 of the current (2002) APA Ethics Code.

◆ ◆ ◆

Commentary: Researchers have found a significantly positive relationship between the level of psychologists' homophobia and the likelihood of breaching the confidentiality of individuals diagnosed with AIDS. They warn that personal bias, rather than clinical factors, may affect professional ethical decision making. See McGuire, J., Nieri, D., Abbott, D., Sheridan, K., & Fisher, R. (1995). Do Tarasoff *principles apply in AIDS-related psychotherapy: Ethical decision making and the role of therapist homophobia and perceived client dangerousness.* Professional Psychology: Research and Practice, 26, *608–611.*

For other helpful articles that discuss the duty to protect third parties from clients who present issues concerning sexually transmitted diseases, see

Gray, L. A., & Harding, A. K. (1988). *Confidentiality limits with clients who have the AIDS virus.* Journal of Counseling and Development, 66, *219–223.*

Harding, A. K., Gray, L. A., & Neal, M. (1993). *Confidentiality limits with clients who have HIV: A review of ethical and legal guidelines and professional policies.* Journal of Counseling and Development, 71, *297–305.*

Kain, C. (1988). *To breach or not to breach: Is that the question? A response to Gray and Harding.* Journal of Counseling and Development, 66, *224–225.*

Knapp, S., & VandeCreek, L. (1990). *Application of the duty to protect HIV-positive patients.* Professional Psychology: Research and Practice, 21, *161–166.*

Lamb, D., Clark, C., Drumheller, P., Frizell, K., & Surrey, L. (1989). *Applying* Tarasoff *to AIDS-related psychotherapy issues.* Professional Psychology: Research and Practice, 20, *37–43.*

Melchert, T., & Patterson, M. (1999). *Duty to warn and interventions with HIV-positive clients.* Professional Psychology: Research and Practice, 30, *180–186.*

Stanard, R., & Hazler, R. (1995). *Legal and ethical implications of HIV and duty to warn for counselors: Does* Tarasoff *apply?* Journal of Counseling and Development, 73, *397–400.*

Totten, G., Lamb, D., & Reeder, G. (1990). Tarasoff *and confidentiality in AIDS-related psychotherapy.* Professional Psychology: Research and Practice, 21, *155–160.*

Stimulated by the disclosure that Anne Sexton's daughter authorized the release of hundreds of audiotapes of the poet's psychotherapy sessions with her psychiatrist so they could be used in a biography, Burke raised interesting but rarely asked questions about the ethicality of releasing confidential information after a patient's death, including whether the possibility of such disclosure should be part of the informed consent process at the start of therapy. See Burke, C. A. (1995). Until death do us part: An exploration into confidentiality following the death of a client. Professional Psychology: Research and Practice, 26, *278–280.*

Burke noted that the 1992 Code omitted standards pertaining to the disposition of the client's records after the death of the client. Review the following provisions in the 2002 Code to see if the problem has been rectified.

Standard 4.03—Recording (psychologists required to obtain consent of clients before recording voices and images)

Standard 5.04—Media Presentations (psychologists provide public advice consistent with the code of ethics)

Standard 6.02(c)—Disposal of Confidential Records (psychologists make plans in advance to facilitate appropriate transfer of records and to protect records in event of psychologists' withdrawal from practice). Interestingly, the parallel provision in the 1992 Code (5.09) specifically referred to the psychologist's death, now deleted in 6.02(c).

In any event, none of these provisions appear to contemplate the disposition of records when the patient dies. For an extensive and excellent analysis of the issue, however, see Berg, J. (2001). Grave secrets: Legal and ethical analysis of postmortem confidentiality. Connecticut Law Review, 34, *81–122. For a helpful, empirically based study of the ethics of publishing case studies generally, see Gavey, N., & Braun, V. (1997).* Ethics and the publication of clinical case material. Professional Psychology: Research and Practice, 28, *399–404. The relevant Ethics Code provision is 4.07.*

Finally, for those who work or plan to work in college counseling centers, the following reference raises some pertinent issues, most particularly, to whom is the clinician primarily responsible (student, student's parent, institution), provides some surprising data about students' desire for confidentiality, and offers some helpful hints in responding to requests for information from parents:

Sharkin, B. (1995). *Strains on confidentiality in college-student psychotherapy: Entangled therapeutic relationships, incidental encounters, and third-party inquiries.* Professional Psychology: Research and Practice, 26, *184–189.*

CHAPTER 5

MULTIPLE RELATIONSHIPS

When Borys and Pope (1989) surveyed 2,352 psychologists, social workers, and psychiatrists, only about 16 of them considered "engaging in sexual activity with a current client" to be ethical. One of the few absolute prohibitions in the 2002 APA Code, as well as in its predecessor, is that barring sexual intimacies with current clients (see Principle 6a, APA, 1990; Standard 4.05, APA, 1992; Standard 10.05, APA, 2002). Yet, the APA Ethics Committee (2006) reported that, "sexual misconduct played a role in 50% of the complaints opened in 2005" (p. 526), by far the most frequent category.

Accusations that professionals in positions of power have engaged in inappropriate sexual intimacies have evoked publicity and absorbed the public's attention, particularly during the past decade. This notoriety has not been limited to mental health practitioners but has touched senators, governors, presidents, and Supreme Court justices.

Although sexual impropriety between clients and clinicians is the most written about and troubling form of multiple relationship, it is a relatively low probability event. Many other potential forms of multiple relationships are more likely to confront not only the therapist but the researcher, tester, supervisor, and professor as well. For example, what if a carpenter cannot afford to pay for a psychological assessment of his or her child and offers to build some bookshelves in lieu of the psychologist's fee? What if a research subject asks the experimenter for a date? Can faculty members invite their graduate students to their houses for social gatherings? What should the chair of an admissions committee do if a close friend applies to the chair's doctoral program and it is the only one in the area that the friend can afford to attend? What if patients want to give their therapists inexpensive gifts? Can a psychologist supervising a graduate student in a practicum also become the supervisee's therapist? These are potentially knotty problems that are not always easily resolved by explicit prohibitory language in the Ethics Code.[1]

In this chapter, then, one of the goals is to delineate the wide variety of multiple relationships that can confront psychologists, regardless of the settings in which they work or the roles they perform. With these readings, I also seek to educate readers about the consequences of engaging in multiple relationships and to provide some guidance in avoiding the harm that such relationships can cause.

But this chapter has more implicit and far-ranging aims. For example, one of the topics the reader considers is the barring of sexual intimacies with former clients. Under Standard 10.08

[1] As an example of really low probability events, consider a case brought before the Arizona Board of Psychologist Examiners. It involved a psychologist, also ordained as a minister, who performed an exorcism on a 10-year-old boy and then billed child protective services for his treatment.

of the 2002 Ethics Code, sexual relationships are absolutely forbidden for 2 years after therapy is terminated and, then, after that, only if the therapist can demonstrate that the relationship is not exploitative. The 1992 Ethical Principles was the first of all the ethics codes that APA has promulgated to contain such a provision, and its inclusion was seen as a major advance. It was retained, as is, in the 2002 Code. Ironically, however, the rule as adopted pleases practically no one (perhaps not even the reluctant majority of the APA Council of Representatives who voted for it as a compromise).

Although the provision barring posttermination sexual relationships for 2 years promotes such moral principles as nonmaleficence, the fact that such relationships are not banned in perpetuity angers those who believe that any possibility of a future nonprofessional relationship will harm therapy and the patient. On the other hand, one could argue that any ban constitutes a form of "ethical imperialism" (Gergen, 1973, p. 910). Because the typical sexual dual relationship involves a male therapist and a female patient, does the ban, in fact, produce a perverse kind of antifeminism, forbidding women to exercise their autonomous right to choose to enter into such a relationship—placing them, therefore, in the role of powerless, passive victims?

Even more broadly, one can ask to what extent a code of ethics should interfere in private relationships, particularly nonsexual ones. Although one can acknowledge that the profession universally condemns sexual relationships with current and former patients and many nonsexual ones—for all the reasons that the following material advances and the vast majority of psychologists adopt—that does not mean that the issue cannot be debated rationally and in good faith. This chapter, because of its intellectually controversial and emotion-arousing content, lends itself well to a debate, for the larger purposes that such a debate can serve.

References

American Psychological Association. (1990). Ethical principles of psychologists (amended June 2, 1989). *American Psychologist, 45,* 390–395.

American Psychological Association. (1992). Ethical principles of psychologists and code of conduct. *American Psychologist, 47,* 1597–1611.

American Psychological Association. (2002). Ethical principles of psychologists and code of conduct. *American Psychologist, 57,* 1060–1073.

APA Ethics Committee. (2006). Report of the ethics committee, 2005. *American Psychologist, 61,* 522–529.

Borys, D. S., & Pope, K. S. (1989). Dual relationships between therapist and client: A national study of psychologists, psychiatrists, and social workers. *Professional Psychology: Research and Practice, 20,* 283–293.

Gergen, K. J. (1973). The codification of research ethics: Views of a doubting Thomas. *American Psychologist, 28,* 907–912.

A Preliminary Look at How Psychologists Identify, Evaluate, and Proceed When Faced With Possible Multiple Relationship Dilemmas

Douglas H. Lamb, Salvatore J. Catanzaro, and Annorah S. Moorman

Psychologists who are in professional roles or relationships with clients, supervisees, or students may intentionally, unintentionally, or unforeseeably find themselves in a second role or relationship with that same individual. Cautions, risks, and other considerations related to these multiple relationships (MRs) have been discussed by a variety of authors (e.g., Bersoff, 1999; Gutheil & Gabbard, 1993; Lamb, 1999; Lamb, Catanzaro, & Moorman, 2003; Lerman & Rigby, 1990; Milgrom, 1992; Pope & Vasquez, 1991; Rubin, 2000; Smith & Fitzpatrick, 1995). Others have challenged the assumption of universal harm or exploitation from nonsexual MRs and boundary crossings (Brown, 1994; Ebert, 1997; Lazarus & Zur, 2002b; Williams, 1997) and have spoken to the potential benefits of such crossings. For example, Lazarus and Zur (2002b) presented arguments against dual relationships and their rebuttals, and Lazarus (2002) argued that certain nonsexual boundaries actually diminish therapeutic effectiveness.

Although MRs with clients, supervisees, and students are discussed from a variety of perspectives, they all appear to have five defining characteristics. First, MRs typically take one or more of the following three forms: (a) sexual relationships (e.g., with clients: Bartell & Rubin, 1990; Gabbard, 1989; Garrett, 1999; Lamb et al., 2003; Pope, 1994; Williams, 1992; with supervisees: Bartell & Rubin, 1990; Lamb & Catanzaro, 1998; Lamb et al., 2003; O'Connor-Slimp & Burian, 1994; with students: Blevins-Knabe, 1999; Lamb & Catanzaro, 1998; Lamb et al., 2003; Stamler & Stone, 1998); (b) nonsexual social or professional relationships, such as having dinner with a former client or employing a current supervisee (Anderson & Kitchener, 1996, 1998; Pipes, 1999); and/or (c) financial-business relationships, particularly as they may occur in a rural practice and small communities (Campbell & Gordon, 2003; Faulkner & Faulkner, 1997; Lamb et al., 1994).

Second, there is some evidence that certain activities within the professional relationship itself (e.g., nonsexual touching, self-disclosure by the psychologist) are associated with and may, depending on the circumstances and context of such activities, increase the likelihood of the development of an explicitly sexual MR (see Brodsky, 1989; Folman, 1991; Gabbard, 1989; Lamb & Catanzaro, 1998). Third, MRs, by definition, may occur concurrently, consecutively, or in an overlapping manner with the established professional relationship. For example, a professional relationship may intentionally be discontinued in order to engage in some form of MR, such as terminating psychotherapy in order to develop a sexual relationship with a client (e.g., American Psychological Association [APA], 1988; Gottlieb, 1993; Lamb & Catanzaro, 1998; Lamb et al., 2003). Fourth, MRs are not restricted to the specific individual in the professional relationship (e.g., client, supervisee, student) but may apply to "a person closely associated with or related to the person with whom the psychologist has the professional relationship" (APA, 2002, p. 1065). An example would be a situation in which a therapist learns, in the context of therapy, that she (the therapist) is dating the former spouse of her client.

Finally, engaging in MRs of the nature identified above may or may not be considered unethical, depending on (a) the nature of the MR (e.g., sexual relationships with current clients are prohibited, whereas other MRs are not), (b) the degree to which the MR may impair the psychologist's effectiveness, or (c) whether there is a risk of exploitation or harm to the person with whom the professional relationship exists (e.g., Brown, 1994; Gabbard, 1989; Lerman & Rigby, 1990). In fact, the APA (2002) ethics code states that "multiple relationships that would not reasonably be expected to cause impairment or risk exploitation or harm are not unethical" (p. 1065).

Although it may be relatively easy to define MRs conceptually, clinical practice suggests that it may be more difficult to recognize potential MR dilemmas as they develop. Further, there is little consensus about the ethicality of engaging in various nonsexual MRs (Anderson & Kitchener, 1998; Lazarus & Zur, 2002a; Lerman & Rigby, 1990).

References

American Psychological Association. (1988). Ethics Committee Report. *American Psychologist, 43,* 897–904.

American Psychological Association. (2002). Ethical principles of psychologists and code of conduct. *American Psychologist, 57,* 1060–1073.

Anderson, S., & Kitchener, K. (1996). Nonromantic, nonsexual posttherapy relationships between psychologists and former clients: An exploratory study of critical incidents. *Professional Psychology: Research and Practice, 27,* 59–66.

Anderson, S., & Kitchener, K. (1998). Nonsexual posttherapy relationships: A conceptual framework to assess ethical risks. *Professional Psychology Research and Practice, 29,* 91–99.

Bartell, P., & Rubin, L. (1990). Dangerous liaisons: Sexual intimacies in supervision. *Professional Psychology: Research and Practice, 21,* 442–450.

Bersoff, D. (1999). *Ethical conflicts in psychology* (2nd ed.). Washington, DC: American Psychological Association.

Blevins-Knabe, B. (1999). The ethics of dual relationships in higher education. In D. Bersoff (Ed.), *Ethical conflicts in psychology* (2nd ed., pp. 263–265). Washington, DC: American Psychological Association.

Brodsky, A. S. (1989). Sex between patients and therapists: Psychology's data and response. In G. Gabbard (Ed.), *Sexual exploitation in professional relationships* (pp. 15–25). Washington, DC: American Psychiatric Press.

Brown, L. (1994). Boundaries in feminist therapy. *Women and Therapy, 15,* 29–38.

Campbell, C., & Gordon, M. (2003). Acknowledging the inevitable: Understanding multiple relationships in rural practice. *Professional Psychology: Research and Practice, 34,* 430–434.

Ebert, B. (1997). Dual-relationship prohibitions: A concept whose time never should have come. *Applied and Preventive Psychology, 6,* 137–156.

Faulkner, K., & Faulkner, T. (1997). Managing multiple relationships in rural communities: Neutrality and boundary violations. *Clinical Psychology: Science and Practice, 4,* 225–234.

Folman, R. (1991). Therapist–patient sex: Attraction and boundary problems. *Psychotherapy, 28,* 168–173.

Gabbard, G. (Ed.). (1989). *Sexual exploitation in professional relationships.* Washington, DC: American Psychiatric Press.

Garrett, T. (1999). Sexual contact between clinical psychologists and their patients: Qualitative data. *Clinical Psychology and Psychotherapy, 6,* 54–62.

Gottlieb, M. (1993). Avoiding exploitative dual relationships: A decision-making model. *Psychotherapy, 30,* 41–48.

Gutheil, T., & Gabbard, G. (1993). The concept of boundaries in clinical practice: Theoretical and risk-management dimensions. *American Journal of Psychiatry, 150,* 188–196.

Lamb, D. (1999). Addressing impairment and its relationship to professional boundary issues. *The Counseling Psychologist, 27,* 702–711.

Lamb, D., & Catanzaro, S. (1998). Sexual and nonsexual boundary violations involving psychologists, clients, supervisees, and students: Implications for professional practice. *Professional Psychology: Research and Practice, 29,* 498–503.

Lamb, D., Catanzaro, S., & Moorman, A. (2003). Psychologists reflect on their sexual relationships with clients, supervisees, and students: Occurrence, impact, rationales, and collegial intervention. *Professional Psychology: Research and Practice, 34,* 102–107.

Lamb, D., Strand, K., Woodburn, J., Buchko, K., Lewis, J., & Kang, J. (1994). Sexual and business relationships between therapists and former clients. *Psychotherapy, 31,* 270–278.

Lazarus, A. (2002). How certain boundaries and ethics diminish therapeutic effectiveness. In A. Lazarus & O. Zur (Eds.), *Dual relationships and psychotherapy* (pp. 25–31). New York: Springer.

Lazarus, A., & Zur, O. (Eds.). (2002a). *Dual relationships and psychotherapy.* New York: Springer.

Lazarus, A., & Zur, O. (2002b). Six arguments against dual relationships and their rebuttals. In A. Lazarus

& O. Zur (Eds.), *Dual relationships and psychotherapy* (pp. 3–24). New York: Springer.

Lerman, H., & Rigby, D. (1990). Boundary violations: Misuse of the power of the therapist. In H. Herman & N. Porter (Eds.), *Feminist ethics in psychotherapy* (pp. 51–59). New York: Springer.

Milgrom, J. (1992). *Boundaries in professional relationships.* Minneapolis, MN: Walk-in-Counseling Center.

O'Connor-Slimp, P., & Burian, B. (1994). Multiple role relationships during internship: Consequences and recommendations. *Professional Psychology: Research and Practice, 25,* 39–45.

Pipes, R. (1999). Nonsexual relationships between psychotherapists and their former clients: Obligations of psychologists. In D. Bersoff (Ed.), *Ethical conflicts in psychology* (2nd ed., pp. 254–257). Washington, DC: American Psychological Association.

Pope, K. (1994). *Sexual involvement with therapists.* Washington, DC: American Psychological Association.

Pope, K., & Vasquez, M. (1991). *Ethics in psychotherapy and counseling: A practical guide for psychologists.* San Francisco: Jossey-Bass.

Rubin, S. (2000). Differentiating multiple relationships from multiple dimension of involvement: Therapeutic space at the interface of client, therapist, and society. *Psychotherapy, 37,* 315–324.

Smith, D., & Fitzpatrick, M. (1995). Patient–therapist boundary issues: An integrative review of theory and research. *Professional Psychology: Research and Practice, 26,* 499–506.

Stamler, V., & Stone, G. (1998). *Faculty–student sexual involvement: Issues and interventions.* Thousand Oaks, CA: Sage.

Williams, M. (1992). Exploitation and inference: Mapping the damaging effects from therapist–patient sexual involvement. *American Psychologist, 47,* 412–421.

Williams, M. (1997). Boundary violations: Do some contended standards of care fail to encompass commonplace procedures of humanistic, behavioral, and eclectic psychotherapies? *Psychotherapy, 34,* 238–249.

◆   ◆   ◆

Commentary: *Sonne (1994) stated that*

> [T]he most comprehensive definition of multiple relationships includes those situations in which the psychologist functions in more than one professional relationship, as well as those in which the psychologist functions in a professional role and another definitive and intended role [as opposed to

a limited and inconsequential role] and which may occur concurrently or consecutively. (p. 336)

Sonne, J. (1994). Multiple relationships: Does the new code answer the right questions? Professional Psychology: Research and Practice, 25, 336–343.

Pope (1991) has provided a similar definition: "A dual relationship . . . occurs when the therapist is in another significantly different relationship with one of his or her patients. Most commonly, the second role is social, financial, or professional" (p. 22). Pope, K. (1991). Dual relationships in psychotherapy. Ethics & Behavior, 1, 22–34. As the definition implies, the second role need not be sexual. Consider the following situations:

1. *The therapist hires his patient to be his records clerk;*
2. *The patient asks his therapist and her spouse to spend a week at the patient's vacation house;*
3. *The therapist, who raises rottweilers as a hobby, sells one of his animals to his patient, a fellow dog lover;*
4. *The therapist is treating a lawyer who is feeling severe stress in her practice. The therapist in the meantime wants to file for a divorce from her husband. They agree to swap professional services; and*
5. *A carpenter, experiencing acrophobia, seeks treatment but cannot afford more than one session of psychotherapy and has no insurance. The therapist suggests the carpenter build him bookshelves for the den of his home in return for several sessions of cognitive-behavioral intervention.*

Identify the multiple roles at issue here and the ethical problems they may try to evoke. For other similar examples, see Koocher, G., & Keith-Spiegel, P. (1998). Ethics in Psychology (2nd ed., pp. 177–195). New York: Oxford University Press.

The Sonne (1994) and Pope (1991) definitions of multiple relationships found in the prior two excerpts are helpful in understanding the concept. For the first time, the 2002 Ethics Code provides the APA's formal definition:

> *A multiple relationship occurs when a psychologist is in a professional role with a person and (1) at the same time is in another role with the same person, (2) at the same time is in a relationship with a person closely associated with or related to*

the person with whom they have the professional relationship, or (3) promises to enter into another relationship in the future with the person or a person closely associated with or related to the person. (Standard 3.05, p. 1065)

American Psychological Association. (2002). Ethical principles of psychologists and code of conduct. American Psychologist, 57, 1060–1073. Not all multiple relationships are unethical under Standard 3.05. Only a multiple relationship that "could reasonably be expected to impair the psychologist's objectivity, competence, or effectiveness . . . or otherwise risks exploitation and harm" (p. 1065) is unethical.

With that definition, decide whether the items below typify improper dual relationships. Rate each one on the following scale: 1 = never ethical; 2 = ethical under rare conditions; 3 = ethical under some conditions; 4 = ethical under most conditions; 5 = always ethical.

- Accepting a gift worth under $10
- Accepting a client's invitation to a special occasion
- Accepting a service or a product as payment for therapy
- Becoming friends with a client after termination
- Selling a product to a client
- Accepting a gift worth over $50
- Providing therapy to an employee
- Engaging in sexual activity with a client after termination
- Disclosing details of current personal stresses to a client
- Inviting clients to an office/clinic open house
- Employing a client
- Going out to eat with a client after a session
- Buying goods or services from a client
- Engaging in sexual activity with a current client
- Inviting clients to a personal party or social event
- Providing individual therapy to a relative, friend, or lover of an ongoing client
- Providing therapy to a current student or supervisee
- Allowing a client to enroll in one's class for a grade

Readers can compare their results with those of a survey of 1,108 mental health professionals. See Borys, D. S., & Pope, K. S. (1989). Dual relationships between therapist and client: A national study of psychologists, psychiatrists, and social workers. Professional Psychology: Research and Practice, 20, 283–293. Only five behaviors were rated as never ethical by a majority of the respondents. Which are they?

In order of greatest perceived unethicality, the five behaviors are: sex with a current client; selling a product to a client; sex with a client posttermination; inviting clients to a social event; and providing therapy to an employee. No behavior was universally considered unethical. What issues do these data raise?

How does one decide or know when a particular multiple relationship is unethical. Sonne (1994), in the article quoted above, provided this perspective:

> A multiple relationship may be considered unethical when, given a primary professional relationship, another relationship with an individual risks impairment of the psychologist's fulfillment of expectations or responsibilities in the professional relationship, risks exploitation of the individual's diminished power, or risks damage to the client's emotional involvement in the professional relationship. . . . [M]ultiple relationships that impose on and impair the dynamics of the professional relationship between psychologists and those with whom they work are simply unethical. (p. 339)

Sonne thus argued that exploitation and risk are at the heart of unethical multiple relationships. The APA Code, as well, makes only those multiple relationships that are exploitative or harmful unethical. But one commentator, defining exploitation as the intent to use someone as a means to an end, takes a contrary view:

> [E]xploitation is a poor term to apply to an ethics standard; it is vague and only indirectly associated with harm to clients. Detriment to clients should be the focus. If there is detriment to a client by a therapist's actions, intent becomes a secondary issue. . . . [T]herapists can do unintentional but avoidable harm to clients through relationships other than the initial treatment relationship. Exploitation, therefore, should not be the focal concept in such

matters, A therapist should not be excused in circumstances where harm done to clients is outside the realm of exploitation. And therapists should not be culpable in cases of harmless exploitation. (p. 6)

Cottone, R. R. (2005). Detrimental therapist–client relationships—Beyond thinking of "dual" or "multiple" roles: Reflections on the 2001 AAMFT Code of Ethics. American Journal of Family Therapy, 33, 1–17. See also Lamb, D. H., Catanzaro, S. J., & Moorman, A. S.

(2004). A preliminary look at how psychologists identify, evaluate, and proceed when faced with possible multiple relationship dilemmas. Professional Psychology: Research and Practice, 35, 248–254: *"What remains ambiguous [about the 2002 Ethics Code] is how psychologists go about determining whether a particular action causes impairment, risks exploitation, or is likely to cause harm" (p. 253). Other authors stress boundary violations as the definitive aspect of multiple relationships, as the following excerpt illustrates.*

The Concept of Boundaries in Clinical Practice: Theoretical and Risk-Management Dimensions

Thomas G. Gutheil and Glen O. Gabbard

. . .

ROLE

Role boundaries constitute the essential boundary issue. To conceptualize this entity, one might ask, "Is this what a therapist does?" Although subject to ideological variations, this touchstone question not only identifies the question of clinical role but serves as a useful orienting device for avoiding the pitfalls of the role violations.

> A middle-aged borderline patient, attempting to convey how deeply distressed she felt about her situation, leaped from her chair in the therapist's office and threw herself to her knees at the therapist's feet, clasping his hand in both of her own and crying, "Do you understand how awful it's been for me?" The therapist said gently, "You know, this is really interesting, what's happening here—but it isn't therapy; please go back to your chair." The patient did so, and the incident was explored verbally.

Although such limit setting may appear brusque to some clinicians, it may be the only appropriate response to halt boundary-violating "acting in" (especially of the impulsive or precipitous kind) and to make the behavior available for analysis as part of the therapy.

. . .

TIME

Time is, of course, a boundary, defining the limits of the session itself while providing structure and even containment for many patients, who derive reassurance because they will have to experience the various stresses of reminiscing, reliving, and so forth for a set time only. The beginnings and endings of sessions—starting or stopping late or early—are both susceptible to crossings of this boundary. Such crossings may be subtle or stark.

> A male psychiatrist came in to the hospital to see his female inpatient for marathon sessions at odd times, such as from 2:00 to 6:00 in the morning, rationalizing that this procedure was dictated by scheduling problems. This relationship eventually became overtly sexual.

. . .

. . . [F]rom a risk-management standpoint, a patient in the midst of an intense erotic transference to the therapist might best be seen, when possible, during high-traffic times when other people (e.g., secretaries, receptionists, and even other patients) are around. . . .

PLACE AND SPACE

The therapist's office or a room on a hospital unit is obviously the locale for almost all therapy; some exceptions are noted in the next section . . .

Some boundary crossings of place can have a constructive effect. . . .

> After initially agreeing to attend his analysand's wedding, the analyst later declined, reasoning that his presence would be inappropriately distracting. Later, after the death of the analysand's first child, he attended the funeral

From *American Journal of Psychiatry, 150*, 188–196. Copyright 1993 by the American Psychiatric Association. Adapted with permission of the publisher.

service. Both his absence at the first occasion and his presence at the second were felt as helpful and supportive by the analysand. They both agreed later that the initial plan to attend the wedding was an error.

A relevant lesson from this example is that boundary violations can be reversed or undone with further consideration and discussion. At times, an apology by the therapist is appropriate and even necessary. . . .

Sorties out of the office usually merit special scrutiny. While home visits were a central component of the community psychiatry movement, the shift in the professional climate is such that the modern clinician is best advised to perform this valuable service with an opposite-sex chaperone and to document the event in some detail.

Sessions during lunch are an extremely common form of boundary violation. This event appears to be a common way station along the path of increasing boundary crossings culminating in sexual misconduct. Although clinicians often advance the claim that therapy is going on, so, inevitably, is much purely social behavior; it does not *look* like therapy, at least to a jury. Lunch sessions are not uncommonly followed by sessions during dinner, then just dinners, then other dating behavior, eventually including intercourse.

Sessions in cars represent another violation of place. Typically, the clinician gives the patient a ride home under various circumstances. Clinician and patient then park (e.g., in front of the patient's house) and finish up the presumably therapeutic conversation. From a fact finder's viewpoint, many exciting things happen in cars, but therapy is usually not one of them.

The complexity of the matter increases, however, when we consider other therapeutic ideologies. For example, it would not be a boundary violation for a behaviorist, under certain circumstances, to accompany a patient in a car, to an elevator, to an airplane, or even to a public restroom (in the treatment of paruresis, the fear of urinating in a public restroom) as part of the treatment plan for a particular phobia. The existence of a body of professional literature, a clinical rationale, and risk–benefit documentation will be useful in protecting the clinician in such a situation from misconstruction of the therapeutic efforts.

MONEY

Money is a boundary in the sense of defining the business nature of the therapeutic relationship. This is not love, it's work. Indeed, some would argue that the fee received by the therapist is the only appropriate and allowable material gratification to be derived from clinical work (28). Patient and clinician may each have conflicts about this distinction (29), but consultative experience makes clear that trouble begins precisely when the therapist stops thinking of therapy as work.

On the other hand, most clinicians learned their trade by working with indigent patients and feel that some attempt should be made to pay back the debt by seeing some patients for free—a form of "tithing," if you will. Note that this *decision*—to see a patient for free and to discuss that with the patient—is quite different from simply letting the billing lapse or allowing the debt to mount. The latter examples are boundary crossings, perhaps violations. . . .

In rural areas even today, payments to physicians may take the form of barter. . . . For the dynamic therapist this practice poses some problems, because it blurs the boundary between payment and gift. . . . The clinician should take a case at a reasonable fee or make a *decision* to see the patient for a low fee (e.g., one dollar) or none. Barter is confusing and probably ill-advised today. Of course, all such decisions require documentation.

GIFTS, SERVICES, AND RELATED MATTERS

A client became very upset during an interview with her therapist and began to cry. The therapist, proffering a tissue, held out a hand-tooled Florentine leather case in which a pocket pack of tissues had been placed. After the patient had withdrawn a tissue, the therapist impulsively said, "Why don't you keep the case?" In subsequent supervision the therapist came to understand that this "gift" to the patient was an unconscious bribe designed to avert the anger that the therapist sensed just below the surface of the patient's sorrow.

This gift was also a boundary violation, placing un-identified obligations on the patient and constituting a form of impulsive acting in. A related boundary violation is the use of favors or services from the patient for the benefit of the therapist, as Simon's (6) startling vignette illustrates:

> Within a few months of starting . . . psy-chotherapy, the patient was returning the therapist's library books for him "as a favor." . . . The patient began having trouble paying her treatment bill, so she agreed—at the therapist's suggestion—to clean the therapist's office once a week in partial payment. . . . The patient also agreed to get the therapist's lunch at a nearby delicatessen before each ses-sion. (p. 106)

The obvious exploitive nature of these boundary violations destroys even the semblance of therapy for the patient's benefit. . . .

> A patient in long-term therapy had struggled for years with apparent infer-tility and eventually, with great diffi-culty, arranged for adoption of a child. Two years later she unexpectedly conceived and finally gave birth. Her therapist, appreciating the power and meaning of this event, sent congratula-tory flowers to the hospital.

In this case, the therapist followed social convention in a way that—though technically a boundary crossing—represented a response appropriate to the real relationship. Offering a tissue to a crying patient and expressing condolences to a bereaved one are similar examples of appropriate responses outside the classic boundaries of the therapeutic relationship.

CLOTHING

Clothing represents a social boundary the transgres-sion of which is usually inappropriate to the thera-peutic situation. . . . Excessively revealing or frankly seductive clothing worn by the therapist may repre-sent a boundary violation with potentially harmful effects to patients. . . .

Berne (32) noted the technical error of the male clinician who, confronting a patient whose skirt was pulled up high, began to explain to the patient his sexual fantasies in response to this event. Berne sug-gested instead saying to the patient, "Pull your skirt down." Similar directness of limit setting appears to be suited to the patient who—either from psychosis or the wish to provoke—begins to take off her clothes in the office. As before, the comment, "This behavior is inappropriate, and it isn't therapy; please put your clothes back on," said in a calm voice, is a reasonable response.

LANGUAGE

As part of the otherwise laudable efforts to human-ize and demystify psychiatry a few decades back, the use of a patient's first name was very much in vogue. While this may indeed convey greater warmth and closeness, such usage is a two-edged sword. There is always the possibility that patients may experience the use of first names as misrepresenting the profes-sional relationship as a social friendship (28). There may well be instances when using first names is appropriate, but therapists must carefully consider whether they are creating a false sense of intimacy that may subsequently backfire. . . .

. . . Last names also emphasize that this process is work or business, an atmosphere which may pro-mote a valuable mature perspective and minimize acting out. In addition, calling someone by the name used by primary objects may foster transference per-ceptions of the therapist when they are not desir-able, as with a borderline patient prone to forming severe psychotic transferences. For balance, how-ever, recall that use of last names may also sound excessively distant, formal, and aloof. . . .

SELF-DISCLOSURE AND RELATED MATTERS

Few clinicians would argue that the therapist's self-disclosure is always a boundary crossing. . . . [W]hen a therapist begins to indulge in even mild forms of self-disclosure, it is an indication for careful self-scrutiny regarding the motivations for departure from the usual therapeutic stance. . . .

Self-disclosure, however, represents a complex issue. Clearly, therapists may occasionally use a neutral example from their own lives to illustrate a point. Sharing the impact of a borderline patient's behavior on the therapist may also be useful. The therapist's self-revelation, however, of personal fantasies or dreams; of social, sexual, or financial details; of specific vacation plans; or of expected births or deaths in the family is usually burdening the patient with information, whereas it is the patient's fantasies that might best be explored. The issue is somewhat controversial: a number of patients (and, surprisingly, some therapists) believe that the patient is somehow entitled to this kind of information. In any case, it is a boundary violation and as such may be used by the legal system to advance or support a claim of sexual misconduct. The reasoning is that the patient knows so much about the therapist's personal life that they must have been intimate. . . .

Finally, the boundary can be violated from the other side. An example would be the therapist's using data from the therapy session for personal gain, such as insider information on stock trading, huge profits to be made in real estate, and the like.

PHYSICAL CONTACT

. . . [Professionals] working with a patient with AIDS or HIV seropositivity often describe wishing to touch the patient in some benign manner (pat the back, squeeze an arm, pat a hand) in every session. They reason that such patients feel like lepers, and therapeutic touch is called for in these cases. But even such humane interventions must be scrutinized and, indeed, be documented to prevent their misconstruction in today's climate.

From the viewpoint of current risk-management principles, a handshake is about the limit of social physical contact at this time. Of course, a patient who attempts a hug in the last session after 7 years of intense, intensive, and successful therapy should probably not be hurled across the room. However, most hugs from patients should be discouraged in tactful, gentle ways by words, body language, positioning, and so forth. Patients who deliberately or provocatively throw their arms around the therapist despite repeated efforts at discouragement should be stopped. An appropriate response is to step back, catch both wrists in your hands, cross the patient's wrists in front of you, so that the crossed arms form a barrier between bodies, and say firmly, "Therapy is a talking relationship; please sit down so we can discuss your not doing this any more." If the work degenerates into grabbing, consider seriously termination and referral, perhaps to a therapist of a different gender.

What is one to make of the brands of therapy that include physical contact, such as Rolfing? Presumably, the boundary extends to that limited physical contact, and the patient expects it and grants consent; thus, no actual violation occurs. Massage therapists may struggle with similar issues, however. In other ideologies the issue may again be the impact of the appearance of a violation:

> A therapist—who claimed that her school of practice involved hugging her female patient at the beginning and end of every session, without apparent harm—eventually had to terminate therapy with the patient for noncompliance with the therapeutic plan. The enraged patient filed a sexual misconduct claim against the therapist. Despite the evidence showing that this claim was probably false (a specious suit triggered by rage at the therapist), the insurer settled because of the likelihood that a jury would not accept the principle of "hug at the start and hug at the end but no hugs in between." If the claim was indeed false, this is a settlement based on boundary violations alone.

At another level this vignette nicely suggests how nonsexual boundary violations may be harmful to a patient in much the same way that actual sexual misconduct is. Instead of engaging the patient in a mourning process to deal with the resentment and grief about the deprivations of her childhood, the therapist who hugs a patient is often attempting to

225

provide the physical contact normally offered by a parent. The patient then feels entitled to more demonstrations of caring and assumes that if gratification in the form of hugs is available, other wishes will be granted as well. . . . When actual physical contact occurs, the crucial psychotherapeutic distinction between the symbolic and the concrete is lost [(21),] and the patient may feel that powerful infantile longings within will finally be satisfied. . . .

References

6. Simon, R. I. (1989). Sexual exploitation of patients: how it begins before it happens. *Psychiatry Annals, 19*, 104–122.

21. Casement, P. J. (1990). The meeting of needs in psychoanalysis. *Psychoanalytic Inquiry, 10*, 325–346.

28. Epstein, R. S., & Simon, R. I. (1990). The exploitation index: an early warning indicator of boundary violations in psychotherapy. *Bulletin of the Menninger Clinic, 54*, 450–465.

29. Krueger, D. W. (Ed.). (1986). *The Last Taboo: Money As Symbol and Reality in Psychotherapy and Psychoanalysis*. New York: Brunner/Mazel.

32. Berne, E. (1972). *What Do You Say After You Say Hello? The Psychology of Human Destiny*. New York: Grove Press.

◆ ◆ ◆

Commentary: Following up on the work of Gutheil and Gabbard (1993, excerpted here), Knapp and Slattery (2004) distinguished between boundary crossings and boundary violations. Boundary crossings, they said, occur "any time a professional deviates from the strictest professional role" (p. 554), for example, by accepting a token gift, and "can be helpful, harmful, or neutral. . . . Boundary crossings can be boundary violations when they place clients at risk for harm" (p. 554), for example, extensive self-disclosure. Knapp, S., & Slattery, J. M. (2004). Professional boundaries in nontraditional settings. Professional Psychology: Research and Practice, 35, 553–558. See also Shapiro, E. L., & Ginzberg, R. (2003). To accept or not to accept: Referrals and the maintenance of boundaries. Professional Psychology: Research and Practice, 34, 258–263 (discussing the dangers of accepting referrals from clients, present and former, and from colleagues).

Other authors believe "that the use of 'boundary' as the exclusive metaphor to guide our conceptualization of ethical connection between professional helper and client/patient is problematic" (p. 78). Austin, W., Bergum, V., Nuttgens, S., & Peternelj-Taylor, C. (2006). A re-visioning of boundaries in professional helping relationships: Exploring other metaphors. Ethics & Behavior, 16, 77–94. Anticipating a view I shall explore later in this chapter (e.g., the Lazurus excerpt), Austin et al. argued:

> *The idea of firm, intractable boundaries as a way to guarantee ethical action in professional helping relationships may be a comforting one. It is, however, a false comfort. Fixed general rules cannot capture the complex reality of therapeutic relationships. Normative principles can be invaluable as guides to ethical practice. They are, nevertheless, insufficient. Practitioners need to follow the ethical codes and standards of their discipline, but they must do more than this. They need to be unceasingly attentive to the way in which they act within the moral context of practice. They must be attentive to their colleagues' behavior as well and to the way in which the discipline is shaping the moral education of future members. (p. 91)*

Psychologists know little empirically about the characteristics of clinicians who have sex with their patients. A decade ago, however, two Israeli psychologists interviewed former patients who disclosed sexual experiences with their therapists. These were some pertinent findings:

> *The former patient's descriptions of the therapeutic techniques included the following: 13 traditional-psychodynamic, 5 expressive, 4 supportive, 3 cognitive-behavioral, and 2 consultative. . . . The average age of the offending therapists was 47.5 (SD = 9.3) and their age span was 30–70. The age range of the patients was 19–46, with a mean age of 32.5 (SD = 8.5). (p. 505)*

Somer, E., & Saadon, M. (1999). Therapist–client sex: Client's retrospective reports. Professional Psychology: Research and Practice, 30, 504–509.

More recently, in a self-report survey sent to 1,000 clinical and counseling psychologists, of whom 368 responded and of those 13 (3.5%) reported at least one sexual boundary violation as a professional, the authors found:

> *Those [13] individuals . . . had been providing psychological services longer than a comparable group of psychologists who did not engage in such behaviors (M = 19.27 years vs. 16.94 years), although that difference was not significantly different. In addition, although a majority of both groups of psychologists were married, those psychologists who engaged in the prohibited relationships were slightly less likely to be married (65% vs. 75%). The two groups did not differ significantly on any other demographic variables. (p. 104)*

Lamb, D. H., Catanzaro, S. J., & Moorman, A. S. (2003). *Psychologists reflect on their sexual relationships with clients, supervisees, and students: Occurrence, impact, rationales, and collegial intervention.* Professional Psychology: Research and Practice, 34, 102–107.

In the same study, Lamb et al. found that 36 (10%) of respondents reported at least one sexual encounter during their own therapy, supervision, or education. However, "only one man reported violations as both participant and professional." (p. 104). More intriguing, the results of a recent study "strongly suggest that a childhood history of severe sexual abuse [in the therapist] is a significant contributory factor in these egregious transgressions" (p. 203). Jackson, H., & Nuttall, R. (2001). A relationship between childhood abuse and professional sexual misconduct. Professional Psychology: Research and Practice, 32, 200–204.

In their survey of 323 social workers, psychiatrists, and psychologists, Jackson and Nuttall found that 8.6% of those surveyed reported sex with clients. Male psychologists led the way, with 15.8% (6 of 38) reporting such behavior. Nevertheless, "The true base rate of sexual misconduct among psychologists is not known" (p. 455). Gottlieb, M. (1990). Accusation of sexual misconduct: Assisting in the complaint process. Professional Psychology: Research and Practice, 21, 455–461. *In part, that is because of the methodological problems involved in gathering data about sexual intimacies with*

clients. See, for example, Williams, M. (1992). Exploitation and inference: Mapping the damage from therapist–patient sexual involvement. American Psychologist, 47, 412–421.

For a summary of data revealing the prevalence of sexual intimacies between psychologists and nonclients, for example, students, supervisees, and advisees, see Lamb et al. (2003,) cited previously; Lamb, D. H., & Catanzaro, S. J. (1998). Sexual and nonsexual boundary violations involving psychologists, clients, supervisees, and students: Implications for professional practice. Professional Psychology: Research and Practice, 29, 498–503; *Sonne, J. (1994). Multiple relationships: Does the new ethics code answer the right questions?* Professional Psychology: Research and Practice, 25, 336–343.

Although in their most recent studies, Lamb & Catanzaro (1998) and Lamb et al. (2003) indicated that 6% and 3.5%, respectively, of self-reporting psychologists admit to at least one act of sexual intimacy, there appears to be a trend toward a lower incidence of these self-reports. Keeping in mind that there are methodological issues with all self-report studies, note the following data:

1. *1977—In a study of 1000 psychologists (return rate = 70%) 12.1% of male therapists and 2.6% of female therapists reported erotic contact with clients. Holroyd, J., & Brodsky, A. (1977). Psychologists' attitudes and practices regarding erotic and nonerotic physical contact with patients.* American Psychologist, 32, 843–849 *(excludes same-sex involvements).*

2. *1979—In a study of 1000 psychologists (return rate = 48%), 12% of male therapists and 3.0% of female therapists reported erotic contact with clients. Pope, K., Levenson, H., & Schover, L. (1979). Sexual intimacy in psychology training.* American Psychologist, 34, 682–689.

3. *1986—In a study of 1000 psychologists (return rate = 58.5%), 9.4% of male therapists and 2.5% of female therapists reported erotic contact with clients. Pope, K., Keith-Spiegel, P., & Tabachnik, B. (1986). Sexual attraction to clients: The human therapist and the (sometimes) inhuman training system.* American Psychologist, 41, 147–158.

4. *1986—In a study of 5574 psychiatrists (return rate = 26%), 7.1% of male therapists and 3.1% of*

female therapists reported erotic contact with clients. Gartrell, N., Herman, J., Olarte, S., Feldstein, M., & Localio, R. (1986). Psychiatrist–patient sexual contact. Results of a national survey, I: prevalence. American Journal of Psychiatry, 143, 1126–1131.

5. *1987—In a survey of 1000 psychologists (return rate = 46%) 3.6% of male therapists and 0.4% of female therapists reported erotic contact with clients. Pope, K., Tabachnik, B., & Keith-Spiegel, P. (1987). Ethics of practice: The beliefs and behaviors of psychologists as therapists. American Psychologist, 42, 993–1006.*

6. *1988—In a survey of 1000 psychologists (return rate = 39.5%) 3.5% of male therapists and 2.3% of female therapists reported erotic contact with clients. Akamatsu, T. (1988). Intimate relationships with former clients: National survey of attitudes and behavior among practitioners. Professional Psychology: Research and Practice, 19, 454–458.*

7. *1989—In a survey of 4800 psychologists, social workers, and psychiatrists (return rate = 56.5%), 0.9% of male therapists and 0.2% of female therapists reported erotic contact with clients. Borys, D., & Pope, K. (1989) Dual relationships between therapist and client: A national study of psychologists, psychiatrists, and social workers. Professional Psychology: Research and Practice, 20, 283–293.*

What explains the apparent downward trend? Is it the result of methodological differences in the studies, the increasing trend toward criminalization of sexual activity between therapists and patients (see subsequent material in this chapter), a genuine diminution of activity, or some other explanation?

In light of the issues and arguments contained so far in this chapter, readers may profit from discussing the sexually oriented dual-relationship vignettes presented in chapters 2 and 3, as well as the following hypothetical but realistic vignette from Hall, J. E. (1987). Gender-related ethical dilemmas and ethics education. Professional Psychology: Research and Practice, 18, 573–579.

> *A psychologist in a full-time, solo private practice advertises that he limits his practice to marital problems. In 20 years in private practice, he has been successful in solving his clients' marital problems but not in saving his own marriage. Because he works 60–70 hours per week, he is able to avoid focusing on his own problems.*
>
> *His secretary schedules his 5:00 opening with a new client, a 35-year-old married woman, and leaves to catch the 5:00 bus. The client impresses him as someone in need of confirmation of her own worth; after several sessions she admits that she was molested as a child by her father and that her sexual relationship with her husband is both unsatisfactory and coerced. After 3 months pass, the psychologist realizes that he is looking forward to seeing his client each week and is beginning to feel sexually attracted to her. (p. 575)*

Hall (1987) suggested several choices that the male psychologist might make:

1. *Deny attraction to the client as well as "their vulnerability to each other" and continue to see the client in therapy;*

2. *Consult with a colleague and ask for peer supervision on the case;*

3. *Tell the client that it is unethical to have a sexual relationship with her and, therefore, that he must terminate the therapeutic relationship immediately;*

4. *Tell the client that it is unethical to have a sexual relationship with her, and suggest that if they terminate therapy and she initiates treatment with another therapist they could see each other socially after a reasonable period of time; or*

5. *Provide a referral to another therapist, and explain to the client that he cannot help her and that the other therapist is better qualified. He then seeks therapy for himself.*

What boundary violations occurred in this situation? What standards of the 2002 APA Ethical Principles are implicated? Which of these options are in accord with those provisions? Which options are unethical? Which simply reflect poor judgment? See the original article for Hall's own perspectives on each option.

It is noteworthy that Hall did not list an option in which the therapist, after careful evaluation, concludes that the client is not psychotic and is capable of making competent judgments, discusses the issue thoroughly with the client, and decides (with the client's consent) to continue therapy while beginning a social and romantic relationship with her. Are there any conditions under which such an option would be ethical? This response by Pope, Sonne, and Holroyd (1993) represents the professional consensus:

> Under no circumstances should a therapist ever engage in sexual intimacies with a patient. No matter what the situation. No matter who the patient. No matter what the patient has said and done. No matter how the therapist or the patient feels. Therapist–patient sexual intimacies are in all instances wrong and must be avoided. (p. 180)

See Pope, K. S., Sonne, J. L., & Holyroyd, J. (1993). Sexual feelings in psychotherapy. Washington, DC: American Psychological Association.

If one wants a tragic example of the dangers of developing a romantic relationship with clients, consider this case. In 1973, a 15-year-old sought treatment from Frank Polk, a therapist 26 years her senior. They began a sexual relationship and eventually married in 1982. In 2001 Susan Polk filed for divorce, but custody of their three children was granted to her husband. A year later she stabbed her husband to death, claiming that he had essentially been raping her from the time she became his patient and that she killed him in self-defense. The jury, however, convicted her and she is now serving 16 years to life in prison. See McKinley, J. (2006, June 17). Conviction concludes bizarre trial for murder, The New York Times, p. A10; Woman is sentenced in stabbing (2007, February 24). The New York Times, p. A13.

Nevertheless, are there any reasonable counterarguments that one can put forth to the consensus that Pope et al. (1993) asserted, under the considerations I have described above?

Although there is near unanimity regarding sexual intimacies with current clients, professional opinions do diverge over the propriety of absolutely preventing sexual intimacies with former clients. In one survey, Sell, Gottlieb, and Schoenfeld (1986) found that of 54 cases before ethics committees and 48 cases before state licensing boards involving sexual intimacies, not one psychologist was exonerated solely because the

adjudicating body agreed that a sufficient amount of time had elapsed between termination of treatment and initiation of sexual relationship. However, they also found that very few of these bodies had developed guidelines to determine whether sexual relationships between psychologists and former clients would be permissible. Sell et al. urged APA to amend the Ethical Principles to create an absolute ban on sexual intimacies between psychologists and either current or former clients. See Sell, J. M., Gottlieb, M. C., & Schoenfeld, L. (1986). Ethical considerations and social/romantic relationships with present and former clients. Professional Psychology: Research and Practice, 17, 504–508.

In a later survey (Akamatsu, 1988) of 394 members of APA Division 29 (Psychotherapy), 44.7% said that intimate relationships with former clients were highly unethical. However, 31.3% felt that such relationships were neither ethical nor unethical, or even felt them to be ethical to some degree; 23.9% felt that such relationships were only somewhat unethical. The primary factor that respondents stated should be taken into account in determining whether posttherapy intimacy was ethical was time since termination. Other factors included the length and nature of therapy, the mental health of the client, whether therapy would resume, and promotion of the patient's freedom of choice. Interestingly, 14.2% of men and 4.7% of women admitted intimate relationships with former patients. The average interval between termination and the commencement of the relationship was 15.6 months. See Akamatsu, T. J. (1988). Intimate relationships with former clients: National survey of attitudes and behavior among practitioners. Professional Psychology: Research and Practice, 19, 454–458. Akamatsu then concluded:

> My results strongly suggest that ethical guidelines be established by the APA. However, because of the divergent interpretations possible for current results, it may be that the recommendations . . . for a blanket prohibition of sexual intimacies with clients and former clients is more conservative than the views of many practitioners. Guidelines clearly are necessary, but they should delineate contingencies or circumstances that might be considered in

determining the ethics of a particular case. This compromise would probably necessitate the individual handling of each case, but the task would be made considerably easier if guidelines were clear to therapists and their state boards or ethics committees. (p. 457)

As events transpired, Akamatsu's (1988) conjecture that an absolute ban on sex with former clients would not gain consensus turned out to be correct. The 2002 Ethical Principles retains an unconditional prohibition on sexual intimacies with current clients (Standard 10.05), but limits the prohibition to 2 years after termination for intimacy with former therapy patients. After that, however, the burden is on the psychologist to show that the development of a sexual relationship is a "most unusual circumstance" and that there has been no exploitation of the former client as a result of the relationship, considering all the factors set out in Standard 10.08.

Is Standard 10.08 sufficiently specific, and does it take into account all the factors that should be balanced in developing a reasonable rule? Does it go far enough to protect psychotherapy clients? Cottone (2005) noted that both the American Psychiatric Association and the International Association for Marriage and Family Counseling have adopted a rule that makes sexual intimacies with former clients unethical in perpetuity. "A perpetuity rule is the most concrete, simplest, and enforceable standard a profession can promulgate on sexual or romantic interactions with former clients," (p. 14), he argued. Cottone, R. R. (2005). Detrimental therapist–client relationships— Beyond thinking of "dual" or "multiple" roles: Reflections on the AAMFT code of ethics. American Journal of Family Therapy, 33, 1–17. On the other hand, does even a 2-year ban interfere with autonomous decision making as long as both parties are adults and there is appropriate disclosure of the risks to the client? Consider the article that follows.

Explicit Ambiguity: The 1992 Ethics Code as an Oxymoron

Donald N. Bersoff

. . .

Gabbard (1994) raised and rebutted "nine arguments frequently set forth as favoring a policy permitting posttermination sexual involvements" (p. 331). He called this permissive policy "premature" (p. 334), however, and urged the APA to permanently bar any sexual intimacies with former therapy clients. In support of his argument, he, as well as many others (Brown, 1988; Gabbard & Pope, 1989; Sell, Gottlieb, & Schoenfeld, 1986; Shopland & VandeCreek, 1991; Vasquez, 1991), provided powerful reasons for such a ban.

There may be excellent reasons for reconsidering the APA's position, and it is worthy of further debate. Certainly, Standard 4.07,[1] as currently written or as it might be revised to bar sexual relations in perpetuity, does reflect such central moral principles as nonmaleficence and beneficence (Beauchamp & Childress, 1989; Bersoff & Koeppl, 1993; Kitchener, 1984). In considering the validity of the current provision or its alternative, however, I suggest that other competing moral or ethical principles be kept in mind. Foremost among those competing principles is autonomy—"forbearing from interfering in the expression of self-determination by those who wish to make decisions for themselves" (Bersoff, 1992, pp. 1569–1570). Society in general and our professional association in particular should be committed to, among other values, respecting each individual's right to choose his or her own fate, even if the choices the individual makes do not serve, in some objective sense, what the majority would consider to be the individual's best interests. . . .

Concern about posttermination sexual intimacies, at least in part, is predicated on the belief that there will always be an unequal relationship between the powerful therapist—usually a man—and the subservient patient—usually a woman (Gabbard, 1994; Vasquez, 1991). Coleman (1988), however, suggested that any permanent bar

> raises fundamental questions about . . . unconscious sexist motivations.
>
> The first such question is the appearance of paternalism. An absolute prohibition means [therapists] are deciding for patients that they will always be incapable of giving informed consent to a sexual relationship with their former therapists. Although such a rule ostensibly applies to both male and female patients, in reality those involved are almost exclusively women. Consequently, an absolute prohibition effectively renders female patients incapable of giving informed consent because they always remain under the influence of their male [therapists]. (p. 48) . . .

That women who were once in therapy will not be able to make an informed, voluntary, and intelligent decision about their sexual partners is precisely the claim proponents make in favor of an absolute ban. There should be more data to support such a hypothesis, however, before it is converted into an ethical rule relegating female clients to the role of passive victims rather than reinforcing their status as autonomous, self-determining, consenting adults. . . .

From *Professional Psychology: Research and Practice, 25*, 382–387. Copyright 1994 by the American Psychological Association.
[1]*Ed. Note:* See Standard 10.08 of the current (2002) APA Ethics Code.

References

Beauchamp, T. L., & Childress, J. F. (1989). *Principles of biomedical ethics.* New York: Oxford University Press.

Bersoff, D. N. (1992). Autonomy for vulnerable populations: The Supreme Court's reckless disregard for self-determination and social science. *Villanova Law Review, 37,* 1569–1605.

Bersoff, D. N., & Koeppl, P. M. (1993). The relation between ethical codes and moral principles. *Ethics & Behavior, 3,* 345–357.

Brown, L. S. (1988). Harmful effects of posttermination sexual and romantic relationships between therapists and their former clients. *Psychotherapy, 25,* 249–257.

Coleman, P. (1988). Sex between psychiatrist and former patient: A proposal for a "no harm, no foul" rule. *Oklahoma Law Review, 41,* 1–52.

Gabbard, G. O. (1994). Reconsidering the American Psychological Association's policy on sex with former patients: Is it justifiable? *Professional Psychology: Research and Practice, 25,* 329–335.

Gabbard, G. O., & Pope, K. (1989). Sexual intimacies after termination: Clinical, ethical, and legal aspects. In G. O. Gabbard (Ed.), *Sexual exploitation in professional relationships* (pp. 115–127). Washington, DC: American Psychiatric Press.

Kitchener, K. S. (1984). Intuition, critical evaluation and ethical principles: The foundation for ethical decisions in counseling psychology. *The Counseling Psychologist, 12,* 43–55.

Sell, J. M., Gottlieb, M. C., & Schoenfeld, L. S. (1986). Ethical consideration of social/romantic relationships with present and former clients. *Professional Psychology: Research and Practice, 17,* 504–508.

Shopland, S. N., & VandeCreek, L. (1991). Sex with ex-clients: Theoretical rationales for prohibition. *Ethics & Behavior, 1,* 35–44.

Vasquez, M. (1991). Sexual intimacies with clients after termination: Should a prohibition be explicit? *Ethics & Behavior, 1,* 45–61.

◆ ◆ ◆

Commentary: Gabbard (1994; cited above), like Cottone (2005), takes the more traditional view:

> *In the absence of data that would persuasively demonstrate such relationships to be harmless, the prudent course of action would be to proscribe posttermination relationships under the same rationale used to prohibit sex with* current [emphasis added] *patients. When one considers that there are 5 billion people on the planet, the choice of a former patient as a sexual partner must raise serious questions about the judgment and ethics of the psychotherapist.* (p. 334)

Rarely discussed or studied is the instigation of sexual intimacies by clients with their therapists. In a survey of 750 licensed female psychologists (354 of whom responded) the author reported that

> *more than half [53%] . . . have experienced sexual harassment by a patient at some point in their clinical practice. However, the incidence of harassment per therapeutic contact can very roughly be estimated at less than 1 in 5,000 [therapy hours]. The types of harassment reported by psychologists ranged from indirect verbal exchanges, to requests for sex, to threats of sexual assault.* (p. 60)

The most severe incidents occurred with male patients (85%) in outpatient settings (80%), although those who reported the greatest number of incidents worked in state prisons, with sex offenders, or both. See deMayo, R. A. (1997). Patient sexual behavior and sexual harassment: A national survey of female psychologists. Professional Psychology: Research and Practice, 28, *58–62. In a more recent survey, 39% of 298 clinician respondents "indicated that the possibility of a sexual relationship was initiated by the other individual (client, supervisee, or student) during the formal relationship," (p. 253) of which 49% of such invitations were made by clients. Lamb, D. H., Catanzaro, S. J., & Moorman, A. S. (2004). A preliminary look at how psychologists identify, evaluate, and proceed when faced with possible multiple relationship dilemmas.* Professional Psychology: Research and Practice, 35, *248–254. Perhaps more troubling is the finding gleaned from a survey of 830 Australian psychologists that*

> *the lifetime prevalence of stalking by clients [defined as 10 or more intrusions persisting for 2 or more weeks] was 20% . . . with 8% . . . of psychologists subjected to this*

level of stalking in the 12 months prior to the study. (p. 539)

Purcell, R., Powell, M. B., & Mullen, P. E. (2005). Clients who stalk psychologists: Prevalence, methods and motives. Professional Psychology: Research and Practice, 36, 537–543. *What implications, if any, can be drawn from these data regarding the assumed power relationship between therapist and client? Given that women now constitute a majority of new doctoral-level psychologists, are there issues related to the training of clinicians that should be taken into account?*

One other finding from the Lamb et al. (2004) survey cited previously is relevant to the power of the APA Ethics Code to guide behavior. The authors sought to discover what rationales psychologists used to decide not to engage in sexual relationships with clients and others with whom they work. In order of frequency, the four most adopted reasons were (a) my personal ethics, values, and morals prohibited me from pursuing it (89%); (b) I believe in the principle of client perpetuity (65%); (c) the situation constituted a dual relationship with negative consequences (55%); and (d) power differential still exists between me and client (44%). In discussing these data the authors concluded:

> The finding that the rationale related to ethics, morals, and values was cited the most . . . suggests the potential value of the Code as a deterrent. . . . Yet the APA Ethics Code is not necessarily a strong deterrent for those individuals who eventually participate in sexual relationships. . . . [T]here is a suggestion that those who offend are aware of ethical prohibitions and that such prohibitions often serve as a deterrent, perhaps for many psychologists. Yet ethics prohibitions alone are not powerful enough to always prevent the sexual relationship from happening. It would be reasonable to assume that the pursuit of a prohibited sexual relationship requires the psychologist to reject, rationalize, or otherwise ignore the relevance of the APA Ethics Code for that relationship that eventually becomes sexual. (p. 253)

Although most research regarding multiple relationships has focused on sexual activity, a few scholars have looked at nonromantic relationships. Using an adaptation of the Borys and Pope scale (1989, excerpted earlier in this chapter), Baer and Murdock (1995) surveyed 223 APA members (56% female; 96% Caucasian) and found that

> overall, therapists thought that nonerotic dual-relationship behaviors were ethical in only limited circumstances at best. The highest rating of all the presented behaviors was 3.49 [providing therapy to friend of ongoing client], *falling in between the scale points of ethical "under some conditions" and "under rare conditions." Therapists judged social and/or financial involvements with their clients as the least ethical of the three classes of nonerotic dual relationships [the other two are incidental, e.g., accepting an inexpensive gift, and dual professional, e.g., allowing client to enroll in one's class].* (p. 143)

Baer, B. E., & Murdock, N. L. (1995). Nonerotic dual relationships between therapists and clients: The effects of sex, theoretical orientation, and interpersonal boundaries. Ethics & Behavior, 5, 131–145. *See also,* DeJulio, L. M., & Berkman, C. S. (2003). Nonsexual multiple relationships: Attitudes and behaviors of social workers. Ethics & Behavior, 13, 61–78.

Given the problems about boundary violations and the findings from the few studies "of nonerotic dual relationships between therapists and clients . . . indicat[ing] that a professionals' (sic) attitude about nonerotic contact is predictive of his or her attitude about and likelihood to have erotic contact with clients (references omitted)" (Baer & Murdock, 1995, p. 132), should we be more concerned about nonerotic contacts and about the possible intrapersonal vulnerabilities that lead to them?

Although prior excerpts reveal the intense debate about romantic liaisons between therapists and former clients, another little studied area is nonerotic relationships with former clients. As a preliminary matter, there is the methodological and ethically relevant issue of defining a former client. If one terminates a professional relationship with a patient for the purpose of developing a social, business, or romantic relationship, is the patient truly a "former patient?" Does the following provide us with a useful definition? "[C]lients for whom there has been a responsible and appropriately documented termination process, who do not anticipate returning to therapy, and who have in no way been led to believe that they are free to return to therapy are . . . former clients" (p. 28). This definition comes from Pipes, R. B. (1997). Nonsexual relationships between psychotherapists and their former clients: Obligations of psychologists. Ethics & Behavior, 7, 27–41. In any event, the following article is one of the few to study the issue in depth.

Nonromantic, Nonsexual Posttherapy Relationships Between Psychologists and Former Clients: An Exploratory Study of Critical Incidents

Sharon K. Anderson and Karen S. Kitchener

[*Ed. Note:* Using the Critical Incident Technique developed by John Flanagan in the 1950s, the authors identified 8 categories of nonromantic, nonsexual posttherapy relationships gleaned from 63 psychologist-respondents. Respondents were also asked about their perspectives concerning the ethicality of these relationships.]

. . .

PERSONAL OR FRIENDSHIP RELATIONSHIPS

. . . In these relationships, the therapists and former clients had moved past the position of social acquaintance to a closer or more intimate relationship, and the therapist appeared to be more personally invested in the relationship. It was likely that more of the therapist's personal life was known by the former client. The incidents included in this relationship category reflected either a personal connection between the therapist and former client that had some unique or special quality such that the therapist's private life was accessible to the former client, or a friendship where there was a sense of camaraderie between the therapist and former client. The nine incidents defined as personal relationships spanned a broad range of contexts from the therapist being a neighbor of the former client to the therapist being the parent of a teenager who dated the former client. The following is an example of these incidents:

> Former client marries friend of psychologist's spouse. Former client's spouse and therapist's spouse want to socialize together as couples. (personal relationship)

A majority of the participants (seven out of nine) who described these incidents perceived the relationships as ethically problematic. Some of these participants suggested that an equal, normal friendship between a therapist and former client is improbable if not impossible. Other participants shared their belief that a multiple relationship would occur because the therapist–client relationship continues after termination.

One of the two participants who did not see these personal relationships as ethically problematic stated that it was really the former therapist's responsibility to maintain the "appropriate boundary" in the relationship. This person, speaking from the perspective of a former client, went on to provide a rationale for the personal relationship:

> I did, however, make a conscious decision that I would never return to this person as a therapist before developing the friendship [with the therapist's family member] . . . this was hard for me but seemed important.

The other nine incidents in this category described a friendship between the therapist and former client. Frequently, the respondents actually used a variation of the word *friend* in their descriptions of the relationships.

. . .

None of the participants who described these relationships saw them as ethically problematic. Their reasons for this perspective included the time lapse since termination, the maturity of both parties, and the discussion by the therapist and former client of the parameters of the new relationship. The following is an example of a response by one of the participants who described a posttherapy incident of friendship:

> Although I had hesitations initially regarding the friendship, I do not see it as ethically problematic because 1) our therapeutic relationship was terminated, 2) it was agreed that if my former client wanted to re-engage in therapy that they would seek a different therapist, and 3) we have discussed in detail and maintain very clear boundaries in our friendship including confidentiality of our previous therapeutic relationship and assuring communication of needs and feelings remains two-way.

SOCIAL INTERACTIONS AND EVENTS

. . . Participants described interactions that ranged from a onetime occurrence (e.g., attending the wedding of former clients) to social activities that could have been more ongoing and ranged from casual (e.g., participating in community or neighborhood activities) to sexual (e.g., participating in "swingers" parties). The circumstantial and intentional subcategories emerged during the sorting process. In the following example, the therapist and former client seemed to have met each other in a social context with little or no prior planning on either person's part.

> Found myself a fellow competitor at a dog show with a former patient. (social interactions and events—circumstantial)

Different from the circumstantial interactions between the therapist and former client, the following example illustrates a type of social activity where the therapist or former client initiated some action to invite contact or ensure interaction with the other in a social context. The former client initiated a majority of these social interactions.

> While coincidentally vacationing in the same resort area, psychologist and family accepted invitation of former client and family to visit at their vacation house along with several other guests. (social interactions and events—intentional)

Six out of the nine participants who described circumstantial social contacts saw these interactions as not ethically problematic. They provided justifications such as the following: the contact was brief and unplanned; confidentiality remained intact; and the psychologist took preventive measures to minimize potential harm in the posttherapy contact. For example, one psychologist who anticipated the possibility of social contact "discussed [with the former client] the potential uncomfortableness of the relationship after discharge."

All of the participants who described incidents of intentional social interactions saw these interactions as ethically problematic. A majority of them shared the belief that the therapist–client relationship continues after termination and that another relationship would create the potential for either exploitation or conflict of role expectations and obligations. The respondent who accepted the invitation to visit the former client at the former client's vacation home shared a slightly different but related reason:

> Clients often idealize their therapist and getting together socially becomes too heavy [a] dose of reality all at once which can be difficult for client, especially when the treatment relationship is over and client may not have a setting to work through this.

BUSINESS OR FINANCIAL RELATIONSHIPS

The common theme in the business or financial category was either (a) exchanging dollars between the therapist and former client for the former client's expertise or assistance or (b) joining areas of expertise that brought in dollars (e.g., hiring a former client, receiving financial assistance or advice from a former client, patronizing the former client's place of business, and having a business together). . . . The following is an example:

> Psychologist hired a former patient to clean house for psychologist's family on a weekly basis. Was later let go because of poor performance, unreliability. (business or financial relationship)

Seven of the twelve participants saw this type of relationship as ethically problematic. Their reasons for this perspective included the following: dual role issues; negative impact on the former client's internalized image of the therapist; special knowledge about the former client influencing the therapist's objectivity; the power differential; and a limit on the former client's option to return to therapy.

. . .

Five participants did not see the incidents they described as ethically problematic. These participants identified the following reasons for their perspective: the relationship remained a professional relationship without two-way exchange of personal information, and the boundaries of the business relationship remained clear.

COLLEGIAL OR PROFESSIONAL RELATIONSHIPS

In these 12 incidents, the therapist and former client held positions or took roles potentially equal in power and the relationship was likely to be more externally focused on professional or business issues or problems. An example follows:

> Professor of psychology served as therapist to university colleague (in another department); the two later occasionally worked on university committees together. (collegial or professional relationship)

Nine out of twelve participants said they saw these new relationships as not ethically problematic. Some of the participants argued they could compartmentalize their roles. For example, one participant wrote: "We all have multiple roles. . . . Some degree of compartmentalization is normal in life . . . dual relationships between [the] therapist and client are sensibly managed this way."

The participants who saw the collegial or professional relationship as ethically problematic suggested that the new relationship could produce problems because of dual role conflicts and transference issues. The following is an example of one participant's point of view: "A therapist [might] overlook transferential material as important deter-

minants of relationships long after the 'treatment' aspect has ended."

SUPERVISORY OR EVALUATIVE RELATIONSHIPS

In 10 incidents, the new relationship was more supervisory or evaluative in nature. Typically, the therapist took or held a role that required overseeing or evaluating the former client's performance in a clinical or academic setting. As with the social interactions and events incidents, the raters judged that some of these relationships occurred because of an external factor somewhat out of the control of either the therapist or the former client. The following description is an example of the incidents in this category:

> As an instructor for a psychology course occasionally, it is not uncommon to have students previously seen at the counseling center by myself or others I supervise. (supervisory or evaluative relationship—circumstantial)

There were supervisory or evaluative relationships that occurred by more intentional action by either the therapist or former client. Frequently, the intentional action was a request or invitation. The following is offered as a sample of the eight incidents in the intentional subcategory of supervisory or evaluative relationships:

> I provided clinical supervision to a private agency who employed a counselor–therapist who had been a client of mine before and during the former client's graduate days. (supervisory or evaluative relationship—intentional)

Half of the participants (five) saw these circumstantial and intentional supervisory or evaluative relationships with former clients as ethically problematic because of conflicting role obligations. For example, a participant who was an administrator of an agency completing a job search commented:

> A former client . . . applied for a . . . clinical position . . . [the former client] was fairly pathological and I felt wouldn't

be good for the job . . . I couldn't acknowledge my role due to confidentiality. I was very worried [the former client] would be selected by the search committee.

More specifically, the struggle for these participants revolved around the special knowledge obtained in the therapist–client relationship that influenced or could influence the therapist's ability to be objective toward the former client in his or her new role. A participant wrote that it was hard to "treat the [former client] with the same unbiasness or biasness as other students."

The five participants who saw the supervisory or evaluative relationships as not ethically problematic offered different perspectives. A few believed that the former therapist–client relationship no longer existed. Other participants stated that the therapist–former client relationship "naturally evolved" into a different, but still supportive, relationship. One shared that the therapist–client relationship still existed, but the new supervisory, evaluative relationship was necessary. For example, a participant commented that he or she was the "only psychologist qualified to provide" the therapy to a superior because of the structure of the organization in which the therapist worked.

RELIGIOUS AFFILIATION RELATIONSHIPS

. . . . Although the main theme of this category was attending the same church, most of these incidents included another type of interaction, such as working together on church committees, social contact after a service, or support and assistance in another part of the former client's life (e.g., campaigning for a public office).

. . .

None of the participants who described these incidents saw the contact or relationship as ethically problematic. Their reasons for this perspective included the following: the therapist–client relationship was over; confidentiality was maintained; the posttherapy relationship was discussed prior to entering it; considerable time had elapsed since termination; and it was unethical to ignore or avoid the former client. More specifically, one participant,

who described a posttherapy incident in a religious context, stated:

Given a small community, it is virtually impossible to attend church or social events without contact with present or former clients. . . . The more I practice . . . the more I recognize flexibility is needed with regard to general, social contact with former clients, especially in small communities.

As a note of caution, one participant suggested:

A great deal depends on the individuals involved. There is always a potential for ethical issues to arise when someone has special knowledge of others gained through therapy and then interacts with them in another capacity. This knowledge may take the form of bias, expectations, pushing the others' buttons, etc.

COLLEGIAL OR PROFESSIONAL PLUS SOCIAL RELATIONSHIP

The difference between this category and the category of collegial or professional relationships is the presence of social contact in addition to the collegial or professional connection. The social contacts between therapists and former clients took place in a variety of settings (e.g., parties, social involvement in the psychology community, and meeting for lunch). The following is an example:

An ex-patient of mine entered training at the same institute where I was a faculty member. . . . Later, this person too became a faculty member of the same institute. We found ourselves on the same committees, at the same faculty meetings and social events. (collegial or professional plus social relationship)

Similar to those participants who described collegial or professional relationships with former clients, a majority of these participants (six out of seven) did not see these relationships as ethically problematic. Their reasons included length of time since termination, the conscious effort to discuss issues related to the new relationship, and the natural evolution of the new relationship from the therapist–former client relationship. Although these six participants did not see the relationships as ethically problematic, two of them did identify the collegial plus social relationships as being "uncomfortable" for them. For example, one participant commented:

> At times [it is] uncomfortable for me (who would like to keep my personal and professional experiences separate) but I see no clear violation of ethical standards. . . . It is extremely important at the outset to discuss potential complications re: overlap of contact with patients in this category.

Four of these seven participants indicated that they worked and lived in small communities and therefore adjusted their behavior because of the greater potential to run into former clients on a frequent, if not regular, basis.

Only one participant saw the collegial plus social relationship as ethically problematic. . . .

WORKPLACE RELATIONSHIPS

In this category, participants described five incidents where the therapist and former client found themselves in the same workplace, either as professional peers or as employees of the same clinical practice. . . . The following is an example of the incidents that were sorted into the subcategory of circumstantial workplace relationships:

> A psychologist left one job to go to work in another setting where a former client had been recently employed as office help. (workplace relationship—circumstantial)

In the other two workplace incidents, the therapist or former client initiated some purposeful action to bring about the workplace relationship. The following is an example:

> A clinic I work at recently hired a former client's parent as office help (over my objections). This parent was involved in

several therapy sessions with the child. Presently, the parent has both computer and file drawer access to our files. (workplace relationship—intentional)

Four out of the five participants saw these workplace relationships as ethically problematic. Some participants identified the ethical problem of dual role relationships; others indicated a strong concern related to "special knowledge" that the therapist might have about the former client and how this could influence the therapist's objectivity in the new relationship or role. For example, one participant stated it might be difficult "to separate work behavior from the psychological knowledge. . . . Anytime [the] employee was late for work or work behavior was decreasing, it would be difficult to remain unbiased." . . .

DISCUSSION

Because of the exploratory nature of the study and the small *n*, only tentative implications can be drawn from the data. Four implications are presented. First, some psychologists practicing psychotherapy seem to be dealing with a variety of nonromantic, nonsexual relationships with former clients. In addition, they are dealing with this complex issue with little or no professional guidance from the current APA Ethical Principles and Code of Conduct. At least some of these relationships arise because of circumstances beyond the control of the psychologist or the former client. . . . Clearly, psychologists cannot be held ethically culpable for circumstantial contact with former clients; however, they may be ethically responsible for how they handle those contacts if, in fact, the posttherapy relationship leads to harmful consequences for the former client or if therapeutic gains are reversed as a result of the posttherapy relationship (Kitchener, 1988).

Other contacts reported in this study appeared to be initiated by former clients or therapists. Former clients appeared to initiate contact with their former therapists for a variety of personal reasons as well as for professional ones, such as supervision, whereas the relationships initiated by the therapists appeared to be linked primarily to some kind of business setting. Although in some cases therapists did not believe that these relationships were ethically problematic, the relationships do require further professional dialogue because the therapist does have some responsibility for actively deciding whether to enter into such relationship or not. Psychologists who are presented with the difficult issue of posttherapy contact might benefit from a decision-making model and from guidelines that are both practical and flexible enough to deal with the complexity of issue.

The second implication of the study is related: There seems to be little consensus among psychologists who participated in the study regarding whether or not nonromantic, nonsexual relationships are ethical. . . . [M]any of the participants in this study did not hold to "once a client, always a client." In fact, a majority of participants who described posttherapy relationships saw these relationships as ethical.

The third notable implication of our study was that participants on both sides of the argument about the ethical nature of these relationships identified a number of different therapeutic issues to support their position. For example, participants who saw posttherapy relationships with former clients as unethical suggested that transference issues might not be fully resolved and that contact too soon after termination might reignite issues that were only partially resolved. Furthermore, they noted that clients sometimes carry idealized images of their therapists and that viewing or interacting with their therapists in a real world context might lead clients to reevaluate the positive influence of the therapist. In addition, respondents noted that the former client would not be able to return to therapy with the therapist. Those who did not see the relationship as ethically problematic suggested that therapeutic issues related to termination of services were important considerations. For example, participants suggested that posttherapy relationships were ethical if an appropriate time lapse since termination had occurred. These participants suggested that a time period of 2 to 10 years was sufficient length to then engage in a new relationship with a former client. Others proposed that the posttherapy relationship was ethical if the former client decided not to return to therapy with the former therapist and the posttherapy interaction

did not seem to hinder subsequent therapy with different therapists. Furthermore, some participants suggested that the therapeutic issue of confidentiality could be better kept by allowing the relationship or interaction to occur instead of steering clear of it.

The fourth implication of our study is related to the current Ethics Code (APA, 1992). The code makes only one reference to former clients, and (as already noted) it focuses on sexual relationships between therapists and former clients. In future revisions, APA may need to consider whether the code should address nonromantic, nonsexual relationships with former clients (S. E. Jones, personal communication, April 1993). According to many of the respondents in this study, some of these relationships are potentially harmful, and others may not be. Furthermore, some may be unavoidable; thus, any new ethical standards should be written with clear knowledge of the breadth of the issues and problems involved. . . .

References

American Psychological Association. (1992). Ethical principles of psychologists and code of conduct. *American Psychologist, 47,* 1597–1611.

Kitchener, K. S. (1988). Dual role relationships: What makes them so problematic? *Journal of Counseling and Development, 67,* 217–221.

◆　　◆　　◆

Commentary: Review the 2002 Ethic Code. Does it contain provisions regarding nonsexual relationships with former clients, as Anderson and Kitchener recommend? In a later article, the authors provide analyses of the data and provide specific questions that the clinician and client should answer before embarking on a posttherapy relationship. See Anderson, S., & Kitchener, K. (1998). Nonsexual posttherapy relationships: A conceptual framework to assess ethical risks. Professional Psychology: Research and Practice, 29, 91–99. *In their survey of almost 300 psychologists, Lamb et al. (2004), using the seven categories delineated by Anderson and Kitchener (1996) in the excerpt provided here, found that the most frequently discussed nonsexual multiple relationships with former clients were social interactions and events and collegial and professional relationships. Lamb, D. H., Catanzaro, S. J., &*

Moorman, A. S. (2004). *A preliminary look at how psychologists identify, evaluate, and proceed when faced with possible multiple relationship dilemmas.* Professional Psychology: Research and Practice, 35, 248–254.

Pipes (1997) provides several reasons why therapists should limit nonsexual relationships with former clients. Among them are the following:

1. They may need to return to therapy.
2. Many of them remain vulnerable following termination and would be susceptible to exploitation by their former therapist.
3. Posttermination relationships may interfere with therapist objectivity and client trust.
4. There is the danger that these relationships will end badly.
5. State laws may prohibit them, creating the danger of licensure loss.

Although Pipes, like Anderson and Kitchener, notes the APA's Ethics Code does not address the issue, one should ask what a provision barring nonromantic relationships would look like. Is there the danger that some innocuous interactions, "such as purchasing a routine item from a business owner" (Pipes, 1997, p. 36), would come to be seen as unethical? See Pipes, R. (1997). *Nonsexual relationships between psychotherapists and former clients: Obligations of psychologists.* Ethics & Behavior, 7, 27–41.

Pulakos (1994) found that 59% of clients seen at a university counseling center experienced incidental encounters with their therapists—not a surprising occurrence on a college campus. When asked how their therapists responded to these chance meetings, 8% said their therapists ignored them, 59% said they briefly acknowledged them, and 22% engaged them in conversation. What is interesting is that although 79% felt that these respective responses were appropriate, 21% wanted more:

> For example if the therapist had ignored the client, the client wanted a brief acknowledgment or engagement in conversation; if the therapist gave a brief acknowledgment, the client wanted engagement in conversation. In no cases did clients want less than the therapist offered. (p. 301)

The author thought that the most striking finding was that in only 29% of cases were these encounters discussed in therapy. See Pulakos, J. (1994). *Incidental encounters between therapists and clients: The client's perspective.* Professional Psychology: Research and Practice, 25, 300–303.

This study raises the much broader question of whether psychologists are more concerned about multiple relationships in therapy than are clients. The following material reveals that the issue can be quite controversial.

How Certain Boundaries and Ethics Diminish Therapeutic Effectiveness

Arnold A. Lazarus

. . .

During my internship in the 1950s I was severely reprimanded by one of my supervisors for allegedly stepping out of role (one type of boundary) and thereby potentially undermining my clinical effectiveness. (In many quarters, clearly demarcated client–therapist roles have been very strongly emphasized in recent years.) It had come to my supervisor's attention that at the end of a session I had asked a client to do me the favor of dropping me off at a service station on his way home. My car was being repaired, and I had ascertained that the client would be heading home after the session and that I would not be taking him out of his way. My supervisor contended that therapy had to be a one-way street and that clients should not be called upon to provide anything other than the agreed-upon fees for service. Given my transgression, my supervisor claimed that I had jeopardized the client–therapist relationship. Interestingly, I recall that my rapport with the client in question was enhanced rather than damaged by our informal chat on the way to the service station.

The extent to which some clinicians espouse what I regard as *dehumanizing* boundaries is exemplified by the following incident. During a recent couples therapy session, the husband mentioned that he had undergone a biopsy for a suspected malignancy and would have the result later that week. Our next appointment was 2 weeks away, so I called their home after a few days to ask about the laboratory findings. The husband answered the telephone, reported that all was well, and expressed gratitude at my interest and concern. The wife, a licensed clinical psychologist, had a different reaction. She told a mutual colleague (the person who had referred the couple to me) that she was rather dismayed and put out at what I had done, referring to it as the violation of a professional boundary. A simple act of human decency and concern had been transformed into a clinical assault.

A different boundary issue was raised in the columns of a state journal. A therapist was treating an adolescent and wanted to arrange a meeting with the boy's mother. A busy professional, the mother's schedule was such that the most convenient time was during a lunch break, and she suggested they meet to discuss the matter at a local restaurant. The position taken by various correspondents was that this would not only transgress various boundaries but constitute a dual relationship. I wondered whether meeting in the park, or at the mother's place of work, in a hotel lobby, or in a car would be similarly discounted. Or could the venue indeed be a restaurant if no food but only coffee were ordered? [footnote omitted].

. . . With some clients, anything other than a formal and clearly delimited doctor–patient relationship is inadvisable and is likely to prove counterproductive. With others, an open give-and-take, a sense of camaraderie, and a willingness to step outside the bounds of a sanctioned healer will enhance treatment outcomes. Thus I have partied and socialized with some clients, played tennis with others, taken long walks with some, graciously accepted small gifts, and given presents (usually books) to a fair number. At times, I have learned more at different sides of a tennis net or across a dining room table than might ever have come to light in my consulting room. (Regrettably, from the viewpoint of present-day risk management, in the face of allegations of sexual impropriety, it has been pointed out

From *Ethics & Behavior, 4,* 255–261. Available at http://www.informaworld.com. Copyright 1994 by Taylor & Francis. Adapted with permission of the author and publisher.

that such boundary crossings, no matter how innocent, will ipso facto be construed as evidence of sexual misconduct by judges, juries, ethics committees, and state licensing boards.)

Out of the many clients that I have treated, the number with whom I have stepped outside the formal confines of the consulting room is not in the hundreds, but give or take a few dozen. And when I have done so, my motives were not based on capriciousness but arose from reasoned judgments that the treatment objectives would be enhanced. Nevertheless, it is usually inadvisable to disregard strict boundary limits in the presence of severe psychopathology; involving passive–aggressive, histrionic, or manipulative behaviors; borderline personality features; or manifestations of suspiciousness and undue hostility. . . .

Let me not be misunderstood. I am *not* advocating or arguing for a transparent, pliant, casual, or informal therapeutic relationship with everyone. Rather, I am asserting that those therapists who always go by the book and apply predetermined and fixed rules of conduct (specific dos and don'ts) across the board will offend or at the very least fail to help people who might otherwise have benefited from their ministrations.

. . .

I remain totally opposed to any form of disparagement, exploitation, abuse, or harassment, and I am against any form of sexual contact with clients. But outside of these confines, I feel that most other limits and proscriptions are negotiable. But the litigious climate in which we live has made me more cautious in recent years. I would not take certain risks that I gave no thought to in the 1960s. For example, I accepted two clients into my home (at different times). One lived with my family for several weeks, the other for several days. Both were men from out of state who had relocated and were looking for a place to live. Similarly, I would have thought nothing of offering a client our spare bedroom on a snowy night or furnishing a couple of aspirins if someone asked for them. But like most of my colleagues, I have attended seminars on how to avoid malpractice suits that have made my blood run cold. It is difficult to come away from those lectures without viewing every client as a potential

adversary or litigant. Fortunately, the effects tended to wear off after a few days, and I regained my spontaneity. But the ominous undertones remain firmly implanted and are reinforced by passages in books that explain how innocent psychologists can protect themselves against unwarranted lawsuits. . . . Consequently, being more guarded has rendered me a less humane practitioner today than I used to be in the 1960s and 1970s.

. . .

It is, of course, safer and easier to go by the book, to adhere to an inflexible set of rules, than to think for oneself. But practitioners who hide behind rigid boundaries, whose sense of ethics is uncompromising, will, in my opinion, fail to really help many of the clients who are unfortunate enough to consult them. The truly great therapists I have met were not frightened conformists but courageous and enterprising helpers, willing to take calculated risks. If I am to summarize my position in one sentence, I would say that one of the worst professional or ethical violations is that of permitting current risk-management principles to take precedence over humane interventions. By all means drive defensively, but try to practice psychotherapy responsibly—with compassion, benevolence, sensitivity, and caring.

◆ ◆ ◆

Commentary: Lazarus's article stimulated an interesting and fiery debate. Although what follows is but a sample of responses, readers are urged to read the more complete versions:

> *Time has demonstrated that many practitioners who fail to acknowledge generally accepted boundaries, regardless of their rationale for breaking the boundary, do not manage their behaviors effectively and eventually violate the client by overstepping a boundary. (p. 265)*

Bennett, B. E., Bricklin, P. M., & VandeCreek, L. (1994). Response to Lazarus's "How Certain Boundaries and Ethics Diminish Therapeutic Effectiveness." Ethics & Behavior, 4, 263–266.

> *The kind of rote, mindless rule-following that Lazarus abhors, and its stultifying*

interpersonal consequences, are likely to occur primarily where therapists fail to understand the rationale behind and various levels of meaning inherent in therapeutic boundaries and ethics. A therapist who is comfortable with these boundaries, and experiences them as promoting effective, safe treatment, will find [sic] to be allies in the process and to be safeguards that actually allow greater levels of spontaneity and warmth by helping to keep nontherapeutic needs and impulses of the clinician within their proper parameters. (p. 273)

Borys, D. S. (1994). Maintaining therapeutic boundaries: The motive is therapeutic effectiveness, not defensive practice. Ethics & Behavior, 4, 267–273.

A disconcerting aspect of Dr. Lazarus's article is his oversimplification of the complexities inherent in dual roles. When he asserts that he has learned more about his patients from playing tennis with them or eating a meal with them than he has in the consulting room, the reader is left to wonder how he handles such situations. Does he bill his patients for his time when he is playing tennis or eating with them? If not, why is he "working" when he is socializing? Moreover, I wonder how he decides when he is playing tennis if he should try as hard as possible to win or allow the patient to win because of the patient's fragile self-esteem. How does the patient react to this unclarity of roles? Does the patient begin to withhold certain material from the therapist for fear that it will damage

their friendship? How does the patient know when therapeutic activities are taking place and when the interaction is purely social? (p. 286)

Gabbard, G. O. (1994). Teetering on the precipice: A commentary on Lazarus's "How Certain Boundaries and Ethics Diminish Therapeutic Effectiveness." Ethics & Behavior, 4, 283–286.

Lazarus is right to remind us that following ethical guidelines and risk management procedures must always be done within the context of good clinical judgment. Yet . . . to argue that following such guidelines may even harm patients is not just an unsubstantiated claim, it is irresponsible. (p. 291)

Gottlieb, M. C. (1994). Ethical decision-making, boundaries, and treatment effectiveness: A reprise. Ethics & Behavior, 4, 287–293.

[I]n none of [Lazarus's examples] does he appear to consider the impact on the patient . . . of that very intervention, no matter how benignly intended. The patient's experience may not be benign. (p. 296)

Gutheil, T. G. (1994). Discussion of Lazarus's "How Certain Boundaries and Ethics Diminish Therapeutic Effectiveness." Ethics & Behavior, 4, 295–298.

The final comment comes from Laura S. Brown, who broadens the discussion to raise issues of more general ethical, professional, philosophical, and theoretical concern, issues that the reader will recognize from chapters 2 and 3. A longer excerpt from her critique of Lazarus's article appears next.

Concrete Boundaries and the Problem of Literal-Mindedness: A Response to Lazarus

Laura S. Brown

. . .

I would like to argue that Lazarus's article locates the problem incorrectly, and does so in a way that potentially endangers thoughtful dialogues on ethical dilemmas and the problem of creating a frame and boundaries in psychotherapy that not only allow for but nourish the human, compassionate, relational encounter between therapist and client. The location of the problem is not in the development of ethical standards requiring care, circumspection, and the elucidation of boundaries in psychotherapy. Rather, the problem lies in three other places.

This first location of this dilemma is in the failure of mainstream mental health disciplines to appreciate the power dynamics of the psychotherapeutic relationship, not merely at the symbolic level (e.g., transference) but in terms of the real social and political context forming the matrix in which any given psychotherapy relationship situates itself. . . . The second location of the problem is in the difficulties that mental health professionals seem to have with conceiving of our ethics code as a series of decision rules that allow for careful, informed consideration of the meanings of our actions in a manner that allows us to avoid abuses of the power of the psychotherapeutic relationship. Our ethical standards are not a concrete wall hemming us in, forbidding us from human connections. Rather, they are a potential ethical methodology, directions about how to *think* about what constitutes ethical actions so that we can respond freshly to each new situation and person. . . . The third aspect of the problem is that ethics are not perceived as core to and integrated into other aspects of clinical practice, such as diagnosis, case conceptualization, and psy-chotherapy. Instead, for the most part, ethics are treated as an add-on—something to worry about, rebel against, or ignore rather than the core and central component of our epistemologies as psychotherapists. This problem is embedded in how ethics are taught in our training programs. When they are explicitly taught at all, they are either an optional course or one in which few clear connections are made between ethics and everything else that a therapist does.

. . .

For opening this discourse, I appreciate Lazarus's candor and willingness to risk the opprobrium of his colleagues. I can only reiterate my wish that his commentary was less an invitation to comply with sadness and more an explication of how he has made ethical decisions in his work. The promulgation of a decision-based rather than rules-based approach to ethics in psychotherapy benefits from the contributions of every therapist, in the manner in which many of our original ethics codes reflected the lived dilemmas of many psychotherapists. The best possible outcome from this discourse will be that therapists will transform their ethical methodologies and depart from the concrete and legalistic themes that pervade both dominant culture and, increasingly, the cultures of psychotherapy.

♦   ♦   ♦

Commentary: Lazarus was given the opportunity to respond to each of these critiques, which he viewed as ranging from cautionary to downright hostile. It is worth reading his response in full but, as Lazarus notes, "A succinct summary of the major differences between my own views and theirs is that whereas, in

From *Ethics & Behavior, 4,* 275–281. Available at http://www.informaworld.com. Copyright 1994 by Taylor & Francis. Adapted with permission of the author and publisher.

terms of 'risk–benefit ratios,' they dwell mostly on potential costs and dangers, I focus on the advantages that may accrue when certain boundaries are transcended" (p. 299). See Lazarus, A. A. (1994). *The illusion of the therapist's power and the patient's fragility: My rejoinder.* Ethics & Behavior, 4, 299–306. See also Lazarus, A., & Zur, O. (2002). (Eds.). Dual relationships and psychotherapy. *New York: Springer.* Zur, O. (2001). *Out of office experience: When crossing office boundaries and engaging in dual relationships are clinically beneficial and ethically sound.* The Independent Practitioner, 21(2), 96–100. For an excellent critical, historical, and legal analysis of multiple relationships, and for an argument for a new standard, see Ebert, E. (1997). *Dual-relationship prohibitions: A concept whose time never should have come.* Applied & Preventive Psychology, 6, 137–156.

The issue of sexual intimacy also confronts those who train psychologists. Pope, Levensen, and Schover (1979), in a survey of 481 APA members, found that almost 10% of respondents reported sexual contact as a student with at least one of their educators. By a significant margin, more women (17%) reported such contact in comparison with men (3%). For women, the bulk of their sexual contact was with teachers, whereas for men it was with their clinical supervisors. See Pope, K. S., Levenson, H., & Schover, L. R. (1979). *Sexual intimacy in psychology training.* American Psychologist, 34, 682–689.

From another perspective, Pope et al. (1979) reported that 12% of psychology teachers, 4% of supervisors, and 3% of administrators disclosed sexual contact with their students (in comparison with about 7% of therapists in the survey who reported such contact with their clients). Only 2% unequivocally endorsed the benefit of educator–trainee sexual relations, 21% thought it might be beneficial, and the remainder indicated that they thought it could not be of benefit.

Based on responses to a questionnaire from 464 female members of the APA's Division 12 (Clinical Psychology), Glaser and Thorpe (1986) found much greater disapproval of sexual intimacy between students and faculty. Seventeen percent of the women reported having had sexual contact with an educator, which was essentially identical to that reported by Pope et al. However, in comparison with 77% of respondents in the Pope et al. study who believed sexual

contact was damaging, Glaser and Thorpe (1986) found that "over 95% of all respondents judged such contact as unethical, coercive, and harmful to the working relationship to a considerable degree" (p. 49), even though at the time of contact most saw no ethical problems or felt coerced or exploited. See Glaser, R. D., & Thorpe, J. S. (1986). *Unethical intimacy: A survey of sexual contact and advances between psychology educators and female graduate students.* American Psychologist, 41, 43–51.

In the most recent study of sexual intimacies between trainers and students the authors studied 1,000 graduates of clinical and counseling doctoral programs (with a 51% return rate). The results tracked the data found 15 years earlier; 15% of women graduates and 2% of men reported having sexual contact, that is, intercourse or genital stimulation, with an educator during training. The authors did find that for former female students, a higher proportion of such contact occurred with those who graduated before 1983 but concluded:

> Nonetheless, these problematic behaviors still occur with disturbing frequency. . . . Attitudes by student participants toward these experiences appear to become more negative over time, with retroactive opinions that such relationships were coerced and had negative consequences for students. The gender and age composition of these liaisons still reflects a great power differential: The modal relationship is between an older male professor and a younger female graduate student. (p. 96)

Hammel, G., Olkin, R., & Taube, D. (1996). *Student–educator sex in clinical and counseling psychology doctoral training.* Professional Psychology: Research and Practice, 27, 93–97.

The 1992 Code provided in Standard 1.19:

> Psychologists do not engage in sexual relationships with students or supervisees in training over whom the psychologist has evaluative or direct authority. . . .

The 2002 Code, now Standard 7.07, states:

> Psychologists do not engage in sexual relationships with students or supervisees who are in their department, agency, or train-

ing center or over whom psychologists have or are likely to have evaluative authority.

Does this mean that an intimate relationship would be precluded between a doctoral student in an organizational psychology program and a faculty member who specializes in animal behavior and who have no other academic contact? Is this overregulating private conduct, or are there other values in barring such liaisons?

Although sexual intimacy is a troubling issue, other kinds of multiple relationships also occur in teaching and training settings. For example:

> [P]rofessors may have a professional colleague, a family member, or a friend who wants to take their class; professors may have a desire to become friends with a member of a class they are currently teaching; professors may want to engage in a business relationship with a member of a current class; professors and their students may be members of the same social organization or church; professors may desire to date their current students; professors may desire to become sexually involved with current students; or professors who are also therapists may have clients who wish to take their courses. (p. 151)

Blevins-Knabe, B. (1992). The ethics of dual relationships in higher education. Ethics & Behavior, 2, 151–163.

How prevalent are sexual relationships between faculty members and students? The next excerpt provides some answers.

Intimate Relationships Between Teaching Assistants and Students: Ethical and Practical Considerations

Sarah E. Oberlander and Jeffrey E. Barnett

Faculty–student relationships are often characterized by multiple and overlapping roles, many of which may be necessary and appropriate, such as professor–advisor, professor–research supervisor, and professor–teaching assistant supervisor (Biaggio et al., 1997). Nonsexual multiple relationships allow faculty members to serve as guides, role models, teachers, and sponsors of graduate students, offering unique opportunities for career and personal development (Johnson & Nelson, 1999).

However, the intimacy and mutuality often present in mentoring relationships also introduces the possibility of exploitation, as in the case of a sexual multiple relationship (Johnson & Nelson, 1999). Although it's difficult to ascertain realistic rates of sexual faculty–student relationships, several studies indicate disturbing trends. Pope, Levenson, and Schover (1979) surveyed 481 faculty members of the American Psychological Association (APA)'s Division of Psychotherapy and found that 13% reported entering into sexual relationships with students.

More than 10% of the sample of 482 APA members working in educational institutions reported becoming sexually involved with a student (Tabachnick, Keith-Spiegel, & Pope, 1991), although 71% of the sample described sexual relationships with students as unquestionably unethical. Nearly 20% of Tabachnick et al.'s sample reported engaging in sexual relationships with a student after a course had ended, and nearly 21% described these relationships as unquestionably unethical. Only 24% reported never having been sexually attracted to a student, and more than 15% believed such an attraction to be unquestionably unethical (Tabachnick et al., 1991). Recent research suggested that rates of sexual relationships between faculty and students

may be declining, and in a survey of 368 APA psychologists, only 3% reported engaging in a sexual relationship with a student (Lamb et al., 2003).

In a retrospective study of faculty–student sexual relationships, Hammel et al. (1996) found respondents to report such relationships during their graduate training to be "coercive, ethically problematic and a hindrance to the working relationship" compared to how they viewed it at the same time it occurred (p. 93). Research has suggested that engaging in sexual relationships during training is correlated with engaging in problematic multiple relationships and exploitive behavior in the future (Biaggio et al., 1997; Pope et al., 1979). Although this finding has not been replicated by all investigators (e.g., Lamb & Catanzaro, 1998; Lamb et al., 2003), 77% of psychologists who reported engaging in a sexual relationship with a client, student, or supervisee noted that the relationship ended undesirably, and 90% reported that they would avoid similar relationships in the future (Lamb et al., 2003).

References

Biaggio, M., Paget, T. L., & Chenoweth, M. S. (1997). A model for ethical management of faculty–student dual relationships. *Professional Psychology: Research and Practice, 28,* 184–189.

Hammel, G. A., Olkin, R., & Taube, D. A. (1996). Student–educator sex in clinical and counseling psychology doctoral training. *Professional Psychology: Research and Practice, 27,* 93–97.

Johnson, W. B., & Nelson, N. (1999). Mentor–protegeé relationships in graduate training: Some ethical concerns. *Ethics & Behavior, 9,* 189–210.

Lamb, D. H., & Catanzaro, S. J. (1998). Sexual and nonsexual boundary violations involving psychologists, clients, supervisees, and students: Implications for professional practice. *Professional Psychology: Research and Practice, 29,* 498–503.

Lamb, D. H., Catanzaro, S. J., & Moorman, A. S. (2003). Psychologists reflect on their sexual relationships with clients, supervisees, and students: Occurrence, impact, rationales, and collegial intervention. *Professional Psychology: Research and Practice: 34,* 102–107.

Pope, K. S., Levenson, H., & Schover, L. R. (1979). Sexual intimacy in psychology training: Results and implications of a national survey. *American Psychologist, 34,* 682–689.

Tabachnick, B. G., Keith-Spiegel, P., & Pope, K. S. (1991). Ethics of teaching: Beliefs and behaviors of psychologists as educators. *American Psychologist, 46,* 506–515.

◆　◆　◆

Commentary: As in universities, there is also the possibility that questionable sexual, social, therapy, and business relationships may occur between interns and their supervisors. See Slimp, A. O., & Burian, B. K. (1994). Multiple role relationships during internship: Consequences and recommendations. Professional Psychology: Research and Practice, 25, 39–45. *Slimp and Burian asserted that such relationships may cause staff to fail to keep intern's training needs primary, impair the intern's professional and personal function-*ing *(particularly in the case of sexual relationships), reduce the possibility of objective evaluations, create conflicts of interest, compromise confidentiality, and risk exploiting the intern.*

The current 2002 Code now contains two new provisions covering student disclosure of personal information and the conduct of mandatory therapy in educational and training settings. See Standards 7.04 and 7.05. As Slimp and Burian advocate, 7.05(b) prohibits faculty from providing therapy to students they are, or will be, evaluating.

For other recent discussions of these issues, see Biaggio, M., Paget, T. L., & Chenoweth, M. S. (1997). A model for ethical management of faculty–student dual relationships. Professional Psychology: Research and Practice, 28, 184–189; *Burian, B., & Slimp, A. (2000). Social dual-role relationships during internships: A decision-making model.* Professional Psychology: Research and Practice, 31, 332–338; *Russell, R. K., & Petrie, T. (1994). Issues in training effective supervisors.* Applied and Preventive Psychology, 3, 27–42.

The final set of materials in this chapter discusses the issue of how to prevent, punish, or remediate unethical multiple relationships. They address training, decision making, and intervention, respectively.

The Current State of Sexual Ethics Training in Clinical Psychology: Issues of Quantity, Quality, and Effectiveness

Linda M. Housman and Jayne E. Stake

A cause for concern is that many students had not developed an adequate understanding of the principles of sexual ethics. In spite of the training reported by students and corroborated by directors, students showed no more understanding of sexual ethics than practicing professionals in earlier studies who had less sexual ethics training (Borys & Pope, 1989; Herman et al., 1987; Pope et al., 1986). Seven percent of the students in the present study did not know that sex with current clients is always prohibited, 34% did not understand that termination or transfer does not free therapists to have sex with their clients, and 68% did not know that sexual feelings for clients are normal and not unethical. Students who had been attracted to a client and did not discuss the attraction with a supervisor were particularly ill informed. They were therefore at risk for mishandling their feelings of attraction and for making therapeutic errors damaging to themselves and their clients.

Given that course hours did not directly relate to knowledge scores, we know that an increase in number of course hours is not the complete answer to improving student understanding. It is important, in addition, to improve the effectiveness of the training provided. One means of more effectively conveying sexual ethics principles was suggested by our findings for supervision. Students who discussed an actual client attraction with their supervisor showed the greatest sexual ethics knowledge. Supervision can be a particularly effective means of developing sexual ethics understanding for several reasons. First, supervisors are in a position to monitor minor boundary violations in the therapy relationship when they begin to appear and can help the supervisee recognize how breaks in maintaining boundaries may lead to, or be an indication of, the sexualizing of the therapy relationship (Gabbard, 1997; Pope, Sonne, & Holroyd, 1993). Second, students can be reassured by their supervisors that feelings of attraction for clients are not uncommon or shameful. Ladany et al. (1997) reported that students who discussed attractions in supervision appreciated supervisors who accepted and normalized their feelings. Moreover, supervisors can help students use their feelings of attraction to understand the client and the therapeutic process. Supervisors can explore with the student the dynamics of the relationship that led to the attraction and identify personal issues for students to address in their own therapy. Finally, supervisors can help students recognize the harm they would cause were they to act on the attraction and can emphasize the imperative that feelings of attraction be resolved outside the therapy relationship. The supervisor is in the best position to convey that no action, including transfer or termination, would ethically justify initiation of a sexual relationship with the client. A model of supervision in which such exploration and teaching could effectively take place was described by Thompson, Shapiro, Nielsen, and Peterson (1989) and Pope et al. (1993). They stressed the importance of mirroring in supervision what is expected of the student therapist, with particular attention to maintaining appropriate boundaries with supervisees and providing the conditions for self-exploration and increased self-awareness.

Despite the benefits of direct supervision, not all students will have the advantage of this method of sexual ethics training. Programs therefore cannot depend on supervisory consultations as the only form of experiential training. Instead, programs should provide all students with some form of planned experiential training. Models of sexual ethics training have been suggested that include experiential components, such as exercises for developing skill in clarifying boundaries and setting limits with clients, discussion of videotaped scenarios portraying client and therapist sexual feelings and ethical dilemmas, role-playing of common scenarios that led to sexual misconduct, and opportunities to discuss personal cases. . . .

In developing a full understanding of how sexual violations occur in treatment, training must focus not only on the treatment setting but more broadly on the social and political context within which the therapy is embedded. Students need to recognize the power differential between themselves and their clients and status differences in gender, race, social class, and education that enhance this power differential. A recognition of gender power dynamics is particularly important for understanding how sexual abuses in therapy occur. . . .

Perhaps even more disturbing, many students who had discussed an attraction with their supervisor still lacked the ethical understanding needed to cope with the attraction. These students were better informed than others, yet 47% thought sexual feelings for clients were unacceptable and 7% believed sex with current clients could be ethical and therapeutic. These results indicate that the supervision some students received did not convey sexual ethics principles effectively. Some who went to supervision were not reassured about their client attraction or were not made sufficiently aware that acting on their feelings was unacceptable. Although directors indicated some awareness that there was room for improvement in their sexual ethics training, they were clearly unaware of the magnitude of the problem. In particular, they overestimated the number of faculty and supervisors with whom students would feel safe discussing sexual attraction for a client.

Given the importance of program atmosphere for effective sexual ethics training, how can it best be improved? First, programs should be directly assessed to identify program weaknesses. Directors should gain information on students' comfort and satisfaction with sexual ethics training and their understanding of sexual ethics principles. Second, recall that greater amounts of training were associ-

ated with student willingness to consult a supervisor. The presence of didactic training was apparently a cue to students that therapist–client sexual issues are a legitimate concern that supervisors would want brought to supervision. Sexual ethics training, placed at multiple points in the program, should help to develop a general program ethos in which students understand the appropriateness, importance, and value of discussing these issues in supervision.

A third step is to establish guidelines for faculty behavior with students that are parallel to expectations of student behavior with clients. . . .

Finally, our findings highlight the importance of addressing sexual issues in therapy early in students' training.

References

Borys, D. S., & Pope, K. S. (1989). Dual relationships between therapist and client. A national study of psychologists, psychiatrists, and social workers. *Professional Psychology: Research and Practice, 20,* 283–293.

Gabbard, G. O. (1997). Lessons to be learned from the study of sexual boundary violations. *Australian and New Zealand Journal of Psychiatry, 144, 164–169.*

Herman, J. L., Gartell, N., Olarte, S., Feldstein, M., & Localio, R. (1987). Psychiatrists–patient sexual contact: Results of a national survey, II: Psychiatrists' attitudes. *American Journal of Psychiatry, 144,* 164–169.

Ladany, N., O'Brien, K. M., Hill, C. E., Melincoff, D. S., Knox, S., & Peterson, D. A. (1997). Sexual attraction toward clients, use of supervision, and prior training: A qualitative study of predoctoral psychology interns. *Journal of Counseling Psychology, 44,* 413–424.

Pope, K. S., Keith-Spiegel, P., & Tabachnick, B. G. (1986). Sexual attraction to clients. The human therapist and the (sometimes) inhuman training system. *American Psychologist, 41,* 147–158.

Pope, K. S., Stone, J. L., & Holroyd, J. (1993). *Sexual feelings in psychotherapy. Explorations for therapists and therapists in training.* Washington, DC: American Psychological Association.

Thompson, P., Shapiro, M., Nielson, L., & Peterson, M. (1989). Supervision strategies to prevent sexual abuse by therapists and counselors. In B. E. Sanderson (Ed.), *It's never OK: A handbook for professionals on sexual exploitation by counselors and therapists* (pp. 19–26). St. Paul: Minnesota Program for Victims of Sexual Assault.

◆   ◆   ◆

Commentary: For other helpful articles on prevention and training (some with discussable vignettes), see:

Anderson, S. K., & Kitchener, K. S. (1998). *Nonsexual post-therapy relationships: A conceptual framework to assess ethical risks.* Professional Psychology: Research and Practice, 29, *91–99.*

Biaggio, M., Paget, T. L., & Chenoweth, M. S. (1997). *A model for ethical management of faculty–student dual relationships.* Professional Psychology: Research and Practice, 28, *184–189.*

Borys, D. S., & Pope, K. S. (1989). *Dual relationships between therapist and client: A national study of psychologists, psychiatrists, and social workers.* Professional Psychology: Research and Practice, 20, *283–293.*

Brodsky, A. (1989). *Sex between patient and therapist: Psychologist's data and response. In G. O. Gabbard (Ed.), Sexual exploitation in professional relationships (pp. 15–25). Washington, DC: American Psychiatric Press.*

For a discussion of trainee characteristics and training factors that may lead to or reduce the potential for future clinicians to engage in sexual misconduct, and for preventative measures, e.g., supervision and workshops, see:

Hamilton, J., & Spruill, J. (1999). *Identifying and reducing risk factors related to trainee–client sexual misconduct.* Professional Psychology: Research and Practice, 30, *318–327.*

Lamb, D. H., & Catanzaro, S. (1998). *Sexual and nonsexual boundary violations involving psychologists, clients, supervisees, and students: Implications for professional practice.* Professional Psychology: Research and Practice, 29, *438–503.*

Lerman, H. (1990). *Sexual intimacies between psychotherapists and patients: An annotated bibliography of mental health, legal and public media literature and relevant legal cases (2nd ed.). Washington, DC: American Psychological Association.*

Rodolfa, E., Hall, T., Holms, V., Davena, A., Komatz, D., Autunez, M., & Hall, A. (1994). *The management of sexual feelings in therapy.* Professional Psychology: Research and Practice, 25, *168–172.*

Vasquez, M. (1988). *Counselor–client sexual contact: Implications for ethics training.* Journal of Counseling and Development, 67, *238–241.*

APA has also sought to educate members of the public who use psychological services. See Committee on Women in Psychology, American Psychological Association. (1989). If sex enters into the psychotherapy relationship. Professional Psychology: Research and Practice, 20, *112–115.*

Managing Risk When Contemplating Multiple Relationships

Jeffrey N. Younggren and Michael C. Gottlieb

One of us (Jeffrey N. Younggren) recently attended an ethics workshop where the presenter, an attorney, said, "All dual relationships in psychotherapy are unethical or at least run the risk of getting you into trouble with your licensing board." This is a common view pervading the mental health professions, although some have taken an opposing stand, arguing that dual relationships do not always cause harm and can sometimes prove helpful (e.g., Lazarus & Zur, 2002). The coexistence of these opposing arguments may cause confusion because both oversimplify a very complex area of professional practice.

Professional practice abounds with the potential for multiple relationships, and the circumstances under which these types of relationships occur are quite varied. Although psychologists frequently choose to enter into these types of relationship, many may actually be unavoidable, and in some situations one can even conceptualize the avoidance of the dual relationship not only as unethical but as potentially destructive to treatment itself (Campbell & Gordon, 2003). For example, consider the solo practitioner in a very small community, who must of necessity maintain some multiple relationships with his or her patients by virtue of proximity and living conditions. To avoid all contact with patients in this situation would require the practitioner to lead the life of a virtual hermit. To make matters worse, this type of unusual conduct could raise questions in the minds of other members of the community as to why the practitioner acts in such a manner. A socially isolated practitioner will attract few patients and arguably will serve them less well by failing to integrate himself or herself into the community. Such examples have forced the profession to accept the logical position that not all multiple relationships are unethical per se (American Psychological Association [APA], 2002).

The key considerations for practitioners who are faced with deciding if they should participate in a multiple relationship, or who inadvertently find themselves already in such a relationship, involve thoughtful analysis of potential hazards. Our purpose is twofold: First, we focus on how to evaluate and manage such relationships to avoid exploitation of and harm to patients, and second, we discuss how to minimize risk for the practitioner.

. . .

This article should not be seen as a definitive or exhaustive checklist of issues that must be addressed when dealing with multiple relationships. The complexities of professional–client relationships dictate guidance by many factors. We present a series of questions with the goal of assisting practitioners in thinking through these issues broadly and in a more systematic fashion. These questions focus on both the welfare of the patient and the practitioner's need to manage risk to both patient and therapist. We make several assumptions in addressing these issues, which are provided below.

ASSUMPTIONS

1. *Engaging in multiple relationships has a high potential for harming patients and, as a general matter, should be avoided* (APA, 1992, 2002). The proscription against multiple relationships has a strong foundation in the prohibition against sexual relations with patients. Although sexual misconduct can unquestionably cause harm to patients, plainly constitutes unethical behavior, and violates the law in some states, the concept of multiple relationships extends more broadly and includes many types of nonsexual relationships that possibly may pose danger to patients or risk to the practitioner. These

From *Professional Psychology: Research and Practice, 35,* 255–260. Copyright 2004 by the American Psychological Association.

more ambiguous situations establish the need for the following guidelines.

2. *Psychologists have many different types of professional relationships; not all of them involve psychotherapy patients.* . . .

The ethical and risk-management issues that arise in other types of professional relationships and with other types of psychotherapy do not necessarily have the same types or degrees of risk. Logically, those who engage in less intimate professional activities such as biofeedback, consultation, forensic services, and some types of assessment need to be aware of the risks associated with multiple relationships, but the relational dynamics in these situations are often different from those of psychotherapy. However, the reader should bear in mind that individuals who perform these types of functions could also ask themselves many of the same questions prior to entering into the additional relationship with a consumer and could work to resolve risks if such relationships inadvertently arise.

3. *Some multiple relationships are completely unavoidable and even obligatory, such as those that occur in the military* (Barnett & Yutrzenka, 1994). Psychologists can be placed in legally mandated dual relationships by virtue of the roles they occupy. For example, military psychologists are frequently placed in situations in which they are required to engage in administrative evaluations of individuals they treat. Because of frequent personnel limitations, combined with the unique nature of the military mission, psychologists must perform these dual functions or risk being found in violation of the Uniform Code of Military Justice. This paradox is a reality attendant to the unique role of the military psychologist, and it is only through informed consent that psychologists in the military, and others in similar situations, manage these potentially risky conflicts. Although highly problematic, such unique issues reach beyond our intended scope.

4. *Practitioners create risk for themselves and their patients when they make decisions in a vacuum.* We assume that consultation with trusted and knowledgeable colleagues should undergird all steps in the decision-making process. Those who give consideration to entering into a dual relationship should make consultation central to that process.

5. *Good risk management also means providing good care, and these notions are not viewed as mutually exclusive.* This article focuses on providing good care to the patient while also protecting the provider. Although achieving both of these objectives becomes impossible in some circumstances, we believe that they constitute realistic goals in the vast majority of the professional situations practitioners encounter. If one is to assume that good care is generally care that is satisfactory to the patient, we know that satisfied consumers become originators of litigation and disciplinary complaints far less often than those who are disgruntled clients (Hickson et al., 2002).

6. *When adjudicatory panels such as ethics committees or state regulatory boards evaluate cases alleging harmful multiple relationships, they must of necessity focus on the clinician's behavior retrospectively.* When practitioners consider entering multiple relationships, they must think prospectively to consider how professional bodies might evaluate the complaint retrospectively. Therefore, when considering whether to enter into a multiple relationship, a wise course will involve evaluating how those in the future, in an entirely different setting and circumstance, would react to the present conduct. . . .

QUESTIONS

1. *Is entering into a relationship in addition to the professional one necessary, or should I avoid it?* Psychotherapy, by its very nature, becomes a uniquely complex interpersonal process. Diagnostic formulations may evolve as more information comes to light, causing treatment planning and goals to change. Simply speaking, one cannot know at the outset where the course of treatment will lead. Seemingly straightforward initial clinical presentations may become highly complex and difficult clinical-treatment situations that even the most experienced practitioner could not have predicted. In these circumstances, participating in dual relationships is fraught with unnecessary risk. Therefore, the best interests of the patient and the practitioner generally dictate avoiding dual relationships whenever possible.

2. *Can the dual relationship potentially cause harm to the patient?* A basic principle of biomedical ethics (Beauchamp & Childress, 1994) is that interventions should not harm patients. In addition, if some harm is a necessary component of treatment, an attempt must be made to minimize it. In this connection, any proposed relationship in addition to the therapeutic one must yield to an analysis of risk of harm (Gottlieb, 1993). That is not to say that a professional entering into a dual relationship must anticipate and prevent all risk, but that professional has a fiduciary obligation to anticipate reasonably foreseeable risks and make every effort to avoid, minimize, and manage them.

Consider the following example. A practitioner in an isolated community agrees to serve on the vestry of the local church. Subsequently, the minister's wife seeks out the practitioner for treatment. The practitioner, knowing that the prospective patient would be forced to travel great distances to obtain services elsewhere, agrees to see her. It would seem that such a decision would benefit the minister's wife, but agreeing to treat this woman has foreseeable risks. What if, sometime after treatment begins, some members of the church become dissatisfied with the minister, and the vestry must decide whether to renew his contract? Because the patient knows of the therapist's position on the vestry, the professional relationship could be seriously damaged even if the practitioner is recused from the vestry's discussions. This example only adds further emphasis to the point that what may seem to be a prudent decision at one time can create risk in the face of subsequent unpredictable events. Although the therapist did not create the problem, the situation must still be managed holding the best interest of the patient paramount.

One may argue that predicting future harm as a function of the additional relationship is an impossibility. The reality is that it is easier to believe that a multiple relationship had risk for harm after harm has occurred and a complaint has been filed. However, adjudicatory bodies will look closely at whether a practitioner considered the possibility of future harm, and if harm were a reasonably foreseeable outcome, the practitioner should assume that sanctions will follow.

3. *If harm seems unlikely or avoidable, would the additional relationship prove beneficial?* This type of dilemma occurs frequently for those who work in isolated communities. For example, what should a practitioner do about purchasing a car from the only automobile dealership in a small town when the owner is also a patient? Could making such a purchase enhance the therapeutic alliance by increasing the patient's trust of the therapist and thereby have a positive effect on the therapy? Or, does purchasing the car increase the patient's sense that the therapist trusts him or her? If the practitioner decided to buy the car from the patient, what is to be done regarding negotiating the price? Should the psychologist pay the vehicle's sticker price? Would doing so lead to resentment on the psychologist's part for being forced to pay more than necessary for the vehicle? On the other hand, would purchasing the vehicle elsewhere cause people to wonder why the therapist avoided the local dealership? This might cause particular problems for the practitioner if strong social pressures exist to support the local economy. In this example, purchasing the car elsewhere not only could raise questions among one's neighbors but also might negatively affect the therapeutic alliance. From this very plausible example, it becomes clear that assessing how patients and practitioners may benefit from additional relationships requires caution, careful thinking, and foresight.

4. *Is there a risk that the dual relationship could disrupt the therapeutic relationship?* This question not only requires careful consideration before treatment but also may require periodic reevaluation throughout the treatment process. Given the need to minimize risk, the practitioner who chooses to enter into a dual relationship with a client must manage the relationships in such a way that the therapeutic relationship is not damaged by the additional one. Whenever possible, the practitioner has an obligation to discuss the issue of potential harm in detail with the patient prior to entering into the additional relationship. Furthermore, both therapist and client should revisit the topic regularly to prevent damage to the therapeutic alliance. In addition, the therapist has the obligation to anticipate the types of situations that could damage the therapeutic alliance, because it seems highly unlikely that the client would recognize them. This type of forethought might even benefit the therapeutic process by offering a starting point for discussion of these types of issues with the client. The client may feel more cared for and protected by the practitioner, and this may lead to enhanced therapeutic effectiveness.

Consider this example. A young, attractive female patient has symptoms that initially suggest a diagnosis of a mild, acute depression. The male practitioner finds himself in the midst of a painful divorce, and he has recently considered joining a dance group to increase his socialization opportunities. In the process of treatment, he learns that his patient loves dancing and belongs to the very club he considered joining. After obtaining consultation from a trusted colleague and discussing his own struggles with that colleague, he decides to join a different group. As therapy progresses, the practitioner begins to suspect that his patient may have borderline personality disorder.

In this example, the practitioner had no reason to believe any problem would necessarily arise if he joined the same dance club as his patient, but the consultant brought two issues to his attention. First, the practitioner's emotional state made him vulnerable and might lead to his projecting feelings onto his patient that could complicate her treatment. Second, given the relative newness of the patient, he had no way of knowing whether his diagnosis would remain unchanged once her depressive symptoms began to remit. Here the practitioner imposed a restriction on himself that many might believe unnecessary. Nevertheless, in this case the judgment proved highly prudent and preserved the professional relationship by putting the therapeutic relationship at the forefront in the decision-making process.

5. *Can I evaluate this matter objectively?* This very difficult question demonstrates a fundamental of good risk management. One must always assume that a compromise in one's objectivity might reach beyond one's awareness. However, when one is confronted with this type of problem, careful self-evaluation is always a good place to start. Standing back from a potential dual relationship and looking at it, oneself, and one's own motivation will surely help lend clarity to the matter. In addition, review-

ing the available literature in this area can also improve one's objectivity and could even provide answers to questions about current professional standards of care.

The only other way to approach answering the question about objectivity begins with obtaining consultation from trusted colleagues. (It is important to note that obtaining consultation from others, such as attorneys, may also be entailed.) The inherent high level of risk associated with acting out unconscious needs, or conscious but neglected ones, makes addressing these types of professional concerns with others extremely valuable. When the answers to questions about personal objectivity are unclear, one should discuss and process them with other individuals to ensure that the answers maximize thoughtful, objective consideration; good clinical care; and sound risk management.

RISK MANAGEMENT

Once a practitioner has addressed the "treatment-oriented" questions above and has decided to proceed with a dual or multiple relationship, he or she should now turn to what we term the "risk-management mode." Because the decision to enter into additional relationships has risk for the patient, the therapy, and the practitioner, he or she must engage in a risk-management strategy that provides protection if charges of unprofessional conduct ever surface as a result of the choice. Although some might see such a strategy as "self-serving," the realities of a litigious society require self-protective conduct. Furthermore, in keeping with our assumptions, we contend that good risk management is also consistent with good clinical and ethical practice. Therefore, when choosing to engage in a dual or multiple relationship, the prudent practitioner should now address the following questions.

1. *Have I adequately documented the decision-making process in the treatment records?* Because the spirit of the law is "If it isn't written down, it did not happen," inadequate documentation can negate the existence and value of the entire decision-making process regardless of how comprehensive and thoughtful it may have been. No matter how well the practitioner may have addressed the questions

raised earlier in this article, if the process was not documented, then the protection afforded by having done so is largely lost. Once a complaint or lawsuit is filed, efforts to explain the process without documentation will result in considerable skepticism and will be viewed as self-serving and as an effort to put one's own interests ahead of the patient's. On the other hand, good record keeping can significantly contribute to a strong defense against allegations of professional misconduct (APAIT [American Psychological Association Insurance Trust], 2002a; Nottingham & Herz, in press). If the record reflects a carefully considered decision-making process that led to the choice to engage in a dual relationship, it can lend great weight to one's defense, even if that choice turned out to be the wrong one.

More specifically, the record should reflect the process by which the choice evolved and demonstrate full consideration of other alternatives. Creating documentation in this manner produces a record that should lead the reader to reach the same conclusion, or at least to have a good understanding of the practitioner's thinking on the matter. To meet this standard, the practitioner should ensure that the record reflects all consultations and logically explains the rationale for the choices made.

Finally, how does the record reflect that the patient has received appropriate information and consents to the additional relationship? Ideally such documentation could take the form of a signed agreement, something that is discussed in the next section, but at the very least this type of consent should consist of a note in the patient's chart. Although a note affords weaker evidence of informed consent, it remains a testament to the fact that some agreement did, in fact, occur. If the record fails to incorporate these considerations, it may leave the practitioner as the only witness who supports the choice. A good record serves almost as a second witness to what actually occurred. If this "witness" provides data supporting the practitioner's choice, it lends great strength to the argument that the choice was a sound one.

Let us once again consider our dancing colleague and assume that he chose to join the club where his patient also danced. Before deciding to join, he spoke with a colleague and discussed his personal

vulnerabilities in the situation as well as the possible harm it could cause his patient. He then reviewed the issue with the patient as a matter of informed consent. She understood and felt that his action would not pose a problem for her. After joining the club, he also periodically inquired regarding the patient's feelings in order to address potential transferential issues and documented each of these inquiries at the time. Now, because this prudent therapist created a very strong record of what happened, if the patient were to file a complaint against him, he would stand on much firmer ground when defending himself.

2. *Did the practitioner obtain informed consent regarding the risks of engaging in the dual relationship?* Patients are in relatively less powerful positions with respect to their psychotherapist (Kitchener, 1988). When a practitioner faces a difficult decision that entails the risk of a multiple relationship, he or she should make sure that the client fully understands the issues, the alternatives, and the advantages and disadvantages of each as a matter of informed consent (APA, 1992, 2002; Beauchamp & Childress, 1994). Informed consent, in the era of HIPAA (the Health Insurance Portability and Accountability Act), is increasingly complex, and many consent forms and therapist–patient contracts are currently available commercially, in the published literature, and as part of free risk-management services offered by various organizations (e.g., Harris & Bennett, 1998; APAIT, 2002b; APA Practice Organization & APAIT, 2003). However, the type of informed consent being addressed here would clearly require a detailed addendum to an existing standard form or a separate agreement that clearly sets out the issues addressed in this article.

Generally, it is a good practice to allow patients time to consider these matters before making a final decision (Gottlieb, 1993). If the patient agrees to proceed with the additional relationship(s), then they may proceed.

We hasten to note that patients cannot give informed consent to something that poses severe risk to them and/or is a violation of the law, because these rights cannot be legally waived. A good example is consent to engage in a sexual relationship with a therapist. Even if attempts to use informed consent as a defense in this type of case were made, they would fail.

3. *Does the record show adequate evidence of professional consultation?* In many circumstances, consultation helps to establish that the standard of care was met. Talking with others supports the argument that the decisions made in a given matter were in accordance with the guidance of others who would have behaved in a similar fashion under comparable circumstances. This view of the standard of care can be found in the 2002 APA Ethics Code, where "reasonable" professional conduct is defined as "the prevailing professional judgment of psychologists engaged in similar activities in similar circumstances given the knowledge the psychologist had or should have had at the time" (APA, 2002, p. 2). Thus, adequate consultation allows the practitioner to say that he or she did what other reasonable psychologists would do under similar circumstances, creating an additional defense against criticism of his or her conduct that is founded on a violation of the standard of care.

As we noted earlier, consultation should not be limited to an exchange that occurred prior to the decision but should occur throughout the treatment process. Finally, as we have emphasized, consultation should always be documented. Too often practitioners fall into the trap of the "hallway consultation" in which neither consultant nor consultee document the conversation. The best practice is to set aside time to meet with a consultant and, for serious matters that potentially have high risk, both should document the consultation (APAIT, 2002a).

4. *Does the record reflect a patient-oriented decision-making process?* Although not an easy task, making notations that reflect a struggle on the part of the practitioner to protect the patient and to make the right choices for the benefit of the patient becomes a strong defense in legal and ethical proceedings. Even if the choices are arguably incorrect based on subsequent events, the visibility of the process of seeking the right, patient-oriented answer when confronted with a choice of entering into a dual relationship is a very helpful defense.

. . .

5. *Are the sources of consultation credible?* Credibility is difficult to measure as it frequently lies in the eye of the beholder. However, having consulted someone with expertise, not only in the treatment modality being utilized but also in the relevant area of ethics and mental health law, can be a very strong defense. If one does not know how to find such a consultant, contact with local or national professional associations for such a referral can frequently be of great assistance. In addition, these types of consultative services are often provided free of charge to individuals who are members of various organizations, to include the APAIT and the APA Office of Ethics. The individual with whom one consults can be quite important, and, if colleagues of this stature request payment for their consulting services, it is our view that this money is very well spent. Another benefit that comes from practicing in this fashion occurs when the psychologist is sued or his or her license is attacked. Under this circumstance, the consultant can be brought as a witness to testify and, because of being removed from the case and arguably being more objective, may be able to make a stronger argument on behalf of the psychologist than the psychologist could himself or herself.

6. *Do the diagnostic issues matter when considering a dual relationship?* In a word, yes! Logically, entering into a dual relationship with a patient who has a fear of public speaking could be viewed by other professionals as having substantially different risks from those of a patient with a complex borderline personality disorder and a history of childhood sexual abuse. In general, it is our contention that risk is inversely related to the general level of integration of the patient. Multiple relations with patients who are well integrated may present various risks, but these risks are substantially lower than those that occur when a therapist chooses to engage in the same type of relationship with a patient who is seriously emotionally compromised. Multiple relationships in the latter circumstance are almost never a good idea.

Second, there is no question that diagnosis is always provisional. The initial diagnosis is often not the diagnosis with which the patient is discharged. Although multiple relationships may be permissible under certain circumstances with some patients who are well integrated, there is no practitioner who cannot be fooled, miss a diagnosis, or simply learn more information about his or her patient later that would have led to a different decision in diagnostic formulation. Again considering our dancing colleague, much of the risk the therapist runs will depend on the developing diagnosis of the patient, and undiagnosed borderline tendencies pose substantial risk.

Finally, regardless of whether a practitioner believes a choice to enter into a dual relationship with a patient who is compromised is the correct one, he or she must consider the prevailing views of the profession regarding this type of conduct, for it is these views that will be encountered in the courtroom and during the resolution of the complaint.

7. *Does knowledge of the patient support the establishment of a dual relationship?* How well one knows a patient has a direct impact on the choice to enter into a dual relationship. Inherent in many of the points made throughout this article is a belief that more, and accurate, information about a patient is helpful in determining whether the choice to enter into a dual relationship is a wise one. . . . Thus, a comprehensive understanding of the patient and the complexity of the patient's life, family, and related issues would be helpful in arriving at the "right choice" in this case. In truth, when faced with the risk (to both client and therapist) that could come from being wrong, logically, more information is always helpful. For example, and simply put, knowing that a patient has a long history of litigious behavior could cause one to pause when considering whether to enter into another relationship with that individual.

8. *Does one's theoretical orientation matter when considering a dual relationship?* Theoretical orientation matters because in some cases it may increase risk. Those who practice from a more traditional, insight-oriented approach are most likely to have patients who develop transferential feelings that must be addressed in therapy. These types of treatment modalities generally call for clear boundaries and, whenever possible, the avoidance of multiple relationships. Conversely, the behavioral modalities could be seen by some as being less prone to the complexities of more traditional treatment relationships.

However, for various reasons, those who practice from a cognitive or behavioral perspective are not immune from the difficulties found in traditional therapies. First, such approaches are not always confined to symptomatic treatment. Second, the treatment itself does not preclude the possibility of perceptual distortions on the part of patients and/or therapists. Third, the type of treatment may be modified as the patient improves and his or her therapeutic needs evolve. Changing treatment modalities may also change the nature of the patient–practitioner relationship (Gottlieb & Cooper, 2002), and multiple relationships appropriate to the initial format may not be appropriate to the new one.

. . .

IMPLICATIONS FOR PRACTICE

Whether one chooses to enter into a multiple relationship with a patient or inadvertently finds himself or herself in one, significant risks arise for both the patient and the professional. We acknowledge that these types of relationships are not necessarily violations of the standards of professional conduct, and/or of the law, but we know enough to recommend that they have to be actively and thoroughly analyzed and addressed, although not necessarily avoided. This process becomes extremely important in light of the aforementioned risks to both parties.

A professional finding himself or herself facing such a dilemma must address the problem based on the best interests of the client. Careful analyses of the risk for conflicts of interest, loss of objectivity, and disruption of the therapeutic alliance must be made. Following this, the professional must review and discuss the potential difficulties with the client, making the client an active part of the decision-making process. If from this analysis it appears that the relationship is appropriate and acceptable, the therapist must document the entire process and, if possible, make the client a part of that process through the use of a signed informed consent.

Following the completion of this patient-oriented evaluation of the contemplated multiple relationship, the professional must now adopt a risk-managed approach to the problem. That is, he or she must view the relationship and the decision-making process from the perspective of a regulatory or a judicial authority called upon to determine if the professional's conduct was consistent with the standard of care. The psychologist must do all that can be done to evaluate whether the decision to enter into the relationship was reasonable conduct that the public should expect from the average professional in the same or similar circumstances. This must be done through a careful review of a variety of important issues such as diagnosis, level of functioning, therapeutic orientation, local standards, and practices, and through consultation with qualified professionals who could support the decision to enter into the relationship as being consistent with the standard of care. Only after having taken all these steps can the professional consider entering into the relationship, and he or she should then do so with the greatest of caution.

References

American Psychological Association. (1992). Ethical principles of psychologists and code of conduct. *American Psychologist, 47,* 1597–1611.

American Psychological Association. (2002). Ethical principles of psychologists and code of conduct. *American Psychologist, 57,* 1060–1073.

American Psychological Association Insurance Trust. (2002a). *Legal and ethical risk management in professional psychological practice—Sequence 1: General risk management strategies* [Workshop presented nationally]. Washington, DC: Author.

American Psychological Association Insurance Trust. (2002b). *Sample Informed Consent Form.* Retrieved from http://apait.org/download.asp?item=INF.doc

American Psychological Association Practice Organization, & American Psychological Association Insurance Trust. (2003). *HIPAA for psychologists* [CD-ROM]. Washington, DC: American Psychological Association.

Barnett, J. E., & Yutrzenka, B. A. (1994). Nonsexual dual relationships in professional practice, with special applications to rural and military communities. *The Independent Practitioner, 14*(5), 243–248.

Beauchamp, T. L., & Childress, J. F. (1994). *Principles of biomedical ethics* (4th ed.). New York: Oxford University Press.

Campbell, C. D., & Gordon, M. C. (2003). Acknowledging the inevitable: Understanding multiple relationships in rural practice. *Professional Psychology: Research and Practice, 34,* 430–434.

Gottlieb, M. C. (1993). Avoiding exploitative dual relationships: A decision making model. *Psychotherapy, 30,* 41–48.

Gottlieb, M. C., & Cooper, C. C. (2002). Ethical and risk management issues in integrative therapies. In J. Lebow (Ed.), *Comprehensive handbook of psychotherapy: Vol. 4. Integrative and eclectic therapies* (pp. 557–568). New York: Wiley.

Harris, E. A., & Bennett, B. E. (1998). Sample psychotherapist-patient contract. In G. P. Koocher, J. C. Norcross, & S. S. Hill (Eds.), *Psychologists desk reference* (pp. 191–199). New York: Oxford University Press.

Hickson, G. B., Federspiel, C. F., Pichert, J. W., Miller, C. S., Gauld-Jaeger, J., & Bost, P. (2002). Patient complaints and malpractice risk. *Journal of the American Medical Association, 287,* 2951–2957.

Kitchener, K. S. (1988). Dual role relationships: What makes them so problematic? *Journal of Counseling and Development, 67,* 217–221.

Lazarus, A., & Zur, O. (2002). *Dual relationships and psychotherapy.* New York: Springer.

Nottingham, E., & Herz, G. (in press). *Promoting practice health: Risk managed documentation in clinical practice.* Sarasota, FL: Professional Resource Press.

◆　◆　◆

Commentary: Younggren and Gottlieb (2004) in the excerpt provided here, discuss multiple relationships in small communities and the military. This issue as it occurs in rural and other circumscribed communities is addressed more fully in chapter 7 (Therapy and Other Forms of Intervention). The role of psychologists in the military is a particularly knotty problem, however, as Younggren and Gottlieb acknowledge. Multiple relationships in military settings go beyond sexual intimacies; they go to the heart of the role of military clinicians and the difficult loyalty and fidelity issues that role raises. For a discussion of these conflicts see, for example, Johnson, W. B. (1995). Perennial ethical quandaries in military psychology: Toward American Psychological Association–Department of Defense Collaboration. Professional Psychology: Research and Practice, 26, 281–287; *Johnson, W. B., Ralph, J., & Johnson, S. J. (2005). Managing multiple roles in embedded environments: The case of aircraft carrier psychology.* Professional Psychology: Research and Practice, 36, 73–81; *Staal, M., & King, R. (2000). Managing a multiple relationship environment: The ethics of military psychology.* Professional Psychology: Research and Practice, 31, 698–705. *See also White, T. W. (2003, September/October). Managing dual relationships in correctional settings.* The National Psychologist, 12, 14–15. *See generally, Knapp, S., & Slattery, J. M. (2004). Professional boundaries in nontraditional settings.* Professional Psychology: Research and Practice, 35, 553–558.

If education and prevention efforts fail, there are a variety of ways to discipline psychologists and other mental health professionals who violate prohibitions on sexual intimacies and other boundaries with their clients. These include actions by APA and state ethics committees, licensing boards, and plaintiffs bringing malpractice suits. Some insurance companies refuse to cover sexual conduct by therapists with clients under professional liability policies or severely limit what they will pay to damaged plaintiffs. For comprehensive and recent reviews, including an intensive discussion of legal remedies available to clients (e.g., civil actions, administrative complaints to licensing boards, and criminal prohibitions), see Bisbing, S. B., Jorgenseon, L. M., & Sutherland, P. K. (1995). Sexual abuse by professionals: A legal guide. Charlottesville, VA: Michie; *Jorgenseon, L. M., Hirsch, A. B., & Wahl, K. M. (1997). Fiduciary duty and boundaries: Acting in the client's best interest.* Behavioral Sciences and the Law, 15, 49–62; *Jorgenson, L., Randles, R., & Strasburger, L. (1991). The furor over psychotherapist–patient sexual contact: New solutions to an old problem.* William and Mary Law Review, 32, 647–732; *and Haspel, K. C., Jorgenson, L. M., Wincze, J. P., & Parsons, J. P. (1997). Legislative intervention regarding therapist sexual misconduct: An overview.* Professional Psychology: Research and Practice, 28, 63–72.

At least 15 states (Arizona, California, Colorado, Connecticut, Florida, Georgia, Iowa, Maine, Minnesota, New Hampshire, New Mexico, North Dakota, South Dakota, Texas, and Wisconsin) have made client–therapist sex a criminal activity, continuing to fuel debate. See Haspel et al. (1997), cited above.

Criminalization of Psychotherapist–Patient Sex

Larry H. Strasburger, Linda Jorgenson, and Rebecca Randles

. . .

ARGUMENTS FOR CRIMINALIZATION

Deterrence

Deterrence is the primary argument in favor of criminalization of psychotherapist–patient sexual activity. A criminal law articulates to everyone the wrongfulness of such behavior. Proponents believe that sexual contact would be restrained by an unmistakable legal message that such behavior is severely damaging and totally unconscionable backed by the threat of a felony conviction and a prison sentence. Controversy exists over the probable effectiveness of this deterrence, but among the categories of exploitative therapists (1, p. 402; 15), those who are naive, uninformed, or undergoing the effects of midlife crisis may well respond to the prospect of punishment.

Retribution

In addition to the utilitarian function of deterrence, retribution is also a primary goal of criminal statutes. . . . This morally justified retaliation constitutes a vindictive justice that metes out suffering to pay back the wrongdoers. One of the strongest arguments for criminalization may now be that sexual exploitation, in the light of the evidence documenting its ill effects on patients, is so outrageous a transgression of societal rules that retribution is called for. Although therapist behavior rooted in the character pathology of impulsive, narcissistic, or sociopathic personalities may not be deterred by criminalization, retribution for such individuals may nonetheless be socially appropriate.

Additional Redress

A criminal statute would augment existing procedures that, for one reason or another, have not functioned effectively. In the past, an exploited victim could obtain redress for sexual exploitation only through complaints to professional societies' ethics committees, complaints to licensing authorities, or lawsuits for civil damages. Each of these routes has presented problems. Ethical procedures are ponderous, often involving long delays and ineffective action from the professional societies, themselves fearful of being sued by therapists. Licensing authorities have often been unresponsive or impotent. A civil lawsuit can be very expensive and may drag on for years. Criminalization, then, provides an additional option for a victim when other avenues fail. Implementing this option, however, may itself be lengthy and be delayed by the motions of a defendant exercising due process rights.

Dealing With Unlicensed Therapists

Although no panacea, criminalization may also provide a practical way to deal with unlicensed therapists and to incapacitate practitioners who continue to practice unregulated after their licenses have been revoked (17). Licensure boards cannot sanction them, and many of them have so few financial resources that a civil suit would be fruitless. . . .

Money to Treat Victims

Proponents of criminalization point out that such laws can provide access to money for both prevention and treatment of victims. Minnesota, for example, has used money from federal criminal justice programs to fund educational efforts dealing with the problem (18). Money may be available to help fund ongoing victim treatment in states where public funds are dedicated to assistance of crime victims. Such financial restitution, however, may represent an unkept promise. Although funds for assistance to crime victims do exist in theory, the current austerity of state budgets has led to large cuts in the funding of such programs.

ARGUMENTS AGAINST CRIMINALIZATION

Obscuring the Issue

Paradoxically, criminalization may cause psychotherapist–patient sex to be reported even less. Colleagues may be less willing than they currently are to report an offending psychotherapist if an ethics complaint would lead to criminal charges. This might be the case despite an ethical duty to report (2) and the statutes on mandatory reporting that some states have passed (19). A patient may also be reluctant to complain, appalled at the idea that the psychotherapist would be subject to criminal sanctions. While some complainants want retribution or restitution, others may want help for their impaired therapists. Although some patients may not be aware of it, criminal prosecutions cannot proceed without their testimony, which they can choose to withhold.

Voiding Malpractice Coverage

One of the gravest concerns of victims of therapist exploitation is that criminalization may void malpractice insurance coverage. Although insurers continue to recognize an obligation to defend accused therapists, the trend has been to exclude paying judgments for sexual exploitation. Criminalization provides additional justification for such exclusion, as most policies specifically exclude criminal acts from coverage. Criminalization, then, may eliminate a resource that victims sorely need to finance continuing treatment. There is no victim compensation fund comparable to the therapist's malpractice policy. Although the victim may be able to reach the personal assets of the psychotherapist, these resources are frequently inadequate or nonexistent.

This concern about loss of malpractice coverage may be exaggerated. There are indications that insurers may be required to indemnify such claims even in states which have criminalizing statutes (20). Successful suits are frequently based on assertions of mishandled transference. One appellate opinion has held that in such circumstances, "It is the mishandling of transference, and not the resulting

sexual conduct, which gives rise to the alleged malpractice. . . . The sexual acts are an incidental outgrowth of the primary malpractice, not the proximate cause" (21). Some plaintiffs have won lawsuits despite these exclusionary policies by alleging concurrent proximate causes for their injuries—where the injuries have been caused by both the excluded risk (sexual misconduct) and an insured risk (such as wrongful or improper termination of therapy).

Impairment of Civil Actions

Criminalization may make it more difficult for patients to win civil suits for damages. The risk of criminal prosecution certainly will make offending therapists less likely to admit their behavior. The therapist may exercise Fifth Amendment rights. This in effect will prevent the process of discovery by civil and administrative boards until the criminal trial is completed. This could delay not only an award of (money) damages but also restriction or revocation of the therapist's license by the licensing board. Even the simple matter of apology, which some victims find healing, becomes difficult in the face of a possible criminal prosecution. . . .

Inappropriate Catharsis

Victims' advocates observe that pursuit of criminal prosecution provides an anodyne to the shame and feeling of powerlessness experienced by victims of sexual exploitation. Whether this emotional relief is greater than that obtained through a civil lawsuit or action before a licensing board is unclear. Nevertheless, it may be inappropriate to use the blunt instrument of criminal law to palliate and enable victims.

. . .

Loss of Control of Process

Many victims of sexual exploitation by psychotherapists feel that they have lost control of their lives, and involvement in criminal prosecution may heighten this feeling. Although some writers believe that a decision to file a criminal complaint helps recover a sense of control, the victim does not control a criminal process and civil process in the same way. Although the victim is free to choose whether or not to come forward with a complaint and a prosecutor cannot proceed if the only witness against the therapist refuses to testify, victims have been concerned that after a complaint is entered the prosecutor's decisions will determine how the case is run.

Unproven Deterrence

Although anecdotal information and common sense suggest that criminalization may act as a deterrent, there is as yet no empirical evidence to demonstrate this premise. In fact, few people even file criminal charges in states where statutes exist. Over 1,600 victims of therapist sexual contact have been seen in the Walk-In Counseling Center in Minneapolis, but Minnesota has prosecuted only nine criminal charges to date.

Absence of Rehabilitation

The absence of a provision for the rehabilitation of offenders is a major omission in the current criminal statutes. Although some sexual exploiters victimize multiple patients, appear to be without conscience, and are probably not treatable, others commit a single offense that may be a response to a situational or life cycle crisis, and these psychotherapists might benefit from treatment and be restored to social productivity. Casting these latter individuals in the role of un-redeemable criminals may not be wise social policy.

SPECIAL CONSIDERATIONS

Consent

Some criminal laws, such as those against rape and indecent assault, already apply to therapist sexual misconduct. As a practical matter these laws cover only the most egregious cases, and consent of the victim is an absolute defense (17). Eliminating consent as an issue by defining psychotherapist–patient sexual contact as a specific crime provides a more effective statute. Most statutes criminalizing patient–therapist sex exclude consent as a defense, defining such contact as a crime regardless of the victim's behavior. This strict liability standard means that the only matter to be adjudicated is whether the sexual contact occurred.

Some commentators believe that removing the defense of consent in effect portrays psychotherapy patients as incompetent "presumptive sillies" (23). If this were to occur, the status of patients would clearly be stigmatized. As a practical matter, in our experience victims are not concerned that they will be demeaned through the removal of the issue of consent. Obviously, competent adults are presumed capable of consent and the law is reluctant to remove this presumption. . . .

It is not that the victim cannot consent or that consent is improperly obtained—as through undue influence of transference or lack of information about risks. Consent is irrelevant. The issue is fiduciary breach and abuse of power in the therapeutic relationship. A fiduciary is in a position of special trust, analogous to that of a trustee, involving "a duty to act primarily for another's benefit" and requiring "scrupulous good faith and candor" (24). Trust and confidence are reposed in the therapist on the basis of a perception of social role. Even a sophisticated patient must place himself or herself in a vulnerable, less powerful position vis-a-vis a therapist who has more knowledge, training, and experience of the therapeutic process. It is the duty of the therapist as fiduciary to attend only to the needs of the patient and to do no harm. Sexual contact is countertherapeutic behavior that will harm patients. The consequences of such acts are so socially deleterious that they call for proscription regardless of consent. Attention should focus entirely on the therapist's behavior, not on that of the victim. . . .

False Accusations

For psychotherapists the possibility of having to defend themselves against false accusations of sexual misconduct is terrifying, and false accusations do occur (26). The criminal law, although it exposes the accused therapist to greater jeopardy, provides better protection against false accusations of sexual exploitation than the civil law. The standard of proof in a criminal trial is "beyond reasonable doubt," whereas in a civil trial a jury can find for the plaintiff on "the preponderance of the evidence." In an ambiguous situation a properly instructed criminal court jury should be less likely to enter a judgment against a therapist than a jury in a civil trial. In actuality the difficulty of proving a criminal case beyond reasonable doubt may make prosecutors hesitant to proceed. The vast majority of these cases involve alleged actions in an office in which only two people were present, and the evidence is limited to one person's word against another's. The narrow and specific definition of behavior in a criminal statute, which is necessary to avoid constitutional challenge of the statute on the basis of vagueness, means that a therapist may avoid criminal conviction for acts that could incur civil liability. The criminal law also offers more due process protection to the accused therapist than proceedings before licensure boards, which may allow testimony that would be excluded under strict rules of evidence and which may not be governed by a statute of limitations. . . .

References

1. Schoener, G., Milgrom, J., & Gonsiorek, J., et al. (1989). *Psychotherapists' sexual involvement with clients: Intervention and prevention*. Minneapolis, MN: Walk-In Counseling Center.

2. American Psychiatric Association. (1989). *The principles of medical ethics with annotations especially applicable to psychiatry*. Washington, DC: Author.

15. Pope, K., & Bouhoutsos, J. (1986). *Sexual intimacy between therapists and patients* (pp. 33–45). New York: Praeger.

17. Jorgenson, L., Randles, R., & Strasburger, L. H. (1991). The furor over psychotherapist–patient sexual contact: new solutions to an old problem. *William and Mary Law Review, 32*, 643–729.

18. Sanderson, B. (ed). (1989). *It's never OK: A handbook for professionals on sexual exploitation by counselors and therapists*. St. Paul: Minnesota Department of Corrections.

19. Strasburger, L., Jorgenson, L., & Randles, R. (1990). Mandatory reporting of sexually exploitative psychotherapists. *Bulletin of the American Academy of Psychiatry Law, 18*, 379–384.

20. Vigilant Insurance Co. v. Kambly, 114 Mich App 683, 319 N.W. 2d 382 (1982).

21. St. Paul Fire and Marine Insurance Co. v. Love, 447 N.W. 2d 5 (Minn Ct App 1989).

23. Leff, A. A. (1967). Unconcionability and the code—the emperor's new clause. *University of Pennsylvania Law Review,115*, 485–559.

24. Black, H. C. (1968). *Black's law dictionary* (4th ed., p. 753). St. Paul, MN: West Publishing.

26. Gutheil, T. G. (1989). Borderline personality disorder, boundary violations, and patient–therapist sex: medicolegal pitfalls. *American Journal of Psychiatry, 146*, 597–602.

Remediation for Ethics Violations: Focus on Psychotherapists' Sexual Contact With Clients

Melissa J. Layman and J. Regis McNamara

. . .

In addition to further ethics education and training, punitive actions, informal support options, and practice oversight, mandatory personal therapy has been suggested as an option for rehabilitation of impaired psychologists and ethics offenders (APA, 1992; Burton, 1973; V. Hedges, Ohio Board of Psychology, personal communication, May 1995; Laliotis & Grayson, 1985; Lamb et al., 1987; Pope, 1987; R. Reaves, ASPPB, personal communication, May 1995; Schoener & Gonsiorek, 1988) . . .

[T]here are several reasons against using mandated therapy for ethics violations. First, although personal therapy is highly valued by the field of psychology, psychologists do not appear to be willing to mandate participation for all therapists in training. Second, several problematic issues exist specifically for the therapist in therapy, which may hinder or even prevent the entry of the professional into a therapeutic setting. Third, there is little clear outcome literature suggesting that personal therapy will improve the psychologist or his or her work with clients, let alone remediate violations of ethics. Finally, variables associated with treatment of sex offenders (insofar as those variables are applicable to this population), such as denial and minimization of actions (Brodsky, 1986; Gabbard, 1995; Hanson et al., 1991; Schoener & Gonsiorek, 1988; Schwartz, 1992; Walzer & Miltimore, 1993), and with mandated psychotherapy seem likely to compromise the effectiveness of therapy in a variety of situations.

In addition to these reasons, the issue of viability for rehabilitation must be raised. In a recent survey, 87% of psychologists responded "absolutely yes" or "probably" to the question of whether licensing boards should "be able to require therapists (e.g., who have violated professional standards) to obtain therapy as a condition of their continuing or resuming practice" (Pope & Tabachnick, 1994, p. 254). However, only 34% responded similarly to the question of whether such an intervention would be effective (Pope & Tabachnick, 1994). . . .

Holroyd and Brodsky (1977) discussed the chronic nature of exploitative therapists' problems, stating that "therapists who disregard the sexual boundary once are likely to repeat" (p. 849); this statement appears to hold true today (Pope, 1994). This finding implies that the level of motivation for change in ethics violators is not likely to be sufficient for remediation through personal therapy. In fact, Pope (1994) stated that "It is difficult to find any published evidence . . . that shows any effectiveness of rehabilitation interventions" for sexually offending therapists (p. 43).

Gonsiorek and colleague (Gonsiorek, 1995; Schoener & Gonsiorek, 1988) indicated that success in intervention with ethics violators depends strongly on the type of deficit involved. Of the six categories of sexually exploitative therapists, these researchers described only one group as potentially remediable—the healthy or mildly neurotic therapist, who is often dealing with situational stresses, recognizes the impact of his or her behavior, and seeks help to end it. In further support of this categorization, several researchers have mentioned that the therapist who recognizes his or her problems and commits himself or herself to address them constructively has a good prognosis for change (Brodsky, 1986; Gabbard, 1995; Keith-Spiegel & Koocher, 1985; Vasquez, 1988). Walzer and Miltimore (1993) further noted that a specific emotional, mental, or situational difficulty leading to sexual offending may be handled through treatment; in these cases, one would expect to be able to prevent repeat offenses.

From *Professional Psychology: Research and Practice, 28,* 281–292. Copyright 1997 by the American Psychological Association.

The uninformed or naive therapist who commits ethics violations may be educated or trained further but may not have the ethical instincts or judgment to counsel even after this education (Schoener & Gonsiorek, 1988). Rehabilitation of the severely neurotic therapist may be possible, but it does not carry as good a prognosis because of denial or rationalization of the unethical behavior (Gabbard, 1995; Gonsiorek, 1995; Schoener & Gonsiorek, 1988). In terms of the other of the three categories of therapists—the character disordered—all the above authors stated that these are not candidates for rehabilitation because of their lack of concern over their behavior. Therefore, it seems that ethics violators who can be categorized by the majority of offender categories are not likely to benefit from mandated personal therapy. . . .

SUGGESTIONS FOR ALTERNATIVE METHODS OF REMEDIATION

If mandated personal therapy is not an appropriate treatment for ethics violators, what can be done in the way of remediation for these therapists? . . .

One general suggestion is to carefully identify, monitor, and intervene with therapists at risk for acting on sexual attraction, if possible (Pope, 1987; Schwebel et al., 1994). These therapists may be identified during training or later during their careers by personal characteristics or by the nature of clientele being served, although the chances of accomplishing this scientifically or ethically are low. Given the low base rate of sexual offending, identification on the basis of possible future offenses would be likely to involve a high number of false positives . . .

Preventative training specifically aimed at sexual misconduct seems to be a topic of current interest (Schwebel et al., 1994). Vasquez (1988) discussed a prevention program that would be implemented during training, where students would be sensitized to ethical issues surrounding sexuality and sexual contact. In this program, knowledge and self-awareness would be emphasized. Vasquez (1988) felt that "most problems . . . are amenable to amelioration in counselors-in-training" (p. 240); this may, in fact, be an excellent

time to identify potential offenders. Another important opportunity for identification of ethics violators is during the internship (Lamb et al., 1987). Lamb et al. indicated that the stresses and situation changes present in transition to full-time clinical practice, concurrent with extensive supervision, present a chance to observe, identify, and treat potential unethical behavior. . . .

Unfortunately, both Vasquez's and Lamb et al.'s approaches are limited in that a relatively small number of cases of therapist–client sexual contact occur during graduate training or internships. Variables commonly associated with the sexually exploitative therapist, such as burnout or depression, may not yet play a role in the training therapist's interactions with clients. Moreover, the low base rate of sexual offending makes it difficult to accurately identify future offenders.

Another intervention that may prove useful is educating clients about therapy boundaries (Gottlieb, Vasquez, Applebaum, & Jorgenson, 1993; Strasburger, Jorgenson, & Sutherland, 1992), for example, presenting a sexual misconduct brochure to clients before they enter therapy (Thorn, Shealy, & Briggs, 1993). This brochure would inform the client of the unethical nature of therapist sexual misbehavior as well as the right to file a complaint (Thorn et al., 1993). Given that many therapists have encountered a client who was sexually involved with a previous therapist (Pope, 1993; Stake & Oliver, 1991), a brochure of this type may be a useful resource to clients. In addition, the knowledge that a client is aware of sexual inappropriateness and potential legal action may act as an external source of control for the clinician's actions.

. . .

Callanan and O'Connor (1988, p. 11) concluded that "prospects for rehabilitation are minimal and it is doubtful that they [sexually exploitative therapists] should be given the opportunity to ever practice psychotherapy again" (cited in Pope, 1994), a provision echoed by Gabbard (1995) and Gonsiorek (1995), particularly when a character disorder is present. Given the need to protect the public, punitive disciplinary action may be the only current avenue for remediation for the character disordered violators of ethical principles until other interventions can be derived, implemented, and evaluated. Even for those not so deeply affected, the jury is still out on the extent to which remedial therapy or education can be of benefit. Only when well-done evaluation of remediation is undertaken can the jury return to render its verdict.

References

American Psychological Association. (1992). Rules and procedures. *American Psychologist, 47,* 1612–1628.

Brodsky, A. M. (1986). The distressed psychologist: Sexual intimacies and exploitation. In. R. R. Kilburg, P. E. Nathan, & R. W. Thoreson (Eds.), *Professionals in distress: Issues, syndromes, and solutions in psychology* (pp. 153–171). Washington, DC: American Psychological Association.

Burton, A. (1973). The psychotherapist as client. *American Journal of Psychoanalysis, 33,* 94–103.

Callanan, K., & O'Connor, T. (1988). *Staff comments and recommendations regarding the report of the Senate Task Force on Psychotherapist and Patients Sexual Relations.* Sacramento, CA: Board of the Behavioral Science Examiners and Psychology Examining Committee.

Gabbard, G. O. (1995). Psychotherapists who transgress sexual boundaries with patients. In J. C. Gonsiorek (Ed.), *Breach of trust: Sexual exploitation by health care professionals and clergy* (pp. 133–144). Thousand Oaks, CA: Sage.

Gonsiorek, J. C. (1995). Assessment for rehabilitation of exploitative health care professionals and clergy. In J. C. Gonsiorek (Ed.), *Breach of trust: Sexual exploitation by health care professionals and clergy* (pp. 145–162). Thousand Oaks, CA: Sage.

Gottlieb, M. C., Vasquez, M. J. T., Applebaum, P. S., & Jorgenson, L. (1993). Sexual contact between psychotherapists and clients. In J. A. Mindell (Ed.), *Issues in clinical psychology* (pp. 153–182). Dubuque, IA: Brown & Benchmark/Wm. C. Brown.

Hanson, R. K., Cox, B., & Woszcyna, C. (1991). Assessing treatment outcome for sexual offenders. *Annals of Sex Research, 4,* 177–208.

Holroyd, J., & Brodsky, A. (1977). Psychologists' attitudes and practices regarding erotic and non-erotic physical contact with patients. *American Psychologist, 32,* 843–849.

Keith-Spiegel, P., & Koocher, G. P. (1985). *Ethics in psychology: Professional standards and cases.* New York: Random House.

Laliotis, D. A., & Grayson, J. H. (1985). Psychologist heal thyself: What is available for the impaired psychologist? *American Psychologist, 40,* 84–96.

Lamb, D. H., Presser, N. R., Pfost, K. S., Baum, M. C., Jackson, V. R., & Jarvis, P. A. (1987). Confronting professional impairment during the internship: Identification, due process, and remediation. *Professional Psychology: Research and Practice, 18,* 597–603.

Pope, K. S. (1987). Preventing therapist–patient sexual intimacy: Therapy for a therapist at risk. *Professional Psychology: Research and Practice, 18,* 624–628.

Pope, K. S. (1993). Licensing disciplinary actions for psychologists who have been sexually involved with a client. Some information about offenders. *Professional Psychology: Research and Practice, 24,* 374–377.

Pope, K. S. (1994). *Sexual involvement with therapists: Patient assessment, subsequent therapy, forensics.* Washington, DC: American Psychological Association.

Pope, K. S., & Tabachnick, B. G. (1994). Therapists as patients: A national survey of psychologists' experiences, problems, and beliefs. *Professional Psychology: Research and Practice, 25,* 247–258.

Schoener, G. R., & Gonsiorek, J. (1988). Assessment and development of rehabilitation plans for counselors who have sexually exploited their clients. *Journal of Counseling and Development, 67,* 227–232.

Schwartz, B. K. (1992). Effective treatment techniques for sex offenders. *Psychiatric Annals, 22,* 315–319.

Schwebel, M., Skorina, J. K., & Schoener, G. (1994). *Assisting impaired psychologists (Rev. ed.): Program development for state psychological associations.* Washington, DC: American Psychological Association.

Stake, J. E., & Oliver, J. (1991). Sexual contact and touching between therapist and client: A survey of psychologists' attitudes and behavior. *Professional Psychology: Research and Practice, 22,* 297–307.

Strasburger, L. H., Jorgenson, L., & Sutherland, P. (1992). The prevention of psychotherapist at sexual misconduct: Avoiding the slippery slope. *American Journal of Psychotherapy, 46,* 544–555.

Thorn, B. E., Shealy, R. C., & Briggs, S. D. (1993). Sexual misconduct in psychotherapy: Reactions to a consumer-oriented brochure. *Professional Psychology: Research and Practice, 24,* 75–82.

Vasquez, M. J. T. (1988). Counselor–client sexual contact: Implications for ethics training. *Journal of Counseling and Development, 67,* 238–241.

Walzer, R. S., & Miltimore, S. (1993). Mandated supervision, monitoring, and therapy of disciplined health care professionals. *The Journal of Legal Medicine, 14,* 565–596.

♦ ♦ ♦

Commentary: Layman and McNamara's (1997) views did not go unchallenged. For example, Gonsiorek (1997) charged that the authors engaged

> . . . *in a puzzling argument: Since the effectiveness of therapy with therapists is not clearly demonstrated one way or the other, it should be viewed as likely ineffective, despite the fact that the literature on therapy outcomes is generally seen as positive. It seems to me that one would need compelling data, not insufficient data, to suggest that therapists, distinct from the general population, are such a suspect class regarding therapy outcome. I have no disagreement that therapy outcome with therapists is insufficiently researched to draw firm conclusions. I believe, however, that in this situation, the best estimate is that we psychologists are probably most akin to other groups studied. (p. 300)*

Gonsiorek, C. J. (1997). Suggested remediations to "Remediation." Professional Psychology: Research and Practice, 28, 300–303.

Brown (1997) thought that the arguments for or against remediation of the offending therapist neglected a more fundamental issue:

> *In my clinical and forensic experience with the victims of offending psychotherapists, I have had ample opportunity to observe that, even when the professional has fulfilled all of the requirements of the regulatory agency, has gone into treatment, has gotten supervision, has attended ethics classes, has paid fines, and has lost privileges, the primary and secondary victims are left in a continuing state of distress. Boundary violations in professional psychology occur in the context of relationships between therapists and clients; rehabilitation plans routinely ignore the relationship. Remediation cannot be considered to have occurred if those who we are attempting to heal from the ravages of a boundary violation have never had*

> *amends made to them in ways that are meaningful to them; nor will remediation happen if the system in which the boundary violation took place is allowed to continue on as before, creating future risks. (p. 297)*

> . . .

> *It is extremely common for a direct victim of an offending therapist to state that she simply wishes to have the therapist apologize directly, in person, and with no excuses; to listen to the client's expressions of pain, anger, and betrayal; and to affirm that she, the victim, had no hand in causing the boundary violation. In other words, what is desired is the clear and unequivocal shouldering of personal responsibility by the professional who has done harm. Fines, loss of a therapist's license, and other more usual punishments are frequently quite secondary considerations (aside from the desire for funding of the victim's own future psychotherapy). Yet psychology's regulatory boards and ethics committees persist in imposing the latter and not the former as penalties for gross violations of ethical standards. (p. 298)*

> . . .

> *I believe that as long as we psychologists do not transform our models of remediation to become paradigms of genuine amends, we engage in a massive case of collective denial about solutions to the problem of serious boundary violations. (p. 299)*

Brown, L. S. (1997). Remediation, amends, or denial? Professional Psychology: Research and Practice, 28, 297–299.

The reader may wish to see Layman and McNamara's (1997) rejoinder to the critiques of their original article by Gonsiorek and Brown: Layman, M. J., & McNamara, J. R. (1997). Remediation revisited. Professional Psychology: Research and Practice, 28, 304–305.

What is your opinion with regard to psychology's response to its members who violate ethical boundaries with clients, students, and trainees? Should these members be treated as criminal perpetrators, as impaired professionals needing treatment, or as requiring remedial ethics training? If they are expelled from APA or delicensed, how will their future conduct be monitored? On the other hand, can the profession afford to have them remain? Perhaps any sanctions are premature at this time. But is it more true that psychology should recognize that the profession "really does not know much at all about boundary violations or violators, that the time for solutions can only come after we have obtained more understanding [and that] it is time for investigation, not for impulsive solutions" (Orr, p. 294)?

Orr, P. (1997). Psychology impaired? Professional Psychology: Research and Practice, 28, 293–296.

CHAPTER 6

PSYCHOLOGICAL ASSESSMENT

Assessment, particularly testing, permeates every facet of people's lives. Almost every subset of psychologists uses tests. Researchers use tests to acquire data from those who participate in their studies. Clinical psychologists administer tests for diagnostic purposes and to monitor the course of psychotherapy. School psychologists assess children to determine their eligibility for possible placement in special education programs. Counseling psychologists use vocational, occupational, and interest tests to guide career development and measure problem-solving skills throughout the life span. Forensic psychologists use tests to help courts determine the best placement for children whose parents are divorcing or to assess whether a criminal defendant is competent to stand trial or should be held responsible for an otherwise criminal act. Industrial and organizational psychologists measure skills and job knowledge of those seeking employment or promotion. And, of course, academics often devise their own instruments to assess what their undergraduate and graduate students have learned.

As the nonexhaustive list above illustrates, assessment can take many forms. Each form may have its own ethical implications. For example, when clinicians use intelligence scales, paper-and-pencil personality tests, or projective techniques, issues of privacy and informed consent arise. When psychologists in employment settings use tests, issues of dual loyalties arise: For whom is the psychologist working and to whom does the psychologist owe the primary obligation of fidelity—the test taker or the employer? When school psychologists assess children for special education placement, who is the client—the child, the parent, or the school system that is paying the evaluator? When a researcher gathers data through tests, questions of informed consent and deception become important (see chap. 8, this volume). When forensic clinicians evaluate a criminal defendant, are they working on behalf of the prosecution, the defense, or the court (see chap. 9, this volume)? And regardless of the assessor's role, the issue of competence becomes pervasive. Are the tests that are used psychometrically sound, and are the interpretations and judgments that psychologists make from the data valid? Finally, the advent of computerized testing in general and the increased use of so-called honesty or integrity tests in employment in particular open such discussions to a whole new set of issues.

This chapter can only provide an introduction to the complex ethical issues inherent to gathering, storing, interpreting, and disseminating information about test takers that is gleaned from assessment. Such technical issues as validity, reliability, norming, and standardization are addressed here only if they are relevant to ethical and social issues. To gain a broader perspective on both technical and social policy questions, see the two special issues of the *American Psychologist* devoted to testing and edited by Amrine (1965) and by Glaser and Bond (1981). In addition, the National Academy of Sciences has produced two major works evaluating standardized tests in general (Heller, Holtzman, & Messick, 1982; Wigdor & Garner, 1982).

The ethical problems raised in this chapter cannot be fully understood if they are examined outside of their historical, social, and legal contexts. Thus, I urge readers to also examine such classical articles as Cronbach's (1975) and Haney's (1981). For recent reviews of some of the more controversial issues, see Elliot's (1987) book and Helms's (1992) article. I, too, have contributed to the legal literature on this topic (Bersoff, 1979, 1981, 1982, 1984).

There is one significant topic in this chapter that has not appeared in prior editions. In June 2005, APA issued its Report of the Presidential Task Force on Psychological Ethics and National Security (PENS Report, 2005), exploring the ethical aspects of psychologists involved in military interrogations. The report aroused considerable critical comment as well as stout defense. Although this controversial topic does not fit neatly in any particular category, I have placed it in this chapter because one can view interrogations as a form of assessment. In any event, I believe it deserves extensive discussion.

References

American Psychological Association. (2005). *Report of the American Psychological Association Presidential Task Force on Psychological Ethics and National Security (PENS)*. Retrieved from http://www.apa.org/releases/PENSTaskForceReportFinal.pdf

Amrine, M. (Ed.). (1965). Testing and public policy [Special issue]. *American Psychologist, 20*(11).

Bersoff, D. N. (1979). Regarding psychologists testily: Legal constraints on psychological testing in the public schools. *Maryland Law Review, 39*, 27–120.

Bersoff, D. N. (1981). Testing and the law. *American Psychologist, 36*, 1047–1056.

Bersoff, D. N. (1982). Larry P. and PASE: Judicial report cards on the validity of individual intelligence scales. In T. Kratochwill (Ed.), *Advances in school psychology* (Vol. 2, pp. 61–95). Hillsdale, NJ: Erlbaum.

Bersoff, D. N. (1984). Social and legal influences on test development and usage. In B. Plake (Ed.), *Social and technical issues in testing* (pp. 87–109). Hillsdale, NJ: Erlbaum.

Cronbach, L. J. (1975). Five decades of public controversy over mental testing. *American Psychologist, 30*, 1–14.

Elliot, R. (1987). *Litigating intelligence: IQ tests, special education, and social science in the courtroom.* Dover, MA: Auburn House.

Glaser, R., & Bond, L. (Eds.). (1981). Testing: Concepts, policy, practice, and research [Special issue]. *American Psychologist, 36* (10).

Haney, W. (1981). Validity, vaudeville, and values: A short history of social concerns over standardized testing. *American Psychologist, 36*, 1021–1034.

Heller, K., Holtzman, W., & Messick, S. (Eds.). (1982). *Placing children in special education: A strategy for equity.* Washington, DC: National Academies Press.

Helms, J. (1992). Why is there no study of cultural equivalence in standardized *cognitive* ability testing? *American Psychologist, 47*, 1083–1101.

Wigdor, A. K., & Garner, W. R. (Eds.). (1982). *Ability testing: Uses, consequences, and controversies* (Vols. 1 & 2). Washington, DC: National Academies Press.

Test Validity and the Ethics of Assessment

Samuel Messick

Fifteen years ago or so, in papers dealing with personality measurement and the ethics of assessment, I drew a straightforward but deceptively simple distinction between the psychometric adequacy of a test and the appropriateness of its use (Messick, 1964, 1965). I argued that not only should tests be evaluated in terms of their measurement properties but that testing applications should be evaluated in terms of their potential social consequences. I urged that two questions be explicitly addressed whenever a test is proposed for a specific purpose: First, is the test any good as a measure of the characteristics it is interpreted to assess? Second, should the test be used for the proposed purpose in the proposed way? The first question is a scientific and technical one and may be answered by appraising evidence for the test's psychometric properties, especially construct validity. The second question is an ethical one, and its answer requires a justification of the proposed use in terms of social values. Good answers to the first question are not satisfactory answers to the second. Justification of test use by an appeal to empirical validity is not enough; the potential social consequences of the testing should also be appraised, not only in terms of what it might entail directly as costs and benefits but also in terms of what it makes more likely as possible side effects.

. . .

. . . Values thus appear to be as pervasive and critical for psychological and educational measurement as is testing's acknowledged touchstone, validity. Indeed, "The root remaining of the word 'validity' is the same as that of the word 'value': both derive from a term meaning strength" (Kaplan, 1964, p. 198). . . .

VALIDITY AS EVALUATION OF IMPLICATIONS

. . .

If test validity is the overall degree of justification for test interpretation and use, and if human and social values encroach on both interpretation and use, as they do, then test validity should take account of those value implications in the overall judgment. . . . If, as an intrinsic part of the overall validation process, we weigh the actual and potential consequences of our testing practices in light of considerations of what future society might need or desire, then test validity comes to be based on ethical as well as evidential grounds. . . .

References

Kaplan, A. (1964). *The conduct of inquiry: Methodology for behavioral science.* San Francisco: Chandler.

Messick, S. (1964). Personality measurement and college performance. *Proceedings of the 1963 Invitational Conference on Testing Problems.* Princeton, NJ: Educational Testing Service.

Messick, S. (1965). Personality measurement and the ethics of assessment. *American Psychologist, 20,* 136–142.

♦   ♦   ♦

Commentary: In 1995, the late Dr. Messick reiterated that validity should be considered a unitary concept rather than be fragmented into the traditional tripartite categories of criterion, content, and construct validity. More relevant for our purposes, he asserted that validity is a social as well as a measurement value: "[I]t is fundamental that score validation is an empirical evaluation of the meaning and consequences of measurement" (p. 742). "The consequential aspect," he said, "appraises the value implications of score interpretation as a basis for action as well as the actual and potential consequences

From *American Psychologist, 35,* 1012–1027. Copyright 1980 by the American Psychological Association. Figures 1 and 2 have been omitted.

of test use" (p. 745) particularly with regard to issues of bias and fairness. Thus, he concluded, "validity and values are one imperative, not two, and test validation implicates both the science and the ethics of assessment, which is why validity has force as a social value" (p. 749). See Messick, S. (1995). Validity of psychological assessment: Validation of inferences from persons' responses and performances as scientific inquiry into score meaning. American Psychologist, 50, 741–749.

Do you think his argument has merit or does considering the consequences of testing as part of validity overburden "an already overburdened concept" (Zimiles, 1996, p. 981) and create "a dangerous intrusion of politics into science" (Lees-Haley, 1996, p. 982)? For the complete responses to Messick's provocative article, see:

Lees-Haley, P. R. (1996). Alice in Validityland, or the dangerous consequences of consequential validity. American Psychologist, 51, 981–983.

Zimiles, H. (1996). Rethinking the validity of psychological assessment. American Psychologist, 51, 980–981.

According to Malgady (1996), "it is estimated that about 40% of the clients in the mental health services system will be members of ethnic minority groups in the year 2000" (p. 73). See Malgady, R. G. (1996). The question of cultural bias in assessment and diagnosis of ethnic minority clients: Let's reject the null hypothesis. Professional Psychology: Research and Practice, 27, 73–77. *Malgady also states that it is imperative that those psychologists providing assessment services understand both the technical and social issues concerning testing.*

The issue of test fairness is so important that the current version of the Test Standards contains four chapters on the issue. See AERA, APA, & NCME. (1999). Standards for educational and psychological testing. *Washington, DC: AERA (Chapters 7–10). In fact, any psychologist involved in the development, administration, scoring, interpretation, or publication of tests should read the* Standards *thoroughly, but particularly the chapters and standards on validity and reliability. As Weiner (1989) stated,*

> *Although it is . . . possible in psychodiagnostic work to be competent without being ethical, it is not possible to be ethical without being competent. Competence is a prerequisite for ethicality, and psychologists who practice or teach psychodiagnosis without being fully informed concerning*

> *what tests can and cannot do are behaving unethically. . . . (p. 830)*

Weiner, I. (1989). On competence and ethicality in psychodiagnostic assessment. Journal of Personality Assessment, 53, 827–831.

The test standards were "formulated with the intent of being consistent with" (p. viii) the then-current (1992) APA Ethics Code. In critiquing the 1992 APA Ethics Code with regard to testing ethnic minority clients, the reviewer concluded:

> *[I]n my judgment, the 1992 code requires supplementation with guidelines for assessment practice with each visible racial and ethnic group. . . . Noncompliance with or violations of the new code can be responded to with educational and remedial efforts to enhance an understanding of the complex nature of ethical dilemmas stemming from diverse belief systems and expectations. (p.353)*

Dana, R. (1994). Testing and assessment ethics for all persons: Beginning and agenda. Professional Psychology: Research and Practice, 25, 349–354.

Review the current Code, particularly General Principles D and E, and Standards 3.01, 9.02(b), and 9.05, and decide whether the 2002 version addresses issues of assessment of ethnic minorities in a more complete and sounder way than the 1992 Code Dana criticized.

Because assessment may infringe on the test taker's sense of privacy and because it has such serious consequences for both society and the individual, there have been constant calls for either its abolition or its strict regulation. But as Messick warned 30 years ago,

> *absolute rules forbidding the use of . . . tests . . . would be an intolerable limitation both to scientific freedom and to professional freedom. . . . [I]n our consideration of possible ethical bases for self-regulation in assessment, it seems imperative that we go beyond ethical absolutism . . . and espouse an "ethics of responsibility" in which pragmatic evaluations of the consequences of alternative actions form the*

*basis for particular ethical decisions. . . .
In this sense, then, we need continual
assessments of ethics as the basis for an
ethics of assessment. (p. 140)*

Messick, S. (1965). Personality measurement and the
ethics of assessment. American Psychologist, 20,
136–142.

*As you read the next group of materials, consider
whether there has been too much self-regulation by the
profession and too much intrusive involvement in
assessment by the federal government and the courts.
On the other hand, given the enormous social consequences of testing, has the plethora of professional and
legal regulation in the past 30 years been insufficient
to deal with the problems?*

The Legal Regulation of School Psychology

Donald N. Bersoff and Paul T. Hofer

TESTING AND EVALUATION

Nondiscriminatory Assessment

While every person in the United States probably has been affected in some way by tests, schoolchildren are its most frequent targets. . . . Undoubtedly, test results have been used to admit, advance, and employ, but for the majority of persons scores derived from psychometric instruments serve as exclusionary devices—to segregate, institutionalize, track, and deny access to desired goals. . . .

While criticism of testing by social, political, and psychological commentators arose within the test industry itself, the legal system seriously began to examine the issue of nondiscriminatory assessment only since the mid-1960s. In part, judicial interest in testing may be explained by the Supreme Court's mandate in *Brown v. Board of Education* (1954) that the public schools must be desegregated. Civil rights advocates view educational and psychological tests as tools to hinder integration and, more broadly, as discriminatory instruments, denying the full realization of the constitutional rights of racial and ethnic minorities. As a result, from the mid-1960s to the 1980s there was an explosion of litigation and legislation affecting the administration, interpretation, and use of psychological tests. . . .

. . . In 1975 Congress passed P.L. 94-142 (20 U.S.C. §§ 1401–1461), the Education for All Handicapped Children Act (EAHCA). Two years earlier it had enacted § 504 of the Rehabilitation Act of 1973 (29 U.S.C. § 794). Implementing regulations for the EAHCA were drafted by the Department of Health, Education, and Welfare (now the Department of Education) and for § 504 by what is now the Department of Health and Human Services, both of which took effect in 1977.

P.L. 94-142 is essentially a grant-giving statute providing financial support to state and local education agencies for special education and related services if they meet certain detailed eligibility requirements. P.L. 94-142 and its implementing regulations reaffirmed earlier mandates concerning nondiscriminatory evaluation and fleshed out the meaning of this requirement. Section 300.532 of the regulations states:

(a) Tests and other evaluation materials:

(1) Are provided and administered in the child's native language or other mode of communication . . .

(2) Have been validated for the specific purpose for which they are used; and

(3) Are administered by trained personnel in conformance with the instructions provided by their producer. . . .

Other provisions also affect psychological and educational assessment. Children with sensory, manual, or speaking impairments are to be given tests that reflect genuine deficits in aptitude or achievement, not those impairments. Further, all assessment is to be comprehensive, multifaceted, and multidisciplinary. Evaluations for placement must be conducted by persons from education, medicine, and psychology who assess children "in all areas related to the suspected disability, including where appropriate, health, vision, hearing, social and emotional status, general intelligence, academic performance, communicative status, and motor abilities." Tests cannot be used which are "merely . . . designed to provide a single general intelligence quotient" nor can one single procedure be "used as the sole criterion for determining an appropriate educational program for a child." In making placement decisions the school is required to "draw upon information from a variety of sources, including aptitude and achievement tests, teacher recommendations, physical condition, social and cultural background and adaptive behavior." Thus, P.L. 94-142 makes it quite clear that assessment and placement decisions are the responsibility not of a school psychologist acting alone, but of a multidisciplinary team. The apparent reasons behind this diffusion of duty are to reduce individual bias and broaden accountability.

To ensure that all these provisions are effectuated, both the statute and the regulations provide mechanisms enabling parents "to present complaints with respect to any matter relating to the identification, evaluation, or educational placement" of their children. The complaints are presented in an impartial administrative hearing in which parents have the right to compel the attendance of, and to cross-examine, witnesses involved in the assessment and programming decisions. The consequence is that psychologists are vulnerable to intense scrutiny of their credentials and performance, including the reliability and validity of the evaluation measures they employ, the interpretations they make from the information gathered, or the recommendations they offer as a result of their evaluation. . . .

With regard to the Rehabilitation Act, a multi-purpose law to promote the education, employment, and training of handicapped persons, Congress declared in § 504 that "no otherwise qualified handicapped individual in the United States . . . shall, solely by reason of his handicap, be excluded from participation in, be denied the benefits of, or be subjected to discrimination under any program or activity receiving federal financial assistance." This section thus represents the first federal civil rights law protecting the rights of handicapped persons and reflects a national commitment to end discrimination on the basis of handicap. Unlike P.L. 94-142, the requirements of § 504 are not triggered by receipt of funds under institutions receiving federal financial assistance. Thus, any school system, public or private, receiving federal monies for any program or activity whatsoever is bound by its mandates.

The regulations implementing the broad right-granting language of § 504 were published in 1977. In addition to general principles already established under P.L. 94-142, it sets forth regulations pertaining to the evaluation of children suspected of being handicapped. The language of those provisions, requiring preplacement evaluations, validated tests, multidisciplinary comprehensive assessment, and periodic reevaluations, are almost identical to that which now appears in the implementing regulations to P.L. 94-142. . . .

◆　　◆　　◆

Commentary: The Education for All Handicapped Children Act was renamed the Individuals With Disabilities Education Act (IDEA). The Rehabilitation Act of 1973 is applicable to employment settings as well as to schools. Section 84.13 of the act's implementing regulations prohibits the use of employment tests that screen out applicants who are disabled, unless the test is job related and there are no alternative selection devices available that do not screen out such applicants. Even more broadly applicable to employers is the Americans With Disabilities Act (ADA). The ADA covers all employers engaged in interstate commerce that have 15 or more employees, even if these employers receive no federal financial assistance. Like the Rehabilitation Act, it prohibits the use of employment tests with an adverse impact on people who are disabled unless the tests are job related and are consistent with business necessity. On July 26, 1991, the Equal Employment Opportunity Commission published detailed regulations implementing the ADA. See the Federal Register, 56, 35726–35753, 1991. The ADA also restricts the use of medical examinations prior to a contingent offer of employment. The question arises whether psychological testing is defined as "medical" under the Act. The EEOC, rejecting most of the APA's recommendations on the issue, published guidelines stating its interpretation of the regulations. See Equal Employment Opportunity Commission. (1994, May). Enforcement guidance: Preemployment disability-related inquiries and medical examinations under the Americans With Disabilities Act of 1990 (EEOC Notice, 915.002). *Washington, DC: Author; Equal Employment Opportunity Commission. (1995, October). ADA enforcement guidance: Preemployment disability-related* questions and medical examinations. *Washington, DC: Author.*

Novick provided a useful history and summary of existing laws, regulations, and guidelines promulgated by the federal government concerning testing. See Novick, M. R. (1981). Federal guidelines and professional standards. American Psychologist, 36, *1035–1046. The most detailed and relevant of these documents is the Uniform Guidelines on Employee Selection Procedures, published in the 1978* Federal Register *(Vol. 43, pp. 38290–38315), and a series of questions and answers designed to clarify and interpret the Uniform Guidelines, published in the 1979* Federal Register *(Vol. 44, pp. 11996–12009).*

For a relatively up-to-date discussion of how the law has affected assessment in educational settings, see Reschly, D., & Bersoff, D. N. (1999). Law and school psychology. In C. Reynolds & T. Gutkin (Eds.), The handbook of school psychology *(3rd ed., pp. 1077–1112). New York: Wiley. See also Jacob-Timm, S., & Hartshorne, T. (1998).* Ethics and law for school psychologists. *New York: Wiley.*

A recent helpful article connects the requirements of IDEA and ADA to the 2002 Ethics Code:

> *In accordance with the new language in Standards 9.02a and 9.02b, selection of test instruments should be limited to those that have established reliability and validity for use with members of the population being tested. If there is no instrument available that is psychometrically appropriate for the child who is being evalu-*

ated, that needs to be explained, as do the adaptations made to standard procedures and the consequent limitations of the data obtained. Standard 9.02c requires that the child's language competence and proficiency be taken into account when selecting assessment tools. Standard 9.06 now requires psychologists to give careful consideration to "situational, personal linguistic, and cultural differences" in the interpretation of assessment results. . . . Thus, the ethical requirement of nonbiased assessment is stated more clearly in the 2002 code; however, it continues to be difficult for practitioners to translate this complex requirement into practice. (p. 438)

Flanagan, R., Miller, J. A., & Jacob, S. (2005). The 2002 revision of the American Psychological Association's ethics code: Implications for school psychologists. Psychology in the Schools, 42, *433–445.*

In addition to test fairness issues, APA has long been concerned about test misuse, particularly by those who may not have the requisite psychometric sophistication to administer and interpret assessment devices appropriately. Formal attention has been paid to this issue since 1981, when APA formed the Test User Qualifications Working Group. The most comprehensive and recent set of guidelines for the use of psychological tests was developed by the Task Force on Test User Qualifications (TFTUQ). Organized in 1996, it published its recommendations in 2001. A lengthy excerpt from that document appears next.

APA's Guidelines for Test User Qualifications: An Executive Summary

Samuel M. Turner, Stephen T. DeMers, Heather Roberts Fox, and Geoffrey M. Reed

. . .

The Task Force on Test User Qualifications (TFTUQ) was established in part because of evidence that some current users of psychological tests may not possess the knowledge and skill that the APA considers desirable for optimal test use (see, e.g., Aiken, West, Sechrest, & Reno, 1990). The phrase *test user qualifications* refers to the combination of knowledge, skills, abilities, training, experience, and, where appropriate, practice credentials that the APA considers desirable for the responsible use of psychological tests. The guidelines in the TFTUQ's report are intended to apply to persons who use psychological tests in a variety of settings and for diverse purposes. The APA's purpose in developing these guidelines is to inform test users as well as individuals involved with training programs, regulatory and credentialing bodies, and the public about the qualifications that promote high professional standards in the use of tests with the public.

. . .

SCOPE OF THE GUIDELINES

. . .

These guidelines describe two types of test user qualifications: (a) generic psychometric knowledge and skills that serve as a basis for most of the typical uses of tests and (b) specific qualifications for the responsible use of tests in particular settings or for specific purposes (e.g., health care settings or forensic or educational decision making). The guidelines apply most directly to standardized tests, such as tests of ability, aptitude, achievement, attitudes, interests, personality, cognitive functioning, and mental health. The guidelines define a psychological test as any measurement procedure for assessing psychological characteristics in which a sample of an examinee's behavior is obtained and subsequently evaluated and scored using a standardized process. The guidelines do not apply to unstandardized questionnaires and unstructured behavior samples or to teacher- or trainer-made tests used to evaluate performance in education or training.

. . .

GENERIC KNOWLEDGE AND SKILLS

The TFTUQ began by conceptually dividing those skills and knowledge considered important for good test use into two main categories: first, core knowledge and skills and, second, context-related qualifications. The core knowledge and skills discussed in this section are deemed essential for all test users who make decisions or formulate policies that directly affect the lives of test takers. This core set of knowledge and skills is considered to be relevant for all test users; however, the level of skill and depth of knowledge in these domains may vary depending on the testing purpose and context.

Psychometric and Measurement Knowledge

In general, it is important for test users to understand classical test theory and, when appropriate or necessary, item response theory (IRT). When test users are making assessments on the basis of IRT, such as adaptive testing, they should be familiar with the concepts of item parameters (e.g., item difficulty, item discrimination, and guessing), item and test information functions, and ability parameters (e.g., theta).

Descriptive statistics. Basic to any test use is the ability to define, apply, and interpret concepts of descriptive statistics. . . . Persons using tests should have sufficient knowledge and understanding of descriptive statistics to select and use appropriate test instruments, as well as to score and interpret results. The most common descriptive statistics relevant to test use include frequency distributions, descriptive statistics characterizing the normal curve (e.g., kurtosis, skewness), measures of central tendency (e.g., mean, median, and mode), measures of variation (e.g., variance and standard deviation), indices of relationship (e.g., correlation coefficient), and scales, scores, and transformations.

Test results frequently represent information about individuals' characteristics, skills, abilities, and attitudes in numeric form. Test users should understand issues related to scaling, types of scores, and methods of score transformation. For example, test users should understand and know when to apply the various methods for representing test information (e.g., raw scores, standard scores, and percentiles). Relevant concepts include types of scales, types of scores (e.g., raw, transformed, percentile, standard, normalized), scale score equating, and cut scores.

Reliability and measurement error. Test users should understand issues of test score reliability and measurement error as they apply to the specific test being used, as well as other factors that may influence test results, and the appropriate interpretation and application of different measures of reliability (e.g., internal consistency, test–retest reliability, interrater reliability, and parallel forms reliability). Similarly, test users should understand the standard error of measurement, which presents a numerical estimate of the range of scores consistent with the individual's level of performance.

Validity and meaning of test scores. The interpretation and uses of test scores, not the test itself, are evaluated for validity. Responsibility for validation belongs both to the test developer, who provides evidence in support of test use for a particular purpose, and to the test user, who ultimately evaluates that evidence, other available data, and information gathered during the testing process to support interpretation of test scores. Test users have a particularly important role in evaluating validity evidence when

the test is used for purposes different from those investigated by the test developer.

Contemporary discussions of validity have focused on evidence that supports the test as a measure of a construct (sometimes called *construct validity*). For example, evidence for the uses and interpretation of test scores may come through evaluation of the test content (content representativeness), through evidence of predictions of relevant outcomes (criterion-related validity), or from a number of other sources of evidence. . . .

Normative interpretation of test scores. Norms describe the distribution of test scores in a sample from a particular population. Test users should understand how differences between the test taker and the particular normative group affect the interpretation of test scores. Issues to be considered include the types of norms and their relevance for interpreting test taker scores, characteristics of the normative group, type of score referent (e.g., domain referenced, self-referenced), and expectancy tables.

Selection of appropriate test(s). Test users should select the best test or test version for a specific purpose and should have knowledge of testing practice in the context area and of the most appropriate norms when more than one normative set is available. Knowledge of test characteristics such as psychometric properties (presented above), basis in theory and research, and normative data (where appropriate) should influence test selection. For example, normative data or decision rules may not be accurate when (a) important characteristics of the examinee are not represented in the norm group, (b) administration or scoring procedures do not follow those used in standardizing the test, (c) characteristics of the test may affect its utility for the situation (e.g., ceiling and floor effects), (d) the test contains tasks that are not culturally relevant to the test taker, or (e) the validity evidence does not support decisions made on the basis of the test scores.

. . . [F]or test users to select an appropriate test for a particular use, it is important that they understand and consider such issues as the intended use of the test score, the method and procedures used to develop or revise the test being considered, the definition of the construct that the test purports to measure, and the definition of the test purpose and its intended context of use.

Test administration procedures. Knowledge about procedural requirements, confidentiality of test information, communication of results, and test security is important for many testing applications, as is familiarity with standardized administration and scoring procedures and understanding a test user's ethical and legal responsibilities and the legal rights of test takers. Similarly, it is important that test users understand the legal and ethical issues related to the release of test materials, including issues of confidentiality, depending on the context of the testing and the characteristics of the test taker. Test users should be able to explain test results and test limitations to diverse audiences. Written communication should include the purpose of the test and the setting in which the testing occurred. In preparing written reports on test results, test users should be aware that test scores might become separated from the interpretive report over time. . . .

Ethnic, Racial, Cultural, Gender, Age, and Linguistic Variables

Consideration of these variables may be important to the proper selection and use of psychological tests. For certain purposes, legal requirements influence or restrict the testing, scoring, interpretation, analysis, and use of test data of individuals in different subgroups. In some cases (e.g., employment testing), the use of gender, race, and ethnicity in test interpretation is illegal. Test users should consider and, where appropriate, obtain legal advice on legal and regulatory requirements to use test information in a manner consistent with legal and regulatory standards. Issues associated with testing individuals from particular subgroups, such as race or ethnicity, culture, language, gender, age, or other classifications, are addressed in greater detail in the 1999 version of the *Standards for Educational and Psychological Testing* (AERA, APA, & NCME, 1999).

. . .

Testing Individuals With Disabilities

Tests are administered to increasing numbers of persons with disabilities in a variety of settings and for a multitude of purposes. The requirement to accommodate an individual with a disability in the testing situation raises many complex issues for test users. Test users must frequently make decisions regarding the use of tests that were not developed and normed for individuals with disabilities. In such circumstances, confidence in the inferences drawn from test results may be diminished. There may be legal requirements concerning the accommodation of individuals with disabilities in test administration and the use of modified tests. Test users should consider and, where appropriate, obtain legal advice on legal and regulatory requirements regarding appropriate administration of tests and use of test data when assessing individuals with disabilities.

Test users should be familiar with several efforts initiated during the 1990s to provide guidance to test users for assessing individuals with disabilities. The APA Task Force on Test Interpretation and Diversity published a book identifying the scientific and policy issues related to the interpretation of tests used with individuals for whom the tests were not developed, standardized, and validated (Sandoval, Frisby, Geisinger, Scheuneman, & Grenier, 1998). . . . Finally, the 1999 *Standards for Educational and Psychological Testing* (AERA, APA, & NCME, 1999) includes a chapter on technical considerations for testing individuals with disabilities. Those who administer tests to individuals with disabilities should be familiar with the legal, technical, and professional issues governing the use of tests with individuals with disabilities. . . .

Supervised Experience

In addition to test users having knowledge and skills needed for appropriate test use, it is important that they have the opportunity to develop and practice their skills under the supervision of appropriately experienced professionals. . . .

. . .

A LOOK FORWARD

The psychological testing process has undergone significant technological change over the past few decades. The use of computers to administer tests and to score and interpret test results is already an important part of everyday testing. Emerging technologies of the Internet and other innovations that expand applications across vast distances may significantly alter the relationship of the test user, the test taker, and the consumer of testing results.

Some of the positive changes resulting from these new technologies include wider availability, greater accuracy, and increased accessibility of tests. Continuing improvements in the development of interpretive algorithms and expert systems are leading to diminishing concurrent human oversight of the testing process. This technology will simplify some aspects of the assessment process. As the application of new technology to the testing arena produces improved but more complex testing services, it may become necessary for the knowledge and skills articulated in this article to be supplemented with increased technological sophistication. Ironically, this increased complexity may mandate more extensive education and training in the fundamentals of test use. The knowledge and skills articulated here will become even more important as test users are required to distinguish technology-based style from science-based substance.

References

Aiken, L. S., West S. G., Sechrest, L., & Reno, R. R. (1990). Graduate training in statistics, methodology, and measurement in psychology: A survey of PhD programs in North America. *American Psychologist, 45*, 725–734.

American Educational Research Association, American Psychological Association, & National Council on Measurement in Education. (1999). *Standards for educational and psychological testing.* Washington, DC: American Psychological Association.

Sandoval, J., Friby, C. L., Geisinger, K. F., Scheuneman, J. D., & Grenier, J. R. (Eds.). (1998). *Test interpretation and diversity: Achieving equity in assessment.* Washington, DC: American Psychological Association.

♦   ♦   ♦

Commentary: TFTUQ's report also includes specific guidelines for test use in employment, educational, career and vocational counseling, healthcare, and forensic contexts. Readers using assessment devices in those domains should refer to those more particular recommendations.

Despite APA's efforts to restrict test purchase and use to qualified practitioners, those efforts may be undermined by the current prevalence of eBay, the electronic auction site. A recent survey found that 82 psychological tests or partial tests were listed for sale during a 3-month period in 2005:

> *The majority of the items (74%) were versions of the Wechsler Adult Intelligence Scale . . . and the Wechlser Intelligence Scale for Children. . . . The Rorschach Inkblot Test was the most frequently listed personality instrument [9.8%]. (p. 69)*

The Thematic Apperception Test and the Minnesota Multiphasic Personality Inventory were also listed, among others. Many tests included the manuals as well. Almost 50% of the auction listings "did not specify that the sale of item was restricted to individuals who met professional or training qualifications" (p. 69). LoBello, S. G., & Zachar, P. (2007). Psychological test sales and Internet auctions: Ethical considerations for dealing with obsolete or unwanted test materials. Professional Psychology: Research and Practice, 38, 68–70. Readers should keep these data in mind when considering material later in this chapter on maintaining test security.

Ethical Issues in Testing and Evaluation for Personnel Decisions

Manuel London and Douglas W. Bray

. . .

ETHICAL OBLIGATIONS OF PSYCHOLOGISTS

Organizational staff members who are responsible for formulating and applying evaluation procedures have ethical obligations to their profession, to the people they evaluate, and to their employers. . . .

Psychologists' Obligations to the Profession

Organizations often employ individuals with advanced degrees in personnel-related fields. Psychologists who are members of APA or who are licensed by a state to practice psychology are expected to abide by the standards and principles for ethical practice set forth by APA, regional professional organizations, and/or state statutes. . . . [T]he federal *Uniform Guidelines on Employee Selection Procedures* sets standards for all personnel experts in organizations subject to federal regulations regarding equal employment opportunity. . . . Desirable behaviors for ethical conduct generally include keeping informed of advances in the field, reporting unethical practices, and increasing colleagues' sensitivity to ethical issues.

Maintaining professional competence is necessary for effective application of evaluation techniques. The *Standards for Educational and Psychological Tests* devotes a section to qualifications of test users. Test users must have a general knowledge of measurement and validation principles and the limitations of test interpretation as well as an understanding of the literature relevant to the evaluation devices they use. The *Ethical Standards of Psychologists* emphasizes the need for continuing education, being open to

new procedures, and remaining abreast of relevant federal, state, and local regulations concerning practice and research. . . .

Psychologists' Obligations to Those Who Are Evaluated

Social and legal influences mandate that career decisions be made with a concern for accuracy and equality in employment opportunity (Division of Industrial and Organizational Psychology, 1975). A concern for the person who is affected by career decisions, however, leads to a number of ethical principles that go beyond improving and maintaining accuracy and ensuring equal employment opportunity. These principles include guarding against invasion of privacy, guaranteeing confidentiality, obtaining employees' and applicants' informed consent before evaluation, respecting employees' right to know, imposing time limitations on data, minimizing false positive and false negative decisions, and treating employees with respect and consideration. . . .

Some organizations routinely provide evaluation results to employees in the hope that knowledge of results will improve performance. Other organizations maintain a policy of secrecy or leave it up to individual supervisors to decide whether to provide feedback. Legislation now guarantees public employees access to this information . . . Research on the effects of access on the quality of information and the behavior and attitudes of the employee is necessary. . . .

Another issue pertaining to the confidentiality of evaluations such as recommendations deals with protecting the identity of individuals providing the information. Specifically, should employees have access to recommendations written about them? . . . .

Allowing employees to decide whether or not to waive their right to access to recommendations and other information in their personnel files may be a viable solution to employee complaints about confidential information they believe may be used against them. Here, as in other areas, there is a conflict between the rights of the individual and the validity of information obtained. An important research question is whether those named as references will supply negative information if they know the applicant will have access to it.

An especially difficult ethical problem involves maintaining the confidentiality of test results within an organization. Typically, many individuals outside the personnel staff have legitimate access to the information. For instance, a manager who is responsible for filling a position vacancy by promotion from within the company may use information about an employee's job experience and performance. Such information is often used without the knowledge of the employee. This raises the issue of informed consent—that is, of informing candidates about the intended use of test results prior to their taking the test. Tests given by an organization for one purpose are often used later for additional purposes. Thus, a score on an employment test may be used later for selection to a training program, assignment to a specific type of work, or promotion to a higher level. A person has the right to be told every potential use of the test results. This does not mean that the individual has to be informed every time a decision is made. Rather, it simply means that he or she should be aware of the types of decisions that may depend in part on the test results. . . .

Ethical treatment of employees during and after evaluation is another obligation of psychologists. How employees or applicants are treated when they are evaluated can influence the results of the evaluation and their acceptance of the ensuing decision. In general, evaluation procedures should be standardized to guarantee equal treatment and to enable examinees to do their best. . . . Standard procedures should include personal and considerate treatment, a clear explanation of the evaluation process, and direct and honest answers to examinees' questions.

Psychologists' Obligations to the Employer

Ethical obligations to the employer . . . include conveying accurate expectations for evaluation procedures, ensuring high-quality test data, implementing and periodically reviewing the adequacy of decision-making procedures, respecting the employer's proprietary rights, and balancing vested interests of the employer with government regulations, with commitment to the psychology profession, and with the rights of those evaluated for personnel decisions. . . .

Psychologists must attempt to provide high-quality information for personnel decisions, namely, reliable, valid, and fair data. However, psychologists are often unable to use the most rigorous scientific methods to ascertain a test's reliability and validity because of limited resources, time pressure, or other constraints imposed by the employer. . . .

Fairness relates to the absence of discrimination on the basis of race, sex, national origin, or other characteristics not related to the job. The law has responded to this issue in the form of legislation and judicial rulings. In general, a reasonably reliable and valid test that does not exhibit differential validity may still be unfair if it results in a substantially smaller proportion of favorable personnel decisions for one or more protected classes than for the majority group. (A substantially smaller proportion is defined in the *Uniform Guidelines* as less than 80% of the majority group selection rate, but this criterion does not necessarily define unfairness.) Therefore, in addition to determining that an evaluation device is reliable and valid, a psychologist must ascertain that it is free from bias. . . .

Psychologists must respect the proprietary rights of the employer as long as it is possible to maintain standards of ethical practice. Many organizations insist that their selection methods remain confidential, and in some cases they maintain this policy even when under review by government agencies. Companies in a competitive environment that invest heavily in personnel methods may be reluctant to publicize the details of their procedures. Moreover, organizations may fear that information given out about their procedures will lead to difficult questions even if the procedures are perfectly proper. . . . Therefore, psychologists working in industry may be constrained from publishing data regarding test development and validation or other research results sponsored by the employer.

Another ethical issue arises when psychologists are constrained from conducting research because the results may in some way be detrimental to their employer. . . . In such a case, the psychologist must abide by the wishes of the employer, try to persuade the employer otherwise, or change jobs. The ethical issue must be resolved by the psychologist. The issue becomes salient when the psychologist believes that proper practice has been hindered. Indeed, this is the crux of many ethical issues in psychology. Ethical responsibility is a personal and individual issue. Although the situation may be constructed by the employer, the psychologist perceives and interprets the situation and must deal with restrictions that he or she believes contribute to unethical practice. . . .

The potential for conflict among the professional's obligations to the employer, the profession, and employees is perhaps most likely in the area of confidentiality. Management's need to know must be satisfied while keeping promises to employees and applicants that evaluation results will remain confidential and while ensuring that the contents of evaluation devices are not disclosed to the extent that they are invalidated. . . .

SUMMARY AND CONCLUSION

. . .

. . . Finally, we must recognize that today's ethical standards are frequently tomorrow's laws. Professional standards are often incorporated into laws and used as the basis for judicial rulings. When published professional standards are insufficient, Congress and the courts do not hesitate to impose their own. Consequently, psychologists must play active roles in lobbying and writing legislation. Recognizing that ethical prescriptions and legal requirements are intertwined and are likely to become more so should be impetus enough for adopting ethical personnel practices and conducting research that will influence legislation.

Reference

Division of Industrial and Organizational Psychology, American Psychological Association. (1975). *Principles for the validation and use of personnel selection procedures.* Dayton, Ohio: Author.

◆ ◆ ◆

Commentary: For a comprehensive analysis of ethical issues in industrial settings, see Lowman, R. (1998). The ethical practice of psychology in organizations. Washington, DC: American Psychological Association. See also Eyde, L. D., & Quaintance, M. J. (1988). Ethical issues and cases in the practice of personnel psychology. Professional Psychology: Research and Practice, 19, 148–154. It contains generalizable vignettes worthy of discussion, including issues related to competence in selecting and interpreting tests, multiple relationships, and failure to use validated instruments.

Although London and Bray did not cite it, in 1979 the U.S. Supreme Court decided a case that raised many of the issues discussed in their article. More important, although the case involved an interpretation of the National Labor Relations Act and the use of tests in employment settings, it had broader ramifications for all psychologists. The case was not only relevant to issues of confidentiality of test results but, in the larger context, it pitted all of APA's Ethics Code against competing legal obligations (see chapter 2). The case started when 10 employees of a local electric company who applied for promotions failed to achieve acceptable scores on a battery of aptitude tests. Under the terms of a collective bargaining agreement union representatives for the aggrieved employees contested the results and claimed the examination procedure was unfair. They requested that the employer submit the tests, the employees' answer sheets, and other test-related data.

The employer argued that disclosing test data would make the battery useless in the future. Furthermore, the employer refused to disclose test data on any particular individual, claiming a confidential relationship between the employee and the psychologist who administered the test. Union representatives asserted they had the right to see these data.

The dispute was first heard by an administrative law judge (ALJ) who ruled that the employees' test results should be turned over to an industrial psychologist chosen by the union. To protect test security, the ALJ barred union representatives from copying or disclosing questions to employees. Nevertheless, the National Labor Relations Board overruled the ALJ's decision and ordered that the test results and raw data be given directly to union representatives. They had the discretion but were not required to use a psychologist if they needed help in interpreting test results.

That decision was reviewed by a federal appellate tribunal. Over the objections of APA (which had filed a friend of the court brief), the court affirmed the Board's order and ruled that test security would be protected adequately through the Board's banning of test data disclosure by union officials. The employer countered by claiming that any disclosure of test questions or scores would cause the psychologists involved in the testing to breach their code of ethics. The appellate court rejected that argument, asserting that the APA code of ethics could not stand in the way of union members exercising their rights to collective bargaining.

The employer asked the U.S. Supreme Court to review the lower court's decision. The Court began its opinion by acknowledging that "psychological aptitude testing is a widely used employee selection and promotion device in both industry and government. Test secrecy is concededly critical to the validity of any such program, and confidentiality of scores is undeniably important to the examinees" (p. 304). The Court held that the National Labor Relations Board's order, enforced by the Court of Appeals, failed to adequately accommodate those concerns. The Board, it said, abused its discretion in ordering the company to turn over the test battery and answer sheets directly to the union. It then addressed the ethical issues.

Detroit Edison Co. v. National Labor Relations Board

. . .

The Company argues that even if the scores were relevant to the Union's grievance (which it vigorously disputes), the Union's need for the information was not sufficiently weighty to require breach of the promise of confidentiality to the examinees, breach of its industrial psychologists' code of professional ethics, and potential embarrassment and harassment of at least some of the examinees. The Board responds that this information does satisfy the appropriate standard of "relevance," . . . and that the Company, having "unilaterally" chosen to make a promise of confidentiality to the examinees, cannot rely on that promise to defend against a request for relevant information. The professional obligations of the Company's psychologists, it argues, must give way to paramount federal law. Finally, it dismisses as speculative the contention that employees with low scores might be embarrassed or harassed.

We may accept for the sake of this discussion the finding that the employee scores were of potential relevance to the Union's grievance, as well as the position of the Board that the federal statutory duty to disclose relevant information cannot be defeated by the ethical standards of a private group. . . . Nevertheless we agree with the Company that its willingness to disclose these scores only upon receipt of consents from the examinees satisfied its statutory obligations under § 8 (a)(5).

. . .

The sensitivity of any human being to disclosure of information that may be taken to bear on his or her basic competence is sufficiently well known to be an appropriate subject of judicial notice [footnote omitted]. . . .

[A]ny possible impairment of the function of the Union in processing the grievances of employees is more than justified by the interests served in conditioning the disclosure of the test scores upon the consent of the very employees whose grievance is being processed. The burden on the Union in this instance is minimal. The Company's interest in preserving employee confidence in the testing program is well founded.

. . . [W]e are unable to sustain the Board in its conclusion that the Company, in resisting an unconsented-to disclosure of individual test results, violated the statutory obligation to bargain in good faith. . . . Accordingly, we hold that the order requiring the Company unconditionally to disclose the employee scores to the Union was erroneous. . . .

◆　◆　◆

Commentary: As Eberlein (1980) noted, the psychologists in this case were employees perceived as part of management. As such, they were bound by collective bargaining agreements between their employer and the union, creating the possibility of a conflict between their ethical duties and the duty to obey the law. Although, as he noted, consulting psychologists face less severe ethical conflicts, they may be obligated to refuse to engage in certain behavior but still face difficult decisions:

> *Psychologists may be called on to deviate from their standard practice in some consulting requests and must be prepared to reject a contract as potentially involving conflict of interest or calling for unprofessional conduct. Ethical standards are only guidelines; psychologists should be prepared to deviate from them when substantial reason exists. A legal requirement or court order provides such a reason, and it becomes a matter of conscience whether a psychologist is willing to suffer the consequences of contempt of court or provide the information required by the appropriate legal process. (p. 754)*

From *Detroit Edison Co. v. National Labor Relations Board,* 440 U.S. 301 (1979).

Eberlein, L. (1980). *Confidentiality of industrial psychological tests.* Professional Psychology: Research and Practice, 11, 749–754.

By far, the overarching point in Detroit Edison *is the Supreme Court's apparent agreement with the National Labor Relations Board that a federal law requiring the disclosure of relevant information cannot be defeated by the ethical standards of a private group like the APA. Thus, the decision in* Detroit Edison *implied that psychologists cannot rely solely on professional ethics and standards to protect them when they are faced with overriding obligations imposed by the law. In what other areas than testing may this conflict create problems for scientists and professionals?*

In any event, Standard 5.7 of the current Test Standards states that "[t]est users have the responsibility of protecting the security of test materials at all times." Similarly, Standard 9.11 of the current Ethics Code requires that psychologists "make reasonable efforts to maintain the integrity and security of test materials and other assessment techniques consistent with law, contractual obligations, and in a manner that permits adherence to this Ethics Code."

Consider the following situation:

> *An attorney for a criminal defendant charged with a serious crime retains a forensic clinician to conduct an evaluation to determine whether the defendant can assert an insanity defense. The psychologist conducts a comprehensive evaluation consisting of a clinical interview and a number of tests. Subsequent to the evaluation, the clinician writes a report and pursuant to the relevant rules of evidence, the defendant's attorney turns over the psychologist's report to the prosecutor. The prosecutor, however, also demands that the psychologist produce the underlying "raw data" from the tests that were administered to the defendant. Is the psychologist ethically barred from complying with that demand?*

In answering this question, the first task of the clinician is to define "raw data." Although the 1992 Code left the term undefined, the current Code is helpful in delineating more precisely its two meanings. Standard 9.04 refers to the release of "test data." This term "refers to raw and scaled scores, client/patient responses to test questions or stimuli, and psychologists' notes and recordings concerning client/patient statements and behavior during examination." Standard 9.11 differentiates test data from "test materials." The latter "refers to manuals, instruments, protocols, and test questions or stimuli." Note, therefore, that those portions of test materials that include client/patient responses are included in the definition of test data.

The second task is to refer to the relevant sections of the 2002 Code and other policy documents. Read Standards 9.04 and 9.11. Also see Guidelines for Child Custody Evaluations in Divorce Proceedings (see chap. 9, Guidelines 9–11); Specialty Guidelines for Forensic Psychologists (see chap. 9, Guidelines V[A][2]; VI[B]; VII[A][2][a,b]); and most particularly Record Keeping Guidelines (see chap. 10).

If readers have interpreted these documents accurately, it is clear that there is no absolute ethical bar to the disclosure of test data and materials. Beyond the professional organizational documents cited above, the Detroit Edison *case shows there are obvious external limits to protecting test security. With the advent of televised trials the situation becomes even more perilous. Consider the position of the psychologist who is compelled by the court to exhibit and discuss questions, results, and interpretation of such materials as IQ scales, personality tests, and projective instruments. And, of course, psychologists have no control over the conduct of judges. For example, in a case challenging the validity of the Wechsler and Stanford-Binet scales—* PASE v. Hannon, *506 F.Supp. 831 (N.D. Ill. 1980)— the judge, in evaluating the tests disclosed all the questions and correct answers to both tests. So even though he held that the tests were not culturally biased, their security had been seriously compromised, if not destroyed. For a more complete discussion of these issues, see Bersoff, D. N. (1982).* Larry P. *and* PASE: *Judicial report cards on the validity of individual intelligence tests. In T. Kratochwill (Ed.),* Advances in school psychology *(Vol. 2, pp. 61–95). Hillsdale, NJ: Erlbaum.*

Given the anxiety-provoking state of affairs with regard to protecting test data and test materials, two of APA's governing bodies provide guidance concerning the release of information gleaned from psychological assessments. The first document was approved by the APA Council of Representatives and is thus considered APA policy.

Statement on the Disclosure of Test Data

Committee on Psychological Tests and Assessment, American Psychological Association

. . .

GENERAL ISSUES

Test data include an individual's test results, raw test data, records, written/computer-generated reports, global scores or individual scale scores, and test materials such as test protocols, manuals, test items, scoring keys or algorithms, and any other materials considered secure by the test developer or publisher.

. . .

Psychologists should be aware that professional standards and practices as well as legal mandates governing the disclosure of test data often differ substantially depending on the setting, intended purpose, and use of testing. At times, this statement, and APA standards, may conflict with legal mandates, organizational or institutional requirements. When such conflicts arise, psychologists should attempt to identify the relevant issues, make known their commitment to relevant standards, and attempt to resolve them in a way that, to the extent feasible, conforms both to law and professional practice as required by the Ethics Code (APA, 1992),[1] licensing regulations, and other relevant standards.

ACCESS TO TEST DATA

Psychologists, and their employing organizations and institutions, may develop formal procedures and policies to address the retention, review, and release of test data. Psychologists generally discuss limitations on confidentiality or disclosure of test data and test results with test takers, individuals, and organizational clients prior to testing. In this way, psychologists can help to minimize any misunderstanding concerning the release of such confidential and secure test data. . . .

. . . When appropriate, psychologists should consider that there may be conflict among the confidentiality rights of test takers, contractual obligations with test publishers, and other relevant parties (e.g., third-party payers).

INFORMING THE TEST TAKER OF THE PURPOSE, USE, AND RESULTS OF TESTING

Psychologists usually obtain informed consent from test takers or their legal representatives prior to the testing, except when the nature of the testing does not require such consent (e.g., some types of employment testing, court-ordered assessment). Even when consent is not required, it may be desirable to obtain it. Consent may also be required when an evaluation is requested by an attorney rather than ordered by the court. Informed consent implies the test taker or his/her representative has agreed to the testing after having been informed, prior to testing, of the reasons for testing, the intended use and its range of possible consequences, what testing information will be released, and to whom testing information will be released.

. . .

Following the completion and scoring of the test, psychologists should also provide test takers with explanations of test results when the psychologist's role does not prevent such explanations and when the psychologist has explained possible limitations to this explanation before testing (APA, 1992; Standards 1.07, "Describing the Nature and Results of Psychological Services," and 2.09, "Explaining Assessment Results"). Both the Ethics

[1]*Ed. Note:* Now see the current (2002) APA Ethics Code.

Code (APA, 1992) and Testing Standards (1985) recognize exceptions to furnishing test results and explanations to clients. Release and explanation of test data may not be required when testing is mandated by law, when testing is conducted as part of an admissions or employment screening process . . . or, in some organizational consulting, security screening and forensic evaluations (APA, 1992, Standard 2.09, "Explaining Assessment Results").[2] When appropriate, psychologists inform individuals of these limitations at the outset of testing.

. . . [W]hen test scores or reports are released to test takers or other persons or institutions (e.g., parents, guardians, teachers, human resource departments, legal authorities), psychologists should make reasonable efforts to provide understandable explanations concerning the nature, purposes, and results of the testing (e.g., an explanation of what the scores mean, their confidence intervals, any significant reservations they have about the accuracy or limitations of their interpretations) and how scores will be used.

RELEASING DATA WITH OR WITHOUT THE CONSENT OF THE TEST TAKER

Test data identified by the names of individual test takers are usually not released to any person, third-party payer, or institution without the informed consent of the test taker, the test taker's parent or guardian, or organizational client or legal representatives. Whether such consent is provided or not required (see Section III above), psychologists may still attempt to limit access to test data to only qualified professionals.

. . .

When the client's intention to waive confidentiality is viewed by the psychologist to be contrary to the client's best interest, the psychologist usually discusses the implications of releasing psychological information. The psychologist usually assists the client in limiting disclosure only to information required by the present circumstances and only to other qualified professionals.

. . .

[2]*Ed. Note*: See Standard 9.10 of the current (2002) APA Ethics Code.

RELEASE OF DATA AND TEST SECURITY

. . .

Disclosure of secure testing materials (e.g., test items, test scoring, or test protocols) to unqualified persons may decrease the test's validity. Availability of test items to an unqualified person can not only render the test invalid for any future use with that individual, but also jeopardizes the security and integrity of the test for other persons who may be exposed to test items and responses. Such release imposes very concrete harm to the general public—loss of effective assessment tools. Because there are a limited number of standardized psychological tests considered appropriate for a given purpose (in some instances only a single instrument), they cannot easily be replaced or substituted if an individual obtains prior knowledge of item content or the security of the test is otherwise compromised.

Development and refinement of items and norms for individual intelligence tests, personality assessment techniques, and achievement tests often require many years of research and considerable effort and expense. Improper disclosure of test items or other test materials also may result in damage to those parties which have developed or have ownership in the test and possibly result in breach of contract claims against psychologists who violate the terms of their test purchase or lease agreements.

RELEASING DATA TO UNQUALIFIED PERSONS

Psychologists usually inform persons or agencies requesting test data of the psychologist's obligations to the Ethics Code (APA, 1992) and professional standards and practices, which includes taking reasonable steps to limit the release of test data to persons qualified to use such information.

Any release of data must conform to the Ethics Code (APA, 1992), which requires psychologists to refrain from misuse of assessment techniques, results, and interpretations and to take reasonable steps to prevent misuse of assessment results by others. . . . The primary concern of releasing test data to individuals who are not competent to interpret them, including the limitations of the data, is that the data will be misused, having potentially harmful effects on the client, patient, or others. In addition, untrained and/or unqualified individuals might make harmful and misguided decisions based on a misunderstanding of the test data. The psychologist's responsibilities extend to raw test materials such as responses to test items or recording of observations during assessment that may be contained in test protocols or testing records.

PROTECTING COPYRIGHT INTERESTS WHEN RELEASING DATA

Tests and test protocols are generally protected by the federal copyright laws and usually may not be copied without permission of the copyright holder. Psychologists mandated by law or regulation to provide copies of a test, test manual, or test protocols need to consider copyright laws which may potentially be violated by releasing such materials.

It is prudent for psychologists to be familiar with the terms of their test purchase or lease agreements with test publishers as well as reasonably informed about relevant provisions of the federal copyright laws. Psychologists may wish to consult with test publishers and/or knowledgeable experts to resolve possible conflicts before releasing specific test materials to ensure that the copyright and proprietary interests of the test publisher are not compromised.

CONFORMING TO FEDERAL AND STATE STATUTES AND RULES, REGULATORY MANDATES, AND INSTITUTIONAL/ ORGANIZATIONAL RULES AND REQUIREMENTS

Federal and state statutes, federal/state rules and regulations, and court precedents address disclosure requirements that vary by the setting, use or purpose of testing, and the party requesting disclosure. Court decisions have been largely case specific, that is, decisions based on the specific facts of a case, usually balancing the rights of participants with the degree to which the protected information is considered necessary for resolution of legal issues. There may also be additional constitutional, statutory, or common-law privacy protections governing test disclosure. Therefore, it is advisable for psychologists to become informed about applicable legal constraints governing requests for test information disclosure in their state and in a specific situation.

RELEASING TEST DATA TO THIRD-PARTY PAYERS

[*Ed. Note:* See also chapter 10]

Third-party payers (e.g., health insurance organizations, health maintenance organizations) and employers (when self-insured or for other purposes such as disability determination or leave approval) sometimes request test data in determining a client's eligibility for services or reimbursement for a psychologist who has provided testing or assessment services. Psychologists often ask clients or their legal guardians to sign a written release which acknowledges consent for the release of such records to appropriate health insurance organizations. Such records often are released in written form and may include or exclude actual test scores. However, psychologists exert special care concerning release of secure test materials (e.g., protocols, test items) and inform the requesting parties of relevant ethical standards and any contractual obligations which restrict the release of such materials.

RELEASING TEST DATA WHEN THE ORGANIZATION IS THE CLIENT

. . .

Psychologists do retain professional responsibilities to test takers even when the client is an organization. In such circumstances, psychologists working for organizational clients should attempt to anticipate possible competing objectives and clarify with both the organizational client and test takers how such conflicts can be resolved or prevented. In many instances the nature of the psychologist's role within the organization (employee or consultant) and organizational policies will prevent disclosure of test data to individual test takers. In circumstances of legally mandated disclosure of tests or test records in organizational contexts, psychologists should consider attempting to assure appropriate protection of any released tests and test records (e.g., materials in possession of government entities could be subject to disclosure under state or federal freedom of information laws).

. . .

ROLE OF PSYCHOLOGISTS IN FORENSIC CONTEXTS

[*Ed. Note:* See also chapter 9]

Legal requirements governing disclosure of test data may vary substantially from state to state. Psychologists faced with demands to produce test data are encouraged to secure advice about the governing law(s) in the state where the problem arises as well as federal and local statutes and regulations applicable to specific contexts. Psychologists are also encouraged to refer to ethical and appropriate professional standards, as well as applicable guidelines.

. . .

ROLE OF PSYCHOLOGISTS IN REQUESTING OR OBTAINING SECURE TEST DATA AND TEST MATERIALS

Psychologists who request the release of test data, or who are affiliated (through employment, paid or unpaid consulting relationships, or other related affiliations) with organizations or agencies making such requests, should be aware of applicable ethical and professional standards. Psychologists requesting test data, or who are affiliated with organizations requesting test data, make reasonable attempts to maintain the integrity and security of requested tests and assessments, to protect the confidentiality of clients and test data, and to take reasonable steps to prevent others from misusing test data. Psychologists may assist organizations requesting test data to appropriately restrict the request to test data that are relevant for a specific purpose and to limit access to qualified professionals with a legitimate interest. . . .

OTHER ISSUES

Reprinting of Test Items

In deciding whether to reprint items, psychologists are encouraged to consider the qualifications of the intended audience, access to the publication by the general public or potential test takers, the intent and use of the publication, the potential for invalidating the assessment technique, and intellectual property/copyright law. The reprinting or description of individual test items in a publication (e.g., popular press, paper presentation, research article, book, technical report, handout) may jeopardize the integrity and security of many standardized tests.

Psychologists generally obtain permission from the copyright holder prior to reprinting test items. . . .

Use of Test Items in Teaching and Training

It is advisable for persons in training who use test materials, or who have access to test data, to be directly supervised by a qualified professional. Academic departments and professors should maintain the security of all test materials under conditions that prevent access by unauthorized individuals . . .

When students are administered a test for demonstration purposes, the instructor assures the security and appropriate use of the test. Because exposure to tests in such demonstrations can invalidate the test for future use with students, simulated test items, film or video demonstrations, or other alternative means are encouraged as alternatives to classroom administration or demonstrations of actual tests, whenever possible.

Retention and Maintenance of Testing Data

The Testing Standards (APA, 1985) state that test protocols and any written reports should be preserved when any test data about a person are retained (Standard 15.9), and data (whether retained on paper, data files, etc.) should be adequately protected from improper disclosure (Standard 16.5). The Ethics Code (APA, 1992) and *Record Keeping Guidelines* (APA, 1993) contain additional information regarding the retention of psychological records. . . .

Reference

American Psychological Association. (1992). Ethical principles of psychologists and code of conduct. *American Psychologist, 47,* 1597–1611.

Strategies for Private Practitioners Coping With Subpoenas or Compelled Testimony for Client Records or Test Data

Committee on Legal Issues, American Psychological Association

. . . This document is not intended to establish any standards of care or conduct for practitioners nor does it establish American Psychological Association (APA) policy or guidelines. Rather, it provides some general information regarding strategies that may be available to psychologists in independent practice for responding to subpoenas or compelled court testimony concerning client records, test data, test manuals, test protocols, or other test information.

As a general principle of law, all citizens are required to provide information necessary for deciding issues before a court. From the perspective of the legal system, the more relevant information available to the trier of fact (i.e., judge or jury), the greater the likelihood of a fair decision being reached. Statutes, rules of civil and criminal procedure, and rules of evidence have established the procedures for the transmittal of such information. In order to obtain this material, *subpoenas* (legal commands to appear to provide testimony) or *subpoenas duces tecum* (legal commands to appear and bring along specific documents) may be issued. Alternatively, the court may issue a *court order* to provide testimony or produce documents. A subpoena requesting testimony or documents, even if not signed by a judge, requires a timely response, but it may be modified or quashed (i.e., made void or invalid).

It is important to differentiate responding to a subpoena from disclosing confidential information. Unless the issuing attorney or court excuses the psychologist, it will be necessary to respond to a subpoena, that is, to be at a particular place at a particular time (with records, if the subpoena is a subpoena duces tecum). Responding to the subpoena, however, does not necessarily entail disclosing confidential information. In order to disclose confidential information, a psychologist will need to ensure that the conditions for disclosing confidential information, such as the client's consent or a judge's order or other legal mandate, are met, in addition to having a valid subpoena. Thus, although a subpoena requires a response, a subpoena alone will generally not be sufficient to warrant a disclosure of confidential information. However, once a court order for testimony or documents is issued and any attempt (made in a timely manner) to have the court vacate or modify its order has been unsuccessful, a psychologist may be held in contempt of court if he or she fails to comply.

The demands of the legal system sometimes conflict with the responsibility of psychologists to maintain the confidentiality of client records. This responsibility arises from tenets of good clinical practice, ethical standards, professional licensing laws, statutes, and other applicable laws. In many contexts, the client material generated in the course of a professional relationship may also fall under an evidentiary privilege, which protects such information from judicial scrutiny. Most state and federal jurisdictions recognize a psychotherapist–patient privilege that allows the client to prevent confidential material conveyed to a psychotherapist from being communicated to others in legal settings. In most jurisdictions, the privilege belongs to the client, not to the therapist. The psychologist has a responsibility to maintain confidentiality and to assert the psychotherapist–patient privilege unless the client has explicitly waived privilege, unless a legally recognized exception to privilege exists, or unless the court orders the psychologist to turn over the client's information. Therapy notes, process notes, client information forms, billing records, and other such information usually may be turned over to the court with an appropriate release by the client or with a court order. Psychological test material presents a more complicated situation because inappropriate disclosure may seriously impair the security and threaten the validity of the test and its value as a measurement tool.

Psychologists have numerous ethical, professional, and legal obligations that touch on the release of client records, test data, and other information in the legal context. Many such obligations may favor disclosure, including, in particular, the general obligation of all citizens to give truthful and complete testimony in courts of law when subpoenaed to do so. But there are often conflicting duties and principles that favor withholding such information. These may include obligations to (a) clients or other individuals who receive treatment and/or are administered psychological tests (e.g., privileged or confidential communications that may include client responses to test items), (b) the public (e.g., to avoid public dissemination of test items, questions, protocols, or other test information that could adversely affect the integrity and continued validity of tests), (c) test publishers (e.g., contractual obligations between the psychologist and test publishers not to disclose test information; obligations under the copyright laws), and (d) other third parties (e.g., employers). Such obligations may, at times, conflict with one another. Under APA's "Ethical Principles of Psychologists and Code of Conduct" (APA, 2002), hereinafter referred to as the APA Ethics Code, psychologists facing a conflict between their ethical and legal responsibilities make known their commitment to the Ethics Code, take steps to resolve the conflict, and may fulfill their legal obligations if the conflict is unresolvable. . . .

There are specific settings (e.g., educational, institutional, employment) in which the legal or ethical obligations of psychologists as they relate to disclosure of client records or test information present special problems. This article does not purport to address disclosure issues in these special contexts, nor does it attempt to resolve dilemmas faced by psychologists in reconciling legal and ethical obligations.

STRATEGIES FOR DEALING WITH SUBPOENAS

Determine Whether the Request for Information Carries the Force of Law

It must first be determined whether a psychologist has, in fact, received a legally valid demand for disclosure of sensitive test data and client records, and consultation with a lawyer may be necessary to make this determination. If a demand is not legally enforceable for any reason, then the psychologist has no legal obligation to comply with it and may have no legal obligation to respond. A subpoena to produce documents generally must allow a sufficient period of time to respond to the demand and provide for some time within which the opposing side may move to quash such a demand. Without this allowed time period, the subpoena may not be valid. Even a demand that claims to be legally enforceable may not be. For example, the court issuing the subpoena may not have jurisdiction over the psychologist or his or her records (e.g., a subpoena issued in one state may not be legally binding on a psychologist residing and working in a different state). Or, the subpoena may not have been properly served to the psychologist (e.g., some states may require service in person or by certified mail or that a subpoena for such records be accompanied by a special court order). It is advisable that a psychologist consult with an attorney in making such a determination. If the psychologist concludes that the demand is legally valid, then some formal response to the attorney or court will be required—either compliance with or opposition to the demand, in whole or in part. A psychologist's obligations in responding to a valid subpoena are not necessarily the same as those under a court order (see section titled File a Motion to Quash the Subpoena or File a Protective Order below). The next step, in most cases, may involve contacting the psychologist's client. However, the psychologist may wish to consider grounds for opposing or limiting production of the demanded information before contacting the client so that the client can more fully understand his or her options (see section titled Possible Grounds for Opposing or Limiting Production of Client Records or Test Data below).

Contact the Client

The client to whom requested records pertain often has a legally protected interest in preserving the confidentiality of the records. If, therefore, a psychologist receives a subpoena or advance notice that he or she may be required to divulge client records or test data, the psychologist, when appropriate, discusses the implications of the demand with the client (or his or her legal guardian). Also when appropriate and with the client's valid consent, the psychologist may consult with the client's attorney. It is important to recognize, however, that the client's attorney's interests and a psychologist's interests may diverge through the course of legal proceeding, and the psychologist may need to seek independent legal consultation and representation to make sure his or her interests are protected.

The discussion with the client will inform the client which information has been demanded, the purpose of the demand, the entities or individuals to whom the information is to be provided, and the possible scope of further disclosure by those entities or individuals. Following such a discussion, a legally competent client or the client's legal guardian may choose to consent to production of the data. It is safest to have such consent in writing, for clarity and if there is a need for documentation in the future. In some states, consent in writing may be required by law. The client's consent may not, however, resolve the potential confidentiality claims of third parties (such as test publishers). For more information, see APA Ethics Code, Ethical Standards, Section 4 (APA, 2002), and *Standards for Educational and Psychological Testing* (1999).

Negotiate With the Requester

If a client does not consent to release of the requested information, the psychologist (often through counsel) may seek to prevent disclosure through discussions with legal counsel for the requesting party. The psychologist's position in such discussions may be bolstered by legal arguments against disclosure, including the psychologist's duties under rules regarding psychotherapist–patient privilege. These rules often allow the psychologist to assert privilege on behalf of the client in the absence of a specific release or court order. (Some possible

arguments are outlined in the section titled Possible Grounds for Opposing or Limiting Production of Client Records or Test Data below.) Such negotiations may explore whether there are ways to achieve the requesting party's objectives without divulging confidential information, for example, through disclosure of nonconfidential materials or submission of an affidavit by the psychologist disclosing nonconfidential information. Negotiation may also be used as a strategy to avoid compelled testimony in court or by deposition. In short, negotiation can be explored as a possible means of avoiding the wholesale release of confidential test or client information—release that may not be in the best interests of the client, the public, or the profession and that may not even be relevant to the issues before the court. Such an option could be explored in consultation with the psychologist's attorney or the client's attorney.

Seek Guidance From the Court

If, despite such discussions, the requesting party insists that confidential information or test data be produced, the safest course for the psychologist may be to seek a ruling from the court on whether disclosure is required. The simplest way of proceeding, and perhaps the least costly, may be for the psychologist (or his or her attorney) to write a letter to the court, with a copy to the attorneys for both parties, stating that the psychologist wishes to comply with the law but that he or she is ethically obligated not to produce the confidential records or test data or to testify about them unless compelled to do so by the court or with the consent of the client. In writing such a letter, the psychologist (or his or her lawyer) may request that the court consider the psychologist's obligations to adhere to federal requirements (e.g., the Health Insurance Portability and Accountability Act of 1996 [HIPAA]), to protect the interests of the client, to protect the interests of third parties (e.g., test publishers or others), and to protect the interests of the public in preserving the integrity and continued validity of the tests themselves. This letter may help sensitize the court about the potential adverse effects of dissemination. The letter might also attempt to provide suggestions, such as the following, to the court on ways to minimize the adverse consequences of disclosure if the court is inclined to require production at all:

1. Suggest that the court direct the psychologist to provide test data only to another appropriately qualified psychologist designated by the court or by the party seeking such information.

2. Suggest that the court limit the use of client records or test data to prevent wide dissemination. For example, the court might order that the information be delivered to the court, be kept under seal, be used solely for the purposes of the litigation, and that all copies of the data be returned to the psychologist under seal after the litigation is terminated. The order might also provide that the requester must prevent or limit the disclosure of the information to third parties.

3. Suggest that the court limit the categories of information that must be produced. For example, client records may contain confidential information about a third party, such as a spouse, who may have independent interests in maintaining confidentiality, and such data may be of minimal or no relevance to the issues before the court. The court should limit its production order to exclude such information.

4. Suggest that the court determine for itself, through in camera proceedings (i.e., a nonpublic hearing or a review by the judge in chambers), whether the use of the client records or test data is relevant to the issues before the court or whether it might be insulated from disclosure, in whole or in part, by the therapist–client privilege or another privilege (e.g., attorney–client privilege).

5. Suggest that the court deny or limit the demand because it is unduly burdensome on the psychologist (see, e.g., Federal Rule of Civil Procedure 45[c][1-3]).

6. Suggest that the court shields from production "psychotherapy notes," if the psychologist keeps separate psychotherapy notes as defined by HIPAA privacy regulations . . . [See chap. 10, this volume].

File a Motion to Quash the Subpoena or File a Protective Order

A *motion to quash* is a formal application made to a court or judge for purposes of having a subpoena vacated or declared invalid. Grounds may exist for asserting that the subpoena or request for testimony should be quashed, in whole or in part. For example, the information sought may be protected by the therapist–client privilege and therefore may not be subject to discovery, or it may not be relevant to the issues before the court (see section titled Possible Grounds for Opposing or Limiting Production of Client Records or Test Data below). This strategy may be used alone or in combination with a motion for a protective order.

A *motion for a protective order* seeks an order or decree from the court that protects against the untoward consequences of disclosing information. A protective order can be tailored to meet the legitimate interests of the client and of third parties such as test publishers and the public. The focus of this strategy first and foremost is to prevent or limit disclosure and the use of sensitive client and test information. The protective order—and the motion—may include any of the elements listed in the preceding section.

If, because of local procedure or other considerations, guidance cannot be sought through the informal means of a letter to the court, it may be necessary to file a motion seeking to be relieved of the obligations imposed by the demand for production of the confidential records. In many jurisdictions, the possible motions include a motion to quash the subpoena, in whole or in part, or a motion for a protective order. Filing such a motion may require the assistance of counsel, representing either the psychologist or the psychologist's client.

Courts are generally more receptive to a motion to quash or a motion for a protective order if it is filed by the client about whom information is sought (who would be defending his or her own interests) rather than by a psychologist who, in essence, would be seeking to protect the rights of the client or other third parties. The psychologist may wish to determine initially whether the client's lawyer is inclined to seek to quash a subpoena or to seek a protective order and, if so, may wish to provide assistance to the client's attorney in this regard. If the client has refused to consent to disclosure of the information, his or her attorney may be willing to take the lead in opposing the subpoena.

PSYCHOLOGIST'S TESTIMONY

If a psychologist is asked to disclose confidential information during questioning at a deposition, he or she may refuse to answer the question only if the information is privileged. If there is a reasonable basis for asserting a privilege, the psychologist may refuse to provide test data or client records until so ordered by the court. A psychologist who refuses to answer questions without a reasonable basis may be penalized by the court, including the obligation to pay the requesting parties' costs and fees in obtaining court enforcement of the subpoena. For these reasons, it is advisable that a psychologist be represented by his or her own counsel at the deposition. A lawyer may advise the psychologist, on the record, when a question seeks confidential information; such on-the-record advice will help protect the psychologist from the adverse legal consequences of erroneous disclosures or erroneous refusals to disclose.

Similarly, if the request for confidential information arises for the first time during courtroom testimony, the psychologist may assert a privilege and refuse to answer unless directed to do so by the court. The law in this area is somewhat unsettled. Thus, it may be advisable for him or her to consult an attorney before testifying.

POSSIBLE GROUNDS FOR OPPOSING OR LIMITING PRODUCTION OF CLIENT RECORDS OR TEST DATA

The following options may or may not be available under the facts of a particular case and/or a particular jurisdiction for resisting a demand to produce confidential information, records, or test data . . . :

1. The court does not have jurisdiction over the psychologist, the client records, or the test data, or the psychologist did not receive a legally sufficient demand (e.g., improper service) for production of records or test data testimony.
2. The psychologist does not have custody or control of the records or test data that are sought, because, for example, they belong not to the psychologist but to his or her employer.
3. The therapist–client privilege insulates the records or test data from disclosure. The rationale

for the privilege, recognized in many states, is that the openness necessary for effective therapy requires that clients have an expectation that all records of therapy, contents of therapeutic disclosures, and test data will remain confidential. Disclosure would be a serious invasion of the client's privacy. The psychologist is under an ethical obligation to protect the client's reasonable expectations of confidentiality. See APA Ethics Code, Ethical Standards, Section 4 (APA, 2002).

4. The information sought is not relevant to the issues before the court, or the scope of the demand for information is overbroad in reaching information not relevant to the issues before the court, including irrelevant information pertaining to third parties such as a spouse.
5. Public dissemination of test information such as manuals, protocols, and so forth may harm the public interest because it may affect responses of future test populations. This effect could result in the loss of valuable assessment tools to the detriment of both the public and the profession of psychology.
6. Test publishers have an interest in the protection of test information, and the psychologist may have a contractual or other legal obligation (e.g., copyright laws) not to disclose such information. Such contractual claims, coupled with concerns about test data devolving into the public domain, may justify issuance of a protective order against dissemination of a test instrument or protocols.
7. Psychologists have an ethical obligation to protect the integrity and security of test information and data and to avoid misuse of assessment techniques and data. Psychologists are also ethically obligated to take reasonable steps to prevent others from misusing such information. See APA Ethics Code, Ethical Standards, Section 2 (APA, 2002).
8. Refer to ethical and legal obligations of psychologists as provided for under ethics codes; professional standards; state, federal, or local laws; or regulatory agencies.
9. Some court rules allow the party receiving the subpoena to object to the subpoena's demand, or ask that the demand be limited, on the basis that it imposes an undue burden on the recipient (see, e.g., Federal Rule of Civil Procedure 45[c][1-3]).

References

American Psychological Association. (2002). Ethical principles of psychologists and code of conduct. *American Psychologist, 57,* 1060–1073.

Definitions, 45 C.F.R. § 164.501 (2005).

Fed. R. Civ. P. 45(c).

Health Insurance Portability and Accountability Act of 1996, Pub. L. No. 104-191, 110 Stat. 1936.

Standards for educational and psychological testing. (1999). Washington, DC: American Psychological Association.

◆　◆　◆

Commentary: See also APA. (1999). Test security: Protecting the integrity of tests [Editorial]. American Psychologist, 54, 1078; Behnke, S. (2006, November). Release of test data and the new ethics code. APA Monitor, 35, 90–91; Michaels, M. H. (2006). Ethical considerations in writing psychological assessment reports. Journal of Clinical Psychology, 62, 47–58 (esp. pp. 51–53).

Much has changed ethically and legally since Berndt (1983) surveyed psychologists who specialized in assessment about their informed consent practices. At that time almost 20% of the respondents indicated they did not obtain any consent prior to testing. As for sharing results, psychologists were least likely to tell clients how they did on so-called projective tests such as the Rorschach, Thematic Apperception Test, and figure drawings and more likely to do so with IQ tests and the Minnesota Multiphasic Personality Inventory. As the author noted, however, "a mood of consumerism also appears on the rise." (p. 585). See Berndt, D. J. (1983). Ethical and professional considerations in psychological assessment. Professional Psychology: Research and Practice, 14, 580–587. The 2002 Ethics Code has now codified this rising consumerism by regulating both informed consent to testing (Standard 9.03) and the sharing of assessment results (Standard 9.10).

Beyond the issue of protecting test materials is a larger one: To what extent should psychologists share test results and interpretations with those they assess? The following material provides descriptive and prescriptive discussions of this controversial topic.

The Ethical Practice of School Psychology:
A Rebuttal and Suggested Model

Donald N. Bersoff

. . .

The following is not meant to be an all-encompassing model, but is limited to the process of assessment. It rests on three assumptions:

1. Test responses are a function not only of the characteristics of the organism to whom the test is administered but also of the stimulus properties of the test and the background or environments (e.g., instructions, setting, nature of the experimenter) in which the test is administered (Fiske, 1967; Hamilton, 1970; Murstein, 1965; Sattler & Theye, 1967).

2. Each person perceives the testing situation differently and thus develops an idiosyncratic style or strategy in responding to test material. Without discerning these strategies, the validity of test interpretation is highly attenuated (Fulkerson, 1965).

3. Parents are at least equally capable as the school staff in deciding what is best for their children (Goldman, 1971).

Accepting these assumptions allows the psychologist to include the client in all aspects of the evaluation. In fact, it makes it imperative that he do so if he wants to obtain data that are not obfuscated by mistrust, misunderstanding, and the inhibition of self-disclosure. Because we have not included the client (both the child and his parents) in the assessment transaction it is possible that most of our test data and their subsequent interpretation may be of doubtful veracity. As Jourard (1971) conjectured,

> the millions of psychometric tests mildewing in agency files might be lies told by untrusting clients and patients to untrustworthy functionaries. If psychologists were serving the interests of bureaucracies, wittingly or unwittingly, in their . . . activities, then it would be quite proper for . . . patients not to trust us; functionaries masquerading as professionals are not to be trusted too far. (p. 2)

If we are to achieve intimate, ethical relationships consonant with the empirical data concerning the interactive nature of test productions, it may be necessary to reconceive of the assessment process as one in which there is mutual disclosure. In a series of papers, Fischer (1970, 1971a, 1971b, 1972a, 1972b, 1973) detailed both the theoretical foundations and the practical expression of just such a relationship in which tester and client become "coevaluators" (Fischer, 1970). Specifically, the following steps are recommended.

1. *Coadvisement.* This is an expansion of the principle of informed consent. The psychologist tells the child and his parents how he functions; informs them of the identity of the referral agent and the purpose for referral; and describes the nature of the assessment devices he will use, the merits and limitations of those devices, what kinds of information will be put in a report, and who might eventually read the report. The psychologist then asks the child to tell how he perceives the purposes of testing and what he feels the consequences of such an evaluation might be. The psychologist secures agreement from the child and his parents to proceed with the assessment subsequent to full and mutual disclosure concerning the purposes of the evaluation.

From *Professional Psychology, 4,* 305–312. Copyright 1973 by the American Psychological Association.

2. *Sharing impressions.* Immediately after the administration of the psychometric instruments the psychologist, the child, and his parents engage in a dialogue in which the psychologist gives his interpretation of the child's test behavior as he has just experienced it. By conferring with the child he further attempts to extrapolate from the testing situation to other situations similar to the one represented by the test stimuli. Such a dialogue provides immediate feedback to the child about how others perceive his behavior and enables the assessor to check out hypotheses about how equivalent the test behavior observed is to actual classroom behavior and to develop possible strategies he may use to intervene in the instructional environment (see Fischer, 1970, for an example of how such an interaction might proceed). It also gives the child a chance to disagree with the psychologist's initial interpretations and to offer his perceptions about his own behavior. Rather than assuming that the behavior observed in the testing situation can be extrapolated to all other situations, the psychologist has an opportunity to discover the situations or contexts in which the behavior does occur. Such an approach has been variously called psychosituational (Bersoff, 1971a; Bersoff & Grieger, 1971) or contextual (Fischer, in press-a) assessment, but whatever its title, such a method prevents the child from being mislabeled and interpretations of his behavior from being over-generalized.

3. *Critique of the written evaluation.* This concludes the sequence of mutually disclosing events. After the evaluation is complete and the psychologist has prepared his report, he shows the child and his parents a copy of the written evaluation. This insures that the report will be recorded so that it is understandable to all concerned. In addition, as Fischer (1970) described,

> This procedure also produces a beneficial side effect: Knowing that his client is going to read his report, the psychologist strives all the more to be true to him, to capture his world as well as words allow, and to avoid overstatements,

unintended implications, and loose descriptions [p. 74].

Then, the child and his parents are given the opportunity to clarify the points made, to add further material, and, if there is disagreement between the psychologist and the clients, to provide a dissenting view (in writing if warranted). . . .

There is no doubt that adopting such an approach requires much rethinking and rebehaving on the part of school psychologists. . . . Admittedly, there may be some difficulty in implementing the approach fully. . . . A comment by Leo Goldman (1971), arguing against psychological secrecy and offering some suggestions for its reduction, may help put the matter in perspective:

> All of this may sound very unappealing to psychologists who would prefer to see themselves as the "good guys" who are there just to help people and make the world a better place. Unfortunately, that just isn't a viable arrangement when one is a member of the staff of a public school serving a community which contains diverse social, ethnic, and political elements. And it certainly is not possible in any pure sense in a setting such as the public schools, where the "clients" are not clients at all but mostly a captive, involuntary audience. We will just have to find a way to work out agreements in each school system . . . so that the professional helpers can do their thing, while the students and their families retain the power to decide *whether* they will be helped, what personal information they will divulge, and what the school may release to anyone. Although this will undoubtedly cramp our style to some extent, it will on the whole make for a healthier social institution than we now have. (p. 11)

The suggestions made in this article for reorienting assessment will hopefully move us toward making the school a healthier social institution. At the very least we will treat the child and his parents as our equals, with the right to participate in the interpretations and decisions that will directly affect their lives. Certainly, the chances of damaging diagnoses and class placements will be lessened. And those diagnoses and placements that are made will have been a "co-constituted" decision, agreed on by those affected, increasing the probability of greater cooperation in making the changes that *all* have deemed appropriate.

References

Bersoff, D. N. (1971). "Current functioning" myth: An overlooked fallacy in psychological assessment. *Journal of Consulting and Clinical Psychology, 37,* 391–393.

Bersoff, D. N., & Grieger, R. M. (1971). An interview model for the psychosituational assessment of children's behavior. *American Journal of Orthopsychiatry, 41,* 483–493.

Fischer, C. T. (1970). The testee as co-evaluator. *Journal of Counseling Psychology, 17,* 70–76.

Fischer, C. T. (1971a, September). Paradigm changes which allow sharing of "results" with the client. In S. L. Brodsky (Chm.), *Shared results and open files with the client: Professional responsibility or effective involvement.* Symposium presented at the annual meeting of the American Psychological Association, Washington, DC.

Fischer, C. T. (1971b). Toward the structure of privacy: Implications for psychological assessment. In A. Giorgi, W. F. Fischer, & R. vonEckartsberg (Eds.), *Duquesne studies in phenomenological psychology.* Pittsburgh, PA: Duquesne University Press.

Fischer, C. T. (1972a). Paradigm changes which allow sharing of results. *Professional Psychology: Research and Practice, 3,* 364–369.

Fischer, C. T. (1972b). A theme for the child-advocate: Sharable everyday life data of the child-in-the-world. *Journal of Clinical Child Psychology, 1,* 23–25.

Fischer, C. T. (1973). Contextual approach to assessment. *Journal of Community Mental Health, 9,* 38–45.

Fiske, D. W. (1967). The subject reacts to tests. *American Psychologist, 22,* 287–296.

Fulkerson, S. C. (1965). Some implications of the new cognitive theory for projective tests. *Journal of Consulting Psychology, 29,* 191–197.

Goldman, L. (1971, September). Psychological secrecy and openness in the public schools. In S. L. Brodsky (Chm.), *Shared results and open files with the client: Professional responsibility or effective involvement.* Symposium presented at the annual meeting of the American Psychological Association, Washington, DC.

Hamilton, J. (1970). Stimulus variables in clinical evaluation. *Professional Psychology: Research and Practice, 1,* 151–153.

Jourard, S. M. (1971, September). Some reflections on a quiet revolution. In S. L. Brodsky (Chair), *Shared results and open files with the client: Professional responsibility or effective involvement.* Symposium presented at the annual meeting of the American Psychological Association, Washington, DC.

Murstein, B. I. (1965). Assumptions, adaptation level, and projective techniques. In B. I. Murstein (Ed.), *Handbook of projective techniques* (pp. 49–68). New York: Basic Books.

Sattler, J. M., & Theye, F. (1967). Procedural, situational, and interpersonal variables in individual intelligence testing. *Psychological Bulletin, 68,* 347–361.

◆　　◆　　◆

Commentary: For more recent explications of the process described in this article, see Fischer, C. T. (1985/1984). Individualizing psychological assessment. *Mahway, NJ: Erlbaum; Fischer, C. T. (2000). Individualized, collaborative assessment.* Journal of Personality Assessment, 74, *2–14; Schleifer, M. R., & McElfresh, P. J. (2005, May). How can the psychological assessment process promote autonomy? APA ethical principles in action.* The Pennsylvania Psychologist Quarterly, 65(5), *11, 21.*

Now, parental involvement in and consent for psychoeducational evaluations conducted on children suspected of being, or already labeled as, disabled are controlled by federal law under the Individuals with Disabilities in Education Act. Regulations under the Act, found in Title 34 of the Code of Federal Regulations (34 C.F.R. 300.504-300.505), now require school systems to notify parents when they propose (or refuse) to evaluate their children for special education placement purposes. Parents must be given the opportunity to consent to a preplacement evaluation, but if they refuse, schools may initiate a hearing conducted by an impartial officer to determine if parents' refusal may be overridden. Parents must also be given a description of evaluation procedures and tests schools propose to use. Although these regulations have salutary benefits in that they compel school systems to involve parents in material decisions, the children themselves do not have the right to notice or consent. Given the preceding material, is this a serious omission or simply recognition that the law gives parents the right to act as children's primary decision makers?

For a more complete explanation of the parental consent and notice rules under Public Law 94-142 and its regulations, see Pryzwansky, W. B., & Bersoff, D. N. (1978). Parental consent for psychological evaluations:

Legal, ethical, and practical considerations. Journal of School Psychology, 16, 274–281.

In the last section of the Task Force on Test User Qualifications report (see excerpt, this chapter), the authors note the use of computers to administer, score, and interpret tests and the emerging use of Internet applications. The following articles address these important issues.

Legal Issues in Computerized Psychological Testing

Donald N. Bersoff and Paul J. Hofer

. . . .

PSYCHOLOGY'S RESPONSE TO CPT

. . .

There are several sources of ethical guidelines relevant to computerized psychological testing (CPT). . . . [T]he 1974 *Standards for Educational and Psychological Tests* (APA, AERA, NCME, 1974), the revised 1985 Standards (APA, 1985),[1] the 1977 *Standards for Providers of Psychological Services* (APA, 1977) and its recently adopted revision, the *General Guidelines for Providers of Psychological Services* (APA, 1987), as well as the 1981 *Specialty Guidelines for the Delivery of Services* (APA, 1981) all contain references to computerized assessment. However, in these latter documents, many CPT issues are subsumed under general standards applicable to all types of testing or psychological practices and the specific implications for CPT may not be clear.

. . .

. . . The American Psychological Association's Board of Directors in January, 1984, instructed the Committee on Professional Standards and the Committee on Psychological Tests and Assessment to develop guidelines specific to CPT. These guidelines . . . were adopted by the APA Council of Representatives in February, 1986. Importantly, at this point, the guidelines are considered advisory. After they have been tested in the real world, the APA may wish to revise them once again and make them binding standards. For now these guidelines are the clearest statement of the requirements of good practice, and professionals should familiarize themselves with them.

RIGHTS AND RESPONSIBILITIES OF PROFESSIONALS

Should there be any legal challenge to the administration, interpretation, and decisions related to computer-based tests, both the testing service and the test user are likely to be named as defendants. Both may be ultimately liable, either as joint wrongdoers or as individuals each responsible for their own negligence. In such cases, it might appear that clinicians could rely on a defense that they were ignorant of the underlying bases for the interpretations they accepted and passed along to their clients. But, such a defense would be an admission that the clinician violated the APA Ethical Principles and engaged in professional negligence. The *Ethical Principles of Psychologists,* Principle 8(e) (APA, 1981, p. 637) states: "Psychologists offering scoring and interpretation services are able to produce appropriate evidence for the validity of the programs and procedures used in arriving at interpretations."[2]

Conversely, testing services will probably not be able to place the entire blame on the user for injurious decisions resulting from negligent interpretations, and they could be held liable under a number of legal theories. Placing the responsibility for the validity of reports entirely on the user might erode the usefulness of CPT as reviewing the validity of each interpretative statement could be comparable with writing the entire report oneself, and most people use CPT to save time and effort. . . .

These considerations suggest that some division of labor and responsibility between developer and user must be found. The gist of the APA guidelines is: The validity and reliability of the computerized version of a test should be established by the developer, but CPT interpretations should be used only in conjunction

[1]*Ed. Note:* Now see the 1999 revision of the Test Standards referenced earlier.

[2]*Ed. Note:* See Standard 9.09 of the APA's current (2002) Ethics Code.

with professional review. This rather general principle might be elaborated into a more specific assignment of responsibilities. The developer seems in the best position to assure that the scales and research on which the report is based are not obsolete or otherwise inadequate. Actuarially based interpretations should use the best research and statistical equations. Developers can stay abreast of relevant research, incorporate new findings into the system, and direct practitioners to research that may assist them in properly using the report. Users can then concentrate on overseeing the context of the testing and evaluating the appropriateness of the norms and validation studies used by the system for interpreting any particular client's scores. They can concentrate on gathering clinical information not used by the CPT system but relevant to clinical decision making. By specializing and working together, developers and users can assure the full advantages of CPT are realized.

. . . A major potential conflict in CPT is the tension between users' needs for sufficient information to review reports, and developers' proprietary interest in their algorithms, software, and other business assets.

. . .

[*Ed. Note:* I have omitted a long section on intellectual property issues—such as copyright, patents, and trade secrets. These problems, although beyond the scope of this text, are extremely important, and readers are referred to the full article for their discussion]

THE RIGHTS OF TEST TAKERS

. . .

A major concern about computer-generated reports is that they may not be as individualized as those generated in the conventional manner. Some information, such as demographic characteristics of the examinee, can be included in interpretation programs so that the computer will use more appropriate norms or base rates if they exist and qualify interpretations to take into account the particular test taker's characteristics. But no program can consider all the unique attributes of each individual and in most cases the same programmed decision rules will be applied to all test scores.

The revised *Standards for Educational and Psychological Testing* (APA, 1985) clearly indicates that test users are ultimately responsible for their test interpretations, no matter from what format the data are derived. Assessing the validity of interpretations requires that a human being observe the testing situation and decide if conditions are present that could invalidate test results. It is imperative that the final act of decision making be that of a qualified practitioner, consistent with state law, ethical principles, and professional standards, who takes responsibility for overseeing the process of testing and judging the applicability of the interpretive report for individual examinees.

There must be an interposition of human judgment between the CPT report and decision making to ensure that decisions are made with full sensitivity to all the nuances of test administration and interpretation, and the unique constellation of attributes in each person is evaluated. Relying solely on test developers' computerized conception of the test taker's responses, isolated from a clinician's trained observation of the test taker's behavior during the administration of the test, may tend to create bland, impersonal, and nonspecific assessments that fail to capture the test taker's cognitive, affective, and behavioral functioning across a variety of situations. . . .

References

American Psychological Association. (1977). *Standards for providers of psychological services*. Washington, DC: Author.

American Psychological Association. (1981). Specialty guidelines for the delivery of services. *American Psychologist, 36,* 640–681.

American Psychological Association. (1985). *Standards for educational and psychological tests*. Washington, DC: Author.

American Psychological Association. (1986). *Guidelines for computerized-based tests and interpretations*. Washington, DC: Author.

American Psychological Association. (1987). *General guidelines for providers of psychological services*. Washington, DC: Author.

American Psychological Association, American Educational Research Association, & National Council of Measurement in Education. (1974). *Standards for educational and psychological tests*. Washington, DC: Author.

♦   ♦   ♦

Commentary: Similarly, Matarazzo (1986) commented

> *that the computer rarely delivers several different but equally plausible clinical interpretations. With almost no exceptions, today's software produces only a single, typically very lengthy, clinical narrative. Another danger of this clinical-appearing product is the aura of seeming validity that surrounds its objectively presented, neatly typed page after page of narrative clinical statements. (p. 20)*

Matarazzo, J. D. (1986). *Computerized clinical psychological test interpretations: Unvalidated plus all mean and no sigma.* American Psychologist, 41, 14–24.

Many psychologists are concerned that unqualified and untrained people in other professions will be sold computerized tests and scoring and interpretive services or may otherwise be given access to these. Is this a genuine concern or merely an argument to eliminate competition? For helpful readings on this problem and other legal and ethical issues, see, for example, these publications:

Eyde, L. D., & Kowal, D. M. (1987). *Computerised test interpretation services: Ethical and professional concerns regarding U.S. producers and users.* Applied Psychology: An International Review, 36, 401–417.

Hartman, D. E. (1986). *On the use of clinical psychology software: Practical, legal, and ethical concerns.* Professional Psychology: Research and Practice, 17, 462–465.

Zachary, R., & Pope, K. (1984). *Legal and ethical issues in the clinical use of computerized testing.* In M. D. Schwartz (Ed.), Using computers in clinical practice (pp. 151–164). New York: Haworth Press.

Computerized testing usually takes place in the clinician's office. Online or electronic assessment usually describes a process in which testing occurs at a distance as through e-mail or the Internet. Technologically mediated remote assessment, as computerized testing before it, is becoming more popular. A recent survey indicated that 15.1% of respondents provided "psychological and neuropsychological assessment" (VandenBos & William, 2000, Table 1, p. 491) through some electronic format. See VandenBos, G., & Williams, S. (2000). The Internet versus the telephone: What is telehealth anyway? Professional Psychology: Research and Practice, 31, 490–492. The following article, prepared by The Task Force on Psychological Testing on the Internet (cosponsored by APA's Board of Scientific Affairs), describes the many forms of online tests, catalogs their potential uses, and describes the strengths of these devices. The portion reprinted here focuses on its potential ethical problems.

Psychological Testing on the Internet: New Problems, Old Issues

Jack A. Naglieri, Fritz Drasgow, Mark Schmit, Len Handler, Aurelio Prifitera, Amy Margolis, and Roberto Velasquez

. . .

ETHICAL AND PROFESSIONAL ISSUES

Ethical issues abound for psychologists who use the Internet in their practice. Many of these issues are being addressed by specific APA committees (American Psychological Association, 1997). Although all of the ethical issues surrounding the use of the Internet in the practice of psychology are important, we confine our discussion to the issues specifically raised around Internet testing. Our discussion is framed by the current APA *Ethical Principles of Psychologists and Code of Conduct* (American Psychological Association, 2002), specifically Section 9, Assessment, which covers most of the issues surrounding Internet testing.

The first ethical issue to be considered is the professional context in which the Internet testing takes place. The associated ethical principle [is . . . 9.01, Bases of Assessment (see chap. 1, this volume)]. . . .

The issue raised by Internet testing is how testing is placed into a professional context when conducted on the Internet. Many tests on the Internet are accompanied by little other than some broad statements about the use of the test. Further, test takers may not read instructions or may ignore disclaimers more than in face-to-face situations (Barak & English, 2002). Under these principles, test materials that are posted for self-administration and interpretation on the Internet should be accompanied by a statement to the test taker that clearly defines the bounds and limitations of the professional relationship with the client that can be achieved through this medium. This may seem a bit counterintuitive given the impersonal nature of Internet communications. However, a potential client who is browsing the Internet for professional advice is seeking a trust relationship. Providing preliminary test materials for diagnostic or evaluative purposes therefore implies an offer to form this trust relationship. Thus, the limitations of the relationship that can be developed through an impersonal medium such as the Internet should be clearly described in an opening statement to the test taker. In addition, test providers may need to make available contact information (e.g., e-mail address, phone number) for those who do not completely understand directions or the purpose of the test. Finally, the limits of the feedback provided to the test taker following the test should be clearly described both before the test and preceding feedback. This description should clearly describe the potential limitations of conclusions and recommendations that can be made as a result of a very limited and potentially nonpersonal Internet approach.

The next area of ethical consideration involves the appropriate use of Internet testing and assessment. The ethical principle [is 9.02, Use of Assessments (see chap. 1, this volume)]. . . .

Internet testing, in many cases, has been simply a process of putting paper-and-pencil or computerized tests onto a new medium. However, although research has explored the equivalence of some forms of computerized and paper-and-pencil tests (e.g., Mead & Drasgow, 1993), very little research has been conducted on the equivalence of Internet testing with these other formats. This may call into question the evidence for the usefulness of these tools. Further, tests that may have been developed and researched in a proctored setting are now often being used in an unproctored context that is facilitated by the Internet and its widening accessibility. This approach calls into question the proper application of the techniques. The effects of both the medium and the context require additional research to ensure appropriate use of tests and assessment on the Internet.

As noted earlier, an advantage to using the Internet to deliver tests is that it may provide greater accessibility and reach than an approach that requires an individual to be at a certain place, at a particular time. This advantage can also create a challenge. Wider access may cause a difference in the populations for which the test was developed versus the ultimate population that has access. For example, a preemployment test may be specifically developed and researched for a management population. Under more traditional conditions, applicants for these management positions may be required to test at a specific location where a significant effort and commitment is involved. However, the Internet may provide easy access to a different population where a nonqualified candidate could decide that he or she might just take the test on the off chance that he or she might gain entry to an otherwise inaccessible position.

Normative issues are also a related concern for Internet test delivery. With good intentions, a test may be placed on a Web site by a psychologist in the United States, but someone in China may have access to it and complete the test. Feedback may be based only on U.S. norms. An inadvertent, but inappropriate, use of norms is the result. This is clearly an area of great potential for the inappropriate use of tests and associated norms. Psychologists will need to make substantial efforts to collect demographic information prior to testing and to provide feedback only to individuals in groups for which normative data are available.

The next area of ethical consideration involves informed consent. The ethical principle [is 9.03, Informed Consent in Assessments (see chap. 1, this volume)]. . . .

Gaining true informed consent through electronic means is likely to create unique challenges for psychologists. As noted earlier, the impersonal and standardized nature of Internet testing programs are not likely to fit all individuals the same. In other words, it may be very difficult to provide true informed consent to all individuals completing tests through the Internet. In many cases, it will not be known whether the person completing the test is capable of giving informed consent or whether permission is required from a legally authorized person. Take, for examples, a preteen who poses as an individual over 18 years old or a patient under the legal guardianship of another who gives consent in order to gain access to testing. Psychologists who wish to use testing on the Internet, other than for excepted practices, will need to find ways to deal with this thorny problem of how to authenticate informed consent over the Internet.

The next area of ethical consideration involves the appropriate release of test data. The ethical principle [is 9.04, Release of Test Data (see chap. 1, this volume)]. . . .

Psychological test data reveal very personal details about human characteristics, behaviors, preferences, and capabilities. This type of data is not only valuable to psychologists, but is also valuable to sales, marketing, political, and other groups who may or may not have the individual's best interest in mind when deciding how to use these data. Therefore, it is imperative that measures be taken to provide secure sites for the collection of psychological test data on the Internet. Without secure sites, test data could be intercepted, corrupted, or changed by unscrupulous data thieves and hackers. There are three major principles of Internet security, and psychologists using the Internet for testing should take proactive steps in each of these areas to protect test takers (Howard, Paridaens, & Gramm, 2001). The first principle is confidentiality, which deals with keeping information from being viewed by unintended readers. Encryption technology is designed to provide confidentiality by scrambling data so that only the appropriate senders and receivers can read the data. The second principle is integrity, which is concerned with keeping information from being altered. Message digests are fingerprints that do not allow the changing of information or at least can detect when information has been changed. The final principle is authentication, which relates to identifying the origins of the data. Digital signatures can provide the authentication through a system of keys that are used both in the sending and receiving of messages to identify the sender as authentic. Given the value and highly sensitive nature of psychological test data, psychologists should use technologies in each of these areas to secure data.

The sharing of data and reports is infinitely easier as a result of Internet-based access to databases. . . . This ease of access provides more opportunity than in the past for both the intentional and the inadvertent release of data to unqualified individuals. Safeguards must be put in place by psychologists, in conjunction with information technologists, to avoid the release of data to those who are unqualified to use it. . . .

The next ethical issue of note in the use of tests on the Internet has to do with test development efforts. The ethical principle [is 9.05, Test Construction (see chap. 1, this volume)]. . . .

Traditional test construction techniques are appropriate for administration over the Internet in proctored test environments. However, as noted earlier, tests developed in a paper-and-pencil format and researched in monitored and controlled situations cannot be assumed to provide equivalent measurement when administered over the Internet in unmonitored and uncontrolled situations. Therefore, additional studies of test equivalence and norming should be conducted over the Internet, with subjects completing the test under conditions that represent those that the intended target population will experience (Epstein, Klinkenberg, Wiley, & McKinley, 2001).

. . . [I]t is incumbent on psychologists to understand the bounds of current psychometric methods and to establish, research, and report on new methods that support emerging technological advances. It would be unethical to develop new measurement tools that cannot be held to existing psychometric standards (American Educational Research Association, American Psychological Association, & National Council on Measurement in Education, 1999) without providing arguments and evidence for new or revised standards. Advances in testing spurred by the Internet should be encouraged, but

associated advances in psychometric theory may be a mandatory part of this advancement (i.e., in cases in which existing models are inappropriate).

The interpretation of Internet test results poses some unique ethical considerations. The relevant ethical principle [is 9.06, Interpreting Assessment Results (see chap. 1, this volume)]. . . . Internet testing will often be conducted in unproctored and in variable environments. Test takers will likely be in unstandardized settings (e.g., home, library, school), and psychologists will have little or no way of knowing exactly what conditions might exist that could influence or limit interpretations. This problem may be alleviated to some extent by the use of instructions to test takers, but it is likely that this will only reduce a small amount of irrelevant variability in scores. Further, when tests are completed in unmonitored situations, there is currently no way to guarantee the true identity of the test taker (Schmit, 2001). Thus, psychologists will need to weigh carefully the importance they place on tests administered over the Internet. Confirmatory methods, administration of equivalent forms, or gathering of data through additional methods will almost always be necessary before making anything other than preliminary evaluations, diagnostic, or predictive decisions.

Gaining an understanding of the test-taking skills and specific personal characteristic of the test taker poses an even greater challenge, given the impersonal approach that characterizes most Internet-based testing and assessment. For example, in preemployment testing situations, a provider may have no way of knowing whether an applicant has a particular disability that might affect the test results and invalidate the possible interpretation of those results. Similarly, a test may be posted in English for use in counseling, but the test taker speaks English only as a second language. Unless the test taker is asked about this condition, the interpretation of results will likely be flawed. The point is that psychologists using Internet testing and assessment must make provisions for understanding the unique needs of test takers that may ultimately affect the interpretation of results.

In addition, test takers must be given information that clearly identifies the purpose of the test so that they can determine whether the test is appropriate for their situation. However, this may not be as easy as providing a purpose statement. The test taker will need help understanding whether the test is a fit for his or her situation. There will likely be a need for prescreening the test taker to help him or her understand whether the test or assessment is right for his or her situation.

The next set of ethical issues to be considered with regard to Internet testing involves the use of Internet tests by unqualified persons. The ethical principle [is 9.07, Assessment by Unqualified Persons (see chap. 1, this volume)]. . . .

The Internet has made it very easy for anyone to publish any kind of material in the public domain. This freedom has led many to assume that anything published on the Internet is in the public domain and can be copied and used by anyone who chooses to do so. . . . Whole tests, scales, and test items posted on the Internet can be copied and used by unqualified people. It is the responsibility of psychological test publishers and authors to keep their works under tight control and to report copyright violations. Most do this well with customers who use appropriate channels to gain access to the materials. However, publishers and authors must scan the Web for whole and partial elements of tests that require professional training for administration or interpretation. Partial tests are likely to be the most difficult to identify, yet they may be the most damaging, as the original psychometric properties are likely denigrated. Consistent with Principle 9.11 . . . publishers must also protect their copyrights on test materials. It is the duty of the psychology profession to protect the public from unscrupulous vendors who exploit the Internet with tests of others or, worse yet, with bad renditions of the original test. . . .

The next ethical principle to be considered [is 9.08, Obsolete Tests and Outdated Test Results (see chap. 1, this volume)]. . . . The Internet is full of obsolete and outdated information. Consumers often have difficulty sorting out the current from the outdated pages available on the Internet. Consistent with the discussion of the previous principle, when partial or whole replication of test materials is made through uninformed or fraudulent acts, these tests materials are likely to become obsolete or outdated, because the original publisher updates the materials. Further, it is quite easy for Web publishers to forget about published pages on the Internet that may be updated in different places, yet the old materials remain available to the public. Finally, psychologists who do not closely watch the literature and other materials from test publishers may inadvertently use outdated materials online. Others may resist change and intentionally use outdated materials. . . .

Third-party vendors of Internet tests and associated services also have a set of ethical issues to consider. The relevant ethical principle [is 9.09, Test Scoring and Interpretation Services (see chap. 1, this volume)]. . . .

The Internet is full of psychological, parapsychological, and pop-psychology tests, as described in earlier sections. Psychologists must find ways to differentiate themselves from the mass of alternatives that do not meet professional standards (American Educational Research Association et al., 1999). Providing the information described in this ethical principle is the first step in overcoming such confusion. Psychologists who provide tools to other trained professionals should go beyond the simple provision of providing basic psychometric information to potential users. Steps could be taken to show the equivalence of Internet testing with traditional forms of the measure (Epstein et al., 2001). Efforts should also be made to provide consultation and training to test users regarding the challenges faced in using tests on the Internet (Barak & English, 2002). The training should be specific to tests and populations that will take the tests. Processional vendors of psychological tests to be used on the Internet may be able to overcome some of the noise of Internet marketing by becoming professional Internet test consultants. Producers of pop-psychology tests should be made to issue more detailed disclaimers, or warnings, describing their tests as entertainment and not as true tests, just as tobacco manufacturers must issue store warnings on cigarette packages.

The advent of technological breakthroughs and the ease of conducting a professional practice that results from these innovations can occasionally blind adaptors to the fundamental qualities that comprise quality tools. Psychologists must learn to discriminate among efficient delivery tools, flashy format, face-valid content, and psychometric quality. All of these qualities may be important to a psychologist in choosing a vendor, but the foundations of psychometrics are still necessary conditions that should be the first hurdle in a multihurdle decision process. Technology advances should not be considered in a vacuum when choosing an Internet test.

Perhaps one of the greatest challenges of Internet testing will involve the explanation of results to test takers. The ethical principle dealing with this issue is [9.10, Explaining Assessment Results (see chap. 1, this volume)]. . . . Providing feedback to test takers over the Internet is a topic of concern to many psychologists. There are at least three major ethical issues to consider. First, there are limited ways to understand the conditions under which the test taker completed the test. Did the individual complete the test or did someone else help or do it for him or her? Under what environmental conditions was the test taken? These and many other questions should be answered in order to provide accurate feedback. Second, it is very difficult to provide feedback, particularly negative feedback, to a test taker without knowing the person's emotional and mental state. The wrong type of feedback could exacerbate the individual's condition. Third, it is difficult to provide test takers with immediate emotional support in cases where the feedback has traumatic effects on an individual. It is also difficult to know the extent of these reactions in the first place. Given these severe limitations and many other possibilities, psychologists should rarely provide feedback over the Internet. When they do provide feedback, processes for resolving these ethical issues either in "real time" or within a reasonable time period should be established. Feedback should generally be limited and should include directions for seeking additional information and help through other means. Ultimately, feedback should rely on multiple methods of evaluation to provide assessment results consistent with professional best practice.

Another rather charged area of ethical concern is the maintenance of test security when tests are delivered over the Internet. The ethical principle covering this set of issues is [9.11, Maintaining Test Security (see chap. 1, this volume)]. . . .

. . . Many psychological tests and assessments are copyrighted because much effort was expended in their development. These instruments constitute much of test publishers' intellectual capital and must be safeguarded. It is unethical and illegal for unauthorized parties to distribute or use such copyrighted materials. In fact, a quick search of www.ebay.com on any given day will produce quick access to many copyrighted and sensitive test materials. For example, a quick search on June 18, 2003, produced the opportunity to bid on an *MMPI Manual for Administration and Scoring* together with unused testing materials as well as the opportunity to purchase Rorschach Psychodiagnostic Plates. . . .

RECOMMENDATIONS FOR THE FUTURE

This examination of the issue of testing on the Internet leads to several conclusions. First, and perhaps most important, is that the current psychometric standards, including test reliability and validity, apply even though the way in which the tests are developed and delivered may be quite different. Unfortunately, because there are many more tests that are now available via the Internet, there is much variability in the quality of these tests. The extent to which there is documented evidence of the reliability and validity of these tests is also quite variable because many Internet tests do not seem to meet standards established by the profession. This puts consumers in the unfortunate position of having the responsibility of evaluating the quality of the information they receive, often with little knowledge and skill to do so. One conclusion is obvious: Internet testing should be subjected to the same defensible standards for assessment tools (American Educational Research Association et al., 1999) as paper-and-pencil tests when their results are used to make important decisions. Still, new methods and combinations of methods that are made possible by emerging technologies will push the boundaries of existing psychometric theory, and it is up to psychologists to test and expand the limits of psychometrics to keep pace with these innovations.

The Internet provides a tremendous opportunity for testing, and with that opportunity comes a corresponding need for the ethical and professional use of these tests and a responsibility to expand our science to test the usefulness of these interventions. Despite the flash and sparkle of Internet testing, critical questions of the validity of the inferences made from test scores must be demonstrated. This is a fundamental issue of test validity that must be weighed in relation to the ease of availability, cost, and convenience of Internet testing. All of these advantages become irrelevant if scores are used in ways that are not supported by evidence of validity. The *Standards for Educational and Psychological Testing* (American Educational Research Association et al., 1999) provides extensive information about what is needed to justify a particular use of a test. Internet test developers and test users should carefully read the Standards and ensure that their tests are used in appropriate ways.

Although the Internet has considerable potential as a means of testing, assessment will require the integration of information obtained via this medium with other relevant information. For this reason, what is typically available on the Internet is testing in contrast to psychological assessment. The test results obtained on the Internet may be inaccurate for a variety of reasons and therefore there must be a professional available to verify the validity of the information and assist in interpretation. Although it is conceivable that future Internet testing methods may approach a psychological assessment, the requirements for appropriate psychological assessment exceed current Internet capabilities. Practitioners must, therefore, be mindful of this distinction and utilize the Internet for its strength and augment it with their assessment skills.

Tests can be placed on the Internet in a manner that suggests authority and conveys confidence, although many of these tests may have little to no documentation of reliability and validity, test takers often ignore disclaimers that might appear, and self-administered tests can yield inaccurate interpretations. What is needed is considerably more accountability of the Internet site authors so that the user receives the same kind of protections obtained in traditional assessment sessions. Similarly, test developers and publishing companies that enter into Internet testing programs should ensure that Internet tests are held to the same psychometric standards as traditional tests. This would include, for example, documentation summarizing standardization samples, reliability, and validity as well as additional evidence, such as equivalence of tests delivered on Internet and paper, uniformity of stimulus quality on different displays, and so forth, to ensure high quality test administration.

There are tremendous opportunities provided by Internet testing. This article has described many of them, and other innovations await discovery. The importance of this new method of testing and assessment is clear, as is the need for formal guidelines for Internet-based tests and the many ways in which psychologists may use this environment for a variety of applications. We encourage psychologists to think creatively about how their research and practice can be improved by Internet testing. Times have changed as the Internet has brought testing out of the secure environment controlled by a licensed professional psychologist or psychometrician. As testing becomes more accessible, it is important to realize that the principles of good testing still apply and the ethical standards for psychologists are still fundamental. Balancing widespread accessibility with good practice presents a critical challenge to psychologists for the new millennium. There are many issues that await resolution. Over the years to come, much research and critical thinking will be required to address these issues. We believe that psychologists should look forward to this work with excitement and enthusiasm.

References

American Educational Research Association, American Psychological Association, & National Council on Measurement in Education. (1999). *Standards for educational and psychological testing*. Washington, DC: Author.

American Psychological Association. (1997). *Services by telephone, teleconferencing, and Internet: A statement by the Ethics Committee of the American Psychological Association*. Retrieved from http://www.apa.org/ethics/stmnt01.html

American Psychological Association. (2002). Ethical principles of psychologists and code of conduct. *American Psychologist, 47*, 1597–1611. Available from the APA Web site: http://www.apa.org/ethics/code1992.html

Barak, A., & English, N. (2002). Prospects and limitations of psychological testing on the Internet. *Journal of Technology in Human Services, 19*, 65–89.

Epstein, J., Klinkenberg, W. D., Wiley, D., & McKinley, L. (2001). Insuring sample equivalence across Internet and paper-and-pencil assessments. *Computers in Human Behavior, 17*, 339–346.

Howard, B., Paridaens, O., & Gramm, B. (2001, 2nd Quarter). Information security: Threats and protection mechanisms. *Alcatel Telecommunications Review*, 117–121.

Mead, A. D., & Drasgow, F. (1993). Equivalence of computerized and paper-and-pencil cognitive ability tests: A meta-analysis. *Psychological Bulletin, 114*, 449–458.

Schmit, M. J. (2001, September). Use of psychological measures for online recruitment and pre-employment selection. In L. Frumkin (Chair), *Internet-based assessment: State of the art in testing*. Symposium conducted at the 109th Annual Conference of the American Psychological Association, San Francisco, CA.

◆　◆　◆

Commentary: For other relevant ethical principles see Standards 4.02c and 6.02a of the 2002 Ethics Code.

Another area of emerging interest is the controversial use of tests to predict dishonesty, usually for purposes of personnel selection. For perhaps the best article on the topic addressing ethical issues, see Camara, W., & Schneider, D. (1994). Integrity tests: Facts and unresolved issues. American Psychologist, 49, 112–119.

Little written about is the penultimate topic in this chapter—ethical issues concerning the teaching of intelligence and personality testing to graduate students. As readers will see, it is worth exploring. The authors of the following excerpt sent surveys to the training directors of APA-accredited doctoral programs in school, counseling, and clinical psychology. Of the 550 forms sent, 138 were usable. The survey asked questions about five topics. In the excerpt I focus on four of these: access to practice subjects, feedback issues, confidentiality, and consent. There was also an open-ended question about ethical dilemmas encountered by instructors while teaching the testing course.

Practical and Ethical Issues in Teaching Psychological Testing

Patricia A. Rupert, Neal F. Kozlowski, Laura A. Hoffman, Denise D. Daniels, and Jeanne M. Piette

. . .

Access to Practice Subjects

Instructors of both adult and child testing courses seemed to turn to a number of sources to find appropriate practice subjects. Of the 64 adult instructors who provided information about sources of nonclient volunteers, a large number reported use of university contacts such as a departmental subject pool (over 50% reported use), university classes (about 42%), or friends of students and faculty (over 50%). The community-at-large (about 31%) and community organizations (about 13%) were also reported as sources of volunteers. Of the 59 child testing instructors who provided information about nonclient child volunteers, many reported use of community resources, including the community at large (about 42%), schools (about 36%), day care centers (about 31%), and community organizations (about 22%). By far, however, the most frequently used source for child volunteers was friends (over 80%).

The use of actual clients as testing subjects was less frequent, perhaps because of the potential tensions between service and training needs plus the difficulty finding clients who may be suitable for beginning level students to test. Interestingly, for both adult (24 instructors reporting) and child (21 instructors reporting) courses, university in-house training clinics were the most frequently noted source of clients (about 63% of adult instructors and about 57% of child instructors reported use). In addition, adult clients were secured from inpatient units (about 42% reported use), outpatient clinics (about 29%), and residential centers (about 17%), and child clients were secured from school system referrals (about 48%), outpatient treatment centers (about 29%), residential centers (about 29%), and inpatient centers (about 24%).

Problems in this area were reported with some frequency; 19 problems described by adult testing instructors and 15 by child testing instructors were coded as being related to this area. These problems seemed to relate primarily to access to appropriate nonclient volunteers. With both adults and children, many problems involved multiple relationship concerns (i.e., testing children of friends or relatives or adults who are known to students through other personal contacts or professional roles) or problems in finding individuals who do not have serious problems, who are not in therapy, or who will not need to be tested at a later time (particularly with children).

These data highlight a number of ethical issues that must be considered in finding appropriate practice subjects. First, the issue of multiple relationships is of concern, particularly given the heavy reliance on friends or university sources. In this regard, the procedure of having students recruit their own volunteers through personal contacts seems especially problematic; in such instances, students create multiple role situations where the potential for breaches of confidentiality and conflicting responsibilities is high. To avoid such problems, it seems important to have a system for securing volunteers that does not rely on students to find their own testing subjects.

To obtain practice subjects, the instructor or program needs to establish contacts necessary to secure appropriate testing subjects. Our data suggest that, for adult volunteers, contacts may be readily established through the use of a departmental subject pool or university classes. To secure child volunteers, contacts with day care centers, schools, and community organizations may be helpful. As an extra safeguard,

From *Professional Psychology: Research and Practice, 30,* 209–214. Copyright 1999 by the American Psychological Association.

it is important to educate graduate students about the ethical issues and potential dangers associated with dual relationships. In this regard, a beginning level testing course provides an excellent opportunity for students to learn to establish and maintain appropriate professional boundaries.

A second ethical issue relates to the freedom of "volunteers" to actually choose to serve as "practice" test subjects. In particular, the use of friends and personal or professional contacts to secure volunteers may result in subtle pressure to say yes to help out a colleague or friend. Children may be especially vulnerable if parents feel such pressure. Eliminating the use of personal contacts to secure volunteers should greatly reduce this problem.

The third ethical concern arises in the tension between the training situation and the needs of volunteers who may be in distress or encountering some difficulty that may require future evaluation and service. Given concerns about student competence and potential harm to volunteers, it seems important that recruitment procedures consider ways to minimize the possibility that an adult or child volunteer requires service. Careful selection of nonclinical settings as sources for volunteers (e.g., classes, schools, agencies that serve individuals in the normal range of functioning) may be an important first step in this regard. Beyond that, a brief screening process through telephone interview or questionnaire may provide a way of identifying individuals who are inappropriate practice subjects and directing them to appropriate services. . . .

Feedback

Feedback policies and procedures varied depending on whether nonclient volunteers or clients were being tested. With nonclient volunteers, only a small percentage of respondents reported giving feedback; about 26% of adult testing instructors and 30% of child testing instructors reported giving feedback on a routine basis. When given, feedback was almost always verbal.

With clients, feedback was much more frequently given on a routine basis; 79% of adult instructors ($n = 24$) and 100% of child instructors ($n = 20$) gave feedback to clients or their parents. With adult clients, feedback was most often verbal (67%), whereas with children, it was most often both written and verbal (59%). With child clients, 50% also reported giving feedback to the child in addition to the parent.

The tension surrounding this area was apparent in the number and types of problems encountered here. Problems related to feedback were the most frequently reported by both adult (34 described problems in this area) and child testing instructors (29 described problems here). In nearly all instances, these problems involved nonclient volunteers, and most centered around no feedback policies. As the data indicated, the majority of instructors adopt no feedback policies when volunteers are tested. In other words, these volunteers are truly seen as "practice" subjects and, given concerns about the validity of testing plus the expectation that these volunteers are relatively intact, results of testing are not shared with the testing subject, parents, or any outside agencies. However, two types of problems were reported with some frequency by both adult and child instructors: (a) volunteers or their parents pressure for feedback, and (b) testing reveals a problem that may require intervention. With adult volunteers, such problems generally took the form of severe distress or psychopathology and suicidal risk. With children, suspected child abuse or learning problems were also noted. . . .

These data highlight two ethical concerns related to the rights and well-being of the practice subjects in testing courses. First, in terms of subjects' rights, the issue of feedback must be considered carefully, and very clear policies must be established and communicated to both students and testing subjects. The APA Ethics Code (Standard 2.09; APA, 1992)[1] states that an explanation of assessment results must be given unless the nature of the assessment precludes such an explanation, and this is clearly explained in advance. When beginning level students are testing nonclient volunteers, two aspects of the testing situation would seem to justify a policy of no feedback: (a) the "subject" is not seeking and, one hopes, does not need, clinical services; and

---

[1]*Ed. Note:* See Standard 9.10 in the current (2002) APA Ethics Code.

(b) the validity of test results is questionable. Such a policy seems both responsible and ethical if communicated in writing in advance for volunteers. When clients are tested and the need and expectation of services exist, however, feedback must be given. In these instances, adequate preparation and supervision of students is critical to ensure that test results are valid and that feedback is given in a sensitive, helpful manner. . . .

Second, even when nonclient volunteers are tested and there is no expectation of feedback, the data underscore that we cannot ignore the well-being of practice subjects. The problem descriptions of our respondents indicate that, even with nonclients, situations occur that challenge the purely "training" nature of the testing and may require some response (e.g., a testing subject expresses suicidal ideation or a child provides evidence of abuse). Thus, a feedback policy must establish criteria for identifying, and procedures for dealing with, emergency situations. These must also be clearly communicated to both students and testing subjects.

Confidentiality and Data Handling

Both child and adult testing instructors indicated that raw test data were reviewed by a number of people. Of the 64 adult instructors and 58 child instructors who provided information about test data from nonclient volunteers, most indicated that test protocols were reviewed by the instructor (about 90% for adult and about 95% for child). Protocols were also frequently reviewed by graduate assistants (about 80% for adult and about 69% for child) and occasionally reviewed by other students in the class (about 27% for adults; about 22% for child). A similar pattern of review was reported when actual clients were tested.

Most respondents seemed sensitive to the confidentiality concerns, particularly with nonclient volunteers. Of the 64 adult instructors and the 57 child instructors providing information about nonclient volunteers, over 80% reported removing names of volunteers from the raw test data and from case presentation materials, and slightly over 90% removed names from test reports. With clients ($n = 25$ for adult and 19 for child testing), names were less fre-

quently removed from both test data and test reports (approximately 50% of adult instructors and approximately 30% of child instructors reported removal). They were more likely to be removed for case presentations, particularly with children (64% for adult and about 84% for child).

Sixty-six adult and 60 child instructors provided information regarding what happened to raw test data when the process of testing and supervision was completed. . . . [I]t appeared that data for clients were often placed in clinical records, whereas volunteer data were more likely to be kept by the student (about 50% of instructors checked this) or destroyed (about 25–30% checked this). Only a small number of respondents reported storing data for research purposes (under 15% for both adult and child instructors) and about 15–18% indicated "other" policies (which typically involved the data being kept by the instructor, field supervisor, or department).

. . .

The APA Ethics Code (Standard 5; APA, 1992)[2] clearly states our "primary obligation" to protect the privacy and confidentiality of those with whom we work. In training settings, special attention to the confidentiality of nonclient volunteers is important; because volunteers and their families may be known to class members through personal or other professional contacts, the potential for unnecessary invasions of privacy or damaging revelations of sensitive information is high. Thus, it is important that data gathered during testing be protected, not only during the training process, but also after training functions have been completed.

More attention may need to be given to what happens to test data and information once training purposes have been served. Obviously, if testing has been done for clinical purposes, test data and reports belong in appropriately managed clinical files. However, if test data are not needed for clinical purposes or if copies of clinical data exist, it seems important that this information either be destroyed or that clear policies be established to guard against careless release of confidential information.

In addition to confidentiality of testing subjects, problem descriptions suggested that instructors

[2]*Ed. Note:* See Standard 4.01 in the current (2002) APA Ethics Code.

must also be concerned about confidentiality of graduate students taking testing courses when these students take tests themselves or test fellow students to gain practice. This was reported as a very common method of providing students with testing experience and seems to be a sound way of introducing students to test administration procedures before asking them to test nonclient volunteers. However, when the testing procedures require students to reveal sensitive information about themselves to their peers or the instructor, this procedure raises ethical concerns about dual roles. . . . In fact, two of the ethical problems reported involved students revealing information about themselves or classmates in write-ups of practice tests. Although practicing with classmates may play an important role in preparing students to administer complex tests, it is important that instructors be aware of the ethical issues involved and institute safeguards to avoid placing students in quasi-client situations that require them to reveal personal information. Such safeguards may include having students practice only parts of tests or setting up the testing situation as a role play in which the student being tested is asked to play a specific role rather than reveal information about himself or herself.

Consent

Formal consent procedures were routinely followed with nonclient volunteers and clients or their parents and guardians. Of the 63 instructors providing information about consent with nonclient adult volunteers, 63% reported that they used written consent, 22% used verbal consent, 6% used a combination of written and verbal, and only 3% reported that they did not have a formal consent procedure. Similarly, of the 59 instructors providing information about child volunteers, 71% secured written consent of the parent or guardian, 19% secured verbal consent, 8% used a combination of written and verbal, and only 1 instructor did not have a formal consent procedure. With actual clients, particularly child clients, consent procedures seemed more formalized. All 20 instructors who provided information about child

clients reported securing formal consent from a parent or guardian; 80% used written consent and 20% used a combination of written and verbal. With adult clients (25 instructors), 60% used a written format, 20% used a combination of written and verbal, and 20% obtained only verbal consent.

With children, an additional ethical issue concerns the child's involvement in the consent process. Both child volunteers and clients were included in the consent process most often by securing their verbal assent to testing; with volunteers, only 25% reported using written consent and, with clients, only 21%.

The concept of informed consent requires that individuals have information necessary to make an informed decision about participation. Respondents were asked to indicate what type of information was provided in the consent process for both adult and child volunteers and clients. Information included most frequently (by at least 80% of the respondents) in the consent process for all included test procedures, confidentiality, how data are used, and feedback policy. Interestingly, freedom to withdraw was also mentioned by at least 80% of the respondents, except with adult clients where only 64% reported covering this. With parents of child clients, risks and benefits were covered by at least 80% of respondents; however, with parents of child volunteers and with adults (either volunteers or clients), they were covered by only 50–60% of the respondents.
. . .

Although the APA Ethics Code (APA, 1992) does not explicitly state that informed consent is required for testing, Canter, Bennett, Jones, and Nagy (1994) noted that such a requirement seems inherent in several standards (e.g., Standards 2.01, 1.14, and 4.02).[3] Obviously, when dealing with minor children, it is the consent of the parent or guardian that must be secured (see Standard 4.02).[4] Most respondents seemed sensitive to the importance of obtaining and documenting such consent, particularly when actual clients are tested. However, it should be noted that a substantial number of instructors reported obtaining only verbal consent with adult

---

[3]*Ed. Note:* But now see Standard 9.03 in the current (2002) APA Ethics Code.

[4]*Ed. Note:* See Standard 9.03 in the current (2002) APA Ethics Code.

clients and with nonclient volunteers or their parents. Given the training nature of the experience, a formal written procedure seems advisable when dealing with all practice subjects. In fact, a written consent procedure that very clearly covers the nature of the test situation, ways in which data will be used, and feedback policy might help minimize problems encountered in these areas. . . .

An additional consent issue with children involves the participation of the child in the consent process. As discussed by Gustafson and McNamara (1987) there is considerable research evidence that children can participate in at least some types of treatment decisions. Indeed, the APA Ethics Code highlights the importance of informing individuals who are legally incapable of giving consent about interventions or procedures and seeking their assent (see Standard 4.02).[5] . . . It was thus encouraging to note that a very high percentage of respondents reported involving the child in the consent process, generally by obtaining the child's verbal assent. Such assent may be particularly important with child volunteers who are not being tested because of any identified need and who have nothing to gain from the testing. To avoid exploiting these children for our training purposes, special efforts need to be made to ensure their willingness to participate and protect their well-being throughout the testing process.

SUMMARY AND CONCLUSIONS

. . .

In summary form, we suggest the following:

1. Students need to be educated about the ethical issues associated with dual relationships and should be cautioned against testing acquaintances, friends, relatives, and any individual or child of an individual with whom they have an established relationship.
2. A formalized procedure for securing volunteers through university or community contacts, schools, day care centers, and so on may be established to avoid many of the problems associated with the use of personal contacts to secure volunteers.

3. Regardless of the source of volunteers, a screening process (either a brief questionnaire or telephone interview) may be instituted to maximize the possibility that volunteers are appropriate for training purposes.
4. Practice with classmates may be a helpful procedure for allowing students to develop some skill in administering tests before they do any testing of practice subjects. However, when this is done, care should be taken to avoid placing students in situations where they are required to reveal personal information.
5. In child testing courses, it is important to keep in mind that some graduate students may have little, if any, experience with children. These students may require special instruction to prepare them to be sensitive to the needs of young children during practice testing. . . .
6. When testing is conducted with nonclinical populations solely for training purposes, a no-feedback policy seems justified. This policy must be clearly thought out, with consideration given to possible exceptions and procedures for handling emergency situations, and must be communicated in writing to testing subjects or their parents.
7. When clients are tested, a procedure for giving feedback should be incorporated into the content of the testing class.
8. A very thorough consent procedure is essential with both nonclient volunteers as well as clients. When children are being tested, it is important that their verbal assent be secured during the consent process.
9. Special care must be taken to protect the confidentiality of practice subjects. Whenever possible, names and identifying data should be removed from test protocols. Policies must be established for either destroying test data or ensuring that it is securely maintained once training purposes have been served.

References

American Psychological Association. (1992). Ethical principles of psychologists and code of conduct. *American Psychologist, 47,* 1597–1611.

[5]*Ed. Note:* See Standard 3.10(b) in the current (2002) APA Ethics Code.

Canter, M. B., Bennett, B. E., Jones, S. E., & Naggy, T. F. (1994). *Ethics for psychologists: A commentary on the APA Ethics Code.* Washington, DC: American Psychological Association.

Gustafson, K. E., & McNamara, J. R. (1987). Confidentiality with minor clients: Issues and guidelines for therapists. *Professional Psychology: Research and Practice, 18,* 503–508.

Commentary: In a follow-up to Rupert et al. (1999), Yalof and Brabender present a number of vignettes related to teaching about personality scales and projective techniques. One issue not raised by Rupert et al. but discussed by Yalof and Brabender is the ethics of making class presentations using clinical data from test subjects. Which ethical principle is at issue here? They conclude their article with this recommendation:

> *We are suggesting that graduate courses in personality assessment provide an opportunity for the cultivation of good ethical judgment. As ethical dilemmas arise in the classroom, they should be identified and discussed in terms of the ethical principles they activate. The course instructor should model a decision-making process that leads to a specific course of action. In this way, students will acquire an organized approach to ethical problems, an approach that they can take beyond the classroom to any of the contemporary venues in which personality assessments are conducted. (pp. 212–213)*

Yalof, J., & Brabender, V. (2001). Ethical dilemmas in personality assessment courses: Using the classroom for in vivo training. Journal of Personality Assessment, 77, *203–213.*

Report of the Presidential Task Force on Psychological Ethics and National Security

American Psychological Association

I. OVERVIEW OF THE REPORT

The Presidential Task Force on Psychological Ethics and National Security (PENS) met in response to the Board of Directors' February 2005 charge, that the Task Force:

> [E]xamine whether our current Ethics Code adequately addresses [the ethical dimensions of psychologists' involvement in national security-related activities], whether the APA provides adequate ethical guidance to psychologists involved in these endeavors, and whether APA should develop policy to address the role of psychologists and psychology in investigations related to national security.

Recognizing the ethical complexity of this work, which takes place in unique settings and constantly evolving circumstances, the Task Force was nonetheless able to set forth 12 clear and agreed-upon statements about psychologists' ethical obligations.

. . .

II. INTRODUCTION TO THE REPORT

. . .

The Task Force addressed the argument that when psychologists act in certain roles outside traditional health-service provider relationships, for example, as consultants to interrogations, they are not acting in a professional capacity as psychologists and are therefore not bound by the APA Ethical Principles of Psychologists and Code of Conduct (hereinafter the Ethics Code).[2] The Task Force rejected this contention. The Task Force believes that when psychologists serve in a position by virtue of their training, experience, and expertise as psychologists, the APA Ethics Code applies. Thus in any such circumstance, psychologists are bound by the APA Ethics Code.

Principle B of the Ethics Code, Fidelity and Responsibility, states that psychologists "are aware of their professional and scientific responsibilities to society." Psychologists have a valuable and ethical role to assist in protecting our nation, other nations, and innocent civilians from harm, which will at times entail gathering information that can be used in our nation's and other nations' defense. The Task Force believes that a central role for psychologists working in the area of national security-related investigations is to assist in ensuring that processes are safe, legal, and ethical for all participants.

The Task Force looked to the APA Ethics Code for fundamental principles to guide its thinking. The Task Force found such principles in numerous aspects of the Ethics Code, such as the Preamble, "Psychologists respect and protect civil and human rights" and "[The Ethics Code] has as its goals the welfare and protection of the individuals and groups with whom psychologists work"; Principle A, Beneficence and Nonmaleficence, "In their professional actions, psychologists seek to safeguard the welfare and rights of those with whom they interact professionally and other affected persons"; Principle D, Justice, "Psychologists exercise reasonable judgment and take precautions to ensure that their potential biases, the boundaries of their competence, and the limitations of their expertise do not lead to or condone unjust practices"; and Principle E, Respect

---

Retrieved from http://www.apa.org/releases/PENSTaskForceReportFinal.pdf. Adapted with permission of the publisher. Issued in June 2005.

[2]American Psychological Association. (2002). Ethical principles of psychologists and code of conduct. *American Psychologist, 57,* 1060–1073. (Also available at http://www.apa.org/ethics/)

for People's Rights and Dignity, "Psychologists respect the dignity and worth of all people." The Task Force concluded that the Ethics Code is fundamentally sound in addressing the ethical dilemmas that arise in the context of national security-related work.

III. TWELVE STATEMENTS CONCERNING PSYCHOLOGISTS' ETHICAL OBLIGATIONS IN NATIONAL SECURITY-RELATED WORK AND COMMENTARY ON THE STATEMENTS

1. **Psychologists do not engage in, direct, support, facilitate, or offer training in torture or other cruel, inhuman, or degrading treatment.** The Task Force endorses the 1986 Resolution Against Torture of the American Psychological Association Council of Representatives,[3] and the 1985 Joint Resolution Against Torture of the American Psychological Association and the American Psychiatric Association[4] (Principle A, Beneficence and Nonmaleficence, and Ethical Standard 3.04, Avoiding Harm). The Task Force emphasizes that the Board of Directors' charge did not include an investigative or adjudicatory role and so the Task Force does not render any judgment concerning events that may or may not have occurred in national security-related settings. The Task Force nonetheless feels that an absolute statement against torture and other cruel, inhuman, or degrading treatment is appropriate.

2. **Psychologists are alert to acts of torture and other cruel, inhuman, or degrading treatment and have an ethical responsibility to report these acts to the appropriate authorities.** This ethical responsibility is rooted in the Preamble, "Psychologists respect and protect civil and human rights. . . . the development of a dynamic set of ethical standards for psychologists' work-related conduct requires a personal commitment and lifelong effort to act ethically [and] to encourage ethical behavior by . . . colleagues,"

and Principle B, Fidelity and Responsibility, which states that psychologists "are concerned about the ethical compliance of their colleagues' scientific and professional conduct" (Ethical Standard 1.05, Reporting Ethical Violations). The Task Force notes that when fulfilling the obligation to respond to unethical behavior by reporting the behavior to appropriate authorities as a prelude to an adjudicatory process, psychologists guard against the names of individual psychologists being disseminated to the public. Inappropriate or premature public dissemination can expose psychologists to a risk of harm outside of established and appropriate legal and adjudicatory processes (Ethical Standard 3.04, Avoiding Harm).

3. **Psychologists who serve in the role of supporting an interrogation do not use health care related information from an individual's medical record to the detriment of the individual's safety and well-being.** While information from a medical record may be helpful or necessary to ensure that an interrogation process remains safe, psychologists do not use such information to the detriment of an individual's safety and well-being (Ethical Standards 3.04, Avoiding Harm, and 3.08, Exploitative Relationships).

4. **Psychologists do not engage in behaviors that violate the laws of the United States, although psychologists may refuse for ethical reasons to follow laws or orders that are unjust or that violate basic principles of human rights.** Psychologists involved in national security-related activities follow all applicable rules and regulations that govern their roles. . . . Psychologists have an ethical responsibility to be informed of, familiar with, and follow the most recent applicable regulations and rules. The Task Force notes that certain rules and regulations incorporate texts that are fundamental to the treatment of individuals whose liberty has been curtailed, such as the United Nations Convention Against Torture and Other Cruel,

---

[3]American Psychological Association Council of Representatives. (1986). *American Psychological Association resolution against torture.* Retrieved from http://www.apa.org/about/division/cpminternatl.html#3

[4]American Psychiatric Association & American Psychological Association. (1985). *Against torture: Joint resolution of the American Psychiatric Association and the American Psychological Association.* Retrieved from http://www.psych.org/edu/other_res/lib_archives/archives/198506.pdf

Inhuman, or Degrading Treatment or Punishment and the Geneva Convention Relative to the Treatment of Prisoners of War.[5]

The Task Force notes that psychologists sometimes encounter conflicts between ethics and law. When such conflicts arise, psychologists make known their commitment to the APA Ethics Code and attempt to resolve the conflict in a responsible manner. If the conflict cannot be resolved in this manner, psychologists may adhere to the requirements of the law (Ethical Standard 1.02). An ethical reason for psychologists to not follow the law is to act "in keeping with basic principles of human rights" (APA Ethics Code, Introduction and Applicability). The Task Force encourages psychologists working in this area to review essential human rights documents, such as the United Nations Convention Against Torture and Other Cruel, Inhuman, or Degrading Treatment or Punishment and the Geneva Convention Relative to the Treatment of Prisoners of War.

5. **Psychologists are aware of and clarify their role in situations where the nature of their professional identity and professional function may be ambiguous.** Psychologists have a special responsibility to clarify their role in situations where individuals may have an incorrect impression that psychologists are serving in a health care provider role (Ethical Standards 3.07, Third-Party Requests for Services, and 3.11, Psychological Services Delivered to or Through Organizations).

The Task Force noted that psychologists acting in the role of consultant to national security issues most often work closely with other professionals from various disciplines. As a consequence, psychologists rarely act alone or independently, but rather as part of a group of professionals who bring together a variety of skills and experiences in order to provide an ethically appropriate service (Ethical Standard 3.09, Cooperating with Other Professionals).

Regardless of their role, psychologists who are aware of an individual in need of health or mental health treatment may seek consultation regarding how to ensure that the individual receives needed care (Principle A, Beneficence and Nonmaleficence).

6. **Psychologists are sensitive to the problems inherent in mixing potentially inconsistent roles such as health care provider and consultant to an interrogation, and refrain from engaging in such multiple relationships. . . .**

7. **Psychologists may serve in various national security-related roles, such as a consultant to an interrogation, in a manner that is consistent with the Ethics Code, and when doing so psychologists are mindful of factors unique to these roles and contexts that require special ethical consideration.** The Task Force noted that psychologists have served in consultant roles to law enforcement on the state and federal levels for a considerable period of time. Psychologists have proven highly effective in lending assistance to law enforcement in the vital area of information gathering and have done so in an ethical manner. The Task Force noted special ethical considerations for psychologists serving as consultants to interrogation processes in national security–related settings, especially when individuals from countries other than the United States have been detained by United States authorities. Such ethical considerations include

- How certain settings may instill in individuals a profound sense of powerlessness and may place individuals in considerable positions of disadvantage in terms of asserting their interests and rights (Ethical Standards 1.01, Misuse of Psychologists' Work, and 3.08, Exploitative Relationships).
- How failures to understand aspects of individuals' culture and ethnicity may generate misunderstandings, compromise the efficacy and hence the safety of investigatory processes,

[5]United Nations. (1987, June 26). *Convention against torture and other cruel, inhuman or degrading treatment or punishment.* Retrieved from http://www.unhchr.ch/html/menu3/b/h_cat39.htm

United Nations. (1950, October 21). *Geneva convention relative to the treatment of prisoners of war.* Retrieved from http://www.unhchr.ch/html/menu3/b/91.htm

and result in significant mental and physical harm (Principle E, "Psychologists are aware of and respect cultural, individual, and role differences, including those based on . . . race, ethnicity, culture, national origin . . . and consider these factors when working with members of such groups"; Ethical Standard 2.01(b), Boundaries of Competence, "Where scientific or professional knowledge in the discipline of psychology establishes that an understanding of factors associated with . . . race, ethnicity, culture, national origin . . . is essential for effective implementation of their services or research, psychologists have or obtain the training, experience, consultation, or supervision necessary to ensure the competence of their services, or they make appropriate referrals"; and Ethical Standard 3.01, Unfair Discrimination, "In their work-related activities, psychologists do not engage in unfair discrimination based on . . . race, ethnicity, culture, national origin").

- How the combination of a setting's ambiguity with high stress may facilitate engaging in behaviors that cross the boundaries of competence and ethical propriety. As behavioral scientists, psychologists are trained to observe, respond to, and ideally correct such processes as they occur (Principle A, Beneficence and Nonmaleficence, and Ethical Standard 3.04, Avoiding Harm).

8. **Psychologists who consult on interrogation techniques are mindful that the individual being interrogated may not have engaged in untoward behavior and may not have information of interest to the interrogator.** This ethical obligation is not diminished by the nature of an individual's acts prior to detainment or the likelihood of the individual having relevant information. At all times psychologists remain mindful of and abide by the prohibitions against engaging in or facilitating torture and other cruel, inhuman, or degrading treatment. Psychologists inform themselves about research regarding the most effective and humane methods of obtaining information and become familiar with how culture may interact with the techniques consulted

upon (Principle E, Respect for People's Rights and Dignity; Ethical Standards 2.01, Boundaries of Competence; 2.03, Maintaining Competence; and 3.01, Unfair Discrimination).

9. **Psychologists make clear the limits of confidentiality** (Ethical Standard 4.02, Discussing the Limits of Confidentiality). Psychologists who have access to, utilize, or share health or mental health related information do so with an awareness of the sensitivity of such information, keeping in mind that "Psychologists have a primary obligation and take reasonable precautions to protect confidential information" (Ethical Standard 4.01, Maintaining Confidentiality). When disclosing sensitive information, psychologists share the minimum amount of information necessary, and only with individuals who have a clear professional purpose for obtaining the information (Ethical Standard 4.04, Minimizing Intrusions on Privacy). Psychologists take care not to leave a misimpression that information is confidential when in fact it is not (Ethical Standards 3.10, Informed Consent, and 4.02, Discussing the Limits of Confidentiality).

10. **Psychologists are aware of and do not act beyond their competencies, except in unusual circumstances, such as set forth in the Ethics Code** (Ethical Standard 2.02, Providing Services in Emergencies). Psychologists strive to ensure that they rely on methods that are effective, in addition to being safe, legal, and ethical (Ethical Standards 2.01, Boundaries of Competence; 2.04, Bases for Scientific and Professional Judgments; and 9.01, Bases for Assessments).

11. **Psychologists clarify for themselves the identity of their client and retain ethical obligations to individuals who are not their clients** (Ethical Standards 3.07, Third-Party Requests for Services, and 3.11, Psychological Services Delivered to or Through Organizations). Regardless of whether an individual is considered a client, psychologists have an ethical obligation to ensure that their activities in relation to the individual are safe, legal, and ethical (Ethical Standard 3.04, Avoiding Harm). Sensitivity to the entirety of a psychologist's ethical obligations is especially important

where, because of a setting's unique characteristics, an individual may not be fully able to assert relevant rights and interests (Principle A, Beneficence and Nonmaleficence, "In their professional actions, psychologists seek to safeguard the welfare and rights of those with whom they interact professionally and other affected persons . . . "; Principle D, Justice, "Psychologists exercise reasonable judgment and take precautions to ensure that their potential biases, the boundaries of their competence, and the limitations of their expertise do not lead to or condone unjust practices"; Principle E, Respect for People's Rights and Dignity, "Psychologists are aware that special safeguards may be necessary to protect the rights and welfare of persons or communities whose vulnerabilities impair autonomous decision making"; and Ethical Standard 3.08, Exploitative Relationships).

12. **Psychologists consult when they are facing difficult ethical dilemmas.** The Task Force was emphatic that consultation on ethics questions and dilemmas is highly appropriate for psychologists at all levels of experience, especially in this very challenging and ethically complex area of practice (Preamble to the Ethics Code, "The development of a dynamic set of ethical standards for psychologists' work-related conduct requires a personal commitment and lifelong effort to act ethically . . . and to consult with others concerning ethical problems," and Ethical Standard 4.06, Consultations).

The Task Force drew several other conclusions:
  . . .

■ Psychologists should encourage and engage in further research to evaluate and enhance the efficacy and effectiveness of the application of psychological science to issues, concerns, and operations relevant to national security. One focus of a broad program of research is to examine the efficacy and effectiveness of information-gathering techniques, with an emphasis on the quality of information obtained. In addition, psychologists should examine the psychological effects of conducting interrogations on the inter-

rogators themselves to explore ways of helping to ensure that the process of gathering information is likely to remain within ethical boundaries. Also valuable will be research on cultural differences in the psychological impact of particular information-gathering methods and what constitutes cruel, inhuman, or degrading treatment.

■ The Task Force noted a potential area of tension between conducting research that is classified or whose success could be compromised if the research purpose and/or methodology become known and ethical standards that require debriefing after participation in a study as a research subject (Ethical Standards 8.07, Deception in Research, and 8.08, Debriefing). APA should identify and further examine the ethical dimensions of such tensions.

■ Psychologists working in this area should inform themselves of how culture and ethnicity interact with investigative or information-gathering techniques, with special attention to how failing to attend to such factors may result in harm.

The Task Force engaged in vigorous discussion and debate and did not reach consensus on several issues:

■ *The role of human rights standards in an ethics code.* While all Task Force members felt that respect for human rights is critical, some task force members felt strongly that international standards of human rights should be built into the ethics code and others felt that the laws of the United States should be the touchstone.

■ *The degree to which psychologists may ethically disguise the nature and purpose of their work.* While all members of the Task Force agreed that full disclosure of the nature and purpose of a psychologist's work is not ethically required or appropriate in every circumstance, members differed on the degree to which psychologists may ethically dissemble their activities from individuals whom they engage directly.

■ *Whether the discussions of the Task Force should have been made available outside the Task Force.* Some members believed that sharing the substance of the discussions, debates, and disagreements of the Task Force would be helpful to others in fostering the development of professional ethics in other areas of national security. Others felt that not sharing information beyond this report and other public statements would facilitate richer and more productive exchanges during the Task Force meeting. The Task Force voted on this issue. By a vote of seven to one, with one abstention, the Task Force voted to limit what information is disclosed concerning its deliberations to this report and other public statements made by the Task Force as a whole.

◆   ◆   ◆

Commentary: Compare the APA's position to that of the American Psychiatric Association whose policy was approved by its Board of Trustees in May 2006 and which follows.

Psychiatric Participation in Interrogation[1] of Detainees

American Psychiatric Association

1. The American Psychiatric Association reiterates its position that psychiatrists should not participate in, or otherwise assist or facilitate, the commission of torture of any person. Psychiatrists who become aware that torture has occurred, is occurring, or has been planned must report it promptly to a person or persons in a position to take corrective action.

2. (a) Every person in military or civilian detention, whether in the United States or elsewhere is entitled to appropriate medical care under domestic and international humanitarian law. (b) Psychiatrists providing medical care to individual detainees owe their primary obligation to the well-being of their patients, including advocating for their patients, and should not participate or assist in any way, whether directly or indirectly, overtly or covertly, in the interrogation of their patients on behalf of military or civilian agencies or law enforcement authorities. (c) Psychiatrists should not disclose any part of the medical records of any patient, or information derived from the treatment relationship, to persons conducting interrogation of the detainee. (d) This paragraph is not meant to preclude treating psychiatrists who become aware that the detainee may pose a significant threat of harm to him/herself or to others from ascertaining the nature and the seriousness of the threat or from notifying appropriate authorities of that threat, consistent with the obligations applicable to other treatment relationships.

3. No psychiatrist should participate directly in the interrogation of persons held in custody by military or civilian investigative or law enforcement authorities, whether in the United States or elsewhere. Direct participation includes being present in the interrogation room, asking or suggesting questions, or advising authorities on the use of specific techniques of interrogation with particular detainees. However, psychiatrists may provide training to military or civilian investigative or law enforcement personnel on recognizing and responding to persons with mental illnesses, on the possible medical and psychological effects of particular techniques and conditions of interrogation, and on other areas within their professional expertise.

♦   ♦   ♦

Commentary: In light of the American Psychiatric Association's policy that none of its practitioners should directly participate as members of behavioral science consulting teams ("biscuits") who aid in the interrogation of detainees, the military announced that it intended to use only psychologists to help interrogators devise strategies to extract information from those held in places like Guantanamo Bay.

Stephen Behnke, director of the American Psychological Association's (APA's) Ethics Office, asserted that the difference between the APA and the American Psychiatric Association is their respective views of their ethical obligations. He stated that psychologists believe that they "have ethical responsibilities to the individual under questioning, as well as to third parties and the public" (Behnke, 2006, p. 66). In contrast, he maintained,

> *The American Psychiatric Association uses a somewhat different analysis in assessing*

[1] As used in this statement, "interrogation" refers to a deliberate attempt to elicit information from a detainee for the purposes of incriminating the detainee, identifying other persons who have committed or may be planning to commit acts of violence or other crimes, or otherwise obtaining information that is believed to be of value for criminal justice or national security purposes. It does not include interviews or other interactions with a detainee that have been appropriately authorized by a court or by counsel for the detainee or that are conducted for or on behalf of correctional authorities with a prisoner serving a criminal sentence.

the appropriate role for its members in interrogations. Rather than deriving its position from two ethical principles—Do No Harm and contribute to society by preventing harm—the psychiatrists appear to focus solely on the first, Do No Harm. (p. 67)

Behnke, S. (2006, July/August). Ethics and interrogations: Comparing and contrasting the American Psychological, American Medical and American Psychiatric Association positions. Monitor on Psychology, 37, 66–67.

In an article published in the New England Journal of Medicine (Okie, 2005), Steven Sharfstein, then president of the American Psychiatric Association, who was an invited visitor to Guantanamo, explaining his association's position, was quoted as saying, "There is a great concern about when you depart from your physician role" (p. 2533). The author of the article went on:

> When a forensic psychiatrist examines a prisoner in a civilian jail, the psychiatrist first explains to the prisoner that the interview may not be to his benefit, and the prisoner is allowed to refuse. "With the detainee situation, there is none of that," Sharfstein said. "The process of interrogating detainees is, by its very nature, deceptive, and that's a major problem . . . [ellipsis in original]. People have to interrogate, but it's really inappropriate to use psychiatrists." (p. 2533)

Okie, S. (2005). Glimpses of Guantanamo—Medical ethics and the war on terror. The New England Journal of Medicine, 353, 2529–2534.

Another physician argued that Department of Defense policies governing biscuit teams enabled "physician participation in coercive interrogation practices" (p. 7). Keram, E. A. (2006). Will medical ethics be a casualty of the war on terror? Journal of the American Academy of Psychiatry and the Law, 34, 6–8. It is noteworthy that the PENS report does not preclude psychologists' involvement in coercive interrogations. Then APA President Gerald Koocher defended APA's position: "The task force declined to

use the words 'coercive' or 'harmful' in describing ethical misconduct, because many legitimate professional roles of psychologists could prove problematic in that regard [e.g., mandated reports of abuse, evaluations to determine a defendant's competency to stand trial]" (p. 5). Koocher, G. P. (2006, February). Speaking against torture. Monitor on Psychology, 37, 5.

Koocher's column stimulated letters, both pro and con, about his views and the PENS report generally. See, for example, letters by Fraenkel (pro), Arrigo (con), and Wessels (con), the latter two members of the PENS task force, in the (2006, May) Monitor on Psychology, 37, 8; Suedfeld (pro) and Shinn & Woolf (con) in the (2006, April) Monitor on Psychology, 37, 4, 8. See also the report of a debate between supporters and detractors of the PENS report at the 2006 APA annual convention: Munsey, C., & Meyers, L. (2006, October). Debating psychologists' wartime roles. Monitor on Psychology, 37, 28–29. At that meeting it was announced that APA's Ethics Committee would develop a detailed commentary/casebook to help psychologists understand their role in interrogations and as adherents to the Ethics Code.

In any event, this debate harkens back to the issues raised by the Tarasoff case discussed in chapter 4, but on a much larger scale. The concerns about the PENS report and the contrasting positions of the American Psychological and American Psychiatric Associations center on the prima facie duty of fidelity. As the court did in Tarasoff, the APA views psychologists as having dual loyalties—to the individual and to the greater society, permitting psychologists to override their duty of fidelity to clients for significant governmental or societal purposes. Psychiatrists seem to view their roles primarily as treaters, acting to benefit their patients' mental health, not as adjuncts to coercive governmental conduct. Which position do readers believe is more ethical, more realistic and practical, and in the long run, more protective of society?

Ed. Note: As this text was going to press, the APA's Council of Representatives reaffirmed its 2006 Resolution Against Torture and, in addition, specified a number of interrogation techniques such as water boarding, sexual humiliation, exploitation of phobias, and psychopathology that psychologists are specifically *prohibited from engaging in. See http://www.apa.org/releases/councilres0807.html. After a lengthy debate, however, the Council defeated a resolution that "would have limited psychologists' role in national security facilities to that of health-care providers" (p. 14). Farberman, R. (October 2007). Council extends its* stance on torture. Monitor on Psychology, 38, 14. *See also Okorodudu, C., Strickland, W. J., Van Hoorn, J. L., & Wiggins, E. C. (November 2007). A call to action: APA's 2007 resolution against torture.* Monitor on Psychology, 38, 22–25. *Does the resolution resolve the ethical issues?*

CHAPTER 7

THERAPY AND OTHER FORMS
OF INTERVENTION

Few human relationships so quickly attain the level of intimacy as a working therapeutic relationship. Although in most instances therapists are complete strangers at the beginning of treatment, clients are expected to reveal their innermost and private feelings, thoughts, and behavior to them, and with them, confront the clients' deepest, darkest, and most distasteful sides of themselves. At times, clients may be asked to do this not only in front of their therapists but also in the company of family members or even strangers who make up their therapeutic group.

To compound the problem, in most cases, people enter therapy only after considerable worry and rumination. They are experiencing such symptoms as debilitating feelings or nonproductive, even self-damaging behavior. Although they may want desperately to understand and ameliorate these indicators of distress, it is likely that they do not know much about the process of therapy.

Despite their anxiety, these potential clients are at least facing the prospect voluntarily. However, not all people come to treatment on their own initiative. Some patients—for example, those involuntarily committed to mental hospitals or forced by a court to seek treatment as a condition of probation or parole—may be compelled to see a psychologist. In either case, therapists are likely to encounter clients who, at their initial consultation, are confused, anxious, needy, and vulnerable—and sometimes, downright hostile and negative.

It is almost inevitable, then, that complex ethical issues will arise in settings where therapy and other forms of intervention take place. Preceding chapters have already explored some of these issues. In chapters 4 and 5, I provided materials in which crucial issues concerning confidentiality and multiple relationships, respectively, were debated. In chapter 10, I introduce some of the more ethically sensitive commercial aspects of providing psychological services. In this chapter, I concentrate on several additional issues that are not covered elsewhere in this book.

The 1989 APA code of ethics contained no divisible set of ethical principles related to therapy. In this regard, the 1992 Code offered significant improvement, with Section 4 devoted to that issue. The current (2002) Code continues this practice, although the standards focusing on therapy are now found mainly in Section 10. It is in Standard 3.10(a), however, that the Code requires psychologists to obtain informed consent. Standard 10.01 mandates that this process occur as early as is feasible in treatment. Standard 3.10(d) stipulates that psychologists "appropriately document written or oral consent." Nevertheless, it does not flesh out this requirement in any explicit way. Thus, many authors have sought to advance their views on how the consent process should take place. Some have even questioned whether consent should be sought at all. Another matter of considerable debate is whether the therapist and the client should enter into a formal written informed-consent contract.

These controversies about the substance and procedure of informed consent to treatment are important in themselves, but they also raise larger, more overarching issues. What does the kind of consent process, if any, say about the nature of the relationship between the professional and the person seeking help? Which of the moral principles discussed in chapter 3 are promoted by consent? Does obtaining consent promote certain values but endanger others? Can in fact obtaining consent damage—if not destroy—the value of certain forms of therapy?

Single client–therapist issues are complex enough; they become geometrically enlarged when therapists engage in couples, family, or group therapy. Confidentiality issues become paramount, of course, and the materials in this chapter on confidentiality amplify the ideas put forth in chapter 4. Added to this, however, is the complicating fact that family therapy often involves children. Should they have the right to consent to therapy? Do they have independent rights to privacy that should be respected? Should one assume that parents represent their children's interests? When, if ever, should therapists act as children's advocates?

It is essential that this chapter cover these traditional (though yet unresolved, and unsolved) problems. However, the world of psychology is not limited to spoken, face-to-face forms of treatment. For example, psychologists are increasingly involved in behavioral medicine, such as stress and pain management. Moreover, it is impossible to ignore the presently raging debate over the effort of many powerful and influential psychologists to obtain the right for licensed psychologists, given proper training, to prescribe antipsychotic and other psychotropic medications. In addition, some psychologists write self-help texts that become bestsellers, whereas others conduct therapy over the telephone or electronic mail (and probably by fax).

Not only do psychologists engage in different forms of treatment, but they are also confronted with a diversity of clients. Women in general, gays and lesbians, ethnic minorities, those from rural communities, and people with disabilities often confront the responsible psychotherapist (still predominantly men who are White and urban) with a plethora of ethical issues. Finally, ethical problems may even survive the death of the therapist. Consider, for example, what ethical obligations psychologists have toward their patients in contemplation of their own deaths?

These are the issues covered in chapter 7. The challenges they represent clearly show that good therapy is more than technique, empathy, and sound theory.

Seeking an Understanding of Informed Consent

Jeffrey E. Barnett

Regardless of the nature of the professional relationship, be it psychotherapy, assessment, research, clinical supervision, consultation, or some other professional role, psychologists are ethically and legally bound to begin these relationships only after initiating a process of informed consent (American Psychological Association [APA], 2002; Knapp & VandeCreek, 2006). *Informed consent* is a shared decision-making process in which the professional communicates sufficient information to the other individual so that she or he may make an informed decision about participation in the professional relationship. . . .

. . .

HISTORICAL PERSPECTIVE

Informed consent has a long history in the health professions, beginning in medicine, and has evolved substantially over the years through case law. Initially, physicians could be seen as benevolent authoritarians who very paternalistically directed each patient's assessment and treatment. Through the 19th and into the 20th century, physicians generally did not first obtain their patients' consent prior to providing services to them and were not seen as under any widely accepted ethical or legal mandate to do so (Grisso & Appelbaum, 1998). This model has been described as the "doctor-knows-best system," in which patients were passive recipients of services (Welfel, 2006). There was little sharing of information, collaboration, or patient involvement in decision making, and as a result, patients may be seen as having been more vulnerable to abuse or harm. Overall, the doctrine of informed consent changed this practice to require that health professionals share information about anticipated treatments sufficient to allow the patient to make an informed decision about participation.

A foundation for informed consent seen in case law is *Schloendorf v. Society of New York Hospital* (1914), in which Judge Cardozo stated that "every human being of adult years and sound mind has a right to determine what shall be done with his own body" (as cited in Stromberg et al., 1988, p. 446). Then, over a number of years beginning in the 1950s, a series of malpractice cases ruled on issues of alleged harm to patients by health care professionals. . . .

In *Salgo v. Stanford* (1957), the California Court of Appeals ruled that a patient must fully comprehend the information shared and that risks and benefits associated with participation must be included in that consent for it to be considered valid. In the landmark case of *Canterbury v. Spence* (1972), it was ruled that merely answering patients' questions is insufficient and that all information necessary must be shared that patients need "for an intelligent decision" (p. 783) regarding participation, and that it must be presented in terms that can be understood by the individual. This is a significant step forward from the previous standard of sharing what health professionals determined patients needed to know to make their decisions. In *Truman v. Thomas* (1980), the California Supreme Court ruled that patients must also be informed of the risks associated with refusing treatment, not just the risks associated with acceptance of the proposed treatment. And, more recently, the case of *Osheroff v. Chestnut Lodge* (1985), although settled out of court, established the precedent that patients must also be informed of reasonably available alternatives and their relative risks and benefits as well. Those familiar with informed-consent standards included in the APA's *Ethical Principles of Psychologists and Code of Conduct*

From *Professional Psychology: Research and Practice, 38*, 179–182. Copyright 2007 by the American Psychological Association.

(referred to as the APA Ethics Code; APA, 2002) will see many of the currently accepted elements of informed consent above in this brief review of its chronological development.

GOALS OF INFORMED CONSENT

Although informed consent is rooted in the medical field and originally concerned specific discrete procedures, it has become widely accepted as an essential aspect of each client's participation in the psychotherapy process as well as in all other services psychologists provide. Authors such as Beahrs and Gutheil (2001) defined informed consent as "the process of sharing information with patients that is essential to their ability to make rational choices among multiple options" (p. 4). But informed consent brings with it several other important benefits, including "promoting client autonomy and self-determination, minimizing the risk of exploitation and harm, fostering rational decision-making, and enhancing the therapeutic alliance" (Snyder & Barnett, 2006, p. 37). Although the psychologist's theoretical orientation may affect one's view of informed consent, in general it can be seen as consistent with psychologists' general goal of establishing a collaborative relationship that is built on trust, openness, and respect. Additionally, the provision of information necessary to make an informed choice also promotes the sharing of decision-making power in the professional relationship, which enhances the professional collaboration, reduces risks of exploitation and harm (Meisel, Roth, & Lidz, 1977), and encourages trust, openness, and sharing in the relationship (Snyder & Barnett, 2006).

Informed consent should be viewed as a process, not as a single event that occurs at the outset of treatment (or supervision, research, or any other professional relationship). It is best implemented if integrated into the professional relationship from its outset through its completion. The APA Ethics Code (APA, 2002) states that psychologists should begin the informed-consent process "as early as is feasible in the therapeutic relationship" (p. 1072), but psychologists should not consider their obligation met at that point. It is important to update the informed-consent agreement throughout the course of the professional relationship as circumstances warrant, such as any proposed significant changes to the treatment to be offered and, thus, changes to the original informed-consent agreement.

With regard to treatment services, the APA Ethics Code (APA, 2002) requires psychologists to include in each informed-consent agreement information about "the nature and anticipated course of therapy, fees, involvement of third parties, and limits of confidentiality" (p. 1072) as well as reasonable alternatives available, their relative risks and benefits, and the right to refuse or withdraw from treatment. Additional requirements are also included for informed consent to supervision, research, assessment, and other services provided by psychologists. Studies (e.g., Sullivan, Martin, & Handelsman, 1993) have found that consumers value having detailed information provided to them at the outset of the professional relationship and even rate those psychologists who engage in an informed-consent process as more expert and trustworthy than those who do not. But just how that information is provided to them can significantly affect the specific information they request (Braaten, Otto, & Handelsman, 1993). Whether informed consent should be provided through use of written documents, verbally, or in combination is unclear, yet many professionals suggest a combination approach. The use of an appropriate written consent agreement can augment all verbal consent discussions. It helps ensure that clients understand what they are agreeing to, provides clients with a written document they may refer to and review over the course of the professional relationship, and allows the psychologist to refer to it as well should there be any confusion or misunderstandings later.

IS THE CONSENT TRULY INFORMED?

Legally, three conditions must be met for informed consent to be considered valid. The client must understand the information presented, the consent must be given voluntarily, and the client must be competent to give consent (Gross, 2001). It is not sufficient to just present the information to the client "using appropriate language understandable to that person" (APA, 2002, p. 1065). In addition, psychologists must actively ensure each client's understanding of the information presented and of that to which he or she is agreeing. Merely asking if clients understand or if they have any questions would not be seen as meeting this obligation. For example, having clients explain their understanding of information shared and of specific agreements would better demonstrate their understanding than simply asking questions as described above. Written informed-consent agreements may be seen as useful in allowing the client to have something to refer to later, and they provide a tangible record of agreements between both parties. But even in conjunction with a verbal review, written informed-consent agreements should be developed with attention to reading level and ease of comprehension. In one study of informed-consent forms used in 114 U.S. medical schools, results found the forms to be written on average at the 10.6 grade level, despite these schools' own requirements for a readability level of 2.8 grade levels lower (Paasche-Orlow, Taylor, & Brancati, 2003). In the popular media, examples of perhaps even greater concern are seen in a review of the readability of notice of privacy forms from a number of prominent health care facilities: percentage of patient privacy forms that in a test were shown to be as easy to read as comics (0%), percentage as easy to read as J. K. Rowling's *Harry Potter and the Sorcerer's Stone* (1%), percentage as easy to read as H. G. Wells's *The War of the Worlds* (8%), and percentage as easy to read as professional medical literature or legal contracts (91%; "The Numbers Game," 2005).

Just how much information to include in the informed-consent process is unclear. Certainly, it is possible to overwhelm a client with too much information, and this could be inimical to the previously stated goals of the informed-consent process. Studies of psychologists' informed-consent practices have found a wide range of variability in the breadth and depth of information shared with clients (e.g., Dsubanko-Obermayr & Baumann, 1998; Otto, Ogloff, & Small, 1991). Certain issues must always be included in informed consent, as has been described earlier. A careful review of issues such as limits to confidentiality is essential, because clients may have very different expectations of the psychologist's obligations in this regard. For example, Miller and

Thelen (1986) found that 69% of consumers surveyed believed and expected that all information shared in psychotherapy would be kept confidential, and 74% stated that there should be no exception to this rule. Finally, 96% expressed wanting to know about any possible limits to confidentiality prior to beginning the psychotherapy relationship. Pomerantz and Handelsman (2004) recommended including issues such as insurance and managed-care details and psychopharmacology, among others. These authors also made recommendations regarding the format for presenting informed-consent information. They offered a written question format that includes a number of questions clients may ask their psychologist to help gather important information relevant to the informed-consent process. They did not suggest one set of questions to be addressed by all clients in all psychotherapy situations. Rather, they offered this as guidance for what Pope (1991) described as a dynamic process that can be tailored to best address each individual client's needs and circumstances.

ISSUES TO CONSIDER

Informed consent is an important aspect of the psychotherapy process and psychotherapy relationship as well as for all professional relationships in which psychologists participate. Whereas standards exist for the minimal information to be included in the informed-consent process, no specific standard exists for when to limit this information and when to know if one is sharing too much. The extent and specificity of information that should be included in this process—as well as how to decide what to include or not to include and how best to present this information—remain unclear. Dilemmas exist regarding competence, understanding, and voluntariness to include obtaining consent from minors, inpatients, prisoners, those with cognitive impairment, and others and knowing when to share information, how much information to share, and when this process may be counterproductive. It is also important to know how best to present the information, be it verbally, through a written document, or in combination. Psychologists should also consider and understand the potential impact of diversity on this process, such as the role that language, age (and developmental level), cultural background, and other factors may play in affecting the informed-consent process. Clinical work with individuals, couples, families, and groups each presents unique challenges with regard to informed consent, as do third-party requests for services, clinical supervision, research, and teaching. Knowing how best to address these challenges is of great importance for protecting clients' rights, promoting their autonomy, and working to achieve the best possible outcomes in the professional relationships we form with them.

References

American Psychological Association. (2002). Ethical principles of psychologists and code of conduct. *American Psychologist, 57,* 1060–1073.

Beahrs, J. O., & Gutheil, T. G. (2001). Informed consent in psychotherapy. *American Journal of Psychiatry, 158,* 4–10.

Braaten, E. B., Otto, S., & Handelsman, M. M. (1993). What do people want to know about psychotherapy? *Psychotherapy, 30,* 565–570.

Canterbury v. Spence, 464 F.2d 772 (D.C. Cir. 1972).

Dsubanko-Obermayr, K., & Baumann, U. (1998). Informed consent in psychotherapy: Demands and reality. *Psychotherapy Research, 8,* 231–247.

Grisso, T., & Appelbaum, P. S. (1998). *Assessing competence to consent to treatment: A guide for physicians and other health professionals.* New York: Oxford University Press.

Gross, B. H. (2001). Informed consent. *Annals of the American Psychotherapy Association, 4,* 24.

Knapp, S. J., & VandeCreek, L. D. (2006). *Practical ethics for psychologists: A positive approach.* Washington, DC: American Psychological Association.

Meisel, A., Roth, L. H., & Lidz, C. W. (1977). Toward a model of the legal doctrine of informed consent. *American Journal of Psychiatry, 134,* 285–289.

Miller, D. J., & Thelen, M. H. (1986). Knowledge and beliefs about confidentiality in psychotherapy. *Professional Psychology: Research and Practice, 17,* 15–19.

Osheroff v. Chestnut Lodge, 490 A.2d 720 (Md. App. 1985).

Otto, R. K., Ogloff, J. R., & Small, M. A. (1991). Confidentiality and informed consent in psychotherapy: Clinicians' knowledge and practices in Florida and Nebraska. *Forensic Reports, 4,* 379–389.

Paasche-Orlow, M. K., Taylor, H. A., & Brancati, F. L. (2003). Readability standards for informed-consent forms as compared with actual readability. *New England Journal of Medicine, 348,* 721–726.

Pomerantz, A. M., & Handelsman, M. M. (2004). Informed consent revisited: An updated written question format. *Professional Psychology: Research and Practice, 35,* 201–205.

Pope, K. S. (1991). Informed consent: Clinical and legal considerations. *Independent Practitioner, 11,* 36–41.

Salgo v. Leland Stanford Jr. Univ. Bd. of Trustees, 154 Cal. App. 2d 560, 317 P.2d 170 (1957).

Schloendorf v. Society of New York Hospital, 211 N.Y. 125, 105 N.E. 92 (1914).

Snyder, T. A., & Barnett, J. E. (2006). Informed consent and the process of psychotherapy. *Psychotherapy Bulletin, 41,* 37–42.

Stromberg, C. D., Haggarty, D. J., Leibenluft, R. F., McMillian, M. H., Mishkin, B., Rubin, B. L., & Trilling, H. R. (1988). *The psychologist's legal handbook.* Washington, DC: Council for the National Register of Health Service Providers in Psychology.

Sullivan, T., Martin, W. L., & Handelsman, M. M. (1993). Practical benefits of an informed-consent procedure: An empirical investigation. *Professional Psychology: Research and Practice, 24,* 160–163.

The numbers game. (April 12, 2005). *The Washington Post,* p. F3.

Truman v. Thomas, 611 P.2d 902 (Cal. 1980).

Welfel, E. R. (2006). *Ethics in counseling and psychotherapy: Standards, research, and emerging issues.* Belmont, CA: Thomson Brooks/Cole.

◆　◆　◆

Commentary: Barnett's excellent overview highlighting the autonomy-based rationale for informed consent echoes the work of others published 30 years ago:

> *The process of providing information and obtaining agreement through the use of contract defines the therapeutic relationship as a mutual endeavor to which the therapist contributes knowledge and skill in psychology and to which the client brings specialized knowledge and a commitment to work on his or her problems. (p. 7)*

Hare-Mustin, R. T., Marecek, J., Kaplan, A. G., & Liss-Levenson, N. (1979). Rights of clients, responsibilities of therapists. American Psychologist, 34, *3–16.*

Similarly, Handelsman and Galvin (1988) asserted that consent forms have roles in "increasing professionals' self-scrutiny, respecting the autonomy of clients, and allowing clients to enhance their welfare by becoming partners with the therapist in their mental health care" (p. 223). Handelsman, M., & Galvin, M. (1988). Facilitating informed consent for outpatient therapy: A suggested written format. Professional Psychology: Research and Practice, 19, *223–225. For an updated format (taking into account the requirements of the federal government's Health Insurance Portability and Accountability Act, see chap. 10, this volume), see Pomerantz, A. M., & Handelsman, M. (2004). Informed consent revisited: An updated written question format.* Professional Psychology: Research and Practice, 35, *201–205.*

Despite the supportive research cited by Barnett in the excerpt provided here, there have been theoretical and practical concerns raised about informed consent, particularly regarding the use of contracts. For example, one commentator has argued that in psychoanalytically oriented psychotherapy . . .

> *such contracts of cure or even contracts outlining the specifics of the treatment process would be wholly inappropriate and, in fact, counterproductive. . . . There is enough built-in resistance to analytic psychotherapy . . . that we should avoid adding more coals to the fire. (p. 258)*

Parker, K. (1976). Comment: On a contractual model of treatment. American Psychologist, 31, *257–258.*

Perhaps the therapeutic technique that raises the most ethical questions is paradoxical intention. Paradoxical strategies usually require the client to maintain or intensify a presenting symptom; for example, a therapist encourages an anxious client to act anxiously in an actual situation. For the strategy to work, it is at times necessary for the therapist to distort his or her rationale for using it. Thus, one could claim that the use of this strategy is unethical. Others respond that the ethical issues are no different in the use of this technique than in any form of psychotherapy. For controversial discussions of this topic, see

Betts, G. R., & Remer, R. (1993). The impact of paradoxical interventions on perceptions of the therapist and ratings of treatment and acceptability. Professional Psychology: Research and Practice, 24, *164–170.*

Brown, J. E., & Slee, P. T. (1986). Paradoxical strategies: The ethics of intervention. Professional Psychology: Research and Practice, 17, *487–491.*

Hunsley, J. (1988). Conceptions and misconceptions about the context of paradoxical therapy. Professional Psychology: Research and Practice, 19, *553–559.*

More generally, some have questioned whether it is clear

> *that the therapist has the capacity to present the necessary information for an informed consent, because the risks and consequences of the treatment and its alternatives are so vast, indeterminate, and complex that they belie adequate presentation. (p. 512)*

Widiger, T. A., & Rorer, J. G. (1984). The responsible psychotherapist. American Psychologist, 39, *503–515.*

One suggestion to deal with the difficulty in communicating the complexities of therapy and the incompatibility of informed consent with certain therapeutic strategies is for clinicians to inform their clients that because of their theoretical orientation they will not discuss the specific techniques or objectives of therapy. See Graca, J. (1985). Whither informed consent to psychotherapy? American Psychologist, 40, *1062–1063. Would Graca's alternative comport with the informed consent provisions of the 2002 Ethics Code?*

Despite the fact that the issue of whether therapists must engage in an informed consent process appears to be settled by the 2002 Ethics Code, important ancillary problems have been noted, as the following excerpts and comments explain.

Informed Consent: Complexities and Meanings

Erica H. Wise

. . . Most often it is not realistic to fully inform potential clients in a manner that allows them total autonomy or equality in making treatment decisions. The APA's [American Psychological Association] Ethics Code (APA, 2002) uses the term *reasonably understandable* to describe the level of complexity and completeness that is expected of psychologists. Barnett (2007) summarizes research suggesting that informed-consent documents may not actually be reasonably understandable to the general population. How might we best determine the precise risks of seeking or failing to seek treatment? Is it realistic for us to fully articulate all reasonable treatment alternatives and risks to clients? Can we truly ensure that potential clients have adequately understood what we have attempted to communicate to them? If the purpose of informed consent is to elicit agreement with our proposed treatment plan, then we are arguably engaging in risk management rather than truly meeting the aspirational goal of informed consent. Although few psychologists would question the value of seeking informed consent, it is, in fact, a surprisingly complex ethical duty to implement effectively. Among many examples, acutely distressed individuals seeking psychological treatment may have little interest in attempting to comprehend the nuances of a long or technically complex informed-consent statement. In addition, clients from differing cultural backgrounds may not feel personally empowered to ask questions of a professional or may actually perceive it to be disrespectful.

Although the profession is in wide agreement with the move toward greater autonomy of those whom we serve, it is not always clear how to most effectively include clients in the process of making active decisions about their treatment. I very much agree with Barnett's (2007) suggestion to provide informed consent both verbally (to foster discussion) and in writing (for later review). Asking ourselves what we would want to know if either we or a loved one were contemplating the proposed course of treatment enables us to more meaningfully take the perspective of the client. Ethical discharge of this duty would also suggest that we take extra time with clients who, for example, are acutely distressed or whose cultural background might make it difficult for them to question a professional. This exercise in perspective-taking enhances the effective discharge of this duty in line with aspirational rather than purely risk-management goals and intentions. We also might want to consider integrating terms such as choice and decision into our ethical discourse to more effectively and accurately portray our commitment to empowering our clients.

References

American Psychological Association. (2002). Ethical principles of psychologists and code of conduct. *American Psychologist, 57,* 1060–1073.

Barnett, J. E. (2007). Seeking an understanding of informed consent. *Professional Psychology: Research and Practice, 38,* 179–182.

Evolving Standards for Informed Consent: Is It Time for an Individualized and Flexible Approach?

Doug Johnson-Greene

. . .

Does the level of intrusiveness associated with psychological services justify informed consent? The answer to that question depends on your definition of intrusiveness. Although psychotherapy does not have the same type of intrusiveness as medicine, in which there is the alteration of the physiology or structure of one's body, there is a highly intrusive quality associated with sharing and altering thoughts and beliefs, assessing mental capabilities and capacities, and providing closely guarded information that would otherwise be kept from the closest of relatives. Also, psychological services are increasingly used as the basis for loss of various freedoms such as the ability to drive, to make financial or medical decisions, to have employment opportunities, and to complete educational programs. They are also used as the basis for determining competency to stand trial and eligibility for imposition of death sentences for convicted criminals. These outcomes are clearly not from the same domain as complications from invasive surgery, but there should be little doubt that they are highly intrusive in their own right.

CONTENT AND CONVEYANCE OF INFORMED CONSENT

Although there are now several ongoing National Institutes of Health-funded studies examining the content and conveyance of informed consent for specific types of research participants (e.g., persons with Alzheimer's disease and multiple sclerosis), there is an appalling lack of empirical investigations of informed consent for clinical services. Thus, recommendations about informed consent are a matter of ethical statements made by professional guilds or based on legal advice, personal beliefs and morals, clinical lore, and educated guesses.

The content of informed consent for research has been well mapped, and several specialties within psychology have addressed this issue (Caplan, 1988; Johnson-Greene, 2005). The latest iteration of the APA [American Psychological Association's] ethics code (APA, 2002) described in Standard 10.01 that informed consent for psychotherapy has several components, including "the nature and anticipated course of therapy, fees, involvement of third parties, and limits of confidentiality" (p. 1072). Despite these recommendations, our profession lacks a consensus about informed consent for psychotherapy patients.

I would argue that informed consent for psychotherapy should include at a minimum all basic parameters such as fees, expected duration, potential consequences that could be reasonably expected, limits to confidentiality, objectives of treatment, and alternatives to the proposed treatment. In addition, there needs to be flexibility in the content and conveyance of informed consent for issues of diversity as described by Barnett (2007) but also flexibility related to the situation and purpose of the treatment. Informed consent would be expected to look much different for psychotherapy services provided to a cognitively impaired patient in a hospital setting being evaluated for capacity to make decisions compared with those provided to a reasonably intact outpatient seeking psychotherapy.

The APA Ethics Code (APA, 2002) describes in Standard 3.1 that written or oral informed consent needs to be documented, which implies that it may be permissible to obtain an oral consent in some circumstances. Use of a written informed-consent document ensures that important items are not

From *Professional Psychology: Research and Practice, 38,* 183–184. Copyright 2007 by the American Psychological Association.

inadvertently omitted by in essence standardizing the process. Thus, important areas are always covered, and it leaves less doubt about whether a specific aspect had been covered should questions about a patient's consent arise later. Perhaps more important, Barnett's (2007) paper suggests that informed consent is not a onetime document signing but rather a process that necessitates an ongoing exchange of information, and one should document that an exchange of information occurred and its content. Barnett suggests that psychologists should "actively ensure" that patients understand the information presented to them, and I wholeheartedly agree. Clinicians may wish to ask questions after providing information to ensure understanding and to increase the opportunity for patients to ask questions. Such techniques will ensure that the informed-consent process is not passive; rather, it is an active interchange of information between psychologists and their patients.

References

American Psychological Association. (2002). Ethical principles of psychologists and code of conduct. *American Psychologist, 57,* 1060–1073.

Barnett, J. E. (2007). Seeking an understanding of informed consent. *Professional Psychology: Research and Practice, 38,* 179–182.

Caplan, A. (1988). Informed consent and patient–provider relationships in rehabilitation medicine. *Archives of Physical Medicine and Rehabilitation, 69,* 2–7.

Johnson-Greene, D. (2005). Informed consent procedures for neuropsychology: Official Statement of the National Academy of Neuropsychology. *Archives of Clinical Neuropsychology, 20,* 335–340.

Increasingly Informed Consent: Discussing Distinct Aspects of Psychotherapy at Different Points in Time

Andrew M. Pomerantz

The current [2002] "Ethical Principles of Psychologists and Code of Conduct" (American Psychological Association [APA], 2002) includes overt guidelines regarding the process of obtaining informed consent to psychotherapy. Ethical standard 3.10 describes a general obligation of psychologists to obtain informed consent to psychotherapy, and ethical standard 10.01a more specifically states that when obtaining this informed consent, "psychologists inform clients/patients as early as is feasible in the therapeutic relationship about the nature and anticipated course of therapy, fees, involvement of third parties, and limits of confidentiality" (p. 1072). . . .

The phrase "as early as is feasible" in ethical standard 10.01a (p. 1072) suggests that in some psychotherapy cases, obtaining informed consent during the first meeting with a client may not be appropriate. In fact, numerous authors have strongly argued that informed consent in psychotherapy should not be an "all-at-once" occurrence, and that instead it should be an ongoing process that necessarily unfolds or evolves over time. . . . Additionally, Fisher (2003) mentioned that specific elements of informed consent may need to be delayed if discussions between the therapist and the third-party payer are necessary, or if the client is in an acute crisis state or has treatment needs that are identified gradually rather than immediately. . . .

When the argument that informed consent to psychotherapy should be obtained on an ongoing, unfolding basis is considered in combination with the breadth of topics to be addressed in the psychotherapy informed consent process, psychotherapists might determine that there are separate "as early as is feasible" points regarding separate elements of informed consent (APA, 2002, p. 1072). In other words, it may be reasonable for therapists to discuss with clients certain aspects of psychotherapy earlier in the psychotherapy process than others. Some facets of psychotherapy may remain relatively constant across clients, presenting problems, and situations, allowing for discussions of these facets at the outset. Other facets of psychotherapy will vary greatly between clients or may emerge more belatedly, requiring a postponement of their discussion. However, no previous empirical research has specifically examined the timing of the discussion of particular pieces of information in the psychotherapy informed consent process. The purpose of this study was to perform such an investigation.

[*Ed. Note:* The author surveyed 400 licensed psychologists in Missouri (return rate = 27%). Respondents were asked to fill out a questionnaire derived from Standard 10.01 of the 2002 ethics code and instructed to respond to the following question regarding each of the 21 items: "What is the earliest point in outpatient psychotherapy at which you feel you could substantively and accurately answer each of the following client questions?" See Table 1 for questions and results.]

DISCUSSION

According to the results of this study, psychologists practicing psychotherapy believe that there is considerable variability in the earliest feasible point in time to address distinct aspects of the informed consent process. Though some information about psychotherapy can be provided to clients immediately at the beginning of the therapy process, it is not feasible to substantively and accurately provide other types of information until at least one therapy session, and

From *Ethics & Behavior, 15,* 351–360. Available at http://www.informaworld.com. Copyright 2005 by Taylor & Francis. Adapted with permission of the publisher.

TABLE 1

Descriptive Statistics for the Earliest Point in Outpatient Psychotherapy at Which Client Questions Can Be Answered

Item	*M*	*SD*
How many sessions will therapy last?	4.28	2.15
What will be the goals of therapy?	2.55	.86
What activities will be involved in the therapy?	2.20	.87
How often will our sessions take place?	2.19	.97
How long has this type of treatment been established in the therapy field?	2.16	1.76
What type of psychotherapy (approach, orientation) will this be?	2.11	.84
How much does my insurance company pay? (percentage, total)	2.06	1.96
What risks are involved in this type of treatment?	2.06	1.48
What alternative treatments are available?	2.05	1.09
What information will my employer be given?	1.37	1.38
What information will my insurance company be given?	2.06	1.96
	2.06	1.96
Can fees go up at some point?	1.33	1.36
How long will each session last?	1.29	.71
Are you being supervised? By whom?	1.28	1.29
What are your policies regarding late payments?	1.22	.98
How often will I need to pay?	1.14	.71
Is everything I say confidential?	1.13	.75
Do you accept my insurance?	1.08	.68
How much does therapy cost?	1.08	.28
What are your policies regarding missed appointments?	1.06	.25
What forms of payment do you accept (cash, credit cards, checks)?	1.02	.13

Note. Rating scale for all items: 1 = at the beginning of the first session; 2 = at the end of the first session; 3 = at the end of the second session; 4 = at the end of the third session; 5 = at approximately the fifth session; 6 = at approximately the tenth session; 7 = at a point later than the tenth session; 8 = never.

possibly several sessions, have taken place. These results support the "process" model of informed consent to psychotherapy as opposed to the "event" model (e.g., Berg et al., 2001; O'Neill, 1998; Stone, 1990), whereby clients become increasingly informed about their therapy as it progresses. The specific data provided by the participants in this study bolster the argument that informed consent to psychotherapy should not take place as a single one-time occurrence at the outset of therapy but instead should constitute an ongoing process between therapist and client.

The aspects of therapy that psychologists appear most comfortable discussing at the outset involve the relatively constant policies or rules of therapy that a given therapist applies immediately to most, if not all, of his or her clients regardless of variations in presenting problem: fees, confidentiality, supervision status, and length of each session. On the other hand, psychologists appear to require about one full session of psychotherapy to feel capable of addressing the many important aspects of psychotherapy that either require customization for particular clients or emerge more gradually. These aspects center around the substance or essence of the therapy, including its basic approach and goals, the activities involved, the risks and alternatives, and the frequency of the sessions.

Psychologists appear to require a relatively extensive amount of time—at least three completed sessions—with the client before feeling capable of addressing the issue of the length of therapy. The issue of therapy duration is particularly complex in that it not only depends on the presenting problem, which may take sessions to unfold and varies widely across clients, but also on the client's responsiveness to the initial treatment attempts, which may require additional time to become apparent. Further complicating the matter is the issue of third-party payment. The initial discussions (or negotiations) between therapist and payer may extend for weeks after the client's first visit. Thus, even if the therapist can estimate how long therapy should last immediately after the first session, the therapist may be hesitant to discuss this estimate with the client until confirming with the payer the financial resources available for treatment. . . .

One specific recommendation strongly suggested by the results of this study is to inform clients at the outset that informed consent is an ongoing process rather than a one-time event, and that answers to certain questions may need to wait until the therapy has a specific appreciation of the client's issues or responsiveness. In other words, if, as these results suggest, therapists may be able to predict that some pieces of information can be addressed with clients earlier than others, therapists should begin the informed consent process by informing clients about this ongoing, staggered nature of informed consent. . . .

References

American Psychological Association. (2002). Ethical principles of psychologists and code of conduct. *American Psychologist, 57,* 1060–1073.

Berg, J. W., Appelbaum, P. S., Lidz, C. W., & Parker, L. S. (2001). *Informed consent: Legal theory and clinical practice* (2nd ed.). New York: Oxford University Press.

Fisher, C. B. (2003). *Decoding the ethics code: A practical guide for psychologists.* Thousand Oaks, CA: Sage.

O'Neill, P. (1998). *Negotiating consent in psychotherapy.* New York: New York University Press.

Stone, A. A. (1990). Law, science, and psychiatric malpractice: A response to Klerman's indictment of psychoanalytic psychiatry. *American Journal of Psychiatry, 147,* 419–427.

Risk Management With the Suicidal Patient: Lessons From Case Law

Dana Royce Baerger

Suicide is the ninth leading cause of death in the United States and the third leading cause of death for Americans between the ages of 15 and 24 (Moscicki, 1997). Empirical research indicates that 20% of psychologists (i.e., those with a doctoral-level degree) and 50% of psychiatrists will lose a patient to suicide during their careers (Chemtob, Hamada, Bauer, Kinney, & Torigoe, 1988; Chemtob, Hamada, Bauer, Torigoe, & Kinney, 1988). Owing to the emotionally devastating aftermath of a suicide and the resultant guilt and anger of family members, suicide continues to account for a comparatively large proportion of all lawsuits filed against mental health professionals. For example, in an analysis of claims brought against psychiatrists between 1980 and 1985, Robertson (1988) discovered that post-suicide lawsuits accounted for both the largest number of suits and the largest monetary settlement amounts. Other commentators have revealed that among psychologists insured by the American Psychological Association's Insurance Trust, patient suicide ranked sixth among claim categories but ranked second in percentage of total costs (Bongar, Maris, Berman, & Litman, 1998). As the number of malpractice suits against practitioners continues to rise, clinicians report a comparable increase in their fear of being sued (see, e.g., Hauser, Commons, Bursztajn, & Gutheil, 1991).

. . .

Despite the prominence of suicide in mental health malpractice litigation, clinicians must resist resorting to defensive clinical practices in an attempt to shield themselves from potential lawsuits. In other words, clinicians must resist relying on excessively restrictive treatments (e.g., involuntary hospitalization, unnecessary medication, unwarranted physical restraint) in an effort to protect themselves from criti-

cism or censure (McQuade, 1991). As Gutheil (1992) has pointed out, the best protection against potential liability for suicide is for the clinician to have followed acceptable standards of practice throughout treatment. Integrating risk management practices into routine clinical care can not only serve to reduce apprehension and misunderstanding regarding malpractice issues (Packman & Harris, 1998) but can also serve as prevention against the possibility of postsuicide liability (Gutheil, 1992). . . . Since general risk management choices should be chosen and incorporated into practice well before a crisis situation arises, this article provides a number of different ways that both outpatient and inpatient clinicians can minimize the risk of liability exposure while treating at-risk patients.

. . .

MALPRACTICE LIABILITY FOR THE MENTAL HEALTH PROFESSIONAL

The term *malpractice* refers to "professional misconduct or unreasonable lack of skill" (Black, 1990, p. 959). Psychiatrists, psychologists, and other mental health professionals must meet a standard of care in the course of their professional duties. Legally, the *standard of care* is defined as "that degree of care which a reasonably prudent person should exercise in same or similar circumstances" (Black, 1990, p. 1405). Hence, in the case of medical or clinical professionals, the standard is typically that of a reasonable or average professional practicing in the same field. The standard of care is violated when a professional fails to render services with the degree of skill or care commonly applied by an average member of the profession (*Matthews v. Walker*, 1973). If an injury or harm results from a failure to meet the

From *Professional Psychology: Research and Practice, 32*, 359–366. Copyright 2001 by the American Psychological Association.

standard of care, then that failure can be considered malpractice.

. . . Simply stated, there are four basic elements that a patient must establish to make a claim of negligence: (a) that the clinician owed a duty of care to the patient, (b) that this duty of care was breached by the clinician, (c) that the patient suffered an injury or harm for which he or she should be compensated, and (d) that the patient's injury was directly caused by the clinician's conduct.

. . .

The two primary legal issues in the situation of patient suicide are *foreseeability* and *causation* (Simon, 1988), that is, whether the clinician should have anticipated the suicide and whether the clinician took sufficient steps to protect the patient (VandeCreek et al., 1987). The issue of foreseeability necessitates a thorough assessment of the risk a patient presents, and the issue of causation necessitates the formulation of a treatment and safety plan based on that risk assessment (Jobes & Berman, 1993). Essentially, these issues require that the clinician use his or her knowledge of risk factors and diagnoses in conducting a thorough assessment of the immediate level of risk presented by an individual patient. Thus, it appears that clinicians will not be considered negligent for a failure to predict suicide but that they will be held negligent for a failure to conduct a comprehensive risk assessment. In practice, this means that clinicians must conduct a two-step evaluation process, first assessing a patient's relative degree of risk for suicide and then implementing a treatment plan to reduce or eliminate that risk (Packman & Harris, 1998).

COMMON FAILURE SCENARIOS AND CASE EXAMPLES

Bongar et al. (1998) have enumerated 12 common failure scenarios in the case of outpatient suicide; however, these scenarios are equally applicable to the inpatient context. Essentially, these scenarios represent a variety of fact patterns in which a clinician would be vulnerable to a lawsuit alleging malpractice in the handling of a patient's level of risk. These scenarios are (a) failure to properly evaluate the need for psychopharmocological intervention or use of unsuit-

able pharmacotherapy, (b) failure to specify criteria for hospitalization and failure to implement hospitalization, (c) failure to maintain appropriate clinician–patient relationship, (d) failures in supervision and consultation, (e) failure to evaluate for suicide risk at intake, (f) failure to evaluate for suicide risk at management transitions, (g) failure to secure records of prior treatments or inadequate history taking, (h) failure to conduct a mental status exam, (i) failure to diagnose, (j) failure to establish a formal treatment plan, (k) failure to safeguard the environment, and (l) failure to adequately document clinical judgments, rationales, and observations.

[*Ed. Note:* The author, then, offers 5 recommendations abstracted here: (a) The clinician must conduct a comprehensive examination of the patient at intake; (b) if the patient is at risk, hospitalization should be seriously considered and only rejected in the event of a comprehensive safety plan; (c) the clinician should review the level of risk a patient presents at particularly stressful times in the patient's life; (d) the clinician should maintain accurate records that explain significant treatment decisions and that clearly delineate the reasons for rejecting hospitalization for at-risk outpatients and the reasons for choosing discharge for at-risk inpatients; and (e) the clinician must take special precautions against suicide when treating the at-risk patient, including—where appropriate—involving the patient's family or friends in safety or discharge plans. The author next addresses some ethical issues.]

. . .

Of course, clinicians' ethical obligation to keep patients' communications confidential can run counter to the legal obligations described above; in turn, these legal obligations can run counter to the guarantee of confidentiality that is necessary for a strong working alliance. Rudd and colleagues (Rudd, Joiner, Jobes, & King, 1999, p. 441) described this as the "paradox" inherent in the "life-and-death nature" of therapeutic work with suicidal patients. A full discussion of the issue of confidentiality in mental health treatment is beyond the scope of this article, but it is important to note that confidentiality is not absolute and that there are circumstances under which breaking confidentiality is both legally and ethically required (Bongar, 1991).

Imminent suicidality is one such circumstance. Indeed, courts have consistently held that clinicians may breach confidentiality in certain justifiable circumstances, the two most common being when such breach is in the public interest (e.g., in the case of possible harm to others) and when such breach is in a patient's own interests (e.g., in the case of harm to self). Thus, clinicians' legal duties to patients essentially constitute a hierarchy in which some responsibilities take precedence over others. The obligation to take all reasonable measures in order to prevent patient suicide clearly supercedes preexisting confidentiality obligations.

As a way of managing this dilemma in practice, Rudd and colleagues (Rudd et al., 1999) highlighted the therapeutic and legal benefits of using informed consent with suicidal patients. Essentially, according to Rudd et al., informed consent serves as a foundation of shared understanding regarding the "ground rules" pertaining to confidentiality and safety within the context of treatment. Rudd and colleagues recommended that clinicians carefully discuss with suicidal patients all relevant aspects of treatment, including treatment options and goals, treatment duration and intensity, threshold rules regarding confidentiality (and, for the outpatient, hospitalization), and emergency availability and procedures, thereby providing the patient with critical front-end information regarding the parameters of the therapy. As these authors noted, once "a potentially suicidal patient has received thorough informed consent about the legal parameters of confidentiality and the importance of . . . physical safety, they can then proceed in good faith with their clinician toward developing an appropriate treatment plan" (Rudd et al., 1999, p. 441).

CONCLUSION

. . .

When dealing with the suicidal patient, as when dealing with any patient, the guiding principle must be "to keep the benefit of the patient foremost in our mind" (Bongar et al., 1998, p. 28). Acting in the patient's best interest constitutes powerful evidence of good faith on the clinician's part, even if the outcome is poor (Hoge & Appelbaum, 1989). Perhaps the best protection against patient suicide is a solid therapeutic alliance in which the clinician is able to enlist in treatment those parts of the patient that want to live. As one commentator noted, "We cannot be so afraid of litigation as to deny our patients their right to learn to live" (Rachlin, 1984, p. 306).

References

Black, H. C. (1990). *Black's law dictionary*. St. Paul, MN: West.

Bongar, B. (1991). *The suicidal patient: Clinical and legal standards of care*. Washington, DC: American Psychological Association.

Bongar, B., Maris, R. W., Berman, A. L., & Litman, R. E. (1998). *Outpatient standards of care and the suicidal patient*. In B. Bongar, A. L. Berman, R. W. Maris, M. M. Silverman, E. A. Harris, & W. L. Packman (Eds.), *Risk management with suicidal patients* (pp. 4–33). New York: Guilford.

Chemtob, C. M., Hamada, R. S., Bauer, G. B., Kinney, B., & Torigoe, R. Y. (1988). Patient suicide: Frequency and impact on psychiatrists. *American Journal of Psychiatry, 145*, 224–228.

Chemtob, C. M., Hamada, R. S., Bauer, G. B., Torigoe, R. Y., & Kinney. B. (1988). Patient suicide: Frequency and impact on psychologists. *Professional Psychology: Research and Practice, 19*, 416–420.

Gutheil, T. G. (1992). Suicide and suit: Liability after self-destruction. In D. Jacobs (Ed.), *Suicide and clinical practice* (pp. 147–167). Washington, DC: American Psychiatric Press.

Hauser, M. J., Commons, M. L, Bursztajn, H. J., & Gutheil, T. G. (1991). Fear of malpractice liability and its role in clinical decision making. In T. G. Gutheil, H. J. Bursztajn, A. Brodsky, & V. Alexander (Eds.), *Decision making in psychiatry and the law* (pp. 209–226). Baltimore: Williams & Wilkins.

Hoge, S. K., & Appelbaum, P. S. (1989). Legal issues in outpatient psychiatry. In A. Lazare (Ed.), *Outpatient psychiatry: Diagnosis and treatment* (2nd ed., pp. 605–621). Baltimore: Williams & Wilkins.

Jobes, D. A., & Berman, A. L. (1993). Suicide and malpractice liability. Assessing and revising policies, procedures, and practice in settings. *Professional Psychology: Research and Practice, 24*, 91–99.

Matthews v. Walker, 34 Ohio App. 2d 128, 296 N.E. 2d 569 (1973).

McQuade, J. S. (1991). The medical malpractice crisis—Reflections on the alleged causes and proposed cures: A discussion paper. *Journal of the Royal Society of Medicine, 84*, 408–411.

Moscicki, E. K. (1997). Identification of suicide risk factors using epidemiologic studies. *Psychiatric Clinics of North America, 20*, 499–517.

Packman, W. L., & Harris, E. L. (1998). Legal issues and risk management in suicidal patients. In B. Bongar, A. L. Berman, R. W. Maris, M. M. Silverman, E. A. Harris, & W. L. Packman (Eds.), *Risk management with suicidal patients* (pp. 150–186). New York: Guilford.

Rachlin, S. (1984). Double jeopardy: Suicide and malpractice. *General Hospital Psychiatry, 6,* 302–307.

Robertson, J. D. (1988). *Psychiatric malpractice: Liability of mental health professionals.* New York: Wiley.

Rudd, M. D., Joiner, T. E., Jobes, D. A., & King, C. A. (1999). The outpatient treatment of suicidality: An integration of science and recognition of its limitations. *Professional Psychology: Research and Practice, 30,* 437–446.

Simon, R. J. (1988). *Concise guide to clinical psychiatry and the law.* Washington, DC: American Psychiatric Press.

VandeCreek, L., Knapp, S., & Herzog, C. (1987). Malpractice risks in the treatment of dangerous patients. *Psychotherapy, Theory, Research, and Practice, 24,* 145–153.

◆ ◆ ◆

Commentary: Packman et al. (2004), in addition to a comprehensive summary of relevant cases, offered recommendations for managing suicide risk, including: (a) good record keeping; (b) consultation with colleagues; (c) knowledge of legal and ethical responsibilities; (d) knowledge of suicide risk factors; (e) thorough evaluation of risk; (f) gathering of historical information, for example, past suicide attempts or ideation; and (g) self-knowledge of competence to deal with suicide. See Packman, W. L., Pennuto, T. O., Bongar, B., & Orthwein, J. (2004). Legal issues of professional negligence in suicide cases. Behavioral Sciences and the Law, 22, 697–713.

For additional readings on legal, ethical, and competency issues in treating clients who threaten suicide, see, for example:

Bongar, B. (2002). The suicidal patient: Clinical and legal standards of care (2nd ed.). Washington, DC: American Psychological Association.

Judge, B., & Billick, S. B. (2004). Suicidality in adolescence: Review and legal considerations. Behavioral Sciences and the Law, 22, 681–695.

Packman, W. L., Marlitt, R. E., Bongar, B., & Pennuto, T. O. (2004). A comprehensive and concise assessment of suicide risk. Behavioral Sciences and the Law, 22, 667–680.

Pope, K., & Vasquez, M. (1991). Ethics in psychotherapy and counseling (pp. 153–168). San Francisco: Jossey-Bass.

Sanchez, H. (2001). Risk factor model for suicide assessment and intervention. Professional Psychology: Research and Practice, 32, 351–358.

Bongar, one of the more prolific and respected writers on suicide intervention has stated: "I believe that clinicians have a professional duty to take appropriate affirmative measures to prevent their patients from harming themselves." (p. 83). Bongar, B. (1992). The ethical issue of competence in working with the suicidal patient. Ethics & Behavior, 2, 75–89. He, and most other authors on this topic thus appear to adopt a beneficence–paternalism model in treating suicidal clients. Is this consistent with the case law discussed in the previous excerpt? Are there any moral principles or provisions in the 2002 Ethics Code that would permit a therapist to abide by a client's wish to die?

Mishara and Weisstub (2005), in fact, identified three broad categories of positions concerning suicide: (a) the moralist position that adheres to the view "that suicide is unacceptable and that there is a pervasive moral obligation to protect life" (p. 25); (b) the libertarian perspective that emphasizes "the freedom of choice by individuals to determine whether or not to live or die" (p. 25); and (c) relativist approaches that evaluate the ethicality of suicide "based upon either contemporary situational and cultural variables or the anticipated consequences of action or inaction" (p. 26). Mishara, B. L., & Weisstub, D. N. (2005). Ethical and legal issues in suicide research. International Journal of Law and Psychiatry, 28, 23–41. See also Szasz, T. (1968). The case against suicide prevention. American Psychologist, 41, 806–812.

Ethical and Legal Considerations in Marital and Family Therapy

Gayla Margolin

. . .

RESPONSIBILITY

The therapist's primary responsibilities are to protect the rights and to promote the welfare of his or her clients. The dilemma with multiple clients is that in some situations an intervention that serves one person's best interests may be countertherapeutic to another. Indeed, the very reason that families tend to seek therapy is because they have conflicting goals and interests. . . .

The family therapist must insure that improvement in the status of one family member does not occur at the expense of another family member. . . . [W]hat sets the family therapist apart from the individual therapist is the family therapist's clear commitment to promoting the welfare of each family member. . . .

To work constructively in the face of conflicting family needs, some therapists identify the family system, rather than one or another individual, as "the patient." The family therapist then becomes an advocate of the family system and avoids becoming an agent of any one family member. Assuming that change by one person affects and is affected by other family members, the system advocate ensures that all problem definitions and plans for change are considered in the context of the entire family. . . . If informed of the therapist's role as an advocate of the system, family members generally understand and accept this position, although at certain moments they still solicit the therapist as a personal ally. . . .

There are certain instances in which working as an advocate of the relationship system and changing patterns of interaction is not advised. Weiss and Birchler (1978) point out that a therapeutic alliance based on the ostensible goal of changing the relationship is countertherapeutic if one spouse seeks therapy as a way to exit from the relationship or to ease the burden of announcing a decision to separate. . . . Similarly, it is misleading to maintain a guise of working on the relationship when the actual objective is to change the behavior of one family member (e.g., to reduce a father's drinking or to increase a child's compliance). If the target individual in those cases is under the mistaken impression that there will be mutual change, she or he may end up feeling deceived by both the therapist and the other family members.

Finally, in addition to clinical considerations, there are legal prescriptions defining when the welfare of an individual takes precedence over relationship issues. The clearest obligation in this regard occurs in the instance of physical abuse among family members. Child abuse reporting laws require therapists to inform authorities if they suspect that a child has been abused, despite the possible consequences for the therapeutic alliance with other family members. Though the legal prescription for action is not quite as obvious for abuse between marital partners, the primary goal still is to reduce the danger of physical harm. If this objective cannot be realized within the context of conjoint therapy, it is the therapist's ethical responsibility to abdicate the role of relationship advocate and help the threatened person find protection (Margolin, 1979). . . .

CONFIDENTIALITY

. . .

How do standard practices of confidentiality translate from the traditional dyadic client–therapist relationship to a therapeutic relationship that includes several family members? There are two divergent positions in this regard. One preference is for the therapist to treat each family member's confidences as though that person were an individual client. That is, information obtained during a private session, during a telephone call, or from written material is not divulged to other family members. Some therapists, in fact, arrange for sessions with individual family members to actively encourage the sharing of "secrets" to better understand what is occurring in the family. The therapist then may work with the individual client in the hope of enabling that person to disclose the same information in the family session. Should that fail to occur, however, the therapist upholds the individual client's confidentiality and remains silent on that issue vis-à-vis other family members.

Other therapists adopt the policy of not keeping secrets from other family members. They explicitly discourage the sharing of any information that might lead to a special alliance with one individual and that excludes the remaining uninformed family members. Contrary to more traditional views of psychotherapy that hold the client–therapist confidence as a crucial factor in the overall effectiveness of therapy, this stance essentially blocks the occurrence of confidences between one family member and the therapist. Therapists who subscribe to this approach generally avoid receiving individual confidences by conducting joint, as opposed to individual, sessions. However, this one safeguard often proves insufficient against the sharing of individual confidences. Unless the client is directly informed of the therapist's policies, the client who seeks to divulge personal information will find a way to do so.

Between these two extreme positions are intermediary steps. Rather than treat all information shared in individual sessions as confidential, the therapist may indicate that (1) in general, confidentiality conditions do not apply, but (2) the client has the right to request that any specific information be kept confidential and the therapist will comply with any such requests. Likewise, it should be recognized that the therapist who does not promise to maintain confidences may, indeed, wish to exercise the option not to divulge certain information. For instance, faced with information that one spouse has had an affair, particularly one that has terminated long since, many therapists find it unnecessary and inadvisable to share such information. In conveying that she or he does not preserve the confidences of individual family members, the therapist should avoid implying that she or he will not conceal anything. Except for legal considerations mentioned previously, it is the therapist's discretion, not his or her responsibility, to divulge confidential information.

One instance that complicates issues of confidentiality is a change in the format of therapy, for example, individual therapy being replaced by marital therapy. How does the therapist handle the information that she or he has obtained during the course of individual therapy? One possibility is to obtain the individual client's permission to use such information, when necessary, in the conjoint sessions. If permission is not granted, however, that information must be kept confidential, a resolution far from desirable for the therapist who prefers not maintaining individual confidences in conjoint therapy. . . .

As in individual therapy, clients must be informed of the limits of their confidentiality. This is particularly important in family therapy, since the limits of confidentiality, vis-à-vis other family members, essentially are left to the therapist's discretion. Therapists who will not keep confidences must inform clients of this policy before any such information has been received. Otherwise, the client, particularly one who has had previous experience in individual therapy, is likely to presume that the therapist will maintain the confidentiality of his or her statements from other family members. The therapist who does keep individual confidences likewise should inform clients of this policy so that family members do not persist in trying to obtain information about one another through the therapist.

Although both sides of the decision about whether or not to maintain confidentiality are ethically defensible, they carry different clinical implications. In certain situations, maintaining one partner's confidences severely limits the therapist's options with another family member. Consider, for example, the situation in which marital therapy has been initiated by the wife on discovering that her husband had been having an affair. While willing to give the relationship one last try, she is adamant about terminating the marriage if the husband does not end his affair and then remain sexually faithful. Although the husband initially agrees to this condition, several months later he reveals to the therapist that he has resumed the extramarital relationship. Desperate to avoid the possibility of his wife's leaving him, the husband refuses to divulge this information in a conjoint session.

What is the therapist's course of action? If confidentiality has been promised, the therapist may find himself or herself in a position of concealing information that is crucial to the wife's decision about remaining both in therapy and in the marriage. When the wife learns about the affair, she may believe that the therapist has neglected her welfare in favor of the husband and may even accuse the therapist of keeping her in therapy for personal gain. Even if the therapist were to terminate the case, an explanation is owed to the wife, which is likely to compromise the husband's confidentiality. Even though the therapist might believe that dealing openly with the husband's behavior would have long-range therapeutic benefit, this course of action is not possible without violating the husband's confidentiality.

The therapist who has not promised confidentiality has more options open and thus must carefully consider the therapeutic ramifications of his or her actions. Deciding not to divulge this information about the husband's affair might be justifiable if (1) the wife had made it clear that she did not want to know about the husband's indiscretions, (2) the affair would not interfere with the ongoing therapy, and (3) the affair had ended, so the therapist's action could not be construed as encouraging the husband's behavior. In view of the specifics of this case, however, in which the wife has clearly stated her preference not to be duped into believing her husband is sexually faithful, open discussion of the husband's affair and the wife's ultimatum is indicated. Such discussion is likely to precipitate a relationship crisis, the long-range effects of which cannot be predicted. One or both spouses may receive the information they need, finally, to pronounce the marriage over. Alternatively, the couple may make certain accommodations despite their divergent values regarding fidelity; for example, the husband could terminate his long-term liaison while not committing himself to sexual fidelity, and the wife could abandon her ultimatum regarding sexual faithfulness as long as there are no long-standing affairs.

The most difficult predicament for the therapist would be if she or he failed to convey a policy on confidentiality. In that case, it is possible that the husband and wife would be functioning under different assumptions, for example, the husband assuming confidentiality would be maintained and the wife assuming that there would be no individual secrets in marital therapy. Neither spouse knows the limits of confidentiality nor has made a conscious decision to accept those limits. . . .

This example . . . illustrates that the therapist's position in terms of confidentiality can have important ramifications for how marital therapy is conducted. By maintaining the confidentiality of individual partners, the therapist is likely to have information that otherwise might not be available. The therapist's options with that information are severely limited, however, and she or he may not find it possible to put the information to therapeutic advantage from a family-system perspective. On the other hand, obtaining permission to discuss conjointly information that either partner chooses to reveal individually poses risks to the spouses (i.e., that there is no safe environment for personal disclosures) and risks to the therapist (i.e., that she or he will not gain access to important information). When this stance is clearly understood, however, individual disclosures to the therapist may simply signal the desire for guidance on how to broach a particularly difficult topic with one's partner. . . .

Confidentiality issues also arise when a therapist has individual sessions with a child. Ethical standards of confidentiality apply to the child as a client just as they do for adult clients. In some states parents have the right to inspect the therapist's records, but they have no legal right to demand that the therapist reveal information to them. The therapist's foremost objective in child therapy is to protect the rights of the child, particularly since the child is less able to understand or guard his or her rights. Yet secondarily the therapist must show sensitivity to the concerns of interested parents, since their help and support is often quite influential in the overall effectiveness of child therapy. Before beginning child therapy sessions, it is important to set up an agreement with both the child and the parents about what, if any, information from the child's sessions will be discussed with the parents. The limits of confidentiality should be determined; for example, can the child specifically request that the parents not be told certain information? The structure of this feedback also should be determined: for example, How often will the therapist meet with the parents? Will the child be present at those meetings? In setting up these conditions, the therapist may wish to indicate that other family members are not to pressure the child to reveal what has transpired in his or her individual sessions. . . .

PATIENT PRIVILEGE

. . .

For the most part, privilege tends to be ill-defined for the situation in which two or more clients are seen simultaneously in therapy. Since privilege only covers communications that are uttered in confidence, the question arises of whether statements made in the presence of another family member indeed are confidential. The question also arises of whether privilege covers client-to-client communications. Since some states extend privilege to persons who aid in the delivery of personal services and are present during the uttering of confidential information (e.g., nurses, technicians), a liberal interpretation of privilege statutes might show that family members (or group members) are agents of the therapist (Bersoff & Jain, 1980). Lacking definitive legislation on these issues, however, family therapists cannot comfortably assume that existing privilege statutes protect the communications that occur during family therapy. In view of the inconsistencies of current laws, the therapist might wish to have a clear understanding with family members on these issues, for example, obtaining a written agreement that none of the members will call on the therapist to testify in litigation.

INFORMED CONSENT AND THE RIGHT TO REFUSE TREATMENT

. . .

Recent reviews of informed consent (Everstine et al., 1980; Hare-Mustin et al., 1979) recommend that the following types of information be provided to clients before therapy is formally initiated: (a) an explanation of the procedures and their purpose, (b) the role of the person who is providing therapy and his or her professional qualifications, (c) discomforts or risks reasonably to be expected, (d) benefits reasonably to be expected, (e) alternatives to treatment that might be of similar benefit, (f) a statement that any questions about the procedures will be answered at any time, and (g) a statement that the person can withdraw his or her consent and discontinue participation in therapy or testing at any time.

Each of these guidelines also applies to marriage and family therapy. Guidelines c and d, for example, deserve special attention inasmuch as risks and benefits are different in family than in individual therapy. Since each family member has less control over the eventual outcome of family than of individual therapy, clients should be warned that marital and family therapy may lead to an outcome viewed as undesirable by one or another of the participants, for example, the decision to divorce or compromises in one's power over other family members.

Data on individual versus family therapy are central to Guideline e, particularly for the person torn between wanting to improve marital/family relationships and wanting the sanctuary of an individual therapeutic relationship. According to Gurman and Kniskern's (1978) comprehensive review, though marital therapy may be risky, individual therapy for marital problems is even riskier: Individual therapy for marital problems yields improvement in less than half of its consumers, whereas therapies that involve both partners yield improvement in approximately two thirds of the clients. . . .

It is typical of most families that some members are more eager to participate in therapy than others, raising the issue . . . of voluntary participation. Obviously, coercion of the reluctant individual by other family members or by the therapist is unethical; however, this does not mean that the therapist cannot strongly encourage a family member to attend at least one session to discover what therapy may offer. Nor does it suggest that the therapist ignore what may be underlying reasons contributing to the person's reluctance, such as feeling threatened. In sorting out whether or not a particular family member will participate in therapy, the therapist should identify the extent to which each person will be expected to participate, for example, whether some persons simply can attend the therapy sessions in the role of observer, learning enough about the therapeutic process so that they do nothing to impede its progress. The therapist also should explain to the reluctant member that if other family members still choose to participate, the family as a whole is likely to change regardless of that individual's lack of participation.

A potential source of coercion surrounding voluntary participation comes from the relatively common therapeutic policy of refusing to see families unless all family members are present. Do other family members go untreated just because one person is unwilling to participate? Does one person's decision to terminate mean that all family members must discontinue contact with the therapist? To avoid the conclusion that one family member denies the others access to therapeutic services, therapists with a strong preference for working with the entire family should inform the family that other therapists do not necessarily share this preference and should have available a list of competent referral sources. . . .

Children's Right to Consent

Recently there has been an increasing ground swell of opinion that children should be allowed to exercise the right to consent to psychological treatment. Generally speaking it is the parent or legal guardian who takes responsibility for providing the child's consent to treatment (Morrison, Morrison, & Holdridge-Crane, 1979). Exceptions to this general policy are found in some state statutes that offer teenagers the right to obtain sexual counseling, abortions, or drug counseling. In view of the legal constraints for children, the psychological community needs to address the issue of informed consent with children. The therapist needs to be sensitive to the fact that children constitute a consumer group who require extra protection, since even those parents who are well intentioned do not always know what is best for their children. It has been recommended that there be a child advocate to examine and protect what is in the best interest of the child client, particularly when a child is adamantly

opposed to therapy (Morrison et al., 1979) or when the child does not have the capacity to give full unpressured consent (Koocher, 1976).

. . . The rationale for obtaining informed consent from children who will be participating in therapy is at least as compelling as that for participating in research. Since the effectiveness of psychotherapy depends on a trusting relationship between the therapist and client, there is much to be gained by explaining what is to occur and having the child become involved in decisions that will contribute to the therapeutic endeavor (LoCicero, 1976). Describing procedures in simplified language that children can understand and questioning the children about what has been said reveals to both the therapist and parents the extent to which each child comprehends what will occur. Children who lack the experiential background or intellectual sophistication to weigh the risks and benefits of an informed decision should not be pressured to give written informed consent (Levy & Brackbill, 1979). Yet even partial understanding without formal consent is preferable to proceeding with therapy in the absence of any explanation. . . .

THERAPIST VALUES

The impact of the therapist's values, inescapable in any therapeutic change process, can play a particularly weighty role in marital and family therapies. . . .

Preservation of the Family

To what extent does a marital or family therapist express personal opinions about whether a couple should separate or divorce? The clearest professional standard on this issue is found in the Professional Code of the American Association for Marriage and Family Therapy (AAMFT), which states, "In all circumstances, the therapist will clearly advise a client that the decision to separate or divorce is the responsibility solely of the client" (AAMFT, 1979). Although appealing in principle, this stance is difficult, if not impossible, to exercise in practice. Certainly one function of marital therapy is to help distressed couples decide whether to stay together. Indeed, most couples who enter marital therapy have considered separation or divorce, and some seek therapy with the express purpose of making that decision. These couples "are primed to be influenced by the therapist and are quite sensitive to the cues which the therapist provides concerning his/her opinions about the relationship" (Jacobson & Margolin, 1979, p. 335).

Though few therapists would deny formulating impressions about whether a couple should remain together, there is substantial variability in how comfortable therapists feel in sharing those opinions. . . .

Several . . . therapists endorse an explicit statement of one's opinion to the clients while claiming that the opinion is a personal one rather than a reflection of professional expertise (Gurman & Klein, 1981; Halleck, 1971). Perhaps by making this influence explicit, clients are better able to choose how much they want to be swayed by the therapist's opinions and to sort out their own reactions as distinct from those of the therapist. . . .

Extramarital Affairs

. . .

Does knowledge that one partner is currently engaging in an extramarital affair alter the course of therapy? Therapists who answer "no" to this question often focus on improving the primary relationship, which if successful may cause the other relationship to dwindle in importance. A small number of therapists even encourage one spouse to initiate or continue an affair for the well-being of that individual or perhaps even for the betterment of the relationship. . . .

There are, however, . . . potential drawbacks to advocating extramarital affairs for clients. First, even if the affair is beneficial to one person, the other is bound to suffer. Second, therapy that is directed toward the relationship is unlikely to work if one spouse is splitting his or her attention between two relationships. . . .

The other alternative is to actively discourage extramarital relationships or even to stipulate that extramarital affairs must be ended for therapy to commence (e.g., Ables & Brandsma, 1977; Jacobson & Margolin, 1979). This stance, typically described as strategic rather than moralistic, assumes that the affair would impede both partners' abilities to commit themselves fully to relationship improvement and

would result in a halting and frustrating course of therapy. Though widely endorsed, this position represents a *professional value,* rather than an empirically derived conclusion. The therapeutic benefit of this stance is that it often prompts termination of an affair as a demonstration of that spouse's desire to work on the relationship. However, the drawback is that a spouse might carefully conceal information about an affair for fear of being excluded from therapy. . . .

Sex Roles

To what extent does the therapist accept the family's definition of sex role identities as opposed to attempting to influence and modify their attitudes in this regard? Recent attention to this question has led to the conclusion that marital and family therapy often tends to reinforce sex role stereotyping (Gurman & Klein, 1981; Hare-Mustin, 1978). Of the sexist attitudes found to characterize psychotherapy in general (APA Task Force on Sex Bias and Sex-Role Stereotyping, 1975), family therapists are particularly vulnerable to the following biases: (1) assuming that remaining in a marriage would result in better adjustment for a woman; (2) demonstrating less interest in or sensitivity to a woman's career than to a man's career; (3) perpetuating the belief that child rearing and thus the child's problems are solely the responsibility of the mother; (4) exhibiting a double standard for a wife's versus a husband's affair; and (5) deferring to the husband's needs over those of the wife.

How does the therapist respond when family members agree that they want to work toward goals that, in the therapist's viewpoint, represent sexist ideologies? By attempting to remain nonjudgmental about the client's objectives, the therapist may unwittingly reinforce these sexist attitudes. But by attempting to reorient them to an egalitarian viewpoint, the therapist might thwart the family from attaining their goals and alienate those individuals whose socialization is such that they are happy with traditional roles (Hare-Mustin, 1978). . . .

A more difficult dilemma arises when the woman challenges traditional sex roles while the husband seemingly is an intractable sexist. As soon as the therapist even privately identifies the husband's sexism as the problem, that therapist has violated guiding principles in marital therapy—balancing alliances with each partner and seeking to understand each spouse's perspective on an issue. What needs to be sorted out is whether the conflict regarding roles reflects vastly divergent ideological positions or whether the ideological differences are accentuated by relationship issues; that is, the wife's demands threaten the husband, who becomes more rigid in his position, which causes the wife to make more demands, and so on. . . .

. . . Since inattention to gender role issues runs the risk of reinforcing sex role inequalities, it is recommended that family therapists examine therapeutic objectives in light of traditional versus nontraditional values. It also is recommended that therapists examine their own behavior for unwitting comments and questions that may imply that the husband and wife command differential roles and status. . . . Finally, it is recommended that the therapist be aware of his or her personal views about sex roles in order to avoid imposing these views on the family or judging the family from a predetermined perspective of how families should function. . . .

References

Ables, B. S., & Brandsma, J. M. (1977). *Therapy for couples*. San Francisco: Jossey-Bass.

American Association for Marriage and Family Therapy. (1979). *Code of professional ethics and standards for public information and advertising*. Upland, CA: Author.

American Psychological Association Task Force. (1975). Report of the Task Force on Sex Bias and Sex-Role Stereotyping in Psychotherapeutic Practice. *American Psychologist, 30,* 1169–1175.

Bersoff, D., & Jain, M. (1980). A practical guide to privileged communication for psychologists. In G. Cooke (Ed.), *The role of the forensic psychologist*. Springfield, IL: Charles C Thomas.

Everstine, L., et al. (1980). Privacy and confidentiality in psychotherapy. *American Psychologist, 35,* 828–840.

Gurman, A. S., & Klein, M. H. (1981). Women and behavioral marriage and family therapy: An unconscious male bias? In E. A. Blechman (Ed.), *Contemporary issues in behavior modification with women*. New York: Guilford.

Gurman, A. S., & Kniskern, D. P. (1978). Research on marital and family therapy: Progress, perspective, and prospect. In S. L. Garfield & A. E. Bergin (Eds.), *Handbook of psychotherapy and behavior change: An empirical analysis* (2nd ed.). New York: Wiley.

Halleck, S. L. (1971). *The politics of therapy*. San Francisco: Jossey-Bass.

Hare-Mustin, R. T. (1978). A feminist approach to family therapy. *Family Process, 17,* 181–194.

Hare-Mustin, R. T., Maracek, J., Kaplan, A. G., & Liss-Levinson, N. (1979). Rights of clients, responsibilities of therapists. *American Psychologist, 34,* 3–16.

Koocher, G. P. (1976). Civil liberties and aversive conditioning for children. *American Psychologist, 31,* 94–95.

Levy, C. M., & Brackbill, Y. (1979, March). Informed consent: Getting the message across to kids. *APA Monitor*, pp. 3; 18.

LoCicero, A. (1976). The right to know: Telling children the results of clinical evaluations. In G. Koocher (Ed.), *Children's rights and the mental health profession*. New York: Wiley.

Margolin, G. (1979). Conjoint marital therapy to enhance anger management and reduce spouse abuse. *American Journal of Family Therapy, 7,* 13–23.

Morrison, K. L., Morrison, J. K., & Holdridge-Crane, S. (1979). The child's right to give informed consent to psychiatric treatment. *Journal of Clinical Child Psychology, 8,* 43–47.

Weiss, R. L., & Birchler, G. R. (1978). Adults with marital dysfunction. In M. Hersen & A. S. Bellack (Eds.), *Behavior therapy in the psychiatric setting*. Baltimore: Williams & Wilkins.

Yoell, W., Stewart, D., Wolpe, J., Goldstein, A., & Speierer, G. (1971). Marriage, morals and therapeutic goals: A discussion. *Journal of Behavior therapy and Experimental Psychiatry, 2,* 127–132.

◆　◆　◆

Commentary: For a fuller exposition of the problems of dealing with extramarital affairs, both in individual and in couples therapy, see Snyder, D. K., & Doss, B. D. (2005). Treating infidelity: Clinical and ethical directions. Journal of Clinical Psychology/In Session, 61, *1453–1465. As they point out,*

> *Treating clients coping with infidelity presents special clinical and ethical challenges. Among these challenges are ensuring professional competence, inherent conflicts of interest when dealing with multiple clients, policies and limitations regarding confidentiality, and responsibility for clarifying implicit values. (p. 1453)*

See also Schneider, T. P., & Levinson, B. (2006). Ethical dilemmas related to disclosure issues: Sex addiction therapists in the trenches. Sexual Addiction & Compulsivity, 13, *1–39.*

One of the criticisms of the pre-1992 ethical codes was that they neglected marriage, family, and group therapy issues. The 2002 Code includes a new provision, 10.03 (Group Therapy), requiring psychologists who conduct groups to "describe the roles and responsibilities of all parties and the limits of confidentiality." See also 10.02 (Therapy Involving Couples or Families), a slightly edited version of 4.03 in the 1992 Code.

Lakin has raised a rarely mentioned concern:

> *The [1992] code does not directly address a significant ethical issue that few practitioners have shown concern about, namely, grouping one's individual clients or patients and adding group sessions on a regular basis. . . . [Practitioners] did not see that concurrent treatment by the identical therapist complicates the already complex therapy relationship, that confidentiality must be further eroded, and, perhaps most worrisome of all, that they could have financial incentives in referring to themselves. (p. 346)*

Lakin, M. (1994). Morality in group and family therapies: Multiperson therapies and the 1992 ethics code. Professional Psychology: Research and Practice, 25, *344–348. Has this problem been rectified in the 2002 Code?*

For other helpful material on group therapy, see

Corey, G., Williams, G. T., & Moline, M. E. (1995). *Ethical and legal issues in group counseling.* Ethics & Behavior, 5, *161–183.*

Hansen, J. C., Green, S., & Kutner, K. B. (1989). *Ethical issues facing school psychologists working with families.* Professional School Psychology, 4, *245–255.*

Lakin, M. (1986). *Ethical challenges of group and dyadic psychotherapies: A comparative approach.* Professional Psychology: Research and Practice, 17, *454–461.*

Patten, C., Barnett, T., & Houlihan, D. (1991). *Ethics in marital and family therapy: A review of the literature.* Professional Psychology: Research and Practice, 22, *171–175.*

Piercy, F. P., & Sprenkle, D. G. (1983). *Ethical, legal, and professional issues in family therapy: A graduate level course.* Journal of Marital and Family Therapy, 9, *393–401.*

For an excellent article supporting Margolin's (prior excerpt) view that therapists should seek children's agreement to participate in family therapy, see Miller, V. A., Drotar, D., & Kodish, E. (2004). Children's competence for assent and consent: A review of empirical findings. Ethics & Behavior, 14, *255–295.*

Other articles related to providing treatment to children include:

Aquino, A., & Lee, S. (2000). *The use of nonerotic touch with children: Ethical and developmental considerations.* Journal of Psychotherapy in Independent Practice, 1, *17–30.*

Jackson, Y. (1999). *Applying APA ethical guidelines to individual play therapy with children.* International Journal of Play Therapy, 7(2), *1–15.*

Yanagida, E. (1998). *Ethical dilemmas in the clinical practice of child psychology. In R. Anderson, T. Needels, & H. Hall (Eds.), Avoiding ethical misconduct in psychology specialty areas (pp. 47–77.) Springfield, IL.: Charles C Thomas.*

For an informative text on ethical issues related to children in general, see Koocher, G., & Keith-Spiegel, P. (1990). Children, ethics, and the law. Lincoln: University of Nebraska Press.

National Survey of Ethical Practices Across Rural and Urban Communities

Craig M. Helbok, Robert P. Marinelli, and Richard T. Walls

Do rural psychologists encounter more ethical dilemmas than their urban counterparts? The present study examined potential differences in ethical practices across rural and urban communities. The goal was to identify whether there are unique ethical problems that arise while practicing psychology in rural communities. Much of the previous literature on rural practice has been anecdotal. Our objective was to quantify differences across communities by gathering baseline data on actual practices.

Ethical problems or dilemmas may arise in rural communities because of limited population density as well as geographical isolation. Rural communities are complex interrelated systems of formal and informal social and political units (Hargrove, 1986). Relationships among community members are interdependent and complex and may have deep historical, social, political, and familial roots (Hargrove, 1986; Sundet & Mermelstein, 1983). Members of the community often have multiple roles within the community, tend to rely on each other and on kinship ties, and prefer to take care of their own problems rather than place any trust in outsiders (Stockman, 1990).

Compared with urban areas, rural communities tend to have scarce resources, high rates of poverty, lack of access to employment, lack of higher formal education, higher illiteracy rates, inadequate health services, limited insurance coverage, higher rates of disabilities, and fewer mental health resources. . . . Persons who live in these communities . . . are less likely to seek mental health services because of the stigma associated with seeking such services and the lack of understanding of what such services entail (Cook, Copans, & Schetky, 1998; Stockman, 1990).

There is considerable evidence that there is a greater prevalence of social and health problems in rural areas than in urban areas (Wagenfeld & Buffum, 1983). . . . Suicide rates in rural areas have been higher than in urban areas for the last 20 years; rural areas have high rates of chronic illness, alcohol abuse, and disability (Roberts et al., 1999; Wagenfeld, 1988).

Most psychologists are trained according to an urban model of psychology, with most of their research performed and practical experience gained at universities in urban areas, where there is access to many services. . . . Because rural areas generally have limited resources, psychologists must be creative and flexible and must make use of existing natural resources such as kin, churches, and other nonprofessional supports (Reed, 1992). Murray and Keller (1991) stated that "there has been a consensus in the literature that this urban model of mental health service delivery is inappropriate to meet the special needs of rural communities" (p. 225). . . . Rural providers often feel that ethics codes, texts, and other literature are so urban biased, or culturally incongruent, that they are not helpful (Roberts et al., 1999). Whether rural practice is distinct from urban practice is an empirical question, one which we hope this study begins to address.

The context for examining differences in practices across communities in this study is the ethics code of the American Psychological Association (APA, 1992, 2002). The ethical issues examined in this study include multiple relationships, competency, burnout, confidentiality, and visibility. (For a more detailed description of how the characteristics of rural communities give rise to these specific ethical issues, see Helbok, 2003, and Barbopoulos & Clark, 2003.)

. . .

From *Professional Psychology: Research and Practice, 37*, 36–44. Copyright 2006 by the American Psychological Association.

SURVEY ON ETHICAL PRACTICES

. . .

[*Ed. Note:* The authors surveyed 500 urban and 500 non-urban clinicians with a response rate of 44.7%. The survey instrument consisted of demographic items plus 120 questions related to the practice of psychology.]

Results for the Primary Research Question

. . .

The first MANOVA, in which the independent variable was community and the dependent variable was multiple relationships, was significant, $F(34, 389) = 3.521$, $p < .01$. Follow-up analyses with ANOVAs revealed that 19 of the 34 questions were significantly different for urban/suburban versus small town/rural. The multiple relationship questions and their significance levels are provided in Table 1.

. . .

The second MANOVA, in which the independent variable was community and the dependent variable was visibility, was significant, $F(11, 420) = 8.91$, $p < .01$. Post hoc analyses with ANOVAs revealed nine significant questions (see Table 2). As predicted, therapists in small towns and rural communities may be more likely to feel they are therapists 24 hours a day, to run into clients in the community, and to participate in activities in which clients are also participating. These results also tend to confirm the reports in the review of the rural literature that a therapist has to be willing to be known as a person in rural communities and that clients are likely to know a great deal about the therapist, whether the therapist is comfortable with this or not.

The third MANOVA, in which the independent variable was community and the dependent variable was competency, was significant, $F(34, 384) = 2.04$, $p < .01$. Contrary to expectations, only three of the individual ANOVAs were significant (those questions are listed in Table 3). We had predicted that psychologists from small towns and rural areas would have difficulty maintaining their competency and that they would struggle with having to take patients who are beyond their scope of training. This was not the case, however, at least according to self-report. Although therapists did not endorse items that concerned their own competency, they were much more likely to be concerned about their colleagues' competency, though this held true across types of community.

The fourth MANOVA, in which the independent variable was community and the dependent variable was burnout, was also significant, $F(26, 404) = 1.67$, $p < .05$, although only two of the individual ANOVAs were significant, as shown in Table 3. Contrary to predictions, small town and rural psychologists did not endorse more items indicative of burnout. In fact, psychologists from both urban/suburban and small town/rural communities endorsed items suggesting that they enjoy their work, feel they have control over their work environment, have autonomy, and find their work professionally and personally satisfying. Urban psychologists appear to be more likely to seek counseling from another therapist, but we cannot determine if this is due to different value systems or to the availability of the resources.

The fifth MANOVA, in which the independent variable was community and the dependent variable was confidentiality, was significant, $F(13, 415) = 5.79$, $p < .01$. Six of the 13 ANOVAs were significant (see Table 3). Urban/suburban therapists are more likely to discuss their work or their clients with friends, colleagues, and other professionals. On the open-ended question at the end of the survey, several respondents emphasized that when discussing clients with others, they do not use client identifying information. As expected, small town/rural psychologists are more likely to prepare their clients for chance encounters, and they are more likely to learn information about the client from sources other than the client.

. . .

Finally, we believe that this research has implications for nonrural practitioners as well. For example, several respondents indicated that they encounter issues addressed in this survey although they live in nonrural towns:

> Although my community is about 50,000 it remains a rather small town. I often feel that I expend a great deal of energy making sure boundaries are not crossed. At times I feel a bit isolated socially because I refrain from activities

TABLE 1

TABLE 1

Community: Significantly Different Multiple Relationship Questions

Question	C	Likert rating					
		1	2	3	4	5	6
Provide therapy to one of your friends	U	87.7	8.4	1.5	0.3	0	2.1
	S*	81.4	13.3	1.8	0.9	0	2.7
Provide therapy to a relative of a friend	U	64.0	24.3	8.4	1.2	0	2.1
	S**	49.1	23.2	23.2	0.9	0.9	2.7
Accept goods or services in lieu of a fee	U	85.9	9.0	2.4	0	0.3	2.4
	S*	70.8	20.4	3.5	0	0	5.3
Purchase goods or services from a place or business where a client works	U	43.4	35.9	16.2	1.5	0.9	2.1
	S**	11.5	27.4	33.6	14.2	9.7	3.5
Work with a client in a community setting (PTA, church group)	U	60.8	29.9	6.0	1.2	0.3	1.8
	S**	38.1	26.5	19.5	4.4	6.2	5.3
Provide individual therapy to a lover of an ongoing client	U	72.3	15.7	8.7	0.3	0.3	2.7
	S*	57.5	24.8	13.3	1.8	0	2.7
Provide therapy to a child of one of your friends	U	79.3	15.0	1.8	0.6	0	3.3
	S*	69.0	18.6	7.1	0	0.9	4.4
Become social friends with parents of a former client	U	86.5	10.8	0.9	0	0	1.8
	S*	71.7	18.6	3.5	0	0	6.2
Find yourself working with two clients who happen to have a relationship with each other	U	21.9	42.0	32.1	2.1	0.9	0.9
	S**	17.7	30.1	35.4	10.6	4.4	1.8
Provide therapy to a relative of an ongoing client	U	39.0	33.3	21.9	3.0	0.3	2.4
	S**	25.7	31.9	29.2	10.6	0.9	1.8
Attend a party or social gathering and run into a client	U	22.2	41.6	31.7	2.4	1.8	0.3
	S**	15.0	25.7	35.4	10.6	12.4	0.9
Find that your children have become friends with a client or a client's children	U	58.7	23.7	6.3	0.9	0.3	10.2
	S**	35.4	18.6	14.2	5.3	4.3	22.1
Provide therapy to a client with whom you have had a previous social relationship	U	77.8	17.7	3.3	0	0	1.2
	S**	54.0	34.5	8.0	0	0.9	2.7
Loan books or other personal possessions to a client	U	28.3	30.1	34.9	4.5	2.1	0
	S**	17.7	33.6	30.1	8.0	9.7	0.9
Socialize with a client after terminating therapy	U	77.2	21.0	1.5	0	0	0.3
	S**	57.5	35.4	3.5	1.8	0	1.8
Provide therapy to a client whom you know of from being in same social sphere	U	46.1	33.1	15.7	2.1	0.6	2.4
	S**	33.0	34.8	19.6	6.3	3.6	2.7
Provide therapy to a friend of a current client	U	34.6	28.0	30.1	4.5	0.9	1.8
	S**	20.5	25.9	36.6	12.5	2.7	1.8
Find yourself working with a client who discusses problems with a person who is also your client	U	35.4	43.2	17.7	1.8	0.3	1.5
	S**	23.2	36.6	31.3	5.4	1.8	1.8
Purchase goods or services from a client	U	76.3	20.1	2.1	0.3	0.3	0.9
	S**	50.4	24.8	15.9	3.5	3.5	1.8

Note. C = community; 1 = *never*, 2 = *rarely*, 3 = *sometimes*, 4 = *fairly often*, 5 = *often*, 6 = *not applicable*; U = urban/suburban; S = small town/rural.
* *p* < .05. ** *p* < .01.

in the community in order to keep what I think is appropriate distance from my clients.

Another reported, "You have described communities our size as suburban. However, we are 2 hours away from the nearest urban area. This is a predominantly rural area. We are careful to define potential conflicts." A third responded, "Although [our town] and [the] surrounding area has 89,000 people, it could not be considered urban . . . [T]his is a rural community [and] . . . dual relationships are impossible to avoid."

		Likert rating					
Question	**C**	**1**	**2**	**3**	**4**	**5**	**6**
Work on same committee in the community as a client does	U	71.7	18.4	5.1	0.9	2.7	1.2
	S**	42.5	23.0	18.6	1.8	8.8	5.3
Run into clients in community	U	5.1	30.5	46.4	11.7	6.3	0
	S**	1.8	9.7	29.2	24.8	32.7	1.8
Work on same committee with a former client	U	77.2	18.0	2.7	0.9	0.3	0.9
	S**	44.6	27.7	16.1	0	5.4	6.3
Feel that you are a therapist 24 hr a day	U	33.0	39.6	20.1	3.3	2.4	1.5
	S*	27.4	34.5	28.3	3.5	4.4	1.8
See your clients in restaurants	U	15.9	42.8	33.2	4.8	2.1	1.2
	S**	8.0	15.9	46.9	15.0	12.4	1.8
Have clients who know more about your personal life than you would prefer	U	34.7	50.3	13.8	0.3	0.3	0.6
	S**	17.7	50.4	24.8	3.5	3.5	0
Belong to or join same club or organization as a former client (e.g., political, religious, social)	U	37.2	40.8	15.3	3.9	2.1	0.6
	S**	23.9	30.1	24.8	8.0	8.0	5.3
Participate in same neighborhood activity as a client (e.g., fundraiser, community project)	U	52.3	33.9	11.7	0.3	0.9	0.9
	S**	31.0	30.1	22.1	6.2	7.1	3.5
Have a client become aware of a personal stressor in your life from a source other than yourself	U	45.6	42.6	10.3	0	0.3	1.2
	S**	29.7	42.3	21.6	1.8	2.7	1.8

Note. C = community; 1 = *never*, 2 = *rarely*, 3 = *sometimes*, 4 = *fairly often*, 5 = *often*, 6 = *not applicable*;
U = urban/suburban; S = small town/rural.
* $p < .05$. ** $p < .01$.

Small communities also often exist within larger communities. For example, one respondent stated, "This item can be very misleading as many of us participate in small communities in large metro areas, such as gays and lesbians, Jews, ethnic groups, etc." Another respondent related the experience of working within the recovery community and being a part of the Alcoholics Anonymous (or 12-step) culture and coping with such norms as hugging each other on greeting. A third reported, "One issue for me is a small community within an urban setting due to my sexual orientation and work with that small community as well as a large urban population." Another respondent who works primarily within the deaf community in a large urban area noted the similarities of trying to maintain boundaries in a rural area and working with a specific population within an urban area. This psychologist cited difficulties with maintaining confidentiality, as many clients know each other, and trying to maintain a balance between letting clients get to know the psychologist as a person in order to be accepted in the community but at the same time attempting to maintain professional boundaries.

CONCLUSIONS

The purpose of this study was to empirically examine the question of whether there are unique ethical dilemmas when practicing psychology in rural communities. Findings suggest that rural psychologists are more likely to encounter specific types of ethical dilemmas, particularly related to multiple relationships. Rural psychologists also struggle with maintaining client confidentiality and issues related to being so highly visible in the community, such as having some clients know a great deal about the psychologist's personal life. These potential ethical dilemmas are likely to have an impact on clinical practice and clinical decision making. We believe it is imperative to have a forum for rural psychologists to discuss the issues related to their practice.

TABLE 3

Community: Remainder of Significantly Different Questions by Category

Question	C	Likert rating					
		1	2	3	4	5	6
		Competency					
Not able to refer clients because of lack of referral services	U	28.3	39.5	25.6	3.0	2.4	1.2
	S**	12.6	28.8	39.6	10.8	6.3	1.8
Have opportunity to discuss problems in work environment with peers	U**	2.4	11.1	37.5	29.4	16.5	3.0
	S	6.2	15.0	34.5	27.4	10.6	6.2
Feel frustrated with lack of alternative resources to help your clients	U	9.0	30.3	45.9	9.6	4.2	0.9
	S**	3.5	23.9	47.8	15.9	7.1	1.8
		Burnout					
Feel you don't do enough to help your clients	U*	5.1	47.6	41.0	3.9	2.1	0.3
	S	10.6	53.1	30.1	5.3	0.9	0
Seek counseling from another therapist	U**	26.7	20.9	33.9	5.2	7.6	5.8
	S	36.3	26.5	24.8	2.7	1.8	8.0
		Confidentiality					
Discuss a client with a psychologist colleague, without informed consent	U**	29.4	26.1	30.3	9.3	3.3	1.5
	S	37.2	33.6	22.1	4.4	0.9	1.8
Discuss clients with friends, without using client names	U**	41.6	40.1	15.6	1.8	0.6	0.3
	S	54.9	32.7	11.5	0	0	0.9
Prepare clients for chance encounters in the community	U	25.5	25.5	24.0	11.7	10.8	2.4
	S**	7.1	18.6	34.5	18.6	18.6	2.7
Discuss a client with other mental health professionals without consent	U**	40.3	34.5	20.3	3.6	0.6	0.6
	S	53.2	29.7	14.4	0.9	0.9	0.9
Discuss with clients how to deal with situation where you may run into each other in public	U	28.1	28.4	25.1	6.9	9.6	1.8
	S**	10.7	25.9	39.3	9.8	10.7	3.6
Unintentionally learn information about client from other resources in community	U	11.7	38.3	41.9	5.1	2.4	0.6
	S**	1.8	17.7	50.4	14.2	13.3	2.7

Note. C = community; 1 = *never*, 2 = *rarely*, 3 = *sometimes*, 4 = *fairly often*, 5 = *often*, 6 = *not applicable*; U = urban/suburban; S = small town/rural.
* $p < .05$. ** $p < .01$.

References

American Psychological Association. (1992). Ethical principles of psychologists and code of conduct. *American Psychologist, 47,* 1597–1611.

American Psychological Association. (2002). Ethical principles of psychologists and code of conduct. *American Psychologist, 57,* 1060–1073.

Barbopoulos, A., & Clark, J. M. (2003). Practising psychology in rural settings: Issues and guidelines. *Canadian Psychology, 44,* 410–424.

Cook, A. D., Copans, S. A., & Schetky, D. H. (1998). Psychiatric treatment of children and adolescents in rural communities. *Child and Adolescent Psychiatric Clinics of North America, 7,* 673–690.

Hargrove, D. S. (1986). Ethical issues in rural mental health practice. *Professional Psychology: Research and Practice, 17,* 20–23.

Helbok, C. (2003). The practice of psychology in rural communities: Potential ethical dilemmas. *Ethics & Behavior, 13,* 367–384.

Maslach, C., & Florian, V. (1988). Burnout, job setting, and self-evaluation among rehabilitation counselors. *Rehabilitation Psychology, 33,* 85–93.

Murray, J. D., & Keller, P. A. (1991). Psychology and rural America: Current status and future directions. *American Psychologist, 46,* 220–231.

Reed, D. A. (1992). Adaptation: The key to community psychiatric practice in the rural setting. *Community Mental Health Journal, 28,* 141–150.

Roberts, L. W., Battaglia, J., & Epstein, R. S. (1999). Frontier ethics: Mental health care needs and ethical dilemmas in rural communities. *Psychiatric Services, 50,* 497–503.

Stockman, A. F. (1990). Dual relationships in rural mental health practice: An ethical dilemma. *Journal of Rural Community Psychology, 11,* 31–45.

Sundet, P. A., & Mermelstein, J. (1983). The meaning of community in rural mental health. *International Journal of Mental Health, 12*, 25–44.

Wagenfeld, M. O. (1988). Rural mental health and community psychology in the post community mental health era: An overview and introduction to the special issue. *Journal of Rural Community Psychology, 9*, 5–11.

Wagenfeld, M. O., & Buffum, W. E. (1983). Problems in, and prospects for, rural mental health services in the United States. *International Journal of Mental Health, 12*(1–2), 89–107.

◆ ◆ ◆

Commentary: For earlier helpful articles on this issue see Hargrove, D. S. (1986). Ethical issues in rural mental health practice. Professional Psychology: Research and Practice, *17, 20–23; Schank, J. A., & Skovholt, T. M. (1997). Dual-relationship dilemmas of rural and small-community psychologists.* Professional Psychology: Research and Practice, *28, 44–49.*

One issue that these authors, as well as Helbok et al. (excerpted here), fail to address is bartering for services, a problem that may confront those who serve rural or poor clients, particularly those enrolled in managed care programs that limit the number of reimbursable visits. In 1982, the APA Ethics Committee approved a policy that proclaimed bartering of services a violation of then Principle 6a (Dual Relationships). That policy was modified in the 1992 Ethical Principles (Standard 1.18) and was retained in Standard 6.05 of the 2002 Ethics Code. That provision generally discourages bartering, permitting it only if it is not clinically contraindicated and is not exploitive. But Sonne (1994) thought that even this broadening might be problematic:

> *Even if the psychologist were able to make the prediction a priori that bartering posed no ethical concerns, at least three other issues remain. First, bartering for services may, in essence, establish an employment relationship. . . . When such conditions of employment are implicit—the potential for harmful effects in the dynamics of the therapist–client relationship is greater.*
>
> *Second, the practitioner needs to consider the position of the state licensing board regarding employing a client and bartering. . . .*
>
> *Third, psychologists need to be aware of the position of the American Professional Agency, whose malpractice insurance policy . . . states, 'This policy does not . . . apply to any claims arising out of any business venture with any prior or current patient or client of the insured' [citation omitted]. Lack of coverage of such acts seems a clear indication of how potentially destructive they can be. (p. 341)*

See Sonne, J. (1994). Multiple relationships: Does the new ethics code answer the right questions? Professional Psychology: Research and Practice, *25, 336–343. In a similar vein, Woody argued that "bartering seems so fraught with risks for both parties that it seems illogical to even consider it as an option" (p. 176). He would use it only as a last resort. See Woody, R. J. (1988). Bartering for psychological services.* Professional Psychology: Research and Practice, *29, 174–178.*

Are these cautionary notes appropriate or do they support the position that ethics codes, licensing boards, and insurers are too rule-bound and neglect the realities of rural practice and the provision of services to certain ethnic and "small-community" groups?

The possibility for therapist self-disclosure may be heightened in rural and small communities, but it is a controversial issue for all practitioners. Psychodynamic theorists generally eschew self-disclosure as a detrimental treatment, but more humanistically oriented therapists argue that disclosure creates a more honest and authentic setting, enhancing greater self-disclosure from clients. A recent small study seems to support the latter view, although in the context of cognitive–behavioral or supportive therapies. Barrett and Berman (2001) found

> *that therapist self-disclosure can influence the outcome of psychotherapy. When therapists were instructed to increase their level of self-disclosure, the clients they treated reported greater reductions in symptom distress than did comparable clients for whom therapists limited their level of disclosure.*

Coupled with reductions in symptom distress, clients also liked their therapists more when therapist disclosure was increased. (p. 602)

Barrett, M., & Berman, J. (2001). Is psychotherapy more effective when therapists disclose information about themselves? Journal of Consulting and Clinical Psychology, 69, 597–603.

Is self-disclosure barred by the 2002 Ethics Code? See Standard 2.06 (Personal Problems and Conflicts). As Garfield (1987) noted,

> *Obviously, self-disclosure that results in harm and exploitation to family members is never justified. Sexual intercourse with patients, physical, or emotional abuse, all suggest that the therapist is operating out of his own narcissistic and/or sadistic needs and not in the interest of the family's well-being. In these situations, the therapist does not make himself vulnerable, but may think so, or rationalize his actions, to avoid facing serious personal problems. The therapist's activities may need to be checked and reviewed by other professionals. (p. 74)*

Garfield, R. (1987). On self-disclosure: The vulnerable therapist. Contemporary Family Therapy, 9, 58–78.

The APA has been reasonably forthcoming in producing documents designed to help therapists deal with such sensitive issues as sexism, racism, and the treatment of gays and lesbians. For example in 1975, an APA task force on sexism in psychotherapy published the following: American Psychological Association. (1975). Report of the task force on sex bias and sex-role stereotyping in psychotherapeutic practice. American Psychologist, 30, 1169–1175. Like many other task force reports, this one has not been adopted by the Council of Representatives as APA policy. But it has raised many issues that are still of concern, such as the treatment of lesbians by therapists who are not fully trained or knowledgeable in this area and the problem of sexual attraction between therapist and patient.

The 1975 report recommended, among other things, that APA develop guidelines for nonsexist psychotherapeutic practice. The APA appropriated funds for this endeavor, and in 1978, these guidelines were published in the American Psychologist, 33, 1122–1123.

More particular guidelines produced under APA auspices follow.

Guidelines for Therapy With Women

Task Force on Sex Bias and Sex Role Stereotyping in Psychotherapeutic Practice

. . .

1. The conduct of therapy should be free of constrictions based on gender-defined roles, and the options explored between client and practitioner should be free of sex role stereotypes.

. . .

2. Psychologists should recognize the reality, variety, and implications of sex-discriminatory practices in society and should facilitate client examination of options in dealing with such practices.

. . .

3. The therapist should be knowledgeable about current empirical findings on sex roles, sexism, and individual differences resulting from the client's gender-defined identity.

. . .

4. The theoretical concepts employed by the therapist should be free of sex bias and sex role stereotypes.

. . .

5. The psychologist should demonstrate acceptance of women as equal to men by using language free of derogatory labels.

. . .

6. The psychologist should avoid establishing the source of personal problems within the client when they are more properly attributable to situational or cultural factors.

. . .

7. The psychologist and a fully informed client mutually should agree upon aspects of the therapy relationship such as treatment modality, time factors, and fee arrangements.

. . .

8. While the importance of the availability of accurate information to a client's family is recognized, the privilege of communication about diagnosis, prognosis, and progress ultimately resides with the client, not with the therapist.

. . .

9. If authoritarian processes are employed as a technique, the therapy should not have the effect of maintaining or reinforcing stereotypic dependency of women.

. . .

10. The client's assertive behaviors should be respected.

. . .

11. The psychologist whose female client is subjected to violence in the form of physical abuse or rape should recognize and acknowledge that the client is the victim of a crime.

. . .

12. The psychologist should recognize and encourage exploration of a woman client's sexuality and should recognize her right to define her own sexual preferences.

. . .

13. The psychologist should not have sexual relations with a woman client nor treat her as a sex object.

. . .

◆　　◆　　◆

Commentary: In 1984, APA's Division 17 (Counseling Psychology) produced a corollary set of precepts titled "Principles Concerning the Counseling and Psychotherapy of Women" that are worth studying (available from Division 17). For more recent texts on this subject, see Brabeck, M. (2000). Practicing feminist ethics in psychology. Washington, DC: American Psychological Association; Rave, E., & Larsen C. (Eds.). (1995). Ethical decision making in therapy: Feminist perspectives. New York: Guilford Press (including a Feminist Therapy Code of Ethics);

From *American Psychologist, 33,* 1122–1123. Copyright 1978 by the American Psychological Association.

Gartrell, N. (Ed.). (1994). Bringing ethics alive: Feminist ethics in psychotherapy. *New York: Haworth Press; and Lerman, H., & Porter, N. (Eds.). (1990). Feminist ethics in psychotherapy. New York: Springer.*

In 1990, a survey conducted as part of a report by the Task Force on Bias in Psychotherapy with Lesbians and Gay Men found that the conduct of many therapists in assessing and treating these client populations violated existing ethical principles, particularly with regard to competence and client welfare. Ten years later, APA adopted and issued guidelines to remedy this problem. These guidelines are reproduced next but, because of space limitations, without the explanatory material.

Following the guidelines for psychotherapy with lesbians and gays are guidelines, also adopted as APA policy, developed by a task force established by the APA's Board of Ethnic Minority Affairs. These guidelines were established to help psychologists better understand cultural and ethnic factors when providing psychological services to diverse populations.

Guidelines for Psychotherapy With Lesbian, Gay, and Bisexual Clients

Division 44/Committee on Lesbian, Gay, and Bisexual Concerns Joint Task Force on Guidelines for Psychotherapy With Lesbian, Gay, and Bisexual Clients

. . .

The specific goals of these guidelines are to provide practitioners with (a) a frame of reference for the treatment of lesbian, gay, and bisexual clients and (b) basic information and further references in the areas of assessment, intervention, identity, relationships, and the education and training of psychologists.

. . .

ATTITUDES TOWARD HOMOSEXUALITY AND BISEXUALITY

Guideline 1. Psychologists understand that homosexuality and bisexuality are not indicative of mental illness.

. . .

Guideline 2. Psychologists are encouraged to recognize how their attitudes and knowledge about lesbian, gay, and bisexual issues may be relevant to assessment and treatment and seek consultation or make appropriate referrals when indicated.

. . .

Guideline 3. Psychologists strive to understand the ways in which social stigmatization (i.e., prejudice, discrimination, and violence) poses risks to the mental health and well-being of lesbian, gay, and bisexual clients.

. . .

Guideline 4. Psychologists strive to understand how inaccurate or prejudicial views of homosexuality or bisexuality may affect the client's presentation in treatment and the therapeutic process.

. . .

RELATIONSHIPS AND FAMILIES

Guideline 5. Psychologists strive to be knowledgeable about and respect the importance of lesbian, gay, and bisexual relationships.

. . .

Guideline 6. Psychologists strive to understand the particular circumstances and challenges faced by lesbian, gay, and bisexual parents.

. . .

Guideline 7. Psychologists recognize that the families of lesbian, gay, and bisexual people may include people who are not legally or biologically related.

. . .

Guideline 8. Psychologists strive to understand how a person's homosexual or bisexual orientation may have an impact on his or her family of origin and the relationship to that family of origin.

. . .

ISSUES OF DIVERSITY

Guideline 9. Psychologists are encouraged to recognize the particular life issues or challenges that are related to multiple and often conflicting cultural norms, values, and beliefs that lesbian, gay, and bisexual members of racial and ethnic minorities face.

. . .

Guideline 10. Psychologists are encouraged to recognize the particular challenges that bisexual individuals experience.

. . .

From *American Psychologist, 55,* 1446–1451. Copyright 2000 by the American Psychological Association.

Guideline 11. Psychologists strive to understand the special problems and risks that exist for lesbian, gay, and bisexual youth.

. . .

Guideline 12. Psychologists consider generational differences within lesbian, gay, and bisexual populations and the particular challenges that lesbian, gay, and bisexual older adults may experience.

. . .

Guideline 13. Psychologists are encouraged to recognize the particular challenges that lesbian, gay, and bisexual individuals experience with physical, sensory, and cognitive–emotional disabilities.

. . .

EDUCATION

Guideline 14. Psychologists support the provision of professional education and training on lesbian, gay, and bisexual issues.

. . .

Guideline 15. Psychologists are encouraged to increase their knowledge and understanding of homosexuality and bisexuality through continuing education, training, supervision, and consultation.

. . .

Guideline 16. Psychologists make reasonable efforts to familiarize themselves with relevant mental health, educational, and community resources for lesbian, gay, and bisexual people.

◆　◆　◆

Commentary: Recently, several excellent publications have addressed a variety of issues concerning the treatment of gay, lesbian, and bisexual clients. Among them are

Anderson, J., & Barrett, R. (Eds.). (2001). Ethics in HIV-related psychotherapy: Clinical decision making in complex cases. Washington, DC: American Psychological Association. (A chapter by Stevenson & Kitchener, pp. 19–42, discusses confidentiality in Tarasoff-like situations and rational suicide.)

Benoit, M. (2005). Conflict between religious commitment and same-sex attraction: Possibilities for a virtuous response. Ethics & Behavior, 15, 309–325. (Reviews ethical arguments for and against sexual reorientation therapy.)

Johnson, W. B., & Buhrke, R. A. (2006). Service delivery in a "don't ask, don't tell" world: Ethical care of gay, lesbian, and bisexual military personnel. Professional Psychology: Research and Practice, 37, 91–98. (Addresses, among other issues, ethical and administrative problems for clinicians who treat gay, lesbian, and bisexual persons in military settings.)

Kessler, L. E., & Waehler, C. A. (2005). Addressing multiple relationships between clients and therapists in lesbian, gay, bisexual, and transgender communities. Professional Psychology: Research and Practice, 36, 66–72.

Lasser, J. S., & Gottlieb, M. C. (2004). Treating patients distressed regarding their sexual orientation: Clinical and ethical alternatives. Professional Psychology: Research and Practice, 35, 194–200.

Guidelines for Providers of Psychological Services to Ethnic, Linguistic, and Culturally Diverse Populations

American Psychological Association

. . .

GUIDELINES

Preamble: The Guidelines represent general principles that are intended to be aspirational in nature and are designed to provide suggestions to psychologists in working with ethnic, linguistic, and culturally diverse populations.

1. Psychologists educate their clients to the processes of psychological intervention, such as goals and expectations; the scope and, where appropriate, legal limits of confidentiality; and the psychologists' orientations.
   a. Whenever possible, psychologists provide information in writing along with oral explanations.
   b. Whenever possible, the written information is provided in the language understandable to the client.
2. Psychologists are cognizant of relevant research and practice issues as related to the population being served.
   a. Psychologists acknowledge that ethnicity and culture impact on behavior and take those factors into account when working with various ethnic/racial groups.
   b. Psychologists seek out educational and training experiences to enhance their understanding and thereby address the needs of these populations more appropriately and effectively. These experiences include cultural, social, psychological, political, economic, and historic material specific to the particular ethnic group being served.

   c. Psychologists recognize the limits of their competencies and expertise. Psychologists who do not possess knowledge and training about an ethnic group seek consultation with, and/or make referrals to, appropriate experts as necessary.
   d. Psychologists consider the validity of a given instrument or procedure and interpret resulting data, keeping in mind the cultural and linguistic characteristics of the person being assessed. Psychologists are aware of the test's reference population and possible limitations of such instruments with other populations.
3. Psychologists recognize ethnicity and culture as significant parameters in understanding psychological processes.
   a. Psychologists, regardless of ethnic/racial background, are aware of how their own cultural background/experiences, attitudes, values, and biases influence psychological processes. They make efforts to correct any prejudices and biases.

   Illustrative statement. Psychologists might routinely ask themselves, "Is it appropriate for me to view this client or organization any differently than I would if they were from my own ethnic or cultural group?"
   b. Psychologists' practice incorporates an understanding of the client's ethnic and cultural background. This includes the client's familiarity and comfort with the majority culture as well as ways in which the client's culture may add to or improve various aspects of the majority culture and/or of society at large.

Illustrative statement. The kinds of mainstream social activities in which families participate may offer information about the level and quality of acculturation to American society. It is important to distinguish acculturation from length of stay in the United States and not to assume that these issues are relevant only for new immigrants and refugees.

c. Psychologists help clients increase their awareness of their own cultural values and norms, and they facilitate discovery of ways clients can apply this awareness to their own lives and to society at large.

Illustrative statement. Psychologists may be able to help parents distinguish between generational conflict and culture gaps when problems arise between them and their children. In the process, psychologists could help both parents and children to appreciate their own distinguishing cultural values.

d. Psychologists seek to help a client determine whether a "problem" stems from racism or bias in others so that the client does not inappropriately personalize problems.

Illustrative statement. The concept of "healthy paranoia," whereby ethnic minorities may develop defensive behaviors in response to discrimination, illustrates this principle.

e. Psychologists consider not only differential diagnostic issues but also the cultural beliefs and values of the client and his/her community in providing intervention.

. . .

4. Psychologists respect the roles of family members and community structures, hierarchies, values, and beliefs within the client's culture.
   a. Psychologists identify resources in the family and the larger community.
   b. Clarification of the role of the psychologist and the expectations of the client precedes intervention. Psychologists seek to ensure that both the psychologist and client have a clear understanding of what services and roles are reasonable.

. . .

5. Psychologists respect clients' religious and/or spiritual beliefs and values, including attributions and taboos, since they affect world view, psychosocial functioning, and expressions of distress.
   a. Part of working in minority communities is to become familiar with indigenous beliefs and practices and to respect them.

Illustrative statement. Traditional healers (e.g., shamans, curanderos, espiritistas) have an important place in minority communities.

b. Effective psychological intervention may be aided by consultation with and/or inclusion of religious/spiritual leaders/practitioners relevant to the client's cultural and belief systems.

6. Psychologists interact in the language requested by the client and, if this is not feasible, make an appropriate referral.
   a. Problems may arise when the linguistic skills of the psychologist do not match the language of the client. In such a case, psychologists refer the client to a mental health professional who is competent to interact in the language of the client. If this is not possible, psychologists offer the client a translator with cultural knowledge and an appropriate professional background. When no translator is available, then a trained paraprofessional from the client's culture is used as a translator/culture broker.
   b. If translation is necessary, psychologists do not retain the services of translators/paraprofessionals who may have a dual role with the client, to avoid jeopardizing the validity of evaluation or the effectiveness of intervention.
   c. Psychologists interpret and relate test data in terms understandable and relevant to the needs of those assessed.

7. Psychologists consider the impact of adverse social, environmental, and political factors in assessing problems and designing interventions.
   a. Types of intervention strategies to be used match the client's level of need (e.g., Maslow's hierarchy of needs).

Illustrative statement. Low income may be associated with such stressors as malnutrition, substandard housing, and poor medical care; and rural residency may mean inaccessibility of services. Clients may resist treatment at government agencies because of previous experience (e.g., refugees' status may be associated with violent treatments by government officials and agencies).

   b. Psychologists work within the cultural setting to improve the welfare of all persons concerned, if there is a conflict between cultural values and human rights.

8. Psychologists attend to, as well as work to eliminate, biases, prejudices, and discriminatory practices.

   a. Psychologists acknowledge relevant discriminatory practices at the social and community level that may be affecting the psychological welfare of the population being served.

Illustrative statement. Depression may be associated with frustrated attempts to climb the corporate ladder in an organization that is dominated by a top echelon of White men.

   b. Psychologists are cognizant of sociopolitical contexts in conducting evaluations and providing interventions; they develop sensitivity to issues of oppression, sexism, elitism, and racism.

Illustrative statement. An upsurge in the public expression of rancor or even violence between two ethnic or cultural groups may increase anxiety baselines in any member of those groups. This baseline of anxiety would interact with prevailing symptomatology. At the organizational level, the community conflict may interfere with open communication among staff.

9. Psychologists working with culturally diverse populations should document culturally and sociopolitically relevant factors in the records. These may include, but are not limited to

   a. number of generations in the country

   b. number of years in the country

   c. fluency in English

   d. extent of family support (or disintegration of family)

   e. community resources

   f. level of education

   g. change in social status as a result of coming to this country (for immigrant or refugee)

   h. intimate relationship with people of different backgrounds

   i. level of stress related to acculturation.

◆   ◆   ◆

Commentary: See American Psychological Association. (2003). Guidelines on multicultural education, training, research, practice, and organizational change for psychologists. American Psychologist, 58, 377–402 *(enacted as APA policy but due to expire by 2009). See also Mailloux, S. L. (2004). Ethics and interpreters: Are you practicing ethically?* Journal of Psychological Practice, 10, 37–44.

The final policy document (Guidelines for Psychological Practice with Older Adults; see following excerpt) deals with older adults. Though enacted as APA policy, it is due to expire by August 31, 2010. Only the guidelines are reproduced; the extensive discussion and reference list have been omitted.

Guidelines for Psychological Practice With Older Adults

American Psychological Association

ATTITUDES

Guideline 1. Psychologists are encouraged to work with older adults within their scope of competence, and to seek consultation or make appropriate referrals when indicated.

Guideline 2. Psychologists are encouraged to recognize how their attitudes and beliefs about aging and about older individuals may be relevant to their assessment and treatment of older adults, and to seek consultation or further education about these issues when indicated.

GENERAL KNOWLEDGE ABOUT ADULT DEVELOPMENT, AGING, AND OLDER ADULTS

Guideline 3. Psychologists strive to gain knowledge about theory and research in aging.

Guideline 4. Psychologists strive to be aware of the social/psychological dynamics of the aging process.

Guideline 5. Psychologists strive to understand diversity in the aging process, particularly how sociocultural factors such as gender, ethnicity, socioeconomic status, sexual orientation, disability status, and urban/rural residence may influence the experience and expression of health and of psychological problems in later life.

Guideline 6. Psychologists strive to be familiar with current information about biological and health-related aspects of aging.

CLINICAL ISSUES

Guideline 7. Psychologists strive to be familiar with current knowledge about cognitive changes in older adults.

Guideline 8. Psychologists strive to understand problems in daily living among older adults.

Guideline 9. Psychologists strive to be knowledgeable about psychopathology within the aging population and cognizant of the prevalence and nature of that psychopathology when providing services to older adults.

ASSESSMENT

Guideline 10. Psychologists strive to be familiar with the theory, research, and practice of various methods of assessment with older adults, and knowledgeable of assessment instruments that are psychometrically suitable for use with them.

Guideline 11. Psychologists strive to understand the problems of using assessment instruments created for younger individuals when assessing older adults, and to develop skill in tailoring assessments to accommodate older adults' specific characteristics and contexts.

Guideline 12. Psychologists strive to develop skill at recognizing cognitive changes in older adults, and in conducting and interpreting cognitive screening and functional ability evaluations.

INTERVENTION, CONSULTATION, AND OTHER SERVICE PROVISION

Guideline 13. Psychologists strive to be familiar with the theory, research, and practice of various methods of intervention with older adults, particularly with current research evidence about their efficacy with this age group.

Guideline 14. Psychologists strive to be familiar with and develop skill in applying specific psychotherapeutic interventions and environmental modifications with older adults and their families, including adapting interventions for use with this age group.

Guideline 15. Psychologists strive to understand the issues pertaining to the provision of services in the specific settings in which older adults are typically located or encountered.

Guideline 16. Psychologists strive to recognize issues related to the provision of prevention and health promotion services with older adults.

Guideline 17. Psychologists strive to understand issues pertaining to the provision of consultation services in assisting older adults.

Guideline 18. In working with older adults, psychologists are encouraged to understand the importance of interfacing with other disciplines, and to make referrals to other disciplines and/or to work with them in collaborative teams and across a range of sites, as appropriate.

Guideline 19. Psychologists strive to understand the special ethical and/or legal issues entailed in providing services to older adults.

EDUCATION

Guideline 20. Psychologists are encouraged to increase their knowledge, understanding, and skills with respect to working with older adults through continuing education, training, supervision, and consultation.

◆　　◆　　◆

Commentary: In the final section of this chapter, I address ethical issues related to more nontraditional forms of therapy. Conventional psychological interventions do not intrude into the client's body. Some psychophysical measurements, like electroencephalography, do involve the corpus of the client but do not "break the skin." Thus, they raise no special legal or ethical issues. But with the development of biofeedback, stress and pain management, aversive conditioning, behavioral medicine, and such "alternative" therapies as diet and nutrition, herbal remedies, aromatherapy, and exercise—as well as psychologists' increasing participation in these fields (see, e.g., Greub, B., & McNamara, J. [2000]. Alternative therapies in psychological treatment: When is consultation with a physician warranted? Professional Psychology: Research and Practice, 31, 58–63)—procedures that involve physical interventions have come under governmental scrutiny.

An APA task force in 1981 issued a report concluding that the use of physical interventions was within the scope of psychological practice when preceded by formal and appropriately supervised training and experience. Presciently, it envisioned the development of courses to qualify psychologists to prescribe psychoactive drugs. In 1992 a comprehensive report on prescription privileges was issued by the APA ad hoc Task Force on Psychopharmacology. Subsequently, the APA Council of Representatives endorsed a policy favoring the securing of prescription privileges for psychologists. Psychologists have now been given those privileges in Guam, Louisiana, and, most notably, New Mexico where regulations implementing the statute allowing licensed psychologists with appropriate training and certification to prescribe psychotropic medication took effect in January 2005. Under the regulations, for psychologists to receive a prescribing certificate they must complete at least 450 hours of classroom instruction; an 80-hour practicum in clinical assessment and pathophysiology; a 400-hour, 100-patient course of practical training under physician supervision; and a national Psychopharmacology Examination for Psychologists. Despite these advances, there is no consensus within the field favoring such privileges, as the next excerpt illustrates.

A Debate on Prescription Privileges for Psychologists

Elaine M. Heiby, Patrick H. DeLeon, and Timothy Anderson

A debate on the American Psychological Association's (APA's) policy on prescription privileges (also referred to as RxP) for psychologists was held at APA's August 22–25, 2002, convention in Chicago. The debate, organized and chaired by Timothy Anderson, was entitled "The Role of Prescription Authority for the Psychologist." Patrick H. DeLeon presented arguments in favor and Elaine M. Heiby presented arguments against APA's policy on RxP.

. . .

OPENING STATEMENTS

The debate began with a proposition stated in the positive for DeLeon and in the negative for Heiby as follows. *Proposed: "The science and practice of clinical psychology will [not] benefit from psychologists having the authority to prescribe medicine."*

Opening Statement: DeLeon

. . .

I believe prescriptive authority is important for psychology because this is the future. The future is holistic health care. The future is educated consumers. The future is ensuring that one's professional training, regardless of discipline, becomes readily available to those in need. It is no longer acceptable to wait a month or 6 weeks to see a specialist. Our nation's health care system must become more responsive to consumer needs.

. . . Pharmacy has "prescription privileges" in 38 states, under varying conditions. Similarly, there are 75,000 advanced practice nurses (nurse practitioners, clinical specialists, nurse midwives) in all 50 states. That profession and others are providing quality primary care. Psychology must accept this professional challenge and become actively engaged in the primary care arena. We must provide high-quality care in community health centers, the true safety net for our nation's uninsured and underinsured. It is our societal responsibility (DeLeon, 2002).

Where Elaine and I absolutely agree, and where we have always agreed, is that psychopharmacology training should be at the postdoctoral level, and not at the undergraduate or even graduate level. It is important for psychologists to be well schooled in the foundation of psychology and the behavioral sciences. We should learn how to accurately diagnose and treat. Our internship experiences are invaluable. The prescribing psychologist must foremost be a psychologist. He or she can then obtain the pharmacology expertise as an additional clinical skill. Once one has obtained his or her primary professional identity (including how one interacts with patients), one sees the world somewhat differently than individuals with other professional identities do. . . . Obtaining prescriptive authority is the future, and with this additional clinical skill, our clinicians will serve society very well. Other nonphysician providers are increasingly obtaining this clinical responsibility. If psychology ever decided not to invest in the future, future generations of the best and brightest undergraduates would no longer seek out psychology (DeLeon, 2003). . . .

Opening Statement: Heiby

I would like to thank APA for holding this debate. First, I believe the proposed statement (*the science and practice of clinical psychology will [not] benefit from having the authority to prescribe medicine*) represents a number of misunderstandings of the issues raised by the opponents to APA policy on prescription privileges. Therefore, I would like to start by pointing out the positions of the opposition to APA policy for RxP.

The first misunderstanding in need of clarification is the belief that the opponents of APA policy object to psychologists obtaining the authority to prescribe. Indeed, prescribing authority is supported under certain conditions. The opponents officially do not, and never have, objected to psychologists obtaining such authority. Rather, opponents support obtaining such authority through already established routes, such as joint or executive track nursing programs. Using established avenues to obtain such authority would not require new laws, would not divide the profession, would not alienate our medical colleagues, and would not cost millions of dollars in lobbying.

What opponents object to is APA policy on Level 3 (independent practice) training in terms of the locus of training (which is at both the doctoral and postdoctoral levels) and the quality of training (which is far less than that of any prescribing profession). Pat just mentioned that he agrees that training should be postdoctoral, but the APA policy places such training at both levels. I'll expand on concerns about the locus and quality of training later in the debate.

A second important misunderstanding in this debate concerns the size and nature of opposition to APA policy on RxP. Opponents include five significant organizations of applied and academic psychologists who are concerned about the preservation and growth of the scientist–practitioner model of clinical practice and university-based departments of psychology. Surveys of rank-and-file psychologists also indicate opposition to RxP.

The following five organizations expressed objection to RxP before it became APA policy in August 1995: (a) the American Association of Applied and Preventive Psychology, (b) the Society for a Science of Clinical Psychology, (c) the Council of University Directors of Clinical Programs, (d) the Council of Graduate Departments of Psychology, and (e) the Committee Against Medicalizing Psychology. While the membership numbers of these five organizations are smaller than the total membership of APA, the roles these organizations play and the people they represent are central to the preservation of clinical science and the raison d'être for professional practice. . . .

The objections of these five organizations obviously were not heeded. According to DeNelsky (2001), the procedure that led to APA's RxP policy suspended council rules "before the vote so that full debate and review of this important policy issue with APA governance did not occur" (p. 5). When APA and some state psychology associations proceeded to introduce RxP-enabling legislation even though they were fully aware that there were organizations of psychologists who objected to these bills, the debate moved from within the profession to state legislatures where psychology is presented as divided in a public forum.

. . .

A third common misunderstanding of the opposition to APA's RxP policy concerns the importance of medical training. Opponents to APA's RxP policy recognize the advantages to psychologists of obtaining medical training outside the discipline of psychology. Opponents have asserted that psychologists are generally very smart people and that many psychologists also obtain a degree in law, nursing, business management, and so on. The positive contributions of these cross-trained psychologists are obvious. The benefits of psychologists obtaining training in medicine through already established avenues are enormous. There could be greater cross-fertilization between the medical and psychological sciences and their applications, which now tends to occur through collaboration and consultation. Psychotropic medications have become a major form of treatment, and psychologists should know about them. Psychologists also would be able to provide empirically supported psychosocial treatments instead of or in addition to medical ones.

Along the same lines, opponents also acknowledge advantages to enhancing the training in psychopharmacology within the discipline. APA's underscoring of the importance of having a background in psychopharmacology has forced departments of psychology to review undergraduate- and graduate-level curricula in terms of the adequacy of what's called Level 1 training (basic psychopharmacology). APA's 1995 Board of Educational Affairs working group and others have argued that Level 1 training would require adding one additional three- or four-semester credit course in psychopharmacology, which many psychology departments already offer. Level 1 training is not opposed by organized psychology, and there are good reasons for APA to include Level 1 training in its accreditation criteria. In addition, APA's underscoring of the importance of making Level 2 training (collaborative practice) available, given that most psychoactive medications are prescribed by nonpsychiatric physicians, would address concerns about consumers having the option for psychological interventions about which a primary care physician may be unaware. Level 2 training builds on Level 1 training. It is recommended to occur at the practicum level, the internship level, and the continuing education level. Level 2 training has not been opposed by organized psychology. There are some practicum and internship sites that are prepared to provide Level 2 training. It would be difficult to make Level 2 training a standard for doctoral and postdoctoral training because the resources are not available at all training sites.

Opponents of APA's RxP policy argue, because of the concerns delineated so far, that it is time for a moratorium on pursuing enabling legislation. Opponents also argue that it is time to explore the implications for the discipline of psychology of adopting RxP Level 3 training, particularly as APA's policy currently recommends this training at both the doctoral and the postdoctoral level.

. . .

SUMMARY AND DISCUSSION: ANDERSON

This debate focused not so much on whether psychologists should attain prescription authority, but on how and when psychology should look to undertake this change in its professional identity. Heiby states that a "misunderstanding in need of clarification is the belief that the opponents of APA policy object to psychologists obtaining the authority to prescribe. Indeed, prescribing authority is supported under certain conditions." While it should be noted that there is a vocal group of psychologists who believe that prescription authority would dilute the uniquely psychological nature of psychological practice, both Heiby and DeLeon generally agree that psychology as a profession could add the authority to prescribe medicine. More in question are the

procedures for training psychologists, which for DeLeon already appear streamlined for immediate implementation, but for Heiby appear to be a poorly planned hodgepodge.

. . .

This debate might best be understood as a choice between two highly meaningful professional values that are in conflict. On the one hand, there are pragmatic issues (too few providers, limitations of practice due to medications). On the other hand, there are more idealistic principles of fidelity to science. The reader will ultimately decide how to cast his or her lot in our profession's continuing struggle with science and practice. . . . The arguments deserve careful consideration. Both debaters are likely to agree even more on one final point: The future of the profession is likely to be shaped more by the outcome of this choice than by any other contemporary issue.

References

DeLeon, P. H. (2002). Presidential reflections: Past and future. *American Psychologist, 57,* 425–430.

DeLeon, P. H. (2003). Foreword: Reflections on prescriptive authority and the evolution of psychology in the 21st century. In M. T. Sammons, R. U. Paige, & R. F. Levant (Eds.), *Prescriptive authority for psychologists: A history and guide* (pp. xi–xxiv). Washington, DC: American Psychological Association.

DeNelsky, G. (2001, July/August). Ten years of psychology through the eyes of *The National Psychologist. The National Psychologist, 10,* pp. 1–7, 11–15.

♦ ♦ ♦

Commentary: Other commentators have been even more negative than Heiby (excerpted here). For example, the late George Albee, former APA president, stated,

> *Despite my longtime friendship with Pat DeLeon, I must state clearly that he and other supporters of prescription privileges for clinical psychology are just plain wrong.*
>
> . . .
>
> *The most important reason is that most mental disorders are not diseases.*
>
> . . .

Successful psychotherapy shows that recovery is possible without organic intervention, and thus gives evidence against the brain disease model. Why then is APA so determined to focus efforts and money on the state by state battle to get the legal right to practitioners to prescribe drugs when the evidence is so much more certain about the damaging effects of poverty, terrible housing, inadequate schools, etc. (Albee, 2005, pp. 11, 23)

Albee, G. W. (2005, Summer). A contrary view about prescription authority. The ABPP Specialist, 24, 11, 23.

For other articles, pro and con, compare the following:

DeLeon, P., Fox, R., & Graham, S. (1991). Prescription privileges: Psychology's next frontier? American Psychologist, 46, 383–393.

DeLeon, P., & Wiggins, J. (1996). Prescription privileges for psychologists. American Psychologist, 51, 225–229.

DeNelsky, G. (1996). The case against prescription privileges for psychologists. American Psychologist, 51, 207–212.

Hayes, S., & Heiby, E. (1996). Psychology's drug problem: Do we need a fix or should we just say no? American Psychologist, 51, 198–206.

Mantell, E. O., & Ortiz, S. O. (2004). What price prescribing? A commentary on the effect of prescription authority on psychological practice. Professional Psychology: Research and Practice, 35, 164–169.

May, W., & Belsky, J. (1992). Response to "Prescription privileges: Psychology's next frontier? or The siren call: Should psychologists medicate?" American Psychologist, 47, 427.

McGrath, R. E., Sammons, M. T., Brown, A., Wiggins, J. G., Levant, R. F., & Stock, W. (2004). Professional issues in pharmacotherapy for psychologists. Professional Psychology: Research and Practice, 35, 158–163.

Reist, D., & VandeCreek, L. (2004). The pharmaceutical industry's use of gifts and educational events to influence prescription practices: Ethical dilemmas and implications for psychologists. Professional Psychology: Research and Practice, 35, 329–335.

See generally, Sammons, M., Paige, R., & Levant, R. (Eds.). (2003). Prescriptive authority for psychologists. Washington, DC: American Psychological Association.

For an excellent review of problems related to prescription privileges for psychologists who work with children, see DeMers, S. T. (1994). Legal and ethical issues in school psychologists' participation in psychopharmacological interventions with children. School Psychology Quarterly, 9, 41–52. *See also Sparks, J. A., & Duncan, B. L. (2004). The ethics and science of medicating children.* Ethical Human Psychology and Psychiatry, 6, 25–38.

Do you think that psychology needs a separate set of guidelines to govern the practice and ethics of administering psychotropic medication? For one suggested set, see Buelow, G. D., & Chafetz, M. D. (1996). Proposed ethical practice guidelines for clinical pharmacopsychology: Sharpening a new focus in psychology. Professional Psychology: Research and Practice, 27, 53–58. *What provisions of the APA's 2002 Ethical Principles and Code of Conduct are already implicated in the controversy over prescription privileges for psychologists?*

An older but still controversial issue concerns interventions that are "totally self-administered without professional consultation" (Rosen, 1976, p. 139) or, more generically, what Jacobs & Goodman (1989) label as "self-care," for example, "self-help groups, do-it-yourself therapies, and other self-change efforts that do not involve direct contact with a professional" (Rosen, 1993, p. 340). See Jacobs, M. K., & Goodman, G. (1989). Psychology and self-help groups: Predictions on a partnership. American Psychologist, 44, 536–544; *Rosen, G. M. (1976). The development and use of nonprescription behavior therapies.* American Psychologist, 31, 139–141; *Rosen, G. M. (1993). Self-help or hype? Comments on psychology's failure to advance self-care.* Professional Psychology: Research and Practice, 24, 340–345. *In 1978, an APA Task Force on Self-Help Therapies concluded that many self-help books were violating the then-extant version of the APA Ethics Code, particularly because they failed to fully inform purchasers of the limitations of the techniques that authors were espousing and to meet recognized standards for evaluating therapeutic procedures. Because some self-help therapies at the time, however, were found to benefit the public, the task force urged APA not to create an ethical bar to their promulgation and dissemination in books, in public lectures, or through the media. In fact, a recent review found that*

Decades of empirical research and dozens of meta-analyses have underscored the effectiveness of self-help programs in general.

The meta-analyses consistently indicate that self-help programs substantially exceed those of wait-list and no-treatment controls.

. . .

Meta-analyses have found that bibliotherapy for depression and anxiety is superior to no treatment and slightly less effective than therapist-administered treatment. . . .

The research on self-help groups is similarly encouraging. (p. 684)

Norcross, J. C. (2006). Integrating self-help into psychotherapy: 16 practical suggestions. Professional Psychology: Research and Practice, 37, 683–693.

Norcross (2006) noted, in fact, that as of 2006

more people will read a self-help book than visit a mental health professional; more people will receive psychological information and advice from the Internet than from a mental health professional; and indeed, Americans will make more visits to self-help groups for addictions and mental disorders than to all mental health professionals combined. (p. 683)

Given these data and the danger of psychologists producing products with exaggerated claims for their effectiveness, to what extent are these and other concerns addressed in the 2002 Ethics Code? What is the cumulative effect of Standards 5.02, 5.03, and 9.01 on the use of self-help therapies and manuals?

Haas et al. (1996) noted that although telephone-only therapy is an emerging area of practice and that the use of the telephone for purposes such as suicide hotlines was reasonably well established, "The use of telephone for the provision of regular ongoing therapy or for diagnosis is not established, nor are such services as teleconferencing, Internet, or similar methods" (p. 160, quoting the APA Ethics Committee's Statement on Psychotherapy by Telephone). Haas, L. J., Benedict, J. G., & Kobos, J. C. (1996). Psychotherapy by telephone: Risks and benefits for psychologists and consumers. Professional Psychology: Research and Practice, 27, 154–160; American Psychological Association. (1995, October). Ethics committee statement on psychotherapy by telephone.

APA Monitor, 27, 15. Review Standards 2.01e, 3.10, and 10.01. What ethical requirements do they impose on psychologists using the telephone for treatment purposes?

Note the reference to the Internet in the Ethics Committee statement quoted in the previous paragraph. Providing therapy over cyberspace is becoming a major point of contention, particularly because it appears that a "growing number of people are using the Internet to provide counseling and therapy to the public, despite the absence of empirical evidence supporting such activities" (p. 484). Maheu, M., & Gordon, B. (2000). Counseling and therapy on the Internet. Professional Psychology: Research and Practice, 31, 484–489. Given the ethical and legal issues they raise, the use of the Internet and e-mail to engage in therapy is sure to be increasingly scrutinized (see, e.g., Koocher, G., & Morray, E. [2000]. Regulation of telepsychology: A survey of state attorneys general. Professional Psychology: Research and Practice, 31, 503–508) and, thus, deserves extended discussion, which the following material begins to provide.

Cybertherapy may refer simply to "bulletin boards, chat rooms, news and discussion groups operated within health-related web pages . . . listservs, . . . and other electronic forums focused on social, health, and psychological issues" (p. 493). Humphreys, K., Winselberg, A., & Klaw, E. (2000). Psychologists' ethical responsibilities in Internet-based groups: Issues, strategies, and a call for dialogue. Professional Psychology: Research and Practice, 31, 493–496. In addition,

in the category of psychotherapy delivery over the Internet there are four modalities: (1) real time, as it occurs in the now popular "chat rooms" where communication occurs through written emails . . . occurring successively on the screen, (2) video teleconferencing in real time, (3) e-mail, a delayed text modality, and (4) web telephony, or phone via Internet. (p. 66)

Landau, B. (2001). Psychotherapy online in 2001: For psychotherapists new to the Internet. Journal of Mental Imagery, 25, 65–82.

In an early article on this topic, Shapiro and Schulman (1996) quoted the following advertisement that appeared on the Internet:

Cyberlink Consulting Inc. Presents: Shrink-Link

Shrink-Link helps people develop judgments and choices concerning human behavior. Shrink-Link allows direct E-Mail access to a staff of top clinical psychologists and psychiatrists ready to review and comment on almost any important question or conflict in your life.

Concerned about your fears? About who you are? Trouble at home or work? Got the blues? Questions about medication? Shrink-Link psychotherapists have been addressing questions such as these in private sessions for years. Whether you need general guidance, are on the verge of a crisis, or are looking for competent peer review, Shrink-Link may be able to help. Panelists also include in their responses useful referral information, when appropriate.

Shrink-Link is not a substitute for face-to-face counseling and may not be appropriate for everyone. However it does focus the attention of a group of highly trained mental health professionals on YOU! The Shrink-Link panel currently includes six psychologists and one psychiatrist, each with 15–40 years of clinical experience. These are the same people who normally charge $100–$200 per 45-or-so-minute session!

And through Shrink-Link, you can direct your query to one of eight specialty areas of psychotherapy, such as family issues, drug/alcohol abuse, etc. (The choices are listed on the form page.) Here are a few sample queries (including routings).

The cost for using Shrink-Link is $20 per valid question and response. You can expect to receive a response via E-Mail within 72 hours (often within 24 hours). Sound interesting? Compose a query!

Shapiro, D. E., & Schulman, C. E. (1996). Ethical and legal issues in e-mail therapy. Ethics & Behavior, 6, 107–124. Before reading the next article, identify the ethical issues involved and ethical standards that may have been violated.

Internet-Mediated Psychological Services and the American Psychological Association Ethics Code

Celia B. Fisher and Adam L. Fried

The use of the Internet has created innovations and opportunities for the provision of psychological services. . . .

. . . In this article, we use the terms *Internet-mediated services, behavioral telehealth,* and *telehealth* interchangeably to describe the delivery of Internet-mediated psychological assessment and therapy, including e-mail therapy, video conferencing, online therapy, Internet chat rooms, Web-based assessment, and Web-based consultation services. This is a narrow use of a broader application of these terms that applies to delivery of services at a distance through, among other technologies, the Internet, telephone, fax, and interactive televideo (Buchanan, 2002; Jerome & Zaylor, 2000; Laszlo, Esterman, & Zabko, 1999; Maheu & Gordon, 2000; Nickelson, 1996; VandenBos & Williams, 2000).

Questions about validity, efficacy, and safety of different Internet-mediated techniques for psychological assessment and therapy remain largely unanswered as the field rapidly evolves. Constant innovation in telehealth continues to outpace the development of specific guidelines for delivery of services. This article highlights aspects of the newly revised American Psychological Association's (APA) Ethical Principles of Psychologists and Code of Conduct (2002; referred to as the Ethics Code throughout the remainder of this article) that are particularly relevant to the ethical practice of Internet-mediated psychological services. . . .

As in previous versions, the most recent Ethics Code applies to all activities, all persons, all settings, and all communication contexts that are conducted, encountered, or used in one's role as a psychologist. Communication contexts explicitly referred to in the 2002 Ethics Code include telephone, Internet, and other electronic transmissions. In reviewing the professions' evolving use of the Internet and other electronic media for behavioral telehealth, psychological assessment, consulting, video conferencing, and research, the ECTF [Ethics Code Task Force] concluded that the broadly worded enforceable standards were applicable to electronic media, and therefore, telehealth did not need a special section or special references. However, the ECTF did decide it was important to explicitly highlight the relevance of four standards for psychologists using the Internet and other electronic media: Standards 3.10a, Informed Consent; 4.02c, Discussing the Limits of Confidentiality; 5.01a, Avoidance of False or Deceptive Statements; and 5.04, Media Presentations.

In this article, we discuss the applicability of the APA Ethics Code to telehealth through the discussion of enforceable standards within six broad categories of ethical conduct: competence, conflicts of interest, informed consent, privacy and confidentiality, public statements and advertising, and test selection and scoring.

COMPETENCE

Training, Education, Consultation, and Experience

Competence is the linchpin enabling psychologists to fulfill other ethical obligations required by the Ethics Code. Several standards under 2.01a–2.01e, Boundaries of Competence, are particularly relevant to the use of the Internet in providing psychological services. Under Standard 2.01a, psychologists must refrain from providing services in areas in which they have not had the education, training, supervised experience, consultation, study, or professional experience recognized by the discipline as

From *Psychotherapy: Theory, Research, Practice, Training, 40,* 103–111. Copyright 2003 by the Educational Publishing Foundation.

necessary to conduct their work competently. Determinations regarding whether psychologists are engaged in activities outside the boundaries of their competence vary with current and evolving criteria in the relevant field. This is especially true for the use of continuously changing equipment and technologies such as the computer and Internet services. Standard 2.01c requires psychologists who wish to expand the scope of their practice to techniques or technologies that are new to them to undertake relevant education, study, consultation, or experiences to obtain the qualifications necessary as established by the field.

Use of Emerging Technologies

Standard 2.01e applies when psychologists wish to develop or implement new practice techniques for which there are no generally agreed upon scientific or professional qualifications. The standard recognizes the value of innovative techniques as well as the added risks that such innovations may place on those with whom psychologists work. Psychologists must take reasonable steps to ensure the competence and safety of their work in new areas. In using the term *competence,* the standard reflects the assumption that to be considered *psychology,* an emerging area must draw on established scientific or professional knowledge of the discipline of psychology (see also Standard 2.04, Bases for Scientific and Professional Judgments). Adherence to this standard thus requires that psychologists have the foundational knowledge and skills in psychology and computer technology necessary to construct or implement novel approaches in Internet-based assessment and psychotherapy and to evaluate their effectiveness.

For example, psychologists using e-mail or chat rooms to provide behavioral health services to clients/patients at a distance are venturing into relatively uncharted territories in which traditional assessment and psychotherapy techniques based on oral and nonverbal cues may not transfer to communication through written text (Nickelson, 1998). Harm to Internet clients/patients may be incurred when psychologists fail to appropriately diagnose a disorder, fail to identify suicidal or homicidal ideation, or reinforce maladaptive behavior, for example, social phobia (see also Standard 3.04, Avoiding Harm). Steps that psychologists using Internet-mediated assessment or therapeutic services might take to ensure the competence of one's work and to protect clients/patients from harm include staying abreast of advances in the field, requiring an in-person initial consultation, and identifying professionals and health and social service agencies that are in the area in which the client/patient lives that can be called in crises situations (Maheu, 2001).

CONFLICTS OF INTEREST

Psychologists strive to benefit and establish relationships of trust with those with whom they work through the exercise of professional and scientific judgments based on their training, experience, and established knowledge of the discipline. Standard 3.06, Conflict of Interest, prohibits psychologists from taking on a professional role when it competes with professional, personal, financial, legal, or other interests or relationships that could reasonably be expected to impair the psychologists' objectivity, competence, or ability to effectively perform this role. An example of a conflict of interest in the use of the Internet sufficient to appear to compromise professional services is when psychologists use their professional Web site to recommend Internet mental health services in which they have an undeclared financial interest.

INFORMED CONSENT

Informed consent is seen by many as the primary means of protecting the self-governing and privacy rights of those with whom psychologists work. In the previous APA (1992) Ethics Code the obligation to obtain informed consent was limited to research and therapy. The broader informed consent requirements introduced into the current revision of the Ethics Code reflect the societal change from a paternalistic to an autonomy-based view of professional ethics. Required elements of informed consent specifically relevant to Internet practice are detailed in Standards 9.03, Informed Consent in Assessments, and in 10.01, Informed Consent to Therapy. The obligations described in Standard 3.10, Informed Consent, apply to these other consent standards. When psychologists provide assessment, therapy, counseling, or consulting services, over the Internet, these psychologists must obtain the informed consent of the individual by providing an appropriate explanation of the nature and purpose of services provided, fees, involvement of third parties, and limits of confidentiality as well as sufficient opportunity for the client/patient to ask questions.

Client/Patient Identification

A unique challenge for psychologists engaged in telehealth activities, and in Internet-mediated services in particular, is client/patient identification. When administering Web-based assessments or providing e-therapy, psychologists need to ensure that the individual who gave consent is in fact the individual completing the assessment or receiving the psychologist's services. Psychologists must also confirm the age and legal status of the service recipient. For example, states vary in terms of the age at which providing services to a minor without parental permission is a violation of law. When minors or older adults with impaired consent capacities are the recipients of services, telehealth providers must ensure that the appropriate guardian's permission and assent is obtained (Standard 3.10b, Informed Consent). To meet these challenges, psychologists might consider the use of client/patient passwords, an initial in-person interview, or video conferencing.

. . .

Fees

Discussion of fees must include the cost of services, the payment schedule, and what form of payment is acceptable (e.g., credit card, checks; Standards 9.03, Informed Consent in Assessments, and 10.01, Informed Consent to Therapy). Telehealth providers need to develop secure procedures for receiving credit card payments if clients/patients are to be billed and/or are to pay for services over the Internet. In addition, psychologists need to determine and inform clients/patients of the payment method as soon as is feasible and, if appropriate, whether their health plan covers Internet health care (see also Standard 6.04, Fees and Financial Arrangements).

Confidentiality

Informed consent to assessment and therapy must provide a clear explanation of the extent and limits of confidentiality, including (a) when the psychologist must comply with reporting requirements such as mandated child abuse reporting or duty to warn laws and (b) in the case of assessments involving minors, the guardian's access to records (see also Standards 4.01, Maintaining Confidentiality, and 4.02, Discussing the Limits of Confidentiality). Psychologists providing services over the Internet must inform clients/patients about the procedures that are used to protect confidentiality and the threats to confidentiality unique to this form of electronic transmission of information. As laws regarding the use of telehealth across state boundaries continue to evolve, psychologists must become knowledgeable about reporting laws on child abuse and neglect, elder abuse, duty to warn, and other mandatory disclosures in the state in which the client/patient is receiving the services. Measures to take to protect confidentiality over the Internet are discussed in the Privacy and Confidentiality section.

Third Parties

Standards 3.10a, Informed Consent; 9.03a, Informed Consent in Assessments; and 10.01a, Informed Consent to Therapy, also require informed consent to include the psychologists' discussion of third party involvement: individuals, health insurance companies, employers, organizations, or legal or other governing authorities requesting the assessment or to whom the results of the assessments or other information may be provided. Psychologists providing assessment or psychotherapy over the Internet need to identify the form in which information will be shared with third parties as well as the form in which the client/patient release for disclosure of information will be acceptable. Federal regulations (see Health Insurance Portability and Accountability Act, HIPAA, below) and good ethical practice do not permit, open-ended release forms. With few exceptions, for example, when services are court ordered, psychologists must have specific and time-limited signed releases or authorizations to disclose information to third parties. Telehealth providers need to ascertain the form in which such releases have legal standing and inform clients/patients of these requirements.

Implications of HIPAA

Psychologists who use, disclose, or provide health services over the Internet are covered entities under the HIPAA (http://www.hhs.gov/ocr/hipaa/finalreg.html). At the beginning of the professional relationship, covered entities are required to provide clients/patients with a written notice of privacy practices that provides information on the uses and disclosures of protected health information (PHI; individually identifiable health information created or received by a health care provider relating to the past, present, or future health, provision of health care, or payment for health care) that may be made by the covered entity, and the individual's rights and covered entity's legal duties with respect to PHI. [*Ed. Note:* See chapter 10 for more on HIPAA].

Treatments for Which Generally Recognized Techniques and Procedures Have Not Been Established

Most techniques that are now accepted practice in the profession of psychology emerged from new technologies or treatment needs unmet by existing therapies. Standard 10.01b, Informed Consent to Therapy, recognizes that innovation in mental health services is critical if a profession is to continue to adequately serve a diverse and dynamic public. The standard also recognizes that during the development and refinement of new therapeutic techniques, the risks and benefits to clients/patients are unknown. Consequently, respect for a client's/patient's right to informed, rational, and voluntary consent requires that when the treatment needs of a client call for innovative techniques, during informed consent, psychologists have the obligation to (a) explain the relatively new and untried nature of the therapy, (b) clearly describe alternative established treatments that may be available, and (c) clarify the client's/patient's right to dissent in favor of more established treatments, whether they are offered by the psychologist obtaining the consent or other mental health professionals.

. . . [T]echniques and procedures to provide therapy over the Internet (e.g., e-mail, chat rooms, video conferencing) and the mental health benefits and risks of different forms of telehealth for different clients/patients are still being explored and debated in the literature. Psychologists developing and using such techniques are pioneers in the field. Under Standard 10.01b for specific aspects of telehealth that remain in this developing state or forms that emerge, psychologists need to inform prospective clients/patients of the following: (a) that the use of the specific telehealth technique is a new and still developing form of therapy; (b) that although there is reason to believe this form of therapy may serve the client's/patient's mental health needs, the extent of such benefits is still largely unknown; (c) that current risks associated with e-mail therapy include, for example, confidentiality concerns and lack of immediacy; (d) that traditional treatments for the client's/patient's presenting problem include, for example, face-to-face therapy at a local clinic; and (e) that if the client/patient prefers to receive a more traditional therapy, the psychologist, for example, is able to offer such therapy or to provide a referral.

PRIVACY AND CONFIDENTIALITY

Protecting Confidentiality

Protecting the confidentiality of the clients with whom psychologists work reflects their obligation to respect the privacy and dignity of persons (Principle E: Respect for People's Rights and Dignity). Standard 4.01, Maintaining Confidentiality, and Standard 6.02, Maintenance, Dissemination, and Disposal of Confidential Records of Professional and Scientific Work, are broadly written and require all psychologists to take reasonable precautions to protect confidential information. The nature of precautions required to protect confidential information differs with respect to (a) the psychologist's role, (b) the purpose of the psychological activity, (c) the legal status of the person with whom the psychologist is working, (d) federal regulations, (e) state and local laws, and (f) institutional and organizational policies. The terms *reasonable precautions* in Standard 4.01 in telehealth pertain to the psychologist's responsibility to become familiar with or obtain assistance when technical expertise is required to protect confidentiality.

The privacy of data and physical security of electronic devices, whether they are housed in a working environment or at home or whether they are portable, is essential. Below are general recommendations for maintaining confidentiality when services are provided over the Internet.

- Use encrypted data transmission, password protected data storage, and firewall techniques.
- Discuss and develop security measures with appropriate personnel when files are stored via a common server or are backed up on an institutional system or hub.
- Include instructions for trainees on appropriate procedures to protect client confidentiality when using the Internet for supervision.
- Keep disks and other data storage devices in safe locations or use passwords to protect computer access.
- Distort voice recordings or mask faces in visual images to protect confidentiality.
- Destroy recordings when they are no longer needed as long as their destruction does not conflict with other ethical or legal obligations to maintain scientific or professional records.
- Do not share passwords and do change them often.
- Be mindful of ways to protect security of wireless devices.
- Avoid use of confidential information in e-mail or instant messaging unless you use encryption.
- Take extra measures to protect physical security of portable devices such as laptop or notebook computers, palmtops, and smart phones whether they are in the office or at home.
- Use privacy screens to protect monitors or other types of screens from viewing by others.
- Update virus protection software and other security measures frequently for both personal and work space computing devices on which PHI is kept.
- Remove all data when disposing or recycling old computers. This will most likely require assistance from technical experts because even after erasing data or using reformatting disks, traces of data may remain.

Discussing the Limits of Confidentiality
Standard 4.02c, Discussing the Limits of Confidentiality, specifically highlights the importance of discussing the limits of confidentiality

when services are provided via electronic media. Psychological services or transmission of records conducted over the Internet and other electronic media are vulnerable to breaches in confidentiality that may be beyond the individual psychologist's control. Under Standard 4.02c, clients/patients must be made aware of the risks to privacy and limitations to protections that the psychologist can institute to guard against violations of consumer confidentiality when information is transmitted electronically. For example,

- Psychologists conducting therapy or assessments via e-mail or through secure chat rooms need to inform clients about the possibility of strangers hacking into secure sites or, when applicable, the extent to which institutional staff has access to secure sites on a hub server.
- Sometimes clients may access their therapist's personal e-mail account and send unsolicited sensitive communications. In these situations, psychologists should inform such clients about the risks of others reading these e-mails and discourage clients from future e-mail communications if appropriate.
- Psychologists providing services on a Web site should include a visible and easy-to-understand privacy statement whenever a consumer's personal information is requested. The privacy statement should advise consumers of how personal information is used (i.e., sold to other sites, used to contact the consumer at a later date) and whether clients can opt out of these uses. Psychologists can download a sample privacy policy statement from the APA's Web site at http://helping.apa.org/dotcomsense/privacy.html.

Implications of HIPAA
Standard 4.05a permits psychologists to disclose confidential information with the appropriate consent of the client/patient. Except as otherwise permitted or required by law, under HIPAA, a covered entity may not use or disclose PHI without valid client/patient authorization. The HIPAA core elements for authorization to provide PHI to others go beyond the information psychologists have typically required for client/patient signed releases, and

telehealth providers must be familiar with these requirements. Psychotherapy notes have special protections under HIPAA. For example, psychologists who work for or with other covered entities are prohibited from requiring patient authorization to disclose psychotherapy notes as a condition for evaluating eligibility. In addition, when appropriate releases and authorizations are obtained, the HIPAA Privacy Rule requires psychologists to share only the minimum amount of information necessary for billing agencies and nonhealth provider internal staff to perform their roles.

HIPAA regulations may require special creativity for telehealth psychologists using the disclosing PHI. In particular, for psychologists to have control over client/patient access to psychotherapy notes, HIPAA requires that these notes must be kept in a separate file from the rest of the client's/patient's designated record set. Similarly, HIPAA requires that authorizations are separate from other informed consent materials. The legal meaning and process of separate files in Internet-mediated services and computer data storage is an important and fruitful avenue for future exploration. Psychologists may wish to use the HIPAA-compliant Notice of Privacy Practices and Authorization model forms developed by the APA Insurance Trust and the APA Practice Directorate (http://www.apa.org/apait).

PUBLIC STATEMENTS AND ADVERTISING

Avoidance of False Statements

Psychologists aspire to promote accuracy, honesty, and truthfulness in the practice of psychology and do not engage in subterfuge or intentional misrepresentation of fact (Principle C: Integrity). Standard 5.01a, Avoidance of False or Deceptive Statements, prohibits false, deceptive, or fraudulent public statements regarding work activities or the activities of persons or organizations with which psychologists are affiliated. . . . Public statements that might appear on the Internet include (a) paid or unpaid advertising or product endorsements; (b) Web brochures or printed matter describing a psychologist's services; (c) directory listings, personal resumes, or curricula vitae; (d) commentary on Internet news sites; or (e) Web-linked advice columns.

Statements by Others

Standard 5.02c, Statements by Others, permits psychologists to run paid advertisements, including those on Web sites, describing their services, as long as it is identified or otherwise clear to consumers that it is a paid advertisement. Canned columns are an example of a paid advertisement that often is presented in a way that can be deceptive to consumers. Canned columns written and paid for by psychologists are typically presented in news or advice Web format intended to lead readers to erroneously believe that the psychologist has been invited or hired by the media outlet to write the column because of his or her expertise. The column usually includes a description of the psychologist's services, picture, and contact information. Canned columns that do not include a clear statement that the column is a paid advertisement are in violation of this standard. In some instances, psychologists do not write the column themselves but purchase it from a writer who sells the columns to psychologists nationwide. In such instances, the column must state that the psychologist is providing—but has not written—the column (see also Standard 5.01a, Avoidance of False or Deceptive Statements).

Media Presentations

Standard 5.04, Media Presentations, only applies to psychologists' public statements in various mediums when the purpose of the statement is information sharing, commenting, or advice giving. It does not apply to therapist–client/patient communications regarding treatment, assessment, or consultation made in video conferencing, e-mail, Web based or other forms in Internet transmission. This standard prohibits psychologists from giving public advice or comment via the Internet or from other forms of communication on topics and issues that are outside the boundaries of the psychologists' competence on the basis of their education, training, supervised experience, or other accepted means of acquiring professional or scientific expertise (see Standard 2.01a, Boundaries of Competence). The standard also prohibits psychologists from giving public comment or advice that significantly deviates from or is otherwise inconsistent with established psychological literature and practice (see Standard 2.04, Basis for Scientific and Professional Judgments).

Psychologists providing public advice in response to questions over the Internet or to published advice columns should clarify the educative versus therapeutic nature of their answers, avoid language that refers personally to the person asking the question, and take steps to avoid repeat communications with the person, which may encourage the mistaken impression that a professional relationship has been established (Shapiro & Schulman, 1996).

References

American Psychological Association. (1992). Ethical principles of psychologists and code of conduct. *American Psychologist, 47,* 1597–1611.

American Psychological Association. (2002). Ethical principles of psychologists and code of conduct. *American Psychologist, 57,* 1060–1073.

Buchanan, T. (2002). Online assessment: Desirable or dangerous? *Professional Psychology: Research and Practice, 33,* 148–154.

Jerome, L. W., & Zaylor, C. (2000). Cyberspace: Creating a therapeutic environment for telehealth applications. *Professional Psychology: Research and Practice, 31,* 478–483.

Laszlo, J. V., Esterman, G., & Zabko, S. (1999). Therapy over the Internet? Theory, research, and finances. *Cyber-Psychology & Behavior, 2,* 293–307.

Maheu, M. M. (2001). *Exposing the risk, yet moving forward: A behavioral e-health model.* Retrieved from http://www.ascusc.org/jcmc/

Maheu, M. M., & Gordon, B. L. (2000). Counseling and therapy on the Internet. *Professional Psychology: Research and Practice, 31,* 484–489.

Nickelson, D. W. (1996). Behavioral telehealth: Emerging practice, research and policy opportunities. *Behavioral Sciences and the Law, 14,* 443–457.

Nickelson, D. W. (1998). Telehealth and the evolving health care system: Strategic opportunities for professional psychology. *Professional Psychology: Research and Practice, 29,* 527–535.

Shapiro, D. E., & Schulman, C. E. (1996). Ethical and legal issues in e-mail therapy. *Ethics & Behavior, 6,* 107–124.

VandenBos, G. R., & Williams, S. (2000). The Internet versus the telephone: What is telehealth, anyway? *Professional Psychology: Research and Practice, 31,* 490–492.

◆　◆　◆

Commentary: As one would expect, the literature on this topic is burgeoning. See, for example:

Barak, A. (1999). Psychological applications on the Internet: A discipline on the threshold of a new millennium. Applied and Preventive Psychology, 8, 231–246.

Barnett, J. E., & Scheetz, K. (2003). Technological advances and telehealth: Ethics, law, and the practice of psychotherapy. Psychotherapy: Theory, Research, Practice, Training, 40, 86–93.

Berg, J. (2002). Ethics and e-medicine. Saint Louis University Law Journal, 46, 61–84. *(an excellent legal perspective)*

Heinlen, K. T., Welfel, E. R., Richmond, E. N., & O'Donnell, M. S. (2003). The nature, scope, and ethics of psychologists' e-therapy Web sites: What consumers find when searching the Web. Psychotherapy: Theory, Research, Practice, Training, 40, 112–124.

Humphreys, K., Winzelberg, A., & Klaw, E. (2000). Psychologists' ethical responsibilities in Internet-based groups: Issues, strategies, and a call for dialogue. Professional Psychology: Research and Practice, 31, 493–496.

Mallen, M. J., Vogel, D. L., & Rochlen, A. B. (2005). The practical aspects of online counseling: Ethics, training, technology, and competency. The Counseling Psychologist, 33, 776–818.

Nickelson, D. (1996). Behavioral telehealth: Emerging practice, research, and policy opportunities. Behavioral Sciences and the Law, 14, 443–457.

Rees, C. S., & Stone, S. (2005). Therapeutic alliance in face-to-face versus video conferenced psychotherapy. Professional Psychology: Research and Practice, 36, 649–653. *(finding therapeutic alliance significantly lower in video therapy)*

Shaw, H. E., & Shaw, S. F. (2006). Critical ethical issues in online counseling: Assessing current practices with an ethical intent checklist. Journal of Counseling & Development, 84, 41–53.

Many authors have also offered recommendations for "safe" cybertherapy. For example, Koocher and Morray (2000) suggested, in addition to those recommendations already noted, that practitioners consult with their professional liability insurance carrier and ascertain in writing whether electronic services will be covered and that practitioners clearly indicate to third parties who are billed for services (like managed care companies) that the services were provided electronically to avoid any question of fraud. See Koocher, G., & Morray, E. (2002). Regulation of telepsychology: A survey of state attorneys general. Professional

Psychology: Research and Practice, 31, 503–508. (see, especially, pp. 507–508)

Shapiro and Schulman (1996), referenced in the excerpt provided here, suggested the following ethical standard specifically related to e-mail therapy:

> Psychologists offering e-mail facilitated therapeutic communication encourage clients to ask general questions that do not refer to a specific individual. Psychologists advertising such services include in advertisements all information necessary for clients to understand (a) The modality is experimental and its usefulness may be unrelated to the success of traditional therapies; (b) the communication is not confidential; (c) no therapist–client professional relationship exists; (d) repeated communications with the same professional are discouraged; and (e) records of the interaction may be stored with no report of such storage available to the client. Psychologists using e-mail to communicate with new clients encourage clients to seek more traditional therapies. Psychologists do not transmit confidential information, including payment information such as credit card data, by e-mail without using encryption programs considered the standard. (pp. 122–123)

Review the 2002 ethical standards. Do they cover all the points that Shapiro and Schulman recommended, or is such a new standard necessary?

Although little discussed, the ethical therapist must contemplate taking appropriate steps to protect clients in case of his or her death or disability. Standard 3.12 of the 2002 Ethics Code requires psychologists to "make reasonable efforts to plan for facilitating services in the event that psychological services are interrupted by . . . illness, death, unavailability, relocation, or retirement. . . ." Standard 6.02c also mandates that "psychologists make plans in advance to facilitate the appropriate transfer and protect the confidentiality of records and data in the event of psychologists' withdrawal from positions or practice." For APA policy regarding records in general, see APA Committee on Professional Practice and Standards. (2007). *Record keeping guidelines* (reprinted in chap. 10, this volume).

Finally, to summarize the entire chapter, researchers interviewed 10 clinicians identified as "master therapists" to discern what ethical values they bring to their work. The most important was a relational connection to their clients. Other consensual ethical values that the authors identified are autonomy, beneficence, nonmaleficence and the avoidance of harm, building and maintaining expertise, acting with humility, professional growth, openness to complexity and ambiguity, and self-awareness. See Jennings, L., Sovereign, A., Bottorff, N., Mussell, M. P., & Vye, C. (2005). Nine ethical values of master therapists. Journal of Mental Health Counseling, 27, 32–47.

CHAPTER 8

ACADEMIA: RESEARCH, TEACHING, AND SUPERVISION

The bricks and mortar of college buildings and the various forms of flora growing on them have long hid conduct of concern to ethicists and those in academia. Researchers, scholars, and supervisors have seemed to be beyond the scrutiny of ethics committees. Academicians, after all, were simply data gatherers, teachers, mentors, and initiators of new theories. They were believed immune to the vagaries of professional practice that often landed their clinical colleagues in trouble, such as setting and collecting fees, mediating the needs of clients and the demands of third-party payors, becoming sexually attracted to patients, or disclosing intimate information gathered in therapy. In fact, there seems to have been no articles in English published on research ethics with human beings before 1951. The first empirical study on this topic was not published until 1967 (McGaha & Korn, 1995).

But science and the public are becoming increasingly aware that donning a white lab coat or a tweed, elbow-patched jacket does not insulate one from unethical behavior. People now know that for more than 60 years academic scientists working for the federal government engaged in risky research that proved harmful to participants, who were never fully informed about the nature, costs, and benefits of the studies. It has also been acknowledged that professors sometimes do appropriate students' ideas and works as their own; that teachers and supervisors develop intimate, sometimes sexual, relations with students and trainees; and that some teachers are often unprepared to face their classes (or continue to lecture from the proverbial time-stained notes) and leave students languishing for months before returning examinations or seminar papers. These issues have become so salient that for the first time in nine revisions, the current (1992) set of APA Ethical Principles contains a specific section of standards (Section 6) that address teaching, training, supervision, research, and publishing. The current 2002 code now contains two sections devoted to those issues: Section 7 (Training) and Section 8 (Research and Publications).

Materials in this chapter introduce the reader to a broadening array of ethical issues within academia, although the bulk of the material is devoted to research. Research is an interesting enterprise from an ethical perspective because its purpose is not necessarily devoted to the betterment of those who participate in it. Psychological assessment and therapeutic interventions are, at the least, processes intended to benefit participants.

Alternatively—although not true of all studies—research usually does not contribute to the welfare of participants at all. It is ironic, then, that subjects of research—animals as well as humans—may be the least well treated of all those with whom psychologists interact. The validity of this hypothesis may be supported by examining the controversy over *deception research*—studies in which the participant is either not fully informed or is misinformed about the purpose of the experiment so as not to contaminate the data. I have chosen to make such studies a focus of this chapter. This ethical dilemma is not only of central importance in research; rather, like other issues I highlight in this text, it evokes more universal conflicts that should be considered.

Issues concerning deception are at the surface of conflict between the interests of science and those of the participant in research:

> The respect for privacy rests on the appreciation of human dignity, with its high evaluation of individual self-determination. . . . In this, respect for human dignity and individuality shares an historical comradeship with the freedom of scientific inquiry, which is equally precious to modern liberalism. The tension between these values, so essential to each other in so many profoundly important ways, is one of the antimonies of modern liberalism. The ethical problems with which we are dealing. . . . arise from the confrontation of autonomy and privacy by a free intellectual curiosity, enriched by a modern awareness of the depth and complexity of the forces that work in us implemented by the devices of a passionate effort to transform this awareness into scientific knowledge. (Shils, 1959, pp. 120–121)

Similar note of this tension was made by psychologist Ross Stagner (*Problems Concerning Federal Support, 1967*) before a Senate subcommittee concerned with government research:

> Social scientists. . . . have a genuine obligation to devise protections for the right of privacy, and to avoid mere psychic voyeurism. At the same time they have a compelling obligation to accumulate data—and meaningful generalizations— about the powerful impulses of loyalty, hostility, fear, and ambition, which shape human history. . . .
>
> . . .
>
> There is an obvious conflict between the need of society to know and the right of the individual to dignity and privacy. (pp. 757–758)

The ambivalence between advancing science and protecting the integrity of the individual is also reflected in the current code. Standard 8.07, dealing with deception, is clearly utilitarian.

Beyond exploring this central conflict in social science research, the material in this chapter covers more mundane but crucial issues: exploitation of graduate students (both academically and socially), authorship issues (including publication credit), clinical supervision, and simply bad teaching. These topics have often been neglected in discussions of ethics. I hope that this compilation of materials reveals the seriousness of such issues and promotes even more extended attention to them.

References

McGaha, A. C., & Korn, J. H. (1995). The emergence of interest in the ethics of psychological research with humans. *Ethics & Behavior, 5,* 147–159.

Problems Concerning Federal Support of Social Science Research: Hearings on S.836 before the Subcommittee on Government Research of the Senate Committee on Government Operations, 90th Cong., 1st Sess. 757 (1967) (testimony of Ross Stagner).

Shils, E. A. (1959). Social inquiry and the autonomy of the individual. In D. Lerner (Ed.), *The human meaning of the social sciences* (pp. 114–148). New York: Meridian Books.

Ethical Perspectives in Clinical Research

David M. Bersoff and Donald N. Bersoff

A group of psychologists working for the military were interested in creating an experimental situation that effectively aroused the fear of death or injury in participants. Using this paradigm, they hoped to identify the determinants of effective performance under the stress of combat. This was the first in the series of experiments they designed and performed as part of their research program.

Sixty-six men ages 18–24 in their first weeks of Army basic training were randomly assigned to one of three groups: an experimental group, a flying control group, and a grounded control group. Subjects in the experimental group boarded a plane for what they were told would be a routine training flight. Once aloft, at 5,000 feet, they completed an irrelevant test then waited for the plane to reach a higher altitude. Suddenly, the aircraft lurched. The passengers saw that one propeller had stopped turning and heard about other malfunctions over the intercom. They were then informed directly that there was an emergency. A simulated pilot-to-tower conversation was provided to the passengers over their earphones to support the deception. As the plane passed within sight of the airfield, the study participants could see fire trucks and ambulances on the airstrip in apparent expectation of a crash landing. After several minutes, the pilot ordered the steward to prepare for ditching in the nearby ocean because the landing gear was not functioning properly.

At this point, the steward distributed to everyone on the plane something called the Emergency Data Form. This was a terribly complicated form the passengers were asked to complete so that the military would know to whom their personal possessions should go in the event of their death. They also were given the Emergency Instructions Test, which asked questions about airborne emergency procedures that

the passengers had been required to read before the flight. The supposed purpose of this second form was to furnish proof to insurance companies that emergency precautions had been properly followed. These two sets of forms were to be put in a waterproof container and jettisoned before the aircraft fell to the ocean. After a specified time, the plane made a safe landing at the airport.

The flying control group was taken up for a flight but was not exposed to the fear-of-death-inducing manipulations. The grounded controls never left the ground. All three groups completed the same set of dependent measures. The participants were then debriefed, interviewed about the experience, and asked for a urine sample. (In the case of the experimental group, collecting the urine sample probably entailed simply wringing out their underwear into a beaker.) As expected, the experimental group rated themselves as being more stressed than the control groups, made more errors when filling out the Emergency Data Form and the Emergency Instructions Test, and had more corticosteroids in their urine, a physiological index of stress.

We present the Ditching study (Berkun, Bialek, Kern, & Yagi, 1962) to make three basic, introductory points. The first is that research ethics is fundamentally a methodological issue; each procedural decision a researcher makes has potential ethical implications. As a consequence, ethics should not be an afterthought and attention to ethical considerations must go beyond preparing a consent form and a debriefing. If the Ditching study is unethical, it is in large part because the researchers failed to temper their methodological decision making with empathy for their participants. Their only apparent concession to moral propriety was refraining from actually crashing the plane into the ocean, and that may have been only because one or more of the researchers were on board. This study demonstrates what can happen when scientific goals drive research methodology unchecked by ethical considerations.

The second point is that ethical problems often arise as a result of scientists viewing research participants as objects to be manipulated, as data on the hoof, or as a means to a publication. Apparently, the researchers who performed the Ditching study placed ecological validity and the scientific goals of their research firmly ahead of the emotional welfare of their subjects. The word "subjects" is used here as opposed to the currently preferred "participants" precisely because the men in this study were treated as subjects, as lab rats might be treated, and not as autonomous beings. Participants are people who have graciously given research scientists their time and attention and often their considerable effort; they have a right to expect nonmaleficence and respect in return. Resisting the temptation to objectify the people in their studies is one of the biggest ethical challenges researchers face. As is true with almost all people-oriented professions, it is hard not to come to have a certain degree of contempt for the people one relies on for his or her livelihood. Just as salespeople often view their customers merely as a means to a commission and wait staffs have a certain degree of disdain for restaurant patrons, researchers also may develop a somewhat jaundiced view of the people in their studies especially because research participants often miss appointments, fail to cooperate, and, on occasion, even render data contrary to their hypotheses. Unfortunately, psychologists cannot afford to indulge in objectifying their participants, nor allow their contempt to influence their methodological choices, because psychologists hold far more sway over people's well-being than do salesclerks and waiters.

The most important point to remember . . . is that you can do damage, that what psychologists say and do to people carries more weight than similar words and deeds on the part of someone who is not a psychologist. If a salesclerk calls a customer an idiot, it is a rude insult. If a psychologist calls a person in a study the equivalent of an idiot (say, in the form of false feedback on a fake intelligence test), it can be construed as a diagnosis based on scientific evidence. . . .

The third point is that ethical considerations will often require making methodological tradeoffs. This fact may make it seem as though good ethics and good science are often adversaries. As a case in point, there is the Ditching study, a methodological masterpiece. One can imagine the researchers growing more pleased with themselves as each little bit of realism was incorporated into their design. They did not just switch off an engine; they allowed the passengers to hear emergency transmissions between the pilot and tower personnel. As a final touch, they allowed the passengers to see emergency equipment lining the runway. If anyone had the presence of mind to wonder why the passengers had to fill out forms that would be as unlikely to survive a crash as they were, the researchers had the clever idea of introducing the notion of a waterproof canister that could be jettisoned before impact. Every methodological decision the researchers made was in service to convincing their subjects that they were in a life-threatening situation. This was also the heart of the study's ethical problems. It made people suffer the experience of being in fear for their lives. But to the extent that the researchers would have included procedural steps designed to ameliorate this fear, there would have been a cost in terms of the scientific goal of the study—to observe the impact of fear of death on psychological functioning.

In situations such as this, in which good ethics seems to stand in the way of good science, there are several possibilities to consider. The first is that the issue being addressed is unworthy of study. Just because a question can be asked does not mean that it should be asked. A case in point is the notorious Tuskegee study on the disease course of untreated syphilis. Surely, medical science could have done without the information gained in that investigation, especially after a cure for the disease was found partway into the study. Closely related is the possibility that the question being examined is not worth the cost in terms of the suffering required to gain the information sought. The pursuit of knowledge is not human kind's highest virtue; there are considerations that carry more weight. Perhaps knowing how people react in the face of life threatening situations is less important than abiding by the right people have not to be put in fear of their lives. Although it may be important for the Army to know how their soldiers will react in the face of possible death, more important considerations may mean that this question will have to be left unasked. Deciding to forgo a study, however, is the most drastic and not always the most desirable way of handling a conflict between ethical concerns and research goals.

A less onerous alternative is to consider the possibility of whether there is a different, more ethical, way to operationalize the variable of interest. Perhaps the researchers in the Ditching study could have caused significant fear without making people think that they were about to be in a plane crash. If fear of death is viewed as merely an extreme point on a continuum of fear, then perhaps subjecting people to a lesser fear would still have allowed the researchers to gather the information they wanted. For example, soldiers about to make their first parachute jump could have been used in the experimental group. Surely, such soldiers are harboring some form of fear resembling a fear of death, but they are experiencing this fear by choice, assuming that being a paratrooper is a job one signs up for, and this fear is probably less acute than that generated in the Ditching study.

A final possibility is that instead of examining the question in a manipulation study, perhaps one can take advantage of a naturally occurring situation. Researchers looking for cancer cures do not give people the disease and then try to cure it; they find people who already have cancer. Instead of simulating a plane crash, the Ditching study researchers could have found a war (there is almost always one occurring someplace in the world) and worked with the soldiers at the front who were already in a position to be fearful for their lives.

These last two possibilities point to another link between methodology and ethics. A skilled and creative methodologist can almost always find a way to research an issue in an ethical manner. Conversely, an inferior methodologist is unlikely to do ethical

research. Poorly designed, even if otherwise quite benign, research is unethical if for no other reason than that it represents a waste of time, effort, and resources that could have been devoted to research that had the potential to be truly informative (Rosenthal, 1994). Poorly designed research also has a greater likelihood of yielding erroneous or artifact-driven results, which, in turn, can lead to harmful consequences such as misbegotten further research, misinformed policy decisions, and misperceptions on the part of the public. . . .

Although ethics and psychological research may seem to be in an adversarial relationship, the relationship is actually more like that of the Supreme Court and Congress. The Court's purpose is not to impede the work of Congress but rather to ensure that Congress does not infringe on the basic rights of the people. Though the Court's judgments may seem at times like unwelcome intrusions to the Congress, in the long run they serve to protect Congress and the government as a whole. Our government, as does psychological research, exists only at the pleasure of the people. If either institution comes to be viewed as immoral, exploitative, or insensitive to the values and concerns of society, it will be sanctioned or eliminated. Institutional review boards (IRBs) were mandated into existence in response to perceived abuses by researchers. The more jaundiced a view society comes to have of psychological research, the tighter funding and regulation will become. In the long run, the benefits of good ethical conduct to psychology as a science more than compensate for the constraints it imposes on research methodology.

References

Berkun, M. M., Bialek, H. M., Kern, R. P., & Yagi, K. (1962). Experimental studies of psychological stress in man. *Psychological Monographs: General and Applied, 76*(15), 1–39.

Rosenthal, R. (1994). Science and ethics in conducting, analyzing, and reporting psychological research. *Psychological Science, 5,* 127–133.

Science and Ethics in Conducting, Analyzing, and Reporting Psychological Research

Robert Rosenthal

. . .

CONDUCTING PSYCHOLOGICAL RESEARCH

Issues of Design

Imagine that a research proposal that comes before an institutional review board proposes the hypothesis that private schools improve children's intellectual functioning more than public schools do. Children from randomly selected private and public schools are to be tested extensively, and the research hypothesis is to be tested by comparing scores earned by students from private versus public schools. The safety of the children to be tested is certainly not an issue, yet it can be argued that this research raises ethical issues because of the inadequacy of its design. The goal of the research is to learn about the causal impact on performance of private versus public schooling, but the design of the research does not permit reasonable causal inference because of the absence of randomization or even some reasonable attempt to consider plausible rival hypotheses (Cook & Campbell, 1979).

How does the poor quality of the design raise ethical objections to the proposed research? Because students', teachers', and administrators' time will be taken from potentially more beneficial educational experiences. Because the poor quality of the design is likely to lead to unwarranted and inaccurate conclusions that may be damaging to the society that directly or indirectly pays for the research. In addition, allocating time and money to this poor-quality science will serve to keep those finite resources of time and money from better quality science in a world that is undeniably zero-sum.

. . .

Issues of Recruitment

. . .

On the basis of several reviews of the literature, my friend and colleague Ralph Rosnow and I have proposed a number of procedures designed to reduce volunteer bias and therefore increase the generality of our research results (Rosenthal & Rosnow, 1975, 1991; Rosnow & Rosenthal, 1993). Employment of these procedures has led us to think of our human participants as another "granting agency"—which, we believe, they are, since they must decide whether to grant us their time, attention, and cooperation. Part of our treating them as such is to give them information about the long-term benefits of the research. In giving prospective participants this information, we have a special obligation to avoid hyperclaiming.

Hyperclaiming. Hyperclaiming is telling our prospective participants, our granting agencies, our colleagues, our administrators, and ourselves that our research is likely to achieve goals it is, in fact, unlikely to achieve. Presumably our granting agencies, our colleagues, and our administrators are able to evaluate our claims and hyperclaims fairly well. However, our prospective participants are not; therefore, we should tell them what our research can actually accomplish rather than that it will yield the cure for panic disorder, depression, schizophrenia, or cancer.

Causism. Closely related to hyperclaiming is the phenomenon of causism. Causism refers to the tendency to imply a causal relationship where none has been established (i.e., where the data do not support it).

. . .

If a perpetrator of causism is unaware of the causism, its presence simply reflects poor scientific training. If the perpetrator is aware of the causism, it reflects blatantly unethical misrepresentation and deception.

. . . When a description of a proposed research study is couched in causal language, that description represents an unfair recruitment device that is at best inaccurate, when it is employed out of ignorance, and at worst dishonest, when it is employed as hype to increase the participation rates of potential participants. . . .

Bad Science Makes for Bad Ethics

Causism is only one example of bad science. Poor quality of research design, poor quality of data analysis, and poor quality of reporting of the research all lessen the ethical justification of any type of research project. I believe this judgment applies not only when deception, discomfort, or embarrassment of participants is involved, but for even the most benign research experience for participants. If because of the poor quality of the science no good can come of a research study, how are we to justify the use of participants' time, attention, and effort and the money, space, supplies, and other resources that have been expended on the research project? . . . For this reason, I believe that institutional review boards must consider the technical scientific competence of the investigators whose proposals they are asked to evaluate. . . .

Costs and Utilities

Payoffs for doing research. When individual investigators or institutional review boards are confronted with a questionable research proposal, they ordinarily employ a cost-utility analysis in which the costs of doing a study, including possible negative effects on participants, time, money, supplies, effort, and other resources, are evaluated simultaneously against such utilities as benefits to participants, to other people at other times, to science, to the world, or at least to the investigator. The potential benefits of higher quality studies and studies addressing more important topics are greater than the potential benefits of lower quality studies and studies addressing less important topics. Any study with low utility and high cost should not

be carried out. Studies in which costs equal utilities are very difficult to decide about.

Payoffs for failing to do research. However, Rosnow and I have become convinced that this cost-utility model is insufficient because it fails to consider the costs (and utilities) of *not* conducting a particular study (Rosenthal & Rosnow, 1984, 1991; Rosnow, 1990; Rosnow & Rosenthal, 1993).

The failure to conduct a study that could be conducted is as much an act to be evaluated on ethical grounds as is conducting a study. . . . The behavioral researcher whose study may have a good chance of reducing violence or racism or sexism, but who refuses to do the study simply because it involves deception, has not solved an ethical problem but only traded in one for another. . . .

This idea of lost opportunities has been applied with great eloquence by John Kaplan (1988), of the Stanford University Law School. The context of his remarks was the use of animals in research and the efforts of "animal rights" activists to chip away "at our ability to afford animal research. . . . [I]t is impossible to know the costs of experiments not done or research not undertaken. Who speaks for the sick, for those in pain, and for the future?" (p. 839). . . .

DATA ANALYSIS AS AN ETHICAL ARENA

Data Dropping

Ethical issues in the analysis of data range from the very obvious to the very subtle. Probably the most obvious and most serious transgression is the analysis of data that never existed (i.e., that were fabricated). Perhaps more frequent is the dropping of data that contradict the data analyst's theory, prediction, or commitment.

Outlier rejection. There is a venerable tradition in data analysis of dealing with outliers, or extreme scores, a tradition going back over 200 years (Barnett & Lewis, 1978). Both technical and ethical issues are involved. The technical issues have to do with the best ways of dealing with outliers without reference to the implications for the tenability of the data analyst's theory. The ethical issues have to do with the relationship between the data analyst's theory and the choice of method for dealing with outliers. For example, there is some evidence to suggest that outliers are more likely to be rejected if they are bad for the data analyst's theory but treated less harshly if they are good for the data analyst's theory (Rosenthal, 1978; Rosenthal & Rubin, 1971). At the very least, when outliers are rejected, that fact should be reported. In addition, it would be useful to report in a footnote the results that would have been obtained had the outliers not been rejected.

Subject selection. A different type of data dropping is subject selection in which a subset of the data is not included in the analysis. In this case, too, there are technical issues and ethical issues. There may be good technical reasons for setting aside a subset of the data, for example, because the subset's sample size is especially small or because dropping the subset would make the data more comparable to some other research. However, there are also ethical issues, as when just those subsets are dropped that do not support the data analyst's theory. When a subset is dropped, we should be informed of that fact and what the results were for that subset. Similar considerations apply when the results for one or more variables are not reported.

Exploitation Is Beautiful

Many of us have been taught that it is technically improper and perhaps even immoral to analyze and reanalyze our data in many ways (i.e., to snoop around in the data). We were taught to test the prediction with one particular preplanned test and take a result significant at the .05 level as our reward for a life well-lived. Should the results not be significant at the .05 level, we were taught, we should bite our lips bravely, take our medicine, and definitely not look further at our data. . . .

. . . [A]ntisnooping dogma is wasteful of time, effort, money, and other resources. If the research was worth doing, the data are worth a thorough analysis, being held up to the light in many different ways so that our research participants, our funding agencies, our science, and society will all get their time and their money's worth. . . .

Meta-Analysis as an Ethical Imperative

Meta-analysis is a set of concepts and procedures employed to summarize quantitatively any domain of research (Glass, McGaw, & Smith, 1981; Rosenthal,

1991). We know from both statistical and empirical research that, compared with traditional reviews of the literature, meta-analytic procedures are more accurate, comprehensive, systematic, and statistically powerful (Cooper & Rosenthal, 1980; Hedges & Olkin, 1985; Mosteller & Bush, 1954). . . .

Retroactive increase of utilities. Meta-analysis allows us to learn more from our data and therefore has a unique ability to increase retroactively the benefits of the studies being summarized. The costs of time, attention, and effort of the human participants employed in the individual studies entering into the meta-analysis are all more justified when their data enter into a meta-analysis. That is because the meta-analysis increases the utility of all the individual studies being summarized. Other costs of individual studies—costs of funding, supplies, space, investigator time and effort, and other resources—are similarly more justified because the utility of individual studies is so increased by the borrowed strength obtained when information from more studies is combined in a sophisticated way.

The failure to employ meta-analytic procedures when they could be used thus has ethical implications because the opportunity to increase the benefits of past individual studies has been foregone. In addition, when public funds or other resources are employed by scientists to prepare reviews of literatures, it is fair to ask whether those resources are being used wisely or ethically. Now that we know how to summarize literatures meta-analytically, it seems hardly justified to review a quantitative literature in the pre-meta-analytic, prequantitative manner. . . .

REPORTING PSYCHOLOGICAL RESEARCH

Misrepresentation of Findings

Mother nature makes it hard enough to learn her secrets, without the additional difficulty of being misled by the report of findings that were not found or by inferences that are unfounded. Although all misrepresentations of findings are damaging to the progress of our science, some are more obviously unethical than others.

Intentional misrepresentation. The most blatant intentional misrepresentation is the reporting of data that never were (Broad & Wade, 1982). That behavior, if detected, ends (or ought to end) the scientific career of the perpetrator. A somewhat more subtle form of intentional misrepresentation occurs when investigators knowingly allocate to experimental or control conditions those participants whose responses are more likely to support the investigators' hypothesis. Another potential form of intentional misrepresentation occurs when investigators record the participants' responses without being blind to the participants' treatment condition, or when research assistants record the participants' responses knowing both the research hypothesis and the participants' treatment condition. Of course, if the research specifically notes the failure to run blind, there is no misrepresentation, but the design is unwise if it could have been avoided.

Unintentional misrepresentation. Various errors in the process of data collection can lead to unintentional misrepresentations. Recording errors, computational errors, and data analytic errors can all lead to inaccurate results that are inadvertent misrepresentations (Broad & Wade, 1982; Rosenthal, 1966). We would not normally even think of them as constituting ethical issues except for the fact that errors in the data decrease the utility of the research and thereby move the cost-utility ratio (which is used to justify the research on ethical grounds) in the unfavorable direction. . . .

Misrepresentation of Credit

. . . .

Problems of authorship. Because so many papers in psychology, and the sciences generally, are multi-authored, it seems inevitable that there will be difficult problems of allocation of authorship credit. Who becomes a coauthor and who becomes a foot-note? Among the coauthors, who is assigned first, last, or any other serial position in the listing? Such questions have been discussed in depth, and very general guidelines have been offered (APA, 1981, 1987; see also Costa & Gatz, 1992), but it seems that we could profit from further empirical studies in which authors, editors, referees, students, practitioners, and professors were asked to allocate authorship credit to people performing various functions in a scholarly enterprise.

. . .

Failing to Report or Publish

Sometimes the ethical question is not about the accuracy of what was reported or how credit should be allocated for what was reported, but rather about what was *not* reported and why it was not reported. The two major forms of failure to report, or censoring, are self-censoring and external censoring.

Self-censoring. Some self-censoring is admirable. When a study has been really badly done, it may be a service to the science and to society to simply start over. Some self-censoring is done for admirable motives but seems wasteful of information. For example, some researchers feel they should not cite their own (or other people's) unpublished data because the data have not gone through peer review. I would argue that such data should indeed be cited and employed in meta-analytic computations as long as the data were well collected.

There are also less admirable reasons for self-censoring. Failing to report data that contradict one's earlier research, or one's theory or one's values, is poor science and poor ethics. . . . A good general policy—good for science and for its integrity is to report all results shedding light on the original hypothesis or providing data that might be of use to other investigators.

. . .

External censoring. Both the progress and the slowing of progress in science depend on external censoring. It seems likely that sciences would be more chaotic than they are if not for the censorship exercised by peers: by editors, by reviewers, and by program committees. All these gatekeepers help to keep the really bad science from clogging the pipelines of mainstream journals.

There are two major bases for external censorship. The first is evaluation of the methodology employed in a research study. I strongly favor such external censorship. If the study is truly terrible, it probably should not be reported.

The second major basis for external censorship is evaluation of the results. In my 35 years in psychology, I have often seen or heard it said of a study that "those results aren't possible" or "those results make no sense." Often when I have looked at such studies, I have agreed that the results are indeed implausible. However, that is a poor basis on which to censor the results. Censoring or suppressing results we do not like or do not believe to have high prior probability is bad science and bad ethics (Rosenthal, 1975, 1994).

References

American Psychological Association. (1981). Ethical principles of psychologists. *American Psychologist, 36*, 633–638.

American Psychological Association. (1987). *Casebook on ethical principles of psychologists.* Washington, DC: Author.

Barnett, V., & Lewis, T. (1978). *Outliers in statistical data.* New York: Wiley.

Broad, W., & Wade, N. (1982). *Betrayers of the truth.* New York: Simon and Schuster.

Cook, T. D., & Campbell, D. T. (1979). *Quasi-experimentation: Design and analysis issues for field settings.* Chicago: Rand McNally.

Cooper, H. M., & Rosenthal, R. (1980). Statistical versus traditional procedures for summarizing research findings. *Psychological Bulletin, 87*, 442–449.

Costa, M. M., & Gatz, M. (1992). Determination of authorship credit in published dissertations. *Psychological Science, 3*, 354–357.

Glass, G. V., McGaw, B., & Smith, M. L. (1981). *Meta-analysis in social research.* Beverly Hills, CA: Sage.

Hedges, L. V., & Olkin, I. (1985). *Statistical methods for meta-analysis.* New York: Academic Press.

Kaplan, J. (1988). The use of animals in research. *Science, 242*, 839–840.

Mosteller, F., & Bush, R. R. (1954). Selected quantitative techniques. In G. Lindzey (Ed.), *Handbook of social psychology: Vol. 1. Theory and method* (pp. 289–334). Cambridge, MA: Addison-Wesley.

Rosenthal, R. (1966). *Experimenter effects in behavioral research.* New York: Appleton-Century-Crofts.

Rosenthal, R. (1975). On balanced presentation of controversy. *American Psychologist, 30*, 937–938.

Rosenthal, R. (1978). How often are our numbers wrong? *American Psychologist, 33*, 1005–1008.

Rosenthal, R. (1991). *Meta-analytic procedures for social research* (rev. ed.). Newbury Park, CA: Sage.

Rosenthal, R. (1994). On being one's own case study: Experimenter effects in behavioral research—30 years later. In W. R. Shadish & S. Fuller (Eds.), *The social psychology of science* (pp. 214–229). New York: Guilford Press.

Rosenthal, R., & Rosnow, R. L. (1975). *The volunteer subject.* New York: Wiley.

Rosenthal, R., & Rosnow, R. L. (1984). Applying Hamlet's question to the ethical conduct of research: A conceptual addendum. *American Psychologist, 39*, 561–563.

Rosenthal, R., & Rosnow, R. L. (1991). *Essentials of behavioral research: Methods and data analysis* (2nd ed.). New York: McGraw-Hill.

Rosenthal, R., & Rubin, D. B. (1971). Pygmalion reaffirmed. In J. D. Elashoff & R. E. Snow, *Pygmalion reconsidered* (pp. 139–155). Worthington, OH: C. A. Jones.

Rosnow, R. L. (1990). Teaching research ethics through role-play and discussion. *Teaching of Psychology, 17*, 179–181.

Rosnow, R. L., & Rosenthal, R. (1993). *Beginning behavioral research: A conceptual primer.* New York: Macmillan.

Tukey, J. W. (1977). *Exploratory data analysis.* Reading, MA: Addison-Wesley.

◆ ◆ ◆

Commentary: Could Rosenthal's litany create the potential for finding almost any piece of research unethical? Would it be appropriate to make methodological flaws an ethical violation if they do not place research participants at risk or harm them? For discussions of these questions, see

Parkinson, S. (1994). Scientific or ethical quality? Psychological Science, 5, *137–138.*

Pomerantz, J. R. (1995). On criteria for ethics in science: Commentary on Rosenthal. Psychological Science, 5, *135–136.*

One of Rosenthal's more controversial proposals was that institutional review boards (IRBs; see the following two excerpts) evaluate the scientific and technical quality of all research, because bad research, even if it causes no palpable harm to participants, still wastes time, effort, and money. How does the proposal comport with self-determination? Does it inappropriately confuse scientific merit with ethics? For some cogent comments on his proposal and Rosenthal's thoughtful reply, see

Colombo, J. (1995). Cost, utility, and judgments of institutional review boards. Psychological Science, 6, *313–319.*

Mordock, J. B. (1995). Institutional review boards in applied settings: Their role in judgments of quality and consumer protection. Psychological Science, 6, *320–321.*

Rosenthal, R. (1995). Ethical issues in psychological science: Risk, consent, and scientific quality. Psychological Science, 6, 322–323.

Rosenthal's considerations are not merely academic. His concern about intentional misrepresentation is illustrated in the publicity about scientific fraud in the physical sciences (see, e.g., Chang, K. [2002, October 15]. On scientific fakery and the systems to catch it. The New York Times, pp. F1, F4) and the social sciences (see, e.g., Murray, B. [2002, February]. Research fraud needn't happen at all. APA Monitor, pp. 27–28). Now see Standard 8.10 (Reporting Research Results) in the 2002 Ethics Code.

The furor over a meta-analysis of the effects of child abuse by Rind, B., Tromovitch, P., & Bauserman, R. (1998). Meta-analytic examination of assumed properties of child sexual abuse using college samples. Psychological Bulletin, 124, 22–53, (finding that not all sexual relations between minors and adults—most particularly between younger adults and older adolescents—were always harmful), exemplifies Rosenthal's concern about censoring. The issue was fully discussed and debated in Albee, G. (Ed.). (2002). Interactions among scientists and policymakers: Challenges and opportunities [Special issue]. American Psychologist, 57. See also Bjork, R. (2000). Independence of scientific publishing: Reaffirming the principle. American Psychologist, 55, 981–984, and the rejoinder, Ondersma, S. (2002). Scientific freedom is not the only issue. American Psychologist, 57, 141–142. The issue reached the U.S. Congress. Of the 434 voting members of the House of Representatives, 355 voted in favor of a resolution condemning the article by Rind et al. Of the 66 absent members, none voted against the resolution. In addition, 13 voted "present," that is, abstained, including Representative Brian Baird and then-Representative Ted Strickland (now Ohio governor), both psychologists. The U.S. Senate then endorsed the resolution by unanimous consent. For a fuller accounting of this history, the response by APA and the American Association for the Advancement of Science, and references to critiques and defenders of the research see Pittenger, D. J. (2003). Intellectual freedom and editorial responsibilities within the context of controversial research. Ethics & Behavior, 13, 105–125.

The biomedical and behavioral sciences have, unfortunately, a long history of a lack of concern for the ethics and morality of conducting research. As noted in Bersoff and Bersoff (1999), excerpted in the previous article in this chapter, probably the most egregious example in the biomedical sciences (not counting the Nazi experiments on concentration camp victims) is the Tuskegee syphilis study. In 1972 the American public was finally told that for 40 years under the leadership, direction, and guidance of the U.S. Public Health Service there had been a continuing study of the effect of untreated syphilis in approximately 400 Black males in Alabama although there was no evidence that consent for participation had ever been obtained. In the social sciences, it was not the Ditching study that aroused policymakers but Milgram's study of obedience. Central to the startling results achieved was the deception, by the experimenter, of the subjects involved. To briefly recount the design, subjects were told that they would be taking part in a learning experiment. Each subject was assigned to a group of four people, three of whom, unknown to the subject, were Milgram's assistants. One of the assistants was the "learner" in the pseudoexperiment. The subject was to play the role of "teacher," whose function it was to instruct the learner by administering an electric shock when the learner made an error in the memory task. The naive subject was put at a control panel that regulated the shock from mild to extremely intense and painful. The teacher was told to deliver the painful stimulus whenever the learner erred. In reality, no electricity was hooked up to the panel and no learning took place. The subject was deceived concerning the purpose of the experiment. Learners deliberately made mistakes and pretended to feel pain so that the real investigators could determine to what levels subjects would raise the amount of electricity. When subjects hesitated, they were urged to continue. Sixty-two percent of over 1,000 subjects obeyed the experimenter's commands fully, raising the intensity level of the painful stimulus to the highest point possible. The experiment achieved notoriety not only because of the results obtained but because of the reactions of the deceived subjects. They expressed shame, revulsion, anxiety, and extreme tension during and after the experiment. See Milgram, S. (1963). Behavioral studies of obedience. Journal of Abnormal and Social Psychology, 67, 371–378.

The other study of significance is the Stanford Prison Experiment (SPE) in which Philip Zimbardo and his graduate students erected a mock prison. They divided 23 volunteers into two groups—"prisoners" and "guards." By the 2nd day of the study the guards became sadistic, denying the prisoners (fellow Stanford students) food, water, and sleep, and among other things, stripping them naked. Although the study was to last 2 weeks, Dr. Zimbardo was pressured into stopping it after 5 days. See Haney, C., Banks, C., & Zimbardo, P. (1973). International Journal of Criminology and Penology, 1, 69–97. In a recent interview, Zimbardo said that Milgram told him, "Your study is going to take all the ethical heat off my back. People are now going to say yours is the most unethical study ever, and not mine." Dreifus, C. (2007, April 3). Finding hope in knowing the universal capacity for evil. The New York Times, p. F2. For a fuller discussion of the ethical implications of the SPE and the current implications of the experiment, see Zimbardo, P. (2007). The Lucifer Effect: Understanding How Good People Turn Evil. New York: Random House.

Among other events, these experiments led the U.S. Department of Health, Education, and Welfare (now the Department of Health and Human Services [DHHS]) to publish in 1974 regulations regarding the protection of human subjects. These regulations govern the activities of those organizations that receive research funds or are accountable to DHHS. Now codified as federal regulations (45 CFR 46), the rules explicitly declare the government's policy that

> Departments and agencies will conduct or support research . . . only if the institution . . . has certified . . . that the research has been reviewed and approved by an IRB [Institutional Review Board] . . . and will be subject to continuing review by the IRB. . . ." (45 CFR 46.103(b)

The relevant portions of these regulations are reprinted in the next excerpt.

Soon after these regulations appeared, Congress established the National Commission for the Protection of Human Subjects in Biomedical and Behavioral Research. In addition to developing ethical principles and defining informed consent generally, particular attention was paid to identifying the requirements for informed consent for those persons whose capacity for giving consent is considered absent or limited: that is, prisoners, children, and institutionalized mental patients. The Commission's rec-

ommendations concerning prisoners and children were revised and promulgated as regulations (see next excerpt). Interestingly, commission recommendations concerning research with people who have been institutionalized as mentally disabled have never been adopted by DHHS. As Dresser (1996) noted:

> The United States has no specific policy on research involving persons with mental disabilities. . . . Instead, federal law assigns . . . IRBs responsibilities for determining whether protective measures for mentally disabled subjects should be added to the basic provisions governing human experimentation. Yet IRBs lack adequate guidance on fulfilling this responsibility. (p. 67)

In the absence of federal regulations and in the light of fundamental ethical principles, Dresser offered the following recommendations:

1. Adopt informed consent procedures that enhance the autonomy of capable subjects but offer them an opportunity to share decision-making with family or friends;
2. When proxy decision-makers are used for incapable participants, instruct proxies on relevant ethical standards;
3. Exclude those who object, including those incapable of decision-making, unless the research provides an exceptional opportunity for direct benefit;
4. Arrange for genuine representation of the relevant subject population in the planning and ethical review of proposed research.

See Dresser, R. (1996). Mentally disabled research subjects: The enduring policy issues. Journal of the American Medical Association, 276, 67–72.

In addition, the National Bioethics Advisory Commission issued recommended rules for conducting research with participants who are mentally disabled, many of which comport with Professor Dresser's suggestions. See National Bioethics Advisory Commission. (1998). Research involving persons with mental disorders that may affect decision-making capacity (Vol. 1). Rockville, MD: National Bioethics Advisory Commission. See also American Psychiatric Association's Task Force on Research Ethics. (2006). Ethical princi-

ples and practices for research involving participants with mental illness, Psychiatric Services, 57, 552–557. *For a helpful manual devoted to participants with mental retardation see Dinerstein, R., Herr, S., & O'Sullivan, J. (Eds.). (1999).* A guide to consent. *Washington, DC: American Association on Mental Retardation. Finally, there is an interesting and informative discussion of three case vignettes in a recent edition of* Ethics & Behavior: *(a) a young schizophrenic woman with fluctuating decisional capacity; (b) a middle-aged mentally retarded man with impaired decisional capacity; and (c) an elderly woman suffering from the beginning stages of Alzheimer's disease with diminishing decisional capacity. See Fisher, C. (Ed.). (2002).* The forum. Ethics & Behavior, 12, 279–293. *For an excellent discussion of studying minority children, see Fisher, C. et al. (2002). Research ethics for mental health science involving ethnic minority children and youth.* American Psychologist, 57, 1024–1040.

In the early 1990s a federal agency scrutinized a study by university researchers involving participants diagnosed with schizophrenia. Some participants complained that the researchers failed to sufficiently inform them of the possibility that the withdrawal of their medication—one of the components of the study—could lead to severe relapses. The agency concluded that the researchers failed to secure sufficient consent to this procedure from participants. It did agree, however, with the university IRB that the methodology of the research was scientifically sound. See Office for Protection From Research Risks, Division of Human Subject Protections. (1994). Evaluation of human subject protections in schizophrenia research conducted by the University of California, Los Angeles. *Los Angeles: UCLA. It is an instructive case study.*

Relevant parts of the regulations for research conducted or funded by DHHS with human participants generally and with prisoners and children specifically are included in the following pages.

Policy for Protection of Human Research Subjects

U.S. Department of Health and Human Services

SUBPART A—BASIC HHS POLICY FOR PROTECTION OF HUMAN RESEARCH SUBJECTS

. . .

§ 46.101 To What Does This Policy Apply?

(a) Except as provided in paragraph (b) of this section, this policy applies to all research involving human subjects conducted, supported or otherwise subject to regulation by any federal department or agency which takes appropriate administrative action to make the policy applicable to such research. . . .

(b) Unless otherwise required by department or agency heads, research activities in which the only involvement of human subjects will be in one or more of the following categories are exempt from this policy:

(1) Research conducted in established or commonly accepted educational settings, involving normal educational practices, such as (i) research on regular and special education instructional strategies, or (ii) research on the effectiveness of or the comparison, among instructional techniques, curricula, or classroom management methods.

(2) Research involving the use of educational tests (cognitive, diagnostic, aptitude, achievement), survey procedures, interview procedures or observation of public behavior, unless:

(i) Information obtained is recorded in such a manner that human subjects can be identified, directly or through identifiers linked to the subjects; and
(ii) any disclosure of the human subjects' responses outside the research could reasonably place the subjects at risk of criminal or civil liability or be damaging to the subjects' financial standing, employability, or reputation.

(3) Research involving the use of educational tests (cognitive, diagnostic, aptitude, achievement), survey procedures, interview procedures, or observation of public behavior that is not exempt under paragraph (b)(2) of this section, if:

(i) The human subjects are elected or appointed public officials or candidates for public office; or (ii) federal statute(s) require(s) without exception that the confidentiality of the personally identifiable information will be maintained throughout the research and thereafter.

(4) Research, involving the collection or study of existing data, documents, records, pathological specimens, or diagnostic specimens, if these sources are publicly available or if the information is recorded by the investigator in such a manner that subjects cannot be identified, directly or through identifiers linked to the subjects.

(5) Research and demonstration projects which are conducted by or subject to the approval of department or agency heads, and which are designed to study, evaluate, or otherwise examine:

(i) Public benefit or service programs; (ii) procedures for obtaining benefits or services under those programs; (iii) possible changes in or alternatives to those programs or procedures; or (iv) possible changes in methods or

From 45 C.F.R. Part 46. Basic H.H.S. Policy for Protection of Human Research Subjects.

levels of payment for benefits or services under those programs. . . .

§ 46.107 IRB Membership.

(a) Each IRB shall have at least five members, with varying backgrounds to promote complete and adequate review of research activities commonly conducted by the institution. The IRB shall be sufficiently qualified through the experience and expertise of its members, and the diversity of the members, including consideration of race, gender, and cultural backgrounds and sensitivity to such issues as community attitudes, to promote respect for its advice and counsel in safeguarding the rights and welfare of human subjects. In addition to possessing the professional competence necessary to review specific research activities, the IRB shall be able to ascertain the acceptability of proposed research in terms of institutional commitments and regulations, applicable law, and standards of professional conduct and practice. The IRB shall therefore include persons knowledgeable in these areas. If an IRB regularly reviews research that involves a vulnerable category of subjects, such as children, prisoners, pregnant women, or handicapped or mentally disabled persons, consideration shall be given to the inclusion of one or more individuals who are knowledgeable about and experienced in working with these subjects.

(b) Every nondiscriminatory effort will be made to ensure that no IRB consists entirely of men or entirely of women, including the institution's consideration of qualified persons of both sexes, so long as no selection is made to the IRB on the basis of gender. No IRB may consist entirely of members of one profession.

(c) Each IRB shall include at least one member whose primary concerns are in scientific areas and at least one member whose primary concerns are in nonscientific areas.

(d) Each IRB shall include at least one member who is not otherwise affiliated with the institution and who is not part of the immediate family of a person who is affiliated with the institution.

(e) No IRB may have a member participate in the IRB's initial or continuing review of any project in which the member has a conflicting interest, except to provide information requested by the IRB.

(f) An IRB may, in its discretion, invite individuals with competence in special areas to assist in the review of issues which require expertise beyond or in addition to that available on the IRB. These individuals may not vote with the IRB. . . .

§ 46.110 Expedited Review Procedures for Certain Kinds of Research Involving No More Than Minimal Risk, and for Minor Changes in Approved Research.

(a) The Secretary, HHS, has established, and published as a Notice in the Federal Register, a list of categories of research that may be reviewed by the IRB through an expedited review procedure. The list will be amended, as appropriate after consultation with other departments and agencies, through periodic republication by the Secretary, HHS, in the Federal Register. A copy of the list is available from the Office for Protection From Research Risks, National Institutes of Health, HHS, Bethesda, Maryland 20892.

(b) An IRB may use the expedited review procedure to review either or both of the following:

(1) Some or all of the research appearing on the list and found by the reviewer(s) to involve no more than minimal risk.

(2) Minor changes in previously approved research during the period (of one year or less) for which approval is authorized.

Under an expedited review procedure, the review may be carried out by the IRB chairperson or by one or more experienced reviewers designated by the chairperson from among members of the IRB. In reviewing the research, the reviewers may exercise all of the authorities of the IRB except that the reviewers may not disapprove the research. A research activity may be disapproved only after review in accordance with the non-expedited procedure set forth in § 46.108(b). . . .

§ 46.111 Criteria for IRB Approval of Research.

(a) In order to approve research covered by this policy the IRB shall determine that all of the following requirements are satisfied:

(1) Risks to subjects are minimized: (i) By using procedures which are consistent

with sound research design and which do not unnecessarily expose subjects to risk, and (ii) whenever appropriate, by using procedures already being performed on the subjects for diagnostic or treatment purposes.

(2) Risks to subjects are reasonable in relation to anticipated benefits, if any, to subjects, and the importance of the knowledge that may reasonably be expected to result. In evaluating risks and benefits, the IRB should consider only those risks and benefits that may result from the research (as distinguished from risks and benefits of therapies subjects would receive even if not participating in the research). The IRB should not consider possible long-range effects of applying knowledge gained in the research (for example, the possible effects of the research on public policy) as among those research risks that fall within the purview of its responsibility.

(3) Selection of subjects is equitable. In making this assessment the IRB should take into account the purposes of the research and the setting in which the research will be conducted and should be particularly cognizant of the special problems of research involving vulnerable populations, such as children, prisoners, pregnant women, mentally disabled persons, or economically or educationally disadvantaged persons.

(4) Informed consent will be sought from each prospective subject or the subject's legally authorized representative, in accordance with, and to the extent required by § 46.116.

(5) Informed consent will be appropriately documented, in accordance with, and to the extent required by § 46.117.

(6) When appropriate, the research plan makes adequate provision for monitoring the data collected to ensure the safety of subjects.

(7) When appropriate, there are adequate provisions to protect the privacy of sub-

jects and to maintain the confidentiality of data.

(b) When some or all of the subjects are likely to be vulnerable to coercion or undue influence, such as children, prisoners, pregnant women, mentally disabled persons, or economically or educationally disadvantaged persons, additional safeguards have been included in the study to protect the rights and welfare of these subjects. . . .

§ 46.116 General Requirements for Informed Consent.

Except as provided elsewhere in this policy, no investigator may involve a human being as a subject in research covered by this policy unless the investigator has obtained the legally effective informed consent of the subject or the subject's legally authorized representative. An investigator shall seek such consent only under circumstances that provide the prospective subject or the representative sufficient opportunity to consider whether or not to participate and that minimize the possibility of coercion or undue influence. The information that is given to the subject or the representative shall be in language understandable to the subject or the representative. No informed consent, whether oral or written, may include any exculpatory language through which the subject or the representative is made to waive or appear to waive any of the subject's legal rights, or releases or appears to release the investigator, the sponsored, the institution or its agents from liability for negligence.

(a) Basic elements of informed consent. Except as provided in paragraph (c) or (d) of this section, in seeking informed consent the following information shall be provided to each subject:

(1) A statement that the study involves research, an explanation of the purposes of the research and the expected duration of the subject's participation, a description of the procedures to be followed, and identification of any procedures which are experimental;

(2) A description of any reasonably foreseeable risks or discomforts to the subject;

(3) A description of any benefits to the subject or to others which may reasonably be expected from the research;

(4) A disclosure of appropriate alternative procedures or courses of treatment, if any, that might be advantageous to the subject;

(5) A statement describing the extent, if any, to which confidentiality of records identifying the subject will be maintained;

(6) For research involving more than minimal risk, an explanation as to whether any compensation and an explanation as to whether any medical treatments are available if injury occurs and, if so, what they consist of, or where further information may be obtained;

(7) An explanation of whom to contact for answers to pertinent questions about the research and research subjects' rights, and whom to contact in the event of a research-related injury to the subject; and

(8) A statement that participation is voluntary, refusal to participate will involve no penalty or loss of benefits to which the subject is otherwise entitled, and the subject may discontinue participation at any time without penalty or loss of benefits to which the subject is otherwise entitled.

(b) Additional elements of informed consent. When appropriate, one or more of the following elements of information shall also be provided to each subject:

(1) A statement that the particular treatment or procedure may involve risks to the subject (or to the embryo or fetus, if the subject is or may become pregnant) which are currently unforeseeable;

(2) Anticipated circumstances under which the subject's participation may be terminated by the investigator without regard to the subject's consent;

(3) Any additional costs to the subject that may result from participation in the research;

(4) The consequences of a subject's decision to withdraw from the research and procedures for orderly termination of participation by the subject;

(5) A statement that significant new findings developed during the course of the research which may relate to the subject's willingness to continue participation will be provided to the subject; and

(6) The approximate number of subjects involved in the study.

(c) An IRB may approve a consent procedure which does not include, or which alters, some or all of the elements of informed consent set forth above, or waive the requirements to obtain informed consent provided the IRB finds and documents that:

(1) The research or demonstration project is to be conducted by or subject to the approval of state or local government officials and is designed to study, evaluate, or otherwise examine: (i) Public benefit or service programs; (ii) procedures for obtaining benefits or services under those programs; (iii) possible changes in or alternatives to those programs or procedures; or (iv) possible changes in methods or levels of payment for benefits or services under those programs; and

(2) The research could not practicably be carried out without the waiver or alteration.

(d) An IRB may approve a consent procedure which does not include, or which alters, some or all of the elements of informed consent set forth in this section, or waive the requirements to obtain informed consent provided the IRB finds and documents that:

(1) The research involves no more than minimal risk to the subjects;

(2) The waiver or alteration will not adversely affect the rights and welfare of the subjects;

(3) The research could not practicably be carried out without the waiver or alteration; and

(4) Whenever appropriate, the subjects will be provided with additional pertinent information after participation.

(e) The informed consent requirements in this policy are not intended to preempt any applicable federal, state, or local laws which require additional information to be disclosed in order for informed consent to be legally effective.

(f) Nothing in this policy is intended to limit the authority of a physician to provide emergency medical care, to the extent the physician is permitted to do so under applicable federal, state, or local law. . . .

SUBPART C—ADDITIONAL PROTECTIONS PERTAINING TO BIOMEDICAL AND BEHAVIORAL RESEARCH INVOLVING PRISONERS AS SUBJECTS

§ 46.302 Purpose.

Inasmuch as prisoners may be under constraints because of their incarceration which could affect their ability to make a truly voluntary and uncoerced decision whether or not to participate as subjects in research, it is the purpose of this subpart to provide additional safeguards for the protection of prisoners involved in activities to which this subpart is applicable. . . .

§ 46.304 Composition of Institutional Review Boards Where Prisoners Are Involved.

In addition to satisfying the requirements in § 46.107 of this part, an Institutional Review Board, carving out responsibilities under this part with respects to research covered by this subpart, shall also meet the following specific requirements:

(a) A majority of the Board (exclusive of prisoner members) shall have no association with the prison(s) involved, apart from their membership on the Board.

(b) At least one member of the Board shall be a prisoner, or a prisoner representative with appropriate background and experience to serve in that capacity, except that where a particular research project is reviewed by more than one Board only one Board need satisfy this requirement.
. . .

§ 46.305 Additional Duties of the Institutional Review Boards Where Prisoners Are Involved.

(a) In addition to all other responsibilities prescribed for Institutional Review Boards under this part, the Board shall review research covered by

this subpart and approve such research only if it finds that:

(1) The research under review represents one of the categories of research permissible under § 46.306(a)(2);

(2) Any possible advantages accruing to the prisoner through his or her participation in the research, when compared to the general living conditions, medical care, quality of food, amenities and opportunity for earnings in the prison, are not of such a magnitude that his or her ability to weigh the risks of the research against the value of such advantages in the limited choice environment of the prison is impaired;

(3) The risks involved in the research are commensurate with risks that would be accepted by nonprisoner volunteers;

(4) Procedures for the selection of subjects within the prison are fair to all prisoners and immune from arbitrary intervention by prison authorities or prisoners. Unless the principal investigator provides to the Board justification in writing for following some other procedures, control subjects must be selected randomly from the group of available prisoners who meet the characteristics needed for that particular research project.

(5) The information is presented in language which is understandable to the subject population; [and]

(6) Adequate assurance exists that parole boards will not take into account a prisoner's participation in the research in making decisions regarding parole, and each prisoner is clearly informed in advance that participation in the research will have no effect on his or her parole[.] . . .

§ 46.306 Permitted Research Involving Prisoners.

(a) Biomedical or behavioral research conducted or supported by DHHS may involve prisoners as subjects only if:

(1) The institution responsible for the conduct of the research has certified to the

Secretary that the Institutional Review Board has approved the research under § 46.305 of this subpart; and

(2) In the judgment of the Secretary the proposed research involves solely the following:

  (i) Study of the possible causes, effects, and processes of incarceration, and of criminal behavior, provided that the study presents no more than minimal risk and no more than inconvenience to the subjects;

  (ii) Study of prisons as institutional structures or of prisoners as incarcerated persons, provided that the study presents no more than minimal risk and no more than inconvenience to the subjects;

  (iii) Research on concerns particularly affecting prisoners as a class (for example, vaccine trials and other research on hepatitis which is much more prevalent in prisons than elsewhere; and research on social and psychological problems such as alcoholism, drug addiction, and sexual assaults) provided that the study may proceed only after the Secretary has consulted with appropriate experts including experts in penology medicine and ethics, and published notice, in the Federal Register, of his intent to approve such research; or

  (iv) Research on practices, both innovative and accepted, which have the intent and reasonable probability of improving the health or well-being of the subject. In cases in which those studies require the assignment of prisoners in a manner consistent with protocols approved by the IRB to control groups which may not benefit from the research, the study may proceed only after the Secretary has consulted with appropriate experts, including experts in penol-

ogy medicine and ethics, and published notice, in the Federal Register, of his intent to approve such research.

  (b) Except as provided in paragraph (a) of this section, biomedical or behavioral research conducted or supported by DHHS shall not involve prisoners as subjects.

SUBPART D—ADDITIONAL PROTECTIONS FOR CHILDREN INVOLVED AS SUBJECTS IN RESEARCH

. . .

§ 46.402 Definitions.

The definitions in § 46.102 of Subpart A shall be applicable to this subpart as well. In addition, as used in this subpart:

  (a) *Children* are persons who have not attained the legal age for consent to treatments or procedures involved in the research, under the applicable law of the jurisdiction in which the research will be conducted.

  (b) *Assent* means a child's affirmative agreement to participate in research. Mere failure to object should not, absent affirmative agreement, be construed as assent.

  (c) *Permission* means the agreement of parent(s) or guardian to the participation of their child or ward in research.

  (d) *Parent* means a child's biological or adoptive parent.

  (e) *Guardian* means an individual who is authorized under applicable State or local law to consent on behalf of a child to general medical care.

§ 46.403 IRB Duties.

In addition to other responsibilities assigned to IRBs under this part, each IRB shall review research covered by this subpart and approve only research which satisfies the conditions of all applicable sections of this subpart.

§ 46.604 Research Not Involving Greater Than Minimal Risk.

HHS will conduct or fund research in which the IRB finds that no greater than minimal risk to children is presented, only if the IRB finds that adequate provisions are made for soliciting the assent of the children and the permission of their parents or guardians, as set forth in § 46.408.

§ 46.405 Research Involving Greater Than Minimal Risk but Presenting the Prospect of Direct Benefit to the Individual Subjects.

HHS will conduct or fund research in which the IRB finds that more than minimal risk to children is presented by an intervention or procedure that holds out the prospect of direct benefit for the individual subject, or by a monitoring procedure that is likely to contribute to the subject's well-being, only if the IRB finds that:

(a) The risk is justified by the anticipated benefit to the subjects;

(b) The relation of the anticipated benefit to the risk is at least as favorable to the subjects as that presented by available alternative approaches; and

(c) Adequate provisions are made for soliciting the assent of the children and permission of their parents or guardians, as set forth in § 46.408.

§ 46.406 Research Involving Greater Than Minimal Risk and No Prospect of Direct Benefit to Individual Subjects, but Likely to Yield Generalizable Knowledge About the Subject's Disorder or Condition.

HHS will conduct or fund research in which the IRB finds that more than minimal risk to children is presented by an intervention or procedure that does not hold out the prospect of direct benefit for the individual subject, or by a monitoring procedure which is not likely to contribute to the well-being of the subject, only if the IRB finds that:

(a) The risk represents a minor increase over minimal risk;

(b) The intervention or procedure presents experiences to subjects that are reasonably commensurate with those inherent in their actual or expected medical, dental, psychological, social, or educational situations;

(c) The intervention or procedure is likely to yield generalizable knowledge about the subjects' disorder or condition which is of vital importance for

the understanding or amelioration of the subjects' disorder or condition; and

(d) Adequate provisions are made for soliciting assent of the children and permission of their parents or guardians, as set forth in § 46.408.

§ 46.407 Research Not Otherwise Approvable Which Presents an Opportunity to Understand, Prevent, or Alleviate a Serious Problem Affecting the Health or Welfare of Children.

HHS will conduct or fund research that the IRB does not believe meets the requirements of § 46.404, § 46.405, or § 46.406 only if:

(a) The IRB finds that the research presents a reasonable opportunity to further the understanding, prevention, or alleviation of a serious problem affecting the health or welfare of children; and

(b) The Secretary, after consultation with a panel of experts in pertinent disciplines (for example: science, medicine, education, ethics, law) and following opportunity for public review and comment, has determined either:

(1) That the research in fact satisfies the conditions of § 46.404, § 46.405, or § 46.406, as applicable, or

(2) The following:

(i) The research presents a reasonable opportunity to further the understanding, prevention, or alleviation of a serious problem affecting the health or welfare of children;

(ii) The research will be conducted in accordance with sound ethical principles;

(iii) Adequate provisions are made for soliciting the assent of children and the permission of their parents or guardians, as set forth in § 46.408.

§ 46.408 Requirements for Permission by Parents or Guardians and for Assent by Children.

(a) In addition to the determinations required under other applicable sections of this subpart, the IRB shall determine that adequate provisions are made for soliciting the assent of the children, when in the judgment of the IRB the children are capable of providing assent. In determining whether children are capable of assenting, the IRB shall take into account the ages, maturity, and psychological state of the children involved. This judgment may be made for all children to be involved in research under a particular protocol, or for each child, as the IRB deems appropriate. If the IRB determines that the capability of some or all of the children is so limited that they cannot reasonably be consulted or that the intervention or procedure involved in the research holds out a prospect of direct benefit that is important to the health or well-being of the children and is available only in the context of the research, the assent of the children is not a necessary condition for proceeding with the research. Even where the IRB determines that the subjects are capable of assenting, the IRB may still waive the assent requirement under circumstances in which consent may be waived in accord with § 46.116 of Subpart A.

(b) In addition to the determinations required under other applicable sections of this subpart, the IRB shall determine, in accordance with and to the extent that consent is required by § 46.116 of Subpart A, that adequate provisions are made for soliciting the permission of each child's parents or guardian. Where parental permission is to be obtained, the IRB may find that the permission of one parent is sufficient for research to be conducted under § 46.404 or § 46.405. Where research is covered by § 46.406 and § 46.407 and permission is to be obtained from parents, both parents must give their permission unless one parent is deceased, unknown, incompetent, or not reasonably available, or when only one parent has legal responsibility for the care and custody of the child.

(c) In addition to the provisions for waiver contained in § 46.116 of Subpart A, if the IRB determines that a research protocol is designed for conditions or for a subject population for which parental or guardian permission is not a reasonable requirement to protect the subjects (for example, neglected or abused children), it may waive the consent requirements in Subpart A of this part and paragraph (b) of this section, provided an appropriate mechanism for protecting the children who will participate as subjects in the research is substituted, and provided further that the waiver is not inconsistent with Federal, state, or local law. The choice of an appropriate mechanism would depend upon the nature and purpose of the activities described in the protocol, the risk and anticipated benefit to the research subjects, and their age, maturity, status, and condition.

(d) Permission by parents or guardians shall be documented in accordance with and to the extent required by § 46.117 of Subpart A.

(e) When the IRB determines that assent is required, it shall also determine whether and how assent must be documented.

§ 46.409 Wards.

(a) Children who are wards of the state or any other agency, institution, or entity can be included in research approved under § 46.406 or § 46.407 only if such research is:

(1) Related to their status as wards, or

(2) Conducted in schools, camps, hospitals, institutions, or similar settings in which the majority of children involved as subjects are not wards.

(b) If the research is approved under paragraph (a) of this section, the IRB shall require appointment of an advocate for each child who is a ward, in addition to any other individual acting on behalf of the child as guardian or in loco parentis. One individual may serve as advocate for more than one child. The advocate shall be an individual who has the background and experience to act in, and agrees to act in, the best interests of the child for the duration of the child's participation in the research and who is not associated in any way (except in the role as advocate or member of the IRB) with the research, the investigator(s), or the guardian organization.

Empirical Studies of Ethical Issues in Research: A Research Agenda

Barbara Stanley, Joan E. Sieber, and Gary B. Melton

. . .

COMPETENCY OF RESEARCH PARTICIPANTS

Competency to give an informed consent recently has been the subject of empirical studies. A major difficulty with conducting research on competency lies in the lack of a uniform standard of competency (Meisel, Roth, & Lidz, 1977; Roth, Meisel, & Lidz, 1977). Three populations are most often identified as having questionable competency: (a) mentally disabled persons, (b) cognitively impaired elderly persons, and (c) children.

MENTALLY DISABLED PERSONS

The empirical evidence that is available with respect to severely disordered persons presents a somewhat mixed picture. One conclusion that can be safely drawn with respect to psychiatric patients is that they do no better than medical patients in the consent process. The evidence that they are less able to give consent is somewhat equivocal and to a certain extent depends on the definition of competency that is used. With respect to comprehension of consent information, a few studies have assessed psychiatric patients' ability to understand consent information (Appelbaum, Mirkin, & Bateman, 1981; Grossman & Summers, 1980; Roth et al., 1982; Soskis & Jaffe, 1979). In general, psychiatric patients do not have a very high level of understanding of consent information. However, when studies of medical patients are compared with studies of psychiatric patients, their understanding seems nearly equal

(Grossman & Summers, 1980; Soskis & Jaffe, 1979). For example, one study found that schizophrenic patients understood only about 50% of the material on a consent form that was read to them (Grossman & Summers, 1980). However, in a direct comparison of psychiatric and medical patients, schizophrenic patients were found to be more aware of the risks and side effects of their medication than were medical patients (Soskis, 1978). On the other hand, medical patients were better informed about the name and dosage of their medication, as well as their diagnosis. Psychiatric patients' poor knowledge of their diagnosis may have been partly the result of a general reluctance by hospital staff to tell patients that they have schizophrenia.

Related to the comprehension level of psychiatric patients are studies that have examined their literacy skills. Although acutely hospitalized psychiatric patients' comprehension of consent information seems to be equal to that of medical patients, research indicates that reading comprehension scores of chronic patients are only at the fifth-grade level (Berg & Hammit, 1980; Coles, Roth, & Pollack, 1978). Thus, hospital documents should be simplified for psychiatric patients (Berg & Hammit, 1980), as some have suggested they be for medical patients. . . .

Overall, the empirical research on informed consent shows that psychiatric patients do have some impairment in their abilities. However, the research also shows that in some respects they do not differ from medical patients. As a result, further studies that use comparison groups, particularly medical patients, are necessary to draw conclusions about the competency of mentally disordered persons as a group to consent to research.

COGNITIVELY IMPAIRED ELDERLY PERSONS

Studies of the elderly have shown some impairment in their ability to comprehend consent information (Stanley, Guido, Stanley, & Shortell, 1984). Impaired recall of consent information has been noted in elderly persons who have poor verbal skills (Taub, 1980). However, it appears that the overall quality of decision making is not affected by age, although comprehension and recall may be (Stanley et al., 1984). In other words, elderly people typically reach decisions regarding agreement to proposed procedures that are similar to those of younger people.

CHILDREN

As with the other groups, the competence of minors to consent to research probably is often underestimated. A large body of research has developed about children's competence in making personal decisions, including consent to treatment (see generally Melton, 1984; Melton, Koocher, & Saks, 1983). Generally, such studies show that even elementary school children commonly are able to express a preference and, indeed, to make the same decision that average adults make (Weithorn & Campbell, 1982). By age 14, for most decisions, minors are as competent as adults to understand and weigh the risks and benefits of the available alternatives.

Few studies have examined minors' competence to consent to research. However, the studies that are available are consistent with the general findings about minors' decision making (Keith-Spiegel, 1983; Keith-Spiegel & Maas, 1981; Lewis, Lewis, & Ifekwunigue, 1978). . . .

References

Appelbaum, P. S., Mirkin, S., & Bateman, A. (1981). Competency to consent to psychiatric hospitalization: An empirical assessment. *American Journal of Psychiatry, 138,* 1170–1176.

Berg, A., & Hammit, K. B. (1980). Assessing the psychiatric patient's ability to meet the literacy demands of hospitalization. *Hospital and Community Psychiatry, 31,* 266–268.

Coles, G., Roth, L., & Pollack, L. (1978). Literacy skills of long-term hospitalized mental patients. *Hospital and Community Psychiatry, 29,* 512–516.

Grossman, L., & Summers, F. (1980). A study of the capacity of schizophrenic patients to give informed consent. *Hospital and Community Psychiatry, 31,* 205–207.

Keith-Spiegel, P. (1983). Children and consent to participate in research. In G. B. Melton, G. P. Koocher, & M. J. Saks (Eds.), *Children's competence to consent* (pp. 179–211). New York: Plenum Press.

Keith-Spiegel, P., & Maas, T. (1981, August). *Consent to research: Are there developmental differences?* Paper presented at the meeting of the American Psychological Association, Los Angeles, CA.

Lewis, C. E., Lewis, M. A., & Ifekwunigue, M. (1978). Informed consent by children and participation in an influenza vaccine trial. *American Journal of Public Health, 68,* 1079–1082.

Meisel, A., Roth, L., & Lidz, C. (1977). Towards a model of the legal doctrine of informed consent. *American Journal of Psychiatry, 134,* 285–289.

Melton, G. B. (1984). Developmental psychology and the law: The state of the art. *Journal of Family Law, 22,* 445–482.

Melton, G. B., Koocher, G. P., & Saks, M. J. (Eds.). (1983). *Children's competence to consent.* New York: Plenum.

Roth, L. H., Lidz, C. W., Meisel, A., Soloff, P. H., Kaufmen, K., Spiker, D. G., & Foster, F. G. (1982). Competency to decide about treatment or research: An overview of some empirical data. *International Journal of Law and Psychiatry, 5,* 29–50.

Roth, L. H., Meisel, A., & Lidz, C. W. (1977). Tests of competency to consent to treatment. *American Journal of Psychiatry, 134,* 279–284.

Soskis, D. A. (1978). Schizophrenic and medical inpatients as informed drug consumers. *Archives of General Psychiatry, 35,* 645–647.

Soskis, D. A., & Jaffe, R. L. (1979). Communicating with patients about antipsychotic drugs. *Comprehensive Psychiatry, 20,* 126–131.

Stanley, B., Guido, J., Stanley, M., & Shortell, D. (1984). The elderly patient and informed consent. *Journal of the American Medical Association, 252,* 1302–1306.

Taub, H. A. (1980). Informed consent, memory, and age. *The Gerontologist, 20,* 686–690.

Weithorn, L. A., & Campbell, S. B. (1982). The competency of children and adolescents to make informed treatment decisions. *Child Development, 53,* 1589–1598.

◆ ◆ ◆

Commentary: For more recent studies on the ability of those persons hospitalized as mentally ill to consent, see

Appelbaum, P. S., & Grisso, T. (1995). *The MacArthur Treatment Competency Study I: Mental illness and competence to consent to treatment.* Law and Human Behavior, 19, *105–126.*

Grisso, T., & Appelbaum, P. S. (1995). *The MacArthur Treatment Competence Study III: Abilities of patients to consent to psychiatric and medical treatments.* Law and Human Behavior, 19, *149–174.*

Grisso, T., Appelbaum, P. S., Mulvey, E. P., & Fletcher, K. (1995). *The MacArthur Treatment Study II: Measures of abilities related to competence to consent to treatment.* Law and Human Behavior, 19, *127–148.*

For a view that the policies and measures advocated in these studies are too paternalistic, see Kirk, T., & Bersoff, D. N. (1996). How many procedural safeguards does it take to get a psychiatrist to leave the light bulb unchanged? A due process analysis of the MacArthur Treatment Competency Study. Psychology, Public Policy, and the Law, 2, *45–72. See also Edwards, S. J., Kirchin, S., & Huxtable, R. (2004). Research ethics committee and paternalism.* Journal of Medical Ethics, 30, *88–91.*

For helpful material on significant issues related to research with children, see:

Brody, J. L., Scherer, D. G., Annett, R. D., & Pearson-Bish, M. (2003). *Voluntary assent in biomedical research with adolescents: A comparison of parent and adolescent views.* Ethics & Behavior, 13, *79–95. (finding great agreement between parent and child but in 17% of cases parents would have consented but children would have declined)*

Brooks-Gunn, J., & Rotheram-Borus, M. J. (1994). *Rights of privacy in research: Adolescents versus parents.* Ethics & Behavior, 4, *109–121.*

Fisher, C. B. (1994). *Reporting and referring research participants: Ethical challenges for investigators studying children and youth.* Ethics & Behavior, 4, *87–95.*

Fisher, C. B., Hoagwood, K., Boyce, C., Duster, T., Frank, D. A., Grisso, T., et al. (2002). *Research ethics for mental health science involving ethnic minority children and youths.* American Psychologist, 57, *1024–1040.*

Hubbard, J. A. (2005). *Eliciting and measuring children's anger in the context of their peer interactions: Ethical guidelines and practical considerations.* Ethics & Behavior, 15, *247–258.*

Miller, V. A., Drotar, D., & Kodish, E. (2004). *Children's competence for assent and consent: A review of empirical findings.* Ethics & Behavior, 14, *255–295.*

Lothen-Kline, C., Howard, D. E., Hamburger, E. K., Worrell, K. D., & Boekeloo, B. O. (2003). *Truth and consequences: Ethics, confidentiality, and disclosure in adolescent longitudinal prevention research.* Journal of Adolescent Health, 33, *385–394. (finding that adolescents who assent to participate in research may be less likely to disclose personal information, e.g., suicidal thoughts, if they know their disclosure may result in a break in confidentiality)*

Scott-Jones, D. (1994). *Ethical issues in reporting and referring in research with low-income minority children.* Ethics & Behavior, 4, *97–108.*

Sterling, C. M., & Walco, G. A. (2003). *Protection of children's rights to self-determination in research.* Ethics & Behavior, 13, *237–247.*

Underwood, M. K. (2005). *Observing anger and aggression among preadolescent girls and boys: Ethical dilemmas and practical solutions.* Ethics & Behavior, 15, *235–245.*

Yan, E. G., & Munir, K. M. (2004). *Regulatory and ethical principles in research involving children and individuals with developmental disabilities.* Ethics & Behavior, 14, *31–49.*

See, generally, Kodish, E. (2005). Ethics and research with children. New York: Oxford University Press; Institute of Medicine. (2004). The ethical conduct of clinical research involving children. Washington, DC: The National Academies Press.

For an excellent series of articles on the capacity to consent in research and treatment for the elderly, persons with schizophrenia, criminal defendants, and children, see Petrila, J. (Ed.). (2006). Capacity to consent: A snapshot of contemporary legal and clinical issues [Special issue]. Behavioral Sciences and the Law, 24(4).

The impact of the Health Insurance Portability and Accountability Act (HIPAA) on psychological practice, as noted earlier, is discussed in more detail in chapter 10. Very briefly, however, regulations effective in 2003 limit the use and release of private health information by health care providers. Fisher (2004) raised the question of the impact of HIPAA on clinical research involving minors. She concluded:

> *Psychologists conducting research involving direct delivery of services or assessments and diagnoses that will be used for a patient's treatment decisions should consider themselves covered entities [e.g., providers who transmit health information in electronic form related to financial information] under HIPAA. (p. 833) [and thus bound by the regulations]*

Fisher, C. B. (2004). *Informed consent and clinical research involving children and adolescents: Implications of the revised APA ethics code and HIPAA.* Journal of Clinical Child and Adolescent Psychology, 33, *832–839.*

A recent decision by Maryland's highest court has created great anxiety for investigators and their sponsoring institutions who do research with children. In Grimes v. Kennedy Krieger Institute, Inc., 782 A.2d 807 (Md. 2001) the court held "that in Maryland a parent . . . or other applicable surrogate, cannot consent to the participation of a child or other person under legal disability in nontherapeutic research or studies in which there is any risk of injury or damage to the health of the subject" (p. 858). In such cases, "the consent of a parent alone cannot make appropriate that which is innately, inappropriate" (p. 855). Thus, parental consent, no matter how informed, is insufficient. Furthermore, the court did not have kind things to say about institutional review boards [IRBs]. It called them "in house organs" (p. 817), "not designed, generally, to be sufficiently objective in the sense that they are as sufficiently concerned with the ethicality of the experiments they review as they are with the success of the experiment" (p. 817). This finding would surprise many researchers whose proposals have been criticized by IRBs for not following ethical guidelines.

What if the researcher is surveying responses of adolescents to a childhood depression scale and discovers that some of the respondents report they are actively considering suicide? Does the researcher have an obligation to identify them, notify their parents, or provide clinical services? For a discussion of this problem, see Bersoff, D. M., & Bersoff, D. N. (2000). Ethical issues in the collection of self-report data. In A. A. Stone, J. S. Turkkan, C. A. Bachrach, J. B. Jobe, H. S. Kurtzman, & V. S. Cain (Eds.), The science of self-report: Implications for research and practice (pp. 9–24). Mahway, NJ: Erlbaum. For differing viewpoints on the responsibility of investigators studying risky behavior in risky populations, see

Becker-Blease, K. A., & Freyd, J. J. (2006). Research participants telling the truth about their lives: The ethics of asking and not asking about abuse. American Psychologist, 61, 218–226.

Fisher, C. B., & Walker, S. (2000). Through the community looking glass: Reevaluating the ethical and policy implications of research on adolescent risk and psychopathology. Ethics & Behavior, 10, 99–118.

Hinshaw, S. P. (2005). Objective assessment of covert antisocial behavior: Predictive validity and ethical considerations. Ethics & Behavior, 15, 259–268. (discussing ethics of evoking and observing fighting and stealing in children in laboratory setting)

Margolin, G., Chien, D., Duman, S. E., Fauchier, A., Gordis, E. B., Oliver, P. H., et al. (2005). Ethical issues in couple and family research. Journal of Family Psychology, 19, 157–167.

O'Sullivan, C., & Fisher, C. B. (1997). The effect of confidentiality and reporting procedures on parent–child agreement to participate in adolescent risk research. Applied Developmental Science, 1, 187–199.

Scarr, S. (1994). Ethical problems in research on risky behaviors and risky populations. Ethics & Behavior, 4, 147–155.

For a debate on whether researchers should be mandated reporters of suspected child abuse, compare Urquiza, A. (2003, June). Yes, there should be mandated reporting for researchers; with Uttal, D. (2003, June). No, researchers should not be mandated reporters of child abuse; in Monitor on Psychology, 34, 28, 30. See also Appelbaum, P. S., & Rosenbaum, A. (1989). Tarasoff and the researcher: Does the duty to protect apply in the research setting? American Psychologist, 44, 885–894. What are the readers' views on this subject. Is it an all or none decision, or would some kinds of research, for example, research on clinical populations, warrant disclosure of these events?

Of the three requirements for legally sufficient informed consent—knowledge, voluntariness, and capacity—the issue related to children concerns competency or cognitive ability to consent. With regard to prisoners, however, as the regulations reveal, the issue is whether incarceration affects their ability to make voluntary and uncoerced decisions. See Kalmbach, K. C., & Lyons, P. M. (2003). Ethical and legal standards for research in prisons. Behavioral Sciences and the Law, 21, 671–686, for a history of the alleged abuses of prisoner-subjects, particularly in biomedical and drug research. Recently, a report by the Institute of Medicine recommended that the U.S. Department of Health and Human Services loosen its regulations to permit more testing of pharmaceutical products on prisoner populations. Does this recommendation comport with a lessening of paternalism and greater trust in prisoners' ability to evaluate for themselves the risks and benefits of volunteering in such research, or does this harken back to the era four decades ago when prisoners were taken advantage of?

Some ancillary research may shed light on this issue. Drug abuse outpatients were randomly assigned to receive payments of $10, $40, or $70 in cash or a *gift certificate for attending a 6-month follow-up assessment. Findings indicated that neither the magnitude nor mode of incentive had a significant effect on rates of new drug use or perceptions of coercion. See Festinger, D. S., Marlowe, D. B., Croft, J. R., Dugosh, K. L., Mastro, N. K., Lee, P. A., et al. (2005). Do research payments precipitate drug use or coerce participation? Drug and Alcohol Dependence, 788, 275–281.*

Despite the Maryland court's disparaging remarks about IRBs in Grimes, as the regulations show, IRBs wield significant power in determining whether biomedical and behavioral research will be approved. Although only research conducted or funded by the federal government must receive IRB review, almost all proposed institutional research now undergoes such review. Some critics have alleged that IRB members are overly cautious and are guided more by personal and sociocultural values than by valid assessments of methodological rigor, risk to participants, and benefit to society. For example, in a provocative study, Ceci, Peters, and Plotkin (1985) found that, when asked to review hypothetical research proposals identical in their proposed treatment of human participants but differing in their sociopolitical sensitivity, IRBs were twice as likely to reject the socially sensitive proposals. Nonsensitive proposals that did not include ethical problems (such as deception or the absence of debriefing) were approved 95% of the time, but comparable, sensitive ones were approved only 40%–50% of the time. On the other hand, researchers asked to judge pairs of deliberately flawed experiments that were identical except for the importance of their subject matter were significantly more likely to overlook methodological problems and to recommend publication when they perceived the topic to be important. Thus, although regulations regarding the protection of human subjects specifically instruct IRBs not to consider the public policy effects of research, these studies show that, in fact, review boards do consider the sociopolitical consequences of the proposed research. See

Ceci, S. J., Peters, D., & Plotkin, J. (1985). Human subjects review, personal values, and the regulation of social science research. American Psychologist, 40, 994–1002.

Rosnow, R. L., Rotheram-Borus, M. J., Ceci, S. J., Blanck, P. D., & Koocher, G. P. (1993). The institutional review board as a mirror of scientific and ethical standards. American Psychologist, 48, 821–826.

Wilson, T. D., DePaulo, B. M., Mook, D. G., & Klaaren, K. J. (1993). Scientists' evaluations of research: The biasing effects of the importance of the topic. Psychological Science, 4, 322–325.

More generally, there has been widespread dissatisfaction with the scrutiny by IRBs of social science research. As one set of critics summarized,

> Social scientists often argue that the federal guidelines for the protection of human participants are better suited to medical research than to SBES [social, behavioral, and economic sciences] research, and that members of IRBs are often unfamiliar with social science research methods and data files. IRBs are faulted for being overprotective, unreasonable in their demands for consent, impractical in their directives for the protection of confidentiality, and excessive in the time required for review. (p. 352)

DeVries, R., DeBruin, D. A., & Goodgame, A. (2004). Ethics review of social, behavioral, and economic research: Where should we go from here? Ethics & Behavior, 14, 351–368. See also Ashcroft, M. H., & Krause, J. A. (2007). Social and behavioral researchers' experiences with their IRB. Ethics & Behavior, 17, 1–17; DuBois, J. M. (2004). Is compliance a professional virtue of researchers? Reflections on promoting the responsible conduct of research. Ethics & Behavior, 14, 383–395.

As is the case with AIDS, research that may both benefit society by promoting human welfare and aid public health efforts to control disease may conflict with research participants' right to privacy. For example, as Melton and Gray (1988) have explained,

> disclosure of participants' status, even if simply as members of a risk group, may result in their being subjected to social stigma and legal sanctions (e.g., quarantine, punishment for engaging in prohibited risky behavior). Thus, participants may have a clear interest in avoiding participation and, if they choose to participate, preventing disclosures of data to third parties.
>
> At the same time, participants, particularly if they are patients themselves or

members of risk groups, have a profound interest in promotion of research on the illness in question. They even have an interest in retention of identifiable data when it might be used for longitudinal research or sharing of data sets crucial to understanding the process of the disease. (p. 60)

Melton, G. B., & Gray, J. N. (1988). Ethical dilemmas in AIDS research. Individual privacy and public health. *American Psychologist, 43,* 60–64.

To some extent, the disclosure of certain sensitive and confidential data gleaned from participation in government-funded mental health research may now be protected by obtaining a Confidentiality Certificate from the Department of Health and Human Services. The certificate, for which one must apply, protects researchers from the compelled disclosure of identifying information obtained from research subjects by any governmental or civil order. See 42 C.F.R. Part 2a (Protection of Identity–Research Subjects); Hoagland, K. (1994). The Certificate of Confidentiality at the National Institute of Mental Health: Discretionary considerations in its applicability in research on child and adolescent mental disorders. Ethics & Behavior, 4, 123–131.

For an informative and extended debate concerning the ethical conflict between protecting the confidentiality of research data generally and the tradition of open sharing in science, see the articles presented in the Adversary Forum of the June 1988 issue (Vol. 12) of Law and Human Behavior *(pp. 159–206) and those in the Forum section of* Ethics & Behavior *(Vol. 3, pp. 311–317). The relevant standard in the APA's 2002 Ethical Principles is 8.14 (Sharing Research Data for Verification).*

Standards 8.01 to 8.15 of the Ethical Principles now control the ethics of conducting and publishing research. Thirty years ago, however, Gergen (1973) argued that "until we can provide scientific answers to questions about deception, coercion, informed consent, and so on, strong APA policies seem unwarranted" (p. 908). See Gergen, K. J. (1973). The codification of research ethics: Views of a doubting Thomas. American Psychologist, 28, 907–912. Since then, researchers have been attempting to answer these questions.

Informed Consent for Psychological Research: Do Subjects Comprehend Consent Forms and Understand Their Legal Rights?

Traci Mann

. . .

According to the American Psychological Association (1992), psychologists must "inform participants of the nature of the research; they [must] inform participants that they are free to participate or to decline to participate or to withdraw from the research; they [must] explain the foreseeable consequences of declining or withdrawing; they [must] inform participants of significant factors that may be expected to influence their willingness to participate" (p. 1608).[1] Research subjects have to understand this information to make an informed decision about whether they wish to participate in an experiment. . . .

Even though it is unknown whether subjects comprehend consent forms, researchers continue to add more information to them. In an analysis of consent form readability, Baker and Taub (1983) found that the average length of consent forms for research in Veterans Administration hospitals doubled over the 7-year time span from 1975 to 1982. They concluded that consent forms increased in length in order to include more information about subjects' rights in accordance with federal guidelines. It is unclear, however, if these statements about rights, liability, and confidentiality are understood by research participants. Indeed, the quasi-legal language may cause research subjects to think they have signed a legal document designed to protect researchers.

This experiment compared psychology subjects' comprehension of two consent forms matched for readability level—a long, detailed form and a shorter, less detailed one. In addition, we looked specifically at the effectiveness of consent forms in conveying to subjects their legal rights by comparing subjects who had signed a consent form with subjects who had read an information sheet, but who had not signed a consent form. . . .

The data support three main conclusions. First, longer consent forms that attempt to describe a procedure fully may be comprehended less well than shorter forms that suppress some relevant details. Accordingly, federal regulations that require information to be added to already lengthy consent forms may end up reducing the amount of information subjects receive from consent forms. If a subject is to understand a consent form, the form should be as short and concise as possible.

Second, the 53 subjects who signed consent forms for an MRI scan did so without understanding important aspects of the experiment. Subjects answered only 60% of the specific questions correctly. These questions covered information crucial for deciding whether or not to participate in an experiment (e.g., risks, benefits, procedures). Because a consent is not considered valid unless the information on the consent form is understood (Beauchamp & Childress, 1989), subjects in this experiment did not give a valid consent.

In addition, subjects answered correctly only 50% of the general questions (which covered information they had presumably been exposed to in other experiments). Less than half of the subjects understood what the researchers would do for them if they got hurt, or could list even two of the four things their signature on the consent form meant. Only 39% of the subjects knew that the consent form included

From *Psychological Science, 5,* 140–143. Copyright 1994 by Wiley. Adapted with permission of the author and publisher. Tables 1–3 have been omitted.

[1]*Ed. Note:* See Standard 8.02 of the current (2002) APA Ethics Code.

any information on what to do if one had complaints about an experiment, and only 1 of the 53 subjects was able to state the procedure for registering complaints about experiments. This last problem is particularly serious because institutional review boards (IRBs) use feedback from subjects to determine whether an experiment can be continued safely. If no subjects complain when they are upset or hurt in experiments, IRBs may be led to believe that there are no problems, even when problems exist.

The third conclusion supported by the data is that the very act of signing a consent form caused subjects to believe that they had lost the right to sue the researcher, even for negligence [footnote omitted]. Subjects who signed a consent form thought they had lost their right to sue the experimenter, whereas subjects who read the same information but did not sign a consent form generally did not think they had lost this right.

According to the U.S. Department of Health and Human Services (1983), "No informed consent, whether oral or written, may include any exculpatory language through which the subject is made to waive or appear to waive any of the subject's legal rights, or releases or appears to release the investigator, the sponsor, the institution, or its agents from liability for negligence" (45 CFR §46.115). The consent forms used in this study were not in violation of this code. They stated explicitly that subjects who signed the forms were not giving up any rights to sue. Despite this explicit statement on the consent forms, subjects thought they had given up their rights to sue. To rectify this problem will require more than a statement about rights on a consent form.

This research suggests an argument for the use of oral consent procedures. . . . Perhaps subjects who consent orally but do not sign a legalistic form will not feel that they have lost their rights. Perhaps subjects simply need to be reminded after signing a consent form that they have not given up any rights by signing it, but have merely consented to go ahead with the research. . . .

References

American Psychological Association. (1992). Ethical principles of psychologists and code of conduct. *American Psychologist, 47*, 1597–1611.

Baker, M. T., & Taub, H. A. (1983). Readability of informed consent forms for research in a Veterans Administration medical center. *Journal of American Medical Association, 250*, 2646–2648.

Beauchamp, T. L., & Childress, J. F. (1989). *Principles of biomedical ethics.* New York: Oxford University Press.

U.S. Department of Health and Human Services. (1983). Protection of human subjects. *Code of Federal Regulations, 45*, §46.115.

◆   ◆   ◆

Commentary: Mann asserted that consent is not valid unless the participant understands the information in the consent form. Is this realistic and practical? In a very recent study the authors evaluated how well participants recalled consent information 2 weeks after a technician explained the informed consent procedure and then asked them to read the form to themselves as the technician read it aloud to them.

> *Results indicated that participants failed to recall over 65% of the consent information. . . . Not a single participant was able to fully relate the reasons for the study, the potential risks or benefits, their rights as a participant, or who they should contact if they have inquiries or have been harmed. (p. 16)*

Festinger, D. S., Ratanadilok, K., Marlowe, D. B., Dugosh, K. L., Patapis, N. S., & DeMatteo, D. S. (2007). Neuropsychological functioning and recall of research consent information among drug court clients. Ethics & Behavior, 17, 1–24. The question then becomes, is it the researcher's ethical obligation to ensure that participants comprehend what the form says, or is the obligation simply limited to a duty to disclose the information? What position does Standard 8.02 of the APA's 2002 Ethics Code take?

One of the most controversial topics in research is the use of deception, which inevitably requires researchers to dilute, if not completely dispense with, the requirement for informed consent from participants. In many areas of psychology, disclosing to subjects the purposes and procedures of the study would significantly alter the data. Thus, researchers may disguise or misrepresent the nature of the experiment or, in some cases, may not even inform participants that they are the subjects of research. These practices have been both pilloried and justified, but "it is clear that over time deception has become normative practice for research in social psychology" (Adair, Dushenko, & Lindsay, 1985, p. 63).

Two recent studies examined the frequency of deception research over the past 75 years. See Nicks, S. D., Korn, J. H., & Manieri, T. (1997). The rise and fall of deception in social psychology & personality research, 1921 to 1994. Ethics & Behavior, 7, 69–77; Sieber, J. E., Iannuzzo, R., & Rodriguez, B. (1995). Deception methods in psychology: Have they changed in 23 years? Ethics & Behavior, 5, 67–85. Sieber et al. found that

> *Uses of confederates and other kinds of role deception [used in the 1960s] tended to be replaced by uses of computers and other kinds of bogus devices to provide false impressions to subjects. Research generally requiring deception, prevalent in 1969, tended to be supplemented extensively with research in areas such as socialization, personality, sex differences, environmental psychology, and attribution, where the use of deception is often unnecessary. However, by 1992, the percentage of deception studies conducted in these five areas increased to 37% as compared to 22% in 1986, and the percentage of deception studies conducted in the rest of the areas increased to 55%, as compared to 44% in 1986. (p. 82)*

Nevertheless, Adair et al. found that, for the studies they examined, researchers rarely reported on matters related to ethics, including informed consent and their attempts to debrief participants about the real purposes

of the experiment after it was concluded. But they agreed with others that psychological research . . . [should] be guided by neither methodological imperialism, in which the dignity and safety of the subject are disregarded in the interests of science, nor an ethical imperialism, in which research progress is thwarted at every turn by an obsession with individual rights. (p. 70)

See Adair, J. G., Dushenko, T. W., & Lindsay, R. C. L. (1985). Ethical regulations and their impact on research practice. American Psychologist, 40, 59–72.

Yet, Diana Baumrind (1985), perhaps the major critic of this position, has adamantly argued that "the use of intentional deception in the research setting is unethical, imprudent, and unwarranted scientifically" (p. 165) and that "effective debriefing does not nullify the wrong done participants . . . and may not even repair their damaged self-image or ability to trust adult authorities" (p. 172). See Baumrind, D. (1985). Research using intentional deception: Ethical issues revisited. American Psychologist, 40, 165–174. But as Fisher (2005) pointed out

> *The requirements of APA . . . Standard 8.07a paradoxically encourage research psychologists to resolve the ethical tension between their fiduciary responsibility to produce scientifically valid data and their obligation to respect the autonomy and privacy rights of research participants by privileging the former. This bias toward the value of scientifically valid and valuable knowledge over individual autonomy reflects the utilitarian meta-ethical values ubiquitous in Western science. . . . (p. 275)*

Fisher, C. B. (2005). Deception research involving children: Ethical practices and paradoxes. Ethics & Behavior, 15, 271–287.

Deception Methods in Psychology: Have They Changed in 23 Years?

Joan E. Sieber, Rebecca Iannuzzo, and Beverly Rodriguez

. . .

WHEN IS DECEPTION ETHICALLY OBJECTIONABLE OR HARMFUL?

. . .

Kind of Failure to Inform

Deception in research involves some kind of failure to inform (e.g., there may be no informing, false informing, or consent to possible deception). Some approaches to not informing are less objectionable ethically and less likely to harm subjects than are other approaches. Indeed, ethically sensitive researchers have developed approaches to not informing that are highly respectful of subjects' autonomy; these are the first three approaches described in the following list. One would hope that these approaches are becoming more widely used. The basic kinds of noninforming are as follows:

1. *Informed consent* to participate in one of several specified conditions without knowing which condition will actually occur (as in placebo studies).
2. *Consent to deception*, in which subjects are warned that some deception may occur. They are told what events they will experience if they agree to participate in the study and are debriefed completely about the purpose of the study afterward.
3. *Waiver of right to be informed*, in which subjects waive informing but are not explicitly forewarned of the possibility of deception.
4. *Consent and false informing*, in which subjects believe they are engaging in a truthful informed consent procedure, but are actually misinformed about some aspect of the nature of the research.

5. *No informing, no consent*, in which subjects do not know that they are participating in research.
6. *Self-deception*, in which the aim of the research is so different from what subjects expect that they behave under incorrect assumptions. For example, in incidental learning experiments, subjects are given a task such as learning pairs of non-sense syllables and are then tested on some attribute of the syllables such as their color.
7. *Deception by a third party*, in which the researcher observes a relationship in which someone deceives someone else; for example, in research on "therapeutic privilege" the researcher would observe physicians lying to patients when the physician believes that the truth would be harmful.

The last four approaches to deception seem more objectionable than the first three—but why? The following are ethical objections (as opposed to actual harms) that seem most pertinent to one or more of these kinds of deception:

1. *Invasion of privacy*. The researcher extracts kinds of information that subjects might not wish to reveal.
2. *No informing*. Subjects are not told what to expect regarding procedures or risks.
3. *No self-determination*. Subjects do not have an opportunity to decide whether to participate in the study.
4. *No debriefing*. The researcher does not explain the deception after the study is completed (and indeed it may be imprudent for him or her to do so).
5. *Researcher lies*. The researcher actively falsifies or misrepresents pertinent information.
6. *Researcher conceals pertinent information.*

From *Ethics & Behavior*, 5, 67–85. Available at http://www.informaworld.com. Copyright 1995 by Taylor & Francis. Adapted with permission of the author and publisher.

[T]he last four approaches to deception are indeed more likely to be ethically objectionable than are the first three. These strong forms of deception deny people the right of self-determination. In contrast, the weaker forms of deception provide varying degrees of accurate information and are respectful of autonomy.

. . .

Topic of the Deception

Subjects may be deceived about various kinds of things:

1. They may be given, or be caused to hold, false information about the main purpose of the study.
2. They may be given false information concerning stimulus materials (bogus devices). . . .
3. The use of a confederate may cause them to misunderstand the actual role of some individual (role deception).
4. They may be given false feedback about themselves.
5. They may be given false feedback about another person.
6. They may be kept unaware of being subjects in research.
7. They may be unaware that a study was in progress at the time of manipulation or measurement, or unaware of being measured (e.g., video-taped).
8. Two related studies may be presented as unrelated.

None of these deceptive events is necessarily unethical or harmful; for example, the popular TV show *Candid Camera* employed all of these devices and was not regarded by the public as wrong or harmful. But in conjunction with certain other aspects of deception, these deceptive events may be harmful or unethical.

Debriefing

Finally, the deception and its effects may be undone or not. Debriefing has two possible parts. *Dehoaxing* means explaining what really happened. *Desensitizing* means removing any emotional harm, thus returning the person to at least as good a condition as before the study. Unfortunately, dehoaxing is not always possible, feasible, or harmless, and it is not always obvious what emotional harm remains or how to remove it. . . .

Deception in Research: Distinctions and Solutions From the Perspective of Utilitarianism

David J. Pittenger

The use of deception has and continues to be a controversial topic in the behavioral sciences, especially psychology. . . . Authors on both sides of this argument tend to directly or indirectly appeal to the principles of utilitarianism to justify their conclusions. Indeed, Baumrind (1985), in her appeal to a utilitarian resolution of the debate, characterized deontological ethical theories as "too dogmatic" (p. 167).

The problem that psychologists face is the fact that the ethical guidelines of the American Psychological Association (APA, 1992) are an attempt to simultaneously reconcile utilitarian and deontological ethical values. For example, Standard 6.15[1] of the APA's ethical principles (1992) provides a utilitarian ethical perspective that permits researchers to use deception. Specifically, to use deceptive practices, the researcher must demonstrate the merit of the anticipated results, that there are no reasonable alternatives for obtaining the data, that potential participants receive an accurate account of the risks involved in the research, and that the researcher debrief the participants at the conclusion of the study. In contrast, Principle D requires that psychologists "respect the rights of individuals to . . . self-determination and autonomy" (p. 1599). This principle represents a deontological ethical perspective, as it establishes, a priori, the value of preserving the autonomy of the individual and does not consider the consequences of applying the principle as a general rule.

The problem is that these principles express conflicting ethical theories for evaluating the permissibility of deception. The first principle represents a teleological perspective, as it determines the permissibility of deception by focusing on the consequences of deception. As such, the utilitarian perspective makes the use of deception in psychological research permissible as long as the ends justify the means. The second principle, which is clearly deontological, establishes as a prior fact that the individual's right to autonomy is a primary ethical claim. Consequently, deception is impermissible in any context to the extent that it violates one's claim to autonomy.

Unfortunately, neither the current nor the proposed APA ethical guidelines provide a clear resolution to the conundrum created by the conflicting principles. Indeed, other parts of the guidelines appear to further confuse the issue. As an example, the preamble of both the current and proposed guidelines (APA, 1992, 2001) imply that psychologists strive to learn more about the causes of behavior and to use this knowledge to improve the quality of life for all people. The values expressed in this ideal suggest that deception is permissible to the extent that it increases knowledge and improves the quality of life of others. At the same time, the preamble requires that psychologists respect the civil and human rights of all people, thus negating the permissibility of deception to the extent that deception denies individuals of their right to be free of a researcher's coercion. Therefore, psychologists continue to face the conflict created by the want to conduct research for which participant deception is the only means of collecting valid data and the want to respect the individual's right to autonomy.

. . . With regard to deception, I believe that psychologists can find a suitable resolution to the conflict between the utilitarian perspective that would allow deception in research and the deontological perspective that would prohibit its use. The result will be a

From *Ethics & Behavior, 12*, 117–142. Available at http://www.informaworld.com. Copyright 2002 by Taylor & Francis. Adapted with permission of the author and publisher.

[1]*Ed. Note:* See Standard 8.07 of the current (2002) APA Ethics Code.

more consistent set of guidelines that protect the researcher's need to use deception in limited circumstances and the researcher's requirement to protect the autonomy of the research participants.

. . .

I focus on the utilitarian ethical theory for the simple reason that it is a ubiquitous feature in the APA ethical guidelines. . . . Utilitarianism is also the standard by which institutional review boards (IRBs) evaluate the appropriateness of research proposals. The federal regulations that govern the protection of human participants (Protection of Human Subjects, 1991) require that researchers justify their research procedures by demonstrating that the benefits to the participants and society outweigh the costs to the participants.

. . .

STUDYING DECEPTION

An essential element of rule utilitarianism is the opportunity to revisit and revise a practice, having considered the consequences of its application. What is paradoxical for psychology is the dearth of available evidence regarding the consequences of using deception in psychological research. Direct empirical research on the consequences of deception is sparse and does not offer the same level of insight afforded by more mature programs of empirical research. Although there have been fluctuations in the use of deception during the past 30 years (e.g., Nicks, Korn, & Mainieri, 1997; Sieber, Iannuzzo, & Rodriguez, 1995), deception of one form or another is still a component of many types of psychological research and shows no sign of abatement. Indeed, as Sieber et al. (1995) suggested, fluctuations in the use of deception in research appear to reflect trends in the phenomena and theories that psychologists chose to study rather than concerns for the ethical permissibility of deception.

Presently, there are three interesting circumstances regarding deception. First, the use of deception in research is a controversial topic and one that regulatory agencies require researchers to confront. Second, the use of deception in research continues as a common practice. Third, researchers who use deception do not typically examine the consequences of their techniques.

The available research on participant's reactions to deception reveals that the dire threats to the profession predicted by Baumrind (1985) and Kelman (1967) have not materialized. Similarly, there is no evidence that former participants have sought sanctions against researchers who used deception as a part of a study. In addition, several research teams (e.g., Collins, Kuhn, & King, 1979; Fisher & Fyrberg, 1994; Korn, 1987) indicated that prospective participants do not find many commonly used deception procedures objectionable. Moreover, prospective participants appear to appreciate the need for deception and find that the cost–benefit ratio of prototypical psychological research favors the data produced by the study.

Other research raises further doubts regarding participants' negative reactions to researchers' use of deception. For example, Smith and Richardson (1983) reported that college students who participated in research using deception perceived the study as more enjoyable than research that did not use deception. In addition, Richardson, Pegalis, and Britton (1992) reported that students had more positive reactions to their participation in research if they engaged in an elaborate debriefing procedure that included writing an essay that examined the purpose of the research.

More recently, Epley and Huff (1998) found little evidence of negative reaction to participation in a study that used deception. Regarding Kelman's (1967) concern that using deception will tarnish the reputation of the profession, Epley and Huff found that their participants did express a short-lived suspicion of future psychological research but did not harbor ill will for the researcher or question the integrity of the profession.

Although these observations appear to alleviate several concerns regarding participants' reactions to deception, they should not be used as an excuse to become sanguine about the continued use of deception. For example, Patton (1977) criticized Milgram's (1974) account of the participants' generally positive reaction to their participation in the obedience studies. Specifically, Patton questioned the credibility of the participants' evaluation of the research by pointing out that these were the people who had acquiesced to the will of the experimenter and had continued to deliver obviously painful shocks to another person. Patton speculated that the participants' positive evaluation of the research could be further evidence of their supplication to the researcher. In terms familiar to psychologists, the participants' positive reactions may reflect their attempt to reduce cognitive dissonance, preserve their definition of self, or both. Thus, research that attempts to examine participants' reactions to deception may require techniques that control for these alternative explanations. Similarly, such research should ensure a sufficiently broad sample of participants and representative deceptive practices.

. . .

Given the expressed concern for the well-being of the participants in the APA ethical guidelines, it is interesting that little is written about the participants' conditions in the typical experiment that incorporates deception. In the conventional research article, the authors will describe in detail the deceptive procedures and the manipulation checks used to ensure that the deception worked, yet provide little or no information regarding the procedures used for the dehoaxing and desensitization process. Correspondingly, it is also noteworthy that researchers rarely, if ever, report the participant's reactions to learning about the deception. Therefore, even if deception were to have negative consequences for the participant, this information may be systematically withheld from the research community (see Oliansky, 1991, for a rare negative report of the consequences of deception). As a result, psychologists have meager empirical information with which to evaluate the effectiveness of the ethical guidelines as a mechanism for limiting the risks to those who participate in the research.

Therefore, I propose that psychologists who conduct research that includes ethically sensitive practices describe in their published reports the ethical rationale for their procedures, the methods used to minimize the harm the participants experienced, the methods used to dehoax and desensitize participants, and the participants' reactions to the deception. . . .

By expanding the scope of the methods and results sections of empirical articles, we will be able to address one of Sieber's (1944) criticisms of the APA's ethical guidelines. Specifically, Sieber critiqued Standard 6.06(d)[2]—that psychologists take reasonable

steps to implement appropriate protections for the rights and welfare of human participants, other persons affected by the research, and the welfare of animal subjects—because the standard is neither educational nor enforceable.

Although the proposed ethical guidelines (APA, 2001) dispense with most of Standard 6, the revisions do not directly address Sieber's (1994) criticism. Indeed, the proposed guidelines continue to use language that is difficult to define, establish principles that cannot be easily enforced, and fail to help readers learn how they might best resolve ethical dilemmas. This problem stems from the fact that the guidelines use broad modifiers, such as *reasonable* and *appropriate,* to describe how psychologists use their professional judgment to determine an ethical course of action in ambiguous situations. The intent of using such modifiers is to eliminate inequities in a practice, generalize to many situations, avoid rigid legalisms, and afford "moral growth in the field" (p. 79). This tactic does little to help one determine how psychologists are to learn what is reasonable and appropriate, or whether they have acted reasonably or appropriately.

. . .

There are at least three potential objections to the requirements I have outlined: (a) It creates an unnecessary burden for the researcher; (b) it fills the journals with superfluous information; and (c) it creates the misperception that the participants' reactions create an ipso facto justification for the use of deception. These concerns may be dispatched, given the following observations.

To begin, the APA ethical guidelines grant the permissibility of deception as a practice, assuming that the intended benefits of the deception are greater than its costs. In addition, because the guidelines require researchers to preserve the participant's well-being, it is incumbent on the researcher to demonstrate in the research proposal and in the final research report that he or she has fulfilled this duty. Also, as I argued previously, including such information is not superfluous to the extent that it provides the community of researchers with objective information regarding the real hazards experienced by participants and the effectiveness of various protections and remedies.

---

[2]*Ed. Note:* Note this standard was deleted in the current (2002) APA Ethics Code.

DETERMINING THE SCOPE OF DECEPTIVE PRACTICES

Regarding deception, I believe that there are four broad features of deception that researchers should weigh when planning their research. These features are (a) the message contained in the false feedback, (b) the type of information withheld by the researcher, (c) the participant's claim to privacy, and (d) the social desirability of the behavior evoked by the dissembling technique. These features cover a broad array of research procedures, and each can be presented as a continuum that ranges from little or no harm to serious harm.

The false feedback feature includes any research procedure that provides participants information that is contrived by the researcher. . . . The potential ethical objection to this feature increases as content of the false message is more harmful to the individual. Specifically, the cost of this procedure increases as the content of the false feedback indicates that the person expresses socially undesirable behaviors, suffers a particular pathological condition, or similar information that would devalue the self-worth of the person.

Withholding information can include the obvious omissions of relevant details as well as provide a cover story that is a subterfuge used to prevent the participant from attending to or learning about specific features of the study. As with the false-feedback procedure, the objection to withholding information increases as the details shift from concealing general aspects of the research design (e.g., whether the individual is in a control or experimental group) to withholding information regarding risks of participating in the study.

The researcher also needs to consider the participant's claim to privacy, with the critical dimension being the degree to which the dependent variable is a generally public, private, or secret component of the person. Although there is nothing inherently wrong in asking a person to disclose information that most would consider private (e.g., frequency of sexual encounters) or secret (e.g., performance of an illegal act), the objection arises when participants are coerced to reveal such information through the researcher's ruse.

Finally, the researcher should consider the social desirability of the behavior evoked by the manipulations. The potential for objections to a deceptive technique increases as it evokes socially undesirable behaviors, especially as the individual is more likely to regret the act and resent being duped. It is also possible that people may resent being tricked into engaging in a prosocial behavior; however, without sufficient evidence, these concerns remain speculative.

. . . By making specific reference to these features of deception, the ethical code of conduct will be better able to offer guidance to researchers regarding the levels of threat to the well-being of the research participant that can be tolerated by the research community.

The changes I have recommended do shift attention away from the utility of individual acts and to the permissibility of practices. As such, the debate focuses on the costs and benefits of broad practices. These changes have not, however, resolved the lingering conflict between two perspectives regarding deception. The first perspective is that deception is unacceptable to the extent that it conflicts with the participants' right to autonomy, as it allows the researcher to surreptitiously control participants' behavior (cf. Baumrind, 1985). The second perspective is that deception is not prima facie immoral and that there are conditions within behavioral research when it is acceptable (cf. Sieber et al., 1995; Wendler, 1996).

. . .

Refinement of the APA's ethical code of conduct may do much to justify the practice of deception within a utilitarian context. The points that I have made thus far, if incorporated into the ethical guidelines, would help psychologists better understand the parameters of the practice of deception. In addition, the recommended procedures would allow the APA to better monitor the consequences of the practice. These changes alone cannot, however, resolve the fact that the APA condones deception as a practice and thus violates its own imperative that people not be treated as a means to an end. Therefore, I propose to review a complementary option that revises the informed consent agreement that researchers use when deception is a part of the research.

EXPANDING THE SCOPE OF INFORMED CONSENT

One way to overcome the lingering problem of the permissibility of deception in research is to change the informed consent agreement. Wendler (1996) recommended that researchers inform potential participants that deception will be used in the research as a part of the process of obtaining informed consent. In other words, as a practice, researchers would treat participants in a study that uses deception as if they were in a study that uses a placebo treatment. . . . As an example, Wendler (1996) recommended the following passage:

> You should be aware that, in order to complete this study, the investigator cannot inform you of all its details. For this reason, certain details have been left out of the description of the study. However, the investigator will be happy to explain these details to you [later]. In addition, you are free to choose not to participate if you do not like the use of deception, or for any other reason. (p. 105)

In justifying this modification, Wendler (1996) described how the revised informed consent procedure addresses the ethical problem with intentional deception. The primary benefit of this procedure is that it ensures the autonomy of the participants. By admitting to the incomplete description of the research, the researcher has fulfilled the obligation to inform the participants of all reasonable risks that may be encountered in the study. As an aside, this procedure probably confirms what most participants expect when volunteering for a psychology experiment—that there is more to the research than meets the eye. Because many researchers already conduct manipulation checks and other procedures to ensure that the participants responded to the critical variables in the design of the study, it seems reasonable to expect that researchers will continue to determine whether the participants correctly recognized the ruse used in the study.

As Wendler (1996) argued, there are two reasons to believe that participants will not be harmed when researchers use the enhanced informed consent procedure. First, use of deception within the context of informed consent does not free researchers from the obligation to mitigate harms created by the deceptive practices. Researchers will still have to demonstrate that the risks of the research protocol are minimal and that the participants understand the gravity of these risks. Second, if the ethical guidelines better articulate the types of deception that can and cannot be used and the boundaries of acceptable risks, then participants will be reasonably protected from objectionable harm.

The primary goal of the enhanced informed consent agreement is to resolve the conflict between the deontological concern for the fundamental rights of research participants and the want to permit circumscribed use of deception. Adopting this requirement will allow the APA to maintain its commitment that researchers respect the autonomy of research participants while allowing researchers the ability to use deception in research when necessary.

Although this practice resolves the deontological concern for the rights of the participants, we can, nevertheless, examine the consequences of the practice from the perspective of utilitarianism. The primary benefit is that the revised informed consent procedure preserves the autonomy of individuals who participate in psychological research and their right to informed consent. The practice also preserves deception as a research procedure that researchers may find indispensable in some circumstances.

The cost of this practice can only be imagined, as there is scant empirical evidence that allows researchers to determine the consequence of adopting this guideline. An obvious objection would be that alerting participants to the potential of deception would confound the results of the study. Participants in such a study may become distracted by their attempt to determine how the researcher is deceiving them. This may well be a valid threat to the integrity of behavioral research. Nevertheless, one would need to show that informing participants of the potential for deception creates a greater level of distraction than experienced by the typical research participant who may already be suspicious of the research's motives.

References

American Psychological Association. (1992). Ethical principles of psychologists and code of conduct. *American Psychologist, 47*, 1597–1611.

American Psychological Association. (2001). Ethical principles of psychologists and code of conduct: Draft for comment. *Monitor on Psychology, 32*(2), 76–89.

Baumrind, D. (1985). Research using intentional deception: Ethical issues revisited. *American Psychologist, 40*, 165–174.

Collins, F. L., Kuhn, I. F., & King, G. D. (1979). Variables affecting subjects' ethical ratings of proposed experiments. *Psychological Reports, 44*, 155–164.

Epley, N., & Huff, C. (1998). Suspicion, affective response, and educational benefit as a result of deception in psychology research. *Personality & Social Psychology Bulletin, 24*, 759–768.

Fisher, C. B., & Fyrberg, D, (1994). Participant partners: College students weigh the costs and benefits of deceptive research. *American Psychologist, 49*, 417–427.

Kelman, H. C. (1967). Human use of human subjects: The problem of deception in social psychological experiments. *Psychological Bulletin, 67*, 1–11.

Korn, J. H. (1987). Judgments of acceptability of deception in psychological research. *Journal of General Psychology, 114*, 205–216.

Milgram, S. (1974). *Obedience to authority*. New York: Harper & Row.

Nicks, S. D., Korn, J. H., & Mainieri, T. (1997). The rise and fall of deception in social psychology and personality research, 1921 to 1994. *Ethics & Behavior 7*, 69–77.

Oliansky, A. (1991). A confederate's perspective on deception. *Ethics & Behavior 1*, 848–852.

Patton, S. C. (1977). The case that Milgram makes. *The Philosophical Review, 86*, 350–364.

Protection of Human Subjects, 56 Fed. Reg. 28003, C.F.R. § 46.101–§ 46.409 (1991).

Richardson, D. R., Pegalis, L., & Britton, B. (1992). A technique for enhancing the value of research participation. *Contemporary Social Psychology, 16*, 11–13.

Sieber, J. E. (1994). Will the new code help researchers to be more ethical? *Professional Psychology: Research and Practice, 25*, 369–375.

Sieber, J. E., Iannuzzo, R., & Rodriguez, B. (1995). Deception methods in psychology: Have they changed in 23 years? *Ethics & Behavior, 5*, 67–85.

Smith, S., & Richardson, D. (1983). Amelioration of deception and harm in psychological research: The important role of debriefing. *Journal of Personality & Social Psychology, 44*, 1075–1082.

Wendler, D. (1996). Deception in medical and behavioral research: Is it ever acceptable? *The Milbank Quarterly, 74*, 87–114.

◆   ◆   ◆

Commentary: For further debate over whether psychology ought to ban deception outright, compare

Broder A. (1998). Deception can be acceptable. American Psychologist, 53, 805–806.

Kimmel, A. J. (1998). In defense of deception. American Psychologist, 53, 803–805.

Korn, J. H. (1998). The reality of deception. American Psychologist, 53, 805.

Ortmann, A., & Hertwig, R. (1997). Is deception acceptable? American Psychologist, 52, 746–747.

Ortmann, A., & Hertwig, R. (1998). The question remains: Is deception acceptable? American Psychologist, 53, 806–807.

In light of the preceding material, it would be helpful to review the Ethical Principles that address consent and deception in psychological research (see Standards 8.02, 8.04, 8.05, and 8.07). Which side of the "scientist versus humanist" ledger do these provisions fall on? Do they address Baumrind's concerns? If you were contemplating doing research that involved deception, would these standards be an adequate guide to help you avoid ethical pitfalls? In this regard how relevant is this comment? "[E]thics can represent a thoughtful, and sometimes courageous, commitment to creating trustworthy human relationships within our research enterprise. . . . What makes research 'ethical' is not a characteristic of the design or procedures, but of our individual decisions, actions, relationships, and commitments" (pp. 146–147). Haverkamp, B. E. (2005). Ethical perspectives on qualitative research in applied psychology. Journal of Counseling Psychology, 52, 146–155.

Designing and conducting psychotherapy research presents special ethical problems, particularly because scientific rigor may conflict with clinical care. A prime example is the controlled clinical trial in which some groups may receive placebo treatment or no treatment at all. The brief excerpt next provides an introduction to the ethical dilemmas that arise when conducting clinical trials.

Informed Consent and Deception in Psychotherapy Research: An Ethical Analysis

Richard T. Lindsey

. . .

One the most problematic of ethical dilemmas . . . is the use of "placebos" in counseling and clinical research. Placebos, by definition, are inert and not expected or designed to do anything really helpful for the subject. By contrast, when people enter treatment and develop a contract with a therapist/agency, it is with the understanding they will receive an active treatment designed to help them. If clients are given a placebo in place of the active treatment they seek, that contract is violated. In addition, if and when clients discover that they have received a placebo rather than the active treatment they sought, they may feel angered and betrayed by a profession committed to their betterment. As a result, their autonomous choice is violated by using inaccurate and insufficient information. The principle of nonmaleficence is also violated because the possibility of deterioration in the absence of psychotherapy cannot be eliminated. Finally, the principle of beneficence is violated, for they may be no better after "treatment" than before. These ethical violations would be all the more severe in cases where effective alternative forms of treatment were available (O'Leary & Borkovec, 1978). These arguments could hold for no-treatment control groups as well.

It is important to point out that there do seem to be alternative designs available that could be used in place of placebos and no-treatment control groups. For example, O'Leary and Borkovec (1978) argue that since placebo conditions are difficult to create, researchers ought to compare a treatment of interest with an alternative treatment which also appears to be effective for a problem.

As long as two treatments are equated for duration of contact time and other nonspecific variables, and as long as independent assessments . . . indicate equivalent generation of expectancy for improvement through the treatment trial, such a design provides control for some of the usual factors addressed by placebo conditions. (p. 826)

Also, by replacing control groups with comparison groups, as O'Leary and Borkovec have argued ought to be done for placebo groups, we avoid the ethical problem of leaving some clients without treatment who stand in need of it.

The one exception to this procedure would be in situations where resources are scarce, such that the relatively large number of clients needing treatment exceed the available psychotherapists. In such a situation, to randomly assign some to no-treatment control groups would be ethically acceptable (Stricker, 1982).

By using comparison groups, the assignment of clients to the various treatment groups becomes important. It would seem that randomization is the wisest choice, with each client being informed that s/he will be randomly assigned to one of a number of treatments, each of which is viewed as potentially capable of being helpful (Stricker, 1982; O'Leary & Borkovec, 1978). The clients could then make an informed choice (O'Leary & Borkovec, 1978) as to whether they would be willing to be randomly assigned or not. At the conclusion of the study, if one particular method proved to be the more effective treatment, then it could be offered to members of the other treatment groups if they still needed assistance (Stricker, 1982). . . .

References

O'Leary, K. D., & Borkovec, T. D. (1978). Conceptual, methodological, and ethical problems of placebo groups in psychotherapy research. *American Psychologist, 33,* 821–830.

Stricker, G. (1982). Ethical issues in psychotherapy research. In M. Rosenbaum (Ed.), *Ethics and values in psychotherapy: A guidebook* (pp. 403–424). New York: Free Press.

◆　　◆　　◆

Commentary: For a more extensive exploration of ethical problems in conducting not only controlled clinical trials but also collaborative research among several institutional sites, see Imber, S. D., Glanz, L. M., Elkin, E., Sotsky, S. M., Boyer, J. L., & Leber, W. R. (1986). Ethical issues in psychotherapy research. American Psychologist, 41, *137–146. They describe a multisite collaborative investigation in which a clinical trials design was used to evaluate the effectiveness and safety of two forms of brief psychotherapy for depression (cognitive–behavioral therapy and interpersonal therapy) in comparison with the administration of imipramine (psychopharmacological medication) and a placebo-controlled condition. What ethical problems are raised by such a protocol? What are the potential conflicts among the demands of science, the traditional reliance on professional judgment, and the ultimate responsibility for patient welfare? In what ways are these problems exacerbated by the fact that, in the Imber et al. example, the patients were depressed? Read the entire article for a helpful discussion of these rarely analyzed questions. For more recent material on this important topic see*

Fleetwood, J. (2001). *Conflicts of interest in clinical research: Advocating for patient–subjects.* Widener Law Symposium Journal, 8, *105–114.*

Street, L., & Luoma, J. (Eds.). (2002). *Control groups in psychosocial intervention research [Special issue].* Ethics & Behavior, 12(1).

There are also many well-regarded texts that address the issues introduced in this chapter in a more detailed and comprehensive way. The following are just a few examples:

Boruch, R. F., & Ceci, J. S. (1983). Solutions to ethical and legal problems in social research: Quantitative studies in social relations. *San Diego, CA: Academic Press.*

Chatain, G., & Landrum, R. (1999). Protecting human subjects: Departmental subject pools and institutional review boards. *Washington, DC: American Psychological Association.*

Elliott, D., & Stern, J. E. (Eds.). (1997). Research ethics: A reader. *Hanover, NH: University Press of New England.*

Kimmel, A. J. (1988). Ethics and values in applied social research. *Newbury Park, CA: Sage.*

Levine, R. J. (1988). Ethics and regulation of clinical research (2nd ed.). *New Haven, CT. Yale University Press.*

Miller, D. J., & Hersen, M. (1992). Research fraud in the behavioral and biomedical sciences. *New York: Wiley.*

Sales, B., & Folkman, S. (Eds.). (2000). Ethics in research with human participants. *Washington, DC: American Psychological Association.*

Sieber, J. E. (1992). Planning ethically responsible research: A guide for students and internal review boards. *Newbury Park, CA: Sage.*

For timely news, updates, and resources regarding scientific ethics, see Professional Ethics Report *published by the American Association for the Advancement of Science.*

Certain behaviors in carrying out research may also lead to legal liability as well as scrutiny by ethics bodies. For a review of civil and criminal penalties, see:

Kuzma, S. M. (1992). *Criminal liability for misconduct in scientific research.* University of Michigan Journal of Law Reform, 25, 357–421.

Sise, C. B. (1991). *Scientific misconduct in academia: A survey and analysis of applicable law.* San Diego Law Review, 28, 401–428.

Of interest is that both articles begin with a discussion of the case of Stephen Bruening, a psychologist, who was indicted and pled guilty to two counts of false grant statements, a federal crime.

In contemplating all the issues raised in this chapter so far it may be well to keep in mind philosopher Hans Jonas's provocative statement:

> *Let us not forget that progress is an optional goal, not an unconditional commitment, and that its tempo in particular, compulsive as it may become, has nothing sacred about it. Let us also remember that a slower progress in the conquest of disease would not threaten society, grievous as it is to those who have to deplore that their particular disease is not yet conquered, but that society would indeed be*

threatened by the erosion of those moral values whose loss, possibly caused by too ruthless a pursuit of scientific progress, would make its most dazzling triumphs not worth having. (p. 28)

Jonas, H. (1970). Philosophical reflections on experimenting with human subjects. In P. Freund (Ed.), Experimentation with human subjects *(pp. 1–31).* New York: Braziller.

In this regard, how relevant is this comment? "[E]thics can represent a thoughtful and sometimes courageous commitment to creating trustworthy human relationships within our research enterprise. . . . What makes research 'ethical' is not a characteristic of the design or procedures, but of our individual decisions, actions, relationships, and commitments" (pp. 146–147). Haverkamp, B. E. (2005). Ethical perspectives on qualitative research in applied psychology. Journal of Counseling Psychology, *52, 146–155.*

McConnell and Kerbs (1993) have offered this reminder:

> *Successful research with human subjects depends on the cooperation of potential subjects and the organizations which they are affiliated with as clients, staff, or administrators. Maintaining viable subject pools requires that researchers be viewed positively by both subjects and nonresearch professionals who are involved in the research process. This is accomplished by adherence to human-subject requirements, including providing appropriate feedback in a timely way. (p. 269)*

See McConnell, W. A., & Kerbs, J. J. (1993). Providing feedback in research with human subjects. Professional Psychology: Research and Practice, *24, 266–270. Yet, they and others have complained that subjects (both those included in the experiment and those screened out by preexperimental procedures), institutions in which the research is conducted, and funding agencies often do not receive information about the results of research. Only a few have viewed this as an ethical issue. In addition to McConnell and Kerbs (1993), see*

Gurman, E. B. (1994). Debriefing for all concerned: Ethical treatment of human subjects. Psychological Science, *5, 139.*

Sieber, J. E., & Saks, M. J. (1989). A census of subject pool characteristics and policies. American Psychologist, *44, 1053–1061.*

An extremely important emerging issue is the use of the Internet to conduct research. As a report of a workshop sponsored by the American Association for the Advancement of Science (AAAS) acknowledged, "Internet research raises a number of complex issues for the scientific community, research subjects, and policy makers" (p. 15). Frankel, M. S., & Siang, S. (1999, June). Ethical and legal aspects of human subjects research on the Internet: A report of a workshop. Retrieved from http://www.aaas.org/spp/dspp/sfrl/projects/intres/main.htm. The next excerpt addresses the complexities.

Psychological Research Online: Report of Board of Scientific Affairs' Advisory Group on the Conduct of Research on the Internet

Robert Kraut, Judith Olson, Mahzarin Banaji, Amy Bruckman, Jeffrey Cohen, and Mick Couper

The Internet and the widespread diffusion of personal computing have the potential for unparalleled impact on the conduct of psychological research, changing the way psychologists collaborate, collect data, and disseminate their results. In this article, we focus on the way the Internet is changing the process of empirical research, identifying both opportunities and challenges. The Internet presents empirical researchers with tremendous opportunities. It lowers many of the costs of collecting data on human behavior, allowing researchers, for example, to run online experiments involving thousands of subjects with minimal intervention on the part of experimenters (Nosek, Banaji, & Greenwald, 2002b). Internet chat rooms and bulletin boards provide a rich sample of human behavior that can be mined for studies of communication (Galegher, Sproull, & Kiesler, 1998), prejudice (Glaser, Dixit, & Green, 2002), organizational behavior (Orlikowski, 2000), or diffusion of innovation (Kraut, Rice, Cool, & Fish, 1998), among other topics. The Internet is also a crucible for observing new social phenomena, such as the behavior of very large social groups (Sproull & Faraj, 1995), distributed collaboration (Hinds & Kiesler, 2002), and identity switching (Turkle, 1997). These phenomena are interesting in their own right and have the potential to challenge traditional theories of human behavior.

At the same time, the Internet raises concerns about data quality and the treatment of research subjects. Researchers often lose control over the context in which data are procured when subjects participate in experiments online. Ensuring informed consent, explaining instructions, and conducting effective debriefings online may be more difficult than in traditional laboratory settings.

Observations in chat rooms and bulletin boards raise difficult questions about risks to subjects, including privacy and lack of informed consent.

This article will discuss both the advantages and the challenges associated with conducting psychological research online. We think the problems in conducting research online can be mastered, and we close with recommendations directed toward both the researcher and the institutional review boards (IRBs) that oversee the protection of human research subjects.

[*Ed. Note:* Sections on opportunities for Internet research and the problem of data quality have been omitted.]

. . .

CHALLENGES OF INTERNET RESEARCH: PROTECTION OF HUMAN SUBJECTS

[C]onducting research online can affect human subjects and the actions that researchers must take to protect their welfare. We believe that online research poses no more risk to human subjects than comparable research conducted through other means, but conducting research online changes the nature of the risks and investigators' ability to assess it. Some of the challenges arise because fundamental concepts that underlie federal regulation for the protection of human subjects, such as the concept of minimal risk and public behavior, change or become ambiguous when research is conducted online. Other challenges arise because it is more difficult to assess subjects' identities or their reactions to the research experience online.

. . .

Identifiable Versus Anonymous Information

Determining whether an individual is identifiable or anonymous has implications for the risks subjects are exposed to, whether the research is exempt from federal human-subjects regulations, and whether the research is even defined as involving human subjects at all. According to the federal regulations (C.R. § 102(f)), research involves human subjects only if data are collected through interaction with a subject or if it collects "identifiable private information." Observations of public behavior, in which individuals cannot be identified directly or indirectly, are exempt from the federal regulations protecting human subjects (C.R. § 101(b)).

As we will discuss, the greatest risk associated with online research centers on breaches of confidentiality, in which private, identifiable information is disclosed outside of the research context. In the case of online survey and experimental research, the researcher can often reduce this risk by explicitly not asking for identifying information or by recording personal identifiers separately from the research data.

In observations of naturally occurring online behavior, however, anonymity is more difficult to achieve, and the very nature of anonymity versus identifiability becomes ambiguous. Suppose one wishes to quote statements made in an online forum. One cannot assume that pseudonyms, often used by individuals to simultaneously mask and express their identities online, render their conversations anonymous, because posters may choose pseudonyms that contain part or all of their real names or disclose information that publicly links their pseudonyms to their real identities (see Bassett & O'Riordan, 2002, for a fuller discussion). Even seemingly anonymous snippets of text posted in an online diary (known as a Web log or blogs) or online forum may be traced back to individual posters through the use of Internet search engines. Therefore, to preserve anonymity, researchers should disguise pseudonyms and alter quoted text.

Public Versus Private Behavior

Some have argued that scientists can record public Internet-based communication without the knowledge or consent of subjects, because this constitutes observation of public behavior (Herring, 1996). Many online communication forums have unrestricted membership, allowing anyone who comes by to participate in conversation or observe it. For example, lurkers (individuals who read messages but don't post them) represent well over 50% of subjects in many e-mail distribution lists (Nonnecke & Preece, 2000). In such cases, we believe that people who post in these groups should have no reasonable expectation of privacy, and researchers and IRBs should be able to treat online communication in them as public behavior.

There are, however, important caveats about when online communication should be treated as public behavior. The federal regulation bases its definition of private information on the expectation of privacy. Whether a person conversing online can reasonably expect the communication to be private depends on legal regulation, social norms, and specific details of implementation, all of which are changing. Implementation details include such features of the online settings as the number of people who subscribe, whether membership is restricted or open, whether membership is static or rapidly changing, whether conversations are ephemeral or archived, whether the presence of lurkers is visible, and whether the forum has posted explicit recording policies. Researchers and IRBs need to take considerations such as these into account on a case-by-case basis when deciding about the status of online communications among individuals on an electronic distribution list (e.g., Baym, 1993) or an Internet chat room (e.g., Bull & McFarlane, 2000).

The ethical considerations should be influenced by relevant legislation, but the laws about the privacy of computer-based electronic communication are still evolving. The Electronic Communications Privacy Act (1986) states that it is illegal to intercept electronic communications. Private e-mail and instant messaging exchanged between individuals are considered protected communication. However, this protection does not include most group-oriented communication, such as bulletin boards, public distribution lists, and chat rooms, even ones where members must enter a password before participating, if the person recording the information is considered a "party to the communication." The communication is also not protected if "the electronic communication system . . . is configured so that such electronic communication is readily accessible to the general public" (Electronic Communications Privacy Act, 1986, 18 U.S.C. § 2511(2)(g)(I)).

Whether behavior should be considered public or private also depends on changing features of technology. For example, many Web sites automatically create logs showing the IP address of the machines that visit the site. When a person has exclusive use of a personal computer with a fixed IP address, knowing the IP address is tantamount to knowing the identity of its user. However, dynamic IP addresses, in which one of a fixed number of addresses is assigned to a machine on the fly, do not translate into individual identifiers. In the case of dynamic IP addresses, tracing the address only identifies the machine pool, not the individual machine or its user.

Preexisting Public Records

Research is exempt from human-subjects regulations if it involves collecting preexisting public data, documents, and records (C.R. § 46.101(b)(4)). . . . In order to be preexisting, all of the data must exist prior to the beginning of the research, such as research on archives of online discussions. Data that are generated during the course of the research, such as postings to a blog (i.e., a Web log or online diary posted for public consumption and comment) or to a live discussion group would not be considered preexisting. Such research would qualify for expedited review: "Research involving materials (data, documents, records, or specimens) that have been collected, or will be collected solely for nonresearch purposes" (Categories of Research That May Be Reviewed by the Institutional Review Board [IRB] Through an Expedited Review Procedure, 1998). Under expedited review, the requirements for informed consent must be considered, but the expedited reviewer can waive those requirements if the regulatory criteria are met.

RISK TO SUBJECTS FROM INTERNET RESEARCH

Both general ethical principles and federal regulation require that the risks to subjects from participating in research be minimized. Although few

psychological studies involve physical risk, they can involve social, psychological, economic, and legal outcomes that may have harmful effects. According to the federal regulations, research has minimal risk when "the probability and magnitude of harm or discomfort anticipated in the research are not greater in and of themselves than those ordinarily encountered in daily life" (C.R. § 102.(i)).

Internet research involves two potential sources of risk:

- harm resulting from direct participation in the research (e.g., emotional reactions to questions or experimental manipulations) and
- harm resulting from breach of confidentiality.

Harm as a Consequence of Participation in Online Research

Much online research involves minimal risk. It exposes subjects to innocuous questions and benign or transient experiences with little lasting impact. In general, online surveys, experiments, or observations are no more risky than any of their offline counterparts. In some respects, they may be less risky, because the reduced social pressure (Sproull & Kiesler, 1991) in online surveys or experiments makes it easier for subjects to quit whenever they feel discomfort. This freedom to withdraw is no trivial benefit, given the strong pressures to continue in face-to-face studies (e.g., Milgram, 1963) and even telephone calls.

Although risk in online settings is typically low, the actual risk depends on the specifics of the study. For example, some questions in a survey or feedback from an experiment may cause subjects to reflect on unpleasant experiences or to learn something unpleasant about themselves (e.g., Nosek et al.'s, 2002b, research on automatic stereotyping). Experiments that deliberately manipulate a subject's sense of self-worth, reveal a lack of cognitive ability, challenge deeply held beliefs or attitudes, or disclose some other real or perceived characteristic may result in mental or emotional harm to some subjects. The concern in online research is not that some subjects are at risk. Risks can be justified if the potential benefits of the research are substantial enough and the cost–benefit analysis is no different in evaluating online research than in medical research or in traditional psychological research. Rather, the special concern is that researchers may have a diminished ability to monitor subjects in online research and remediate any harm caused by the research.

. . . [R]esearch subjects may be harmed if the welfare of the online groups in which they participate is damaged by the research. Consider online social-support groups, where people who confront a common health or other problem share information, empathy, and advice. King (1996) quoted a member of an online support group who wrote that she was not going to participate actively because of a researcher's presence in the group: "When I joined this I thought it would be a *support* group, not a fishbowl for a bunch of guinea pigs" (p. 122; see Eysenbach & Till, 2001, for similar concerns). When conducting cost–benefit analyses for research, investigators and IRBs alike must consider these subtle consequences of their decisions.

Debriefing

American Psychological Association (2002) ethical guidelines call for debriefing subjects—providing an explanation of the nature, results, and conclusions of the research—as soon after their participation as practical. If deception was involved, the researcher needs to explain the value of the research results and why deception was necessary. If investigators become aware during the debriefing that research procedures have caused harm to a subject, they are to take steps to ameliorate the harm.

When conducting research online, researchers can post debriefing materials at a Web site, can automatically update these materials as new results become available, and can tailor debriefing materials to particular experimental conditions or even individual subjects. There are even methods to provide debriefing materials to those who leave before completing the research (Nosek, Banaji, & Greenwald, 2002a). For example, researchers can deliver debriefing material through a link to a "leave the study" button or through a pop-up window, which executes when a subject leaves a defined Web site. As suggested earlier, however, appropriate debriefing in online research may be

difficult. The absence of a researcher in the online setting makes it difficult to assess a subject's state and therefore to determine whether an individual has been upset by an experimental procedure or understands feedback received.

Breach of Confidentiality

We believe that a greater risk of harm in online research comes from possible disclosure of identifiable private information outside of the research context, not from the experience of participating in the research itself. The identifying information can include records of statements, attitudes, or behaviors coupled with names, e-mail addresses, partially disguised pseudonyms, or other identifying information. Researchers must ensure adequate provisions to protect the privacy of subjects and to maintain the confidentiality of data.

Identifying information may be inadvertently disclosed either as the data are being collected or, more commonly, when they are stored on a networked computer connected to the public Internet. Data in transit are vulnerable, for example, if a subject or automated process sends data to the investigator by e-mail. The store-and-forward nature of e-mail means that the message may rest in temporary directories on intervening computers before it is finally delivered to the addressee. The danger is less for data collected through automated Web surveys, although "sniffing" programs can eavesdrop on data in transit to search for known patterns, such as social security numbers, credit card numbers, or e-mail addresses. These risks can be avoided by not collecting identifying information or by separating these data from other research data. Although analogous risks can occur with paper forms, they are higher when data are shipped over the Internet, because of the openness of the networks and the possibility of automated pattern detection.

Greater risks to confidentiality result from outsiders gaining access to stored data files, either through deliberate hacking or because researchers mistakenly distributed them. This risk is not unique to online research but is a challenge for all data stored on networked computers. The standard approach to dealing with problems of confidentiality is to separate personal identifiers from other data describing subjects. Thus, one should keep identifying information, such as names and addresses, in one file and data in a second, with an arbitrary code number to link the two. Tourangeau, Couper, and Steiger (2003) illustrated some techniques used to maintain separation of identity from data in survey research involving sensitive data.

Maintaining the confidentiality of data stored on computer systems may require psychologists to become more sophisticated about computer technology than many currently are. Researchers should configure their computers so that only those with a need to know have access to directories containing research data and should regularly check the permissions. They should routinely keep abreast of the security alerts issued by their vendors and apply security updates when these are released. For sensitive data, directories can be password protected, and sensitive files can be encrypted. Many investigators, however, fail to take these precautions to protect their data.

. . .

Paying online subjects for their participation may also link subjects' responses to their identities when sending a payment requires a mailing address or accounting regulations require a social security number. Some researchers have severed this link by buying gift certificates from online retailers, such as Amazon.com, and displaying the unique certificate number to a respondent at the completion of a questionnaire. Thus, subjects can redeem their certificates without revealing their identity.

The degree of concern over confidentiality and steps taken to ensure it should be directly related to the sensitivity of the data being collected. One is less concerned when subjects are anonymous or when the information about them is innocuous (i.e., its revelation would bring no harm or embarrassment to subjects). Many online surveys and experiments fall into one or both of these categories. In these cases, use of passwords, encryption, or strong assurance to research subjects is not needed and may harm the research. For example, as Singer, Hippler, and Schwarz (1992) demonstrated, overly elaborate assurances of confidentiality may actually heighten rather than diminish respondents' concern, causing subjects to be less

willing to provide sensitive information. Strong security measures (e.g., using secure socket layer protocols) may prohibit some research subjects from participating.

However, when subjects are identifiable and the research involves data that place them at risk of criminal or civil liability or that could damage their financial standing, employability, insurability, reputation, or could be stigmatizing, investigators must be especially concerned about breaches of confidentiality. Under these circumstances, standard security measures in place for electronic commerce, such as encryption and secure protocols, are likely to be sufficient. Numerous tutorials outline the options (e.g., Garfinkel, Spafford, & Russell, 2002).

Informed Consent

Investigators must typically obtain and document voluntary informed consent from research subjects, in which subjects freely agree to participate after they understand what the research involves and its risks and benefits (C.R. § 116). Federal human-subjects regulation also requires that informed consent be documented by the use of a "written consent form approved by the IRB and signed by the subject" (C.R. § 117). It is difficult to obtain legally binding signatures online. However, IRBs can waive the requirements for written documentation of informed consent for minimal-risk research either when the research would not require informed consent outside a research context or when the documentation is the only link between the research data and a subject's identity (C.R. § 117(c)). In the case of much online research involving adults, these conditions for waiving documentation of informed consent are met, and we recommend that IRBs should waive the document and allow a procedure in which subjects click a button on an online form to indicate they have read and understood the consent form.

As we have indicated earlier, the lack of interactivity in online research means that the investigator often cannot tell whether a subject understood the informed consent statement. As a result, online research may require more pretesting of these statements than research conducted in other venues.

Researchers can increase the likelihood that subjects are granting truly informed consent by requiring feedback from subjects about their level of understanding, for example, by requiring a "click to accept" for each element in an informed consent statement or even administering short quizzes to establish that a subject understood. As with efforts to protect confidentiality, however, these extra efforts to ensure informed consent may reduce response rates, increase nonresponse to sensitive items (Singer, 1978), and possibly produce biased data (Trice, 1987). Therefore, these techniques are recommended only for research involving more than minimal risk to the subject.

These simple procedures for research involving competent adults may not be appropriate for online research involving children and other vulnerable groups, such as the mentally handicapped. According to federal regulation, these populations are not empowered to give consent for themselves. Their parent or guardian must consent, and the child may optionally be asked to assent. Here the inability to establish the subjects' identity is especially problematic, because researchers cannot easily determine whether online subjects are revealing their true age and because children can easily pretend to be their parents. Researchers can institute procedures to more reliably distinguish children from adults by having subjects enter information that is generally available only to adults (e.g., credit card numbers) or by requiring that they register with a trusted authority, such as VeriSign (http://www.verisign.com/products/asb/). Depending on the risk involved, the researcher and IRB must either accept the possibility that unidentified minors participated in the research or that they forged parental consent or insist that a legally verified signature accompany the consent form, by conducting the research offline. Note that researchers working with children online are subject not only to human-subjects regulations, but also to the Children's Online Privacy Protection Act (1998; see http://www.ftc.gov/ogc/coppa1.htm). Researchers are prohibited from collecting personal information from a child without posting notices about how the information will be used and without getting verifiable parental consent.

ADVICE TO RESEARCHERS AND INSTITUTIONAL REVIEW BOARDS

. . .

When Risk Is Low, Use Sensible But Not Extreme Protections

No purpose is served when researchers or their IRBs place hurdles in front of research involving minimal risk. One should not use overelaborate informed consent statements, extensive assurances of confidentiality, encryption, or digital signatures when risks are minimal. Instead, one can guard against risk with lower keyed approaches. IRBs should waive documentation of informed consent, for example, by agreeing to a "click to assent" button for experiments and by permitting continued participation to signal consent for minimal-risk online surveys. For low-risk surveys and experiments, debriefing material can be customized to subjects' behavior and delivered as an updated set of frequently asked questions, if necessary. Because the most likely risk for data collected online is the breach of confidentiality, investigators should use good data-management practices to lessen this risk. In particular, stripping identifiers from data, storing identifiers and data in separate files, auditing the security of data directories, and installing security patches on operating systems should be routine practice for all research involving human subjects, whether conducted online or off.

When Risk Is High, Use Stronger Safeguards or Do Not Use the Internet

Research that places human subjects at greater risk, either as a direct consequence of the research experience itself or from disclosure of sensitive data, requires stronger safeguards or may not even be appropriate for the Internet. Because investigators have reduced ability to assess a subject's state or to respond to evidence of distress when conducting online research, deception experiments and research that exposes subjects to stressful events may be problematic if conducted online. Researchers should screen respondents, either through sample selection or through preliminary data collection, to screen out vulnerable populations. The greater freedom of subjects to withdraw from online research is a mixed benefit. Subjects can more easily leave online settings before experiencing severe distress than they can in phone interviews or laboratory settings, but they can also leave before being adequately debriefed. To counteract early withdrawal, researchers can arrange their study so that subjects are sent to a debriefing site automatically at the end of a session, and debriefing material can be customized to their behavior.

If the data collection involves highly sensitive information, engage extra precautions. In addition to the standard practice of separating identifying information from the data itself, a researcher might consider engaging an outside service to acquire subjects, collect the data, and arrange for payment, if appropriate. In this way, the researcher is never in possession of the identifying information that would harm the subject.

With sensitive topics, such schemes as certified digital signatures for informed consent, encryption of data transmission, and technical separation of identifiers and data may be warranted. Research with sensitive topics may require strong verification that the assent is from the person who purports to be answering, including digital signatures or mailed consent. There are special difficulties if the research involves minors. Depending on the sensitivity of the information collected, parental consent may have to be acquired on paper, to ensure the parents are fully informed about the experience their child will have in the research.

Take Special Precautions When Dealing With Research Involving Minors

The Internet may appeal to researchers conducting research on children and adolescents because of the large numbers of minors using it. Research involving minors requires parental consent. Because of the difficulty of verifying the age and identity of people online, researchers will need to take special steps in conducting research with minors. For example, to ensure parental consent, they may need to ask for data that only an adult would have (e.g., a portion of a driver's license).

Even if the research targets adults, if the research also appeals to minors (e.g., research about an online game), researchers may need to program their site to screen out self-identified minors or to place more effortful guards around the site.

. . .

References

American Psychological Association. (2002). *Ethical principles of psychologists and code of conduct, Draft 7.* Washington, DC: Author.

Bassett, E. H., & O'Riordan, K. (2002). Ethics of Internet research: Contesting the human subjects model. *Journal of Ethics and Information Technology, 4,* 233–247.

Baym, N. (1993). Interpreting soap operas and creating community: Inside a computer-mediated fan culture. *Journal of Folklore Research, 30,* 143–176.

Bull, S., & McFarlane, M. (2000). Soliciting sex on the Internet: What are the risks for sexually transmitted diseases and HIV? *Sexually Transmitted Diseases, 27,* 545–550.

Categories of Research That May Be Reviewed by the Institutional Review Board (IRB) Through an Expedited Review Procedure 63 Fed. Reg. 60364-60367 (Nov. 9, 1998).

Children's Online Privacy Protection Act 13 U.S.C. §§ 1301–1308 (1998).

Electronic Communications Privacy Act 18 U.S.C. § 2511 (1986).

Eysenbach, G., & Till, J. E. (2001). Ethical issues in qualitative research on Internet communities. *British Medical Journal, 323,* 103–105.

Galegher, J., Sproull, L., & Kiesler, S. (1998). Legitimacy, authority, and community in electronic support groups. *Written Communication, 15,* 493–530.

Garfinkel, S., Spafford, G., & Russell, D. (2002). *Web security, privacy and commerce.* Cambridge, MA: O'Reilly & Associates.

Glaser, J., Dixit, J., & Green, D. P. (2002). Studying hate crime with the Internet: What makes racists advocate racial violence? *Journal of Social Issues, 58,* 177–193.

Herring, S. (1996). Linguistic and critical analysis of computer-mediated communication: Some ethical and scholarly considerations. *The Information Society, 12,* 153–168.

Hinds, P., & Kiesler, S. (Eds.). (2002). *Distributed work.* Cambridge, MA: MIT Press.

King, S. (1996). Researching Internet communities: Proposed ethical guidelines for the reporting of results. *The Information Society, 12,* 119–127.

Kraut, R. E., Rice, R. E., Cool, C., & Fish, R. S. (1998). Varieties of social influence: The role of utility and norms in the success of a new communication medium. *Organization Science, 9,* 437–453.

Milgram, S. (1963). Behavioral study of obedience. *Journal of Abnormal and Social Psychology, 67,* 371–378.

Nonnecke, B., & Preece, J. (2000). Lurker demographics: Counting the silent. *CHI 2000, ACM Conference on Human Factors in Computing Systems, CHI Letters, 4*(1), 73–80.

Nosek, B. A., Banaji, M. R., & Greenwald, A. G. (2002a). E-research: Ethics, security, design, and control in psychological research on the Internet. *Journal of Social Issues, 58,* 161–176.

Nosek, B. A., Banaji, M., & Greenwald, A. G. (2002b). Harvesting implicit group attitudes and beliefs from a demonstration web site. *Group Dynamics, 6,* 101–115.

Orlikowski, W. J. (2000). Using technology and constituting structures: A practice lens for studying technology in organizations. *Organizational Science, 11,* 404–428.

Singer, E. (1978). Informed consent: Consequences for response rate and response quality in social surveys. *American Sociological Review, 43,* 144–162.

Singer, E., Hippler, H., & Schwarz, N. (1992). Confidentiality assurances in surveys: Reassurance or threat? *International Journal of Public Opinion Research, 4,* 256–268.

Sproull, L., & Faraj, S. (1995). Atheism, sex, and databases: The net as a social technology. In B. Kahin & J. Keller (Eds.), *Public access to the Internet* (pp. 62–81). Cambridge, MA: MIT Press.

Sproull, L., & Kiesler, S. (1991). *Connections: New ways of working in the networked organization.* Cambridge, MA: MIT Press.

Tourangeau, R., Couper, M. P., & Steiger, D. M. (2003). Humanizing self-administered surveys: Experiments on social presence in Web and IVR surveys. *Computers in Human Behavior, 19,* 1–24.

Trice, A. D. (1987). Informed consent: VIII. Biasing of sensitive self-report data by both consent and information. *Journal of Social Behavior and Personality, 2,* 369–374.

Turkle, S. (1997). *Life on the screen.* New York: Touchstone Books.

◆ ◆ ◆

Commentary: For other helpful articles stressing the ethical components of online research see

Keller, H. E., & Lee, S. (2003). Ethical issues surrounding human participants research using the Internet. Ethics & Behavior, 13, 211–219.

Kralik, D., Warren, J., Price, K., Koch, T., & Pignone, G. (2005). The ethics of research using electronic mail discussion groups. Journal of Advanced Nursing, 52, 537–545.

Pittenger, D. J. (2003). Internet research: An opportunity to revisit classic ethical problems in behavioral research. Ethics & Behavior, 13, 4–60.

Varnhagen, C. K., Gushta, M., Daniels, J., Peters, T. C., Parmar, N., Law, D., Hirsch, R., Takach, B. S., & Johnson, T. (2005). How informed is online informed consent? Ethics & Behavior, 15, 37–48. (finding little difference between online informed consent and that obtained by paper presentation)

For a helpful article on cyberspace research methodology, see Hewson, C., Laurent, D., & Vogel, C. (1996). Proper methodologies for psychological and sociological studies conducted via the Internet. Behavior Research Methods, Instruments, and Computers, 28, 186–191.

Finally, interested readers have certainly become aware that experimentation with human participants is not the only kind of research that has engendered controversy. As Galvin and Herzog (1992) have noted, "The use of animals as subjects in behavioral and biomedical research has become a major issue with social, political, philosophical, and psychological ramifications" (p. 263). See Galvin, S. L., & Herzog, H. A. (1992). The ethical judgment of animal research. Ethics & Behavior, 2, 263–286; Saucier, D. A., & Cain, M. E. (2006). The foundations of attitudes about animal research. Ethics & Behavior, 16, 117–133. Because of these ramifications as well as pressure from animal activists, like human research, animal research conducted at universities is scrutinized by review boards called Institutional Animal Care and Use Committees. *In addition to the provisions in the 2002 Ethical Principles, the APA has developed its own policies concerning animal research (reprinted next).*

Guidelines for Ethical Conduct in the Care and Use of Animals

American Psychological Association

. . .

The following guidelines were developed by the American Psychological Association (APA) for use by psychologists working with nonhuman animals. They are based on and are in conformity with Section 6.20 of the *Ethical Principles of Psychologists and Code of Conduct* of APA.[1] In the ordinary course of events, the acquisition, care, housing, use, and disposition of animals should be in compliance with applicable federal, state, local, and institutional laws and regulations and with international conventions to which the United States is a party. APA members working outside the United States are to follow all applicable laws and regulations of the country in which they conduct research.

. . .

I. JUSTIFICATION OF THE RESEARCH

A. Research should be undertaken with a clear scientific purpose. There should be a reasonable expectation that the research will a) increase knowledge of the processes underlying the evolution, development, maintenance, alteration, control, or biological significance of behavior; b) determine the replicability and generality of prior research; c) increase understanding of the species under study; d) provide results that benefit the health or welfare of humans or other animals.

B. The scientific purpose of the research should be of sufficient potential significance to justify the use of animals. Psychologists should act on the assumption that procedures that would produce pain in humans will also do so in other animals.

C. The species chosen for study should be best suited to answer the question(s) posed. The psychologist should always consider the possibility of using other species, nonanimal alternatives, or procedures that minimize the number of animals in research, and should be familiar with the appropriate literature.

D. Research on animals may not be conducted until the protocol has been reviewed by an appropriate animal care committee, for example, an institutional animal care and use committee (IACUC), to ensure that the procedures are appropriate and humane.

E. The psychologists should monitor the research and the animals' welfare throughout the course of an investigation to ensure continued justification for the research.

II. PERSONNEL

A. Psychologists should ensure that personnel involved in their research with animals be familiar with these guidelines.

B. Animal use procedures must conform with federal regulations regarding personnel, supervision, record keeping, and veterinary care. [footnote omitted]

C. Behavior is both the focus of study of many experiments and a primary source of information about an animal's health and well-being. It is therefore necessary that psychologists and their assistants be informed about the behavioral characteristics of their animal subjects, so as to be aware of normal, species-specific behaviors and unusual behaviors that could forewarn of health problems.

[1]*Ed. Note:* See Standard 8.09 of the current (2002) APA Ethics Code.

D. Psychologists should ensure that all individuals who use animals under their supervision receive explicit instruction in experimental methods and in the care, maintenance, and handling of the species being studied. Responsibilities and activities of all individuals dealing with animals should be consistent with their respective competencies, training, and experience in either the laboratory or the field setting.

III.   CARE AND HOUSING OF ANIMALS

The concept of "psychological well-being" of animals is of current concern and debate and is included in Federal Regulations (United States Department of Agriculture [USDA], 1991). As a scientific and professional organization, APA recognizes the complexities of determining psychological well-being. Procedures appropriate for a particular species may be inappropriate for others. Hence, APA does not presently stipulate specific guidelines regarding the maintenance of psychological well-being of research animals. Psychologists familiar with the species should be best qualified professionally to judge measures such as enrichment to maintain or improve psychological well-being of those species.

A. The facilities housing animals should meet or exceed current regulations and guidelines (USDA, 1990, 1991) and are required to be inspected twice a year (USDA, 1989).

B. All procedures carried out on animals are to be reviewed by a local animal care committee to ensure that the procedures are appropriate and humane. The committee should have representation from within the institution and from the local community. In the event that it is not possible to constitute an appropriate local animal care committee, psychologists are encouraged to seek advice from a corresponding committee of a cooperative institution.

C. Responsibilities for the conditions under which animals are kept, both within and outside of the context of active experimentation or teaching, rest with the psychologist under the supervision of the animal care committee (where required by federal regulations) and with individuals appointed by the institution to oversee animal care. Animals are to be provided with humane care and healthful conditions during their stay in the facility. In addition to the federal requirements to provide for the psychological well-being of nonhuman primates used in research, psychologists are encouraged to consider enriching the environments of their laboratory animals and should keep abreast of literature on well-being and enrichment for the species with which they work.

IV.   ACQUISITION OF ANIMALS

A. Animals not bred in the psychologist's facility are to be acquired lawfully. The USDA and local ordinances should be consulted for information regarding regulations and approved suppliers.

B. Psychologists should make every effort to ensure that those responsible for transporting the animals to the facility provide adequate food, water, ventilation, space, and impose no unnecessary stress on the animals.

C. Animals taken from the wild should be trapped in a humane manner and in accordance with applicable federal, state, and local regulations.

D. Endangered species or taxa should be used only with full attention to required permits and ethical concerns. . . .

V.   EXPERIMENTAL PROCEDURES

Humane consideration for the well-being of the animal should be incorporated into the design and conduct of all procedures involving animals, while keeping in mind the primary goal of experimental procedures—the acquisition of sound, replicable data. The conduct of all procedures is governed by Guideline I.

A. Behavioral studies that involve no aversive stimulation to, or overt sign of distress from, the animal are acceptable. These include observational and other noninvasive forms of data collection.

B. When alternative behavioral procedures are available, those that minimize discomfort to the animal should be used. When using aversive conditions, psychologists should adjust the parameters of stimulation to levels that appear minimal, though compatible with the aims of the research. Psychologists are encouraged to test painful stimuli on themselves, whenever reasonable. Whenever consistent with the goals of the research, consideration should be given to providing the animals with control of the potentially aversive stimulation.

C. Procedures in which the animal is anesthetized and insensitive to pain throughout the procedure and is euthanized before regaining consciousness are generally acceptable.

D. Procedures involving more than momentary or slight aversive stimulation, which is not relieved by medication or other acceptable methods, should be undertaken only when the objectives of the research cannot be achieved by other methods.

E. Experimental procedures that require prolonged aversive conditions or produce tissue damage or metabolic disturbances require greater justification and surveillance. These include prolonged exposure to extreme environmental conditions, experimentally induced prey killing, or infliction of physical trauma or tissue damage. An animal observed to be in a state of severe distress or chronic pain that cannot be alleviated and is not essential to the purposes of the research should be euthanized immediately.

F. Procedures that use restraint must conform to federal regulations and guidelines.

G. Procedures involving the use of paralytic agents without reduction in pain sensation require particular prudence and humane concern. Use of muscle relaxants or paralytics alone during surgery, without general anesthesia, is unacceptable and should be avoided.

H. Surgical procedures, because of their invasive nature, require close supervision and attention to humane considerations by the psychologist. Aseptic (methods that minimize risks of infection) techniques must be used on laboratory animals whenever possible.

1. All surgical procedures and anesthetization should be conducted under the direct supervision of a person who is competent in the use of the procedures.

2. If the surgical procedure is likely to cause greater discomfort than that attending anesthetization, and unless there is specific justification for acting otherwise, animals should be maintained under anesthesia until the procedure is ended.

3. Sound postoperative monitoring and care, which may include the use of analgesics and antibiotics, should be provided to minimize discomfort and to prevent infection and other untoward consequences of the procedure.

4. Animals cannot be subjected to successive surgical procedures unless these are required by the nature of the research, the nature of the surgery, or for the well-being of the animal. Multiple surgeries on the same animal must receive special approval from the animal care committee.

I. When the use of an animal is no longer required by an experimental protocol or procedure, in order to minimize the number of animals used in research, alternative uses of the animal should be considered. Such uses should be compatible with the goals of research and the welfare of the animal. Care should be taken that such an action does not expose the animal to multiple surgeries.

J. The return of wild-caught animals to the field can carry substantial risks, both to the formerly captive animals and to the ecosystem. Animals reared in the laboratory should not be released because, in most cases, they cannot survive or they may survive by disrupting the natural ecology.

K. When euthanasia appears to be the appropriate alternative, either as a requirement of the research or because it constitutes the most humane form of disposition of an animal at the conclusion of the research:

1. Euthanasia shall be accomplished in a humane manner, appropriate for the species, and in such a way as to ensure immediate death, and in accordance with procedures outlined in the latest version of the "American Veterinary Medical Association (AVMA) Panel on Euthanasia." [footnote omitted]

2. Disposal of euthanized animals should be accomplished in a manner that is in accord with all relevant legislation, consistent with health, environmental, and aesthetic concerns, and approved by the animal care committee. No animal shall be discarded until its death is verified.

VI. FIELD RESEARCH

Field research, because of its potential to damage sensitive ecosystems and ethologies, should be subject to animal care committee approval. Field research, if strictly observational, may not require animal care committee approval (USDA, 1989, p. 36126).

A. Psychologists conducting field research should disturb their populations as little as possible—consistent with the goals of the research. Every effort should be made to minimize potential harmful effects of the study on the population and on other plant and animal species in the area.

B. Research conducted in populated areas should be done with respect for the property and privacy of the inhabitants of the area.

C. Particular justification is required for the study of endangered species. Such research on endangered species should not be conducted unless animal care committee approval has been obtained and all requisite permits are obtained (see IVD).

VII. EDUCATIONAL USE OF ANIMALS

Laboratory exercises as well as classroom demonstrations involving live animals can be valuable as instructional aids. APA has adopted separate guidelines for the educational use of animals in precollege education, including the use of animals in science fairs and demonstrations. For a copy of APA's "Ethical Guidelines for the Teaching of Psychology in the Secondary Schools," write to: High School Teacher Affiliate Program, Education Directorate, APA, 750 First St., NE, Washington, DC 20002-4242.

A. Psychologists are encouraged to include instruction and discussion of the ethics and values of animal research in all courses that involve or discuss the use of animals.

B. Animals may be used for educational purposes only after review by a committee appropriate to the institution.

C. Some procedures that can be justified for research purposes may not be justified for educational purposes. Consideration should be given to the possibility of using nonanimal alternatives.

References

U.S. Department of Agriculture. (1989, August 21). Animal welfare; Final rules. *Federal Register.*

U.S. Department of Agriculture. (1990, July 16). Animal welfare; Guinea pigs, hamsters, and rabbits. *Federal Register.*

U.S. Department of Agriculture. (1991, February 15). Animal welfare; Standards; Final rule. *Federal Register.*

◆   ◆   ◆

Commentary: The federal regulations referenced in the APA's Animal Guidelines concerning the well-being of primates and dogs were printed in the Federal Register, 56, 6425–6505 (February 15, 1991), and they also appeared in the Code of Federal Regulations (Animal Welfare Standards, 9 C.F.R. Part 3). However, in 1993 a federal court ordered the United States Department of Agriculture (USDA) to rewrite these regulations. In overturning the 1991 regulations, the court said that they did not provide the minimum standards that Congress had intended under the Animal Welfare Act. However, the court of appeals later reversed this decision, allowing the USDA regulations to stand. These developments have made it difficult for researchers constructing animal facilities to conform their conduct to the law and ethical demands.

Obviously, there have been strong reactions to many of the restrictions on animal research advocated by those who identify themselves as protectors of animal rights. For some critiques of the animal rights movement, see, for example:

King, F. A. (1991). Animal research: Our obligation to educate. In M. A. Novak & A. J. Petto (Eds.), Through the looking glass: Issues of psychological well-being in captive nonhuman primates (pp. 212–230). Washington, DC: American Psychological Association.

Lansdell, H. (1993). The three Rs: A restrictive and refutable rigamarole. Ethics & Behavior, 3, 177–185.

Volume 7, No. 2 (1997) of Ethics & Behavior *is entirely devoted to articles on ethical issues in the use of animals in research. The entire special issue is worth reading, but especially relevant is: Orlans, F. B. (1997). Ethical decision-making about animal experiments.* Ethics & Behavior, 7, 163–171. The APA Committee on Animal Research Ethics has prepared a video titled, *"Guidelines for the Use of Animals in Behavioral*

Projects in Schools." It is available from the APA Science Directorate. For the latest word on the topic see NIMH. (2002). Methods and welfare considerations in behavioral research with animals. Report of a National Institutes of Health Workshop *(NIH Publication No. 02-5083). Washington, DC: U.S. Government Printing Office.*

The most notorious case in the annals of animal activism concerned psychologist Edward Taub and his laboratory monkeys, whose nerves he cut in an experiment at the Institute for Behavioral Research in Maryland. For an extensive and reasonably balanced discussion of that case, see Fraser, C. (1993, April 19). The raid at Silver Spring. The New Yorker, *66–74, 76–84. Partly in response to violent disruptions by those opposed to biomedical and behavioral research using animal subjects, Congress in 1992 passed the Animal Enterprise Protection Act, amending the U.S. Criminal Code (18 U.S.C. § 43). It provides, in relevant part:*

SEC. 2. ANIMAL ENTERPRISE TERRORISM

(a) In General.—Title 18, United States Code, is amended by inserting after section 42 the following: . . .

§ 43. Animal Enterprise Terrorism

"(a) Offense.—Whoever—

"(1) travels in interstate or foreign commerce, or uses or causes to be used the mail or any facility in interstate or foreign commerce, for the purpose of causing physical disruption to the functioning of an animal enterprise; and

"(2) intentionally causes physical disruption to the functioning of an animal enterprise by intentionally stealing, damaging, or causing the loss of, any property (including animals or records) used by the animal enterprise, and thereby causes economic damage exceeding $10,000 to that enterprise, or conspires to do so; shall be fined under this title or imprisoned not more than one year, or both.

"(b) Aggravated Offense.—

"(1) Serious Bodily Injury.—Whoever in the course of a violation of subsection (a) causes serious bodily injury to another individual shall be fined under this title or imprisoned not more than 10 years, or both.

"(2) Death.—Whoever in the course of a violation of subsection (a) causes the death of an individual shall be fined under this title and imprisoned for life or for any term of years.

"(c) Restitution.—An order of restitution under section 3663 of this title with respect to a violation of this section may also include restitution—

"(1) for the reasonable cost of repeating any experimentation that was interrupted or invalidated as a result of the offense; and

"(2) the loss of food production or farm income reasonably attributable to the offense."

Ethical Issues in the Supervision of Student Research: A Study of Critical Incidents

Rodney K. Goodyear, Clyde A. Crego, and Michael W. Johnston

[*Ed. Note:* In this study, 57 well-published and experienced professional psychologists were asked to describe, in free-response form, up to three instances of ethical problems related to student–faculty research collaboration. Respondents reported 114 critical incidents. The results are summarized by category in Table 1. Under the heading "Applicable APA Ethical Principles," provide the appropriate standards in the 1992 Ethical Principles. Then continue with the authors' consideration of each of the categories.]

. . .

Incompetent supervision. Psychologists recognize that, because of the risk of harm to clients, it is unethical to practice outside their areas of competence when they provide client services. This same principle should extend to the research supervisor, though this application of it has received scant discussion in the literature. Although the critical incidents addressed only the supervisor's methodological competence, another area of competence that is important in research supervision is that of subject matter.

Subject matter competence seems to arise most often as an issue in the supervision of dissertation or thesis research. The ethical tension is between that of respecting the student's autonomy, on the one hand, and that of being able to benefit the student and act faithfully, on the other. In fact, it seems possible to array the ways in which faculty have responded to this matter along a continuum. At one end of the continuum are faculty who would allow each student whom they supervise to follow his or her own interests, regardless of faculty knowledge of that area. Often these seem to be faculty who believe that conducting "independent" research means that the student is to have complete freedom in topic choice. On the other end of the continuum are faculty who define specific areas of expertise for themselves and refuse to supervise any student research that does not fall into one of these areas.

Neither of these extreme solutions is wholly satisfactory. The second approach, however, probably offers the better balance of the competing ethical principles as long as students have the freedom within a program to pair with the faculty member whose interests are closest to their own: Students who feel coerced into research on a topic of little interest to them lose perceived autonomy and may suffer harm (e.g., in their attitudes toward research, in the quality of their work).

The second issue of competence concerns the research supervisor's mastery of research methodology and statistics. Competence, of course, exists on a continuum, and few people are as competent as they could be. However, in the words of one respondent, "Ultimately the authors of articles must assume sole responsibility for all aspects of their scholarly product and their interpretations. It is insufficient to simply say 'Because the statistician said so.' " There does seem to be a point at which the supervisor's lack of expertise impairs his or her ability to benefit the supervisee or to act faithfully in that relationship; conceivably, it also could cause actual harm to the supervisee.

. . . Fortunately, by tradition there is a committee to whom thesis and dissertation students answer. This can moderate many, though not all, effects of incompetent supervision.

Inadequate supervision. It is possible, of course, for a research supervisor to be competent but still leave students to fend for themselves, with neither

TABLE 1

Ethical Problems in Faculty Supervision of Student Research

Category	Examples of critical incidents	Applicable APA Ethical Principles
Incometent supervision	(a) Faculty member knows so little about statistics that he refers his students to consultants or other faculty for even the most basic information. (b) Data analysis for a thesis conducted by a statistician without the student's or advisor's knowledge of the statistics being used.	
Inadequate supervision	(a) The faculty advisor to a senior honors thesis was only peripherally involved in the student's research, did not read her thesis draft, and was unavailable prior to the day of her defense meeting. The resulting paper was awful and the student was humiliated. (b) A faculty member participated little in a thesis project and provided minimal supervision. Just before the defense, the faculty member berated the student for the topic as well as the obtained results. (c) Dissertation chair sets inadequate standards for student performance, fails to have the student follow-through on suggestions made by the dissertation committee, and argues that "no one is going to read it anyway."	
Supervision abandonment	(a) "I have seen students dropped in the middle of research projects either because the faculty weren't interested, had moved away, or some other reason." (b) Three years ago, I was, as an intern, part of a research team that conducted a large treatment outcome study. None of the several papers we outlined have yet been done—and despite my repeated offers to assist in writing/analysing/editing, I am told my held is not needed." (c) Faculty member gets research teams together, makes then to do a great deal of work, says she will write it up, then doesn't.	
Intrusion of supervision values	(a) Faculty member refused to chair her advisee's dissertation because she was an atheist and the sudent wanted to study a religious issue. (b) Faculty member insisted her student employ a radical feminist perspective in his dissertation study of campus date rape even though the student did not find the perspective useful.	
Abusive supervision	(a) A student's advisor verbally and emotionally abused her, leading to her hatred of research, self-doubt, and thought of leaving the program. (b) To gain access to needed data, a student was required to join a research team, do work she was not interested in—and to be ridiculed as incompetent in front of the group (her contribution, which ultimately resulted in a publication with the faculty member, was minimized and ridiculed). (c) Professor took student off as coauthor after she confronted his sexual harassment behavior.	
Exploitive supervision	(a) Professor requires graduate assistants to assist in the teaching of his courses. They are afraid to confront him for fear of reprisals. (b) Professor consistently exploited a student's time and regularly insisted that she work on a research project during a time she was scheduled to be in class with another professor.	

TABLE 1

Ethical Problems in Faculty Supervision of Student Research *(Continued)*

Category	Examples of critical incidents	Applicable APA Ethical Principles
Dual relationships	(a) Dissertation advisor and student were involved romantically, but the relationship went sour, they broke up, and he gave her a hard time on her dissertation research and written document. (b) A professor provided research assistantships and authorships to a student who was in a sexual relationship with him.	
Encouragement to fraud	(a) Faculty member urged students to skew a report of data analyses that failed to support his preferred theory. (b) Student was an RA for a faculty member, doing house-to-house survey: Faculty member told the student to make up data if no one was home.	
Authorship issues		
1. Plagiarism	(a) A GA (graduate assistant) essentially ghost wrote several chapters of a faculty member's book, but received no credit. (b) A professor published the ideas of one of his students without crediting her. (c) Student wrote a critique of a book; it then was published with the professor who assigned the task as the sole author.	
2. Failure to give (expected) credit	(a) Student and faculty member collaborate on a project; unbeknownst to the student, the faculty member submitted it for convention presentation. (a) A PI wrote up the results of a study and submitted it for publication without inviting the RA (who had been substantially involved) to coauthor. (c) The senior author dropped the 3rd author from authorship on page proofs without notifying 2nd or 3rd authors—who found out after publication.	
3. Giving unwarranted credit	(a) I have observed faculty giving students authorship for activities that likely do not fall under the rubric of authorship. (b) A student conducted a thesis, relying primarily on faculty other than his advisor for guidance and support—then in a nice gesture, gave his advisor second authorship of a resulting article (though uncomfortable, the advisor consented). (c) Faculty member and student are sole collaborators on an article. But when galleys arrive, faculty member adds spouse as third author.	

---

the support nor the skills they will need for truly successful completion of their research project. There is no way of knowing what percentage of research supervisors provide consistently inadequate supervision. But it is likely that even the most conscientious of us occasionally is guilty of a less serious version of this type of behavior: providing students with tardy responses to or inadequate critiques of their work (see, e.g., Magoon & Holland, 1984). Of Kitchener's (1984) ethical principles, the one that seems to apply most to inadequate research supervision is that of acting faithfully, although the principles of being fair, benefiting others, and doing no harm apply as well.

Supervision abandonment. Occasionally, a supervisor will fail to fulfill an implicit or explicit contract with the student to see a research project through to completion. The supervisor has not acted faithfully or provided benefit to these supervisees. In fact, she or he actually may cause them some degree of harm (e.g., in graduation delays, in time invested that could have been used more profitably elsewhere).

There seem to be two qualitatively different manifestations of this ethical problem category. In one version, the students participate in a research project, often as members of a research group. They may have done a great deal of work, but the supervising faculty member fails to follow through with his or her promised efforts, and the project is not completed. Because of the power differential or because the faculty member has physical possession of the data, research supervisees are unable to reap the expected (and deserved) rewards of their efforts.

A second type of abandonment occurs when the faculty member leaves the student midway through his or her thesis or dissertation. Although faculty occasionally will do this when they take a sabbatical, this seems to occur more often when faculty move to another university. The degree to which this is a breach of ethical principles (especially those of faithfulness and doing no harm) is moderated by such factors as the stage of the student's research and the extent to which he or she has been given prior information about the likelihood of the supervisor leaving.

. . . [I]nstitutional context, institutional policies and norms have a great deal to do with how research supervision is handled if a faculty member leaves that setting. Some universities, for example, will provide the travel costs and even some stipend to a departing faculty member in order to see a dissertation through to completion. But if the situation will not permit the department faculty member to continue as the student's primary research supervisor, he or she should be active in helping to arrange the student's transition to another faculty supervisor (just as a psychologist would arrange a client's referral under parallel circumstances).

Intrusion of the supervisor's values. Certainly most people have beliefs about what is important to study and the perspective or perspectives from which that should be done. Research supervision can be no less value free than psychotherapy. There is, though, a fine line between merely sharing those values and actively imposing them on students, a behavior that violates the principles of autonomy and fairness. It is possible to provide reasonable protection to students from this problem by ensuring that the students (a) are clear about strongly held values of faculty members, and (b) have freedom within their training program not to work with faculty members whose guiding values would prove problematic to them.

Abusive and exploitive supervision. Although abusive and exploitive supervision share some similar characteristics, the raters judged that they were sufficiently different to merit separate clustering. The difference seemed to be one of the supervisor's intent: Whereas with exploitive supervision the research supervisor subjects the supervisee to inconvenience for some selfish end, in abusive supervision the supervisor's motive seems to be punishment of the supervisee for some real or imagined "shortcoming." In either case, the offending supervisor is likely to have violated the principles of fairness and of doing no harm.

Dual relationships. Dual relationships apparently constitute a problem in research supervision just as in other areas of psychological practice. Goodyear and Sinnett (1984) have noted that people who choose the same occupation tend to share common values and beliefs, and that such similarities can provide the basis for the mutual attraction that sometimes occurs between faculty and students. Moreover, in contrast to therapist–client relationships, faculty and students interact in multiple contexts and therefore experience fewer boundary constraints on their behaviors. In fact, as Tabachnick et al. (1991) have observed, "sometimes, what with so many social and other types of activities available to both students and faculty on and off campus, boundary blurring seems practically built into the academic system" (p. 514).

The salient issue, though, is one of protecting the student from exploitation, for the power differential is such that the student is at greater risk in these relationships than the faculty member—no matter how well intentioned the involved parties might be. . . . The principles of faithfulness and of doing no harm are at issue in these cases.

Encouragement to fraud. Encouraging students to engage in such fraudulent research activity as faking data or results seems especially reprehensible. To the extent that these efforts are "successful," science is tainted and students are exposed to unfortunate role models who have failed to behave faithfully. As important, though, is the fact that students are placed at risk of harm by such behaviors. . . .

Authorship issues. Finally, there is the important and often-troublesome matter of authorship credit: Who should be an author and in what order? This matter often emerges as a basis of disputes between or among well-intentioned people who have honest disagreements about authorship. A number of the reported incidents were of this type. It was difficult, however, to identify ethical principles that would justify these situations as being ethically problematic.

It was possible, though, to identify three subcategories of authorship problems that were ethically problematic. The first two of these subcategories involve supervisee exploitation, with consequent harm to the supervisee and a breach of faithfulness on the part of the supervisor. These subcategories differ, though, in that with the first category, plagiarism, the person from whom the ideas of work was taken may either be unaware of the infraction or actually have colluded in it. Although in the second category, failure to give credit, one or more persons who expected author credit did not receive it.

Some of the more contentious problems arise in determining what authorship, if any, a faculty member can take on an article developed from a dissertation. This, in turn, seems grounded in assumptions about what a dissertation is or should be: If it literally is independent research in which the student has formulated the problem, developed the design, gathered data, and conducted analyses with relative independence, the authorship certainly is the student's. Some faculty apparently believe this is how all dissertations are to be developed. . . .

In practice, few dissertations would meet such a rigorous standard of independence. This is so because students approach their dissertations with differing levels of preparation and therefore faculty often must assume substantial roles in the conceptualization and execution of the projects. Moreover, students often participate in larger research projects, from which they obtain real benefits.

One element in the debate about what level of authorship, if any, a faculty member should have on dissertation-based articles likely derives from psychology's failure to adopt uniform guidelines for the research preparation of students. Compare this situation, for example, with the practitioner training that students receive in professional psychology programs. For this training, students participate in a series of practica and internship experiences; APA accreditation guidelines provide some general consistency across training programs for these experiences. No such uniformity exists, however, in the research training of students, even in those programs that espouse a scientist–practitioner model. . . . Thus, whereas a dissertation is for some students akin to an internship in research, for many others it is more akin to a first practicum. That is, whereas some students have multiple experiences in conducting research prior to undertaking a dissertation, for too many it is their first research project. In the latter case, it is difficult for the faculty supervisor to avoid making major contributions to the project, thereby earning eventual authorship.

Another cause of authorship uncertainties seems to come from the common use of the implicit metaphor of authorship as a type of currency to purchase resources. Researchers often offer junior authorship as compensation for any of a variety of possible contributions that might be made to a research project, from conducting literature searches to providing access to existing databases. But this metaphor can become a source of problems for the many students who engage in supervised research as graduate assistants and are receiving real currency as compensation. The results of several critical incidents have suggested that the question in many such cases is whether receiving a paycheck adequately compensates for research participation. Perhaps the alternative question is, Does receiving both a paycheck and a junior authorship constitute "double-dipping." (Faculty, of course, receive both salary and authorship for their contributions with no such questions being raised.) In the absence of clear norms for these matters, the best way of handling such issues probably is to have the ground rules for research participation clear to all parties at the outset of a project.

443

In contrast to the possible "theft" involved in the first two of these authorship subcategories, the third subcategory involves unwarranted gifts of credit. A real difficulty in this case is that the psychologist may operate with the best of motives. He or she may, for example, wish to help promote the career of a mentee. In this way, the supervisor actually is adhering to the principle of benefiting another. A possible difficulty, though, is that if others are involved as coauthors on the basis of having made real contributions to the project, their benefits are "diluted" with the inclusion of the noncontributor (i.e., generally, the greater the number of authors, the less the perceived contribution of each). This raises both the principle of fairness and that of doing no harm. . . .

References

Goodyear, R. K., & Sinnett, E. R. (1984). Current and emerging ethical issues of counseling psychologists. *The Counseling Psychologist, 12,* 87–93.

Kitchener, K. S. (1984). Intuition, critical evaluation, and ethical principles: The foundation for ethical decisions in counseling psychology. *The Counseling Psychologist, 12,* 43–45.

Magoon, T. M., & Holland, J. L. (1984). Research training and supervision. In S. D. Brown & R. W. Lent (Eds.), *Handbook of counseling psychology* (pp. 682–715). New York: Wiley.

Tabachnick, B. G., Keith-Spiegel, P., & Pope, K. S. (1991). Ethics of teaching: Beliefs and behaviors of psychologists as educators. *American Psychologist, 46,* 506–515.

◆ ◆ ◆

Commentary: Although the APA Ethics Committee receives very few complaints concerning authorship credit (see chap. 1, this volume), a recent survey of 604 APA members and student affiliates found that over 27% of respondents believed they had been involved in unethical or unfair authorship assignment with non-tenured faculty members, and women were more likely to be involved in such incidents compared with tenured faculty and men. No reliable data were available for students because only 4% responded to the survey. See Sandler, J. C., & Russell, B. L. (2005). Faculty–student collaborations: Ethics and satisfaction in authorship credit. Ethics & Behavior, 15, *65–80.*

For a more extended discussion of the assignment of publication credit in student–faculty collaborations see also Nguyen, T., & Nguyen, T. D. (2006). Authorship ethics: Issues and suggested guidelines for the helping professions. Counseling and Values, 50, *208–216. See, particularly, Costa, M. M., & Gatz, M. (1992). Determination of authorship credit in publishing dissertations.* Psychological Science, 3, *354–357. Using vignettes distributed to all students and faculty at seven geographically diverse doctoral-level psychology departments, Costa and Gatz found that students were given more credit by faculty on published dissertations than on nondegree research but that second authorship credit by the faculty member for dissertations was almost automatic. Contrary to expectations, students were more generous to advisors than advisors were to themselves, with senior faculty giving greater credit to graduate students than did junior faculty. Another helpful resource is Fine, M. A., & Kurdek, L. A. (1993). Reflections on determining authorship credit and authorship order on faculty–student collaborations.* American Psychologist, 48, *1141–1147. This article was particularly educational because it contained four realistically based but hypothetical cases involving authorship credit, suggested ethical principles to guide decision making, proposed some decision rules, and then applied these principles and rules to the four cases. Readers may not agree with the outcomes, but these cases will surely provoke useful discussion. For three published comments on Fine & Kurdek, see the Comment section of 1994* American Psychologist, 49, *1094–1096. For a study, also using vignettes, that correlates gender and differences in the appraisal of authorship credit, see Rose, M. R., & Fischer, K. (1998). Do authorship policies impact students' judgments of perceived wrongdoing?* Ethics & Behavior, 8, *59–79.*

Although guidelines for authorship credit appear in the fifth edition of the Publication Manual of the American Psychological Association *(2001), an enforceable provision concerning assignment of publication credit is now found in Standard 8.12 of the 2002 Ethical Principles. Other relevant standards are 8.10 (Reporting of Research Results), 8.11 (Plagiarism), 8.13 (Duplicate Publication of Data), and 8.14 (Sharing Research Data for Verification). For a rare discussion of ethical issues related to the peer review* of manuscripts, see Rogers, R. (1992). *Investigating psychology's taboo: The ethics of editing. Ethics & Behavior, 2, 253–261. For an extended discussion of academic dishonesty generally and cheating particularly see Keith-Spiegel, P., & Whitley, B. (Eds.). (2001). Academic dishonesty [Special issue]. Ethics & Behavior, 11.*

The conduct, reporting, and publishing of research are not the only arenas within the academic environment that engender ethical concerns. Yet, with the exception of the problem of multiple relationships between faculty and students (see chap. 5, this volume), few writers have paid attention to a host of ethical dilemmas that may arise in the university. There is, however, beginning to be some literature on the ethics of supervision and mentoring. As Johnson and Nelson (1999) explain,

> Though no specific ethical guidelines have been drafted specifically for mentoring relationships, [but see Standards 7.06 and 7.07 of the 2002 Ethics Code] several essential principles serve as a reasonable starting point. . . . Psychologists who mentor may consider the principles of (a) Autonomy (How can I strengthen my protégé's knowledge, maturity, and independence?), (b) Nonmaleficence (How can I avoid intentional or unintended harm to those I mentor?), (c) Beneficence (How can I contribute to the welfare of my protégé and facilitate his or her growth?), (d) Justice (How will I ensure equitable treatment of protégés regardless of . . . race, age, and gender?), and (e) Fidelity (How can I keep promises and remain loyal to those students I mentor?). (p. 195)

Johnson, W. B., & Nelson, N. (1999). *Mentor–protégé relationships in graduate training: Some ethical concerns.* Ethics & Behavior, 9, 189–210.

See also, for example:

Barnett, J. E., & Carter, J. A. (Eds.) (2007). *Clinical supervision issues in professional psychology [Special section].* Professional Psychology: Research and Practice, 38, 221–275.

Bernard, J., & Goodyear, R. (1992). *Fundamentals of clinical supervision.* Boston: Allyn & Bacon.

Russell, R., & Petrie, I. (1994). *Issues in training effective supervisors.* Applied and Preventive Psychology, 3, 27–42.

Sullivan, L., & Ogloff, J. (1998). *Appropriate supervisor–graduate–student relationships.* Ethics & Behavior, 8, 229–248.

Vacha-Haase, T., Davenport, D. S., & Kerewsky, S. D. (2004). *Problematic students: Gatekeeping practices of academic professional psychology programs.* Professional Psychology: Research and Practice, 35, 115–122.

Vasquez, M. (1992). *Psychologist as clinical supervisor: Promoting ethical practice.* Professional Psychology: Research and Practice, 23, 196–202.

Although these articles focus on supervisor behavior, a recent article investigated unethical conduct by supervisees. See Worthington, R. L., Tan, J. A., & Poulin, K. (2002). *Ethically questionable behaviors among supervisees: An exploratory investigation.* Ethics & Behavior, 12, 323–351. *What do readers believe are the most flagrant violations of the APA Ethics Code among trainees?*

Black and White and Shades of Gray:
A Portrait of the Ethical Professor

Mary Birch, Deni Elliott, and Mary A. Trankel

. . .

UM SURVEY OF ETHICS

The survey described in this article represents an attempt to identify expectations of ethical behavior shared by members of a single institution from a variety of teaching disciplines. From these expectations we developed a portrait of an ethical professor.

. . .

METHOD

A survey questionnaire was sent to all UM (Univ. of Montana) faculty who were identified as full-time tenured teaching faculty as of the Spring semester of 1997 ($N = 336$). Respondents in this survey were asked to rate 64 behaviors in terms of perceived ethical appropriateness. The 5-point rating scale ranged from 1 (*unquestionably not ethical*) to 5 (*unquestionably ethical*). The last item on the survey asked, "Do you have any other comments to offer with regard to ethical behaviors of professors?" Respondents were also requested to indicate their sex and whether they taught an ethics course.

LIMITATIONS

Survey results must be viewed with care. The concern most frequently expressed by respondents, and the most serious limitation of this research, is the lack of context for the behaviors listed in the survey. That is several comments from respondents indicated that some behaviors could be considered ethical under certain circumstances but unethical under others. . . .

. . .

RESULTS

Surveys were returned by 154 of the 336 faculty on the mailing list (a response rate of 46%). One hundred and forty-seven provided useable data.

. . .

In developing this portrait of the ethical professor we combined the two ratings on either end of the scale—that is, ratings of *unquestionably not ethical* and *most likely not ethical* were combined to discuss perceptions of what the faculty perceived as *not ethical*. Similarly, *unquestionably ethical* and *most likely ethical* were combined in discussing what was perceived as *ethical* behavior. Behaviors rated "3" and behaviors not rated were combined in the "unsure" category. A high-percentage response in the extremes of the continuum constitutes the "black and white" area of our portrait. Those behaviors that did not have high rating agreement at either extreme and/or higher percentage of ratings in the "unsure" category constitute the gray area of the portrait. These are the behaviors that may or may not be ethical, depending on the specifics of any given situation, or they may be considered "undesirable" but not necessarily "unethical." Table 1 shows the percentage response for each of the 5-point ratings for the 64 behaviors on the survey. Items are presented in descending order according to the percentage who rated them as unethical (i.e., the combined responses for ratings of 1 and 2). The combined percentages falling into this "unsure" category appear in the final column of Table 1.

The first column of Table 1 also contains designations for assignment of each item into overall categories of behaviors. Sixteen items on the survey ("G" designation) appear to tap faculty perceptions of behaviors related to grading and testing. Eighteen

TABLE 1

Percentage of Professors Responding in Each Category

Category	Survey items	M	% Unethical	1	2	3	4	5	% Unsure
G	Giving lower grades to students who strongly oppose your views.	1.12	98.6	88.4	10.2	0	.7	0	.7
G*	Ignoring evidence of cheating.	1.21	98.0	79.6	18.4	1.4	0	0	2.1
S*	Telling a student, "I'm sexually attracted to you."	1.12	98.0	87.8	10.2	.7	0	0	2.1
S*	Becoming sexually involved with a student enrolled in one of your classes.	1.14	97.9	89.1	8.8	.7	1.4	0	.7
G*	Giving easy grades to avoid negative evaluations from students.	1.27	96.6	76.2	20.4	2.0	.7	0	2.7
T*	Teaching under the influence of alcohol or recreational drugs.	1.18	95.9	82.3	13.6	.7	0	.7	3.4
S	Failure to acknowledge significant student participation in research publication.	1.24	95.3	76.2	19.1	.7	0	.7	4.1
T*	Teaching that certain races are intellectually inferior.	1.17	93.8	85.0	8.8	2.0	1.4	0	4.7
G	Lowering course demands for student athletes.	1.37	93.2	66.7	26.5	2.7	1.4	0	5.4
S*	Belittling students' comments in class.	1.48	89.1	60.5	28.6	5.4	1.4	.7	8.8
G*	Allowing a student's likeability to influence your grading.	1.61	88.4	51.0	37.4	4.8	2.0	1.4	8.2
G	Lowering course demands for minority students.	1.65	83.7	48.3	35.4	9.5	2.7	0	13.6
G	Relaxing rules (e.g., late papers, attendance) so students will like you.	1.66	83.0	49.0	34.0	10.2	.0	.7	14.3
S*	Sharing with colleagues confidential disclosures told to you by student.	1.54	82.3	60.5	21.8	10.2	2.0	.7	15.0
M	Using university supplies and equipment for personal use.	1.82	81.7	45.6	36.1	7.5	6.1	2.7	9.5
G	Lowering course demands for students who have too many work or family demands.	1.71	81.0	44.9	36.1	14.3	1.4	0	17.7
G	Failure to provide negative comments on a paper or exam when these comments reflect your honest assessment of the student's performance.	1.85	81.0	35.4	45.6	12.9	4.1	0	14.9
G	Grading on criteria not included in course syllabus.	1.93	78.2	33.3	44.9	11.6	5.4	1.4	15.0
T	Failure to keep up-to-date on recent research and scientific findings in one's field of academic/professional expertise.	1.89	78.2	34.0	44.2	11.6	4.8	.7	16.4
U*	Ignoring a colleague's unethical behavior.	1.88	76.8	33.3	43.5	13.6	2.0	1.4	19.7
G	Not providing alternative teaching and testing procedures for students who have learning disabilities.	1.90	74.1	36.7	37.4	17.7	4.8	0	21.1
S*	Ridiculing a student in a faculty-only discussion.	1.89	72.8	40.1	32.7	12.9	7.5	.7	19.0
U	Failure to challenge remarks by students or colleagues that are racist, sexiist, or otherwise derogatory to particular groups of people.	2.16	67.3	23.1	44.2	19.7	6.1	2.0	24.5
T*	Failing to present views that differ from your own.	2.15	66.0	23.1	42.9	19.0	8.2	.7	25.1
T*	Criticizing all theoretical orientations except those you personally prefer.	2.18	63.9	34.0	29.9	14.3	10.2	5.4	20.4
T	Failure to maintain regularly scheduled office hours.	2.27	63.2	19.0	44.2	20.4	10.2	1.4	25.2
S	Using your role to influence students to support causes in which you have an interest.	2.14	63.2	29.9	33.3	23.1	6.1	2.7	27.9
S*	Reluctance to help a student file an ethics complaint against another instructor when you believe that the complaint might be justified.	2.22	61.9	26.5	35.4	27.2	3.4	4.8	29.9

(continued)

TABLE 1

Percentage of Professors Responding in Each Category (*Continued*)

Category	Survey items	M	% Unethical	1	2	3	4	5	% Unsure
T	Teaching a class in ethics while engaging in unethical behavior in one's personal life.	2.12	61.2	38.8	22.4	22.4	10.9	2.0	25.8
S*	Avoiding negatives in writing a letter of reference for a questionable student or colleague.	2.35	58.5	17.0	41.5	27.2	9.5	1.4	30.6
T	Differing significantly from materials or content listed in course syllabus or college catalog.	2.40	57.1	17.0	40.1	22.4	10.9	3.4	28.5
T*	Teaching a class without adequate preparation for the day.	2.46	56.5	17.0	39.5	24.5	11.6	4.8	27.2
G	Leaving graded papers and exams outside one's office in an area of public access.	2.46	56.4	26.5	29.9	20.4	8.2	11.6	23.8
TS*	Teaching in settings that do not accommodate students with disabilities.	2.30	55.8	23.1	32.7	23.7	9.5	2.7	31.9
G	Giving passing grades to students who could not pass tests, but who put forth considerable effort to meet course standards.	2.31	54.55	25.2	29.3	27.2	12.9	.7	32.0
S	Discussing your personal problems with a student.	2.36	53.0	19.0	34.0	33.3	4.8	3.4	38.7
U	Avoidance of departmental/university committees and associated responsibilities.	2.55	51.0	19.0	32.0	24.5	13.6	6.8	28.6
G	Returning grade papers without comments.	2.59	49.0	14.3	34.7	25.9	16.3	4.1	30.7
M	Giving priority to one's research interest over the students' educational experience.	2.66	47.0	14.3	32.7	22.4	19.7	4.8	28.5
M*	Selling unwanted complimentary texts to used book buyers.	2.70	46.9	19.7	27.2	25.2	14.3	11.6	27.2
S*	Allowing students to withdraw from or drop a class when they are technically not eligible to do so.	2.54	45.6	14.3	31.3	34.0	13.6	1.4	39.4
U	Failure to maintain a collegial atmosphere among faculty, students, and other memfbers of the university community.	2.67	44.9	10.2	34.7	32.0	10.2	6.8	38.1
G*	Grading on a strict curve regardless of class performance level.	2.70	42.9	13.6	29.3	30.6	12.9	7.5	36.7
U	Unwillingness to engage in discussion with colleagues with whom you diagree over issues of departmental or university policy.	2.68	41.5	16.3	25.2	33.3	12.2	7.5	38.7
S*	Becoming sexually involved with a student only after the course is completed and the grades filed.	2.66	41.4	22.4	19.0	30.6	15.0	8.2	35.4
M*	Using school resouraces to create a "popular" trade book.	2.69	40.1	20.4	19.7	26.5	19.7	6.1	34.0
M*	Giving academic credit instead of salary for student assistants.	2.81	36.7	15.6	21.1	31.3	18.4	8.2	36.7
TS*	Teaching in classes so crowded your ability to teach effectively is impaired.	2.77	36.1	11.6	24.5	36.7	15.0	5.4	43.5
U	Failure to support (teach in accordance with) the stated educational mission of the university.	2.74	33.3	8.8	24.5	38.8	15.0	2.0	49.7
U	Failure to publicly voice concerns over university policies or procedures about which you disagree.	3.04	29.2	5.4	23.8	39.5	13.6	12.2	44.9
S	Going to a bar with students after class.	3.09	27.2	12.9	14.3	28.6	27.2	10.9	34.7
T*	Teaching material that you had not yet mastered.	3.15	27.2	8.2	19.0	27.9	27.2	10.9	34.7
S*	Selling goods—your car, insurance, books—to one of your students.	3.19	24.4	8.8	15.6	30.6	29.9	10.9	34.7
S*	Hugging students.	3.14	24.4	8.8	15.6	36.1	23.8	11.6	40.2

TABLE 1

Percentage of Professors Responding in Each Category (*Continued*)

Category	Survey items	M	% Unethical	1	2	3	4	5	% Unsure
G	Giving the same test you used in previous semesters.	3.30	23.8	5.4	18.4	28.6	25.9	15.6	34.7
T*	Using same lecture notes from last term without updating them.	3.41	19.7	5.4	14.3	25.9	28.6	17.0	34.7
TS*	Teaching a setting lacking in racial/ethnic/gender diversity among the faculty.	3.59	17.6	2.0	15.6	27.9	19.0	27.2	36.1
S	Beginning an ongoing friendship with student who is enrolled in your class.	3.64	15.6	2.0	13.6	23.8	33.3	22.4	28.6
T*	Teaching that homosexuality per se is an acceptable alternative lifestyle.	3.84	12.9	7.5	5.4	19.0	26.5	37.4	23.1
S	Hiring a student to work for you—babysit, paint your house, type something.	3.74	10.9	6.1	4.8	24.5	31.3	27.9	29.9
S*	Accepting a student's invitation to a party.	3.70	10.2	4.1	6.1	26.5	36.7	22.4	30.6
M	Encouraging the elimination of programs that cannot be maintained at an appropriate level of excellence or that lack financial resources.	3.67	9.5	2.0	7.5	32.0	30.6	21.8	38.1
M	Accepting payment for speeches/consultant work while contracted full-time with the university.	3.98	8.2	3.4	4.8	17.0	35.4	34.7	21.8
T*	Encouraging competition among students.	3.84	8.2	1.4	6.8	25.2	33.1	27.9	30.6

Note. N = 147. Items appear in descending order by percentage who rated the behavior as Unethical. % Unethical = percentages answering 1 and 2; % Unsure = percentages answering 3 or leaving item blank (not rated); 1 = *Unquestionably not ethical*; 2 = *Most likely not ethical*; 3 = *Not sure*; 4 = *Most likely ethical*; 5 = *Unquestionably ethical*. * = Items on 1991 study; G = Grading and Testing; S = Student–Faculty Relationships; T = Teaching Activities; M = Miscellaneous; U = University Responsibility; TS = Teaching Settings.

items related specifically to teaching activities are designated with a "T." The items marked "TS" for "teaching settings" were separated from the overall "T" category because responses to those behaviors were not consistent with the others in the teaching category. Relationships between students and faculty formed a third category of 18 questions designated with an "S." Activities extending beyond the immediate classroom included interactions with colleagues and responsibilities related to overall functioning of the university (eight items with a "U" designation). . . . A final miscellaneous dimension ("M") was used to categorize a scattering of items that did not fit easily into any of the major category themes.

PORTRAIT OF THE ETHICAL PROFESSOR

In composing this portrait of the ethical professor, we identified nine behaviors that 90% or more of all faculty rated as unethical (i.e., *unquestionably not ethical* or *most likely not ethical*). Eight additional behaviors reached at least 80% agreement as being unethical. Highest on the list of these characteristics are the qualities of equity and fairness in assigning grades and applying course requirements. Equally important is the need to maintain clear boundaries in sexual relationships with students while they are in the professor's class.

The portrait that emerges is of a faculty member who does not do any of the following: punish students by assigning lower grades to those who hold views opposing their own, ignore evidence of cheating, give easy grades as a way of avoiding negative student evaluations, or relax rules to gain student approval. The ethical professor does not lower demands for student athletes, minority students, or students who have too many work or family demands. Objectivity is required in grading, and likability cannot influence the grading procedure. In addition, the ethical professor does not compromise objectivity by failing to provide negative comments on papers or exams when these comments reflect an honest assessment of the student's performance.

When students make important contributions to faculty research and publications, the ethical faculty member acknowledges such contributions. Professors show respect for students by not belittling their comments in class and by maintaining confidences that students disclose to faculty. The ethical professor does not compromise the quality of the students' educational experience by teaching under the influence of alcohol or recreational drugs or by presenting course material that portrays certain races as intellectually inferior. This professor also demonstrates ethical integrity by using university supplies and equipment for professional tasks only.

The ethical professor maintains clear sexual boundaries with students: He or she does not become sexually involved with students and does not tell students that he or she is sexually attracted to them. Although ethical sexual boundaries are well-defined for students in the professor's classes, these boundaries become less distinct once the student is no longer attending the professor's class.

The aforementioned features of our portrait were constructed from ratings of strong agreement among four-fifths of faculty respondents. There were six additional behaviors on which at least two-thirds of all faculty agreed were ethically inappropriate. In this extended picture, which begins to enter the "gray zone," the ethical professor is expected to: grade on the criteria delineated in the course syllabus, provide alternative teaching and testing procedures for students with learning disabilities, and keep up-to-date on recent research and scientific findings in his or her field of expertise. Respect for the student now extends to avoiding ridicule of students within faculty-only discussions. Two university-related items also fell into this slightly gray picture. The ethical professor does not ignore colleagues' unethical behavior and does challenge derogatory remarks made by students or colleagues.

CONCLUSIONS

Equity and fairness in applying course requirements and in assigning grades is essential for maintaining ethical integrity in academia, according to the respondents in this survey. Similarly, clear and irrefutable boundaries prohibiting sexual conduct with students enrolled in classes are required of the ethical professor.

However, faculty are far less certain about other areas of ethical behavior in academia. Considerable disagreement and uncertainty is evident in expectations concerning nonsexual relationships with students. This lack of clarity about the ethical appropriateness of dual relationships with students, such as developing friendships, may threaten the clearly agreed on ethical mandate of equity and fairness in treatment of all students.

Ethical responsibilities concerning involvement in the university community is a second area of considerable uncertainty. Professors who teach ethics courses are, however, significantly more likely than those who do not teach ethics to view these activities as part of their ethical responsibility. Willingness to engage in discussions with colleagues with whom the professor disagrees, publicly voicing concerns over problematic university policies, maintaining collegiality among members of the university community, and participating in committee responsibility were viewed by the ethics faculty as part of their ethical responsibilities.

. . . Two areas worthy of additional study identified by this survey are: clarification of the ethical expectations concerning faculty-student relationships outside the classroom, and clarification of ethical expectations that define and guide interaction among faculty colleagues and the university community as a whole. Furthermore, this study did not address some of the newer areas that may become concerns of the future—for example, reliance on electronic distance learning, use of part-time faculty, and efforts to diversify the student and faculty population along different lines.

. . .

Such attempts to clarify areas of ethical uncertainty may ultimately lead to debates about the desirability and the potential content of a Code of Ethics for academia. Indeed, a few potential respondents refused to fill out our survey because they feared such an inevitability. Their written comments suggested that professors should be left alone to determine their own personal code of ethical behaviors, just as they are free to determine class content and mode of presentation. However, we maintain that discussions of ethical responsibility in academia will clarify and energize what faculty believe is essential in maintaining educational institutions of high integrity worthy of public support, and these discussions and further research ought to be pursued.

References

Keith-Spiegel, P., Tabachnick, G., & Allen, M. (1993). Ethics in academia: Students' views of professors' actions. *Ethics & Behavior, 3,* 149–162.

Tabachnick, B., Keith-Spiegel, P., & Pope, K. (1991). Ethics of teaching, beliefs and behaviors of psychologists as educators. *American Psychologist, 46,* 506–515.

♦   ♦   ♦

Commentary: For a similar study surveying the judgments of graduate assistants in psychology doctoral programs, see Branstetter, S., & Handelsman, M. (2000). Graduate teaching assistants: Ethical training, beliefs, and practices. Ethics & Behavior, 10, 27–50.

CHAPTER 9

FORENSIC SETTINGS

The American legal system is complex. One of the complicating factors is that there are two parallel sets of courts: one national network of federal courts and 51 sets of separate state courts (including the District of Columbia). Furthermore, within each there is a criminal justice system and a civil justice system. State courts also have a hybrid criminal–civil system that deals with matters affecting juveniles. Forensic psychologists are called on to provide these systems and divisions within them with useful expert information that, it is hoped, will lead to more informed decisions by judges and juries about human behavior.

As Otto and Heilbrun (2002) note, psychologists have long provided therapeutic services in forensic settings such as prisons and juvenile detention centers. Newer conceptions of forensic psychology focus more on direct involvement in legal proceedings: A "forensic psychologist refers to any psychologist, experimental or clinical, who specializes in producing or communicating psychological research or assessment information intended for application to legal issues" (Grisso, 1987, p. 831; see also Committee on Ethical Guidelines for Forensic Psychologists, 1991). More forensic psychologists, however, engage in forensic psychological assessment, conducting evaluations at the behest of judges or attorneys (Otto & Heilbrun, 2002), than do research.

For example, in the criminal system, a forensic psychologist's traditional role may include evaluating criminal defendants (a) to determine whether they are competent to stand trial, (b) to determine what their mental state was at the time of the crime, or (c) to help the judge or the jury determine the proper sentence, including, in capital cases, whether the defendant should suffer the death penalty. In the civil system, a forensic psychologist may testify about the mental capacity and propensity for violence of someone that the state wishes to involuntarily hospitalize (civilly commit) and then offer recommendations for appropriate inpatient treatment. In the juvenile system, the forensic psychologist may offer an opinion, after an assessment, about whether a minor should be tried in juvenile court or waived for trial to an adult court (e.g., when the minor has allegedly been involved in a serious crime, particularly a violent one). Finally, a more academically oriented psychologist may consult with a party in litigation about legal tactics, jury selection, or the influence of pretrial publicity on jury objectivity.

Many of these, as well as other, functions are performed by psychologists who identify themselves as *forensic specialists*. They may belong to Division 41 (American Psychology–Law Society) of the American Psychological Association, or they may have been awarded a diploma by the American Board of Forensic Psychology—signifying that they meet certain educational, experiential, and evaluative criteria identifying them as having forensic expertise (see Otto & Heilbrun, 2002). They usually are employed by state-run institutions, but they are also found in community mental health centers and in independent practice (Grisso, 1987). These psychologists, primarily clinicians, spend a great deal of time in the courtroom and are frequent visitors to the witness stand.

It would be a mistake, however, to believe that only those psychologists who identify themselves as *forensic mental health professionals* will find themselves involved with the law. Every psychologist—whether clinician, scientist, or academician—is a potential expert witness (Otto & Heilbrun call them "accidental experts" [p. 15]), and each must be prepared to interact with the legal system. For example, clinicians who see children or families may be called to testify in divorce, child custody, or abuse litigation. A therapist whose client is in a serious automobile accident and claims to have been traumatized by it may be called to testify by the plaintiff–client or by the defendant about the client's mental or emotional condition before the accident. A neuropsychologist may be asked to give an opinion about the capacity of an elderly client to make a will or the extent of brain injury suffered by a worker in an industrial accident. An industrial psychologist who has developed a preemployment screening test claimed to discriminate against, for example, people with disabilities, may be compelled to explain how the instrument was constructed and validated. An academician conducting studies on adolescent gang violence or on other socially sensitive issues may be ordered by a judge to reveal otherwise confidential data concerning some or all of the participants in those studies. Likewise, a researcher who specializes in perception may be called by the defense in a criminal matter to inform a jury about the vagaries of eyewitness identification. Finally, psychologists, whatever their training, may wish to inform legislative or regulatory bodies about pending enactments or to lobby for a certain measure.

The psychologist's part in each of these scenarios is guided by ethical considerations. Although lawyers are obligated to champion their clients' causes through zealous and unbridled representation, different ethical imperatives may guide the behavior of psychologists who enter the hallowed halls of the law. This chapter examines the ethical dimensions of three major questions that face forensic psychologists: (a) Should an expert witness be an advocate or an objective teacher? (b) When performing psychological services at the behest of the court, who is the psychologist's ultimate client? and (c) Are there forensic functions that an ethical psychologist should refuse to perform?

Finally, a note about the 2002 Ethics Code and forensic psychology. The 1992 Code contained a separate component (Section 7) devoted to forensic activities. The 2002 Code no longer does so, although there are separate sections for education and training, research, assessment, and therapy. As Behnke (2004) explained, the task force decided to write its ethical standards broadly. Thus, "in keeping with this principle, the task force did not include a separate section on Forensic Activities in the revised code" (p. 84). Rather, it sprinkled provisions from Section 7 of the 1992 code throughout the 2002 Code. I have identified the following standards of the 2002 Code that are relevant to forensic psychology: 1.05, 2.01e, 2.04, 3.05a and c, 3.07, 3.10c, 4.05b, 5.01a, 9.01, 9.02–9.04, 9.10–9.11, and 10.02b.

References

Behnke, S. (2004, May). Forensic matters and the new APA Ethics Code. *Monitor on Psychology, 35*, 84–85.

Committee on Ethical Guidelines for Forensic Psychologists. (1991). Specialty guidelines for forensic psychologists. *Law and Human Behavior, 15*, 655–665.

Grisso, T. (1987). The economic and scientific future of forensic psychological assessment. *American Psychologist, 42*, 831–839.

Otto, R., & Heilbrun, K. (2002). The practice of forensic psychology: A look toward the future in light of the past. *American Psychologist, 57*, 5–18.

Use and Then Prove, or Prove and Then Use? Some Thoughts on the Ethics of Mental Health Professionals' Courtroom Involvement

David Faust

. . .

The psychology–law interface obviously involves two systems or institutions in which, however, psychology and law are not equal partners. Rather, in the legal arena, psychology is subsumed under law. It is not the judge who enters the clinician's office and lies down on the couch but the psychologist who enters his or her honor's home field. The legal system dominates in determining not only whether participation occurs but, when allowing it, the rules and procedures under which it takes place.

The court's authority, however, is incomplete. Most important, the potential psychologist–expert usually is not compelled to participate but rather does so voluntarily. For example, although the judge may allow testimony on the likelihood of future violent behavior, a psychologist asked to assist in the determination can refuse the request. The choice to not participate when one could paves the way for the expression of personal or professional (i.e., internal) standards and eases or alleviates the pressure to defer to the court's external standards. Usually, one can make the choice of nonparticipation without violating the rules of the dominant authority structure or without creating legal jeopardy. In contrast, if the law required professionals to serve as expert witnesses whether they wanted to or not, and one's own standards dictated noninvolvement, this would create an immediate legal conflict and put one at risk for official sanction. Of course, one can still live by personal standards under such circumstances, but it is more difficult to do so, and the balance of pluses and minuses may shift dramatically.

Obviously, the court's standards, which are external to the psychologist, and the psychologist's internal or professional standards may clash. At opposing ends of the spectrum are psychologists who always follow external standards and those who always follow internal standards, and in between are various possible combinations. . . .

◆ ◆ ◆

Commentary: Faust posits that law and psychology operate under two different systems. In what ways is this true, particularly with regard to their respective searches for the "truth" and their tolerance for indecision? Given these differences, one "basic concern is that the ethical standards of the psychologist can be jeopardized in the courtroom setting because of the psychologist's failure to recognize that the basic tenets of the legal system and the science of psychology are often at odds" (pp. 764–765). Anderten, P., Staulcup, V., & Grisso, T. (1980). On being ethical in legal places. Professional Psychology, 11, 764–773.

Reclaiming the Integrity of Science in Expert Witnessing

Bruce D. Sales and Daniel W. Shuman

. . .

Critics complain that many experts who testify abandon their scientific integrity and that the legal system stimulates this result. . . .

Given the importance of expert testimony and the pool of competent attorneys and scientists, what explains the perceived problems with expert witnessing? An important reason lies in the inherent conflicts between the goals of attorneys and the goals of scientists/experts (Champagne, Shuman, & Whitaker, 1991 . . .). Because the legal system is an adversarial system and science is not, the goals of the attorneys and the goals of the scientists/experts differ. Attorneys need partisan experts to persuade the trier of fact (judge or jury), which weighs in favor of the selection of the most articulate, understandable, presentable, and persuasive expert rather than the best scientist. Even when there are good scientists who fit the bill, attorneys have a strong incentive to choose the person whose presentation and interpretation of the data are most sympathetic to the attorney's cause. As Champagne et al. (1991) noted in their empirical study of the use of experts, "lawyers seemingly want articulate, partisan experts with integrity" (p. 387).

Science, on the other hand, demands that scientists focus only on scientific knowledge without the influence—whether subtle or explicit—of the attorney's goals. Of equal concern is that the attorneys respond to current cases, which causes them to pressure experts to reach firm conclusions on the witness stand, even if the science on the issue and the scientific enterprise are tentative and iterative in nature or if the scientific information is available. . . .

Although the law has attempted to address some of these problems (e.g., through the rules of evidence and the cases interpreting them), its solutions have neither quieted the legal debate nor provided helpful guidance to the dilemmas scientists experience as expert witnesses. . . . Thus, to the extent that scientists have placed their hopes for a resolution of this dilemma on the legal system, they have been disappointed. Perhaps the law should not be expected to be overly concerned about the needs of science given that it is not the law's focus; the law focuses on the resolution of disputes between parties.

Prior discussions of these problems by scientists are not terribly helpful. . . . The intervention of a rule or principled analysis could provide a systematic approach to generating insights and guidelines for solutions. To the extent that ethics governs all scientific and professional behavior—which it does—it is only appropriate that it becomes the first metric against which to judge the expert witnessing of scientists and professionals.

. . . [B]ecause psychologists have a well-developed system of ethics that bears on their activities . . . an ethical analysis of expert testimony by psychologists is informative. . . .

References

Champagne, A., Shuman, D. W., & Whitaker, E. (1991). The use of expert witnesses in American courts. *Judicature, 31,* 375–392.

When Is an "Expert" an Expert?

Kirk Heilbrun

THE QUESTION

As a newly-licensed doctoral-level clinical psychologist, you have recently begun working at a forensic hospital which evaluates and treats individuals committed by the courts as Incompetent to Stand Trial and Not Guilty by Reason of Insanity. As part of the orientation for new clinical staff, you have received information about the relevant applicable law for assessing trial competence and criminal responsibility, but you have not yet had the opportunity to perform any evaluations (under supervision or otherwise). You receive a request from an attorney to evaluate her client on these two issues as part of your private practice.

- Do you accept the referral?
- More generally, how do you decide when you are "sufficiently expert" to provide such evaluations?

THE RESPONSE

The response is from Kirk Heilbrun.

There are two levels on which these questions can be addressed: legal and ethical. . . . On the first level, the main question posed in this vignette involves how the law defines expertise in mental health for the purpose of providing forensic evaluation or testimony in litigation. We might begin with the definition of expertise provided by the *Federal Rules of Evidence*: a witness qualified "by knowledge, skill, experience, training, or education" may testify as an expert (Rule 702). Further elaboration is provided in the *Criminal Justice Mental Health Standards* published by the American Bar Association. Under Standard 7-3.10, qualifications for appointment by the court to perform a forensic evaluation should include:

1. sufficient professional education and sufficient clinical training and experience to establish the clinical knowledge required for the specific type(s) of evaluation(s) being conducted; and

2. sufficient forensic knowledge, gained through specialized training or an acceptable substitute therefore, necessary for understanding the relevant legal matter(s) and for satisfying the specific purpose(s) for which the evaluation is being ordered. (1989, p. 130)

Relevant state statutes, administrative code, and case law may provide further elaboration of these criteria.

For ethical guidance, one can look to APA's *Ethical Principles and Code of Conduct* (1992) and to the *Specialty Guidelines for Forensic Psychologists* (1991). The *Ethical Principles* indicate that "Psychologists . . . recognize the boundaries of the particular competencies and the limitations of their expertise. They provide only those services . . . for which they are qualified by education, training, or experience" (1992, p. 1599).[1] The *Specialty Guidelines* also emphasize the role of "specialized knowledge, skill, experience, and education" (1991, p. 658), the obligation to present to the court "the factual bases (knowledge, skill, experience, training, and education) for their qualifications as an expert, and the relevance . . . on the specific matters at issue" (1991, p. 658). Finally, the *Specialty Guidelines* note the responsibility for "a fundamental and reasonable level of knowledge and understanding of the legal and professional standards that govern their participation as experts in legal proceedings" (1991, p. 658).

In this case, there is fairly close agreement between relevant law and ethical standards regarding the basis for expertise (for a more detailed discussion of this relationship, see, e.g., Bersoff, 1995; Golding, 1990). The issue then becomes how we operationalize "knowledge, skill, experience, training, and education" in the context of the present

From *American Psychology–Law Society News*, 16(3), 5–6. Copyright 1996 by Division 41 of the American Psychological Association.

[1]*Ed Note*: See Standard 2.01 of the current (2002) APA Ethics Code.

example. One useful framework was discussed at the 1995 "Villanova Conference" on training in law and psychology, in which one working group considered the distinction between "informed," "proficient," and "specialized" in the forensic context. The informed clinician would be sufficiently aware of relevant law in important areas (e.g., informed consent, duty to protect) to practice in a legally sensitive way; such information could be obtained through a course at the graduate or internship level, or ongoing CE. However, this level of expertise was not envisioned as sufficient to provide forensic evaluation services. Elsewhere (Heilbrun, 1995), I have offered a two-part test to determine whether a given clinician has sufficient expertise to perform such evaluations: (1) whether the clinician has *substance expertise* with a given population, and (2) whether this expertise has been *applied in forensic contexts.* This test could be applied to the present question, if we assume that a psychologist should be at least *proficient* in a given area to provide forensic assessment services. Proficiency would require a substantive expertise with mentally disordered offenders, obtained through relevant training and experience with individuals with severe mental disorders and other kinds of psychopathology that are seen in correctional and forensic populations. Proficiency would also require that this substantive expertise had been applied in forensic contexts, particularly to the kind of issues (trial competence and criminal responsibility) there were to be decided as part of the present referral.

How might we decide whether a psychologist is sufficiently "proficient" in both substantive and applied forensic areas to reasonably accept this case? For the first part, we might ask whether the psychologist has obtained didactic training and supervised experience in clinical work with mentally disordered offenders. For the second (typically the part that is more likely to be overlooked), we might ask whether the psychologist has an awareness of law, ethics, and behavioral science research that is relevant to the forensic context. We might also look to determine whether the psychologist had received supervised experience in at least 5–10 similar cases during practicum, internship, postdoctoral, or CE training, had attended "forensic evaluator training" if it is available (in states such as Virginia and Florida), and had been certified as a forensic evaluator if available (in states such as Massachusetts).

Finally, there is a certain amount of judgment that should be exercised, depending on the nature of the referral. Cases of a certain kind (complex or highly visible, with a good deal of media exposure, or involving very serious offenses) require experience and competence beyond the proficient level. It would be preferable for a mental health professional, faced with a referral involving this kind of case, to refrain from accepting it until it seems clear that they can comfortably deal with the basics and the complexities presented by such forensic evaluations.

References

American Bar Association. (1989). *Criminal justice mental health standards.* Washington, DC: Author.

American Psychological Association. (1992). Ethical principles of psychologists and code of conduct. *American Psychologist, 47,* 1597–1611.

Bersoff, D. (Ed.). (1995). *Ethical conflicts in psychology.* Washington, DC: American Psychological Association.

Committee on Ethical Guidelines for Forensic Psychologists. (1991). Specialty guidelines for forensic psychologists. *Law and Human Behavior, 15,* 655–665.

Golding, S. (1990). Mental health professionals and the courts: The ethics of expertise. *International Journal of Law and Psychiatry, 13,* 281–307.

Heilbrun, K. (1995). Child custody evaluation: Critically assessing mental health experts and psychological tests. *Family Law Quarterly, 29,* 63–78.

◆　　◆　　◆

Commentary: Unfortunately, as the next excerpt indicates, the principles explicated by Heilbrun are not always honored.

Competence and Quality in the Performance of Forensic Psychologists

Leonard J. Haas

. . .

[J]udging by the sort of complaints that reach ethics committees and licensing boards, more professional attention needs to be addressed to the issues of competence and quality in psychological courtroom work. The need for this inquiry can be shown by referring to a case:

> Dr. F, a psychologist with essentially no forensic experience, was contacted by a former client and asked to write a letter in support of her attempt to obtain custody of the child after a divorce. The psychologist complied, writing a report to the mother's attorney, describing the father in a consistently negative light, alleging inferior school performance on the part of the child as a result of the father's influence, and suggesting that the son's intellectual capacity would have been better fostered under his mother's care. The letter was written without the psychologist having interviewed the son. The father obtained the services of another psychologist who evaluated all parties. This psychologist recommended that the father receive custody, in large part because the son had lived with the father and his current wife for the previous 12 years. In court testimony, Dr. F strenuously insisted that the mother showed no evidence of psychopathology, that she would be a superior parent, and that the father was destructive to the son. He was unable to provide evidence for any of these conclusions. When ethics charges were brought against Dr. F, he responded by attacking the ethics committee for its protectionist guild stance, alleging that to censure him would be to deprive him of free speech; further, he insisted that the adversary situation in the courtroom allowed him to advocate for the mother because the father had the benefit of his own counsel and psychologist.

The case illustrates a number of concerns that are examined later in this article. Consider first Dr. F's apparent attitudes toward his role, the courtroom context, and his professional peers. There is a certain amount of hubris in accepting the request of a former client in the first place, given that one has no prior experience in forensic work and given the problems of advocating for one side when it is necessary to have an equally complex understanding of the other side to competently render an assessment. Consider also the cavalier attitude toward the courtroom; "anything goes" when the other side can defend itself. Further, consider the attitude toward peers who try to critique Dr. F's behavior; they have nothing to teach him but rather are trying to restrict the exercise of what he obviously considers his enormous skills. Also consider the technical aspects of Dr. F's performance. He evaluates blindly on third party reports, which is less than competent even in a noncourtroom situation. He makes legal judgments (the mother should be awarded custody) rather than giving expert psychological testimony. In fact, his testimony is flawed in that it consists of opinions that are ordinarily based on assessment evidence; but he does not have the evidence. He also fails to indicate any awareness of alternative interpretations of the facts (e.g., the boy does not do well in school—

From *Ethics & Behavior, 3,* 251–256. Available at http://www.informaworld.com. Copyright 1993 by Taylor & Francis. Adapted with permission of the author and publisher.

although clear evidence would be helpful here also, and this could stem from a number of other causes but poor fathering). There is also a deceptive element in his lack of concern with the apparently successful adjustment the boy has made while living with the father for a number of years. Overall, this psychologist failed to appreciate that he was not really being recruited as an expert witness (who testifies about scientific findings and reviews the facts of the case in light of scientific knowledge not available to the court) or as a fact witness (who testifies as to what he has observed in his direct experience relevant to the case). Rather, the psychologist has been recruited as an advocate for the mother, illegitimately using his professional credentials to support what amounted to unvalidated opinions that could potentially harm the father, the boy, and perhaps others affected by this case. . . .

Obviously, the mere possession of generic professional psychology credentials cannot be claimed to give evidence of the necessary and sufficient skill to perform competently as a forensic psychologist. In addition to problems already noted, the performance pressures of being on the witness stand and the seductions of highly compensated evaluations and testimony can lead to enormous temptations to be a "hired gun" for the side that obtains one's services. It is ironic that in a forum supposedly designed to ferret out "the truth," psychologists at times find it hard to adhere to this standard. Consider the following case:

> Psychologist Q offered his services as an expert witness in a fitness-to-stand-trial case. He indicated that he was a "registered psychologist, APA" and that he was a professor at a college in another state. His vitae listed department chairmanship in one section, although in another he is listed as department chair during a different time period. In fact, he was neither licensed nor an ex-department chair, and the American Psychological Association (APA) does not "register" psychologists. When confronted with the inconsistencies on cross-examination, he admitted to the inaccurate representation of his credentials. He claimed that he wanted to testify

> out of concern for the client and that the errors were made by a secretary.

Examining the problems with this case, we find that it exemplifies, at its root, multiple levels of dishonesty. First, the psychologist misrepresents his credentials, and then attempts to misrepresent the cause of the misrepresentation. And, again, this is done in a setting designed to ensure that statements are factual. Granted, this may be an extreme example; nonetheless, a number of observers (Fersch, 1980; Shapiro, 1990) have noted that the demand characteristics of the forensic arena seem to exert considerable pressure on even well-trained psychologists to make more absolute statements than they can justify, to find classic examples, . . . and to abandon the standards of competence and quality they might espouse in more tranquil environments.
. . .

COMPETENCE IN RELATION TO THE PURPOSE OF COURTROOM TESTIMONY

The competent expert witness must know when his or her opinion is truly that of an expert and when it is no more informed than the opinion of an educated layperson. It is useful to note that the rules of evidence prohibit lay witnesses from testifying regarding their opinions. Rather, witnesses are required to testify about the facts. Experts, on the other hand, whose opinions may be based on special knowledge not available to the court or to the layperson, are entitled to give their opinions. However, those opinions must be given only within the area of their expertise.

In addition, with regard to obtained facts, the competent forensic psychologist clearly describes limitations and qualifications of findings, not just when they are based on third-hand report. . . .

In other words, competent experts should also know the strengths and limitations of their data and decision making. It is remarkable that so often this threshold is not reached, especially as the competent forensic psychologist should know that opposing counsel (and their experts) will exert their efforts (sometimes unfairly it seems) to highlight the inadequacies and deficiencies in the psychologist's evaluation findings. Rather, there seems to be a widely noted temptation in forensic work to go beyond the limits of one's competence (Fersch, 1980; Shapiro, 1990) and to "render opinions in areas in which either the psychologist has no particular training or the state of knowledge is so meager that opinions should not be rendered" (Shapiro, 1990, p. 746). Shapiro also noted the "classic example" problem: The expert witness describes the (far from conclusive) findings as revealing a classic example of Syndrome X. A case example illustrates this only too well:

> Dr. Q, a highly experienced forensic psychologist, was asked by the mother of two boys (the custodial parent) to evaluate them to determine if they were suffering psychological or physical damage from visitation with her estranged husband. The psychologist saw the mother and saw the boys each for approximately 2 hr, and later he testified in court regarding visitation issues. He recommended no visitation. In his testimony, the psychologist repeatedly stated that the father was physically, psychologically, and verbally abusive; his source for this was verbal allegations by the sons, reports by the mother, and suggestions in the report of a previous psychologist who had evaluated the family. Asked about his confidence in his opinions, based upon only 2 hr with each child and no contact with the father himself, the psychologist stated "this is one of the clearest cases I've ever seen." He also indicated that he had no reservations about the validity and reliability of his opinions, diagnosis, and prognosis.

This is another extreme, yet telling, example of the apparently irresistible urge to go beyond one's data and to use strong language to cover up lack of evidence. This psychologist's work represents the offering of opinions without adequate data. There was no indication that the psychologist was alert to pressure that could have led to the misuse of his influence. He apparently felt that it was his duty to protect these boys and in that regard went forward despite the inadequacy of his factual base. In addition, by

diagnosing the father as abusive solely on the basis of the boy's allegations, the psychologist was using inadequate assessment techniques. Again, "psychologists must remain scrupulously close to the data, present only material that is solidly documented, and present only conclusions that can be firmly supported by the data" (Shapiro, 1990, p. 746). . . . If an expert witness cannot make more valid judgments than a judge or jury, then it is unlikely that the expert will be able to help a judge or jury improve the accuracy of their judgments.

. . .

Competence also requires the ability to recognize who is the client. This awareness may sharpen some of these ethical problems. If the psychologist considers that his or her client is the court or the justice system in the abstract, it would seem clear that the best way to serve the interests of the client is to be as honest and careful as possible (Fersch, 1980) . . . . It is incumbent on psychologists to become aware of the limits of their roles. They must also attempt to communicate these limitations to the relevant participants in the legal proceeding.

There may be an additional ethical dilemma for the psychologist in the courtroom who believes that there is an ethical obligation to attempt to prevent misuse of his or her work (Fersch, 1980). It appears unlikely that this is a resolvable dilemma, largely because it is not clear how this obligation could be carried out in the courtroom environment. In the courtroom, the ethics of the jurisprudence system demand an adversarial proceeding, in which opposing attorneys will attempt to present only aspects of the testimony that support their respective sides and where control over the testimony heavily resides with attorneys and the questions they pose.

THREATS TO COMPETENCE

The seductive power of the courtroom and the subtle gratification of being on stage as the expert can sometimes blind the psychologist to the need for particular skills and particular frames of mind necessary to both serve the court system and do justice to the complexity and integrity of the psychological profession. This section identifies several difficulties that interfere with competent practice.

Failure to Understand the Justice System

As noted, it is important to recognize when one is entitled to give one's opinion in court rather than simply testifying about the facts. It is also important to know when one is rendering a legal opinion versus a professional opinion that is within one's area of expertise. Although these problems are more common among psychologists who are less experienced in courtroom work, they are certainly not unknown among psychologists with many years of experience in the justice system.

A problem that also appears, regardless of experience, is that of not preparing adequately; numerous cases have been demolished by the expert psychologist not having access to his or her records, not having reviewed the findings carefully, or overlooking or omitting key material. This type of problem reflects a lack of understanding that the justice system requires evidence to support conclusions and that careful preparation is required.

Ironically, much of the effectiveness of courtroom work by psychologists hinges on their persuasive or performance skills rather than their skills at doing the psychological job. . . . Potentially, one could argue that the witness who fails to clearly carry his or her point across to the jury is not as competent as the expert showman. Clearly this is not a dichotomous judgment of competence; there is both a content dimension and a process dimension to competent expert testimony, but the testimony, regardless of the flair with which it is delivered, must be scientifically valid and germane to the issues at hand.

Unfortunately, the emphasis on style over substance can lead to cynicism about the justice system; assuming that the most dazzling presentation will sway the naive jury or dumbfound the poorly prepared opposition can lead psychologists to forget the ethic of competence. On the other hand, cynicism and incompetence can result from the psychologist feeling overwhelmed by the legal arena, assuming that the deck is stacked, and not bothering to prepare adequately. This can be compounded by the psychologist getting away with such behavior; more than one ethics complaint has elicited the response "but this is the way I did it in my previous three cases and no one complained."

Professional Arrogance

Although this is more commonly a threat to the competence of senior forensic psychologists than more junior ones, it is not unknown even among psychologists who are complete novices in the courtroom. The arrogant psychologist often relies completely on his or her superb memory, thus ignoring standards of recordkeeping or documentation and exhibiting an almost complete certainty about conversations and observations that occurred long ago.

The problem of diagnosis in absentia can be considered a result of arrogance as well, although, in the many ethics complaints arising from this problem, it is simply characterized as incompetence. The psychologist who is willing to make a diagnostic statement based solely on the report of a third party is making a diagnosis based on hearsay, and with the publication of the revised "Ethical Principles of Psychologists and Code of Conduct" (APA, 1992) is likely to be committing an ethical breach. The ethical principles place the burden for diagnosis in absentia squarely on the psychologist's shoulders; it is permissible only if one can justify such a deviation from standard assessment practice.

The reliance of some senior forensic psychologists on their clinical savvy also reflects professional arrogance, and this often leads to inadequate assessment. Judgments based on intuition following a brief interview, although they may be useful as working hypotheses in ongoing treatment, can be damaging when used as the basis for expert testimony.

Advocating Rather Than Testifying

The belief that as a psychologist one knows more than anyone in the justice system about the proper outcome for a case can be a major threat to competence. Wasserstrom (1975) referred to "role-differentiated behavior" that allows the professional to suspend certain moral considerations that would hold for individuals in general. . . . Applying this logic to the arena of forensic psychologists, it is easy to see how the demand characteristics of the legal arena might sway psychologists from their position of scientific objectivity to an advocacy position. A related problem may have more to do with a displaced faith in the adversary system; the psychologist freely advocates for his or her side and assumes that the other side can protect itself. This logic leads to greatly underestimating the potential that one's testimony might do harm to one or more participants in the process. A trenchant example of this is a recent ethics complaint in which the psychologist defended himself by noting that the court failed to follow his recommendations (which were based on inadequate assessment); therefore, no harm was caused.

Failure to Attend to Changes in the Knowledge Base

It is perhaps tautological to point out that deficient knowledge is a major threat to competence (Peterson & Bry, 1980), and yet it is important to consider the fluid nature of competence in this regard. Competence is always a relative term, especially in a field that is based on empirical findings and that is evolving at a rather rapid rate. . . . This is a strong argument for continuing education and continuing self-examination. A considerable number of ethics and malpractice complaints could be avoided if the psychologist were to become acquainted with (and use) current, well-validated assessment instruments, for example.

. . .

Greed

Unfortunately, forensic work is seen as a lucrative line of work, and this comprises a threat to competence. In a rational world, highly rewarded activities might generate greater efforts to become competent, but a number of ethics complaints demonstrate that a small proportion of psychologists view the opportunity to provide expert testimony as an opportunity to over-assess, perform lengthy reviews of material, and generally inflate their expenses. In addition, psychologists who hope to enrich themselves by showing how they can win cases may misstate their credentials or their findings.

. . .

CONCLUSION

In large part, the discussion has only elaborated on principles contained in the "Ethical Principles of Psychologists and Code of Conduct" (APA, 1992). But these standards must be elaborated by an awareness of the relevant substantive literature in one's area(s) of forensic practice; the obtaining of ongoing education in one's field of practice; and the possession of sufficient education, training, or experience to make one competent. Clearly, the skills to perform well in the courtroom are not automatically gained when one is granted a license to practice psychology or a doctoral degree.

References

American Psychological Association. (1992). Ethical principles of psychologists and code of conduct. *American Psychologist, 44,* 1597–1611.

Fersch, E. A. (1980). Ethical issues for psychologists in court settings. In J. Monahan (Ed.), *Who is the client?* (pp. 43–62). Washington, DC: American Psychological Association.

Peterson, D. R., & Bry, B. H. (1980). Dimensions of perceived competence in professional psychology. *Professional Psychology, 11,* 965–971.

Shapiro, D. L. (1990). Problems encountered in the preparation and presentation of expert testimony. In E. Marginal (Ed.), *The encyclopedic handbook of private practice* (pp. 739–758). New York: Gardner.

Wasserstrom, R. A. (1975). Lawyers as professionals: Some moral issues. *Human Rights, 5,* 1–24.

♦ ♦ ♦

Commentary: One hundred years ago, an author writing on expert testimony quoted this from an unidentified trial lawyer's closing statement: "Gentlemen of the jury," the attorney began, "there are three kinds of liars—the common liar, the damned liar, and the scientific expert" (p. 169). See Foster, W. L. (1897). Expert testimony—Prevalent complaints and proposed remedies. Harvard Law Review, 11, 169–186.

There is some evidence that lawyers do frequently coach experts; that experts are generally receptive to this process; and as a result, that these "hired guns" vary their testimony to suit the needs of the side by which they have been retained. See, for example:

Buckshot, R. (1986). Personal values and expert testimony. Law of Human Behavior, 10, 127–144.

Champagne, A., Shuman, D. W., & Whitaker, E. (1991). The use of expert witnesses in American courts. Judicature, 31, 375–392.

Guthrie, T. G., Hauser, M., White, M. S., Spruill, G., & Strasburger, L. H. (2003). "The whole truth" versus "the admissible truth": An ethics dilemma for expert witnesses. Journal of the American Academy of Psychiatry and the Law, 31, 422–427.

Hagen, M. (1997). Whores of the court: The fraud of psychiatric testimony and the rape of American justice. New York: HarperCollins.

Human, R. J., & Kennedy, D. B. (1987). Subjective factors in clinicians' judgments of insanity: A comparison of a hypothetical and an actual case. Professional Psychology: Research and Practice, 18, 439–446.

Mossman, D. (1999). "Hired guns," "whores," and "prostitutes": Case law references to clinicians of ill repute. Journal of the American Academy of Psychiatry and the Law, 27, 416–425.

Otto, R. K. (1989). Bias and expert testimony of mental health professionals in adversarial proceedings: A preliminary investigation. Behavioral Sciences and the Law, 7, 267–273.

For a general review of biases to which forensic clinicians are subject, see Bersoff, D. N. (1992). Judicial deference to nonlocal decision-makers: Imposing simplistic solutions on problems of cognitive complexity in mental disability law. Southern Methodist Law Review, 46, 327–370.

Haas's article, excerpted above, raises a number of crucial ethical issues for forensic psychologists: dual relationships, testifying as to the ultimate issue, the difference between fact and expert witnesses, competence, and the distinction between the expert as advocate and educator, among others. The following article provides some guidance in dealing with the competing tensions expert witnesses face.

The Expert Witness, the Adversary System, and the Voice of Reason: Reconciling Impartiality and Advocacy

Daniel W. Shuman and Stuart A. Greenberg

The ethical codes that guide psychologists' behavior in the courtroom seek to ensure that psychologists are impartial providers of reliable information to the courts in their field of competence. The rules of evidence that determine the admission of expert testimony seek to ensure that expert testimony assists the judge or jury in its decision making. The adversary system, and more particularly the attorneys who shape its operation, demand that the experts whom they retain assist them in their obligation to provide diligent representation to their clients. Partisanship is often an implicit condition of expert employment, and it may also result unintentionally from empathy or identification with a party or litigation team loyalty.

Although the evidentiary and ethical codes are both intended to result in the presentation of reliable evidence that assists in ascertaining truth, they exert competing tensions when applied within the adversary system. In perhaps the most common of such conflicts, experts complain that they are pressured by the attorneys who retain them to support the attorney's advocacy by testifying beyond their professional standards. The courts provide little direct assistance to experts desiring to resist this pressure and rarely consider ethical standards in judging the admissibility of expert testimony (Shuman & Greenberg, 1998). Even when a judge overrules an objection grounded in the violation of an ethical rule and permits experts to testify, that does not exempt experts from professional discipline for behaving in a judicially acceptable but an ethically problematic manner. Nor does a judge's failure to exclude expert testimony exempt experts from malpractice suits by parties harmed by ethically problematic testimony. These disparities leave experts vulnerable to ethical sanctions and malpractice actions, even when the behavior did not result in the court's exclusion of the problematic testimony.

Experts perceive that they are often trapped between discordant ethical and legal concerns. Consequentially, experts may perceive that they must choose between integrity and advocacy. This article explains why pitting integrity against advocacy is a false choice. It . . . describes an alternative, integrated approach to advocacy that permits experts to be concurrently ethical, persuasive, impartial, and helpful.

THE RULES OF THE COURTS AND THE PROFESSIONS

The legal system has adopted a series of rules that govern the qualifications, reliability, basis, and form of expert testimony. These rules impose preconditions for the admissibility of expert testimony, superimposed on civil and criminal liability schemes designed to deter testimony that frustrates the interests of the legal system. The core legal rule that governs the admissibility of expert testimony in most jurisdictions in the United States is expressed in Federal Rule of Evidence (Fed. R. Evid.) 702 and its state equivalents. The federal rule provides that "if scientific, technical, or other specialized knowledge *will assist the trier of fact to understand the evidence or to determine a fact in issue* [italics added], a witness qualified as an expert by knowledge, skill, experience, training, or education, may testify thereto in the form of an opinion or otherwise." It is this language that cases like *Daubert v. Merrell Dow Pharmaceuticals, Inc.* (1993) have interpreted in order to consider the evidentiary reliability proffered experts must achieve to

From *Professional Psychology: Research and Practice, 34,* 219–224. Copyright 2003 by the American Psychological Association.

be admitted. Thus, in the first instance, the admissibility of expert testimony turns on the assistance that experts may provide to the judge or jury.

Similarly, the professional system of regulation of the conduct of psychologists, as well as psychiatrists and other mental health professionals, creates a detailed system of ethical norms that governs their behavior as experts. These ethical norms govern the methods and procedures to be used in providing a forensic opinion to the legal system. The core ethical principle for psychological expert witnesses requires that "psychologists refrain from taking on a professional role when personal, scientific, professional, legal, financial, or other interests or relationships could reasonably be expected to (1) impair their objectivity, competence, or effectiveness in performing their functions as psychologists" (American Psychological Association [APA], 2002, Standard 3.06). This principle is embellished in the Specialty Guidelines for Forensic Psychologists (APA, Committee on Ethical Guidelines for Forensic Psychologists, 1991, Section VII B): "Forensic psychologists realize that their public role as 'expert to the court' or as 'expert representing the profession' confers upon them *a special responsibility for fairness and accuracy* [italics added]."

The legal rules and ethical norms express the compatible and comparable intent of encouraging expert witness reliability. However, the evidentiary rules are applied through the adversary system. This system delegates to the parties the decision to invoke or waive the rules of evidence and to judges the authority to admit challenged evidence, leaving to the jury the weight to afford it. Thus, if a party chooses not to object to the testimony of an unqualified witness, neither the witness nor the judge is ordinarily constrained to do so. Unlike the legal system's rules, however, the application of ethical norms is not bounded by the adversary system. For example, at least when it is possible to do so, "psychologists provide opinions of the psychological characteristics of individuals only after they have conducted an examination of the individuals adequate to support their statements or conclusions" (APA, 2002, Standard 9.01b). The decision of an opposing attorney not to object to an unfounded opinion in the absence of an examination waives the

legal objection but not the malpractice liability of the psychologist or the ethical complaint for the psychologist doing so. Neither does the judge's overruling such an objection.

Ethical guides (e.g., the Ethical Guidelines for the Practice of Forensic Psychiatry [American Academy of Psychiatry and the Law, 1996]; the Ethical Principles of Psychologists and Code of Conduct [APA, 2002]) suggest that forensic experts approach their role in a neutral, impartial manner, even when they are retained by one party. Psychologists may refuse the request of the attorneys who retained them to offer unfounded opinions. However, experts who do not respond to the adversarial needs of the parties who retain them risk their ire, risk not being retained again, and risk developing a reputation for uncooperativeness in the legal community. Experts face other risks if they succumb to the pressure or temptation of advocacy and go beyond what is adequately supported. Although a judge may rule that such overzealous testimony is admissible, experts may nevertheless be subject to civil liability and ethical complaints. Expert witnesses who offer inadequately reliable testimony may find themselves in a precarious legal and ethical position.

THE ROLES THAT EXPERTS PLAY

Tension in the roles that experts are expected to play is fundamental to the way in which experts are used in the legal system. Yet their use has become routine and, in some cases, almost unavoidable: "Expert testimony often adds an aura of reliability to a party's theories and claims. Many cases could not be tried without expert witnesses to testify as to the applicable standard of care, the reconstruction of accidents, or the value of a plaintiff's damages" (Richmond, 2000, p. 909).

It is often assumed that the major role problem presented by expert testimony is the conflict between serving therapeutic and forensic functions for the same client (Greenberg & Shuman, 1997; Heilbrun, 1995; Simon, 1995; Strasburger et al., 1997). It is easy to ignore the problems of intrarole conflicts and assume that each role is clear and manageable in its own right. However, the forensic expert is beholden to multiple masters. Integrating the demands of these masters is inherently complex. This requires reconciliation of a system of mental health professional regulation that demands impartiality and a system of legal dispute resolution that demands partisanship.

Attorneys are ethically required to be diligent advocates for their clients. Implicitly, all aspects of an attorney's conduct, including the presentation of experts, should further that role of diligent advocacy rather than disinterested neutrality. Most attorneys "would go into a lawsuit with an objective uncommitted independent expert about as willingly as [they] would occupy a foxhole with a couple of noncombatant soldiers" (Jensen, 1993, p. 192).

This concern is all the more powerful for those who work full time as forensic experts. Experts are aware that they are retained to assist in partisan advocacy that their ethics appear to prohibit. Experts are also aware that those who criticize the use of partisan experts complain that, for the right price, it is almost always possible to retain an expert to testify favorably in a case, regardless of the consensus of professional opinion on an issue.

Is there a role dictated by the "voice of reason" for the retained expert who responds to the demands of the adversary system yet still fulfills the expert's obligations to the court to be neutral? How can a retained testifying expert, operating within the constraints of these tensions, satisfy the adversarial imperatives, avoid malpractice liability, provide testimony that meets the highest standards of the profession, and be regularly employed?

LICENSURE AND ETHICAL JEOPARDY

Psychologists' behavior while providing expert testimony is governed by their professional ethical rules and guidelines. Violations of these rules and guidelines may result in exclusion of their testimony or a breach of contract or malpractice action (*Murphy v. A. A. Mathews,* 1992). However, experts are often granted immunity from civil claims for their conduct as experts. Nonetheless, no state extends that immunity to proceedings before state licensing boards or professional ethics committees (*Budwin v. American Psychological Association,* 1994). In two cases of first impression, Washington and Pennsylvania courts

declined to extend immunity to ethical complaints lodged with state licensing boards for the actions of health care professionals while serving as expert witnesses. The Washington Supreme Court refused to extend the broad grant of immunity it recognized for expert witnesses from civil liability to disciplinary proceedings (*Deatherage v. Examining Board of Psychology,* 1997). The court reasoned that the threat of professional discipline is an important check on the conduct of professionals who are otherwise immune from civil liability. In *Huhta v. State Board of Medicine* (1998), a Pennsylvania appellate court also held that immunity from civil liability for expert witnesses is not a defense in disciplinary proceedings before the State Board of Medicine because it would hamper the licensing board's fulfilling its responsibility to ensure the competence and fitness of physicians to practice medicine (Trimmer, 1999).

The grant of immunity from civil liability while retaining liability for professional disciplinary actions leaves experts subject to substantial risk. The necessity of defending oneself before a licensing board or ethics committee carries dire consequences for experts that are similar to those involved in the defense of a civil suit. Prevailing in either forum may nonetheless leave the expert's reputation tainted. Experts can and should carry insurance against a licensing board complaint in addition to insurance against a civil claim for damages arising out of their forensic activities. However, the economic costs of legal and professional sanctions are borne by the licensee. Lost income as the result of the suspension or revocation of a license or the harm to reputation suffered with a tort malpractice judgment remains a cost to be borne by the professional.

. . .

BEYOND COMPETENCY: IMPARTIALITY AS THE BEST ADVOCACY

Expert witnesses face evidentiary demands imposed by courts, ethical demands imposed by professional licensing agencies, liability demands imposed by disgruntled litigants, and economic demands imposed by the attorneys who employ them. How should experts respond to these demands, which seem to ask them to play both neutral and partisan roles?

Our proposal, *impartiality as the best advocacy*, does not ask experts to choose between these roles but offers guidance on how to fulfill both roles simultaneously. The crucial assumption that guides this proposal is that an expert's credibility is an essential component of being an effective advocate and that credibility derives from the expert's impartiality. An expert's absence of impartiality is fatal not only for its impact on neutrality but also for its impact on advocacy.

In the sections that follow, we address the question of how to reconcile these demands. . . .

Competence

The application of the Ethical Principles of Psychologists and Code of Conduct (APA, 2002) and the Specialty Guidelines for Forensic Psychologists (APA, 1991) in a world that seems hostile to them emphasizes what we regard as their core concern: "Forensic psychologists [should] provide services only in areas of psychology in which they have specialized knowledge, skill, experience, and education" (APA, 1991, p. 658). Unlike the clinical setting in which the psychologist's competence may be an issue that forms a part of the process of informed consent, forensic psychological services are imposed on individuals who do not necessarily consent or accede to the psychologist's competence. The competence of psychologists to provide forensic services is issue specific and contextual. Experts are pressured by advocates to offer opinions beyond the bounds of their competence. The tensions of the context, however, are never a basis for experts to offer opinions on subjects about which they are not competent. . . .

Experts should first identify each legal question on which their opinion is being sought and then determine if and how their competence permits them to offer an expert opinion to assist in the resolution of these legal questions. This may entail an initial conversation with the retaining attorney about the issues on which they might testify, followed up with a retaining letter from the attorney documenting the issues that the attorney anticipates will be addressed by the forensic examination. As the research or examination proceeds, the task of experts is to anticipate, as much as possible, the

opinions about which they are likely to offer testimony and to identify all of the evidence that is relevant to those opinions.

Relevance

The rules of evidence define relevant evidence as "evidence having any tendency to make the existence of any fact that is of consequence to the determination of the action more probable than it would be without the evidence" (Fed. R. Evid. 401). We speak here of a narrower concept of relevance to the opinion that the expert has been asked to address that is more tailored to Rule 705, which addresses the disclosure of the "facts or data underlying expert opinion" (Fed. R. Evid. 705). This principle applies to any evidence that has any tendency to add or subtract weight from the expert's opinion.

When testifying, experts should attempt to disclose to the parties all information relevant to their proffered opinion testimony on those questions, even when the issues change during the course of trial. Conversely, although they must answer all questions asked fully and truthfully, we maintain that experts have no obligation to attempt to disclose information that is not relevant to the issues questioned, whether that information or those opinions might be relevant to other legal issues in the case or not. We suggest that this careful selection and omission of opinion testimony by the attorney and the retained expert is both a legitimate and an effective means of advocacy. Although experts may be compelled by the court to disclose nonprivileged information that is relevant to the case whether or not they were initially requested to address that issue, we maintain that to integrate the role of neutrality and advocacy, the expert's unilateral obligation of disclosure only applies to information relevant to issues on which the expert's opinions have been sought.

The obligation of the retained expert to the party who retained the expert provides the starkest contrast between the demands of impartiality and partisanship. The obligation of the witness's oath to tell the truth, the whole truth, and nothing but the truth does not obligate the expert to offer opinions about which the expert is not asked at trial. Consider a fairly common question that arises with retained experts: May a retained testifying expert advise an attorney how to examine the expert to avoid disclosure of information that casts a negative light on the client/party? Certainly a litigant will appreciate being informed before the trial that "if you ask me X, this is how I would answer. Of course if you asked the question somewhat differently, I would not answer it in that fashion." The retaining attorney may be more likely to retain the expert in the future and be less likely to sue or file an ethics complaint if provided such an advance warning. . . .

Applying the principle of relevance to this situation, we suggest that the retained expert may not participate with the retaining attorney in efforts to shield evidence that is relevant to the expert's opinion. It is, however, appropriate for experts to participate with the attorney in shielding information that is not relevant to the expert's opinion. For example, if the expert is called to testify in a personal injury case solely on the issue of damages, the expert may not shield information that bears on the expert's opinion about damages. In the course of the examination in which the expert has also acquired information about a breach of the standard of care, we suggest there is no limitation on the expert's suggesting that a question be rephrased to avoid disclosure of information that is not relevant to the expert's opinion on damages. Of course, if the expert is asked about information that the expert considers irrelevant to the opinion being offered but the court concludes is relevant and not privileged, the expert must provide all information that is relevant to the opinion.

Consider the implications of this approach in terms of the various roles of the expert and the tensions that the expert must face. In terms of the risk of a malpractice complaint, an ethics complaint, or future retention by this attorney, assisting in avoiding the disclosure of information that is irrelevant furthers the interest of the attorney and the expert. It also furthers the expert's neutral role. We have discovered no reported opinions in which an expert was found liable or disciplined for disclosing non-privileged information relevant to the expert's opinion.

The decision about how experts should behave is based on a neutral principle that turns on the expert's opinion about an issue, not on who will benefit from it. It does not compromise advocacy through neutrality, nor does it compromise neutrality through advocacy. Honesty about information relevant to the expert's opinion is an effective tool for attorney advocacy. It casts the expert in a more neutral role in the eyes of the fact finder, giving experts greater credibility; it forces the attorney to address the disclosure of information that will invariably come out anyway; and it serves the interests of the court in helping to achieve accurate fact finding.

Perspective

To integrate neutrality and advocacy effectively, experts have an obligation to test their opinions on the issues they have been asked to address from the perspective of the parties' competing versions of the case, without insulation from opposing views. Any case has at least two conflicting perspectives on some relevant question or it would have been resolved. To be effective, experts must require the attorneys who retain them to provide, at minimum, the pleadings and legal memorandums describing the competing versions of the case, as well as all reports of other experts. Balancing the demands of lawyers, litigants, judges, and licensing boards requires that forensic experts maintain a realistic appreciation of the adversarial context in which forensic examinations occur. This realistic perspective requires experts to identify the evidence that might support or refute each party's perspective. An expert witness who is uninformed of the parties' differing perspectives can hardly be expected to be a credible witness.

. . .

Consider the implications of this approach for the competing tensions on the expert. Maintaining perspective plays an important role in the presentation of testimony that is candid and forthright, furthering the court's interest in the fact-finding process. Although some attorneys may at first balk at the expert's attempt to maintain perspective, it not only assists in presenting more persuasive expert testimony but also forces the attorney to consider plausible alternate theories of the case. This perspective also reduces the risk of tort and ethical complaints against the expert, as well as increases prospects for future retention, because testimony that accounts for competing perspectives is more persuasive and assists in the attorney's advocacy.

Balance

Having identified each perspective, the expert has an obligation to assign a fair weight to each, not to engage in confirmatory or hindsight bias, and not to allow the inherent pressures of the situation to influence this decision making. The expert's approach to the litigants' differing perspectives on the relevance issue is critical to integrating neutrality and advocacy effectively. Experts who fail to balance the parties' perspectives fairly are unlikely to help the fact finder reach accurate conclusions on the issues they have been asked to address, and the fact finder is unlikely to perceive them as credible. Looking at issues disproportionately from the perspective of the litigant who hired the expert violates this principle because this absence of balance renders the expert an ineffective advocate for whatever opinions the expert reaches.

Experts are obligated to weigh all perspectives fairly. By this we mean that they must consider the rival hypotheses in an even-handed manner. Experts and attorneys are familiar with the tendency to invoke a bunker mentality in which their side's perspective is given greater weight and the other side's perspective is minimized. Failing to provide appropriate weight to the perspective of each litigant violates this principle.

One factor that threatens the expert's ability to balance all litigants' perspectives fairly is the psychologist's role conflicts. In addition, these conflicts may increase the risk of a complaint by a disgruntled patient-litigant. A psychologist who develops a therapeutic alliance with a patient is less likely to be able to consider fairly a perspective that rejects the accuracy of the facts that the patient and psychologist developed in the course of their therapeutic work together. Additionally, the therapist is unlikely to have unfettered access to all of the parties' perspectives and to be able to balance them fairly (Greenberg & Shuman, 1997).

. . .

Candor

By *candor* we refer to the forthrightness with which psychological experts present their analysis. Experts who selectively disclose relevant information about an opinion to aid or disadvantage a party frustrate the search for accuracy and impair their own credibility. Thus, having identified the issues they have been asked to address and having considered them fairly from the perspective of all parties, experts have an obligation to present all perspectives considered candidly and explain the weight assigned to each in presenting their findings.

In our discussions of the first four principles, we considered the way in which experts should go about reaching an opinion. But in any legal proceeding there is much filtering of the facts and opinions. Aside from the well-recognized phenomenon of "wood shedding" or, more politely phrased, "negotiating opinions" (Gutheil, 2001), attorneys formulate questions to which experts have no legal right to object or demand that supplemental questions be asked. Nonetheless, experts have certain latitude in responding to the questioning process (Brodsky, 1991). We contend that experts should, to the maximum extent provided by law, candidly present the results of their fact finding and analysis, as described previously. The role of the expert is not to deliver favorable testimony as a matter of contract. The obligation is to render services at the relevant professional standard of care. . . . One clear benefit of this approach is that it is exactly what courts expect of witnesses—candid and forthright testimony.

Without doubt, this principle may present the hardest case to defend to the retaining attorney in that it might appear to risk disappointment, increasing the risk of tort and ethical complaints, and reducing chances for reemployment. For many attorneys, the benefits achieved by this approach in terms of the enhanced credibility of the expert with the fact finder are consistent with the attorney's litigation strategy. For other attorneys, this candor seems a betrayal of the partisan loyalty that attorneys expect of experts. We recognize that for work with those attorneys, our suggestion may not result in harmonizing all of the competing tensions and may even conflict with the attorney's brand of advocacy. For some experts, this may require that a decision be made regarding with which attorneys they wish to work. For the attorney who demands a "combatant" as his expert, the expert may choose to seek employment elsewhere. Similarly, attorneys with a combatant style are likely to seek experts who employ a similar approach. Yet even these experts must face their ethical obligations as experts and the risk that experts failing to meet these obligations may be held accountable by their licensing board. Even in jurisdictions granting absolute immunity for expert witnessing, the complaint to a licensing board or an ethics body that an opinion was not based on adequate scientific foundation looms large for experts who have shaded their testimony in a partisan manner.

CONCLUSION

What is the value of our principles in resolving these potential conflicts? Although the APA Ethics Code addresses forensic issues and describes ethical standards that govern the behavior of psychologists when testifying, our principles explain how psychologists can integrate the idealistic Ethics Code in the rough-and-tumble adversary system. The APA Ethics Code and the Specialty Guidelines for Forensic Psychologists appear to direct psychologists to a standard of behavior that is destined to collide with the reality of the judicial world. Attorneys are ethically obligated to advocate for their clients while experts are ethically obligated to examine issues objectively and advocate accordingly. Our principles reconcile these conflicts and offer psychologists a path that is both ethical and practicable to provide assistance to the courts.

. . .

If the testimony of mental health experts is not based on the principles of competence, relevance, perspective, balance, and candor, it is unlikely to be trustworthy. If the testimony of mental health experts is not trustworthy, it is unlikely to be beneficial to the courts, the professions, or the litigants who retain them. If the testimony of mental health experts is not trustworthy, it is unlikely to help mental health experts to shed the characterization of "hired gun."

References

American Academy of Psychiatry and the Law. (1996, November 13). *Ethical guidelines for the practice of forensic psychiatry.* Retrieved January 17, 2001, from http://www.emory.edu/AAPL/ethics.htm

American Psychological Association. (2002). *Ethical principles of psychologists and code of conduct.* Retrieved October 18, 2002, from http://www.apa.org/ethics/code2002.html

Committee on Ethical Guidelines for Forensic Psychologists, American Psychological Association. (1991). Specialty guidelines for forensic psychologists. *Law and Human Behavior, 15,* 655–665.

Brodsky, S. L. (1991). *Testifying in court: Guidelines and maxims for the expert witness.* Washington, DC: American Psychological Association.

Budwin v. American Psychological Association, 29 Cal. Rptr. 2d 453 (1994).

Daubert v. Merrell Dow Pharmaceuticals, Inc., 509 U.S. 579 (1993).

Deatherage v. Examining Board of Psychology, 948 P. 2d 828 (Wash. 1997).

Fed. R. Evid. 401.

Fed. R. Evid. 702.

Fed. R. Evid. 705.

Greenberg, S. A., & Shuman, D. W. (1997). Irreconcilable conflict between therapeutic and forensic roles. *Professional Psychology: Research and Practice, 28,* 50–57.

Gutheil, T. G. (2001). Adventures in the twilight zone: Empirical studies of the attorney–expert relationship. *Journal of the American Academy of Psychiatry and the Law, 29,* 13–17.

Heilbrun, K. (1995). Child custody evaluation: Critically assessing mental health experts and psychological tests. *Family Law Quarterly, 29,* 63–78.

Huhta v. State Board of Medicine, 706 A. 2d 1275 (Pa.Commw. Ct. 1998), appeal denied 727 A. 2d 1124 (Pa. 1998).

Jensen, E. (1993). When "hired guns" backfire: The witness immunity doctrine and the negligent expert witness. *University of Missouri at Kansas City Law Review, 62,* 185–207.

Murphy v. A. A. Mathews, 841 S.W. 2d 671 (Mo. 1992).

Richmond, D. R. (2000). Expert witness conflicts and compensation. *Tennessee Law Review, 67,* 909–948.

Shuman, D. W., & Greenberg, S. A. (1998). The role of ethical norms in the admissibility of expert testimony. *The Judges' Journal: A Quarterly of the Judicial Division, 37,* 4–43.

Simon, R. I. (Ed.). (1995). Toward the development of guidelines in the forensic psychiatric examination of posttraumatic stress disorder claims. In R. Simon (Ed.), *Post-traumatic stress disorder in litigation:*

Guidelines for forensic assessment (pp. 31–34). Washington, DC: American Psychiatric Publishing.

Strasburger, L. H., Gutheil, T. G., & Brodsky, A. (1997). On wearing two hats: Role conflict in serving as both psychotherapist and expert witness. *American Journal of Psychiatry, 154*, 448–456.

Trimmer, M. A. (1999). Annual survey of Pennsylvania administrative law: Survey of selected court decisions: Licensing: Huhta v. State Board of Medicine. *Widener Journal of Public Law, 8*, 843–855.

◆　◆　◆

Commentary: The issue of biased advocacy versus neutral testimony arises in many contexts, most often surfacing in testimony by professional psychologists, as in cases involving the insanity defense, emotional damages for victims of abuse, the appropriate placement of children needing special education, the validity of employment tests, and, as will be addressed later, child custody. But, it is also an issue for experimental psychologists, particularly those who testify concerning the vagaries of eyewitness identification in criminal cases.

In the 1980s, a conference was held at The Johns Hopkins University to discuss the issue:

> Most conference participants agreed that the most desirable role for the expert is that of impartial educator, and some held that this is the only ethically defensible position. It is clear that the law defines the role of the expert as that of an impartial educator called to assist the trier of fact. (p. 5)

McCloskey, M., Egeth, H., & McKenna, J. (1986). The experimental psychologist in court: The ethics of expert testimony. Law and Human Behavior, 10, 1–13.

Loftus (1986), who has testified in many eyewitness cases, took a somewhat different position:

> The view that psychologists may serve as advocates, presenting only the beneficial side of the case, begins with the argument that the trial is an adversary process in which each side has the right to make the best possible case. As a participant in this process, experts may limit their testimony to points that support the arguments of one side, leaving the opposing attorneys the task of presenting evidence and arguments favoring their position. The opposition can resort to vigorous cross-examination to bring out weaknesses in the testimony offered by the other side. . . . (p. 71)

Loftus, E. F. (1986). Experimental psychologists as advocate or impartial educator. Law and Human Behavior, 10, 63–78.

Elliot criticized Loftus's position. Specifically, he remarked that the notion that

> as between the expert as educator-scientist and the expert as an advocate we can settle claims to merit by waiting to see which survives seems to me to be both misplaced Darwinism and bad advice. Lawyers and other policy actors will almost always choose advocates over impartial scientists, which only means that the adversary system is not a fit environment for science. Why let the world of policy be the touchstone of the value of science? (pp. 433–434)

See Elliot, R. (1993). Expert testimony about eyewitness identification. Law and Human Behavior, 17, 423–448.

The danger of accepting Loftus's argument is reflected in the views of one judge, as the next excerpt exemplifies.

Psychologists and the Judicial System: Broader Perspectives

Donald N. Bersoff

. . .

. . . In June 1980, Judge John Grady of the federal district court in northern Illinois, issued his opinion in *PASE v. Hannon* (1980). The plaintiffs had challenged the use of individual intelligence scales to place black children in classes for the educably mentally retarded. A disproportionate number of black children had been misclassified as retarded, they claimed, because the tests upon which the determinations were based were racially and culturally biased. During the three-week trial on this controversial issue, Judge Grady heard the testimony of several prominent psychologists, including a past president of the American Psychological Association, a former member of its Board of Directors, and other acknowledged experts who would comprise a veritable Who's Who of American Measurement, if such a compendium existed. Some of the experts agreed with the plaintiffs that, indeed, there were data to support the assertion that the tests unduly favored those from the white middle-class culture; others concurred with the defendant school system that there was no evidence that the tests disfavored blacks because of inherent bias in their construction.

Actually, the gathering of the experts in *PASE* was something of a reunion. Many of these same witnesses had appeared earlier in San Francisco in a much more heralded case, *Larry P. v. Riles* (1972; 1979). There Judge Robert Peckham found in favor of the minority plaintiffs on both statutory and constitutional grounds. He concluded the tests were culturally biased and permanently enjoined the defendant state of California "from utilizing, permitting the use of, or approving the use of any standardized tests . . . for the identification of black EMR children or their placement into EMR classes, without first securing prior approval by this court" (p. 989).

The plaintiffs in *PASE* apparently expected a replay of the trial in *Larry P.* However, rather than ruling that the tests in question were culturally biased, Judge Grady held that individual intelligence tests "do not discriminate against black children in the Chicago public schools" (p. 883). Judge Grady's reference to *Larry P.* occupied a bit less than one page of his 52-page opinion, and he virtually rejected its tenability out of hand. "The witnesses and the arguments," Judge Grady said, "which persuaded Judge Peckham have not persuaded me" (p. 882).

One of the most intriguing aspects of Judge Grady's decision was his almost utter rejection of the testimony of expert psychologists who testified on behalf of both parties. The reason for this rejection is, at the same time, illuminating, instructive, and very troublesome:

> None of the witnesses in this case has so impressed me with his or her credibility or expertise that I would feel secure in basing a decision on his or her opinion. In some instances, I am satisfied that the opinions expressed are more the result of doctrinaire commitment to a preconceived idea than they are the result of scientific inquiry. I need something more than the conclusions of the witnesses in order to arrive at my own conclusions. (p. 836)

This perception of the behavior of the expert witnesses who testified before Judge Grady raises some formidable and disturbing, if not painful, ethical issues. If he is correct in that perception, each of the psychologists who offered opinions out of a "doctrinaire commitment to a preconceived idea" rather than as a "result of scientific inquiry" may be guilty

From *Law and Human Behavior, 10,* 151–165. Copyright 1986 by Springer. Adapted with permission of the author and publisher.

of violating several important provisions of the Ethical Principles of Psychologists. . . .

These are genuinely serious concerns. If the ethical integrity and scientific objectivity of experimental psychologists begin to be questioned, the significant and potentially useful information they produce may be permanently neglected by the judicial system. This will be detrimental not only to the just resolution of legal disputes between parties that involve empirical issues, but to the advancement of social policy in general. It is imperative, therefore, that social scientists remain true to the primary role they serve in society. . . .

[W]hile unbridled advocacy may be a moral imperative for attorneys, it may be directly antagonistic to the ethical principles that control the behavior of psychologists. Social scientists must continually be conscious of the fact that their data, interpretations, and opinions will be tested in the crucible of courtroom cross-examination whose very purpose it is to destroy credibility and evoke evidence of bias. Although the distillation of that process may yield testimony of great consequence and weight to the court, it can be highly anxiety provoking for psychologists who act as injudicious advocates, pleading for a position, rather than as cautious scientists presenting data in an evenhanded manner. I am not suggesting that it is inappropriate to testify on behalf of a particular party in a legal dispute, but, in doing so, psychologists should exhibit the prudence of a circumspect, rational, scrupulous scientist.

Through their publications, collaboration with attorneys and judges, participation in the drafting of *amicus* briefs, testimony before legislative committees, and administrative agencies, as well as serving as expert witnesses, there are many ways social scientists can influence public policy effectively. . . . Within the bounds of scientific and professional ethics, these are important, if not crucial roles. But, if experimental psychologists are to be respected by the courts and treated as more than mere numerologists attempting to convince the judiciary of doctrinaire positions, they must offer more situation-specific, ecologically valid, objective data that serve science, not a particular adversary. In that way, perhaps, courts may finally arrive at, not only

judicially sound but, empirically justified decisions that will withstand both appellate and scientific scrutiny.

References

Larry P. v. Riles, 343 F.Supp. 1306 (N.D. Cal. 1972) (order granting preliminary injunction) *aff'd* 502 F.2d 963 (9th Cir. 1974); 495 F.Supp. 926 (N.D. Cal. 1979) *appeal docketed* No. 80–4027 (9th Cir., Jan. 17, 1980).

PASE v. Hannon, 506 F.Supp. 831 (N.D. Ill. 1980).

◆　　◆　　◆

Commentary: Perhaps the most succinct summary of the consensus position comes from Adams, K. M., & Putnam, S. H. (1994). Coping with professional skeptics: Reply to Faust. Psychological Assessment, 6, 5–7:

> *Psychologists called to court are best advised to act as psychologists first and best, allowing the legal arena to evolve as it must and will. Psychologists and lawyers are professionals with different goals, cultures, and rules and who operate in epistemologically diverse ways. (p. 6)*

As a middle-ground position, consider Hastie's (1986) recommendations:

> *I would like to suggest a concrete image in place of Loftus's teacher–advocate dichotomy. I think that the psychologist should assume the role of watchdog.*
>
> *When he or she honestly believes, based on scientific findings, that, for example, eyewitness testimony is unreliable, then he or she should take the witness stand to testify against the eyewitness. If any other expert improperly applies scientific findings to impugn eyewitness testimony, then the psychologist should testify against the expert. My watchdog image is meant to exclude two other roles. The psychologist should not be a timid lapdog who never believes there is sufficient reason to leave the comfort of the laboratory to challenge an unreliable eyewitness or misleading expert in the courtroom. Nor should*

the psychologist be a rabid attack dog who assaults every eyewitness who appears in the courtroom. (p. 80)

Hastie, R. (1986). *Notes on the psychologist expert witness.* Law and Human Behavior, 10, 79–82.

In any event, despite attempts to seek help from the then-current version of the APA code of ethics to resolve the advocacy–educator issue, by the 1980s there began to be a call for specific guidance to be provided for psychologists who enter the legal arena:

> As a profession psychology must decide for itself the standards and level of quality that should apply to its forensic assessments. The most important reason for doing this is consumer and public welfare. Moreover, every industry knows that a high level of internally imposed standards and quality control is important to ensure a high-quality product and to avoid personal and corporate liability.

Both APA's Division 41 and the ABFP can play a role in the development of such standards. The standards should reflect the values not only of psychological practitioners, but also of researchers in psychology and law and scientific psychology in general. The standards should reflect these values because psychologists who perform forensic assessments represent psychology—not merely forensic clinical psychology—when they enter the courtroom. Furthermore, as noted earlier, experimental psychologists themselves are entering the courtroom in increasing numbers. They are facing the same questions regarding the limits of their testimony. (p. 837)

See Grisso, T. (1987). *The economic and scientific future of forensic psychological assessment.* American Psychologist, 42, 831–839.

Four years later, the call was answered.

Specialty Guidelines for Forensic Psychologists

Committee on Ethical Guidelines for Forensic Psychologists

The *Specialty Guidelines for Forensic Psychologists* were adopted by majority vote of the members of Division 41 [American Psychological Association] and the American Psychology–Law Society. They have also been endorsed by majority vote by the American Academy of Forensic Psychology. The Executive Committee of Division 41 and the American Psychology–Law Society formally approved these *Guidelines* on March 9, 1991.

The *Specialty Guidelines for Forensic Psychologists*, while informed by the *Ethical Principles of Psychologists* (APA, 1990) and meant to be consistent with them, are designed to provide more specific guidance to forensic psychologists in monitoring their professional conduct when acting in assistance to courts, parties to legal proceedings, correctional and forensic mental health facilities, and legislative agencies. The primary goal of the *Guidelines* is to improve the quality of forensic psychological services offered to individual clients and the legal system and thereby to enhance forensic psychology as a discipline and profession. The *Specialty Guidelines for Forensic Psychologists* represent a joint statement of the American Psychology–Law Society and Division 41 of the American Psychological Association and are endorsed by the American Academy of Forensic Psychology. The *Guidelines* do not represent an official statement of the American Psychological Association.

The *Guidelines* provide an aspirational model of desirable professional practice by psychologists, within any subdiscipline of psychology (e.g., clinical, developmental, social, experimental), when they are engaged regularly as experts and represent themselves as such, in an activity primarily intended to provide professional psychological expertise to the judicial system. This would include, for example,

clinical forensic examiners; psychologists employed by correctional or forensic mental health systems; researchers who offer direct testimony about the relevance of scientific data to a psycholegal issue; trial behavior consultants; psychologists engaged in preparation of *amicus* briefs; or psychologists, appearing as forensic experts, who consult with, or testify before, judicial, legislative, or administrative agencies acting in an adjudicative capacity. Individuals who provide only occasional service to the legal system and who do so without representing themselves as *forensic experts* may find these *Guidelines* helpful, particularly in conjunction with consultation with colleagues who are forensic experts.

While the *Guidelines* are concerned with a model of desirable professional practice, to the extent that they may be construed as being applicable to the advertisement of services or the solicitation of clients, they are intended to prevent false or deceptive advertisement or solicitation and should be construed in a manner consistent with that intent.

I. PURPOSE AND SCOPE

A. Purpose

1. While the professional standards for the ethical practice of psychology, as a general discipline, are addressed in the American Psychological Association's *Ethical Principles of Psychologists,* these ethical principles do not relate, in sufficient detail, to current aspirations of desirable professional conduct for forensic psychologists. By design, none of the *Guidelines* contradicts any of the *Ethical Principles of Psychologists;* rather, they amplify those *Principles* in

the context of the practice of forensic psychology, as herein defined.

2. The *Guidelines* have been designed to be national in scope and are intended to conform with state and Federal law. In situations where the forensic psychologist believes that the requirements of law are in conflict with the *Guidelines*, attempts to resolve the conflict should be made in accordance with the procedures set forth in these *Guidelines* [IV(G)] and in the *Ethical Principles of Psychologists*.

B. Scope

1. The *Guidelines* specify the nature of desirable professional practice by forensic psychologists, within any sub-discipline of psychology (e.g., clinical, developmental, social, experimental), when engaged regularly as forensic psychologists.

   a. "Psychologist" means any individual whose professional activities are defined by the American Psychological Association or by regulation of title by state registration or licensure, as the practice of psychology.

   b. "Forensic psychology" means all forms of professional psychological conduct when acting, with definable foreknowledge, as a psychological expert on explicitly psycholegal issues, in direct assistance to courts, parties to legal proceedings, correctional and forensic mental health facilities, and administrative, judicial, and legislative agencies acting in an adjudicative capacity.

   c. "Forensic psychologist" means psychologists who regularly engage in the practice of forensic psychology as defined in I(B)(1)(b).

2. The *Guidelines* do not apply to a psychologist who is asked to provide professional psychological services when the psychologist was not informed at the time of delivery of the services that they were to be used as forensic psychological services as defined above. The *Guidelines* may be helpful, however, in preparing the psychologist for the experience of communicating psychological data in a forensic context.

3. Psychologists who are not forensic psychologists as defined in I(B)(1)(c), but occasionally provide limited forensic psychological services, may find the *Guidelines* useful in the preparation and presentation of their professional services.

C. Related Standards

1. Forensic psychologists also conduct their professional activities in accord with the *Ethical Principles of Psychologists* and the various other statements of the American Psychological Association that may apply to particular subdisciplines or areas of practice that are relevant to their professional activities.

2. The standards of practice and ethical guidelines of other relevant "expert professional organizations" contain useful guidance and should be consulted even though the present *Guidelines* take precedence for forensic psychologists.

II. RESPONSIBILITY

A. Forensic psychologists have an obligation to provide services in a manner consistent with the highest standards of their profession. They are responsible for their own conduct and the conduct of those individuals under their direct supervision.

B. Forensic psychologists make a reasonable effort to ensure that their services and the products of their services are used in a forthright and responsible manner.

III. COMPETENCE

A. Forensic psychologists provide services only in areas of psychology in which they have specialized knowledge, skill, experience, and education.

B. Forensic psychologists have an obligation to present to the court, regarding the specific matters to which they will testify, the boundaries of their competence, the factual bases (knowledge, skill, experience, training, and education) for their qualifications as an expert, and the relevance of those factual bases to their qualification as an expert on the specific matters at issue.

C. Forensic psychologists are responsible for a fundamental and reasonable level of knowledge and understanding of the legal and professional standards that govern their participation as experts in legal proceedings.

D. Forensic psychologists have an obligation to understand the civil rights of parties in legal proceedings in which they participate, and manage their professional conduct in a manner that does not diminish or threaten those rights.

E. Forensic psychologists recognize that their own personal values, moral beliefs, or personal and professional relationships with parties to a legal proceeding may interfere with their ability to practice competently. Under such circumstances, forensic psychologists are obligated to decline participation or to limit their assistance in a manner consistent with professional obligations.

IV. RELATIONSHIPS

A. During initial consultation with the legal representative of the party seeking services, forensic psychologists have an obligation to inform the party of factors that might reasonably affect the decision to contract with the forensic psychologist. These factors include, but are not limited to

  1. the fee structure for anticipated professional services;

  2. prior and current personal or professional activities, obligations, and relationships that might produce a conflict of interests;

  3. their areas of competence and the limits of their competence; and

  4. the known scientific bases and limitations of the methods and procedures that they employ and their qualifications to employ such methods and procedures.

B. Forensic psychologists do not provide professional services to parties to a legal proceeding on the basis of "contingent fees," when those services involve the offering of expert testimony to a court or administrative body, or when they call upon the psychologist to make affirmations or representations intended to be relied upon by third parties.

C. Forensic psychologists who derive a substantial portion of their income from fee-for-service arrangements should offer some portion of their professional services on a *pro bono* or reduced fee basis where the public interest or the welfare of clients may be inhibited by insufficient financial resources.

D. Forensic psychologists recognize potential conflicts of interest in dual relationships with parties to a legal proceeding, and they seek to minimize their effects.

  1. Forensic psychologists avoid providing professional services to parties in a legal proceeding with whom they have personal or professional relationships that are inconsistent with the anticipated relationship.

  2. When it is necessary to provide both evaluation and treatment services to a party in a legal proceeding (as may be the case in small forensic hospital settings or small communities), the forensic psychologist takes reasonable steps to minimize the potential negative effects of these circumstances on the rights of the party, confidentiality, and the process of treatment and evaluation.

E. Forensic psychologists have an obligation to ensure that prospective clients are informed of their legal rights with respect to the anticipated forensic service, of the purpose of any evaluation, of the nature of procedures to be employed, of the intended uses of any product of their services, and of the party who has employed the forensic psychologist.

1. Unless court ordered, forensic psychologists obtain the informed consent of the client or party, or their legal representative, before proceeding with such evaluations and procedures. If the client appears unwilling to proceed after receiving a thorough notification of the purposes, methods, and intended uses of the forensic evaluation, the evaluation should be postponed and the psychologist should take steps to place the client in contact with his/her attorney for the purpose of legal advice on the issue of participation.

2. In situations where the client or party may not have the capacity to provide informed consent to services or the evaluation is pursuant to court order, the forensic psychologist provides reasonable notice to the client's legal representative of the nature of the anticipated forensic service before proceeding. If the client's legal representative objects to the evaluation, the forensic psychologist notifies the court issuing the order and responds as directed.

3. After a psychologist has advised the subject of a clinical forensic evaluation of the intended uses of the evaluation and its work product, the psychologist may not use the evaluation work product for other purposes without explicit waiver to do so by the client or the client's legal representative.

F. When forensic psychologists engage in research or scholarly activities that are compensated financially by a client or party to a legal proceeding, or when the psychologist provides those services on a *pro bono* basis, the psychologist clarifies any anticipated further use of such research or scholarly product, discloses the psychologist's role in the resulting research or scholarly products, and obtains whatever consent or agreement is required by law or professional standards.

G. When conflicts arise between the forensic psychologist's professional standards and the requirements of legal standards, a particular court, or a directive by an officer of the court or legal authorities, the forensic psychologist has an obligation to make those legal authorities aware of the source of the conflict and to take reasonable steps to resolve it. Such steps may include, but are not limited to, obtaining the consultation of fellow forensic professionals, obtaining the advice of independent counsel, and conferring directly with the legal representatives involved.

V. CONFIDENTIALITY AND PRIVILEGE

A. Forensic psychologists have an obligation to be aware of the legal standards that may affect or limit the confidentiality or privilege that may attach to their services or their products, and they conduct their professional activities in a manner that respects those known rights and privileges.

1. Forensic psychologists establish and maintain a system of record keeping and professional communication that safeguards a client's privilege.

2. Forensic psychologists maintain active control over records and information. They only release information pursuant to statutory requirements, court order, or the consent of the client.

B. Forensic psychologists inform their clients of the limitations to the confidentiality of their services and their products (see also Guideline IV [E]) by providing them with an understandable statement of their rights, privileges, and the limitations of confidentiality.

C. In situations where the right of the client or party to confidentiality is limited, the forensic psychologist makes every effort to maintain confidentiality with regard to any information that does not bear directly upon the legal purpose of the evaluation.

D. Forensic psychologists provide clients or their authorized legal representatives with access to the information in their records and a meaningful explanation of that information, consistent with existing Federal and state statutes, the *Ethical Principles of Psychologists, the Standards for Educational and Psychological Testing,* and institutional rules and regulations.

VI. METHODS AND PROCEDURES

A. Because of their special status as persons qualified as experts to the court, forensic psychologists have an obligation to maintain current knowledge of scientific, professional, and legal developments within their area of claimed competence. They are obligated also to use that knowledge, consistent with accepted clinical and scientific standards, in selecting data collection methods and procedures for an evaluation, treatment, consultation, or scholarly/empirical investigation.

B. Forensic psychologists have an obligation to document and be prepared to make available, subject to court order or the rules of evidence, all data that form the basis for their evidence or services. The standard to be applied to such documentation or recording *anticipates* that the detail and quality of such documentation will be subject to reasonable judicial scrutiny; this standard is higher than the normative standard for general clinical practice. When forensic psychologists conduct an examination or engage in the treatment of a party to a legal proceeding, with foreknowledge that

their professional services will be used in an adjudicative forum, they incur a special responsibility to provide the best documentation possible under the circumstances.

1. Documentation of the data upon which one's evidence is based is subject to the normal rules of discovery, disclosure, confidentiality, and privilege that operate in the jurisdiction in which the data were obtained. Forensic psychologists have an obligation to be aware of those rules and to regulate their conduct in accordance with them.

2. The duties and obligations of forensic psychologists with respect to documentation of data that form the basis for their evidence apply from the moment they know or have a reasonable basis for knowing that their data and evidence derived from it are likely to enter into legally relevant decisions.

C. In providing forensic psychological services, forensic psychologists take special care to avoid undue influence upon their methods, procedures, and products, such as might emanate from the party to a legal proceeding by financial compensation or other gains. As an expert conducting an evaluation, treatment, consultation, or scholarly/empirical investigation, the forensic psychologist maintains professional integrity by examining the issue at hand from all reasonable perspectives, actively seeking information that will differentially test plausible rival hypotheses.

D. Forensic psychologists do not provide professional forensic services to a defendant or to any party in, or in contemplation of, a legal proceeding prior to that individual's representation by counsel, except for persons judicially determined, where appropriate, to be handling their representation *pro se.* When the forensic services are pursuant to court order and the client is not represented by counsel, the forensic psychologist makes reasonable efforts to inform the court prior to providing the services.

1. A forensic psychologist may provide emergency mental health services to a pretrial defendant prior to court order or the appointment of counsel where there are reasonable grounds to believe that such emergency services are needed for the protection and improvement of the defendant's mental health and where failure to provide such mental health services would constitute a substantial risk of imminent harm to the defendant or to others. In providing such services the forensic psychologist nevertheless seeks to inform the defendant's counsel in a manner consistent with the requirements of the emergency situation.

2. Forensic psychologists who provide such emergency mental health services should attempt to avoid providing further professional forensic services to that defendant unless that relationship is reasonably unavoidable [see IV(D)(2)].

E. When forensic psychologists seek data from third parties, prior records, or other sources, they do so only with the prior approval of the relevant legal party or as a consequence of an order of a court to conduct the forensic evaluation.

F. Forensic psychologists are aware that hearsay exceptions and other rules governing expert testimony place a special ethical burden upon them. When hearsay or otherwise inadmissible evidence forms the basis of their opinion, evidence, or professional product, they seek to minimize sole reliance upon such evidence. Where circumstances reasonably permit, forensic psychologists seek to obtain independent and personal verification of data relied upon as part of their professional services to the court or to a party to a legal proceeding.

1. While many forms of data used by forensic psychologists are hearsay, forensic psychologists attempt to corroborate critical data that form the basis for their professional product. When using hearsay data that have not been corroborated, but are nevertheless utilized, forensic psychologists have an affirmative responsibility to acknowledge the uncorroborated status of those data and the reasons for relying upon such data.

2. With respect to evidence of any type, forensic psychologists avoid offering information from their investigations or evaluations that does not bear directly upon the legal purpose of their professional services and that is not critical as support for their product, evidence, or testimony, except where such disclosure is required by law.

3. When a forensic psychologist relies upon data or information gathered by others, the origins of those data are clarified in any professional product. In addition, the forensic psychologist bears a special responsibility to ensure that such data, if relied upon, were gathered in a manner standard for the profession.

G. Unless otherwise stipulated by the parties, forensic psychologists are aware that no statements made by a defendant, in the course of any (forensic) examination, no testimony by the expert based upon such statements, nor any other fruits of the statements can be admitted into evidence against the defendant in any criminal proceeding, except on an issue respecting mental condition on which the defendant has introduced testimony. Forensic psychologists have an affirmative duty to ensure that their written products and oral testimony conform to this Federal Rule of Procedure (12.2[c]), or its state equivalent.

1. Because forensic psychologists are often not in a position to know what evidence, documentation, or element of a written product may be or may lend to a "fruit of the statement," they exercise

extreme caution in preparing reports or offering testimony prior to the defendant's assertion of a mental state claim or the defendant's introduction of testimony regarding a mental condition. Consistent with the reporting requirements of state or federal law, forensic psychologists avoid including statements from the defendant relating to the time period of the alleged offense.

2. Once a defendant has proceeded to the trial stage, and all pretrial mental health issues such as competency have been resolved, forensic psychologists may include in their reports or testimony any statements made by the defendant that are directly relevant to supporting their expert evidence, providing that the defendant has "introduced" mental state evidence or testimony within the meaning of Federal Rule of Procedure 12.2(c), or its state equivalent.

H. Forensic psychologists avoid giving written or oral evidence about the psychological characteristics of particular individuals when they have not had an opportunity to conduct an examination of the individual adequate to the scope of the statements, opinions, or conclusions to be issued. Forensic psychologists make every reasonable effort to conduct such examinations. When it is not possible or feasible to do so, they make clear the impact of such limitations on the reliability and validity of their professional products, evidence, or testimony.

VII. PUBLIC AND PROFESSIONAL COMMUNICATIONS

A. Forensic psychologists make reasonable efforts to ensure that the products of their services, as well as their own public statements and professional testimony, are communicated in ways that will promote understanding and avoid deception, given the particular characteristics, roles, and abilities of various recipients of the communications.

1. Forensic psychologists take reasonable steps to correct misuse or misrepresentation of their professional products, evidence, and testimony.

2. Forensic psychologists provide information about professional work to clients in a manner consistent with professional and legal standards for the disclosure of test results, interpretations of data, and the factual bases for conclusions. A full explanation of the results of tests and the bases for conclusions should be given in language that the client can understand.

   a. When disclosing information about a client to third parties who are not qualified to interpret test results and data, the forensic psychologist complies with Principle 16 of the *Standards for Educational and Psychological Testing*. When required to disclose results to a nonpsychologist, every attempt is made to ensure that test security is maintained and access to information is restricted to individuals with a legitimate and professional interest in the data. Other qualified mental health professionals who make a request for information pursuant to a lawful order are, by definition, "individuals with a legitimate and professional interest."

   b. In providing records and raw data, the forensic psychologist takes reasonable steps to ensure that the receiving party is informed that raw scores must be interpreted by a qualified professional in order to provide reliable and valid information.

B. Forensic psychologists realize that their public role as "expert to the court" or as "expert representing the profession" confers upon them a special responsibility for fairness and accuracy in their public statements. When evaluating or commenting upon the professional work product or qualifications of another expert or party to a legal proceeding, forensic psychologists represent their professional disagreements with reference to a fair and accurate evaluation of the data, theories, standards, and opinions of the other expert or party.

C. Ordinarily, forensic psychologists avoid making detailed public (out-of-court) statements about particular legal proceedings in which they have been involved. When there is a strong justification to do so, such public statements are designed to assure accurate representation of their role or their evidence, not to advocate the positions of parties in the legal proceeding. Forensic psychologists address particular legal proceedings in publications or communications only to the extent that the information relied upon is part of a public record, or consent for that use has been properly obtained from the party holding any privilege.

D. When testifying, forensic psychologists have an obligation to all parties to a legal proceeding to present their findings, conclusions, evidence, or other professional products in a fair manner. This principle does not preclude forceful representation of the data and reasoning upon which a conclusion or professional product is based. It does, however, preclude an attempt, whether active or passive, to engage in partisan distortion or misrepresentation. Forensic psychologists do not, by either commission or omission, participate in a misrepresentation of their evidence, nor do they participate in partisan attempts to avoid, deny, or subvert the presentation of evidence contrary to their own position.

E. Forensic psychologists, by virtue of their competence and rules of discovery, actively disclose all sources of information obtained in the course of their professional services; they actively disclose which information from which source was used in formulat-

ing a particular written product or oral testimony.

F. Forensic psychologists are aware that their essential role as expert to the court is to assist the trier of fact to understand the evidence or to determine a fact in issue. In offering expert evidence, they are aware that their own professional observations, inferences, and conclusions must be distinguished from legal facts, opinions, and conclusions. Forensic psychologists are prepared to explain the relationship between their expert testimony and the legal issues and facts of an instant case.

◆   ◆   ◆

Commentary: The Specialty Guidelines are presently undergoing revision, and an updated edition should be published when that process is completed.

If there is one category of cases that most frequently evokes the accusation of "hired gun," it is the assessment of children during custody disputes between divorcing parents. It is here that the confluence of incompetence, multiple relationships, role conflicts, and biased advocacy is most rampant. Unless these disputes are settled amicably, there are always going to be parents who feel aggrieved by the clinician's recommendation. Thus, "[f]rom a risk management perspective, misunderstandings in child custody evaluations pose significant risk to the examiner. Compared to other forensic examinations [they] have achieved some notoriety as a minefield of board complaints and lawsuits" (citations omitted). (p. 446). Connell, M. (2006). Notification of purpose in custody evaluation: Informing the parties and their counsel. Professional Psychology: Research and Practice, 37, *446–451.*

As Karras and Barry (1985) acknowledged, the child custody "evaluator is frequently confronted with ethical pitfalls, such as . . . overstepping the boundary of research-supportable recommendations for custody arrangements [and failing to] . . . avoid the adversarial evaluator role" (p. 83). Karras, D., & Berry, K. K. (1985). Custody evaluations: A critical review. Professional Psychology: Research and Practice, 16, *76–85. See also Brodzinsky, D. (1993). On the use and misuse of psychological testing in child custody evaluations.* Professional Psychology: Research and

Practice, 24, 213–219. *In fact, it was recently argued that psychologists should refrain from making custody recommendations because they are unqualified to do so. See Wittman, J., & Tippins, T. (2005). Empirical and ethical problems with custody recommendations: A call for clinical humility and judicial vigilance.* Family Court Review, 43, 193–222.

Nevertheless, psychologists remain the primary forensic evaluators in custody disputes. As a result, there was consensus that an institutional response by APA to the ethical issues raised by child custody evaluations was necessary to reduce the number of ethical complaints by parents and to educate its members. Thus, APA developed the following document, which is now APA policy.

Guidelines for Child Custody Evaluations in Divorce Proceedings

American Psychological Association

These guidelines were drafted by the Committee on Professional Practice and Standards, a committee of the Board of Professional Affairs, with input from the Committee of Children, Youth, and Families. They were adopted by the Council of Representatives of the American Psychological Association in February 1994.

INTRODUCTION

Decisions regarding child custody and other parenting arrangements occur within several different legal contexts, including parental divorce, guardianship, neglect or abuse proceedings, and termination of parental rights. The following guidelines were developed for psychologists conducting child custody evaluations, specifically within the context of parental divorce. These guidelines build upon the American Psychological Association's *Ethical Principles of Psychologists and Code of Conduct* (APA, 1992) and are aspirational in intent. *As guidelines, they are not intended to be either mandatory or exhaustive. The goal of the guidelines is to promote proficiency in using psychological expertise in conducting child custody evaluations.*

Parental divorce requires a restructuring of parental rights and responsibilities in relation to children. If the parents can agree to a restructuring arrangement, which they do in the overwhelming proportion (90%) of divorce custody cases (Melton, Petrila, Poythress, & Slobogin, 1987), there is no dispute for the court to decide. However, if the parents are unable to reach such an agreement, the court must help to determine the relative allocation of decision-making authority and physical contact each parent will have with the child. The courts typically apply a "best interest of the child" standard in determining this restructuring of rights and responsibilities.

Psychologists provide an important service to children and the courts by providing competent, objective, impartial information in assessing the best interests of the child; by demonstrating a clear sense of direction and purpose in conducting a child custody evaluation; by performing their roles ethically; and by clarifying to all involved the nature and scope of the evaluation. The Ethics Committee of the American Psychological Association has noted that psychologists' involvement in custody disputes has at times raised questions in regard to the misuse of psychologists' influence, sometimes resulting in complaints against psychologists being brought to the attention of the APA Ethics Committee (APA Ethics Committee, 1985; Hall & Hare-Mustin, 1983; Keith-Spiegel & Koocher, 1985; Mills, 1984) and raising questions in the legal and forensic literature (Grisso, 1986; Melton et al., 1987; Mnookin, 1975; Ochroch, 1982; Okpaku, 1976; Weithorn, 1987).

Particular competencies and knowledge are required for child custody evaluations to provide adequate and appropriate psychological services to the court. Child custody evaluation in the context of parental divorce can be an extremely demanding task. For competing parents the stakes are high, as they participate in a process fraught with tension and anxiety. The stress on the psychologist/evaluator can become great. Tension surrounding child custody evaluation can become further heightened when there are accusations of child abuse, neglect, and/or family violence.

Psychology is in a position to make significant contributions to child custody decisions. Psychological data and expertise, gained through a child custody evaluation, can provide an additional source of information and an additional perspective not otherwise readily available to the court on what appears to be in a child's best interest, and thus can increase the fairness of the determination the court must make.

GUIDELINES FOR CHILD CUSTODY EVALUATIONS IN DIVORCE PROCEEDINGS

I. **Orienting Guidelines: Purpose of a Child Custody Evaluation**
    1. **The primary purpose of the evaluation is to assess the best psychological interests of the child.** The primary consideration in a child custody evaluation is to assess the individual and family factors that affect the best psychological interests of the child. More specific questions may be raised by the court.
    2. **The child's interests and well-being are paramount.** In a child custody evaluation, the child's interests and well-being are paramount. Parents competing for custody, as well as others, may have legitimate concerns, but the child's best interests must prevail.
    3. **The focus of the evaluation is on parenting capacity, the psychological and developmental needs of the child, and the resulting fit.** In considering psychological factors affecting the best interests of the child, the psychologist focuses on the parenting capacity of the prospective custodians in conjunction with the psychological and developmental needs of each involved child. This involves (a) an assessment of the adults' capacities for parenting, including whatever knowledge, attributes, skills, and abilities, or lack thereof, are present; (b) an assessment of the psychological functioning and developmental needs of each child and of the wishes of each child where appropriate; and (c) an assessment of the functional ability of each parent to meet these needs, including an evaluation of the interaction between each adult and child.

The values of the parents relevant to parenting, ability to plan for the child's future needs, capacity to provide a stable and loving home, and any potential for inappropriate behavior or misconduct that might negatively influence the child also are considered. Psychopathology may be relevant to such an assessment, insofar as it has impact on the child or the ability to parent, but it is not the primary focus.

II. **General Guidelines: Preparing for a Child Custody Evaluation**
    4. **The role of the psychologist is that of a professional expert who strives to maintain an objective, impartial stance.** The role of the psychologist is as a professional expert. The psychologist does not act as a judge, who makes the ultimate decision applying the law to all relevant evidence. Neither does the psychologist act as an advocating attorney, who strives to present his or her client's best possible case. The psychologist, in a balanced, impartial manner, informs and advises the court and the prospective custodians of the child of the relevant psychological factors pertaining to the custody issue. The psychologist should be impartial regardless of whether he or she is retained by the court or by a party to the proceedings. If either the psychologist or the client cannot accept this neutral role, the psychologist should consider withdrawing from the case. If not permitted to withdraw, in such circumstances, the psychologist acknowledges past roles and other factors that could affect impartiality.
    5. **The psychologist gains specialized competence.** A. A psychologist contemplating performing child custody evaluations is aware that special competencies and knowledge are required for the undertaking of such evaluations. Competence in performing psychological assessments of children, adults, and families is necessary

but not sufficient. Education, training, experience, and/or supervision in the areas of child and family development, child and family psychopathology, and the impact of divorce on children help to prepare the psychologist to participate competently in child custody evaluations. The psychologist also strives to become familiar with applicable legal standards and procedures, including laws governing divorce and custody adjudications in his or her state or jurisdiction.

B. The psychologist uses current knowledge of scientific and professional developments, consistent with accepted clinical and scientific standards, in selecting data collection methods and procedures. The *Standards for Educational and Psychological Testing* (APA, 1985) are adhered to in the use of psychological tests and other assessment tools.

C. In the course of conducting child custody evaluations, allegations of child abuse, neglect, family violence, or other issues may occur that are not necessarily within the scope of a particular evaluator's expertise. If this is so, the psychologist seeks additional consultation, supervision, and/or specialized knowledge, training, or experience in child abuse, neglect, and family violence to address these complex issues. The psychologist is familiar with the laws of his or her state addressing child abuse, neglect, and family violence and acts accordingly.

6. **The psychologist is aware of personal and societal biases and engages in nondiscriminatory practice.** The psychologist engaging in child custody evaluations is aware of how biases regarding age, gender, race, ethnicity, national origin, religion, sexual orientation, disability, language, culture, and socioeconomic status

may interfere with an objective evaluation and recommendations. The psychologist recognizes and strives to overcome any such biases or withdraws from the evaluation.

7. **The psychologist avoids multiple relationships.** Psychologists generally avoid conducting a child custody evaluation in a case in which the psychologist served in a therapeutic role for the child or his or her immediate family or has had other involvement that may compromise the psychologist's objectivity. This should not, however, preclude the psychologist from testifying in the case as a fact witness concerning treatment of the child. In addition, during the course of a child custody evaluation, a psychologist does not accept any of the involved participants in the evaluation as a therapy client. Therapeutic contact with the child or involved participants following a child custody evaluation is undertaken with caution.

A psychologist asked to testify regarding a therapy client who is involved in a child custody case is aware of the limitations and possible biases inherent in such a role and the possible impact on the ongoing therapeutic relationship. Although the court may require the psychologist to testify as a fact witness regarding factual information he or she became aware of in a professional relationship with a client, that psychologist should generally decline the role of an expert witness who gives a professional opinion regarding custody and visitation issues (see Ethical Standard 7.03) unless so ordered by the court.

III. Procedural Guidelines: Conducting a Child Custody Evaluation

8. **The scope of the evaluation is determined by the evaluator, based on the nature of the referral question.** The scope of the custody-related evaluation is determined by the nature of the question or issue raised by the referring person or the court, or is inherent in the situation. Although comprehensive child custody evaluations generally require an evaluation

of all parents or guardians and children, as well as observations of interactions between them, the scope of the assessment in a particular case may be limited to evaluating the parental capacity of one parent without attempting to compare the parents or to make recommendations. Likewise, the scope may be limited to evaluating the child. Or a psychologist may be asked to critique the assumptions and methodology of the assessment of another mental health professional. A psychologist also might serve as an expert witness in the area of child development, providing expertise to the court without relating it specifically to the parties involved in a case.

9. **The psychologist obtains informed consent from all adult participants and, as appropriate, informs child participants.** In undertaking child custody evaluations, the psychologist ensures that each adult participant is aware of (a) the purpose, nature, and method of the evaluation; (b) who has requested the psychologist's services; and (c) who will be paying the fees. The psychologist informs adult participants about the nature of the assessment instruments and techniques and informs those participants about the possible disposition of the data collected. The psychologist provides this information, as appropriate, to children, to the extent that they are able to understand.

10. **The psychologist informs participants about the limits of confidentiality and the disclosure of information.** A psychologist conducting a child custody evaluation ensures that the participants, including children to the extent feasible, are aware of the limits of confidentiality characterizing the professional relationship with the psychologist. The psychologist informs participants that in consenting to the evaluation, they are consenting to disclosure of the evaluation's findings in the context of the forthcoming litigation and in any other proceedings deemed necessary by

the courts. A psychologist obtains a waiver of confidentiality from all adult participants or from their authorized legal representatives.

11. **The psychologist uses multiple methods of data gathering.** The psychologist strives to use the most appropriate methods available for addressing the questions raised in a specific child custody evaluation and generally uses multiple methods of data gathering, including, but not limited to, clinical interviews, observation, and/or psychological assessments. Important facts and opinions are documented from at least two sources whenever their reliability is questionable. The psychologist, for example, may review potentially relevant reports (e.g., from schools, health care providers, child care providers, agencies, and institutions). Psychologists may also interview extended family, friends, and other individuals on occasions when the information is likely to be useful. If information is gathered from third parties that is significant and may be used as a basis for conclusions, psychologists corroborate it by at least one other source wherever possible and appropriate and document this in the report.

12. **The psychologist neither overinterprets nor inappropriately interprets clinical or assessment data.** The psychologist refrains from drawing conclusions not adequately supported by the data. The psychologist interprets any data from interviews or tests, as well as any questions of data reliability and validity, cautiously and conservatively, seeking convergent validity. The psychologist strives to acknowledge to the court any limitations in methods or data used.

13. **The psychologist does not give any opinion regarding the psychological functioning of any individual who has not been personally evaluated.** This guideline, however, does not preclude the psychologist from reporting what an evaluated indi-

vidual (such as the parent or child) has stated or from addressing theoretical issues of hypothetical questions, so long as the limited basis of the information is noted.

14. **Recommendations, if any, are based on what is in the best psychological interests of the child.** Although the profession has not reached consensus about whether psychologists ought to make recommendations about the final custody determination to the courts, psychologists are obligated to be aware of the arguments on both sides of this issue and to be able to explain the logic of their position concerning their own practice.

   If the psychologist does choose to make custody recommendations, these recommendations should be derived from sound psychological data and must be based on the best interests of the child in the particular case. Recommendations are based on articulated assumptions, data, interpretations, and inferences based upon established professional and scientific standards. Psychologists guard against relying on their own biases or unsupported beliefs in rendering opinions in particular cases.

15. **The psychologist clarifies financial arrangements.** Financial arrangements are clarified and agreed upon prior to commencing a child custody evaluation. When billing for a child custody evaluation, the psychologist does not misrepresent his or her services for reimbursement purposes.

16. **The psychologist maintains written records.** All records obtained in the process of conducting a child custody evaluation are properly maintained and filed in accord with the APA *Record Keeping Guidelines* (APA, 1993) and relevant statutory guidelines.

All raw data and interview information are recorded with an eye toward their possible review by other psychologists or the court, where legally permitted. Upon request, appropriate reports are made available to the court.

References

American Psychological Association. (1985). *Standards for educational and psychological testing.* Washington, DC: Author.

American Psychological Association. (1992). Ethical principles of psychologists and code of conduct. *American Psychologist, 47,* 1597–1611.

American Psychological Association. (1993). *Record keeping guidelines.* Washington, DC: Author.

American Psychological Association: Ethics Committee. (1985). *Annual report of the American Psychological Association Ethics Committee.* Washington, DC: Author.

Grisso, T. (1986). *Evaluating competencies: Forensic assessments and instruments.* New York: Plenum.

Hall, J. E., & Hare-Mustin, R. T. (1983). Sanctions and the diversity of ethical complaints against psychologists. *American Psychologist, 38,* 714–729.

Keith-Spiegel, P., & Koocher, G. P. (1985). *Ethics in psychology.* New York: Random House.

Melton, G. B., Petrila, J., Poythress, N. G., & Slobogin, C. (1987). *Psychological evaluations for the courts: A handbook for mental health professionals and lawyers.* New York: Guilford Press.

Mills, D. H. (1984). Ethics education and adjudication within psychology. *American Psychologist, 39,* 669–675.

Mnookin, R. H. (1975). Child-custody adjudication: Judicial functions in the face of indeterminacy. *Law and Contemporary Problems, 39,* 226–293.

Ochroch, R. (1982, August). *Ethical pitfalls in child custody evaluations.* Paper presented at the 90th Annual Convention of the American Psychological Association, Washington, DC.

Okpaku, S. (1976). Psychology: Impediment or aid in child custody cases? *Rutgers Law Review, 29,* 1117–1153.

Weithorn, L. A. (Ed.). (1987). *Psychology and child custody determinations: Knowledge, roles, and expertise.* Lincoln: University of Nebraska Press.

♦ ♦ ♦

Commentary: Apparently, not all forensic clinicians follow the guidelines when conducting custody evaluations. An analysis of the content of such evaluations in one court in a Midwestern state found a lack of consistency between the guidelines and clinical practice. See

Horvath, L., Logan, T., & Walker, R. (2002). Child custody cases: A content analysis of evaluations in practice. Professional Psychology: Research and Practice, 33, 557–565.

Although the guidelines specifically assert they are aspirational and are not intended to be mandatory, at least two states, West Virginia and Florida, have passed legislation providing psychologists immunity from malpractice suits if their evaluation is consistent with the guidelines. There is no indication that following them would insulate evaluators from ethics complaints.

Comparable guidelines for evaluating children suspected to be victims of neglect and abuse have also been adopted as APA policy. See American Psychological Association Committee on Professional Practice and Standards. (1998). Guidelines for psychological evaluations in child protection matters. American Psychologist, 54, 586–593. For one model that may be useful in assessing suspected sexual abuse, see Bow, J., Quinnell, F., Zaroff, M., & Assemany, A. (2002). Assessment of sexual abuse allegations in child custody cases. Professional Psychology: Research and Practice, 33, 566–575.

Child custody evaluations are not the only area fraught with ethical problems. The forensic psychologist must anticipate such concerns in all assessment contexts. See, for example,

Archer, R. A. (Ed.). (2003). Editor's introduction to a special issue on the topic of forensic assessment [Special issue]. Assessment, 10(4).

Butcher, J., & Pope, K. (1993). Seven issues in conducting forensic assessments: Ethical responsibilities in light of new standards and new tests. Ethics & Behavior, 3, 267–288. (focusing on versions of the MMPI)

Christy, A., Douglas, K. S., Otto, R. K., & Petrila, J. (2004). Juveniles evaluated incompetent to proceed: Characteristics and quality of mental health professionals' evaluations. Professional Psychology: Research and Practice, 35, 380–388.

Goldstein, A. M. (2007). Forensic psychology: Toward a standard of care. In A. M. Goldstein (Ed.), Forensic Psychology (pp. 3–41). New York: Wiley.

Grote, C. L., & Parsons, T. D. (2005). Threats to the livelihood of the forensic neuropsychological practice: Avoiding ethical misconduct. Journal of Forensic Neuropsychology, 3, 79–93.

Guilmette, T., & Hagen, L. (1997). The ethical neuropsychologist/courting the clinical: Ethical considerations in forensic neuropsychological consultation. The Clinical Neuropsychologist, 11, 287–290.

Haag, A. M. (2006). Ethical dilemmas faced by correctional psychologists in Canada. Criminal Justice and Behavior, 33, 93–109.

Heilbrun, K. (2001). Principles of forensic mental health assessment. New York: Kluwer Academic/Plenum Publishers.

Knapp, S., & VandeCreek, L. (2001). Ethical issues in personality assessment in forensic psychology. Journal of Personality Assessment, 77, 242–254.

Lipsitt, P. D. (2007). Ethics and forensic psychological practice. In A. M. Goldstein (Ed.), Forensic Psychology (pp. 171–189). New York: Wiley.

Malina, A. C., Nelson, N. W., & Sweet, J. J. (2005). Framing the relationships in forensic neuropsychology: Ethical issues. Journal of Forensic Neuropsychology, 4, 21–44.

For an excellent comprehensive analysis of difficult cases facing forensic clinicians, see Heilbrun, K., Marczyk, G., & DeMatteo, D. (2002). Forensic mental health assessment: A casebook. New York: Oxford University Press.

Pfeifer and Brigham (1993) surveyed 37 academic forensic psychologists to identify ethical issues that they had encountered while consulting in pretrial phases of litigation or as experts during trials. Every one of the respondents reported that they had never "resolved their current ethical dilemmas by referring either to the APA's ethical principles or the [Committee on Ethical Guidelines for Forensic Psychologist's] specialty guidelines" (pp. 341–342). See Pfeifer, J. E., & Brigham, J. C. (1993). Ethical concerns of nonclinical forensic witnesses and consultants. Ethics & Behavior, 3, 329–343. Many of the respondents suggested that ethical conflicts should be resolved through personal choice, beliefs, and values. What do these findings say about the utility of these two documents for scientists who serve as experts?

Even if one followed ethical standards, as Sales and Simon (1993) point out, "By their very nature ethics documents do not specifically address all issues and conundrums that experts will face in the courtroom" (pp. 244–245). Sales, B., & Simon, L. (1993). Institutional constraints on the ethics of expert testimony, Ethics & Behavior, 3, 231–249.

Forensic psychologists, like their colleagues who provide treatment, face important issues concerning dual relationships:

[P]roviders of forensic services must be aware of, and sensitive to, the potential conflicts between the psychological roles of examiner, therapist, and consultant; between the legal roles of expert witness and fact witness; and between the roles of advocate for the client and advocate for the professional opinion.

. . .

The identification of who is the client has important ramifications in the determination of what service is to be provided, who is to have access to the information, what information is to be confidential, what product is to be generated by the psychologist, to whom the psychologist is to report, and who is to pay the fee for the service. (pp. 377–378)

Perrin, G., & Sales, B. (1994). *Forensic standards in the American Psychological Association ethics code.* Professional Psychology: Research and Practice, 25, 376–382. *Standard 3.05c provides some guidance but the issues are much more complex than the standard contemplates. Some of their complexities are addressed in the next set of materials.*

Irreconcilable Conflict Between Therapeutic and Forensic Roles

Stuart A. Greenberg and Daniel W. Shuman

With increasing frequency, psychologists, psychiatrists, and other mental health professionals are participating as forensic experts in litigation on behalf of their patients. . . . [T]his practice constitutes engaging in dual-role relationships and often leads to bad results for patients, courts, and clinicians.

. . .

This article contrasts the role of therapeutic clinician as care provider and the role of forensic evaluator as expert to the court, acknowledges the temptation to engage in these two roles in the same matter, explains the inherent problems and argues strongly against doing so, and discusses the ethical precepts that discourage the undertaking of the dual roles, as well as the legal and professional responses to this dilemma. The specific problem addressed here is that of the psychologist or psychiatrist who provides clinical assessment or therapy to a patient–litigant and who concurrently or subsequently attempts to serve as a forensic expert for that patient in civil litigation.

Expert persons may testify as fact witnesses as well as either of two types of expert witnesses: treating experts and forensic experts. No special expertise beyond the ability to tell the court what is known from first-hand observation is required to be a fact witness. Being an expert person, however, does not preclude one from simply providing to the court first-hand observations in the role of a fact witness. What distinguishes expert witnesses from fact witnesses is that expert witness have relevant specialized knowledge beyond that of the average person that may qualify them to provide opinions, as well as facts, to aid the court in reaching a just conclusion. Psychologists and psychiatrists who provide patient care can usually qualify to testify as treating experts, in that they have the specialized knowledge, not possessed by most individuals, to offer a clinical diagnosis and prognosis. However, a role conflict arises when a treating therapist also attempts to testify as a forensic expert addressing the psycholegal issues in the case (e.g., testamentary capacity, proximate cause of injury, parental capacity).

. . .

ROLE CONFLICT

In most jurisdictions, a properly qualified therapist testifies as a fact witness for some purposes, as he or she is expected to testify to information learned first hand in therapy, and as an expert witness for some purposes, as he or she is permitted to testify to opinions about mental disorder that a layperson would not be permitted to offer. Thus, a therapist may, if requested to do so by a patient or ordered to do so by a court, properly testify to facts, observations, and clinical opinions for which the therapy process provides a trustworthy basis. This testimony may include the history as provided by a patient; the clinical diagnosis; the care provided to a patient; the patient's response to that treatment; the patient's prognosis; the mood, cognitions, or behavior of the patient at particular times; and any other statements that the patient made in treatment. A therapist may properly testify, for example, that Ms. Jones reported the history of a motor vehicle accident (MVA) 2 weeks prior to the start of therapy and that the therapist observed the patient to be bruised, bandaged, tearful, and extremely anxious. The therapist may properly testify that he or she observed, and that Ms. Jones reported, symptoms that led to a diagnosis of posttraumatic stress disorder (PTSD). The therapist may also describe the particular type

From *Professional Psychology: Research and Practice, 28*, 50–57. Copyright 1997 by the American Psychological Association.

of treatment used, the patient's response to that treatment, and her prognosis. The therapist may properly testify that the primary focus for the therapy was the MVA, or the PTSD secondary to the MVA. The therapist may even properly testify that, for treatment purposes, the operating assumption was that the MVA rather than her impending divorce or recent job termination or the death of a family member was what caused the patient's distress.

To be admissible, an expert opinion must be reliable and valid to a reasonable degree of scientific certainty (a metric for scrutinizing the certainty of expert testimony as a condition of its admissibility). It is improper for the therapist to offer an expert opinion that the MVA was the proximate cause of her impairments rather than the divorce, job termination, or bereavement. This is true for two reasons. First, the type and amount of data routinely observed in therapy are rarely adequate to form a proper foundation to determine the psycholegal (as opposed to the clinically assumed) cause of the litigant's impairment; nor is therapy usually adequate to rule out other potential causes. Second, such testimony engages the therapist in conflicting roles with the patient. Common examples of this role conflict occur when a patient's therapist testifies to the psycholegal issues that arise in competency, personal injury, worker's compensation, and custody litigation.

These concerns do not apply when the treating expert witness stays within the boundaries of facts and opinions that can be reliably known by the treating professional. Indeed, the treating therapist can be compelled to testify to information perceived during the therapeutic process and to opinions previously formed for the purpose of therapy but cannot be compelled to do a forensic examination or analysis (Shuman, 1983). Clinical, ethical, and legal concerns arise when the treating expert offers psycholegal assessment—an assessment for which the treating expert does not have adequate professional basis, for which there are inherent role conflicts, and for which there will almost certainly be negative implications for continued therapy.

The temptation to use therapists as forensic experts falls on fertile ground because clinical psychology and psychiatry graduate students often do not receive adequate training in forensic ethics.

Although graduate training in ethics has vastly improved in general, most graduate ethics courses teach clinicians in training about the dual roles that most often get therapists in difficulties: mainly, sexual and other nonprofessional relationships with patients. The legal arena is sufficiently foreign to most academicians and their students that ethics training primarily focuses on licensing laws and ethical codes for general practice. For example, few psychologists receive training in the Specialty Guidelines for Forensic Psychologists (Committee on Ethical Guidelines for Forensic Psychologists, 1991) because few see themselves as forensic psychologists. When these clinicians eventually testify in court, they see themselves as benignly telling the court about their patients and perhaps even benevolently testifying on behalf of their patients. Therapists are not typically trained to know that the rules of procedure, rules of evidence, and the standard of proof are different for court room testimony than for clinical practice.

The temptation to use therapists as forensic experts on behalf of patient–litigants exists because of erroneous beliefs about efficiency, candor, neutrality, and expertise. Using a therapist to provide forensic assessment appears efficient because the therapist has already spent time with the patient and knows much about him or her that others are yet to learn and not without substantial expenditures of time and money for an additional evaluation. A therapist appears to gain candid information from a patient–litigant because of the patient's assumed incentive to be candid with the therapist to receive effective treatment. Although litigants may learn much about themselves as a consequence of receiving thorough forensic evaluations (Finn & Tonsager, 1996), the same treatment incentive does not exist in a forensic examination. Thus, the facts forming the basis for a therapist's opinion may initially appear more accurate and complete than the facts that could be gathered in a separate forensic assessment.

In addition, a therapist does not appear to be the attorney's hired gun who came into the case solely to assist in advancing or defeating a legal claim or defense. Thus, a therapist's forensic assessment may appear more neutral and less immediately subject to financial incentives to reach a particular result than does a separate forensic evaluation. And, it is sometimes assumed that if a therapist has the expertise to be trusted to treat the condition for which a patient seeks compensation, surely the therapist has the expertise to testify about it. Indeed, in many ways it would appear from this analysis that one would have to be foolish not to have therapists also testify as forensic experts. Nevertheless, examining the differences between the therapeutic and forensic relationships, process, and expertise reveals that such foolishness is the mirror image of sensibility.

TEN DIFFERENCES BETWEEN THERAPEUTIC AND FORENSIC RELATIONSHIPS

As can be seen from Table 1, the therapeutic and forensic roles demand different and inconsistent orientations and procedures (adapted from Greenberg & Moreland, 1995). The superficial and perilous appeal of using a therapist as a forensic examiner is debunked by examining the conceptual and practical differences between the therapist–patient relationship and the forensic examiner–litigant relationship.

The first and perhaps most crucial difference between the roles is the identification of whose client the patient–litigant is. As implied by the name, the patient–litigant has two roles, one as therapy patient and another as plaintiff in the legal process. The patient–litigant is the client of the therapist for the purposes of treatment. The patient–litigant is as well the client of the attorney for guidance and representation through the legal system.

The nature of each relationship and the person who chooses to create it differs for therapy and forensic evaluation. The therapist is ultimately answerable to the client, who decides whether to use the services of a particular therapist; the forensic evaluator is ultimately answerable to the attorney, or the court in the case of a court-appointed expert, who decides whether to use the services of a particular forensic evaluator. The patient retains the therapist for treatment. The attorney (or the court)

TABLE 1

Ten Differences Between Therapeutic and Forensic Relationships

		Care provision	Forensic evaluation
1.	Whose client is patient/litigant?	The mental health practitioner	The attorney
2.	The relational privilege that governs disclosure in each relationship	Therapist–patient privilege	Attorney-client and attorney work-product privilege
3.	The cognitive set and evaluative attitude of each expert	Supportive, accepting, empathic	Neutral, objective, detached
4.	The differing areas of competency of each expert	Therapy techniques for treatment of the impairment	Forensic evaluation techniques relevant to the legal claim
5.	The nature of the hypotheses tested by each expert	Diagnostic criteria for the purpose of therapy	Psycholegal criteria for purpose of legal adjudication
6.	The scrutiny applied to the information utilized in the process and the role of historical truth	Mostly based on information from the person being treated with little scrutiny of that information by the therapist	Litigant information supplemented with that of collateral source and scrutinized by the evaluator and the court
7.	The amount and control of structure in each relationship	Patient structured and relatively less structured than forensic evaluation	Evaluator structured and relatively more structured than therapy
8.	The nature and degree of "adversarialness" in each relationship	A helping relationship: rarely adversarial	An evaluative relationship; frequently adversarial
9.	The goal of the professional in each relationship	Therapist attempts to benefit the patient by working within the therapeutic relationship	Evaluator advocates for the results and implications of the evaluation for the benefit of the court
10.	The impact on each relationship of critical judgment by the expert	The basis of the relationship is the therapeutic alliance, and critical judgment is likely to impair that alliance	The basis of the relationship is evaluative, and critical judgment is unlikely to cause serious emotional harm

retains the forensic evaluator for litigation. This arrangement allows for the relationship that is most straightforward and free of conflict of interest. It best protects the parties' interests as well as the integrity of the therapist and the forensic evaluator.

Second, the legal protection against compelled disclosure of the contents of a therapist–patient relationship is governed by the therapist–patient privilege and can usually only be waived by the patient or by court order. Society seeks to further the goal of treatment through recognition of a privilege for confidential communications between a therapist and patient in most jurisdictions under a physician–, psychiatrist–, psychologist–, or psychotherapist–patient privilege (Shuman & Weiner, 1987).

Legal protection against compelled disclosure of the contents of the forensic evaluator–litigant relationship is governed by the attorney–client and attorney–work-product privileges. Because the purpose of a forensic relationship is litigation, not treatment nor even diagnosis for the purpose of planning treatment, communications between a forensic examiner and a litigant are not protected under a physician–, psychiatrist–, psychologist–, or psychotherapist–patient privilege. The forensic evaluator, however, having been retained by the attorney, is acting as an agent of the attorney in evaluating the party or parties in the legal matter. This legal agency status puts the forensic evaluator under the umbrella of the attorney–client privilege and usually protects privileged information until such time that the evaluator is declared to be a witness at trial. Until that time, most states, especially in civil matters, allow the attorney to prevent access to that attorney's retained expert by opposing counsel, thus best protecting the party's interest should the evaluator's independent opinion not favor the party of the attorney who has retained him or her. Because it would not be a therapeutic relationship, no such potential protection is available if the forensic evaluator were to be retained directly by the party, thereby creating the onus of one's own expert who was hired to evaluate some potential merit to the case instead being used to discredit the retaining side. Because parties, through their attorneys, need to be able to evaluate the merits of their case candidly without such jeopardy, the attorney–work-

product privilege covers such trial-preparation use of experts retained by counsel.

The main practice point to be made here is that the logic, the legal basis, and the rules governing the privilege that applies to care providers are substantially different from those that apply to forensic evaluators. Given this, the duty to inform forensic examinees of the potential lack of privilege and the intended use of the examination product is embodied in case law (*Estelle v. Smith,* 1981) and the Specialty Guidelines for Forensic Psychologists (SGFP) adopted by the American Psychology–Law Society (APA Division 41) and the American Board of Forensic Psychology in 1991 [see Guideline IV(E)]. . . .

The third difference is evident in the evaluative attitude of each of the experts. The therapist is a care provider and usually supportive, accepting, and emphatic; the forensic evaluator is an assessor and usually neutral, objective, and detached as to the forensic issues. A forensic evaluator's task is to gain an emphatic understanding of the person but to remain dispassionate as to the psycholegal issues being evaluated. For therapists, empathy and sympathy—generating a desire to help—usually go hand-in-hand. For forensic evaluators, the task is a dispassionate assessment of the psycholegal issues.

Fourth, to perform his or her task, a therapist must be competent in the clinical assessment and treatment of the patient's impairment. In contrast, a forensic evaluator must be competent in forensic evaluation procedures and psycholegal issues relevant to the case. A therapist must be familiar with the literature on diagnoses and treatment interventions, knowing from among which diagnostic categories and treatment interventions the patient's difficulties would be best identified and treated. The forensic evaluator must know the basic law as it relates to the assessment of the particular impairment claimed.

Fifth, a therapist then uses this expertise to test rival diagnostic hypotheses to ascertain which therapeutic intervention is most likely to be effective. . . . A forensic evaluator must know the relevant law and how it relates to a particular psychological assessment. A forensic evaluator then uses this expertise to test a very different set of rival psycholegal hypotheses that are generated by the elements of the law applicable to the legal case being adjudicated. . . .

The sixth difference is the degree of scrutiny to which information from the patient–litigant is subjected. Historical truth plays a different role in each relationship. At least with competent adults, therapy is primarily based on information from the person being treated, information that may be somewhat incomplete, grossly biased, or honestly misperceived. Even when the therapist does seek collateral information from outside of therapy, such as when treating children and incompetent adults, the purpose of the information gathering is to further treatment, not in the pursuit of validating historical truth. In most instances, it is not realistic, nor is it typically the standard of care, to expect a therapist to be an investigator to validate the historical truth of what a patient discusses in therapy. Indeed, trying to do so by contacting family members, friends, or coworkers and by requesting corroborating documentation may frustrate therapy even if the patient has signed a release of information. Further, this corroboration is usually unnecessary. Effective therapy can usually proceed even in the face of substantial historical inaccuracy. . . .

The more important question for most psychotherapeutic techniques is how a patient perceives or feels about the world—what is real to that patient—not factual or historical truth (Wesson, 1985). . . . Thus, the historical truth of matters raised during therapy cannot, simply on that basis alone, be considered valid and reliable for legal purposes. This is not a criticism of therapy. . . .

In contrast, the role of a forensic examiner is, among other things, to offer opinions regarding historical truth and the validity of the psychological aspects of a litigant's claims. The accuracy of this assessment is almost always more critical in a forensic context than it is in psychotherapy. A competent forensic evaluation almost always includes verification of the litigant's accuracy against other information sources about the events in question. These sources may include collateral interviews with coworkers, neighbors, family members, emergency room personnel, or a child's teacher or pediatrician and a review of documents such as police reports, school records, military records, medical records, personnel files, athletic team attendance, credit card bills, check stubs, changes in one's resume, deposi-

tions, witness statements, and any other possible sources of information about the litigant's pre- and postincident thoughts, emotions, and behaviors. . . .

Seventh, the need for historical accuracy in forensic evaluations leads to a need for completeness in the information acquired and for structure in the assessment process to accomplish that goal. Therapeutic evaluation, in comparison, is relatively less complete and less structured than a forensic evaluation. Moreover, a patient provides more structure to a therapeutic evaluation than does a litigant to a forensic evaluation. Ideally, a patient and therapist work collaboratively to define the goals of a therapeutic interaction and a time frame within which to realize them. The time frame and goals of a forensic evaluation are defined by the legal rules that govern the proceeding, and once these are determined, the forensic evaluator and litigant are usually constrained to operate within them. To make maximum use of the time available, forensic evaluators usually conduct highly structured assessments using structured interviews supplemented with a battery of psychological tests and forensically oriented history and impairment questionnaires. . . .

Eighth, although some patients will resist discussing emotionally laden information, the psychotherapeutic process is rarely adversarial in the attempt to reveal that information. Forensic evaluation, although not necessarily unfriendly or hostile, is nonetheless adversarial in that the forensic evaluator seeks information that both supports and refutes the litigant's legal assertions. This struggle for information is also handled quite differently by each expert: The therapist exercises therapeutic judgment about pressing a patient to discuss troubling material, whereas a forensic evaluator will routinely seek information from other sources if the litigant will not provide it or to corroborate it when the litigant does provide information. In the extreme, when presented with excessive underreporting or overreporting of critical information, the forensic evaluator might even decide that the litigant is dissembling.

Ninth, consider the goals of each of these relationships. Therapy is intended to aid the person being treated. A therapist–patient relationship is predicated on principles of beneficence and nonmaleficence—doing good and avoiding harm. A therapist attempts to intervene in a way that will improve or enhance the quality of the person's life. Effective treatment for a patient is the reason and the principal defining force for the therapeutic relationship. . . .

Forensic examiners strive to gather and present objective information that may ultimately aid a trier of fact (i.e., judge or jury) to reach a just solution to a legal conflict. A forensic examiner is obligated to be neutral, independent, and honest, without becoming invested in the legal outcome. A forensic evaluator advocates for the findings of the evaluation, whatever those findings turn out to be. Thus, the results of a forensic examination may well be detrimental to the legal position of an examinee (American Psychiatric Association, 1984) and contrary to basic therapeutic principles.

Tenth, the patient–litigant is likely to feel differently about expert opinions rendered by therapists than those rendered by forensic experts. Consider the role of judgment in therapeutic relationships. There is a robust, positive relationship between the success of the therapist–patient alliance and success in therapy (Horvath & Luborsky, 1993). To develop a positive therapist–patient alliance, a therapist must suspend judgment of the patient so that the therapist can enter and understand the private perceptual world of the patient without doing anything that would substantially threaten that relationship. . . .

In contrast, the role of a forensic examiner is to assess, to judge, and to report that finding to a third party (attorney, judge, or jury) who will use that information in an adversarial setting. To assess, a forensic examiner must be detached, maybe even skeptical, and must carefully question what the litigant presents. Because a forensic psychologist or psychiatrist has not engaged in a helping relationship with the litigant, it is less likely that his or her judgment-laden testimony would cause serious or lasting emotional harm to the litigant than would that of the psychologist or psychiatrist who has occupied a therapeutic role.

WAIVING THE DUAL-ROLE CONFLICT

These role differences are not merely artificial distinctions but are substantial differences that make inherently good sense. Unless these distinctions are respected, not only are both the therapeutic and forensic endeavors jeopardized for the patient–litigant but as well the rights of all parties who are affected by this erroneous and conflictual choice. Unlike some conflicts of interest, this role conflict is not one that the plaintiff can waive, because it is not the exclusive province of the plaintiff's side of the case. The conflict affects not only the plaintiff but also the defense and the court. This conflict not only poses therapeutic risks to the patient–litigant but also risks of inaccuracy and lack of objectivity to the court's process and to all of the litigants.

[*Ed. Note:* The authors now cite principles from various documents that bar dual and conflicting professional roles with patient–litigants, the most relevant of which are already reprinted in this text.] . . .

CONCLUSION

. . .

. . . Therapists need to acknowledge the limits of what they can accurately and reliably say on the basis of therapeutic relationships. Although it is difficult, when asked psycholegal questions, therapists must be willing to testify "I cannot answer that question given my role in this case," "I do not have an adequate professional basis to answer that question," "I did not conduct the kind of evaluation necessary to reliably answer that question," "I can only tell you what I observed," or "I can only tell you what my patient told me." No matter how laudable their motives might be, therapists who venture beyond these limits and into the arena of psycholegal opinion are deceiving themselves and others. Engaging in an irreconcilable role conflict and lacking an adequate professional basis for their testimony, they can be neither neutral, objective, nor impartial.

References

American Psychiatric Association. (1984). *Psychiatry in the sentencing process: A report of the task force on the role of psychiatry in the sentencing process.* Washington, DC: Author.

Committee on Ethical Guidelines for Forensic Psychologists. (1991). Specialty guidelines for forensic psychologists. *Law and Human Behavior, 15,* 655–665.

Estelle v. Smith. 451 U.S. 454 (1981).

Finn, S. E., & Tonsager, M. E. (1996). *Therapeutic assessment: Using psychological testing to help clients change.* Manuscript submitted for publication.

Greenberg, S. A., & Moreland, K. (1995). *Forensic evaluations and forensic applications of the MMPI/MMPI-2.* Unpublished manuscript, University of Minnesota, Department of Continuing Education and Conference Services, Minneapolis, and The American Academy of Forensic Psychology.

Horvath, A. O., & Luborsky, L. (1993). The role of the therapeutic alliance in psychotherapy. *Journal of Consulting and Clinical Psychology, 61,* 561–573.

Shuman, D. W. (1983). Testimonial compulsion: The involuntary medical expert witness. *Journal of Legal Medicine, 4,* 419–446.

Shuman, D. W., & Weiner, M. F. (1987). *The psychotherapist–patient privilege: A critical examination.* Springfield, IL: Thomas.

Wesson, M. (1985). Historical truth, narrative truth, and expert testimony. *Wash. L. Rev., 60,* 331–354.

◆   ◆   ◆

Commentary: More recently, Shuman, Greenberg, and their colleagues proposed that therapists should be prohibited from testifying about their patients in all legal contexts, arguing that all such dual-relationship testimony harms the judicial system as well as treatment. See Shuman, D. W., Greenberg, S., Heilbrun, K., & Foote, W. E. (1998). An immodest proposal: Should treating mental health professionals be barred from testifying about their patients? Behavioral Sciences and the Law, 16, *509–523.*

Compatibility of Therapeutic and Forensic Roles

Terence Heltzel

Psychologists are becoming increasingly aware of ethical responsibilities and risks associated with their interactions with the legal system. For instance, an article by Greenberg and Shuman (1997) takes the position that there are irreconcilable role conflicts for therapists attempting to also serve as forensic experts, providing "psycholegal opinions" to the court system regarding their clients and that for psychologists to attempt to do so involves serious ethical hazards. . . .

It would thus appear that many mental health professionals are, according to Greenberg and Shuman (1997), violating ethical standards. Their important and influential article was more recently given even more national exposure by its inclusion in the American Psychological Association (APA) publication *Ethical Conflicts in Psychology* (Bersoff, 2003). The alleged ethical conflicts described by Greenberg and Shuman are not of only academic interest. The professional careers of many psychologists are being threatened by the application of the concepts they espoused. For instance, the State Board of Psychology of Ohio (2003), hereinafter referred to as the *Ohio Board,* published the newsletter *Alert!,* warning psychologists regarding ethical violations when therapists attempt to provide expert testimony. In this publication, the Ohio Board (2003) identified the article by Greenberg and Shuman as one of three specific recommended resources "for the competent psychologist" (p. 2). The clear inference is that the Ohio Board, which adjudicates charges of ethics violations against Ohio psychologists, regards this article as an authoritative reference to be used in their deliberations.

. . .

APPLICABLE ETHICAL STANDARDS

. . .

Greenberg and Shuman's (1997) position relies heavily on a false and misleading . . . distinction that they make between a "forensic expert" and a "treatment expert." It should be noted that The [Specialty] Guidelines make no such distinction, and specifically define *treatment* as a forensic activity when psycholegal issues are involved. The Guidelines explicitly state forensic psychologists "are obligated to use that knowledge, consistent with accepted clinical and scientific standards, in selecting data collection methods and procedures for an evaluation, *treatment* [italics added], consultation or scholarly/empirical investigation" (Committee on Ethical Guidelines for Forensic Psychologists, 1991, Section VI, A). Also,

> When forensic psychologists conduct an examination or *engage in the treatment of a party to a legal proceeding* [italics added], with foreknowledge that their professional services will be used in an adjudicative forum, they incur a special responsibility to provide the best documentation possible under the circumstances. (Committee on Ethical Guidelines for Forensic Psychologists, 1991, Section VI, B)

Furthermore, "As an expert conducting an evaluation, *treatment* [italics added], consultation, or scholarly/empirical investigation, the forensic psychologist maintains professional integrity by examining the issue at hand from all reasonable perspectives, actively seeking information that will differentially test plausible rival hypotheses"

From *Professional Psychology: Research and Practice, 38,* 122–128. Copyright 2007 by the American Psychological Association.

(Committee on Ethical Guidelines for Forensic Psychologists, 1991, Section VI, C). These statements from The Guidelines clearly contradict Greenberg and Shuman's (1997) premise that there is a fundamental distinction between a forensic and treatment expert—a distinction upon which they base their conclusions regarding an "irreconcilable conflict between therapeutic and forensic roles" (p. 50). It is evident that a treatment expert is also a forensic expert. The clear inference is that The Guidelines consider treatment and expert testimony to be compatible roles.

It reasonably follows that as soon as a treating psychologist recognizes that a patient's mental state may be an issue in a legal proceeding, it is clear that answering psycholegal questions and serving as a witness may be required. With this "definable fore-knowledge," the psychologist ought to realize that, in addition to the traditional diagnostic and treatment roles, he or she can reasonably anticipate being called upon to provide expert testimony. Anticipating this additional role, the psychologist should conduct himself or herself with the duties of this role in mind. If the psychologist does not have the requisite competence, or the willingness, to assume these duties, then the psychologist should protect the patient's interests by, in consultation with the patient's attorney, making an appropriate referral or obtaining a supplemental forensic assessment.
. . .

Greenberg and Shuman (1997) argued that one of the primary reasons that the therapist role is incompatible with a forensic expert role is that a therapist is unlikely to conduct an evaluation sufficient to provide a valid and reliable basis for testimony on psycholegal issues—and that the therapist is therefore functioning outside of his or her boundaries of competence when attempting to provide expert opinions regarding psycholegal issues. They stated that the "evaluative attitude" (Greenberg & Shuman, 1997, p. 53) of the typical therapist is insufficiently neutral or objective, and a therapist is not usually as concerned about historical truth as is the forensic expert. However, there is no justifiable reason why a competent psychologist cannot and should not conduct an objective and appropriate evaluation of a patient seeking clinical services as a

basis for the treatment. Greenberg and Shuman in effect have erected a straw man with their position that a therapist is an inadequate diagnostician. The contention here is that the therapist must first and foremost be a competent diagnostician and is ethically required to objectively evaluate his or her patient as a basis for both effective treatment and expert testimony. Of course, most therapy patients do not present with pressing legal issues for which a need for testimony would be anticipated. Competent and objective assessment of each patient should be tailored to the needs and issues of that patient. When psycholegal issues are identified as an important aspect of the patient's presenting complaints and circumstances, the therapist must ensure that the issues are competently addressed. Having conducted an evaluation objectively addressing relevant psycholegal issues, the diagnostician-therapist can appropriately provide expert opinions on these issues.

. . . Greenberg and Shuman (1997) defined *psycholegal issues* as the province of the forensic expert. . . . However, the issues which are the subject of a psycholegal opinion are not the exclusive province of the legal system. For instance, a patient's diagnosis and the etiology of the condition have both psycholegal relevance as well as clinical relevance. The extent of impairment and prognosis have both clinical and psycholegal relevance. A competent and thorough diagnostician-therapist does not find issues of judgment, foundation, and historical truth problematic.
. . .

In an adversarial system, neutrality or independence of expert testimony is not required. Honesty is required. For instance, the plaintiff's attorney and the defendant's attorney can each retain an expert to evaluate the plaintiff, and each expert can then offer an honest opinion, and yet these honest opinions by the experts can differ (perhaps on the basis of different facts, observations, or weight given to variables and reasoning), and it is up to the trier-of-fact to weigh the value and credibility of each opinion. Likewise, the treatment expert can also offer a psycholegal opinion, the weight and credibility of which is up to the trier-of-fact to determine. If either the plaintiff's evaluator-therapist or the defendant's consultant-evaluator selectively presents only favorable or distorted facts, or makes a weak argument, this will usually become evident to the trier-of-fact. The legal system does not assume unbiased or neutral testimony. It should be up to the court, not a preemptive state board position, to assess the extent and importance of any bias in expert testimony.

. . . When a psychologist's activities are judged with respect to competency, they are normally compared with the prevailing standard of care. . . . Although their article clearly articulates their own view, Greenberg and Shuman did not provide much evidence regarding prevailing standards of care. Other than a few references to "Existing Professional Guidelines" (p. 54), which only tangentially address the issue, Greenberg and Shuman (1997) provided very little information beyond their own writings regarding professional acceptance of their position. Several articles (e.g., Berger, 2004; Strasburger, Gutheil, & Brodsky, 1997) have been identified which were theoretical discussions in agreement with Greenberg and Shuman. Strasburger et al. (1997) was noteworthy because they at least made an effort to determine prevailing opinions regarding the ethics related to a therapist providing testimony. What is especially instructive is that the survey evidence they referenced indicated that only a small minority of forensic psychiatrists agree with the position that it is a significant ethical problem for a therapist to provide expert testimony regarding a patient (Weinstock, 1986, 1989; Weinstock, Leong, & Silva, 1991). The survey results dramatically support a finding that there is no violation of a prevailing standard of care for a therapist providing expert witness testimony.

Greenberg and Shuman (1997), as indicated above, make reference to "Existing Professional Guidelines," that might be regarded as including recommended standards of care. None of the referenced guidelines provide a coherent prohibition against a therapist providing expert testimony, other than in child custody or visitation cases. The reference to a single statement in the Ethical Guidelines for the Practice of Forensic Psychiatry (American Academy of Psychiatry and the Law, 1989, as cited in Greenberg & Shuman, 1997) comes closest: "A treating psychiatrist should generally avoid agreeing to be an expert witness or to perform an evaluation of his patient for legal purposes because a forensic evaluation usually requires that other people be interviewed and testimony may adversely affect the therapeutic relationship."

The reasons given for avoiding the dual roles have been discredited here: To the extent that interviewing others is necessary to form an expert opinion, then a treating psychologist can and should do so, and the potential for testimony to adversely affect the therapeutic relationship is remote and is ethically addressed with appropriate informed consent, as discussed in detail below.

. . .

Limits of Confidentiality

Issues related to limits of confidentiality are important to Greenberg and Shuman's (1997) position that there are irreconcilable conflicts between the therapeutic role of a treatment provider and the role of the expert witness answering psycholegal questions. They argue that a psychologist evaluating a patient with respect to forensic issues sacrifices the privilege of confidential communication between a therapist and patient. They claim that, by inquiring regarding psycholegal issues, the psychologist establishes "a forensic relationship" and "communications between a forensic examiner and litigant are not protected" (Greenberg & Shuman, 1997, p. 52). However, the competent and thorough evaluation recommended here, encompassing forensic and clinical issues, and to be used as a basis for treatment and anticipated forensic testimony, surely would enjoy traditional psychologist–patient privileges. In any case, it is well-known that a patient filing a legal claim involving his or her mental state waives the privilege of confidentiality. Furthermore, there are probably circumstances in which the patient's mental state becomes an issue before a court, regardless of whether the patient initiates a claim, and it is certainly conceivable that the patient's therapist may be required to offer testimony due to circumstances beyond either the patient's or therapist's control.

Therefore, it should be clear that the ideal of complete confidentiality as a feature of the therapeutic relationship is simply not capable of being guaranteed and that all therapy carries inherent risks to confidentiality because of legal requirements. It follows that the risks related to limits of confidentiality cannot reasonably render treatment an unethical professional activity. EPPCC [Ethics Code (2002)] simply requires that recipients of psychological services be informed and give consent regarding these limits to confidentiality.

Avoiding Harm

Regarding avoiding harm, the EPPCC (2002) states, "Psychologists take reasonable steps to avoid harming their clients/patients, . . . and others with whom they work, and to minimize harm where it is foreseeable and unavoidable" (Standard 3.04). Greenberg and Shuman (1997) asserted that harm occurs when a therapist provides forensic testimony because the therapist's duty of beneficence and nonmaleficence to the patient conflicts with the forensic expert's duty to testify truthfully, regardless of the effect on the patient's legal position—thus potentially causing harm. They stated,

> A forensic evaluator advocates for the findings of the evaluation, whatever those findings turn out to be. Thus, the results of a forensic evaluation may well be detrimental to the legal position of an examinee . . . and contrary to basic therapeutic principles. (Greenberg & Shuman, 1997, p. 54)

The competent diagnostician-therapist can best limit the risk of testimony damaging to the patient's legal position by conducting a thorough and objective evaluation. The psychologist is ethically obligated to carefully assess and probe for circumstances and issues which would harm the patient's legal position, and openly discuss any evident problems with the patient. It is clearly in the patient's best interest to be advised of any weaknesses of his or her legal position before he or she decides to file a claim. If, after conducting a thorough, competent evaluation, and determining that the facts and clinical data support rendering opinions favorable to a claim, the psychologist can confidently proceed without reasonable anticipation of having to provide damaging testimony.

The harm described by Greenberg and Shuman (1997) is also relatively infrequent because the patient normally has the option of whether to file a claim leading to the psychologist's expert testimony. This decision is based on the patient and his or her

attorney first having the opportunity to review the treating psychologist's evaluation report. It is reasonable to presume that a claim will not be filed unless the evaluation supports the patient's legal position. If the diagnostician-therapist's evaluation report does not support a claim, the patient is not harmed because the findings may persuade the patient not to pursue a claim of doubtful validity. Or, the patient, with the advantage of legal counsel, can search for a diagnostician-therapist whose evaluation may be more favorable. In any event, a properly informed patient should never be surprised by unfavorable forensic testimony from his or her therapist.

If, in the course of treatment, the psychologist's opinions evolve unfavorably to the patient's legal position, this patient must be informed and the issues discussed as an important aspect of the therapeutic process. Proper anticipation of adverse legal determinations can go a long way to mitigate against harm. Who better than a patient's therapist to provide "bad news" regarding lack of support for a claim? It would appear that Greenberg and Shuman's (1997) position is that a therapist should avoid addressing issues that negatively impact a patient's legal position for fear of harming the therapeutic relationship; however, a good case could be made that their approach constitutes the very harm that they claim a therapist is obligated to avoid. Would it not be far more ethical for a therapist to acknowledge any adverse facts or professional opinions and process these in therapy?

An even more basic flaw with Greenberg and Shuman's (1997) argument regarding the alleged role conflict pertains to their misapplication of the concept of the therapist's duty of beneficence and nonmaleficence, by which they indicate that the potential for unfavorable testimony constitutes harm that must be ethically avoided. However, the duty to do no harm pertains to the therapist's intentions, competence, and treatment goals, not the potential outcome of the interventions and services. The potential for a bad outcome cannot reasonably be interpreted as implying a violation of the duties of beneficence and nonmaleficence. Clinicians (e.g., surgeons) routinely—and with beneficence and nonmaleficence—provide services involving much greater known and predictable risks than those associated with expert testimony. So long as the patient has been informed of the risks and decides that the potential benefits outweigh those risks, then provision of the services is ethical, even in the event of a poor outcome.

It is also questionable whether a resulting adverse legal ruling constitutes "harm." For instance, a denial of benefits or damage award is simply a legal determination that the individual was not entitled to those benefits or award—and therefore is not truly harmed by not receiving an award to which he or she was not entitled anyway. Furthermore, if a patient can be harmed by a legal outcome, then it would follow that successful treatment would become unethical because of the harm to the patient's legal position— that is, reduced benefits or awards for damages. It would also follow that a consultant would be harming his or her client (the attorney for either the plaintiff or defense) by testifying contrary to the client's legal position.

Impaired Objectivity and Bias

Reasonable expectation of impaired objectivity is identified in the EPPCC as a basis for a finding of unethical multiple relationships (3.05) or conflict of interest (3.06). Greenberg and Shuman (1997) and the Ohio Board clearly refer to impaired objectivity and bias as reasons which would render testimony by a therapist ethically hazardous. . . . This is a particularly poorly considered position, which could have very damaging effects to the practice of psychotherapy.

It is probably reasonable to assume and expect that a therapist will have the "supportive, accepting, and empathic" attitude toward his or her patient, as described by Greenberg and Shuman (1997). What is not reasonable is to equate this attitude with impaired objectivity. A diagnostician-therapist, whether or not providing testimony, is ethically required to maintain reasonable professional objectivity, which should not be incompatible with a supportive, accepting, and empathic attitude. To assert otherwise is to condemn psychotherapy as a professional activity. A therapist whose required professional objectivity is impaired by his or her "evaluative attitude," is probably not fit to provide diagnostic services or therapy. Absolute or perfect objectivity is not possible, and less than absolute objectivity is not equivalent to impaired objectivity.

A competent diagnostician-therapist does not gullibly accept as factual all statements made by a patient. Also, the appropriate level of skepticism need not be made offensive to a patient. Most patients readily understand and appreciate the need for careful, objective evaluation when explained to them in the context of legal requirements. It is also important to emphasize to the patient that important background information presented as "fact" is subject to scrutiny by a legal adversary.

Imperfect objectivity is not unique to a therapist. A diagnostician-consultant engaged by an attorney also manifests an evaluative attitude and experiences emotional reactions to the litigant being evaluated as well as toward the attorney-client. Thus, this psychologist has one relationship as a consultant to the attorney, who pays the psychologist's fees and whose opinions regarding the benefits of the psychologist's services are likely to contribute to or detract from the psychologist's reputation with the attorney and his or her colleagues. This psychologist also has another relationship to the litigant whom he or she evaluates and also has an evaluative attitude. This is not a relationship "most straightforward and free of conflict of interest," as purported by Greenberg and Shuman (1997, p. 52).

. . . Ethical practice is determined not by the presence of absolute impartiality or perfect objectivity. Ethical practice is determined more by competence and integrity. Integrity requires honest effort to fairly evaluate the psycholegal issues, with appropriate consideration to alternative, competing explanations for the problems assessed.

In the Public Interest

The Greenberg and Shuman (1997) arguments appear designed to persuade state boards to enforce prohibitions against therapists offering expert testimony on psycholegal issues to protect several public interests (reliable testimony and protection of the therapy relationship). It is worth noting that the authors extended their positions in a subsequent article (Shuman, Greenberg, Heilbrun, & Foote, 1998) in which they argued that even testimony from treatment experts should be disallowed. They described their opposition to such testimony as "radical," and "an immodest proposal." They stated,

On what basis and by what mechanisms do we propose to bar therapists from testifying about their patients? On the basis of conflict of interest, lack of foundation, and potential for unfair prejudice, we propose that a rule of law disqualify treating therapists from offering testimony about their patients. On the basis of harm to the therapist–patient relationship, we propose that professional codes of conduct condemn treating mental health professionals testifying about their patients. (Shuman et al., 1998, p. 510)

Their positions are indeed radical and immodest and would involve an overhaul to our current system of justice, to the detriment of the public interest.

It has been argued here that a therapist can and should conduct an evaluation sufficient to both guide treatment and serve as a basis for credible testimony. The option also exists for a therapist to seek consultation or make referral for a specialized assessment if desired, but in any case it would seem reasonable that a therapist should have a well-informed opinion regarding the legal challenges faced by his or her patient. There are already ethical standards regarding impaired objectivity for therapists, and the legal system safeguards against bias by permitting vigorous cross-examination and introduction of testimony by other experts. It has also been shown that a therapeutic relationship founded on informed consent, a competent evaluation, and candor between therapist and patient minimizes, and mitigates against, potential harm to the therapeutic relationship. Thus, it would seem especially imprudent to radically alter the current system or to adopt the immodest proposal to restrict testimony from therapists regarding psycholegal issues.

Furthermore, for state boards of psychology to define a therapist's expert opinions as inherently unethical would be to usurp a prerogative and responsibility of a court to weigh the credibility of any expert testimony. Such an approach would deny clients the use of the opinion of the therapist, which might be regarded as a free speech or civil rights issue. Certainly, the patient and court would lose access to an important source of vital information if a patient's therapist is prevented from expressing well-founded expert opinions. It should also be considered that several important administrative and judicial bodies (e.g., Social Security Administration, Workers Compensation, Probate Court) rely heavily on the testimony of treatment providers. To deny treatment providers the ability to testify would impose significant costs on patients and the judicial system because of the necessity of requiring additional assessments from high-priced specialists.

References

American Psychological Association. (2002). Ethical principles of psychologists and code of conduct: 2002. *American Psychologist, 57,* 1060–1073.

Berger, S. H. (2004). Ethics and dual agency in forensic psychiatry. *Psychiatric Times, 15,* 6.

Bersoff, D. N. (Ed.). (2003). *Ethical conflicts in psychology* (3rd ed.). Washington, DC: American Psychological Association.

Committee on Ethical Guidelines for Forensic Psychologists. (1991). Specialty guidelines for forensic psychologists. *Law and Human Behavior, 15,* 655–665.

Greenberg, S. A., & Shuman, D. W. (1997). Irreconcilable conflict between therapeutic and forensic roles. *Professional Psychology: Research and Practice, 28,* 50–57.

Shuman, D. W., Greenberg, S., Heilbrun, K., & Foote, W. E. (1998). Special perspective an immodest proposal: Should treating mental health professionals be barred from testifying about their patients? *Behavioral Sciences and the Law, 16,* 509–523.

State Board of Psychology of Ohio. (2003, Fall). *Alert!* Available at http://psychology.ohio.gov/pdfs/ALERT2003revised.pdf

Strasburger, L. H., Gutheil, T. G., & Brodsky, B. A. (1997). On wearing two hats: Role conflict in serving as both psychotherapist and expert witness. *American Journal of Psychiatry, 154,* 448–456.

Weinstock, R. (1986). Ethical concerns expressed by forensic psychiatrists. *Journal of Forensic Science, 31,* 596–602.

Weinstock, R. (1989). Perceptions of ethical problems by forensic psychiatrists. *Bulletin of the American Academy of Psychiatry and the Law, 17,* 189–202.

Weinstock, R., Leong, G. B., & Silva, J. A. (1991). Opinions by AAPL forensic psychiatrists on controversial ethical guidelines: A survey. *Bulletin of the American Academy of Psychiatry and the Law, 19,* 237–248.

When Worlds Collide: Therapeutic and Forensic Roles

Stuart A. Greenberg and Daniel W. Shuman

. . .

MUTUALLY EXCLUSIVE CHOICES

[T]he decision to provide therapeutic services and forensic services requires mutually exclusive professional choices. Providing each service requires the expert to establish a mutually exclusive choice of priorities between that of patient welfare and assistance to the court. Providing each service requires a mutually exclusive choice between a relationship with the patient-litigant based on trust and empathy or one based on doubt and distance. Providing each service also requires a mutually exclusive level of involvement in the fabric of the patient-litigant's mental health, either trying to better it or dispassionately evaluating it for the court.

. . .

The provision of therapeutic services and forensic services involves a specialized set of tasks, each asks substantially different questions, and each requires a substantially different area of competency. The same person can possess both sets of expertise. The core problem in role conflicts is not a lack of expertise. Most therapists are competent diagnosticians for therapeutic purposes, and many may also possess the skill and expertise to examine a patient-litigant for forensic purposes. Therapists (and for that matter, forensic examiners) may also possess the skill and expertise, and be appropriately licensed, to drive a motorcycle, give massages, style hair, broker real estate, and sell their own artistic creations. Possessing that competency and licensure does not argue that therapists should provide therapy to their patients on motorcycles, give them massages, style their hair, or sell them homes or art. This is not because they are not competent to do so. This is because, professionally, the tasks are irreconcilably mutually exclusive. No matter how dually competent, a professional cannot ethically and adequately accomplish both sets of tasks with the same patient-litigant. Possessing the dual competencies necessary to provide both therapy and examination services to the same individual does not explain why a psychologist should provide both services to the same individual. In our humble opinion, prudent psychologists will not.

♦ ♦ ♦

Commentary: In any event, there may be a middle-ground position, particularly for "treating experts" in divorce and custody situations:

> *Treating therapists may become involved in the legal system in at least two different ways. A psychologist may be retained to provide treatment to the children of separating or divorcing families or to a divorcing parent. Mental health professionals may also be directed by the courts to provide treatment for a specific purpose. (p. 470)*

Greenberg, L., & Gould, J. (2001). The treating expert: A hybrid role with firm boundaries. Professional Psychology: Research and Practice, 32, 469–478. As the authors point out, in contrast to the breadth of the forensic evaluator, the treating expert's focus, although narrower, is more intimate and longitudinal:

> *Treating experts may therefore be well qualified to render expert clinical opinions on a client's diagnosis, behavior patterns observed in treatment . . . and other issues. However, the treating therapist does not have the distance, fact-finding focus, or breadth of information considered by the child custody evaluator. (p. 473)*

Thus, "the treating expert should not express opinions on psycholegal issues which are the province of the child custody evaluator and the court (e.g., parental fitness or custody recommendations)" (Greenberg & Gould, 2001, p. 476).

A little-considered factor in forensic assessment is that of restrictions on interjurisdictional practice. A majority of jurisdictions do permit a forensic clinician licensed in one state to perform an evaluation in another. But a number of jurisdictions bar such practice, with dis-ciplinary consequences for noncompliance. For excellent articles reviewing this problem, see Shuman, D. W., Cunningham, M. D., Connell, M. A., & Reid, W. M. (2003). Interstate forensic psychology consultations: A call for reform and proposal of a model rule. Professional Psychology: Research and Practice, 34, 233–234; and Tucillo, J., Fillipis, N., Denney, R., & Dsurney, J. (2002). Licensure requirements for inter-jurisdictional forensic evaluations. Professional Psychology: Research and Practice, 33, 377–383.

Role Conflicts in Coercive Assessments: Evaluation and Recommendations

Jose M. Arcaya

. . .

BACKGROUND CONSIDERATIONS

Psychologists normally are trained to administer evaluations in situations in which the clients freely present themselves for testing or examination. These settings—for example, mental health clinics, hospitals, and private practice offices—generally operate according to administrative philosophies that are consistent with the psychologist's own ethical standards to respect the client's privacy and confidentiality. . . .

However, when traditionally trained psychologists—who are thus taught to be protective of the client's privacy, freedom, and integrity—are hired by the various agencies of the criminal justice system (e.g., courts, police departments, prisons, community treatment centers) to conduct assessments, they are required to establish a different kind of professional understanding with their client–offenders. These agencies require that psychologists diversify their professional allegiances. They expect the psychologists to be concerned not only about their clients' welfares, but also about the practical exigencies facing these forensic employers (e.g., maintaining institutional order, upholding court-ordered legal standards, fulfilling governmental mandates) and the general safety of the community.

In the criminal justice system, psychologists are necessarily expected to share their assessment results with many more individuals (e.g., lawyers, administrators, probation-parole officers) than in the free-world situation. Because by definition all criminal justice cases are adversarial, the readership of such forensic reports must be inevitably composed of parties opposed to one another, representing the concerns of the client–offender, the criminal justice system, and the community. Therefore, forensic psychologists automatically find themselves in the midst of controversy whenever they submit their results as neutral professionals, having displeased somebody along the way (e.g., displeasing a prosecutor by advocating lenient treatment, the client by recommending the denial of parole).

These two differences—role diversity and role conflict—are the bases for the role confusion of psychologists working in the criminal justice system. As noted by the American Psychological Association's (APA) Task Force Report on the Role of the Psychologist in the Criminal Justice System (American Psychological Association, 1980), "What psychology appears to lack at the present time is an effective way to differentiate obligations owed to organizational as opposed to individual clients" (p. 2). It indicates, for example, that of 203 criminal justice psychologists surveyed by the Task Force, 75% reported that one of the major ethical issues that they faced concerned confidentiality: how much and what kind of information should be revealed to their criminal justice employers. . . .

THE COERCIVE SETTING

The coercive setting differs markedly from the voluntary situation mainly because client–offenders do not hire their psychologists. They are forced to undergo the evaluation under penalty of law or deprivation of certain rights and privileges. These client–offenders, therefore, are in no position to dictate their terms to their examiners. They must submit to their psychologists' tests and inquiries whether they like it or not, knowing that if they refuse, such intransigency might result in possible negative consequences (e.g., denial of parole, more stringent sentencing, loss of institutional perquisites).

Because client–offenders have been pressured to go to their psychologists, they avoid having to take responsibility for this participation and for solving the problems that are the focus of the evaluation. Instead, they tend to approach their psychologists warily and resistively. The psychologists, therefore, have the task of penetrating these facades of self-sufficiency and denial before being able to reliably assess their client–offenders' true strengths and vulnerabilities.

In portraying themselves in as positive a light as possible, client–offenders tend to exclude from view anything that would block them from attaining their goals (e.g., outright freedom, less severe sentencing, day passes from a locked facility to the community). This guardedness arises, of course, because the evaluation results are not confidential but are used to decide important matters about the clients–offenders' lives. Indeed, in many forensic settings the psychologists are required to warn their client–offenders that whatever they divulge may be used against them in court (see Principle 5, *Ethical Standards of Psychologists*; American Psychological Association, 1981).[1]

Because an assessment report is a legal document that is subject to perusal by a variety of individuals in the criminal justice system, the psychologist in the forensic agency has little control over how the findings will be used and understood. Many judges, lawyers, administrators, counselors, and probation officers associated with a particular client–offender's case have the right to read its contents. This fact makes it difficult for psychologists to tailor their comments to particular individuals or suit the needs of specific referral sources. It also makes it difficult to establish rapport with their client–offenders. However, because forensic psychologists are paid to conduct their evaluations by their agency employers, there exists less incentive to build a working alliance with the typical criminal justice client than with the voluntary subject. Such forensic evalua-

tions are conducted primarily for the benefit of various criminal justice personnel, insofar as they, not the examinees, are the main critics of the psychologists' work.

Despite this reality, forensic psychologists are typically still concerned about their client–offenders' plights. However, they worry about the social institutions with which client–offenders might eventually become involved (such as employers in the case of employment screening), the safety of the community (in the case of probation or parole evaluations), and the well-being of other involved third parties (such as the offspring of mothers charged with child neglect). Thus divided in their concern—to their client–offenders (e.g., "How will my decision affect the long-term interest of this person?"), the community (e.g., "Will this individual pose a threat to other people?"), and the criminal agency for which they are employed (e.g., "Is this agency properly equipped to handle this kind of individual?")—thoughtful forensic psychologists find themselves forced to consider many more variables in making their determinations than are their free-world counterparts.

Obviously, different kinds of cases tend to demand different kinds of priorities among these competing interests. . . . However, sometimes forensic psychologists can adopt one way of approaching all criminal justice clients. When such a way is predictable and habitual, it can stem from unconscious motives and is analogous to the kinds of countertransference encountered in psycho-therapy. . . .

THE HELPER BIAS

. . . This stance leads the psychologist to side with the client–offender in practically every instance. According to this person-centered, humanitarian perspective, the needs of the client–offender are more important than the agency's needs or the concerns of the community. The helper bias is based on a kind of antibureaucratic and antiorganizational philosophy, and its followers tend to be oblivious to dimensions of the evaluation other than the offenders' viewpoints. . . .

---

[1]*Ed. Note:* See Standard 9.03 of the current (2002) APA Ethics Code.

THE PROSECUTORIAL BIAS

The prosecutorial bias is relatively rare in comparison with the helper bias; the psychologist adopting the prosecutorial bias considers client–offenders with suspicion and tends to make negative value judgments about their conduct. This position is identified closely with the feelings of the community, and the client–offender is considered more from a moral than from a humanitarian perspective. This bias is prosecutorial because the psychologist is assumed to be an extension of the judicial system. The psychologist is more likely to consider the offender's behavior in a condemning rather than in a clinical fashion. . . .

Because the prosecutorial evaluators tend to adopt a negative view about the future of the client–offender, their recommendations are likely to be conservative and guarded. These evaluators predictably tend to favor the interests of the community over the welfare of their client–offenders. . . .

THE UNCOMMITTED BIAS

This bias reflects the classic bureaucratic mentality. It is more responsive to the implicit demands of the institution for which the evaluator works than to the needs of the client–offender or of the community. These psychologists avoid taking risks because they dislike conflict and controversy. Psychologists personifying this attitude tend to write their evaluations in terms of the preferences of the agency administrators reading their reports, rather than in terms of their true convictions. . . .

ADVERSARIAL MODEL

The adversarial model is proposed to help avoid the biases inherent in the previous stances. . . .

Following the same rationale as the legal system itself, the adversarial evaluator assumes that final judgments and recommendations about forensic clients are best decided after all opposing viewpoints have been considered. In effect, the adversarial model extends this rationale into the assessment process itself; the report is to be organized and communicated as though it were a courtroom debate between hypothetical psychologists representing opposed vested interests (i.e., the defendant, the prosecutor). Only after these viewpoints are fully discussed could psychologists present their final recommendations.

This model requires psychologists to act as "devil's advocates" who, instead of trying to fit disparate findings about their client–offenders into a consistent narrative (possibly because they want to convey a sense of scientific certainty to the reader), disclose these contradictions honestly. . . . [A]s a result of exposure to diverse and opposed information, the readers of reports written from this perspective would be in a better position to evaluate the merits of the evaluator's final recommendations.

Rather straightforward in its format, this model requires forensic psychologists to subdivide their reports into as many sections as there are legal perspectives on their client–offenders. They would then consider their clients from each one of these viewpoints. . . . After presenting all of the relevant information appropriate to these subsections, psychologists would then make their final recommendations and conclusions.

The standard forensic assessment format, on the other hand, makes it easy for psychologists to present their data impersonally, thereby obscuring their biases. It helps them to avoid dealing with the legal context in which the assessment takes place, in which there is no single truth . . . and in which radically different views of reality are in contention. . . . The adversarial model, in contrast, forces psychologists to be more reflective and to think through their rationales before reaching their conclusions. . . .

References

American Psychological Association. (1980). *Who is the client? The psychological intervention in the criminal justice system.* Washington, DC: Author.

American Psychological Association. (1981). Ethical principles of psychologists. *American Psychologist, 36,* 633–638.

Role Conflict in Forensic Clinical Psychology: Reply to Arcaya

Dewey G. Cornell

. . .

The various roles of clinical psychologists in the criminal justice system cannot be characterized in the same way. . . . Arcaya's concerns about the psychologist–client relationship need more careful explication for each different role. . . .

For purposes of this discussion, attention will be focused on psychologists who conduct pretrial evaluations of criminal defendants. Typically, these evaluations concern one or both of two legal issues: competency to stand trial or criminal responsibility (legal insanity). An evaluation of competency to stand trial concerns the defendant's present mental state: whether the defendant suffers from a mental condition that impairs his or her ability to defend himself or herself at the trial. Criminal responsibility concerns the defendant's mental state at the time of the alleged offense: whether the defendant suffered from a mental condition that would exculpate him or her from criminal charges. Specific legal criteria and guidelines for these evaluations vary from state to state.

However, the psychologist–defendant/client relationship differs in important ways for these two legal issues. For example, . . . a defendant has no choice about submitting to an evaluation of competency to stand trial. Although the evaluation is usually conducted on an outpatient basis, the defendant could be committed for inpatient evaluation. If adjudicated incompetent to stand trial, the defendant could be committed involuntarily for a period as long as 15 months.

The circumstances are quite different for evaluations of criminal responsibility. Here the defendant is the one initiating the claim of insanity, and the defendant retains complete authority to refuse or cancel an evaluation. Contrary to Arcaya's global characterization of forensic evaluations, there are important differences according to the legal issue involved, and the defendant does retain voluntary status in some circumstances. Last, the defendant who disagrees with a psychologist's clinical opinion in a pretrial evaluation retains the right to request an independent evaluation by another professional.

As this example indicates, it is misleading for Arcaya to contrast evaluations conducted for the criminal justice system with all other evaluations by describing the former as "coercive" and the latter as "free-world" evaluations. Moreover, many evaluations outside the criminal justice system are far from fully voluntary. Probably the most "coercive" evaluation in mental health today occurs when an individual is evaluated for involuntary commitment, a civil court matter. A close second would be evaluations of adolescent minors whose parents are seeking to have them admitted for inpatient treatment. Psychologists also face less-than-willing subjects when they conduct child custody evaluations or when they are hired by the defense to examine the complainant in personal injury cases. . . .

. . .

PROPOSALS FOR CHANGE

Arcaya's (partial) solution to the problem of psychologist bias was to modify the format for psychological reports. He proposed that psychologists write their reports in a manner more consistent with the legal system's adversarial model. Evidence supporting each side of the case would be presented and weighed before the psychologist expressed a final opinion.

There are several problems with this approach. First, if Arcaya was correct in stating that psychologists are biased because of unconscious personality conflicts and countertransference reactions to the defendant, it is highly unlikely that any change in report format would be effective. . . .

If bias is primarily a result of institutional pressures and professional role conflict, again it seems that merely changing report format would be too weak an intervention. The legal system, rather than the individual, would be the appropriate target for intervention. . . .

Last, many of Arcaya's concerns about bias and role conflict can be addressed from the standpoint of the Ethical Principles of the American Psychological Association. . . . Psychologists are *already* obligated to assume an objective and evenhanded approach in their report of psychological findings. . . .

ALTERNATIVES

Psychologists should not attempt to cope with the adversarial pressures of the legal system by mimicking an adversarial approach in their report writing. Instead, psychologists need to resist being co-opted by the system and to reassert their professional identity as scientist-practitioners. Forensic psychologists need to make clear, as often as is necessary, that their role is objective and neutral, and that although they may reach clinical opinions favorable to either defense or prosecution, they are never advocates of one side or the other in legal proceedings. . . .

. . .

◆　◆　◆

*Commentary: Despite their differences, Arcaya and Cornell did agree that forensic clinicians experience significant role conflicts, particularly when they con-*duct court-compelled evaluations in criminal prosecutions. These role conflicts not only create the potential for ethical violations but also may impair the defendant's rights under the U.S. Constitution as well. The Fifth Amendment states in relevant part: "no person shall be compelled in any criminal case to be a witness against himself." Also, the Sixth Amendment provides that "in all criminal prosecutions, the accused shall enjoy the right. . . . to have the assistance of counsel for his defense." Consider how these constitutional protections might be endangered under the following scenario:*

> *When Smith was indicted for murder, the state announced that it would seek the death penalty. The trial judge ordered Dr. Grigson, a psychiatrist, to evaluate whether Smith was competent to stand trial. After a 90-minute interview, Dr. Grigson determined that Smith was competent. Smith was then tried and convicted of murder. Subsequently, a separate sentencing proceeding was held before a jury to decide whether Smith should be executed. One of the issues the jury had to determine in the positive, if it were to give Smith a death sentence, was the probability that Smith would commit violent criminal acts again. At the sentencing hearing, Dr. Grigson was called by the state to testify about Smith's proclivity toward future violence. Basing his testimony on the pretrial competency evaluation, Dr. Grigson stated that Smith would be a danger to society. The jury then sentenced Smith to death. Smith charged this procedure violated his rights under the Fifth and Sixth Amendments. The Supreme Court agreed to review his claims, with the following result.*

Estelle v. Smith

. . .

. . . [W]e turn first to whether the admission of Dr. Grigson's testimony at the penalty phase violated respondent's Fifth Amendment privilege against compelled self-incrimination because respondent was not advised before the pretrial psychiatric examination that he had a right to remain silent and that any statement he made could be used against him at a sentencing proceeding. . . .

The fact that respondent's statements were uttered in the context of a psychiatric examination does not automatically remove them from the reach of the Fifth Amendment. . . . The state trial judge, *sua sponte,* ordered a psychiatric evaluation of respondent for the limited, neutral purpose of determining his competency to stand trial, but the results of that inquiry were used by the State for a much broader objective that was plainly adverse to respondent. Consequently, the interview with Dr. Grigson cannot be characterized as a routine competency examination restricted to ensuring that respondent understood the charges against him and was capable of assisting in his defense. Indeed, if the application of Dr. Grigson's findings had been confined to serving that function, no Fifth Amendment issue would have arisen.

Nor was the interview analogous to a sanity examination occasioned by a defendant's plea of not guilty by reason of insanity at the time of his offense. When a defendant asserts the insanity defense and introduces supporting psychiatric testimony, his silence may deprive the State of the only effective means it has of controverting his proof on an issue that he interjected into the case. Accordingly, several Courts of Appeals have held that, under such circumstances, a defendant can be required to submit to a sanity examination conducted by the prosecution's psychiatrist. . . .

Respondent, however, introduced no psychiatric evidence, nor had he indicated that he might do so. Instead, the State offered information obtained from the court-ordered competency examination as affirmative evidence to persuade the jury to return a sentence of death. Respondent's future dangerousness was a critical issue at the sentencing hearing, and one on which the State had the burden of proof beyond a reasonable doubt. . . . To meet its burden, the State used respondent's own statements, unwittingly made without an awareness that he was assisting the State's efforts to obtain the death penalty. In these distinct circumstances, the Fifth Amendment privilege was implicated.

. . . *Miranda v. Arizona*[1] . . . held that "the prosecution may not use statements, whether exculpatory or inculpatory, stemming from custodial interrogation of the defendant unless it demonstrates the use of procedural safeguards effective to secure the privilege against self-incrimination." . . . Thus, absent other fully effective procedures, a person in custody must receive certain warnings before any official interrogation, including that he has a "right to remain silent" and that "anything said can and will be used against the individual in court." . . .

The considerations calling for the accused to be warned prior to custodial interrogation apply with no less force to the pretrial psychiatric examination at issue here. Respondent was in custody at the Dallas County Jail when the examination was ordered and when it was conducted. That respondent was questioned by a psychiatrist designated by the trial court to conduct a neutral competency examination, rather than by a police officer, government informant, or prosecuting attorney, is immaterial. When Dr. Grigson went beyond simply reporting to the court on the issue of competence and testified for the prosecution at the penalty phase on the crucial issue of respondent's future dangerousness, his role changed and became essentially like that of an agent of the State recounting unwarned statements made in a postarrest custodial setting. During the psychiatric evaluation, respondent assuredly was "faced

From *Estelle v. Smith,* 451 U.S. 459 (1981).

[1]See *Miranda v. Arizona,* 384 U.S. 436 (1966).

with a phase of the adversary system" and was "not in the presence of [a] perso[n] acting solely in his interest." . . . Yet he was given no indication that the compulsory examination would be used to gather evidence necessary to decide whether, if convicted, he should be sentenced to death. He was not informed that, accordingly, he had a constitutional right not to answer the questions put to him. . . .

A criminal defendant, who neither initiates a psychiatric evaluation nor attempts to introduce any psychiatric evidence, may not be compelled to respond to a psychiatrist if his statements can be used against him at a capital sentencing proceeding. Because respondent did not voluntarily consent to the pretrial psychiatric examination after being informed of his right to remain silent and the possible use of his statements, the State could not rely on what he said to Dr. Grigson to establish his future dangerousness. If, upon being adequately warned, respondent had indicated that he would not answer Dr. Grigson's questions, the validly ordered competency examination nevertheless could have proceeded upon the condition that the results would be applied solely for that purpose. In such circumstances, the proper conduct and use of competency and sanity examinations are not frustrated, but the State must make its case on future dangerousness in some other way.

"Volunteered statements . . . are not barred by the Fifth Amendment," but under *Miranda v. Arizona* we must conclude that, when faced while in custody with a court-ordered psychiatric inquiry, respondent's statements to Dr. Grigson were not "given freely and voluntarily without any compelling influences" and, as such, could be used as the State did at the penalty phase only if respondent had been apprised of his rights and had knowingly decided to waive them. . . . These safeguards of the Fifth Amendment privilege were not afforded respondent and, thus, his death sentence cannot stand [footnote omitted].

When respondent was examined by Dr. Grigson, he already had been indicted, and an attorney had been appointed to represent him. The Court of Appeals concluded that he had a Sixth Amendment right to the assistance of counsel before submitting to the pretrial psychiatric interview. . . . We agree. . . .

Here, respondent's Sixth Amendment right to counsel clearly had attached when Dr. Grigson examined him at the Dallas County Jail [footnote omitted], and their interview proved to be a "critical stage" of the aggregate proceedings against respondent. . . . Defense counsel, however, were not notified in advance that the psychiatric examination would encompass the issue of their client's future dangerousness [footnote omitted], and respondent was denied the assistance of his attorneys in making the significant decision of whether to submit to the examination and to what end the psychiatrist's findings could be employed. . . .

Therefore, in addition to Fifth Amendment considerations, the death penalty was improperly imposed on respondent because the psychiatric examination on which Dr. Grigson testified at the penalty phase proceeded in violation of respondent's Sixth Amendment right to the assistance of counsel [footnote omitted]. . . .

◆　◆　◆

Commentary: Shuman and Greenberg (1998) quoted a 1995 news release from the American Psychiatric Association (No. 95–25, July 20, 1995) that stated that the Association voted to expel Dr. Grigson from membership "for arriving at a psychiatric diagnosis without first having examined the individual in question, and for indicating, while testifying in court as an expert witness, that he could predict with 100 [per cent] certainty that the individual would engage in future violent acts" (p. 6) in connection with his testimony in Barefoot v. Estelle, 463 U.S. 880 (1983), among other cases. See Shuman, D. W., & Greenberg, S. A. (1998, Winter). The role of ethical norms in the admissibility of expert testimony. The Judges' Journal, 37, 4–9; 42–43.

Apparently, the American Medical Association (AMA) is going even further. According to the online site of the journal, Lawyer's Weekly, *the AMA has ruled that physicians are practicing medicine when they testify as experts and that they are subject to reprimand or revocation of their AMA membership if their testimony is judged to fall outside accepted scientific standards. Subsequent to a judgment that the testimony is unsound, the AMA will register violations in a national databank that is discoverable by attorneys and hospitals where physicians apply for privileges.*

If a psychologist were to act as Grigson did, what provisions of the APA's 2002 Ethical Principles would the clinician violate? What sections of the Specialty Guidelines would be implicated? For a discussion of the implications of Estelle v. Smith for psychologists and their obligations to the defendant, defense counsel, and the prosecution, see Cunningham, M. D. (2006). Informed consent in capital sentencing evaluations: Target and content. Professional Psychology: Research and Practice, 37, 452–459; see also, Foote, W. E., & Shuman, D. W. (2006). Consent, disclosure, and waiver for the forensic psychological evaluation: Rethinking the roles of psychologist and lawyer. Professional Psychology: Research and Practice, 37, 437–445.

Is it not the psychologist's duty to disclose at the initiation of therapy such important information as limits to confidentiality (i.e., in a manner equivalent to the police officer's Miranda warnings)? As chapter 4 illustrated, the legal system compels psychologists at times to act as agents of the state, such as when they are required to report child abuse or to protect a private third party from a patient's violent threats. In instances like these, should not psychologists, regardless of the setting in which they work, inform their clients of those situations in which they feel obligated to serve society and in which, like Grigson, they determine that the duty of fidelity has shifted from their clients to the state?

Role conflicts are an inevitable fact of life for academicians and practitioners, but they occur more often—as Estelle v. Smith proves—when the client is an involuntary participant in assessment or treatment. In many such cases, the forensic clinician is asked to predict whether the involuntary client might engage in an act of violence. This is usually the most crucial criterion in determining whether a capital development should be executed. Such predictions are not restricted to death penalty cases, however, but are also requested in more commonplace instances, with regard to civil commitment, bail and parole hearings, detention of juveniles, and child abuse.

Recently, a federal appellate judge asserted that "the scientific community virtually unanimously agrees that psychiatric testimony on future dangerousness is, to put it bluntly, unreliable and unscientific" (p. 463). Flores v. Johnson, 210 F.3d 456 (5th Cir. 2000), a view that Tolman and Mullendore (2003) called "not valid" (p. 227). Tolman, A. O., & Mullendore, K. B. (2003). Risk evaluations for the courts: Is service quality a function of specialization? Professional Psychology: Research and Practice, 34, 225–232. The next set of materials addresses this most serious controversy.

Is It Unethical to Offer Predictions of Future Violence?

Thomas Grisso and Paul S. Appelbaum

THE NATURE OF THE PREDICTIVE TESTIMONY

Let us presume that when critics have spoken against "predictions of dangerousness," they have been referring to "predictions of future violent behavior." Expert testimony about future violence can take several forms, all of which might be considered predictions as the term is used broadly in the behavioral and social sciences. We can cite no authority for the forms of testimony that such predictions take, but the following are examples from our experience:

a. *Dichotomous:* Statement that a particular behavior (or type of behavior) will or will not occur in the future. ("In my opinion, he will engage in serious violent behavior in the future.")

b. *Dichotomous With Qualified Confidence:* Dichotomous statement, with additional testimony concerning expert's confidence in his or her opinion. ("In my opinion, he will engage in a serious violent behavior in the future, and I believe that it is more likely than not [or 'reasonably certain' or 'very certain'] that my judgment would prove accurate.")

c. *Risk, Individual-Based:* Statement of the degree of likelihood that this individual will engage in a particular behavior (or type of behavior) in the future. ("In my opinion, there is a 40% probability that he will engage in serious violent behavior in the future.")

d. *Risk, Class-Based:* Statement of likelihood or probability, but offered in reference to a class of persons of which the individual is alleged to be a member. ("In my opinion, about 25% of people with this individual's characteristics engage in violent behavior after release from a mental hospital.") May be combined with individual-based.

("... but I believe that he presents somewhat greater/less risk than that group" [e.g., based on future environmental circumstances].)

All of these forms of testimony may be construed as predictions [footnote omitted]. They attempt to inform the listener about the clinician's professional opinion concerning behaviors that may occur in the future. Statements of risk are no less predictions than statements in dichotomous form; they simply provide additional information concerning the likelihood that others will be right or wrong in drawing their own dichotomous conclusion.

Broad arguments for a ban on predictions of violent behavior appear not to have been limited to dichotomous statements of prediction, but would prohibit all types of predictive testimony involving questions of future violence and restriction of liberty. . . . If one intends to condemn all forms of predictive testimony as unethical, and if the basis for this conclusion is inadequate scientific support for predictions, then the conclusion is wrong if there is reasonable scientific support for any of the above forms of predictive testimony. It would seem that there is.

Let us consider first the evidence as it relates to dichotomous predictive testimony, our types *a* and *b*. Research demonstrating the lack of scientific support for the validity of predictions of future violence is derived primarily from publications in the 1970s, which have been reviewed extensively (e.g., Monahan, 1981; Webster & Menzies, 1987). . . . Reviews of the literature concluded that clinicians have no ability, or no special ability, to predict whether or not a person will engage in a violent act in the future and that they would be right in at best about one in three cases in which they made such predictions (e.g., Cocozza & Steadman, 1976, 1978; . . . Ennis & Litwack, 1974) [footnote omitted].

From *Law and Human Behavior, 16,* 621–633. Copyright 1992 by Springer. Adapted with permission of the author and publisher.

. . . Dichotomous predictions of future violence . . . remain vulnerable to arguments that they violate ethical propriety.

Turning now to predictive testimony of types *c* and *d*, some of the same studies of the 1970s that challenged the validity of dichotomous predictions provided the earliest scientific support for offering predictive testimony in the form of probabilistic or comparative risk statements. . . .

Much more sophisticated research during the 1980s significantly augmented the scientific support for identification of groups with relatively high base rates of future violence (e.g., Binder & McNiel, 1988; Klassen & O'Connor, 1988, 1990; Link, Cullen, & Andrews, 1990; Swanson, Holzer, Ganju, & Jono, 1990). . . .

These newer studies, of course, do not provide scientific evidence with which to claim validity for predictive testimony in dichotomous form (predictive testimony of types *a* and *b* in our characterization above). They merely provide research support, in some cases, for predictive testimony that offers courts a sense of the relative risk of violence associated with individuals in question (predictive testimony of types *c* and *d*). Yet this is enough to contradict the generalized assertion that *all* predictive testimony regarding future violence is unethical for lack of a scientific basis. . . .

THE FOUNDATION OF THE PREDICTIVE TESTIMONY

[T]he scientific basis for predictions of future violence is derived from studies identifying particular characteristics of research subjects who subsequently engaged in violent behavior. This suggests three important limitations on the appropriateness even of predictive risk statements, consistent with a general standard of competence in clinicians' performance of evaluations. . . .

First, the person about whom the estimate of risk is being made must be similar to the research subjects in the studies from which the predictive model is derived. Second, the estimate of risk must be based on types of data comparable to those available in the studies that are being relied upon. Third, the expert's evaluation process and methods by which

data are gathered must be sufficiently reliable to assure accurate identification of the relevant characteristics of the individual in question.
. . .

THE LEGAL CONSEQUENCES OF THE PREDICTION

. . .

When we participate in legal proceedings in which our predictive testimony results in decisions with high false-positive rates and their consequences, do we practice unethically? There are at least three ways that one might address the question. First, one can argue that *any* restriction of liberty based on predictive testimony about risk involving large false-positive rates constitutes a misuse of psychological or psychiatric information by the legal system. This position would be based on either of two views: (1) that it is wrong for society to restrict liberties on the basis of less than 0.5 probability of future violence, and that to do so demeans the rights of the individual, is "unjustifiable," and does not "promote human welfare" . . . ; or (2) that even with an expert's attempts to inform the court about the limits of testimony based on probabilities with high false-positive rates, there is an unacceptable potential for misunderstanding or misuse of the information in the legal forum. Experts who testify about risk probabilities with high false-positive rates, therefore, would be perceived as participating unethically in the process.

A second approach would leave questions of justification to the courts and society to determine, not the mental health professional. Statutes and procedures of law define the conditions under which society "justly" restricts the liberties of its citizens. The expert who provides reliable risk probability information (and clearly explains its limitations) to courts within that legal framework engages in ethical practice, according to this view, even if the legal outcome deprives the individual of liberty "mistakenly." The duties of the forensic expert are different in this regard from those of the clinician in a doctor–patient relationship, wherein the obligation to maximize the welfare of the patient is paramount. Therefore, the consequences of a court's restrictions of liberty present no ethical burden for the expert beyond that of presenting reliable testimony and clearly explaining its limitations.

A third position is intermediate in relation to the other two. It would not leave questions of justification only to the courts. On the other hand, it would observe that not all types of liberty restrictions are of equal consequence, especially given variability across circumstances (e.g., civil commitment vs. capital sentencing) in potential, counterbalancing benefits to the person whose liberty is restricted. This position might also recognize variability in the quality of legal justice across jurisdictions (e.g., known patterns of racial bias in sentencing in certain jurisdictions). This perspective would see predictive testimony about risk probabilities with high false-positive rates as neither ethical nor unethical per se. Instead, it would encourage professional debate regarding the circumstances (e.g., degree and type of liberty restrictions associated with the legal questions, types of benefits that may accrue) in which the various magnitudes of false-positive error resulting from risk probability testimony would be ethically acceptable or unacceptable in relation to the balance of consequences for the individual and society.

Our purpose here is not to evaluate, endorse, or refine any of these approaches. We merely observe that they reach different answers to the questions of ethical propriety in predictive testimony about risk probabilities. The second approach would not consider such predictive testimony unethical, and the third might consider it unethical for certain types of legal proceedings, but not for all.

The first approach would, indeed, see all such testimony as unethical. . . .

References

Binder, R., & McNiel, D. (1988). Effects of diagnosis and context on dangerousness. *American Journal of Psychiatry, 145,* 728–732.

Cocozza, J., & Steadman, H. (1976). The failure of psychiatric predictions of dangerousness: Clear and convincing evidence. *Rutgers Law Review, 29,* 1084–1101.

Cocozza, J., & Steadman, H. (1978). Prediction in psychiatry: An example of misplaced confidence in experts. *Social Problems, 25,* 265–276.

Klassen, D., & O'Connor, W. (1988). A prospective study of predictors of violence in adult male mental health admissions. *Law and Human Behavior, 12,* 143–158.

Klassen, D., & O'Connor, W. (1990). Assessing the risk of violence in released mental patients: A crossvalidational study. *Psychological Assessment, 1,* 75–81.

Link, B., Cullen, F., & Andrews, H. (1990, August). *Violent and illegal behavior of current and former mental patients compared to community controls.* Paper presented at the meeting of the Society for the Study of Social Problems.

Monahan, J. (1981). *The clinical prediction of violent behavior.* Rockville, MD: National Institute of Mental Health.

Swanson, J., Holzer, C., Ganju, V., & Jono, R. (1990). Violence and psychiatric disorder in the community: Evidence from the Epidemiologic Catchment Area Surveys. *Hospital and Community Psychiatry, 41,* 761–770.

Webster, C., & Menzies, R. (1987). The clinical prediction of dangerousness. In D. Weisstub (Ed.), *Law and mental health: International perspectives,* Vol. 3 (pp. 158–208). New York: Pergamon.

Conducting Risk Evaluations for Future Violence: Ethical Practice Is Possible

Anton O. Tolman and Andrea L. Rotzien

In civil and criminal court, judges and juries routinely face the task of considering an individual's risk for future violence, often relying on psychological experts to help them. For example, civil cases might involve consideration of a restraining order to prevent harm to a potential victim, evaluation of a mentally ill individual's danger to others, and deliberation regarding an ex-spouse's potential harm to his children in a custody determination. Criminal cases involve consideration of future risk throughout the adjudication process, including setting bail, jail classification and housing, potential juvenile transfers, sentencing decisions involving violent offenders, management of violence risk on probation or parole, and, in some jurisdictions, opinions regarding a person's status as a "sexually violent predator."

However, early research on the effectiveness of clinical predictions of violence decreased confidence in clinical evaluations of risk and therefore in testimony by psychologists. These early risk evaluations mostly used clinical "intuition," nonstandardized clinical techniques and lore, and psychological instruments not specifically developed to assess future risk. The seminal review of this type of risk evaluation (Monahan, 1981) concluded that these methods were weak in predicting future violence. Monahan (1984) later called for a "second generation" of research to guide practice and policy development.

This second generation of risk research continues, focusing on identified risk factors associated with various forms of violence (e.g., physical, sexual, domestic) and on the development of actuarial and guided clinical instruments to assist clinicians in improving their ability to assess the level of risk posed by a given individual. Evaluations of the reliability, validity, and utility of these instruments generally reach favorable conclusions and indicate that these methods represent a significant advance over unguided clinical inference. For example, regarding one of these second-generation instruments, the Historical, Clinical, Risk Management—20 (HCR–20; Webster, Douglas, Eaves, & Hart, 1997), a recent report concluded, "Research on the HCR–20 generally supports claims that . . . its items can be scored reliably and are related to violence. . . . interrater reliability coefficients have been found to be acceptable and encouraging for the responsible use of the HCR–20" (Webster & Douglas, 2001, p. 3). Hanson (2005) stated, "The validation research has typically found that all these measures [second-generation instruments] show moderate accuracy in predicting violent recidivism" (p. 214). . . .

Despite these significant advances in the understanding of risk factors related to violence and the creation of specific risk-related instruments, some have criticized risk evaluations as part of professional practice. Several past authors evaluated published concerns about statistical base rates and other considerations (e.g., Grisso & Appelbaum, 1992; Saks & Kidd, 1986), universally concluding that the techniques were not perfect but had value in conducting evaluations for legal decision makers. More recently, additional critics have claimed that it is unethical to perform risk evaluations and that the evidentiary basis for these techniques is insufficient to permit their use in court (Berlin, Galbreath, Geary, & McGlone, 2003; Campbell, 2000, 2003). From the perspective of an expert witness to the courts, psychologists conducting risk evaluations should be aware of these criticisms to respond to them effectively. This article examines these recent criticisms . . . through the functional perspective of ethical practice and the tasks facing the legal system. . . .

RISK EVALUATIONS: ADDRESSING THE CONCERNS

. . .

[S]ome have worried (Campbell, 2000, 2003; Cunningham & Reidy, 2002) that courts will be unduly influenced by experts testifying about risk, particularly using actuarial data; the concern is that this increases the potential damage caused by purportedly "unscientific" risk evaluations and fosters the implication that such practice is unethical. However, in practice, the courts are not passive recipients of expert testimony. The courts are built on an aggressive adversarial system and assume that the fact finder is capable of sorting out bad science from good science through means available to them (e.g., discovery, cross-examination). . . . Obviously, this does not reduce the ethical burden of the psychologist to present his or her conclusions as objectively and clearly as possible in accordance with ethical principles and highlights the need for experts to not only inform but also educate the court and court officers on matters relevant to risk (e.g., psychopathy).

. . .

CONDUCTING ETHICAL RISK EVALUATIONS

In summary, the goal of ethical practice is not to categorically predict with a high rate of accuracy the likelihood that a given offender will commit a future violent crime. The goal of ethical practice is to provide the court with information on risk factors, describe whether or not those factors apply in the current context, describe and elaborate the person's history of previous violent behaviors and relate those previous contexts to the person's current and reasonably estimated future situations, and suggest strategies to reduce risk. Ethical and effective risk evaluations are highly responsive to the legal context in which the evaluation is performed (e.g., sentencing evaluations vs. release evaluations in a forensic hospital), consistent with the review by Heilbrun (1997). Ethical practice in this area is based on competent and relevant forensic assessment using modern instruments and methods; education of legal decision makers, if necessary,

regarding the elements of the report; careful delineation of the limits of our technology and knowledge; and effective use of scientific reasoning. The role of the risk evaluator as a neutral party and educator for the court on risk issues is consistent with the role of an expert witness and appears to be one of the defining characteristics of forensic evaluators versus clinicians (Tolman & Mullendore, 2003). . . .

It seems obvious to recommend that a mental health professional be competent in the field of risk assessment before stepping into a courtroom, but unfortunately there is evidence that professionals become involved in these cases without adequate preparation (Haag, 2006; Tolman, 2001; Tolman & Mullendore, 2003). Given that the field of risk assessment is rapidly developing and changing, any professional practicing in this field must stay abreast of the evolving guidelines and methods of evaluation. For professionals conducting forensic evaluations, ethical standards have existed for some time, as reflected in the Specialty Guidelines (Committee on Ethical Guidelines for Forensic Psychologists, 1991). These guidelines are currently under revision, but they originally built on and supported the American Psychological Association's Ethical Standards at the time. . . . Ethical forensic evaluations emphasize the role of the psychologist as an objective evaluator, not an advocate, regardless of which side retained the expert. Practicing psychologists should be aware of and adhere to these ethical principles in conducting evaluations (see also American Educational Research Association, 1999; American Psychological Association, 2002).

Apart from ethical standards, practitioners should be aware that even a cursory review of the scientific risk assessment literature indicates some broad areas of agreement on practice standards for ethical risk evaluations. First, there is almost universal agreement that unstructured clinical techniques are insufficient (e.g., Monahan, 1981). Second, given the strength and stability of the relationship between psychopathy and recidivism, this is a factor that should probably be assessed when evaluating a person's risk for future violence, using an instrument designed for that purpose (e.g., Hare, 2003) and after having received training in its use (see also Gacono, 2000; Hart, 1998; Monahan et al., 2001). . . .

Third, risk evaluations should review other known risk factors related to the context of the evaluation (e.g., Hanson & Bussiere, 1998; Harris et al., 2003; Quinsey et al., 1998), a task that is enhanced through the use of actuarial (e.g., Quinsey et al., 1998) and guided clinical instruments (e.g., Webster et al., 1997), and not rely solely on traditional clinical instruments and techniques. Earlier we provided several comprehensive resources for more information on these instruments.

Fourth, an expert should consider dynamic risk factors as well as potential protective factors and base rates (Douglas & Skeem, 2005; Rogers, 2000; Webster, Hucker, & Bloom, 2002) in evaluating risk; it should be noted that the guided clinical instruments such as the HCR–20 already enjoin consideration of dynamic factors as part of the instrument. The impact of treatment on dynamic factors and consequently recidivism is not yet clear (Miller et al., 2005). However, Douglas and Skeem (2005) provided an excellent review of the most promising dynamic factors with regard to violence risk assessment.

Fifth, forensic evaluators should make use of collateral data sources and assess multiple domains of functioning, as well as address issues of risk management and risk reduction (e.g., Hart, 2001). We acknowledge that integrating these sources and variables can be difficult. We have found Heilbrun (2001), Heilbrun et al. (2002), and Gacono (2000) particularly helpful with regard to synthesizing report information.

References

American Educational Research Association. (1999). *Standards for educational and psychological testing.* Washington, DC: Author.

American Psychological Association. (2002). Ethical principles of psychologists and code of conduct. *American Psychologist, 57,* 1052–1059.

Berlin, F. S., Galbreath, N. W., Geary, B., & McGlone, G. (2003). The use of actuarials at civil commitment hearings to predict the likelihood of future sexual violence. *Sexual Abuse: A Journal of Research and Treatment, 15,* 377–382.

Campbell, T. W. (2000). Sexual predator evaluations and phrenology: Considering issues of evidentiary reliability. *Behavioral Sciences and the Law, 18,* 111–130.

Campbell, T. W. (2003). Sex offenders and actuarial risk assessments: Ethical considerations. *Behavioral Sciences and the Law, 21,* 269–279.

Committee on Ethical Guidelines for Forensic Psychologists. (1991). Specialty guidelines for forensic psychologists. *Law and Human Behavior, 15,* 655–665.

Cunningham, M. D., & Reidy, T. J. (2001). A matter of life or death: Special considerations and heightened practice standards in capital sentencing evaluations. *Behavioral Sciences and the Law, 19,* 473–490.

Douglas, K. S., & Skeem, J. L. (2005). Violence risk assessment: Getting specific about being dynamic. *Psychology, Public Policy, and Law, 11,* 347–383.

Gacono, C. B. (Ed.). (2000). *The clinical and forensic assessment of psychopathy: A practitioner's guide.* Mahwah, NJ: Erlbaum.

Grisso, T., & Appelbaum, P. S. (1992). Is it unethical to offer predictions of future violence? *Law and Human Behavior, 16,* 621–633.

Haag, A. M. (2006). Ethical dilemmas faced by correctional psychologists in Canada. *Criminal Justice and Behavior, 33,* 93–109.

Hanson, R. K. (2005). Twenty years of progress in violence risk assessment. *Journal of Interpersonal Violence, 20,* 212–217.

Hanson, R. K., & Bussiere, M. T. (1998). Predicting relapse: A meta-analysis of sexual offender recidivism studies. *Journal of Consulting and Clinical Psychology, 66,* 348–362.

Hare, R. D. (2003). *Psychopathy Checklist—Revised (2nd ed.) technical manual.* Toronto, Ontario, Canada: Multi-Health Systems.

Harris, A. J. R., Phenix, A., Hanson, R. K., & Thornton, D. (2003). *Static–99 coding rules revised.* Ottawa, Canada: Office of Public Safety and Emergency Preparedness. Retrieved November 8, 2005, from http://www.sgc.gc.ca/corrections/publications_e.asp#2003

Hart, S. D. (1998). Psychopathy and the risk for violence. In D. J. Cooke, A. E. Forth, & R. D. Hare (Eds.), *Psychopathy: Theory, research, and implications for society* (pp. 355–373). Dordrecht, the Netherlands: Kluwer Academic.

Hart, S. D. (2001). Assessing and managing violence risk. In K. S. Douglas, C. D. Webster, S. D. Hart, D. Eaves, & J. R. P. Ogloff (Eds.), *HCR–20 violence risk management companion guide* (pp. 13–26). Burnaby, British Columbia: Simon Fraser University, Mental Health, Law, and Policy Institute.

Heilbrun, K. (1997). Prediction versus management models relevant to risk assessment: The importance of legal decision-making context. *Law and Human Behavior, 21,* 347–359.

Heilbrun, K. (2001). *Principles of forensic mental health assessment*. New York: Kluwer Academic/Plenum Publishers.

Heilbrun, K., Marczyk, G. R., & DeMatteo, D. (2002). *Forensic mental health assessment: A casebook.* Oxford, England: Oxford University Press.

Miller, H. A., Amenta, A. E., & Conroy, M. A. (2005). Sexually violent predator evaluations: Empirical evidence, strategies for professionals, and research directions. *Law and Human Behavior, 29,* 29–54.

Monahan, J. (1981). The clinical prediction of violent behavior. In *Crime and delinquency issues: A monograph series* (Publication No. ADM 81-921). Washington, DC: U.S. Government Printing Office.

Monahan, J. (1984). The prediction of violent behavior: Toward a second generation of theory and policy. *American Journal of Psychiatry, 141,* 10–15.

Monahan, J., Steadman, H. J., Silver, E., Appelbaum, P. S., Robbins, P. C., Mulvey, E. P., et al. (2001). *Rethinking risk assessment: The MacArthur Study of Mental Disorder and Violence.* Oxford, England: Oxford University Press.

Quinsey, V. L., Harris, G. T., Rice, M. E., & Cormier, C. A. (1998). *Violent offenders: Appraising and managing risk.* Washington, DC: American Psychological Association.

Rogers, R. (2000). The uncritical acceptance of acceptance of risk assessment in forensic practice. *Law and Human Behavior, 24,* 595–605.

Saks, M. J., & Kidd, R. F. (1986). Human information processing and adjudication: Trial by heuristics. In H. R. Arkes & K. R. Hammond (Eds.), *Judgment and decision making: An interdisciplinary reader* (pp. 213–242). New York: Cambridge University Press.

Tolman, A. O. (2001). Clinical training and the duty to protect. *Behavioral Sciences and the Law, 19,* 387–404.

Tolman, A. O., & Mullendore, K. B. (2003). Risk evaluations for the courts: Is service quality a function of specialization? *Professional Psychology: Research and Practice, 34,* 225–232.

Webster, C. D., & Douglas, K. S. (2001). Purpose of the companion guide. In K. S. Douglas, C. D. Webster, S. D. Hart, D. Eaves, & J. R. P. Ogloff (Eds.), *HCR–20 violence risk management companion guide* (pp. 1–12). Burnaby, British Columbia, Canada: Simon Fraser University, Mental Health, Law, and Policy Institute.

Webster, C. D., Douglas, K. S., Eaves, D., & Hart, S. D. (1997). *HCR–20: Assessing risk for violence* (Version 2). Burnaby, British Columbia, Canada: Simon Fraser University, Mental Health, Law, and Policy Institute.

Webster, C. D., Hucker, S. J., & Bloom, H. (2002). Transcending the actuarial versus clinical polemic in assessing risk for violence [Special issue: Risk assessment]. *Criminal Justice and Behavior, 29,* 659–665.

◆　　◆　　◆

Commentary: Although predictions of violence and risk assessment permeate almost all areas of forensic psychology, "No other consultation . . . has greater life-or-death implications than capital sentencing evaluations" (p. 473). Cunningham, M., & Reidy, T. (2001). A matter of life or death: Special considerations and heightened practice standards in capital sentencing evaluations. Behavioral Sciences and the Law, 19, *473–490. Forensic psychologists may be asked by defense counsels to evaluate their clients for the purposes of providing evidence that sentences should be mitigated from death to life imprisonment. On the other hand, prosecutors may ask clinicians to provide evidence that capital defendants present a continuing threat of violence, the major criterion for imposing the death penalty.*

As a result of the U.S. Supreme Court's decision in Atkins v. Virginia, 536 U.S. 304 (2002), *forensic clinicians have been given a role in death penalty litigation beyond that of mitigation. In that case the Court held that capital punishment of people with mental retardation violates the cruel and unusual punishment clause of the Eighth Amendment and is, therefore, unconstitutional. Thus, psychologists have been employed by both the defense and the prosecution for the purpose of either establishing or negating a claim that the defendant in a first degree murder case is mentally retarded. Unfortunately, there is no consistent definition of mental retardation among the states, and several definitions may contradict those developed by professional associations such as the American Association on Mental Retardation and the American Psychiatric Association in its* Diagnostic and Statistical Manual of Mental Disorders *(4th ed., text rev.). As one article pointed out, if state law contradicts clinical definitions, and Standard 1.02 of the APA Ethics Code allows a psychologist to follow the law even if it conflicts with the code, "by following the law the psychologist will be violating the basic foundations of psychological testing principles and practices" (p. 664). Duvall, J. C., & Morris, R. J. (2006). Assessing mental retardation in death penalty cases: Critical issues for psychology and psychological practice.* Professional Psychology: Research and Practice, 37, *658–665. There is now a burgeoning literature on this interesting topic. See, for example,*

Brodsky, S. L., & Galloway, V. A. (2003). *Ethical and professional demands for forensic mental health professionals in the Post-Atkins era.* Ethics & Behavior, 13, 3–9.

Ceci, S. J., Scullin, M., & Kanaya, T. (2003). *The difficulty of basing death penalty eligibility on IQ cutoff scores for mental retardation.* Ethics & Behavior, 13, 11–17.

Kessler, D. B. (2003). Atkins v. Virginia: *Suggestions for the accurate diagnosis of mental retardation.* Jurimetrics, 43, 415–426.

Watt, M. J., & MacLean, W. E. (2003). *Competency to be sentenced and executed.* Ethics & Behavior, 13, 35–41.

Young, B., Baccaccini, M. T., Conroy, M. A., & Lawson, K. (2007). *Four practical and conceptual assessment issues that evaluators should address in capital case mental retardation evaluations.* Professional Psychology: Research and Practice, 38, 169–178.

In declaring the execution of persons with mental retardation unconstitutional, the Supreme Court's majority found them less culpable because of their "diminished capacities to understand and process information, to communicate, to abstract from mistakes and learn from experience, to engage in logical reasoning, to control impulses, and to understand the reaction of others" (Atkins v. Virginia, 2002, p. 321). This language echoed statements APA made in its amicus curiae brief it submitted in support of Mr. Atkins. Nevertheless,

> *If we accept the concept of blanket incapacity, we relegate people with mental retardation to second-class citizenship, potentially permitting the state to abrogate the exercise of such fundamental interests as the right to marry, to have and to rear one's children, or such everyday entitlements such as to enter into contracts or to make a will. (p. 90)*

Bersoff, D. N. (2004). *The differing conceptions of culpability in law and psychology.* Widener Law Review, 11, 83–94. See also

Bersoff, D. N. (2002). *Some contrarian concerns about law, psychology, and public policy.* Law and Human Behavior, 26, 565–574.

Greenspan, S., & Switzky, H. N. (2003). *Execution exemption should be based on actual vulnerability, not disability label.* Ethics & Behavior, 13, 19–26.

Kane, H. (2003). *Straight talk about IQ and the death penalty.* Ethics & Behavior, 13, 27–33.

As Bonnie (1990) points out, strong moral opposition to the death penalty may distort the clinician's opinion about the defendant's candidacy for execution; so too may a clinician's strong support for the death penalty. In both cases, the principle of nonmaleficence would hold that the forensic psychologist should decline to participate. See Bonnie, R. (1990). Dilemmas in administering the death penalty: Conscientious abstention, professional ethics, and the needs of the legal system. Law and Human Behavior, 14, 67–90.

In any event, if forensic clinicians opt to participate in death penalty cases it is incumbent on them to use psychometrically sound instruments. Unfortunately, this is not always the case. Two popular instruments being used to determine a capital defendant's proclivity for violence are the Psychopathy Checklist Revised (PCL-R) and the Violence Appraisal Guide (VRAG). But

> *elevations on these scales have not been demonstrated to reliably predict serious violence in the context of American prisons. . . . Such misuse is particularly problematic with the PCL-R as the label of "psychopath" [is] . . . so profoundly pejorative as to equate with the sentence of death. . . . Employment of measures that have not been validated for applications they are being purported as demonstrating is in violation of Specialty Guidelines of responsibility (SGFP: II), competence (SGFP: VI.A, C), and communications (SGFP: VII.D). (Cunningham & Reidy, 2001, pp. 479–480)*

I raise similar issues in a later article.

Some Contrarian Concerns About Law, Psychology, and Public Policy

Donald N. Bersoff

My penultimate concern relates to an increasingly invidious practice; the use of the PCL–R [Psychopathy Checklist—Revised] in the penalty phase of capital murder cases. You may recall that in 1995 the American Psychiatric Association expelled from its membership James Grigson, the notorious Texas psychiatrist, better known as Dr. Death. He was tossed out "for arriving at a psychiatric diagnosis without first having examined the individual in question, and for indicating, while testifying in court as an expert witness, that he could predict with 100 [percent] certainty that the individual would engage in future violent acts" (quoted in Shuman & Greenberg, 1998). Much of the same kind of behavior is, unfortunately, being engaged in, in my opinion, by a few misguided, ignorant, and unethical forensic psychologists who are using the PCL-R to testify, to a reasonable psychological certainty, that capital defendants comprise a continuing threat of violence, even while confined in maximum security prisons. The problem is compounded by the fact that, unlike psychiatric diagnoses propounded on the basis of interviews, the PCL–R is widely regarded as a psychometrically sound instrument. Although it may have some usefulness in predicting future violence, recent articles (Edens, in press; Edens, Petrila, & Buffington-Venum, 2001; Freedman, 2001) indicate that it is not a valid predictor of the most pertinent forms of violence relevant to determining future dangerousness in capital cases. For example, Sorenson and Pilgrim (2001) reported that of a sample of 6,390 convicted murderers in the Texas prison system, the incidence of homicides over a 40-year period was about 0.2%. Given that the base rate of psychopathy is about 20%–30% of the prison population, approximately 1,600 of the prisoners would be psychopaths as defined by the PCL–R. As Edens et al., who cited this study in their about-to-be published article, state, "[e]ven if all of the 13 homicides estimated to occur over this [40 year] time period . . . were to be committed by psychopaths—a highly questionable assumption—the overwhelming majority of these offenders (99%) will not kill again." A table summarizing almost a dozen studies in Freedman's 2001 article in the *Journal of the American Academy of Psychiatry and Law* indicates that false positive rates for violent recidivism are uniformly at or above 50%. The use of the PCL–R in death penalty cases to offer an expert opinion about future lethal violence is therefore, in my humble opinion, negligent, unethical, and inadmissible under any reasonable interpretation of *Daubert v. Merrell Dow Pharmaceuticals, Inc.* (1993) and *Kumho Tire Co., Ltd. v. Carmichael* (1999) [see next excerpts].

Let me also warn, that attorneys who defend death penalty cases are well aware of this literature. I strongly urge all forensic psychologists to read this literature as well. In the unbridled defense of their clients, defense counsel are ready, willing, and able to attack on cross-examination those unwary psychologists who misuse the PCL–R or any psychological instrument and to report this conduct to the appropriate professional associations.

References

Daubert v. Merrell Dow Pharmaceuticals, Inc., 509 U.S. 579 (1993).

Edens, J. (2001). Misuses of the Hare Psychopathy Checklist—Revised in court: Two case examples. *Journal of Interpersonal Violence, 16,* 1082–1093.

From *Law and Human Behavior, 26,* 565–574. Copyright 2002 by the American Psychology–Law Society/Division 41 of the American Psychological Association.

Edens, J., Petrila, J., & Buffington-Vollum, J. K. (2001). Psychopathy and the death penalty: Can the Psychopathy Checklist—Revised identify offenders who represent "a continuing threat to society?" *Journal of Psychiatry and Law, 29,* 433–481.

Freedman, D. (2001). False prediction of future dangerousness: Error rates and the Psychopathy Checklist—Revised. *Journal of the American Academy of Psychiatry and Law, 29,* 89–95.

Kumho Tire Co., Ltd. v. Carmichael, 526 U.S. 137 (1999).

Shuman, D., & Greenberg, S. (1998, winter). The role of ethical norms in the admissibility of expert testimony. *The Judges' Journal, 37,* 4–9; 42–43.

Sorenson, T. R., & Pilgrim, R. L. (2001). Criminology: An actuarial risk assessment of violence posed by capital murder defendants. *Journal of Criminal Law and Criminology, 90,* 1251–1270.

◆　◆　◆

Commentary: There is a growing literature on the assessment of the risk of violence, what Grisso and Tomkins (1996), called "a required professional ability for every clinical psychologist" (p. 928). See Grisso, T., & Tomkins, A. J. (1996). Communicating violence risk assessments. American Psychologist, 51, 928–930. *Much of this literature has been supported and promulgated by the Research Network on Mental Health and the Law of the John D. and Catherine T. MacArthur Foundation. For recent reviews (containing valuable references) see*

Borum, K. (1996). Improving the clinical practice of violence risk assessment: Technology, guidelines, and training. American Psychologist, 51, 945–956.

DeMatteo, D., & Edens, J. F. (2006). The role and relevance of the Psychopathy Checklist—Revised in court. Psychology, Public Policy, and Law, 11, 347–383.

Douglas, K. S., & Skeem, J. L. (2005). Violence risk assessment: Getting specific about being dynamic. Psychology, Public Policy, and Law, 11, 347–383.

Edens, J. D., Buffington-Vollum, J. K., Keilen, A., Roskamp, P., & Anthony, C. (2005). Predictions of future dangerousness in capital murder trials: Is it time to "disinvent the wheel?" Law and Human Behavior, 29, 55–86.

Heilbrun, K. (1997). Prediction versus management models relevant to risk assessment: The importance of legal decision-making context. Law and Human Behavior, 21, 347–360.

Heilbrun, K., Dvoskin, J., Hart, S., & McNeil, D. (1999). Violence risk communication implications for research, policy, and practice. Health, Risk, & Society, 1, 91–106.

Litwack, T. R. (1994). Assessments of dangerousness: Legal, research, and clinical developments. Administration and Policy in Mental Health, 21, 361–378.

Melton, G., Petrila, J., Poythress, N., & Slobogin, C. (1997). Psychological evaluation for the courts: A handbook for mental health professionals and attorneys (2nd ed.). New York: Guilford.

Menzies, R., Webster, C., McKain, S., Staley, S., & Scaglione, R. (1994). The dimensions of dangerousness revisited: Assessing forensic predictions about violence. Law and Human Behavior, 18, 1–28.

Monahan, J., & Steadman, H. J. (1996). Violent storms and violent people: How meteorology can inform risk communication in mental health law. American Psychologist, 51, 931–938.

Monahan, J., Steadman, H., Silver, E., Appelbaum, P., Robbins, P., Mulvey, E., et al. (2001). Rethinking risk assessment. New York: Oxford.

Mossman, D. (1994). Assessing predictions of violence: Being accurate about accuracy. Journal of Consulting and Clinical Psychology, 62, 663–668.

Schopp, R. F. (1996). Communicating risk assessments: Advocacy, efficacy, and responsibility. American Psychologist, 51, 939–944.

In discussing the scientific bases for risk assessment and whether predictions of violence are ethical, are scholars neglecting fundamental moral issues? Contrast the preceding series of articles with the following, from Goldman (1986):

> *The psychologist ought to weigh directly the probable moral consequences of his testimony and use his full powers of moral reasoning in deciding whether and how to testify as an expert. It is not sufficient from a moral point of view that he tell the truth and do what the court asks of him. He must also desist from contributing directly to outcomes to which he is morally opposed on good grounds.*
>
> *There are many areas in which psychologists might be called as experts. A preliminary example that can be cited here relates to the predictability of violent behavior. Suppose that methods for prediction improve until a high degree of reliability is achieved and that courts increasingly use such predictions as bases for imposing the death penalty. . . . In my view a psychologist who is morally opposed to capital*

punishment cannot rightly agree to provide testimony that will lead to its imposition on grounds that he is only telling the truth and providing "ethically neutral" scientific knowledge that the judge has the authority to seek and use. Rather than usurping the role of the judge, the psychologist who refuses to testify in such a case is taking a stand as an individual against what he perceives to be unjustifiable homicide. Since individual psychologists cannot themselves determine the law on the matter, such input into the system does not represent the usurpation of lawmaking authority. Just as citizens in general need not support on moral grounds or contribute to the enforcement of laws they consider seriously unjust, so here the psychologist need not aid the imposition of a morally abominable sentence. (p. 37)

Goldman, A. H. (1986). Cognitive psychologists as expert witnesses: A problem in professional ethics. Law and Human Behavior, 10, 29–45.

Goldman also raised this question: Are there some functions that an ethical psychologist should refuse to perform? This question has been broached most poignantly in the debate over implementation of the death penalty. Specifically, in Ford v. Wainwright, 477 U.S. 399, (1986), the U.S. Supreme Court held that the execution of a psychotic and incompetent death row inmate would violate the Eighth Amendment ban on cruel and unusual punishment. Do mental health professionals act unethically if they participate in treating seriously mentally ill criminals so that they may become competent enough to be executed? The American Medical Association has advised physicians that they should not take part in legally authorized executions. Although in 1992 the Louisiana Supreme Court held that it is unconstitutional for the state to forcibly medicate condemned inmates with antipsychotic drugs so that they can become competent enough to be executed, a federal court of appeals in 2003 upheld the constitutionality of such "treatment." See Hensl, K. (2004). Restored to health to be put to death:

Recognizing the legal and ethical dilemmas of medicating to execute in Singleton v. Norris. Villanova Law Review, 49, 291–328.

With the exception of a few clinicians in the military, Guam, New Mexico, and Louisiana psychologists are not yet entitled to prescribe psychotropic medication, but they are qualified to either assess whether a death row inmate is competent to be executed or design and implement psychotherapeutic and behavioral interventions to achieve competency. Should psychologists participate in such endeavors? Readers whose immediate reaction is no should consider this: What about prisoners who choose to be executed rather than live in a psychotic state during a lifetime in prison? For a variety of perspectives on these issues, see

Bonnie, R. (1990). Dilemmas in administering the death penalty: Conscientious abstention, professional ethics, and the needs of the legal system. Law and Human Behavior, 14, 67–90.

Brodsky, S. L. (1990). Professional ethics and professional morality in the assessment of competence for execution: A response to Bonnie. Law and Human Behavior, 14, 91–97.

Freeman, S. (2002). Objectivity versus beneficence in a death row evaluation. Ethics & Behavior, 12, 295–298.

Heilbrun, K., Radelet, M. L., & Dvoskin, J. (1992). The debate on treating individuals incompetent for execution. American Journal of Psychiatry, 149, 596–605.

Salguero, R. G. (1986). Medical ethics and competency to be executed. Yale Law Journal, 96, 167–186.

White, W. S. (1987). Defendants who elect execution. University of Pittsburgh Law Review, 48, 853–877.

What guidance, if any, do the APA Ethical Principles and the Specialty Guidelines give the forensic practitioner about these issues? What are the relevant provisions in these documents? What moral principles, described in chapter 3 (e.g., justice and nonmaleficence), should prevail? Is there any place for virtue ethics here?

In 1993, the Supreme Court issued an opinion that clarified the rules for the admissibility of scientific evidence in federal courts. The decision, Daubert v. Merrell Dow Pharmaceutical Co., 509 U.S. 579 (1993), excerpted in relevant part next, will not only have an impact on the admissibility of risk assessment evidence, but on all other forensic psychological evidence as well.

Daubert v. Merrell Dow Pharmaceuticals, Inc.

. . .

[U]nder the [Federal] Rules [of Evidence] the trial judge must ensure that any and all scientific testimony or evidence admitted is not only relevant, but reliable.

The primary locus of this obligation is Rule 702, which clearly contemplates some degree of regulation of the subjects and theories about which an expert may testify: "*If scientific,* technical, or other specialized *knowledge will assist the trier of fact* to understand the evidence or to determine a fact in issue" an expert "may testify *thereto.*" (Emphasis added.) The subject of an expert's testimony must be "scientific . . . knowledge."[8] The adjective "scientific" implies a grounding in the methods and procedures of science. Similarly, the word "knowledge" connotes more than subjective belief or unsupported speculation. The term "applies to any body of known facts or to any body of ideas inferred from such facts or accepted as truths on good grounds." *Webster's Third New International Dictionary* 1252 (1986). Of course, it would be unreasonable to conclude that the subject of scientific testimony must be "known" to a certainty; arguably, there are no certainties in science. . . . But, in order to qualify as "scientific knowledge," an inference or assertion must be derived by the scientific method. Proposed testimony must be supported by appropriate validation—i.e., "good grounds," based on what is known. In short, the requirement that an expert's testimony pertain to "scientific knowledge" establishes a standard of evidentiary reliability.[9]

Rule 702 further requires that the evidence or testimony "assist the trier of fact to understand the evidence or to determine a fact in issue." This condition goes primarily to relevance. "Expert testimony which does not relate to any issue in the case is not relevant and, ergo, non-helpful." 3 Weinstein & Berger 702[02], pp. 702–18. . . . The consideration has been aptly described by Judge Becker as one of "fit." *Ibid.* "Fit" is not always obvious, and scientific validity for one purpose is not necessarily scientific validity for other, unrelated purposes. . . .

Rule 702's "helpfulness" standard requires a valid scientific connection to the pertinent inquiry as a precondition to admissibility.

That these requirements are embodied in Rule 702 is not surprising. Unlike an ordinary witness, see Rule 701, an expert is permitted wide latitude to offer opinions, including those that are not based on firsthand knowledge or observation. See Rules 702 and 703. Presumably, this relaxation of the usual requirement of firsthand knowledge—a rule which represents "a 'most pervasive manifestation' of the common law insistence upon 'the most reliable sources of information,' " Advisory Committee's Notes on Fed. Rule Evid. 602, 28 U.S.C. App., p. 755 (citation omitted)—is premised on an assumption that the expert's opinion will have a reliable basis in the knowledge and experience of his discipline.

Faced with a proffer of expert scientific testimony, then, the trial judge must determine at the outset . . . whether the expert is proposing to testify to (1) scientific knowledge that (2) will assist the trier of fact to understand or determine a fact in issue [footnote omitted]. This entails a preliminary assessment of whether the reasoning or methodology underlying the testimony is scientifically valid and of whether that reasoning or methodology properly can be applied to the facts in issue. We are confident that federal judges possess the capacity to undertake this review. Many factors will bear on the inquiry, and we do not presume to set out a definitive checklist or test. But some general observations are appropriate.

From *Daubert v. Merrell Dow Pharmaceuticals, Inc.*, 509 U.S. 579 (1993).

[8]Rule 702 also applies to "technical, or other specialized knowledge." Our discussion is limited to the scientific context because that is the nature of the expertise offered here.

[9]We note that scientists typically distinguish between "validity" (does the principle support what it purports to show?) and "reliability" (does application of the principle produce consistent results?). . . . In a case involving scientific evidence, *evidentiary reliability* will be based upon *scientific validity*.

Ordinarily, a key question to be answered in determining whether a theory or technique is scientific knowledge that will assist the trier of fact will be whether it can be (and has been) tested. "Scientific methodology today is based on generating hypotheses and testing them to see if they can be falsified; indeed, this methodology is what distinguishes science from other fields of human inquiry." Green 645. See also C. Hempel, *Philosophy of Natural Science* 49 (1966) ("[T]he statements constituting a scientific explanation must be capable of empirical test"); K. Popper, *Conjectures and Refutations: The Growth of Scientific Knowledge* 37 (5th ed. 1989) ("[T]he criterion of the scientific status of a theory is its falsifiability, or refutability, or testability") (emphasis deleted).

Another pertinent consideration is whether the theory or technique has been subjected to peer review and publication. Publication (which is but one element of peer review) is not a *sine qua non* of admissibility; it does not necessarily correlate with reliability, . . . in some instances well-grounded but innovative theories will not have been published. . . . Some propositions, moreover, are too particular, too new, or of too limited interest to be published. But submission to the scrutiny of the scientific community is a component of "good science," in part because it increases the likelihood that substantive flaws in methodology will be detected. . . . The fact of publication (or lack thereof) in a peer reviewed journal thus will be a relevant, though not dispositive, consideration in assessing the scientific validity of a particular technique or methodology on which an opinion is premised.

Additionally, in the case of a particular scientific technique, the court ordinarily should consider the known or potential rate of error . . . and the existence and maintenance of standards controlling the technique's operation. . . .

Finally, "general acceptance" can yet have a bearing on the inquiry. A "reliability assessment does not require, although it does permit, explicit identification of a relevant scientific community and an express determination of a particular degree of acceptance within that community." *United States v. Downing*, 753 F. 2d, at 1238. . . . Widespread acceptance can be an important factor in ruling particular

evidence admissible, and "a known technique which has been able to attract only minimal support within the community," *Downing*, 753 F. 2d, at 1238, may properly be viewed with skepticism.

The inquiry envisioned by Rule 702 is, we emphasize, a flexible one. Its overarching subject is the scientific validity—and thus the evidentiary relevance and reliability—of the principles that underlie a proposed submission. The focus, of course, must be solely on principles and methodology, not on the conclusions that they generate.

◆　　◆　　◆

Commentary: As a result of this decision, Rule 702 of the Federal Rules of Evidence was amended to read (with the new text appearing in the enumeration):

> *If scientific, technical, or other specialized knowledge will assist the trier of fact to understand the evidence or to determine a fact in issue, a witness qualified as an expert by knowledge, skill, experience, training, or education, may testify thereto in the form of an opinion or otherwise, if (1) the testimony is based upon sufficient facts or data, (2) the testimony is the product of reliable principles and methods, and (3) the witness has applied the principles and methods reliably to the facts of the case.*

Readers should note that Daubert *only addressed the federal rules, not the rules of evidence of the states. Many states decided to adopt the federal rule, but many have not, retaining the requirement that admissibility of novel scientific evidence be predicated merely on its general acceptance in the field. What are the weaknesses of this evidentiary test? For a catalog of states adopting* Daubert *or retaining the general acceptance test, see Parry, J. W. (2004, March/April). Expert evidence and testimony: Daubert versus Frye. Mental and Physical Disability Law Reporter, 28(2), 136–140.*

Daubert *spoke only to the question of what test should be applied to the admissibility of scientific knowledge under Rule 702. Some analysts argued that the decision did not reach "technical, or other specialized knowledge" in the rule. Furthermore, some psychologists asserted that forensic clinical psychology was more technical than scientific, and was thus not bound by Daubert. Others adamantly disagreed. The matter was settled in a subsequent case. In 1999, the Supreme Court held that the obligation of judges to inquire into the validity of expert testimony applied to all expert testimony, whether scientific, technical, or other specialized knowledge. See Kumho Tire Co., Ltd v. Carmichael, 526 U.S. 137 (1999).*

These two decisions, along with Joiner v. General Electric Corp., 522 U.S. 136 (1997), have already had a major impact on social science testimony. See, for example:

Berger, M. A. (2005). *What has a decade of* Daubert *wrought?* American Journal of Public Health, 95(Suppl.), S59–S65.

Breyer, S. (2000). *Science in the courtroom.* Issues in Science and Technology, 16(4), 52–56.

Campbell, T. (1999). *Challenging the evidentiary reliability of the DSM-IV.* American Journal of Forensic Psychology, 17, 47–68.

Cecil, J. S. (2005). *Ten years of judicial gatekeeping under* Daubert. American Journal of Public Health, 95(Suppl.), S74–S80.

Faigman, D., Kaye, D., Saks, M., & Sanders, J. (2002). *Science in the law: Social and behavioral science issues.* St. Paul, MN: West Group.

Gatowski, S. I., Dobbin, S. A., Richardson, J. T., Ginsburg, G. P., Merlino, M. L., & Dahir, V. (2001). *Asking the gatekeepers: A national survey of judges on judging expert evidence in a post-Daubert world.* Law and Human Behavior, 25, 433–458.

Groscup, J. L. (2004). *Judicial decision making about expert testimony in the aftermath of* Daubert *and* Kumho. Journal of Forensic Psychology Practice, 4, 57–66.

Grove, W. M., Barden, C., Garb, H. N., & Lilienfeld, S. O. (2002). *Failure of Rorschach-comprehensive-system-based testimony to be admissible under the Daubert-Joiner-Kumho standard.* Psychology, Public Policy, and Law, 8, 216–234.

Gutheil, T. G., & Bursztajn, H. (2003). *Avoiding ipse dixit mislabeling: Post-Daubert approaches to expert clinical opinions.* Journal of the American Academy of Psychiatry and the Law, 31, 205–210.

Medoff, D. (2003). *The scientific basis of psychological testing: Considerations following* Daubert, Kumho, *and* Joiner. Family Court Review, 41, 199–213.

Ritzler, B., Erard, R., & Pettigrew, G. (2002). *Protecting the integrity of the Rorschach expert witness: A reply to Grove and Barden (1999) Re: The admissibility of testimony under Daubert/Kumho analyses.* Psychology, Public Policy, and Law, 8, 201–216.

Studebaker, C., & Goodman-Delahunty, J. (Eds.). (2002). *Expert testimony in the courts: The influence of the* Daubert, Joiner, *and* Kumho *decisions, Part 1* [Special issue]. Psychology, Public Policy, and Law 8(2).

Studebaker, C., & Goodman-Delahunty, J. (Eds.). (2002). *Expert testimony in the courts: The influence of the* Daubert, Joiner, *and* Kumho *decisions, Part 2* [Special issue]. Psychology, Public Policy, and Law 8(3).

Studebaker, C., & Goodman-Delahunty, J. (Eds.). (2002). *Expert testimony in the courts: The influence of the* Daubert, Joiner, *and* Kumho *decisions, Part 3* [Special issue]. Psychology, Public Policy, and Law 8(4).

Yanez, Y. T., & Fremouw, W. (2004/5). *The application of the* Daubert *standard to parental capacity measures.* American Journal of Forensic Psychology, 22, 5–28.

See also Berger, M. (2000). Expert testimony: The Supreme Court rules. Issues in Science and Technology, 16(4), 57–63:

> [T]he Supreme Court's trilogy is most useful in emphasizing that expert witnesses may not make claims in court that they would never make in the context of work in their professional fields. It is to be hoped that the S&T [science and technology] community will also take this pronouncement to heart and voice some disapproval of members of their disciplines who are willing to offer conclusions in the context of judicial proceedings that they would never make outside the courtroom. After Kumho, courts are less likely to tolerate such behavior, and the expert who does not take the lessons of the trilogy to heart may find that his services as an expert witness will no longer be required. (p. 63)

On Being Ethical in Legal Places

Patricia Anderten, Valerie Staulcup, and Thomas Grisso

. . .

SAFEGUARDING ETHICAL STANDARDS

Given that the courtroom presents ethical difficulties and professional conflicts for psychologists, one need not conclude that psychologists should avoid either the courtroom or consultation to attorneys and their clients. A weighing of the potential benefits and liabilities of placing psychological information at the disposal of courts would probably find the potential benefits weighing heavier in the balance. The focus, then, should be on how we can offer our services within the legal system in the most effective and professional manner. An examination of the dynamics of the situations we have discussed suggests several general recommendations for psychologists who would wish to reduce the chances of ethical malfeasance in their participation in legal cases.

First, knowledge of the legal process and of the problems inherent in psychological testimony is essential to maintaining competent and ethical practice as an expert witness. Acquiring this knowledge is presently a matter of individual initiative. Few graduate courses on professional and ethical issues deal more than cursorily with the complexities of psychologist–attorney relationships or the expert witness role. However, workshops in these areas are increasing in number. . . .

Second, especially if one is inclined to actively seek involvement in legal cases, it is important to examine seriously one's needs and motives in relation to this intent. . . . [E]xcessive influence by altruistic motives and self-serving motives alike can easily cloud one's judgment. Clinical psychologists will recall similar admonitions by their supervisors in the early stages of psychotherapy training. For most psychologists, the role of expert witness is as foreign and complex as was the psychotherapist's role in their earlier training and, therefore, requires no less by way of awareness of personal motivations if competent and ethical practice is to prevail.

Third, psychologists who have passed beyond that period of professional development in which they obtained case consultation from another psychologist may wish to reinstate that practice. Peer review of assessment data can provide a hedge against bias during one's initial explorations into legal casework when the threat to autonomous objectivity may be greatest because of one's initial insecurity in a new professional situation.

Finally, we urge psychologists to be assertive concerning the establishment of a truly collaborative relationship with the attorney and the client (be this an individual or a court). . . . Careful joint preparation will reduce the number of "surprises" encountered by psychologists in the courtroom and allow the psychologists to avoid various ethical pitfalls. It is also through active involvement with the attorney that the psychologist can best educate the attorney regarding ethical problems as they arise and can attend closely to events that may unduly jeopardize the psychological well-being of the client.

As more psychologists take the witness stand, the courtroom may become a major source of information with which the public forms its impressions of psychology as a science and a profession. There is a commensurate responsibility for psychologists to adequately prepare themselves to meet the special ethical demands of the expert witness role, not only because they represent the profession in the public's eye but also for the welfare of the clients who are served.

From *Professional Psychology, 11,* 764–773. Copyright 1980 by the American Psychological Association.

◆   ◆   ◆

Commentary: As the final substantive words in this chapter, I can find no more eloquent or elegant summary than this, by Butcher and Pope (1993):

> The psychologist who conducts forensic assessments holds a sometimes overwhelming power over the lives of others. The results of a forensic assessment may influence—perhaps even determine—whether a person receives custody of his or her child, is forced to pay damages to another litigant, returns home from the courtroom, or spends years in prison. In some cases, the assessment results may literally determine whether a person accused of a capital crime lives or dies. Whatever other implications this power has, it mandates that we never take it for granted or treat it carelessly. The explicit ethical and professional standards reviewed . . . are the profession's attempt to ensure that this power is used competently, carefully, appropriately, and responsibly. Our responsibility as forensic practitioners includes not only upholding these standards in our own work of conducting assessments but also constantly rethinking the nature of these standards, their presence in our education and training, the degree to which the profession ensures accountability or, alternatively, passively tolerates and tacitly accepts or encourages violations, and the care with which we spell out responsibilities that fit the current and constantly evolving demands of forensic assessment. (p. 285)

See Butcher, J. N., & Pope, K. S. (1993). *Seven issues in conducting forensic assessments: Ethical responsibilities in light of new standards and new tests. Ethics & Behavior, 3, 267–288.*

CHAPTER 10

THE BUSINESS OF PSYCHOLOGY

During the time that I first wrote this chapter, there was a joke being bandied about by disgruntled mental health professionals. Relating it to the reader in an attempt at humor may be a dubious reward for wending one's way through the world of ethics reflected in this book, but it will also serve a useful purpose in making the point of this chapter.

> Three physicians happened to die on the same day and arrived at the proverbial Pearly Gates, waiting to be interviewed by St. Peter to determine whether they would be allowed to enter the Kingdom of Heaven.
>
> "And who are you?" asked St. Peter of the first candidate.
>
> "I'm Jonas Salk," he replied meekly.
>
> "Oh, the discoverer of the vaccine that saved so many children from the perils of polio. Come right in."
>
> Turning to the second healer, St. Peter asked the same question. "I'm Benjamin Spock. I wrote a book on children's health and development," the second physician responded authoritatively.
>
> "Ah, yes, and a wise counselor to millions of otherwise anxious and worried parents. We welcome you to Heaven for the remainder of eternity." He then turned to the third supplicant, saying "And who might you be?"
>
> "Well, I'm Gordon Smiley."
>
> "Don't think I recognize the name. What have you done?"
>
> "I," Smiley said proudly, "invented the concept of managed health care."[1]
>
> "Really?" St. Peter said, "Okay. You're approved for 3 days."

The logistics of doing professional psychology no longer simply involves renting an office; buying an oriental rug, an aquarium, and comfortable couches and chairs; and exercising independent professional discretion. Psychology is becoming, and will very likely be for the foreseeable future, a business. Psychologists are no longer therapists or doctors; they are health service providers (or, worse yet, vendors). Those who receive treatment are no longer patients or clients; they are consumers of psychological services. Patients no longer remit fees; bills are submitted for reimbursement to third-party payors. For good or ill, and regardless of this kind of "new speak," these are the realities that psychologists face.

---

[1]For those still innocent, managed health care involves, among other things, attempts by health care systems and third-party payors (like insurance companies) to control costs. They do this in a variety of ways, including requiring permission before certain procedures, such as surgery or psychotherapy, are undertaken and determining length of treatment, such as limiting a hospital stay to 1 day or therapy to 8–10 sessions.

The changing world of professional psychology confronts the concerned clinician with an array of ethical issues. The modern psychologist must traverse the metaphorical minefield in which are hidden such explosive and competing values as controlling the quickly rising costs of health care, exercising proper professional autonomy, and serving what are perceived to be the needs and best interests of the patient. Even more generally, the health care revolution raises the question of what effects the commercialization of psychology will have on such fundamental moral principles as beneficence, autonomy, fidelity, and justice.

Another part of the new environment for psychologists is the specter of malpractice. Although psychologists rarely are successfully sued for professional negligence, the threat still looms. Performing incompetent child custody evaluations, invading the boundaries of professional relationships through sexual relationships with clients, damaging patients by improperly administering psychotropic medication (increasingly possible as prescription privileges for psychologists become more likely), and committing other vagaries of practice all may lead to malpractice claims. In an attempt to prevent such claims from succeeding and to alert readers to the concurrent ethical problems that may arise from malpractice suits, this chapter presents material on such important issues as proper record keeping (including an edited version of the new Record Keeping Guidelines passed in 2007) and keeping one's financial "house" in order. It also contains a comprehensive summary of the Health Insurance Portability and Accountability Act (HIPAA) that took effect on April 14, 2003, and will have a significant impact on record keeping and dissemination.

Finally, because the federal government views the provision of psychological services as a commercial, competitive enterprise, it has sought to regulate both the profession and its professionals. In particular, the Federal Trade Commission (FTC) has scrutinized ethical principles of such associations as APA to see if they restrict competition inappropriately. As a result, there are now fewer controls on setting fees, advertising, and soliciting clients. These changes may increase competition within and between professions (e.g., psychology and psychiatry), but they may also lead to dubious ethical conduct. I hope that the material in this chapter helps readers to discern the differences among sleazy behavior, bad form, illegal actions, and unethical conduct.

The Commerce of Professional Psychology and the New Ethics Code

Gerald P. Koocher

Increasingly . . . successful practice demands a sophisticated understanding of commercial issues not routinely addressed in graduate training. The increasing prevalence of managed mental health care, the range of payment mechanisms, and economic hard times contribute to compounding the complexity of the business aspects of running a mental health practice, whether it is done on a solo basis or as part of a large agency. . . .

RECORDS

New specifics on record maintenance . . . , preservation . . . , ownership . . . , and withholding records for nonpayment . . . are provided in the new code. It is now clear, for example, that protection of the confidentiality of records demands consideration of all media (e.g., magnetic, electronic, and optical computer storage, as well as paper and ink records). The new code reiterates the obligation of clinicians to plan in advance for the protection of confidential records in the event of their death or incapacity. Similarly, psychologists must ensure the continuing availability of records and data that may be needed to serve the best interests of their clients. . . . The . . . code also clearly addresses the issue of withholding records solely because of nonpayment. . . . [I]t is clear that records that are needed to serve the client's imminent welfare cannot be held hostage to unpaid bills. At the same time, however, there is no clear requirement that the psychologist prepare reports or summaries that require additional professional work to produce when a bill for prior services remains

unpaid. The . . . code addresses only preexisting records under this provision. . . .[1]

Although not specifically cited in the . . . code, the so-called electronic superhighway of communications calls for special cautions. The dissemination of records . . . by electronic mail and facsimile requires special caution. For example, confidential records should not be transmitted to E-mail accounts or fax destinations that are not secure or appropriately monitored. Similarly, it is important to recognize that conversations on cellular or cordless telephones are not quite as private as those on standard wired phones. . . .

Some psychotherapists have occasionally asserted with misguided pride that they keep no records other than those needed to issue bills (e.g., dates of appointments, charges, and payments). One such psychologist attempted to argue to a state licensing board investigating concerns about her record keeping practices that case records would be of little use to anyone else because, in her opinion, the only truly important aspect of the treatment was the transference, and that could not be picked up using written notes. The standards explicit in both the new code and the *Record Keeping Guidelines* [see next excerpt] ensure that her practice of not keeping more detailed notes would be deemed negligent (Standards 1.23 and 1.24). . . .[2]

FEES AND FINANCIAL ARRANGEMENTS

[T]he key point in the ethics of financial arrangements, aside from basic honesty and fairness . . . is disclosure. As stated in Standard 1.25(a),[3] the client

---

From *Professional Psychology: Research and Practice, 25,* 355–361. Copyright 1994 by the American Psychological Association.

[1]*Ed. Note:* See Section 6 of the current (2002) APA Ethics Code for specific standards addressing all these record keeping issues.

[2]*Ed. Note:* See Standard 6.01 in the current (2002) APA Ethics Code.

[3]*Ed. Note:* See Standard 6.04 in the current (2002) APA Ethics Code.

should know from the initiation of the professional relationship what to expect in terms of fees and payments. In addition, the psychologists are warned in Standard 1.25(c) that they must be mindful that their practices (even solo practices) are businesses and, as a result, are regulated by many state and local laws. For example, a psychologist might think it is a good idea to charge interest or late payment penalties on client bills; however, such practices may well run afoul of state debtor and creditor laws without special legally approved credit agreements. . . .

Discussing fees up front and taking into account the client's ability to pay, restrictions imposed by third-party payers, and similar issues are very important matters. The psychologist's goal should be to thoughtfully avoid the risk of abandoning the client for financial reasons, to obey applicable laws on financial matters, to be nonexploitative, to make no misrepresentation, to anticipate limitations, to discuss collection practices, and to make accurate reports to payers (Standard 1.26).[4] Although not mentioned in the code, it would be wise for psychologists' special fee requirements (e.g., billing for missed appointments or appointments that were cancelled late) to secure clients' agreement on this point at the start of the relationship. . . .

Providing bribes or kickbacks in exchange for referrals has never been acceptable. However, from the FTC's perspective, some ethics panels or licensing boards interpreted such prohibitions as forbidding participation in health maintenance organizations, preferred provider organizations, or certain referral services. The FTC regards referral services as procompetitive, and barring them per se was regarded as a significant problem. Unfortunately, what constitutes a bribe, as opposed to a legitimate fee reduction or membership payment, is open to a wide range of opinion. The key to discriminating between an appropriate and an inappropriate payment will depend on the rationale and justification for the charges or fee reductions and the openness of information on these arrangements to the consumers of the services.

In the new code it is clear that payments for referrals and dividing of fees must be based on services rather than the referral per se (Standard 1.27).[5] . . . Both their payers and recipients of referral fees should be prepared to document the actual costs of services provided (e.g., office space rental, secretarial costs, or utilities) and the qualifications of the recipient of the referral to meet the particular needs of the client. . . .

Fraud or lying about services actually provided is illegal under most circumstances and has always been unethical. In Standard 1.26,[6] the . . . code, however, specifically addresses the issue of accuracy in reporting to payers and funding sources. This would include giving accurate accounts of fees charged and copayments made. Similarly, it is clearly unethical to misrepresent the identity of the actual service provider (e.g., failing to disclose that a service was provided by an assistant) or the actual diagnosis (e.g., exaggerating symptoms to ensure insurance coverage). . . .

The most common business issue that leads to ethical disputes between colleagues involves departures from a practice. This may mean leaving an institution for private practice, leaving a partnership or group practice to strike out on one's own, or simply moving on. Often such career transitions are either not entirely voluntary or not uniformly welcomed by those departing and those staying behind. At such times clients can too often be lost in the shuffle or used as pawns with each side claiming to righteously respect the needs of the client with its own proposed solution.

The new code addresses this issue in Standard 4.08[7] by focusing appropriately on the client's needs with respect to interrupted services. Psychologists are cautioned to carefully consider how they will resolve their clinical responsibilities on departure at the time they propose to enter an employment or

---

[4]*Ed. Note:* See Standard 6.06 in the current (2002) APA Ethics Code.

[5]*Ed. Note:* See Standard 6.07 in the current (2002) APA Ethics Code

[6]*Ed. Note:* See Standard 6.06 in the current (2002) APA Ethics Code.

[7]*Ed. Note:* See Standards 3.12 and 10.09 in the current (2002) APA Ethics Code.

contractual relationship. In this way, the client's best interests can be focused on hypothetically (i.e., before they are actually the new hire's clients), and the sensitive issue of parting can be addressed during a period of maximal goodwill between employer and employee.

The paramount issue to be considered is client welfare. The client's needs must never be held hostage to a practitioner's business or personal interests. . . .

♦ ♦ ♦

Commentary: In their survey, Fulero and Wilbert (1988) found wide variability in psychologists' record-keeping policies and practices. They strongly recom- *mended the promulgation of "a specific set of guidelines propounded under the auspices of the APA" that, they speculated, "could help to reduce the variability in record-keeping practices found in [their] study" (p. 660). Fulero, S. M., & Wilbert, J. R. (1988). Record-keeping practices of clinical and counseling psychologists: A survey of practitioners.* Professional Psychology: Research and Practice, 19, 658–660. *In 1993, the APA responded to this and similar suggestions with its Record Keeping Guidelines. They were substantially revised and lengthened in 2007. As of this writing they were not yet formally published but a shortened version is provided next. Readers are urged to review the entire document, which can be retrieved from http://www.apa.org/practice/recordkeeping.pdf.*

Record Keeping Guidelines

Committee on Professional Practice and Standards, Board of Professional Affairs, American Psychological Association

INTRODUCTION

These guidelines are designed to educate psychologists and provide a framework for making decisions regarding professional record keeping. State and federal laws, as well as the American Psychological Association's (APA, 2002) "Ethical Principles of Psychologists and Code of Conduct" (hereafter referred to as the Ethics Code), generally require maintenance of appropriate records of psychological services. The nature and extent of the record will vary depending upon the purpose, setting, and context of psychological services. Psychologists should be familiar with legal and ethical requirements for record keeping in their specific professional contexts and jurisdictions. These guidelines are not intended to describe these requirements fully or to provide legal advice.

Records benefit both the client[2] and the psychologist through documentation of treatment plans, services provided, and client progress. Record keeping documents the psychologist's planning and implementation of an appropriate course of services, allowing the psychologist to monitor his or her work. Records may be especially important when there are significant periods of time between contacts or when the client seeks services from another professional. Appropriate records can also help protect both the client and psychologist in the event of legal or ethical proceedings. Adequate records are generally a requirement for third-party reimbursement for psychological services.

. . .

INTERACTION WITH STATE AND FEDERAL LAWS

Specific state and federal laws and regulations govern psychological record keeping. To the extent possible, the document has attempted to provide guidelines that are generally consistent with these laws and regulations. In the event of a conflict between these guidelines and any state or federal law or regulation, the law or regulation in question supersedes these guidelines. It is anticipated that psychologists will use their education, skills, and training to identify the relevant issues and attempt to resolve conflicts in a way that conforms to both law and to ethical practice.

HIPAA. Psychologists who are subject to the Health Information Portability and Accountability Act of 1996 (HIPAA) should be aware of certain record-keeping requirements and considerations under HIPAA's Security Rule and Privacy Rule (HIPAA Administrative Simplification Regulation Text, 45 CFR [Code of Federal Regulations] Parts 160, 162, and 164). These guidelines indicate some key areas in which HIPAA requirements or considerations impact record keeping. However, detailed coverage of the requirements for HIPAA compliance is beyond the scope of this document, and the rules related to HIPAA and their interpretation may change over the lifetime of these guidelines. Accordingly, consultation with other sources of information regarding the implications of HIPAA for psychologists is recommended.[3]

Adopted by the APA Council of Representatives February 2007. Full text available from http://www.apa.org/practice/recordkeeping.pdf

[2]The term client is used throughout this document to refer to the child, adolescent, adult, older adult, family, group, organization, community, or other population receiving psychological services. Although it is recognized that the client and the recipient of services may not necessarily be the same entity (APA Ethics Code, Standard 3.07), for economy the term client will be used in place of service recipient.

[3]Resources regarding HIPAA, and HIPAA compliance for psychologists, are available at the Health and Human Services website (http://www.hhs.gov/ocr/hipaa/) and in documents prepared by the APA Practice Organization (APAPO), solely or in collaboration with the APA Insurance Trust (APAIT; APAPO, 2006a, 2006b; APAPO & APAIT, 2006).

EXPIRATION

These guidelines are scheduled to expire 10 years from February 16, 2007 (the date of adoption by APA Council of Representatives). After this date, users are encouraged to contact the APA Practice Directorate to determine whether this document remains in effect.

. . .

GUIDELINES

1. **Responsibility for records.** Psychologists generally have responsibility for the maintenance and retention of their records.
   Rationale. Psychologists have a professional and ethical responsibility to develop and maintain records (Ethics Code 6.01). The psychologist's records document and reflect his or her professional work. In some circumstances, the records are the only way that the psychologist or others may know what the psychologist did and the psychologist's rationale for those actions. As a consequence, the psychologist aspires to create records that are consistent with high quality professional work. If the psychologist is later questioned about services or billing, the availability of accurate records facilitates explanation and accountability.

   . . .

2. **Content of records.** A psychologist strives to maintain accurate, current, and pertinent records of professional services as appropriate to the circumstances and as may be required by the psychologist's jurisdiction. Records include information such as the nature, delivery, progress, and results of psychological services, and related fees.
   Rationale. The Ethics Code (6.01) sets forth reasons why psychologists create and maintain records. Based on various provisions in the Ethics Code, in decision-making about content of records, a psychologist may determine what is necessary in order to (a) provide good care; (b) assist collaborating professionals in delivery of care; (c) ensure continuity of professional services in case of the psychologist's injury, disability, or death or with a change of provider; (d) provide for supervision or training if relevant;

(e) provide documentation required for reimbursement or required administratively under contracts or laws; (f) effectively document any decision-making, especially in high risk situations; and (g) allow the psychologist to effectively answer a legal or regulatory complaint.

. . .

Considerations regarding the level of detail of the record:
A psychologist makes choices about the level of detail in which the case is documented. Psychologists balance client care with legal and ethical requirements and risks. Information written in vague or broad terms may not be sufficient if more documentation is needed (e.g., for continuity of care, mounting an adequate defense against criminal, malpractice, or state licensing board complaints). However, some clients may express a desire for the psychologist to keep a minimal record in order to provide maximum protection and privacy. Although there may be advantages to keeping minimal records, for example, in light of risk management concerns or concerns about unintended disclosure, there are alternately legitimate arguments for keeping a highly detailed record. Those may include such factors as improved opportunities for the treatment provider to identify trends or patterns in the therapeutic interaction, enhanced capacity to reconstruct the details of treatment for litigation purposes, and more effective opportunities to use supervision and consultation. The following issues may provide a guide to assist the psychologist in wrestling with these tensions:

> *The client's wishes.* For a variety of reasons, clients may express a wish that limited records of treatment be maintained. In some situations, the client may require limited record keeping as a condition of treatment. The psychologist then considers whether treatment can be provided under this condition.
> *Emergency or disaster relief settings.* When psychologists provide crisis intervention services to people on emergency relief basis, the records that are created may be less substantial because of the situational demands. The psychologist

may be guided by the oversight agency regarding necessary elements for the record. For example, disaster relief agencies may require only cursory identifying information, the date of service, a brief summary of the service provided, and the provider's name. There may be limited opportunity to keep as detailed records as would be kept in a less urgent situation, particularly in the short-term or immediate crisis. In some situations, such as disaster relief following an airplane crash or a hurricane, no further intervention beyond the on-site contact may occur and, given the brevity and sheer number of services provided, highly detailed records may be impossible to construct even after the crisis.

Alteration or destruction of records. Many statutes, regulations, and rules of evidence prohibit the alteration or removal of information once a record has been made. In the context of litigation, addition or removal of information from a record that has been subpoenaed or requested by court order may create liability for the psychologist. Psychologists may wish to seek consultation regarding relevant state and federal law before changing an existing record. It is recommended that later additions made to a record be documented as such.

Legal/regulatory. Some statutes and regulations mandate inclusion or prohibit exclusion of particular information. For example, an institutional rule for record keeping may prohibit reference to sealed juvenile records or to HIV test results, or a statute may govern disclosure of information about treatment for chemical dependency. The psychologist takes into account the statutes and regulations that govern practice and heeds mandates in making decisions about record detail.

Agency/setting. Psychologists providing psychological services within an institution consider institutional policies and procedures in making decisions about the level of detail in the record (See Guideline 10).

Third-party contracts. The psychologist considers whether the decision to maintain less detailed records deviates from contracts between the psychologist and third-party payors. Many third-party payors' contracts require specific information to be included within the record. Psychologists who sign but do not abide by contracts with such payors will potentially experience a number of adverse consequences (e.g., required reimbursement of previously received funds, legal actions).

The record of psychological services may include information of three kinds.

Information in the client's file:

- identifying data (e.g., name, client ID number);
- contact information (e.g., phone number, address, next of kin);
- fees and billing information;
- where appropriate, guardianship or conservatorship status;
- documentation of informed consent or assent for treatment (Ethics Code 3.10);
- documentation of waivers of confidentiality and authorization or consent for release of information (Ethics Code 4.05);
- documentation of any mandated disclosure of confidential information (e.g., report of child abuse, release secondary to a court order);
- presenting complaint, diagnosis, or basis for request for services;
- plan for services, updated as appropriate (e.g., treatment plan, supervision plan, intervention schedule, community interventions, consultation contracts);
- health and developmental history.

For each substantive contact with a client:

- date of service and duration of session;
- types of services (e.g., consultation, assessment, treatment, training);

- nature of professional intervention or contact (e.g., treatment modalities, referral, letters, e-mail, phone contacts);
- formal or informal assessment of client status;

The record may also include other specific information, depending upon circumstances:

- client responses or reactions to professional interventions;
- current risk factors in relation to dangerousness to self or others;
- other treatment modalities employed such as medication or biofeedback treatment;
- emergency interventions (e.g., specially scheduled sessions, hospitalizations);
- plans for future interventions;
- information describing the qualitative aspects of the professional/client interaction;
- prognosis;
- assessment or summary data (e.g., psychological testing, structured interviews, behavioral ratings, client behavior logs);
- consultations with or referrals to other professionals;
- case-related telephone, mail, and e-mail contacts;
- relevant cultural and sociopolitical factors.

3. **Confidentiality of records.** The psychologist takes reasonable steps to establish and maintain the confidentiality of information arising from service delivery.
   Rationale. Confidentiality of records is mandated by law, regulation, and ethical standards (Ethics Code 4.01; 6.02). The assurance of confidentiality is critical for the provision of many psychological services. Maintenance of confidentiality preserves the privacy of clients and promotes trust in the profession of psychology.
   . . .

4. **Disclosure of record keeping procedures.** When appropriate, psychologists inform clients of the nature and extent of record keeping procedures (including a statement on the limitations of confidentiality of the records; Ethics Code 4.02).

Rationale. Informed consent is part of the ethical and legal basis of professional psychology procedures (Ethics Code 3.10, 8.02, 9.03, & 10.01), and disclosure of record keeping procedures may be a part of this process.
. . .

5. **Maintenance of records.** The psychologist strives to organize and maintain records to ensure their accuracy and to facilitate their use by the psychologist and others with legitimate access to them.
   Rationale. The usefulness of psychological service records often depends on the record being systematically updated and logically organized. Organization of client records in a manner that allows for thoroughness and accuracy of records, as well as efficient retrieval, both benefits the client and permits the psychologist to monitor ongoing care and interventions. In the case of the death or disability of the psychologist or of an unexpected transfer of the client's care to another professional, current, accurate, and organized records allow for continuity of care (see Guideline 13).
   Application. . . . The psychologist may consider dividing client files into two or more sections. Psychotherapy notes, as defined by HIPAA, are necessarily kept apart from other parts of the record.
   . . .

6. **Security.** The psychologist takes appropriate steps to protect records from unauthorized access, damage, and destruction.
   Rationale. Psychologists proceed with respect for the rights of individuals to privacy and confidentiality (Ethics Code, Principle E). Appropriate security procedures protect against the loss of or unauthorized access to the record, which could have serious consequences for both the client and psychologist.[6] Access to the records is limited in order to safeguard against physical and electronic breaches of the confidentiality of the information. Advances in technology, especially in electronic record keeping, may create new challenges for psychologists in

---

[6]For psychologists who are subject to HIPAA and keep electronic records, the Security Rule requires a detailed analysis of the risk of loss of, or unauthorized access to, electronic records and detailed policies and procedures to address those risks . . . .

their efforts to maintain the security of their records (see Guideline 9).

Application. The psychologist strives to protect the security of the paper and electronic records he or she keeps and is encouraged to develop a plan to ensure that these materials are secure.[7] In the security plan, two elements to be considered are the medium on which the records are stored and access to the records.

Maintenance. Psychologists are encouraged to keep paper records in a secure manner in safe locations where they may be protected from damage and destruction (e.g., fire, water, mold, insects). Condensed records may be copied and kept in separate locations so as to preserve a copy from natural or other disasters. Similarly, electronic records stored on magnetic and other electronic media may require protection from damage (e.g., electric fields or mechanical insults; power surges or outages; and attacks from viruses, worms, or other destructive programs). Psychologists may plan for archiving of electronic data including file and system backups and off-site storage of data (See Guideline 9).

Access. Control of access to paper records may be accomplished by storing files in locked cabinets or other containers housed in locked offices or storage rooms. Psychologists protect electronic records from unauthorized access through security procedures (e.g., passwords, firewalls, data encryption and authentication). Consistent with legal and regulatory requirements and ethical standards (e.g., Ethics Code 6.02; HIPAA Privacy Rule and Security Rule), psychologists employ procedures to limit access of records to appropriately trained professionals and others with legitimate need to see the records.

7. **Retention of records.** The psychologist strives to be aware of applicable laws and regulations and to retain records for the period required by legal, regulatory, institutional, and ethical requirements.

   Rationale. A variety of circumstances (e.g., requests from clients or treatment providers, legal proceedings) may require release of client records after the psychologist's termination of contact with the client. Additionally, it is beneficial for the psychologist to retain information concerning the specific nature, quality, and rationale for services provided. In addition to the interests of the client and psychologist, the retention of records may serve not only the interests of the client and the psychologist, but also society's interests in a fair and effective legal dispute resolution and administration of justice, when those records are sought to illuminate some legal issue such as the nature of the treatment provided for the psychological condition of the service recipient at the time of services.

   Application. In the absence of a superseding requirement, psychologists may consider retaining full records until 7 years after the last date of service delivery for adults or until 3 years after a minor reaches the age of majority, whichever is later. In some circumstances, the psychologist may wish to keep records for a longer period, weighing the risks associated with obsolete or outdated information, or privacy loss, versus the potential benefits associated with preserving the records (See Guideline 8).

8. **Preserving the context of records.** The psychologist strives to be attentive to the situational context in which records are created and how that context may influence the content of those records.

   . . .

9. **Electronic records.** Electronic records, like paper records, should be created and maintained in a way that is designed to protect their security, integrity, confidentiality, and appropriate access, as well as their compliance with applicable legal and ethical requirements.

   . . .

10. **Record keeping in organizational settings.** Psychologists working in organizational settings (e.g., hospitals, schools, community agencies, prisons) strive to follow the record-keeping

---

[7]If the psychologist is subject to HIPAA and maintains electronic records, the HIPAA Security Rule will generally *require* the development of security policies and procedures for those records. . . .

policies and procedures of the organization, as well as the Ethics Code.

Rationale. Organizational settings may present unique challenges in record keeping. Organizational record-keeping requirements may differ substantially from procedures in other settings. Psychologists working in organizational settings may encounter conflicts between the practices of their organization and established professional guidelines, ethical standards, or legal and regulatory requirements. Additionally, record ownership and responsibility is not always clearly defined. Often, multiple service providers access and contribute to the record. This potentially affects the degree to which the psychologist may exercise control of the record and its confidentiality.

Application. . . . Record keeping practices may depend upon the nature of the psychologist's legal relationship with the organization. In some settings, the physical record of psychological services is owned by the organization and does not travel with the psychologist upon departure. However, in consultative relationships, record ownership and responsibility may be maintained by the psychologist. It is therefore helpful for psychologists to clarify these issues at the beginning of the relationship in order to minimize the likelihood of misunderstandings.

. . .

It is important to note that multidisciplinary records may not enjoy the same level of confidentiality generally afforded psychological records. The psychologist working in these settings is encouraged to be sensitive to this wider access to the information and to record only information congruent with organizational requirements and necessary to accurately portray the services provided. In this situation, if permitted by institutional rules and legal and regulatory requirements, the psychologist may keep more sensitive information, such as therapy notes, in a separate and confidential file.[11]

11. **Multiple client records.** The psychologist carefully considers documentation procedures when conducting couple, family, or group therapy in order to respect the privacy and confidentiality of all parties.

. . .

12. **Financial records.** The psychologist strives to ensure accuracy of financial records.

Rationale. Accurate and complete financial record keeping helps to assure accuracy in billing (Ethics Code 6.04; 6.06). . . .

Application. . . . Special consideration may be given to: fee agreements and policies, barter agreements, issues relating to adjusting balances, issues concerning co-payments, and concerns about collection.

Fee agreement or fee policy. The financial record for services may begin with a fee agreement or fee policy statement that identifies: the amount to be charged for service and the terms of any agreement for payment. The record may potentially include who is responsible for payment, how "missed appointments" will be handled, acknowledgement of any third-party payor pre-authorization requirements, any agreement regarding co-pay and adjustments to be made, payment schedule, interest to accrue on unpaid balance, suspension of confidentiality when collection procedures are employed, and the methods by which financial disputes may be resolved (Ethics Code 6.04).

Barter agreements and transactions. Accurately recording bartering agreements and transactions helps ensure that the record clearly reflects how the psychologist was compensated. Designation of the source, nature, and date of each financial or barter transaction facilitates clarification, when needed, regarding the exchange of goods for service. Because of the potential for the psychologist to have greater power in the negotiation of bartering agreements, careful documentation protects both the psychologist and the client. Such documentation may reflect the psycholo-

---

[11]In order for therapy notes to have heightened protection as "psychotherapy notes" as defined by the HIPAA Privacy Rule, the notes must be kept separate from the rest of the record. If they are psychotherapy notes, only the psychologist who took the notes can access them, absent a HIPAA complaint authorization from the client (for more details regarding the Privacy Rule see referenced resources).

gist's basis for concluding, at the onset, that the arrangement is neither exploitative nor clinically contraindicated (Ethics Code 6.05).

Adjustments to balance. It is helpful to designate the rationale for, description of, and date of any adjustments to the balance that are made as a result of agreement with a third-party payor or service recipient. This may reduce potential misunderstanding or perceived obligations that might affect the relationship.

Collection. Psychologists may consider including in the record information about collection efforts, including documentation of notification of the intention to use a collection service.

13. **Disposition of Records.** The psychologist plans for transfer of records to ensure continuity of treatment and appropriate access to records when the psychologist is no longer in direct control and, in planning for record disposal, the psychologist endeavors to employ methods that preserve confidentiality and prevent recovery.

Rationale. Client records are accorded special treatment in times of transition (e.g., separation from work, relocation, death). A record transfer plan is required by both the Ethics Code (6.02), and by laws and regulations governing health care practice in many jurisdictions. Such a plan provides for continuity of treatment and preservation of confidentiality. Additionally, the Ethics Code (6.01; 6.02) requires psychologists to dispose of records in a way that preserves their confidentiality.

Application. The psychologist has two responsibilities in relation to the transfer and disposal of records. In anticipation of unexpected events, such as disability, death, or involuntary withdrawal from practice, the psychologist may wish to develop a disposition plan in which provisions are made for the control and management of the records by a trained individual or agency. In other circumstances, when the psychologist plans in advance to leave employment, close a practice, or retire, similar arrangements may be made or the psychologist may wish to retain custody and control of client records. In some circumstances, the psychologist may consider a method for notifying clients about changes in the custody of their records. This may be especially important for those clients whose cases are open or who have recently terminated services. The psychologist may consider including in the disposition plan, in accordance with legal and regulatory requirements, a provision for providing public notice about changes in the custody of the records, such as placing notice in the local newspaper. . . .

◆　◆　◆

Commentary: For another helpful resource, see Knapp, S. J., & VandeCreek, L. D. (2006). Confidentiality, privileged communications, and record keeping. In Practical ethics for psychologists: A positive approach *(pp. 111–128). Washington, DC: American Psychological Association.*

HIPAA: Federal Regulation of Healthcare Records

Donald N. Bersoff

The record-keeping landscape has changed materially as a result of promulgation by the U.S. Department of Health and Human Services of rules implementing the Health Insurance Portability and Accountability Act (HIPAA) of 1996. There are three major rules: (a) the transaction rule, which focuses on creating a standard format for electronic transactions related to health care claims, plan eligibility, and plan coverage; (b) the security rule, which focuses on the health care provider's physical infrastructure to ensure confidentiality of patient information; and (c) most relevant for psychologists, the privacy rule, which focuses on policies, procedures, and business service agreements used to control access to patient information. The privacy rule took effect in April 2003, for most large health plans; those with less than $5 million in annual receipts had 1 additional year to comply (see 45 CFR part 160 and Subparts A & E of Part 164).

The HIPAA privacy rule applies to data called Protected Health Information (PHI), defined as information, whether oral, written, typed, or electronic, that relates to the past, present, or future physical or mental health condition of an identifiable individual; the provision of health care to such an individual; and the past, present, or future payment for the provision of health care to such an individual.

The privacy rule is triggered when a covered entity (e.g., a health care provider) transmits PHI in electronic form (e.g., Internet, CDs, faxes) in connection with health care claims for reimbursement, payments, enrollment in health plans, and status, among other transactions. Once triggered, however, the privacy rule applies to psychologists' entire operation, not solely to information in electronic form. With certain limited exceptions the rule protects PHI regardless of whether the patient is dead or alive. Only those involved (a) directly with patient care, (b) with record keeping or billing, and (c) with quality assurance and training are permitted access to PHI.

Originally, the privacy rule required patient consent prior to using PHI to carry out treatment, payment, and health care operations. But this requirment was eliminated as too burdensome and disruptive of patient care. As a substitute all patients must be provided a Notice of Disclosure informing them "about what information is designated as personally identifiable, how their private health information will be protected, and how disclosures will be made" (Benefield, Ashkanazi, & Rozensky, 2006, p. 274). A signed copy of this Notice is then placed in the patient's record. Patients may request access to their records, review their records, ask for them to be duplicated, and amend records to correct any perceived inaccuracies.

The notice requirement does not pertain, however, to psychotherapy notes. The psychologist must obtain additional authorization for process notes to be released to third parties. The authorization must define specifically the information to be disclosed, indicate to whom the information is going and for what purpose, specify an expiration date, and inform patients that they have a right to refuse authorization or revoke authorization once given. In that light, it is highly recommended that clinicians keep psychotherapy process notes in a secure file separate from more routine PHI, such as diagnoses, prognosis, and treatment plan, to which third-party payors have legitimate access. The regulations, in fact, contain a provision that will gladden the hearts of therapists who must deal with managed care companies (see material later in this chapter). Such companies and other third-party payors are barred from conditioning eligibility for, or payments of, benefits on the disclosure of psychotherapy notes.

With regard to children receiving psychological services, in general, parents, as their personal representatives, have the right of access to their minors' mental health records unless state law permits minors access without parental consent, a court authorizes someone other than parents to make health care decisions for a minor, or a parent agrees to confidentiality between the child and the psychologist.

As defined in regulations adopted in March 2006, there are three escalating penalties for failing to comply with HIPAA. At present, DHHS may take administrative action; the psychologist may be fined up to $100 for each violation with a cap of $25,000 per year; and for wrongful disclosure of PHI there may be fines up to $250,000 and/or imprisonment for up to 10 years. Readers should note that as of the date of the regulations, DHHS received close to 19,000 HIPAA compliance complaints, most from patients of private health entities.

Finally, the privacy rule merely establishes a minimum set of mandates for the protection of PHI. It takes precedence over state law only when it is more stringent than state law. But, when state law is more protective of PHI, then state law takes precedence.

This is but a brief educational summary of the major requirements under privacy rule regulations. Because the operations of all practitioners and the facilities within which they work (and some researchers who use PHI, see Fisher, 2004), are affected, it is helpful to obtain formal legal advice, review the regulations in the *Federal Register* (December 28, 2000), and gain access to the American Psychological Association's (APA's) Practice Organization material referenced in the Commentary that follows to be better informed about its nuances and to apply successfully all the regulations. Although under Standard 1.02 of the Ethics Code (APA, 2002), psychologists can attempt to resolve conflicts between the code and the law, as the standard also indicates, "if the conflict is unresolvable via such means, psychologists may adhere to the requirements of the law, regulations, or other governing legal authority."

References

American Psychological Association. (2002). Ethical principles of psychologists and code of conduct. *American Psychologist, 57,* 1060–1073.

Benefield, H., Ashkanazi, G., & Rozensky, R. H. (2006). Communication and records: HIPPA [sic] issues when working in health care settings. *Professional Psychology: Research and Practice, 37,* 273–277.

Fisher, C. B. (2004). Informed consent and clinical research involving children and adolescents:

Implications of the revised APA ethics code and HIPAA. *Journal of Clinical Child and Adolescent Psychology, 33,* 832–839.

◆ ◆ ◆

Commentary: The APA's Practice Organization has created several documents designed to apprise clinicians of the substance of the three basic rules and models for compliance. As of this writing they are retrievable at no cost for APA members who pay the special assessment. See

American Psychological Association Practice Organization. (2003). Getting ready for HIPAA: What you need to know: A psychologist's guide to the transaction rule. *Retrievable at http://www.apapractice.org/apo/hipaa/trans*

American Psychological Association Practice Organization. (2005). The HIPAA security rule primer. *Retrievable at http://www.apapractice.org/apo/hipaa/hipaa_security_rule.html#*

American Psychological Association Practice Organization & American Psychological Association Insurance Trust. (2002). Getting ready for HIPAA: What you need to know now: A primer for psychologists. *Retrievable at http://www.apapractice.org/apo/hipaa/apapractice.html#*

See also

American Psychiatric Association. (2002). Psychotherapy notes provision of the Health Insurance Portability and Accountability Act (HIPAA) privacy rule resource document. *Retrievable at http://www.psych.org/edu/other_res/lib_archives/200201/pdf*

In an important article, Erard (2004) argued that under HIPAA the protection of "raw test data" (see definitions in chap. 6, this volume), including patient responses to test materials, is no longer viable, although he recommended a number of measures that can still be adopted to maintain a reasonable degree of test security. Rogers (2004), in a rejoinder, lamented the softening of protections of test data and materials under HIPAA and the 2002 APA code and saw serious and harmful erosion of test security. Compare Erard, R. E. (2002). Release of test data under the 2002 ethics code and the HIPAA privacy rule: A raw deal or just a half-baked idea? Journal of Personality Assessment, 82, 23–30, with Rogers, R. (2004). APA 2002 ethics, amphibiology, and the release of psychological test records: A counterperspective to Erard. Journal of Personality Assessment, 82, 31–34.

In recent years, the Federal Trade Commission (FTC) has scrutinized the business practices of health care entities. It has charged that these entities have placed restrictions on professionals that both reduce competition among practitioners and reduce the free flow of truthful information to consumers. Among the entities scrutinized are state boards that license health care professionals and professional associations that regulate the ethical conduct of their members. As the APA Ethics Committee noted in the following excerpt from its annual report, the APA has not been immune to FTC scrutiny:

In July 1986, the Federal Trade Commission (FTC) began an investigation charging that APA's Ethical Principles of Psychologists were in violation of the federal antitrust laws. In particular, the Federal Trade Commission expressed concern about Principles 4.b.iii, 4.b.v, 4.b.vi, 4.b.vii, 4.b.viii, and portions of Principles 6.d and 7.b. The APA voluntarily placed a moratorium on the adjudication of complaints of unethical conduct under the challenged principles and informed the APA membership of this action. Thereafter, a long series of letter exchanges took place between APA and the FTC, and in June 1989, the APA Board of Directors, on advise [sic] of legal counsel, declared an emergency and voted to rescind the challenged ethical principles. In October 1989, on the advise [sic] of legal counsel, the Board of Directors authorized APA to sign the renegotiated complaint, consent agreement, and order.

In the opinion of expert legal counsel, the portions of APA's Ethical Principles of Psychologists in question were clearly in violation of the antitrust laws. Similar principles to those rescinded by the APA Board of Directors contained in the American Medical Association's ethical code were declared in violation of the antitrust laws by the federal district and appellate courts. (p. 874)

See APA Ethics Committee. (1990). *Report of Ethics Committee, 1988*. American Psychologist, 45, 874. For a more complete history, see also *Koocher, G. P. (1994). APA and the FTC: New adventures in consumer protection*. American Psychologist, 49, 322–328 (some of which is reprinted on the following pages).

As a result of negotiations with the FTC, the following sections from the 1981 ethical principles were deleted in 1989:

4(b)(iii) Public statements by psychologists do not contain a testimonial from a patient regarding the quality of a psychologists' services or products . . . ; (v) a statement implying unusual, unique, or one-of-a-kind abilities; (vi) a statement intended or likely to appeal to a client's fears, anxieties, or emotions concerning the possible results of failure to obtain the offered services; (vii) a statement concerning the comparative desirability of offered services; (viii) a statement of direct solicitation of individual clients.

6(d) [Psychologists] neither give nor receive any remuneration for referring clients for professional services.

7(b) If a person is receiving similar services from another professional, psychologists do not offer their own services directly to such a person.

In what ways could these deleted standards be said to restrict competition and the free flow of information to the clients of psychologists? In what ways does the deletion of these standards disserve client welfare and interfere with the goals of effective assessment, therapy, and research?

APA and the FTC: New Adventures in Consumer Protection

Gerald P. Koocher[1]

. . .

THE NATURE OF RESTRICTIONS ON ADVERTISEMENTS

If the general goals of the FTC were to make useful information available to the general public, it is understandable that clinging to vestiges of sameness in public statements for the sake of a sense of professionalism would not survive. However, some limits on advertising may well serve legitimate public interests. This is especially true in professions such as psychology, in which the consumers are often particularly vulnerable to undue influence because of their intellectual or emotional status. . . .

Is Commercial Speech Free Speech Too?

Do restraints imposed by professional association restrictions on advertising violate commercial free speech? Although it is not the same as political free speech, in the constitutional sense, the concept is still highly relevant and has often been an issue in efforts to limit advertising by lawyers. Commercial speech is protected under the First and Fourteenth Amendments, just as political speech is protected (*Virginia State Board of Pharmacy*, 1975); however, the courts have ruled that it is still reasonable to demand substantiation in the face of alleged false or deceptive advertising. The FTC's thrust has been to expand access to truthful information in the marketplace, although there are some exceptions that are discussed later as "in-your face'" solicitations. A good example of the commercial free speech argument involved an enterprising Kentucky lawyer named Shapero.

In *Shapero v. Kentucky Bar Association* (1988), the Supreme Court dealt with the case of a young lawyer who wanted to solicit business by sending truthful, nondeceptive letters to potential clients known to be confronting certain legal problems. The letter in question was to go to "potential clients who have had a foreclosure suit filed against them" and advised "you may be about to lose your home" and that "federal law may allow you to . . . ORDER your creditor to STOP." Potential clients were invited to "call my office for FREE information . . . it may surprise you what I may be able to do for you" (p. 1919).

Mr. Shapero had the foresight to ask the Kentucky state bar whether his proposed letter to people facing foreclosure was acceptable. Although the state bar commissioners ruled that the letter was not misleading, they said no to Shapero, citing a then existing Kentucky Supreme Court rule prohibiting the direct solicitation of individuals (i.e., as opposed to members of the general public) as a directed result of some specific event. Shapero appealed to the U.S. Supreme Court and won. The key point in the decision was that the content of his notice was not false or deceptive and held genuine potential interest for the intended recipients—which they could then choose to act on or ignore.

"In-Your-Face" Solicitation

What if the nature of the commercial exercise of free speech involves a more intense approach than Attorney Shapero's letter or takes advantage of a client in a vulnerable position? The bottom line seems to be that so-called in-your-face solicitation of clients, especially vulnerable ones, will not be tolerated.

From the *American Psychologist, 49,* 322–328. Copyright 1994 by the American Psychological Association.

[1]For the author's latest discussion of this topic see Koocher, G. P., & Keith-Spiegel, P. (1998). *Ethics in psychology: Professional standards and cases* (2nd ed., pp. 259–283). New York: Oxford University Press.

Consider the case of an enterprising attorney named Ohralik from Montville, Ohio (*Ohralik v. Ohio State Bar Association*, 1978). . . .

. . .

[*Ed. Note:* Ohralik visited two young women who had been injured in an auto accident. One was still in the hospital; the other had just been released. He was sanctioned by the state bar and appealed to the state's highest court, which agreed that direct solicitation was inconsistent with the ideals of the legal profession. He then appealed to the U.S. Supreme Court.]

[T]he U.S. Supreme Court (*Ohralik v. Ohio State Bar Association*, 1978) ruled that Ohralik's conduct posed "dangers that the state has a right to prevent" (p. 449), noting that the "appellant not only foisted himself upon these clients; he acted in gross disregard for their privacy" (p. 469).

Testimonials

The use of testimonials by "satisfied users" has a kind of inherent face validity that appeals to the FTC. Unfortunately, like many forms of face validity, the true predictive potential of a testimonial endorsement is far more complex so far as psychological services are concerned. If psychotherapy research has taught us anything, it is that any given psychotherapist is not equally efficacious with all potential clients.

One ironic inconsistency in the latest version of the *EP* [Ethical Principles] is obvious when one contrasts the two-year interval during which sexual intimacies with former psychotherapy clients are absolutely proscribed . . . with the instant availability of the client as a testimonial provider upon the moment of terminating therapy. Psychotherapists know very well that their influence in the life of their clients does not end at the close of the last treatment session. The FTC did allow APA to bar the use of testimonials from "current psychotherapy patients" or from "persons who because of their particular circumstances are vulnerable to undue influence." Apparently, the FTC does not regard the lingering influence of the transference relationship and its potential consequences as an automatic barrier to testimonial advertising (e.g., potentially unfair and deceptive endorsements provided in the glow of a positive transference).

Although most private practitioners know that satisfied clients and the people who referred those clients are their best sources of future referrals, there are few data to suggest that the public will rely on commercially advertised testimonials in selecting medical care providers. . . .

Appeals to Fear

Many psychologists wondered why the FTC would object to APA's ban of advertising that appealed to potential clients' fears. After all, some of our clients are emotionally insecure and may be even more vulnerable to inappropriate duress than [the young women in *Ohralik*]. From the FTC's perspective, global bans on advertising that "appeals to fear if services are not obtained" were simply unacceptable in general. Lots of effective advertising appeals to emotions and fears at some level (e.g., fear of tooth decay if you don't brush, fear of accidental injury or death if you ride in a car without benefit of seat belts and air bags, or fear of AIDS as a result of not practicing "safe sex"). In fact, social psychology has taught us that an "appeal to fear" coupled with a designated course of action is highly effective in evoking attitude change.

How might an ethics committee have become involved in such complaints? In one instance, actual complaints were filed when consumers objected to advertising by psychologists running programs to help people quit smoking. The advertisements powerfully cited potential death from lung cancer and other pulmonary diseases. A more troubling example is the coupling of an appeal to fear with so-called in-your-face solicitation. . . . Imagine the situation in which a psychologist arrives unsolicited at the home of a child who witnessed a playground shooting and urges the parents to subscribe to a course of therapy to prevent inevitable posttraumatic stress syndrome in their as-yet asymptomatic child.

It is interesting that FTC Commissioner Azcuenaga disagreed with her colleagues on this point. She supported APA's wish to continue a ban on scare advertising. . . . She cited the FTC's lack of expertise concerning psychotherapy and noted that "nothing, even hypothetically, suggests that the [APA's] justification is either implausible or invalid" (Azcuenaga, 1990, p. 2). She was outvoted.

Fee Splitting

Providing bribes or kickbacks in exchange for referrals was never an acceptable practice, but from the FTC's perspective some ethics panels or licensing boards were interpreting prohibitions on this point as forbidding psychologists' participation in health maintenance organizations, preferred provider organizations, or referral services during the 1980s. The FTC regards referral services as procompetitive, and barring them per se was regarded as a significant problem. Unfortunately, what constitutes a bribe, as opposed to a legitimate fee reduction or membership payment, is open to a wide range of opinion. The FTC consent order does permit APA to issue "reasonable" principles requiring disclosures to consumers regarding fees paid to referral services or similar entities. The key to discriminating between reasonable and inappropriate payment will have to depend on the rationale for the charges or fee reductions and the openness of information on these arrangements to the consumers of the services.

1992 APA ETHICS CODE

. . .

. . . What does all of this mean for the psychologist who wants to consider advertising in light of the current code? How about the state licensing board that wants to impose restrictions greater or more specific than those adopted by APA?

The following guidelines summarize the key factors to focus on.

1. Advertising by psychologists is clearly acceptable and cannot be banned, although the content of advertisements should ideally focus on facts of meaningful interest to the potential consumer.

2. One must take great care when listing affiliations, degrees, and other data so as to assure that the public is not misled, confused, or otherwise deceived. Both intentional deception and inadvertent errors that are not corrected can be prosecuted.

3. Once completely prohibited, soliciting testimonials or quotes from "satisfied users" is now permissible, so long as they are not solicited from current psychotherapy clients or others subject to "undue influence." The effectiveness of such advertising for psychologists is unknown.

4. The uninvited, direct, in-your-face solicitation of individuals as clients is also prohibited to the extent that it subjects the potential client to "undue influence," as opposed to mass solicitation through media advertising. However, this does not include barriers to inviting the significant others of current clients for collateral treatment.

5. Psychologists who serve organizational or industrial clients are entitled to broader latitude than those who serve individuals (e.g., current organizational clients could be solicited for endorsements), lay groups, and families; however, they too must observe factual validity-based criteria and avoid deception in their advertising claims.

6. Fees may be mentioned in advertisements but must also be reasonably honored for the reasonable life of the announcement.

7. Referral services may ethically charge a fee to clients, therapists, or both, although this should not be secret from the client, and the fee should not be the primary basis for making the specific referral. When portions of fees are paid to others parties, such fees should be in payment for services actually rendered (e.g., referral service, consultation, supervision, office space rental).

8. Although there is no longer any prohibition to offering treatment to a client who is receiving services from another professional, specific discussion with the client of the potential risks and conflicts is now required. It would also be wise to seek authorization from the client to contact the other professional and to consult with that person.

9. Psychologists must consider their style of presentation-of-self and public statements carefully in any public context, whether or not advertising per se is involved.

10. States may impose more stringent restrictions on professional advertising than do professional associations, so long as a legitimate state's interest is documented and so long as that state's

interest does not violate a customer's access to useful information.

References

Azcuenaga, M. L. (1990). *Separate statement of Commissioner Mary L. Azcuenaga concurring in part and dissenting in part in American Psychological Association File 861–0082.* Washington, DC: Federal Trade Commission.

Ohralik v. Ohio State Bar Association, 436 U.S. 447 (1978).

Shapero v. Kentucky Bar Association, 486 U.S. 466 (1988).

Virginia State Board of Pharmacy et al. v. Virginia Citizens Consumer Council, Inc., et al., 425 U.S. 747 (1975).

◆ ◆ ◆

Commentary: Koocher correctly stated that the 1992 Ethical Principles bar uninvited in-person solicitation of actual or potential psychotherapy clients who are vulnerable to undue influence (see Standard 3.06; now see Standard 5.06). The FTC approved old Standard 3.06 on the basis of the Supreme Court's decision in Ohralik v. State Bar Association, 436 U.S. 447 (1978), concerning in-person solicitation by lawyers of clients suffering personal injuries (such as in auto accidents, like the case summarized by Koocher in the preceding excerpt). However, in 1993, the Supreme Court struck down a Florida rule precluding certified public accountants from engaging in direct in-person solicitation. The Court noted that it had not banned all such attempts to garner business and that distinctions among professions were significant in assessing whether such bans were reasonable and constitutional. In Edenfield v. Fane, 507 U.S. 761 (1993), the Court ruled that solicitation by certified public accountants was different than solicitation by lawyers because lawyers are trained in the art of persuasion, whereas accountants' training emphasizes independence and objectivity, not advocacy. Who are psychologists more like—lawyers or accountants? Should not the proper analysis involve examining the nature of the client, not the nature of the profession? From that perspective, is the APA's Standard 5.06 appropriate?

Consider the following advertisement:

> *Premature ejaculation, impotence and vaginismus, cured by World's Who's Who psychotherapist. Ninety-five percent*

success, revolutionary short term program, compassionate, scientific, sincere. All anxieties treated between 11:00 a.m. and 1 p.m. Area code. . . .

This ad, quoted by Frisch and Rebert (1991, p. 176), in their article, appeared in the Village Voice *in 1989. The authors argued that such self-advertising is not in the best interest of psychology. Instead, they advocated "that psychology should, in fact, expand its efforts to advertise the profession as a whole, bringing the public information about the use of psychological services and where to find those services" (p. 179). Such collective public education programs, they believed, offer a more positive image of the profession. See Frisch, G. R., & Rebert, D. (1991). Effects of advertising on psychology. Canadian Psychology, 32, 176–180. In any event, is the ad that they quoted in violation of the APA Ethical Principles?*

For a more extensive history of restrictions on advertising by psychologists and a discussion of ethical standards related to claims of unusual, unique, or one-of-a-kind abilities and statements appealing to clients' fears and anxieties, see Shead, N. W., & Dobson, K. S. (2004). Psychology for sale: The ethics of advertising professional services. Canadian Psychology, 45, 125–136.

With regard to another controversial matter, Koocher correctly stated that Standard 1.27 of the 1992 Ethical Principles (now Standard 6.07) does not bar referral fees as long as the fees are based on services provided and are not simply "kick-backs" for the referral itself. But the line between a kickback and a proper referral fee may be difficult to draw. Furthermore, under the statutes regulating Medicare (nationwide health insurance for the elderly) and Medicaid (state medical assistance programs for the poor), "whoever knowingly and willfully solicits or receives any remuneration" or "whoever knowingly and willfully offers to pay any remuneration (including any kickback, bribe, or rebate) directly or indirectly, overtly or covertly, in cash or in kind in return for referring an individual to a person for the furnishing of [Medicare or Medicaid] service" is guilty of a felony, punishable by a fine of up to $25,000 and imprisonment of up to 5 years. See Social Security Spending Reduction Act of 1984, 42 U.S.C. § 1320a–7b(b). Thus, *although some referral-fee practices may be ethical, they may be illegal within federal health systems. Furthermore, some state ethics codes, incorporated into their licensure laws, may be more restrictive than the APA code of ethics. The APA Ethics Committee issued a statement intended to clarify old Standard 1.27. It says that the Standard*

> *does not prohibit an independent contractor from paying a percentage of a fee to a colleague as long as the payment is within a reasonable range of the fair market value of the services provided. Services are broadly defined and include, for example, mentoring and promotional activities.*
> *(p. 713)*

See APA Ethics Committee. (1995). Report of the Ethics Committee, 1994. American Psychologist, 50, *706–713. Although this clarification is helpful, the prudent practitioner will obtain sound legal advice before offering or receiving referral fees. For an informative and cautionary article concerning fraud in federal programs generally, see Geis, G., Pontell, H. N., Keenan, C., Rosoff, S. M., O'Brien, M. J., & Jesilow, P. D. (1985). Peculating psychologists: Fraud and abuse against Medicaid.* Professional Psychology: Research and Practice, 16, 823–832.

Finally, in reviewing the 1981 APA code of ethics, Faustman (1982) raised another difficult money related concern:

> *The ethical standards seem somewhat vague on the act of referring [delinquent accounts] to an external collection service. Under the intent of the standards, the use of a collection agency may be ethical if the therapist, prior to the initiation of therapy, obtains the expressed consent (e.g., written and/or verbal consent) of the client to release information should the client not pay the fee. (p. 209)*

See Faustman, W. O. (1982). Legal and ethical issues in debt collection strategies of professional psychologists. Professional Psychology, 13, 208–214.

Standard 6.04(e) of the 2002 Ethics Code is much clearer on this issue. Psychologists planning to use collection agencies may do so, provided that they "first

[inform] the person that such measures will be taken and [provide] that person an opportunity to make prompt payment." However, a collection agency's "aggressive attempts to obtain payment . . . may result in the client's bringing suit against the therapist" (Faustman, 1982, p. 210). For a helpful guide to all these knotty matters, see Yenney, S. L., & American Psychological Association Practice Directorate. (1994). Business strategies for a caring profession. *Washington, DC: American Psychological Association.*

When the first edition of this book was published, President Clinton's attempt to revolutionize health care delivery and achieve health insurance coverage for all Americans had just failed. As this is being written there is still no consensual solution to the health care crisis.

The complexities of health care reform are far beyond the scope and intent of this text. For two good background pieces, however, the reader may profit from reviewing:

Higuchi, S. A., & Newman, R. (1994). *Legal issues for psychotherapy in a managed care environment.* Psychoanalysis and Psychotherapy, 11, *138–153.*

Petrila, J. (1996). *Ethics, money, and the problem of coercion in managed behavioral health care.* Saint Louis University Law Journal, 40, *359–405.*

The relevant question for practitioners is whether the provision of mental health services under the rubric of managed care will create a significant number of ethical conflicts for psychologists and other mental health professionals. Many practitioners appear to think so. In a 1997 survey sponsored by Division 42 of APA (Independent Practice), 57.8% of 442 respondents (of 1,000 surveyed) reported experiencing ethical dilemmas in managed care organizations not addressed in the 1992 Ethics Code, and 60.6% stated that the code inadequately helped psychologists solve ethical issues encountered in managed care organizations. See Murphy, M. J., DeBernardo, C. R., & Shoemaker, W. E. (1998). Impact of managed care on independent practice and professional ethics: A survey of independent practitioners. Professional Psychology: Research and Practice, 29, 43–51. *In what appears to be the most recent survey of clinical and counseling psychologists the authors found that respondents (N = 365 of 1,200 surveyed) with high managed care caseloads worked longer hours, had more client contact, received less supervision, reported more negative client behaviors,* experienced more stress, were less satisfied with their incomes, and scored higher on emotional exhaustion than those with low managed care involvement. There also appeared to be a significant diminution in psychological testing referrals and rates of reimbursement for the evaluations. *See Rupert, P. A., & Baird, K. A. (2004). Managed care and the independent practice of psychology.* Professional Psychology: Research and Practice, 35, *185–193. See also Turchik, J. A., Karpenko, V., Hammers. D., & McNamara, J. R. (2007). Practical and ethical assessment issues in rural, impoverished, and managed care settings.* Professional Psychology: Research and Practice, 38, *158–168. See also Field, R. I. (1998). New ethical relationships under health care's new structure: The need for a new paradigm.* Villanova Law Review, 43, *467–498.*

Whatever the eventual course of health care legislation and whatever attempts are made to reform managed care, it is clear, as Kiesler and Morton (1988)

presciently observed, that "health policy is in a state of upheaval in the United States. . . . The rapid evolution of health policy has potentially dramatic implications for psychologists, as scientists, professionals, and advocates" (p. 993). Kiesler, C. A., & Morton, T. L. (1988). Psychology and public policy in the "health care revolution." American Psychologist, 43, *993–1003. What was true 15 years ago is decidedly more true today.*

The following set of materials provides some education concerning the emotional nature of the debate concerning managed mental health care structures. It also provides some guidance for resolving ethical conflicts to those who provide mental health services in these uncertain and changing times. It may be helpful while reading these materials to consider the obligations of psychologists in temporal terms. That is, what should be the responsibilities of therapists prior to becoming involved with managed care companies, to the patient before therapy begins, and to the patient during the course of therapy?

Practicing Psychology in the Era of Managed Care: Implications for Practice and Training

Lisa M. Sanchez and Samuel M. Turner

MANAGED BEHAVIORAL HEALTH CARE: HISTORY OF DEVELOPMENT

Prior to the advent of managed care, the primary vehicle for reimbursement for behavioral health care was based on indemnity insurance plans. In this fee-for-service system, the insurance plan would reimburse the patient or mental health care provider for services, typically an hour of psychotherapy. There were few cost controls and, in most cases, individuals were free to choose their health care provider (Hayes, Barlow, & Nelson-Gray, 1999). Providers generally treated small numbers of patients for long periods of time and were not financially accountable for outcome or length of treatment. This system became untenable as health care costs skyrocketed in the 1980s. Between 1987 and 1992, the average premium for mental health and substance abuse benefits increased by almost 100% (Strosahl, 1994), and national health care costs composed nearly 11% of the U.S. gross national product (Levit, Freeland, & Waldo, 1990). This increase impacted the ability of the health insurance industry to maintain profits and of individuals to purchase health insurance (Hayes et al., 1999). As a result, insurance companies began to increase premiums to businesses, governments, and individuals.

The concept of merging managed care with national health care policy was expressed in President Nixon's 1971 Message to Congress (as cited in DeLeon, VandenBos, & Bulatao, 1991) and subsequently adopted into effect by the HMO Act of 1973. This law provided federal funding for the development of nonprofit and for-profit HMOs (DeLeon et al., 1991). To qualify for federal subsidies, HMOs were required to provide a set of services, including outpatient mental health care and treatment and referral services for substance abuse ("HMO Law," 1974). Partly because of the restrictive qualifications, which made it difficult for HMOs to compete with traditional insurance plans, the implementation of the act was slow. Subsequent amendments in 1976 and 1978 encouraged the growth of HMOs through a series of financial and administrative incentives (DeLeon et al., 1991). Managed care systems increased in numbers as a result.

Since the 1980s, it has become common to manage mental health care through behavioral health carve-out plans. In a carve-out plan, mental health and/or substance abuse benefits are separated out from general medical benefits and managed separately. Carve-outs typically have separate budgets and administrative and provider networks (Grazier, Eselius, Hu, Shore, & G'Sell, 1999). Currently, it is estimated that 88% of the insured managed care population is enrolled in a managed mental health carve-out program. The development of this separate system was partly due to a belief that behavioral health care was inferior to medical health care (Cummings, 1995; Drum, 1995). However, the primary motivation for the development of carve-out plans was the escalating costs of mental health care relative to medical health care. From 1980 to 1995, mental health care costs doubled relative to the overall health care dollar (American Psychological Association [APA], 1992).

Several factors contributed to this phenomenon. New and costly technology was introduced into the mental health care system, including psychotropic drugs and psychological and biological assessment procedures (Cummings, 1995; Hayes et al., 1999; Strosahl, 1994). Although new technology also was introduced into the medical sector, psychotropic medications often were more expensive than other

From *American Psychologist, 58,* 116–129. Copyright 2003 by the American Psychological Association.

types of drugs (Docherty, 1999). The inclusion of mental health services in the 1965 Medicare and Medicaid programs and the 1973 HMO Act increased the number of people treated by mental health care providers (Frank, 2000). Also, demand for psychological services increased as they became more culturally acceptable. Private (and expensive) psychiatric hospitals and addiction treatment centers proliferated because of increased demand and readily available reimbursement (Hayes et al., 1999). The result was that the mental health care system became extremely expensive and thus encouraged the mostly artificial distinction between mental and physical health care services.

CURRENT MANAGED CARE SYSTEMS

Managed care today extends far beyond the HMO as originally conceptualized in 1973. The majority of health care delivery in this country now occurs within a managed care system. Among those who are insured, 75% are in a managed care plan, and 88% of these are enrolled in a managed mental health carve-out program (Kiesler, 2000). . . .

The term *managed care* refers to the management of a prepaid health care delivery system to control input and output (Docherty, 1999). In other words, it is a system for rationing health care services to the population (Cummings, Budman, & Thomas, 1998; I. J. Miller, 1996). Methods used to offset costs include utilization review (after a predetermined number of sessions, the utilization reviewer evaluates the patient profile and treatment plan and must authorize the continuation of treatment), practice profiling (the monitoring of clinicians' costs and effectiveness), session limits, reduced inpatient stays, patient risk sharing (copayments and/or deductibles), "gatekeeping" (e.g., a primary care physician must authorize referral to a mental health specialist), use of less trained providers, and provider risk sharing (capitation). In a capitated arrangement, the demand for services is predicted by the provider and negotiated ahead of time (Kiesler, 2000). As an example, a managed care company may agree to pay a provider a given fee for treating 100 patients in a given year (i.e., the claims target). If the provider fails to meet the claims target, or if actual costs were higher than the claims target, then the provider risks financial loss.

Several types of managed care organizations differ in the extent to which they use these cost-control strategies. HMOs contract with employers to provide health services for employees for a set fee per year, typically based on the number and characteristics (e.g., age and sex) of employees. It is to the advantage of the HMO to bid the lowest cost per employee and to provide fewer services (Hayes et al., 1999). Often, providers are salaried by the HMO and provide services only to those patients who are under the given plan. Therefore, the HMO model relies heavily on capitation, limits on care, and gatekeeping. Preferred provider organizations (PPOs) are composed of clinicians who agree to provide services at reduced fees in exchange for a consistent referral base from the insurance company. PPOs manage care primarily through patient risk sharing (copayments) and utilization reviews (Dana, Conner, & Allen, 1996). In an individual practice association (IPA) model, providers contract directly with employers or other groups, using capitated arrangements and copayments. Employee assistance programs (EAPs) are provided by companies and emphasize cost savings through prevention by identifying mental health or substance abuse problems in their early stages and arranging for referral (Hayes et al., 1999). Together, the HMO, PPO, IPA, and EAP models account for the majority of health care delivery in this country.

. . .

IMPACT OF MANAGED CARE ON THE DELIVERY OF BEHAVIORAL HEATH CARE

. . .

New Patterns in Service Delivery and Organizational Structure

Because the majority of the American insured population is under a managed behavioral health care plan, many practitioners have been forced to work with managed care companies (Hayes et al., 1999). In a 1996 national survey of APA Division 42 (Psychologists in Independent Practice; $N = 1,000$, respondents = 442), 84% of the respondents indicated they were members of HMO or PPO panels (Murphy, DeBernardo, & Shoemaker, 1998). The modal number of panel memberships was in the category of nine or more. In response to demands imposed by this new relationship, many mental health care providers have been forced to reorganize their practices and methods for treating patients in order to maintain profits.

Prior to managed care, most clinicians in private practice carried a relatively small caseload and treated each patient over a long period of time (Shore & Beigel, 1996). Generally, patients who had indemnity insurance and who pursued long-term therapy were young, educated, and affluent persons who sought help for problems in living (Cummings et al., 1998). Cummings et al. (1998) noted that during the peak of solo fee-for-service practice, 20% of patients accounted for 70% of the total mental health care expenditures. In the current system, session limits often are imposed by the managed care organization, and the goal of treatment is functional improvement and symptom reduction in the context of short-term therapy (Bedell, Hunter, & Corrigan, 1997; Shore & Beigel, 1996).

Previously, the individual clinician attracted patients on the basis of reputation, visibility, or advertising (Drum, 1995). In contrast, providers are now more obliged to recruit patients and secure referrals by competing for membership on managed care panels. Currently, most mental health benefits are provided only if patients receive treatment from a clinician on their insurance plan panel of providers. Benefits for treatment received by an out-of-network provider will typically be denied or subject to higher copayments. Therefore, those who offer effective services at lower prices can more successfully bid for panel membership and obtain a secure referral base (Hayes et al., 1999). This competition for patients has resulted in reduced fees because, as previously noted, managed care organizations reimburse services at lower rates (Hayes et al., 1999). . . .

In addition to changing patterns of service delivery, managed care policies also have impacted the organization of clinician practices. The survey of APA Division 42 members (Murphy et al., 1998) revealed that 21% of the respondents had moved from solo practice to a larger integrated network, and an additional 23% anticipated joining a group or network in the future. Because clinicians have more adminis-

trative responsibilities in the current system, many have reduced their clinical hours or have added salaried clerical staff to manage administrative tasks. Therefore, one change in practice patterns as a result of managed care is increased attention to administrative responsibilities and, as a result, the shift toward larger networks of providers with support staff.

A second change in practice patterns relates to treatment outcome and efficacy. Utilization reviewers typically require documentation of treatment efficacy before offering reimbursement. One strategy adopted by practitioners for dealing with these requirements has been the increased use of outcome measures. A 1995 national survey of all APA members who had been billed for special practice assessment as part of their APA dues ($N = 47,119$, respondents = 15,918) revealed a small but consistent trend for more recently licensed providers to use outcome measures in clinical practice (Phelps, Eisman, & Kohout, 1998). Twenty-three percent of those licensed through 1969 reported using outcome measures, compared with 27% licensed in 1970–1979 and 31% licensed in 1990–1995. This trend likely reflects the increasing need of providers to be accountable for treatment efficacy and to offer inexpensive services in order to retain managed care referrals and be reimbursed for services.

Similarly, new reimbursement requirements may have fostered increased use of and adherence to practice guidelines. In response to the need to prove treatment efficacy and greater accountability, in the late 1980s, the federal government sought the construction of clinical practice guidelines (Hayes et al., 1999). *Best practice standards* are now typically part of the utilization review process, and providers may be dropped from managed care panels and subject to legal action if they are not followed. Although some consider the guidelines to create more uniformity in services delivered and to provide an empirical basis for assessing and treating mental health problems, others view psychotherapy as too complex and individualized to be subjected to standardized interventions. Again, it is unclear what effect guidelines have had on treatment outcome.

Finally, social workers and other master's-level clinicians have assumed a more prominent role in the current behavioral health care market

(Cummings, 1995). Eighty-three percent of respondents in the 1995 national survey of APA members indicated they believed ("to a great extent") that managed care has led to an increased use of non-doctoral-level providers, such as social workers, for service delivery (Phelps et al., 1998). It has been argued that the delivery of services by less trained and less educated practitioners results in poorer standards of care. However, this has yet to be subjected to empirical study.

. . .

Quality of Behavioral Health Care in the Managed Care Environment

. . .

One of the ways the managed care system has altered patient access to psychological services is by requiring primary care physicians to authorize a mental health referral. In a 1986 national survey of all operating HMOs, 75% ($N = 473$, respondents = 286) indicated that the approval of a patient's primary care physician was required for any mental health service to be obtained (Shadle & Christianson, 1988). One concern with respect to the increasing reliance on primary care physicians for the detection of and referral for mental health problems is that patients will be deflected from mental health settings to primary care settings and treated primarily pharmacologically. The influx of patients into the primary care setting also is feared to promote the conceptualization of mental disorders in an overly biological and reductionistic manner (Dana et al., 1996). There is some evidence to support this concern. For example, in recently created clinical practice guidelines for depression, there is a strong emphasis on pharmacological treatment (American Psychiatric Association, 1993; Barlow, 1996). . . .

. . .

Perhaps the chief concern regarding the quality of treatment provided in a managed care system is related to the imposition of third-party payers into the traditional dual relationship between patient and clinician. Specifically, these concerns relate to the increasing control of managed care companies in determining treatment decisions and limiting the supply of services available to enrollees. . . .

In addition, the results of several surveys suggest that treatment may be terminated prematurely as a result of managed care practices. In a Colorado survey of 223 responding psychologists, 64% reported incidents of managed care companies discontinuing treatment prematurely (Hipp, Atkinson, & Pelc, 1994). In a national survey of psychologists in APA Division 39 (Psychoanalysis; $N = 3,956$, respondents = 718), 49% reported that their patients experienced adverse consequences due to treatment delay or denial (Tucker & Lubin, 1994). Adverse outcomes included the need for hospitalization, suicidal or homicidal ideation and behavior, medical illness, severe anxiety and depression, and increased rates of relapse. However, it was not specified what percentage of patients experienced these outcomes, and it is not clear that such outcomes were the direct result of treatment delay or denial. Furthermore, these data reflected opinion and were not the result of systematic empirical study.

This cost-driven system may also adversely impact quality by relying on utilization reviewers, who typically have less knowledge and education than do the providers, to authorize or deny treatment (I. J. Miller, 1996). . . .

Quality of Behavioral Health Care Revisited

Although survey data indicate that the majority of clinicians believe that managed care has adversely impacted quality by placing restrictions on care, using gatekeepers as a mandatory referral source, and imposing unqualified reviewers into the decision-making process, others have argued that it has created an opportunity to make psychotherapy more efficient. . . .

In terms of limits on services, Cummings and colleagues have argued that shorter term and more efficient therapy actually produces greater overall access to and quality of mental health services. They stated that when "brief, dynamic, and active psychotherapy" (Cummings & VandenBos, 1981, p. 169) was provided to individuals in the Kaiser Permanente Health Plan, 85% of patients responded to therapy in a mean of 8.6 sessions and only 10% required long-term therapy (Cummings, 1977; Cummings et al., 1998; Cummings & Follette, 1976; Cummings &

VandenBos, 1979, 1981). Specifically, patients receiving either 1 session (in the very brief psychotherapy condition) or 2 to 8 sessions (in the brief psychotherapy condition) did not require additional sessions to maintain a significant decrease in medical utilization over five years (in comparison to a matched control group). A reduction in medical utilization was purported to reflect a decrease in somatization and hence a diminution in emotional distress. The authors interpreted this result to mean that brief psychotherapy provides satisfactory therapeutic effectiveness as well as cost savings through the reduction of both mental health and medical visits. Therefore, they concluded that when brief therapy is provided to short-term therapy responders, the health system has the ability to finance the psychotherapy for patients needing more intensive long-term treatment. . . .

However, interpretation of the results from the series of studies by Cummings and colleagues (Cummings, 1977; Cummings et al., 1998; Cummings & Follette, 1976; Cummings & VandenBos, 1979, 1981) is hampered by a lack of clarity in methodological, conceptual, and data analytic strategies, and this may impact the validity of these conclusions. . . .

Given the lack of empirical data on the impact of cost-cutting measures on mental health outcomes and access to appropriate care, including provider availability, delays in care, referral rules, and utilization management, there currently is not enough evidence to support conclusions regarding the impact of managed care on quality of care. What clearly is missing from the literature is analysis of patient outcomes for different types of mental health problems, treated by different types of providers, before and after the introduction of managed care. In the few studies examining such outcomes, results indicated no quality compromise from managed care practices. However, because of the methodological deficiencies in these studies, it is premature to draw definitive conclusions regarding the impact of managed care on quality of mental health services.

Confidentiality of Patient Information in the Managed Care Environment

Another primary concern for psychologists, particularly those in independent practice, is the extent to which the informational requirements of managed care interfere with the confidential relationship of psychotherapy. During utilization review, managed care staff collect patient information from the therapist to authorize treatment and payment. One concern is that this intrusion may impact the quality of the therapeutic relationship. Analogue studies examining confidentiality have found that patients prefer conditions of absolute confidentiality over conditions of limited confidentiality. Under conditions of limited confidentiality, subjects report they are less willing to self-disclose (Haut & Muehleman, 1986; Nowell & Spruill, 1993).

In a second study, Kremer and Gesten (1998) compared the impact of three different descriptions of therapeutic confidentiality on students' and therapy patients' self-reported willingness to disclose. Results indicated that patients and students in the managed care condition were significantly less willing to disclose than were subjects in the standard limits or rationale conditions ($p < .05$; see Kremer & Gesten, 1998). The effect size of the managed care condition versus the standard limits condition was especially large for psychotherapy patients ($n = 92$, $d = .93$). These data suggest that limits to confidentiality imposed by managed care companies can reduce patients' willingness to self-disclose.

To date, there are limited data on the impact of less self-disclosure on treatment outcome. However, the implication is that patients' reluctance to disclose sensitive and potentially therapeutically relevant information will adversely affect treatment by resulting in improper or inadequate diagnosis and treatment (Kremer & Gesten, 1998; McGuire, Toal, & Blau, 1985). In addition, the quality of the therapeutic relationship is widely considered to be a major factor in treatment outcome (e.g., Beutler, Machado, & Neufeldt, 1994), and managed care informational requirements may interfere with this relationship by introducing an element of distrust. Ambivalence regarding managed care limits to confidentiality may even prevent patients from pursuing treatment in the first place. Then again, it is not clear that self-disclosure as a global construct in psychotherapy is specifically related to clinical outcome. Thus, arguments have been based on the a priori notion that self-disclosure is important to treatment outcome, but in reality this is a complex variable that needs to be examined in a more specific fashion.

. . .

A second issue relating to confidentiality is the extent to which the managed care environment affects clinicians' reporting practices. In a survey of APA Division 42 practitioners in 1996, 75% of the 442 respondents indicated that concerns regarding confidentiality and reimbursement have compromised patient confidentiality and reporting practices (Murphy et al., 1998). Fifty-three percent strongly disagreed that the vast majority of managed care companies would keep their patients' information confidential, and 63% felt that there was a high potential that information provided to managed care companies could be used to harm patients. These concerns apparently have resulted in some rather disturbing developments. For example, 63% of clinicians in this survey believed that to a large extent, psychologists alter diagnoses or Current Procedural Terminology codes to protect patients' confidentiality, future employment, or future medical insurance. Sixty-one percent believed that psychologists submit the lowest level of diagnosis that is reimbursable and leave off an Axis II diagnosis if a patient has a reimbursable Axis I diagnosis. In addition to the ethical and legal implications of misreporting, this behavior may result in the collection of inaccurate information on the epidemiology of treated disorders and outcome of treatment. If this were to occur, it could result in the development of inaccurate treatment guidelines that could subsequently affect the treatment of patients.

References

American Psychiatric Association. (1993). Practice guideline for major depressive disorder in adults. *American Journal of Psychiatry, 150*(4, Suppl. 1), 1–26.

American Psychological Association. (1992). Ethical principles of psychologists and code of conduct. *American Psychologist, 47,* 1597–1611.

Barlow, D. H. (1996). Health care policy, psychotherapy research, and the future of psychotherapy. *American Psychologist, 51,* 1050–1058.

Bedell, J. R., Hunter, R. H., & Corrigan, P. W. (1997). Current approaches to assessment and treatment of persons with serious mental illness. *Professional Psychology: Research and Practice, 28,* 217–228.

Beutler, L. E., Machado, P. P., & Neufeldt, S. A. (1994). Therapist variables. In A. E. Bergin & S. L. Garfield (Eds.), *Handbook of psychotherapy and behavior change* (4th ed., pp. 243–244). New York: Wiley.

Cummings, N. A. (1977). Prolonged (ideal) versus short-term (realistic) psychotherapy. *Professional Psychology: Research and Practice, 8,* 491–501.

Cummings, N. A. (1995). Unconscious fiscal connivance. *Psychotherapy in Private Practice, 14,* 23–28.

Cummings, N. A., Budman, S. H., & Thomas, J. L. (1998). Efficient psychotherapy as a viable response to scarce resources and rationing of treatment. *Professional Psychology: Research and Practice, 29,* 460–469.

Cummings, N. A., & Follette, W. T. (1976). Brief psychotherapy and medical utilization. In H. Dörken & Associates (Eds.), *The professional psychologist today* (pp. 165–174). San Francisco: Jossey-Bass.

Cummings, N. A., & VandenBos, G. R. (1979). The general practice of psychology. *Professional Psychology: Research and Practice, 10,* 430–440.

Cummings, N. A., & VandenBos, G. R. (1981). The twenty year Kaiser-Permanente experience with psychotherapy and medical utilization: Implications for national health policy and national health insurance. *Health Policy Quarterly, 1*(2), 159–175.

Dana, R. H., Conner, M. G., & Allen, J. (1996). Quality of care and cost-containment in managed mental health: Policy, education, research, advocacy. *Psychological Reports, 79,* 1395–1422.

DeLeon, P. H., VandenBos, G. R., & Bulatao, E. Q. (1991). Managed mental health care: A history of the federal policy initiative. *Professional Psychology: Research and Practice, 22,* 15–25.

Docherty, J. P. (1999). Cost of treating mental illness from a managed care perspective. *Journal of Clinical Psychiatry, 60* Suppl. 3., 49–53.

Drum, D. D. (1995). Changes in the mental health service delivery and finance systems and resulting implications for the National Register. *Register Report, 20,* 4–10.

Frank, R. G. (2000). The creation of Medicare and Medicaid: The emergence of insurance and markets for mental health services. *Psychiatric Services, 51,* 465–468.

Grazier, K. L., Eselius, L. L., Hu, T., Shore, K. K., & G'Sell, W. A. (1999). Effects of a mental health carve-out on use, costs, and payers: A four-year study. *Journal of Behavioral Health Services & Research, 26,* 381–389.

Haut, M. W., & Muehleman, T. (1986). Informed consent: The effects of clarity and specificity on disclosure in a clinical interview. *Psychotherapy, 23*(1), 93–101.

Hayes, S. C., Barlow, D. H., & Nelson-Gray, R. O. (1999). *The scientist practitioner: Research and accountability in the age of managed care.* Boston: Allyn & Bacon.

Hipp, M. L., Atkinson, C., & Pelc, R. (1994). *Colorado Psychological Association legislative survey.* Denver: Colorado Psychological Association.

HMO Act of 1973, 42 U.S.C. § 300e (1973).

HMO law includes mental health services as basic benefit. (1974). *Hospital and Community Psychiatry, 25,* 257–261.

Kiesler, C. A. (2000). The next wave of change for psychology and mental health services in the health care revolution. *American Psychologist, 55,* 481–487.

Kremer, T. G., & Gesten, E. L. (1998). Confidentiality limits of managed care and clients = willingness to self-disclose. *Professional Psychology: Research and Practice, 29,* 553–558.

Levit, K. R., Freeland, M. S., & Waldo, D. R. (1990). National health care spending trends, 1988. *Health Affairs, 9*(2), 171–184.

McGuire, J., Toal, P., & Blau, B. (1985). The adult client's conception of confidentiality in the therapeutic relationship. *Professional Psychology: Research and Practice, 16,* 375–384.

Miller, I. J. (1996). Managed care is harmful to outpatient mental health services: A call for accountability. *Professional Psychology: Research and Practice, 27,* 349–363.

Murphy, M. J., DeBernardo, C. R., & Shoemaker, W. E. (1998). Impact of managed care on independent practice and professional ethics: A survey of independent practitioners. *Professional Psychology: Research and Practice, 29,* 43–51.

Nowell, D., & Spruill, J. (1993). If it's not absolutely confidential, will information be disclosed? *Professional Psychology: Research and Practice, 16,* 385–397.

Phelps, R., Eisman, E. J., & Kohout, J. (1998). Psychological practice and managed care: Results of the CAPP practitioner survey. *Professional Psychology: Research and Practice, 29,* 31–36.

Shadle, M., & Christianson, J. B. (1988). Organization of mental health care delivery in HMOs. *Administration in Mental Health, 15,* 201–225.

Shore, M. F., & Beigel, A. (1996, January 11). The challenges posed by managed behavioral health care. *New England Journal of Medicine, 334*(2), 116–119.

Strosahl, K. (1994). Entering the new frontier of managed mental health care: Gold mines and land mines. *Cognitive and Behavioral Practice, 1,* 5–23.

Tucker, L., & Lubin, W. (1994). *National survey of psychologists* (Report from Division 39, American Psychological Association). Washington, DC: American Psychological Association.

Legal Liability and Managed Care

Paul S. Appelbaum

. . .

LIABILITY IMPLICATIONS
FOR CLINICIANS

. . .

In a managed care system . . . clinicians are not always able to provide or obtain care that they believe is necessary for patients, even when that care would appear to be covered by patients' insurance. If a reviewer for the entity managing the insurer's mental health benefits concludes that the recommended care is not "medically necessary" (the standard ordinarily applied), coverage may be denied, despite the patient's not having exhausted available benefits (Hall & Anderson, 1992). Although mental health professionals have always had to deal with the problem of limited benefits, denial of coverage is now a potential problem for every insured patient, and may occur early in the course of treatment.

To demonstrate the issues that can arise for clinicians in such circumstances, consider the following hypothetical (but, as will be seen, not unimaginable) case. A depressed, suicidal patient is hospitalized, then followed in psychotherapy for two months by an outpatient clinician. The clinician believes long-term treatment is indicated to help the patient remain stable, even though the acute symptoms of depression have resolved. Adequate coverage remains under the patient's insurance plan, but the patient has no personal resources to pay for further care. An employee of the managed care entity overseeing the treatment, on the basis of a record review and a telephone discussion with the clinician, determines that further treatment is not medically necessary. Because of recent cutbacks in state funding, no public sector resources are available for patients of this sort.

What should a clinician do in a case like this? Should one continue treatment of the patient without compensation? If one is expected to extend free care to this patient, how much of one's caseload must be nonpaying before it is permissible to decline to offer such services? Or should one simply terminate the patient's care, despite one's belief that further treatment is needed to prevent relapse? If so, who will bear responsibility if the patient again becomes suicidal and injures himself or herself severely?

Such questions are usually answered by reference to the "standards of care" of the mental health professions, which evolve from the collective experience of clinicians, shaped by the recommendations of educators and experts in the field. Failure to conform to a recognized standard of care can be the basis for a finding of malpractice. Thus, clinicians concerned about reducing risks of liability naturally will want to know what their colleagues and the courts have accepted as reasonable standards of practice in situations like these.

The task of identifying appropriate standards in this case, however, is complicated by the limited opportunities clinicians and the courts have had to deal with these questions. Standards addressing previously unprecedented situations often crystallize at an agonizingly slow pace, with both the professional literature and appellate court decisions taking a decade or more to catch up to changes in practice. Moreover, standards of care are not static, but are modified continuously as new treatment techniques are developed and innovations are introduced in the delivery of care. Early data suggest that the introduction of managed care itself has led to modifications in professional standards, including marked shifts from inpatient to outpatient treatment (Thompson, Burns, Goldman, & Smith, 1992) and reductions in the number of outpatient sessions per episode of treatment (Norquist & Wells, 1991). As the approaches to mental health treatment reflected in these data become widely practiced, it is likely

From *American Psychologist, 48,* 251–257. Copyright 1993 by the American Psychological Association.

that the professions and the courts will recognize them as constituting legitimate alternative standards of care (Hall, 1989; Hirshfeld, 1990a).

. . .

Duty to Appeal Adverse Decisions

At a minimum, a clinician whose patient has been denied payment for care that he or she believes is indicated may have an obligation to contest, on the patient's behalf, the decision of the managed care entity. All such systems have some appellate procedures, and the new generation of state statutes regulating managed care practices often sets certain parameters for their availability and speed of response (American Medical Association, 1990). . . .

Even if one accepts a general obligation to advocate for patients' needs, however, several questions remain. How far must appeals be pursued? Managed care companies and insurers usually have several levels of review. Must every case be taken through the entire process? Because managed care entities are often accused of creating time-consuming procedural obstacles to discourage appeals, does the extent of a caregiver's obligation to spend uncompensated time on this process depend on the amount of time required?

Must appeals be taken in every case? Is this obligation limited to urgent or emergent situations, or does it include cases in which treatment merely would be beneficial to the patient? Perhaps most important, does the likelihood of success affect the duty? If previous appeals have always, or almost always, been rejected . . . , is a clinician obligated to try again every time? In Virginia, for example, Blue Cross/Blue Shield has a 4.6% rate of approving appeals (Task Force on Managed Health Care, 1991). Is that sufficiently high to justify a requirement that appeals always be pursued?

The answers to these questions are unclear, but there does seem to be an evolving belief that clinicians are obligated to undertake at least some efforts to obtain approval for needed treatment. Moreover, lawyers advising managed care entities on how to avoid liability for their actions (discussed more fully below) recommend that they never discontinue coverage when caregivers feel adamantly that further care is needed. Instead, they suggest the reviewers authorize care for an interim period while additional review

(perhaps by a neutral third party) takes place (Hinden & Elden, 1990). If this advice is followed, appeals are likely to have greater potency, at least over the short term, making imposition of a duty to appeal more meaningful.

What constitutes a reasonable approach from a clinician's point of view? At least an initial appeal of adverse decisions should be undertaken when a clinician believes that the treatment in question is necessary for a patient's well-being. Further levels of appeal probably should be pursued only after consultation with the patient, taking into consideration the likelihood of success, whether the patient still desires to proceed with treatment, and the availability of alternative means of paying for care. Clinicians, to this point, generally have assumed the burden of these procedures without directly seeking compensation for their time, although that may change in the future, particularly with patients who can afford to defray the cost of exceptional periods of time spent contesting adverse decisions. Many mental health professionals, in response to the greater bureaucratic demands of working with managed care systems, including appellate procedures, have shortened the standard length of treatment sessions (e.g., treatment "hours" have dropped from 50 to 45 minutes in many places) while maintaining fees at a constant level.

Duty to Disclose

Morreim (1991) has suggested that the entry of managed care into the clinical setting creates an additional obligation on caregivers to discuss with patients the economic implications of their treatment. This duty could be based on clinicians' fiduciary duties, contractual obligations, or the underlying duty to disclose information relevant to obtaining patients' informed consent.

What might such a duty include? At the initiation of therapy, clinicians might want to discuss with patients the potential effects of managed care on the course of treatment, including the possibility that payment for therapy might be terminated before either the patient or the clinician believes that the goals of treatment have been achieved. Patients who are about to embark on therapy involving painful self-disclosure and the activation of disturbing affects might well find such information important to their decision to proceed. Disclosure of the nature and extent of information that may have to be released to managed care reviewers may also be useful to patients.

When further coverage is denied, clinicians will probably need to enter into a full discussion of patients' options. Denial of coverage does not in itself mean that treatment must end. Patients may elect to pay for care out of pocket, or to proceed with therapy during the appeals process, risking in the interim being held responsible for charges accrued. Referral to alternative sources of care that are free or less expensive may also be an option.

The duty to disclose this information to patients seems neither onerous nor unreasonable. Nonetheless, it is not a duty that the courts have yet had an opportunity to rule on, and thus its legal status remains unclear.

Duty to Continue Treatment

When coverage for further treatment has been denied by a managed care entity, a clinician always retains the option of continuing to care for a patient without payment or at a reduced rate. This is obviously not an attractive option from the clinician's perspective, but there may be circumstances in which it is required, and others in which its status is unclear.

Most authorities would probably agree that when clinicians believe an emergency exists—such as in the case example above, if the patient had been acutely suicidal—there is an obligation to continue with treatment until the emergent state resolves or until an alternative provider of care can be found (Appelbaum & Gutheil, 1991). The same is true when insurance coverage is exhausted completely ("Court Finds," 1992). In principle, these situations should arise infrequently, because coverage should not be refused in such cases.

The nature of clinicians' obligations in nonemergent situations, such as in the case example, is less evident. Some court cases dating from before the managed care era indicate that, once accepting a patient for treatment, clinicians and hospitals must provide all necessary care (Marsh, 1985). Such language can be found in more recent cases as well. One opinion, rejecting the attempt of a group of psychiatrists to abrogate a managed care agreement because of alleged negative effects on patient care, noted,

"Whether or not the proposed treatment is approved, the physician retains the right and indeed the ethical and legal obligation to provide appropriate treatment to the patient" (*Varol v. Blue Cross and Blue Shield of Michigan,* 1989, p. 833).

As a matter of public policy, however, this approach makes no sense, and it is clearly not sustainable over the long run. Clinicians and hospitals cannot simply be required to provide unlimited amounts of uncompensated care. What then of the duty not to abandon patients whose care one has undertaken? It should be evident that this duty is not absolute, particularly in nonemergent situations. As has always been the case when insurance benefits expired and patients could not or would not assume responsibility for the costs of care, clinicians' obligations are limited to referral (if free or low-cost care is available) or appropriate termination. Depending on the length of time that therapy has gone on, termination may require from one to several sessions to wrap up and consolidate the gains of treatment. Inpatients, of course, will need enough time to make discharge plans. No more can be reasonably required, although it is noteworthy that this is another issue that the courts have yet to address.

The new economic realities embodied in managed care in all likelihood have created a new set of obligations for clinicians, including advocacy of their patients' interests and disclosure of the economic consequences of their treatment decisions. Unlimited responsibilities for the provision of uncompensated care, however, are not likely to be part of clinicians' duties. . . .

References

American Medical Association. (1990). Utilization review. *State Health Legislation Report, 18*(2), 30–35.

Appelbaum, P. S., & Gutheil, T. G. (1991). *Clinical handbook of psychiatry and the law* (2nd ed.) Baltimore: Williams & Wilkins.

Court finds Charter negligent in discharge of suicidal teen: Hospital will appeal. (1992, March 20). *Psychiatric News,* p. 1.

Hall, M. A. (1989). The malpractice standard under health care cost containment. *Law, Medicine, and Health Care, 17,* 347–355.

Hall, M. A., & Anderson, G. F. (1992). Health insurers' assessment of medical necessity. *University of Pennsylvania Law Review, 140,* 1637–1712.

Hinden, R. A., & Elden, D. L. (1990). Liability issues for managed care entities. *Seton Hall Legislative Journal, 14,* 1–63.

Hirshfeld, E. B. (1990a). Economic considerations in treatment decisions and the standard of care in medical malpractice litigation. *JAMA: The Journal of the American Medical Association, 264,* 2004–2012.

Institute of Medicine. (1989). *Controlling costs and changing patient care? The role of utilization management.* Washington, DC: National Academy Press.

Marsh, F. H. (1985). Health care cost containment and the duty to treat. *Journal of Legal Medicine, 6,* 157–190.

Morreim, E. H. (1991). Economic disclosure and economic advocacy: New duties in the medical standard of care. *Journal of Legal Medicine, 12,* 275–329.

Norquist, G. S., & Wells, K. B. (1991). How do HMOs reduce outpatient mental health care costs? *American Journal of Psychiatry, 148,* 96–101.

Task Force on Managed Health Care, Board of Health Professions. (1991). *Report to the Commission on Health Care for all Virginians.* Richmond: Virginia Department of Health Professions.

Thompson, J. W., Burns, B. J., Goldman, H. H., & Smith, J. (1992). Initial level of care and clinical status in a managed mental health program. *Hospital and Community Psychiatry, 43,* 599–603.

Varol v. Blue Cross and Blue Shield of Michigan, 708 F. Supp. 826 (E.D. Mich. 1989).

◆ ◆ ◆

Commentary: The hypothetical that Appelbaum presents does not suggest, in attempting to secure further treatment, the option is to exaggerate the diagnosis. In a survey of physicians reported in The New York Times, *45% of internists said that they would lie about diagnosis if an insurance company refused to pay for what the physicians considered medically necessary treatment. The more life-threatening the illness the higher the percentage of doctors who would deliberately lie. Support for deception was 32% to obtain psychiatric treatment for severe depression. See* The ethics of lying. *(1997,*

August 2). The New York Times, *p. C9. See also Buckloh, L., & Roberts, M. (2001). Managed mental health care. Attitudes and ethical beliefs of child and pediatric psychologists.* Journal of Pediatric Psychology, 26, *193–202.*

In the most relevant survey of independent practitioners, the impact of managed care was clear:

> *Results of this study suggest that the method by which a client pays for psychological services has a very strong influence on the diagnostic decisions of the psychologist providing the services. Specifically, . . . relative to clients who pay out of pocket, clients who pay via managed care are far more likely to be diagnosed with a DSM–IV disorder and are more likely to receive an adjustment disorder diagnosis in particular. (p. 192)*

Kielbasa, A. M., Pomerantz, A. M., Krohn, E. J., & Sullivan, B. F. (2004). How does clients' method of payment influence psychologists' diagnostic decisions? Ethics & Behavior, 14, *187–195.*

What provisions in the APA code would make a deliberate misdiagnosis, even for laudable ends, unethical? And would the ends always be laudable? Although increasing the severity of diagnosis to secure extended services may be seen as a proper and short-term resolution of a choice-of-evils, there may be long-term negative effects for patients. They will have official records in which they are diagnosed more severely than their condition warrants. This may affect their ability to secure certain employment positions or enter certain professions. An additional side effect comes because psychologists' reports and hospital records may contain inaccurate renditions of clinical history, current functioning, and diagnosis, making hospital records useless in supporting research.

Managed Outpatient Mental Health Plans: Clinical, Ethical, and Practical Guidelines for Participation

Leonard J. Haas and Nicholas A. Cummings

. . .

MANAGED MENTAL HEALTH CARE: UNIQUE THREAT?

. . .

There are various means to limit the access of prospective insurance policyholders or patients to a plan or to a service. These means may be examined from clinical, fiscal, and ethical perspectives, because these are the usual types of concerns expressed about such policy decisions. . . . A description of the options and relevant ethical concerns follows:

1. A plan may simply impose limitations on treatment. These limitations are for the present purposes being called *time limits,* although they are most clearly so primarily in HMOs. In other plans, time limits are translated into dollar limits. Thus, a plan could offer (as many do) a $2,000 yearly maximum for outpatient mental health coverage, occurring in a maximum of 50 sessions. In many HMOs, the limit is 20 sessions annually, with annual and lifetime cost caps. From a clinical perspective, this policy may be risky: Patients may be denied needed care that extends beyond their benefits. From a fiscal perspective, this policy is sensible. There is a known cap on the amount of financial risk the program takes (although there is the fiscal risk that patients may, justly or unjustly, accuse the program of depriving them of needed care). From an ethical perspective, the policy is problematic: It shifts the risk to the therapist, because therapists are ethically bound to care for their patients and not abandon them. Thus, to provide care to patients whose benefits have been exceeded puts the therapist in the position of needing to make a referral of the patient if

continued treatment is appropriate. Alternatively, therapists could provide *pro bono* service, although doing this frequently might eventually lower the therapist's income to an unacceptable level.

2. A plan may institute no time limits but may carefully select its policyholders so that they are unlikely to exceed some (actuarially derived) time limits or expenditure limits. This is called *skimming* (McGuire, 1989), or selecting to insure those individuals who are least likely to make a claim. . . . Ethically, the primary problem involves informed consent; as long as the program gives policyholders clear information on the limits of coverage and they are free to choose other plans, there is no coercion into inappropriate service. However, there is the more abstract ethical concern that by selecting only low-utilization patients, the plan unfairly burdens other health insurers with higher utilization patients.

3. A plan may opt for the policy of limiting access to treatment, and limiting access to the policy itself through selection criteria or marketing strategies. There is little data on this option; however, it is likely to be fiscally the safest; a clearly known financial risk is involved. It is, on the other hand, clinically risky: Unless very clear diagnostic criteria are specified, the situation is similar to Paragraph 2, just discussed; it poses the danger that a patient who needs treatment will be denied it. Such a plan is potentially ethically problematic in the same way as other treatment limits are, because it changes the therapist's role to one of resource rationer and restricts his or her ability to act in the best interests of the patient.

4. A program may impose no limitations on outpatient treatment and may offer reimbursement

(minus the copayment) to any policyholder. Although this is not a widespread policy (Cummings, 1988), it has proven viable when carefully implemented. Presumably, most plans avoid this arrangement out of fear that it expands their risks uncontrollably. This policy option is clinically safe (patients who need more extensive treatment will get it); it is economically risky (the plan has no way of limiting the amount of expenses it is exposed to); and it is ethically sound (the competent and ethical provider decides in conjunction with the patient what treatment is indicated).

. . .

CONSIDERATIONS BEFORE JOINING A MANAGED-CARE SYSTEM

First and foremost, the prospective provider in a managed-care plan must know exactly what the plan involves and what constraints it will impose. Beyond this, several features of mental health care plans should raise questions.

1. *Who takes the risks?* In the usual arrangement, the insurer takes the risks: The plan and its benefits assume a probability of particular treatment needs, and if the patient should need more treatment, the plan reimburses for it. In managed-care plans, some of this risk is shifted to the patient: If costs go above a certain level, the patient pays. In other plans, notably HMOs, some of the risk is shifted onto providers: If costs go above the limits, or if referrals to specialists become necessary, the provider's reimbursement drops. One side effect of the shifting of risk to providers is that this tempts them to hoard resources (Morreim, 1988), in the sense that they may be reluctant to refer or extend treatment if it costs them too much.

2. *How much does the plan intrude into the patient–provider relationship?* The professional who agrees to participate in a mental health care plan incurs obligations both to the plan provider and to the patient. In the traditional doctor–patient relationship, there is substantial contractual freedom. The prototypical consumer experiences a need for a service, chooses a provider from among some alternatives, and has some degree of participation in the treatment planning process (e.g., selection of procedures if alternatives are available, agreement to follow the doctor's orders if called on to do so, and informing provider if treatment appears to be working). For the prototypical provider, the relationship involves loyalty to the patient; that is, the provider has the freedom to accept or decline to treat the patient, to select appropriate treatment or treatments from among those in which he or she is competent, and then to honor his or her duty to treat the patient until the presenting problem is resolved, a referral is made, or the patient discontinues treatment. In theoretical terms, the principles of beneficence, autonomy, and justice are relevant (Beauchamp & Childress, 1988). In more conventional language, the relationship is marked by freedom and responsibility; freedom to treat as the provider sees fit, and responsibility, primarily to the patient, to resolve the presenting problem. Although some commentators have argued that this arrangement provides incentives to offer more care than necessary, others (e.g., Nelson et al., 1989) argue that it also highlights the primary loyalty of provider to consumer. The risk to the clinician participating in managed-care arrangements becomes that of balancing loyalty to the patient with responsibilities as an agent of the mental health program. If the program takes on undue risks from a particular case (e.g., the patient's care becomes too costly), the program may suffer damage, as may the therapist and other potential patients of the program.

3. *What provisions exist for exceptions to the rules?* A provider who is willing to incur the financial risk (or who works in a noncapitated arrangement) may want to continue providing treatment to a particular patient who has exceeded benefits. The provider may be tempted to change the diagnosis or the description of treatment so that the patient can be reimbursed. These maneuvers are possible in any third-party paid arrangement, of course. However, they illustrate that tightening limits on benefits may simply challenge the creativity of clinicians loyal to their patients and that the risks of altering that loyalty extend beyond simply the escalation of costs.

4. *Are there referral resources if patient needs should exceed plan benefits?* Psychologists, like other mental health professionals, have a duty to treat the patient until the presenting problem is resolved, a referral is made, or the patient discontinues treatment. To do otherwise is to abandon the patient, and this is unethical (American Psychological Association, 1990). Thus, a key question before joining a plan that limits benefits may well become, How do practitioners avoid abandoning their patients without going bankrupt?

5. *Does the plan provide assistance or training in helping the provider to achieve treatment goals?* An alternative to the dilemma just mentioned involves the clinician in becoming more knowledgeable about short-term treatment options. . . . If prospective providers have not been trained in these approaches, plans should either not select them or should make provisions to train them appropriately.

6. *Does the plan minimize economic incentives to hospitalize patients?* The "perverse incentives" noted above operate in many plans. Providers should carefully investigate their existence and perhaps lobby for alternative incentive systems.

7. *Are there ways in which the plan is open to provider input?* Given the proliferation of benefit options and plan arrangements, it is essential that some feedback mechanisms be built into these plans. Otherwise, the provider becomes simply an employee rather than a professional treating patients.

8. *Do plans clearly inform their policyholders of the limits of benefits?* Just as providers have loyalties to both other parties in the system, they should avoid being trapped in the middle, having to explain benefit limits to naive patients after the benefit limits have been reached.

Of course, the ideal policy for a managed mental health care program is one that does not create dual loyalties among therapists and that provides benefits both to specific patients in need of services and to potential patients who may require program resources in the future. This is a difficult policy option to implement because pressing immediate needs are those most likely to claim our loyalties even though alleviating present needs may increase the suffering of patients who will have needs in the future. . . .

ADDITIONAL ETHICAL ISSUES

Consideration of additional ethical issues in managed mental health care plans brings several to the forefront. First. . . . the issue of competence is crucial. Consistent with the ethical obligation to offer services within the domain of their competence, psychologists must be capable of delivering service in a time-limited context if they are to be involved in managed-care plans.

Second is the issue of informed consent. The prospective patient must be given clear information about the benefits to which he or she is entitled and clear information about the limits of treatment as the clinician envisions them.

A third issue of ethical importance concerns divided loyalties. Third-party payment arrangements always elicit such issues, but never so clearly as in managed mental health care plans. The principal of fidelity (Beauchamp & Childress, 1988) demands that the provider or professional be loyal to those with whom he or she has a contractual relationship. Thus, if a therapist agrees to work in a managed health care program, he or she should believe in the service philosophy it endorses. If the therapist agrees to work with a particular patient, he or she should be loyal to that patient's interests (this is part of what is meant by a fiduciary relationship). The Ethical Principles of Psychologists . . . focuses on fidelity . . . in terms of the psychologist's obligation to obtain informed consent from consumers, and on avoiding relationships in which there is a conflict of interest that may impair his or her objectivity. On this last point, the Ethical Principles of Psychologists . . . is also clear. When demands of an organization conflict with the ethics code, psychologists attempt to bring the conflict to the attention of relevant parties and resolve it. In this case, the conflict would likely be between the demands of the plan that reimbursement for treatment cease or change versus the needs of the patient and the psychologist's ethical responsibility to act for the benefit of the client ("welfare of the consumer"). Psychologists may have a corollary obligation to ensure that plans with which they are associated have mechanisms to receive their input and recommendations for change. . . .

References

Beauchamp, T., & Childress, W. (1988). *Principles of biomedical ethics* (3rd ed.). Baltimore: Johns Hopkins University Press.

Cummings, N. A. (1988). Emergence of the mental health complex: Adaptive and maladaptive responses. *Professional Psychology: Research and Practice, 19,* 308–315.

Haas, L. J., & Malouf, J. L. (1989). *Keeping up the good work: A practitioner's guide to mental health ethics.* Sarasota, FL: Professional Resource Exchange.

McGuire, T. G. (1989). Outpatient benefits for mental health services in Medicare: Alignment with the private sector? *American Psychologist, 44,* 818–824.

Morreim, E. H. (1988). Cost containment: Challenging fidelity and justice. *Hastings Center Report, 18,* 20–25.

Considerations for Ethical Practice in Managed Care

Catherine Acuff, Bruce E. Bennett, Patricia M. Bricklin, Mathilda B. Canter, Samuel J. Knapp, Stanley Moldawsky, and Randy Phelps

[*Ed. Note:* This article contains many references to provisions in the 1992 Ethics Code. To make the article current, I have substituted for those, the numbers of the equivalent or substantially similar 2002 Ethics Code standards.]

. . .

The business emphasis in the current health care marketplace on "units of work" (therapy hours) and "commodity prices" (fees) by the "provider" (psychologist) represents a language and set of values that are alien to many practitioners. Many psychologists experience considerable discomfort over their professional roles and organizational expectations when business standards and incentives conflict with professional values and ethics.

. . .

We review general considerations in ethical decision making and problem solving. . . . We also examine four areas, or domains, in which ethical dilemmas most commonly arise for psychologists working in or with organized systems of care: informed consent, confidentiality, abandonment, and utilization management–utilization review. Hypothetical examples are provided to illustrate many of the issues and dilemmas encountered in the managed care environment.

GENERAL CONSIDERATIONS

Many practitioners are experiencing dilemmas or are raising questions about their ethical obligations because some MCOs [managed care organizations] deny authorization for needed treatment, fail to respect patient privacy, restrict communications between psychologists and their patients, or are perceived as attempting to intimidate psychologists through the use of "no cause termination" clauses.

Although these practices are not engaged in by every MCO, they are clearly problematic when they occur. In addition, psychologists who are increasingly entering into capitated contracts or working on a case-rate basis face the problem of delivering quality health care services within a very limited budget. And, one impact of marketplace changes in general, and of managed care in particular, has been to curtail drastically the availability of psychological assessment and long-term therapy, two of psychology's most significant modalities. Finally, the competitiveness embodied in the managed care marketplace has changed the tenor of professional relationships within the health care industry. Psychologists face competing demands as they try to meet their ethical obligations while providing services in a changing environment.

The following vignette illustrates a dilemma regarding the competing demands of capitation and one way in which a hypothetical group of psychologists may deal with these demands.

VIGNETTE 1

Situation

The Acme Psychological Center, a private corporation owned by 10 psychologists, has just been awarded a large capitated contract, which starts in 1 month. When the new plan takes effect, 30% of the Center's patient caseload will be either entirely self-pay or under fee-for-service insurance, 30% will be under other managed care plans, and 40% will be under the new capitated plan.

Issue

The owners, being ethical psychologists, are concerned that they do not put profits above patient welfare in the capitated contract. They have assigned

From *Professional Psychology: Research and Practice, 30,* 563–575. Copyright 1999 by the American Psychological Association.

one of the practice partners, Dr. Anne Ethical, to propose internal procedures to ensure that patient welfare will not be compromised.

Discussion and Response

Dr. Ethical wants to ensure that the recommendations will reduce the temptation to compromise patient care. In the proposal she sent to the other group members, Dr. Ethical recommended that (a) all patients will be given access to an internal utilization review process if they are dissatisfied with the treatment plan or services offered to them. The utilization review process includes input from a respected outside psychologist who has no financial ties to the group practice; (b) the informed consent brochure given to incoming patients informs them of the potential for conflict of interest and of the internal utilization review process; (c) the practice will develop an internal monitoring system that looks at the length of patient care in the nonmanaged care and managed care (capitated) reimbursement systems. The owners will monitor their behavior to ensure that the capitated patients are not subjected to a systematic downgrading of their treatment; (d) outcome measures and satisfaction forms will be used for both the capitated and noncapitated patient populations; and (e) the owners will agree that the sharing of profits depends, in part, on the results of the outcomes and patient satisfaction data.

A CRITICAL DISTINCTION

The terms *ethics* and *ethical* can have various connotations depending on the context in which they are used. For example, the term *ethical* may refer to overarching moral principles, such as autonomy, beneficence (doing good for others), nonmaleficence (doing no harm), fidelity, and justice.

In a more narrow sense, the term *ethical* may refer to the "APA Ethical Principles of Psychologists and Code of Conduct" . . . or to codes of ethics adopted by state boards of psychology. These codes of conduct mandate or prohibit specific actions and they may have the force of law. MCOs' actions often seem to offend the "ethics" of many practitioners and the public in the first sense of the term; that is, they are seen as morally outrageous. In this article we

evaluate psychologists' ethical questions in the second sense of the word; that is, in the context of managed care in accordance with the APA Ethics Code.

No code of ethics, however well written, can anticipate all of the various situations in which psychologists may confront ethical dilemmas, and no code of ethics may be able to specify concrete actions for the psychologist to follow in all situations. Consequently, some of the possible ethical conflicts faced by psychologists have no clear solution and require psychologists to engage in an ethical decision process involving the balancing of competing ethical standards. The challenges presented by MCOs make it more important than ever for psychologists to familiarize themselves with the APA Ethics Code and relevant state laws.

Several studies reveal that a majority of practitioners believe managed care has created ethical dilemmas for most psychologists (Murphy, DeBernardo, & Shoemaker, 1998; Phelps, Eisman, & Kohout, 1998; Rothbaum, Bernstein, Haller, Phelps, & Kohout, 1998). Despite these beliefs, our task force found, on the basis of our own survey of state licensing boards and state association ethics committees, that there have been few adjudicated cases dealing specifically with alleged violations arising from psychological practice related to managed care. This suggests that psychologists who participate in managed care arrangements may use the term *ethics* to refer to their personal moral outrage toward the rules and limitations imposed by the managed care system, rather than to actual violations of the APA Ethics Code. In other words, an MCO's requirements may create limitations for the client and difficult situations for the psychologist, but these problems may not always rise to the level of an actual violation of the APA Ethics Code.

. . .

VIGNETTE 2

Situation

Dr. F. Russ Stration is working with a patient who consulted him following an initial panic attack. At the first session, as part of his normal consent procedure, Dr. Stration reviewed with the patient her MCO benefit. He informed her that this particular MCO requires treatment reports every third session, which might include disclosure of his session notes and treatment summaries. He developed a treatment plan that he reviewed with the patient before submitting it to the MCO.

Several days before the second session, Dr. Stration called the MCO about the status of his request for approval of the treatment plan. The MCO case manager explained that the normal response time for nonemergent care approval was 2 weeks but that he would try to have an answer for Dr. Stration as soon as possible. By the time of the second session, Dr. Stration still had not heard from the MCO and found himself unable to tell the patient whether their third session would be the last under her benefit or whether additional sessions would be allowed. As of the third session, the patient appeared to be benefiting from the treatment interventions; she reported no further panic attacks and said she felt an increased sense of well-being. Dr. Stration told her he would call her when he heard from the MCO, scheduled a tentative fourth session contingent on plan approval, and discussed with her the availability of a local support group should further treatment be denied.

Issue

Dr. Stration was angry over this situation and feared that the uncertainty of further treatment would be detrimental to therapy. Although he felt that he had done all he could for this patient, he believed that the MCO case manager was acting unethically and he was outraged.

Discussion

Dr. Stration's feelings of distress over this situation may be familiar to many psychologists. Despite these feelings, Dr. Stration has dealt effectively with the ethical issues that could have arisen. By conducting an extensive discussion with the patient at the outset of therapy, Dr. Stration has met his obligation in structuring the relationship (Standard 10.10), providing informed consent to treatment (Standard 3.10), explaining the limits of confidentiality (Standard 4.02), and disclosing information appropriately (Standard 4.05). He has also planned for facilitating care in the event that psychological services are interrupted (Standard 3.12), and offered an appro-

priate alternative (Standard 10.10) should treatment terminate because of the MCO's refusal to authorize continued care.

Response

Dr. Stration should review his contract with the MCO regarding response time for treatment requests. If the MCO has violated the contract, he could protest the lack of timely response, as well as support the patient in protesting to her employer's benefits manager. Otherwise, his response to the MCO's procedures may best be categorized as moral outrage, and one course of action may be to engage in advocacy efforts to make known his feelings to legislators and others who can affect managed care policies and procedures.

. . .

VIGNETTE 3

Situation

Dr. R. E. Search evaluates a 10-year old hyperactive boy with behavioral problems in school. He also interviews the parents. Dr. Search then recommends therapy for the child, a referral for evaluation of specific medication as an adjunct to treatment, and adjunctive therapy for the parents. The parents agree to the plan. During utilization review, the MCO's reviewer states that medication should be prescribed for the boy and that psychotherapy will not be authorized.

Issue

Dr. Search is faced with a denial of the treatment plan that, in his professional judgment, is in the best interest of the patient.

Discussion

Dr. Search has an ethical obligation to his patient within the context of the professional relationship that has been established. The highest aspirational goals of the profession call him to act according to the patient's welfare (Principle E). To the extent that he believes the MCO's recommended treatment will harm the patient, Standard 1.14 is applicable.

Response

Dr. Search's response may include any of the following: (a) submitting a written appeal to the MCO,

(b) presenting literature to the reviewer indicating that medication without psychotherapy is not as effective as combined therapy, (c) explaining to the parents that he does not agree with the reviewer's recommendation and that the parents may wish to appeal the decision as well, and (d) engaging in advocacy efforts such as writing a letter to the editor of a newspaper, calling the MCO to task for just trying to save costs and not attending to the quality care needed for the patient.

If the MCO's utilization reviewer is a psychologist, he or she should review the relevant data and information regarding appropriate treatment for the described disorder. The issue is whether the recommendation to prescribe medication only would be considered to be below the prevailing "standard of care." If so, then the reviewer is behaving unethically by recommending a treatment plan that is below the standard and not supported by the professional literature or community.

VIGNETTE 4 [OMITTED]

. . .

AN ETHICAL DECISION-MAKING PROCESS

The drastic change in the context of psychological practice over the past decade has made it necessary for psychologists to renew their familiarity with the APA Ethics Code and to use a deliberative process in applying it to current dilemmas. However, ethical dilemmas all too often lack clear-cut right or wrong answers. In fact, different solutions, all of them appropriate to the individual circumstances, may well be arrived at by different people at different times.

Moreover, there are times when, after a search for answers in the Ethics Code, professional guidelines, and related documents, and through consultation with colleagues, no clear resolution to a dilemma is apparent. This is one reason for developing decision-making processes for ethical problem solving. . . .

Because decision making is so important, below are a series of questions that a psychologist facing a managed care dilemma of ethical dimensions might ask himself or herself and their answers, which may help the psychologist to decide on a possible course of action.

1. What are my personal ethics on similar issues?
2. What is my gut-level opinion on a possible course of action? Awareness of personal ethics and understanding of gut-level or intuitive responses to any given situation are necessary before the psychologist can proceed to examine rationally the next seven questions.
3. Is this truly an ethical dilemma, or is it a business, technical, or other problem?
4. Is this a dilemma that I cannot resolve? Does it require systems change and/or organizational advocacy, or legal or legislative action? The answer to these questions may direct the psychologist to the importance of consultation and group advocacy in resolving many dilemmas of managed care. This question is particularly important in managed care settings. If the psychologist's answer to this question is *yes*, then the recognition that this is not a dilemma the psychologist alone can solve is helpful and frees the psychologist to consult or participate in advocacy or other actions more likely to lead to resolution of the dilemmas.
5. If it is an ethical dilemma, who are the persons who have a legitimate stake in the resolution of the dilemma?
6. What are the relevant ethical standards or principles?
7. Is a psychological or legal consultation needed?
8. Are there compelling reasons to deviate from the ethical standard?
9. What are the overarching ethical principles involved (e.g., patient autonomy, doing good for others, doing no harm, justice or fidelity)? . . . It is at this point that prioritization of those major principles is critical: the patient's rights to make autonomous decisions versus a psychologist's belief about what is good for the patient versus issues of trust, confidentiality, and truthfulness versus the overriding "above all, do no harm."

Depending on the answers to these questions, the final steps involve generating possible courses of action, evaluating, and choosing among them. At this point the psychologist asks two questions: Is this plan of action ethical and Is it implementable? Above all, psychologists must recognize which dilemmas are beyond the power of an individual acting alone. . . .

DOMAINS

We have identified four domains in which ethical dilemmas most commonly arise for psychologists working in or with organized systems of care: (1) informed consent, (2) confidentiality, (3) abandonment, and (4) utilization management.

Informed Consent

. . .

The patient's confidence and trust in the psychologist constitute an essential component of successful psychotherapy. In this context, it is not surprising that confusion on the part of the patient may easily lead to dissatisfaction and anger. Misunderstandings and miscommunications between the psychologist and the patient may interfere with the course of therapy and may lead the patient to develop ill feeling toward the psychologist.

Regardless of the type of health care service provided—or the setting in which the service is delivered—informed consent is an essential aspect of modern-day practice. Informed consent is such a fundamental part of health care that it is now required by APA Ethics Code. . . . Because some MCOs do not provide full, complete, and accurate information to their subscribers, many patients are not fully aware of the complexities of managed care arrangements and how these arrangements affect their benefits and rights. Psychologists must be especially attentive to informed consent issues when working with these patients. However, individual psychologists cannot be held accountable for the array of managed care arrangements in the current marketplace. Psychologists may need to turn to APA or their state organizations for advocacy to ensure that benefits provided by an MCO are those that are publicly declared in the patient's contracts.

. . .

Informed consent, fees, and financial arrangements. To avoid confusion or misunderstanding, it is important that the psychologist reach an agreement with the patient specifying the compensation and the billing

arrangements to be used (Standard 6.04 [a]). The agreement should address the psychologist's billing practices for ancillary services, such as testing, report writing, professional consultation, voluntary or required court appearances, and other related procedures that may be provided by the psychologist.

The psychologist is also required by the Ethics Code to discuss any limitation on services that may be anticipated due to limitations in financing (Standard 6.04 [d]). Such limitations may result from contractual obligations in the patient's managed care program. It is helpful for psychologists to understand and be able to convey to their patients such information as: (1) the MCO's provisions related to the number of authorized sessions, (2) the method and timing of utilization review, (3) the nature of the information required by the MCO to authorize services, (4) the amount of reimbursement provided, (5) the patient's share of any expenses (deductible or copayment), (6) the services that are covered or excluded, (7) the responsibility for payment if the MCO determines that a particular service is not covered under the patient's plan, and (8) any other foreseeable financial matters.

Informed consent and role clarification. Frequently, psychologists find themselves in conflicting roles when providing professional services, especially in a managed care setting. For example, psychologists who provide services under a capitated arrangement may feel increased pressure to limit treatment in order to sustain profits. When such conflicts occur or are foreseeable, the psychologist should attempt to clarify the situation with the parties involved and delineate the role(s) that the psychologist can and cannot perform. These role clarification issues take on greater significance when providing couples, marital, or family therapy because of the increased complexity when multiple parties are involved (Standards 3.07, 10.02, and 3.05).

Informed consent and confidentiality. Confidentiality is an essential ingredient in the therapeutic relationship. It is important that the patient be fully informed about professional and legal obligations that may require the psychologist to release sensitive patient information to the MCO as a part of utilization review or for determination of necessity of treatment

(Standard 5.05). If it is foreseeable that the information obtained in the course of delivering services may be used for these or other purposes, the patient should be made aware of this fact. The discussion of confidentiality should occur at the initial stages of treatment and thereafter as new issues arise in therapy. Special confidentiality provisions are involved when the psychologist is providing couples, marital, family, or group therapy (Standard 4.02).

Informed Consent Recommendations

The following are specific recommendations regarding informed consent. Standards of the APA Ethics Code are referenced where appropriate.

1. Psychologists should be aware that informed consent is an ethical requirement (Standard 3.10).
2. Psychologists should provide informed consent, which, at a minimum, includes (a) information regarding fees and other potential costs of services . . . ; (b) responsibility for payment . . . ; (c) type of service and anticipated number of sessions (Standards 3.11 and 10.01); (d) any contractual limitations on the services provided (Standard 6.04 [d]); (e) record keeping, including electronic storage and transfer, release of information, and confidentiality (Standards 6.01 and 4.02); and (f) the roles that the psychologist can and cannot play (Standards 3.05, 3.07, and 10.02).
3. When working with a patient who is part of a managed care arrangement, the psychologist should review with the patient any information that will be provided to the MCO for purposes of utilization review or quality assurance (Standard 4.05).
4. Because informed consent is an ongoing process, issues should be addressed at the onset of services and thereafter, as appropriate. For example, the patient should be informed if his or her MCO requires reauthorization information.
5. Psychologists may want to consider using a written document for establishing informed consent. An example is the "Psychotherapist–Patient Informed Consent Contract" (Harris & Bennett, 1998). Psychologists are advised to consult with an attorney prior to using such a document to ensure that it is in compliance with local and state statutes.

Confidentiality

. . .

Exceptions to confidentiality have always existed. For decades, even under indemnity arrangements, insurance companies have required the psychologist to provide the patient's diagnosis and, at times, the treatment plan prior to paying for the service. The legal system similarly places limits on confidentiality to serve the interests of justice and the public welfare. For example, mandatory child-abuse-reporting statutes are found in all states. Nevertheless, the strong demand for patient information inherent in managed care systems far exceeds these previous provisions and threatens the confidentiality of the psychologist–patient relationship, potentially reducing the quality of patient care.

MCOs, for example, may require patients to reveal sensitive and affect-laden information to case managers or intake workers before authorizing initial or additional treatment, or when transferring a patient from one provider to another. It is not unheard of for an MCO to require a practitioner to submit all treatment records before payment is made. More often, MCOs use standard forms that may solicit more information than is typically required for the development of an effective treatment plan. Some MCO policies require certain information from all patients on the premise that they need access to this information to monitor patient care. This requirement may lead psychologists reluctantly to place more information in the records than may be necessary.

It is assumed that the patient has consented to release this type of information because insureds will typically have signed release forms when first enrolled in the managed care plan (except in the case where the MCO requires the provider to obtain the release). However, the insured rarely understands the extent to which the release permits private information to be shared, so it is incumbent on the psychologist to inform the patient in this regard. Unless the release is revoked by the patient, it will probably be effective, so the psychologist may release the information if required by law. Psychologists should be aware of the applicable confidentiality laws specific to their state.

MCOs sometimes demand inspection of a psychologists' records of nonbeneficiaries before they will credential the psychologist as a member of the

MCO panel. Although psychologists risk exclusion from panels for failure to comply with this standard, there are no exceptions to confidentiality that allow client information to be revealed without written consent under these circumstances. In this situation, redacted records should be acceptable to the MCO. If not, the psychologist may want to pursue other alternatives with the MCO, such as challenging the request on ethical grounds, offering to provide a fictitious sample record, or offering to share an MCO's patient record after becoming a member of the MCO panel and receiving the referral, following patient consent.

Some MCO contracts state that the MCO owns the patient's records. The psychologist is advised to review all managed care contracts related to record ownership. Again, the psychologist should be aware of applicable state confidentiality laws.

With ongoing buyouts and mergers in the health care industry, no one has assurances regarding the ultimate disposition of confidential patient information. Information that a psychologist might have once been able to hold in confidence may now be open to review or entry into databases. The mental health information may be comingled with other health care information. The disclosure of mental health information may be more problematic than the disclosure of general health information because of the risk of greater stigmatization.

Confidentiality Recommendations

The following are specific recommendations regarding confidentiality. Standards of the APA Ethics Code are referenced where appropriate.

1. Psychologists should inform patients as soon as feasible at the outset of treatment about the relevant limits of confidentiality under their managed care policy. Patients should be made aware that psychologists have no control over confidential information after it leaves their offices. . . .
2. It may not be clinically indicated or feasible in all situations for psychologists to share with patients all information that will be released to the MCO. However, the usual rule of thumb is that patients should know generally what is being released. There should be appropriate consent prior to the release of this information. . . .
3. Because of the potential for abuses of confidential information by MCOs, psychologists need to consider what they place in clinical records. Psychologists can obtain guidance on record keeping from the APA's "Record Keeping Guidelines" . . . , regulations from their state boards of psychology, or various ethics texts and articles (Standards 4.04 and 6.02).
4. Psychologists who perform utilization reviews are held to the same ethical standards as psychologists who provide direct treatment. They may not share patient information without written consent and are entitled only to as much information as is necessary to fulfill their professional duties (Standards 4.04 and 4.06).
5. Psychologists should be aware of and make accommodations for the threats to confidentiality inherent in newer modes of information transmission and storage such as fax and electronic mail communication, computerized databases, and so forth (Standards 6.02).
6. Psychologists should read managed care contracts carefully to determine their obligations related to confidential information including who, under the terms of the contract, owns the records and has control over their release. Psychologists also should be aware of the limits on confidentiality governed by applicable state laws. . . .
7. Without written permission from the patient, psychologists may not allow MCOs to inspect patient records (Standard 4.05). Psychologists should be aware that the patient may have signed a waiver to permit records inspection by the MCO.[1]

VIGNETTE 5 [OMITTED]

ABANDONMENT

Abandonment, the abrupt or unwanted discontinuation of treatment during a time of need, is a potential ethical and legal cause of action and may lead to harm

---

[1]Ed. Note: See discussion of psychotherapy notes in HIPAA excerpt.

of the patient. Although current marketplace trends limiting treatment may affect continuity of care, thereby increasing the potential for abandonment, it should be noted that the issue of abandonment also predates managed care. Abandonment can include the precipitous termination of a patient in crisis because of nonpayment for services. Abandonment may also arise if psychologists do not have sufficient coverage during weekends, out-of-office hours, vacations, or educational leaves. The APA Ethics Code provides guidance on these issues (Standards 10.09 and 10.10).

Although the cost containment practices of MCOs are not inherently unethical, they have led to increased concerns about patient abandonment. Psychologists working in organized systems of care are often concerned that the institution or the MCO's session limit will necessitate termination with patients who need more treatment. Psychologists are also concerned that such terminations may be violations of legal and ethical standards that prohibit patient abandonment. Moreover, many MCOs have closed panels, and psychologists face dilemmas when their patients change health care coverage to a company in which the psychologist is not an impaneled provider. And, as companies consolidate or as new MCOs enter the market, psychologists must be concerned about disruption of treatment with existing patients.

Unfortunately, the industrialization of health care has created financial incentives to limit treatment even when, in the psychologist's opinion, treatment is clinically indicated and the patient desires more treatment. These arrangements may limit the ability of psychologists and patients to work collaboratively to complete treatment successfully within a realistic time frame. Overly restrictive limits on sessions or benefits may result in the interruption of needed services to a particular patient. These incentives to limit care may occur when (a) MCOs contract directly with psychologists as providers, (b) MCOs limit the ability of psychologists to contract independently with patients covered under the MCO contract, or (c) psychologists work under a capitated contract with an MCO.

MCOs Contract Directly With Psychologists

Even when psychologists have directly contracted as providers for MCOs, they should only accept patients whom they believe they can benefit. That decision may depend on the match between the needs of the patient and the expertise of the psychologist (Standards 2.01 and 2.03), as well as the ability of the patient (or the patient's insurer) to meet the financial requirements of the treatment. One factor to consider is whether the benefit will allow the psychologist sufficient time to diagnose and treat the problem or otherwise benefit the patient. Such decisions may be difficult because the primary issue for which the person sought treatment may not turn out to be the primary focus of therapy. External stressors may lead to a precipitous decline in the functioning of the patient, or the true nature of the problem may not be discernible until therapy has been underway for some time. Nevertheless, to the extent feasible, the psychologist and patient need to discuss the anticipated needs of the patient and the ability of the MCO or the patient to pay for needed services.

Even after a patient is accepted into therapy, an MCO may discontinue reimbursement for a variety of reasons. At these times, if in the psychologist's opinion the patient still needs treatment, the psychologist may be obligated to appeal, or to encourage a patient to appeal, those decisions (see section on Utilization Management–Utilization Review).

When patients without financial resources require additional treatment, psychologists may refer them to public agencies or self-help groups, develop a deferred or reduced payment plan, schedule sessions less frequently or of shorter duration if clinically appropriate, or use other strategies to ensure access to care. Bartering may also be a consideration, but psychologists should be familiar with Standard 1.18 of the APA Ethics Code. The exact nature of the psychologist's recommendations involves both clinical and financial considerations.

Regarding coverage situations, an MCO contract may not permit the psychologist a full range of colleagues to use for coverage while the psychologist is absent. For example, coverage arrangements may be restricted to the MCO's provider panel. In that instance, arranging coverage can be particularly challenging when a psychologist's caseload consists of patients from several MCOs. Psychologists need to consider this possible issue when deciding to sign a managed care contract.

Prohibition on Private Fee Arrangements

Most MCOs permit psychologists who are network providers to enter into private fee arrangements with patients for noncovered services. However, some do not. Psychologists should look for these clauses in MCO contracts and should consider them when making long-term plans for the care of patients.

Psychologists Directly Hold Capitated Contracts

Some MCOs hire psychologists and other mental health professionals on a fee-for-service basis. Other MCOs may "carve out" behavioral health care services through capitated arrangements with subcontractors, including group practices in which psychologists have a personal financial risk that may depend, in part, on the type and length of treatment provided patients. The very nature of these arrangements places the psychologist in a potential conflict of interest with his or her patients because the psychologist's business interests may be advanced to the detriment of the patient through the withholding of care. Psychologists should inform patients when they are involved in any financial arrangements that might serve as an incentive to potentially limit care (see earlier section on Informed Consent).

Abandonment Recommendations

The following are specific recommendations regarding abandonment. Standards of the APA Ethics Code are referenced where appropriate.

1. Patients should not be abandoned during periods of crisis. . . .
2. Psychologists are aware that emergency, weekend, or after-hours coverage may be required for some patients . . . , and they should make necessary arrangements for this coverage. Particularly

for managed care patients, it may be necessary to consider other impaneled providers when making coverage arrangements.

3. When patients without financial resources need more treatment, psychologists should attempt to help them find alternative ways to receive the needed treatment (Standards 6.05 and 10.10).
4. Psychologists should read MCO contracts carefully to understand any limits on coverage. They should also be aware of the appeal mechanism(s) in the contract and pay attention to any other clauses that could limit patient care (Standards 1.02, 10.01, 3.10, and 1.03).
5. Psychologists should inform patients if the contract includes financial incentives to limit care. Although capitation arrangements are not inherently unethical, psychologists with financial incentives to deny care are advised to develop quality control mechanisms that minimize the likelihood that patient welfare would be compromised (Standards 2.06, 3.04, and Principle A). (See Vignette 1 for examples.)

VIGNETTE 6

Situation

Dr. Greatheart and her patient are close to reaching their therapy goals when the patient is diagnosed as having breast cancer and becomes emotionally distraught. The therapist requests authorization for additional sessions, but the MCO denies the request because the patient's benefits have been exhausted. The patient suggests that Dr. Greatheart continue to see her by naming her husband as the patient, because he had not used his benefits at all.

Issue

Dr. Greatheart knows that continued psychological treatment could make a significant difference for the patient during this difficult time and is aware that the APA Ethics Code makes it clear that psychologists may not abandon patients in crisis (Standard 4.09).[2] The issue for Dr. Greatheart is how to meet her ethical and professional responsibilities to her patient given the MCO's denial.

---

[2]*Ed. Note:* But now see Commentary following this excerpt.

Discussion

Initially, Dr. Greatheart is frustrated with the MCO, but she realizes that the denial of additional sessions is based on her patient reaching the contractual benefit limit. This is a different situation than one where an MCO denies sessions for other reasons (e.g., additional treatment does not meet their definition of *medical necessity*) and is an issue that psychologists have faced many times in the past (e.g., with uninsured patients or when patients with indemnity insurance reached the benefit limit). Therefore, the situation is not limited to managed care arrangements.

Even though the benefit is exhausted, it is possible that an appeal may be successful, and Dr. Greatheart may wish to consider this option. MCOs often have a multistage appeals process, ranging from the utilization reviewer to a clinical peer or equivalent and finally to the clinical director.

If the MCO contract permits, Dr. Greatheart could also consider seeing the patient on a private basis at her usual and customary fee, a reduced fee, or on a pro bono basis. She may also consider making a referral to an appropriate community resource for therapy. Additionally, she may refer the patient to the local American Cancer Society chapter for assistance and available peer support groups. In the absence of community resources, she may involve herself in advocacy efforts within her state or local psychological association or other community groups (e.g., United Way, city council, and other arenas) for funding for the development of appropriate community resources.

Response

In this situation, Dr. Greatheart should make arrangements to see that the patient's needs for continuity of care are considered to the extent feasible. Psychologists should not falsify information in the interests of providing patient care. This patient's suggestion that the psychologist continue to see her, but name her husband as the patient, is not acceptable. For Dr. Greatheart to collude in this fashion could be considered fraud.

UTILIZATION MANAGEMENT–UTILIZATION REVIEW

Utilization management (UM), in the broadest sense and under different names, is not new to psychol-ogy. Psychologists have been making UM decisions ethically and professionally for decades. UM involves making decisions regarding types of treatment, setting, and treatment duration in the delivery of professional services, and has occurred in both the public and the private sectors. UM also involves other such clinical functions as supervision, consultation, case staffing, peer review, and case studies.

Utilization review (UR), one form of UM, is in and of itself neither ethical nor unethical. In the past, the primary focus of utilization management was to serve the best interests of the patient or client. For years, public mental health agencies have engaged in heroic efforts to provide quality services to patients with limited budgets and serious financial restrictions. Today, there is a legitimate need to control health care costs, and some MCOs are interested in the quality of care provided while being responsive to this need. However, the high profits awarded CEOs of some MCOs and the emphasis on earnings within the for-profit MCOs suggest that the normal outrage of many psychologists who decry UR does have some rational basis. Also, some psychologists working as utilization reviewers within managed care systems may face a built-in conflict-of-interest as pressures for cost containment and profit motives compete with, and may well override, quality of care priorities in their decision making.

The applicability of the APA Ethics Code to UM-UR functions depends on the financial incentives involved and the issues to be considered in the decision-making process. When psychologist–reviewers exercise professional judgment in performing UR services they may be performing a health care procedure as opposed to a benefits management procedure. Thus, the type of service performed (e.g., health care vs. benefits decisions) will determine the ethical obligations of the psychologist. When professional judgment is required, and the psychologist is free to exercise discretion determining the number of sessions allowed—as opposed to purely routine administrative functions such as determining the number of sessions remaining in the plan benefit—ethical obligations to the patient ensue.

Psychologist–reviewers and providers are in the most precarious situation when the UR procedures provide financial incentives to deny treatment (e.g., in capitated arrangements or when the reviewer is employed by an MCO where the primary goal of the UR may be cost saving, rather than quality service provision). If the employer's benefit package limits the benefit to a specific number of sessions, the psychologist–provider should offer the best service possible, given the limits of the benefit.

On the other hand, if the design of the benefit is unlimited, or the limit of benefits has not yet been reached when UR is instituted, the psychologist–reviewer is exercising professional judgment in authorizing or denying treatment. Whereas containing costs may be one of the MCO's objectives, it is only one of many criteria that should guide the reviewer's decision to deny or continue care. Patient needs should remain paramount, though they should be met in a cost-effective manner.

RECOMMENDATIONS FOR PSYCHOLOGISTS PERFORMING UTILIZATION MANAGEMENT AND REVIEW

As noted earlier, UR may involve a primarily administrative function, such as determining if a particular service is covered by the MCO contract. However, UR often requires psychologists to exercise professional judgment to determine if the treatment is "medically necessary," or to determine the type of service or number of sessions needed to help the patient. Such clinical decision making in UR is a professional service and is subject to ethical standards and requirements for ethical practice. Relevant sections of the Ethics Code include all under Standard 3.0, particularly 3.04, Avoiding Harm.

1. Psychologists are advised to be cautious about entering into employment with MCOs that appear to base UR decisions primarily or solely on cost containment or profit motives, rather than on quality of care.
2. Prior to accepting employment with an MCO, psychologists are advised to read carefully both their contracts and the MCO's UR-UM policies. They are also cautioned to review renewal contracts and policy changes (Standards 1.02 and 1.03).

3. When psychologists who are functioning as utilization reviewers respond to requests for additional care of patients, they should be flexible in applying criteria for continuing care. Their decisions should be based on patient needs within the framework of the benefits stipulated in the contract (Standards 3.04, Principle A, and 6.04).
4. When performing UR that requires professional judgment and allows discretion, psychologists may be providing professional services. They should perform these services within the boundaries of their competence. Because the reviewer is called on to make clinical judgments without having direct contact with the patient, it is particularly important to attend to the basis on which "medical necessity" is determined in reaching these decisions (Standards 2.01, 2.03, 2.04, and 9.02).

. . .

RECOMMENDATIONS FOR PSYCHOLOGISTS DELIVERING PROFESSIONAL SERVICES SUBJECT TO UTILIZATION REVIEW

Many psychologists are not employed by MCOs but have contracted to provide professional services to patients with health care benefits administered by MCOs. The following specific recommendations are provided for these psychologists. Standards of the APA Ethics Code are referenced where appropriate.

1. When an MCO denies needed care, psychologists should assist the patient in trying to obtain the needed services. This may require working with the patient to appeal the decision or writing to the clinical director to notify the MCO of the potential adverse consequences to the patient. It may also involve exploring other options available outside of the MCO (Standards 3.04, 3.10, 3.12, and 10.10).
2. When psychologists believe that an MCO's authorization for treatment is less than appropriate care, they should consider other available options and possible consequences for the patient's welfare and should act in the best interests of the patient within their ethical obligations. It is

577

important to inform and discuss with the patient the implications of any decisions being made. The decision may be to appeal the MCO's decision or to accept the UR determination and proceed with the authorized treatment. Of course, it is essential that the treating psychologist has an adequate clinical basis for the appeal. Whatever the psychologist and patient decide to do, it should be based on helping and not harming the patient (Standards 3.04, 3.10, and 3.12).

SUMMARY

. . .

In trying to sort out whether there is an actual or potential violation of the APA Ethics Code, the individual psychologist will have to seek his or her answer through careful application of a systematic problem-solving and decision-making process, including consultation with peers who are knowledgeable about the Code. The psychologist should acknowledge that there is no mandated "right" course of action in many circumstances and that there may be more than one possible appropriate solution. In fact, different solutions, all of them appropriate to the individual circumstances, may well be arrived at by different people at different times.

Finally, psychologists facing managed care dilemmas must recognize which of them are beyond the power of an individual acting alone. This is one reason for the recurrent recommendation that consultation with knowledgeable colleagues should be sought, and for our belief that all psychologists should be involved in systemic advocacy.

References

Harris, E., & Bennett, B. E. (1998). Sample psychotherapist–patient contract. In G. P. Koocher, J. C. Norcross, & S. S. Hill (Eds.), *Psychologist's desk reference* (pp. 191–196). London: Oxford University Press.

Murphy, M. J., DeBernardo, C. R., & Shoemaker, W. E. (1998). Impact of managed care on independent practice and professional ethics: A survey of independent practitioners. *Professional Psychology: Research and Practice, 29,* 43–51.

Phelps, R., Eisman, E. J., & Kohout, J. (1998). Psychological practice and managed care: Results of the CAPP practitioner survey. *Professional Psychology: Research and Practice, 29,* 31–36.

Rothbaum, P. A., Bernstein, D. M., Haller, O., Phelps, R., & Kohout, J. (1998). New Jersey psychologists report on managed mental health care. *Professional Psychology: Research and Practice, 29,* 37–42.

♦ ♦ ♦

Commentary: Among other issues, Acuff and colleagues raise the problem of abandonment. In discussing the issue they refer to Standard 4.09 in the 1992 Ethics Code. A subprovision of that standard (4.09[a]) stated, "Psychologists do not abandon patients or clients." That was one of the few deontological absolutes in that Code. Interestingly, that standard has been deleted and does not appear in the current 2002 Code. In its place are a more equivocal standard (10.09) and a more controversial one (10.10). Standard 10.09 states,

> *When entering into employment or contractual relationships, psychologists make reasonable efforts to provide for orderly and appropriate resolution of responsibility for client/patient care in the event that the employment or contractual relationship ends, with paramount consideration given to the welfare of the client/patient.*

Standard 10.10(c) states, "Except where precluded by the action of clients/patients or third party payors, prior to termination psychologists provide pretermination counseling and suggest alternative service providers as appropriate." What makes this controversial, at least to psychologists who have negative perceptions of managed care companies, is that psychologists are not ethically bound to provide pretermination advice and information if they are prohibited from doing so by third party payors. What does this imply with regard to the code's purported adherence to the principle of fidelity to one's clients?

In 1989, APA's policy making body, the Council of Representatives, adopted the following resolution concerning managed care:

> *Therefore, be it resolved that the American Psychological Association urges consumers, subscribers, and psychologists to review carefully the mechanisms, procedures, practices, and policies of managed care programs before deciding to partici-*

pate. Although such programs may offer the potential to expand access to appropriate mental health care, they may also restrict the availability of necessary psychological services.

It is further recommended that providers may wish to require as a condition of their participation that such managed health care delivery systems adequately and concretely demonstrate provisions to serve the consumer's interest with sufficient quantity and highest quality of health care based on the available scientific evidence of efficacy.

It is further recommended that consumers, subscribers and psychologists, as a condition of their participation, require that these programs practice truth in advertising regarding the range and duration of psychological services available through the plan and that these programs provide patients access to diversity of psychological health care competencies

based on the available scientific evidence of efficacy.

It is also recommended that providers require that such systems operate in accordance with prevailing standards of care and prevailing scientific knowledge, applicable ethical principles, and that the systems have sufficient economic resources to cover the delivery system's liability.

Finally, individual members, state psychological associations and divisions are strongly urged to monitor and inform themselves of the legal and regulatory requirements imposed on managed health care systems and to advocate that such requirements meet the principles enumerated herein. (APA, Council of Representatives, 1989, p. 1024)

American Psychological Association, Council of Representatives. (1989). Proceedings of the American Psychological Association, Incorporated, for the year 1988. American Psychologist, 44, 996–1028.

Index

AAAS (American Association for the Advancement of Science), 425

AAMFT (American Association for Marriage and Family Therapy), 350

Abandonment, patient, 88
  APA Ethics Code on, 578
  APA recommendations concerning, 575
  and managed care, 561, 573–576

Abortion, 161

"Above all, do no harm," 36, 136

Absolutists, 134

Academia
  issues in, 385
  and supervision of student research, 439–445
  and teaching, 446–451

Academic settings, 11

Acceptance
  of expulsion recommendation, 61
  of reprimand/censure recommendation, 60
  of stipulated resignation recommendation, 53, 54, 59
  widespread, 527

Access to data, 86–87
  in child psychology, 93
  from employment testing, 283
  in school psychology, 300
  by third parties, 162

Access to practice subjects, 313–314

"Accidental experts," 454

Accountability, 145

Acculturation, ethics training by, 122–127
  assimilation strategy in, 123–124
  Berry's model of, 123–124
  continuing, 126–127
  and culture of psychology, 122–123
  defined, 122

and ethics courses, 125–126
implications/applications of, 124–127
integration strategy in, 123
marginalization strategy in, 124
and practicum supervision, 126
separation strategy in, 124
and trainee selection, 125
and training programs, 126

Acculturation stress, 125, 126

Accuracy, 16
  of expert witnesses, 466, 482–483
  of forensic evaluations, 496
  in reporting to payers, 23, 534
  in teaching, 24

"Acting in," 222, 224

Activities within professional relationship, 217

ADA. *See* Americans With Disabilities Act

Adherence to treatment plan, 183

Ad Hoc Committee on Psychology and AIDS (APA), 204

Adjudication, 41, 65

Adjustments to charges, 542

Administrative regulations, 4n2

Admissibility, of evidence, 525–528

Adolescents
  and confidentiality, 192
  lesbian/gay/bisexual, 364
  reporting risk-taking behavior of, 197–201

Adult development, 368

Adversarial evaluator, 509

Adversary system, of courts, 465, 472, 500, 507, 519

Advertising
  APA Ethical Standards on, 21–22
  APA Ethics Code on, 548–549
  appealing to fear in, 547

avoidance of false/deceptive statements in, 21–22
dilemmas with, 106
and fee splitting, 548
and free speech, 546
and in-person solicitation, 22
and Internet-mediated psychological services, 381
"in-your-face," 546–547
and media presentations, 22
percentage of psychologists using, 81
restrictions on, 546–548
solicitation vs., 85
and statements by others, 22
and testimonials, 22
testimonials as, 547
of workshops/non-degree-granting educational programs, 22

Advocacy
  impartiality as best, 468
  in managed care setting, 560
  testimony vs., 459–460, 462–463, 467, 472

Affidavit
  failure to return, 52
  of resignation, 39, 47, 53

Age
  of minor clients, 194
  and test user qualification, 281

Aging, 368

AIDS cases, number of diagnosed, 203

AIDS research, 410–411

Alcohol
  adolescent use of, 200
  doing therapy while under influence of, 67, 81, 82
  survey of understanding of principles relating to problems with, 69–73

Alcohol and Drug Abuse Amendments of 1983, 154
Alcoholics Anonymous, 357
Alert! newsletter, 499
Alteration, of records, 538
Alternative action, 57
Alternative therapies, 369
Ambiguity, 12, 68, 92, 231
American Academy of Forensic Psychology, 476
American Association for Marriage and Family Therapy (AAMFT), 350
American Association for the Advancement of Science (AAAS), 425
American Association of Applied and Preventive Psychology, 371
American Association on Mental Retardation, 521
American Bar Association, 457
American Board of Forensic Psychology, 453
American Board of Professional Psychology, 44
American Counseling Association, 32
American Medical Association, 170, 172, 525
American Professional Agency, 359
American Psychiatric Association, 171, 193, 230, 320, 325
  Dr. Grigson expelled by, 513
American Psychological Association (APA), 205, 220, 320
  founding of, 10
  legal counsel for, xxi
American Psychological Association Insurance Trust (APAIT), 257, 258, 342, 381
American Psychologist, 10, 272
American Psychology–Law Society, 476
Americans With Disabilities Act (ADA), 277–278
American Veterinary Medical Association (AVMA) Panel on Euthanasia, 436
Analysis, data. *See* Data analysis
Anesthesia, 436
Anger, discussing, 86
Animal Enterprise Protection Act, 438
Animal enterprise terrorism, 438
Animal rights activists, 391, 437, 438
Animal subjects
  acquisition of, 435
  care/housing of, 435
  commentary on use of, 437–438
  educational use of, 437

experimental procedures involving, 435–436
field research involving, 437
guidelines for care/use of, 434–438
justification for research involving, 434
personnel involved with, 434–435
welfare of, 16, 26, 433
Animal Welfare Act, 437
Anonymous complaints, 54–55
Anonymous information, 427
Antipsychotic drugs, 525
Antisodomy statutes, 161, 164–165
Anxiety baselines, 367
APA. *See* American Psychological Association
APA Association Rules (ARs), 13
APA Board of Directors
  action by, 64
  and Ethics Committee, 38, 39
  and membership recommendations, 51
  proceedings before, 63–64
  referral to, 63–64
  review by, 53
  show cause review by, 53
  and stipulated resignation, 53–54, 59, 60
APA bylaws, 38–39
APA Code of Ethics
  1952 version, 12
  1981 version, 12, 115
  1989 version, 68, 329
  1992 version, 11–13, 113, 114, 231, 246, 274, 329
  2002 version. *See* 2002 APA Code of Ethics
  activities covered by, 14
  on advertising, 548–549
  applicability of, 42
  aspirational principles/enforceable standards of, 153
  and boundaries, 31–37
  categories in, 10
  and commerce of professional psychology, 533–535
  confidentiality provisions of, 165, 315
  and confidentiality with HIV clients, 211–212
  on deception research, 417–420
  development of, 7–8, 10–13
  enforcement of, 8
  and Ethics Committee. *See* APA Ethics Committee

on family/marital/group therapy issues, 353
on forensic psychology, 454
general principles of, 16–17
as guidance, 15
on informed consent, 337, 339
intent of, 15–16
on Internet-mediated psychological services, 376
and legal/ethical conflicts, 294
and multiple relationships, 218–220
and personal/professional behavior, 35
preamble to, 15–16
sections of, 14
Standard 1.02, 109–110
standards of, 17–30
on therapy, 329
wording of, 10–11
APA Committee on Animal Research Ethics, 437–438
APA Committee on Ethical Standards for Psychology, 10
APA Committee on Psychological Tests and Assessment, 289
APA Committee on Scientific and Professional Ethics, 7, 10
APA Council of Representatives, xvii, 10, 13, 578–579
APA Ethics Committee, 13, 545
  adoption/application of rule/procedures of, 41–43
  on bartering for services, 359
  bylaws pertaining to, 38–39
  commentary on rule/procedures of, 64–65
  complaints of violation of ethics code to, 54–64
  cooperating with, 17
  general operating rules for, 42–50
  general operating rules of, 42–50
  general provisions, 40
  of Hearing Committee's decision, 63
  and membership, 50–51
  objectives/authority of, 42
  powers of, 38
  processing/review of complaints by, 40–41
  as resource for regulating psychology, 88
  rules/procedures of, 40–65
  show cause procedures for, 51–54
  statement by, 53
  statement of, 60, 64
APA ethics probe, 154

APAIT. *See* American Psychological Association Insurance Trust
APA Office of Ethics, 258
APA policy adoption, 13
APA Practice Directorate, 381
APA Rules and Procedures, 8, 15, 40–65
    2001 version, 15
    adoption/application of, 41–43
    commentary on, 64–65
    general operating rules (part II), 42–50
    general provisions, 40
    membership (part III), 50–51
    objectives/authority of Ethics Committee (part I), 42
    processing/review of complaints by Ethics Committee, 40–41
    show cause procedures (part IV), 51–54
    violation of ethics code, complaints alleging, 54–64
APA Task Force on Interpretation and Diversity, 281
Appealing adverse decisions, 560
Appeals to fear, 547
Applications, for readmission, 50–51
Applications, membership, 40, 50
Applied ethics, 133–134
"Appropriate," 135
"Appropriateness," 114
Appropriateness of colleagues actions, 106
Arizona Board of Psychologist Examiners, 215*n*1
Arrogance, professional, 462
ARs (APA Association Rules), 13
Aseptic techniques, 436
ASPBB. *See* Association of State and Provincial Psychology Boards
Aspirational principles, 13, 16, 35, 153
Assent, 403
Assessment(s)
    APA Ethical Standards on, 27–28
    applications for, 27
    bases for, 27
    coercive. *See* Coercive assessments
    of competence in ethics, 130–131
    competence with, 82–83
    cultural bias in, 473
    explaining results of, 28
    forensic vs. therapeutic, 495
    informed consent in, 27
    interpreting results of, 28
    and obsolete test/outdated test results, 28

psychological. *See* Psychological assessment
    and release of test data, 27–28
    rising costs due to, 552
    scoring/interpretation services, 28
    security of, 28
    of student/supervisee performance, 24
    and test construction, 28
    by unqualified persons, 28
Assimilation strategy, 123–124
Association of Psychology Postdoctoral and Internship Centers, 128
Association of State and Provincial Psychology Boards (ASPPB), 37, 44, 154
Association Rules (ARs), 13
Atkins v. Virginia, 521, 522
Attendance, at Ethics Committee meetings, 43
Attitudes
    about older adults, 368
    and acculturation strategy, 123
    minor clients and professional, 193–194
    toward homosexuality/bisexuality, 363
    toward "impaired" peers, 72–73
Attorney–client collaboration, 529
Audiotapes, 48–49, 63
Audits, of risk policy, 185
Authentication, 307–308
Authority
    of court system, 455
    of Ethics Committee, 42
Authorship, 393, 441, 443–444
Automatic expulsion(s)
    notice of, 52
    number of, 65
    response to, 52
Autonomy, 36, 37
    balancing, with other interests, 138
    beneficence vs., 150–151
    and deception research, 421
    of HIV clients, 211
    and posttermination sexual involvements, 231
    respect for, 134
Aversive conditioning, 369
Aversive stimulation, 435, 436
AVMA (American Veterinary Medical Association) Panel on Euthanasia, 436
Avoiding harm, 19
Awareness, lack of, 14

Back-dating, 185–186
Bad science, 391
Baird, Brian, 395
Balance, of expert testimony, 470
Barefoot v. Estelle, 513
Barter agreements, 541–542
Bartering for services
    and boundaries, 223
    with clients/patients, 23
    dual relationships with, 85
    record keeping about, 541–542
    in rural communities, 359
Bases for assessments, 27
Battered spouses, 190
Behavior(s)
    and acculturation strategy, 123
    and beliefs, 80
    minor clients and professional, 193–194
    nearly universal, 80
    personal vs. professional, 31–32
    public vs. private Internet, 427–428
    rare, 80–81
    reporting dangerous, 93
    social desirability of, 420
Behavioral health carve-out plans, 552
Behavioral medicine, 369
Behavioral science consulting teams ("biscuits"), 325, 326
Behaviorist ideologies, 223
Beliefs, 80
Bellah v. Greenson, 176
Beneficence, 16, 36, 134, 319
    autonomy vs., 150–151
    as moral duty, 135
    in research, 150
Bentham, Jeremy, 131
Best interest of child, 193, 485, 489
Best practice standards, 554
Bias(es), 17, 213
    awareness of, 487
    in coercive assessments, 508–509
    and forensic–therapeutic interests, 503
    helper, 508
    prosecutorial, 509
    sex-role, 351
    and test validity, 274
    uncommitted, 509
Bibliotherapy, 374
Billing records, 294
Biofeedback, 369
Biomedical ethics, 134, 135
"Biscuits." *See* Behavioral science consulting teams
Bisexual clients, 363–364

Black men, 395
Blogs, 427, 428
Blue Cross/Blue Shield, 560
Blurred relationships, 11
Bodily injury, 177
Borrowing money, 81
Boundaries, 31–37, 222–230
  in child psychology, 92, 95
  client education about, 267
  clothing, 224
  commentary on, 36–37, 226–230
  of competence, 18–19
  fuzzy, 34–35
  and gifts/services/related matters,
    223–224
  importance of, 34
  language, 224
  money, 223
  personal/professional, 31–34
  and physical contact, 225–226
  place/space, 222–223
  role, 222
  and self-disclosure, 224–225
  in small communities, 357
  and therapeutic effectiveness,
    242–247
  time, 222
Boundary crossings, 226
Bowers v. Hardwick, 161, 164–165
Bribes, 534, 548
Brief psychotherapy, 555–556
Brown v. Board of Education, 276
Bulletin boards, online, 426, 427
Burden of proof, 63
Burnout, 355, 358
Business of psychology, 531–579
  commentary on, 535
  and consumer protection, 546–551
  ethics in, 533–535
  fees/financial arrangements in,
    533–535
  and HIPAA, 543–545
  and managed health care, 552–579
  record keeping in, 536–542
  record maintenance in, 533
Business relationship with client, 81, 85,
  236–237
Bylaws, APA. *See* APA bylaws

*C*aesar v. Mountanos, 161
California Court of Appeals, 331
California Supreme Court, 160, 166, 168,
  171, 176, 331
Canadian Code of Ethics for
  Psychologists, 32, 37, 148–151

Canadian Psychological Association, 135,
  148
Candid Camera (TV show), 416
Candor, 470–471
Canned columns, 381
Canterbury v. Spence, 331
Capital punishment, 524–525
Capitated contracts, 575
Capitation, 553
Capricious complaints, 54
Care
  duty of, 171
  providing good, 254
Care ethic, 133
Caring, responsible, 37
Cars, sessions in, 223
Carve-out plans, 552
Case conferences, 183
Case files, 61
Case histories, 139
Case investigation, for violation of ethics
    code, 57–58
  documentation, 58
  information from other sources, 58
  issuance of charge letter, 57
  referral to Committee, 58
  response from respondent, 57–58
Case law, 154–155
Case studies, 140
Categorical Imperative, 132
Catharsis, 263
Causation, 343
Cause for action, 56, 57
Causism, 390–391
CDC (Centers for Disease Control and
    Prevention), 203
Cease and desist order, 49
Censoring
  external, 393–395
  self-, 393
Censure, 49
Censure recommendation, 59–61
  acceptance of, 60
  Board acceptance of, 54
  by Committee, 53, 59
  independent adjudication following,
    60–61
  respondent's acceptance of, 60
Centers for Disease Control and
    Prevention (CDC), 203
Certification, laws pertaining to, 4n2
Chair of Ethics Committee
  Director's concurrence with, 50
  election/duties of, 43
  evaluation of complaints by, 41, 56–57

Chair of Hearing Committee, 62, 63
Chair of independent adjudication panel,
    60–61
Character, 34, 140, 142, 145–146
Charge letter, 57
Chart notes, 87, 182
Chat rooms, 374, 380, 426, 427
Child abuse
  allegations of, 487
  breaking confidentiality of, 86
  meta-analysis of effects of, 395
  and privileged communication laws,
    159
  suspicions of, 490
Child abuse reporting, 174, 346, 378
Child advocates, 405
Child clinical psychology survey. *See*
    Minnesota Child Psychologists'
    survey
Child custody evaluations, 81, 83, 93,
    485–491
  commentary on, 489–491
  conducting, 487–489
  difficulties presented in, 483–484
  dual role of therapist in, 505–506
  introduction, 485–486
  preparing, 486–487
  purpose of, 486
  scope of, 487–488
Child development, 192–193
Childhood sexual abuse, 227
Children
  competence of, 407–408
  confidentiality issues with, 348–349
  consent of, 316–317
  Internet-based research involving,
    431, 432
  as research subjects, 403–405
  right to consent of, 350
Children's Online Privacy Protection Act,
    431
Child sexual abuse
  duty to warn of threat of, 105
  law–ethics conflicts with reporting,
    110–111
Choice of procedures, 48
Cigarette smoking, 199, 200
Civil actions, 263
Civil commitment, 179, 188, 453
Civil commitment hearings, 159
Civil court system, 453
Civil disobedience, 31n3, 68, 111
Civil liability, 15
Civil penalties, 154
Civil rights, 15

Clarity, 12, 129
Class-based risk predictions, 516
"Classic example" problem, 461
Classified research, 323
"Click to assent" button, 431
Client(s)
 asking, about violent behavior, 181
 educating, about boundaries, 267
 and forensic psychology, 480–481
 interests of, 98, 100
 knowledge of, 259
 as research participants, 25
 served by others, 29, 548
 sexual intimacies with current, 29
 sexual intimacies with former, 29–30
 sexual intimacies with relatives/signifi-
  cant others of current, 29
 testimonials from, 547, 548
Client identification
 in agencies/employers, 154
 in court cases, 461, 494, 495
 and Internet-mediated psychological
  services, 378
 and interrogation of detainees,
  322–323
Client information forms, 294
Client–offenders, 507–509
Client preferences, 105
Client records
 grounds for opposing/limiting production of, 297
 subpoenas/compelled testimony for,
  293–298
Client relationships, ethical standards in,
 10
Client's wishes, 537
Clinical education, 180
Clinical perception and judgment, 153
Clinical training, assessing for ethical
 competence in, 131
Closed investigations, reopening of, 48
Clothing, 224
Coadvisement, 299
Coercive assessments, 507–511
 adversarial model for, 509
 alternatives to, 511
 background considerations in, 507
 commentary on, 511
 helper bias in, 508
 proposals for change of, 510–511
 prosecutorial bias in, 509
 setting for, 507–508
 uncommitted bias in, 509
Cognitive capacity, 194
Cognitively impaired elderly persons, 407

Colleagues
 consultations with, 110, 111, 148,
  153, 254, 256, 258, 323, 355,
  358
 discussions with, 106
 sexual conduct of, 106
Collection agencies, 84, 550
Collective bargaining agreement, 285,
 286
College counseling centers, 213
Collegial relationships, 237–239
Commercial speech, 546
Committee Against Medicalizing
 Psychology, 371
Committee's statement, in show cause
 procedures, 53
Common law, 155, 171
Communication(s)
 of forensic psychologists, 482–483
 for investigation, 45
 online, 427–428
 patient/family, 176–177
 privileged. *See* Privileged
  communication
 in risk assessment, 182
Communitarian values, 145
Community, interests of, 98, 100
Compassion, 133
Compelled testimony, 293–298
Competence
 APA Ethical Standards on, 18–19
 with assessments, 82–83, 495,
  500–501
 as bases for scientific/professional
  judgments, 18
 boundaries of, 18
 of client to give consent, 332
 clinical/cultural considerations in, 153
 and delegation of work, 18
 dilemmas with, 105–107
 of expert witness, 468
 and Internet-mediated psychological
  services, 376–377
 and interrogation of detainees, 322
 maintaining, 18
 and managed care, 565
 and personal problems/conflicts,
  18–19
 practice only with, 82–83
 in psychological testing, 274
 in risk assessment, 519
 of rural vs. urban psychologists, 355,
  358
 services outside areas of, 82

 of student research supervision, 439,
  440
 of supervisors in ethics, 120
Competence, of forensic psychologists,
 459–464, 478
 in child custody evaluations,
  486–487
 commentary on, 463–464
 for courtroom testimony, 460–461
 specialty guidelines on, 478
 threats to, 461–463
Competence in ethics, 128–131
 assessment of, 130–131
 core components of, 128
 modeling of, 129
 trainee selection/adjudication for,
  128–129
 training for, 129–130
Competencies Conference, 122
Competency of research participants,
 406–411
 children, 407
 commentary on, 407–411
 impaired elderly persons, 407
 mentally disabled persons, 406
Competency to stand trial, 510–512
Competition, 532, 545
Complainant, notification to, 44, 45
Complaints
 anonymous, 54–55
 capricious/malicious, 54
 consecutive, 55
 conversion to *sua sponte* action from,
  48
 counter-, 54
 "do no harm" and filing, 82
 improper, 17
 and investigations of unethical conduct, 40
 and membership matters, 40
 by members/nonmembers, 54
 against nonmembers, 55
 preliminary evaluation by Director,
  55–56
 procedures for filing, 55
 processing/review of, 40–41
 and show cause proceedings, 40–41
 simultaneous, 55
 sua sponte action, 54
 time limits on, 46–47
 of unethical conduct, 15
 and unfair discrimination, 15
 and violation of Ethics Code, 41
 of violation of ethics code, 54–55
Complaints procedure, 54–55

Compliance
    with risk policy, 185
    with time requirements, 43
Comprehension, of consent forms,
    412–414
Computerized psychological testing
    (CPT), 303–305
    commentary on, 305
    professional's rights/responsibilities
      with, 303–304
    psychology's response to, 303
    test taker's rights with, 304
Computerized psychological test interpre-
    tations, 83
Concurrence, of Chair and Director of
    Ethics Office, 50
Concurrent jurisdiction, 47
Concurrent litigation, 47
Concurrent relationships, 217
Conducting research, 390–391
    and bad science, 391
    commentary on, 395–397
    cost-utility analysis of, 391
    design issues in, 390
    recruitment issues in, 390–391
Confidential information
    client control of, 105
    disposal of, 213
    in managed care environment,
      556–557
    responding to subpoena vs. disclosing,
      293
Confidentiality, 11, 16–17, 159–213
    and access by staff/legal counsel/duly
      appointed persons, 44
    and adolescent risk-taking behavior,
      197–202
    APA Ethical Standards on, 21
    breaking, 86, 188–189, 429–430
    in child psychology, 93, 94, 96
    commentary on, 164–165, 168
    and consultations, 21
    and dangerous clients, 187–191
    dilemmas with, 106, 107
    and disclosures, 21
    discussing limits of, 21, 200, 210, 322,
      380, 488, 514
    and duty to warn, 166–167, 170–174
    and employment testing, 283–285
    of ethics files, 45
    within families/couples, 105
    in family therapy, 346–349
    and forensic psychology, 479–480,
      501–502
    and HIV-positive clients, 203–213

importance of, 173
and informed consent, 571–572
and Internet-based psychological
    testing, 307
and Internet-based research, 429–430
with Internet-mediated psychological
    services, 378–380
issues of, 67
limits of, 117–118, 169–170, 188,
    190–191
maintaining, 21
and managed care, 572–573
mandatory, 206
with minor clients, 192–195
obstacles to preservation of, 162–163
patient expectations of, 163
principle of, 134
and privacy issues, 161–162
privacy vs., 162
and privilege issues, 163–164
protecting, 86
and public policy, 175–179
recommendations about, 167–168
and recordings, 21
of records, 539
requirement of, 43–44
and risk management, 180–186
in rural vs. urban settings, 355, 358
study of decision making about, 98,
    100
and suicidality, 343–344
and teaching of psychological testing,
    315–316
and trust, 167
and writings/publication/lectures, 21
Confidentiality certificates, 178, 411
Confidential records
    disposal of, 22–23, 213
    maintenance/dissemination/disposal
      of, 22–23
Conflicts of interest, 19
    dilemmas with, 106
    with Internet-mediated psychological
      services, 377
Conflictual relationships, 11
Consecutive relationships, 217
Consent
    children's right to, 350
    to deception, 415
    and psychotherapist–patient sex, 264
    and teaching of psychological testing,
      316–317
    and test-data release, 290
    and therapy, 329–330

Consent forms, 412–413
Consultation(s)
    with affected parties, 148
    with colleagues, 110, 111, 148, 153,
      254, 256, 258, 323, 355, 358
    and confidentiality, 21
    credible sources of, 258
    and feedback, 130
Consumer protection, 546–551
    and advertising restrictions, 546–548
    APA Ethics Code on, 548–549
    commentary on, 549–551
Contact and participation dimension, 123
Content
    of information, 184
    of records, 537–539
Context, of records, 540
Contextual approach, 300
Contingency fees, 85
Continuing education courses, 107, 130,
    180
Contraceptives, 161
Control of process, loss of, 263–264
Conversion of procedures
    of action initiated by complainant to
      sua sponte action, 48
    choice of procedures, 48
    to show cause action, 48
    show cause action to *sua sponte* action,
      48
Converted cases, notification of, 45
Cooperate with ethics process, failure to,
    49
Cooperation
    with ethics committees, 17
    with other professionals, 20
Copayments, 553
Copyright interests, of testing materials,
    291, 309, 310
Core components of competence in
    ethics, 128
Corrective actions, 50
Correspondence (Ethics Committee)
    delivery of, 49
    personal response, 48
    use of, 48
Corticosteroids, 387
Cost-utility analysis, 391
Council for the National Register of
    Health Service Providers, 44–45
Council of Graduate Departments of
    Psychology, 371
Council of Representatives, 44
Council of University Directors of Clinical
    Programs, 371

Countercomplaints, 54
Countertransference, 85, 211
Couples therapy, 29, 105, 541
Court-compelled testimony
    for client records/test data, 293–298
    grounds for opposing, 297
Courtesy or etiquette, issues of, 11
Court orders, 293
CPT. *See* Computerized psychological
    testing
Credentials, of expert witness, 460
Credibility, of consultation sources, 258
Credit
    failure to give, 441, 443
    misrepresentation of, 393
    publication, 26
    unwarranted giving of, 441, 444
Credit card payments, 378
Criminalization of
        psychotherapist–patient sex,
        262–265
    advantages of, 262–263
    civil action impaired by, 263
    and consent, 264
    as deterrence, 262, 264
    disadvantages of, 263–264
    and false accusations, 264–265
    as inappropriate catharsis, 263
    issue obscured by, 263
    loss of control of process with,
        263–264
    malpractice coverage voided by, 263
    and money to treat victims, 262–263
    as redress, 262
    rehabilitation absent with, 264
    as retribution, 262
    and unlicensed therapists, 262
Criminal Justice Mental Health Standards
    (American Bar Association), 457
Criminal justice system, 453
Criminal offenses, show cause proceed-
    ings based on, 51–52
Criminal penalties, 154
Criminal responsibility, 510
Critical incident method, 11, 131
Cruel and unusual punishment, 521, 525
Crying, 86
Cultural context, 73
    and legal–ethical conflicts, 153
    and test validity, 274
Cultural maintenance, 123
Culture(s)
    diverse, 365–367
    and interrogation of detainees,
        321–323

and test user qualification, 281
Culture of psychology, 122–123
Current treatment records, 181
Custody evaluations. *See* Child custody
    evaluations
Cyberlink Consulting Inc., 375
Cybertherapy, 374–375, 382–383

Damage control, 185–186
Damages, award of, 155
Dangerous-clients, decision-making
        model for working with, 187–191
    case illustrations, 187–189
    commentary on, 190–191
    intervention selection, 187
Dangerousness, predictions of, 516
Data, Internet, 429–432
Data access. *See* Access to data
Data analysis, 391–392
    commentary on, 395
    data dropping, 391–392
    meta-, 392
    thoroughness of, 392
Data compilations
    for formal hearings, 63
    transcription of, 48–49
Data dropping, 391–392
Data gathering, 488
Data storage devices, 380
Data subset selection, 392
Date of information, 184
Daubert v. Merrell Dow Pharmaceuticals,
    Inc., 465, 523, 525–528
Death
    of client, 213
    fear of, 387–389
    of member, 45
    of therapist, 383
Death sentence hearings, 511, 513,
    521–523
Debriefing, 25, 415, 416, 418, 429, 432
Deception
    determining scope of, 420
    in research, 25
    studying, 418–419
Deception research, 385–386, 395
    and debriefing, 416
    ethical analysis of, 423–425
    and failure to inform, 415–416
    frequency of, 413–414
    types of, 416
    utilitarian perspectives on, 417–422
Deceptive statements, in advertising,
    21–22
Decertification, 52

Decision-based ethics, 245
Decisionism, 139
Decision-making model(s)
    adopting a personal, 128
    for dangerous-client confidentiality.
        See Dangerous-clients,
        decision-making model for
        working with
    for HIV-client confidentiality. *See* HIV-
        positive clients, confidentiality
        and
    K. S. Kitchener's two-level, 130
    J. R. Rest's, 130
Decision-making process(es), 146
    and Canadian Code of Ethics,
        148–149
    documentation of, 257
    for law–ethics conflicts, 109–110
    in managed care, 570–571
    patient-oriented, 258
    teaching of, 149
Decision making study, 98–100
Deductibles, health-insurance, 553
Degree of willingness, 69
Dehoaxing, 416
Delegation of work, 18
Deliberateness, measured, 142
Delivery, of documents, 49
Denial of coverage, 559
Deny readmission recommendation,
    51
Deontological ethics, 132, 140, 207, 209,
    210, 417
Departure, from practice, 534–535
Depression, 367, 424
Descriptions, of education and training
    programs, 23
Descriptive ethicists, 3n1
Descriptive statistics, 279–280
Desegregation, school, 276
Desensitizing, 416
Design
    of education and training programs,
        23
    research, 390
Destruction, of records, 538
Detail, or records, 537–538
Detainees, interrogation of. *See*
    Interrogation of detainees
Deterrence, of psychotherapist–patient
    sex, 262, 264
Detroit Edison Co. v. National Labor
    Relations Board, 287–288
Developmental status of client, 94
"Devil's advocate," 509

DHHS. *See* U.S. Department of Health and Human Services
Diagnosis
 in absentia, 462
 access to, 86–87
 altering, for insurance criteria, 84, 557, 562
 dilemmas with, 106, 107
Diagnostic and Statistical Manual of Mental Disorders (DSM–IV–R), 521
Diagnostic issues, 259
Dichotomous predictions, 516–517
Dichotomous with qualified confidence predictions, 516
Digital signatures, 308, 431, 432
Dignity
 and deception research, 386
 respect for, 16–17, 37, 85–86, 320
Dinner, sessions during, 223
Direct contracting, 574–575
Directives (Ethics Committee), 49–50
 cease and desist order, 49
 corrective actions, 50
 education/training/tutorial requirement, 50
 evaluation/treatment requirement, 50
 probation, 50
 supervision requirement, 50
Director of Ethics Committee
 Committee's concurrence with, 50
 evaluation of complaints by, 41, 55–57
 notification by, 44–45
Direct solicitation, 546–547
Disabilities
 of lesbian/gay/bisexual clients, 364
 testing individuals with, 276, 277, 281
Disappointment, discussing, 86
Disaster relief settings, 537–538
Discernment, 133
Disciplinary actions, 154
 for boundary violations, 261
 by other bodies, 47
Disclosure(s), 145
 and confidentiality, 21, 190
 of economic implications of treatment, 560–561
 of fact of investigation, 45
 and HIV clients, 204
 permissive, 205
 professional ethics guidelines on, 204–205
 of psychological information, 159
 of record keeping procedures, 539
 required, 205–206
 state guidelines on, 205–206

by students, 24
 of test data, 289–298
Discrimination
 against complainants/respondents, 15
 unfair, 19
Discussion(s)
 of clients by name, 81, 86
 with colleagues, 106
 with supervisors, 126
Dishonesty, 312
Dismissal, of case, 52, 58–60
 insufficient evidence, 59
 no action warranted, 59
 no violation, 58
Disposal
 of confidential records, 22–23, 213
 of euthanized animals, 436
Disposition, of records, 542, 573
Dissemination, of confidential records, 22–23
Dissertations, 443
Distributive justice, 136
Ditching study, 387–389
Diversity
 of lesbian/gay/bisexual clients, 363–364
 in older adults, 368
Divorce, and child custody. *See* Child custody evaluations
"Doctor-knows-best system," 331
"Doctor's dilemma," 166
Documentation
 of bartering for services, 223
 of child custody evaluations, 489
 of colleague consultations, 258
 of cultural/sociopolitical factors, 367
 of decision-making process, 257
 by Ethics Committee, 48–49
 of forensic psychology outcomes, 480
 and HIV-client confidentiality, 205–206
 of investigation, 58
 and malpractice, 87
 of professional/scientific work, 22
 public domain, material from, 49
 of reasons for civil disobedience, 111
 and risk containment, 183–184
 service of documents, 49
 transcription, 48–49
Documents
 failure to provide, 63
 for Hearing Committee, 62–63
"Do no harm," 16, 82, 136, 326
"Double-dipping," 443
Drug abuse research, 409–410

Drug use, adolescent, 200
DSM–IV, rev (*Diagnostic and Statistical Manual of Mental Disorders*), 521
Dual relationships, 11, 85. *See also* Multiple relationships
Due process, 8, 12, 52
Due Process Clause (of U.S. Constitution), 165
Duty of care, 171
Duty to appeal adverse decisions, 560
Duty to continue treatment, 561
Duty to disclose, 560–561
Duty to warn
 and HIV clients, 205
 and Internet-mediated psychological services, 378
 psychotherapist's, 170–179
 of threatened violence, 105, 118, 166–167

EAHCA. *See* Education for All Handicapped Children Act
EBay, 282
Economic incentives, 565
ECTF (Ethics Code Task Force), 376
Editor's Notes (Ed. Notes), xxii
Educably mentally retarded (EMR) children, 473
Education
 about older adults, 369
 clinical, 180
 directive for, 50
 legal, 180
 on lesbian/gay/bisexual issues, 364
 policy for staff, 184, 185
 and risk assessment, 180
Educational use, of animals, 437
Education and training programs
 and accuracy in teaching, 24
 APA Ethical Standards on, 23–24
 and assessing student/supervisee performance, 24
 descriptions of, 23
 design of, 23
 and legal–ethical conflicts, 155–156
 and mandatory individual/group therapy, 24
 perceived utility of, 102
 professional, 107
 and sexual relationships with students/supervisees, 24
 and student disclosure of personal information, 24
 types of, 106

Education for All Handicapped Children Act (EAHCA), 276–277
Educative letter, 57, 59
EEOC (Equal Employment Opportunity Commission), 277
Eighth Amendment (of U.S. Constitution), 521, 525
Eisenstadt v. Baird, 161
Electroencephalography, 369
Electronic assessment, 305
Electronic communications, 427–428, 533, 573
Electronic Communications Privacy Act, 427–428
Electronic media, 376
Electronic records, 540
E-mail, 374, 375, 380, 533
E-mail therapy, 383
Emancipated minors, 192
Emergency settings, 537–538
Emergency treatment
    of minors, 192
    pretrial, 481
Emerging technologies, 377
Emerich v. Philadelphia Center for Human Development, 176
Emotional distress, 176
Empathic attitude, 503
Empathy, 387
Empirical approach, 10, 11
Employee assistance plans (EAPs), 553
Employees
    dual relationships with, 85
    providing therapy to, 220
Employer policies, 153–154
Employers
    psychologists' obligations to, 284–285
    sanctions by, 8
Employment settings
    personnel testing/evaluation in, 283–288
    and testing, 277–278
Employment tests, 277
EMR (educably mentally retarded) children, 473
Encryption, 430, 432
Encryption technology, 307, 380, 383
Endangered species, 435, 437
Endorsements, 105
EPPCC. *See Ethical Principles of Psychologists and Code of Conduct*
Equal Employment Opportunity Commission (EEOC), 277
Equity, promoting, 87–88
Erotic activity, 80, 83, 228

Erotic contact, 232
Erotic transference, 222
Erroneous findings of fact, 64
Estelle v. Smith, 512–514
Ethical, ethics vs., 568
Ethical acculturation, 122, 125
Ethical behavior, integrating knowledge into, 118–119
Ethical dilemmas
    limitations of, 139–140
    recognizing, 128
    training concentrating on, 121
Ethical dilemmas national survey, 101–108
    commentary on, 107–108
    discussion, 105–106
    implications, 106–107
    method, 101–104
    results, 102–105
Ethical environment, 126
Ethical floor, 125
"Ethical Guidelines for the Teaching of Psychology in Secondary Schools" (APA), 437
Ethical imperialism, 216
Ethical import, issues with clear, 10
Ethical integrity, 131
Ethical narratives, 126
Ethical obligations, understanding of, 110, 111
Ethical principles, graduate students' understanding of, 69–73
Ethical Principles of Psychologists and Code of Conduct (EPPCC) (APA). *See* APA Code of Ethics
Ethical professor, portrait of, 449–450
Ethical role models, 126
Ethical standards
    research-based, 10
    safeguarding, 529
Ethical Standards of Psychologistsical (APA), 10, 283
Ethical Standards section (of APA Code of Ethics), 14, 17–30
    advertising/public statements, 21–22
    assessment, 27–28
    competence, 18–19
    education/training, 23–24
    human relations, 19–20
    privacy/confidentiality, 21
    record keeping/fees, 22–23
    research/publication, 24–27
    resolving ethical issues, 17
    therapy, 28–30

Ethical violations
    informal resolution of, 17
    remediation for, 266–270
    reporting, 17
Ethics
    defined, 3, 7
    dilemmas in, 4
    ethical vs., 568
    perspectives on, 67
Ethics autobiography, 125, 126
Ethics codes, 7–65. *See also* APA Code of Ethics; Canadian Code of Ethics for Psychologists
    ambiguity of, 114
    development of, 7
    failings of, 112
    importance of, 7
    limited moral authority of, 113
    as political compromise, 7
    purposes of, 13
Ethics Code Task Force (ECTF), 376
Ethics Complaint Form, 57
Ethics courses, 125–126
Ethics ethnograms, 125–126
Ethics of care, 133
Ethics theory(-ies)
    applied ethics, 133–134
    care ethics, 132
    deontological ethics, 131
    feminist ethics, 132
    meta-ethics, 132
    modern Western, 131
    Utilitarian ethics, 131–132
Ethics training
    by acculturation. *See* Acculturation, ethics training by
    complexities of, 122
    current state of, 250–252
    by osmosis, 120
Ethnic minorities
    guidelines for providers of psychological services to, 365–367
    and test user qualification, 281
    and test validity, 274
Euthanasia, 436
Evaluation for treatment
    critique of written, 300–301
    directive for, 50
Evaluation of complaints
    cause for action defined, 56
    by Chair and Director, 56–57
    decision to open a case, 57
    determination of cause for action, 57
    Director's preliminary, 55–56
    educative letter, 57

Evaluation of complaints (*continued*)
   insufficient information, 56–57
   preliminary investigation, 56–57
   reconsideration of decision to open, 57
   supplementary/alternative action, 57
Evaluative relationships, 237–238
Event model, of informed consent, 340
Evidence, rules of, 63, 457, 465–466, 481
Evidentiary privilege, 293
Ewing v. Goldstein, 176, 177
*Ewing v. Northridge Hospital Medical
   Center,* 177
Excessive sanction or directives, 64
Exorcism, 215*n*1
Expected conduct, 129
Expedited review procedure, 399, 428
Experimental procedures, animal subjects
   and, 435–436
Expert testimony
   rules for, 465–466
   scientific knowledge as subject of, 526
   validity of, 528
Expert witness(es), 85, 465–472
   accidental, 454
   balance of, 470
   candor of, 470–471
   commentary on, 472
   competence of, 468
   impartiality of, 467–471
   knowledge/limitations of, 457–458
   licensure and ethical jeopardy of, 467
   perspective of, 469–470
   predictions of violence by, 524–525
   relevance of, 468–469
   roles of, 466–467
   scientific integrity of, 456
   treatment vs. forensic, 492
Explaining results, of assessments, 28
Exploitation, 218, 220–221
   avoiding, 83–85
   and boundary violations, 224
Exploitative relationships, 20
Expression, freedom of, 15
Expulsion(s), 8, 49, 153, 154
   automatic. *See* Automatic expulsion(s)
   and felony convictions, 31*n*3
   notice of automatic, 52
   number of, 65
   recommendation for, 41
   show cause proceedings based on, 52
Expulsion recommendation, 53, 59,
   61–64
   acceptance of, 61
   board of directors' proceedings follow-
     ing, 63–64

formal hearing following, 61–63
   notification of, 64
   reconsideration of, 64
External censoring, 393–395
External review, of risk policy, 185
Extramarital affairs, 351

Face masking, 380
Facsimile (fax), 533
Faculty
   ethics of, 446–451
   multiple relationships of, 129
Faculty–student collaborations, 441, 444
Failure
   to pay, 117–118
   to report findings, 393–394
   to return affidavit, 52
Fairness, 8, 16
   and employment testing, 284
   of expert witnesses, 466, 482–483
   and justice, 136
   test, 274
False accusations, 264–265
False feedback, 420
False grant statements, 424
False informing, 415
False or fraudulent pretense allegations
   about membership, 51
   board of directors' action, 51
   Committee's recommendation, 51
   review procedures, 51
   specific jurisdiction, 51
   void membership recommendation, 51
False statements
   in advertising, 21–22
   and Internet-mediated psychological
     services, 381
Family(-ies)
   confidentiality within, 105
   involvement of, in minor-client treat-
     ment, 194–195
   of lesbian/gay/bisexual clients, 363
   preservation of, 350–351
Family meetings, 194, 195
Family members
   asking, about violent behavior, 181
   threat communicated by, 176–177
Family therapy, 29, 346–353
   commentary on, 352–353
   confidentiality in, 346–349
   informed consent/right to refuse treat-
     ment in, 349–350
   multiple relationships in, 93
   patient privilege in, 349
   record keeping in, 541

therapist's responsibility in, 346
   and therapist's values, 350–352
Fear
   appeals to, 547
   of being sued, 88
   of death, 387–389
"Feasible," 114
Federal courts, 453
Federal laws, 536
Federally funded programs, 154
Federal Rules of Evidence, 457, 465, 526,
   527
Federal statutes, 154
Federal Trade Commission (FTC), 12,
   532, 534, 545–549
Fee agreement or policy, 541
Fee arrangements, private, 575
Fee collection, 84–85, 159, 542, 550
Feedback
   from assessments, 310
   and consultation, 130
   false, 420
   to practice test subjects, 314–315
   to research participants, 388
   from research subjects, 431
Fees
   and accuracy in reports to
     payors/funding sources, 23
   advertisements mentioning, 548
   APA Ethical Standards on, 22–23
   bartering over, 23
   and boundaries, 223
   charging, 87–88
   collecting, 159
   disclosure of, 533–535
   filing lawsuits to collect, 84–85
   and financial arrangements, 23
   of forensic psychologists, 478
   information about, 137
   with Internet-mediated psychological
     services, 378
   and managed care, 571
   with minor clients, 194
   raising, 84
   referral, 23, 81, 534, 548–550
   and referrals, 23
   as taboo subject, 84
Fee-splitting, 85, 548
Felony convictions, 31*n*3, 35, 51–52, 154
Female psychologists, 231
Feminist ethics, 133
Feminist psychology, 33
Feminist Therapy Code of Ethics, 33
Fidelity, 16, 36
   avoiding harm vs., 150

in ethics of care, 133
and interrogation of detainees, 319, 326
and managed care, 565
as moral duty, 135
principle of, 134
Field research, 437
Fifth Amendment (of U.S. Constitution), 263, 511–513
Filing complaints, 55
Final adjudication, 41
Financial arrangements
for child custody evaluations, 489
with clients, 81
disclosure of, 533–535, 560–561
and fees, 23
and managed care, 571
Financial barriers, 87–88
Financial-business relationships, 217, 236–237
Financial issues
and exploitation, 84–85
study of decision making about, 98, 100
Financial records, 541–542
Findings, misrepresentation of, 392–393
Firewalls, 380
First Amendment (of U.S. Constitution), 546
Firsthand knowledge, 526
"Fit," 526
Force of law, 294
Ford v. Wainwright, 525
Forensic evaluator training, 458
Forensic issues, in child psychology, 93, 97
Forensic psychologists, 477
Forensic psychology, 453–530
and advocating vs. testifying, 462–463
and child custody evaluations, 485–491
and coercive assessments, 507–509
competence/quality in performance of, 459–464
contingency fees in, 85
and courtroom involvement, 455
and current knowledge, 463
Daubert v. Merrell Dow Pharmaceuticals, Inc., 526–528
defined, 453, 477
Estelle v. Smith, 512–514
and ethics in legal system, 529–530
and expert witnesses, 456–458
and greed, 463
impartiality vs. advocacy in, 465–472

issues in, 11
and judicial system, 462, 473–475
power of, 530
and professional arrogance, 462
and Psychopathy Checklist Revised, 523–525
risk evaluations for future violence, 518–522
specialty guidelines for, 476–484
and therapeutic role, 492–511
and violence predictions, 515–517
Forensic specialists, 453
Forensic–therapeutic roles, 492–511
and anticipation of testimony, 500
in child custody cases, 505–506
in coercive assessments, 507–511
commentary on, 498, 505–506
compatibility of, 499–504
conflict of, 492–498
ethical standards applying to, 499–504
examples of conflict in, 492–494
and limits of confidentiality, 501–502
as mutually exclusive choices, 505
relationship differences in, 494–497
waiving conflict of, 497
Foreseeability, 343
Formal ethics coursework, 106, 149
Formal hearing(s), 41
after expulsion recommendation, 61–63
burden of proof in, 63
Chair of, 62
committee for, 62
date of, 62
documents/witnesses for, 62–63
procedures for, 63
request for, 62
Forms
client-information, 294
for documenting actions, 184, 185
Ethics Complaint, 57
informed-consent, 333
Notice of Privacy Practices and Authorization, 381
Fourteenth Amendment (of U.S. Constitution), 546
Fraud
about services, 534
encouragement to, 441–443
scientific, 395
Fraudulent pretense allegations about membership, 51
Freedom of expression, 98, 100
Freedom of inquiry and expression, 15
Free sessions, 223, 559

Free speech, 546
Free therapy, 88
Freud, Sigmund, 85, 87
Friends, dual relationships with, 85
Friendships, with former clients, 235–236
FTC. *See* Federal Trade Commission
Funding sources, reporting to, 23
Fund-raiser items, 92
Fuzzy boundaries, 34–35

Gatekeeping, 553
Gay men, 362–364
Gender differences
in student/supervisee sexual intimacy, 246
and test user qualification, 281
Gender power dynamics, 251
Gender-related behaviors, 78, 80, 87
"General acceptance," 527
General Counsel of the Association, 63
General Guidelines for Providers of Psychological Services (APA), 86, 87, 303
Generalized beneficence, 135–137
General operating rules (Ethics Committee), 42–50
Board of Directors' Standing Hearing Panel, 49
choice/conversion of procedures, 48
concurrence of Chair and Director of Ethics Office, 50
confidentiality/notifications, 43–45
correspondence/documentation, 48–49
directives, 49–50
failure to cooperate, 49
general provisions, 42–43
jurisdiction, 45–48
meetings/officers, 43
records, 45
reopening a closed investigation, 48
sanctions, 49
General Principles section (of APA Code of Ethics), 14, 16–17
General provisions (Ethics Committee), 40, 42–43
APA documents, 42
applicable ethics code, 42
compliance with time requirements, 43
computation of time, 43
rules/procedures, 42–43
Geneva Convention Relative to the Treatment of Prisoners of War, 321
Genograms, 125–126

Genuineness, 141–142
Gifts
   accepting, 80
   boundaries with, 223–224
   giving, 81, 92
   of unwarranted credit, 441, 444
Government agencies, 367
Government research, 386
Graduate coursework in ethics, 107, 117
   and boundaries, 34–35
   change required in, 72
   effectiveness of, 120–121
Graduate students, multiple relationships
   with, 248–249
Graduate students' understanding of ethi-
   cal principles study, 69–73
   commentary on, 71–73
   discussion, 70–71
   method, 69–70
   results, 70
Grand rounds, 183
Grant statements, 424
Gratitude, 135
"Greatest happiness" principle, 132
Greed, 463
Grigson, James, 511–513, 523
Grimes v. Kennedy Krieger Institute, Inc.,
   408
Griswold v. Connecticut, 161
Groundwork of the Metaphysics of Morals
   (Kant), 132
Group therapy, 24, 29, 353, 541
Group variability, 92
Guam, 369, 525
Guantanamo Bay detainees, xv
Guardians, 403–405
"Guidelines for Formal Hearings" (APA
   Ethics Office), 61
*Guidelines for Providers of Psychological
   Services to Ethnic, Linguistic, and
   Culturally Diverse Populations*
   (APA), 153
"Guidelines for the Use of Animals in
   Behavioral Projects in Schools"
   (APA), 437–438

Hahnemann University, xxii
Handshaking, 80, 83, 225
Harassment, 19
Harm. *See also* Threat(s)
   avoiding, 19, 136, 150, 502–503
   confidentiality and preventing, 86
   do no. *See* "Do no harm"
   expulsion recommendation due to,
      59

Internet-based research participation
   leading to, 428–429
   minimizing, 110, 112
   in multiple relationships, 253–255
   in research, 389
   to students, 33
Hate speech, 33–34
Hawaii Psychiatric Society v. Ariyoshi,
   162
HCR-20. *See* Historical, Clinical, Risk
   Management–20
Health care costs, 552
Health insurance, 552
Health Insurance Portability and
   Accountability Act (HIPAA), xvii,
   257, 295, 296, 379–381, 407, 532,
   536, 543–545
Health maintenance organizations
   (HMOs), 552
Hearing, formal, 41
Hearing Committee, 61–63
   decision of, 63
   designation of, 62
   documents/witnesses for, 62–63
   legal counsel for, 63
   officers of, 63
   rules of evidence for, 63
   voir dire of members for, 62
Hearsay, 462, 481
Hedlund v. Superior Court, 176
Helper bias, 508
Helpfulness standard, 526
HIPAA. *See* Health Insurance Portability
   and Accountability Act
Hippocratic Oath, 82
Historical, Clinical, Risk Management–20
   (HCR-20), 518, 520
HIV/AIDS Office for Psychology
   Education (APA), 204, 205
HIV exposure, 203
HIV-positive clients
   adolescent, 199
   and physical contact, 225
HIV-positive clients, confidentiality and,
   203–206
   and breaking confidentiality,
      209–212
   commentary on, 206, 213
   decision-making model for, 203–206
   determining need for disclosure
      (step 1), 204
   and duty to warn, 207–213
   ethical issues with, 203
   referring to professional ethical guide-
      lines (step 2), 204–205

referring to state guidelines (step 3),
   205–206
   sexually-active, 207–212
HMO Act of 1973, 552, 553
HMOs (health maintenance organiza-
   tions), 552
Holistic health care, 370
"Holy trinity" (assessment, intervention,
   research), xvii
Home visits, 223
Homicidal clients, 86
Homicide rate, 523
Homophobia, 213
Homosexuality, 87, 161, 164–165, 363
Honesty, 16, 312, 500
Honor code commandment, 144
Hospitalization, 565
Hospitalization, involuntary, 87, 179
Housing, of animal subjects, 435
Hugging, 83, 92, 225–226, 357
Huhta v. State Board of Medicine, 467
Humane treatment, of animals in
   research, 26
Human relations
   APA Ethical Standards on, 19–20
   avoiding harm, 19
   conflicts of interest, 19
   cooperation with other professionals,
      20
   exploitative relationships, 20
   harassment, generally, 19
   informed consent, 20
   interruption of psychological services,
      20
   multiple relationships, 19
   psychological services delivered
      to/through organizations, 20
   sexual harassment, 19
   third-party requests for services, 19–20
   unfair discrimination, 19
Human research subjects
   in Internet-based research, 426–433
   policy for protection of, 398–405
   protecting, 426–428
   risks to, 428–431
   treatment of, 396
Human rights, 15, 212, 319, 321, 323
Hyperclaiming, 390

IACUCs. *See* Institutional Animal Care
   and Use Committees
IDEA. *See* Individuals With Disabilities
   Education Act
Identifiable third party (term), 208, 209,
   212

Identity as ethical psychologist, 122
Imipramine, 424
Immunity
    from civil liability, 467
    from malpractice suits, 490
Impaired performance, 82
Impartiality, of expert witnesses, 467–471
Impressions, sharing, 300
Improper complaints, 17
In camera proceedings, 296
Incapacitation, 182
Incarceration, involuntary, 169
Income level, 366
Incorrect application of ethical standards,
    64
Independent adjudication, 41
    after reprimand/censure recommenda-
        tion, 60–61
    and Committee statement, 60
    panel selection for, 60–61
    request for, 60
    respondent's response to, 60
Independent adjudication panel
    case file provided to, 61
    Chair of, 60–61
    consideration/vote by, 61
    decision of, 61
    designation of, 60
    on expulsion cases, 62
    finality of decision by, 61
    and notification of respondent, 61
    on reprimand/censure cases, 60–61
    selection of, 60–61
Indifference, 132
Individual-based risk predictions, 516
Individual practice association (IPA), 553
Individual rights, 98, 100
Individuals With Disabilities Education
    Act (IDEA), 277, 278, 301
Individual therapy, 24
Individual uncertainty, 92
Inducements, for research participation, 25
Industrial psychologists, 285–287
Inform, failure to, 415–416
Informal resolution, of ethical violations,
    17
Information
    access to, 44
    content of, 184
    current treatment records as, 181
    date of, 184
    free flow of, 545
    insufficient, 55–57
    Internet, 427

from other sources, 56, 58
past treatment records as, 181
from patient, 181
in risk assessment, 180–181
from significant others, 181
source of, 184
withholding, 420
Informed consent, 20, 331–335
    acting only with, 86–87
    in assessments, 27
    for child custody evaluation, 488
    client's understanding of, 332–333
    and coadvisement, 299
    commentary on, 334–335
    complexities/meanings of, 336
    and confidentiality, 571–572
    considerations with, 333–334
    content/conveyance of, 337–338
    defined, 331, 332
    dispensing with, 25
    and dual relationships, 257–258
    and employment testing, 284
    evolving standards for, 337–338
    exceptions to requirement for, 137
    expanding scope of, 421
    in family/marital therapy, 349–350
    and fidelity, 137
    and forensic psychology, 479
    goals of, 332
    historical perspective on, 331–332
    with Internet-based psychological test-
        ing, 307
    and Internet-based research, 430–431
    with Internet-mediated psychological
        services, 377–379
    and legal–ethical conflicts, 154
    legality of, 332–333
    and managed care, 565, 571–572
    with minor children/families, 192–193
    as ongoing process, 340
    to recordings, 25
    study of decision making about, 98, 100
    with suicidal clients, 344
    to therapy, 28–29
    timing of discussion of, 339–340
    and virtue ethics, 140–141
Informed-consent forms, 333
Informed consent to research
    and comprehension, 412–414
    and deception. *See* Deception research
    general requirements for, 400–402
    from mentally disabled subjects,
        396–397
    standards on, 24–25

Initiation of legal action, 45
Innocence, 322
Innovative treatments, 379
Inpatient stays, reduced, 553
In-person solicitation, 22
Inquiry, freedom of, 15
Insanity defense, 510, 512
Instant messaging, 380
Institute for Behavioral Research, 438
Institute of Medicine, 409
Institutional Animal Care and Use
    Committees (IACUCs), 433, 434
Institutional approval, of research, 24
Institutional review boards (IRBs), 389,
    394, 396
    composition of, 399, 402
    consent procedure approval by,
        401–402
    criteria for approval by, 399–400
    duties of, 403
    expedited review by, 399
    feedback from subjects to, 413
    Maryland court on, 408
    power of, 410
    and prisoners as subjects, 402–403
    and social science research, 410
    utilitarian standard for, 418
Insufficient evidence, case dismissal due
    to, 59
Insufficient information, 55–57
Insurance companies, settlement by, 155
Insurance coverage
    for electronic services, 382
    and minor clients, 194
    and sexual misconduct, 261
    and waiver of rights, 159
Insurance fraud, 84
Integration strategy, 123
Integrity, 16
    of expert witnesses, 456
    of Internet-based psychological test-
        ing, 307
    in relationships, 37
Intelligence quotient, 276
Intensified treatment, 182
Intentional misrepresentation, 392–393,
    395
Interest, on late payments, 534
International Association for Marriage
    and Family Counseling, 230
Internet-based psychological research,
    426–433
    commentary on, 433
    identifiable vs. anonymous informa-
        tion in, 427

precautions for, 431–432
and preexisting public records, 428
protection of human subjects in, 426–428
and public vs. private behavior, 427–428
risks to subjects from, 428–431
Internet-based psychological testing, 306–312
appropriate use of, 306–307
commentary on, 312
context of, 306
development of, 308–309
ethical/professional issues with, 306–310
explaining results of, 310
and informed consent, 307
normative issues with, 307
obsolete/outdated information in, 309
qualifications of test users of, 309
recommendations for future use of, 310–311
release of test data from, 307–308
security of, 310
third-party vendors of, 309–310
Internet-mediated psychological services, 374–383
avoiding false statements with, 381
commentary on, 382–383
competence issues with, 376–377
and confidentiality, 378–380
conflicts of interest with, 377
emerging technologies used with, 377
and fees, 378
and HIPAA, 379–381
and identification of client, 378
and informed consent, 377–379
and innovative treatments, 379
and media presentations, 381–382
and privacy, 379–381
public statements/advertising of, 381–382
and third parties, 378–379
Internet security, 307–308
Interns, 249
Interpretation services, for assessments, 28
Interpreting results, of assessments, 28
Interrogation of detainees
American Psychiatric Association's position on, 325
APA's Presidential Task Force on, 319–324
commentary on, 325–327
and Miranda v. Arizona, 512

Interruption, of therapy, 20, 30
Interventions, 329–383
APA Code of Ethics on, 329
against client's wishes, 87
with culturally diverse populations, 365–367
and informed consent, 331–340
Internet-mediated, 376–383
with lesbian/gay/bisexual clients, 363–364
marital/family therapy, 346–353
with older adults, 368–369
and prescription privileges for psychologists, 370–375
in rural vs. urban communities, 354–360
and suicidal-patient risk management, 342–345
with women, 361–362
Introduction section (of APA Code of Ethics), 14
Intrusions, minimizing, 21
Intuition, 518
Investigation(s)
disclosure of fact of, 45
of readmission application, 51
in show cause procedures, 52
of unethical conduct, 40, 41
Investigation files, 45
Involuntary commitment, 510
Involuntary hospitalization, 87, 179
Involuntary incarceration, 169
"In-your-face" solicitation, 546–549
IPA (individual practice association), 553
IP address, 428
IRBs. See Institutional review boards
Item response theory (IRT), 279
IV drug use, 204, 205

Jaffee v. Redmond, 174, 175, 177, 178
Judgment(s)
bases for scientific/professional, 18
difficult, 81
and legal–ethical conflicts, 153
role of, 498
therapist's, 98, 100
Judicial system, 453, 473–475
authority of, 455
failure to understand, 462
Jurisdiction
concurrent disciplinary proceedings, 47
concurrent litigation, 47
of Ethics Committee, 45–48
lack of, 55

for membership application/ readmission, 50
persons, 45–46
referral/retention of, 48
resignation barred, 47
subject matter, 46
time limits for complaints/show cause notices, 46–47
Justice, 16, 36
as moral duty, 135
principle of, 134
promoting, 87–88
theory of, 133
Juvenile court system, 453

Kaiser Permanente Health Plan, 555–556
Kant, Immanuel, 131
Kentucky Bar Association, 546
Kentucky Supreme Court, 546
Kick-backs, 85, 534, 549
King, Martin Luther, 68
Kissing, 83
Knowledge
of client, 259
of expert witnesses, 526–527
keeping current on, 463
of legal process, 529
of older adults, 368
Kumho Tire Co., Ltd. v. Carmichael, 523, 528

Language(s)
boundaries with, 224
diverse, 365–367
native, 276
and test user qualification, 281
Larry P. v. Riles, 473
Late payments, interest on, 534
Law(s)
ethical responsibilities in conflict with, 15, 17
licensure/certification/administrative regulation, 4n2
and school psychology, 276–278
study of decision making about, 98, 100
understanding of, 110
Lawrence v. Texas, 165
Lawyer's Weekly, 513
Learning ethics, 117–156
by acculturation, 122–127
and Canadian Code of Ethics for Psychologists, 148–151
with competency training, 128–131
historical overview of, 132–134

and matrix of considerations, 152–156
by osmosis, 120–121
principle-based approach to, 135–138,
144–147
virtue-based approach to, 139–143
Lectures, 21
Legal action, initiation of, 45
Legal counsel, 185
Legal Counsel for Association, 62
Legal Counsel for Hearing Committee, 63
Legal education, 180
Legal–ethical conflict(s), 109–115,
152–156
and agency/employer policies,
153–154
and case law, 154–155
with child sexual abuse, 110–111
and clinical/cultural factors, 153
commentary on, 112–115
court participation as, 454
decision-making process in, 109–110
disobeying law in, 111
and federal/state/local statutes, 154
of forensic psychologists, 479
and implications for ethics educators,
155–156
and interrogation of detainees, 321
matrix of considerations for, 152–155
and moral principles/personal values,
152–153
obeying law in, 111–112
and professional code of ethics, 153
recognizing, 128
and rules/regulations, 154
Legal liability, managed care and,
559–562
commentary on, 562
duty to appeal adverse decisions, 560
duty to continue treatment, 561
duty to disclose, 560–561
"Legal Liability Related to Confidentiality
and the Prevention of HIV
Transmission" (APA), 209
Lending money, to clients, 82
Lesbians, 360, 362–364
Liability, managed care and. *See* Legal liability, managed care and
Liars, 463
Libertarian perspective, 345
Liberty restrictions, 516–517
License, revocation of, 12, 15, 52, 154
Licensing boards
and expert testimony, 467
notification by Ethics Director to, 44
and psychotherapist–patient sex, 262

references to, 43*n*3
sanctions by, 8, 12
Licensure
hours required for, 67
laws pertaining to, 4*n*2
Life-threatening situations, 388
Limit setting, 224
Literacy, 406
Literal-mindedness, in ethics interpreta-
tion, 242–247
Litigation, 47
Loss of membership, 45
Lost opportunities, 391
Louisiana Supreme Court, 525
Love, 133
Loyalty, 137, 565
Lunch sessions, 223
Lurkers, 427

MacArthur Project, 175
Maintenance, of records, 22–23, 539
Majority rule, 43
Malicious complaints, 54
Malpractice, 155, 342, 532
Malpractice insurance, 263, 359
Malpractice liability, 342–343
Malum in se, 144
Managed behavioral health care
confidential information in, 556–557
history of development of, 552–553
quality of, 555–556
service delivery/organizational structures in, 553–555
Managed care, ethical practice in,
567–579
abandonment, 573–576
approved treatment below standard of
care, 569–570
commentary on, 578–579
confidentiality, 572–573
decision-making process for, 570–571
ethics vs. ethical, 568
general considerations, 567
informed consent, 571–572
profits vs. patient welfare, 567–568
response time for treatment requests,
568–569
utilization management, 576–578
Managed care companies, 153–154
Managed care organizations (MCOs), 567
Managed health care, 552–557
confidentiality of patient information
in, 556–557
current systems of, 553

history of development of, 552–553
joke about, 531
and legal liability, 559–562
mental health services under, 550–551
new patterns in service delivery/orga-
nizational structure of, 553–555
percentage of insured under, 553
quality of behavioral health care in,
555–556
Managed mental health care, 563–566
and assistance/training in achieving
treatment goals, 565
considerations in joining, 564–565
and economic incentives to hospitalization, 565
ethical issues with, 565–566
and information to policyholders of
limits, 565
marketing strategy option, 563
no treatment limitations option,
563–564
and patient–provider relationship,
564
policyholder selection option, 563
and provider input, 565
and provisions for exceptions to rules,
564
and referral resources, 565
and risk assignment, 564
treatment limitations option, 563
Mandatory confidentiality, 206
Mandatory personal remediation therapy,
266–267
Mandatory reporting laws, 105, 112, 162,
174, 178, 190–191, 409
Mandatory therapy, 24
Marginalization strategy, 124
Marijuana, 199
Marital therapy
confidentiality in, 347–348
and extramarital affairs, 351
and preservation of family, 350–351
and sex roles, 351–352
Marketing strategy, 563
Massage therapists, 225
Master therapists, 383
Materiality rule, 169
Mature minors, 192
Maturity level, of profession, 134
Mayhem, threats of, 177
Measured deliberateness, 142
Measurement error, 280
Measurement knowledge. *See*
Psychometric and measurement
knowledge

Media presentations
and confidentiality, 213
dilemmas with, 106
and Internet-mediated psychological
services, 381–382
public statements in, 22
Medicaid, 162, 549, 553
Medical examinations, for hiring, 277
Medical patients, competency of, 406
Medical records, 320
Medical training, 371
Medicare, 549, 553
Meetings (Ethics Committee), 43
attendance, 43
authority, 43
designation of responsibilities, 43
frequency/quorum, 43
majority rule, 43
selection of officers, 43
Member complaints, 46, 54
Membership
determination of, 46n6
expert testimony and AMA, 513
loss of, 45
notification by Ethics Committee to, 44
Membership rules and procedures, 50–51
applications, 50
false/fraudulent pretense allegations,
51
readmission applications, 38, 50–51
Mentally disabled persons, 396–397
Mental retardation, 521, 522
Mental state, testimony about, 481–482
Mentoring, 445
Message digests, 307
Meta-analysis, 392, 395
Meta-ethics, 133
Military academies, 144
Military interrogations, 272
Military psychologists, 254, 261
Mill, J. S., 131–132
Minnesota Board of Psychology, 91
Minnesota Child Psychologists' survey
clinical boundary issues, 92, 95
confidentiality issues, 93, 96
findings of, 92–93
forensic issues, 93, 97
implications of, 93–95
professional relationship issues,
92–93, 95–96
Minnesota Multiphasic Personality
Inventory, 282
Minor clients
access to records of, 543–544
and confidentiality, 192–195

and determining best interest of child,
193
developmental considerations in consent to treatment, 192–193
evaluation of, 510
guidelines for, 194–195
Internet-based research involving, 432
and Internet-mediated psychological
services, 378
legal considerations in consent to
treatment, 192
and professional attitudes/behaviors,
193–194
treatment planning/evaluation and
involvement of, 193, 194
Miranda v. Arizona, 512, 513
Mirroring, 250
Misrepresentation
of credit, 393
of findings, 392–393
intentional, 392–393, 395
unintentional, 393
Missed appointments, charging for, 84
Misunderstanding, 14
Misuse, of psychologists' work, 17
Modeling moral behaviors, 129
"Model Law of Confidentiality" (APA), 193
Money
boundaries of, 223
lending to client, 82
for treatment of victims of
psychotherapist–patient sex,
262–263
Monkeys, 438
Moral action, 147
Moral authority, of code of ethics, 113
Moral behavior
components of, 146
teaching, 130
Moral discourse, 140
Moralist position, 345
Morality, standards of, 98, 100
Moral reasoning, 130, 147
Moral sensitivity, 146
Motion for protective order, 296
Motion to quash subpoena, 296
Motivation, of expert witness, 529
MRs. *See* Multiple relationships
Multicultural issues, 129–130
Multidisciplinary records, 541
Multiple client records, 541
Multiple relationships (MRs), 19,
215–270
and access to practice testing subjects,
313

and activities within professional relationship, 217
ambiguity of 1992 Ethics Code on,
231–234
boundary issues with. *See* Boundaries
characteristics of, 217–218
in child custody evaluations, 487
in child psychology, 92–93
commentary on, 258
concurrent/consecutive/overlapping,
217
considerations with potential,
254–256
criminalization of sexual, 262–265
decision-making questions about
potential, 254–256
define, 219
and exploitation/harm, 218
of faculty and students, 129
in family therapy, 346
of forensic psychologists, 478
forms of, 217
with graduate assistants/students,
248–249
harm in, 253–255
identifying/evaluating/resolving dilemmas with, 217–221
and implications for practice, 256–257
and interrogation of detainees, 321
nature of, 217–218
nonromantic/nonsexual, 235–241
with related persons, 217
remediation for violations of, 266–270
risk management with potential,
256–261
in rural vs. urban settings, 355, 356
and sexual ethics training, 250–252
in student research supervision, 441,
442
and therapeutic effectiveness, 218,
242–247
unavoidable, 254
Muscle relaxants, 436

Names, use of, 224
National Academy of Sciences, 272
National Bioethics Advisory Commission,
396
National Commission for the Protection
of Human Subjects in Biomedical
and Behavioral Research, 396
National Labor Relations Act, 285
National Labor Relations Board, 286, 288
National security, 319–324
Native language, 276

Naturally occurring situations, 389
Negative nature of behavior factor, 198–200
Neglect, 490
Negligence, 303, 343
Networks, 130, 554
Nixon, Richard, 552
Nonacceptance, of Ethics Committee's recommendation, 41, 64
Noncompliance, with treatment plan, 183
Non-degree-granting educational programs, 22
Nonmaleficence, 16, 36, 134, 135, 319
Nonmembers
    complaints against, 55
    complaints by, 46, 54
Nonparticipation, in court, 455
Nonpayment, withholding records for, 23, 533
Nonromantic, nonsexual posttherapy relationships with former clients, 217, 235–241
    APA members' views on, 233–234
    business/financial, 236–237
    collegial/professional, 237–239
    commentary on, 240–241
    personal/friendship, 235–236
    reasons for limiting, 241
    religious-affiliation, 238
    and social interactions/events, 236
    supervisory/evaluative, 237–238
    workplace, 239
Normative ethicists, 3n1
Normative interpretation of test scores, 280
Notice of Disclosure (HIPAA), 543
Notice of Privacy Practices and Authorization model forms, 381
Notification(s)
    of Board of Director's decision, 64
    and communication, 45
    by Ethics Committee, 44–45
    of impending disclosure, 205
    and initiation of legal action constitutes waiver, 45
    of investigation/final disposition, 44–45
Notification to respondent
    of Hearing Committee's decision, 63
    of independent adjudication panel's decision, 61
    of insufficient information, 56

in show cause procedures, 53
of stipulated resignation recommendation, 59
Nursing notes, 181

Obedience studies, 395, 418–419
Objectivity, 256, 503
Obsolete tests, 28
Office for Protection From Research Risks, 399
Officers (Ethics Committee), 43
    authority of, 43
    and meeting attendance, 43
    responsibility of, 43
    selection of, 43
Ohio State Bar Association, 547
Ohio State Board of Psychology, 499, 503
Ohralik v. Ohio State Bar Association, 547, 549
Older adults
    assessment of, 368
    attitudes about, 368
    clinical issues with, 368
    commentary on working with, 369
    competency of cognitively-impaired, 407
    education about, 369
    general knowledge about, 368
    guidelines for psychological practice with, 368–369
    intervention/consultation/service provision for, 369
    lesbian/gay/bisexual, 364
Online assessment, 305
Online communication, 427–428
Online social-support groups, 429
Open-ended questions, 181
Opening cases
    decision for, 57
    reconsideration of, 57
Opinions, of expert witnesses, 460–461
Oral consent, 413
Ordering or principles, 150
Organization(s)
    as clients and release of test data, 291–292
    of clinical practices, 554
    conflicts between ethics and demands of, 17
    psychological services delivered to/through, 20
    record keeping within, 538, 540–541
Osheroff v. Chestnut Lodge, 331
Osmosis, ethical training by, 120
Outcome measures, increased use of, 554

Outdated test results, 28
Outlier rejection, 391–392
Out-of-network providers, 554
Overlapping relationships, 217

Pain and suffering, 155
Pain management, 369
Paradoxical intention, 335
Paralytic agents, 436
Paratroopers, 389
Parental consent
    and Internet-based research, 431, 432
    professional attitudes/behaviors regarding, 193–194
    to research with children, 409
    seeing minors without, 86
    and teaching of psychological testing, 316–317
Parenting capacity, 486
Parents
    and access to child's data, 93, 543–544
    and children's right to consent, 350
    confidentiality issues with, 348–349
    defined, 403
    permission of, in research with children, 404–405
    and school psychology model, 299–302
Participants. *See* Research subjects or participants
Participatory framework for ethics, 113
Paruresis, 223
PASE v. Hannon, 288, 473
Password protection, 380
Past treatment records, 181
Paternalism, 211, 231
Patient communication, 176
Patient expectations, 163
The Patient or His Victim (Fleming and Maximov), 172
Patient-oriented decision-making process, 258
Patient rights, 163–164
Patient risk sharing, 553
Patients. *See* Client(s)
Patient welfare, profits vs., 567–568
Payment, for research participation, 409–410, 430
Payment issues, 11
Payor for services
    accuracy in reports to, 23
    and legal–ethical conflicts, 154
Peck v. Counseling Service of Addison County, 176
Peer consultation-study groups, 130

Peer review, 527, 529
Peer-reviewed journals, 527
PENS *See* Psychological Ethics and National Security
Permission, 403–405
Permissive disclosure, 205
Perpetuity rule, 230
Personal appearance, of respondent, 58
Personal behavior, professional vs., 31–35
Personal development, 35
Personal freedom, 98, 100
Personal information, student disclosure of, 24
Personal problems, competence and, 18–19
Personal relationships, with former clients, 235–236
Personal response, 48
Personal therapy, mandated, 266–267
Personal values, 109, 152–153
Personnel, animal research subjects and, 434–435
Personnel testing and evaluation, 283–288
    commentary on, 285–286
    and employer's interests, 284–285
    and evaluee's interests, 283–284
    and professional obligations, 283
Perspective, of expert witness, 469–470
Perverse incentives, 565
PHI (protected health information), 379
Philosophy, 121
Phobia treatments, 223
Physical contact, boundaries and, 225–226
Placebo treatment, 421, 423, 424
Place boundaries, 222–223
Plagiarism, 26, 441, 443
Planning, risk, 182–183
Poddar, Prosenjit, 166, 168, 171–175
Policy(-ies)
    agency's/employer's, 153–154
    external review of, 185
    and forms, 185
    risk-related, 184–185
    and staff education/compliance, 185
    written guidelines in, 184
Policyholders
    informing, of benefit limits, 565
    selection of, 563
Politics, 33
Portable devices, 380
Posttraumatic stress disorder (PTSD), 492–493
Powerlessness, 321

Practice, issues of good, 11
Practice profiling, 553
Practicum supervision, 126
Preamble section (of APA Code of Ethics), 14–16
Predicates for use of show cause procedures, 51–52
    expulsion/suspension/unlicensure/decertification, 52
    felony/equivalent offense, 51–52
Predictive-violence testimony, 514–517
    foundation of, 516
    legal consequences of, 516–517
    nature of, 515–516
    reliability of, 514
Preferred provider organizations (PPOs), 553
Preliminary evaluation, of complaints by Director, 55–56
    insufficient information, 55
    lack of jurisdiction, 55
    time limit, process with respect to applicable, 55–56
Prescription privileges for psychologists (RxP), 369–375
    commentary on, 372–375
    debate on, 370–372
    opposition to, 370–372
    support for, 370
Preservation, of family, 350–351
Presidential Task Force on Psychological Ethics and National Security. *See Report of the Presidential Task Force on Psychological Ethics and National Security* (APA)
Preventative training, 267
Prima facie duties, 36, 135, 137, 138, 144
Primary care physicians, referrals from, 555
Primum non nocere, 36, 136
Principle-based ethics, 135–137, 144–147
    and balancing moral principles, 137
    beneficence, 136
    and character/community, 145–146
    commentary on, 146–147
    decision-making process of, 111
    fidelity, 136–137
    focus of, 130
    generalized beneficence, 137
    justice, 136
    and legal–ethical conflicts, 152–153
    limitations of, 139–140
    nonmaleficence, 136
    prima facie duties in, 144
    respect for client autonomy, 136

Principles of Medical Ethics (American Medical Association), 170, 172
Principles of Medical Ethics with Annotations Especially Applicable to Psychiatry, 32
Prisoners. *See also* Interrogation of detainees
    mock study of, 395–396
    as research subjects, 402–403, 409
Prisoners of war, 321
Privacy, 16
    APA Ethical Standards on, 21
    commentary on, 164–165
    concept of, 161
    confidentiality vs., 162
    constitutional right to, 161–162
    deception and invasion of, 415, 420
    and Internet-mediated psychological services, 379–381
    minimizing intrusions on, 21
    of patient information, 543
    and recordings, 21
    and research, 386
    Supreme Court on, 159
    and testing, 274–275
Privacy rule (HIPAA), 543, 544
Privacy screens, 380
Privacy statement, 380
Private fee arrangements, 575
Privilege
    concept of, 163
    and court testimony, 495
    criticism of, 164
    evidentiary, 293
    in family/marital therapy, 349
    legal conditions for breach of, 167
    waiver of, 164
Privileged communication
    breaking of, 178–179
    and coercive assessments, 508
    dilemmas with, 106
    and patient's rights, 163–164
    testimony about, 297
Privileged communication laws, 159
Probation, 50
Problem-solving approach, 146, 149
Procedural errors, 64
Procedural justice, 136
Process model, of informed consent, 340
Process notes, 293–294
Professional arrogance, 462
Professional behavior
    personal vs., 31–35
    regulation of, 13

Professional ethics
    and client confidentiality, 204–205
    development of, 133–134
    and legal–ethical conflicts, 153
Professional ethics education, 107
Professionalism, 142
Professional relationships
    in child psychology, 92–93, 95
    ethical standards in, 10
    with former clients, 237–239
    types of, 254
Professional services agreement, 194
Professional value, 351
Professors' ethics survey, 446–451
    conclusions of, 450–451
    limitations of, 446
    method of, 446
    and portrait of ethical professor,
        449–450
    results of, 446–449
Profits, patient welfare vs., 567–568
Prosecutorial bias, 509
Protected health information (PHI), 379,
    543, 544
Protecting third parties from harm, 118
Protection, of human research subjects,
    398–405
    applications, 398–399
    with children, 403–406
    and criteria for IRB approval, 399–400
    and expedited review procedures, 399
    and informed consent requirements,
        400–402
    and IRB membership, 399
    with prisoners, 402–403
Protective order, motion for, 296
Provider input, 565, 566
Provider risk sharing, 553
Proximate cause, 155
Prudence, 144, 145
Psychoeducational decisions, involvement
    of minor clients in, 193
Psycholegal assessment, 493
Psycholegal issues, 500
Psychological assessment, 271–327
    and access to test data, 289
    computerized, 303–305
    conforming to rules/regulations for, 291
    copyright interests of, 291
    *Detroit Edison Co. v. National Labor
        Relations Board*, 287–288
    disclosure of test data, 289–298
    and informed consent, 290
    informing test taker of purpose/use/
        results of, 289–290

Internet-based, 306–312
    and interrogation of detainees,
        325–327
    and national security, 319–324
    of older adults, 368
    and organizational clients, 291–292
    personnel testing/evaluation, 283–288
    releasing data from, 290–292
    and reprinting of test items, 292
    and retention/maintenance of testing
        data, 292
    role of psychologists with, 292
    school psychology laws, 276–278
    school psychology model of practice,
        299–302
    subpoenas/compelled testimony for
        client records/test data,
        293–298
    teaching of, 313–318
    and teaching/training, 292
    test user qualifications, 279–282
    test validity, 273–275
Psychological Ethics and National
    Security (PENS), 272, 319
Psychological services
    delivered to/through organizations, 20
    interruption of, 20
    organizational delivery of, 20
Psychological well-being, of animal sub-
    jects, 435
Psychologists
    capitated contracts held directly by,
        575
    defined, 477
    MCOs contracting directly with,
        574–575
Psychologists' ethical beliefs and behav-
    iors study, 73–88
    acting only with informed consent
        (principle 6), 86–87
    behavior–beliefs relationship, 80
    demographic characteristics of partici-
        pants, 75
    difficult judgments, 81
    discussion, 78, 80–88
    do no harm (principle 1), 82
    do not exploit (principle 3), 83–85
    ethical framework, 81–88
    gender-related behaviors, 78, 80
    method, 74
    near-universal behaviors, 80
    practice only with competence (princi-
        ple 2), 82–83
    promoting equity and justice (princi-
        ple 7), 87–88

    protect confidentiality (principle 5),
        86
    rare behaviors, 80–81
    resources for regulating psychology,
        75, 79, 88
    results, 75–79
    survey questionnaire, 74
    theoretical orientation of participants,
        75
    treat people with respect for their
        dignity as human beings (prin-
        ciple 4), 85–86
    validity/interpretation issues, 78, 80
Psychology
    business of. *See* Business of
        psychology
    culture of, 122–123
Psychology departments, ethical orienta-
    tion in, 126
Psychometric and measurement knowl-
    edge, 279–281
    descriptive statistics, 279–280
    normative interpretation of test scores,
        280
    reliability/measurement error, 280
    selection of appropriate tests,
        280–281
    test administration procedures, 281
    validity/meaning of test scores, 280
Psychopath, 522
Psychopathy, 519, 523
Psychopathy Checklist Revised (PCL–R),
    522, 523
Psychopharmacology, 371–372
Psychopharmacology Examination for
    Psychologists, 369
Psychosituational approach, 300
Psychotherapist–client privilege, 167,
    174, 175, 177
"Psychotherapist–Patient Informed
    Consent Contract," 572
Psychotherapists
    and duty to warn, 169–174
    and right to privacy, 161–162
    values of, 350–352
Psychotherapy, brief, 555–556
Psychotropic medication, 183, 525,
    552–553
PTSD. *See* Posttraumatic stress disorder
Publication
    APA Ethical Standards on, 24–27
    and confidential information, 21
    credit in, 26
    duplicate publication of data, 26
Publication credit, 26

Publication Manual of the American Psychological Association, 444
Public behavior, 427–428
Public domain
    and anonymous complaints, 54–55
    material from, 49
Public education programs, 549
Public forum psychology, 86
Public interest, 503–504
Public Interest Directorate (APA), 212
Public peril, 160, 167
Public policy, 98, 100, 175
Public records, 428
Public responsibility
    ethical standards for, 10
    and general beneficence, 137
Public statements, 32–33
    APA Ethical Standards on, 21–22
    avoidance of false/deceptive statements in, 21–22
    and in-person solicitation, 22
    and Internet-mediated psychological services, 381
    and media presentations, 22
    and statements by others, 22
    and testimonials, 22
    of workshops/non-degree-granting educational programs, 22
Public welfare, threats to, 45

Qualifications, test-user. *See* Test user qualifications
Qualifying language, 114
Quandary ethics, 139, 140
Quorum, 43

Racial variables, 281
Radio, 86
Rationale for action, 184
Raw data, 288, 544
Rawls, John, 132
Readability, 333, 412
Reading, 106
Readmission applications, 38, 50–51
Readmission of member
    after stipulated resignation, 53, 59
    records concerning, 45
Readmit recommendation, 51
"Reasonable," 114–115, 135
Reasonableness, 15
Reasonable precautions (term), 379
Reasonably understandable (term), 336
Reasoning processes, 107
Rebuttal documents and witnesses, 63

Recommendations, of Ethics Committee, 41
Reconsideration, of case, 57, 64
Recordings
    destruction of, 380
    informed consent to, 25, 213
    masking of voice, 380
    permission for, 21
Record keeping, 22–23, 535
Record Keeping Guidelines (APA), xv, 292, 489, 533, 535–542
    commentary on, 542
    on confidentiality of records, 539
    on content of records, 537–539
    on context of records, 540
    on disclosure of procedures, 539
    on disposition of records, 542
    on electronic records, 540
    expiration of, 537
    and federal/state laws, 536
    on financial records, 541–542
    introduction to, 536
    on maintenance of records, 539
    on multiple-client records, 541
    on organizational settings, 540–541
    on responsibility for records, 537
    on retention of records, 540
    on security, 539–540
Records
    advantages of keeping, 536
    confidential, 22–23
    confidentiality of ethics files, 45
    death of member, 45
    disposal of, 22–23
    dissemination of, 22–23
    documentation of professional/scientific work/maintenance of, 22
    for educative purposes, 45
    of Ethics Committee, 45
    investigation files, 45
    maintenance of, 22–23, 533
    membership loss, files involving, 45
    ownership of, 573
    readmission of member, 45
    tampering with, 185–186
    withholding records for nonpayment, 23
Recruitment
    and causism, 390–391
    and hyperclaiming, 390
    of volunteer subjects, 313–314
Redress, 262
Referral(s)
    to Board of Directors, 63–64
    of case to Committee, 58

    of jurisdiction, 48
    payment for, 23, 81, 534, 548–550
    from primary care physicians, 555
    to therapists, 105
Referral services, 548
Referral sources, 565
Refuse treatment, right to, 349–350
Regulating psychology
    effectiveness of sources for, 79
    resources for, 75, 79, 88
Rehabilitation, 264
Rehabilitation Act of 1973, 276, 277
Reimbursement requirements, 554, 557
Rejection, of stipulated resignation, 54, 59–60
Relationships
    blurred/dual/conflictual, 11
    with current clients, 218
    exploitative, 20
    forensic vs. therapeutic, 494–497
    with former clients, 218
    integrity in, 37
    of lesbian/gay/bisexual clients, 363
    multiple. *See* Multiple relationships
Relatives, dual relationships with, 85
Relativists, 134, 345
Release
    of Internet-based test data, 307–308
    of test data, 27–28, 290–292
Relevance, of expert testimony, 468–469
Reliability, 280
Religious affiliation relationships, 238
Remand, 52, 54, 58
Remediation for psychotherapist–patient sex, 266–270
    and client education about boundaries, 267
    commentary on, 269–270
    effectiveness of, 267–269
    and identification/preventative training, 267
    mandatory personal therapy as, 266–267
Remote assessment, 305
Reopening investigations, 47, 48
Reporting
    of acts of torture, 320
    of diagnosis for managed care, 557
    of ethical violations, 17
    of psychotherapist–patient sex, 263
Reporting adolescent risk-taking behavior, 197–201
    commentary on, 201–202
    ethical dilemmas in, 197–198
    negative nature of behavior, 199–200

and therapeutic process, 200
training/practice implications for, 198, 199
Reporting research, 26, 392–394
commentary on, 394–395
and failing to publish or report, 393–394
and misrepresentation of credit, 393
and misrepresentation of findings, 392–393
Report of the Presidential Task Force on Psychological Ethics and National Security (APA), xv, 272, 319–324
and classified research, 323
and competence, 322
and consultant roles, 321–322
and consulting with others, 323
and culture/ethnicity, 323
discussion of, 326
and identifying client, 322–323
introduction to, 319–320
and limits of confidentiality, 322
and medical records, 320
and multiple relationships, 321
overview of, 319
and participation in torture, 320
and possible innocence of detainee, 322
and reporting of torture, 320
and research, 323
and role of psychologists, 321
and U.S. laws/human rights, 320–321, 323
Reprimand, 49
Reprimand recommendation
Board acceptance of, 54
by Committee, 53, 59
independent adjudication following, 60–61
respondent's acceptance of, 60
Reprinting, of test items, 292
Request for review, 52–53
Required disclosures, 205–206
Research, 385–445
and animal welfare, 26, 434–438
APA Ethical Standards on, 24–27
beneficence in, 150
with client/patient/student/subordinate, 25
on competency, 406–411
conducting/analyzing/reporting, 390–397
and debriefing, 25
on deception, 415–425
deception in, 25

and duplicate publication of data, 26
ethical perspectives in, 387–389
ethical standards in, 10
inducements for participation in, 25
and informed-consent comprehension, 412–414
informed consent to, 24–25
institutional approval of, 24
Internet-based, 426–433
issues in, 385–386
justification of, 434
on national security issues, 323
and plagiarism, 26
and publication credit, 26
and recordings, 25
reporting results of, 26
and reviewers, 26–27
sharing research for verification, 26
supervision of student, 439–445
and welfare of human subjects, 398–405
Researcher lies, 415
Research Network on Mental Health and the Law (MacArthur Project), 175, 524
Research subject pools, 425
Research subjects or participants
access to practice, 313–314
competency of, 406–411
in Ditching study, 388
feedback to practice, 314–315
policy for protection of human, 398–405
treatment of human, 396
Resignation(s)
after charge letter issuance, 57–58
under ethics investigation, 40–41, 47, 65
and insufficient information, 56
number of, 65
right of, 64–65
under scrutiny, 38–39
stipulated. *See* Stipulated resignation
Resignation barred, 47, 52
Resolution Against Torture, 320, 326–327
Resolutions Related to HIV/AID (APA), 212
Resolving ethical issues, 17
Respect
for dignity of persons, 37, 85–86, 320
for patient autonomy, 135, 136
for people's rights/dignity, 16–17
for self and others, 132
Respond, failure to, 40
Respondent(s)
legal representation for, 63

notification by Ethics Committee to, 44
rights of, 63
show cause notification of, 53
Respondent's response
to automatic expulsion notice, 52
to Board of Directors referral, 64
to Ethics Committee statement, 60
to recommendation, 51, 53
time limits for, 57
Response, personal, 48
Response time, for treatment requests, 568–569
Responsibility(-ies)
of Ethics Committee officers, 43
principle of, 16
for records, 537
to society, 37
Responsible caring, 37
Restraining clients, 92
Restraints, 436
Restriction of liberty, 516–517
Rest's decision-making model, 130, 146
Retention
of jurisdiction, 48
of records, 540
Retribution, 262
Review
of applications for membership, 50
by Board of Directors in show cause procedures, 53
of false/fraudulent membership, 51
of readmission applications, 51
of risk policy, 185
Review and recommendation by Ethics Committee, 52–53
dismissal of matter, 52
expulsion, 53
remand, 52–53
reprimand/censure with/without directives, 53
Review and resolution by Ethics Committee, 58–60
dismissal of charges, 58–59
educative letter, 59
expulsion recommendation, 59
remand, 58
reprimand/censure recommendation, 59
stipulated resignation recommendation, 59–60
Reviewers, research, 26–27
Revocation of license, 12, 15, 52, 154
Rewarding clients, 92
Right action, principles of, 133

Rights of people, respect for, 16–17
Right to counsel, 511, 513
Right to refuse treatment, 349–350
Risk assessment, 175, 180–182
    commentary on, 521–522
    communication used in, 182
    conducting, 518–522
    education used in, 180
    individual-based vs. class-based, 516
    information used in, 180–181
Risk assignment, 564
Risk containment
    assessment for risk in, 180–182
    and damage control, 185–186
    and documentation, 183–184
    management of risk in, 182–183
    policy for, 184–185
Risk management, 182–183
    adherence to plan in, 183
    planning in, 182–183
    with potential multiple relationships,
        256–261
    with suicidal patient, 342–345
Risk research, 518
Risk-taking behavior, of adolescents,
    197–201
Roe v. Wade, 161
Role boundaries, 222
Role clarification, 321, 571
Role-differentiated behavior, 462
Role fidelity, 134
Rules and Procedures, APA. *See* APA
    Rules and Procedures
Rules and regulations, legal–ethical con-
    flicts and, 154
Rules-based ethics, 245
Rules of evidence, 63, 457, 465–466, 481
Rural and urban psychologists, ethical
    practices survey of, 354–360
    burnout issues, 355, 358
    commentary on, 359–360
    competency issues, 355, 358
    confidentiality issues, 355, 358
    multiple relationship issues, 355, 356
    peer-consultation issues, 355, 358
    results, 355–358
    visibility issues, 355, 357
RxP. *See* Prescription privileges for psy-
    chologists

Salgo v. Stanford, 331
Sanctions, 8
    by APA, 15
    economic, 12
    and federal/state/local statutes, 154

forms of, 49
    reasons for, 144
SBES (social, behavioral, and economic
    sciences), 410
Scare advertising, 547
Schizophrenia research, 397
Schizophrenic subjects, competency of,
    406
*Schloendorf v. Society of New York
    Hospital,* 331
School desegregation, 276, 473
School placement decisions, 277
School psychology laws, 276–278
    commentary on, 277–278
    nondiscriminatory assessment,
        276–277
School psychology model, 299–302
    coadvisement in, 299
    commentary on, 301–302
    critique of written evaluation in,
        300–301
    sharing impressions in, 300
Science, bad, 391
Science and technology (S&T), 528
Scientific Integrity, 456
Scientific knowledge, 526–527
Scoring, assessment, 28
Scrutiny
    in forensics, 496
    member under, 39
Second generation, of risk research, 518
Second opinions, 182–183
Secretary of Health and Human Services,
    178
Security
    of credit card payments, 378
    with Internet-based psychological test-
        ing, 307–308
    of Internet data, 429–431
    of Internet-mediated psychological
        services, 380
    national. *See Report of the Presidential
        Task Force on Psychological
        Ethics and National Security*
    of records, 539–540
    of test materials, 28, 310
Security rule (HIPAA), 543
Seductive clothing, 224
Self-care, 373
Self-censoring, 393
Self-deception, 35, 415
Self-determination, 17, 145, 415–417
Self-disclosure
    boundaries with, 224–225
    by HIV clients, 205, 211

and managed care, 556
    of minor clients, 193
    as nearly universal therapy technique,
        80
    and respect for dignity of clients, 86
    in small communities, 359–360
Self-help books and programs, 373–374
Self-improvement, 135
Self-incrimination, 511–513
Self-knowledge, 35
Self-reflection, 35
Self-rule, 136
Selling goods, to clients, 81
Separation strategy, 124
September 11, 2001 terrorist attacks, 159
Service(s)
    bartering. *See* Bartering for services
    boundaries with, 223–224
    of legal documents, 49
Sessions
    length of, 560
    limits on number of, 553, 563
Settlement out of court, 155
Sexism, 360, 361
Sex roles, 351–352, 361
Sexton, Anne, 213
Sexual activity
    of adolescents, 199
    of HIV clients, 204, 205, 207–212
Sexual attraction, to client, 80, 84, 228
Sexual boundary violations, 227
Sexual conduct of colleagues, 106
Sexual ethics, 250–252
Sexual fantasies, 84, 224
Sexual harassment, 19, 231
Sexual intimacies/relationships, 11
    with clients, 217
    with current client, 29, 80–81, 215,
        220, 226, 229, 230
    with former client, 29–30, 83,
        215–216, 220, 229–232
    and insurance coverage, 83, 261
    with relatives/significant others of cur-
        rent clients, 29
    with students/supervisees, 24, 84, 217,
        246
    survey of understanding of principles
        relating to, 69–73
Sexual orientation, 357, 363
Sexual partners, therapy with former, 29
Sexual surrogates, 81, 83
Shapero v. Kentucky Bar Association, 546
Sharing research, 26
Show cause notices, time limits on, 46
Show cause procedures, 51–54

automatic expulsion, 52
Committee's statement, 53
due process lacking in prior proceeding, 52
failure to return affidavit, 52
investigation, 52
notification of respondent, 53
predicates for use of, 51–52
respondent's final response, 53
respondent's response, 53
review by Board of Directors, 53
review/recommendation by Committee, 52–53
stipulated resignation, 53–54
sua sponte conversion to/from, 48
Shrink-Link, 375
Significant others, information from, 181
Situational variability, 92
Sixth Amendment (of U.S. Constitution), 511, 513
Skimming, 563
Smith (prisoner), 511–514
Sniffing programs, 429
Social, behavioral, and economic sciences (SBES), 410
Social desirability, of behavior, 420
Social events
    interaction with former client at, 236
    inviting client to, 220
Social isolation, of therapist, 253, 355, 356
Social science research, 410
Social stigmatization, 363
Social workers, 554–555
Society, responsibility to, 37, 135–137, 170
Society for a Science of Clinical Psychology, 371
Sociopolitical contexts, 367
Solicitation
    of clients, 81, 85
    direct, 547–549
    in-person, 22
Sophocles, 111
Source of information, 184, 483
Space boundaries, 222–223
SPE. *See* Stanford Prison Experiment
Special education services, 276, 301
Specialty Guidelines for Forensic Psychologists (APA), 457, 468, 471, 476–484, 519, 522
    commentary on, 483–484
    on competence, 478
    on confidentiality/privilege, 479–480
    on methods/procedures, 480–482

on public/professional communications, 482–483
purpose of, 476–477
and related standards, 477
on relationships, 478–479
responsibilities identified in, 477
scope of, 477
Specificity, 12
Speech, freedom of, 33–34
Speech codes, 33–34
S&T (science and technology), 528
Stalking, by clients, 231–232
Standard of care, 342, 559, 569–570
Standards, decision making and availability of, 100
Standards for Educational an Psychological Testing (AERA), 274, 281, 283, 288, 292, 303, 304, 311, 487
Standards for Providers of Psychological Services (APA), 303
Standing Hearing Panel, 41, 49, 60, 62
Stanford-Binet scale, 288
Stanford Prison Experiment (SPE), 395–396
State courts, 453
State guidelines, on HIV/AIDS-client confidentiality, 205–206
State laws, 536
State licensure board sanctions, 12
Statements by others
    and Internet-mediated psychological services, 381
    in public statements, 22
State statutes
    on advertising, 548–549
    client–therapist sex prohibited by, 261
    and legal–ethical conflicts, 154
    and minor-client confidentiality, 195
Statutes
    antisodomy, 161, 164–165
    on client–therapist sex, 261
    and legal–ethical conflicts, 154
    on minor-client confidentiality, 195
Stipulated resignation(s)
    acceptance by respondent, 53, 59
    action of board of directors, 54
    and Board of Directors, 59, 60
    bylaws concerning, 38
    notification of respondent, 53, 59
    number of, 65
    offer of, 53, 59
    rejection by respondent, 54, 59–60
    and reports to membership, 45

and Standing Hearing Panel, 49
    transmittal to board of directors, 53–54
Stress, 322
Stress management, 369
Student affiliate complaints, 46
Student disclosure of personal information, 24
Student research supervision, 439–445
    abandonment of, 440–442
    abusive, 440, 442
    authorship issues in, 441, 443–444
    commentary on, 444–445
    dual relationships in, 441, 442
    exploitive, 440, 442
    fraud encouraged in, 441–443
    inadequate, 439–441
    incompetent, 439, 440
    intrusion of values into, 440, 442
Students
    assessing performance of, 24
    attitudes of, 69–73
    avoiding harm to, 33
    multiple relationships of, 129
    multiple relationships with, 248–249
    as research participants, 25
    sexual intimacies with, 246
    sexual relationships with, 24
Sua sponte action
    and anonymous complaints, 54–55
    charge letter issued in, 57
    and concurrent disciplinary proceedings, 47
    and due process, 52
    initiation of, 54
Sua sponte complaints, 41, 46
Subjects. *See* Research subjects or participants
Subordinates, as research participants, 25
Subpoena(s)
    for client records/test data, 293–298
    contacting client regarding, 295
    disclosing confidential information vs. responding to, 293
    filing motion to quash, 296
    and force of law, 294
    and negotiating with requester, 295
    seeking court guidance on, 295–296
    waiver of right to, 55
Subpoenas duces tecum, 293
Substance abuse programs, 154, 552
Substance expertise, 458
Sued, fear of being, 88
Suffering, cost in terms of, 388

Suicidal clients
accepting decisions of, 87
adolescent, 199, 200
breaking confidentiality of, 86
and duty to warn, 176
risk management with, 342–345
Suicide rates, 354
Supervised experience, 281
Supervisees
assessing performance of, 24
dishonesty in helping degree/licensing of, 81
dual relationships with, 85
sexual intimacies with, 246
sexual relationships with, 24, 81, 84
signing for unearned hours by, 82
Supervision
abandonment of, 440–442
abusive, 440, 442
competence of, 439, 440
directive for, 50
ethical acculturation and practicum, 126
ethical training in context of, 120
exploitive, 440, 442
inadequate, 439–441
sexual ethics training during, 250
of student research, 439–445
values imposed during, 440, 442
Supervisory relationships, with former clients, 237–238
Supplemental information, request for, 55, 56
Supplementary action, 57
Surgical procedures, 436
Survey of Ethical Dilemmas in Reporting Adolescent Risk-Taking Behavior, 197–198
Suspension, 52
Sympathy, 133
Syphilis, 388, 395

Tabachnick, B. G., 97, 442
Tampering with records, 185–186
Tarasoff, Tatiana, 166, 168, 174
Tarasoff II, 168, 170–175
Tarasoff v. Regents of the University of California, 160, 166–170
Target hardening, 182
Task Force on Bias in Psychotherapy with Lesbians and Gay Men (APA), 362
Task Force on Confidentiality of Children's and Adolescents' Clinical Records (APA), 193

Task Force on Psychopharmacology (APA), 369
Task Force on Test User Qualifications (TFTUQ), 278, 279, 282
Task Force Report on the Role of the Psychologist in the Criminal Justice System (APA), 507
Teaching
accuracy in, 24
dilemmas in, 11
ethical standards in, 10
of moral reasoning/behavior, 130
Teaching, of psychological testing, 313–318
and access to practice subjects, 313–314
commentary on, 318
and confidentiality/data handling, 315–316
and consent, 316–317
and feedback, 314–315
Teams, communication among, 182
Telehealth, 376–383
Telephone therapy, 374
Television, 86
Terminating therapy, 30, 88, 578
Termination of APA membership, 15, 65
Terrorism, animal enterprise, 438
Test administration procedures, 281
Test construction, 28
Test data
and consent of test taker, 290
defined, 288
disclosure of, 289–298
grounds for opposing/limiting production of, 297
qualifications of recipients of, 290–291
retention/maintenance of, 292
security of test and release of, 290
subpoenas/compelled testimony for, 293–298
and teaching of psychological testing, 315–316
and third-party payers, 291
Test developer, 303, 304, 311
Test development, 308–309
Testimonials, 22, 547, 548
Testimony
advocacy vs., 459–460, 462–463, 467, 472
court-ordered, 297
Testing materials
copyright interests of, 291
defined, 288
reprinting of, 292

security of, 290
subpoenas for, 294
teaching/training using, 292
Testing services, 303
Test results, disclosing, 298
Test scores
normative interpretation of, 280
validity/meaning of, 280
Test security, 290, 310, 482, 544
Test selection, 280–281
Test taker(s)
consent of, 290
disclosing results to, 298
explaining Internet-based testing results to, 310
informing, of purpose/use/results of testing, 289–290
rights of, 304
Test user qualifications, 278–282, 309
APA guidelines for, 279–282
commentary on, 282
defined, 279
with employment testing, 283
and ethnic/racial/cultural/gender/age/linguistic variables, 281
future changes in, 281–282
psychometric/measurement knowledge, 279–281
and release of test data, 290–291
and supervised experience, 281
and testing individuals with disabilities, 281
Test User Qualifications Working Group, 278
Test users, rights and responsibilities of, 303, 304
Test validity, 273–275
Texas prison system, 523
Texas Supreme Court, 176, 208
TFTUQ. *See* Task Force on Test User Qualifications
Thapar v. Zezulka, 175, 176, 208
Thematic Apperception Test, 282
Theoretical orientation, 259
A Theory of Justice (John Rawls), 133
Therapeutic effectiveness
and boundaries, 242–247
multiple relationships and impairment of, 218
Therapeutic leverage, 98, 100
Therapeutic process, 200
Therapeutic relationship
and coercive assessments, 508, 510
and confidentiality, 163, 167
and dual relationships, 255–256

and managed care, 564
power of, 245, 264
and violence risk, 187–189
Therapeutic touch, 225
Therapist–client contract, 141
Therapist–Patient Sex Syndrome, 81
Therapy. *See also* Interventions
APA Ethical Standards on, 28–30
couples/family, 29
with former sexual partners, 29
group, 29
informed consent to, 28–29
interruption of, 30
and sexual intimacies, 29–30
terminating, 30
to those served by others, 29
Therapy notes, 293, 296, 381, 543
Third parties
access to information by, 162
deception by, 415
disclosure of information to, 543
and forensic psychology, 481
and Internet-mediated psychological
services, 378–379, 382
notification by Ethics Director to, 45
obligations to, 160
requests for services by, 19–20
threats to, 162, 166, 170–173, 189
as vendors of psychological testing,
309–310
Third-party payers/payments, 84, 291,
538, 555
Thoreau, Henry David, 68
"Thou shalt not lie, cheat, or steal," 144
Threat(s). *See also* Duty to warn
to public welfare, 45
to third parties, 160, 162, 166,
170–173, 189
360-degree-type evaluations, 131
Time
boundaries of, 222
elapsed, for readmission, 50
Time limit(s)
for charge letter, 57
for complaints/show cause notices,
46–47
compliance with, 43
computing, 43
on documentation of investigation,
58
on filing complaints, 55
for respondent's response, 56, 57
superseding, 55–56
waiver of, 41
Tissue damage, 436

Toileting, assisting preschoolers with, 91,
92
Torts, 155
Torture
reporting acts of, 320
resolution against, 320, 326–327
Trading therapeutic services, for other
professional services, 105
Trainee selection, 34, 125, 128–129
Training. *See also* Education and training
programs; Ethics training
to achieve treatment goals, 565
dilemmas in, 11
directive for, 50
and ethical acculturation, 126
for ethics competence, 129–130
for prescriptive privileges, 370, 371
in psychological testing, 292
Transaction rule (HIPAA), 543
Transcription, 48–49
Transference, 224, 533, 547
Translators, 366
"Treating witnesses," 492
Treatment. *See also* Interventions
directive for, 50
duty to continue, 561
managed-care limitations on, 563
of victims of psychotherapist–patient
sex, 262–263
Treatment planning and evaluation, 193,
194
Treatment records
and risk assessment, 181
tampering with, 185–186
Truman v. Thomas, 331
Trust
and breaking confidentiality, 189
and fidelity, 16, 137
of minor clients, 193
and patient expectations, 163
therapeutic relationship based on, 174
Truthfulness, 16, 136, 142
Tuskegee study, 388, 395
Tutoring, 50
2002 APA Code of Ethics
adoption of, 13
applicability of, 31, 32
commentary on, 138
criticism of, 36–37
on documentation of informed consent, 337
on forensic psychology, 454
on group therapy confidentiality, 353
on informed consent, 339
on limits of confidentiality, 117

on mandatory therapy, 249
on multiple relationships, 219–220
on multiple relationships with students, 249
prima facie duties in, 36
principle-based analysis of, 135–137
reasonable/appropriate/potentially
terms used in, 114–115
on reasonable professional conduct,
258
on sexual relationships with
students/supervisees, 246
on sharing testing results with test takers, 298
on telehealth, 376
on therapy standards, 329
on trainee selection, 129, 249

UM. *See* Utilization management
Uncommitted bias, 509
"Under ethics investigation," 40–41, 47
"Under scrutiny," 39
Understanding, lack of, 69
"Undue influence," 547–549
Unearned hours, 82
Unethical behavior, of other profession-
als, 105
Unethical conduct investigations, 40
Unfair discrimination, 19
Uniform Code of Military Justice, 254
*Uniform Guidelines on Employee Selection
Procedures,* 278, 283, 284
Unintentional misrepresentation, 393
Unions, 285–287
United Nations, 320–321
United Nations Convention Against
Torture and Other Cruel,
Inhuman, or Degrading Treatment
or Punishment, 320–321
United States, laws of, 320, 323
United States v. Downing, 527
Universal Law, 132
Unlicensed therapists, 262
Unqualified persons, assessments by, 28
UR. *See* Utilization review
Urban psychologists. *See* Rural and
urban psychologists, ethical prac-
tices survey of
Urine sample, 387
U.S. Congress, 389, 395, 396
U.S. Constitution, 511
U.S. Department of Agriculture (USDA),
437
U.S. Department of Defense, 326
U.S. Department of Education, 276

U.S. Department of Health and Human
  Services (DHHS), 178, 276, 396,
  409, 411, 413, 543, 544
U.S. Department of Health and Human
  Services Regulations, 154
U.S. Public Health Service, 395
U.S. Senate, 395
U.S. Supreme Court, 159, 161, 164–165,
  174, 175, 177, 276, 285–288, 389,
  521, 525, 528, 546, 547, 549
USDA (U.S. Department of Agriculture),
  437
Utilitarianism, 132–133, 207, 209–210,
  212, 417–422
Utilitarian principles, 108
Utilization management (UM),
  576–578
Utilization review (UR), 576–578
Utilization reviewers, 553–555, 573

Validity
  of expert testimony, 528
  and meaning of test scores, 280
  of psychological tests, 273–275
Values, of psychotherapists, 350–352
  on extramarital affairs, 351
  on preservation of family, 350–351
  on sex roles, 351–352
Values, of supervisors, 440, 442
*Varol v. Blue Cross and Blue Shield of
  Michigan*, 561
Veracity, 134
Verification, sharing research for, 26
VeriSign, 431
Vermont Supreme Court, 176
Vice Chair of Ethics Committee, 43, 56
Victim compensation fund, 263
Victims
  remediation for, 269
  treatment of, 262–263
Videotapes, 48–49, 63
Video teleconferencing, 374
Vignettes of ethical issues
  and decision-making study, 99
  and national survey, 103–104
Villanova Conference, 458

Violation(s) of ethics code, 54–64
  case investigation, 57–58
  complaints, 54–55
  Director's preliminary evaluation of
    complaints, 55–56
  dismissal of case, 60
  evaluation of complaints by Chair and
    Director, 56–57
  expulsion recommendation, 61–64
  initiation of actions, 54
  procedures for filing complaints, 55
  reprimand/censure recommendation,
    60–61
  review/resolution by Committee,
    58–60
Violence. *See also* Dangerous-clients,
  decision-making model for working with
  clients who are victims of, 361
  defining, 177
  planning for potential, 182–183
  predicting, 171–174
Violence Appraisal Guide (VRAG), 522
Violence Risk X Alliance Strength table,
  187–189
Virtue-based ethics
  and character, 142
  commentary on, 143
  decision-making process of, 111
  focus of, 130
  genuineness, 141–142
  and history of moral discourse, 140
  informed consent, 140–141
  and legal–ethical conflicts, 152–153
  in psychology, 140–142
Virus protection software, 380
Visibility issues, in rural and urban settings, 355, 357
Voice recording distortion, 380
Voir dire, 62
Volunteered statements, 513
Volunteers, 313–314
VRAG (Violence Appraisal Guide), 522

Waiver
  initiation of legal action as, 45
  of privilege, 164

  of right to be informed, 415
  of right to subpoena, 55
  of time limit, 41
Walk-In Counseling Center (Minneapolis,
  Minnesota), 264
Wards of state, 405
Warn, duty to. *See* Duty to warn
Washington Supreme Court, 467
"Weasel words," 114
Web telephony, 374
Wechsler Adult Intelligence Scale, 282,
  288
Wechsler Intelligence Scale for Children,
  282, 288
Welfare, of animal subjects, 16
Whalen v. Roe, 161
Whistleblowing, 107
*White v. North Carolina State Board of
  Examiners of Professional
  Psychologists*, 115
Whitree v. State, 87
Wild animals, 435–437
Wilkinson v. Vesey, 169
Willingness, degree of, 69
Wireless devices, 380
Wisconsin, 261
Withholding information, 420
Withholding records, for nonpayment,
  23, 533
Witnesses, 63
Women
  guidelines for therapy with,
    361–362
  sexual contact reported by, 246
Workers' Compensation claim, 164
Workplace relationships, with former
  clients, 239
Workshops, public statements about,
  22
Worthiness, of study, 388
Writing and publishing, ethical standards
  in, 10
Writings, confidential information and,
  21
Written guidelines, for risk policy,
  184

About the Author

DONALD N. BERSOFF recently joined the faculties of Drexel University's College of Law and Department of Psychology, where he serves as director of the JD–PhD Program in Law and Psychology. He also consults with attorneys and mental health professionals on ethical issues. He received his PhD from New York University in 1965 and his JD in 1976 from Yale Law School, where he was an editor of the *Yale Law Journal*. Between his PhD and his JD degrees, Dr. Bersoff served as a clinical psychologist in the U.S. Air Force (1965–1968), spending two of those years in Southeast Asia. He then taught at three universities, training future psychologists while maintaining a part-time private practice. In 1976 he joined the faculties of the University of Maryland School of Law and the Johns Hopkins University Department of Psychology, where he developed the nation's second Law and Psychology Program.

In 1979, Dr. Bersoff became the first general counsel of the American Psychological Association (APA). Two years later he helped found the law firm of Ennis, Friedman, Bersoff and Ewing. In his capacity as APA legal counsel (1979–1989), he prepared more than 25 briefs in the U.S. Supreme Court and an equal number in lower federal and state courts, informing these courts of social science evidence relevant to the issues before them. During this time he also served as legal consultant to the APA Ethics Committee, drafted a precursor of its current Rules and Procedures, and participated in all of the 30 meetings the committee held for the decade.

Dr. Bersoff is the author of over 100 chapters, articles, and papers on ethics and the interaction of law, psychology, and public policy. An APA fellow and an ABPP diplomate in school psychology, he has been elected to three terms as a member of the APA Council of Representatives, the APA's legislative body. During the first two of these terms (1977 and 1992), he participated in passing a revised ethics code. From 1994 to 1997 he served on the APA Board of Directors, which functions in one capacity to independently review the work of the Ethics Committee in cases resulting in recommendations to assess the most serious of sanctions. In 1999, he served as chair of APA's Policy and Planning Board.

Dr. Bersoff has served as president of the American Psychology–Law Society, on the American Bar Association's Commission on the Mentally Disabled, and as chair of the Section on Mental Disability Law of the Association of American Law Schools. He is a member of the Pennsylvania, District of Columbia, and Maryland Bars as well as of the Bar of the U.S. Supreme Court. He was given the Arthur Furst Ethics Lectureship Award for "Outstanding Contributions to the Field of Ethics" in 1997, the Pennsylvania Psychological Association's Ethics Educator of the Year Award in 2000, and on his retirement, the American Psychology–Law Society's Lifetime Achievement Award in 2002. In 2007, Dr. Bersoff served as an invited participant in a week-long symposium on Ethical Sentiments: The Waning Trust in Government, at Pembroke College, Oxford University, England.